Telecommunications Law and Regulation

Third Edition

EDITED BY

Ian Walden

OXFORD
UNIVERSITY PRESS

OXFORD

UNIVERSITY PRESS

Great Clarendon Street, Oxford OX2 6DP

Oxford University Press is a department of the University of Oxford.
It furthers the University's objective of excellence in research, scholarship,
and education by publishing worldwide in

Oxford New York

Auckland Cape Town Dar es Salaam Hong Kong Karachi
Kuala Lumpur Madrid Melbourne Mexico City Nairobi
New Delhi Shanghai Taipei Toronto

With offices in

Argentina Austria Brazil Chile Czech Republic France Greece
Guatemala Hungary Italy Japan Poland Portugal Singapore
South Korea Switzerland Thailand Turkey Ukraine Vietnam

Oxford is a registered trade mark of Oxford University Press
in the UK and in certain other countries

Published in the United States
by Oxford University Press Inc., New York

British Library Cataloguing in Publication Data

Data available

Library of Congress Cataloging in Publication Data

Data available

Typeset by Cepha Imaging Private Ltd, Bangalore, India
Printed in Great Britain
on acid-free paper by
CPI Antony Rowe

ISBN 978–0–19–955935–0

1 3 5 7 9 10 8 6 4 2

Contents Summary

Contents

Preface

The origins of this book lie in a University of London LLM course in Telecommunications Law, for which I became responsible and taught on when I joined the Centre for Commercial Law Studies, Queen Mary, University of London, in 1992. One problem faced by our students in those early days was the lack of a suitable textbook, as those targeted at the professional adviser market were priced appropriately. The first edition, published by Blackstone in 2001, was the affordable and accessible single work that we felt was missing in the market. A second edition was published in 2005 by Oxford University Press. For this third edition, my co-editor, John Angel, has stepped down from the role due to his current commitments as Chair of the Information Tribunal. However, I would like to record my thanks to John for his invaluable input to this project since its inception.

This edition substantially updates and extends the scope of the second edition. In terms of new material, all the chapters have again changed and grown significantly, reflecting the ongoing legal and regulatory developments occurring in the sector. New chapters have been included on Communications Technology, Markets, and Services (Sharpe) and Capacity Agreements (Williams and Maguire). The organization of the book has also been restructured into six parts: Fundamentals; Regulatory Regimes; Key Regulatory Issues; Telecommunications Transactions; Communications Content; and International Regulatory Regimes.

The telecommunications sector continues to be of strategic importance to states, both as an activity in its own right as well as an infrastructure over which trade is carried out. Rapid technological and market developments confront the legal frameworks that are designed to regulate the sector, challenging legislators, regulators, and advisers. This book attempts, but inevitably fails, to keep up with such developments and the challenges they generate. While the law should be correct up to July 2008, the issues discussed will continue to occupy law students and professional advisers in the coming years.

Professor Ian Walden
Institute of Computer and Communications Law
Centre for Commercial Law Studies, Queen Mary, University of London
Of Counsel, Baker & McKenzie
August 2008

Contributors

THE EDITOR

Dr Ian Walden is Professor of Information and Communications Law and head of the Institute of Computer and Communications Law in the Centre for Commercial Law Studies, Queen Mary, University of London. His publications include *EDI and the Law* (1989), *Information Technology and the Law* (1990), *EDI Audit and Control* (1993), *Cross-border Electronic Banking* (1995, 2000), *Telecommunications Law Handbook* (1997), *E-Commerce Law and Practice in Europe* (2001), *Telecommunications Law and Regulation* (2001, 2005, 2009), *Computer Crimes and Digital Investigations* (2007) and *Media Law and Practice* (forthcoming 2009). Ian has been involved in law reform projects for the World Bank, the European Commission, UNCTAD, UNECE, and the European Bank of Reconstruction and Development, as well as for a number of individual states. In 1995–96, Ian was seconded to the European Commission, as a National Expert in electronic commerce law, and he is a member of the Legal Advisory Board to the Information Society Directorate-General of the European Commission. Ian has held visiting positions at the Universities of Texas and Melbourne. Ian is a solicitor and is Of Counsel to the global law firm Baker & McKenzie (www.bakernet.com) and is a Trustee and Vice-Chair of the Internet Watch Foundation (www.iwf.org.uk).

THE CONTRIBUTING AUTHORS

John Angel is a solicitor. He is chairman of and presides over the Information Tribunal. He has been appointed interim judicial lead of the General Regulatory Chamber. He is a Visiting Professor at the Institute of Computer & Communications Law, Centre for Commercial Studies, Queen Mary, University of London and has a number of publications to his name including being consultant editor to *Electronic Business Law*, Butterworths LexisNexis, joint editor and author of both *Computer Law (6th edn)* and *Telecommunications Law (2nd edn),* Oxford University Press and general editor and author of *Technology Outsourcing*, Law Society Publishing. He was formerly Head of Online Legal Services at Clifford Chance, practised technology law at Theodore Goddard and previous to that held a number of senior (non-legal) management positions in the IT industry.

Ann Buckingham holds LLB(Hons) and BA degrees from Victoria University of Wellington, New Zealand, and a BCL degree from Oxford University, where she was

awarded the Vinerian Scholarship. She is qualified in California, England and Wales, and New Zealand, and is a lawyer in Latham & Watkins' top-ranked communications and corporate groups, based in San Diego, California. Ann has advised numerous companies, investment banks, governments, and regulators on regulatory restructuring, licence auctions, corporate transactions, and privatizations in the communications sector, with a particular focus on developing countries. Email: ann.buckingham@lw.com.

Camilla Bustani holds a BA (Hons) from Harvard University and a Masters in International Affairs from Columbia University, as well as a BA (Hons) in Jurisprudence from Oxford University. She worked at Clifford Chance for eight years, focusing primarily on telecommunications sector regulatory reform in developing countries, and public international law aspects of telecommunications regulation and sector liberalization. She has been at Ofcom since 2006, where she is project managing Ofcom's involvement in the review of the European framework for the regulation of electronic communications markets, and in the European Regulators' Group (ERG).

Lisa Correa is a visiting research fellow at Queen Mary & Westfield College, University of London and holds a PhD in economics. She currently works as a Senior Economist in Ofcom's Chief Economist Team and has worked on, amongst many other regulatory and competition projects, the Strategic Review of Telecommunications. Prior to joining Ofcom, she worked as a consultant for NERA Economic Consulting where she worked on numerous telecoms projects covering competition, tariff, and public/social policy issues. In addition, she has worked in the UK telecommunications industry as an economist at Mercury Communications, now called Cable & Wireless Communications. Some of the projects she worked on there include the 1997 Retail and Network Price Cap, the Labour Party proposals for Regulation, Mobile Interconnection, Fixed/Mobile Convergence, Number Portability and Numbering where she was the Chair of the Industry Steering Group for the Year 2000 Numbering Change Implementation.

Alan Cunningham, previously Herchel Smith Research Fellow, Queen Mary, University of London, completed his PhD in 2007. Currently living in Berlin, researching for work regarding how rationality (including legal thought), in ignoring context and disregarding personal/emotional/holistic involvement, separates, isolates, and individualizes, with negative effect. Email: cunningham.am@gmail.com.

Anne Flanagan, BA (St John's, New York), JD (Brooklyn Law School, New York), LLM (Lond), is Senior Lecturer of Communications Law, Queen Mary, University of London, Centre for Commercial Law Studies. Anne lectures on the QMUL LLM courses in Information Law and Communications Law. She also teaches distance learning LLM courses in Privacy and Data Protection Law, International Telecommunications Law, European Communications Law, and Information and Communications Technology and Competition Law. She is the author and chief

examiner of the University of London External LLM Telecommunications course. Anne has been involved in law reform projects for the European Commission and the European Bank for Reconstruction and Development. She was Visiting Professor at the Institute of Comparative Law 'Angelo Sraffa', Bocconi University of Milan and visiting scholar at Brooklyn Law School.

Anne is a New York State licensed attorney. She has practised law in the financial services industry at Wilson, Elser, Moskowitz, Edelman and Dicker, and at TIAA-CREF, one of the largest financial services companies in the United States where she served as counsel to the IT divisions. She also served as Director, State Government Relations for the National Association of Insurance Brokers.

Nicholas Higham works independently as a solicitor and consultant based in a small village in Gloucestershire sustained by broadband and the Internet. Nicholas' practice focuses on telecommunications, IT, the Internet, and digital media and includes regulatory and licensing projects in the telecommunications sector, where he acts for governments, regulatory authorities, and leading professional firms. Nicholas also represents small and medium-sized enterprises on commercial matters in his sectors. He has advised regulators in more than 40 countries, from Western Europe through the Middle East and Africa to the Far East. Nicholas has been a Director of PhonepayPlus and of the Independent Mobile Contents Board, regulating content over mobile networks. He is a co-author of a textbook on Digital Media and a Senior Visiting Research Fellow at the Centre for Studies in Commercial Law at Queen Mary, University of London where he lectures on broadcasting law.

Helen Kemmitt is a solicitor in England. She has worked both in-house and in private practice and has been advising clients in the telecommunications sector for more than 15 years. Between 1992 and 1996 she was a legal adviser for Kingston Communications. She joined Baker & McKenzie in 2000 where she is currently a Senior Associate in the IT/Communications Group focusing on telecommunications regulation and compliance. She is co-author of the UK Telecoms and EU Privacy Chapters of Telecommunications Law in Europe (5th edn). Email: helen.kemmitt@bakernet.com.

Gary Lea is an Associate of Buchanan Law, Canberra, Australia, a commercial law firm with a focus on intellectual property, information technology, and telecommunications. Gary is currently working on software acquisition and services development for the firm, dealing daily with a variety of technical standards issues. Previously, he was a Senior Lecturer in Law at UNSW@ADFA, Canberra (2004–2007) and, before that, a Research Fellow and Lecturer at Queen Mary, University of London (1997–2004). Gary's interests in legal aspects of technical standards development and deployment is long-standing (he wrote his first piece on the subject way back in the mid 1990s), especially in the context of the intersection between intellectual property and competition/antitrust law.

Karen Lee is a lecturer at the School of Law of the University of New England (Australia) and a PhD candidate at the University of New South Wales. Her thesis involves an in-depth study of self-regulatory rule making in the Australian telecommunications sector. Prior to joining the law faculty at UNE, she worked for Denton Wilde Sapte (London) in its technology, media, and telecommunications department, where she specialized in telecommunications regulation (1996–2003). She was seconded to the Office of Telecommunications in 1998 and to the Department of Trade and Industry in 2002, where she was a member of the team responsible for the Communications Act 2003. She was the Senior Managing Editor of the *Federal Communications Law Journal* from 1995 to 1996. She is a qualified lawyer in New South Wales, Illinois, and England and Wales and is a member of the Australian Communications and Media Authority's specialist expert resource list in the areas of rural and remote issues. Email: karen.lee@une.edu.au.

Graeme Maguire is a partner within Bird & Bird's international Communications Group. He holds an MA in Law from the University of Cambridge and a diploma in IP Law & Practice from Bristol University. His practice covers commercial and regulatory communications and technology work and has a strong international flavour. He regularly advises on complex outsourcing projects and also has particular experience in satellites, e-commerce, data protection, and privacy. He has spoken and written widely on related topics. Recent publications include the 'Communications and Broadcasting Regulation' chapter of the 4th edition of Graham Smith's *Internet Law and Regulation* (2007). Graeme has spent time on secondment in a competition policy role at Oftel (now Ofcom) and British Telecommunications and prior to joining Bird & Bird in 2005 was a partner in Linklaters TMT group. Email: graeme. maguire@twobirds.com.

Christopher Millard (LLB, MA, LLM) is Professor of Privacy and Information Law at the Centre for Commercial Law Studies, Queen Mary, University of London and is a Senior Research Fellow of the Oxford Internet Institute at the University of Oxford. He is also Of Counsel to Bristows where he is a consultant to the information technology, privacy, and data protection teams. He has 25 years experience in the technology and communications law fields and has led many multi-jurisdictional information governance and data protection compliance projects. He is the author of many articles and book chapters on privacy, technology, and communications law, is a General Editor of the *International Journal of Law and Information Technology* (Oxford University Press), and is a founding editor of Data Protection Laws of the World. He was a member of the OECD's Steering Group on Contractual Solutions for Transborder Data Flows (2000–2001) and since 2002 he has been a member of the International Chamber of Commerce's Task Force on Privacy and Protection of Personal Data. Before he joined Bristows in 2008, Christopher was a partner at Linklaters for six years and head of that firm's global privacy practice. Prior to that he was at Clifford Chance for 18 years, including 10 years as a partner. In 2008, the

International Who's Who of Business Lawyers designated him Internet & eCommerce Lawyer of the Year. Email: c.millard@qmul.ac.uk.

Robin Morton-Fincham is a Senior Legal Advisor within the Legal Team at Visa Europe, advising on competition law. Prior to joining Visa Europe in 2008, Robin was a Managing Associate in the Competition Team at Addleshaw Goddard where he advised extensively on a broad range of competition law matters, including both domestic UK and EU behavioural Article 81 and 82 EC Treaty cases, as well as national, EU, and multinational merger control cases. Robin has particular experience in advising on competition and regulatory related issues within the telecommunications sector, having also been seconded to Openreach (a BT group business) shortly after its creation in 2006. Robin trained at Slaughter and May before joining Theodore Goddard.

Edward Pitt is a partner in the Competition Trade and Regulation Group at Addleshaw Goddard. He has spent more than 25 years in private practice in London and Brussels. Edward joined the firm in 1998 from the Office of Telecommunications (Oftel), where he was Senior Legal Adviser. In that role he was particularly involved with enforcement of telecoms regulation and the control of anti-competitive practices by telecoms operators; he also advised on reform to the UK telecoms regulatory regime. He then spent a period with the UK Department of Trade and Industry, advising on competition policy and on the then UK Competition Bill. In addition to telecommunications, Edward's experience lies primarily in the sphere of EC and UK competition and international trade law, and corporate commercial law.

He has acted for multinational clients before the EU Commission, both in competition investigations and in joint venture and merger clearances. He has also handled cases before the UK Competition Commission and the Office of Fair Trading. Edward is an occasional guest lecturer at both commercial conferences and on university courses. Email: edward.pitt@addleshawgoddard.com.

Jamison Prime is an attorney with the US Federal Communications Commission in Washington, DC. As chief of the Spectrum Policy Branch of the Office of Engineering and Technology, he works primarily on rule-making proceedings that pertain to spectrum allocation and use. Previously, he worked in the agency's Wireless Telecommunications Bureau on matters ranging from the review of transfer and assignment applications in major merger cases to inter-agency coordination of antenna tower regulations. A 1996 graduate of the Indiana University School of Law, he served as managing editor on and was published in the *Federal Communications Law Journal*. He has been an active member of the Federal Communications Bar Association, where he has served on the law journal and nominations committees. He received a BA in History from DePauw University in 1993. Mr Prime's contribution was prepared independently from his employment and should not be read as an official statement of FCC policy. Email: primej@gmail.com.

David Satola is Senior Counsel in the World Bank Legal Department where he has global responsibility for legal aspects of reforms in information and communications technologies, including telecommunications, the Internet, and e-Commerce. His work focuses on advising governments on legal aspects of the enabling environment for ICT infrastructure and services, telecommunications licensing, and new market entry, Internet governance, new technologies, competition regulation involving ICTs, Critical Infrastructure/Network Security, and Alternative Dispute Resolution. His project work at the Bank spans more than 80 countries across all the Bank's regions. Prior to joining the Bank in 1997, Mr Satola was in-house counsel for a major global telecommunications company responsible for its investments in Asia, Europe, and Latin America, and was in private legal practice in both North America and Europe advising on telecommunications joint ventures and mobile licensing. He has published articles, chapters, and books on legal aspects of ICT reforms.

Tim Schwarz is a partner and the Global Head of Telecoms, Media, Technology, and Intellectual Property at Linklaters. Tim advises telecoms operators, equipment manufacturers, investment banks, private equity houses, governments, and regulators on a wide range of global telecoms projects. Between 1995 and 1997, Tim served as the main telecoms lawyer at the World Bank in Washington DC, working on telecoms projects throughout the emerging markets. Since then he has continued to work on emerging markets telecoms projects and has particular experience in the Middle East, North Africa, sub-Saharan Africa, Central and Eastern Europe, and Asia. Tim studied English law at Oxford University and European Union law at the University of Brussels.

Andrew Sharpe is a Partner in the Competition and Regulatory Group at Charles Russell LLP. Andrew practises information technology, intellectual property, and telecommunications law. He regularly lectures on regulatory and commercial aspects of telecommunications, as well as on information technology, data protection, and freedom of information issues. In addition to extensive European Union experience, Andrew has advised on telecommunications issues in Africa, the Caribbean, and the Middle East. Prior to qualifying as a solicitor, Andrew was a Royal Air Force engineering officer. He was a communications-electronics specialist, responsible for the maintenance of airfield radio, radar, telecommunications, and information technology systems. Andrew has both a BSc in Electronic Engineering and an LLB (First Class) from Southampton University. Andrew qualified in 1999 and prior to joining Charles Russell in 2002 was a telecommunications regulatory lawyer at Clifford Chance. He was made a partner in 2007. Email: andrew.sharpe@charlesrussell.co.uk.

Michael Sinclair is a partner and London head of the Information, Communications, and Technology Group at Simmons & Simmons. He advises on global communications services outsourcings with suppliers such as BT, AT&T, Orange Business

Services, and Verizon Business. He has a PhD in Law (Gonville & Caius College, Cambridge) and is co-author of several texts on outsourcing.

Mark Williams is a Senior Economist in the Global ICT group of the World Bank in Washington DC where he specializes in the reform and regulation of telecommunications networks. At the World Bank, he has been closely involved in the design and implementation of open-access regimes for telecommunications infrastructure in developing countries, particularly in Africa and the Middle East. Prior to joining the World Bank, Mark was a professional economist at Frontier Economics Ltd in London. In this role, he advised governments, regulators, and private companies around the world on the economics and regulation of the telecommunications and postal industries. He regularly publishes articles in journals and contributes to books on the subject.

Rhys Williams is a partner within Bird & Bird's International Communications Group. He holds an MA in Law from the University of Cambridge and he has also studied at the University of Manchester and the University of North Carolina, Chapel Hill. He has specialized for over 14 years in providing commercial and regulatory advice to clients in the communications and technology sectors, both in the UK and internationally, ranging from entrepreneurial start-ups to major multinational corporations. He regularly advises on complex outsourcing projects and also has particular experience in e-commerce, data protection, and privacy. He has advised a number of clients on the implementation and roll-out of innovative new technologies, including mobile micro-payment systems, WiFi solutions, and VoIP services. Rhys has twice spent time on secondment to clients. Email: rhys.williams@twobirds.com.

Table of Cases

Tables of Legislation

EUROPEAN LEGISLATION

Regulations

INTERNATIONAL TREATIES, CONVENTIONS AND AGREEMENTS

Abbreviations

21CN	21st Century Network
3G3P	Patent Platform Partnership
ABA	Australian Broadcasting Authority
ACA	Australian Communications Authority
ACCC	Australian Competition and Consumer Commission
ACMA	Australia Communications and Media Authority
ADB	Asian Development Bank
ADC	Access Deficit Charge (Chapter 3)
ADCs	access deficit contributions
ADR	alternative dispute resolution mechanism
ADSL	asymmetrical digital subscriber line
AfDB	African Development Bank
AI	alternative interface
AIP	Administrative Incentive Pricing
ANSI	American National Standards Institute
APEC	Asia-Pacific Economic Co-operation Forum
API	application programme interface
ARPA	Advance Research Projects Agency
ARPANET	US Department of Defense Advanced Research Projects Agency Network
ARPU	average revenue per user
ASA	Advertising Standards Authority
ASP	application service provision
ATIS	Alliance for Telecommunications Industry Solutions
ATM	asynchronous transfer mode
ATVOD	Association for TV on Demand
AUC	authentication centre
AWS	advanced wireless services
B2B	business-to-business
B2C	business-to-consumer
BABT	British Approvals Board for Telecommunications
Basbof	Broadcast Advertising Standards Board of Finance
BBC FtV	BBC Free to View Limited
BBFC	British Board of Film Classification
BBS	Bulletin Board Service
BCC	Broadcasting Complaints Commission

BCR	binding corporate rules
BIT	bilateral investment treaty
BNSC	British National Space Centre
BOO	build-operate-own
BOT	build-operate-transfer
BPO	business process outsourcing
BRAN	Broadband Radio Access Networks
BRAS	broadband remote access server
BS	base station
BSC	Broadcasting Standards Council
BSI	British Standards Institute
BTO	build-transfer-operate
BTS	Base Transceiver Station
C4C	Channel 4 Corporation
CALEA	Communications Assistance for Law Enforcement Act of 1994
CAP	Committee of Advertising Practice
CAT	Competition Appeals Tribunal
CATV	community antenna television
CC	Competition Commission
CCIR	Comité Consultatif International des Radiocommunications
CCITT	Comité Consultatif International Télégraphique et Téléphonique (Cumulative Committee on International Telephone and Telegraph)
CDB	common database
CDMA	Code Division Multiple Access
CDPA 1998	Copyright, Design and Patents Act 1998
CEI	comparably efficient interconnection
CEPT	Conférence Européene des Administrations des Postes et des Télécommunications (Conference on Postal and Telecommunications Administrations)
CID	Civil Investigative Demand
CIDA	Canadian International Development Agency
CLEC	competitive local exchange carrier
CLI	call line identifier
CMRS	commercial mobile radio service
Cocom	Communications Committee
Comsat	Communications Satellite Corporation
CPA	Coalition Provisional Authority
CPNI	customer proprietary network information
CPNP	calling party network pays
CPP	calling party pays
CPS	carrier pre-selection
CSI	customer sited interconnection

DANIDA	Danish International Development Agency
DAS	directory assistance system
DBS	Direct Broadcast Satellite
DCMS	Department for Culture, Media and Sport
DDI	direct dialling inward
DfID	UK Department for International Development
DG	Directorate General of the European Commission
DGT	Director General of Telecommunications
DID	direct inward dialling
DLE	digital local exchange
DMCA 1998	Digital Millennium Copyright Act 1998
DMT	discrete multi-tone
DoJ	Department of Justice
DPA 1998	Data Protection Act 1998
DQ	Directory Enquiries
DRM	Digital Rights Management
DSB	Dispute Settlement Body
DSL	digital subscriber line
DSLAM	digital subscriber line access multiplexer
DTI	Department of Trade and Industry
DWDM	dense wavelength division multiplexing
EAB	Equality of Access Board
EBRD	European Bank of Reconstruction and Development
ECMR	European Community Merger Regulation
ECN	electronic communications network
ECO	effective competitive opportunities
ECPR	Efficient Component Pricing
ECS	Electronic Communications Services
EDGE	Enhanced Data Rates for GSM Evolution
EDI	Electronic Data Interchange
EECMA	European Electronic Communications Market Authority
EGO	external gateway operator
EIB	European Investment Bank
ENISA	European Network and Information Security Agency
EOI	Equivalence of Input
EPC	European Patent Convention
EPG	electronic programme guide
EPO	European Patent Office
ERG	European Regulators Group
ESA	Endangered Species Act
ESO	emergency services organizations
ETNO	European Telecommunications Network Operators Association
ETNS	European Telephony Numbering Space

ETSI	European Telecommunications Standards Institute
FBI	Federal Bureau of Investigations
FCC	Federal Communications Commission
FDMA	frequency division multiple access
FISA	Foreign Intelligence Surveillance Act
FPS	fax preference service
FRIACO	Flat Rate Internet Access Call Origination
FTC	Federal Trade Commission
FTTC	fibre to the corner
FTTH	fibre to the home
FWS	US Fish and Wildlife Service
GATS	General Agreement on Trade in Services
GCC	General Consumer Code of Practice
GEO	geostationary system
GMSK	Gaussian minimum-shift keying
GPD	general permitted development
GPO	General Post Office
GPRS	General Packet Radio Service
GSM	Global system for mobile communications
HDTV	high-definition television
HIPAA	Health Insurance Portability and Accountability Act of 1996
HIPERMAN	High Performance Radio Metropolitan Area Network
HLR	Home Location Register
HSDPA	High Speed Downlink Packet Access
HTTP	hyper text transfer protocol
IA	indirect access
IADB	Inter-American Development Bank
IBRD	International Bank for Reconstruction and Development
ICANN	Internet Corporation for Assigned Names and Numbers
ICE	Institution of Civil Engineers
ICRA	Internet Contents Rating Association
ICRT	International Communications Round Table
ICSID	International Centre for the Settlement of Investment Disputes
ICSTIS	Independent Committee for Standards in Telephone Information Services
IDA	International Development Association
IDD	international direct dialing
IEC	International Electrotechnical Commission
IETF	Internet Engineering Task Force
IFC	International Finance Corporation
IFI	international financial institution
IGF	Internet Governance Forum
IGU	International Geographical Union

ILEC	incumbent local exchange carrier
IMCB	Independent Mobile Classification Body
IMEI	international mobile equipment identifier
IMT-2000	international mobile telecommunication in the year 2000
*info*DEV	Information for Development Grant programme
Inmarsat	International Mobile Satellite Organization
Intelsat	International Telecommunications Satellite Organization
IP	intellectual property (Chapter 10)
IP	Internet Protocol (Chapters 1, 2, 12)
IP/MPLS	Internet Protocol/MultiPrococol Label Switching
IPLC	International Private Leased Circuit
IPOs	initial public offerings
IPRs	intellectual property rights
IRU	indefeasible rights of use
IS	information systems
ISDN	Integrated Services Digital Networks
ISI	in-span interconnection
ISO	International Organization for Standards
ISOC	Internet Society
ISP	Internet Service Provider
ISPA	Internet Service Providers' Association
IT	information technology
ITC	Independent Television Commission
ITFS	instructional television fixed service
ITT	invitation to tender
ITTOIA	Income Tax (Trading and Other Income) Act 2005
ITU	International Telecommunications Union
IWF	Internet Watch Foundation
IXP	Internet exchange point
KPI	key performance indicator
LAN	local area networks
LEO	low earth orbit
LINX	London Internet Exchange
LLU	local loop unbundling
LRAIC	long-run average incremental costs
LRIC	long-run incremental cost
LUS	Light User Scheme
MCMC	Malaysian Communication Multimedia Commission
MDF	main distribution frame
MDG	Millennium Development Goal
MEO	medium earth orbit
MFJ	Modification of Final Judgment
MFN	Most-Favoured-Nation Treatment

MI	market influence
MIGA	Multilateral Investment Guarantee Agency
MMC	Monopolies and Mergers Commission
MNO	mobile network operator
MPLS	multi-protocol label switching
MPP	mobile party pays
MSAN	multi-service access node
MSC	mobile switching centres
MVNO	mobile virtual network operator
MVPD	multichannel video programming distributor
NARUC	National Association of Regulatory Utility Commissioners
NCC	Network Charge Controls
NEPA	National Environmental Policy Act
NGN	next generation network
NHPA	National Historic Preservation Act
NRA	national regulatory authority
NRF	New Regulatory Framework
NSFNet	US National Science Foundation Network
NTC	National Telephone Company
NTIA	National Telecommunications and Information Administration
OECD	Organisation for Economic Cooperation and Development
OECS	Organization of Eastern Caribbean States
Ofcom	Office of Communications
OFT	Office of Fair Trading
Oftel	Office of Telecommunications
ONA	Open Network Access
ONP	Open Network Provision
ORBIT	Open-Market Reorganization for the Betterment of International Telecommunications Act
OSA	Outer Space Act 1986
OSIS	operator services information system
OSS	operations support systems
PABX	private automatic branch exchange
PATS	publicly available telecommunications services
PBX	Private Branch Exchange
PCB	public call box
PCN	personal communication network
PCS	personal communication system
PDH	plesiosynchronous digital hierarchy
PECN	public electronic communications networks
PECS	public electronic communications services
PFI	private finance initiative
PIDA 1998	Public Interest Disclosure Act 1998

PMG	Postmaster General
PNR	Passenger Name Record
PPC	partial private circuits
PPP	public–private partnership
PRS	premium rate service
PSB	public service broadcasting
PSP	Public Service Publisher
PSTN	public switched telecommunications network
PTO	public telecommunications operator
PTT	post, telegraph, and telephone
PUC	Public Utility Commission
PVR	personal video recorder
QAM	quadrature amplitude modulator
QoS	Quality of Service
RACC	Radio Advertising Clearance Centre
RAND	reasonable and non-discriminatory
RANs	radio access networks
RAO	Recognized Operating Agency
RBOCs	Regional Bell Operating Companies
RBS	radio base station
RCS	relevant connectable system
RCU	remote concentrator unit
RFP	request for proposal
RIO	reference interconnection offer
RIPA 2000	Regulation of Investigatory Powers Act 2000
ROA	Regulatory Option Appraisal
RPI	Retail Price Index
RPM	Resale Price Maintenance
RPP	receiving party pays
RRs	Radio Regulations
RSA	recognized spectrum access
SDH	synchronous digital hierarchy
SDO	standard development organization
SGA 1979	Sale of Goods Act 1979
SGSA 1982	Supply of Goods and Services Act 1982
SIDA	Swedish International Development Agency
SIM	subscriber identification module
SLA	service level agreement
SLC	significant lessening of competition
SME	small and medium-sized enterprises
SMP	significant market power
SMR	Specialized Mobile Radio
SNO	second national operator

SONET	synchronous optical network
SPL	self-provision licence
SSNIP Test	small but significant non-transitory increase in price
STM	synchronous transport module
TBT	technical barriers to trade
TC 97	Technical Committee 97
TCAM	Telecommunication Conformity Assessment and Market Surveillance Committee
TCPA	Telephone Consumer Protection Act of 1991
TCP/IP	Transmission Control Protocol/Internet Protocol
TD-CDMA	time-division CDMA
TDM	time-division multiplexing
TDMA	time-division multiple access
TI	traditional interface
TPS	telecommunications preference service
TRIPs	Trade Related Aspects of Intellectual Property Rights
TSL	telecommunications services licence
TTBE	Technology Transfer Block Exemption
TTTA	Trinidad and Tobago Telecommunications Authority
TUPE 1981	Transfer of Undertakings (Protection of Employment) Regulations 1981
TWF	Television Without Frontiers
TX	tandem exchange
UCTA 1977	Unfair Contract Terms Act 1977
UKCPC	UK Cable Protection Committee
UMTS	Universal Mobile Telecommunications System
UNCITRAL	United Nations Commission on International Trade Law
UNCLOS	United Nations Convention on the Law of the Sea 1982
UNE	unbundled network element
UNESCO	United Nations Educational, Scientific and Cultural Organization
USAC	Universal Service Administrative Company
USAID	US Agency for International Development
USO	universal service obligation
USPTO	United States Patent and Trademark Office
UTP	unshielded twisted pair cables
VABE	Vertical Agreements Block Exemption
VAN	Value Added Network Service
VoIP	voice over Internet protocol
VPN	virtual private network
VSAT	very small aperture terminal
WAN	wide area network
WAP	wireless application protocol

WCDMA	wideband code division multiple access
WDM	wavelength division multiplexing
WiBro	Wireless Broadband
Wi-Fi	wireless fidelity
WiMax	worldwide interoperability for microwave access
WIPO	World Intellectual Property Organization
WirelessMAN	wireless metropolitan area network
WISP	Wireless (LAN) Internet Service Provider
WLANs	Wireless Local Area Networks—often known as 'WiFi'
WLR	wholesale line rental
WRC	World Radiocommunications Conference
WSIS	World Summit on the Information Society
WTO	World Trade Organization
WTSA	World Telecommunication Standardization Assembly

Glossary

3G	generic term for third generation mobile telephone networks
ADSL	Asynchronous Digital Subscriber Line—broadband access using existing copper telephone wiring to the house
analogue	where the signal being transmitted is an 'analogue' of the information—for example, an analogue signal carrying voice would have the voltage waveform following the air pressure waveform of the speech
codec coder/ decoder	used to code and decode signals (including voice and video)
DHCP	Dynamic Host Configuration Protocol—a protocol for dynamically assigning IP addresses and other attributes to computers on an IP network
digital	where the signal being transmitted is transformed into a series of discrete values (usually 1s and 0s)
DNS	Domain Name Service—translation of domain names to IP addresses
DSL	Digital Subscriber Line—digital connection over telephone connection to the home
DSLAM	DSL Access Multiplexer—terminates an ADSL line in the network exchange, a switch in a telephone network that is used to route calls (UK terminology); local exchange is at entry to the network; trunk exchange provides transit in the core network
GPRS	General Packet Radio Service—packet data connection on GSM networks
GSM	Global System for Mobile communications—second generation cellular mobile communications system
HTML	HyperText Mark-up Language—computer language used to generate web pages
IEE802.11	standard for WLAN technology
IMAP	Internet Message Access Protocol—a protocol for listing and retrieving email messages; more complex functions supported than in POP
ISDN	Integrated Subscriber Digital Network (legacy)—narrowband digital access to the home over a standard telephone line
modem	modulator/demodulator—used to convert signals into a form suitable for transmitting across a network (e.g. from a computer across the telephone network)

MSC	Mobile Switching Centre—an exchange in a GSM network
PBX	Private Branch Exchange—telephone exchange on customer's premises
POI	Point of Interconnection between two operators
PoP	Point of Presence—point to which a user connects
POP	Post Office Protocol—a protocol used to download email from a mail server
POTS	Plain Old Telephone System
QoS	Quality of Service—specific measures for determining the performance of a network connection
RTP	Real-time Transport Protocol—a protocol for transmitting real-time services (like voice) over IP networks
SMTP	Simple Mail Transfer Protocol—a protocol for sending email messages
TCP	Transmission Control Protocol—a protocol that runs over IP to allow connection-oriented exchange of information
UDP	User Datagram Protocol—a protocol that runs over IP and provides connectionless services
VoIP	Voice-over IP—a technique for transmitting voice signals over IP networks
WAP	Wireless Application Protocol—a standard for information services on wireless terminals like digital mobile phones
WiFi	*see* WLAN
WLAN	Wireless Local Area Network—commonly IEE802.11b
WML	Wireless Mark-up Language—the language used to create pages to be displayed in a WAP browser
xDSL	generic form of DSL
XML	eXtensible Mark-up Language—XML was designed to describe data and to focus on what data is rather than to display it (as HTML does)

Part I

THE FUNDAMENTALS

1

TELECOMMUNICATIONS LAW AND REGULATION: AN INTRODUCTION

Ian Walden

1.1 THE SUBJECT MATTER

This third edition of the book continues to be entitled 'telecommunications' rather than 'communications', despite the best attempts of the European Commission to recast the terminology to reflect the fact that the legal and regulatory framework embraces all forms of infrastructure, services, and equipment supplied for the transmission of data and information, whether traditionally viewed as broadcasting or voice telephony. Telecommunications remains the preferred term for a number of reasons. First, the

change of regulatory terminology is still not reflected in industry discourse, let alone among the wider general public. Second, the book is intended as a text for a global audience, not just the UK or Europe, so it does not seem appropriate for EU terminology to be imposed on our readers. Third, the many historical and cross-jurisdictional aspects of the book recommend consistency as an aid to comprehension. The book does, however, use the terms 'telecommunications' and 'communications' interchangeably.

1.2 THE TELECOMMUNICATIONS SECTOR

The World Trade Organization's (WTO) 'Basic Agreement on Telecommunications', in 1997, can be seen as a defining moment in the international community's commitment to the structural evolution of the sector from a primarily monopolistic environment to a competitive marketplace. Such acceptance has been driven by a recognition that telecommunications is a strategic economic sector, in terms of it being both a tradable service in its own right as well as the infrastructure over which other goods and services are traded and, in an age of electronic commerce, delivered. There is no doubting the continuing dynamic nature of the telecommunications sector within the global economy, despite the massive downturn experienced by the sector following the bursting of the 'dotcom' bubble. By 2000, world stock markets rose and fell in large part based on perceptions of the health and wealth of the telecommunications sector. Indeed such was the dependency that financial regulators expressed concern over the exposure of the banking system to the fortunes of telecommunications companies.[1] Since then, the market has seen large-scale bankruptcies, such as Global Crossing, the exposure of fraudulent trading practices, such as WorldCom, and massive sectoral restructuring. While the 1990s saw a proliferation of new market entrants, the first few years of the 21st century saw many of these disappear without trace or become collections of devalued assets awaiting a bargain-hunter.

However, over the past four years the sector has begun to expand again, as the global economy has recovered, and the strategic role of the telecommunications sector has once again come to the fore although the recent downturn may again reverse this trend.

While the financial environment for the telecommunications industry fluctuates, the rapid developments in technology that underpin the sector and the consequent introduction of new products and services into the market has continued at the same frantic pace. As in any area of law, telecommunications involves use of a particular set of terminology with which a practitioner or student needs to become familiar. Such terminology relates, in large part, to the technology being used, the structure of the industry, and the products and services being supplied. These issues are examined in the next section and in detail in Chapter 2.

---

[1] See Financial Services Authority Press Release, 'Telecoms lending—firms must remain vigilant', FSA/PN/153/2000, 7 December 2000.

1.3 TECHNOLOGY AND TERMINOLOGY[2]

Only a few years ago, the scope of telecommunications technology would have been easy to define: telephony, fax, and mobile. However, now there is a rapidly changing technological environment, which means even systems that we use every day, like the telephone, are now regarded as being 'legacy' technology (see Chapter 2). The current drivers for change are simple: the ever increasing use of the mobile and the Internet. In many countries we already see 'fixed-mobile substitution', where users prefer to use their mobile telephone to make a call, even though they have a landline available; while in developing countries, mobile is by far the most dominant technology. Voice over the Internet has also meant that it is technically possible to make very cheap telephone calls from anywhere in the world by connecting over the Internet to a service provider in the destination country, who then routes the telephone call locally. Going even further, instant messaging systems (like Microsoft's MSN Messenger) provide the capability of making voice and video calls directly between PCs free of charge.

However, while these services and capabilities are evolving rapidly, a lot of the underlying technologies are common. In all systems there are fundamental categories of equipment that the telecommunications network, of whatever type, must use. These are:

- transmission systems;
- switching or routing equipment;
- terminal equipment;
- network management systems; and
- billing systems.

In addition, it is often useful to distinguish between the 'access network' (the connection from the customer to the network) and the 'core network' (connections between network elements).

Transmission systems transfer information from one location to another, with as low probability of error as possible, over wireline (i.e. physical) or wireless (i.e. radio) links. Nowadays most transmission systems in the core network use optical fibres, although some legacy systems using copper cables still exist. Fixed point-to-point radio links are also used where the terrain is difficult or where the network node (particularly a base station in mobile networks) is isolated.

At the level of the 'access network' there is a wide variety of different transmission systems. One of the challenges in getting broadband services to residential customers is the cost of replacing the old 'twisted metallic pair' telephone cables, and much

---

[2] Professor Laurie Cuthbert, Head of the Department of Electronic Engineering at Queen Mary, University of London, drafted this section.

effort has been spent in improving the technology to allow higher bit rates over these copper cables, since the cost of replacing them is prohibitive. ISDN was the first solution, but now this is regarded as obsolete and ADSL (Asynchronous Digital Subscriber Line) allows broadband to be offered to residential customers over their existing telephone lines, at least to those who are close enough to the telephone exchange. Other fixed access transmission systems use coaxial cables (cable TV and cable modems), optical fibres (generally to business customers), or point-to-point radio links.

In mobile networks, the access network is the link between the mobile handset and the network base station (or BTS—Base Transceiver Station—as it is called in GSM (Global system for mobile communications) networks). The type of network (GSM, CDMA (Code Division Multiple Access), 3G) defines the type of transmission used over the radio link. Another radio access method that is becoming very common is that for WLANs (Wireless Local Area Networks), often known as 'WiFi'. The common standard for this is IEEE 802.11b but the newer version IEEE 802.11g provides about five times as much capacity over the same radio link. Almost all laptop computers now being produced include built-in 802.11g wireless access. Within organizations the predominant access technique for computer communications is 'Ethernet' using Unshielded Twisted Pair (UTP) cables, although WLANs are increasingly being implemented now that the security of such systems is being improved.

While transmission systems get information from A to B, users want to be able to connect to different people, or to different websites—this means that connections have to be 'switched' or 'routed' to the right destination. With telephone networks this was done using switches (called 'exchanges' in the UK) but with Internet-type networks (IP networks) the devices performing that function are called routers. The reason for this difference is that telephone networks are traditionally 'circuit-switched', whereas IP networks are 'packet-switched'. Circuit-switched means that a connection is set up for the whole duration of a telephone call; in packet switching, information is broken into units called 'packets' that are independently routed across the network. The important differences between the two techniques are that:

- circuit-switched networks need to have a method of setting up a connection from A to B before any information is sent, and packet networks do not;
- the routing decision for every packet increases the flexibility and reliability of the network as packets can even be re-routed *during* a call, but does increase the overhead;
- the delay in a circuit-switched network is fixed, but in packet networks the nature of the packet routing means that delays between packets can be very variable;
- it is much harder to guarantee 'Quality of Service' (QoS) over packet networks.

Overall this means that packet-switched networks are generally better suited for data connections and circuit-switched networks for voice (which is particularly sensitive

to delay and variations in delay). However, the predominance of packet-based IP (Internet Protocol) for computer communications has led to a major change in how networks are structured, with telephony networks moving to using IP rather than circuit switching. Indeed 3G mobile networks will eventually use IP for all traffic within the network. This change has been enabled as a result of several years of intense research effort to get good quality voice communications with IP. The difference between routers and switches is in fact much more complex (and confusing) than the simple explanation above. IP traffic often passes through equipment called 'switches' in the local area network—and these have a different function.

To complicate matters even further, new architectures for IP networks introduce the concept of 'switched routers'; the new architecture that is most likely to succeed is MPLS (multi-protocol label switching).

In the business world, the local telephone system (PBX—Private Branch Exchange) has evolved from being a traditional telephony switch to a fully IP system with IP phones, or even with 'soft phones' on the workstation. Of course, no network would work if the user did not have any equipment to use with it and it is often the capabilities of the terminal equipment that attracts users rather than that of the underlying network. For instance, in GSM networks the codecs (the devices that convert speech to digital signals and back again) were improved some years ago to make the speech sound more like that on a landline; however, almost no users would have upgraded their mobile handset for that reason.

An important aspect of any communications network is its reliability and availability, particularly when congestion occurs. Ensuring this is a function of network management systems, i.e. complex software programs that control the operation and performance of the various network elements; this is true of all types of network, whether telephony, mobile, or Internet.

Also of crucial importance is the billing system—no network operator could survive in business without one! Modern telephony billing systems are very complicated, recording the details of every transmission and applying a wide range of tariffs based on the type of network user (e.g. retail or wholesale customer or interconnecting operator) and type of communication services (e.g. text messaging and voice calls). The Internet has utilized very different tariff structures from traditional telephone networks, such as flat rate rather than minute-based tariffs, which has enabled the implementation of much simpler (and cheaper) billing systems. However, there are now signs that volume-based charging (where the user pays for the overall amount of data transferred) are starting to appear for Internet use, so billing systems to capture that information are becoming increasingly important.

1.4 TELECOMMUNICATIONS LAW AND REGULATION

This book is primarily concerned with the rules and regulations governing the provision of telecommunications equipment, network infrastructure, and services

(e.g. the carriage of voice and data traffic), rather than the law governing the content of the traffic being sent across telecommunication networks. The latter is generally perceived as the domain of 'media law'[3] or 'Internet law' rather than 'telecommunications law'. However, one recurring issue in telecommunications law is the problem of distinguishing clearly between issues of carriage and issues of content, particularly with the emergence of new services such as Internet telephony. In this edition, therefore, a specific section addresses content issues, in respect of personal data (Chapter 13), as well as broadcasting and related regulatory regimes for content (Chapter 14). Even the categorization of carriage as a service is evolving, with the development of commodity markets for trading carriage in terms of telecommunication minutes.[4] Such economic recategorization may have profound implications for policy makers and regulators.

The various aspects of telecommunications law addressed in this book can be broadly distinguished into competition issues and non-competition public policy issues. Competition law is primarily concerned with establishing and ensuring the sustainability of competitive markets, at a national, regional, and global level. Telecommunications as a sector capable of establishing a comparative advantage in international trade was recognized by the UK government at the outset of liberalization, in the early 1980s. In the Telecommunications Act 1984, for example, four of the ten general duties imposed upon the regulator addressed trade-related aspects of telecommunications, from encouraging the provision of transit services, traffic being routed through the UK, to the supply of telecommunications apparatus (s 3(2)). For developing countries, the prospect of becoming a regional hub in the emerging information economy is promoted as an opportunity arising from market liberalization.

Non-competition public policy issues have historically focused on the provision of telecommunication services to the population as a whole: the issue of universal service. Current concerns about the growth of a 'digital divide' between the information rich and poor is the latest manifestation of such political imperatives. However, other non-competition issues include consumer protection, environmental concerns, health and safety matters, as well as the protection of personal privacy.

It is inevitable that the seismic shifts in the structure of the telecommunication sector are reflected in a complex and rapidly changing legal framework. The liberalization of the sector has usually required significant legal intervention, the classic exemption to the rule being New Zealand, which initially simply opened up the sector to competition without the imposition of a regulatory framework, but has subsequently had to establish a regulatory authority.[5] In parallel with the pursuance of liberalization, the telecommunications sector has experienced rapid and dramatic developments in

---

[3] Walden, I, *Media Law and Practice* (Forthcoming 2009).

[4] e.g. RouteTrader <http://www.routetrader.com>.

[5] All restrictions on the supply of services were removed in 1989. However, by 2001, a Telecommunications Commissioner was appointed within the Commerce Commission, with substantial further enforcement powers being granted to the Commissioner in 2006.

the technology, which has compounded the problems faced by policy makers, legislators, and regulators when trying to establish legal clarity and certainty for an industry undergoing convergence with other industries.[6] The Internet, with the availability of services such as voice telephony and web-casting, is the classic example of this technological phenomenon. The existence of a clear legal and regulatory distinction between issues of carriage, the primary focus of the book, and issues of content is therefore dissolving in the face of such technological change.

This chapter introduces some of the key themes present within the field of telecommunications law. These themes are then considered in greater detail in one or more of the following substantive chapters.

1.5 LIBERALIZATION AND REGULATION

The telecommunications industry has undergone a fundamental change in structure, from that of monopoly to one of competition. Many of the laws and regulations examined in this book are concerned with this process of change: regulating for competition. However, the notion of what type of competition is being sought has sometimes distinguished the response of legislators and regulators.

The telecommunications market can be very crudely divided into equipment, networks, and services. Liberalization of the market for telecommunications equipment has been subject to the broadest consensus among policy makers, reflecting conditions in the broader IT products market. The provision of telecommunications services has experienced a similar general consensus, except in respect of voice telephony.

It is at the level of the network, constructing the physical communications infrastructure, that debate over liberalization continues to be heard. Historically it was argued that telecommunications networks were natural monopolies, that replicating the physical infrastructure was inevitably uneconomic. Whilst such arguments seem arcane in most developed economies, there continue to be those that argue that some form of single network platform is a feasible policy alternative, particularly in developing countries and partly driven by environmental concerns. In addition, the natural monopoly position continues to have relevance in the provision of broadcast networks and wireless telecommunication services. Although technological developments are continually improving our exploitation of the radio frequency spectrum, the market for wireless services may remain oligopolistic if not monopolistic, with associated competition concerns.

One of the historic myths of telecommunications liberalization was that it would arise through market deregulation, a feature of the related and, indeed, converging IT industry. To date, however, the reality has been quite the opposite. The telecommunications sector has become a heavily regulated sector in order to ensure the transition

---

[6] However, see also Standage, T, *The Victorian Internet* (Phoenix, 1998), which describes the revolutionary impact of the telegraph.

to competition, as manifested in part by the increasing scope and amount of material covered in this book. Such regulation has focused primarily on controlling the activities of the incumbent operator in order to facilitate market entry for new providers. However, public policy concerns in respect of universal service and consumer protection issues are also present.

As markets become fully competitive, deregulation has reappeared as a policy objective, sometimes embodied in legislation. Again, as with the sector as a whole, the shift towards deregulation has arisen not only because competitive markets are maturing, but also through technological developments, such as the Internet. In the US, for example, the Telecommunications Act 1996 imposes a general obligation upon the Federal Communications Commission to both forbear from the imposition of regulations under certain conditions, as well as engage in biennial reviews of the existing regulatory framework to remove those regulations identified as 'no longer necessary in the public interest as the result of meaningful economic competition between providers of such service' (47 USC § 160–161). Similarly, in the UK, a specific duty has been placed upon Ofcom, the UK regulatory authority, to review the regulatory framework and remove any unnecessary burdens (Communications Act 2003, s 6).

Complementing the move towards deregulation, some jurisdictions have also given explicit statutory recognition to the role of industry self-regulation in certain areas. In Australia, for example, the Telecommunications Act 1997 states:

The Parliament intends that telecommunications be regulated in a manner that . . . promotes the greatest practicable use of industry self-regulation. (s 4)

Similarly, in the UK, the Communications Act 2003 requires Ofcom to have regard to the possibility of addressing regulatory matters through 'effective self-regulation' (s 6(2)). The technical complexity of the telecommunications market has always meant that much of the regulatory input on particular issues, such as interconnection, simply consisted of the convening and oversight of particular industry groups, intervening only in the event of impasse. However, as regulators reduce or withdraw from market intervention, then increasingly reliance is likely to be made upon the industry to regulate itself.

1.6 LIBERALIZATION AND PRIVATIZATION

A third concept often linked in the past with liberalization and deregulation was that of privatization: the conversion of the incumbent operator from being a state-owned public body to a privately owned entity. As with deregulation, the nature of the relationship with the process of liberalization has been far from straightforward. The policy drivers behind privatization of the incumbent have tended to be based around state revenue concerns rather than the objective of liberalization. The provision of a modern telecommunication infrastructure requires massive capital investment, a funding burden which governments are no longer prepared to shoulder.

Attracting some degree of private sector finance is generally seen as the only feasible mechanism for meeting the policy objective of modernizing this strategic economic sector. Concerns that a state-owned incumbent might inhibit market entry have come a clear second to such revenue-raising concerns. Indeed, governments have remained remarkably attached to the 'national champion', with the majority of the OECD countries continuing to have some stake in the incumbent. However, the process of privatization has, itself, sometimes acted as a barrier to the process of liberalization. In the UK, for example, the divestiture of BT occurred in three stages, 1984, 1991, and 1993. However, at the time of the second sale, the government was also undergoing a comprehensive review of the market, the 'Duopoly Review', in order to promote further liberalization (see Chapter 4). During this process, it was generally perceived that BT used the need to maintain share price for the forthcoming sale as an effective tool in its negotiations with the government. Government stakeholdings in incumbent operators have also been an international trade issue. In the US, for example, concerns were raised in the US legislature about Deutsche Telekom's proposed merger with Voicestream, on the basis that the German government continued to have a stake in its incumbent. After privatization, a government may continue to be concerned about the performance of the incumbent, particularly where, as in the UK, a significant proportion of the shares are held by the general public, i.e. the electorate to which the government is always accountable. In many countries, the need to attract international investment into the telecommunications sector, either through the sale of a strategic stake in the incumbent, through Build–Operate–Transfer schemes or financing new entrants, has actually driven the adoption of a comprehensive legal framework for the provision of telecommunications networks and services. A lack of legal certainty is seen as a significant discouragement to financial investment and therefore to market entry (see Chapters 16 and 17).

1.7 POLICY, LAW, AND REGULATION

The shift from monopolistic telecommunications markets to liberalized competitive markets arose due to a number of different policy drivers, from the need to modernize existing infrastructure, to extending the reach of the national network. In addition, the process of liberalization was made subject to certain other public policy objectives, such as maintenance of universal service, protection of consumer interests, and individual privacy.

Universal service is concerned with the making available of the provision of a certain defined set of telecommunications services as widely as possible, both geographically and socially. Historically, such provision was seen as lying with the incumbent, however successful they were perceived to be in terms of meeting this obligation! In a liberalized market, such service provision needs to continue to be guaranteed through a mechanism that will not distort the competitive conditions

under which providers operate. The scope of universal service will also inevitably evolve over time, as politicians try to ensure that the benefits of the new technologies are made available to the society as a whole.

Governments generally set the broad policy objectives governing the telecommunications market, whether independently, within regional bodies such as the European Union, or through international agreement and institutions. These objectives are then enshrined in national and international legal instruments, conferring rights and obligations upon the various parties. The extent to which a market entrant may rely upon, hold up for reference, and enforce such rights and obligations against others will obviously depend on the legal nature of the instrument. Such legal instruments may impose obligations directly upon operators to address the policy objectives, or lay down principles to which the regulator should have reference when intervening in the market.

Another aspect of telecommunications law concerns the legal relationships that exist between licensor and licensee, between operators and service providers and their customers. An operator's licence may be used to provide for legal certainties absent in the statutory framework, or contain detailed obligations controlling every aspect of an operator's activities (see Chapter 7). Some commercial agreements, such as interconnection agreements and those involving consumers, are often subject to significant regulatory intervention (see Chapters 5 and 8). Others, such as capacity and outsourcing agreements, are substantially left to the freedom of the parties (see Chapters 11 and 12).

The third component of the governing framework is the establishment of a regulatory authority with a specific remit to intervene in the operation of the telecommunications sector and independent from vested interests, whether from operators or the government, when it is a shareholder in the incumbent. Nearly all countries have adopted such an institutional approach to the telecommunications sector.

In the long term, the sustainability of a sector-specific regulator may come under examination. The phenomenon of convergence has already led to a reassessment of the appropriate regulatory structures for issues of carriage and content. In 1999, the European Commission proposed that there be a single regulatory framework for all forms of communications infrastructure, whether voice telephony, data, or broadcasting.[7] In 2003, the UK government created the Office of Communications (Ofcom) through a merger of five existing regulatory bodies, with responsibility for both infrastructure and content. At the same time, it has been argued that once a fully competitive market matures then the need for intervention may simply rest upon traditional competition law principles, enforced by the national competition authority rather than a telecommunications-specific regulator. To date, however, no country has felt in a position to take such a decisive step.

---

[7] See Commission Communication, 'Towards a new framework for electronic communications infrastructure and associated services: The 1999 Communications Review', COM 1999, 539, 10 November 1999.

1.8 REGULATORY FRAMEWORK

The regulatory framework for the telecommunications sector is multifarious, both horizontally and vertically. At a national level, states may divide the regulation of the sector between different authorities. In the UK, for example, the Communications Act 2003 places concurrent jurisdiction upon the Office of Fair Trading and Ofcom for competition matters. In Federal legal systems, such as the United States, such jurisdictional complexities are multiplied, sometimes requiring recourse to the courts to establish rights to regulate (see Chapter 6). Regulatory multiplicity, with regulators exercising concurrent as well as exclusive jurisdiction, may in itself constitute a barrier to market entry, as operators try to work their way through the maze of procedures and peculiarities presented by each of the various institutions.[8]

Vertically, an operator may also need to look to regional organizations, whether as a legislative body to whom representations may be made, such as the European Commission, Parliament, and Council; or in terms of standards-making, where participation in the decision-making process may be a commercial imperative, such as the European Telecommunications Standards Institute (ETSI). At an international level, there exists another layer of laws and regulations under the World Trade Organization's (WTO) multilateral trade agreements and the regulations, recommendations and standards of the International Telecommunications Union (ITU) (see Chapter 15).

The construction of global communication systems, such as Globalstar's satellite network, will require large-scale regulatory activity at both a national and international level. Applications for appropriate orbital slots will need to be made through the ITU, while operating licences may have to be obtained in every jurisdiction into which the services are provided. In contrast, a service provider could offer a voice telephony service over the Internet without needing to acquire any regulatory approval or go through any notification process.

Such a layering of regulatory bodies inevitably raises important questions of legal order: the applicability and enforceability of the rights and obligations arising under various legal instruments, before national and supranational judicial or dispute settlement bodies; and against either governments or market competitors.

In less developed countries, much developmental assistance from organizations such as the World Bank, the International Finance Corporation (IFC), or the European Bank of Reconstruction and Development (EBRD) is directed towards the telecommunications sector, as a strategic part of a country's economic infrastructure. Usually these lending institutions will impose conditions upon any such financial assistance, which may require the recipient jurisdiction to adopt a pro-competitive

---

[8] See generally Coates, K, 'Regulating the telecommunications sector: Substituting practical cooperation for the risks of competition', in McCrudden (ed), *Regulation and Deregulation* (Clarendon Press, Oxford, 1998), at 249–274.

legislative and regulatory framework for the telecommunications market.[9] Indeed, conditional financial assistance to developing countries has been an extremely influential tool in the international harmonization of telecommunications law.

1.9 REGULATORY POWERS

What powers does a regulatory authority have to intervene in the operation of a telecommunications market? The key authority is that of authorization or licensing: granting the right to build, operate, and supply telecommunications equipment, networks, and/or services. Liberalization is about the entry of competitors into a market, therefore the process by which a new entrant can obtain the necessary authorizations may itself be critical to the liberalization process.

Most jurisdictions distinguish between authorizing those wanting to provide telecommunications services and those wanting to provide the networks or infrastructure for the carriage of such services. The nature of the activities associated with the latter category, such as digging up the streets to lay cables, has tended to mean more substantial legal obligations being placed upon such operators. In addition, the incumbent will fall into this category. It is also generally the case that barriers to market entry are greater for the provision of networks than services and, therefore, there is often more scope to engage in anti-competitive practices. With regard to telecommunications equipment, regulatory intervention tends to be limited to procedures ensuring that such equipment is unlikely to cause harm to either the user or the networks to which it is connected.

Allied to the issue of authorization is that of access to scarce resources. Where scarce resources are an element of the service provision, then such resources need to be distributed on an appropriate basis that will not unduly restrict or distort competition. The key scarce resource in telecommunications is the electromagnetic spectrum for use in wireless communications. Historically, spectrum was distributed between the incumbent, the military, and various related public service providers, such as the police and emergency services. With liberalization, access to the spectrum available for commercial usage becomes a key regulatory control. As a scarce resource, spectrum is also usually seen as a public asset that should be utilized and managed in the best interests of society as a whole.

One current trend is to auction spectrum on the basis that this is the most economically efficient mechanism for distributing such scarce and public resources. In the UK and Germany, auctions for the third generation mobile spectrum netted their governments $30 billion and $50 billion respectively; while in the US similar auctions have been run for both the broadcasting and telecommunications markets (see Chapter 6). However, as with much economic theory, rational actors often act irrationally, paying

---

[9] See generally Stigilitz, J, *Globalisation and its Discontents* (Penguin Books, London, 2003).

sums through fear of market reaction as much as the business rationale. As a result, serious questions have been raised about whether the benefits in terms of public revenue will be achieved at the expense of the development of the market itself: through delayed roll-out and higher charges for third generation services.

Another important scarce resource is telephone numbers. Access to a number and the right to control access to numbers needs to be subject to regulatory control in order to facilitate market liberalization. However, strategic national planning for the use and distribution of telephone numbers into the future can be an extremely difficult task and one which, if mistakes are made, can generate substantial adverse public feeling towards the national regulatory authority. The domain name and IP addressing scheme utilized for Internet-based communications has also generated regulatory issues, relating to its management, scarcity, and trade marks.[10]

The right to access or utilize the private property of another for the provisioning of networks and services is an issue that has sometimes been viewed as similar in nature to the use of a scarce resource. Whilst the granting of rights of way need not be limited, the exercise of a statutory right to interfere with another's property has such potentially significant consequences for the owner and/or occupier of the property that regulatory controls are inevitably necessary. Not least, the exercise of such rights interferes with an individual's right of privacy, as enshrined in national and international law.[11]

As telecommunications networks proliferate in a competitive market, it is possible that people challenging the exercise of statutory rights may increasingly raise such human rights concerns against operators building networks across private land. Recognized limitations to an individual's right of privacy on grounds such as the 'economic well-being of the country'[12] may be sustainable as a basis upon which to interfere during the process of liberalization, but would seem less 'necessary' once a market is fully competitive.

The construction of international telecommunications networks raises issues of access to public resources, both state-based, such as the electromagnetic spectrum, as well as resources recognized under public international law as the 'property of all mankind', specifically outer space and the high seas (see Chapter 15).

Public policy makers and regulators are also giving greater consideration to environmental concerns, such as the siting of transmitters for wireless communications systems. Co-location and facility-sharing obligations address environmental as well as competition concerns (see Chapter 8). One critically important area of regulatory intervention is that of dispute resolution. Disputes may arise between service providers and their customers and between competing providers. In the former situation, a regulator is essentially redressing an inevitable imbalance that exists between the

---

[10] See generally Reed, C, *Internet Law: Text and Materials*, (2nd edition, CUP, London, 2004).
[11] e.g. the European Convention for the Protection of Human Rights and Fundamental Freedoms, Art 8(1).
[12] Ibid, at Art 8(2).

two parties, providing easier access to justice and redress for the customer. Intervening in disputes between providers, however, would only seem important whilst a market is undergoing liberalization, primarily because of the position of the incumbent. Once the market is fully competitive, such regulatory intervention may be seen as an unnecessary use of public money when the parties have equal recourse to traditional legal processes. The manner in which a regulator exercises its powers will be an issue of relevance to a telecommunications lawyer. As with any public authority, the regulator will be continuously required to exercise its discretion in respect of when, where, and how it intervenes in the operation of the market. Such intervention will then be subject to judicial review along administrative grounds, e.g. irregularity, irrationality, illegality, and, in respect of EU law, proportionality. However, the complex nature of regulatory decisions in the telecommunications sector will require that operators have the right to appeal against decisions on substantive as well as procedural grounds.

The frequency and manner in which decisions are challenged will also impact on the operation of the whole regulatory framework. Legal activism by operators, frequently challenging the decisions made by the regulator, may effectively slow down the decision-making process, as regulators become cautious and excessively procedural in order to stem legal challenges and the associated commitment of public resources. Legal interventions in regulatory decision-making are generally more often of benefit to the incumbent, than new entrants.

1.10 REGULATORY MODELS AND METHODS

The importance of the regulatory authority in the telecommunications market requires consideration to be given to the structure and the manner of working of the authority being established. Generally, regulatory authorities can be distinguished into one of four models:

- an autonomous quasi-judicial commission (e.g. the US Federal Communications Commission (FCC));
- an independent official or office outside a government ministry (e.g. the Autorité de Régulation des Télécommunications in France);
- an independent official or office inside a government ministry (e.g. PTS in Sweden); or
- a government ministry (e.g. Cambodia).[13]

Regulatory authorities often initially experience a number of problems in the telecommunications sector. First, the inevitable lack of expertise amongst the regulator's

---

[13] See generally Gillick, D, 'Telecommunications policies and regulatory structures: new issues and trends' in *Telecommunications Policy*, December 1992, 726–731. See also Chapter 14 at section 14.7.

staff, particularly in the early years, may render the authority excessively dependent on information and even personnel supplied by the incumbent operator. Such dependency obviously raises accusations of regulatory capture from new entrants.

Second, as with any dynamic sector of the economy, the large differential in remuneration rates between public authorities and private sector operators means staff retention can be a significant concern for a regulator trying to build and retain institutional experience.

Personalities are always likely to influence the prevailing regulatory environment and the manner in which policies are pursued. Where the regulatory authority is invested in a single individual, the influence of personality is likely to be greater. Some countries vest authority in a committee, generally representative to varying degrees of relevant interest groups, such as consumers, operators, and general business end-users. In the UK, the background and interests of the Director General of Telecommunications (DGT) were seen as being critically important in setting the overall direction of regulatory policy. Don Cruickshank (DGT 1989–97), for example, came from the airline Virgin Atlantic and was perceived as being pro-new entrant and naturally untrusting towards BT as the incumbent. Conversely in a committee or commission-based structure, interpersonnel rivalries may surface and render the authority ineffective or undermine its credibility in the eyes of the industry, such as the FCC in the US.

The tools of regulation policy are various; however, a feature of a liberalizing market is the need to direct regulatory controls towards the activities of the incumbent operator and other operators with similar market influence, such as in the mobile sector. Within Europe, such asymmetric regulatory controls are placed on organizations designated as having 'significant market power' (see Chapter 5); while at an international level, the equivalent term in the WTO's Reference Paper is 'major supplier' (see Chapter 15).

Much of the literature in the field adopts a fundamental distinction between so-called *ex ante* and *ex post* regulatory controls. For the purpose of this book, the phrase *ex ante* is used in respect of regulatory measures that proactively control the structure and/or behaviour of market players going forward; while *ex post* refers to measures that arise in reaction to the decisions and activities of entities.

Establishing the costs associated with the provision of telecommunications networks and services is key to their effective regulation. Interconnection charges can represent from a third to a half of a new entrant's costs; therefore regulatory control over such charges through 'cost-orientation' requirements is critical to enabling competition (see Chapter 8). Likewise, universal service policy requires the identification of those service elements that are 'provided at a loss or provided under cost conditions falling outside normal commercial standards',[14] before regulators provide appropriate financial support mechanisms. However, determining and verifying such cost-based obligations is often an extremely controversial regulatory process, in

---

[14] Directive 2002/22/EC on universal service and users' rights relating to electronic communications networks and services (OJ L 108/7, 24 April 2002), at Art. 12 and Annex IV, Part A.

terms of attribution, calculation methodology, e.g. whether historical or forward-looking, and the establishment of appropriate cost accounting systems by incumbent operators (see Chapter 3).

Tariff controls are present under most regimes, whether at a retail or wholesale level. Such controls are generally perceived as being the most appropriate mechanism for ensuring that the incumbent is controlled whilst providing sufficient incentives to encourage economic efficiency. Such controls are, however, notoriously difficult to get right in terms of balancing the interests of customers, new entrants, and the incumbent.

Related to tariff controls are requirements upon an incumbent operator to disclose information about various aspects of their business activities, either to the regulator, competitors, or consumers: e.g. tariff filings and technical standards for interconnection. Information asymmetry is an inevitable regulatory problem in a complex sector such as telecommunications. Transparency obligations are designed to remove the likelihood of anti-competitive practices and to provide a certain degree of legal certainty, for example, through obligations to publish standard contractual terms and conditions (e.g. a Reference Interconnection Offer). The publication of information also helps develop international regulatory best practice in the sector, by enabling regulatory authorities to use benchmarks based on figures made available from comparative jurisdictions.

1.11 REGULATION AND COMPETITION LAW

. . . competition should be the organizing principle of our communications law and policy.[15]

Competition law is inevitably an important component of telecommunications law. However, a distinction needs to be made between the reactive *ex post* application of traditional competition law principles to activities in the telecommunications sector, and proactive *ex ante* regulatory intervention in the operation of the telecommunications market to achieve a competitive market. Both are of interest to a telecommunications lawyer and are examined in this book; however, it is the latter aspect that comprises much of the unique terrain of telecommunications law.

The only example of a jurisdiction that initially pursued market liberalization through reliance solely on the application of traditional competition law has been New Zealand. It is widely accepted, however, that such an approach simply led to delays in the process of liberalization through the need for the lengthy and ineffective recourse to judicial intervention.[16] Competition law can be effective against blatant anti-competitive practices, such as a refusal to supply interconnect services; but is less effective against minor but persistent obstructive tactics, such as delaying

---

[15] FCC Report, 'A New Federal Communications Commission for the 21st Century', 1999.
[16] See case *Telecom Corporation of NZ Ltd v Clear Communications Ltd* (1992) 4 NZBLC.

negotiations, or where ongoing oversight of commercial relationships is required; as noted by the US Supreme Court:

No court should impose a duty to deal that it cannot explain or adequately and reasonably supervise. The problem should be deemed irremedia[ble] by antitrust law when compulsory access requires the court to assume the day-to-day controls characteristic of a regulatory agency.[17]

In such circumstances, *ex ante* regulatory intervention by a specialist regulatory authority has proved critical. It is interesting to note that in the European Commission's review of the regulatory framework for the telecommunications sector, the '1999 Communications Review', significant emphasis was placed on shifting from the current *ex ante* controls to a more hands-off *ex post* competition law regime. However, during the consultation exercise, new entrants express strong reservations that such a move was premature and would enable incumbent operators to entrench their existing positions.[18] As a result, the EU's 2003 regulation framework retained many of the *ex ante* controls (see Chapter 5).

The interest of competition authorities in the telecommunications market can be subdivided into issues of anti-competitive agreements and practices, mergers and joint ventures, abuses of a dominant position, and, to a lesser degree, state aids. A feature of the telecommunications sector is clearly the possibility for an abuse of a dominant position, arising from the position of national incumbent operators. Notification procedures imposed upon certain types of agreements and mergers enable the authorities to exercise prior restraint over players in the market. In addition, the nature of the telecommunications industry as a 'networked' industry, with parallels in industries such as airlines and power, give rise to certain characteristics that raise particular competition concerns, such as issues relating to 'essential facilities', 'network effects', and 'collective dominance'.[19]

Finally, it is important to note that in many jurisdictions, such as the Asian 'tiger' economies, competition law is a relatively underdeveloped discipline. As a consequence, domestic operators, regulators, and the courts have little experience of the application of competition principles and practices. In such jurisdictions, foreign operators will often be more reliant on telecommunications-specific regulations, whether statutory or licence-based, for the protection of their commercial rights.

---

[17] The words of Professor Areeda, quoted with approval in *Verizon Communications Inc. v Law Offices of Curtis V. Trinko* (02-682) 540 U.S. 398 (2004) at 15.

[18] Communication from the Commission, 'The results of the public consultation on the 1999 Communications Review and orientations for the new regulatory framework' COM(2000)239, Brussels, 26 April 2000.

[19] See generally Shapiro, C, and H Varian, *Information Rules: A Strategic Guide to the Network Economy* (Harvard Business School Press, Harvard, 1999).

1.12 REGULATION AND STANDARDS

In our information society, more and more technical standards are used in formulating laws, regulations, decisions etc . . . standards are becoming more important in drafting contractual obligations and interpreting the meaning thereof, whether or not in the courtroom.[20]

The nature of the communications process requires that the various parties adhere to a certain agreed standard, whether in terms of language, protocol, numbers, or physical connection. The need for standardization to communicate across national boundaries gave rise to the establishment of the International Telecommunications Union, one of the oldest intergovernmental organizations. As the quote highlights, there is proliferation of standards within the laws, regulations, and agreements governing the telecommunications market.

Standards are critical to the process of liberalizing a market. New entrants will be as dependent on the technical certainty that arises from the existence of published standards, as they require legal certainty upon which to base their investments. The absence of appropriate standards has been used by incumbents to delay the introduction of competing services. Within the European Union, standards have been critical in the establishment of an Internal Market for telecommunications equipment, networks, and services (see Chapter 5).

Numerous standards-making bodies operate in every aspect of the telecommunications market, as well as at a national, regional, and international level. Historically, such bodies have tended to operate in accordance with complex bureaucratic procedural mechanisms, which led to inevitable delays in decision-making. With the appearance of new technologies and environments, such as the Internet, such institutions have increasingly faced competition from new entities, such as the Internet Engineering Task Force (IETF), operating under more flexible and rapid processes. Participation in the work of such bodies can require operators to devote significant financial and management resource, while failure to participate may effectively hand control over the development of a particular market to competitors.

One important aspect of standards in the technology field is the possibility that a particular standard may constitute the intellectual property of a company, such as a patented process. In 1999, a dispute arose between Ericsson and Qualcomm over the ownership of certain patents related to Code Division Multiple Access (CDMA) technology, which underpins third generation mobile telephony. In such circumstances, competition law principles may be applicable, particularly the 'essential facilities' doctrine.[21] However, regulators may be concerned to ensure that *ex ante* measures are in place to prohibit such practices (see Chapter 10).

---

[20] Stuurman, C, 'Legal aspects of standardization and certification of information technology and telecommunications: an overview', in *Amongst Friends in Computers and Law* (Computer/Law Series, Netherlands, No 8, 1990), at 75–92.

[21] e.g. Cases C-241 and 242/91, *RTE v Magill* [1995] 4 CMLR 718.

1.13 REGULATING IN THE GLOBAL ECONOMY

As discussed above, the inherently global nature of telecommunications has meant that the sector has been the subject of international agreements since its beginnings. It is also worth noting, however, that the transnational nature of the industry is also reflected at various levels in national regulatory policy. Mention was made above of the use of benchmarks as a mechanism for regulating the behaviour of the incumbent in areas such as tariffing, by reference to prices available under prevailing market conditions. Such benchmarks may be based on figures obtained within the national market, but equally regional or international figures may be utilized.[22] Through such mechanisms, the national regulatory framework can come to reflect and embody international 'best practice', particularly where the benchmark reference sites are those markets considered most advanced or liberalized.

Conversely, the imposition of benchmarks on national operators may be used as a tool to encourage further liberalization in other national markets, raising issues relating to the exercise of extraterritorial jurisdiction. The classic example of this is the FCC's 1997 Benchmark Order for International Settlements, which required US-licensed operators to only pay international settlements rates laid down by the FCC, on the basis of country-by-country benchmarks, rather than reached through normal commercial negotiations between operators (see Chapter 15). The objective of the Order was to prevent operators from non-liberalized markets leveraging their domestic monopolistic position to the detriment of the US consumer.

Another feature of the telecommunications market is the amount of joint venture and merger activity taking place, as companies try to position themselves to take advantage of the increasingly global economy. Such agreements inevitably give rise to competition concerns at a national and regional level. To address such industry globalization, competition authorities have entered into their own agreements in order to coordinate their response to such developments; for example, between the United States and the European Community.[23] Such regulatory cooperation has already proved effective in a number of telecommunications cases, such as the WorldCom/MCI merger and the BT/AT&T joint venture.

National concerns about the impact of the transnational merger activity on the national incumbent may also be the subject of regulatory intervention. For example, during BT's abortive attempt to merge with MCI in 1997, the Director General of Telecommunications in the UK expressed concerns that one of the potential consequences were the merger to be successful was that BT may end up with a substantial proportion of its assets residing overseas, as well as its investments, at the expense

---

[22] e.g. Commission Recommendation, 'On leased lines interconnection pricing in a liberalized telecommunications market', C(1999)3863, 24 November 1999.
[23] See Agreement between the European Communities and the Government of the United States of America on the application of positive comity principles in the enforcement of their competition laws, OJ L 173/28, 18 June 98.

of the domestic market.[24] To address this concern, BT's licence was modified to include an annual reporting requirement whereby BT would effectively guarantee that sufficient resources were maintained to meet its domestic obligations.

1.14 CONCLUDING REMARKS

For many countries, the pursuance of a policy of market liberalization coupled with the pace of technological development has meant that the telecommunications sector has gone from an environment of scarcity to one of relative or actual abundance. The legal framework governing such abundance should become less complex than that required during the process of transition from a monopolistic environment. Indeed, a number of jurisdictions are currently addressing the problem of scaling down the regulatory framework for telecommunications. Competition law is likely to provide the core principles upon which this 'second generation' of telecommunications law will be based.

However, the pace of change in some sectors of the market, such as the local loop, has proven more stubborn to competition than anticipated, which has required renewed regulatory intervention (see Chapter 8). Oligopolistic markets also seem a defining feature of a mature telecommunications industry, whether through spectrum limitations imposed on mobile telephony or the impact of globalization on merger activity,[25] which may require traditional competition law principles to be reconsidered.

At the same time, governments are examining the implications of convergence, which raises important issues of content regulation, for which little international consensus has been reached. Regulating content may become an increasingly prominent aspect of a telecommunications lawyers' work, compared to issues of establishment and operation.

Telecommunications law is evolving rapidly in parallel with the market it purports to govern. Any book is therefore destined to date quickly in respect of some details. However, the process of liberalization in Europe and the US, as well as in many other countries, is sufficiently well advanced to provide us with a clear outline of some of the key aspects of international best practice in law and regulation for the telecommunications or communications sector over the next five to ten years.

---

[24] See Oftel publication 'Domestic Obligations in a Global Market', July 1997.

[25] e.g. in the UK, for example, three of the five mobile network operators are owned by incumbent from other European countries, i.e. Orange (France Telecom), T-Mobile (Deutsche Telekom AG), and O₂ (Telefónica SA).

2

COMMUNICATIONS TECHNOLOGIES, SERVICES, AND MARKETS

Andrew Sharpe

This chapter is intended to give an introduction to communications technologies for a lay reader. An understanding of the basic technology behind modern electronic communications networks is important to understand how the technology influences market developments and this in turn is crucial for a proper understanding of telecommunications law and regulation. Given the scope of this book, the technologies discussed chiefly concern voice and data traffic services and not narrowcasting or broadcasting, even though the barriers between these types of services and delivery are becoming increasingly blurred.

In order to give this technology introduction, this chapter first sets out some of the fundamental theory behind electronic communications that shapes their deployment. It then goes on to show how fixed, mobile, and satellite networks are established.

2.1 INTRODUCTION TO COMMUNICATIONS TECHNOLOGIES

The essence of all communications systems is that a message is exchanged between a sender and one or more receivers. How efficient and effective the system is at passing

messages therefore depends upon all the elements that make up the system as well as the nature of the message to be exchanged and the distance over which it is to be exchanged. There are always a number of physical and technological constraints that limit what any communications system can achieve.

Using normal human speech as an example of a communications system, the system is bound by the physical constraint of using air as a medium for the transmission of messages and the audible range of frequencies of the human voice. Air is a poor transmission medium; not only is the energy within speech dissipated in all directions, unless it is focused in some way such as by a speaking tube or hearing trumpet, but there can be high background noise over which the message must be heard. Fortunately, the human brain is an excellent speech processor. Our speech patterns are complex, with our listening ability readily able to compensate for missed syllables or misheard sounds. In communications terms, we have enhanced message coding for transmission of complex messages, with sophisticated error correction at the receiver end to compensate for transmission losses.

For most electronic communications we have dispensed with pressure waves through air as the transmission medium for the communications, instead using electrical energy carried by electrical conductors or the transmission of electromagnetic energy. How effective these electronic communications systems are therefore depends upon the signal processing carried out to deliver messages through the chosen transmission medium and the physical constraints of the medium itself. An understanding of some of the physical and technological constraints that limit the efficiency and effectiveness of electronic communications systems therefore helps to understand the economics behind particular technologies or systems and how the associated markets have developed.

This introduction to communications technologies therefore looks at the constraints that limit how an electronic message or signal can be processed so that it can be delivered over an electronic transmission medium or channel and the limitations of the various transmission channels. This requires dipping into some basic telecommunications engineering theory to understand the origins of these constraints and how they affect the development and deployment of electronic communications systems. In particular, the engineering limitations of electronic communications channels, (digital) signalling processing and processing a signal so that it can be carried over a channel are introduced.

2.1.1 Transmission channels: wire and wireless—fixed and mobile

Electronic communications principally rely on three forms of energy to form communications channels. The oldest is the simple use of electrical energy in conducting elements—the wire, closely followed by using electromagnetic energy for radio—wireless. More recently light has been used as an alternative to both, with laser light used in fibre optics cables or in free space optics (laser light used in the open air). Which method prevails in any electronic communications system depends upon the

economics of the relevant choice or the end application. Obviously, mobile applications will involve wireless technologies, but may include fixed or wireline elements, where these are a more efficient means of carrying traffic.

Spectrum is clearly a limited resource. In many instances spectrum cannot practically be shared between operators. There is also the question of the usability of any given spectrum—in addition to the transmission characteristics of radio channels at any given frequency, the wavelength is also an important feature. Antennae must be multiples of the radiated wavelength for optimal performance, with half-length and quarter-length antennae common. Frequency and wavelength are related as follows:

$$\text{speed of light } (3 \times 10^8 \text{ ms}^{-1}) = \text{frequency} \times \text{wavelength}$$

Clearly, practical mobile terminal equipment needs to operate in spectrum where antenna lengths are manageable (e.g. a 1800MHz GSM mobile handset has a quarter-length monopole antenna of about 4cm).

As a result, certain spectrum is considered more valuable, with the result that it attracts large licence or usage fees from national spectrum authorities.

However, in fixed networks the cost of civil works (ducts, poles, street cabinets, etc.) can have a material impact on the use of wireline technology, particularly in rural areas. Where there is no legacy of a fixed access network in a dispersed population (i.e. no network of a former state monopoly telecommunications operator with physical access to a majority of subscribers or end users), it is often more economic to deploy wireless access, where mobile technologies as are used in static or nomadic environments, such as the use of GSM networks in rural Africa. There can also be significant regulatory issues concerning access to land in order to install electronic communications infrastructure, which result in mobile or wireless technologies being preferred to wireline, such as the use of microwave radio for mobile backhaul (see explanation on networks below) in many emerging markets.

The most basic transmission cable is the simple pair of copper wires, but these are susceptible to electromagnetic interference and cross-talk. Cross-talk is, as its name implies, the interference that occurs between adjacent circuits. These effects can be reduced by twisting the copper wire pair, giving the most common form of telecommunications line, the unshielded twisted pair (or UTP). Almost all analogue local loop circuits are made up of cables of UTPs. UTPs have limited performance over a long distance, but can be extremely efficient and a cheap option over shorter distances. Ethernet computer networking technology systems often use UTPs to pass data at up to 1Gbit/s, but generally limit UTPs for cable runs of tens of metres.

For longer cable runs or for high frequency signals, the standard transmission cable is the coaxial cable. This is most commonly used as the type of cable for radio, satellite and TV antennae. It is typically made up of an inner copper wire surrounded by an insulating spacer of polyethylene, which is then surrounded by an outer shield made up of copper braid and the final cable insulating sleeve. Coaxial cables have now largely been replaced by fibre optic cables in telecommunications networks.

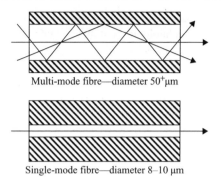

Multi-mode fibre—diameter 50⁺μm

Single-mode fibre—diameter 8–10 μm

Figure 2.1 Optical fibres

Telecommunications fibre optic cables are made of glass and use laser light to pass signals. Each fibre is in effect a waveguide, with light internally reflected along the fibre. As they are immune to electromagnetic interference and can be designed to have extremely low cross-talk, signals travel down fibre optics with very little deterioration. Multi-mode fibres are used for short distances (hundred of metres) and more expensive single-mode fibres for long distance links—see Figure 2.1.

An alternative to cable infrastructure, or wireline, is radio or wireless channels. The properties of radio channels are highly dependent upon the frequencies being used and the method of propagation of the radio signals. Figure 2.2 shows the ITU radio frequency designations and Figure 2.3 the common methods of propagation.

	Designation	Frequency Range	Wavelengths	Typical Uses
ELF	Extremely low frequency	3Hz to 30Hz	100Mm to 10Mm	Submarine communications
SLF	Super low frequency	30Hz to 300Hz	10,000km to 1,000km	Submarine communications
ULF	Ultra low frequency	300Hz to 3kHz	1,000km to 100km	Mine communications
VLF	Very low frequency	3kHz to 30kHz	100km to 10km	Submarine communications, avalanche beacons, wireless heart monitors, geophysics
LF	Low frequency	30kHz to 300kHz	10km to 1km	Navigation, time signals, AM broadcasting
MF	Medium frequency	300kHz to 3MHz	1km to 100m	AM (medium wave) broadcasting
HF	High frequency	3MHz to 30MHz	100m to 10m	Short wave broadcasting, amateur radio, long range aviation and military communications
VHF	Very high frequency	30MHz to 300MHz	10m to 1m	FM broadcasting, television, ground-to-air and air-to-air communications
UHF	Ultra high frequency	300MHz to 3GHz	1m to 10cm	Television, mobile phones, wireless LAN, Bluetooth, microwave ovens
SHF	Super high frequency	3GHz to 30GHz	10cm to 1cm	Wireless LAN, radar
EHF	Extremely high frequency	30GHz to 300GHz	1cm to 1mm	Radio astronomy, high-speed microwave radio

Figure 2.2 ITU radio frequency designations

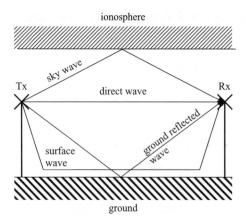

Figure 2.3 Radio transmission paths

In the Very Low Frequency (VLF) band, wavelengths are so long that they are comparable to the height of the ionosphere (approximately 50km), so that the space between the earth and the lower ionosphere acts as a waveguide, enabling worldwide coverage. In the Low Frequency (LF) band, the main means of propagation is by surface wave, which is stable over distances of up to 1,500km. The Medium Frequency (MF) band also uses surface wave propagation, but at shorter ranges as the strength of surface waves is inversely proportional to the frequency. However, sky waves can also be used for MF, particularly at night when losses into the ionosphere are at a minimum. In the High Frequency (HF) band surface waves have limited utility and HF is mainly propagated by means of sky waves. The ionosphere is created by ultraviolet and X-ray emissions from the sun ionizing molecules in the upper atmosphere, which absorb and refract lower order electromagnetic waves. As the ionosphere is created by solar energy, its characteristics change from hour to hour, and from day to day. HF transmitters and receivers therefore need to retune regularly in order to maintain an HF radio channel. Listeners to Short Wave radio will be used to this requirement to retune regularly. Above 30MHz radio waves are not refracted enough by the ionosphere, so escape through it. So for Very High Frequency (VHF) bands and above, propagation is by direct free-space or line-of-sight waves. Such waves are not true line-of-sight waves, as they are refracted by the troposphere, but can be considered to be line-of-sight with an effective earth radius of four thirds (4/3) of the actual radius.

2.1.2 Information theory—Nyquist, Shannon, and Baudot

There are a number of fundamental information theory principles that underpin modern telecommunications.

The Shannon sampling theorem states that if a signal contains no frequency components greater than a certain maximum f_{MAX}, then in order for it to be completely determined, i.e. fully recovered by any coding and transmission system, it must be sampled at intervals of time $1/(2\ f_{MAX})$ apart. The sampling rate, which is known as the Nyquist rate, is then:

$$f_N = 2\ f_{MAX}$$

This is important as it defines the bandwidth that a circuit needs in order to transmit a digital signal. For example, although the normal frequency range of the human voice is between 80Hz (a bass singer's bottom E) to 1100Hz (a soprano's top C), a standard speech signal has a much higher frequency range. A speech signal limited to about 4kHz bandwidth is intelligible, so as the signal has no components greater than 4kHz (i.e. f_{MAX}= 4kHz), a Nyquist rate of 8kHz is required. If this 8kHz sampled signal were to be converted from analogue to digital by means of an 8-bit code, then a circuit capable of transmitting 8-bits x 8kHz, or 64 kbit/s, would be required in order to recover the original signal. This is the reason why the standard bandwidth for voice channel for digital telecommunications is 64 kbit/s.

In order to understand the efficiency of a particular transmission system to pass useful information, telecommunications engineers use the standard unit of symbol rate, the baud (Bd), named after Emile Baudot, inventor of the first internationally accepted telegraphy code (see below), to represent the signalling rate, or the rate at which the communication channel changes. The baud is often confused with the transmission rate of bits, expressed in bits/s or bit/s, of a channel. Conveying more than one bit per symbol allows systems to take into account channel bandwidth, desired information rate, noise characteristics of the channel, and receiver/decoder complexity. A typical modern modem transmits bits at twice the baud (i.e. uses two bits per symbol). Where a channel is very noisy, or subject to jamming, then coding techniques may use more symbols per bit, despite then using more bandwidth to carry the same bit rate than the minimum bandwidth required according to Shannon and Nyquist.

2.1.3 Modulation

Telecommunications systems must be able to pass voice messages, data and/or video signals. This is routinely done by modulating a carrier signal with the input signal to form a signal that can be transmitted (and received). There are essentially three components of any carrier signal that can be modulated by an input signal: its amplitude, frequency, or phase.

Amplitude modulation (AM) has the advantage that it only requires a simple receiver to recover the input signal from the carrier, but the disadvantage that it is susceptible to noise as it is inefficient, with the majority of the transmitted power being contained in the carrier rather than in the input/message signal. It is therefore

ideal for relatively low bandwidth applications such as radio broadcasting. As stated above, a signal with a bandwidth of 4kHz can be used to reproduce sound of satisfactory quality. You may have noticed that AM radio therefore has channels that are 9kHz or 10kHz apart (for example, 9kHz channel bandwidth for Medium Wave and Long Wave broadcast radio in Europe—in the UK, BBC Radio 4 LW is at 198kHz, BBC Radio 5 Live is at 693kHz or 909kHz).

Frequency Modulation (FM) is more bandwidth hungry than AM, with the approximate bandwidth required being set by Carson's Rule:

$$W = 2\,F_m\,(1 + \beta)$$

Where: F_m = maximum baseband frequency
β = modulation index

However, FM is more efficient in terms of distribution of transmitted power, which means it has better signal-to-noise characteristics (an improvement over AM by a ratio proportional to the square of the modulation index ($3\beta^2$)). This makes it preferable for transmission whenever sufficient bandwidth is available.

FM is used in telephone circuits in switched telephone networks for data traffic, where it is known as frequency-shift keying (FSK). Where digital signals are frequency modulated, only a low modulation index is required. The device which *mo*dulates (or *dem*odulates) a digital signal onto an analogue carrier signal is known as a 'modem'. A typical 600 baud FM modem uses 1.3kHz and 1.7kHz tones, and a 1200 baud FM modem uses 1.3kHz and 2.1kHz tones. These are the tones you hear when using dial-up Internet or fax over a standard telephone line.

Phase modulation (PM) is more frequently used for digital signals, where it is known as phase-shift keying (PSK). The carrier is switched to a number of possible values, commonly 0°, 90°, 180°, or 270° for a four-state system. A receiver in standard PM systems needs to have a highly stable reference carrier signal to compare with the incoming signal, so advanced PM systems compare the phase of an incoming signal with the previous interval signal for differential phase-shift keying (DPSK), and dispense with a locally-generated reference carrier signal.

The diagrams at Figure 2.4 show the effect of modulating a simple sinusoidal carrier signal by a digital pulse and a sine wave (a single musical note). For AM, the carrier's amplitude is shaped to follow the input signal. For FM, the frequency of the carrier changes with the input signal. This can most easily be seen for the digital pulse. Similarly for PM, the phase changes with the input signal; when the pulse is '0' the modulated signal is the same as the carrier, when the pulse is at '1', it is at a phase shift of 180°.

The other common modulation technique used in telecommunications is a hybrid AM and PM system. A digital signal can be subject to a combination of AM to give 4 levels of amplitude and a 4-state PM. The result is a 16-state signal known as quadrature amplitude modulation (QAM), capable of sending a 4-bit symbol.

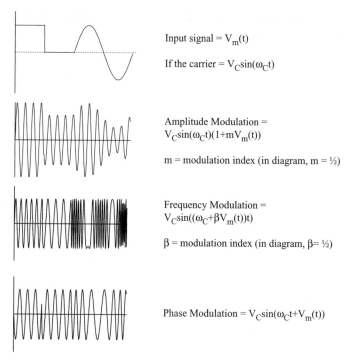

Input signal = $V_m(t)$

If the carrier = $V_C \sin(\omega_C t)$

Amplitude Modulation =
$V_C \sin(\omega_C t)(1+mV_m(t))$

m = modulation index (in diagram, m = ½)

Frequency Modulation =
$V_C \sin((\omega_C + \beta V_m(t))t)$

β = modulation index (in diagram, β= ½)

Phase Modulation = $V_C \sin(\omega_C t + V_m(t))$

Figure 2.4 Modulation techniques

QAM is used to provide 2.4 kbit/s data transmission over telephone circuits with only 600 baud signalling rate, or 9.6 kbit/s over 2400 baud circuits.

Where the carrier signal for an AM system is a pulsed (analogue) signal, the resulting pulsed-amplitude modulation (PAM) signal can be processed by an analogue-to-digital converter to give a digital signal. This modulation technique is called pulse code modulation (PCM). However, the PCM system does introduce quantization distortion, as there is often a small difference between the input and output signals, particularly for low amplitude signals. This can be overcome by using non-linear quantizing of the input signal so that low amplitude signals are amplified, using a device known as a 'compandor'. In telecommunications there are two non-linear encoding international standards (or laws): the A law used in Europe, which gives a 24dB advantage; or the μ law, used in North America and Japan, which gives a 30dB advantage. Decibel, or dB, is a logarithmic scale to measure something relative to a specified or implied reference level (0dB). A measurement twice the reference would therefore be at 3dB; ten times, 10 dB; one hundred times, 20dB (dB is often used when discussing sound levels, where in that context the reference is the smallest sound a human ear can detect at a pressure level of 20 microPascals

(20 μPa)—so a pneumatic drill at 100dB is in fact 10 billion times louder than the quietest sound you can hear, or at a sound pressure level of 200kPa).

2.1.4 Multiplexing

As a PAM signal consists only of a series of pulses, it is possible to interleave other PAM signals onto the same channel. This is called time-division multiplexing (TDM), or time-division multiple access (TDMA). The combined signal is known as a 'frame', which in a standard telecommunications system with an 8kHz sampling rate, has 125 μs duration. In Europe, frames are arranged in 30 channel systems, whereas in North America and Japan, 24 channel systems are used. These primary blocks of 30 or 24 channels are then combined by high-order multiplexing.

Interleaving of channels is achieved either by bit interleaving (taking a bit from each channel in turn), or word/byte interleaving (taking an 8-bit word/byte from each channel in turn—see below). Bit interleaving is simpler to carry out, and so was used for first-generation high-order multiplexers, in plesiosynchronous digital hierarchy (PDH) systems.

European 30 channel (or E-carrier) PDH systems are made up of 32 time slots of 8 digits, giving a total of 8 x 8 x 32 = 2.048 Mbit/s. Slot 0 is a frame-alignment word. Slots 1–15 and 17–31 are speech channels. Slot 16 is a signalling channel, but it can be used to allocate each other channel 4-bits to give four signalling channels at 500bit/s in each direction.

North American 24 channel (or T-carrier) PDH systems are made up of frames of 193 bits, with 24 x 8-bit speech channels and a spare frame alignment bit, giving a total of 8 x 193 = 1.544 Mbit/s. The eighth bit of frames 6 and 12 are used for signalling, as although this 'bit stealing' increases quantization noise, this is only within acceptable limits.

Second generation higher-multiplexing systems multiplex by word or byte interleaving rather than bit interleaving. These are known a synchronous digital hierarchy (SDH) systems in Europe, or synchronous optical network (SONET) systems in North America. The basic SDH signal is the synchronous transport module at level 1 (STM-1). These systems are commonly used, with compatible switches at network nodes, in high-order fibre optic networks.

Figure 2.5 shows the common PDH and second generation SDH/SONET carrier systems in use.

2.1.5 Voice telephony

Voice telephony began around the 1870s. There is increasing controversy over whether Alexander Graham Bell, Elisha Gray, or Antonio Meucci invented the telephone, with Bell's patent of 1876 (the first patent granted) being questioned as to its novelty. Whilst the history is unclear, it shows that telecommunications patent disputes are as old as telecommunications itself. Essentially what the early pioneers had discovered

PDH T & E Carrier Systems	North American			Japanese			European (CEPT)		
	Bit rate	Unit	Channels	Bit rate	Unit	Channels	Bit rate	Unit	Channels
Level 0	64 kbit/s	DS0	1	64 kbit/s		1	64 kbit/s		1
Level 1	1.544 Mbit/s	DS1	24	1.544 Mbit/s		24	2.048 Mbit/s	E1	32
Intermediate	3.152 Mbit/s	DS1C	48	US only			US only		
Level 2	6.312 Mbit/s	DS2	96	6.312 or 7.7786 Mbit/s		96/120	8.448 Mbit/s	E2	128
Level 3	44.736 Mbit/s	DS3	672	32.064 Mbit/s		480	34.368 Mbit/s	E3	512
Level 4	276.176 Mbit/s	DS4	4032	97.728 Mbit/s		1440	139.264 Mbit/s	E4	2048
Level 5	400.352 Mbit/s	DS5	5760	565.148 Mbit/s		8192	565.148 Mbit/s	E5	8192

SONET Optical Carrier Level	SONET Frame Format	SDH level and Frame Format	Payload bandwidth (Mbit/s)	Line Rate (Mbit/s)
OC-1	STS-1	STM-0	48.960	51.840
OC-3	STS-3	STM-1	150.336	155.520
OC-12	STS-12	STM-4	601.344	622.080
OC-24	STS-24	STM-8	1,202.688	1,244.160
OC-48	STS-48	STM-16	2,405.376	2,488.320
OC-96	STS-96	STM-32	4,810.752	4,976.640
OC-192	STS-192	STM-64	9,621.504	9,953.280

Figure 2.5 Telecommunications carrier systems

was a method of converting sound into an electrical signal via a microphone, which signal could then be conveyed over a wire and reconverted into sound by a speaker. Bell's first devices used soft iron reeds attached to stretched membranes. Sound vibrating the membrane within the transmitter device vibrated the reed within a double electromagnet, inducing a corresponding current in the electromagnet. In receivers, these currents in similar double electromagnets created a magnetic field that vibrated soft iron reeds attached to membranes, which then acted as speakers.

Having found a method of converting voice into electrical signals that were passed over simple copper wires between a fixed pair of users, systems gradually developed that enabled the lines to be exchanged between users. At first callers rang a local telephone exchange, where an operator manually connected the call via a jack and plug board to the called party. Such plug and jack telephone exchanges existed until very recently; I last acted as a telephone operator on such an exchange, albeit a private one, in 1991. Long-distance calls were arranged by the operator booking connections with other exchange operators.

Electromechanical telephone switching was introduced in the 1880s, with the most widespread switching system, the Strowger, being invented by the Kansas City undertaker Almon Strowger in 1888. Apocryphally, it is claimed that he sought a system that would replace human operators. He suspected that his local telephone

operator, the wife of a competitor, was diverting business enquiries to her husband. At the heart of a Strowger switch is a stepper motor, working with either vertical or rotary stepping, and being stepped by the number of pulses equal to the dialled digit, hence pulse dialling. The dial pulses were created in a handset by means of a circular finger plate, hence the term 'rotary dialling'.

The first exchanges were small, only requiring two or three digits to differentiate between subscribers. Local exchanges were also known by name, initially being reached by dialling on alphanumeric diallers the first three letters of the name, then later with phone directories giving dialling codes for the exchange—my first telephone number was 'Leuchars 340'. This is the origin of geographic numbering.

Strowger exchanges persisted until late in the last century. BT's last Strowger exchange in Crawford, Scotland, was decommissioned on 23 June 1995. It should be noted that incumbent operators who had Strowger exchanges inherited from former state-owned telecommunications operators significant real estate. A typical Strowger local exchange frame room for 30,000 lines was of the order of 1,000m^2, but has been replaced by equipment that can be contained in standard equipment racks in about 100m^2. This means that these incumbent operators arguably had the necessary free space in local exchanges to enable them to allow access to other operators for local loop unbundling and the associated collocation (see below for description of fixed networks and local loop unbundling). However, these incumbents often made other arguments against allowing access or permitting local loop unbundling, such as issues concerning physical security of equipment, availability of sufficient power supplies and integrity of the incumbents' equipment and network, given the introduction of the other operator's local loop unbundling equipment.

2.1.6 Telex and telegraph

It can be argued that telegraph was the first true telecommunications technology.[1] Wheatstone and Cooke's five-needle telegraph was patented in 1837. It used a diamond grid of 20 letters (c, j, q, u, x, and z were omitted), with five needles arranged in the middle of the grid. The deflection of any two needles would point to specific letters. Using the five-needle telegraph, the Great Western Railway introduced a public telegrams service between London and West Drayton (13 miles west of London) in 1839.

However, the need for five wires to send a signal meant that it was an expensive system, which was soon replaced by single wire systems that used the first universal form of a digital code, the Morse Code, first with single-needle systems and then with audio repeaters. Experienced operators could pass messages at around 40–50 words per minute (which, using the modern ASCII 8-bit code, would equate to a transmission rate of up to 33bit/s).

---

[1] For a good general introduction to telegraphy, see Standage, T, *The Victorian Internet* (Phoenix, 1999).

The history of data transmission from these earliest telegraph systems is then one of increasing transmission rates as encoding techniques became more efficient and telecommunications systems became able to operate at higher frequencies and with greater capacity.

Developments in code enabled fully automated teletypewriters to operate. The first international standard, the Baudot (or International Telegraph Alphabet 1) code, was a 5-bit code, able to represent 32 characters ($2^6 = 32$). This was refined into a second version, the Murray or ITA2 code—see Figure 2.6.

For early telex systems, it was not possible to synchronize the sender's bit rate with the receiver's bit rate, even though the telex systems relied on mechanical commutators (rotating switches) driven by motors set to a common, precise speed. Telex systems are therefore early examples of asynchronous serial communications systems. One channel linked the sender and receiver, hence serial. In order for some synchronization to occur for the receiver to read the transmitted character, a start signal was required, or 'start bit', to prepare the receiver mechanism for reception and a stop signal, or 'stop bit', to return the receiver mechanism to its rest position. Initially the stop bit lasted for 1.42baud, later 2, so that a 5-bit character required 7.42 and then 8baud times to transmit. This represents a loss of performance over a true synchronous system, which could transmit the character in 5baud times.

Given that transmission was usually the most expensive part of the telex system, messages were prepared offline, with the output being a 5-bit (5 hole) paper tape. Message tapes were then passed through a reader attached to a transmitter.

Telex systems including mechanical switching using pulse-dialling for circuit switching, similar to voice telephony to enable routing between teletypes, were introduced in the late 1930s, to give fully automatic data transmission systems.

00000	00001	00010	00011	00100	00101	00110	00111
NUL	E 3	LF	A -	SP	S '	I 8	U 7
01000	01001	01010	01011	01100	01101	01110	01111
CR	D ENQ	R 4	J BEL	N ,	F !	C :	K (
10000	10001	10010	10011	10100	10101	10110	10111
T 5	Z +	L)	W 2	H £	Y 6	P 0	Q 1
11000	11001	11010	11011	11100	11101	11110	11111
O 9	B ?	G &	FIGS	M .	X /	V ;	LTRS

ITA2 uses two code sub-sets. The FIGS character signals the following code is a figure, until reset by the character LTRS. CR is a carriage return, LF is a fine feed, BEL is the bell character to sound a bell in the receiver, SP is space and NUL is a null character (blank). ENQ is a signal to the receiver to send its answerback.

Figure 2.6 Murray ITA2 Code

These 'type A' telex systems operated at 45.45baud, with up to 25 telex channels able to use a single long-distance telephone channel. They persisted into the 1970s.

With the convergence of data and telephony bearer networks, following the conversion of PSTNs to digital networks, the need for separate telex and telegraph systems evaporated. In addition, email systems, which were first messaging systems between accounts on the same (mainframe) computer, adopted more universal coding methods so that eventually email systems become fully standardized and interoperable, superseding telex and telegram systems.

2.1.7 Data networks

High speed and high capacity data networks were originally developed for computing applications. These were extensions of the data networks and their associated protocols used to link mainframe computers with their peripheral devices and terminals. As computing speeds and power increased, so did the need for high speed communications networks. In addition, computers and peripheral devices began to be networked using shared communications, with local area networks (LANs) using protocols such as token ring and Ethernet, which were adapted for interconnection with other LANs to form wide area networks (WANs).

In telecommunications, the most commonly used protocols used for data and computer networks are Ethernet, Frame Relay and Asynchronous Transfer Mode (ATM).

Ethernet is essentially a family of frame-based computer networking technologies for LANs that has been in use since the 1980s. Each device on an Ethernet network has access to a shared communications channel. A device wishing to send a frame of data detects whether the channel is idle and transmits. If the frame collides with another sender's frame, this is detected and the sender waits for a random backoff period and resends. This is often compared to a dinner party, where guests use a common communication channel, the air. A guest wishing to speak waits for the current speaker to finish then speaks. If two guests start speaking at the same time, both stop and wait for a short random time before trying to speak again. As the Ethernet protocol provides for frames with a destination and source address, it has been possible to develop switched Ethernet networks. The protocol has developed from the first 3Mbit/s system described in the first experimental Ethernet network to the still relatively new 10Gbit/s standard (IEEE 802.3ae, which has yet to be formally incorporated into the Ethernet IEEE 802.3 standard). WiFi is usually implemented using a wireless Ethernet standard (IEEE 802.11).

The oldest common technique/standard in common use is frame relay, which was first mooted to the Cumulative Committee on International Telephone and Telegraph (CCITT), the forerunner of ITU-T, in 1984. Frame relay was itself a development of a packet-data standard known as X.25, which was a signalling protocol designed to provide error-free delivery over copper and coaxial cable telecommunications networks that had high error rates. Frame relay stripped down the error-correcting elements

of X.25 so that it was 20 times faster. It also sends data in variable-sized frames rather than packets, with frames containing errors simply dropped (and retransmitted by the sender if requested by the receiver). Frame relay is designed for use on common-access shared-use networks, but for most services provides a permanent virtual circuit between access/termination points. It is commonly used for speeds of between 56kbit/s and 45Mbit/s.

The most common data network standard is asynchronous transfer mode (ATM), which is a development of frame relay in that it is a cell relay, packet switching network, and data link layer protocol. Data is encoded by ATM into small fixed-sized cells (53 bytes, of which 48 bytes are data). It is also known as a connection-orientated technology, in that a logical signalling connection must be made between access/termination points before data is exchanged. It is capable of passing data at speeds of up to 622.080Mbit/s, being designed for SDH links at 155.520Mbit/s. The size of ATM cells is not set by reference to any technological requirements, but is the result of political compromise. The conventional wisdom is that the United States wished to have a cell size of 64 bytes, as this would have made data handling easier (the cell size being a power of 2), but Europe wanted a cell size of 32 bytes. The smaller 32 byte cell size (and therefore shorter transmission times) would have simplified voice applications in Europe—most European countries would have been able to deploy ATM-based voice networks with no requirement for echo cancellation with cells of 32 bytes. The ugly compromise was 48 data bytes.

2.1.8 Converged or integrated networks and the Internet

The first technology that attempted to provide an integrated voice and data network was ISDN (Integrated Services Digital Network, a backronym, as it was originally *Integrertes Sprachund Datennetz*, the German for 'integrated speech and data net'). ISDN is a circuit-switched digital telephone system that was introduced in the 1980s to provide the first broadband, at 128kbit/s, and high quality speech and video conferencing capability. The 'integrated' part of ISDN refers to the protocol's ability to send two or more simultaneous connections in any combination of speech, video, data, or fax, over a single line. Whilst digital subscriber line (DSL) services can now provide better broadband speeds than ISDN, it remains common in some countries where it was effectively rolled out or in rural or outlying areas where high speed DSL is not possible. For example, in Germany there were as many as 25 million ISDN channels (29 per cent of all subscribers) in 2003. ISDN is also widely used in the radio broadcasting industry to link studios. Frame relay was also developed to facilitate transport of traffic in ISDNs.

However, the development of the packet-switched Transmission Control Protocol/Internet Protocol (TCP/IP) model has provided a computer network protocol that is able to carry real time as well as high speed data traffic. TCP/IP was developed for the US Department of Defense Advanced Research Projects Agency Network (ARPANET), a military WAN, which was the predecessor to the Internet. ARPANET

was replaced in 1989 by the US National Science Foundation Network (NSFNet), a US universities' WAN, which was finally shut down on 30 April 1995 as the Internet became a private enterprise.

The network layer of the protocol, the Internet Protocol (IP) is a 'best efforts' delivery protocol for the routing of packets of data through a network. The IP packet header identifies the source and destination by means of an IP address, and the packet length can be variable (compared to the fixed length of frame in Frame Relay and ATM). Routers in the network use the TCP/IP routing algorithms to determine the route each packet takes over the network from source to destination, and they can loosely be considered to be the equivalent of switches in switched networks. The adaptability of IP means that it can use other technologies for data links (e.g. ATM, Frame Relay, ISDN, WiFi, GPRS), but with the advent of multiple protocol label switching nodes, these data link layers can be dispensed with.

One other important feature of TCP/IP networks is that they are interconnected by a hierarchy of peering and transit arrangements. In traditional fixed telephony networks the principle of calling party pays means that the calling party network pays a termination fee to the network of the called party (or transit fee(s) to intermediate network(s)). In data networks, peering and transit are used. Peering is used between data networks who consider that there will be a symmetric data flow between them, so that there will be zero settlement (i.e. they agree to connect their networks at no cost). There is no overall Internet authority, so no formal definition of the Internet's hierarchy. However, it is generally accepted that the Internet consists of Tier 1 networks, being a network that only enters into peering agreements with other networks to reach the Internet, Tier 2 networks who both peer and purchase IP transit, and Tier 3 networks who solely purchase IP transit to reach the Internet. IP transit is the sale of wholesale Internet bandwidth to Internet service providers (ISPs) and content providers.

At the top of the TCP/IP Internet are so-called Tier 1 networks, being those networks that do not purchase IP transit from any other network in order to reach any other Internet point. Tier 1 networks peer with all other Tier 1 networks, who then form a self-regulating group, whose behaviour may be compared to a cartel.[2] A Tier 1 operator considered by the others to be selling IP transit capacity too cheaply, for example, could be threatened with de-peering, which would result in downstream customers of the de-peered Tier 1 operator with no alternative Internet routing, and therefore being isolated until the de-peered operator purchases IP transit capacity or until the network operators of the isolated parts of the Internet resume peering. Tier 1 networks can be considered to be the backbone of the Internet.

It should be noted that the status of Tier 2 and 3 networks is often misrepresented in Internet marketing, as networks often wish to claim Tier 1 status when they are not

---

[2] For a competition-based examination of Tier 1 networks, see *WorldCom and MCI* (Case IV/M.1069; OJ L 116/1, 4 May 1999).

true peering-only networks. In particular, networks are often stated to be 'regional Tier 1', in that it is a network that only peers within a region, but is not IP transit free globally. As with genuine Tier 1 networks, regional Tier 1 networks can exhibit cartel-like behaviour within a region. It should not be a surprise to hear that many regional Tier 1 networks, strictly dominant Tier 2 networks in a region, are those of incumbent operators.

2.2 FIXED (TELEPHONY) NETWORKS

Most fixed telecommunications operators have inherited switched-circuit networks from former state monopoly telecommunications service providers that were designed principally for the carriage of voice telephony. These are the public switched telecommunications networks (PSTNs)—see Figure 2.7.

PSTNs typically comprise of UTP connections between subscribers, via distribution points mounted on telegraph poles and street cabinets, and the main distribution frame (MDF), which is where the individual UTPs are patched to a switch which also multiplexes the switched channels onto higher order PDH cables. This switch is known as the digital local exchange (DLE), which is the lowest switch in the PSTN hierarchy, i.e. the switch physically closest to the subscriber. In some PSTNs, the MDF for some individual subscriber lines is located away from the DLE. In this case the channels on the switch-side of the MDF are multiplexed onto high capacity cables by a remote concentrator unit (RCU). This cable is then connected to the DLE. All these cables between subscribers and the MDFs/DLEs are known as the local loop or 'last mile'.

DLEs are connected to at least one higher level of switch known as a tandem exchange (TX). Various names are given to TXs, depending upon how many DLEs or TXs, if any, are connected to them. For example, the British Telecom PSTN consists of:

(1) digital main switching units, which are the set of tandem exchanges that are all connected to each other;

(2) wide area tandems, which are connected to some other tandem network switches but not all of them;

(3) digital junction switching units, which are an additional layer of switches within the London area above the DLEs to allow calls to be routed without using any other tandem network switches; and

(4) some next generation switches.

DLEs can also be linked. This gives rise to a number of different types of call (see Figure 2.8):

i. own exchange calls, where the call is routed from a calling party to a called party on the same DLE;

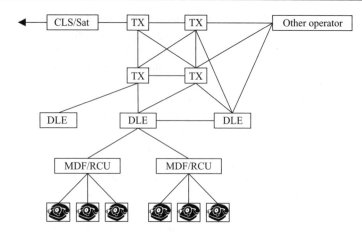

Figure 2.7 PSTN

ii. linked exchange calls, where the calling party is on a DLE linked to the DLE of the called party;

iii. single tandem calls, which route from the calling party's DLE via a tandem exchange to the called party's DLE; and

iv. double tandem calls, which go over more than one tandem exchange.

These various routes become important when determining the conveyancing and other costs to a PSTN operator of routing a call, or the termination costs for inter-connection purposes (where the termination fee of an operator with significant market power or dominance in the voice telephony market is often required to be cost-orientated).

Capacity/cables between RCUs, DLEs, and TXs are often collectively known as the backhaul to the trunk or core network, being the mesh network between TXs.

PSTNs can be interconnected at the DLE or TX switching levels, but typically interconnection is at the TXs' level, via in-span interconnection (ISI) or customer sited interconnection (CSI). For ISI the interconnection is made by a cable that runs between the interconnecting PSTN operators' tandem switches located on the operators' own sites, with each operator notionally owning and maintaining half the link cable. For CSI, interconnection is made via tie cables connecting the interconnecting PSTN operators' switches which are collocated at one of the operators' sites. International interconnection is made with an operator of either a submarine cable or satellite earth station, with the place of interconnection known as an international gateway. The place where the submarine cable terminates is known as the cable landing station, which is usually owned and operated by the submarine cable operator. Submarine cables are expensive to lay and maintain—it is not uncommon for cables to be

broken by ships dragging their anchors, with the cost of repair running to over US$1 million (the cost of the charter of a submarine cable laying ship is of the order of not much less than US$100,000 per day). In order to be economic, these cables have to carry significant levels of traffic. They are therefore usually capable of carrying traffic of the order of STM-64.[3]

Where operators interconnect, each can originate traffic that is terminated on the other and vice versa. As traditional fixed voice telephony in most of the world is billed upon the calling party pays (CPP) principle, the network of the calling party must pay the network of the called party a network termination fee (known as calling party network pays (CPNP)).[4] In most markets the former state monopoly network operator owns a dominant share of the local loop. As duplicating the local loop is prohibitively expensive, alternative means are sought to give non-dominant operators the ability to provide telecommunications services. This is often achieved by requiring the dominant network operator to provide carrier selection (also known as indirect access) or carrier pre-selection services.[5] These services enable a subscriber on either a call-by-call basis or for all calls to determine which network operator will carry the subscribers' calls. This requires either that the calling party dial a selection code (for carrier selection/indirect access, the dialling code also being known as an access code), or that the network should recognize the subscriber as having pre-selected that its calls be switched to the chosen network, so that in either case the switched network diverts the call as soon as technically possible to the relevant interconnection point.

PSTNs do carry some data traffic in the form of dial-up Internet traffic, fax, and telex, but fixed telecommunications operators usually operate separate fixed networks for data traffic. These are typically frame relay and asynchronous transfer mode (ATM) networks, but increasingly operators use IP networks for backhaul of data. These data networks reach the end user either via direct means, such as termination points for switched digital networks such as BT's Integrated Switched Digital Network (ISDN) or over the same UTPs used for the PSTN. This is done by a form of frequency division multiplexing—the data is modulated onto a high frequency carrier by a digital subscriber line access multiplexer (DSLAM) located at the DLE or RCU on the switch-side of the MDF, which then uses the same UTP as the voice telephony. The voice telephony signal, being at a lower frequency than the data signal, can easily be filtered out of the combined signal by small and cheap low pass filters. It is these filters that are used with asynchronous digital subscriber line

---

[3] See Figure 2.5.
[4] There are some significant territories, such as North America, where receiver party pays (RPP). Also, the introduction of NGN networks may force other territories to consider changing from CPP to RPP, as at the wholesale level there are good arguments for operators moving from CPNP to 'bill and keep', where each network bears the cost of terminating traffic coming from other carriers.
[5] See further Chapter 5, at 5.3, and Chapter 9, at 9.5.

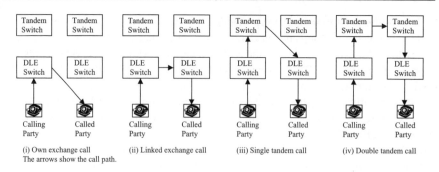

(i) Own exchange call
The arrows show the call path.

(ii) Linked exchange call

(iii) Single tandem call

(iv) Double tandem call

Figure 2.8 Types of PSTN call

(ADSL) services. DSL services are normally configured to give higher download bandwidth from the DSLAM to the DSL subscriber than upload bandwidth from the subscriber to the DSLAM, hence asynchronous.

Figure 2.9 shows DSL access to a subscriber. To the left of the DSLAM in the diagram is the transport network for the data services, usually ATM or Frame Relay, with a higher IP network. Both the IP network and ATM/Frame Relay network are via an Internet service provider (ISP) or broadband remote access server (BRAS) to the Internet (www on the diagram).

There are two important features of DSL services that impact on the deliverable bandwidth and hence data rates that a subscriber can obtain. The first is the distance between the DSLAM and the subscriber, as high frequency signals deteriorate markedly over UTPs with distance. The second is the contention ratio of the DSLAM, or in other words the number of DSL subscribers that can potentially share the DSLAM backhaul via the ATM transport network to the relevant ISP or BRAS. The higher the contention ratio (i.e. the number of potential DSL subscribers that can share a connection to an ISP), the potentially lower the achievable speed. It really does depend upon the number of DSL subscribers online at any one time. It is for this reason that ISPs using DSL connectivity often advertise their services with speed 'up to' a declared maximum that may, for many potential subscribers, never be achievable.

The network of cables from subscribers to the MDF is known as the local loop or 'last mile'. Local loop unbundling is therefore the label to describe the access by other operators to the local loop owned and operated by another operator. The usual form of unbundling, or half-unbundling, is where the local loop operator continues to provide switched voice telephony whilst another service provider delivers DSL services. This is normally done by collocating at the DLE the DSLAMs of the other operator, with the DSLAM operator providing its own backhaul to its own frame relay, ATM, or IP transport network. Alternatively, in full unbundling the other operator may take the PSTN line as well as the DSL.

Where the local loop operator provides a wholesale service for the provision of fully unbundled local loop and backhaul from multiple subscribers to a point of presence, this is known as wholesale line rental. Where the wholesale service is only for broadband access for DSL services, with the service using the DSLAMs and backhaul of the local loop operator, this is known as bitstream access.

An alternative to bitstream access or half-unbundling is sub-loop unbundling. This is where the local loop operator provides access to the unbundling operator at the street cabinet/RCU level, with the DSLAM of the unbundling operator being sited in a nearby cabinet joined to the local loop street cabinet by a tie cable. There is growing interest in sub-loop unbundling, as the close proximity of the DSLAM to the subscriber enables extremely fast DSL services to be provided.

Most incumbent fixed network operators have inherited a PSTN and will almost certainly have at least one data network, either Frame Relay or ATM. Although there was a suggestion that ISDN could provide for a single converged network, it has been overtaken by the ability of IP networks to carry both real time and high speed data applications. As a result, many operators who use multiple networks are converging them onto one Internet Protocol/MultiPrococol Label Switching (IP/MPLS) network, commonly known as a next generation network (NGN), to benefit from the obvious savings in rationalizing transport network provision. In place of a DLE with DSLAMs, an NGN has a multi-service access node (MSAN), which is connected to a metro node to the IP/MPLS core network. This is shown in Figure 2.10.

As an example of the effect of convergence onto NGNs, BT announced in its early presentations of its plans for its NGN, known as 21CN or 21st Century Network, that by converting to an IP/MPLS network it would be able to rationalize

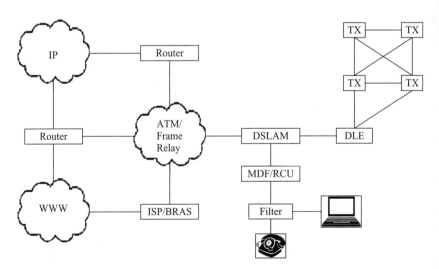

Figure 2.9 DSL and unbundling

approximately 3,500 physical sites and points of presence for its existing IP, Frame Relay, ATM, and PSTN sites down to approximately 100 IP/MPLS metro nodes.

2.3 MOBILE NETWORKS

Mobile networks are often known as cellular networks as they are made up of a tessellation of cells, designed so that the network can use its allocated frequency spectrum in the most efficient way possible. This is shown in Figure 2.11.

A cell is defined as the area of coverage of a base station (BS). Adjacent cells use different frequencies to ensure that there is no channel interference, but the frequencies are reused in the tessellation pattern. In rural areas the cells can cover an extensive area, whereas in built-up areas, the area can be quite small (hence femtocells). Unlike Figure 2.11, therefore, cell sizes are dependent upon local geography and capacity requirements and are not uniform in size or shape.

2.3.1 GSM networks

Global system for mobile communications (GSM, another backronym, being originally *Groupe Spécial Mobile*) is the most ubiquitous standard, being claimed by the

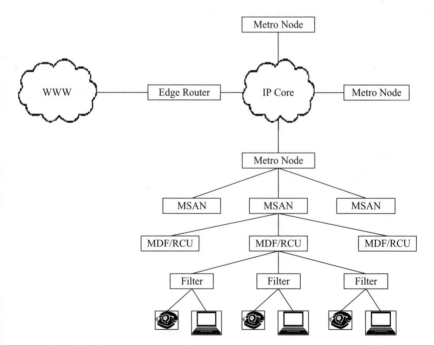

Figure 2.10 IP only networks (NGNs)

GSM Association, the trade association for GSM network operators and equipment suppliers, to cover 82 per cent of the mobile phone market in 2007, with over 2 billion subscribers in over 212 countries and territories. It is also widely known as 2G (second generation, the first being analogue mobile networks). It has continued to develop from the system first deployed in 1991, with the release of standard added packet data capabilities, by means of the General Packet Radio Service (GPRS) in 1997 (hence '2.5G'), with enhanced packet data possible from 1999 with the Enhanced Data Rates for GSM Evolution (EDGE) standard (hence '2.75G', although sometimes claimed to be a 3G technology—see below). GPRS enables data transmission of rates from 56 to 114kbit/s, whereas EDGE gives up to 236.8kbit/s (with a theoretical maximum of 473.6kbit/s).

The GSM standard defines uplinks and downlinks with 25MHz bandwidth subdivided into 124 carrier frequency channels, each spaced 200kHz apart; this is frequency division multiple access (FDMA). By means of FDMA, eight full-rate or sixteen half-rate speech channels can be interleaved onto each radio frequency channel. GSM uses Gaussian minimum-shift keying (GMSK), which can be described as a form of continuous-phase FSK, where the signal to be modulated is smoothed by a Gaussian low-pass filter, which reduces adjacent channel interference.

In GSM networks, the base station controls the transmitters and receivers (mobile phone masts) that communicate directly with handsets, using frequencies in the 900MHz or 1800MHz bands for most GSM standard networks. Base stations are normally linked by fixed backhaul to mobile switching centres (MSCs) when such backhaul is commercially available, or by wireless backhaul (typically microwave links). All MSCs are connected to a customer and billing database, the Home Location Register (HLR), which holds all subscriber information. This includes all security information, which is held in the authentication centre (AUC) (i.e. details of all the subscriber identification module (SIM) cards and device international mobile equipment identifiers (IMEIs)). A simplified diagram of a GSM network is shown at Figure 2.12.

The IMEI is a number unique to every mobile phone. As this information is held by the GSM network, it can be used to verify access by valid devices and can block access to invalid, usually stolen, devices.

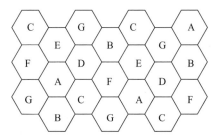

Figure 2.11 Cellular network—reuse of frequencies (for frequencies A to G)

SIM cards are smart cards that allow subscribers to transfer information between handsets, or to change operators and reuse the handset by changing the SIM card. However, some operators block the reuse of handsets by tying the use of a handset to a single SIM card issued by them. This is known as 'SIM locking', and is normally done as the operator subsidizes the price of the handset, in some cases to zero. Clearly, it would not want to have these subsidized or free handsets open to be used on other operators' networks. This practice is, however, illegal in some countries (e.g. Belgium, Costa Rica, India, Indonesia, Pakistan, and Malaysia).

On switching on a GSM handset, it communicates with the nearest base station, which uploads the SIM card and IMEI details to the base station's MSC. Incorporated within each MSC is a Visitor Register, which holds subscription information on every handset in its coverage area, as well as the handset's location data. For handsets of subscribers of the MSC's network, this information is copied from the HLR, and the AUC confirms that the subscriber is authorized to use the network (via the SIM card) and that the device has not been reported as stolen or is otherwise locked (via the IMEI). For other handsets, the MSC communicates with the subscriber's network HLR to carry out authentication, where the networks have a roaming agreement in place to enable the MSC to do so. If there is no roaming agreement, the handset will not be authenticated and registered, other than for emergency calls only.

The MSC therefore knows in which cell and under which base station the handset is operating in order to route calls to it. This is known as switch-on registration. The handset monitors the signal strength of the broadcast channel from the base station to which it is registered, so that if the signal strength deteriorates below a certain level, it will seek the strongest signal on other broadcast channels (from adjacent cells). If necessary, it will select the adjacent cell and re-register (known as forced registration).

On initiating a call, the MSC will allocate a channel to the calling handset. The MSC sets up the call path, either within the network to another mobile handset (including allocating a radio channel in the called party's cell) or to an interconnection point for routing and termination on the called party's network. A similar process to registration takes place if a handset moves across cell boundaries during a call, in a process known as 'handover' or 'handoff' (handover is the UK English/3GPP term). Base stations periodically monitor the signal strength of mobile handsets within their range with a call in progress, under the control of the MSC. If the signal strength at an adjacent cell is determined by the MSC to be better than in the cell handling the call, then the MSC allocates a radio channel in the new cell, sets up the call path to that channel, and directs the handset to retune. Once the handset has retuned, the old channel is released.

2.3.2 3G/UMTS Networks

In order to facilitate multimedia and data mobile applications a third generation of mobile network technologies (or 3G) have been developed to meet the requirements set out by the ITU in its specification for 3G networks (IMT-2000).

The European standard is the Universal Mobile Telecommunications System (UMTS), also known as 3GSM.

UMTS uses a combination of wideband code division multiple access (WCDMA) and time-division CDMA (TD-CDMA). WCDMA is a so-called 'spread spectrum' technique that enables each user to access the whole of the available bandwidth of a wide spectrum (2 x 5MHz for uplink and downlink) in order to set up a call channel (compared to time slots in TDMA or small allocated sub-bandwidths in FDMA). For TD-CDMA, the channel available for CDMA is more limited, usually to channel with 5MHz bandwidth.[6]

CDMA works by giving each call a unique code, which is used to modulate that call. A simple analogy that is often used to explain CDMA is the dinner party. Unlike the Ethernet solution, which is based upon determining if the room is quiet and then speaking etc., mobile networks use more control. GSM uses TDMA on each channel, which is like each person at the party being given a time slot in which to speak, and FDMA for its separate channels, which is like the dinner party guests speaking at different pitches—you would be able to pick out the person speaking after inhaling helium over the general party conversation. CDMA can be likened to the dinner party guests speaking in different languages—guests speaking the same language would be able to filter out other conversations in other languages.

WCDMA can theoretically pass data at up to 14Mbit/s, using an enhanced technology known as High Speed Downlink Packet Access (HSDPA), but this depends upon the signal strength of each user. HSDPA uses adaptive modulation and coding, so that signals with good signal strength adapt from initial QPSK to 16QAM, doubling the data rates.

UMTS/3G is essentially the deployment of more advanced 'air interfaces'.[7] The 3G base station, MSC, and associated backhaul infrastructure has a similar configuration as for standard GSM, with parts of a 3G network known as the circuit-switched domain (essentially the voice traffic sub-system) and the other part the packet-switched domain—see Figure 2.13.

2G with EDGE also have these circuit-switched and packet-switched domains, but use the 2G GMSK modulation for the radio access network. The use of a common radio access network for a circuit-switched domain and a packet-switched domain therefore has parallels with the use of the local loop in fixed networks providing common access for traditional circuit-switched telephony (PSTNs) and data networks. 2G GMSK air interfaces can therefore be considered to be the copper wire parallel for fixed networks, with 3G CDMA/HSDPA air interfaces being the fibre to the curb/fibre to the street cabinet parallel.

---

[6] The other IMT-2000 3G standard in common use is CDMA2000, which uses CDMA over 2×1.25 MHz bandwidth radio channels. CDMA2000's narrower bandwidth makes it easier to use in crowded spectrum.

[7] Under EU law, the 'air interface' represents the regulatory boundary between the network and the terminal equipment of the user. See further Chapter 5, at 5.2.

For operators with UMTS and GSM networks, much of the infrastructure can be shared.

2.4 SATELLITE NETWORKS[8]

The late Sir Arthur C Clarke famously proposed the use of geostationary satellites for communications purposes in the magazine *Wireless World* in 1945. This became a reality on 6 April 1965, with the launch of Intelsat 1 'Early Bird'. However, other types of orbits are also used, particularly elliptical and low (polar and non-polar) orbits. In fact, the first active, direct relay communications satellite, Telstar, owned and operated by a multinational consortium that included AT&T, Bell Telephone Laboratories, NASA, the British General Post Office, and French National PTT, was placed in an elliptical orbit (completed once every 2 hours and 37 minutes), rotating at a 45° angle above the equator, on 10 July 1962.

A satellite in an equatorial circular orbit at a distance of approximately 35,787km (22,237 miles) above mean sea level remains geostationary over the same point on the Earth's equator. Ground stations for such a satellite do not need expensive satellite tracking equipment and can fix the position of their ground antennas, but launching a satellite into a relatively high orbit is more expensive.

Low orbit satellites typically use a circular orbit at around 400km above the earth's surface, giving a rotational period of about 90 minutes. As these satellites are only visible from within a footprint of about 1,000km radius and change their position relative to the ground quickly, a series of low orbit satellites are needed to maintain connectivity, and sophisticated tracking equipment is needed at the earth station. However, these satellites are less expensive to launch and can operate with a lower signal strength. A group of satellites providing continuous coverage is known as a satellite constellation. Two such constellations were intended for satellite phone services, for Iridium and Globalstar.

The Iridium system comprises 66 active low orbit satellites, giving whole-earth coverage (the atomic number for Iridium is 77, the original planned number of satellites). The Iridium service was launched on 1 November 1998, but although it went into Chapter 11 bankruptcy in 1999, has been profitable since 2004. One of its major customers is the US Department of Defense.

The Globalstar system comprises of 40 active satellites that, unlike Iridium, act as repeaters only and have no interlinking. A network of ground stations provides connectivity, with the result that there are areas of the world that are not covered by the system, even though satellites overfly them. However, the unexpectedly rapid deterioration of some of the satellites' amplifiers means that Globalstar will loose duplex (two-way) communications during 2008. Eight spare satellites were launched

---

[8] For a discussion of satellite regulation, see Chapter 15, at 15.2.1.

and a constellation of 48 second-generation satellites was announced in 2007, but it remains to be seen whether Globalstar can maintain a service with these difficulties. Thuraya is an example of a geostationary satellites telecommunications operator, with its first operational satellite, Thuraya 2, capable of handling 13,750 simultaneous voice calls and with a footprint covering most of Europe, the Middle East, and Africa. Thuraya 3 was only launched on 15 January 2008, in order to provide a footprint to cover China, South East Asia, and most of Australasia.

Satellites were initially commercially viable for the provision of intercontinental connectivity for long distance voice telephony. PSTNs routed international calls to an earth station, where they were transmitted via an uplink to a geostationary satellite. The downlink followed a similar path. However, with the introduction of cheaper submarine fibre optic cables, satellites continue to be economic only for remote islands where there is no submarine cable services (for example, Ascension Island, Saint Helena, the Falkland Islands) or for broadcasting applications.

2.5 WIRELESS NETWORKS

The following sections describe technologies that are currently specified for fixed use only. However, they are not truly fixed, in that end user terminal equipment can be moved in a limited coverage area without loss of service. The distinguishing feature between them and the mobile technologies described above is ability to transfer a call or connection between one area of coverage and another. In other words, can the relevant technology handle instantaneous 'hard handovers', where the connection to the first cell is released and only then is a channel in the second cell established, or 'soft handovers', where the connection to the first cell is maintained whilst the connection to the second cell is established.

2.5.1 Wi-Fi

Wi-Fi is the brand name of the Wi-Fi Alliance,[9] a trade association (formerly the Wireless Ethernet Compatibility Alliance), for the wireless technologies implementing the IEEE standards 802.11b and 802.11g, which are commonly deployed in the 2.4GHz band. Wi-Fi is commonly used to enable devices to connect to the Internet when within range of a wireless network access point, or hotspot. Backhaul to the core or transport network is usually provided by fixed networks, WiMAX mesh networks or microwave links. Wi-Fi adapters are now built into most laptops and increasingly other user terminal devices, and the price of Wi-Fi chipsets continues to fall.

---

[9] See Wi-Fi Alliance website at <http://www.wi-fi.org/>.

Wi-Fi hotspots have limited range. A typical hotspot with a standard antenna might have a range of 32m (120ft) indoors and 95m (300ft) outdoors. Range also varies with frequency. Wi-Fi in the most common 2.4GHz spectrum has better range than Wi-Fi in 5GHz spectrum. However, Wi-Fi is frequently used in mesh networks to provide city-wide coverage, even though the system uses contention access. This means that all subscribers that use a particular wireless access point or Wi-Fi hotspot are competing for the hotspot's access on a random interrupt basis, so that Wi-Fi terminal devices nearer to the hotspot access point can more easily interrupt the point than those further away, so that applications that require a constant quality of service, such as voice over IP or IP TV, cannot easily be supported.

2.5.2 WiMAX

WiMAX (Worldwide Interoperability for Microwave Access) has been developed to provide a technology for wireless data networks, or strictly, wireless local loop. The technology is the implementation of the IEEE standard 802.16-2004.[10] In fixed WiMAX there is no ability for handover between base stations, so that there is no true mobile service. However, users can roam within a base station coverage area and can receive services from any base station. As a result, these are sometimes referred to as 'nomadic services'. Mobile WiMAX allows base station handover during a connection.

WiMAX is different to Wi-Fi in that a scheduling algorithm is used to provide multi-user access to a wireless AP and base station. Once assigned, a subscriber maintains an access slot on a TDMA basis. The time slot can expand and contract as other users access the AP, but the continuous connection means that it is more stable and the base station can control the subscribers' quality of services, so permitting voice over Internet (VoIP) applications to be used successfully.

WiMAX can be deployed in the 2 to 66GHz frequency range, but there is no global licensed spectrum set aside for it. The WiMAX Forum,[11] a trade association of WiMAX operators and suppliers, has published spectrum profiles for WiMAX deployment in 2.3GHz, 2.5GHz, and 3.5GHz, in an effort to promote these bands and enable mobile phones and WiMAX-embedded laptops to be produced with a lower unit cost. WiMAX is also deployed in the parts of the 5GHz band that are unlicensed in many countries. WiMAX may also benefit from the so-called 'digital dividend', i.e. the freeing up of spectrum currently used for analogue TV broadcasting with the switchover to digital TV.

Early wireless metropolitan area network (WirelessMAN) standards such as the European standard HIPERMAN (High Performance Radio Metropolitan Area Network), a European Telecommunications Standards Institute (ETSI) Broadband

---

[10] Commonly referred to as '802-16d' or 'fixed WiMAX', and IEEE 802.16e-2005, which amends IEEE 802.16-2004, known as '802.16e' or 'mobile WiMAX'.

[11] See <http://www.wimaxforum.org/home/>.

Radio Access Networks (BRAN) group standard for wireless network communication in the 2 to 11GHz bands, and the Korean standard WiBro (*Wi*reless *Bro*adband), originally deployed in South Korea in the 2.3–2.4GHz band, have been harmonized as part of WiMAX.

2.6 NUMBER PORTABILITY

There is one *ex ante* regulatory measure that ought to be technologically explained, so that its difficulties should not be underestimated.[12] That is number portability. Number portability is the regulated facility that enables subscribers of a publicly available telephone network to change their service provider whilst keeping their allocated telephone number. This is often considered an important step in newly liberalized markets to facilitate ease of switching between service providers. Essentially there are two main types of technical solution to number portability: on-switch and off-switch solutions.

2.6.1 On-Switch

On-switch number portability is so called because the solution depends upon the switches in a switched network rerouting ported calls, or call forwarding, to the new destination of the relevant subscriber. It is a standard method of implementing fixed-to-fixed network number portability. To an extent the ability to implement on-switch number portability also depends upon the relevant numbering plan. For example, where a numbering plan includes local geographic numbering, such as in the UK for fixed telephony, then number portability may be restricted to local areas.

Call forwarding increases the conveyance costs of any ported call and is an inefficient use of network resources such as switching and backhaul capacity, particularly as a result of 'tromboning', and use of allocated numbers. Tromboning is the name given to the effect of the donor network sending back a call to a ported number to the transit switch, which then forwards the call to the gaining network—see Figure 2.14.

Simple call forwarding, where standard switch features are used to reroute calls to ported numbers, can be implemented by assigning to the ported number subscriber a second number. This loses the subscriber's correct call line identifier (CLI) and rapidly consumes numbering resources, but is simple to implement using number translation capabilities of the network software-controlled switches. Alternatively, a generic number can be used to identify ported numbers, but although this uses fewer number resources, it requires modification to all DLEs and is therefore not simple to implement.

---

[12] For a discussion of the UK regulatory approach to number portability, see Chapter 5, at 5.2.

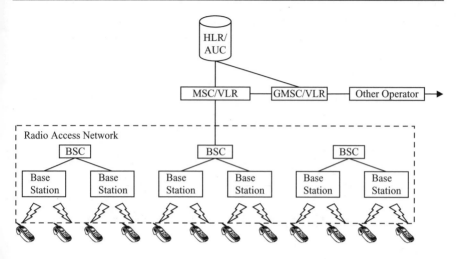

KEY

HLR:	Home Location Register
AVC:	Authentication Centre
MSC:	Mobile Switching Centre
GMSC:	Gateway MSC
VLR:	Visitor Location Register
BSC:	Base Station Controller

Figure 2.12 2G/GSM network

Modified call forwarding is more complex, as it involves enhanced donor switch software to free up resources within the donor switch. However, the call setup and transmission path continues to require involvement of the donor operator. Typical examples are call drop-back, where tromboning between DLEs and TXs is eliminated, and routing table modifications. For trunk or tandem exchange routing table modifications, processing of ported calls takes place at the TX level, so that there is no tromboning to DLEs and no changes are required to DLEs. However, extra analysis of geographic called numbers is required at the tandem exchange.

2.6.2 Off-Switch

Off-switch solutions require the originating switch to refer to a network or national level number portability database to determine whether a called number is to a ported number. If it is, then the originating switch immediately routes it correctly, without first routing the call to the donor switch. Off-switch solutions are either all call query, which, as it name suggests, requires every call to require a query to be made to the number portability database, or query on release, which is a modified call-forwarding technique. The query to a number portability database is only made when the donor switch signals back that the called number has ported.

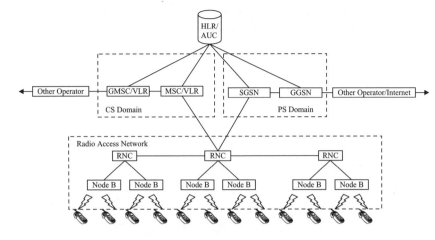

KEY

CS Domain:	Circuit switched domain/network (essentially for voice traffic)
GGSN:	Gateway GRRS Support Node
SGSN:	Service GPRS Support Node
PS Domain:	Packet switched domain/network (essentially for data/IP/internet traffic)
RNC:	Radio Network Controller
Node B:	3G base station

For 3G Networks, there is a common set of abbreviations for various network backhaul.

IuB:	RNC to Node B interface
IuR:	Inter-RNC interfaces (note that in GSM networks there are no equivalent BSC to BSC interfaces)
IuCS:	RNC to CS Domain interface
IuPS:	RNC to PS Domain Interface

Figure 2.13 3G Network

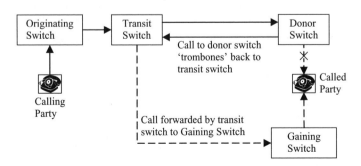

Figure 2.14 Tromboning

All call forward is more efficient if the number of ported numbers increases to an extent that at least 20–25 per cent of the call traffic is to ported numbers. It does not require access to the donor network and reduces conveyancing costs. However, it is expensive to implement in standard PSTNs, and is only likely to be attractive in NGNs.

Mobile number portability is achieved via off-switch solutions, as the HLR and MSC/VLR already have some of the features of a look-up system for an all-call query solution. However, there are significant billing issues, as routing may mean calls of a roaming user may not enter a gaining network, which can then log the origin, destination, and duration of a call for billing purposes, as the calls may be routed by a donor network direct to the roaming user's network. Signalling systems dependent solutions are therefore required, known as signal relay function solutions. All call query via a central database of ported numbers is the common method used for mobile number portability in the European Union, the notable exception being the UK, which uses a unique signal relay function solution.

2.7 CONCLUSIONS

Having spent a long chapter to explain electronic communications, one increasing feature of modern telecommunications regulation suggests that regulatory lawyers will have less reason to try to understand the technical background to any new electronic communications network or service—the increasing application of the principle of technological neutrality. This regulatory principle suggests that 'legislation should define the objectives to be achieved, and should neither impose, nor discriminate in favour of, the use of a particular type of technology to achieve those objectives'.[13] However, international regulatory best practice states that it is essential to determine that there has been or will be a market failure to warrant ex ante regulation. In the European Union the criteria to determine whether a market should be subject to ex ante regulation includes the presence of high and non-transitory barriers to entry.[14] The European Regulators Group guidance on the Commission's criteria suggests that, amongst other factors that national regulatory authorities (NRAs) ought to consider when evaluating high and non-transitory barriers to entry, NRAs ought to assess the magnitude of the barriers to entry indicated by technological advantages or superiority.[15] It is hard to see how a regulatory lawyer could make such an assessment without some understanding of the technology involved.

---

[13] 'Towards a new framework for electronic communications infrastructure and associated services. The 1999 Communications Review', European Commission, COM(1999)539.
[14] Article 2(a) of the Commission Recommendation of 17 December 2007 on relevant product and service markets within the electronic communications sector susceptible to ex ante regulation in accordance with Directive 2002/21/EC of the European Parliament and of the Council on a common regulatory framework for electronic communications networks and services, C(2007) 5406.
[15] ERG Report on Guidance on the application of the three criteria test, June 2008, ERG (08) 21.

3

THE ECONOMICS OF TELECOMMUNICATIONS REGULATION

Lisa Correa[1]

[1] The author would like to thank Federica Maiorano for comments. Any views expressed in this paper are those of the author and do not necessarily reflect the views of the various institutions for which she works.

3.1 INTRODUCTION

This chapter is primarily intended as a work of reference, providing an overview of the economics of telecommunications regulation and summarizing the key economic regulatory concepts of the industry. While the focus is mainly on the economic regulatory developments in the UK, the conclusions and discussion should be relevant to all countries which are embarking or have embarked on telecommunications liberalization.

Before describing the system of economic regulation, it is useful to place it within a basic analytical framework. Increasingly, regulatory agencies and the courts focus on more complete and complex analyses of markets, and on how the behaviour of firms—their actions or conduct—are likely to affect competition. Lawyers need to be familiar with the language of economic theory; economic jargon increasingly shows up in legal briefs, court, and regulatory decisions. It should be noted though that the nature of economics is complex and there is not a 'one size fits all' theory. This complexity can be infuriating for regulatory and competition lawyers who like 'bright-line' tests of anti-competitive behaviour as this provides legal certainty for participants in the industry. Economists believe though that 'bright-line' tests are risky. Different facts about the institutional environment that is under investigation directs what economic theory is used for in each case. Facts in one case might be consistent with one economic model but inconsistent with the model that is appropriate for a different case with different facts. And real-world cases are often (but not always) more complex than off-the-shelf economic models. Therefore, while it is clearly essential for those who work in regulation—whether in companies, government, or regulatory bodies themselves—to be familiar with the content of telecommunications law and licences, it is also important that practitioners should understand the concepts of telecommunications economic regulation and in particular what it is intended to do.

3.2 RATIONALE FOR REGULATION

Traditionally throughout the world, telecommunications services were provided in each country by one monopoly carrier. Such carriers were almost always owned by the government and operated as state agencies, often as part of the postal service.

Beginning in the 1980s and continuing into the 1990s, the telecommunications industry in almost all countries experienced privatization or at least some degree of corporatization. This has generally been accompanied with the newly privatized companies being exposed to market forces and being forced to become more efficient and competitive. The privatization of these previously large state-owned carriers involved, however, serious problems of remaining monopoly power or market failure due to the accreted advantages conferred upon these carriers by their history

and position as compared with those of potential competitors. In particular, these newly privatized companies benefited from having:

- 100 per cent share of the market at the time of privatization and thus 100 per cent control of customers;
- the accumulated assets, and economies of scale[2] and experience of the telecommunications market;
- ownership of vital networks or privileged use of public rights of way to which competitors must perforce have access if they are to be able to compete.

In light of this, it was recognized that without efficient entry and growth of new rivals or the threat of entry, competitive disciplines on the newly privatized incumbent firms would not be exerted and hence these firms would be able to exploit their dominant position at the expense of consumers. However, given the extent of the accreted advantages conferred upon these carriers, it was acknowledged that there could be a difficult transition period before the privatized company could become competitive, and during this time it could use its substantial power to charge customers monopoly prices as well as engage in strategic games to deter new entrants. For this reason, it was considered essential that economic regulation of the incumbent should be implemented so as to prevent monopolistic abuse and anti-competitive behaviour.

3.3 THE PRINCIPLES OF ECONOMIC REGULATION

Before discussing the alternative forms of economic regulation and their subsequent implementation in the UK, the principles which are basic to economic regulation should be addressed at the outset. Different emphases are possible, but the following list is normally considered when evaluating different forms of economic regulation:

- The possible abuse of monopoly power should be prevented. Such abuse may arise if prices were very high in relation to costs so that super-normal profits[3] were earned. Abuse may also arise if costs were higher than they ought to be, or were likely to be in a competitive situation.
- Economic regulation should not distort business decisions. Only where there is a demonstrable competitive or market failure[4] is there a need for regulatory

---

[2] This relates to the situation where an increase in output is associated with a less than proportionate increase in costs.

[3] Super-normal profits relate to the concept of monopoly profits. In a competitive situation, it is assumed that any excess profit will be competed away by competition. However, in a monopoly environment, this is not the case and hence super-normal or excess profit is earned.

[4] The rationale for imposing regulatory measures is generally based on the notion of market failure. This situation exists when a market fails to function properly. Market failure can arise under various circumstances. In such cases the introduction of appropriate regulatory measures can provide a way of

intervention as economic regulation will always be inferior to effective competition. For example, if regulation were to cover both competitive and monopoly elements of the industry, there would be strong incentives on the incumbent to focus its efforts against the competition whilst continuing to earn high profits in the monopoly part of the business. It is important to thus recognize that the competitive playing field can be distorted by economic regulation and so due care must be taken in its implementation.

- The costs of regulation should be limited to that which is essential. In view of the clear disadvantages in practice, of excessive control of nationalized industries by government departments, an important part of the rationale for privatization is to reduce detailed control over essentially business decisions. Therefore, economic regulation should ensure that excessive control under a nationalized industry scenario is not replicated.

- Regulation should try to 'mimic' the likely operation of a competitive market. If this can be achieved, it means that resources will be used as efficiently and as well in one case as in the other.

3.4 FORMS OF ECONOMIC REGULATORY CONTROL

In light of the above principles, at the time of privatization, the favoured form of economic regulation outside the UK was Rate-of-Return regulation. This offered the solution that prices should be such that an allowed 'fair' rate of return on capital could be earned. In other words, under this rule, a ceiling was placed on the profits that a company could keep from its regulated business which would be based on the company's required rate of return on capital.[5]

The problem with this solution, however, is that (as Averch and Johnson[6] revealed) setting a rate of return on the capital base distorts firms' business decisions by encouraging them to expand their capital base so as to achieve a greater absolute level of profit whilst remaining within their regulatory constraints. Thus, the Rate-of-Return regulation rule proved to be fundamentally flawed since the firm, although it has no direct benefit from cost inefficiency, achieves a strategic gain by influencing the permitted price. In addition, this rule covers the whole business and so does not allow regulation to be focused explicitly on the particular services where monopoly power and public concern are greatest. Many have argued, therefore, that this is the worst sort of regulation: both shareholders and customers are worse off!

---

eliminating, or at least reducing, the market failures, thereby providing protection to citizens and consumers, and businesses.

[5] The required rate of return on capital can be considered as a hurdle rate for capital budgeting decisions.

[6] Averch, H and L Johnson, 'Behaviour of the firm under regulatory constraint' (1962) *American Economic Review* 52, 1052–1069.

To address the failings of the Rate-of-Return rule and to more accurately meet the objectives of economic regulation, Professor Stephen Littlechild developed the now well-known 'RPI – X' formula. This formula caps a selected basket of the incumbent's prices for a period of four to five years. These prices can then increase annually by the Retail Price Index (RPI) minus the X factor, with the latter being set by the regulator in the light of the presumed movement of productivity and costs within the industry. Within this four-to-five-year period, the regulated company can then keep any extra profits generated by increased efficiency. And at the end of the review period, new price controls can be implemented which take account of the efficiency gains in the previous period.

The rule was deemed extremely attractive by many economists because it was easy to implement, it encouraged cost-reducing activities, and (via the basket of services) it could be used to target those aspects of the business where regulation was most needed. Furthermore, it was viewed as a regulatory tool that could be decreasingly used as effective competition[7] developed. This latter point was a key argument used by Littlechild. In his own words, he believed:

> Competition is indisputably the most effective means—perhaps the only effective means—of protecting consumers against monopoly power. Regulation is essentially a means of preventing the worst excesses of monopoly; it is not a substitute for competition. It is a means of 'holding the fort' until the competition arrives. Consequently, the main focus of attention has to be on securing the most promising conditions for competition to emerge, and protecting competition from abuse. It is important that regulation in general . . . does not prejudice the achievement of this overall strategy.[8]

Littlechild's vision was, therefore, that competition, rather than regulation, should be the main goal to be aimed for in developing a regulatory framework.

3.5 SETTING THE PRICE CAP

Although, price cap regulation has achieved a considerable positive response, the setting of a price cap requires a large amount of information about the future structure of the market. Figure 3.1 sets out the schematic for the financial model for setting the cap in a monopoly environment. It can be seen that it is essential not only for the regulatory authority to have a clear steer over the potential output and pricing structure of the company, but it also needs to take account of the company's movements of costs and productivity over the life of the price cap.

---

[7] Effective competition can be considered as being in operation when a customer can make a decision independent of any operator across the whole telecommunications industry, or when a customer can choose from a multitude of services and/or deal directly with a large number of service providers without regard to the infrastructure that carries the chosen service from the service provider to the customer.

[8] Regulation of British Telecommunications' Profitability, Report by Stephen C Littlechild, Professor of Commerce, University of Birmingham, to the Secretary of State for Industry, HMSO, 1983, para 4.11.

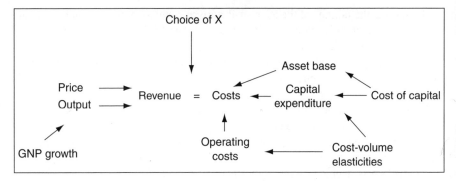

Figure 3.1 The financial model for setting the cap—monopoly

Forecasting growth and efficiency rates in an industry, such as telecommunications, driven so strongly by technological and regulatory developments, is a highly complex exercise. Due to the importance of these parameters in setting X, it is imperative, though, that the regulator ensures that assumptions are robust.

The complexity of this operation is further magnified when competition is introduced into the market. As illustrated by Figure 3.2, the regulator not only needs to forecast the growth and efficiency rates of the incumbent, it also needs to take into account the impact of competitors' outputs and pricing strategies on the incumbent's output and prices and vice versa.

This difficult exercise is compounded by the *asymmetry of information problem* that exists between the regulator and the firm. If the regulator has as much knowledge about industry conditions and behaviour as the regulated firm, it could simply direct the firm to implement its chosen plan. But, of course, decision-makers within the firm are far more knowledgeable than regulators can ever be about circumstances facing them, and the regulator can neither observe nor infer all aspects of the firm's behaviour. In this situation, the regulator can therefore only condition its policy on what it knows and try and design an incentive mechanism so that the firm can be induced to act in accordance with the public interest.

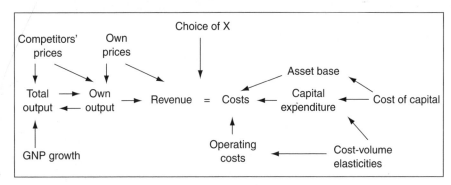

Figure 3.2 The financial model for setting the cap—competitive

3.5.1 Other considerations when setting a price cap

Besides the factors above, it is also important for the regulator, when designing a price cap, to consider whether there is need for additional price control where the emphasis is not to force prices down but to provide a regulatory safety net for customers in case competition does not deliver for them. There are a number of possibilities, such as a median residential bill control which focuses on the customer's total bill, and a limit on the change in the bill for those customers on a light user scheme.[9]

Another factor that needs to be considered is related to capital costs. Given the importance of capital costs in setting the price cap, its measurement plays a key role in the modelling exercise. In particular, the manner in which the asset base is valued can have a major impact on the cost structure of the incumbent. For example, assets can be measured either historically[10] or using current costs.[11] Generally on a total cost basis, the two measures do not differ significantly. The construction costs of trenches and ducts measured in current terms have gone up, but the price of electronic equipment such as switches has declined substantially due to technological progress. One could, therefore, conclude that either measure is appropriate. This assumption is, however, wrong because if prices were set using historic costs, incorrect entry signals may be provided to firms in the industry. In other words, if prospective entrants were considering the costs of entry and existing costs were based on historical costs, then from a business planning perspective 'skewed cost signals' would be provided. From an economic perspective, there is thus a preference for the use of current costs because it ensures that correct, current, and efficient entry signals are provided to all market players.

The duration of the cap is another issue that needs to be reflected on as it can have an enormous impact on the workings of price control. In particular, if it is set for too short a period, it could deliver inappropriate incentives for the incumbent to undertake cost-reducing activities which pay back within the designated timescales. On the other hand, if the control is set for too long a period, the incumbent may benefit from too lax a control and consumers could suffer as a result.

Designing an appropriate price cap is thus an extremely difficult operation; an inappropriate price cap could have a significant negative impact on the development of competition. An erroneous segmentation of industry services and customer segments that need to be covered by the price cap could impose substantial distortions on the market through its impact on other operators. This will be discussed further

---

[9] A Light User Scheme (LUS) is a specialized package that caters to the needs of low spending customers. In the UK, BT have introduced a LUS which is specifically designed to help those people who need a phone to stay in touch but make very few calls themselves. The less calls, the more rebate. BT phone customers are charged the normal quarterly rental for their telephone line and additional charges for any BT equipment they may be renting. Calls are charged at the normal rate, but they could receive a rebate if their call charges fall below a certain threshold per quarter.

[10] Historic costs relate to what the assets cost in the first place, minus depreciation.

[11] Replacement or current costs relate to what it costs to replace old assets with modern equivalent assets of equal remaining life. This reflects general inflation, plus specific effects such as technical progress.

in sections 3.9.1 and 3.9.2. If price cap regulation is pursued then getting the price cap right is crucial if regulatory control is to be effective.

3.6 STRUCTURE OF THE REGULATED INDUSTRY

The implementation of economic regulation has taken various forms in different industries and countries. This is partly because each industry/country has an individual regulator, allowing personal differences to manifest themselves. More fundamental, however, are the underlying differences in the structure of the regulated industry. For effective regulation to occur, it is important that an effective model or industry structure is developed so as to enable effective competition to emerge. As mentioned in section 3.2, a newly privatized company could retain its dominance because the underlying structure of the market flowing from the history of privatization could preclude the development of effective competition. To address this issue, the regulator might therefore at the outset intervene in the market to address the underlying structural obstacle. Three potential ways used to minimize the asymmetry of information problem, regulate dominance, and promote effective competition are: structural separation of the incumbent; accounting separation of the incumbent; and functional separation of the incumbent.

Restructuring of this kind can enhance the effectiveness of competition and regulation by altering incentives and information conditions in such a way that private motives are directed more towards social ends. Below, we discuss these three potential methods.

3.6.1 Structural separation

In the United States, the US authorities conceived that if AT&T continued to operate in the marketplace as a vertically integrated player, it would, through its 'bottleneck' control of the relationship with customers, be able to erect barriers to prevent competition developing naturally. Moreover, based on the structure of costs of a telecommunications network within a static equilibrium framework, the view was that there would be wasteful duplication if households had telephone wires from several suppliers.[12] As a consequence, the US authorities in 1982 put forward a divestiture decree which resulted in the structural separation of the Regional Bell Operating Companies (RBOCs), which handled local telephone networks and services, from AT&T, which handled the long distance network and services.[13]

This type of structural adjustment of dividing the incumbent into smaller, more supposedly manageable organizations was a radical measure to regulate dominance and break the monopoly of information, and increased the debate about whether

---

[12] This implies that the local loop will not become sufficiently competitive. In other words, it was believed that it was a natural monopoly.
[13] See further Chapter 6.

structural separation actually solves the inherent problem of dominance. In most cases, experience appears to indicate that the problem is not solved.

Separated parts of the business can still be dominant and so still require a high degree of regulatory scrutiny to ensure that monopolistic abuse does not occur. In the case of the US, the division of AT&T from the RBOCs created competition in long-distance traffic but left a monopoly in the local network. The arguments about interconnection thus continued and it has been argued that incorrect signals have been provided to long-distance entrants which resulted in efficient entry into the marketplace being discouraged, inefficient bypass being encouraged, and short-term arbitrage opportunities being created.[14]

Moreover, it has subsequently been argued that the implementation of structural separation in the US ignored the potential for competition in the local loop. In particular, as cited by Peter Huber, the dominance of a fully integrated AT&T could have been effectively challenged by technological innovation, by, for example, the use of radio-based technology. It has therefore been argued that because of structural separation, technical innovation in providing competition to the local loop was essentially constrained by the regulatory authorities managing the market, thereby impeding the development of effective competition.[15]

Given the above, it has been suggested that over time, structural separation may have an adverse impact on the development of effective competition. Structural separation can institutionalize a structure that could become obsolete because of technological advances, regulatory changes, and differing trading patterns.

3.6.2 Accounting separation

Accounting separation, in contrast, is much less draconian and comparatively simpler to implement. This method of structurally differentiating the business components of a company by simulating separation via accounting structures is flexible to technological and regulatory change. It provides a means by which relevant costs can be identified for interconnect charging purposes, and the presence of separated accounts means that the reconciliation of costs to financial accounts is much easier to implement. Moreover, for purposes of identifying cross-subsidies, and the use to which they are being put, the separated accounts can prove to be invaluable to regulatory authorities. Nonetheless, accounting separation still suffers from the asymmetry of information problem.[16]

---

[14] Huber, PW, Kellog, MK, and Thorne, J, *The Geodesic Network II* (The Geodesic Company, 1992).

[15] To address this issue, the US Authorities introduced the 1996 Telecommunications Act which aimed to introduce competition into the local network. Unfortunately, arcane rules were put in place which could make the achievement of this objective difficult.

[16] The asymmetry of information problem relates to the fact that the regulator has less information than the regulated firm and therefore it is possible for the regulated firm to manipulate the regulatory situation such that it is able to benefit. This problem does, however, decrease in importance as the regulator gains experience of the environment.

While accounting separation meets the requirement for ensuring flexibility in market changes, it still does not significantly alter the underlying incentives of the vertically integrated incumbent. Specifically, the vertically integrated incumbent still has an incentive and an ability to non-price discriminate against competitors in downstream markets. While price discrimination may be easier to detect, verify, and enforce, non-price discrimination (such as delaying access to key inputs to competitors etc.) is not.

3.6.3 Functional separation

In light of this, in recent years, the notion of functional separation has been proposed as a possible solution. This solution comprises aspects of both structural and accounting separation. Under functional separation, the bottleneck assets to which access is required by competitors and the downstream division of the vertically integrated firm are placed into a 'ring-fenced' separate division of the incumbent company. Rules and procedures that prevent the flow of sensitive information between this division and the retail division of the vertically integrated firm are put in place and accounting separation requirements are also put in place. This separate division is then subjected to a stronger non-discrimination obligation which obliges it to supply a range of upstream inputs to downstream rivals and its own downstream division on the same timescales, terms and conditions (including price), and by the same systems and processes. In addition, the incentives of the managers of the functionally separated division are modified. Specifically, their remuneration is tied to the performance of the functionally separated division rather than the group (comprised of the downstream and upstream divisions of the vertically integrated firm). The aim is thus to increase transparency of the processes and transactions within the relevant incumbent divisions so that the ability of the regulator or downstream rivals to detect and therefore deter anti-competitive behaviour is increased. Further, this approach is relatively flexible to technological and market changes such that as the market develops and competition is introduced into the bottleneck assets, these can be easily moved out of the ring-fenced division.

3.7 THE ECONOMICS OF TELECOMMUNICATIONS

Before discussing the actual implementation of economic regulation in the UK telecommunications industry, it is worthwhile for purposes of economic policy analysis to briefly consider the important economic features of the industry. These include its multi-product nature, the non-storability of its services, stochastic time-varying demands, capacity constraints and sunk costs,[17] the existence of externalities between

---

[17] Sunk costs are defined by the US horizontal merger guidelines as 'the acquisition costs of tangible or intangible assets that cannot be recovered through redeployment of these assets outside the relevant

users, natural monopoly elements, and the complex vertical structure of the industry. The first five factors deserve discussion because they influence the tariffing procedures of the industry, whilst the last three factors merit particular attention because externalities and natural monopoly elements are the market failures that provide the main rationale for policy intervention and vertical issues affect the ease with which regulation is carried out.

On the supply side, the telecommunications industry provides many products and services. These include customer premises equipment, ranging from telephones to private automatic branch exchanges (PABXs), and services provided by the network which range from the supply of telephone calls to various locations at different times of the day to the monthly leasing of dedicated private lines. The nature of telecommunications is, however, such that there is a lump sum cost of providing the consumer's connection or access to the network, a cost that is independent of the number of call minutes used, and a variable cost representing the actual usage of the network. Given this cost structure, it is thus convenient and justifiable to charge customers a two-part tariff comprising a lump sum and a variable component.[18]

The setting of this two-part tariff can, however, have huge implications for competitive activity. The reason is that access and usage are complementary. There are cross price effects in both directions, which means that the price for access to the telephone network has an influence on the number of telephone users. If the number of users increases, usage is likely to rise. Similarly, changes in usage charges heavily influence access demand. If the usage charges increase to a level where an individual's utility of using the network is lower than the costs of the phone calls made and the price of access, then access demand is likely to decrease. There is therefore a significant level of interdependence in telecommunications between access and usage.

On the demand side, although it appears that telecommunication users' demands are stochastic (i.e. random), customers' demands exhibit strong regular and weekly patterns. For example, business users only want to make calls during business hours and therefore their demands are relatively insensitive to price (i.e. less elastic), whereas residential users prefer to make calls during evenings and weekends and have more elastic demands. Given these variations, there is therefore much opportunity for various kinds of price discrimination. The degree to which this is possible is,

---

market' (see <http://www.ftc.gov/bc/docs/horizmer.htm>). Clearly, large portions of the telecommunications infrastructure should, by this definition, be considered sunk. Not only that, but there are also the intangible sunk costs of building a brand and customer acquisition which are no less significant.

[18] Telecommunications networks generally exhibit both economies of scale—see section 3.23; and common fixed costs—costs that are common to multiple services and that cannot be attributed directly to any particular service. The existence of the latter raises important cost recovery issues especially in the context of how local loop fixed costs that are common to exchange lines and DSL (broadband) should be recovered in the prices of the different services. In considering how common fixed costs might be recovered, it is possible to identify a spectrum of alternative approaches. At one end of the range there are approaches that have underpinnings based on economic theory, while at the other end there are more pragmatic methods used by accountants.

however, dependent on each operator's individual constraints, its customers, and its knowledge. Despite what economic theory may say,[19] competition in telecommunications appears to encourage increased price discrimination, as is evidenced by the proliferation of different pricing packages.

The preponderance of sunk costs in a dominant incumbent's overall cost base means that short run variable costs are small. The non-storability of services coupled with low short run variable costs means that up to the available capacity, additional output can be produced at nearly zero marginal cost.[20] Conversely, when demand exceeds capacity levels, output must be rationed which results in a negative externality as additional call attempts cause some high-valued demands not to be served.[21] This factor together with the above-mentioned systematic variation of demand over time often makes the use of peak-load pricing[22] schemes prevalent and justifiable for many services.

Although, as mentioned above, capacity constraints can result in negative externalities, the two-way nature of telecommunications demand also gives rise to an important positive network externality. A fundamental characteristic of telecommunications is that new customers joining a network not only benefit themselves, but create extra opportunities for existing customers.[23] There is, moreover, evidence of dynamic benefits for the economy arising from the development of the telecommunications sector.[24] The relationship between economic development and the

---

[19] Price discrimination often features in economic theory as a manifestation of monopoly power. In theory, therefore, the more competitive the market becomes, the less scope there should be for it to take place. In telecommunications, however, the presence of economies of scale and/or scope can mean that if prices were set at marginal costs, the firm would not be able to efficiently recover its costs and so would not be able to break even. Firms may therefore have to set their prices above their incremental costs so that, for example, common costs (i.e. costs incurred in the production of one or more products that cannot be directly attributed to an individual product) can be recovered. However if the price of the product was in excess of incremental costs, some customers whose valuation of the service exceeded the cost, but not the price, would be deterred from using it. Price discrimination between different customer groups (depending on its structure) may thus provide a means of not only allowing the firm to recover its costs, but it could also lead to an increase in output and to customers who might have otherwise been priced out of the market, being served.

[20] Marginal cost refers to the increase in the total cost of an enterprise when the output of a product or service that it supplies increases by one unit. In other words, it is the increase in the firm's total cost caused by the single-unit output expansion.

[21] The likelihood that a given call is made successfully is an important aspect of the quality of the service. If demand exceeds capacity and the network is therefore congested, a negative externality prevails.

[22] Firms that deal in markets with fluctuating demands such as peak and off-peak periods will incur some costs that are common to both periods and other costs which are separable to whichever is served. In the case of telecommunications, due to the level of sunk costs in the network, costs are low in off-peak periods hence resulting in low prices whilst in peak periods; prices are high because of lower available capacity.

[23] If there is only one customer on a telecommunications network, there is not much point as one would not want to call oneself. If, however, other individuals join the network, the calling opportunities increase and so, from a social viewpoint, everyone benefits.

[24] For a non-technical exposition of the early literature in this area, see the ITU World Telecommunications Development Report 1994 and Saunders, RJ, Warford, JJ, and Wellenius, B, *Telecommunications and*

development of telecommunications infrastructure appears to be reciprocal with growth in one encouraging growth in the other.

The presence of these externalities therefore, has important policy implications for pricing structures as it provides a justification for subsidizing line rentals so as to encourage new users to join the network. Moreover, it also has important implications for policy on interconnection between rival networks, for without interconnection, a small network could be severely disadvantaged relative to the larger one.[25] It is worthwhile noting, however, that, even if there is competition for attracting customers to operators' networks with a great deal of choice over the network on which their call terminates, that choice is made by the called party. There is no incentive for the called party to be connected to more than one network operator and in the unlikely event that this did occur, it would entail wasteful duplication. In essence, the called party network has control over a bottleneck monopoly, in which it can gain monopoly profits by inflating the call termination fees. As a consequence, there is a strong case for regulation of this service and its charges, not only today, but for some considerable time to come on those operators with significant market power or those operators who can act independently of competitors and consumers in the market.

The vertical structure of the industry means that in order for a call to be made, a customer must be linked to a local exchange and in order to complete a call, a customer's call must terminate on a local exchange. As discussed above, local termination of a call is a bottleneck monopoly but what of local origination of a call?

In the past, policy makers have generally assumed that because call termination is an essential facility, call origination is also an essential facility. In other words, the view has been taken that the local loop comprising a home connected to a local exchange is a natural monopoly. In fact, for this reason, as discussed above, the US authorities decided to structurally separate the RBOCs from AT&T. However, in recent years the designation of the local call origination network component as a natural monopoly is being challenged by the rapid development of telecommunications technology. Telecommunications is moving from analogue to digital. The growing deployment of broadband, ICT solutions, and 3G mobile, as well as the design of core networks from analogue switched voice to digital IP-based data, means that the way in which services such as telephone and Internet access are provided will change. In particular, this move from analogue to digital will deliver convergence between the traditional world of public switched telephone networks, and the new world of data networks. This will enable the delivery of substantial cost savings due to the economies of scope inherent in a single converged network and so could mean

---

Economic Development (Johns Hopkins University Press, Baltimore, MD, 1983).

[25] If there are two networks, one large with many customers and another which is just starting up, then no-one would want to join the smaller network, unless the two networks were interconnected, because without interconnection, there would be no communication between the two networks and so the value of joining the smaller network would be small.

that competitive delivery of services to consumers via competing networks becomes more prevalent.

3.8 THE PRIVATIZATION OF BT IN THE UK[26]

The early debate on liberalization in the UK began with customer premises equipment, followed by services, and quickly spread to the beginnings of network competition in response to intense demand for leased circuits in the UK. Cable & Wireless and Barclays Bank were exploring this market and joined together, with subsequent financial support from British Petroleum to form Mercury Communications, in response to the government's offer to license network competitors in this area. The consortium quickly decided that leased circuits alone did not provide a viable business and sought extension of its remit, under its original 1982 licence, to the provision of national and international switched services. The very large investment required for this purpose persuaded the group that it needed a period as the single alternative switched network if it was to develop as an effective competitor to BT. This duopoly policy was adopted by the government in the autumn of 1983 ahead of the sale of the second tranche of shares in the, by then, privatized Cable & Wireless and the reintroduction of what became the 1984 Telecommunications Act, under which BT would be privatized and Oftel was set up as the independent regulatory body.

The duopoly policy, to which the government committed itself for seven years from the date of its announcement, thus set the tone of the subsequent comparatively slow and cautious development of network competition in the UK. The government, right from the start, however, determined to introduce competition into all segments of the market and to foster development of broadband cable television networks in the UK to open up the possibility of local network competition, licensing cable operators to provide all forms of telecommunications services in addition to television programme services. In deference to the duopoly policy, the provision of switched voice telephony, however, could only be undertaken in association with BT or Mercury. Since BT was not keen to compete with itself, this meant that in practice local switched voice telephony services could only be developed by agreement with Mercury during the duopoly period.

In 1984 BT was privatized. Given extensive debate about the structure of the industry encompassing the arguments above in section 3.6, the government shunned the vertical separation policy adopted in the US and instead privatized BT as a vertically integrated company. BT's dominant position throughout the industry meant, however, that there was a clear need for a framework of regulation to contain BT's market power, in particular, regulatory intervention was necessary to ensure that Mercury—and any other subsequent licensed telecommunications operator—had

---

[26] See further Chapter 4.

access to actual and potential customers via BT's local circuits at a non-monopolistic price, in order to be able to mount any effective competition. Herein, therefore, lies the eternal debate on call origination and termination charges, otherwise known as *interconnection*.[27]

In addition to the requirement for regulation over interconnection, there was also a requirement to protect consumers against BT's monopoly power. As such considerable discussion occurred as to the appropriate vehicle for price control in the UK. Given the substantial arguments against rate-of-return regulation, discussed in section 3.4, Littlechild's proposal of RPI – X was adopted.

At the same time as the above, the government also sought to encourage the development of competition in mobile services by licensing in 1985 competing cellular operators, Vodafone and Cellnet (a part BT subsidiary). This was followed in 1991 by the decision to license competing personal communication networks (PCNs) in order to extend the reach of competition in this broad category of service. Then, in 2000, five licences for 3G mobile services were issued. Four of these went to the existing mobile companies but the fifth was awarded to a new entrant. As with fixed services, interconnection has been a key issue—in particular between the mobile operators and fixed operators. This is discussed briefly in section 3.13.2.

In 2003, soon after Ofcom was created (from the merger of five different regulatory agencies dealing with communication services including Oftel), it launched the Strategic Review of Telecommunications.[28] Its aim was to assess whether the then current regulatory approach governing both fixed and mobile services was still appropriate.

The main conclusion from this review was that although liberalization led to a number of downstream retail markets being opened to competition, most competitors still rely on upstream wholesale inputs provided by the incumbent BT. BT's market power in the provision of fixed infrastructure and its vertically integrated structure into the downstream markets for which that infrastructure is a critical input meant that BT (given its then current structure) would always have an incentive and the ability to engage in discriminatory behaviour against its competitors. In particular, as discussed in section 3.6, it considered that while price discrimination may be easier to detect, verify, and enforce, non-price discrimination (such as delaying access to key inputs to competitors etc.) is not. Ofcom believed that its then current powers did not suffice to deal with the problem. Consequently, it put forward a proposal to introduce a form of functional separation and to strengthen the then current non-discrimination rules (as per section 3.6). These measures were later adopted and implemented.[29]

---

[27] See further section 3.13 below and Chapter 8.

[28] Strategic Review of Telecommunications Phase 2 consultation document available at <http://www.ofcom.org.uk/consult/condocs/telecoms_p2/>.

[29] A notice under s 155(1) of the Enterprise Act 2002, available at <http://www.ofcom.org.uk/consult/condocs/sec155/>.

3.9 RETAIL PRICE REGULATION IN THE UK

As recorded above, the presumption of the Littlechild doctrine was that the need for, and intensity of, price cap regulation would wither away in those elements of the telecommunications industry particularly amenable to the opening up of effective competition. Given the government's determination to introduce competition into all segments of the market, it is worthwhile reviewing how in reality the price cap regime in UK telecommunications evolved since its inception.

In 1984, the first price cap was set at RPI − 3 per cent and the basket of controlled services included rental of local exchange lines, and tariffs for directly dialled local and national calls (except for phone boxes). In addition, BT volunteered not to increase residential line rentals by more than RPI + 2 per cent. These controls covered approximately half of BT's revenues and were set for five years.

In the subsequent Price Review of 1988, Oftel tightened the price cap to RPI − 4.5 per cent, and added operator assisted UK calls to the basket. BT maintained its voluntary cap on residential line rentals and connection charges were also made subject to the RPI + 2 per cent restriction, but kept outside the basket.

New controls over domestic private circuits[30] were, however, implemented and were subject to a separate price cap of RPI − 0 with the basket including connection and rental charges for digital and analogue private circuits. This price cap was deemed necessary to increase BT's efficiency in the domestic private circuit market, as Mercury's competition alone was insufficient. In addition to the RPI − 0 price cap, BT committed to improve the quality of their service, backed up by a customer compensation scheme.

These arrangements were supposed to stand for a duration of four years but the Duopoly Review in 1990 meant that these commitments were jettisoned and new arrangements were substituted for them. The result was that the cap was tightened further from RPI − 4.5 per cent to RPI − 6.25 per cent. Furthermore, due to routine monitoring of BT's international calls showing profits were rising sharply, instead of being eroded by Mercury's competition, the Review brought out-going international call charges under control by adding them to the price cap basket for the first time. BT also agreed to reduce their international prices on a one-off basis by 10 per cent, and to an increase of the line rental and connection charge restraint to RPI + 5 per cent (from RPI + 2 per cent) on multi-line business exchange lines only.

Some greater flexibility, subject to certain Oftel monitored conditions, was also given to BT in setting its tariffs, enabling it to offer the option of quantity discounts (with a higher rental charge) to larger users of its services. International resale constraints were, moreover, relaxed in order to put additional pressure on international call charges and settlement rates. To achieve this effect, however,

---

[30] Private circuits are dedicated, permanently open digital transmission channels between two fixed points. They are often used as part of a corporate network.

International Private Leased Circuit (IPLC) prices were restrained. In 1991 therefore, IPLCs were incorporated into BT's domestic private circuit basket, subject to the RPI − 0 cap, due to expire in July 1993.

Whilst the greater flexibility in setting tariffs, above, could be viewed as a movement in the direction of greater regulatory freedom for BT, the overall verdict on the direction of change in telecommunications price cap regulation resulting from the Review indicated both a tightening of the main price cap and an extension of the coverage and complexity of UK telecommunications price cap controls. In fact, Oftel itself calculated that the controls emanating from the Review resulted in about 70 per cent of BT's revenues being subject to regulatory scrutiny as compared with around 50 per cent in 1989.

Oftel's review of the BT price cap, in 1993 resulted in the limit on average price increases for switched services being tightened further from RPI − 6.25 per cent to RPI − 7.5 per cent, with individual price caps of RPI − 0 on most services included in the basket (except exchange line rentals, which remained subject to RPI + 2 per cent for residential and most business customers, and wholesale exchange lines, subject to RPI + 5 per cent). And for the first time connection charges were added to the basket. A price cap of RPI − 0 was also placed on three separate private circuit baskets: national analogue private circuits, national digital private circuits, and international private circuits.

This further evolution of UK price cap controls thus represented a further strengthening of regulation. This evolution, however, dramatically changed in 1997 when Oftel, after conducting a study of the extent of competition[31] in the marketplace decided that retail control should only be implemented where consumer protection was required. The impact of this view was that it limited the price cap to the lowest spending 80 per cent of residential customers and loosened the cap from RPI − 7.5 per cent to RPI − 4.5 per cent. This meant that 26 per cent of BT's group revenues were now subject to retail price caps compared with nearly 70 per cent previously. In February 2001, Oftel determined that the 1997 price controls on BT should be extended until July 2002. Then in June 2002, Oftel loosened the price controls further with a safeguard cap of RPI + 0 for the lowest 80 per cent of residential customers. As an incentive on BT, Oftel added, however, that if BT developed an effective wholesale line rental product,[32] this cap could then be further reduced to RPI + 0 per cent.

In July 2006, Ofcom announced the removal of retail price controls. This significant deregulation followed both the conclusion of Ofcom's Strategic Review of

---

[31] See sections 3.14–3.17 for a discussion about how the extent of competition in telecommunications markets are examined for the purposes of deciding whether regulatory controls are required or not.

[32] Wholesale line rental (WLR) is intended to stimulate competition by allowing suppliers to provide an integrated service comprising calls and access, renting the exchange line from BT, and sending customers a single bill.

Telecommunications[33]—discussed earlier—and the specific public consultation, launched in March 2006, on removing retail price controls.[34] Ofcom stated that this deregulation was enabled by, and reflected, the rapid growth of competition and continued reductions in the cost of phone services to customers. Despite the deregulation, however, BT gave a number of assurances to offer additional protection to customers on low incomes and vulnerable groups. In particular, the company agreed to limit increases on its basic line rental product, which for many represented the overwhelming majority of their bill.

It appears, therefore, that Littlechild's Doctrine is finally being pursued and that Littlechild's vision of a regulatory framework based on the view that the dynamics of competition will eventually render retail regulation redundant is still valid today.

3.9.1 The operation of price caps in the UK

As detailed above, excluding recent developments in price caps, the workings of the price cap regime within the UK telecommunications industry tended to intensify over time. Firstly, the coverage of the price cap, in terms of the goods and services that were subject to regulatory control, tended to expand, and secondly the severity of X, the deduction factor, was typically tightened at successive review periods.

This led to an enforced decline in real prices, which in the short term is of immediate benefit to consumers. A question mark, however, hangs over the matter of whether such increasingly tightening price caps are to the benefit of consumers in the longer term.

Over the longer term, the competitive process forces efficiency on operators and leads to lower prices, particularly through longer-term dynamic efficiency gains.[35] This process, however, has wider dimensions. Competition leads to choice for customers both between operators and in the range of services that are available to them. An effectively competitive market would be characterized by a rich choice of differentiated services that meet the needs of each customer segment.

Given the true benefits of the longer-term competitive process, it is important that any regulatory actions taken do not undermine inter-firm competition or its resultant technological and service innovation. If competition is to flourish, operators will have to extend their investments in the development of new services and their deployment of lower cost technologies. The question that therefore needs to be asked is whether a price cap regime of increasing deduction factors weakens this process?

---

[33] Final statements on the Strategic Review of Telecommunications, and undertakings in lieu of a reference under the Enterprise Act 2002. Available at <http://www.ofcom.org.uk/consult/condocs/statement_tsr/statement.pdf>.

[34] Retail Price Controls: Explanatory Statement and Proposals. Available at <http://www.ofcom.org.uk/consult/condocs/retail/prc.pdf>.

[35] Dynamic efficiency gains result from the degree of rivalry that exists as well as the technological dynamism that is generated by firms within the industry in their competitive struggles.

Price caps imply a particular view of the market. With their focus on lower prices and improved efficiency, they could be considered consistent with a 'utility' view of the telecommunications market which emphasizes a position of lowest cost operator providing highly efficient *but* undifferentiated basic utility services. A price cap based on a utility model could, therefore, impose distortions on a competitive market. These are enshrined in the market through the influence of the price cap on other operators, with the result that these operators could be constrained from offering new service packages and possibly from moving their existing prices in line with their costs. In addition, entry signals can be distorted by regulatory definitions of markets. The shape of the market is by its very nature very difficult to predict. Static regulatory definitions therefore inevitably lead to arbitrarily defined markets and industry segments.[36]

In a monopoly environment, the setting of a price cap is a relatively simple exercise. The regulator sets X commensurate with an efficient operator level of profit. The regulated firm then sets prices according to the RPI − X formula and the resultant profit level is then greater or less than forecast depending on cost control and volume changes.

In contrast, in a potentially competitive environment, designing an appropriate cap is an extremely difficult operation. BT in the UK telecommunications market is the dominant operator and, prior to recent price caps, was the price leader within the industry. Increasingly severe price caps imposed on BT by Oftel and broader baskets would have had the consequence of also forcing competitors such as Mercury etc. to parallel any BT-led price cuts in order to gain and penetrate the market. However, because of BT's dominance, BT had significant freedom to target its required price cuts so as to hurt competitors in a potentially predatory and anti-competitive manner. It is important to recognize, therefore, that the distortionary impact of the price cap can perversely retard the very development of competition that the regulatory structure is supposed to promote over the longer term.

3.9.2 Other flaws of the price cap approach

Although the use of price caps is appropriate in a monopoly environment, when there is potential competition in the marketplace, for the reasons outlined above, it is imperative that the regulator takes deregulatory actions. Prolonging a broad price cap beyond the stage at which competition could become effective is extremely dangerous to nascent competition.

---

[36] It is inevitably the case that regulators will need to define markets in such a way so as to decide whether regulation is required or not. It is important, however, that these definitions are considered in a dynamic manner. In other words, they must take account of the changing nature of the industry otherwise erroneous regulatory decisions could be made which could distort the workings of the sector. For a discussion about the issues that need to be considered in defining the market, see sections 3.14 and 3.15.

The price cap approach considers only one variable: price. In ignoring or failing to capture properly the other issues, whilst tightly constraining one variable, one could severely distort all the others. Some of the issues that therefore need to be considered are:

- quality
- diversity
- evolution of competition
- choice
- 'dynamic efficiency'
- consumer 'irrationality'
- differentiation
- innovation

3.9.2.1 *Quality*

Quality is the scale by which each characteristic of the service is measured. In UK telecommunications, the regulator, in setting a price cap, is implicitly making an assumption about quality. If through the regulatory regime, the regulator is emphasizing or focusing solely on the price variable, then this could be at the expense of quality. In fact (as noted by Mercury Communications in April 1996 in response to Oftel's second consultative document on BT price controls and interconnection charging) examining past performance of BT's quality of service reveals the following:

Service indicator	'X' < 4.5%	'X' > 6.25%
Call failure	Improved	Improved
Network/customer reported faults	Improved	Flat
Fault repair	Improved	Declined
Installation time	Improved	Declined
Operator services	Improved	Declined
Payphone serviceability	Improved	Declined

In summary, it therefore appears that BT's quality of service declines the tighter the price cap. The only exception has been network services, where quality has generally improved. This, though, is due to network modernization and digitization, which would have happened regardless of the level of X.

3.9.2.2 *Evolution of competition*

A dominant firm, as discussed above, will focus price cuts on those sectors of the market where competition is greatest, whilst attempting to earn monopoly profits in sectors where there is the least amount of competition.

Under a broad cap that, on average, eliminates monopoly profits, it is obvious that it would be profit-maximizing behaviour for the dominant firm to cut prices below the level which earns normal profits in a competitive sector whilst keeping them above the normal profit level in a less competitive sector. Such behaviour could completely destroy existing competition and foreclose the market and would be, of course, predatory.

Predatory pricing can occur in both a capped and an uncapped market but the point here is that under a broad cap, there is an additional incentive on the dominant firm to engage in predation. If a broad cap is to be implemented, measures need to be designed to prevent this from occurring.

3.9.2.3 'Dynamic efficiency'
The focus of price cap regulation on the price variable assumes a static view of the industry cost structure. As discussed above, competitive industries improve unit costs over time by companies trying to better each other.

However, in the telecommunications industry, due to the preponderance of sunk or fixed costs in running the network, a static analysis would conclude that the existence of fixed costs in each company is 'wasteful'. Costs of the industry could be lowered, at a given point in time, by reducing the industry to a monopoly environment. This one-off gain could, however, be at the expense of the dynamic efficiency of the market.

3.9.2.4 Differentiation, diversity, and choice
Another fundamental characteristic of a competitive market is the product and firm-specific differentiation that evolves, as competing firms strive to meet the needs of consumers. In relegating competition to the simple role of price competition and via the arbitrary nature of static regulatory definitions of the market, no value is attributed to differentiation, diversity, or choice.

3.2.9.5 Consumer 'irrationality'
While a consumer's failure to behave as predicted can always be justified after the event by some new factor,[37] the regulator must recognize that customers are not always rational. In a regulated utility environment, it is the regulator's role to protect consumers from this. In a normal environment, there is no such protection other than general consumer protection legislation. The regulator, therefore, should not continue with concerns from the old monopoly world and use them to prevent the transition to a competitive world unless of course there are justifiable reasons for doing so.

---

[37] E.g., a failure to buy a product at lowest available price could be rationalized by inventing a 'search cost' parameter that varied over time.

3.2.9.6 *Innovation*

Innovation is a key element in the development of effective competition but is also the most intangible as it is impossible to predict the nature of the market. This therefore highlights a stark choice for the regulator between:

• the dynamic, diverse, innovative, but risky world of a competitive market; or
• the simple, featureless, basic, but predictable world of a regulated utility.

3.9.3 Key issues—price caps

In summary, one can conclude that the asymmetric nature of a price cap, in that it prevents price rises but allows price decreases, while being irrelevant in a monopoly market, becomes a critical failing when potential competition is prevalent. A price cap designed to simulate competition could prevent that very competition from emerging. The dominant operator will make a commercial virtue out of a regulatory necessity and target any required price cuts against the competition. The regulator must hence decide whether he or she wants real competition or perpetual price control. Running both together for any period of time is unsustainable.

Price caps and competition do not mix: price caps must be removed to give nascent competition a chance. As outlined in section 3.3, regulatory intervention should only be initiated if there is a demonstrable competitive or market failure. As a consequence, when reviewing a price cap regime, the regulator must examine the competitiveness and potential competitiveness of the market and should ensure that if the price cap regime is to continue, that it does not impede the development of an effectively competitive market. This will be considered more fully in sections 3.14 to 3.17.

This is exactly what occurred in the UK for the 1997 Review of BT's Price Controls. A report prepared by NERA estimated that by the start of the new price cap period 62 per cent of all business customers would have a choice of three or more direct access operators and 39 per cent would have a choice of five or more. It also estimated that 51 per cent of residential customers would have a choice of two or more direct access operators and, given the coverage of indirect access throughout the country, this meant that there would be considerable choice for an increasing range of customers.

Given these estimates and the fact that the industry has economies of density,[38] Oftel decided that retail control should only be implemented where consumer protection was required. The impact of this view was that it limited the price cap to the lowest spending 80 per cent of residential customers and loosened the cap from RPI − 7.5 per cent to RPI − 4.5 per cent and then to RPI − RPI. Since then, as mentioned above, there has been rapid growth of competition and continued reductions in the cost of phone services to customers. In particular, in 2006, it was announced

---

[38] An industry exhibiting economies of density is one where the more closely packed together the customers are, the lower the unit costs. This is far from being unique to telecommunications: it exists in any industry where geographic location of customers is significant.

that more than 10.7 million UK households and small businesses now used a tele-coms provider other than BT—among them, more than 4.6 million cable customers—and (according to regulatory research) they enjoyed some of the cheapest phone calls in the world. As such, in 2006 Ofcom (formerly Oftel) announced the removal of the retail price controls on BT.

3.10 REBALANCING

In section 3.7, the economic characteristics of the telecommunications industry were briefly discussed. In particular, the interdependence of access and usage meant that BT, in setting the two-part tariff for customers, coupled with the price cap restrictions, could influence, through its balance of charges, the social aspects of telecommunications as well as the level of competitive activity in the market place.

Historically, the pricing structure of dominant operators, inherited from the public sector era, has been driven by history, politics, and social policy. Governments generally feel it desirable, on political grounds, that individuals should have access to communications facilities, so as to exercise their political rights, and on social grounds, so as to avoid a gulf emerging between 'information-rich' and 'information-poor' groups. The above, combined with the existence of externalities and dynamic benefits for the economy, as discussed in section 3.7, means that dominant operators have been encouraged in monopoly environments to subsidize line rental and local call charges so as to stimulate demand, funding this via long distance and international call charges. This has, however, led to tariffs being out of balance with costs which, with the introduction of privatization and liberalization policies, has meant that competitive activity has been targeted to wherever these imbalances have occurred.

In terms of economic efficiency, an unbalanced price structure has a number of adverse effects. Firstly, it provides incorrect signals to potential entrants and may thus result in inefficient entry. Secondly, it results in a loss of economic welfare. Where the price of a service is in excess of long-run marginal cost,[39] potential customers, whose valuation of the service exceeds the cost, but not the price, are deterred from using it. Where price is below long-run marginal cost, there will be consumers whose valuation of the service falls below its cost, but use it because price is below cost. The potential economic welfare benefits from rebalancing can hence be substantial.

Before discussing rebalancing in more depth, it is worthwhile considering exactly what is meant by the concept of rebalancing. Tariffs for two services are said to be balanced if they are set at levels which give equal returns on capital for the supply of the services. This generally means price changes in the direction of balanced tariffs and in terms of telecommunications, applies to line rental prices and call charges. Within this concept of rebalancing, however, lies substantial complications.

---

[39] See section 3.13.1 for a discussion about marginal costs.

The first relates to the difficulty of separately defining costs where two services are closely linked. The second and more significantly important, relates to the political aspects of rebalancing. Rebalancing of charges comprises the reduction of long distance and international charges and the increase of local and line rental charges. Given that the majority of businesses and the better-off are typically the big spenders on long distance and international, rebalancing would, however, mean that these people would pay less whilst the majority, the voters, would pay more.

The issue of rebalancing became prominent in the UK when BT made its first price changes as a private company. It was keen to rebalance quickly, as having tariffs out of balance exposed it to competition targeted exclusively at the high margin calling business. It argued that line rentals priced below cost 'distorts the market and encourages inefficient and misplaced investment'.[40] It was, however, limited in its rebalancing actions via a restriction on line rentals of RPI + 2 per cent. Nonetheless, BT managed to carry out some rebalancing actions but these tended to favour large users over smaller users and involved price cuts in areas where competition was prevalent and price increases where it was not. (The incentives on BT for rebalancing are therefore similar to the incentives produced from price regulation as discussed in sections 3.9.1 and 3.9.2.)

Rebalancing, if pursued too vigorously, could therefore undermine the liberalization process. As a consequence, Oftel investigated this and concluded in 1986 that no further rebalancing between local and long-distance charges should occur. The view was that the liberalization process needed to be protected and if effective would lead to natural cost reductions and rebalancing over a number of years. This would mean that in any one year no one would actually face price rises while the economic welfare benefits of rebalancing could continue to be protected.

3.11 ACCESS DEFICIT CHARGES

In 1991, as mentioned above, the Duopoly Review occurred. This marked an end to the fixed-link Duopoly, and opened up the UK market to competition. With the network externality characteristic of telecommunications and the advent of competition, this meant that each telecommunications operator needed access to the networks of other operators in order that calls made to customers of those networks could be delivered. Given the resultant increase in new entrants and the fact that BT retained an effective monopoly over local access, BT claimed that due to the restriction on rebalancing via the RPI + 2 per cent price cap on line rentals, user subscriptions would be inadequate to cover the costs involved. It argued that interconnecting operators should therefore contribute toward the resultant loss: the 'access deficit'. BT reported the size of this loss through its 'Financial Results by Service' publication,

---

[40] BT's response to Oftel's statement 'Effective Competition: Framework for Action' (para 7.1).

moderated by Oftel under condition 13.5A of BT's licence, and claimed that it cost approximately £1.5 billion per annum.

It is in the consumers' interest to use the most efficient (least cost) operator for each component part of their call. At the time, BT claimed it needed to earn super-normal profits on calls in order to fund the deficit. This (according to BT) thus effectively enabled a higher cost or less efficient operator to carry the long distance or international component of a call, and still make a profit. In order to avoid this inefficiency, BT claimed, therefore, that some contribution must be made by competing operators to cover the access deficit.

As a consequence, in the Duopoly Review, BT's licence was amended. A provision was added that interconnection payments must include an 'Access Deficit Charge' (ADC) in addition to covering BT's cost of conveyance. Effectively, this meant that the industry was economically rationalized by the rule of 'Efficient Component Pricing (ECPR)'.[41] Under this rule, opportunity cost is included as a business cost to BT, and so if BT loses retail revenue in allowing local access to competitors, it must be compensated. The idea behind this concept is that a rational operator would only provide competitors' access to its services if the amount it lost in retail revenue was paid back as interconnection payments. Consequently, the argument is that less efficient operators would be unable to enter the market.

In the first phase of ADC introduction, Oftel deemed the deficit be funded equally by all competitors in proportion to their traffic volume. However, this presented a huge barrier to entry. In the second phase, therefore, Oftel was given the power to waive ADCs wholly or partially using its own discretion and a set of rules relating to market share rates of entrants was put in place.

It was argued, however, that the imposition of ADCs in the UK market led to severe market distortions that acted as a reinforcement mechanism of BT's dominance in the marketplace. As stated above, ADCs are strongly based on the ECPR. The ECPR is a controversial concept which is far from being universally accepted in the world of economics. It derives from the theory of contestable markets and so many consider that it is only relevant in this framework. Contestable market theory hinges on three elements:

- market entry is free and without limit;

- entry is absolute so that the entrant can establish itself before the incumbent can make any price response;

- entry is perfectly reversible so that the firm can leave the market and recoup all the costs of entry.

---

[41] The application of ECPR to telecommunications in the UK was originally advocated by William Baumol in *Modified Regulation of Telecommunications and the Public Interest Standard* (Mimeo, 1991). A detailed exposition appears in Baumol, WJ and Sidak, JG, *Towards Competition in Local Telephony* (MIT Press, 1994).

It is clear that each of these assumptions is invalid in the case of telecommunications and so the use of the ECPR in this industry could be deemed to be inappropriate.

Under the ECPR, market entry would only occur when the entrant can provide services more efficiently than the incumbent, who, via the interconnect rate, is able to charge the entrant the 'opportunity cost' of business it has lost to it. In a contestable market, the incumbent is assumed to be perfectly efficient because an efficient entrant will always be able to drive out an inefficient incumbent.

However, it is possible that the entrant could be more efficient than the incumbent but not by enough to ensure that its total cost of supplying the product is lower than the incumbent's incremental cost. If this were the case, under the ECPR, market entry would not occur. The product would therefore not be provided by the most efficient producer, which the ECPR is supposed to guarantee. The ECPR could therefore turn out to be internally inconsistent because, although it is supposed to ensure production by the most efficient carrier, it can generate conditions under which this is unlikely to hold.

A further major problem with the theory relates to dynamic efficiency gains. Because the incumbent firm in a perfectly contestable market is assumed to be perfectly efficient before a competitor enters the market, then it follows that market entry will not have an impact on the incumbent's costs which are supposed to be already minimized. There is, however, a great deal of evidence to show that this is not necessarily the case. Competition can be expected to cause the incumbent to become more efficient, improve its quality of service, bring its prices more into line with its costs, and develop more innovative services which would increase demand for telecommunications services. However, because the ECPR takes no account of these potential dynamic effects of competition, it undervalues the benefits of entry and so could reinforce the incumbent's inefficiency.

Given that it can be argued that the ECPR/ADC regime:

- enables the incumbent operator to carry a substantial margin of inefficiency;
- fails to take account of the dynamic gains brought about by competition thereby leading to interconnect charges that distort the make or buy decision faced by entrants; and
- encourages firms to behave in other ways that misallocate resources.

The Director General concluded in 1995 that the regime was at odds with the policy objective of obtaining 'the best possible deal for the end user in terms of quality, choice and value for money'.[42] As a result, in 1996, BT's licence was modified and the RPI + 2 per cent line rental constraint was lifted resulting in the access deficit regime being removed. It was envisaged that given that BT had claimed for so long the efficiency of rebalancing that it would raise line rentals accordingly so as to

---

[42] Oftel Consultative Document, *Interconnection and Accounting Separation*, June 1993, HMSO, para 1, p 1.

collect the extra £1.5 billion to finance the 'access deficit'. In practice though, it did not increase them the 80 per cent required to collect this extra amount.[43]

3.12 SOCIAL OBLIGATIONS AND FURTHER CONSTRAINTS ON RETAIL PRICES

As detailed above, BT, in setting its prices, is subject to a combination of regulatory constraints. In sections 3.10 and 3.11 the issues surrounding a rebalancing constraint on BT were presented. A further restriction on BT and on most incumbent operators, however, also relates to the non-de-averaging of geographical tariffs and the requirement to provide service to all customers demanding service (otherwise known as the Universal Service Obligation or USO). This constraint, like that on rebalancing, has the effect of making access unprofitable, although the uncertainties in the demand for telecommunications services makes it difficult to ascertain how a profit-maximizing operator would set prices.

Under the averaging constraint, it is normally claimed that due to the economics of density of the industry[44] certain classes of customers become profitable to serve whilst others become unprofitable. In a pure competitive market, if this occurred, it would mean that those customers who were unprofitable would be excluded from the feasible market for service. However, the fact that the incumbent has a USO means that this cannot occur and therefore to fund this there is cross-subsidization between profitable and unprofitable classes of customers. This subsidization by profitable customers to unprofitable customers, like the subsidization by long distance and international call charges to line rental and local call charges, has historically been encouraged by governments. The rationale for imposing a USO is both social and economic. The social policy goal, as discussed above, is to provide individuals with access to communications facilities so as to avoid a gulf emerging between 'information-rich' and 'information-poor' groups. The economic rationale, on the other hand, relates to the presence of externalities, not taken into account by individuals in their private decision-making. New customers joining a network not only benefit themselves, but create extra opportunities for existing customers. There is, moreover,

---

[43] Even if the line rental constraint is removed, it is not in BT's interest to rebalance quickly. In a competitive market place, a company's products and services are often deliberately priced out of balance, especially when the sale of one service is linked to the sale of the other. An example of this is mobile telephony, where handset subsidies help establish the customer and secure future revenue. It could be argued that this is not strictly comparable to fixed telephony, as a BT access customer can choose to send long distance and international traffic via an indirect supplier. However, in attracting the line rental customer, the local call and interconnect revenue, at least, is also secured, so the principle is fundamentally the same.

[44] An industry exhibiting economies of density is one where the more closely packed together the customers are, the lower the unit costs. This is far from being unique to telecommunications: it exists in any industry where geographic location of customers is significant.

evidence of dynamic benefits for the economy arising from the development of the telecommunications sector.

The presence of these externalities and the social and political considerations mentioned above thus create a case for imposing a USO-sharing mechanism as long as it can be proven that costs outweigh benefits. It should, however, be recognized that the main aim of the obligations will differ at different periods. More precisely, at the time of network build-out and mass-market take-up, the objective of universal service obligations is likely to be primarily economic. Once the network is completed, however, the goal of universal service will shift to being primarily a social one. In the former stage, it is desirable to keep installation prices etc. low so as to stimulate demand and to take account of the network externality. In the latter stage, the emphasis is likely to be upon targeting subsidies to ensure that the telephone is affordable to all and adapted to those with special needs.

Traditionally in a monopoly environment, as mentioned above, the costs of the USO have been covered by a cross-subsidy. When competition has been introduced, however, the incumbent has asserted, as with rebalancing, that having a USO exposes it to competition targeted exclusively at the profitable business thereby resulting in it having inadequate funds to cover the costs of serving unprofitable customers. As a consequence, it claims that the costs of this should be shared amongst operators in order to ensure competition on equal terms.

3.12.1 Costing the Universal Service Obligation

The costs of meeting the USO should comprise the sum of the losses incurred by the USO operator in serving customers whom it is obliged to serve but whom it would not otherwise serve had it not been a USO operator. The calculation must be made on the basis of the costs of an efficient operator, as it is imperative that operators do not subsidize embedded inefficiencies within the USO operator.

The computation of the cost of the USO therefore involves detailed examination of the costs and revenues associated with customers. Given that only a few customers are likely to impose net USO costs, the method for estimation should be focused on the costs of provision to loss-making customers on an avoidable basis. In other words, the calculation should ascertain how much would be saved (i.e. costs) and how much would be lost (i.e. revenues) if loss-making customers were detached from the network.

The calculation of the cost side of the equation comprises detailed economic modelling which should aim to determine the maximum number of customers that can be served economically. Once this has been identified, it should then be possible to derive and cost the shortfall or the cost of serving loss-making customers using avoidable costs.

Once the avoidable costs of delivering universal service have been costed, any commercial benefits, such as good public relations, perception of marketplace ubiquity, reduced churn, or simplified credit procedures arising from serving remaining customers must be quantified. All incremental revenues emanating from

loss-making customers must also be included on the revenue calculation. This should comprise call charges, line rental charges, as well as revenue of incoming calls to loss-making customers. This is of key importance to the calculation as this would be lost to the operator if the customer left the network.

The cost of delivering universal service is then the amount by which the cost of serving loss-making customers exceeds the benefits and incremental revenues associated with serving these same customers.

3.12.2 Funding the Universal Service Obligation

As detailed in section 3.12, if costs outweigh benefits there is then a case for imposing a sharing system so that competition occurs on an 'even playing field'. A number of mechanisms exist for funding and sharing the costs of meeting the need of unprofitable customers or services. If it is deemed that the rationale for the USO is social policy, so that the cost of funding the USO ultimately represents a tax on customers to fund extended services for others, then it is appropriate for the costs to be met by general taxation. However, governments generally find this option unpalatable and therefore it is usually the case that the costs of USO are financed from within the telecommunications sector. This can be done in several ways. The first method relates to a fund or virtual fund where the costs of the universal service are shared out between carriers according to the size of each operator's traffic share, as is the case in Australia. Alternatively, costs could be divided to reflect service revenues minus payments to other operators. A further method involves the tampering of interconnection charges such that there is a surcharge on interconnection which covers USO costs.

It is important that the way in which USOs are allocated and financed minimizes market distortions. It should be recognized that the mode of implementation can influence longer term resource allocation decisions, such as entry and exit, investments in networks and technology choices, and so can impact dynamic efficiency. In the case of a specific USO interconnection surcharge, the distortions would be similar to that of ADCs and could result in tariffs being further unbalanced from underlying costs, as the interconnecting operator would undoubtedly recover the surcharge from the generality of its customers and not only from those making calls to uneconomic areas and customers.

In the UK, a study of the USO was conducted in 1996[45] and was eventually costed at less than £0.05 billion. Oftel thus concluded that since the cost of delivering universal service was more or less insignificant and it was unlikely that the transaction cost of administering and funding the mechanism would exceed the delivery cost, it was decided that the delivery of the USO should not be funded by the industry

---

[45] Universal Telecommunications Services, Statement, Oftel, 1997.

as a whole. Ofcom, however, has stated that the costs and burden of universal service will be kept under review.[46]

The funding of the USO can be carried out using the methods outlined above. Funding via a fund or virtual fund could, however, be further enhanced by the fact that alternative service providers are present in the market. In other words, permitting the incumbent to contract out the USO to the most efficient service provider or, equally, franchising the USO to the most efficient service provider and then making the appropriate transfers could potentially improve the efficiency of USO delivery.

3.12.2.1 *Competitive tendering*

Competitive tendering could operate by segmenting the market into different customer classes and/or regions, and auctioning the obligation to supply each of these. Under one possible competitive franchising arrangement, operators would be invited to bid to supply a USO in a particular region subject to satisfying minimum quality of service standards. Contracts would then be awarded to the lowest cost operator or the operator who requested the lowest subsidy. This would potentially ensure that the costs of providing universal service were minimized and hence the contributions required. It would also avoid the need to measure the costs of the USO, since these would be determined by a competitive bidding process.

An alternative would be to limit the franchise award with estimates of the current cost of USO provision in a particular region or for a customer class. This may be one way of ensuring that lack of competition does not lead to increases in the costs of providing USOs.

The efficacy of employing a particular competitive franchising scheme will, however, depend upon the extent of potential competition for each USO. This will partly depend upon the form of auctioning mechanism used, and the incentives provided by it. However, no franchising scheme will work well where the incumbent or another operator is the only bidder, or uniquely advantaged by virtue of its ownership of the network.

3.12.2.2 *Subcontracting*

An alternative to franchising would be to allocate USOs to different operators, perhaps on the basis of their market shares or some other criterion, making them responsible for USO provision in a particular area. This scheme has the advantage of avoiding the need to levy other operators. It also has the potential to ensure that the overall costs of providing universal service are minimized. Each operator would then have an incentive to seek to meet its USO at the lowest possible cost, and to subcontract the supply of customers to other operators when they are more efficient.

However this scheme suffers from similar problems as a franchising scheme where there is a lack of potential competition. Moreover, and perhaps equally important, since different parts of the country are more profitable than others, the initial

---

[46] *Notification of Proposals for the Designation of Universal Service Providers and Setting of Conditions*, Consultation Document, 12 March 2003. Under the Communications Act 2003, s 65 *et seq* Ofcom have the right to review such matters for the purpose of making a universal service designation.

allocation process could not be conducted fairly without first calculating the costs of the USO in each region.

3.12.2.3 *'Pay or Play'*

Another method that could be used is 'Pay or Play'. In the UK, BT is obliged to provide a special service called the 'Light User Scheme', which is catered to the needs of loss-making customers. Under Pay or Play, competing carriers in loss-making areas could offer a special package or packages on terms similar to that offered by BT and agreed by Ofcom. If loss-making subscribers chose to take service from the alternative operator, that operator would then be credited with the net cost of providing universal service, payable from the fund or virtual fund.

All the alternative mechanisms above have some merit, it is important, however, for any regulator, should it be necessary to fund the USO, to ensure that the way in which USOs are allocated and financed minimizes market distortions. The regulator should also try to secure the introduction of competition in USO provision so as to achieve the USO at minimum cost.

3.13 THE NEED FOR AN EFFECTIVE INTERCONNECTION REGIME[47]

As detailed in section 3.7, a defining characteristic of all network industries, of which telecommunications is one, is that the value of belonging or being connected to the network increases with the number of people on the network. This means that competition between separate networks is unlikely to be sustainable, as the larger any one network gets the greater becomes its advantage over the others.

The solution to this problem is for networks to interconnect, in effect forming one single network. Now, while this solution is in the overall interest of society, if the market is characterized by one dominant network, it will be in that individual network's interest not to interconnect, in order to defend its position. An obligation to interconnect is therefore required to be imposed by regulators.

There is substantial confusion as to what the term interconnection refers to. The true definition of interconnection relates to members of one network calling members of another. In other words, it refers to call completion so as to attain the 'any-to-any' principle of a competitive telecommunications system. In the UK there are many other network services that BT is obliged to provide at a regulated price that are also treated as 'interconnection' or 'access' services.[48] While this is the correct

---

[47] See also Chapter 8.
[48] In the case of the UK, because BT held a monopoly over virtually all aspects of network operation and service provision, Oftel obliged BT to provide call origination services to competitors at regulated prices. So, for instance, in the early years of Mercury's competition with BT, if a customer connected to BT's local network wished to use Mercury's long-distance services, they could either dial an access code or use a pre-programmed telephone ('blue-button' telephone) to dial automatically into Mercury's network. This type of access thereby allowed customers connected to BT's network at the local end to

response to a market failure, it is not the interconnection market failure that has made this necessary.

Nonetheless, if the market is characterized by a dominant network, the effectiveness of an entrant's competitive challenge to the incumbent will depend crucially on the agreed terms of interconnection.[49] Interconnection charges are a key cost component of entrants' tariffs. If high interconnection charges are set so that the incumbent is favoured, new entrants in evaluating their entry business case could conclude that business is not viable and therefore may not enter the market. The very development of competition that the regulatory structure is supposed to promote could therefore be perversely retarded, with the incumbent not only being insulated from competition but also being allowed to prolong its cost inefficiencies, thereby adversely impacting consumers via continued higher tariffs. In this situation, existing entrants' behaviour, with regard to future investment decisions, could also be affected. In particular, the decision about whether entrants should continue to purchase network services from the incumbent or whether they should build it themselves, hence bypassing the incumbent's charges, will be strongly influenced by inflated interconnect charges. If interconnect is kept at inflated levels, existing entrants in the market place are likely to try to minimize costs by bypassing the incumbent's network and building their own network components to compensate. However, if these network components have natural monopoly properties[50] this duplication of network may be inefficient and so consumers could suffer as a result.

In contrast, if interconnect charges are set too low, inefficient entry could be enabled which in the long term could be detrimental to consumers and the industry. Moreover, if charge levels are too low, the incumbent will not be able to efficiently recover its network costs. If this is the case, it could result in investor uncertainty and therefore a corresponding decrease in investment and innovation in the industry. As a result, future network build-out may be less robust because capital funding that might otherwise have been used for network and service construction may not readily be available. In addition, technology choices may be driven by a short-term focus on recovery of network costs rather than a long-term focus on overall industry growth.

---

benefit from competition, albeit in a limited form, whilst at the same time enabling Mercury to gain presence in the market place, as well as 'incentivizing' it to continue its network build-out.

[49] The effectiveness of an entrant's challenge will also be influenced by the non-price terms of interconnection. As discussed in section 3.6, the incumbent has an incentive to impede the entrant via price and non-price mechanisms. Sections 3.6 and 3.7 briefly discussed the approach to deal with the non-price issues. In this section, we discuss the price issues.

[50] A natural monopoly is defined by economists as an activity which exhibits economies of scale throughout the entire stretch of its unit cost curve. Such a condition could make but one firm—the largest and lowest cost one—the inevitable winner and only survivor in any competitive contest with others in that line of activity which exhibits natural monopoly features. It is important to note that it is quite possible for a firm to exhibit natural monopoly properties in one activity but not in others. See Vickers, J and Yarrow, G, *Privatisation: An Economic Analysis* (MIT Press, 1988) for further discussion of this issue in relation to UK privatization and utility regulation.

This may thus have potentially irreversible consequences for service provision and the development of competition in the industry.

Given the complexities in setting interconnect charges, as outlined below in section 3.13.1, striking the appropriate balance of interconnect charge levels is crucial to ensure the efficient development of competition and of the industry. The role of the regulator in setting these charges is critical in establishing a sustainable interconnect regime. To prevent the dominant operator from abusing its position, the regulator must have the appropriate powers and penalty mechanisms to control for this.[51] The importance of these powers cannot be overstated. They are vital both for creating the conditions for effective competition and also for a system of minimum regulatory intervention.

3.13.1 Interconnection cost methodologies

Establishing the right arrangements for setting interconnection charges is probably the most important element in the competitive framework in telecommunications. Economic principles of telecommunication pricing to ensure the efficient use and development of the network dictate that prices should be set in relation to costs. Given that the effectiveness in the development of a competitive telecommunications environment is heavily reliant on the agreed terms of interconnection, it is imperative that the regulatory regime ensures that interconnecting operators pay for the specific services they use, and only for those specific services. The underlying costs of the network are therefore of utmost importance in setting these charges and for the emergence of viable competition, detailed cost of service information is required.[52]

3.13.1.1 *Fully allocated costs*

Historically, regulators and telecommunication operators have used fully allocated costs, which values asset at historic prices,[53] when setting interconnect charges. Fully allocated costs are calculated by attributing to any service whatever costs are directly determined or caused by that service. So, for example, large parts of the local loop can be associated with the provision of access to customers, or an international switch can be associated with the provision of international calls. There are, however, a great many costs that are 'common' to a number of services that cannot be allocated on a causative basis. For example, switching exchange costs are influenced by the number of subscribers attached to the exchange as well as the usage

---

[51] This was one of the key issues that arose of the Strategic Review of Telecommunications.

[52] Determining such costs has been subject to judicial consideration in a number of jurisdictions. See, for example, *Telecom Corporation of NZ Ltd v Clear Communications Ltd* (1992) 4 NZBLC; *Verizon v FCC* 535 US 467, 122 SCt 1646, and most recently the European Court of Justice decision in Case C-55/06, *Arcor AG & Co KG v Bundesrepublik Deutschland*, 24 April 2008.

[53] See section 3.5 for a brief discussion on the valuation of assets and their influence on telecommunication operators.

which each subscriber makes of the telephone. To ensure recovery of these common costs, these are normally allocated to the respective service on the basis of either the output, gross revenues, or direct costs of each service.

Although the use of fully allocated costs for the purposes of interconnect charging appears to be relatively simple to implement and it ensures that all costs are recovered, the procedures for deriving the costs are subject to difficulties. The first problem relates to the asymmetric information problem discussed in earlier sections. The derivation of fully allocated costs is heavily reliant on information that the incumbent dominant operator supplies the regulator. 'Strategic' cost allocations, on the part of the incumbent operator, can thus allow it to raise competitors' costs and so keep them at a permanent cost disadvantage. These 'strategic' cost attribution procedures can be highly complex and hence scrutiny of them by the regulator can prove to be difficult. Another criticism of the use of fully allocated costs is the fact that many costs cannot be allocated on a causative basis and hence must be attributed using some arbitrary rule, i.e. the output, gross revenues, direct costs of each service. The arbitrariness of this rule structure means that changing the rule can change the results.

Given the above arguments in relation to fully allocated costs, many have suggested that the use of these costs for the purposes of interconnect charging is likely to be inefficient. Further, because costs of assets are valued at historic prices, the charges set would not reflect the true replacement cost of the assets and so would not signal to buyers the costs that their actual demands impose on suppliers. Consequently, recent discussions about cost information for the purposes of interconnection charges have shifted towards incremental or marginal costs.

3.13.1.2 *Marginal and incremental costs*

Marginal costs represent the forward-looking costs associated with the provision of an additional unit of output of any particular good or service. Hence the marginal cost of access would be the costs associated with attaching a new subscriber to the local loop and the marginal cost of a long distance call would be the marginal costs of local conveyance at both ends, the marginal cost of switching and the marginal cost of long distance conveyance.

In a perfectly competitive market, economic theory states that setting price equal to marginal or incremental cost is a necessary requirement if resources are to be allocated in an economically efficient way. The reason for this is because if price was above marginal cost, it would always be profitable for firms to enter the market. Excess profits would hence be bid away by the new entry, so that eventually price would equal marginal cost. If, however, price was below marginal cost, firms would be making a loss and hence would exit the market so only efficient and sustainable competition would prevail. Marginal costs thus represent the costs of the marketplace, which will emerge if effective competition develops successfully.

The notion of marginal cost provides a measure of the costs of producing a single unit of output. In contrast, incremental costs provide a measure of the costs per unit

of producing a larger increase in service output. So, for example, the incremental cost of long distance calls could be computed on the basis of the extra costs of providing all long distance calls given the availability of access and would be expressed on a per unit basis. Thus with the same time horizon and output increment, marginal and incremental costs may be regarded as the same.

Marginal and incremental costs can be calculated in two ways. The first, known as 'bottom-up' cost modelling, involves the construction of an engineering/economic model of an optimal telecommunications network. The idea is to try to design and cost an efficient and optimal network which can meet any given set of demands.[54] By changing certain demand parameters for individual services, it is then possible to calculate the marginal or incremental costs of that service. The alternative approach, known as 'top-down' cost modelling, starts from the incumbent's management accounts or fully allocated costs. The first step involves revaluing the assets on the basis of their replacement costs. The non-incremental costs, such as non-attributive 'common' costs, are then removed from the accounts and the remaining costs are used to calculate the incremental costs of service on a per unit basis.

It is normal for both methods to be used in determining incremental or marginal costs; indeed the European Court of Justice has held that 'the national regulatory authorities *have* to take account of actual costs, namely costs already paid by the notified operator and forward looking costs, the latter being based, where relevant, on an estimation of the costs of replacing the network . . .'(italics added).[55] The reason is that the two models act as an auditing mechanism for each other. Each has strengths and weaknesses that ensure that the reconciliation between the two models allows for only efficient costs to be recovered. If the regulator relied exclusively on the top-down model derived from the fully allocated costs of the incumbent, the resulting incremental costs could include significant asymmetric information effects, thereby leading to a heavily skewed outcome in favour of the incumbent where inefficiencies in the incumbent's cost structure could be passed on to competitors in interconnection charges. The bottom-up model, in contrast, has the important advantage of being derived in an open and transparent way so that the confidence of the entire industry can be gained. However, because, the model uses a theoretically efficient network rather than the actual network in place, it may be the case that the assumptions in deriving the model may be unrealistic. As a consequence, the use of both models yields advantages and allows the regulator to scrutinize more closely the cost structure of the dominant operator.

---

[54] The bottom-up model in designing an optimal telecommunications network rather than using the actual network in place removes the margin of inefficiency implicit in most incumbent's network, thereby allowing only efficient costs to be recovered through interconnect charges.

[55] See *Arcor AG*, n 52 above.

3.13.1.3 *Mark-ups*

The use of pure incremental costs in a network industry in transition towards competition, however, will rarely cover the total cost of service of even an efficient operator. Examples of this include the costs of access and the costs of geographic averaging. This, therefore, raises three important issues: whether or not mark-ups on incremental costs to cover these 'common' costs are justified and, if so, which costs should be included in any mark-up system and how the mark-ups should be implemented.

It is already recognized that in a normal competitive market, the costs of interconnect would simply be incremental costs: there would be no need for a system of mark-ups. Where, however, the market is characterized by large common and fixed costs, this issue needs to be considered further. The key criterion for judging the case for or against mark-ups should hence be the impact they would have on the development of effective competition. Mark-ups should only be justified when it can be demonstrated that this regulatory action is of benefit and where it can be shown that unintended consequences are avoided.

It can be argued, however, that distortionary effects are likely to result as all the methodologies for calculating mark-ups entail significant problems. The ECPR is one such method. The flaws with this approach have already been discussed in section 3.11 with regard to ADCs. The use of this rule for the imposition of ADCs was considered to result in a situation where the dominant operator was given substantial scope for inefficient production without the threat of market entry as it encouraged firms to behave in ways that misallocated resources.

Another method for calculating mark-ups is Ramsey pricing. Ramsey pricing entails marking-up services where demand is not responsive to price. In other words, it involves varying the price to incremental cost ratio in inverse proportion to the elasticity of demand. The principle generally implies, therefore, the highest mark-up for access charges followed by local, national, and international calls.

The typical Ramsey pricing formula for calculating the extent of the mark-up depends strongly on the type of competition between the incumbent operator and its competitors, the relative sizes of the firms, the differences in the costs of supplying the final output, and the cost of interconnection. The complexity of the information required to put Ramsey prices into practice means, though, that it is impossible to see them being used at a practical level. The problems of estimating the various elasticities which are required in the Ramsey approach are considerable if not insuperable, particularly when dynamic effects have to be factored in somehow. Therefore, this means that whatever appeal the approach has at a theoretical level, in practice, Ramsey pricing has little to commend itself.

The practical problems which make it virtually impossible to use either the ECPR or Ramsey pricing to calculate mark-ups means that the alternative might be to use equal mark-ups. These are effectively used in the calculation of fully allocated costs to cover 'common' costs. In the incremental cost case, these are calculated by type

of service, with the ratio of mark-up to incremental cost being the same for each service. The immediate problem with this approach is that it lacks any of the theoretical economic justifications which, despite the practical problems associated with their implementation, the ECPR and Ramsey pricing at least partly possess. The rules governing equal mark-ups can be considered completely arbitrary and take no account of customers' preferences. It means that the charges for interconnect may not be the cost of interconnect, and instead operators could be in a position where price signals are distorted so that inefficient behaviour could be encouraged. According to some economists, an interconnection system comprising incremental costs plus equal mark-ups could be deemed to constitute little more than the fully allocated regime. Since it is generally acknowledged that the fully allocated regime has failed to engender effective competition, it might therefore be difficult to see how such a replacement would fare any better.

3.13.2 Interconnection regulation in the UK

In light of the above theoretical discussion on interconnection and the importance of an effective interconnection regime how has the UK regulatory regime dealt with this requirement? The following section is divided into two. The first part describes the developments in interconnection regulation in fixed telecommunications. The second then proceeds to describe the situation for the mobile sector.

3.13.2.1 *Fixed telecommunications interconnection regulation in the UK*
The need for a clear interconnection policy became prevalent when Mercury was licensed for operation. As discussed above, BT had no incentive to provide interconnect to Mercury. However, BT's licence stated that it had an obligation to interconnect. Nonetheless, the licence did not specify how the interconnect charges should be set and since the effectiveness of an entrant's competitive challenge depended crucially on the level of charges agreed, from 1982 to 1984, BT played out an effective series of interconnection negotiations with Mercury to meet its regulatory requirements whilst at the same time postponing Mercury's entry into the market. Given these obstacles, in early 1985 Mercury sought determination from Oftel. The determination delivered in October 1985 embodied the following main elements:

- stipulation that any customer of one system should be able to call any customer of the other, whether or not this involved a choice of network operator by the calling customer (call termination services);
- interconnection at local and trunk level (call origination services). At the local level the interconnecting links between the systems were to be provided by BT on the basis of full tariff business exchange lines; for trunk interconnections, Mercury was given the right to take its system up to the BT exchange;

- restructuring of call and connection payments as follows: national call charges were time and distance related, mirroring the basic BT customer tariff structure; international calls were based on fully published BT tariffs; connection payments payable by Mercury for system interconnection were to be wholly cost related and comprise two components: direct costs of material and labour, and a portion of BT's 'consequential incremental costs' (i.e. all costs increased or expected to increase because of the provision of the point of connection).

The 1985 Interconnection Determination, which provided the basis for the March 1986 Interconnection Agreement between BT and Mercury was essentially a successfully pragmatic effort to facilitate market entry into an overwhelmingly dominated marketplace.

Interconnect prices were set with an RPI – 3 per cent index, the same as the basket of BT's regulated retail prices at the time. BT had already adopted the economic principle of peak-load pricing coupled with distance-related pricing, to maximize utilization of its network. It hence seemed logical to transfer this rationale to the pricing of interconnect. At the time, margins were very high, and the prospect of their erosion received little contemplation. There was thus no reason for Mercury to question this interconnect pricing structure, and it was keen to settle negotiations quickly, as it was reliant upon interconnect in order to commence business.

BT's pricing structure of interconnection with its network, however, effectively placed it in full control over the structure of retail prices offered by its competitors. The use of distance-related pricing meant that interconnect was not cost-related to the number of network components involved in the call; instead, it depended on an arbitrary distance factor. The impact of this was that any form of competitor pricing innovation was effectively constrained to mimic BT's pricing structure. Furthermore, interconnect prices had not fallen in line with BT's costs. Competitors were thus essentially over-charged for their interconnection.

BT's retail prices fell in accordance with their price controls, which in turn eroded the differential with their wholesale interconnect prices leading to margin squeezes. If this had continued *ad infinitum*, competitors (whose prices were materially affected by the underlying wholesale prices) would not have been able to provide a price-competitive alternative service.

Over the period, BT had little interest in reaching agreement over interconnect. It is only when forced to do so by the regulator on an annual basis, following the breakdown in commercial negotiations, that BT reluctantly supplied the minimum access to its interconnect 'bottleneck'. It did not, however, ask Mercury for interconnect to enable BT customers to call those directly connected to Mercury's network. This, therefore, added an additional obstacle for Mercury's market entry as it meant that, given BT's dominance of the market, directly connected customers had to have the inconvenience of continuing to require separate BT incoming lines if they wanted to receive calls.

Given these difficulties, in June 1992 Oftel issued a statement concluding that in the case of BT, detailed 'Accounting Separation' between its different businesses was

necessary—for the continuing development of competition, and for public confidence that BT was not abusing its dominant position.[56] The application of accounting separation to BT's business was in the form of BT's 'retail' and 'network' arms. BT-Network was responsible for the sale of wholesale network services to all retailers including BT-Retail at non-discriminatory regulated prices, determined on an annual basis using the fully allocated costing approach outlined above. BT-Retail, in contrast, was responsible for selling on these services to final customers. Other results of the Accounting Separation process were a set of standard interconnection charges and a methodology for determining undue discrimination (in terms of BT's retail prices versus interconnection prices). Via this approach to accounting separation, BT's costs were therefore expected to be exposed to ensure transparency, non-discrimination, and the revelation of unfair pricing.

It is of course debatable quite how transparent any system based on BT's own accounts can be given the asymmetric information effects in the provision of information. This is one of the reasons why Mercury lobbied hard for a move to incremental costing.

In 1996/97, the change in network costing from fully allocated costs, based upon historic cost accounts, to a system of forward-looking incremental costs, reflecting the replacement cost of capital assets, finally got underway. In addition, Oftel proposed a move away from the need of annual interconnection determinations and instead opted for a more flexible approach based on a network price cap.[57]

Traditionally, price caps were only used for retail services; Oftel, however, felt that the methodology for the setting of retail price caps could also be applied to network and wholesale prices.[58] This new approach marked a significant departure from the norm, since in other countries regulators were just starting to get more deeply involved in the direct regulation of interconnection. In the UK, in contrast, it could be argued that Oftel was pulling back from regulation as competition developed and was transforming its role from a prescriptive regulator to more that of a competition authority.

In setting the network price cap, Oftel stated that it intended to allow BT to recover in its wholesale prices the incremental costs of providing the relevant service which would include an appropriate return on capital and a proportion of common costs. The requirement for incremental cost measures provoked Oftel to undertake work, in conjunction with the industry, to develop the incremental cost models—the bottom-up model based on an economic/engineering approach to the costs of the network, and the top-down model, based on costs derived from BT's Current Cost Accounts. A detailed analysis of differences between the model then led to a

---

[56] This policy is to be contrasted with the more radical policy in the US of structural separation of the RBOCs from AT&T. See section 3.6 for a discussion of structural separation versus accounting separation.

[57] *Network Charges From 1997*, Oftel Consultative Document, December 1996.

[58] See section 3.5 for a discussion on the methodology for setting price caps.

reconciliation between them which produced 'hybrid' figures as the best measure of the relevant incremental costs.

Given that under the new network charge controls, charges would no longer be determined annually but would be set by BT within the confines of network price caps, it was important that Oftel set a new framework of rules. If BT was to set the charges, the extent of its flexibility needed to be dependent upon the competitiveness of the relevant interconnection market so that abuse of dominance could be avoided and so that the Littlechild rule of minimum regulatory intervention could be pursued.

3.13.2.2 New network charge controls

In the event, this is exactly what occurred with Oftel proposing the following arrangements to commence from 1 October 1997 and ending in September 2001:[59]

- For competitive services, BT would be free to set the charges, subject only to general competition legislation, and the conditions of BT's licence, including the Fair Trading Condition and the non-discrimination condition.

- For prospectively competitive services, BT would set charges subject to a safeguard cap of RPI + 0 per cent on each discrete charge, in addition to the general competition legislation and the conditions of BT's licence.

- For non-competitive services, BT would set charges within three network baskets, each subject to a charge cap formula of RPI − 8 per cent, calculated as discussed in section 3.5, in addition to the general competition legislation and the conditions of BT's licence.

To allay fears of BT's ability to manipulate charges, Oftel further proposed that reasoned complaints that the charges set by BT are anti-competitive, unduly discriminatory, or unfair would be investigated. Anti-competitive behavioural investigations would normally involve the comparison of the tariff for a particular service with its cost estimates, with the use of price floors and ceilings playing a significant role in the investigation. If prices were below price floors, set at incremental costs, then (subject to there being no objective justifications) one may assume that prices were predatory. In contrast, if prices were above price ceilings, set at the stand alone cost[60] of providing the particular service in question, then it could be assumed that monopoly profits were being earned at the expense of consumers.

---

[59] *Network Charges From 1997*, Oftel Statement, May 1997.

[60] Stand-alone costs refer to the costs that would be incurred by an efficient entrant if it were to decide to produce only a specified set of commodities. E.g. if an entrant were to produce only access lines, then the costs relating to the production of access lines would refer to stand alone costs. Similarly, if an entrant were to produce only call minutes, then the costs involved in producing these minutes would entail stand-alone costs.

3.13.2.3 *The level of competition of services*

In the case of the services that fell into the competitive, prospectively competitive and non-competitive service categories, Oftel concluded the following:

- **Competitive Services**
  - Operator Assistance
- **Prospectively Competitive Services**
  - Long Distance Conveyance
  - International Calls
  - Directory Enquiry Services
  - Phonebooks

- **Non-Competitive Services** will be grouped into 3 baskets
  - Call Termination basket
    - >> Local exchange segment
  - General Network basket
    - >> Call Origination
    - >> Local to tandem conveyance (origination and termination)
    - >> Single transit
  - Specific Interconnection Services
    - >> Connections & rental of circuits
    - >> Certain Data Amendments

The requirement to judge the competitiveness of the services provided meant that the classification of conveyance services under the new regime needed to be more disaggregated than under the old. There were now two local exchange segment services; one for call termination and one for call origination. A single tandem segment was now composed of two services: a local exchange segment (either call origination or call termination) and local-tandem conveyance. A double tandem segment was made up of three services: a local exchange segment (either call origination or call termination), local-tandem conveyance, and inter-tandem conveyance. These services are shown in Figure 3.3.

The local exchange segment involved the use of the concentrator, the local switch, and transmission between the concentrator and local switch known as remote-local conveyance. Local-tandem conveyance comprises the use of the tandem switch and transmission between the local and tandem switches, known as local-tandem transmission. Inter-tandem conveyance involved the use of a tandem switch and

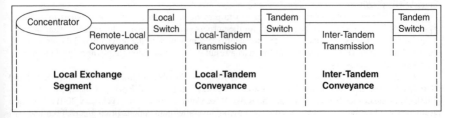

Figure 3.3 Main inland conveyance interconnection services

transmission between two tandem switches, known as inter-tandem transmission and was sub-divided into three distance bands.[61]

All these components form the basis of inland conveyance interconnection services and are used in varying degrees by operators for the provision of service.[62]

Oftel's attempt to judge the level of competition that existed and/or would exist in respect of the provision of each of the services provided by BT raised a substantial level of debate. In particular, the view that Directory Enquiries (DQ) was prospectively competitive raised significant objections. BT had control of access to the numbering database required for DQ. This in the industry's view represented a substantial barrier to entry and so it was felt that it was inappropriate to categorize DQ as a competitive service.[63] Nonetheless, in spite of this opposition, although Oftel acknowledged that there were barriers, it continued to hold this view and felt that the use of ceilings and floors would act as sufficient triggers to avoid anti-competitive behaviour.

During 2000, Oftel began its review for the future structure of the network charge controls and in February 2001, it set out its conclusions.[64] In the light of responses received by Oftel and its own market analysis, Oftel concluded that competition had not increased sufficiently to remove the controls introduced in 1997. Oftel determined, therefore, that new charge controls should be introduced which would run from 1 October 2001 to 30 September 2005. Again, like the previous controls, these were based on the extent of competition in the relevant interconnection market. Specifically, interconnection services were classified into one of the following categories:

• Competitive Standard Services;

• New Standard Services;

• Prospectively Competitive Standard Services; or

• Non-Competitive Standard Services.

Oftel proposed that the services (as designated for the 1997 controls) should remain in their current categorizations of competitiveness until the Director General

---

[61] See also Chapter 2, at section 2.2.

[62] Further details are provided in Oftel's May 1997 Statement 'Network Charges From 1997' in Annex C. Available at: <http://www.ofcom.org.uk/static/archive/oftel/publications/1995_98/pricing/nccannex.htm#ANNEX%20C>.

[63] Since January 1999, BT has been required to provide access to its operator services information system (OSIS) database to service providers for the purposes of providing directory products and services including phone books. This increased the prospects for competition in the provision of DQ services, the potential for which has been further enhanced as a result of Oftel's decision (September 2001) to liberalize DQ enquiry access codes.

[64] For more information see: (1) Price Control Review—Possible Approaches for Future Retail and Network Charge Controls, Consultation March 2000; (2) Price Control Review, Consultation October 2000; (3) Proposals for Network Charge and Retail Price Controls from 2001. (February 2001). These are available at (1) <http://www.ofcom.org.uk/static/archive/oftel/publications/pricing/pcr0300.htm>; (2) <http://www.ofcom.org.uk/static/archive/oftel/publications/pricing/pcr1000.htm>; (3) <http://www.ofcom.org.uk/static/archive/oftel/publications/pricing/pcr0101.htm>.

determined otherwise. The only exceptions to this was international call conveyance and access to the directory assistance system (DAS).[65]

As before, Oftel concluded that controls should not be applied to competitive services. For new interconnection services, however, Oftel proposed to retain the power to 'charge control' new services before they are introduced or subsequent to their introduction. For prospectively competitive services, Oftel concluded that the 'safeguard' cap of RPI + 0 per cent should be maintained. However, the expectation was that competition rather than the safeguard cap would be the binding constraint on the charges for these services.

In the case of non-competitive services, Oftel concluded that interconnection services currently classified as non-competitive should continue to be subject to charge controls. Oftel proposed, however, that they should be grouped into five 'baskets of services' rather than the previous three. Table 3.1 sets out the non-competitive 'basket' structure from 1 October 2001 to 30 September 2005.

Table 3.1 Non-competitive basket structure from 1 October 2001

Basket	Services
Call Origination	Call Origination
Call Termination	Call Termination
Tandem Layer Basket	Local-Tandem Conveyance
	Single Transit
Interconnect Specific Basket	Connections and Rentals of Circuits
	Data Management Amendments
	Product Management, Policy and Planning[66]
Flat Rate Internet Access Call Origination (FRIACO) Basket	FRIACO at the DLE[67]

For each basket, Oftel introduced a different value of 'X'. For charges for originating and terminating calls, the value of 'X' was set at 10 for each basket. For the Tandem Layer Basket, the value of 'X' was set at 13. For the Interconnect Specific Basket, covering the charges made to physically connect with BT, the value was set at 8.25, and finally for the FRIACO Basket, Oftel proposed a charge control for each element of the charge to be set at RPI − 7.5 per cent.

---

[65] The reason for this was because international call conveyance is now provided by Concert. BT offers international direct dialing (IDD) services via Concert but BT's conveyance services to Concert are controlled separately from Concert's IDD control. In the case of DAS, this service is no longer provided.

[66] Product Management, Policy and Planning (PPP) is a surcharge that is levied by BT on each outgoing conveyance minute. It contributes to interconnect specific costs such as billing and management relationship costs.

[67] Flat Rate Internet Access Call Origination (FRIACO) is an unmetered call origination interconnection service which has been available from BT since June 2000. It is used in the provision of internet access over the public switched telephony system.

By introducing a different value of 'X' for each of the baskets (which was now more narrowly defined), Oftel ensured that regulation was targeted on those areas where it was required. The Littlechild principle of minimum regulation was thus still being pursued.

In 2005, following the Strategic Review of Telecommunications and a review of the extent of competition in the relevant interconnection market, Ofcom set new controls for the four years from 1 October 2005. Specifically, it completely deregulated inter-tandem conveyance and inter-tandem transit—by removing charge controls and all other regulations. This followed Ofcom's finding that BT no longer had Significant Market Power status in that market.[68] Furthermore, Ofcom loosened regulation by moving BT's charge control on local-tandem conveyance to a 'safeguard cap' that would limit charge increases for that service to below inflation. Table 3.2 sets out the network charge controls that apply to BT for the four years from 1 October 2005.

As can be observed, Ofcom has disaggregated the baskets such that currently there are eight non-competitive baskets—each with a different value of 'X'. Further, for most of the non-competitive baskets, the value of 'X' has been reduced in comparison with the previous controls. Therefore, again, it suggests that a policy of withdrawing regulation as competition takes hold is being adopted.

As mentioned above, these controls run until 2009. During this period, it is clear that many operators and in particular BT will start to adopt and invest in IP-based telecommunications networks. This means that new interconnect products are likely to be introduced. As such, the current baskets or markets as set out above may not directly correspond to these new products. Ofcom will thus have to consider the

Table 3.2 Network Charge Controls 2005–2009[69]

Service	Network Charge Controls 2005–9
Call termination	RPI − 5%
Call origination	RPI − 3.75%
Single transit	RPI − 11.5%
Local-tandem conveyance	Safeguard cap of RPI − 0%
Interconnection circuits (ISB)	RPI − 5.25%
Product management, policy and planning (PPP)	RPI + 0.75%
DLE FRIACO	RPI − 8%
Single Tandem FRIACO	RPI − 8.5%
Inter-tandem conveyance and Inter-tandem transit	No control as no Significant Market Power

[68] See section 3.14.
[69] For further information of this – see <http://www.ofcom.org.uk/consult/condocs/charge/statement/>.

impact in terms of how markets are defined and how these new wholesale services should be regulated, i.e. via a network charge control or via some other means. This is currently the subject of much debate. What is clear, though, is that whatever occurs, the underlying principles of ensuring investment incentives, the likelihood of competition, and the need for direct consumer protection where competition is not effective or sustainable will need to continue to be respected.

3.13.2.4 *Mobile interconnection regulation in the UK*

As mentioned above in section 3.8, the government sought to encourage the development of competition by licensing a number of mobile operators. As with fixed services, interconnection has been a key issue. In particular, the charges offered to fixed operators to enable their customers to call mobile networks has often been the subject of much debate.

In 1990, Mercury asked Oftel to determine the interconnect charges it should pay to Vodafone and to Cellnet, because these had not been agreed between the parties. These determinations were made in 1991 and included provision for an annual indexation of the charges by Oftel. It should be noted, though, that these interconnect rates only applied to Mercury. The charges paid by BT to the mobile operators had been agreed between the parties, and Oftel had not been asked to determine them.

In subsequent years, residential and business consumer organizations expressed concern to Oftel about the prices for calling mobile phones. Oftel recognized that due to the Calling Party Pays arrangement in the UK, all network operators have a monopoly position over the 'termination' of calls on their own networks. When someone wants to make a call to a mobile, or any other phone, then the calling party has no choice but to call the network to which the called party has subscribed. This means that mobile operators, in common with other network operators, are able to set charges for call termination, without reference to significant competitive pressures. Given this, Oftel initiated an investigation. The main preliminary finding from this work was that BT's prices for calls to Vodafone and Cellnet customers were too high and were mainly caused by Vodafone's and Cellnet's high termination charges. Oftel had the option to impose price controls but it recognized that such action would have a significant impact on the whole of the mobile market. This is especially so, given that the commercial strategy of most UK mobile operators was to subsidize handsets to encourage take-up of service. Any potential price control on termination rates could thus be expected to have an effect on the pricing structure for handsets and calls from mobile networks. Given this, in March 1998, Oftel referred the issue of prices of calls to Vodafone and Cellnet to the Monopolies and Mergers Commission (MMC).[70]

---

[70] Prices of Calls to Mobiles Statement, March 1998 available at <http://www.ofcom.org.uk/static/archive/oftel/publications/1995_98/pricing/ctm0398.htm>.

In December 1998, the MMC completed its investigation and concluded that there was an insufficient competitive constraint on termination charges.[71] It considered that the only effective means of remedying or preventing any adverse effects would be to impose a price control on termination. It thus proposed that Cellnet and Vodafone should reduce their weighted average termination charge for 1999/2000 to 11.7ppm and then in 2000/01 reduce it further by RPI − 9 per cent and by RPI − 9 per cent again in 2001/02.

In February 2001, Oftel carried out a review of the price controls imposed on Cellnet and Vodafone by the MMC (now the Competition Commission).[72] It noted that since the control was set, the mobile market had grown rapidly and at a rate much greater than that predicted by the Competition Commission (CC). However, it stated that:

the key fact remains that when a call is made to the mobile network, it is the calling party which pays for the call, not the person being called. This means that there is a greatly reduced incentive for the network operators to lower the charges which they make for incoming calls to a competitive level, as it is not their customers who pay for the call. Further, research by Oftel suggests that most residential and business mobile phone owners are not generally concerned by incoming call prices, and that their choice of network is unlikely to be influenced by the charges made by that network for incoming calls. To some extent, the reduced incentive to price at the competitive level may be mitigated by closed user groups (i.e. groups which all subscribe to the same network) but this is likely to be of marginal impact.[73]

In light of this, Oftel concluded in September 2001 that controls on charges for termination of calls on the four main mobile networks—O2 (formerly Cellnet), Vodafone, Orange, and T-Mobile (formerly One2One)—were appropriate and justified in order to protect consumers and proposed a charge control of RPI − 12 per cent each year for the four years until March 2006.[74] The mobile network operators (MNOs) objected to this proposal. In particular, they submitted that it was inappropriate to view call termination as a separate market, as it was just one of a bundle of interconnected services purchased by customers; that there was a single market for the provision of all mobile services in the UK; that that market was competitive; and that none of the MNOs had the ability to earn excessive profits from call termination because the competitive pressures they all faced in respect of the totality of the services they offered competed away any such profits. Given these objections, Oftel referred the matter to the CC who published its findings in December 2002.[75]

---

[71] Reports on references under s 13 of theTelecommunications Act 1984 on the charges made by Cellnet and Vodafone for terminating calls from fixed-line networks. Available at <http://www.ofcom.org.uk/static/archive/oftel/publications/1995_98/pricing/cmmc1298.htm>.

[72] Review of the Price Control on Calls to Mobiles, February 2001 available at <http://www.ofcom.org.uk/static/archive/oftel/publications/mobile/ctom0201.htm>.

[73] See Paragraph S3 of Review of the Price Control on Calls to Mobiles, February 2001.

[74] Review of the Charge Control on Calls to Mobiles—26 September 2001, available at <http://www.ofcom.org.uk/static/archive/oftel/publications/mobile/ctm0901.htm>.

[75] Reports on references under s 13 of the Telecommunications Act 1984 on the charges made by Vodafone, O2, Orange, and T-Mobile for terminating calls from fixed and mobile networks. Available at

The CC agreed with Oftel on the matter of call termination being a separate market. As such, it concluded that competitive pressures at the retail level did not constrain termination charges. Reviewing the termination charges offered by the MNOs, the CC submitted that they operated against the public interest. Accordingly, it recommended that:

- for each of O2, Vodafone, Orange, and T-Mobile, there should be two price caps, set at the same level, one regulating termination charges for fixed-to-mobile calls, and the other termination charges for mobile-to-mobile calls. In this way, the MNOs cannot load charges disproportionately on to one or other call type;

- O2, Vodafone, Orange, and T-Mobile should each be required to reduce the level of its average termination charge by 15 per cent in real terms before 25 July 2003;

- O2 and Vodafone should be subject to further reductions in their average termination charges of RPI – 15 per cent in each of the periods 25 July 2003 to 31 March 2004; 1 April 2004 to 31 March 2005; and 1 April 2005 to 31 March 2006;

- Orange and T-Mobile should be subject to further reductions in their average termination charges of RPI – 14 per cent in each of the periods 25 July 2003 to 31 March 2004; 1 April 2004 to 31 March 2005; and 1 April 2005 to 31 March 2006.

Therefore, as can be observed, the reference to the CC resulted in tighter charge controls on the MNOs in comparison with what they would have got under Oftel.

A new European framework for telecommunications regulation in 2003 meant, however, that Ofcom had to carry out an early review of the situation.[76] In June 2004, it published its market review of wholesale voice calls terminated on individual mobile networks.[77] This covered not only the four MNOs discussed above but also calls terminated on Hutchison 3G UK ('H3G')—a 3G MNO. Taking into account the European Commission's Guidelines on market analysis and the assessment of significant market power, Ofcom's view was that each MNO in the UK had significant market power in a separate market for voice call termination on its network. As such it proposed that in respect of Vodafone, O2, T-mobile, and Orange for their 2G call termination services, that they should:

(1) provide network access for the purposes of 2G call termination;

(2) not unduly discriminate in the provision of such access;

<http://www.ofcom.org.uk/static/archive/oftel/publications/mobile/ctm_2003/index.htm>.

[76] See further section 3.14 and Chapter 5.

[77] Review of mobile wholesale voice call termination markets—EU Market Review, available at <http://www.ofcom.org.uk/static/archive/oftel/publications/eu_directives/2003/ctm/ctm0503.pdf> and Wholesale Mobile Voice Call Termination: Proposals for the identification and analysis of markets, determination of market power and setting of SMP Explanatory Statement and Notification 19 December 2003 conditions available at <http://www.ofcom.org.uk/consult/condocs/mobile_call_termination/mct_consultation/>.

(3) publish a Reference Offer;

(4) give prior notification of price changes; and

(5) reduce termination charges in line with the proposed charge controls by the CC.

In respect of 3G voice call termination services, however, it recommended that there should be no *ex ante* regulation although H3G was required to give advance notification of price changes and provide Ofcom with details of call volumes.

Given that Ofcom effectively designated all five MNOs as having significant market power, H3G subsequently appealed its SMP designation to the Competition Appeals Tribunal (CAT) on the grounds, among others, that Ofcom did not carry out a sufficient analysis of prices to entitle it to come to a decision that H3G had significant market power and, failed to take account, or sufficient account, of the ability of BT to restrain pricing, in reaching its conclusions.[78] The CAT, in November 2005, found that Ofcom erred in its SMP determination since it did not conduct a full assessment of the extent to which BT had countervailing buyer power—see section 3.16.3. As such the CAT remitted the decision back to Ofcom to reconsider. At the same time, December 2005, Ofcom put forward a proposal to extend the charge controls on 2G voice call termination for a further year after 31 March 2006 when they would otherwise expire.[79] The main reason for doing this was because it was carrying out a review of mobile voice call termination on 2G and 3G networks after 31 March 2007 and did not want to limit the range of conclusions which may be drawn from this review.

In March 2007, Ofcom concluded its assessment of whether H3G holds a position of significant market power in the market for wholesale mobile voice call termination on its network and at the same time also concluded its review of mobile voice call termination on 2G and 3G networks.[80] The main conclusions were the following:

• There are separate markets for the provision of wholesale mobile voice call termination in the UK to other Communications Providers by each of Vodafone, O2, Orange, T-Mobile, and H3G.

• Each of the five MNOs has SMP in the market for termination of voice calls on its network(s).

• Charge controls should be imposed on the supply of mobile call termination by each of the five MNOs, and those controls should apply without distinction to voice call termination, whether on 2G or 3G networks.

---

[78] See the CAT's judgment, para 35, available at <http://www.catribunal.org.uk/>.

[79] Wholesale mobile voice call termination: Statement and notification extending the charge controls. Available at <http://www.ofcom.org.uk/consult/condocs/wholesale/wmvct_statement/statement.pdf>.

[80] Mobile Call Termination Statement, March 2007 available at <http://www.ofcom.org.uk/consult/condocs/mobile_call_term/statement/>; and Assessment of whether 3G holds a position of SMP in the market for wholesale mobile voice call termination on its network, March 2007, available at <http://www.ofcom.org.uk/consult/condocs/h3gsmp/>.

- The charge control should apply for four years from 1 April 2007.[81]
- Average charges of H3G should be reduced to 5.9ppm (2006/07 prices) by the final year of the charge control (1 April 2010 to 31 March 2011). This level reflects exogenous cost differences between H3G and the 2G/3G MNOs. The change to be implemented by an initial reduction to 8.5ppm (2006/07 prices) followed by three reductions each of equal (percentage) change across the next three years (i.e. from April 2008 to March 2011).
- Average charges of Vodafone, O2, Orange, and T-Mobile should be reduced to 5.1ppm (2006/7 prices) by the final year of the charge control period (1 April 2010 to 31 March 2011). The reduction should be implemented in four equal (percentage) steps across the four years.
- Further conditions should be imposed requiring provision of voice call termination on fair and reasonable terms and conditions (including contract terms), prohibiting undue discrimination, and requiring charge transparency. Ofcom has concluded, however, that the proposed obligation to publish contracts is not proportionate.

In response to these proposals, however, H3G lodged a legal appeal to the CAT against Ofcom. H3G's appeal covered three main areas:

(1) the findings of SMP in each of the Reassessment Statement and the 2007 Statement;

(2) Ofcom's decision to impose a price control in the form imposed by the 2007 Statement;

(3) the level of the price control fixed both for H3G and for the 2G/3G MNOs in the 2007 Statement.

In May 2008, the CAT produced its judgment in the case.[82] The conclusions arrived at by the Tribunal were that:

- the appeal against the finding of significant market power in the Reassessment Statement was dismissed;
- the appeal against the 2007 Statement in so far as it comprised matters which are not specified price control matters was also dismissed; and
- the Tribunal said that Ofcom was correct in deciding to set a price control for H3G as well as for the 2G/3G MNOs in the 2007 Statement.

---

[81] Given that the then existing charge controls were due to expire less than one week after publication of the Ofcom statement, Ofcom decided to impose new controls from 1 April 2007 but to adjust the level of the year-one (1 April 2007 to 31 March 2008) controls by weighting them as though they applied for only 10 of the 12 months of the year-one control and as though for two of the 12 months the present average charges applied.

[82] See <http://www.catribunal.org.uk/documents/Judgment_1083_1085_20052008.pdf>.

3.13.3 Key issues—interconnect

The effectiveness in the development of a competitive telecommunications environment is heavily reliant on the agreed terms of interconnection. Establishing a sustainable interconnect regime is hence probably the most important task in developing a competitive framework for telecommunications.

The role of the regulator in setting these charges, is critical in ensuring that the industry has confidence in the interconnect charge levels. To prevent the dominant operator from abusing its position, the regulator must have the appropriate powers and penalty mechanisms to control for this. The importance of these powers can not be overstated. They are vital both for creating the conditions for effective competition and also for a system of minimum regulatory intervention.

Economic theory states that prices should be set in relation to costs. The traditional use of fully allocated costs, although simple to implement, meant, however, that interconnecting operators could receive the wrong price signals since the charges did not reflect the true replacement costs of the assets and hence distortionary incentives could be allowed to develop with respect to the efficient allocation of resources. The general shift towards the use of incremental costs hence represents an improvement on the status quo although it can be argued that it is difficult to implement and to monitor.

The UK interconnection regime has gone through several stages of development and the liberalization of the market has necessitated the need for a fresh approach. This has been provided by the landmark introduction of the new Network Charge Controls (NCC). NCC has a number of potential advantages for operators and for the market as a whole. The system could be considered to better serve the industry as it maximizes the degree to which markets decide charges and hence reduces as far as possible the inevitable distortionary intervention by the regulator.

However, in relation to termination charges on mobile networks—as can be seen from the above discussion—there has been considerable debate and resistance from the mobile operators to accept charge controls on termination. Developments in this sector inevitably mean that the debate is likely to continue for some time to come.

3.14 OTHER MARKET DEVELOPMENTS

As discussed in previous sections, the UK regulatory regime has undergone significant changes to meet the evolving nature of the sector. In recent years, given the increasing convergence between telecommunications, broadcasting, and information technology, five new EC Communications Directives were introduced which took effect on 25 July 2003.[83]

---

[83] See further Chapter 5.

Under the new regulatory framework for electronic communications networks and services, national regulatory authorities (NRAs)—Ofcom in the UK—have to carry out reviews of competition in communications markets, to ensure that regulation remains proportionate in the light of changing market conditions. This process is subject to scrutiny by the Commission under the Community consultation mechanism established under Article 7 of the Framework Directive.[84] Essentially, the aim of this is to (i) ensure consistency across the EU; (ii) limit regulation to markets where there is a persistent market failure; and (iii) ensure transparency in the regulatory process.

The markets where regulation may be justified, and the criteria used to identify such markets, are listed in a Commission Recommendation.[85] The aim of the Recommendation is to promote harmonization across the European Union by ensuring that the same markets are subject to a market analysis in all the EU Member States. Ofcom, however, can regulate markets that differ from those identified in the Recommendation where this is justified by national circumstances and where the Commission does not raise any objections. In other words, Ofcom can define relevant markets appropriate to national circumstances, provided that the utmost account is taken of the markets listed in the Recommendation. The European Commission has also issued guidelines on market analysis and the assessment of significant market power (the 'SMP Guidelines').[86] Ofcom is required to take the utmost account of these guidelines when identifying a market and when considering whether to make a market power determination. The EC process can thus be considered to be quite thorough. For this reason, it is usually the case that market reviews practically can only occur every two to three years. With increasing developments in technology and the adoption in particular of IP-based networks, the risk with this process, however, is that if market developments happen rapidly, the analysis could become obsolete more quickly and so market reviews may need to occur more frequently.

---

[84] Article 7 of the Framework Directive requires NRAs to notify the Commission and other NRAs of their findings as to market definition and SMP analysis and the regulatory obligations they intend to impose (or remove). The Commission then has one month in which to assess the notification of the proposed measures (the 'phase one' procedure). In cases where the Commission considers that, in terms of market definition or SMP analysis, the proposed measures would create a barrier to the single market or if it has serious doubts as to the measures' compatibility with Community law (and in particular the common policy objectives that all NRAs should pursue), it can conduct a more detailed investigation lasting a further two months ('phase two'). Following this in-depth investigation, should its concerns be confirmed, the Commission may require the NRA to withdraw the draft measures ('veto' decision) and possibly resubmit the market analysis in question at a later stage.

[85] Commission Recommendation (2003/311/EC) of 11 February 2003 on relevant product and service markets within the electronic communications sector susceptible to *ex ante* regulation in accordance with Directive 2002/21/EC (OJ L 114/45, 8 May 2003); superseded by Commission Recommendation (2007/879/EC) of 17 December 2007 (OJ L 344/65, 28 December 2007)

[86] Commission guidelines on market analysis and the assessment of significant market power under the Community regulatory framework for electronic communications networks and services (OJ C 165/6, 11 July 2002).

Where a market is found to be effectively competitive, then this should lead to the NRA withdrawing any existing obligations and not imposing any new ones under the Significant Market Power (SMP) process. On the other hand, if the market is found not to be effectively competitive, NRAs need to designate the dominant operator(s) as having SMP and impose on them the appropriate obligations. Regulation, under the EC rules, should thus only be focused on areas which require regulatory control.

As mentioned in previous sections, Oftel already carried out market definition reviews as part of its regulatory strategy covering retail pricing and interconnection so as to focus controls on only those areas which require regulation. These changes under the new EC Directives do, however, involve some changes as to how Ofcom evaluates competition.

3.15 MARKET DEFINITION[87]

Under the new regime, markets are defined based on competition law principles, specifically upon the principle of the 'hypothetical monopoly. This concept is already well established in antitrust legislation, both in the EU and in the US,[88] and provides the standard framework for market definition analysis in competition policy cases.

The principle states that a product (or geographic) market should be defined as the minimum set of products (or areas) which would be 'worth monopolizing'. In other words, it refers to a range of products whose provision, if it were in the hands of a single firm, could be profitably restricted. This principle is also known as the SSNIP test (small but significant non-transitory increase in price) and involves an iterative procedure covering both a product market and a geographic market dimension. Essentially, the idea is to find both a set of products and geographic dimensions that meets the SSNIP so that a 'hypothetical monopolist'[89] could profitably and permanently raise the price of these products above the competitive level by 5 to 10 per cent. A detailed case-by-case assessment is thus usually required.

The starting point is to consider the products or services of the type supplied by the firm under investigation and ask whether a hypothetical monopolist with control over these products could profitably and permanently raise the price of these products above the competitive level by 5 to 10 per cent, assuming that the price of all other goods remained constant. If the hypothetical monopolist were to be prevented from doing so by a readily available substitute, then this substitute would need to be

---

[87] See further Chapter 9.

[88] See the Notice on the definition of the relevant market (European Commission, 1997) and the Horizontal Merger Guidelines in the US (FTC, 1997)—see <http://www.usdoj.gov/atr/public/guidelines/horiz_book/hmg1.html>.

[89] The term 'monopolist' merely means that the undertaking is the only supplier of these products and services, not that it necessarily possesses any market power.

included into the relevant market. This procedure would then need to be repeated until a set of products is reached where such a price increase, above the competitive level, would be profitable. The smallest set of products that meets the SSNIP test is then defined as the relevant market.[90] Defining the relevant market in this way ensures that all products which pose a significant competitive constraint on the product market under investigation are taken into consideration.

The economic concept of substitution in this process is of key importance in defining the relevant market. It is essential not only to judge the extent to which consumers consider other products as effective substitutes—demand-side substitution—but also to consider the ability of productive assets outside the control of the hypothetical monopolist to be redirected for the production of directly competing products—supply-side substitutes.

3.15.1 Demand-side substitution

Demand-side substitution occurs whenever a rise above the competitive level in the price of the product or service under investigation causes consumers to switch their purchases, from the product whose price has risen, to other products. It should be noted that it is not necessary for all customers to switch. It is sufficient simply that enough switching occurs so that a 5 per cent increase in price is not profitable. In this case, the attempt by a hypothetical supplier to increase price is likely to result in a loss of sales sufficient to render the price increase unprofitable. The products in question would not therefore be worth monopolizing and so would not define a relevant market. In fact, if the relevant market was defined as consisting of this product only, any market power assessment based on market shares would be an overstatement. Any regulatory controls, in this instance, could thus impose considerable distortions on the market.

In assessing the potential for demand-side substitution, consideration must also focus on non-price competition. In many hi-tech industries, firms compete through product innovation, i.e. differences in quality and variety. Applying the SSNIP test to these markets will tend to define markets which are too narrow, since in these industries, consumer demand is driven by a set of performance variables rather than price. Without changes in performance, there might not be substitutability across products even for significant price increases. Given this, it is essential that the analysis also examines non-price factors so as to ensure that erroneous market segmentation is avoided.

---

[90] E.g. if we were to consider the market for bottled waters and found that via the SSNIP test, the monopolist was able to charge a small but significant non-transitory price premium above the competitive level then the relevant market, in this case, would be bottled waters. However, if the SSNIP test showed that the monopolist was prevented from charging a small but significant non-transitory price premium above the competitive level then we would need to repeat the test with the inclusion of the closest substitute such as all non-alcoholic beverages etc.

Barriers to switching must also be included in the analysis. Limited customer ability to switch between providers increases the extent to which providers can act independently of their existing customers. Barriers might exist on the demand side or be maintained by suppliers. The former include the practical difficulty of switching relative to the potential benefits, and customers' awareness of both their ability to switch and the procedures involved. Other potential barriers are the perceived quality of service and reputation of alternative suppliers, and customers' reluctance to take risks with alternative providers. All of these issues must be examined, otherwise it is possible that an erroneous market segmentation will be defined and thus distortive regulatory controls.

3.15.2 Supply-side substitution

Substitution may also take place via alternative suppliers. If other producers respond to a price increase above the competitive level by swiftly switching production facilities to produce the collection of products/services, the increased level of supply may render any attempted price increase unprofitable. In this case, the products in question would not define a relevant market because of the potential for supply-side substitution and the test would therefore need to be repeated, taking into account the goods that these alternative firms produce.[91]

From the above, it is therefore important to note that for supply-side substitution, it is not sufficient for a firm to just have the technical ability to switch production. It must also be necessary for production of the relevant products to be possible without the need for new investments and it must also be possible within a relatively short period of time i.e. a year.

3.15.3 The SSNIP test

As discussed above, the SSNIP test is well established in antitrust legislation and provides a standard framework for market definition analysis. The data requirements to apply the test precisely are, however, onerous and so, in general, it is not a directly operational technique.

The main reason for this is because the SSNIP test asks whether a hypothetical monopolist could profitably implement a small but significant non-transitory increase in price above *the competitive level*.

---

[91] An example is the supply of paper for use in publishing. Here the Commission defined the market based upon supply-side substitution in *Torras/Sarrio* Case IV/M166 OJ (1992) C58/20 [1992] 4 CMLR 341. Paper is produced in various different grades dependent on the coating used. From a customer's point of view, the different types of paper are not viewed as substitutes, but because they are produced using the same plant and raw materials, it is relatively easy for manufacturers to switch production between different grades. If a 'hypothetical monopolist' in one grade of paper tried to set prices above competitive levels, manufacturers currently producing other grades could easily start supplying that grade—the ability to exploit market power is thus constrained by substitution by suppliers.

In sectors with a very large number of providers, the prevailing price level could be used as a proxy for the competitive price level. However, in markets that are served either by only one firm or by a few firms, the current price cannot be assumed to be a proxy for a 'competitive' price. The reason is because any profit-maximizing firm will always set prices at a level where demand for its products is elastic, i.e. at the highest price the market can bear or alternatively where a further increase in price would be unprofitable. In this instance, therefore, if there is market power in the sector under investigation and current prices are assumed to be at the 'competitive' price level then at this price level, the 'relevant' market may be defined too widely. To clarify, using current prices in this instance may show that many products appear to be close substitutes, i.e. if prices are increased, sufficient switching occurs for it to become unprofitable[92] and so the relevant market under the SSNIP test would be widened. At a 'true' competitive price level, however, substitution may not take place and so if 'current' prices were used as proxies for 'competitive' prices the SSNIP test could lead to a situation where the market was erroneously defined. This is known in competition policy analysis as the 'Cellophane Fallacy' after the case of *United States v E I du Pont De Nemours & Co* (1956).[93] In that case, Du Pont argued that cellophane did not constitute a separate market since it competed directly and closely with other flexible packaging materials such as aluminium foil, wax paper, and polyethylene. The problem with this argument, however, was that Du Pont, as the sole supplier of cellophane, is likely to have set the prices for its products at a level where alternative products only provided a constraint on the pricing of cellophane if the prevailing price was used as the 'competitive' price. Given this, wherever there is a suspicion that market power exists, the prevailing price level should be treated with care.

3.15.4 The 'competitive' price level

In the light of the above discussion, the competitive price is sometimes derived from cost information. As discussed in section 3.13.1, in a perfectly competitive market, economic theory states that setting price equal to marginal cost is a necessary requirement if resources are to be allocated efficiently. However, in telecommunications, which is characterized by high fixed costs, it is difficult to determine the appropriate cost to be used.

As discussed in that section, to take account of the issue of high fixed costs in telecommunications, an equal proportional mark-up is normally added to the pure incremental costs of services. This measure, known as long-run incremental costs (LRIC), is then often used in telecommunications as a proxy measure for the 'competitive' price. However, in applying the SSNIP test for market definition purposes

---

[92] This is what we would expect in a sector with market power because if the price rise was profitable, the firm would have implemented it already.
[93] *United States v E I du Pont de Nemours & Co* 351 US 377 (1956); 76 SCt 994; L Ed 1264.

using this as the competitive benchmark, it is important to recognize that bias may be introduced into the process. Specifically, if prices are above pure incremental costs, own elasticities are likely to be higher and so a hypothetical price increase is likely to generate significantly more substitution than if the price increase was on pure incremental costs. This is to do with the fact that at a higher price, the degree of substitutability increases—see the Cellophane Fallacy—and so does the 'own price elasticity'. Under this scenario, the market could be defined too widely. Given this, it is essential that the competitive benchmark is considered carefully so as to ensure that the upward biases in the definition of the market and thus the competitiveness of the market are minimized.

3.16 DESIGNATION OF DOMINANCE

Once the market is defined using the principles outlined above, the next step is to consider whether there is a dominant firm in that market. The European Court has defined a dominant market position as:

a position of economic strength enjoyed by an undertaking which enables it to prevent effective competition being maintained on the relevant market by affording it the power to behave to an appreciable extent independently of its competitors, customers and ultimately of consumers.[94]

An undertaking is unlikely to be dominant if it does not have substantial market power. Market power is not, however, an absolute term but a matter of degree; the degree of market power will depend on the circumstances of each case. In assessing whether there is dominance, a case-by-case review of:

- the structure of the market and the nature of competition prevailing in the market;
- barriers to entry into the market; and
- countervailing buyer power

would need to be conducted.[95]

3.16.1 The importance of market structure

'Market structure' refers to the number and relative size of firms in the market or sector.

---

[94] Case 27/76 *United Brands v Commission*, [1978] ECR 207, [1978]1 CMLR 429.

[95] For a more detailed exposition on the criteria that are considered by Ofcom in market power assessments, see 'Oftel's Market Review Guidelines: Criteria for the Assessment of Significant Market Power', Issued by the Director General of Telecommunications 5 August 2002.

When there are fewer firms in the market, there is a danger that competition may be weak and that one or more firms may have a degree of market power; that is, they may be able to behave without proper regard to their competitors or to customers. Nonetheless, if firms within the market all have low market shares (that is, each serves a relatively small segment of the market) there is less of a chance that any will have market power. If, however, one or more firms have a higher market share, there will be a greater risk that these firms have at least some market power and competition may therefore be weaker.[96]

Given this, market shares (of both the undertaking and competitors) are commonly used as a preliminary indicator of dominance. Although, they are not conclusive on their own, the European Court has stated that dominance can be presumed in the absence of evidence to the contrary if an undertaking has a market share persistently above 50 per cent.[97] Market shares between 40 per cent and 50 per cent could also be considered consistent with dominance if other factors (i.e. weak position of competitors) are also indicative of it. However, in the case of market shares below 40 per cent, the EC considers it unlikely that an undertaking will be individually dominant if its market share is below this threshold, although dominance could be established below that figure if other relevant factors (i.e. the degree of vertical integration or the firm's control of essential inputs that are required by its competitors— see discussion below) provided strong evidence of dominance.

Market shares may be assessed by volume or value of sales. The appropriate measure will vary between markets, although it is likely that the most appropriate measures will be volume for bulk products such as wholesale conveyance minutes, and value for differentiated products such as retail products. Where a firm has a higher market share by value than by volume, it may indicate that it can price above rivals due to market power.

In using market shares for the assessment of dominance, it is important that the history of the market shares of all undertakings within the relevant market are considered. This is more informative than considering market shares at a single point in time, partly because such a snapshot might hide the dynamic nature of a market. For example, where markets are growing fast, high market shares are less indicative of market power than in a more mature or slow-growth market. It is important in these types of markets to thus have a proper picture of the structure of the market so as to ensure that any designation of dominance does not prevent innovative activity from occurring.[98]

---

[96] E.g. if a firm has 35% of the market, it might still be dominant if it has 65 competitors each with 1%. Where two firms have roughly equal market shares, even if they are high, then single firm dominance is unlikely to be found but collective dominance, whereby a group of firms jointly occupies a dominant position, may be found under EC law.

[97] Case C62/86 *AKZO Chemie BV v Commission* [1993] 5 CMLR 215.

[98] In many fast-growing industries, it is often the case that a particular firm takes the innovating initiative which involves considerable up-front investment and so becomes the market leader. Other firms then enter the market and adopt the practices of the first-mover firm. Now because of customer inertia

3.16.2 Barriers to entry

As mentioned above, high shares in a relevant market need not necessarily indicate dominance. This is particularly so if there are low barriers to entry into the market. If there are no barriers, attempts to exploit a large market position via, for example, excessive pricing would attract new entrants so that prices and services would be restored to their competitive levels.

Barriers to entry are defined as a cost that must be borne by a firm entering a market that does not need to be borne by an incumbent already operating in the market. The existence of entry barriers can thus reduce the scope for competition, so that incumbents are able to raise prices above competitive levels.[99]

Entry and exit conditions are thus important in assessing whether a firm possesses market power. To get a better picture of the state of the market, it is important that the regulator has hard evidence of the recent history of the market. Such evidence might include a historical record of entry into and exit from the market (or closely related markets) or, if possible, fully documented evidence of plans to enter.

Growth, or prospective growth, in a market could also have a bearing on the likelihood of entry, as entry will usually be more likely in a growing market than in a static or declining one. The reason is because it will be easier in a growing market for an entrant to be accommodated without any significant declines in prices and profits. The rate of innovation may also be important. In markets where high rates of innovation occur, or are expected, innovation may overcome barriers to entry relatively quickly. Indeed, any profits that result from an entry barrier created by successful innovation may be an important incentive to innovate.

All of these issues would need to be examined as part of a market review of competition and dominance. The existence of fully informed customers should also be considered. If customers are fully aware of the options open to them then this could restrict the leveraging of market power by a firm.

The Office of Fair Trading (OFT) distinguishes between three types of entry barrier:

- absolute advantages;
- strategic advantages; and
- exclusionary behaviour.

(i.e. customers take time to switch their allegiances), initially, the first-mover firm is likely to have a higher market share. This may not, however, reflect a dominant position because if it is relatively easy to enter the market then over a short period of time market shares could be eroded quickly. Now if the undertaking with a high market share was designated as dominant, then this could be detrimental for competition and the development of the industry in the long run as there would be negative incentives on firms to innovate and become the first-mover in an industry.

[99] An exit barrier is a similar concept: a cost borne by a firm leaving a market that a firm remaining in the market does not have to bear. The existence of exit barriers can be important when considering sunk costs since exit costs reduce the disposal value of an incumbent's assets if it chooses to leave a market and may therefore equally deter new entry.

At times they will overlap: exclusionary behaviour by an incumbent might, for example, have the effect of strengthening a pre-existing absolute or strategic advantage.

3.16.2.1 *Absolute advantages*

In some markets an incumbent owns or has access to important assets or resources which are not accessible to the potential entrant. This could therefore bestow an absolute advantage on the incumbent so that the entrant cannot gain access to an asset or resource at any cost or only at a cost substantially higher than that of the incumbent.

One example of this relates to the granting of licences. When the numbers of licences are restricted, such as spectrum, there may be an absolute limit to the number of firms that can operate in the market. This could thus act as an entry barrier unless licences are tradeable in a competitive market, in which case a potential entrant could purchase a licence and enter the market if a profitable opportunity arose.

Another example is when entry to a market might require the use of an essential facility. If access to it is indispensable in order to compete in the market and duplication of the facility is impossible or extremely difficult owing to physical, geographic, or legal constraints, or is highly undesirable for reasons of public policy, then such control may represent a significant barrier to entry.

And finally, intellectual property rights (IPRs) may provide an incumbent with an absolute cost advantage.[100] Assessing the effects of IPRs on competition, however, is complex when dynamic competition is considered. The reason for this is because even though an IPR is likely to constitute an entry barrier in the short term, in the long term a rival may be able to overcome it by its own innovation. What this means, therefore, is that the short-term profit which the IPR provides can act as an incentive to innovate and so can promote competition in innovation. Innovation lies at the heart of the competitive process so when making entry barrier assessments based on IPRs, it is important not to create disincentives on innovation, otherwise, the longer term competitive process could be disadvantaged.

3.16.2.2 *Strategic advantages*

The second source of entry barriers arises when a firm gains an advantage from being in the market first, sometimes called a 'first-mover advantage'. First-mover advantage can allow a firm to shape the way the market develops, by, for example, reducing or completely deterring the potential for others to enter the market.

When a firm contemplates entering a market, it needs to weigh up its expected revenue from entering against the expected costs of entering and exiting. Expected revenues depend on how the entrant expects the incumbent to react when it enters the market. If the potential entrant believed that the incumbent would, for example, aggressively reduce prices if it entered and so reduce the prospective revenue

---

[100] See further Chapter 10.

available from entering the market, then this might pose a significant entry barrier. This is particularly pertinent if an incumbent has previously adopted a predatory strategy against and driven out a new entrant (or existing competitor). Any future potential entrants to this market (or any other market where the incumbent operates) might then attach a higher likelihood to facing an 'aggressive' response, where the incumbent reduces prices significantly in response to entry.

The presence of sunk costs could also affect entry into the market. These are costs that are needed to enter an industry but which cannot be recovered on exit. Specifically, if the incumbent, via its first-mover advantage, has already incurred its sunk investments then it might not need to earn as high a rate of return as a new entrant who will have to make these investments so as to enter the market. This means that it could set prices at a level which may not allow the entrant to recover these sunk costs and compete.

Similarly, if the incumbent excessively invests in sunk assets, then strategically, it could send out a signal to potential entrants which states that it has significant spare capacity. This might imply, therefore, that should an entrant enter the market, it could flood the market with large quantities of the product at a very low cost which could thus adversely affect the entrant's business. The entrant might therefore decide not to enter the market if it thought that this aggressive response may prevail.

Given this, in any assessment of dominance, these issues would need to be considered so as to examine to what extent sunk costs give an incumbent cost advantages over potential new entrants and to what extent sunk costs might affect entry barriers. The mere existence of sunk costs in any particular industry, however, does not necessarily mean that entry barriers are high.

Economies of scale and economies of scope would also need to be considered in any assessment of dominance. Economies of scale arise when increasing production causes average costs to fall.[101] Economies of scope, in contrast means that average costs fall as more types of products are produced.[102] What this means, therefore, is that entry by a potential entrant could be riskier because the incumbent, via its scale and scope, could respond aggressively to the entrant in the marketplace thus adversely affecting its business.

Access to finance is another criterion that may need to be considered as part of a dominance assessment. Entry into an industry requires considerable financing. New entrants may, however, lack the same access to finance as incumbents.

• An incumbent may be a lower risk investment if it can present a proven track record in the market. It may also have better information about the market and therefore be able to present a more convincing business case;

---

[101] Economies of scale are common when the production processes involve high fixed costs.
[102] Economies of scope are common where networks exist as the capacity of the network can be shared across multiple products.

- Any fixed costs involved in raising finance will bear disproportionately on smaller firms, although this need not deter entry by subsidiaries of larger firms.

A potential entrant may therefore face a higher cost of finance (whether obtained from borrowing or sales of equity) than an incumbent. This could thus act as a deterrent on new entry, even when costs of raising finance are not sunk.

3.16.2.3 *Exclusionary barriers*

The third source of entry barrier is created by exclusionary behaviour by the incumbent such as vertical integration, predatory behaviour, and refusal to supply.

Vertical integration can promote dominance in two ways. The first is by making new market entry harder due to control of upstream or downstream markets. The second is through the potential ability to lever market power into upstream or downstream markets, thereby adversely affecting competition.

Predation might deter entry if a firm secured a reputation for aggressive behaviour. Thus, successful predation may confer a dominant position on the firm.

Refusal to supply may also constitute a barrier to entry. If, for example, an upstream firm were the sole supplier of inputs to a downstream industry and if there were barriers to entering the upstream market, the firm's refusal to supply a potential entrant in the downstream market could constitute a barrier to entry in the downstream market, even if no other entry barriers existed at that level.

3.16.3 Countervailing buyer power

Another aspect that should be assessed in a market assessment is countervailing buyer power. Buyer power exists where buyers have a strong negotiating position with their suppliers, which weakens the potential market power of a seller. Thus, even if firms have very high market shares, they may not be in a position to significantly impede effective competition, in particular by acting to an appreciable extent independently of their customers, if the latter possess countervailing buyer power. In assessing whether buyer power exists, the OFT notes a number of factors in its guideline on the assessment of market power.[103] In particular, if the following conditions hold then a buyer's bargaining strength may be enhanced:

(a) the buyer is well informed about alternative sources of supply and could readily, and at little cost to itself, switch substantial purchases from one supplier to another while continuing to meet its needs;

(b) the buyer could commence production of the item itself or 'sponsor' new entry by another supplier (e.g. through a long term contract) relatively quickly and without incurring substantial sunk costs;

---

[103] See <http://www.oft.gov.uk/shared_oft/business_leaflets/ca98_guidelines/oft415.pdf>.

(c) the buyer is an important outlet for the seller (i.e. the seller would be willing to cede better terms to the buyer in order to retain the opportunity to sell to that buyer;

(d) the buyer can intensify competition among suppliers through establishing a procurement auction or purchasing through a competitive tender.[104]

It should be noted, though, that while the conditions mentioned above are important to analyse in a market assessment, buyer power does not always benefit the final consumer. For this reason, a careful analysis of vertical relationships in the market, on a case-by-case basis, is often also required.

3.17 MARKET REVIEWS

In conducting these market reviews, Ofcom has thus had to undertake considerable analysis of the market involving:

• market definition exercises;

• examining the structure and level of competition prevalent in the market;

• investigating possible entry barriers; and

• investigating whether countervailing buyer power is present in the market.

As discussed above, market definition exercises involve substantial information requirements, which means that the SSNIP test is in general not a directly operational technique. However, in order to assess whether market power exists, it is necessary to establish a benchmark against which the actual situation can be assessed. The use of the SSNIP test for the definition of the relevant market thus allows for this benchmark to be established.

Once this benchmark has been ascertained, the assessment of dominance can then occur.[105] As discussed, however, market shares are not conclusive on their own. For this reason, the nature of competition in the market, potential barriers to entry, and buyer power must also be examined. Assessing the effects of entry barriers and the advantages they give to incumbents as well as whether there is an countervailing buyer power is, however, complex.

3.18 CONCLUSIONS

This chapter has provided an overview of the economics of telecommunications regulation encompassing the economic theory of regulation as well as the application of this theory to the UK telecommunications industry.

---

[104] Ibid, at 6.2.
[105] See section 3.16 and Chapter 9.

In years to come, there is little doubt that the 1980s and 1990s will be seen as a landmark era in the history of telecommunications. This is not because of the important technological changes that have occurred or the growing number of services and applications now available to consumers, noteworthy though these are, but because of the steps taken along the road to liberalization. Where once telecommunications was seen as the monopoly preserve of State-owned enterprises, it is now recognized as an industry where competition can and should be allowed.

Through liberalization there has been a constant changing force on the UK telecommunications industry and a constant force on price. As the market develops and convergence takes hold there will be a multitude of pricing packages on the market offering consumers more choice than ever before. Competitors will enter and exit and the fight for market share will continue.

The evolutionary forces of competition and technological developments, alongside the emergence of new innovative economic regulatory policies, means that the future of communications continues to be very exciting!

Part II

REGULATORY REGIMES

4

THE TELECOMMUNICATIONS REGIME IN THE UNITED KINGDOM

Helen Kemmitt and John Angel

4.1 EARLY HISTORY OF THE DEVELOPMENT AND REGULATION OF THE TELECOMMUNICATIONS INDUSTRY

4.1.1 The first monopoly

In a sense, the beginning of telecommunications in England started in 1660 when King Charles II was restored to the throne in England and Scotland. He was acutely mindful that his father had lost his head and he did not want to suffer the same fate. To maintain his position as king he needed to prevent a new Great Rebellion; he decided that he needed to know who was writing letters to whom, what people were saying about events, and what people were saying about him. He decided, therefore, to nationalize postal services and create a monopoly. This was the General Post Office (GPO).[1] The decision to establish a monopoly over the conveyance of communications was taken for reasons of state. Not surprisingly there was no consideration of 'economic efficiency' or 'natural monopolies'. The GPO was a government organ and was established under the Royal Prerogative.

---

[1] As an institution, however, the 'General Post Office' was established by Oliver Cromwell in 1657.

The basic GPO monopoly was over 'letters'. However, for over 300 years there was no statutory definition of a letter. It was not until 1981, under the British Telecommunications Act, that a statutory definition of a 'letter' was laid down.[2]

4.1.2 The telegraph[3]

The first real difficulty with the old letter monopoly arose with the 'telegraph'. Telegraph messages are conveyed over distances, but for most of the way the messages are not conveyed in written form, because they take a non-material form.

Early telegraphs relied on flashes of light from heliographs, or on the movement of flags or signalling arms on telegraph towers. Chains of telegraph towers seem to have been established by the time of the Napoleonic Wars. Where a telegraph was run on a formal or organized basis, a message which started out as a written letter (or signal) was then conveyed over a distance in code and then converted back into written format at the far end.

In economic and regulatory terms the early telegraphs were not significant and the GPO did not seem to have worried about them. Then came the railways in 1825. These were large organizations with a need for communications. Their signalling systems were a specialized form of telegraph, and they were initially large generators of written messages conveyed by hand by guards on trains.

Meanwhile, electricity had been discovered and with it the electromagnet. Between 1835 and 1844 the electric telegraph was introduced,[4] as was the Morse Code. Electric telegraphs made it possible to send letter-like objects in non-material form and the technology made it possible to send 'telegrams' on a commercial and affordable basis.

The railways had a continuing demand for telegraphs and their expanding national networks gave them the physical way-leaves over which to convey messages for others.[5]

Letters suddenly left their infancy and the years of telecommunications began.

4.1.3 Regulation of telegraphs

The development of the electric telegraph threatened to move control away from the government and into commercial hands. The Telegraph Act 1863 was therefore introduced as a means of controlling the activities of these privately owned companies.

---

[2] Section 66(5).

[3] See generally Standage, T, *The Victorian Internet* (Phoenix, 1999).

[4] Wheatstone and Cooke patented their invention in 1837 based on electromagnetic impulses travelling over wires.

[5] The introduction of the Railway Regulation Act 1844 brought electric telegraphs within the legislative domain.

Subsequently, the Telegraph Acts of 1868 and 1869 nationalized those telegraph services originally provided by private companies.

The Telegraph Act of 1869, although introduced before the invention of the telephone, played a significant part in the history of the setting up of telephone systems in the UK. The 1869 Act conferred a monopoly on the Postmaster General (PMG) of all telegraph business. From that time no other body could operate such a business without a licence from the PMG.

The key points which arise from the early Telegraph Acts were:

- the Acts were founded on the principle that telegrams were letters over which the GPO had a monopoly;

- companies and individuals were allowed to run their own telegraph systems on their own land for their own internal purposes but not to provide services to others;

- there were arrangements for licensing companies and individuals to run their own telegraph systems;

- there were rules about the conduct of telegraphs including, for example, the confidentiality of what was conveyed, interference with telegraphs; and

- there were provisions about the construction and installation of telegraphs (especially telegraph poles), compulsory acquisition of land, arrangement for digging up streets, provision for running wires over private land, rights to cross railways and canals, etc.

In the infancy of any telecommunications technology when networks are being installed there are powerful arguments for monopoly. There are reasons for concentrating resources in one organization, using its revenues to develop the business extensively and intensively, and sharing overheads. The infant telegraph business shared facilities with the postal business and each benefited from the economies this generated by using common investment and personnel. Also, the concept of a 'public service' took a powerful hold in the minds of those who thought about telecommunications. Not surprisingly, the GPO took a monopoly of telegraphs and set up its own telegraph network.[6] A few organizations, such as Lloyds and the railways, seemed to have run their own telegraphs under strict GPO supervision.

The Telegraph Act[7] arrangements for the construction and installation of telegraphs were to last. It was not until 1984 that the legal system in the UK formally recognized the concept of a 'telecommunication system' or of a 'telephone network'.

---

[6] The Telegraph Acts of 1868 and 1869 granted the Postmaster General the authority to purchase those commercial companies conducting telegraph business within the UK. In addition, the 1869 Act granted the PMG exclusive privilege in the transmission of telegrams.

[7] The early Telegraph Acts were largely codified in 1863 and 1868, with a series of amendments over the years.

The public switched telephone network was installed on the basis that it was a telegraph. Ground stations communicating with satellites in synchronous orbits 22,000 miles above the earth were legally no different from a person with a Morse key tapping away in the back office of an 1840s post office. Most of the principles remained as before, although the language needed to be changed to bring it into the twentieth century.

4.1.4 The beginnings of the telephone industry

In 1876 the telephone was invented by Alexander Graham Bell.[8] The first public telephone exchange opened in London in 1879.[9]

Initially, the GPO did not regard the telephone as a threat to their national telegraph network and were prepared to watch telephone systems develop in local areas. However, in 1880 it was held that a telephone conversation was a form of telegraph and that a telephone conversation was a telegram, and therefore all telephone companies were required to have licences under the Telegraph Act.[10]

Faced with a choice of either operating the telephone system itself or licensing firms to do so the PMG decided to issue licences to existing telephone companies, such as the National Telephone Company (NTC), to operate telephone systems under certain conditions and restricted to the areas in which they were already operating. The licences required the payment of a royalty to the PMG and gave the PMG an option to purchase the telephone undertaking at the end of a specified term.

This policy was further relaxed in 1882 when the PMG decided to grant licences to operate telephone systems to all responsible persons who applied for them, even where a Post Office system was established, reversing the previous policy 'on the ground that it would not be in the interest of the public to create a monopoly in relation to the supply of telephone communication'.[11]

There was a change in the position of the PMG when he realized that the developing telephone systems were seriously affecting the revenue of the telegraph service. There were also complaints about the quality of the NTC's service and the accumulation of its overhead wires in towns. In 1892, the government decided that the trunk line system should be owned by the state, and in 1896 the PMG took over the trunk lines of the NTC. The NTC was restricted to providing services in local exchange areas and it was decided that no further national licences would be issued. Intercommunications were established between exchange customers of the Post Office in one area and those of the NTC in another.

---

[8] On 14 February 1876 Bell filed an application in America for an apparatus for transmitting vocal sounds.
[9] See generally BT Archives, available at <http://www.btplc.com/Thegroup/BTsHistory/BTgrouparchives/index.htm>.
[10] In *AG v Edison Telephone Company of London* (1880) 6 QBD 244, the Edison Telephone Company failed to show that the telephone and the telegraph were technically different.
[11] Henry Fawcett, Postmaster-General, 17 July 1882.

In 1905, the PMG and the NTC agreed conditions for the transfer of the NTC's undertakings to the Post Office. From this time the Post Office and the NTC began to work towards the unification of their two systems. Intercommunication was possible between subscribers to both systems in the same local area throughout most of the country. On 1 January 1912, the PMG took over the system of the NTC and from this date the Post Office became the monopoly supplier of telephone services throughout most of Britain, with a few exceptions. In 1951 the first statute which recognized telephones as a separate instrument from the telegraph came into force. The Telephone Act 1951 enabled the PMG to set rental charges by means of statutory regulation.

4.1.5 The situation in Hull

The telecommunications market in Hull has developed in a different way from the rest of the UK. The reason for this can be, in part, traced back to the Telegraph Act of 1899. This Act had conferred powers on municipalities to borrow money for the establishment of local telephone systems under licence from the PMG. The PMG maintained the right to purchase any local authority system after a period of years. Thirteen authorities took out licences but only six set up telephone systems. One of these authorities was Hull Corporation (the forerunner of Hull City Council) which was granted its licence on 8 August 1902. This licence was conditional upon it embracing the same exchange area as that covered by the NTC.[12] All of these licences, with the exception of the one granted to the Hull Corporation, lapsed within a few years. Hull Corporation's licence was due to expire in 1911 together with that granted to the NTC. By this time the Post Office network was so small within the Hull area that the Post Office[13] had limited local commercial interest within the area and was content to grant a new licence to Hull Corporation on the condition that it acquired the plant and equipment used in the NTC network.[14] This occurred and a new licence was finally issued in 1917 expiring on 31 December 1932. A succession of licences followed, the only substantial change being the replacement of Hull Corporation by Hull City Council in 1974. In 1984, the City Council was granted a licence under the Telecommunications Act 1984. The licence was transferred to Kingston Communications (Hull) PLC in 1987, a company wholly owned by the City Council.[15]

---

[12] Some local telephone users discovered that competition sometimes meant having to rent two telephones.

[13] In 1911, the following telephone systems were operating in Hull: Post Office System—less than 50 subscribers; Hull Corporation—3,000 subscribers; and National Telephone Company—9,000 subscribers. Source: The History and Development of Kingston Communications—1904–1987, at <http://www.kcom.com/centenary/historyinwords/default.asp?NavID=3>.

[14] Hull Corporation paid £192,423 for the plant and equipment of the NTC.

[15] The Group was partially floated in 1999 with the City Council retaining a 44.9% stake. The City Council announced its intention to sell its remaining shares in May 2007.

This rather unique situation in Hull has been very important to telecommunications regulation in a number of ways, including:

- it showed that a small operation that did not enjoy economies of scale could provide an efficient and cost-effective service; and
- Kingston Communications had a working interconnect which enabled messages sent via one operator's system (i.e. Hull's) to be conveyed by another operator's system (i.e. BT's) and this provided the critical precedent for the Mercury/BT interconnect.[16]

Kingston Communications no longer has a monopoly but the company has remained popular locally and is in some senses a symbol of local pride, although some argue that the reason this unique situation has endured for so long is at least partly because it is simply not worth other service providers coming into the area and interconnecting. There have recently been signs of a rebellion of sorts. In the 2007 Ofcom consultation on the wholesale broadband access by far the greatest number of responses were from residents in Hull complaining about the lack of choice for broadband users.[17]

4.1.6 Evolution of the General Post Office

The first half of the twentieth century saw the development of the GPO Public Switch Telephone Network (the PSTN) and the steady atrophy of the original GPO's telegraph business. Technology advanced significantly with automatic switching, i.e. mechanical telephone exchanges in place of people with earphones putting plugs in holes, long distance conveyance, undersea cables, and the application of radio.

In the 1950s, it became apparent that the position of the GPO as a government department headed by a political PMG was unsatisfactory. Decisions were being taken for political reasons and money was controlled by the Treasury on a public expenditure basis, not on a business basis. There were no proper accounts, only records on what public money had been collected as call charges and when that money had been spent.

In the mid-1960s, the GPO as a whole was converted into a government 'trading fund', which meant that it produced rudimentary commercial accounts, a balance sheet, etc. This produced a radical change within the organization but there was no legislation as such to implement the change. In March 1965, the PMG, Anthony Wedgwood Benn, wrote to the Prime Minister proposing that studies be undertaken to look at converting

---

[16] See further Chapter 7.
[17] A petition on the Downing Street website to scrap the monopoly that Kingston Communications has in Hull for broadband users received 3,222 signatures. See also <http://www.ofcom.org.uk/consult/condocs/wbamr07/responses/>.

the Post Office into a nationalized industry.[18] It was decided that there should be one corporation split into two divisions: Post and Telecommunications.

Under the Post Office Act 1969, the Post Office ceased to be a government department and on 1 October 1969 it became established as a statutory corporation headed by a chairman appointed by the government. The position of PMG was abolished.

The independence of the GPO in 1969 could be viewed as the start of the long process of liberalization which continued until the end of the century. The Act formalized the telecommunications monopoly by giving the new Post Office 'exclusive privilege' to run telecommunication systems. It defined exclusive privilege in terms of the 'running' of 'telecommunication systems'. The word 'running' was never defined. However, 'telecommunication systems' were defined as:

a system for the conveyance through the agency of electric, magnetic, electromagnetic, electrochemical or electro-mechanical energy of—
(a) speech, music or other sounds;
(b) visual images;
(c) signals serving for the impartation (whether as between persons and persons, things and things or persons and things) or any matter otherwise than in the form of sounds or visual images; or
(d) signals serving for the actuation or control of machinery or apparatus.

The 1969 Act was innovative in attempting to define what was meant by the running of a telecommunication system. This definition was introduced in 1969 but remained in section 4(1) of the Telecommunications Act 1984. The concept of running a telecommunication system remained the foundation of the regulatory system until the introduction of the Communications Act 2003.

The next logical step was for the government to take over the licensing function. However, the government did not do this. Instead it appeared to have regarded licensing not as a regulatory issue, but an aspect of the exclusive privilege. It surrendered all licensing powers to the new Post Office which, although essentially a commercial organization, was given powers to license and run other telecommunication systems.

The labour-intensive, low-tech, and traditional postal business had little in common with the high-tech, capital-intensive, and dynamically expanding telecoms business. The common ground was a shared history, common pool of employees, and vested interests in protecting its position.

In 1977, the Carter Committee, commissioned by the government, recommended a further separation of the postal and telecommunications services of the Post Office and their relocation under two individual corporations. The findings in the report led to

---

[18] The idea of converting the Post Office into a nationalized industry had first been raised as early as 1932. A committee under the chairmanship of Lord Bridgeman had been set up to investigate the issue.

the renaming of the Post Office Telecommunications as British Telecom (BT[19]) in 1980 and to the introduction of the British Telecommunications Act 1981.

4.1.7 Radio and mobile communications

The early part of the twentieth century saw the introduction of radio. This was an important technological advance which significantly expanded the scope of telecommunications activities. Initially, however it had a minimal regulatory impact.

Legally in the UK radio is referred to as 'wireless telegraphy'. To the GPO radio was just another form of telegraphy. It therefore fell inside the GPO monopoly, and, apart from specialized regulatory requirements, for example to deal with frequency allocation, the GPO treated radio like any other form of telecommunications.

The legislation regulating radio was consolidated into the Wireless Telegraphy Act 1949.[20] This Act conferred licensing powers on the GPO which then licensed the use of radio for entertainment and allocated frequencies for national purposes, for example the police and the armed forces. The GPO retained for itself a monopoly over the uses of radio frequencies for third-party communications.

The special characteristic of radio is that it makes mobility possible: with radio, telecommunication users can move around. Various transport operators, in particular the large nationalized industries and also smaller firms like taxi operators, were licensed to run radio links. Some of these developed into 'closed user groups' where one operator handled communications on behalf of several different people and took messages on their behalf. Paging was also authorized. All the licensed operators were on a small scale and the GPO ran the main national radio and telephone networks.

Some of these radio licences permitted connections into the public switched telephone network, but these were normally indirect connections through human operators to private 'call handling' services. By 1979, the GPO woke up to the fact that these small operators were threatening its own operations and started to develop its own telephone systems. The GPO systems began to enjoy the economies of scale by using facilities installed for 'telegraphs' and as a result the competition struggled.

4.2 DEVELOPMENT OF THE INDUSTRY

This brings us to the last two decades of the twentieth century. During this period the UK telecommunications market experienced a period of unprecedented growth. Since the 1980s the telecommunications industry has changed almost beyond

---

[19]   We refer to BT throughout this chapter although British Telecom only started trading as BT in 1991.
[20]   The Wireless Telegraphy Act 1949 and subsequent amendments were repealed and replaced by the Wireless Telegraphy Act 2006.

recognition. In particular, since the 1990s the pace of technological change has led to huge changes with the growth in the use of high capacity broadband networks, in particular, over the Internet. We are all used to having an ever expanding range of media available on many different platforms from a wide choice of providers.

Highlighted below are some of the main developments throughout this period.

4.2.1 Developments in the fixed market

4.2.1.1 *The duopoly period (1984–1991)*

In 1979, a Conservative government led by Margaret Thatcher came to power with a commitment to reduce waste and bureaucracy. Nationalized industries were seen as prime examples of inefficiency. It was within this political climate that the British Telecommunications Act 1981 came into force. The 1981 Act allowed the licence of the second fixed network and in July 1981 an application to provide a business transmission system was made by Cable & Wireless,[21] Barclays Bank, and British Petroleum. This new venture was called Mercury Communications Limited and it was licensed in February 1982.

Mercury was intended to be a complete direct fixed network competitor to BT. The government did recognize that the creation of a new network required a very large investment and there would be a long period before the investment would yield a return. It felt that Mercury needed time to install and consolidate its national network; it also felt that BT needed time to adjust to competition. The government therefore gave an assurance that for the foreseeable future it would not licence any additional national public telecommunication network.

It hoped that Mercury would become sufficiently strong to provide competition to BT at all levels. Mercury's first competitive telecommunications services were provided in 1983. The strategy of Mercury quickly appeared to be to connect directly only a limited number of large business users and to attract smaller users to its network for long distance and international calls. It showed little motivation to invest in a national network. By 1991 Mercury had secured only three per cent of the market.

4.2.1.2 *The early 1990s and beyond*

This situation changed dramatically over the next decade with the duopoly review and the decision to issue licences to other operators. As from the early 1990s a number of new national public telecommunications operators (PTOs) were licensed. From the end of the duopoly period to the end of September 2000, the government received 823 applications for licences to run new telecommunications systems. It had granted 632 licences and 102 were under consideration.[22] There were 140 PTOs providing domestic and international services.

---

[21] The government sold all of its shares in Cable and Wireless in three stages starting in October 1981.

[22] Communications Liberalisation in the UK, March 2001, Department of Trade and Industry.

A number of ISPs, in addition to BT, had also entered the market and were providing internet access including AOL and Freeserve.[23]

4.2.1.3 *The cable networks*

Nationwide roll out of the cable network first began in the early 1980s with the licensing of cable TV networks. The country was divided into geographical franchises and licences were awarded on the basis of tenders. Initially, the operators of these licences were not allowed to provide telecommunications services such as voice telephony; this changed with the duopoly review.

Progressive consolidation between individual franchisees (which were licensed by the Cable Authority and then the Independent Television Commission) culminated in the market being served by two major operators, ntl and Telewest.[24] These two operators merged in March 2006. Shortly after this, in July 2006, the merged entity ntl:Telewest announced its acquisition of Virgin Mobile and its relaunch as Virgin Media.

4.2.2 The development of mobile[25]

The development of cellular technology opened the way to the expansion of mobile telephony in the 1980s. The first national cellular radio network licences were granted to Cellnet[26] (jointly owned by BT and Securicor) and Racal Vodafone[27] (now Vodafone) in May 1983, although they did not launch their analogue services until 1985, creating another duopoly.

There were initially restrictions on the retailing of mobile airtime by the mobile operators directly to the public. This led to a growth in the importance of High Street retailers, including Dixons, Currys, and the Carphone Warehouse. These dealers were primarily sellers of mobile hardware and did not themselves offer airtime contracts to their customers. However, because of the expectations of customers buying a mobile phone to complete all the necessary contractual arrangements at the same time, it became the dealer who 'arranged' the airtime contract. Mobile operators became increasingly reliant on the High Street chains to market their services.

In 1993, two further licences were granted to Orange and Mercury One-2-One,[28] allowing these companies to operate 2nd Generation (2G) or GSM (global system

---

[23] Now Orange Home.

[24] A small number of franchises remained independent, including Wight Cable covering the Isle of Wight and Small World in Scotland.

[25] In addition to the mobile network operators, a number of established retail brands, such as Tesco, have entered the market as MVNOs (mobile virtual network operators).

[26] Securicor sold its stake in Cellnet to BT in 1999. BT Cellnet was demerged from BT and floated in 2001 when it changed its name to mmO2. mmO2's UK brand is O2.

[27] Vodafone began as a division of Racal Electronics plc in the early 1980s. 20% of its shares were floated in 1988. The remaining shares were issued in 1991.

[28] Now T-Mobile.

for mobile communications) networks.[29] To allow the mobile operators to compete on an equal basis Vodafone and Cellnet were granted reissued licences which were modified in order that they could provide their services via 2G networks.[30]

In 2000, the government held an auction for licences to operate 3rd Generation (3G) spectrum. 3G networks are aimed at supporting higher speed call services and higher speed mobile data services. The auction process resulted in five 3G licences being granted in 2000, with one to a new entrant TIW UMTS (UK) Ltd (now operating as 3). The process raised over £22 billion. Those who bid successfully were required to provide a 3G network that would cover at least 80 per cent of the UK population by 2007.[31]

The significance of mobile continues to grow. In 1997 in the UK only 14 per cent of the population had a mobile phone, by 2007 there were more mobiles than people.[32]

4.2.3 The broadband market

One of the key issues for the early part of the twenty-first century is broadband. Broadband is seen as key driver of economic growth and competitiveness. The government's expressed aim is to create the most extensive (or widely available) and competitive broadband market within the G7 States.

Broadband is the technology that allows permanent or 'always on' access to electronic communications services, particularly the Internet, at much faster speeds than were available with traditional dial-up narrowband connections. The services offered by the telecommunications industry have changed dramatically over the last few years and this is in large part due to the introduction of broadband access.

Whilst broadband is a term that is much used, there has been some disagreement over what it actually means. Oftel initially defined it by reference to speed, but Ofcom now seem to have abandoned attempts to specify speeds and it is now defined as having three distinguishing features:

- the service is always on, i.e. no dial up is required. This enables the users to have a permanent connection to the network and allows real time delivery of services such as TV;

- it is possible to use both voice and data services simultaneously;

- it has faster downstream speed than a dial up connection.[33]

---

[29] T-Mobile and Orange launched DCS 1800 networks in September 1993 and May 1994 respectively.

[30] Vodafone and Cellnet launched GSM 900 networks in December 1991 and July 1994 respectively.

[31] All five mobile operators have demonstrated that they are in compliance with this condition. Ofcom had threatened to shorten O2's licence by four months if it did not comply. See <http://www.ofcom.org.uk/media/news/2008/05/nr_20080502a>.

[32] Source: BERR next generation broadband review.

[33] See Ofcom Review of Wholesale Access Markets, November 2007.

Broadband can be accessed by a variety of means, such as DSL,[34] cable modems, satellite, broadband wireless, 3G mobile, and digital TV. However, most of these technologies have disadvantages, for example, expense and limitations in geographical coverage which historically have prevented them from being serious rivals to the fixed telephony network. In practice, therefore, the mass market for broadband has been confined to ADSL[35] via BT's telephony infrastructure and to cable.[36]

Initially, take up of broadband in the UK was an area of concern, although there are now signs that this is improving. BT's market share in this area is also slowly eroding. A number of key players such as AOL, Orange Home, and Tiscali have entered the market using BT's wholesale products.

4.3 DEVELOPMENT OF REGULATION IN THE LATE TWENTIETH CENTURY

4.3.1 The start of competition—the British Telecommunications Act 1981

The government started the liberalization of the telecommunications sector in 1980 in a rather cautious manner. One of the first steps was to relax the Post Office monopoly over value added services and terminal equipment.[37] This gave customers choice over the apparatus which they could connect to the network. This ranged from simple telephones to more sophisticated equipment such as private branch exchanges. The British Approvals Board for Telecommunications (BABT) was established to provide independent evaluation and approval of such privately provided equipment and the British Standards Institute (BSI) was given a new role in respect of setting independent standards. The Post Office was required to allow connection to its network of any equipment approved by BABT after testing and approval against defined standards.

The 1981 Act separated the Post Office's functions of telecommunications and postal carrier and BT was created.[38] The government became the licensing authority for telecommunications operators.

---

[34] DSL allows broadband to be delivered via the telephony network once the local exchanges have been suitably enabled.

[35] ADSL is Asymmetric DSL meaning that download speeds are quicker than upload speeds.

[36] The cable operator Virgin Media is not deemed to be nationally dominant and so the regulator cannot force them to open up their network to other service providers in the same way that BT has had to.

[37] Terminal equipment or apparatus liberalization is concerned only with customer premises apparatus. For regulatory purposes the boundary has been drawn at the socket, or test jack frame, where a connection can be made between the chain of apparatus on a customer's premises and the chain of apparatus back to the telephone exchange and beyond the telephone networks. Apparatus liberalization is concerned with the customer side of this boundary.

[38] The formal separation occurred on 1 October 1981, known as Vesting Day.

The British Telecommunications Act 1981 also authorized the licensing of customer premises, or branch systems.[39] Unfortunately the Act did not include a power to limit BT's exclusive privilege, the Post Office having previously run all systems on customer premises under its exclusive privilege. As a result, the 1981 Act powers were never exercised.

As mentioned above, Mercury was granted a licence as the first competitor to BT. This licence gave Mercury the right to provide every form of digital telecommunications service, including leased circuits, switched services to business and domestic premises, and the full range of international services. Mercury was not, however, allowed to lease elements of BT's infrastructure (except for interconnection for call termination). This was in line with the government's policy to encourage infrastructure-based competition. In its 1983 Duopoly Statement[40] the government made it clear that it did not intend to license operators other than BT or Mercury to provide the basic telecommunications service of converting messages over fixed links, whether cable, radio, or satellite, both domestically and internationally for seven years. In return for its protection, Mercury undertook some mild obligations to expand its network.

It soon became clear that the 1981 Act was not a suitable vehicle to promote competition. It had no provision for the licensing of telecommunication services. It allowed BT to retain its exclusive privilege. The Act did not give Mercury powers to dig up the streets or to erect telegraph poles. It included licensing provisions which were seriously flawed, for example BT was to be consulted about all licences and could find out about competitors' plans. It had no provisions to force BT to connect Mercury's network and BT refused to agree to do this, proposing that Mercury should build an overlay network with every customer having two phone points and phone lines, one BT and one Mercury. Overall the issues had not been thought through from the perspective of a competitor.

4.3.2 The duopoly period (1984–1991)

4.3.2.1 *Privatization*

On 19 July 1982, the government made a formal announcement that it intended to privatize BT. BT needed to modernize the public telecommunications network and required finance to do this. Huge sums of money were required and this conflicted with government policy which required that a nationalized industry should not borrow from the government and should where possible pay money to the government.

---

[39] An example of a branch system is a Private Automatic Branch Exchange (PABX) which is a private switch or exchange often found within an organization. The PABX will perform the switching of local calls, usually automatically, within the organization as well as setting up external connections with the local operator or carrier.

[40] Government Statement of 17 November 1983 by Kenneth Baker MP, Minister for Information Technology to the Standing Committee on the Telecommunications Bill.

The calling of a general election in 1983 caused a slight delay to the process. In its manifesto for the 1983 election, the Conservative Party provided a list of enterprises which it intended to return to private ownership, including BT. The Conservatives won the 1983 election with an increased majority, and a bill to privatize BT was introduced.

4.3.2.2 The Telecommunications Act 1984
4.3.2.2.1 Main objectives

The Telecommunications Act 1984 gained Royal Assent on 12 April 1984.[41] The main focus was to transfer BT into private ownership. This sale by the government of 50.2 per cent of its shares was revolutionary in its scale. The concept of privatization had become an election issue and so it was crucial for the government that the sale of its shares in BT was a success and it embarked on a huge marketing campaign. In this respect the policy was successful with full share subscription.[42] The government made clear at this time that it would dispose of the remainder of its shareholding in BT when the circumstances of the company and market conditions permitted.[43]

The main provisions of the 1984 Act included:

- establishing the Director General of Telecommunications (DGT) as the independent regulatory authority. The DGT was head of and supported by Oftel;
- establishing regulatory arrangements based on the concept carried forward from the Post Office Act 1969 and the British Telecommunications Act 1981 of licensing operators to run telecommunications systems;
- abolishing the exclusive right of BT to provide services. This meant that BT finally lost its monopoly in running telecommunication systems. It now needed a licence in the same way as any other telecommunications operator.

The 1984 Act also had the aims of:

- bringing about a complete liberalization of customer apparatus to crack BT's dominance and to remove BT's control over the connection, running, and maintenance of

---

[41] In November 1984, Mercury was issued a licence under the Telecommunications Act 1984. The transfer to British Telecommunications plc of the business of BT took place on 6 August 1984.

[42] The November 1984 share offer was oversubscribed by 3.2 times with shares being issued to applicants on a pro rata basis.

[43] A second share issue took place on 21 November 1991 when 1,598 million shares were sold, reducing the government's stake to 21.8%. A further issue followed in July 1993 with the government selling off virtually all of its remaining shares. In July 1997 the government relinquished its so-called golden share which allowed it to block a takeover of the company and to appoint two non-executive directors to the Board.

customer premises apparatus, in short to repair the defects in these respects of the 1981 Act;

- giving Mercury a better licence than was possible under the 1981 Act;

- improving the licences for cellular and local cable networks where the 1981 licensing regime had proved inadequate in detailed respects;

- empowering Mercury and cable operators to dig up streets, etc. which meant modernizing and extending code powers to other entities;

- authorizing private branch systems and removing them from BT's control;

- controlling BT's charges[44] to prevent monopoly profits; and

- introducing controls on anti-competitive practices by BT including in particular the ending of BT's ability to prevent interconnect.

4.3.2.2.2 Code powers
The 1981 Act had not granted the rights that operators required to construct infrastructure and therefore prevented effective competition in this respect. The Telecommunications Code (generally referred to as 'Code Powers') contained in the Telecommunications Act 1984, s 10 and Sch 2, allowed operators to install apparatus under or over the street, dig up the street, and open sewers,[45] among other works. Where apparatus was constructed to the height of three metres or more a landowner could object to the installation where it affected their enjoyment of the land. This matter could be dealt with in a number of ways: compensation could be paid to the landowner, the apparatus could be required to be modified, or a court could declare that the landowner's agreement be dispensed with. It was imperative for cable companies, as well as PTOs, to be granted code powers so that they could operate and compete in the marketplace.

4.3.2.2.3 The Director General of Telecommunications
As mentioned above, the 1984 Act also introduced an independent regulator known as the DGT. The DGT was appointed by the Secretary of State for Trade and Industry and was an unelected, independent position. He was appointed for a fixed but renewable term of office and could be removed from office only as provided for in his contract. The DGT was head of a non-ministerial government department, known

---

[44] Safeguards on BT's prices were imposed. The Littlechild Report proposed price cap regulation. Prices for call charges were capped at inflation (calculated by the previous year's revenue shares from a basket of various products) minus some X% for a period of 5 years. From 1984 to 1989, BT's retail prices were regulated at RPI – 3% and at RPI – 4.5 % until 1991. An important exception was line rentals, which had previously been cross-subsidized through call charges, which BT was required not to increase by more than RPI + 2% in any year.

[45] Sch 2 para 9. Sch 2 of the 1984 Act has been incorporated into the Communications Act 2003, under s 106, and renamed the 'electronic communications code'. See further Chapter 7, at 7.3.3.4.

as Oftel. Oftel was subject to treasury control so far as expenditure was concerned and accountable to Parliament like any other government department.

4.3.2.2.4 Duties under the 1984 Act

The 1984 Act split regulatory competence between the Secretary of State and the DGT. It imposed primary duties on the Secretary of State and the DGT to exercise their functions with a view to ensuring:

- that so far as reasonably practicable, there are provided throughout the UK such telecommunication services as satisfy all reasonable demands for them, including, in particular, emergency services, public call box services, directory information services, maritime services, and services in rural areas; and
- that the persons responsible for providing telecommunications services are able to finance the provision of those services.[46]

Subject to these overriding duties, the Secretary of State and the DGT were required to exercise their functions in the manner they considered best calculated:

- to promote the interest of consumers, purchasers, and others users in respect of the prices charged for, and the quality and variety of, telecommunication services provided and telecommunications apparatus supplied;
- to maintain and promote effective competition between persons engaged in commercial activities connected with telecommunications in the UK;
- to promote efficiency and economy on the part of such persons; and
- to promote research into and the development and use of new techniques by such persons.[47]

There were also other duties designed to encourage investment, promote international transit services, and enable providers of telecommunication services and producers of telecommunication apparatus to compete overseas.[48]

In addition to these functions the DGT also had a duty to consider complaints under section 49 and had the power to make monopoly and competition references to the Monopolies and Mergers Commission (MMC).[49]

4.3.2.2.5 Power to issue, enforce, and change licences

The Secretary of State was responsible for issuing licences.[50] In practical terms this meant the licensing process was handled by an executive agency of the Department of Trade and Industry[51] the Radiocommunications Agency.

---

[46] Telecommunications Act 1984, s 3(1).
[47] Ibid, s 3(2).
[48] Ibid, s 3(2).
[49] Renamed the Competition Commission under the Competition Act 1998.
[50] Telecommunications Act 1984, s 7.
[51] Now BERR.

The DGT was responsible for enforcement of the licences. The DGT was also obliged to enforce the observance of conditions included in licences granted to telecommunications operators. This could be done by the making of orders under sections 16 to 18 of the 1984 Act. Where the DGT was satisfied that a licence holder was contravening or had contravened and was likely to contravene again the conditions of their licence, he was obliged to make such provision as was requisite to secure compliance with the condition. The DGT was required to follow a number of procedural steps. In practice, in the early days, these sections were rarely used as the threat of enforcement seemed to have the desired affect. There were more orders made in the 1990s. Any person who suffered a loss or damage as a result of a breach of a final or confirmed provisional order could bring an action for damages against the licensee.[52] Failure to comply with a final order could also result in the revocation of a licence.[53]

The DGT also had the power to modify the conditions included in a telecommunication licence. The 1984 Act set out two mechanisms for implementing changes, neither of which was particularly efficient. The first was through a voluntary agreement of licensees under section 12. This meant that in the case of a class licence, all licensees had to agree to a proposed modification.[54] The second mechanism was through a compulsory modification against the wishes of the licensee under section 15 following an MMC investigation. Modifications by this means would generally take a minimum of six months. The difficulties in pursuing licence modifications under both of these mechanisms led to a revision of section 12.[55]

Another important function was to give directions and determinations in relation to matters reserved for the DGT's decision under licences granted to telecommunication operators. This power, derived under sections 7(5) and (6) of the 1984 Act, was used extensively in relation to interconnect.[56]

4.3.2.2.6 Challenges to decisions of the Director General of Telecommunications

These various duties referred to above governed the way that the DGT was required to exercise his functions. The DGT, in common with other regulators, was given a large amount of discretion in making decisions and had a high level of autonomy, although his decisions were open to judicial review.[57] If leave for judicial review was granted, the High Court would review the decision. The court could not, however, review the merits of the decision itself. In practice it was very difficult to challenge any decision where the DGT could argue that he had exercised a judgment under section 3 'in a

---

[52] Section 18(5).
[53] Section 18 (6).
[54] The cumbersome nature of this process meant that in practice class licences were rarely if ever modified. Instead they tended to be revoked and reissued in a modified form by the Secretary of State.
[55] Electronic Communications Act 2000, ss 11–12.
[56] See further Chapter 2, at 2.1.
[57] The main grounds for judicial review to be granted are quite narrow and are limited to grounds such as that the decision maker acted outside the scope of their powers, acted unreasonably, did not follow procedures that they were obliged to follow, or made an error of fact or law.

manner which he considers is best calculated' to undertake his duties. There were some challenges to his decisions but the courts generally allowed the DGT wide discretion, thus successful claims against him were rare. *R v Director General of Telecommunications, ex p Cellcom Ltd and others* [1999] ECC 314 is a prime example of an unsuccessful attempt by Cellcom to seek judicial review of the DGT's decision to modify licence terms. There was a general feeling that the courts in any event would be unwilling to interfere with the decision of a sector-specific regulator.[58]

The 1984 Act continued in force for almost 20 years until it was replaced by the Communications Act 2003. Significant changes did occur in the intervening period, primarily reflecting evolving European Union law.[59] Successive governments chose to transpose the various EU Directives into UK law through statutory instruments made under the European Communities Act 1972, section 2(2), rather than through amendments to the 1984 Act. This secondary regulation imposed a broad range of new functions and duties upon the Secretary of State and DGT in areas such as interconnection, licensing, and voice telephony.[60]

4.3.3 The end of the duopoly period

The results from direct competition were disappointing. The underlying rationale for the duopoly policy was the belief that if there were a number of new entrants to the market they would compete against each other and not the incumbent, whereas it was hoped that a single competitor to the incumbent would build up market share more rapidly. However, Mercury did not manage to introduce a significant degree of competition into the market and in late 1990 the government's commitment not to licence any other operators expired.

The duopoly policy has been criticized by industry observers on the grounds that it effectively delayed the introduction of effective competition.[61] At the time that the policy was introduced in the UK there were no precedents to guide the government and indeed at that time only the USA had managed to introduce competition into its telecommunications sector.[62]

4.3.4 The duopoly review

The first major policy change since the introduction of the Telecommunications Act 1984 was the duopoly review. The government issued a Green Paper in November

---

[58] Graham, G, *Regulating Public Utilities; A Constitutional Approach* (Hart, Oxford, 2000).

[59] See further Chapter 5.

[60] E.g. Telecommunications (Voice Telephony) Regulations 1997, SI 1997/1886; Telecommunications (Licensing) Regulations 1997, SI 1997/2930; and Telecommunications (Interconnection) Regulations 1997, SI 1997/2931.

[61] See OECD Reviews of Regulatory Reform, Regulatory Reform in the UK.

[62] OECD report referred to above.

1990[63] leading up to the White Paper 'Competition and Choice; Telecommunications Policy for the 1990s',[64] published in March 1991. The main conclusions of the White Paper were:

- to end the duopoly policy. This meant that anyone who could show a need for a licence and who had the necessary financial resources could become a public telecommunications operator;

- to introduce equal access as soon as possible;

- to strengthen the arrangements for interconnection in operators' licences including provisions to extend the DGT's power of direction to cover all aspects of interconnection agreements and to enable the DGT to apportion the direct costs of interconnection fairly between operators;

- to allow simple resale. Fixed operators would be required to permit people other than themselves to retail telecommunications services;

- to license international simple resale services on routes to countries whose regulatory regimes were liberalized;[65]

- to allow cable operators to provide voice telephony services;

- that Oftel should control numbering and oversee an integrated numbering plan and have the power to introduce number portability, provided it was technically feasible and justified on cost benefit analysis; and

- to introduce changes in the price control formula.[66]

The restrictions which prevented BT conveying cable programme services under its main licence continued. The government felt that even the prospect of BT entering the market might deter cable companies from investing. As referred to above the country was divided into geographical areas for the purpose of cable licences. BT was free to apply for licences in these individual areas and was authorized, as it always had been, to convey video on demand.

In 1993, a new DGT was appointed, Don Cruickshank. He introduced a much more consultative, open, and transparent regime of regulation. Almost immediately he published a consultative document on interconnection and accounting separation,[67] setting out proposals on how BT's businesses should be divided for regulatory accounting purposes.

---

[63] Cm 1303.
[64] Cm 1461.
[65] In 1996 the government licensed an initial batch of 44 companies to provide international telecommunications services on any route they chose over their own facilities. At the same time the restrictions which limited international simple resale to certain routes were removed.
[66] See further Chapter 3.
[67] Accounting separation was introduced in March 1994.

Oftel published a policy statement in July 1995 (Effective Competition: Framework for Action) which considered the path regulation should take towards the goal of a competitive market place, recommending *inter alia* that:

- the RPI 2 per cent constraint on line rental price increases would be lifted encouraging BT to introduce a more flexible range of service and tariff offerings to meet the needs of different groups of customers;

- Oftel would improve its handling of investigations into complaints of anti-competitive behaviour; and

- new arrangements for universal service provision and funding would be introduced.

Since then extensive use of consultation has been used to deal with such matters.

4.3.5 A change in regulatory policy

The end of the 1990s and the early twenty-first century saw the regulatory balance shift away from promoting infrastructure competition. The goal of promoting infrastructure competition became complicated by three major events.[68] These were:

- EU law encouraged national regulators not to discriminate between providers that were building networks and those that were not;

- the collapse of investor confidence in the telecoms market which led to alternative network providers increasingly demanding access to BT's infrastructure to enable them to offer retail products to end-users; and

- the growth of the Internet. BT was the only operator able to provide an end-to-end service across the UK. This led to a new demand for wholesale products from BT.

4.3.6 Convergence

In July 1998, the DTI published a Green Paper: Regulating communications: approaching convergence in the Information Age.[69] The Green Paper recognized that digital technologies were already changing the way that services were delivered, blurring the boundaries between types of service operation and means of delivery,

---

[68] Ofcom, Strategic Review of Telecommunications, Phase 1 consultation document, Research Annexes, Annex G, Review of Regulatory Policy in the Telecoms Sector.

[69] CM 4022. Also see the Culture, Media and Sport Select Committee: The Multi-Media Revolution (Session 1997–98) (Fourth Report) which first raised the issue of convergence to which the Green Paper was the government's response. Also the Green Paper was a response to the EC's own *Green Paper on Convergence of the Telecommunications, Media and Information Technology Sectors, and the implications for regulation towards an information society approach* (EC COM (97) 623, 3 December 1997).

and eroding the technological distinctions. The main issues arising from convergence identified by the Green Paper were:

- overlap between regulators, particularly where broadcast services are carried over telecommunications networks;

- the direct impact of competition decisions by one regulator on the responsibilities of another as interdependencies across markets increased;

- basing regulatory systems on means of transmission would become increasingly difficult to justify; and

- control of newly emerging gateways (e.g. set-top boxes, integrated digital TV sets, electronic programme guides (EPGs)) were likely to be important to prevent them becoming a barrier to market entry.[70]

Broadcasting, both content and delivery, had been regulated by the Independent Television Commission (ITC)[71] and the BBC. Spectrum was regulated by the Radiocommunications Agency. Bodies like the Broadcasting Standards Commission (BSC)[72] and the Radio Authority[73] were also part of the regulatory landscape, as well as Oftel.

The Green Paper raised a number of questions and, following a consultation period, the government published *Regulating Communications: The Way Ahead* in 1999 setting out the results of the consultation. The report suggested a number of options, including the possibility of creating a radically new regulatory structure to avoid barriers to competitiveness. The government decided to take the evolutionary approach and let the existing structures stay for the present but required them to work closer together.

However, following EU moves for reform, which eventually resulted in the Framework Directive (2002/21/EC) and an appreciation that convergence was gathering pace, the government introduced a White Paper, *A New Future for*

---

[70] See further Chapter 6.

[71] The Independent Television Commission (ITC) was the statutory body which licensed and regulated independent television services in the UK, including cable and satellite. Operating under powers derived from the Broadcasting Acts 1990 and 1996, their responsibilities included setting and maintaining the standards for programmes, economic regulation, public service obligations, research, TV advertising regulation, and technical quality.

[72] The Broadcasting Standards Commission, a non-departmental public body which had statutory responsibilities for standards and fairness in broadcasting. It had three main tasks, established by the Broadcasting Act 1996. These were to produce codes of conduct relating to standards and fairness; to consider and adjudicate on complaints; and to monitor, research, and report on standards and fairness in broadcasting.

[73] The Radio Authority was the statutory body responsible for regulation and licensing of independent radio broadcasting in the UK, that is to say all non-BBC radio services. Operating under powers derived from the Broadcasting Acts 1990 and 1996, their responsibilities included frequency planning, the awarding of licences, the regulation of programming and radio advertising, and the supervision of the radio ownership system.

Communications[74] (the Communications White Paper) to create a new regulatory structure. The proposal was that a new regulator, Ofcom[75] would be created.

4.3.7 The Communications Act 2003

4.3.7.1 *Main provisions*

The Communications Act 2003[76] gave effect to the government's proposals for the reform of the regulatory framework for the communications sector as set out in the Communications White Paper and also covers four of the Directives contained in the EU's new regime:[77]

- Directive 2002/21/EC on a common regulatory framework for electronic communications networks and services (OJ L 108/33, 24 April 2002), the 'Framework Directive';

- Directive 2002/20/EC on the authorization of electronic communications networks and services (OJ L 108/21, 24 April 2002), the 'Authorisation Directive';[78]

- Directive 2002/19/EC on access to, and interconnection of, electronic communications networks and associated facilities (OJ L 108/7, 24 April 2002), the 'Access and Interconnection Directive';[79] and

- Directive 2002/22/EC on universal service and users' rights relating to electronic communications networks and services (OJ L 108/7, 24 April 2002), the 'Universal Services Directive'.

Ofcom took over the regulatory functions of the DGT. It is responsible for the regulation of electronic communication networks and services and for the licensing of broadcasting services. The aim was to reduce the regulatory burden upon communications providers by using general authorizations rather than individual licences wherever possible. Under the new regime, communications providers must comply with general conditions and (as relevant) specific conditions of entitlement. General conditions, as set out in the 'Notification under section 48(1) of the Act' published by Ofcom,[80] apply to all communication providers, whilst specific conditions apply only to certain communications providers in certain situations.

---

[74] Cm 5010 published on 12 December 2000.

[75] This resulted in the Office of Communications Act 2002.

[76] The Office of Communications Act 2002 enabled the government to formally establish Ofcom before the Communications Act came into force. The existing regulators were placed under a duty to assist Ofcom to prepare.

[77] See further Chapter 5.

[78] See further Chapter 5.

[79] See further Chapter 6.

[80] A consolidated version of the general conditions as at 15 August 2007 is available at <http://www.ofcom.org.uk/telecoms/ioi/g_a_regime/gce/cvogc150807.pdf>.

Communications providers are responsible for ascertaining which of the general conditions apply to them and their operations. The obligations themselves are similar to those formerly contained in individual and class licences. The whole area of licensing is discussed in more detail in Chapter 7.

4.3.7.2 *Functions*

Ofcom replaced the DGT, Oftel, the ITC, the BSC, and the Radio Authority. Ofcom also took over responsibility for the allocation, management, and supervision of the UK radio spectrum from the Radiocommunications Agency.[81]

Ofcom consists of a chairman, chief executive, and various other members not totalling more than six.[82] It acts as a board and not, like the DGT, as a single individual.

Ofcom's principal duties when carrying out its functions are:

• to further the interests of citizens in relation to communications matters; and

• to further consumer interests in relevant markets, where appropriate by promoting competition.[83]

In addition, the Communications Act sets out a list of objectives which Ofcom is required to secure, including:

• the optimal use of the radio spectrum;

• the availability throughout the UK of a wide range of electronic communications services;

• the availability in the UK of a wide range of TV and radio services, comprising high-quality services of broad appeal; and

• the maintenance of a sufficient plurality of providers of different television and radio services.[84]

Ofcom has a duty to act in accordance with the six Community requirements set out in the Framework Directive.[85] These are:

• to promote competition;

• to ensure that Ofcom's activities contribute to the development of the European internal market;

• to promote the interests of all persons who are citizens of the European Union;

---

[81] In addition, Phonepay Plus (formerly the Independent Committee for the Supervision of Standards of Telephone Information Services which was generally known as ICSTIS), an independent industry-funded body, regulates premium rate telephone calls. See Chapter 14.

[82] The Office of Communications Act 2002, s 1.

[83] Section 3 (1).

[84] Section 3(2).

[85] Section 4.

- to take account of the desirability of carrying our their functions in a manner which, so far as practicable, does not favour one form of network, service, or associated facility, or one means of providing or making available such a network, service, or facility over another;
- to encourage the provision of network access[86] and service interoperability; and
- to encourage compliance with international standards to the extent necessary to facilitate service interoperability,[87] and to secure a freedom of choice for customers.

Details of the Communications Act are discussed elsewhere in this book, but Ofcom has been given improved duties to make its processes more transparent and efficient and to encourage deregulation as the sector becomes more and more competitive.

4.3.7.3 *Dispute resolution*
Ofcom has specific duties as regards the resolution of disputes.[88] A dispute is the failure of commercial negotiation about a matter which falls within the scope of section 185 of the Communications Act.[89]

4.3.7.4 *Right of appeal*
Previously, the appeals process (including the body) which heard an appeal differed depending upon whether the decision being appealed was taken under the Competition Act 1998 or the 1984 Act. Appeals and reviews of decisions taken under the 1984 Act were to the normal courts whereas appeals of decisions taken under the Competition Act were to the Competition Appeal Tribunal (CAT).[90] The Communications Act made the CAT the appellate body for communications sector matters in general. Decisions by the OFT and/or Ofcom as to whether there has been an infringement of Chapter I and II prohibitions in the Competition Act (or Articles 81 and 82) are still appealable to the CAT. To this has been added decisions made by Ofcom under Part 2 of the Communications Act (Ofcom's sectoral powers) and most

---

[86] Section 151 defines 'network access' as meaning (1) interconnection of public electronic communications networks; or (2) any services, facilities, or arrangements (other than interconnection) by means of which a communications provider or a person making associated facilities available is able, for the purposes of the provision of an electronic communications service (whether by him or by another), to make use of any network or apparatus comprised in a network, or any service or facility capable of being used to provide a service.

[87] 'Service interoperability' is defined in s 151 as interoperability between different electronic communications services.

[88] Communications Act, s 185.

[89] Ofcom: Guidelines for the handling of competition complaints and complaints and disputes about breaches of conditions imposed under the EU Directives, July 2004.

[90] The CAT is a specialist judicial body with cross-disciplinary expertise in law, economics, business, and accountancy. The function of the CAT is to hear and decide appeals and other applications or claims involving competition or economic regulatory issues.

decisions under the Wireless Telegraphy Act 2006.[91] This includes decisions taken pursuant to the exercise of powers to set, modify, revoke, and enforce General and Specific Conditions, including access related conditions. Certain decisions are not appealable to the CAT, including, for example, the decision to designate an undertaking as a provider of a universal service and the making of regulations authorizing spectrum trading.[92]

A peculiar mechanism exists for price control matters (i.e. matters relating to the imposition of any form of price control on a significant market power (SMP) service). These must be referred by the CAT to the Competition Commission for determination. The CAT must follow the determination of the Competition Commission[93] unless it decides that, applying the judicial review principles, the determination of the Competition Commission would fall to be set aside.

An appeal to the CAT can be on the grounds that the decision was based on an error of fact, was wrong in law, or both, or against the exercise of discretion by Ofcom or the government or another person. Appeals from decisions of the CAT are on points of law only and are to the Court of Appeal. Such appeals are only allowed with the permission of the CAT or Court of Appeal.[94]

A widely held criticism of the previous appeals system was that the courts were less well equipped than a specialist regulatory body to understand complex technical and economic issues and consequently were often reluctant to overturn the decision of a industry-specific regulator. Under the old appeals system no decision taken by the DGT was ever successfully challenged in the UK courts. The CAT is proving to be a more effective appeals tribunal than the courts. The first case appealed to the CAT in the telecommunications sector (the *Freeserve*[95] case) resulted in part from the DGT's decision being struck down. Since then there have been numerous cases referred to the CAT.[96]

4.3.8 Ofcom's strategic review of the telecommunications industry

One of the first things Ofcom did when it took over from the DGT at the end of December 2003 was to announce a major strategic review of the telecommunications market. This was the first wide ranging analysis of the telecommunications sector for 13 years. Ofcom set out five fundamental questions:

• In relation to the interests of citizen-consumers, what are the key attributes of a well functioning telecoms market?

---

[91] Communications Act, s 192.
[92] Although it has not been considered as to how this complies with the Framework Directive.
[93] Communications Act, s 193.
[94] Ibid, s 196(4).
[95] [2003] CAT 5.
[96] For copies of judgments see <http://www.catribunal.org.uk/judgments/default.aspx>.

- Where can effective and sustainable competition be achieved in the UK telecoms market?
- Is there scope for a reduction in regulation or is the market power of the incumbents too entrenched?
- How can Ofcom incentivize timely and efficient investment in next generation networks?
- At varying times since 1984, the case has been made for the structural or operational separation of BT or the delivery of full functional equivalence. Are these still relevant questions?[97]

Some of the key issues from the results of Phase 1[98] of the review were:

- a frustration with the continued dominance of BT in the fixed line market. In terms of revenues, market capitalization, and investment, BT Group plc remained larger than most of its competitors put together;
- a recognition of the failure of past regulatory interventions to secure fair access at the wholesale level to BT's networks and services: 20 years of telecoms regulation had failed to overcome problems of enduring bottlenecks. There was little appetite for investment to compete with BT at the local access level;
- from the late 1990s, telecoms regulation had aimed to promote service-based and infrastructure-based competition but both proved slow to take root: infrastructure operators had failed to achieve scale; whereas service providers were frustrated by delays and inadequacies in wholesale access products;
- Ofcom concluded that regulation had failed to overcome the problems of enduring bottlenecks combined with lack of access to those parts of the network. It acknowledged that those who relied on BT to provide access have experienced 20 years of slow product development, inferior quality wholesale products, poor transactional processes, and a general lack of transparency; and
- an increasingly detailed regulation had been introduced by Oftel. This had created what Ofcom referred to as a 'regulatory mesh' which placed a series of obligations on BT both at the wholesale and the retail level. Ofcom referred to 'micro-management' of BT by its predecessor, Oftel.

Ofcom concluded that it should focus regulation to deliver equality of access beyond the levels of infrastructure where competition will be effective and sustainable.

---

[97] See <http://www.ofcom.org.uk/static/telecoms_review/index.htm> for the strategic review consultation documents and statements.

[98] The review did cover mobile but the results of Phase 1 showed that in terms of competitive market structures mobile was strong with five competitive operators and more virtual network operators. Ofcom felt that in all respects the mobile sector displayed the features of a competitive market.

Ofcom's preferred approach to deliver this was what they referred to as 'equality of access'. There were two elements to this:

- equivalence at the product level. This meant that in parts of the network where BT has SMP and which are enduring bottlenecks, BT must offer the same or similar wholesale products to wholesale customers as it offers to itself, at the same prices and using the same or similar transactional processes; and

- supporting organizational changes within BT. This would involve changes in BT's management structures, incentives, business processes, and information flows necessary to support equivalence at the product level.

Ofcom wanted a new regulatory contract with BT: not a real contract but a settlement with the industry to try to obtain real equality of access. It wanted the rules setting out such an approach to be legally enforceable. It found the means to achieve this under the Enterprise Act 2002. The Enterprise Act gives regulators, including Ofcom, the power to make a referral to the Competition Commission of markets where there are reasonable grounds for suspecting:

that any feature, or combination of features of a market in the UK for goods or services prevents, restricts or distorts competition in connection with the supply or acquisition of any goods or services in the UK . . .[99]

Any such investigation would be wide ranging and the Competition Commission would have the power to order structural separation of BT's wholesale network operations and its retail service provision. The majority of respondents to the review had expressed caution about the prolonged uncertainty and disruption to the industry of a reference to the Competition Commission. There were concerns that such an investigation would paralyse the industry for up to two years. However, the Enterprise Act also provides that instead of making a market investigation reference to the Competition Commission, a regulator may accept undertakings to take such action as it considers appropriate.[100] These undertakings must be for the purpose of remedying, mitigating, or preventing any adverse effect on the competition concerned.

4.3.8.1 *The BT undertakings*

On 21 June 2005 BT's board agreed in principle to offer to the Ofcom Board legally binding[101] undertakings which would commit BT to substantive changes in its organization and behaviour.[102] On 22 September 2005 Ofcom decided to accept with some modifications the BT undertakings in lieu of making a reference to the Competition Commission.[103]

---

[99] Enterprise Act 2002, s 131.
[100] Ibid, s 154.
[101] A breach of the undertakings is ultimately enforced through normal courts.
[102] Ofcom news release, 'A new regulatory approach for fixed telecommunications' dated 25 June 2005.
[103] If in practice the undertakings do not deliver the solution required Ofcom may still open an investigation with a view to making a Market Investigation Reference to the Competition Commission.

The incentives on BT to agree to the undertakings were not only to avoid an investigation which could have led to a potential break up, but also to achieve the reduction in regulation at the retail level offered by Ofcom. Ofcom set out its proposals and a timetable for a staged withdrawal of regulation. This started with the withdrawal of much of the existing regulation from fixed retail voice markets.[104]

In terms of BT's organization, the undertakings required BT to establish an operationally separate access service division, Openreach,[105] and to operate this division in accordance with the undertakings. The role of Openreach is to deliver certain access products on an open and even-handed basis to all external wholesale customers, including BT's own downstream divisions, that is BT Wholesale, BT Retail, and BT Global Services.

The undertakings provide that Openreach will not supply any product to any other part of BT unless it also offers that product to other communications providers on an Equivalence of Inputs basis.[106] Equivalence of Input (EOI) is defined in the undertakings as meaning:

that BT provides, in respect of a particular product or service, the same product or service to all Communications Providers (including BT) on the same timescales, terms and conditions (including price and service levels) by means of the same systems and processes, and includes the provision to all Communications Providers (including BT) of the same Commercial Information about such products, services, systems and processes. In particular, it includes the use by BT of such systems and processes in the same way as other Communications Providers and with the same degree of reliability and performance as experienced by other Communications Providers.[107]

Under the concept of EOI, BT's wholesale customers should be able to use exactly the same set of regulated products, at the same prices, and using the same systems and transactional processes as BT's own retail activities.

The Oftel approach had been to try to ensure that wholesale products specifically designed by BT under regulatory pressure were as close to being fit for purpose as possible. Differences in product and processes were tolerated as long as there was no material difference in overall outcome. There were, however, a number of problems with this approach, including the fact that BT had little incentive to produce products for its competitors which it had no interest in using itself.

In theory the advantage of the Ofcom approach is that it provides an immediate incentive on BT to remedy any deficiencies, as it is required to offer exactly the same products to its wholesale customers as to its own retail division.

The undertakings define a number of current products to which equivalence of input must be applied including wholesale line rental, shared and full metallic

---

[104] As from 31 July 2006, all retail price controls on line rental and call charges were removed: Retail Price Controls, explanatory statement, 19 July 2006.
[105] Section 5 of the Undertakings. The Undertakings are on the Ofcom website at <http://www.ofcom. org.uk/telecoms/btundertakings/btundertakings.pdf>.
[106] Undertakings, section 5.46. There are some exceptions to this section.
[107] Undertakings, section 2.

path facility, backhaul extension service, and IPStream.[108] As from June 2008 Openreach is required to compensate all communications providers (including BT's own retail divisions) where it fails to provide and repair services according to agreed services.[109]

Openreach is required to have a separate CEO who reports solely to the BT Group CEO but is not a member of the BT group operating committee.[110] Openreach's annual operating plan must be approved by the BT Board but within that plan Openreach has considerable autonomy. The undertakings set out detailed requirements for the operation of Openreach: it was required to rebrand its website, stationery, buildings, and vehicles and clothing of employees; employees of Openreach remain BT employees (Openreach is not a separate legal entity) but incentives for Openreach employees must solely reflect the performance of Openreach.

Most of the attention tends to focus on the creation of Openreach, however, the undertakings also subject BT Wholesale to a number of obligations. It was required to establish two separate internal divisions for the product management of SMP products not supplied by Openreach and non-SMP products of significance to competing providers (such as wholesale calls and IPStream). BT was also required to implement organizational separation between its downstream and upstream (other than Openreach) divisions. In particular, to maintain a strong organizational separation of people, commercial information, and sales functions.

4.3.8.2 *Equality of Access Board*

Both Openreach and BT Wholesale are subject to monitoring by the Equality of Access Board (the EAB).[111] The EAB consists of five people: three independent members, one BT senior manager, and one BT group non-executive director.[112]

The EAB is supported by the Equality of Access office. The role of the EAB is one of monitoring, reporting, and advising BT on compliance with the undertakings. The EAB is obliged to report any breaches of the undertakings to Ofcom. The EAB is also required to report regularly to the BT board on BT's compliance with the undertakings and can escalate matters of concern directly to the BT board. There were calls from some in the industry for the EAB to be wholly independent of BT or include an industry member. Ofcom felt that it was important that the EAB was internal to BT. It felt that this way it would be able to effectively monitor and it would have a free rein to look at issues which are highly confidential to BT. If it were external it was felt that there would be a risk that it would be able to do nothing more than Ofcom.

---

[108] Section 3.1 of the Undertakings.

[109] See Ofcom Statement and Directions, Service level guarantees: incentivising performance, 20 March 2008.

[110] Sections 5.25 and 5.26 of the Undertakings.

[111] Undertakings, section 10. See <http://www.btplc.com/Thegroup/Theboard/Boardcommittees/EqualityofAccessBoard/EqualityofAccessBoard.htm>.

[112] The initial membership of the board includes Sir Bryan Carsberg a former DGT.

It is probably still too early to come to any firm conclusion about the success or otherwise of functional separation as a solution to the traditional lack of competition in the fixed line market. Currently Ofcom seems to be cautiously optimistic. The European Commission has included it amongst the possible remedies available to other national regulatory authorities (NRAs).[113] Ofcom has said that their experience of functional separation has been sufficiently positive that they fully support this proposal.[114]

4.3.9 Radio and mobile communications

4.3.9.1 *Expansion of mobile telephony*

As mentioned above, there were initially only two mobile licensees: Vodafone and Cellnet. The government decided, for competition reasons, that the retailing of mobile airtime should not be conducted by the operators themselves but by a separate tier of airtime retailers or resellers known as service providers. The two mobile operators were not allowed to sell services or apparatus direct to end users, but were required to provide it wholesale on request to any service provider who was willing to enter into a standard form contract.[115] Consumers wanting to use a mobile phone would buy it from and have a contract with a service provider and not the network operator. The intention behind this decision was to encourage the emergence of competing airtime retailers fully independent of the network operators and, indeed, many such businesses were established. However, network operators were not prevented from owning parallel service provision businesses[116] as long as these businesses were run as separate companies and at arm's length from the network licensees. Cellnet and Vodafone were prohibited from showing undue preference or discrimination and so were not allowed to treat businesses which were associated with them more favourably than competing service providers.[117]

---

[113] See further Chapter 8, at 8.5.1.9.

[114] Speech by David Currie at LBS Global Communications Consortium Conference, November 2007.

[115] Both Cellnet and Vodafone were designated as having market influence (MI)—the ability to raise prices above the competitive level for a non-transitory period without losing sales to such a degree as to make this unprofitable. A designation of MI triggered additional obligations in an operator's licence, including the obligation to provide airtime to qualifying service providers, to provide separate accounts for various activities, and to publish charges, terms, and conditions for services. Vodafone and Cellnet were also designated with SMP for the purposes of the interconnection directive. Operators with SMP were subject to additional obligations, including to meet all reasonable requests for access to the network including points other than the network termination points offered to the majority of end users.

[116] BT's Mobile Communications division and Securicor acted as resellers of Cellnet's airtime and Vodac as a reseller of Vodafone's airtime.

[117] The relationship between the networks and their service providers came increasingly under strain from the beginning of the 1990s for mainly commercial reasons. The difficulties came to a head in 1992 when an independent service provider, Talkland International, made a complaint alleging unfair cross subsidy of the service providers owned by or closely linked to operators of the mobile networks. On 17 May 1994 the DGT produced a statement, Fair Competition in Mobile Service Provision, setting out his conclusions and measures to remedy the situation.

In 1993, two further licences were granted to Orange and Mercury One-2-One. These licences did not include a prohibition on the direct retailing of airtime, although Orange and Mercury One-2-One were obliged to sell wholesale to service providers on request, they had the freedom to sell their services directly to the public.[118] The same freedom was extended to Vodafone and Cellnet when they received new licences in December 1993 and March 1994 respectively.[119]

4.3.9.2 Competition in the mobile market

The mobile market has been subject to regulatory review several times over the last ten years. The particular circumstances of this market, with spectrum as a finite resource, cause concern about lack of competition. A ring-fenced market of this kind affords considerable opportunity for abnormally high profits (and the temptation to engage in collusive behaviour to restrict competition, whether by formal agreement or not).

Imposition of charge controls

In its 1998–99 review of the mobile market[120] the DGT concluded that although the mobile market was not fully competitive, competition was developing, and despite the entry barrier of obtaining spectrum, the mobile market had the potential to become effectively competitive.

The DGT defined a separate market for mobile voice call termination. He considered that all of the mobile operators have SMP in the market for mobile voice termination on their network. The market definition is linked to the calling party pays (CPP) arrangement. This is whereby the calling party pays the entire price for a mobile voice call and so there is a disconnection between the person paying for the calling and the termination charge. The issue of SMP in the market for call termination and subsequent charge controls in this area has been subject to a high degree of scrutiny by the DGT, Ofcom, the CAT, and the MMC. In 1999 the MMC concluded that the mobile call termination charges of Vodafone and Cellnet might be expected to operate against the public interest and recommended the imposition of price controls.[121]

In 2004 charge controls were imposed in respect of mobile voice call termination charges in respect of Vodafone, O2, Orange, and T-Mobile.[122] At this time the price

---

[118] This condition was removed from the licences of One-2-One and Orange in April 1997: Fair Trading in the Mobile Telephony Market. The licences retained the obligations to complete the geographical roll-out of their networks by the end of 1999 and to enable the provision of mobile services in the specified areas.

[119] Fair Trading in Mobile Service Provision, May 1996, Oftel. This obligation was finally removed from the licences of Vodafone and Cellnet on 5 April 2002: Determination to remove the determinations have market influence under condition 56 of their respective licences, Oftel.

[120] Oftel's Review of the mobile market: Statement (July 1999).

[121] See <http://www.competition-commission.org.uk/rep_bpub/reports/1999/index.htm>.

[122] Ofcom statement, Wholesale Mobile Voice Call Termination, June 2004. In September 2006 Consultation, Ofcom set out its proposals for regulating wholesale termination charges on 3G mobile networks.

control was imposed on termination charges using the 2G spectrum. There was no price control on termination using 3G spectrum and, although Ofcom considered that all of the mobile operators including 3 had SMP[123] in the market for call termination, the regulatory obligations on 3 did not include charge controls either for termination on its 3G spectrum or via its roaming arrangements on 2G spectrum. In 2007 Ofcom decided to extend these charge controls to 3. It said that the controls should apply to each of the five network operators without distinction to voice call termination on 2G or 3G networks.[124] This decision has been appealed.

Introduction of the fifth mobile operator
As mentioned above, the government decided that for the 3G mobile networks the most efficient allocation of spectrum would be to sell licences through an auction system. The government argued that auctioning would allow the possession of spectrum to be determined by those who valued the spectrum most, as the cost was set by the market. The licences were awarded to the existing four mobile networks and a new entrant, 3.

The new entrant, 3, faced disadvantages. The 2G operators had the ability to use their 2G networks to provide their 3G services pending the build-out of their 3G networks. The new entrant, however, would be forced to offer only a limited service while it developed its network, thus producing a competitive disparity. For this reason the 2G operators who succeeded in obtaining 3G spectrum were required to accept a condition[125] obliging them to offer roaming services to the new entrant.[126]

Roaming is the term used when the customer of one mobile operator uses another operator's network. In this context it allowed the customers of 3, to use the 2G networks of the existing operators for voice, facsimile, and short message services, where the customer was outside the range of their mobile operator's base station.

4.3.9.3 *Spectrum licensing and management*
As mentioned above it was the Radiocommunications Agency that had the responsibility of managing the civil radio spectrum. The Agency granted licences on behalf of the Secretary of State under the Wireless Telegraphy Act 1949 and allocated specific frequencies. Mobile telecommunication services therefore required two licences to operate: one under the Wireless Telegraphy Act 1949 and one under the Telecommunications Act 1984.

---

[123] 3 appealed against the decision that it has SMP. The CAT found that Ofcom had erred in its decision-making process and remitted the case back to Ofcom. On 27 March 2007 Ofcom published a reassessment and confirmed its earlier conclusion that 3 has SMP—see Ofcom mobile call termination statement, March 2007.

[124] See March 2007 Ofcom statement referred to above. 3 is likely to be the hardest hit by these arrangements as it has relatively more incoming calls from the other operators' networks. Both 3 and BT have appealed to the CAT, which has referred to the Competition Commission (CC) the price control matters in these appeals brought against Ofcom.

[125] Wireless Telegraphy Act 1998, s 3. See further Chapter 5.

[126] 3 reached a commercial national roaming agreement with O2 without using the regulatory backstop. Ofcom reviewed the roaming condition in 2004/2005 and decided to retain the condition.

Historically, spectrum was managed in the UK through an approach known as 'command and control'. The Radiocommunications Agency decided on both the use of a particular band and the users who were allowed to transmit in the band. This system was suitable when the supply and demand for spectrum were in balance and the dominant users of spectrum were public sector. When there are few users and uses, the spectrum manager can have a reasonably good understanding of the best use of spectrum and can sensibly make decisions on spectrum allocation. However, the environment has changed. Economic and technological developments have led to an increasing variety of applications using spectrum and an imbalance between supply and demand.

The Wireless Telegraphy Act 1998 allowed for the first time licence fees to reflect the market value of the spectrum rather than it being associated with the administrative costs of spectrum management by the Radiocommunications Agency.[127] This meant that spectrum pricing could potentially reflect market demand and even out areas of disproportion, as those companies possessing smaller amounts of spectrum would pay less than those with more.

However, despite this change, much of the spectrum was badly managed and there existed little incentive for users to relinquish their unused spectrum or to develop technology to ensure that all spectrum was used to its full potential.

In 2001, the government commissioned an independent review of radio spectrum management issues. The objective of the review was to advise on the principles that should govern spectrum management and the changes required to ensure that all users are focused on using spectrum in the most efficient way possible. The review made many recommendations and concluded that the UK needed to radically change the way in which spectrum was allocated.[128] The report was endorsed by the government. Generally, the recommended approach was the need to make more use of economic mechanisms in order to secure optimal use of the spectrum.

Following this independent report, Ofcom carried out its own review of spectrum management and set out its intentions for the management of spectrum in its Spectrum Framework Review.[129] Ofcom has introduced a series of measures with the aim of deregulating spectrum. This includes reducing the number of restrictions both in terms of who can use spectrum and what it can be used for. This new approach is being implemented primarily through:

- spectrum trading;[130]
- spectrum liberalization; and

---

[127] See various consultation papers on the Agency's website: <http://www.ofcom.gov.uk/regulators_archives/>.

[128] Review of Radio Spectrum Management: An independent review for Department of Trade and Industry and HM Treasury by Professor Martin Cave, March 2002.

[129] Ofcom: A Statement on Spectrum Trading—Implementation in 2004 and beyond, 6 August 2004.

[130] Ofcom introduced spectrum trading for some licences towards the end of 2004. The number of trades remains low. In 2006, 11 assignments were traded which were independent of other commercial activity (e.g. merger): Ofcom, The Communications Market 2007, section 1.6.2.5.

- prompt release of unused spectrum into the market allowing maximum flexibility as to subsequent use.[131]

Ofcom has also been consulting on how the digital dividend[132] should be awarded to interested parties. It has decided that almost all of the digital dividend will be auctioned. This means that new entrants will have an opportunity to bid for the newly released spectrum alongside current spectrum users.[133]

4.4 KEY ISSUES

In this section we focus on a number of key issues that have arisen over the last decades of regulation, some of which are still providing challenges for Ofcom and the industry, for example number portability and universal service. We have also included some of the important regulatory interventions, such as local loop unbundling and the introduction of wholesale line rental which have had an important affect on the market today. Finally we have looked at how Ofcom is facing the challenges of new technologies in terms of voice over internet protocol services (VoIP) and next generation networks.

4.4.1 Continuing issues

4.4.1.1 *Number portability*[134]

Number portability is the facility which allows customers to keep their telephone number when they change network provider. There is clear evidence that customers are reluctant to change network provider if this means that they will have to change their telephone number, and therefore number portability is seen as a key issue in the development of network competition. From 1996, infrastructure competition was a key policy for the DGT and the lack of number portability was seen as a major barrier to access infrastructure competition, so it became a high regulatory priority for the DGT.

Number portability is not the same as number mobility. Number mobility allows a consumer to retain the geographic number when they change address. Any service offered by operators to allow a customer to keep his geographic number when he

---

[131] Timetable for spectrum award programme: <http://www.Ofcom.org.uk/radiocomms/spectrumawards/timetable/>.

[132] This is the spectrum that will be made available by the switch from analogue to digital television broadcasting.

[133] See <http://www.ofcom.org.uk/radiocomms/ddr>.

[134] Originally BT administered the numbering scheme but this was viewed as a barrier to entry to other telecommunication providers. From 1994 Oftel managed the national numbering scheme under which they allocate numbers to operators.

changes address, e.g. within the same local exchange area, is up to the operator concerned.

Operators in the UK began offering numbering portability for geographic services (ordinary telephone numbers of customers located at specific geographic locations) in 1996 and for other fixed services in 1997. Number portability for mobile services became available in January 1999. Number portability was initially provided between operators on a reciprocal basis. Where operators decided to provide number portability their customers could benefit from this arrangement. However, operators were not *required* to provide number portability to their customers until the implementation of the Numbering Directive. From 1 January 2000 customers of fixed services were allowed to retain their existing telephone numbers.[135]

The MMC enquiry[136] on portability held that the DGT had the power to determine the charges for providing portability. The referral was made by the DGT when BT refused to accept a modification to its licence, which had the effect of granting the power of determining the cost of portability to the DGT. The MMC found that the DGT did have the power to alter BT's licence and stipulate what BT was entitled to charge. BT argued that the cost of providing number portability should be borne by the operator requesting the service, while other operators, and at that specific time Videotron, argued that operators should bear their own costs. The MMC determined that the costs should be allocated between the parties with BT bearing the greater proportion.

Since the introduction of number portability in the UK, both fixed and mobile networks have used a system referred to as onward routing to route calls to ported numbers. With onward routing, calls are first routed to the network to which the customer originally subscribed, known as the donor network. The donor network is responsible for routing the call onward to the network to which the consumer now subscribes. There are a number of weaknesses in onward routing. For example, the dependence on the donor network leaves consumers exposed in the event of network failure by the donor network.[137] There are also issues of inefficiency associated with the additional capacity required for the onward routing of calls.

In November 2007[138] Ofcom issued a statement which provided that the industry should cooperate to establish a common database (CDB) to allow direct routing of calls to fixed and mobile ported numbers. Ofcom set out ambitious milestone dates, for example, the CDB was required to be ready to be populated with data by 31 December 2008 and mobile providers were required to directly route all calls to ported mobile numbers by 1 September 2009.

---

[135] Oftel Numbering Directive: Number Portability Requirements (October 1999 and January 2000).
[136] Inquiry by the Monopolies and Mergers Commission into Telephone Number Portability: Explanatory Statement from the Director General of Telecommunications (27 April 1995).
[137] In 2001 the insolvency of Atlantic Telecom resulted in Atlantic customers and customers of other communications providers who had ported numbers from Atlantic losing service on those numbers.
[138] Ofcom, Concluding statement. Telephone number portability for consumers switching suppliers.

The UK porting group[139] was set up by Ofcom to work with the industry on the establishment of the CDB.

Ofcom was also requiring mobile providers to implement quick and simple processes for porting mobile numbers.[140]

4.4.1.2 *Universal service*

As well as trying to open up the market to competition, regulation has also aimed to ensure that everyone has access to telecommunications services. With a monopoly, service is provided by a single operator and lower charges for connection, line rentals, and local calls can be subsidized out of higher revenues generated by, for example, long distance call charges. With liberalization, questions were raised about the willingness and ability of existing and new operators to guarantee this safety net of services. The rationale behind universal service is to provide a safety net: 'to ensure that those telecommunications services which are used by the majority and which are essential to full social and economic inclusion are made available to everybody upon reasonable request in an appropriate fashion and at an affordable price'.[141]

The universal services obligation (USO) aims to ensure that in a liberalized environment the safety net is maintained. In the UK, the USO was initially placed in the licence of BT (and Kingston Communications for the Hull area).

BT (and Kingston Communications) was obliged under its licence to provide a basic level of service at geographically averaged prices. In addition, they had to provide a network of public telephone boxes and schemes for low-income households.

BT was also obliged to ensure that people were connected and that the infrastructure was maintained. This was in contrast to Mercury and other operators whose licence did not require them to provide universal service. The obligation was subject to the opinion of the DGT who had to first interpret the meaning of 'reasonable demand' in the PanAmSat dispute.[142] It was his ruling that 'reasonable demand is primarily demonstrated in the market: reasonable demand exists if one or more customers will pay a fair price for the service', suggesting that the DGT had extensive powers in respect of BT's licence.

---

[139] See <http://www.ukporting.org.uk>.

[140] Vodafone have issued a notice to appeal this decision to the CAT—case number 1094/3/3/08. On 18 September 2008 the CAT issued its judgment upholding the appeal and remitting the whole matter to Ofcom for reconsideration. See www.catribunal.org.uk/documents/Judgment_1094.180908.pdf.

[141] *Universal Telecommunication Services: A Consultative Document issued by the Director-General of Telecommunications* (London, Oftel, July 1999). In respect of EU policy and law on universal service, see further Chapter 5.

[142] 22 March 1988.

Subsequent conditions placed further obligations on BT. For example, Condition 2 required that the company provide services in rural areas, a responsibility inherited from the Post Office. There was an obligation on all public telecommunication operators to provide access to the Public Emergency Call Service by dialling 999 or 112.[143]

The focus for the 1990s and into the 2000s is on bringing benefits to those with low incomes, those with disabilities who need particular services, and customers in rural areas for whom the actual cost for the provision of services might otherwise be prohibitively expensive. Longer term questions surrounding universal service include whether the USO should be extended to include the provision of broadband and the use of mobile services to fulfil universal service obligations. The European Commission has been keen to prevent a 'two-tier-society'[144] whereby some people have access to the new broadband information services while the rest of society is excluded. In 1999, Oftel concluded that although the concept of universal service should not be extended at the present time, the matter should remain under review. It concluded that when the majority of the population were taking advantage of higher broadband services and they were 'essential for full economic and social inclusion'[145] then the universal service obligation might be extended.[146]

With the abolition of licences in 2003, the basis for imposing the universal service requirements changed. It is now the government, and not Ofcom, that determines the specific universal service requirements.[147] Ofcom decides how these should be implemented. The services which must be available include:[148]

- a connection to the public telephone network, able to support voice telephony, fax, and data at rates sufficient to support functional Internet access.[149] The government has not set a specific connection speed in the legislation. Guidelines provide that a connection speed of 28.8 kbit/s is a reasonable benchmark although this may need to be revised over time;[150]

---

[143] Telecommunications (Single Emergency Call Number) Regulations 1992, SI 1992/2875. This has now been repealed and the issue is governed by the General Conditions of Entitlement, Condition 4, issued under the Communications Act 2003. See further Chapter 5.

[144] *Communication to the European Parliament, The Council, the Economic and Social Committee and the Committee of the Regions: Universal Service for Telecommunications in the Perspective of a Fully Liberalised Environment* (1996).

[145] *Communications Regulation in the UK* (London, Oftel, July 2000).

[146] See Oftel *Review of Universal Telecommunications Services* (London, Oftel, September 2000).

[147] Communications Act, s 65.

[148] The Electronic Communications (Universal Service) Order 2003 No 1904.

[149] Article 4 (2) The Universal Services Directive.

[150] Ofcom reviewed this as part of its 2006 review and concluded that these guidelines should be retained.

- the provision of at least one comprehensive directory and directory enquiry facility which must be updated once a year;

- the provision of public pay phones[151] to meet the reasonable needs of end users including the ability to use the emergency call number free of charge;

- billing and payment options to enable subscribers to monitor and control their expenditure and appropriate tariff options for those on low incomes or with special social needs; and

- special measures for end users with disabilities.

In reality the scope and delivery of the USO has changed only slightly since 1984. The current USO still falls on BT and Kingston Communications and is implemented by a number of specific conditions on these two organizations. In addition, a number of General Conditions impose obligations on all publicly available telephone service providers. For example, General Condition 8 requires the provision of directory information and General Condition 18 requires the provision of certain facilities for end users with disabilities.[152]

Ofcom looked at questions surrounding universal service as part of its Strategic Review and it carried out a further review of the USO in 2006[153] to ensure that it continues to meet the needs of customers. In particular it looked at the question of whether the USO should be extended to include broadband and mobile. It concluded that neither were currently appropriate. It considered that exclusion from broadband services did not currently result in social exclusion sufficient to warrant universal service measures being introduced and that in addition imposing a USO for broadband would be inappropriate whilst the market for broadband is still developing. It did feel that it would not be appropriate to rule out the possibility of imposing a USO for broadband at a future date. It also concluded that increased fixed mobile convergence means that at some stage mobile may replace fixed as the primary means of connection and that a universal service obligation defined in terms of access to voice services could be delivered via a mobile connection, rather than the imposition of a separate mobile USO.

Another recurring issue relating to universal service relates to funding. BT (and Kingston Communications) bears the cost of the USO because it was considered that BT obtained benefit from providing the service in the form of positive brand image and the fact that uneconomic customers were likely to remain with BT when they became 'economic customers'. As competition continues to erode margins, at some

---

[151] Ofcom has agreed to BT's request to non-uniform charging for public payphone tariff trials over the next three years: Ofcom statement, 4 June 2007, Public Call Boxes—Consent for non-uniform charging for geographic tariff trials.

[152] See further Chapter 7 at 7.4.4.3.1.

[153] Review of Universal Service Obligation, Statement, 14 March 2006.

point the provision of the USO may become an 'unfair burden'[154] on BT (and Kingston Communications). Ofcom has the power[155] to put in place alternative methods of provision or funding if there is a net cost—that is, a cost (once the benefits have been taken into account) that imposes an unfair burden on the providers with the USO. Ofcom has said that the more effective competition in the telecoms market becomes, the faster some kind of universal service fund will become necessary. This fund could be implemented by a number of means including:

- a direct levy on all consumers of certain communications services (e.g. a fixed amount that appears directly on the bill);
- an indirect levy on consumers via a levy on communications providers and services (this model is used in the USA and France); or
- direct government funding.[156]

As part of its 2006 review, Ofcom set out indicative estimates for 2003/04 costs to BT at £56–74 million and £59–64 million for benefits. It was felt that these estimates did not warrant a full scale review and it was suggested that currently there was not an unfair burden on BT.

4.4.2 Regulatory interventions

4.4.2.1 *Carrier pre-selection*

A mechanism that allowed new operators to compete was equal access or carrier pre-selection (CPS). CPS allows users to select alternative operators in advance without dialling additional codes on the telephone, as customers of Mercury were required to do in the early 1980s.[157] The customer subscribes to the services of one or more CPS operators and chooses the type of calls that will be routed through the alternative operator.

Initially CPS involved the consumer dialling an access code prior to each call in order that another operator could carry the particular call (known as indirect access). The disadvantage of this was that BT would automatically carry the call where the code was not dialled.

In 1996, the DGT issued a statement in which it recognized that indirect access was appropriate over BT's network given its dominant position but that it was concerned that imposing indirect access requirements on non-SMP operators would discourage the development of competing networks. At this time Oftel also looked at the concept of allowing direct connection to BT's access network—which would involve BT leasing the exchange line to another operator who would then

---

[154] The concept of unfair burden originates from EU directives. See Directive 2002/22/EC on universal service and users' rights.
[155] Communications Act 2003, s 70.
[156] Strategic Review of Telecommunications—Phase 2 consultation document.
[157] Although this was achieved through the use of the so-called 'Blue Button'.

take ownership of the BT customer—the second operator's bills would cover calls and line rental. Oftel's conclusion was that 'this would adversely affect the development of competition and would not be in the interest of the UK consumer'.[158] This was a reflection of the DGT's feeling at that time that competition through infrastructure should be the main policy; something that changed with the demand to facilitate the roll-out of broadband Internet access services.

The EC Numbering Directive[159] required that after an initial selection the chosen carrier would automatically carry all calls, thereby eliminating the need to dial the access code every time. The system allowed various options, for example national and international calls could be carried by different operators.

The technology for CPS was required to be implemented by those companies with SMP by 1 January 2000, although BT successfully sought a deferral on technical grounds. CPS was viewed by the European Commission as a means of facilitating more competition largely through service providers. Oftel reluctantly accepted this approach, although the UK regulator favoured infrastructure development as the main means of competition, which is perhaps why Oftel agreed to BT's deferral.[160]

4.4.2.2 *Local loop bundling*[161]

In March 1998, David Edmonds was appointed as the new DGT. His appointment seemed to signal a change in the policy direction referred to above, away from the goal of infrastructure competition. In December 1998, he issued a consultation paper putting forward alternatives for promoting competition in the provision of higher bandwidth services, and in December 1999[162] he concluded that BT should make its local loops available to other operators to allow them to compete directly with BT in providing higher bandwidth access, and that it would be delivered through a form of local loop unbundling.[163] This would be achieved by local access lines or 'unbundled loops' and co-location being made available to operators with interconnection rights and obligations. Oftel set out clearly the requirements on BT through a new condition in BT's licence[164] with a timetable for implementation of July 2001.

---

[158] Oftel, Policy on Indirect Access, Equal Access and Direct Connection to the Access Network—Statement, July 1996.

[159] Directive 98/61/EC of the European Parliament and of the Council of 24 September 1998 amending Directive 97/33/EC with regard to operator number portability and carrier pre-selection, OJ L 268/37, 3 October 1998, implemented in the UK by the Telecommunications (Interconnection) (Number Portability, etc.) Regulations 1999 No 3449.

[160] Now regulated under s 90 of the Communications Act 2003.

[161] *Access to Bandwidth—Delivering Competition for the Information Age* (London, Oftel, November 1999). See further Chapter 6.

[162] This decision was taken in advance of the EU Regulation EC 2887/2000.

[163] Local loop unbundling (LLU) is the process where the incumbent operator (BT and Kingston in the UK) makes its local network (the copper cables that run from customers' premises to the telephone exchange) available to other companies. Operators are then able to upgrade individual lines using DSL technology to offer services, such as always-on high speed Internet access, direct to the customer.

[164] Condition 83 of BT's licence which required BT to provide LLU continued in effect after the commencement of the Communications Act 2003 pursuant to para 9 of Sch 18 of the Act. It ceased with

This was a key decision for the development of telecoms in the UK. It set a framework for the competitive delivery of information age services to consumers.

When LLU was first raised by Oftel in 1998 there was considerable enthusiasm for it, with many companies expressing an interest. However, it is generally accepted that the initial process of LLU was not a success. The actual implementation date of July 2001 was not met. Initial forecasts predicted a huge demand for space in the local exchanges from different operators and so a process for allocation was devised; this became known as the 'Bow Wave' process. Ultimately many of the operators withdrew from the process. Oftel placed the blame for this on the financial climate.[165] The government's select committee was damning of the whole process and said it was in danger of becoming farcical. It referred to BT dragging their feet and was critical of Oftel for not intervening earlier.[166] An OECD report concluded that BT 'found practical ways to resist policy'.[167]

In 2004 there were two key developments:

- the appointment of an independent Telecoms Adjudicator to work with industry to accelerate the implementation and delivery of fit for purpose LLU products and processes;[168] and

- the introduction of price ceilings for a number of LLU products in 2004.

After a notoriously shaky start the process of LLU is generally seen as having been a success. There are now more than 5 million unbundled lines across the UK and Ofcom views the process as having provided consumers with greater choice and lower prices.[169]

4.4.2.3 *Wholesale line rental*

In 2002, the DGT required BT to provide a new wholesale line rental (WLR) product to other operators on cost-based and non-discriminatory terms.[170] Its review of the fixed telephony market had identified that a significant inhibitor of competition and innovation was the inability of alternative service providers to provide a single bill to their customers.[171] Customers who use indirect access or CPS services receive two

---

effect from 16 December 2004 following the imposition of remedies on BT in the wholesale local access market: Review of Wholesale Local Access Market, Ofcom, 16 December 2004.

[165] Other factors which may have affected the withdrawal of many of the operators included a lack of resources and a slower than hoped for uptake of broadband by the general public.

[166] The Select Committee on Trade and Industry, Sixth Report.

[167] OECD Regulatory Reform in the Telecoms Industry, Paris (2002) p 61.

[168] See <http://www.offta.org.uk>. See also Chapter 8, at 8.3.4.6.

[169] See <http://www.ofcom.org.uk/media/features/llufigure>.

[170] Protecting consumers by promoting competition, Oftel's conclusions, 20 June 2002.

[171] At the end of 2001 BT still had a very strong market position: its market share for volume of calls for residential coasters was 78.4%. Its volume of lines was 80.2%. See protecting consumers by promoting competition above.

bills—one from BT for the line rental and one from the service provider for calls. The DGT felt that WLR might encourage larger numbers of customers to consider whether they are receiving the best deal available to them for their expenditure.

The DGT required BT to introduce a new line rental product to enable alternative suppliers to provide a single bill that covers both line rental and telephone calls. In order to give an additional incentive for BT to introduce the WLR product as quickly and efficiently as possible.[172] The DGT said that it would modify retail price controls on BT to RPI + 0[173] per cent once a commercially viable WLR product had been fully implemented by BT in line with the determined product specification and it being taken up by service providers.

Ofcom's Annual Plan, April 2004–March 2005, identifies WLR as a key operating priority under the objective to promote competition. The annual plan states that Ofcom will promote 'competition in all communications markets, via wholesale line rental'.

4.4.3 The challenge of new technologies

4.4.3.1 *Voice over Internet Protocol Services*
VoIP (voice over internet protocol services) is a generic term for the conveyance of voice, fax, and related services, partially or wholly over packet switched, IP-based networks. VoIP services are expected to increase competition as they have a number of advantages over traditional PSTN telephony services, including lower infrastructure deployment costs and more efficient network utilization. Although to date there is little evidence that VoIP is substituting entirely for other voice networks.[174]

The regulatory challenge for Ofcom and indeed other regulators around the world is to find a balance between the often competing objectives of promoting competition and promoting the interests of the consumer.

Most consumers in the UK expect to get a certain level of service from both their traditional home phone line and their mobile.[175] The vast majority of these traditional voice services (both fixed and mobile) fall within the definition of PATS (publicly available telephone services[176]) and therefore these facilities are provided

---

[172] BT introduced a basic WLR product (WLR1) at the beginning of September 2002. The functionality of the product was similar to that of its Calls and Access product. WLR1 required further development for it to be a 'fit-for-purpose' product in the mass market and operate efficiently at large volumes and seamlessly with other product such as carrier pre-selection (CPS).

[173] On 15 December 2005 Ofcom determined that BT's WLR product was fit-for-purpose, reflecting a range of factors including the fact that the product had had a significant impact in the market with over one million WLR lines used by residential consumers. Accordingly, the RPC was relaxed to RPI + 0% with effect from 1 January 2006.

[174] Ofcom, The Communications Market 2007. Ofcom research in Q1 2007 found that 18% of households with broadband were using VoIP services.

[175] The main obligations which apply to PATS are discussed further in Chapter 7.

[176] PATS are services available to the public for originating and receiving national and international calls and access to emergency organizations through a number or numbers in a national or international telephone numbering plan (General conditions of entitlement).

as a result of regulatory intervention, in particular the ability to make calls to the emergency services, free of charge. Access to emergency services is seen as being extremely important from a social responsibility and consumer protection perspective. Although some VoIP services have the potential to look and feel like traditional telephone services they may not be fall within the definition of a PATS service and so are not regulated as such and are not able to deliver features such as access to emergency services. This has the potential to cause confusion amongst consumers.

In interim advice,[177] Ofcom set out its initial view that it was better to offer less reliable access to emergency services than no access at all and it set out its forbearance policy i.e. that it would forbear from enforcing PATS obligations against new services entering the market even if they offered access to 999 services. Voice providers were, however, expected to provide sufficient information at the point of sale *and* at the point of use so that both consumers and users are fully aware of any limitations of the service.

This view was made pending clarification from the European Commission on its position. At that time, Ofcom's understanding of the Commission's position was that providers should be able to choose whether or not they were providing PATS even if they offered the four core elements of PATS, including access to emergency services. This would mean that a service provider could offer access to emergency services, without being subject to the full rigour of the PATS obligations.

It was not until March 2007 and following a period of heavy lobbying by some parts of the industry that Ofcom issued its final statement.[178] The main decisions in the March statement were:

- to discontinue Ofcom's interim forbearance policy;
- to establish guidelines on how Ofcom will investigate potential contraventions of obligations in relation to network integrity and emergency calls; and
- to mandate a code in respect of certain providers which specifies the information that providers must offer to certain customers to ensure they are well informed about the capability of VoIP services.

When Ofcom set out its forbearance policy it was partly on the basis that this reflected the view of the Commission. The Commission did, however, clarify its view and stated that where a service meets all the gating criteria it automatically becomes and must be regulated as a PATS.[179]

---

[177] Ofcom: New voice services, A consultation and interim guidance, 6 September 2004.

[178] Regulation of VoIP Services, Statement and publication of statutory notifications under section 48(1) of the Communications Act 2003 modifying General Conditions 14 and 18.

[179] Expert Group on Emergency Access working document: Regulatory clarification of ECS/PATS and Fixed/Non-Fixed, 23 May 2006.

Ofcom issued a further consultation over the summer and in December 2007[180] announced that as from 8 September 2008:

- VoIP Out services which allow customers to make calls over the Internet to the PSTN but not receive calls from the PSTN; and

- VOIP In and Out services which allow customers to make calls over the Internet to the PSTN and receive calls from the Internet over the PSTN

will be required to provide access to emergency services at no charge and to meet requirements on providing caller location information to the emergency organizations handling the calls.

4.4.3.2 Next generation networks

Next generation networks (NGNs) pose significant opportunities and challenges for regulators and the industry as a whole. As mentioned above the government recognizes the crucial importance of broadband to maintaining the position of the UK within the global economy and therefore the government is keen to avoid a situation that may impact adversely on the UK's ability to match international competitors' performance in delivery of services and applications over broadband.

NGNs can be used to upgrade the capabilities of fixed line telephony networks. Plans to develop these networks are in response to the fact that consumers are changing the way that they use their broadband connections. The take up of services, such as high definition video, will require faster connections and place increasing demands on current networks.[181] There are two types of next generation network upgrade:

- next generation core networks (NGNs)–these are internet protocol based core or backbone networks which can support a variety of existing and new services. Typically they replace multiple legacy core networks with a single IP-based network for the provision of all services. BT's investment in its 21st Century Network (21CN) is an example of an investment in a core NGN;[182] and

- next generation access networks—these are broadband access networks which connect the user to a core network capable of a bandwidth quantity and quality significantly in excess of current levels, for example, the provision of 'fibre to the curb'. This enables new services such as HDTV over broadband to be delivered to end users.

---

[180] Regulation of VOIP services: Access to Emergency Services, December 2007.

[181] The launch of the BBC's iPlayer (its on-demand TV service) has reportedly put a strain on existing networks. More than 42 million programmes were accessed in its first three months. A US analyst firm Nemertes Research has predicted a drastic slow down as networks struggle to cope with the amount of data: see <http://www.nemertes.com>.

[182] Cable and Wireless, Carphone Warehouse, and Tiscali are also upgrading their core networks. Others such as Thus and Easynet invested in next generation core networks at the time when they built their networks (Ofcom, Impact of the Telecoms Strategic Review, December 2007).

It is the provisioning of the latter that has raised the more significant policy and regulatory issues.

There are a number of issues associated with these new networks and in particular with the access networks.[183] For current access network owners, next generation access deployments offer the prospect of very high end customer bandwidths, but they require significant investment in infrastructure. For market competitors and new entrants, these new networks may result in changes to the wholesale products and services that they can purchase.

Ofcom has recognized that the development of the new networks presents it with the opportunity to influence the competitive landscape in years to come. The challenge for governments and regulators is to encourage investment in these new networks and at the same time maintain the benefits of competition, avoiding the issues of regulatory bottlenecks which have plagued the industry over the last 20 years. The current regulatory framework was designed to open up access to a legacy infrastructure (essentially paid for by the tax payer and inherited by BT). It may not be appropriate to regulate one designed to enable investment in a whole new infrastructure and at the same time to maintain the benefits of competition.

At the beginning of 2008,[184] the government announced a review of broadband to look at a number of questions around the potential barriers to deployment of high speed broadband, possible barriers to any new models of investment. At the moment the UK is in what Ofcom describes as a pre-investment stage with respect to next generation access.[185] Many organizations are in the stage of considering how best to address developments in broadband services, but no operator has announced any intention to make wide scale next generation access investments. This is in contrast to the situation in many other countries; for example in Japan, Korea, and the US a significant number of broadband customers already use next generation access. A number of reasons have been put forward as to why this is so—including the higher cost of deployment in the UK as opposed to some other countries, and the capabilities of the existing copper access network infrastructure to deliver services. Ofcom has said that it does not propose incentivizing operators to deploy next generation access networks, neither does it think there is a case for withdrawing regulation from next generation access networks. The challenge for Ofcom and indeed industry as a whole is to ensure that the right level of investment is made in the right type of networks.

---

[183] Broadband Stakeholder Group, Pipe Dreams? Prospects for next generation broadband deployment in the UK.

[184] Announced on 22 February 2008. See <http://www.berr.gov.uk>.

[185] Ofcom, Future Broadband, Policy approach to next generation access, 29 September 2007.

5

EUROPEAN UNION
COMMUNICATIONS LAW

Ian Walden

5.1 INTRODUCTION

The past 20 years and more has seen an extraordinary level of policy, legal, and regulatory activity in the telecommunications sector within the European Union (EU); with well over 100 different directives, decisions, regulations, recommendations and resolutions, relating to every aspect of the industry, having been adopted since 1984.[1] Such activity illustrates clearly that market liberalization should not be confused with concepts of market deregulation. While from a UK perspective, initial EU regulatory intervention in the telecommunications sector seldom impinged on

---

[1] Council Recommendation (84/549/EEC) concerning the implementation of harmonization in the field of telecommunications (OJ L 298/49, 16 November 1984).

the wider public consciousness, largely due to developments already commenced domestically,[2] some Member States experienced significant political fall-out from Commission initiatives in the area, such as public sector industrial action.

The chapter is broadly divided in two: the first part reviews the historical development and key components of the EU regulatory framework; the second part examines particular elements addressed by the framework. It is not the objective of this chapter to provide a detailed analysis of every legal instrument in the field, in part because such a treatment would require a complete book on its own; but also because many aspects are examined in depth in other chapters of the book, particularly Chapter 7, 'Authorization and Licensing'; Chapter 8, 'Access and Interconnection'; Chapter 9, 'Competition Law in Telecommunications'; and Chapter 13, 'Communications Privacy'. Rather, this chapter is designed to place the mass of EU laws, decisions, and regulations into a comprehensible contextual framework.

5.2 EVOLVING POLICY AND THE REGULATED SPHERE

The development of EU policy and legislation in the telecommunications sector can be broadly distinguished into three phases. In the first phase, between 1987 and 1993, the objective was the liberalization of telecommunications equipment and certain service sectors, whilst preserving for the incumbent the provision of network infrastructure, seen by many as a natural monopoly. In order to protect the network, it was believed that it was necessary to safeguard the revenues of the incumbent. As the provision of voice telephony services constituted the incumbent's main source of income, such services were categorized as a 'reserved service', not subject to the process of liberalization. The Commission outlined its initial position on the role of telecommunications in the creation of the Single Market in a Green Paper of 1987.[3] This paper set out three basic principles upon which the regulatory framework would be established:

- liberalization of areas currently under a monopoly provider;
- opening access to telecommunication networks and services, through harmonization and the development of minimum standards; and
- full application of the competition rules.

In the second phase, from 1993 to 2002, full market liberalization became politically acceptable as concerns about the impact of liberalization failed to materialize. The key commitment on liberalization came on 22 December 1994, when the Council of

---

[2] See further Chapter 4.

[3] Commission, 'On the Development of the Common Market for Telecommunications Services and Equipment', COM(87) 290 final of 30 June 1987. See also Commission, 'On the Way to a Competitive Community-Wide Telecommunications Market in the Year 1992', COM (88) 48 final of 9 Feb 1988.

Ministers committed themselves to the target date of 1 January 1998 for full liber-alization of the voice telephony monopoly and telecommunications infrastructure in the majority of Members States.[4] The fact that such a fundamental change in the legal framework governing a market was undertaken and substantially achieved in a relatively short period of time illustrates the considerable degree of consensus between Member States, the Community institutions, and industry itself. However, the reality of a fully competitive market is taking considerably longer, as the divergent interests involved emerge and are fully expressed during the process of implementation.

A third phase of EU telecommunications policy commenced on 25 July 2003, when the new 'Framework Directive'[5] and the specific measures came into force, the 'New Regulatory Framework' (NRF):

- The 'Authorisation Directive';[6]
- The 'Access and Interconnection Directive';[7]
- The 'Universal Services and User's Rights Directive';[8] and
- The 'Communications Privacy' Directive.[9]

This new regulatory regime emerged from the Commission's 1999 Communication Review,[10] which was itself designed to respond to a range of pressures for reform. First, from a legal perspective, the adoption in 1997 of the World Trade Organization (WTO) agreement on 'basic telecommunications' and associated Reference Paper[11] required certain transposition into European law, even though it represented in large part existing EU regulatory principles. Second, from a regulatory perspective, the flexibility within the existing regime had resulted in considerable divergences in practice between the Member States, inhibiting the development of a single market in the telecommunications sector.[12] Third, competition had been introduced or

---

[4] Council Resolution of 22 December 1994 on the principles and timetable for the liberalization of telecommunications infrastructures (OJ C 379/4, 31 December 1994).

[5] Directive 2002/21/EC on a common regulatory framework for electronic communications networks and services (OJ L 108/33, 24 April 2002).

[6] Directive 2002/20/EC on the authorization of electronic communications networks and services (OJ L 108/21, 24 April 2002).

[7] Directive 2002/19/EC on access to, and interconnection of, electronic communications networks and associated facilities (OJ L 108/7, 24 April 2002).

[8] Directive 2002/22/EC on universal service and users' rights relating to electronic communications networks and services (OJ L 108/7, 24 April 2002).

[9] Directive 2002/58/EC concerning the processing of personal data and the protection of privacy in the electronic communications sector (OJ L 201/37, 31 July 2002).

[10] See Commission Communication, 'Towards a new framework for Electronic Communications infra-structure and associated services: The 1999 Communications Review', COM(1999)539, 10 November 1999; at p vi.

[11] See further Chapter 15, at 15.4.

[12] See the Reports on 'Implementation of the Regulatory Framework in the Member States', from 1998–2007, available at <http://ec.europa.eu/information_society/policy/ecomm/implementation_enforcement/index_en.htm>.

existed in all areas of the telecommunications market and there was a recognized desire to simplify the regulatory framework by moving towards greater reliance on the application of *ex post* European competition rules, and away from the array of *ex ante* measures.[13] Fourth, at a technical and market level, the phenomenon of convergence between previously distinct industries has blurred and undermined existing regulatory schemes, as noted in the Framework Directive:

> The convergence of the telecommunications, media and information technology sectors means all transmission networks and services should be covered by a single regulatory framework. (Recital 5)

The new regime is designed, therefore, to embrace all forms of communication or transmission technology, whether used to carry voice calls, Internet traffic, or television programmes; while the concept of telecommunications has been replaced by the concepts of 'electronic communications networks' and 'electronic communications services', defined in the following terms:

- 'electronic communications network' means transmission systems and, where applicable, switching or routing equipment and other resources which permit the conveyance of signals by wire, by radio, by optical, or by other electromagnetic means, including satellite networks, fixed (circuit- and packet-switched, including Internet) and mobile terrestrial networks, electricity cable systems, to the extent that they are used for the purpose of transmitting signals, networks used for radio and television broadcasting, and cable television networks, irrespective of the type of information conveyed;

- 'electronic communications service' means a service normally provided for remuneration which consists wholly or mainly in the conveyance of signals on electronic communications networks, including telecommunications services and transmission services in networks used for broadcasting, but exclude services providing, or exercising editorial control over, content transmitted using electronic communications networks and services; it does not include information society services, as defined in Article 1 of Directive 98/34/EC, which do not consist wholly or mainly in the conveyance of signals on electronic communications networks. (Framework Directive, at Articles 2(a) and (c)).

As with any regulatory regime, definitions constitute the boundaries that determine what falls within and outside the regulated sphere. Such definitions attempt to reflect, not describe, the marketplace to which they apply, since an undertaking's activities may result in concurrent application of different regimes. However, clear and comprehensive definitions contribute towards legal certainty, which in turn reduces potential barriers to market entry. While the NRF establishes a single regime for the

---

[13] For the purpose of this chapter, the phrase *ex ante* ('before the fact') is used in respect of regulatory measures that proactively control the manner in which entities operate going forward; while *ex post* ('after the fact') refers to measures that arise in reaction to the decisions and activities of entities.

provision of conveyance or conduit services, the provision of content services over such networks and services is governed under EU law by at least two, currently, distinct regimes for the provision of 'audiovisual media services' and 'information society services'. The former involves 'providing, or exercising editorial content' and falls under the 'Television without Frontiers' Directive;[14] while the latter consists of services that are more than 'wholly or mainly in the conveyance of signals', and are primarily regulated under the 'Electronic Commerce' Directive.[15] The boundary between this latter activity and the provision of electronic communication services is particularly blurred, given the potential variety of approaches that could be adopted for interpreting the phrase 'mainly in the conveyance of signals'; from quantitative to qualitative measures, including the imputed intention of suppliers or the perception of consumers; all of which can create uncertainty for market participants and new entrants.

As well as excluding content services, the NRF does not currently include rules that govern the provision of 'telecommunications terminal equipment', the physical kit or any other components that are connected to an electronic communications network or service by end-users, which is subject to a separate regime.[16] Reform proposals published by the Commission in November 2007 would amend the Framework Directive to bring certain aspects of terminal equipment into the NRF. The regulatory boundary between a network and equipment is referred to as the 'interface', which comprises either the 'network termination point' for fixed network access or the 'air interface' for wireless access.[17] So, for example, the use of software of a user's computer to make a voice call over the Internet does not fall within the scope of the NRF if no ongoing transmission service is supplied in addition to the software provision.[18] However, certain end-user equipment or components may be categorized as an 'associated facility':

- 'associated facilities' means those facilities associated with an electronic communications network and/or an electronic communications service which enable and/or support the provision of services via that network and/or service. It includes conditional access systems and electronic programme guides (Framework Directive, Article 2(e)).

---

[14] Directive 89/552/EEC of 3 October 1989 of the European Parliament and of the Council on the coordination of certain provisions laid down by law, regulation or administrative action in Member States concerning the provision of audiovisual media services ('Audiovisual Media Services Directive'), as amended by Directive 97/36/EC (OJ L 202/60, 30 July 1997) and Directive 07/65/EC (OJ L 332/27, 18 December 07).

[15] Directive 2000/31/EC on certain legal aspects of information society services, in particular electronic commerce, in the Internal Market (OJ L 178/1, 17 July 2000).

[16] Framework Directive, Arts (1)4. See further section 5.4.3 below.

[17] Directive 99/5/EC at Art 2(e).

[18] See Commission Staff Working Document on 'The Treatment of Voice over Internet Protocol (VoIP) under the EU Regulatory Framework', 14 June 2004, at 3.

'Conditional access systems' control access to encrypted radio or television broadcast signals[19] a content service, and are generally contained with a set-top box or 'enhanced digital television equipment'.[20] We therefore have another blurred regulatory boundary, whereby an item of consumer equipment, the set-top box, contains components that fall within the NRF, while other equipment and systems for accessing content services would lie outside the regulated sphere.

A further distinction is made in the NRF between 'public' electronic communication networks and services and non-public, the former being subject to the bulk of the regulatory obligations and attention. Despite the importance of this regulatory boundary, the NRF does not further define what distinguishes public from private, except to state that the former is 'available to the public'. It is therefore left to national implementing legislation or national regulators to clarify. In the UK, for example, Ofcom has stated that a service is 'publicly available' if it is 'available to anyone who is both willing to pay for it and to abide by the applicable terms and conditions'; as distinct from a bespoke service provided to a restricted group of customers.[21] However, this is another area where some regulatory ambiguity and uncertainty may arise.

While the current regime was intended to be future-proofed, the NRF Directives also contain a review procedure obliging the Commission to report to Council and Parliament about the 'functioning' of the Directives.[22] The first such review took place in 2006 ('the 2006 Review'). Overall, the conclusions of the review were that the NRF was operating successfully, with only relatively minor amendments and improvements being proposed.[23] In November 2007, the Commission published a series of legislative proposals to amend the NRF, key areas for reform being in respect of spectrum management and the procedural burden in respect of the market reviews and the resultant *ex ante* remedies.[24] Adoption of the final texts is expected in early 2009. The proposed amendments to the NRF are discussed throughout the rest of this and the other relevant chapters.

---

[19] Framework Directive, Art 2(f). See further Chapter 8, at 8.3.4.7.

[20] Ibid, Art 2(o).

[21] Oftel, Guidelines for the interconnection of public electronic communications networks, 23 May 2003, at para 6.1 *et seq*; as endorsed in Ofcom's Guidelines on the General Conditions of Entitlement, see <http://www.ofcom.org.uk/telecoms/ioi/g_a_regime/gce/gcoe/>.

[22] E.g. Framework Directive, at Art 25.

[23] Communication from the Commission to the Council, the European Parliament, the European Economic and Social Committee and the Committee of the Regions on the Review of the EU Regulatory Framework for electronic communications networks and services, COM(2006) 334 final (28 June 2006); and accompanying Commission Staff Working Document, SEC(2006) 816.

[24] See Commission Communication, Report on the outcome of the Review of the EU regulatory framework for electronic communications networks and services in accordance with Directive 2002/21/EC and Summary of the 2007 Reform Proposals, COM(2007)696 rev 1 ('2007 Reform Proposals').

5.3 SOURCES OF LAW

The basis for Community involvement in the telecommunications market has primarily been founded on two different strands of European Treaty law: competition law (Articles 81–89) and the establishment of the 'Internal Market' (Article 95). The former articles have been primarily used to open up national markets to competition; whilst the latter has primarily addressed competition issues between national markets, through harmonization measures. Initiatives within each area have been the responsibility of different departments of the European Commission; harmonization measures originating within the Information Society Directorate-General and liberalization issues residing primarily with the Competition Directorate-General.[25]

The role of the Commission's Competition Directorate-General in the development of EU policy in the telecommunications sector has been very considerable. Indeed, the manner in which EU competition law has been applied to the telecommunications sector provides a case study of the significance of competition law within the *acquis communautaire*. In particular, Article 86(3) of the Treaty establishing the European Community (TEC) bestows a supervisory function upon the Commission, supported by special law-making powers:

3. The Commission shall ensure the application of the provisions of this Article and shall, where necessary, address appropriate directives or decisions to Member States.

Therefore, in addition to the more traditional forms of regulatory intervention by a competition authority against undertakings engaged in anti-competitive practices, the Commission could require Member States to fundamentally alter the terms of entry into a particular market.

In 1988, the Commission took the almost unprecedented step of issuing a Directive under Article 86(3), on competition in the market for telecommunications terminal equipment, followed by a further Directive on telecommunication services in 1990. The scope of such 'Commission' directives was viewed by a number of Member States as an illegal exercise of the Commission's competence. Both directives were challenged before the Court of Justice, but were decisively upheld as legitimate measures.[26] As such, European competition law grants the Commission legislative as well as regulatory competence in the telecommunications sector. By contrast, Internal Market measures, under Article 95, are adopted through the co-decision procedure, by the Council and Parliament.

While the majority of measures have taken the form of Directives, the Commission has utilized the full range of legal instruments available under the TEC: Regulations, Decisions, and Recommendations.[27] Regulations are obviously the most significant

---

[25] Formerly known as DG-XIII and DG-IV respectively.

[26] Case C-202/88: *France v Commission* [1992] 5 CMLR 552; and Case C-271/90 *Spain v Commission* [1992] ECR I-5833.

[27] TEC, Art 249.

instrument of harmonization, since they are 'directly applicable' in Member States. To date, only two Regulations have been adopted in the sector, addressing the issue of local loop unbundling[28] and mobile roaming.[29] The first measure was adopted in 2000, during the height of the 'dot.com' boom, when it was viewed as imperative that rapid progress be made in upgrading the fixed access network to exploit the potential of the Internet.[30] At that time there was significant public clamour for action, which seemed to galvanize the institutions to adopt a more interventionist regulatory approach.[31] Similarly, the second measure, 'roaming on public mobile telephone networks', was also a high profile issue among the general public. The stated justification for this choice of instrument was the 'urgency and persistence of the problem';[32] and followed on from a sectoral inquiry carried out by the Competition Commission in 2000,[33] and subsequent investigative raids carried out against nine European mobile operators based in the UK and Germany.[34] A proposal for a further regulation addressing the cost of SMS roaming was announced by the Commission in July 2008.[35]

The Commission has also made extensive use of 'soft law' measures, both formal Recommendations,[36] which have no binding legal force,[37] and informal guidelines and notices.[38] Such documents have been used both to further harmonization among Member States, providing a benchmark of good practice for national regulatory authorities, particularly in respect of the complex but critical areas of pricing and cost accounting; as well as providing assistance to undertakings, both market players and potential entrants, about how the Commission views particular matters, particularly in terms of competition analysis.

However, while 'soft law' had been used by the Commission to pursue its competition agenda, it is pertinent to note that the NRF does not expressly acknowledge the use of co- or self-regulation as an element of the regulatory regime. This is in contrast

---

[28] Regulation 2887/2000 of the European Parliament and Council of 18 December 2000 on unbundled access to the local loop (OJ L 336/4, 30 December 2000).

[29] Regulation 717/2007 of the European Parliament and of the Council of 27 June 2007 on roaming on public mobile telephone networks within the Community and amending Directive 2002/21/EC (OJ L 171/32, 29 June 2007).

[30] The measure was designed to bridge the gap until the NRF was adopted. In the 2006 Review, the Commission has proposed its repeal (Staff Document, n 23 above, at 8.3).

[31] Under the Commission's 2007 Reform Proposals, the Regulation would be repealed.

[32] COM(2006) 382 final, 12 July 2006, at p 8.

[33] See <http://ec.europa.eu/comm/competition/sectors/telecommunications/archive/inquiries/roaming/index.html>.

[34] Commission Press Release, 'Statement on inquiry regarding mobile roaming', MEMO/01/262, 11 July 2001.

[35] Commission Press Release, '"Texting without borders": Commission plans ending roaming rip-offs for text messages abroad', IP/08/1144, 15 July 2008.

[36] E.g. Commission Recommendation 2005/698/EC on accounting separation and cost accounting systems under the regulatory framework for electronic communications (OJ L 266/64, 11 October 2005).

[37] TEC, Art 249.

[38] E.g. Guidelines on the Application of EEC Competition Rules in the Telecommunications Sector (OJ C 233/2, 6 September 1991).

to the position adopted in some Member States, such as the UK,[39] and other non-EU regimes such as Australia,[40] where industry self-regulation is viewed as a natural complement to the move towards deregulation as competitive markets become established. The technical complexity of the telecommunications market has always meant that much of the input on certain issues, such as interconnection, primarily consisted of the convening and oversight of particular industry groups; intervening only in the event of impasse. As regulators reduce or withdraw from *ex ante* intervention in the market, as they are obliged to do under the NRF,[41] then increasing reliance is likely to be made upon industry to regulate itself. This failure to address the role of self-regulation runs counter to general EU policy reflected in an Interinstitutional Agreement on Better Law-making, which expressly acknowledges the potential role of self-regulation,[42] as do measures in related areas, specifically the provision of audiovisual media services.[43]

The Directorate-General (DG), Internal Market, has also been responsible for some initiatives relating directly or indirectly to the telecommunications sector. It is responsible for electronic commerce issues, including regulating the provision of 'information society services',[44] which will generally be offered by telecommunication services providers. The DG Internal Market was also responsible for data protection issues, which included sectoral measures imposing special obligations in the telecommunications sector; although the responsibility has subsequently been transferred to the DG for Freedom, Security and Justice.[45]

The Court of Justice has inevitably played a role in the development of European telecommunications law as the ultimate arbiter of European legal instruments. Proceedings have come before the court based on one of four legal grounds provided for under the TEC:

- *Infringement proceedings* (Article 226)—As part of its role to ensure implementation of Community measures, the Commission has brought proceedings against certain Member States for non-implementation or incorrect implementation of telecommunication measures.[46]

---

[39] I.e. The Communications Act 2004, s 6(2), requires Ofcom to have regard to whether policy could be achieved through 'effective self-regulation', which is further defined as s 6(3).

[40] I.e. Telecommunications Act 1997, s 4, states that 'that telecommunications be regulated in a manner that . . . promotes the greatest practicable use of industry self-regulation'.

[41] See Framework Directive, at Art 16(3).

[42] OJ C 321/1, 31 December 2003, at paras 22–23.

[43] See n 14 above at Art X.

[44] Directive 98/48/EC amending Directive 98/34/EC laying down a procedure for the provision of information in the field of technical standards and regulations (OJ L 217/18, 5.8.1998), at Art 1(2)(a): 'any service normally provided for remuneration, at a distance, by electronic means and at the individual request of a recipient of services'.

[45] See further Chapter 13.

[46] E.g. Case C-411/02, ECJ, 16 March 2004 (Austria); Case C-500/01, OJ C 47/6, 21 February 2004 (Spain); Case C-97/01, OJ C 184/4, 2 August 2003 (Luxembourg); Case C-221/1, OJ C 274/14, 9 November

- *Judicial review proceedings* (Article 230)—Member States have challenged the Commission's right to legislate on particular matters; as discussed above in respect of Article 86(3) measures.

- *Annulment proceedings* (Article 230)—Persons have a right of appeal to the Court of Justice where they have been affected by a decision, such as a refusal to permit a merger;[47] against the fees payable for the granting of a GSM licence,[48] and against having been found to have infringed EU competition provisions.[49]

- *Preliminary rulings* (Article 234)—The court has been required to consider questions of interpretation in respect of telecommunications measures referred to it by national courts,[50] often in the form of challenges made against decisions taken by a national regulatory authority.[51]

Finally, it should be noted that the WTO agreements addressing the telecommunications sector, such as the Annex of Telecommunications and the Reference Paper[52] comprise a potential source of EU law in terms of interpretation and application, if not a basis for initiating proceedings before the Court of Justice.[53]

5.4 LIBERALIZATION OF THE EU TELECOMMUNICATIONS MARKET

As noted above, the basis for the liberalization of Member State markets was the application of European competition law. The first indication of the potential impact of these rules arose in a Commission decision against the UK incumbent, British Telecommunications (BT), for an 'abuse of dominant position' under Article 82 of the TEC. The decision concerned a 'scheme' adopted by BT prohibiting private message-forwarding agencies in the UK from relaying telex messages received from and intended for relay to another country.[54] The Commission's decision was appealed by

---

2002 (Belgium); Case C-146/00, OJ C 84/23, OJ 6 April 2002 (France); Case C-396/99 [2001] ECR I-7577 (Greece); Case C-429/99, OJ C 369/3, 22 December 2001 (Portugal).

[47] E.g. Case T-310/00, *MCI Inc v Commission and France*, [2004] 5 CMLR 26, against the Commission's decision to prohibit the merger of *MCI WorldCom/Sprint*.

[48] *max.mobil Telekommunikation Service GmbH v Commission* [2002] 4 CMLR 32.

[49] E.g. *France Telecom SA v Commission* [2007] 4 CMLR, and *Deutsche Telekom AG v Commission*, CFI Judgment, 10 April 2008.

[50] E.g. Case C-18/88 *RTT v GB-Inno-BM SA* [1991] ECR I-5941; Case C-79/00 *Telefónica de España SA v Administración General del Estado* [2002] 4 CMLR22 and Case C-369/04, *Hutchison 3G UK Ltd & ors v Commissioners of Customs and Excise*, 26 June 2007 re: payment of VAT on spectrum auction transactions.

[51] E.g. Cases C-152/07 and C-154/07, *Arcor AG & Co. KG and others v Bundesrepublik Deutschland*, 17 July 2008.

[52] See n 11 above.

[53] See further Chapter 15.4.4.

[54] Decision 82/861 (OJ L 360/36, 21 December 1982).

the Italian government to the Court of Justice, whilst the British government intervened in support of the Commission.[55]

One issue for the court to decide was whether BT, as a public body, was subject
to the competition rules of the Treaty of Rome. The court found that despite its public sector status, BT was operating as an 'undertaking' for the purposes of Article 82.
It noted that any regulatory powers that had been given to BT were strictly limited
and, therefore, the particular scheme in question 'must be regarded as forming an
integral part of BT's activities as an undertaking' (paragraph 20). In a subsequent
decision, the court confirmed that Article 82 was applicable to 'undertakings' holding a dominant position even where that position arose through law rather than the
activities of the undertaking itself.[56]

The Italian government also argued that BT was exempt from the competition
rules by virtue of being entrusted with the provision of services of 'general economic
interest', under Article 86(2), which could be threatened by the loss of revenue
resulting from the provision of private message-forwarding services. The court held
that it was for the Commission, under Article 86(3), to ensure the application of this
provision and there was no evidence that such activities would be detrimental to the
tasks assigned to BT (paragraphs 28–33). The court also noted that BT's statutory
monopoly only extended to the provision and operation of telecommunication networks, not the supply of services over such networks (paragraph 22). The *British
Telecom* case was a landmark decision in the development of EU policy in the telecommunications sector and led to further investigations by the competition authorities
into the activities of Europe's incumbent operators.

The Commission has applied European competition law to the activities of telecommunications operators through behavioural and structural controls. The former have
been imposed both in *ex ante* legislative instruments, as well as *ex post* decisions
imposing behavioural undertakings as conditions for the approval of certain commercial agreements. Structural controls have been imposed primarily through *ex post*
competition investigations and decisions relating to agreements, joint ventures,
merger activities, and even State aid[57] in every aspect of the sector. Such regulatory
intervention has extended to alliances and mergers between national incumbents;[58]
in the mobile sector;[59] concerning Internet infrastructure;[60] and with providers of

---

[55] Case 41/83 *Re British Telecommunications: Italy v Commission* [1985] 2 CMLR 368.
[56] Case 311/84 *Centre Belge d'Etudes de Marché-Télé-Marketing v Compagnie Luxembourgeoise de
Telediffusion SA and Information Publicite Benelux SA* [1986] 2 CMLR 558.
[57] E.g. *France Télécom* [2003] OJ C 57/5, 12 March 2003. On 20 July 2004, the Commission ordered
France Télécom to repay up to £1.1bn in back taxes, estimated savings that the firm had made from the
granting of exemptions from local taxes that constituted a form of state aid. *Mobilcom* [2003] OJ C 80/5,
3 April 2003 and [2003] OJ C 210/4, 5 September 2003.
[58] E.g. *France Telecom and Deutsche Telekom* (Case No IV/35.337—Atlas; OJ L 239/23, 19 September
1996); *Telia and Telenor* (Case IV/M.1439; OJ L 40/1, 9 February 2001).
[59] E.g. *Vodafone Airtouch and Mannesmann* (Case No Comp/M.1795; OJ C 141/19, 19 May 2000).
[60] E.g. *WorldCom and MCI* (Case IV/M.1069; OJ L 116/1, 4 May 1999).

content services.[61] In all these cases, the Commission has been concerned to protect the interests of European consumers and industry against the inevitable commercial pressures created by the developing global economy. The Commission, as competition authority, has also fined undertakings for abusive practices in the market, including Deutsche Telekom AG,[62] Wanadoo Interactive,[63] and Telefónica SA.[64]

During the first two phases of telecommunications liberalization in Europe, the process has been underpinned by two key legal concepts, that of 'special or exclusive rights' and 'essential requirements'.

5.4.1 'Special or exclusive rights'

As discussed above, Article 86(1) of the EC Treaty concerns 'public undertakings or undertakings to which Member States grant special or exclusive rights'. The primary mechanism by which the Commission decided to liberalize national telecommunications markets, under the Equipment and Services Directives, was by requiring Member States to withdraw the grant of any 'special or exclusive rights' in respect of such activities. Rather than simply addressing the *exercise* of such rights, the Commission went further and challenged the continued *existence* of such rights. Their existence was seen as distorting competition within the markets at Community level; whilst their abolition would not 'obstruct, in law or in fact, the performance' of any service of 'general economic interest' (Article 86(2)), such as universal service, which had been entrusted to undertakings granted such 'special or exclusive rights'.

Member States challenged both directives before the European Court of Justice.[65] The court found in the Commission's favour in respect of the withdrawal of exclusive rights, but upheld the claims of the Member States in respect of the limitation imposed on the granting of special rights, on the grounds that the directives' failed to specify what 'special rights' were or the reasons that such rights were contrary to the provisions of the Treaty. Such provisions were therefore void. As a consequence, the Commission amended the Services Directive to clarify the distinction between 'exclusive rights' and 'special rights',[66] which the Court of Justice subsequently endorsed.[67] 'Special rights' would include powers of compulsory purchase

---

[61] E.g. *AOL and Time Warner* (Case No COMP/M.1845; OJ L 268/28, 9.10.2001).

[62] OJ L 263/9, 14 October 2003, imposing a fine of €12.6m.

[63] Decision of 16 July 2004, imposing a fine of €10.35m.

[64] Decision of 4 July 2007, imposing a fine of €151m.

[65] See n 26 above.

[66] See Art 2(1) of Commission Directive (94/46/EC) of 13 October 1994 amending Directive 88/301/EEC and Directive 90/388/EEC in particular with regard to satellite communications, OJ L 268/15, 19 October 1994.

[67] Case C-302/94, *R v Secretary of State for Trade and Industry, ex parte British Telecommunications plc*, ECR I-6417, at para 34.

and derogations from laws on town and country planning[68] that are granted to undertakings 'otherwise than according to objective, proportional, and non-discriminatory criteria'.[69] During the liberalization process, the procurement practices of telecommunication operators operating under special or exclusive rights were also subjected to regulatory controls.[70]

Despite full market liberalization, Article 86(3) may continue to be relevant to the European telecommunications market. First, in a number of Member States the incumbent operator continues to be a 'public undertaking', through full or partial State ownership, and as such could be subject to State measures which infringe EU competition law. Second, where an operator has been granted 'special or exclusive' rights in a different sector of activity, such as broadcasting or water supply, the exercise or existence of such rights might be perceived as distorting the competition in the telecommunications market.[71] As a consequence, *ex ante* controls may be imposed on such undertakings, to ensure structural separation between the activities.[72]

5.4.2 Essential requirements

A key element in the Commission's liberalization directives was reference to the concept of 'essential requirements'. The free movement of goods (i.e. telecommunications equipment) and the freedom to provide services was achieved by restricting the ability of a Member State to prohibit the supply of equipment and services except for 'non-economic reasons in the general public interest', otherwise referred to as the 'essential requirements'. Such reasons reflect the derogations expressly provided for in the Treaty, i.e. 'on grounds of public policy, public security or public health' (Article 46), and recognized in Court of Justice case law:

. . . Member States retain . . . the power to examine whether the said equipment is fit to be connected to the network in order to satisfy the imperative requirements regarding the protection of users as consumers of services and the protection of the public network and its proper functioning.[73]

---

[68] See n 66, at Recital 11.

[69] Commission Directive 2002/77/EC on competition in the markets for electronic communications networks and services (OJ L 249/21, 17 September 2002).

[70] I.e. Directive 93/38/EEC coordinating the procurement procedures of entities operating in the water, energy, transport and telecommunication sectors (OJ L 199/84, 9 August 93), as amended by Directive 98/4/EC, (OJ L 101/1, 1 April 1998).

[71] For the application of Art 86 to the broadcasting sector see Case C-260/89, *Elliniki Radiophonia Tileorassi* (1991) ECR I-2925.

[72] Framework Directive, Art 13. This represents an extension of an earlier Commission Directive 1999/64/EC amending Directive 90/388/EEC in order to ensure that telecommunications networks and cable TV networks owned by a single operator are separate entities (OJ L 175/39, 10 July 1999).

[73] Case C-18/88, *Régie des Télégraphes et des Téléphones v GB-Inno-BM SA* [1991] ECR I-5941.

The 'essential requirements' obviously differ between telecommunications equipment and services, and have been amended over time to reflect evolving public policy concerns and market conditions:

Telecommunications equipment[74]	Telecommunications services[75]
1. Health and safety of user and any other person	1. Security of network operations
2. Electromagnetic compatibility requirements	2. Maintenance of network integrity
3. Effective use of radio frequency spectrum	3. Interoperability of services*
4. Interworking of apparatus via the network	4. Data protection*
5. Protection of the network from harm or misuse of network resources	5. Effective use of radio frequency spectrum*
6. Features protecting the privacy of subscribers and users†	6. Avoidance of harmful interference*
7. Features ensuring avoidance of fraud†	7. Protection of the environment*
8. Features ensuring access to emergency services†	8. Town and country planning objectives*
9. Features facilitating use by users with disabilities†	
†where proposed by the Commission with the approval of a committee of Member State representatives	*conditions imposed under such reasons are only permissible 'in justified cases'

Over the years public policy concerns broadened to encompass the protection of personal data and environmental issues, impacting on the building of network infrastructure, such as mobile transmitters and digging up streets to lay cable.

In the first stages of liberalization, much concern was directed towards the impact on the 'national' (i.e. incumbent) network of new operators connecting 'unregulated' telecommunications equipment and generating substantial volumes of additional traffic. The network, as a strategic component of Member State economies, was viewed as being vulnerable in a competitive environment. Over time such concerns for the 'national' network have generally proven to be greatly overstated.

Incumbent operators have, however, continued to use the terminology of the 'essential requirements' as grounds for imposing restrictive conditions on new entrants. In the UK, for example, BT used concerns about 'network security' as a justification for requiring separate co-location rooms for operators implementing ADSL at BT's local exchanges, which had an impact on operators' timescales and costs for the introduction of competing services. At times, new entrants have expressed concern that national regulatory authorities have not always scrutinized fully the evidence for some of these 'essential requirement' claims.[76]

---

[74] As defined at Art 3 of Directive 1999/5/EC on radio equipment and telecommunications terminal equipment and the mutual recognition of their conformity, OJ L 91/10, 7 April 1999.

[75] As defined by Art 1(1) of Directive 90/388 (as amended by Directive 96/19/EC) and Art 2(6) of Directive 90/387.

[76] See Commission Communication, 'Sixth Report on the Implementation of the Telecommunications Regulatory Package', COM(2000) 814, 7 December 2000, at p 16 *et seq*.

While the concept of 'essential requirements' continues to be utilized in respect of telecommunications equipment, its use as a distinct regulatory concept in respect of telecommunication networks and services has disappeared; although some of the elements that comprise the concept continue to be specific EU regulatory objectives under the Framework Directive,[77] and all of the elements comprise conditions that may be attached to an authorization granted by a Member State under the Authorisation Directive.[78]

5.4.3 Telecommunications equipment

Telecommunications equipment encompasses a vast array of hardware, software, and related devices used both within the network, for the conveyance of signals, and at the edges of the network, to enable end-users to initiate and receive communications. As noted above, 'telecommunications terminal equipment', that used by end-users, falls outside the NRF and is subject to a different legal regime. Once distinct and stand-alone, most obviously in the form of the traditional telephone, such 'consumer' equipment has merged with the information technology (IT) industry, which has historically always been a highly competitive market sector in stark contrast with telecommunications. As such, liberalization of the market for terminal equipment, and indeed of all forms of telecommunications equipment, has occurred very rapidly and successfully within Europe, with the emergence of strong global players, such as Nokia and Ericsson, and with relatively light regulatory intervention.

At the outset, liberalization of the telecommunications terminal equipment market primarily focused on the application of the principle of the free movement of goods, under Articles 28 to 31 of the TEC. In 1985, for example, the Commission intervened on the basis of Article 37 against Germany in respect of a proposed regulation extending the Bundespost's monopoly over telecommunications equipment to cordless telephones.[79] As with other product areas, mutual recognition was the initial vehicle for the achievement of a 'Single Market'. The first legislative initiative was a Council Directive in 1986 that called upon Member States to implement mutual recognition in respect of conformity tests carried out on mass-produced terminal equipment.[80]

A more comprehensive, and controversial, measure was taken by the Commission in 1988 when it adopted a directive, under Article 86(3), calling upon Member States

---

[77] E.g. Art 8(3)(b) 'interoperability of services', Art (4)(f) 'ensuring that the integrity and security of public communications networks are maintained'.

[78] See Annex at A. 'Conditions which may be attached to a general authorisation' and B. 'Conditions that may be attached to rights of use for radio frequencies'. See further Chapter 7.

[79] *Re Cordless telephones in Germany* [1985] 2 CMLR 397. See also Case C-18/88, *Régie des télégraphes et des téléphones v GB-Inno-BM SA* (1991) ECR I-5941, where it was held that Art 30 of the Treaty precludes an undertaking from having the power to approve telephone equipment for connection to the public network without being susceptible to legal challenge.

[80] Council Directive of 24 July 1986 on the initial stage of the mutual recognition of type approval for telecommunications terminal equipment (86/361/EEC; OJ L217/21, 5 August 1986).

to withdraw any 'special or exclusive' rights that may have been granted to undertakings relating to telecommunications terminal equipment.[81] The Directive stated that the only grounds upon which a Member State could restrict or regulate economic operators from importing, marketing, operating, and maintaining terminal equipment was where such equipment could either be shown to have failed to satisfy the 'essential requirements' or the economic operator failed to possess the necessary technical qualifications in relation to the equipment.[82]

The mutual recognition process, first established under the 1986 Directive and extended under a series of measures addressing terminal equipment,[83] comprised a number of interlinked principles and procedures:

- the notification and publication by Member States of technical specifications relating to the terminal equipment, commonly referred to as 'type approval specifications';

- equipment meeting relevant harmonized standards (published in the Official Journal) is presumed to be compliant with the 'essential requirements';

- the establishment of independent 'notified bodies' (designated by Member States[84]) to carry out an *a priori* examination and assessment of conformity of a specimen of the proposed equipment with the 'essential requirements', and the issuance of an 'EC type-examination certificate' in relation to the particular piece of equipment;

- declaration obligations imposed upon manufacturers that (a) all equipment produced is in compliance with the certificate, and (b) that such equipment was produced under a quality assured system; and

- the adoption of a 'CE conformity marking' scheme to enable identification of terminal equipment that is suitable for connection to the public telecommunications network:

[81] Commission Directive of 16 May 1988 on competition in the markets of telecommunications terminal equipment (88/301/EEC; OJ L131/73, 27 May 1988), Art 2.

[82] Ibid, Art 3.

[83] E.g. Council Directive 91/263/EC on the approximation of the laws of the Member States concerning telecommunications terminal equipment including the mutual recognition of their conformity, OJ L128/1, 23 May 1991 (repealing 86/361); and Directive 98/13/EC relating to telecommunications terminal and satellite earth station equipment, including mutual conformity recognition, OJ L 74, 12 March 1998 (repealing 91/263).

[84] In the UK, there are 13 such bodies, such as the British Approvals Board for Telecommunications. For a complete listing, see <http://ec.europa.eu/enterprise/newapproach/legislation/nb/en99-5-ec.pdf>.

These procedures have been further simplified under a consolidated regime which came into force in April 2000, intended to better reflect the 'pace of technology and market development' by making it easier for manufacturers to place products on the market.[85] This is achieved primarily by removing the requirement for equipment to be tested by 'notified bodies' prior to its manufacture. Instead, greater emphasis is placed upon manufacturers documenting their compliance with 'Conformity Assessment Procedures' relevant to the particular type of equipment.

In June 2008, the Commission codified its rules for competition in the markets for telecommunications terminal equipment, replacing the 1988 Directive and the subsequent measures amending it.[86] In addition, under the Commission's 2007 Reform Proposals 'consumer premises terminal equipment' would be brought within the NRF, specifically in respect of measures designed to improve access to and use of such equipment by disabled users, such text relay services.[87]

5.4.4 Telecommunications services

Historically, the Commission's approach to liberalization has been focused on the competitive provision of services, rather than network infrastructure over which such services are carried. The Commission's 1990 'Services Directive' was limited only to liberalization of the provision of non-voice telephony services, and did not include 'telex, mobile radiotelephony, paging and satellites services'.[88] However, the 'Services Directive' addressed for the first time the need for objective, transparent, and non-discriminatory licensing and declaration procedures for operators wishing to enter the market.

In order to be able to enter the market for the provision of telecommunications services, new entrants need to have access to leased transmission circuits from the providers of network infrastructure, traditionally the incumbent operator. The 'Services Directive' therefore required Member States to ensure that requests for leased circuits are met within a reasonable period of time and any increase in charges are justified, partly through an obligation on Member States to inform the Commission of the factors responsible for any increase (Article 4). The use of any leased circuits could not be restricted, although prohibitions on offering simple resale to the public were permissible until 31 December 1992, in order to protect the incumbent's rights in respect of the provision of voice telephony.

---

[85] Directive 1999/5/EC, n 74 above, at Recital 7.

[86] Commission Directive 2008/63/EC of 20 June 2008 on competition in the markets in telecommunications terminal equipment (OJ L 162/20, 21 June 2008).

[87] Proposal for a Directive amending Directive 2002/22/EC on universal service and users' rights relating to electronic communications networks, Directive 2002/58/EC concerning the processing of personal data and the protection of privacy in the electronic communications sector and Regulation (EC) No 2006/2004 on consumer protection cooperation, SEC(2007) 1472.

[88] Commission Directive 90/388/EEC on competition in the markets for telecommunications services; OJ L192/10, 24 July 1990.

Following the Court of Justice decision to uphold the Commission's right to liberalize the services market, the Commission adopted a series of directives amending the 'Services Directive' to encompass a broader range of telecommunications services:

- satellite services;[89]
- use of cable TV networks;[90]
- mobile and personal communications;[91] and
- 'Full Competition Directive'.[92]

The Full Competition directive required Member States to withdraw all 'exclusive rights for the provision of telecommunications services, including the establishment and the provision of telecommunications networks required for the provision of such services' (Article 1(2)). This removed the 'reserved service' exception that had been granted over the provision of voice telephony services because it was viewed as an integral component in the provision of network infrastructure (Recital 4).

The Full Competition Directive committed the Member States to the 1 January 1998 deadline. This timetable corresponded with the international liberalization process achieved under the Fourth Protocol of the WTO's General Agreement on Trade in Services, to which the Community and Member States were party.[93] Transitional periods were granted to countries considered as having less developed or very small networks: Ireland, Spain, Portugal, Greece, and Luxembourg. Greece was the final EU Member State to fully liberalize its market by 1 January 2001. Full market liberalization was required of the ten States that joined the Union in May 2004[94] and the further two in 2007.[95]

With the implementation of the Full Competition Directive by Greece, the market for telecommunication services was fully liberalized at a regulatory level. The Commission adopted a consolidating directive at part of the NRF, repealing all the previous Commission directives,[96] as it has recently also done in respect of

---

[89] Commission Directive 94/46/EC amending Directive 88/301/EEC and Directive 90/388/EEC in particular with regard to satellite communications; OJ L268/15, 19 October 1994.

[90] Commission Directive 95/51/EC amending Commission Directive 90/388/EEC with regard to the abolition of the restrictions on the use of cable television networks for the provision of already liberalized telecommunication services; OJ L256/49, 26 October 1995.

[91] Commission Directive 96/2/EC amending Directive 90/388/EEC with regard to mobile and personal communications; OJ L20/59, 21 January 1996.

[92] Commission Directive 96/19/EC amending Commission Directive 90/388/EEC regarding the implementation of full competition in telecommunications services; OJ L74/13, 22 March 1996.

[93] Council Decision (97/838/EC) of 28 November 1997 concerning the conclusion on behalf of the European Community, as regards matters within its competence, of the results of the WTO negotiations on basic telecommunications services; OJ L 347/45, 18 December 1997.

[94] I.e. Cyprus, Czech Republic, Estonia, Hungary, Latvia, Lithuania, Malta, Poland, Slovakia, Slovenia.

[95] I.e. Romania and Bulgaria.

[96] See n 86 above.

telecommunications terminal equipment.[97] Even with the progressive enlargement of the EU, we are unlikely to see further Commission directives in the area, since the liberalization framework is clearly set out for future Member States. However, Article 86 directives may continue to have a role to play in the liberalization of the European broadcasting market, which through convergence may impact on the telecommunications market.

5.5 HARMONIZATION OF THE EU TELECOMMUNICATIONS MARKET

While liberalization initiatives aimed at opening up national markets to competition, harmonization measures were required to address competition across markets in the EU. Indeed, the first specific EU measure in the telecommunications sector, in 1984, was a Council Recommendation calling for harmonization in respect of technical standards.[98] The Commission has pursued harmonization across a broad range of issues, from technical standards to the applicable tax regime.

The need for common standards is obviously a critical ingredient in the development of an Internal Market in telecommunications. At an institutional level, the Commission encouraged the establishment of the European Telecommunications Standards Institute (ETSI), by the Conference on Postal and Telecommunications Administrations (CEPT),[99] in 1988.[100] The introduction of Europe-wide numbers, within a so-called 'European Telephony Numbering Space' (ETNS), was viewed as an important harmonization measure towards the achievement of a Single Internal Market.[101] In 1991, a common emergency call number (112) was adopted; and in the following year a common international access code (00).[102] In 2007, the number range beginning with '116' was reserved for the provision of services of social value, such as hotlines and helplines.[103] It was envisaged that further Europe-wide numbers would enable companies to utilize non-geographic European codes for the provision

---

[97] See section 5.4.3 above.
[98] See n 1 above.
[99] CEPT is a body comprising the postal and telecommunications 'administrations' of European Countries, not limited to the EU: <http://www.cept.org>.
[100] E.g. Council Resolution of 27 April 1989 on standardization in the field of information technology and telecommunications, OJ C 117/1, 11 May 1989.
[101] Council Resolution of 19 November 1992 on the promotion of Europe-wide cooperation on numbering of telecommunications services, OJ C 318/2, 4 December 1992.
[102] Council Decision (91/396/EEC) of 29 July 1991 on the introduction of a single European emergency call number, OJ L 217/31, 6 August 1991; Council Decision (92/264/EEC) of 11 May 1992 on the introduction of a standard international telephone access code in the Community, OJ L 137/21, 20 May 1992. Both measures have been repealed under Framework Directive, at Art 26, and are consolidated under the Universal Services Directive at Art 26 and Art 27 respectively.
[103] Commission Decision 2007/116/EC on reserving the national numbering range beginning with '116' for harmonized numbers for harmonized services of social value (OJ L 49/30, 17 February 2007); subsequently amended by Decision 2007/698/EC (OJ L 284/31, 30 October 2007).

of pan-European services, such as the provision of mobile services. Such a scheme has failed to materialize, however, and the Commission has recently proposed its removal from the NRF.[104]

In the mobile sector, the development of European-wide services has been pursued through the adoption of a series of legislative measures reserving common frequency bands within Member States, most importantly in respect of second generation GSM digital mobile services and third generation Universal Mobile Telecommunication Systems (UMTS).[105] The former can be seen as a particular success story for the EU, facilitating the take-up of GSM as the de facto worldwide standard and placing European telecommunications companies at the forefront of the global mobile industry.

In parallel with the Commission's 'Services Directive' in 1990, the Council adopted a directive, under Article 95 of the TEC, establishing the concept of 'Open Network Provision' (ONP). The so-called 'ONP framework' programme was conceived to provide the regulatory basis for imposing harmonization:

This Directive concerns the harmonisation of conditions for open and efficient access to and use of public telecommunications networks and, where applicable, public telecommunications services.[106]

Reflecting the liberalization process, the scope of the ONP programme was initially limited to issues of access to the network infrastructure and 'reserved services' provided by the incumbent operator. As such, the harmonization framework envisaged the drafting of proposals on ONP conditions across a range of issues of concern to providers of non-reserved services:

• the development of technical interfaces between open network termination points;

• the identification of additional service features;

• harmonized supply and usage conditions, such as maximum periods for provision and conditions on the resale of capacity; and

• tariff principles, such as the unbundling of individual service elements.

Such conditions were subject to basic principles concerning the use of objective criteria, transparency, and non-discrimination; whilst any restrictions placed on access would be limited to reasons based on the 'essential requirements'. Subsequent ONP measures were adopted in a number of areas, including the provision of

---

[104] Staff Document, n 23 above, at 8.2.

[105] I.e. Council Directive 87/372/EEC on the frequency bands to be reserved for the co-ordinated introduction of public pan-European cellular digital land-based mobile communications in the Community (OJ L 196/85, 17 July 1987); and Council Decision 128/1999/EC of the European Parliament and of the Council on the coordinated introduction of a third-generation mobile and wireless communications system (UMTS) in the Community (OJ L 17/1, 22 January 1999).

[106] Directive 90/387/EEC on the establishment of the internal market for telecommunications services through the implementation of open network provision; OJ L192/1, 24 July 1990.

leased lines; packet-switched data services;[107] Integrated Services Digital Networks (ISDN);[108] voice telephony, and interconnection[109] and universal service.

In 1995, the ONP framework was applied to voice telephony.[110] Under this measure, the national regulatory authorities were given a broad range of obligations to ensure that the provision of 'fixed' voice telephony to users, which included residential customers as well as competing service providers, was under harmonized conditions. Such conditions included the connection of terminal equipment; targets for supply time and quality of service; service termination; user contracts and the provision of advanced facilities, such as call line identification (CLI). Further market liberalization led to the replacement of the Voice Telephony Directive in 1998, extending certain provisions to mobile voice telephony.[111]

Harmonization between Member State markets has inevitably involved greater complexity and detailed regulatory intervention than that required for the liberalization of national markets. Such detail arises both from the scope of the issues addressed, as well as the imposition of asymmetric obligations on market participants. One feature of the harmonization process is the key role played by the national regulatory authorities in implementing and complying with the principles contained in the harmonization measures. Such reliance on national regulators generated, in some cases, new areas of divergence between market conditions and practices in the Member States.[112] This is reflected, in part, by the fact that the Commission pursued considerably more infringement proceedings against Member States, under Article 226 of the Treaty, in respect of the harmonization directives, as compared with the liberalization directives.

5.6 'SIGNIFICANT MARKET POWER'

With the extension of the liberalization process to infrastructure as well as services, the Leased Lines Directive was amended to reflect the new environment, introducing

---

[107] Recommendation 92/382/EEC on the harmonized provision of a minimum set of packet-switched data services (PSDS) in accordance with open network provision (ONP) principles; OJ L200/1, 18.7.1992.

[108] Recommendation 92/383/EEC on the provision of harmonized integrated services digital network (ISDN) access arrangements and a minimum set of ISDN offerings in accordance with open network provision (ONP) principles; OJ L/200/10, 18 July 1992.

[109] Directive 97/33/EC of the European Parliament and of the Council on Interconnection in Telecommunications with regard to ensuring Universal Service and Interoperability through Application of the Principles of Open Network Provision; OJ L 199/32, 26 July 1997.

[110] Directive 95/62/EC on the application of open network provision to voice telephony (OJ L321/6, 30 December 1995).

[111] Directive 98/10/EC on the application of ONP to voice telephony and on universal service for telecommunications in a competitive environment; OJ L 101/24, 1 April 1998.

[112] See generally the Sixth Implementation Report, n 76 above.

ex ante regulations for certain telecommunications operators.[113] In particular, Member States were required to designate operators within their national markets who were required to provide the 'minimum set', usually comprising 'organizations with significant market power' (SMP) defined in the following terms:

... an organisation shall be presumed to have significant market power when its share of the relevant leased-lines market in a Member State is 25% or more. The relevant leased-lines market shall be assessed on the basis of the type(s) of leased line offered in a particular geographical area. The geographical area may cover the whole or part of the territory of a Member State.[114]

National regulatory authorities (NRAs) were required to notify the Commission that organizations had been so designated.[115] They also had the discretion to determine that an organization on either side of the 25 per cent figure fell outside the presumption, based on factors such as an operator's access to financial resources and its experience in the market. The concept of the so-called 'SMP operator' was subsequently applied in the ONP measures on interconnection and voice telephony, imposing *ex ante* obligations on certain participants in each national market, generally the incumbent.

The SMP concept was recognition that liberalization and harmonization of the telecommunications sector did not simply mean the removal of barriers to market entry and the establishment of a level playing field between participants. The legacy of national incumbents and the particular nature of the sector as a 'network' industry required a more interventionist stance, tipping the playing field by imposing asymmetric regulatory obligations upon incumbents to positively assist new entrants.

The 25 per cent market share trigger represented a lower threshold than the traditional competition law concept of 'dominance', which has generally been considered to exist somewhere over 40 per cent of market share; although market share is not usually the sole factor in determining market power for competition purposes. The potential discrepancy between the 25 per cent SMP regulatory trigger and the concept of 'dominance was the subject of much criticism and, indeed, the German government refused to use the 25 per cent trigger for the application of the SMP obligations arguing:

... if the definitions used in the Directive resulted in a treatment of companies concerned, that is not in line with EC competition law, the question arises whether such a sector-specific special provision is legally admissible.[116]

---

[113] Directive 97/51/EC of the European Parliament and of the Council of 6 October 1997 amending Council Directives 90/387/EEC and 92/44/EEC for the purpose of adaptation to a competitive environment in Telecommunications (OJ L 295/23, 29 October 1997).

[114] Ibid, at Art 2(3).

[115] Ibid, at Art 11(1a).

[116] Letter from Dr Sidel, German Economic Ministry to Mr Cockborne, DG-XIII, dated 13 July 1998; quoted in Tarrant, A, 'Significant market power and dominance in the regulation of telecommunications markets', *European Competition Law Review*, vol 21, no 7, 2000, pp 320–325.

Justifying the lower threshold, the Commission argued that traditional competition law principles are not adequate to deal with some of the unique features of the telecommunications market, whilst the trigger also reduced the burden upon national regulatory authorities to assess 'dominance' on a case-by-case basis.[117]

However, as a result of the Commission's desire to deregulate the sector, as well as addressing legitimacy concerns and the EU's commitments under the WTO Reference Paper, the NRF redefines the concept of an operator with 'significant market power' in the following terms, based on Court of Justice jurisprudence:[118]

An undertaking shall be deemed to have significant market power if, either individually or jointly with others, it enjoys a position equivalent to dominance, that is to say a position of economic strength affording it the power to behave to an appreciable extent independently of competitors, customers and ultimately consumers.[119]

In addition, recognizing the peculiar nature of 'network' industries and the oligopolistic structure of various telecommunications markets, such as mobile, express reference was made to the possibility of two or more undertakings being in a 'joint dominant position in a market', a complex and developing area of EU competition law.[120]

As under the previous regime, NRAs are required to designate operators as having 'significant market power' (Article 14(1)). However, to address the concern about divergent approaches being taken by Member States, the designation procedure is subject to certain harmonization provisions at each stage of the process: market definition, market analysis, and remedies (i.e. imposition of *ex ante* obligations).

First, the Commission issued a Recommendation on the 18 product and service markets, present at either a retail or wholesale level, in which it considered '*ex ante* regulation may be warranted', and to which NRAs are required to give 'utmost account' when defining their national markets (Article 15(3)).[121] This was subsequently revised in a further recommendation in December 2007, reducing the number of markets to seven,[122] which is indicative of the progress that has been achieved towards a fully liberalized sector.

Second, when NRAs analyse the defined markets to establish whether any participant has SMP, they should also give 'utmost account' to guidelines concerning

[117] Ibid.
[118] E.g. Case 322/81 *Michelin BV v Commission* [1983] ECR 3461, para 6.
[119] Framework Directive, Art 14(2).
[120] E.g. Commission decision: Case IV/M. 1524 *Airtours/First Choice* [2000] OJ L 93/01 and Court of First Instance decision: Case T-342/99 *Airtours v Commission*, [2002] 5 CMLR 7.
[121] Commission Recommendation (2003/311/EC) of 11 February 2003 on relevant product and service markets within the electronic communications sector susceptible to *ex ante* regulation in accordance with Directive 2002/21/EC (OJ L 114/45, 8 May 2003).
[122] Commission Recommendation (2007/879/EC) of 17 December 2007 (OJ L 344/65, 28 December 2007).

the analysis procedure issued by the Commission (Article 16).[123] The intention behind the 'utmost account' provisions is clear; however the enforceability of such provisions is less certain. When a NRA carries out a market definition, it must do so 'in accordance with the principles of competition law'. The Recommendation sets out three criteria which it considers central to such an analysis:

• the presence of high and non-transitory entry barriers;
• the dynamic state of competitiveness behind entry barriers; and
• the sufficiency of competition in the absence of *ex ante* regulation.[124]

Where the criteria are not shown to be present, the application of *ex ante* regulation would be considered inappropriate. Following such an analysis, were a NRA to identify a particular market and then to vary that definition to align with a market defined in the Recommendation, it is arguable that the validity of the NRA's final determination could be judicially reviewed.[125]

Once a designation has been made, the NRA must then determine whether to maintain, amend, or withdraw existing obligations (Article 16(2)) and/or, which obligations to impose in respect of access and interconnection (i.e. Access Directive, Articles 9 to 13) or universal service (i.e. Universal Services Directive, Articles 17 to 19), as determined appropriate. Where an SMP finding has been made, a NRA is required to impose at least one of the *ex ante* remedies (Article 16(4)). To ensure harmonization at this stage of the process, the European Regulators Group, in conjunction with the Commission, has adopted a Common Position 'on the approach to appropriate remedies in the new regulatory framework'.[126] This elaborates a typology of 27 potential competition problems based around four market scenarios:

• *Vertical leveraging:* This occurs where a dominant firm seeks to extend its market power from a wholesale market to a vertically related wholesale or retail market.
• *Horizontal leveraging:* This applies where an SMP operator seeks to extend its market power to another market that is not vertically related.
• *Single market dominance:* The problems which may occur within the context of a single market are entry deterrence, exploitative pricing practices, and productive inefficiencies.
• *Termination (Two-way access):* This relates to the link between price setting in termination markets and in the related retail markets that may be competitive.

---

[123] Commission guidelines on market analysis and the assessment of significant market power under the Community regulatory framework for electronic communications networks and services (OJ C 165/6, 11 July 2002).
[124] Ibid, at Recital 9.
[125] Under the Communications Act 2003, Ofcom is only required to 'take due account' of the Commission's Recommendation and Guidelines (s 79(2)).
[126] ERG (03) 30rev1 (April 2004).

Once the competition problem(s) has been identified, the NRAs should follow certain principles in determining the appropriate remedy. First, the decision must be adequately reasoned, with full consideration of alternatives and representing the least burdensome option. Second, where infrastructure competition is not feasible, sufficient access to wholesale inputs should be ensured. Third, where infrastructure replication is feasible, the remedies should assist transition to such a situation, for example through investment incentives. The final principle is that remedies should be 'incentive compatible', in terms of compliance by the designated SMP operator rather than evasion.

The fourth harmonization element in the Framework Directive concerns the notification regime, whereby the NRA is required to notify the Commission and other Member State NRAs about a decision, to enable comments to be made (Article 7(3)), which if received, the NRA is obliged to take 'utmost account' of (Article 7(5)). The legal nature of such comments have twice been subject to challenge by operators dissatisfied with the impact that such comments, specifically from the Commission, have had on subsequent NRA decisions. In both cases, the Court of First Instance ruled that such comments did not have a binding effect and, therefore, could not be challenged under Article 230 of the TEC.[127]

More significantly, the Commission also has the power to overturn a remedy decision of a NRA (Article 7(4)). Relevant decisions are market definitions that differ from those contained in the Recommendation and decisions whether or not to designate an operator as having SMP. Such decisions must also be considered to affect trade between Member States by creating a barrier to market entry. The Commission has the right to require Member States to suspend adoption of the measure (Article 7(4)), pending modification, or even withdraw the measure (in accordance with the procedure at Article 22(2)). To date, the Commission has taken the decision to veto notifications made by the NRAs from Austria, Finland, Germany, and Poland.[128]

The Article 7 procedures have generated significant criticism and are one of the key areas for proposed reform following the first Commission review. Firstly, achieving greater harmonization has proved somewhat illusory, as a significant degree of variation between Member States exists due to specific features of national market structure. Second, the inherent case-by-case analysis required by NRAs has been carried out with widely differing levels of competence, reflecting in part experience and resource issues. In some cases it would appear that those NRAs with least experience and resource have most slavishly followed the Commission Recommendation on Markets; while at the other end of the spectrum, some NRAs, such as Ofcom, have elaborated a much more detailed market schematic than the Commission. Third, the notification procedures themselves have proved complex, burdensome,

---

[127] Case T-109/06 *Vodafone* (12 December 2008) and Case T-295-06 *Base NV v Commission* (22 February 2008).
[128] See Commission Communication 'on market reviews under the EU Regulatory Framework (2nd Report)', SEC(2007) 962, 11 July 2007.

and time-consuming both for the NRAs and the Commission, so the process is going to be further streamlined.[129]

5.7 REGULATORY AUTHORITIES

As discussed above, the Competition Directorate-General of the Commission has treaty-based authority to impose behavioural and structural controls on the activities of telecommunications operators, subject to the jurisdictional requirement that the anti-competitive practice 'may affect trade between Member States'.[130] Otherwise, such anti-competitive practices will have to be addressed by the competent authorities within a Member State, whether a specific telecommunications regulator, a general competition authority, or both.

The *ex ante* controls were transposed into national law by the Member States, often through secondary legislation. Prior to the introduction of the NRF, the Commission only exercised a monitoring role based on information supplied by the NRAs through notification and reporting obligations. The Commission's ability to intervene was significantly enhanced under the NRF, with the power to require Member States to withdraw measures in certain circumstances. However, key aspects of EU telecommunications policy continue to be dependent on being appropriately implemented by the NRAs.

One of the central features present in the Member States prior to liberalization of the telecommunications market was the fact that the regulatory institution responsible for regulating the market, often a Ministry of Communications, was usually also responsible for controlling the commercial activities of the incumbent operator. It was recognized that such merged functions would not be appropriate in a competitive market and that independent regulatory authorities for the sector would need to be established.

5.7.1 National regulatory authorities

Under the 'Equipment Directive' the Commission required that the requirements imposed by the directive be 'entrusted to a body independent of public or private undertakings offering goods and/or services in the telecommunications sector'.[131] The interpretation of this provision has been the subject of a significant amount of Court of Justice case law, primarily because those bodies entrusted with the

---

[129] Staff Document, n 23 above, at 4.

[130] Since 1 May 2004, jurisdiction is shared with Member States: Council Regulation No 1/2003 on the implementation of the rules on competition laid down in Articles 81 and 82 of the Treaty (OJ L1/1, 4 January 2003).

[131] Commission Directive (88/301/EEC) of 16 May 1988 on competition in the markets of telecommunications terminal equipment; OJ L131/73, 27 May 1988, at Art 6. This position had previously been taken by the Court of Justice in *GB-Inno-BM*, n 79 above.

responsibilities under the Directive did not generally have the necessary technical expertise to carry out the required examinations and tests on terminal equipment. Regulators tended, therefore, to be dependent on the incumbent to carry out such activities on their behalf, which gave rise to plenty of scope for abuse. As a consequence, the Court of Justice was required to clarify that Article 6:

must be interpreted as precluding the application of national rules which prohibit economic agents from, and penalize them for, manufacturing, importing, stocking for sale . . . terminal equipment without furnishing proof, in the form of a type-approval or another document regarded as equivalent, that such equipment conforms to certain essential requirements . . . where there is no guarantee that a test laboratory responsible for technically monitoring the conformity of the equipment with the technical specifications is *independent from economic agents offering goods and services in the telecommunications sector.*[132]

The 'Services Directive' reiterated the need for Member States to ensure that 'a body independent of the telecommunications organizations' carried out the regulatory functions.[133] What this formulation does not adequately address is the issue of regulatory independence from the government as owner, in part or whole, of the incumbent operator.

Where a government is concerned to maintain the value of its stake in the incumbent, with an eye to some form of future asset divestiture, then it has a natural incentive to inhibit the emergence of competition into the market. Phased divestiture of the government shareholding, as has occurred in most Member States, extends this dependency relationship over a longer period of time. Privatization will generally have a direct impact on government borrowing which, in an era of monetary union, may be of critical importance to a government. Even post-divestiture, particularly in the short term, a government may show continued concern in the performance of the 'national champion's' share price, as new shareholders among the general public represent future electorate.

The issue of independence from government, as owner of the incumbent, was first addressed within the context of the ONP initiative. Initially, indirect reference is made to the need to conform to the 'principle of separation of regulatory and operational functions'.[134] Direct reference is subsequently made to the establishment of a 'national regulatory authority' (NRA) 'legally distinct and functionally independent of the telecommunications organizations'.[135] However, it is not until 1997 that the

---

[132] See *Thierry Tranchant and Téléphone Store SARL* [1995] Case C-91/94, ECR I-3911, [OJ 96/16/6]. See also *Procureur du Roi v Lagauche & Others, Evrard* [1993] Cases C-46/90 and C-93/91, ECR I-5267, [OJ 93/C316/3]; *Ministere Public v Decoster* [1993] Case C-69/91, ECR I-5335, [OJ 93/C332/7]; *Ministere Public v Taillandier-Neny* [1993] Case C-92/91, ECR I-5383, [OJ 93/C338/6].

[133] Commission Directive (90/388/EEC) of 28 June 1990 on competition in the markets for telecommunications services; OJ L192/10, 24 July 1990, at Art 7.

[134] Council Directive 92/44/EEC, of 5 June 1992, on the application of open network provision to leased lines; OJ L165/27, 19 June 1992; at recital 14.

[135] See Council Directive 95/62/EC, of 13 December 1995, on the application of open network provision to voice telephony; OJ L321/6, 30 December 1995; at Art 2(2).

issue of independence from government becomes the subject of a specific legislative provision:

In order to guarantee the independence of national regulatory authorities:
• national regulatory authorities shall be legally distinct from and functionally independent of all organizations providing telecommunications networks, equipment or services,
• Member States that retain ownership or a significant degree of control of organizations providing telecommunications networks and/or services shall ensure effective structural separation of the regulatory function from activities associated with ownership or control.[136]

In addition, the decisions of a NRA must be capable of being appealed by any affected party to 'a body independent of the parties involved' (Article 5a(3)). Under the NRF, the concept of independence through structural separation has been extended to include local authorities that retain 'ownership or control' over operators and are involved in the granting of rights of way.[137] In the UK, such a provision would be applicable to the Hull City Council, which has a controlling shareholding in KCOM Group plc.

Another aspect of the position of any regulatory authority is that such a body must be given the resources to carry out its assigned tasks. The effectiveness of a regulator depends to a considerable degree on the resources made available to it. This issue was indirectly addressed through the recitals of some of the ONP measures. Initially reference is simply made to an authority having 'the necessary means to carry out these tasks fully',[138] although this was subsequently elaborated:

whereas the national regulatory authorities should be in possession of all the resources necessary, in terms of staffing, expertise, and financial means, for the performance of their functions.[139]

To meet this objective, the NRA must either look to government or the regulated industry for the necessary resources. In an era of public sector spending restraint, sufficient resources from government must always appear doubtful. In terms of the providers of telecommunications networks, equipment, or services, one source of income is through the operation of the licensing regime. However, under the Authorisation Directive, NRAs are only permitted to charge fees that cover 'the administrative costs which will be incurred in the management, control and enforcement of the general authorization scheme' and related matters (Article 12(1)(a)), effectively a form of

---

[136] Directive 97/51/EC of the European Parliament and of the Council of 6 October 1997 amending Council Directives 90/387/EEC and 92/44/EEC for the purpose of adaptation to a competitive environment in Telecommunications, OJ L 295/23, 29/10/1997: at Art 1(6), inserting Art 5a into Directive 90/387/EEC.
[137] Framework Directive, at Art 11(2).
[138] See Council Directive 95/62/EC, at recital 10.
[139] Directive 97/51/EC, at recital 9.

cost-accounting obligation placed on the regulator rather than the regulated, which clearly emphasizes the need to minimize the costs of regulation.[140]

Member States have adopted a diversity of models in establishing regulatory institutions, with some countries dispersing the regulated authority among a number of separate institutions, which is seen as significantly weakening the exercise of such powers. Regulatory dependency on the incumbent for the provision of information, as well as expertise, continues to be perceived as a problem by some new entrants in a number of jurisdictions. In terms of resources, the main reported problem is the retention of staff in such a fast moving well remunerated employment market, which leads to over-reliance on seconded personnel from operators including the incumbent.

In the Commission's 1999 Communications Review of the regulatory framework, it continued to express concern in respect of a number of areas of NRA activity:

(i) strengthening the independence of NRAs, (ii) ensuring that the allocation of responsibilities between institutions at national level does not lead to delays and duplications of decision making, (iii) improving co-operation between sector specific and general competition authorities, and (iv) requiring transparency of decision making procedures at a national level.[141]

To address these concerns, the NRF consolidated existing provisions on regulatory independence,[142] and sets out in some detail both the obligations of national regulatory authorities in the regulation of the provision of electronic communications networks and services,[143] as well as the manner in which such functions should be carried out, including obligations to consult. However, the Commission's ongoing review of Member State implementation of the NRF continues to highlight concern about issues of NRA powers and resources, independence, and appeals.[144] As a consequence, the 2007 Reform Proposals would impose further detailed provisions on how Member States must ensure the independence, impartiality, and transparency of a NRA, by requiring that they do not seek or receive instructions from any other body in relation to the day-to-day performance of its obligations; only permit NRA decisions to be suspended or overturned by the designated appeal body (see below), and limiting the circumstances under which the head of the NRA can be dismissed.[145]

Member States are required to publish procedures for consultation and cooperation between different NRAs, particularly competition and consumer law authorities.[146] In the UK, for example, the Office of Communications (Ofcom) exercises certain functions concurrently with the Director General of Fair Trading in respect of

---

[140] Under the 2007 Reform Proposals, NRAs would be required to have 'separate annual budgets', in addition to the current obligation to 'publish a yearly overview of their administrative costs' (Authorisation Directive, at Art 12(2)).

[141] See the 1999 Communications Review, n 10 above, at section 4.8.3.

[142] Framework Directive, at Art 3(2).

[143] Ibid, at Chapter III, 'Tasks of National Regulatory Authorities'.

[144] E.g. see 13th Implementation Report, at p 10 *et seq.*

[145] Proposed Directive at Art 2(3) amending Framework Directive at Art 3(3).

[146] Ibid, at Art 3(4).

competition law and consumer protection issues;[147] as well as the Office of the Information Commissioner in respect of the enforcement of the communications privacy regulations.[148]

It is also a requirement that any NRA decision be capable of appeal to an independent body, with the 'appropriate expertise available';[149] although the decision of the NRA should stand unless the appeal body decides otherwise, in order to prevent operators using the appeals mechanism to delay compliance with an obligation. Despite this provision, however, the Commission reported that judicial practice in the Member States continues to involve the routine suspension of regulatory decisions.[150] To address this continuing problem, the 2007 Reform Proposals would strengthen the provision in respect of interim measures, stating that such measures may be granted only 'if there is an urgent need to suspend the effect of the decision in order to prevent serious and irreparable damage to the party applying for those measures and the balance of interests so requires',[151] which reflects established Court of Justice case law.[152] Furthermore, Member States would be required to collect information on the occurrence of appeals and the granting of interim measures in order to inform the Commission.[153]

Under the Framework Directive, NRAs are obliged to consult with the Commission and the NRAs of other Member States prior to the adoption of measures on certain issues, such as market definition and imposition of universal service obligations, through a notification procedure.[154] The consulting NRA is then obliged to take 'utmost account' of any comments received from the other NRAs. On matters related to market definition and the designation of operators as SMP, which would affect trade between Member States, the NRA could be required by the Commission 'to withdraw the draft measure' (Article 7(4)). This provision represents a significant enhancement of the Commission's authority, enabling intervention in national implementation of the directives.

In the exercise of their regulatory functions, the NRAs must take 'all reasonable measures' to ensure that certain fundamental objectives are met:

- 'promote competition in the provision of electronic communications networks, electronic communications services and associated facilities and services' (Article 8(2));

---

[147] Communications Act 2003, s 370 (functions under Part 4 of the Enterprise Act 2002) and s 371 (functions under the Competition Act 1998).
[148] I.e. Privacy and Electronic Communications (EC Directive) Regulations 2003. See further Chapter 13.
[149] Framework Directive, Art 4.
[150] 2006 Review, Staff Document, n 23 above at 5.3.2.
[151] Proposed Directive amending the Framework Directive, at Art 2(4).
[152] See, e.g., Order of the President of the Court of First Instance of 30 April 1999 [1999] ECR II-1427.
[153] Proposed new Art 4(3).
[154] Framework Directive at Art 7(3). See also Commission Recommendation 2003/561/EC 'on notifications, time limits and consultations . . .' (OJ L 190/13, 30 July 2003).

- 'contribute to the development of the Internal Market' (Article 8(3)); and
- 'promote the interests of the citizens of the European Union' (Article 8(4)).

Inevitably, these principles may, in particular situations, be in conflict or require different courses of action from which the NRA will be obliged to choose.[155]

A final aspect of NRA responsibility concerns their role in intervening and resolving disputes between market participants. Under pre-NRF, NRAs were required to make decisions in respect of disputes between undertakings, such as interconnection arrangements. However, the speed of NRA decision-making is seen as a potential barrier to entry in some jurisdictions. Inexperience, insufficient powers and appeal procedures often resulted in significant delays, which usually disadvantaged the market entrant. The Framework Directive therefore imposes an obligation upon NRAs to reach a binding decision within four months.[156]

The centrality of Member State NRAs in the regulation of the electronic communications sector continues to be a defining feature of EU law and regulation. National divergences in NRAs as institutions and personalities would seem an inevitable outcome of the unique historical, political, and juridical characteristics of the various Member States; as much as they are a result of market differences in each national market. However, the expression of these differences impacts on the realization of a single European market for the electronic communications sector and, as such, is the concern of the Commission. Striking a balance between independent NRAs and a harmonized EU regulatory approach remains an ongoing challenge.

5.7.2 European regulatory bodies

One proposal to address issues of NRA independence and harmonization of decision-making between Member States has been the establishment of a European regulatory authority to take responsibility for aspects of the regulatory regime. After funding two separate studies,[157] the Commission decided, at the time when the NRF was being developed, that there was an insufficient case for the establishment of a European telecommunications authority. However, in the course of the 2006 Review, the Information Society Commissioner, Viviane Reding, called for the establishment of a European Communications regulator:

For me it is clear that the most effective and least bureaucratic way to achieve a real level playing field for telecom operators across the EU would be to replace the present game of 'ping pong' between national regulators and the European Commission by an independent

---

[155] See *R v Director General of Telecommunications (Respondent), ex p Cellcom*; [1999] ECC 314, with respect to reconciling the principles contained in s 3(2) of the Telecommunications Act 1984.

[156] Framework Directive, at Art 20.

[157] Report by NERA and Denton Hall, 'Issues Associated with the Creation of a European Regulatory Authority for Telecommunications' (March 1997); also 'Report on the value added of an independent European Regulatory Authority for telecommunications' (Sept 1999).

European telecom authority that would work together with national regulators in a system similar to the European System of Central Banks.[158]

Subsequently, as part of the 2007 Reform Proposals, the Commission have proposed the establishment of the European Electronic Communications Market Authority (EECMA).[159] However, as currently drafted, the EECMA does not have anything like the independence and exclusive decision-making powers of the European Central Bank, as called for by Commissioner Reding, which is an indication of the controversial nature of this proposal and the need to reach a political compromise. While the proposed institution is likely to be strenuously resisted by some Member States, others, such as the Portuguese, have welcomed the proposal.[160]

Under the 2007 Reform Proposals, the EECMA would replace the current body representing the NRAs, the European Regulators Group; maintain regulatory oversight for the operation of the regulatory procedures for SMP operators, especially where the market is considered transnational; and other information and advisory functions to the Commission. The only area where it would be able to take decisions would be in respect of the administration and development of the European Telephony Numbering Space (ETNS), i.e. numbers using a single EU-wide prefix. The EECMA would also subsume the tasks of the existing European Network and Information Security Agency (ENISA),[161] which has advisory, information and coordination roles in respect of network and information security.

Under the current regime, the Commission is assisted in the process of developing policy and legislative and regulatory measures, by a range of advisory committees, representing Member State governments as well as the NRAs. Under the pre-2003 Regime, the Commission was primarily advised by the 'ONP Committee' and the 'Licensing Committee';[162] and an ad hoc group composed of the regulatory authorities in the Member States.[163] Under the NRF, the Commission currently has the following bodies to advise it:

• the 'Communications Committee' (Cocom), composed of representatives of the Member States;[164]

---

[158] Speech of Viviane Reding, 'From Service Competition to Infrastructure Competition: the Policy Options Now on the Table' at ETCA Conference, Brussels, 16 November 2006.

[159] Proposal for a Regulation of the European Parliament and of the Council establishing the European Electronic Communications Market Authority, COM(2007)699 rev 2.

[160] *The Independent*, 'Portugal plans to launch telecoms regulator during its EU presidency', 10 May 2007.

[161] Regulation (EC) No 460/2004 of the European Parliament and of the Council of 10 March 2004 establishing the European Network and Information Security Agency; OJ L 77/1, 13 March 2004. See also <http://www.enisa.europa.eu/>.

[162] Established under Directive 90/387, Art 9 and Directive 97/13/EC on a common framework for general authorizations and individual licences in the field of telecommunications services (OJ L 117, 7 May 1997), Art 14, respectively.

[163] Established by the Commission under Council Resolution of 17 December 1992 on the assessment of the situation in the Community telecommunications sector, OJ C 2/5, 6 January 93.

[164] Framework Directive at Art 22 and Recital 34.

- the 'European Regulators Group' (ERG), composed of representatives designated by the national regulatory authorities,[165] supported by a permanent secretariat in Brussels;

- the 'Radio Spectrum Committee', composed of Member State representatives,[166] as well as a 'Radio Spectrum Policy Group';[167] and

- the 'Telecommunications Conformity Assessment and Market Surveillance Committee' (TCAM), to assist the Commission in respect of telecommunications equipment and comprising Member State representatives.[168]

Each of these institutions plays a role in the formulation of future EU policy in the communications sector. The ERG, in particular, is best placed to promote a greater degree of harmonization in the implementation of the NRF. However, to date, it has not proved very effective in carrying out this role, which has resulted in the Commission's proposal for a new EU authority. One of the problems has been that the ERG has sought consensus before adopting any final common positions on issues, which, given the inevitable divergence of experience, attitude and interest between 27 NRAs, has proved problematic.[169]

To effectively monitor and lobby these different bodies, as well as the Commission Directorate-Generals, industry players have also established a range of EU-wide representative bodies and associations, such as the European Telecommunications Network Operators' Association (ETNO).[170]

Subject to the outcome of the EECMA initiative, there will continue to be institutional asymmetry in the regulation of the electronic communications sector in the EU, in stark contrast to the coexistence of Member State and European Union competition authorities.

5.8 UNIVERSAL SERVICE

One key area of ongoing concern of Member States towards the policy of market liberalization has been the ability to preserve and pursue the potentially conflicting public policy objective of 'universal service': the provision of access to telecommunications services for all the State's citizens. In many jurisdictions, the belief that

---

[165] Commission Decision 2002/627/EC establishing the European Regulators Group for Electronic Communications Networks and Services (OJ L 200/38, 30 July 2002), as amended by Commission Decision 2004/3445/EC (OJ L 293/30, 16 September 2004). See <http://erg.eu.int/>.
[166] Decision No 676/2002/EC of the European Parliament and of the Council on a regulatory framework for radio spectrum policy in the European Community (OJ L 108/1, 24 April 2002), at Art 3.
[167] Commission Decision 2002/622/EC establishing a Radio Spectrum Policy Group; OJ L 198/49, 27 July 2002. See <http://rspg.groups.eu.int/>.
[168] Directive 99/5/EC at Art 13.
[169] N 159 above, at 3.1.
[170] See <http://www.etno.be>.

the telecommunications market was one of natural monopoly was closely allied with this need to ensure 'universal service'.

Article 86(2) of the TEC recognizes that undertakings may be entrusted 'with the operation of services of general economic interest' and that the competition rules may be not be applicable to such undertakings where they 'obstruct the performance, in law or in fact, of the particular tasks assigned to them': the so-called 'public service defence'.[171]

The initial liberalization process envisaged under the 1987 Green Paper was not seen as greatly disturbing the policy of universal service, since the provision of voice telephony (as a 'reserved service') and network infrastructure remained with the national incumbent operator. However, the issue came to the forefront of EU telecommunications policy with the Commission's 1992 telecommunication review, which proposed extending the liberalization process from services to network infrastructure.[172] The endorsement of this policy by the Member States was therefore qualified by the need to protect universal service, as noted by the European Parliament:

... the process of liberalization has to be accompanied by maximum protection of the universal service ... especially that of weaker consumers and that of peripheral and disadvantaged countries and regions.[173]

In response, the Commission adopted a Communication addressing the importance of protecting universal service in a liberalized environment and outlined some of the key issues that comprise a policy on universal service.[174]

The legislative framework for the EU's policy on universal service was initially set out in the ONP Voice Telephony Directive (95/62/EC), which detailed the various tiers that comprise the policy. First, a basic voice telephony service must be offered and provided on request without discrimination to all users. Second, this service must be supplied under certain harmonized conditions, including the quality of service, provision of information to consumers, and billing procedures. Third, certain advanced voice telephony facilities, such as CLI, should be made available. Subsequent measures addressed mechanisms to achieve the objectives of universal service, which were then consolidated under the NRF in the Universal Services Directive.

---

[171] See Taylor, SM, 'Article 90 and telecommunications monopolies', *European Competition Law Review*, Vol 15, No 6, 1994, at p 332 *et seq*.

[172] Commission Communication to the Council and European Parliament, '1992 Review of the situation in the telecommunications services sector', SEC(92) 1048, 21 October 1992.

[173] European Parliament Resolution of 20 April 1993 on the Commission's 1992 review of the situation in the telecommunications services sector; OJ C 150/39, 31 May 1993.

[174] Commission Communication to the Council and the Council and European Parliament, 'Developing universal service for telecommunications in a competitive environment', COM(93) 543, 15 November 1993.

As a regulatory concept, the 'universal service obligation' (USO) continues to comprise a number of different elements:

• the provision of certain services throughout the Union;
• provided to a certain quality;
• available 'to all end-users in their territory, independently of geographical location'; and
• at an affordable price.[175]

The regulatory challenge is to achieve this social policy objective without distorting competition between market participants, the objective of liberalization.

Of the specified services, the fundamental requirement is the provision of a connection at a fixed location. This connection may be wireline or fixed wireless, but does not extend to the provision of mobile telephony. The connection must enable access to 'publicly available telephone services', which, as a minimum, means 'a service available to the public for originating and receiving national and international calls and access to emergency services through a number or numbers in a national or international telephone numbering plan' (Article 2(c)). The additional services include directory enquiry services and directories (Article 5), the provision of public pay telephones (Article 6), and special measures for disabled users (Article 7). Member States are given the right to mandate services beyond this minimized harmonized list, to reflect different national conditions and the principle of subsidiarity, such as ensuring that schools have Internet access (Recital 46). However, such services are not part of the USO and may not be funded through the imposition of a 'compensation mechanism involving specific undertakings' (Article 32).

It is recognized that what comprises this minimum list of services within the concept of the USO will need to evolve over time to reflect the pace of technological and market developments. For example, under the 1999 Communications Review, consideration was given to extending the scope of the 'universal service' connection from 'narrowband' to include the provision of 'broadband services'. This was eventually dismissed as premature in terms of market development and potentially detrimental to competition. However, a step in the direction of recognizing the importance of Internet connectivity was made in the Universal Services Directive, where the obligation on Member States to ensure the provision of a 'connection at a fixed location to the public telephone network and for access to publicly available telephone services' encompasses the ability to support data communications 'at data rates that are sufficient to permit Internet access' (Article 4(2)).[176]

---

[175] Universal Services Directive, Art 3(1).
[176] The provision of an Integrated Services Digital Network (ISDN) connection is expressly excluded from the concept of the universal service 'connection' obligation (Recital 8). Under the pre-2003 regime, Germany included such connections within its USO regime.

The Universal Services Directive also provides for a process of periodic review of the scope of 'universal service', to be carried out by the Commission. A first review was carried out in 2005[177] and the Commission has embarked on a second review in 2008;[178] although the 2007 Reform Proposals contain no planned amendment. The reviews take into account a range of factors, such as whether the majority of consumers use the specific service and whether 'non-use by a minority of consumers result in social exclusion' (Annex V). The scope is likely to expand over time, as the Internet becomes the ubiquitous communications platform, although the recent entry of the 12 Accession States may delay somewhat the raising of the threshold.

In respect of the second element of USO, quality, Member States must ensure that all designated operators publish information regarding their performance against certain parameters (Article 11(1)), addressing such matters as the supply time for initial connection, fault repair time, and complaints concerning the correctness of bills (Annex III). NRAs may also set additional quality of service parameters in respect of the provision of services to disabled end-users and consumers (Article 11(2)). NRAs may set and monitor performance against certain targets, with the right to take measures where an operator persistently fails to meet such targets (Article 11(4)–(6)).

In terms of 'affordability', the cost of access is as critical an element as the actual provision of a connection. Under the Universal Services Directive, NRAs may require designated operators to offer tariff options or packages targeted specifically at those on low incomes or with special social needs (Article 9(2)). In addition, common tariffs, such as geographic averaging, may be imposed or price caps (Article 9(3)–(4)). In reality, geographic averaging was the traditional mechanism for funding the USO, which has been retained in all Member States.

The NRAs have the right to designate which operators are required to ensure provision of the 'set' of services (Article 8(1)). While in most Member States the obligation will primarily lie with the incumbent operator, as markets become fully competitive USO may be imposed on a number of operators, including the provision of different service elements by different operators in different geographical areas. Indeed, in a fully competitive market, operators may perceive positive benefits in being designated as having USOs, and therefore Member States are required to ensure that 'no undertaking is *a priori* excluded from being designated' (Article 8(2)).

In addition to designation, an NRA may also impose certain obligations upon those operators determined as having SMP in particular retail markets (Article 16). In contrast to the obligations imposed under the Access Directive,[179] NRAs have certain flexibility in respect of the nature of the regulatory controls placed on retail services, but could, for example, include individual tariff controls (Article 17(2)). However, such retail remedies should only be imposed where wholesale remedies under the Access

---

[177] European Commission, *Communication On the Review of the Scope of Universal Service in accordance with Article 15 of Directive 2002/22/EC*, 24 May 2005, COM(2005) 203.

[178] Universal Services Directive, at Art 15. See COM(2008) 572 Final, 23 September 2008.

[179] See further Chapter 8 at 8.5.1.6.

Directive have not, or would not, prove effective (Article 17(1)). Controls over the provision of a minimum set of leased lines and carrier selection and pre-selection should also be imposed on operators identified as having SMP (Articles 18–19).

Defining the scope of universal service enables regulators to determine the costs associated with its provision and, therefore, mechanisms for ensuring that adequate and appropriate financing is present within a competitive market. The Full Competition Directive was the first to address the issue of the cost of universal service and related funding mechanisms. In particular, the burden could only be placed upon undertakings providing 'public telecommunications networks', i.e. transmission infrastructure, rather than all telecommunication service providers.[180] This contrasted with the position adopted in the US, where '[e]very telecommunications carrier that provides interstate telecommunications services' is required to contribute.[181] EU companies felt such an approach effectively meant that EU network providers were subsidizing US operators supplying services into the EU. As a consequence, the Universal Services Directive provides that funding mechanisms levied on operators should be shared between providers of electronic communication networks and services (Article 13(1)(b)).

The Full Competition Directive also addressed the need for incumbent operators to rebalance their tariffs in order to reduce the burden of universal service. Within the broader debate on universal service, the issue of rebalancing has been one of the most politically sensitive issues for Member State governments to tackle. Historically, incumbent operators have cross-subsidized the cost of installation (i.e. line rental) from future call revenues, particularly long distance and international. This approach was partly justified on the grounds of ensuring universal service. Indeed, Court of Justice jurisprudence has recognized that the performance of such tasks of 'general economic interest' (under Article 86(2)) may involve cross-subsidization between service elements and could justify the restriction of competition in the profitable market sectors.[182] However, with market liberalization the incumbent was required to remove such cross-subsidies as potential barriers to entry, and to move towards cost-based tariffs. The consequences for customers is that they will often experience significant price rises in line rental and local call charges, whilst the cost of international and long-distance calls falls.[183] However, the price rises may impact on government policies, particularly inflation targets, as well as being unpopular with the electorate. Therefore to counter any potential reticence at Member State level, the Full Competition Directive mandated that:

Member States shall allow their telecommunications organizations to rebalance tariffs taking account of specific market conditions and of the need to ensure the affordability of a universal service. (Directive 96/19/EC, Article 6)

[180] Directive 96/19/EC, Art 6, inserting Art 4c into Directive 90/388/EC.
[181] 47 USC § 254(d).
[182] Case C-320/91 *Corbeau* [1993] ECR I-2533, at para 17 *et seq.*
[183] See Sixth Implementation Report, n 76 above, at p 27.

The term 'universal service' is supposed to have been originally coined by Theodore Vail, Chairman of AT&T, in 1907;[184] although the concept he was promoting was that of universal interconnection, rather than universal access. However, there is an important relationship between network interconnection and the promotion of universal service. If an operator is providing elements of a universal service policy, such as full national network coverage, and also has an obligation to interconnect to any new entrant operator, then the former operator may be placed in a disadvantageous competitive position. In the absence of a regulatory obligation to provide such services, the operator would inevitably withdraw from the provision of any uneconomic universal service elements. This connection was recognized by the Council in its 1994 Resolution on universal service,[185] and was given explicit recognition in the Interconnection Directive.[186]

Under the Interconnection Directive, where a Member State determined that meeting any universal service obligations represents an unfair burden upon an operator, the Member State could establish a mechanism to share the net cost. However, new entrants inevitably have concerns that any compensation mechanism may operate as a barrier to market entry, benefiting the incumbent. Calls have therefore been made for the cost of universal service, as a social policy objective, to be borne by governments through general taxation, rather than imposed on operators.

Responding to such concerns, the Universal Services Directive states that Member States shall decide to fund any unfair burden resulting from the provision of the universal service obligation either by introducing a mechanism for compensating the designated undertaking 'from public funds' or by sharing the cost between providers of electronic communication networks and services.[187] The former option, however, was always unlikely to be enthusiastically embraced by governments! The latter may be in the form of a separately administered scheme, such as a 'universal service fund'; or the levy of a supplementary charge. To date, most Member States have deemed that the provision of universal service is not an unfair burden; while of those that have, such as the Czech Republic, Italy, and France, only the last of these has a fully operational compensation transfer scheme.[188]

As with many aspects of telecommunications regulation, a key issue is the determination of 'net costs' involved in meeting the universal service obligations, i.e. the additional costs attributable to the obligations. The Universal Services Directive details the means by which such cost should be calculated, specifically through the identification of those services provided, or categories of persons served, 'at a loss

---

[184] Stated by Garnham, N, 'Universal Service', at 207, in Melody (ed), *Telecom Reform* (Technical University of Denmark, 1997).
[185] Council Resolution of 7 February 1994 on universal service principles in the telecommunications sector, at 'Recognizes' (e).
[186] See n 109 above.
[187] USD, at Art 13(1).
[188] See 12th Implementation Report, Commission Staff Working Document Annex, Vol 1, SEC(2007) 403, 29 March 2007, at p 62.

or provided under cost conditions falling outside normal commercial standards'.[189] Any revenues accruing from the service should be incorporated into the calculation of net cost on a 'forward-looking' basis, since revenues from line rentals, call charges, interconnection, and international transit charges may, over the lifetime of the customer, render a service economic. In addition, the NRAs should take into account any market benefits, both tangible and intangible, which accrue from the provision of universal service, such as the perception of ubiquity in the marketplace.

An alternative proposed mechanism for determining the net cost of 'universal service' is through the operation of public tenders or auctions. Under such an approach operators would be asked to bid for the level of public subsidy that they would require in order to meet the 'universal service' obligation or specific elements of it. The bidder requesting the lowest subsidy would then be 'awarded' the obligation under a service agreement.[190]

To date, Member State experience would not appear to reflect the historic concern shown towards the threat posed by a competitive market to the provision of universal service. Instead, the perception of universal service provision is in the process of being transformed from a burden into an opportunity for market players.

5.9 END-USER RIGHTS AND CONSUMER PROTECTION

Closely linked to the issue of universal service, European telecommunications law also addresses the quality of services being provided to end-users and related consumer protection issues. In contrast to universal service, the introduction of competition is seen as being clearly beneficial to consumers in terms of choice, cost, and quality. Concerns about consumers were, therefore, perhaps initially seen as being an issue during the process of liberalization, before markets are fully competitive and operators with 'significant market power' continue to be prevalent. In a fully competitive market, it could therefore be argued, there would be no need for sector specific rules. However, consumer protection issues remain a central constituent of the EU regime, based on a recognition 'that competition alone may not be sufficient to satisfy the needs of all citizens and protect users' rights', particularly that of 'an inclusive Information Society'; therefore further measures to strengthen and improve such protections form part of the 2007 Reform Proposals.[191]

Part of the liberalization process commenced under the 'Equipment' and 'Services' directives addressed provisions regarding customer contracts. From the Commission's

[189] Universal Services Directive, at Art 12 and Annex IV, Part A.
[190] See further Chapter 3, at 3.12.2.
[191] Proposal for a Directive of the European Parliament and the Council amending Directive 2002/22/EC on universal service and users' rights relating to electronic communications networks, Directive 2002/58/EC concerning the processing of personal data and the protection of privacy in the electronic communications sector and Regulation (EC) No 2006/2004 on consumer protection cooperation, COM(2007) 698, at 1.

perspective, such provisions were necessary to facilitate the opening up of the markets by granting customers of telecommunications operators a right to terminate long-term contracts, subject to minimum notification periods.[192] However, the Court of Justice annulled these provisions on the basis that such private contractual arrangements were not 'State measures' to which Article 86(3) was applicable.[193] Any legal measures against such agreements would need to be the subject of case-by-case decisions made under competition law principles. Subsequently, provisions governing subscriber contracts and quality of service issues were introduced under the ONP framework.

In pursuance of ensuring quality of service, significant powers of intervention were granted to NRAs, such as the right 'to require alteration of the conditions of contracts'.[194] It would seem questionable whether such powers of intervention should continue to be available in a competitive market. In its 1999 Review, the Commission has recognized this point, noting:

. . . good quality services are more likely to be provided as a result of competition between suppliers rather than from regulation, and consumers may demand services of different quality at different prices. (at 4.5.5)

However, the Commission concluded:

it is considered prudent to maintain some reserve powers for NRAs to take action in the event of market failure, particularly to deal with issues of end-to-end quality in a multi-network environment where no single operator has overall control.

The latter reference is clearly applicable to the growth of the Internet as a communications environment.

Under the NRF, Chapter IV of the Universal Services Directive addresses 'end-user interests and rights'. Certain minimum terms must be specified in consumer contracts (Article 20), related transparency obligations are imposed (Article 21, Annex II), as well as compliance with NRA-specified quality of service parameters (Article 22, Annex III). Member States are also required to ensure that 'transparent, simple and inexpensive out-of-court' dispute settlement procedures are established (Article 34).[195] It is debatable, however, whether some of these matters are more appropriately addressed through horizontal measures, such as rules governing unfair contract terms, distance sales, and electronic commerce,[196] rather than sector-specific regulation.

---

[192] Respectively, Art 7 of Directive 88/301 (minimum notice 1 year) and Art 8 of Directive 90/388 (minimum notice 6 months).

[193] See n 26 above, at paras 53–57.

[194] ONP Voice Telephony Directive, at Art 7(3).

[195] In the UK, such services are being offered by two different industry-funded bodies, the Telephone Ombudsman (Otelo) and the Communications & Internet Services Adjudicators Service (CISAS).

[196] E.g. Directive 93/13/EC 'on unfair terms in consumer contracts' (OJ L 95/29, 21 April 1993); Directive 97/7/EC 'on the protection of consumers in respect of distance contracts' (OJ L 144/19, 4 June

Under the 2007 Reform Proposals, a series of amendments are suggested to further enhance the position of consumers in general and especially that of disabled
users.[197] The level of price transparency remains a concern and therefore greater
powers would be given to NRAs to require operators to publish and supply tariff
information to enable and facilitate comparisons by end-users. Where such compara-
tor guides and services are not produced in the market, the NRA has an obligation
to make them available. In terms of ensuring greater use and access for disabled
users, Member States would be obliged to take specific measures, rather than being
able to decide whether such measures are appropriate.

Although the NRF creates a single tier of regulation for the provision of transmission services, rather than the content being transmitted over such services, this distinction is not a clear-cut one, and the 2007 Reform Proposals contain a number of
content-related provisions not previously addressed under the NRF. The first
addresses contractual limitations placed on the ability of users to access or distribute
lawful content or operate lawful applications. There have been concerns that some
service providers have suspended or degraded services for users exhibiting particular
profiles, such as those distributing content using P2P applications, without notice or
explanation. The provision does not prohibit such practices, but does require transparency by the service provider, either prior to the conclusion of the contract or
subsequently, where new restrictions are imposed. Second, rights-holders have lobbied for the insertion of two provisions designed to facilitate the enforcement of their
intellectual property rights. Service providers would have an obligation to inform
their customers, on a regular basis, of the need 'to respect copyright and related
rights';[198] while NRAs would have the right to impose compliance obligations in
respect of IP enforcement, as a general condition for the authorization to provide
services. Third, the debate over 'net neutrality' gets its first airing under EU law, with
the Commission being given the right to adopt measures designed to ensure that a
minimum quality of service is provided over public communications networks, in
order 'to prevent degradation of service and slowing of traffic over networks'. These
provisions implicitly recognize that content impacts on conduit, as the economics of
the former can impact directly on the market conditions of the latter.

1997) and Directive 2000/31/EC 'on certain legal aspects of information society services, in particular
electronic commerce, in the Internal Market' (OJ L 178/1, 17 July 2000). See Universal Services
Directive at Recital 30 and Art 20(1).

[197] Proposal for a Directive amending Directive 2002/22/EC on universal service and users' rights
relating to electronic communication networks, Directive 2002/58/EC concerning the processing of
personal data and the protection of privacy on the electronic communications sector and Regulation (EC)
No 2006/2004 on consumer protection cooperation, COM(2007) 698.

[198] In July 2008, six of the leading UK ISPs signed a voluntary MOU with representatives of the
content industry (e.g. MPAA), Ofcom, and the government establishing a regime to tackle unlawful file-
sharing. The scheme will include, on a trail basis, a process whereby the ISPs will notify subscribers
identified as having engaged in such activities. See BERR Consultation 'on legislative options to address
illicit peer-to-peer (P2P) file sharing', July 2008.

Directory enquiry services are addressed from a number of different perspectives under the new regime. The provision of such services is an element of universal service (Article 5); while the right to be entered into a directory and access to such services is an end-user right (Article 25). As personal data, however, the subscriber data included in a directory is also regulated under the Communications Privacy Directive (Article 12), which addresses the different privacy relationships that arise within a communications environment: between subscribers and service providers, subscribers and users, the parties to the communication and between the user and the state.[199]

5.10 FUTURE DIRECTIONS

This chapter has attempted to examine the development of EU communications law over the past 24 years, culminating in the NRF. As the third distinct phase of development, the 2003 Regime inevitably raises the question whether it will be the final phase of regulatory evolution or whether a fourth, fifth, or even sixth phase can be envisaged.

The NRF embodies a range of different regulatory initiatives. Perhaps the most significant and revolutionary of which is the idea that a single regulatory regime or framework should govern all forms of communications infrastructure and services, irrelevant of the content being communicated. Such an idea is based on current technological and market developments, generally referred to as convergence, which, although reflecting reality to an extent, also anticipates a process that has a long and unpredictable way to go. A truly converged environment should enable the removal of certain legacy regulatory concepts, such as the 'must-carry' obligation in relation to broadcasting, and yet it may require others to be extended, such as the scope and nature of universal service. In addition, as the provision of network becomes a commodity, bundled into the cost of the content being transmitted, the bright line between carriage and content may become more problematic or an irrelevant and meaningless regulatory distinction.

A second objective of the NRF was to move from *ex ante* regulatory intervention towards *ex post* reactive regulation. The rationale being that, with the successful introduction of competition, traditional market mechanisms will control anti-competitive practices, with traditional competition law rules operating as a backstop against abusive practices and situations. This is the model that operates in the information technology sector, whether successfully or not, and was viewed as an inevitable consequence of both liberalization and convergence. However, during the consultation on the 1999 Review, new entrants made it very clear that the current market was not yet sufficiently competitive and was unlikely to be in certain market segments

---

[199] See further Chapter 13.

for some time to come, if ever. Hence the NRF continues to include a broad range of *ex ante* measures. While we can anticipate a further withering away of such measures, most commentators recognize that the unique features of the communications sector, as a networked industry is likely to mean and require a base level of proactive regulatory intervention for the foreseeable future.

Finally, a unique feature of EU communications law is the parallel pursuit of the objectives of liberalization and harmonization. National electronic communications markets continue to exhibit a high degree of variation, both in terms of market development, as well as regulatory structures and intervention. The NRF attempts to address the worst of the variabilities and inconsistencies, through greater Commission oversight. However, issues of subsidiarity and Member State political manoeuvring have prevented this process from going as far as wanted by the Commission. We can therefore anticipate a continuing struggle between the Commission and the Member State NRAs over the theory and practice of regulating the electronic communications sector, which may simply be an inevitable outcome of the European project, rather than being specific to the sector.

6

US TELECOMMUNICATIONS LAW

Karen Lee and Jamison Prime

6.1 INTRODUCTION

This chapter focuses on the regulation of the provision of telecommunications services and the operation of telecommunications networks in the US, principally in the fixed, cable, and mobile sectors, but satellite regulation is briefly touched upon. The chapter

begins by giving a brief history of US telecommunications regulation, and provides an overview of the numerous governmental bodies involved in the regulation of the US telecommunications market. It summarizes the licensing requirements under the Communications Act of 1934, and briefly explains the US approach to certain key regulatory issues in the EU: access and interconnection, spectrum management, broadband, universal service, the application of competition law to the sector, and communications privacy. It concludes with a discussion of the Federal Communications Commission (FCC)'s regulation of IP-enabled services.

6.2 REGULATORY LAW AND POLICY: HISTORY AND DEVELOPMENTS

Today, the mantra of US telecommunications policy is to promote the 'public interest' through the promotion of vigorous competition in all markets for telecommunications services and between all modes of service delivery, with consumer safeguards where appropriate. The FCC, the federal body primarily responsible for overseeing the implementation of this policy, has removed many regulatory restrictions and, broadly speaking, chooses not to regulate industry players unless they acquire dominance in a relevant market or other market failures occur. This deregulatory and technology-neutral approach is in response to the convergence of traditional telephony and broadcasting media. It also follows more than a century of technology- and service-specific regulation and micro-management of the communications markets. Despite the new approach, there continue to be some differences in the regulatory treatment of certain communications technologies and services. This section briefly traces the history of US regulation of terrestrial, cable, mobile, and satellite networks, and the factors that led to the adoption of a pro-competitive framework.

6.2.1 Terrestrial networks

As in the EU, the introduction of full competition in the US fixed market occurred via incremental changes. The process towards a competitive market began in the late 1960s with the introduction of competition in long-distance services. Arguably, the adoption of the Telecommunications Act of 1996, which mandated competition in the local market, was the final step in the process. However, the FCC's implementation of the Act's obligations on incumbent local exchange carriers to offer unbundled network elements provoked lengthy and costly litigation which was only finally resolved in 2006.

6.2.2 Pre-Communications Act 1934

6.2.2.1 *Initial federal regulation*
Early federal regulation of the telegraph and, later, the telephone helped to establish the basic framework of common carrier regulation for terrestrial networks. In 1866, Congress allowed telegraph operators rights of way along post roads and public lands.

In return, the operators agreed to the basic tenet of common carrier regulation—that they would provide service to any customer without discrimination. By the time the telegraph and telephone were formally subjected to federal regulation in 1910, both courts and lawmakers had long regarded the telegraph and telephone to be common carriers akin to railroads and ferry boats. The First Amendment and its restrictions on government regulation of speech played no part in the development of these policies. Instead, regulation of the telephone flowed from regulation of the telegraph, the growth of which coincided with the growth and regulation of America's railroad networks.

6.2.2.2 Evolution of the Bell network

With Alexander Graham Bell's development of the telephone, the Bell Company (Bell)—the company that later became known as AT&T—benefited from its 1876 patent monopoly. The growth of Bell's systems was accelerated by a Supreme Court ruling interpreting the patent broadly, and an agreement whereby Bell would not enter the telegraph business in exchange for Western Union dropping pending patent disputes and litigation. After the Bell patent expired, however, competition flourished, beginning in the mid-1890s. Although independent companies eventually provided up to half of the telephone stations, they were unable to form a nationwide network and service remained primarily local in nature. In addition, many local systems were not interconnected, and it was not unusual for businesses to subscribe to two or more local telephone networks utilizing separate lines and equipment. Bell, meanwhile, successfully reorganized into a vertically integrated company and began to acquire the independent phone companies at a rapid pace. By the 1910s, the first era of telephone competition was in decline.

6.2.2.3 The Kingsbury Commitment and universal service

In 1913, AT&T responded to the threat of federal antitrust litigation by agreeing to the Kingsbury Commitment. Under this agreement, AT&T agreed to interconnect with the independent phone companies and to obtain approval before it acquired any competing companies. Although the agreement aided the development of a nationwide interconnected telephone network, it did little to prevent AT&T's growth. Exploiting loopholes in the agreement, AT&T continued to acquire local phone systems and eliminate competition. In addition to its local and long-distance telephone infrastructure, AT&T also dominated equipment manufacture through its Western Electric unit and communications research via Bell Telephone Laboratories. By the time of the adoption of the Communications Act of 1934, regulators had concluded that the telephone was a natural monopoly that was best served by a single firm. AT&T, with its local operating companies and long-distance lines, appeared to be that firm.

6.2.3 Communications Act of 1934

The Communications Act of 1934 (1934 Act) is significant in that it established the FCC as the primary US communications regulatory body and, thus, is the basis for modern

federal communications regulation. The text of the 1934 Act, which is codified at 47 USC, generally replicated and consolidated existing legislation. Telecommunications carriers are regulated by Title II of the Act, which was patterned after the 1910 Mann-Elkins Act.[1] The Mann-Elkins Act, in turn, was based on the Interstate Commerce Commission Act of 1877,[2] which set forth common carrier regulation for railroads. Title III of the 1934 Act, which pertains to regulation of radio stations, replaced the Radio Act of 1927,[3] which governed the assignment of radio frequencies and radio interference. The 1934 Act confers to the FCC broad authority to act on the basis of 'public interest, convenience, and necessity', which serves as the foundation of FCC action and is a basic principle of US telecommunications regulation. Today, most US telecommunications companies own facilities that are subject to both Title II and Title III of the 1934 Act, although Title II continues to serve as the basis for common carrier regulation.

6.2.4 The evolution of competition: 1950–1996

For several decades, the FCC allowed AT&T to retain its monopoly on telecommunications in order to secure 'rapid, efficient and nationwide communications service with adequate facilities at reasonable charges'; in turn, AT&T subsidized the cost of line rentals and free local calls by charging heavy mark-ups on national and international calls. Over time, the view that the provision of telecommunications services was a natural monopoly was challenged by the courts and Congress. Judicial and legislative intervention eventually led to the gradual introduction of full competition in long-distance and other service markets. This evolution towards full competition can be broken down into roughly three stages:

1) the introduction of competition into the long-distance market;

2) the divestiture of the Bell Operating Companies from AT&T; and

3) the introduction of competition into the local exchange markets.

6.2.4.1 *Long-distance competition*
In 1969, the FCC granted a licence to Microwave Communications, Inc (MCI) to install and operate microwave facilities that would enable limited inter-office communications to subscribers. The grant of such a licence put MCI in competition with AT&T services, and a myriad of applications for similar licences was then filed. In 1971, the FCC in its Specialized Common Carrier decision (*Decision in MCI Telecommunications Corp*, 60 FCC 2d 25 (13 July 1976)) then determined that point-to-point communications by private line services (which would effectively

---

[1] Ch 309, 36 Stat 539 (1910) (repealed).
[2] Ch 104, 24 Stat 379 (1887) (codified as amended in scattered sections of 49 USC).
[3] Ch 169, 44 Stat 116 (1927) (repealed).

allow MCI and others to compete for long-distance business customers) were in the 'public interest'.

Despite permitting competition in private line services, the FCC staunchly opposed the entry of additional common carriers in the public voice telephony market. This ended, however, in 1977, when the United States Court of Appeals for the District of Columbia (the DC Circuit Court) overturned the FCC's order requiring MCI to cease operation of its Execunet division, which essentially provided interstate long-distance services to the public (*MCI Telecommunications Corp v FCC*, 561F 2d 365 (DC Cir 1977)).

6.2.4.2 *Interconnect access and charges*

Having won the right to provide publicly available long-distance services, MCI and other operators also needed the right to interconnect to AT&T's long-distance and local access facilities. In the Specialized Common Carrier decision (see section 6.2.4.1 above), the FCC had ruled that carriers such as AT&T had to provide interconnection services on reasonable terms and conditions to new entrants. Reluctant to enable the new entrants to compete for its customers, AT&T permitted access to residential customers but resisted providing access to its lucrative business customers. MCI and other carriers challenged AT&T, and the FCC ruled in their favour, arguing that new entrants were entitled to interconnection services similar to those enjoyed by AT&T, provided they were technically feasible. The FCC subsequently overturned its own order, but the DC Circuit Court in *Execunet II* later ruled that new entrants were legally entitled to interconnection (*MCI Telecommunications Corp v FCC*, 580F 2d 590 (DC Cir 1978)).

In parallel with these rulings, the FCC also reviewed the charges interstate common carriers paid to local exchange operators to terminate long-distance calls, which were at the time determined by a complicated settlement rate system. The FCC had endorsed the industry's attempt to reach a settlement, but in the early 1980s it was forced to review the issue in its entirety. The results of the FCC's review are too detailed to summarize here; however, they focused on AT&T's need to rebalance tariffs in line with costs in order to remove the market distortions and artificial arbitrage opportunities which arose as a result of the funding of universal service.

6.2.4.3 *Divestiture of AT&T and the Modification of Final Judgment*

In 1974, the US Department of Justice brought a suit against AT&T, Western Electric, and Bell Telephone Laboratories, Inc alleging that the monopoly held by the defendants in several telecommunications service areas and equipment manufacturing violated the Sherman Anti-trust Act.[4] The case was pending for eight years until Judge Harold Greene of the DC Circuit Court entered the Modification of Final

---

[4] Ch 647, 26 Stat 209 (1892) (codified as amended at 15 USC §§1–7).

Judgment (MFJ), which slightly modified divestiture provisions voluntarily agreed to by the parties (*US v AT&T Corp*, 552 F Supp 131 (DC Cir 1982), *aff'd sub nom Maryland v US*, 460 US 1001 (1983)). The MFJ ordered AT&T to divest itself of its 22 Regional Bell Operating Companies (RBOCs), which resulted in the separation of local and interexchange (long-distance) markets, and established procedures for the implementation of divestiture.

Under the provisions of the MFJ, the 22 RBOCs, which by 2008 had been consolidated into three main holding companies—the 'new' AT&T (see section 6.2.7), Qwest, and Verizon—would provide communication in 'exchange areas' (also known as local access and transport areas (LATAs)). Exchange areas referred to geographic areas that encompassed one or more contiguous local exchange areas serving common social, economic, and other purposes. Within these exchange areas, RBOCs could originate and terminate calls, while AT&T and other long-distance providers, such as MCI, would carry calls between exchange areas.

In exchange for retaining their monopolies within these exchange areas, RBOCs were prohibited from providing some types of communications services. RBOCs and any affiliated enterprises could provide neither interexchange telecommunications services nor information services. Although the original settlement provisions sought to restrict the manufacture and provision of customer premises equipment, the MFJ allowed RBOCs to market equipment once they divested from AT&T. However, they could not 'provide any other product or service . . . that [was] not a natural monopoly service actually regulated by tariff'. These three stipulations limited RBOCs to the provision of toll, private line, and 'intercity' services.

The MFJ also sought to ensure that all interexchange service providers (e.g., MCI and Sprint) obtained equal access to RBOC services. The judgment imposed a duty on local exchange carriers to provide service on an 'unbundled, tariffed basis' that was equal in quality, type, and cost to that provided to AT&T and its affiliates. In addition, RBOCs were prohibited from discriminating against other service providers in favour of AT&T in the following areas: procurement, establishment and dissemination of technical information, interconnection standards, interconnection, and provision of new services and facilities.

Although RBOCs retained monopolies in local exchange services under the MFJ, they did remain subject to state regulators who did, in some cases, attempt to introduce competition in the local exchange market. In certain jurisdictions, GTE (now part of Verizon) and rural telcos competed with RBOCs for the provision of local exchange services. However, it was not until the passage of the Telecommunications Act of 1996 that the US formally adopted, at a national level, an aggressive competition policy for local-exchange services.

6.2.5 Competitive carrier rule-making

With the growing emphasis on market competition in the late 1980s, the FCC initiated a series of proceedings examining how best to adapt the regulatory framework

to promote competition among interexchange carriers. Prior to the FCC's investigation, new entrants were subject to the same regulatory obligations under §214 of the 1934 Act as was AT&T. For example, new entrants were required to (among other things) obtain prior FCC approval for all new tariffs and construction of facilities and file all interconnection agreements. These obligations made market entry less desirable. The FCC therefore sought to minimize the regulatory burden on new entrants while imposing requirements designed to facilitate pricing transparency and curb anti-competitive behaviour by entrenched market players, such as AT&T.

In a series of rulings, the FCC distinguished between common carriers with market power ('dominant' carriers) and common carriers without market power ('non-dominant' carriers). Dominant carriers were subject to all of the requirements of Title II of the 1934 Act, including the need to provide 90-days notice for new tariffs and to notify decisions to roll out network infrastructure. Such restrictions on non-dominant carriers, on the other hand, were no longer to be applied and enforced by the FCC. However, non-dominant carriers had to ensure that their service charges were not 'unjust or unreasonable'. To determine whether a common carrier had market power, the FCC defined certain relevant markets, utilizing traditional antitrust analysis. These markets were the provision of all interstate, domestic, and interexchange services in the US, including Hawaii, Alaska, and the US territories. Unsurprisingly, it declared AT&T and local exchange operators dominant, citing their control of local access facilities and their share of the residential market. Resellers and other companies, such as MCI, were deemed non-dominant.

In subsequent proceedings in the early 1990s, the FCC again examined AT&T's position in the long-distance market and found that the business long-distance market was 'substantially competitive'. It removed the regulatory requirements on this aspect of AT&T's business but retained the regulatory obligations (including price caps) on AT&T's residential long-distance services. In a controversial order made in 1995, the FCC reclassified AT&T as a non-dominant carrier in all service markets (*Motion of AT&T to be Re-classified as a Non-dominant Carrier*, 11 FCC Rcd 327 (1995)). Subsequently, the obligations on dominant carriers have been reduced further in light of biennial regulatory reviews mandated by the Telecommunications Act of 1996 to reflect the state of competition in relevant markets.

6.2.6 Value-added services

In addition to promoting fixed network competition in the 1970s, the FCC also advocated competition in the value-added or 'enhanced' services area. In *Computer Inquiry I* (*Regulatory Pricing Problems Presented by the Interdependence of Computer and Communication Facilities*, Final Decision and Order, 28 FCC 2d 267 (1971)), the FCC considered the need to regulate common carriers that were beginning to provide data-processing services over traditional telephony lines and, more broadly, the need to regulate the data-processing industry as a whole. The FCC declined to regulate data-processing by drawing artificial distinctions between 'hybrid communications'

which were regulated and 'hybrid data processing' which was not. The FCC did, however, mandate that any common carrier whose turnover exceeded US$1 million and who wished to offer data-processing services, had to do so by a separate corporate entity. In addition, common carriers could not discriminate in favour of their data processing facilities. In practice, these requirements affected only AT&T and its operating companies, and were imposed to minimize their ability to use telephony revenue to cross-subsidize their data-processing businesses to the detriment of their fixed telecommunications subscribers.

In *Computer Inquiry II (Amendment of §64.702 of the Commission's Rules and Regulations, Second Computer Inquiry*, Final Decision, 77 FCC 2d 384 (1980)), the FCC revisited the issue of value-added services following the inevitable confusion that arose as a result of *Computer Inquiry I.* The FCC distinguished between so-called 'basic' and 'enhanced' services. 'Basic' services consisted of the provision of transmission capacity and were regulated by Title II of the Communications Act. 'Enhanced' services were basic transmission services coupled with computer processing applications and were regulated under the FCC's ancillary jurisdiction under Title I of the Communications Act. In *Computer Inquiry II*, the FCC also removed the structural separation requirements from all carriers with the exception of AT&T and its operating companies. However, all carriers who owned their own transmission facilities and provided enhanced services had to acquire the basic services needed for those enhanced services pursuant to tariff. Moreover, they had to make available basic services to competing enhanced service providers on the same rates, terms, and conditions. Both obligations continue to apply to dominant and non-dominant common carriers providing enhanced services using their own wire-line services and facilities, although exemptions have been granted for specified broadband services (see section 6.11).

Following the implementation of the MFJ, during which it strongly advocated structural separation, the FCC issued *Computer Inquiry III (Amendment of §64.702 of the Commission's Rules and Regulations, Third Computer Inquiry*, Report and Order, 104 FCC 2d 958 (1986)). Although AT&T and RBOCs remained free to offer enhanced services through separate subsidiary companies, *Computer Inquiry III* gave them the flexibility to integrate their basic and enhanced services, provided they comply with specified cost-allocation methods and targeted regulations designed to prevent RBOCs from abusing their market power in basic services. Initially, RBOCs were expected to comply with 'comparably efficient interconnection' (CEI) requirements. In the longer term, RBOCs had to comply with certain Open Network Access (ONA) obligations which required them to unbundle their basic services into 'basic service elements' for purchase by enhanced service providers. In addition, quality, installation, and maintenance reporting requirements were imposed. Like other carriers, RBOCs had to offer the basic services used in their enhanced service offerings pursuant to tariff and on a non-discriminatory basis. Because of procedural errors some aspects of the FCC's decision in *Computer Inquiry III* were overturned on appeal (*People of the State of California v FCC*, 905F 2d 1217 (9th Cir 1990)), but CEI requirements and some ONA obligations were eventually imposed.

6.2.7 Local-exchange competition and the Telecommunications Act of 1996

The Telecommunications Act of 1996[5] (the 1996 Act) marked the first time Congress established policy objectives for the wireline sector since the adoption of the 1934 Act. The 1996 Act was significant in that it declared invalid all state regulation that prohibited or restricted the entry of competitors into intrastate telecommunications services. The 1996 Act overturned the MFJ provisions[6] which allowed RBOCs to retain monopolies in the lucrative local market. In addition, the 1996 Act removed the MFJ's restrictions on the provision of interstate telephony services by RBOCs, provided they comply with a 15-point 'competitive' checklist set out in §271 of the 1996 Act to the satisfaction of the FCC. This checklist included a number of resale, access, and interconnection obligations, including the provision of non-discriminatory access to unbundled network elements, which are discussed in section 6.9.1.1. In December 1999, Bell Atlantic was the first RBOC permitted by the FCC to offer interstate telephony services, provided it met certain conditions in the State of New York and complied with other safeguards in §272 of the 1996 Act. By 2003, the RBOCs had received approval to provide long-distance services in all of their regional areas.

The entry of the RBOCs into the long-distance market has been one of a number of factors which in recent years has contributed significantly to the restructuring of the US telecommunications market and the return of vertically integrated intrastate and long-distance network operators. In 2005, the FCC approved SBC's merger with AT&T and Verizon's merger with MCI. SBC adopted AT&T's name and, in 2006, AT&T merged with BellSouth following FCC approval. In 2007, SBC's merger with AT&T and Verizon's merger with MCI were finally approved after the federal court in Washington, DC entered consent decrees requiring the parties to divest certain assets. Despite the mergers, RBOCs owned by Verizon and AT&T providing interstate telephony services must continue to comply with the competitive checklist in the 1996 Act and other requirements.[7]

6.2.8 Cable

Since its inception in the 1950s, cable television has evolved from a video transmission service to a competitor for advanced voice and data services. Throughout this evolution, the FCC has applied varying degrees of regulation to this medium, first in response to cable's role as a distribution channel for video programming and, most

---

[5] Pub L No 104-104, 110 Stat 56 (1996) (codified in scattered sections of 47 USC).
[6] The MFJ was officially terminated on 11 April 1996 following the enactment of the 1996 Act.
[7] For further discussion of the obligations on RBOCs, see Section 272(f)(1) Sunset of the BOC Separate Affiliate and Related Requirements, Report and Order and Memorandum Opinion and Order, WC Docket No 02-122, CC Docket No 00-175, WC Docket No 06-120, FCC No 07-159, 22 FCC Rcd 16440 (2007)). With the exception of §272(e) of the Telecommunications Act of 1996, the obligations in §272 of the Act ceased to have effect three years from the date the FCC authorized a RBOC to provide long-distance services.

recently, to address the increasing number of broadband services that are delivered by cable. While industry consolidation has created large cable companies such as Comcast, Cox, and TimeWarner, individual cable systems are primarily local in nature due to their design and regulation. Typically, a cable 'head end' facility receives over-the-air broadcast and satellite signals via a series of antennae and dishes. These signals are then transmitted via wire throughout the community the cable provider serves, usually on telephone poles or along streets and other public rights of way. An individual cable line runs to each subscriber. Because a cable signal weakens the further it is from a head end, there is a technological limit to the scope of an individual cable system. Also, due to their use of local rights of way, cable systems have traditionally been subject to local regulation.

6.2.8.1 The development and regulation of cable
The first cable systems served as community antenna television (CATV) systems, and allowed households in mountainous regions to view local television stations whose signals would otherwise be unavailable. Later, cable service expanded into metropolitan areas that could receive over-the-air broadcasts. In the late 1970s and throughout the 1980s, cable began to provide programming unavailable through over-the-air broadcast stations. These services included specialized channels, such as CNN (news) and MTV (music videos), and 'pay cable' services such as HBO and 'pay-per-view' sporting events, and movies, for which the subscriber paid a premium above the normal monthly cable fee.

Initially, the FCC declined to regulate cable. However, as cable evolved beyond simple community antenna systems, the FCC and state regulators became concerned that cable's carriage of free-to-air broadcast signals could fragment audiences and harm local broadcasters' revenue bases. In the 1960s, without specific statutory authority to do so, the FCC began its regulation of cable by adopting policies designed to protect free-to-air broadcasters. Despite the FCC's initial hostility toward cable, the medium continued to grow. By 1980, the FCC had relaxed many of its initial cable regulations and Congress passed the first laws specifically addressing the medium.

The Cable Communications Policy Act of 1984 (the 1984 Cable Act)[8] served a dual purpose: while it furthered efforts to deregulate cable, it set forth the first statutory framework for cable regulation. The 1984 Cable Act explicitly gave the FCC authority to regulate cable, but it removed issues such as subscriber rates and programme carriage from its jurisdiction. Similarly, the 1984 Cable Act limited state and local regulation, which at that time was viewed as an impediment to the growth of cable. Cable rates rose rapidly after deregulation, and both the FCC and Congress soon faced public pressure to do something about the situation. Congress acted by passing

---

[8] Pub L No 98-549, 98 Stat 2779 (1984) (codified as amended in 47 USC §521 et seq).

the Cable Television Consumer Protection and Competition Act of 1992,[9] which repealed many provisions of the 1984 Cable Act. Congress greatly expanded the FCC's role in cable regulation. This legislation was a departure from the previous approach, which emphasized less regulation and greater competition, particularly in rate regulation.

Only a few years later, as part of its broad review of communications law and policy in the Telecommunications Act of 1996, Congress again modified cable regulation. The 1996 Act repealed certain cable-specific regulation, and adopted policies designed to encourage the broad provision of telecommunications services. To that end, the 1996 Act removed restrictions that had limited telephone companies from providing cable services, while concurrently, over a three-year period, phased out many of the cable rate regulations adopted in 1992. The 1996 Act further limited local and state regulation of cable, although municipalities continue to play an important role in granting and renewing local cable franchises.

Throughout the evolution of cable, the courts have generally upheld efforts to regulate the medium. In 1968, the Supreme Court acknowledged the FCC's right to regulate cable, concluding that it was 'interstate commerce by wire or radio' subject to the FCC's authority under the broad provisions of the 1934 Act (*United States v Southwestern Cable Co*, 392 US 157 (1968)). Although cable providers are akin to broadcasters and newspapers, in that they select programming for distribution, they are also similar to common carriers in that they mostly transmit, unaltered, content originated by third parties. Courts have been deferential to cable regulation, but have been unwilling to afford the types of First Amendment protection for regulation offered to newspapers and, to a lesser extent, to broadcasters.

6.2.8.2 *Expansion of cable services*
In part due to cable's potential to provide non-video programming, many cable systems began upgrading their systems in the 1990s by spending more than US$85 million and promising hundreds of channels of specialized programming and advanced voice and data services. In addition, the industry as a whole has undergone a rapid consolidation and evolution since passage of the Telecommunications Act of 1996. Small and regional cable companies have been acquired by cable conglomerates. For example, AT&T acquired cable giant TCI and, later, cable provider Comcast acquired all of AT&T's cable assets. The spectacular failure of Adelphia Communications in 2002 broke apart what was then the fifth largest cable company, but also provided the opportunity for Time Warner and Comcast to grow even larger by acquiring Adelphia's cable systems. Taken together, the combination of capital investment and industry consolidation has given industry players the infrastructure and size to compete directly with traditional telephone carriers.

---

[9] Pub L No 102-385, 106 Stat 1460 (1992) (codified as amended in scattered sections of 47 USC).

Because cable is physically wired into each subscriber's home or office, it offers an enviable conduit for the delivery of broadband services beyond basic video programming, including cable-based telephony using voice over Internet Protocol technology. Cable has been particularly successful at marketing high-speed Internet access, with estimates of the number of cable modem customers rising from 1.9 million at the start of 2000 to 34.7 million by 2008. Strong competition continues to exist from telephone companies that provide residential digital subscriber line (DSL) services, which were estimated to account for 29.5 million subscribers in 2008. To a lesser degree, cable also competes against fibre-to-the-home applications (such as Verizon's Fibre Optic Service), satellite broadband, fixed wireless, and broadband over power line providers in the still-growing market for broadband services.

At the same time cable worked to become a legitimate competitor in the larger telecommunications marketplace, it also had to devote resources to maintaining its traditional role as a provider of video programming. For example, cable companies need to find sufficient capacity to carry both bandwidth-intensive analogue cable channels as well as digital television broadcasts (known as high-definition television or HDTV in the US) during the digital television transition, and will likely continue to offer analogue feeds to households using legacy television sets for some time to come. Similarly, video-on-demand and other interactive video programming services that cable companies are developing to be competitive with digital video recorders and other new technologies create intensive bandwidth demands on the cable infrastructure. Cable continues to be the leading multichannel video programming distributor (MVPD) with more than two-thirds of the market, but satellite-based Direct Broadcast Satellite (DBS) systems, which allow consumers to receive video via pizza box-size dish antennae, are gaining market share and held more than a fourth of the market in 2008. While the remaining market share for multichannel video remains small, the services provided by fibre to the home are growing rapidly and present additional challenges to cable providers.

Cable systems have traditionally been local in nature, with entities having to obtain and periodically renew a local franchise licence in order to operate. However, this is changing in response to concerns that this process can be cumbersome and complaints that it has made it more difficult for new video service providers to enter markets. Some states have allowed cable and telecommunications entities to obtain a single franchise from the state, bypassing the need to negotiate individual local agreements. The FCC began a rulemaking on franchising in 2005, and in a controversial Report and Order[10] found evidence that local authorities had acted unreasonably to delay the entry of new competitors. It established rules regulating how local franchise authorities can act by, among other things, setting strict time limits for local governments to act on new applications to provide video services. In 2008,

---

[10] Implementation of Section 621(a)(1) of the Cable Communications Policy Act of 1984 as amended by the Cable Television Consumer Protection and Competition Act of 1992, Report and Order and Further Notice of Proposed Rulemaking, MB Docket No 05-311, FCC No 06-180, 22 FCC Rcd 5101 (2007).

the US Court of Appeals for the 6th Circuit upheld these rules, finding that the Commission's broad ability to regulate cable also gives it authority to limit the actions of state and local authorities.[11]

6.2.9 Wireless

The regulation of radio communications has long been a part of the FCC's mission, and government interest in this area can be traced back to before the agency's founding. Similarly, the development of commercial wireless telephone systems can trace its roots to the development of cellular networks in 1947. Under the cellular concept, the use of geographically small service areas (cells) allows a limited number of frequencies to be reused across a larger geographic area, which in turn increases the capacity of a mobile network to process a large number of telephone calls using relatively few frequencies. At the time the cellular system was envisioned, however, the technology did not exist to deploy widespread wireless networks.

From 1947 until 1968, the FCC sharply limited the number of frequencies available for cellular-type telephone operations, and thus there was little research or development in the area. The modern cellular radiotelephone service was authorized in 1981. Cellular systems in each market area were divided into two channel blocks, Block A and Block B, each consisting of 20 MHz of spectrum. Block B licences were initially limited to a local wireline carrier. Block A licences were limited to non-wireline cellular systems and were issued by comparative hearings for the initial markets, and later, by lottery. This wireline/non-wireline distinction no longer exists. Due to the growth in demand for cellular service, the FCC allocated an additional five MHz of spectrum to each cellular system in 1986, increasing the spectrum designated for each block to 25 MHz.

In 1994, the FCC began the auction of broadband personal communication system (PCS) spectrum, which consists of 120 MHz of spectrum in the 1850–1910 MHz and 1930–1990MHz bands and is divided into six blocks. The FCC broadly defined PCS as mobile and fixed communications offerings that serve individuals and businesses, and can be integrated with a variety of competing networks. As a practical matter, however, the services that were developed under broadband PCS were essentially marketed as and were widely perceived to be an advanced version of cellular service. In order to deploy PCS, it was necessary to relocate incumbent 2 GHz microwave licensees, which consisted of public utilities, railroads, and other entities who had employed point-to-point microwave links in their private internal radio networks. The FCC's Emerging Technologies relocation principles, which set forth a negotiation process that consists of multiple negotiation phases and which provide incentives for incumbent users to quickly vacate the band, were developed at this

---

[11] *Alliance for Community Media v FCC*, 529 F3d 763 (6th Cir 2008).

time and have since been used as a model for the relocation of incumbent users from other spectrum bands.[12]

A third type of mobile radio service is that provided by Specialized Mobile Radio (SMR) licensees. This service was first established by the FCC in 1979 to provide land mobile communications on a commercial basis. Although traditional SMR configurations provide dispatch-like services and can be found in business settings, several companies have used their licences to provide cellular-like services. The best known, Sprint Nextel, was founded in 1987 under the name Fleet Call. All three of these services (cellular, PCS, and Sprint Nextel's SMR services) are often collectively referred to as 'mobile telephone services'.

The FCC significantly increased the amount of spectrum set aside for wireless services with the allocation of 130 MHz of spectrum between 2002 and 2004 for 'advanced wireless services' (also known as AWS or 3G, for the 'third generation' technologies to follow cellular and PCS deployments). This spectrum consists of the 1710–1755 MHz, 1915–1920 MHz, 1995–2000 MHz, 2020–2025 MHz, and 2110–2180 MHz bands. This effort followed work at the World Radiocommunication Conference 2000, which had identified spectrum for 'next generation' technologies under the general label of 'IMT-2000'. Although existing US military uses prevented the AWS allocation from being fully harmonized with the international IMT-2000 spectrum, the US allocation nevertheless represents a large amount of spectrum that can be used to support new mobile video and broadband applications. The first 90 MHz of this spectrum was licensed by auction in 2006.

The deployment of PCS in the mid 1990s represented a technological improvement in mobile telephone networks, as these systems incorporated digital technology. The original cellular radio systems, which were first deployed using analogue technology,[13] were then incrementally upgraded to support this 'second generation' digital technology. These technical advancements, as well as the additional PCS spectrum, led to the development of a robust, competitive market for mobile telephone services in the US. As the FCC's annual reports on the state of mobile service competition[14] indicate, mobile telephony dramatically and quickly transformed from an expensive service used by a relatively small percentage of the American population to a widely accepted medium that was marked by falling prices, increased service areas, and such innovations as free night and weekend calling, no long-distance charges, and pricing plans that included extensive 'buckets' of minutes. Prior to this

[12] See generally Redevelopment of Spectrum to Encourage Innovation in the Use of New Telecommunications Technologies, ET Docket No 92–9.

[13] On 18 February 2007, the Commission eliminated the requirement for cellular service licensees to provide analogue service. This completed a five-year sunset period established as part of the FCC's Year 2000 biennial regulatory review.

[14] These reports are docketed under the caption 'In the matter of Implementation of Section 6002(b) of the Omnibus Budget Reconciliation Act of 1993; Annual Report and Analysis of Competitive Market Conditions With Respect to Commercial Mobile Services' and are maintained on the FCC's website at <http://wireless.fcc.gov/index.htm?job=cmrs_reports>.

time, the use of mobile telephone services in the US lagged behind that of many other countries, including much of Europe. Notably, by 2008 as many as one in eight American households were estimated to have 'cut the cord' by dropping their wireline telephone carrier in favour of a wireless provider.

6.2.10 Satellite

The provision of domestic and international communications services by satellite in the US has increased dramatically since the 1960s. Historically, domestic satellite services in the US have been provided by private entities; however, international satellite communications services in the US were offered exclusively by the Communications Satellite Corporation (Comsat), a government-controlled entity established under the Communications Satellite Act of 1962 (1962 Act).[15] Comsat was the US signatory to the International Telecommunications Satellite Organization (Intelsat) and the International Mobile Satellite Organization (Inmarsat) and resold Intelsat's services to US telecommunications carriers. Users and service providers were not permitted to access Comsat services directly. To ensure the economic viability of Inmarsat and Intelsat, the FCC did not authorize the operation of other international satellite systems until 1984 when President Ronald Reagan determined that competing systems were in the national interest.[16] However, the newly-licensed satellite operators were precluded from interconnecting to the PSTN, so commercial providers focused on broadcasting and international private communications. The FCC gradually lifted the interconnection restrictions and by 1997 they were removed. As a result, a number of satellite operators now offer integrated packages of traditional telephony and video programming services to their customers.

The desire to encourage greater competition in the US and other foreign markets for international satellite services and to establish a level playing field for competitors also led to the elimination of state control over Comsat, Intelsat, and Inmarsat. In 2000, the Open-Market Reorganization for the Betterment of International Telecommunications Act[17] (ORBIT) was enacted by Congress which amended the 1962 Act by mandating that Intelsat and Inmarsat privatize. If they failed to privatize, the FCC was directed to refuse to grant them the authorizations necessary to provide specified mobile and broadcasting services in the US.[18] ORBIT removed many of the privileges and immunities granted to Comsat and, in particular, the private sector ownership restrictions on Comsat. It also gave customers and service providers direct access to Intelsat services. Although the purpose of ORBIT was to establish a competitive global market for satellite communications services, ORBIT highlights

---

[15] Pub L No 87-624, 76 Stat 419 (1962).
[16] Presidential Determination No 85-2.
[17] Pub L No 106-180, 114 Stat 48 (2000).
[18] Inmarsat was privatized on 15 April 1999, prior to the enactment of ORBIT; Intelsat was privatized on 18 July 2001. See further Chapter 15.

an inconsistency in the US's current technology-neutral approach to regulation. Section 647 of ORBIT prohibits the FCC from awarding spectrum used for the provision of international satellite services even though wireless carriers have incurred significantly higher costs for their spectrum because it was auctioned.

Satellite providers now offer competition to traditional terrestrial and mobile networks in many fields, including radio programming, television, broadband, and telephony. Satellite communications are increasingly being viewed as vital to the provision of public safety services during times of emergency when terrestrial networks may be unavailable. Another trend has been the expansion of the types of mobile satellite terminals that can provide two-way communications, as well as the integration of terrestrial infrastructure (under the general term 'ancillary terrestrial component') that is authorized as part of the satellite licence.

6.3 OVERVIEW OF KEY US REGULATORY BODIES AND PROCEDURAL PRINCIPLES

Telecommunications regulation occurs at both state and federal levels in the US and the number and different types of regulatory bodies reflect the diversity of the 50 states and the federal government, as well as the involvement of the executive and legislative branches of government in this area.

At the federal level the FCC is principally responsible for all interstate and foreign telecommunications issues, and, following the passage of the Telecommunications Act of 1996, for certain intrastate issues. It is the most well-known US regulatory body. The FCC's jurisdiction covers numerous sectors, including fixed, mobile, satellite, and broadcasting, as well as licensing, enforcement, and consumer outreach functions. The FCC's broad authority is similar in size and scope to that afforded to the UK's Office of Communications. The work of the FCC is complemented by that of other federal government entities, most notably the National Telecommunications and Information Administration of the Department of Commerce, the Department of Justice, and the Federal Trade Commission. Unlike other countries, the US has never attempted to combine the offering and regulation of telecommunications services into a single state-run postal telegraph and telephone entity. Telephony and radio broadcasting have always been run by private-sector entities, subject to separate government regulation. At the state level, each of the 50 states and the District of Columbia has a public utility or public commission responsible for all telecommunications issues, including policy, licensing, and enforcement, arising within its jurisdiction. Having said that, state jurisdiction in certain areas has been reduced by the Telecommunications Act of 1996 and the use of the federal pre-emption doctrine (see section 6.7 below). The work of the state regulators is also coordinated by the National Association of Regulatory Utility Commissioners (commonly known by its acronym, NARUC). The FCC is significant in that it wields a significant amount of policy-making authority. It has expansive jurisdiction over telecommunications issues, despite certain statutory

limitations contained in the Communications Act of 1934. It exercises its authority via its rulemaking and order functions, but like all federal government agencies, remains subject to certain restrictions and key procedural principles contained in the Administrative Procedure Act.[19]

6.4 FEDERAL BODIES

6.4.1 The Federal Communications Commission

6.4.1.1 *Role and jurisdiction*

The FCC has full jurisdiction over all issues surrounding interstate and foreign communications which originate and/or are received in the US, including all aspects of fixed, mobile, cable, satellite, broadcasting, and commercial radio spectrum, and, in particular, tariffs and the transfer of 1934 Act licences in the context of mergers and acquisitions of authorized communications providers. The FCC's jurisdiction covers both service providers and facilities-based operators. Within its jurisdiction, the FCC has broad authority to ensure compliance with federal telecommunications law, subject to the requirement that any action taken be 'consistent with the public interest, convenience, and necessity', and is specifically granted the power to 'perform any and all actions, make such rules and regulation, and issue such orders . . . as may be necessary in the execution of its functions'. It is important to note that the regulatory power is conferred to the FCC as a whole rather than to an individual.

6.4.1.2 *Commissioners*

The FCC currently consists of five Commissioners (it originally had seven), each of whom is appointed by the President. The US Senate must, however, confirm the President's selections, and potential candidates are usually subject to a public confirmation hearing. Commissioners serve five-year terms, and Commissioners may be reappointed. Commissioners who are appointed to fill vacant positions must serve the remaining term (as opposed to starting a five-year term), and Commissioners who are not reappointed are limited in how long they may remain in office even if a replacement has yet to be confirmed. Accordingly, the Commission can and often will operate with fewer than five Commissioners if there are delays in the nomination and confirmation process. All Commissioners must be US citizens, and a maximum of three Commissioners may have the same political party affiliation. On a practical level, the Commissioners are responsible for formulating key policy initiatives, implementing new legislation, and adopting agency rules and regulations. However, the Commissioners delegate the day-to-day running of the FCC to its bureaux and offices.

---

[19] Ch 324, 60 Stat 237 (1946) (codified as amended at 5 USC).

One of the five Commissioners is designated by the President to serve as chairman, whose general duty is to coordinate the 'prompt and efficient disposition of all matters within the jurisdiction of the Commission'. The Chairman presents the views of the FCC as a whole and derives significant power from his ability to set the agency's agenda and to direct the work of the Commission's bureaux. Each Commissioner, including the Chairman, is entitled to present his own non-binding views on any particular issue.

6.4.1.3 Bureaux and offices

The 1934 Act confers on the FCC the general power to organize its staff in integrated bureaux and/or other divisional organizations as it deems necessary. It may also (in the interests of efficiency and cost-effectiveness) delegate its powers to its employees. The Commissioners may not delegate certain functions, such as evaluating the lawfulness of tariffs and the resolution of complaints, but, effectively, the bureaux share with the Commissioners the duties of conducting the FCC's business. The FCC is staffed by approximately 2,000 employees, the vast majority of whom work in the FCC's Washington, DC headquarters. The FCC also operates a technical laboratory in Maryland, a licensing office in Pennsylvania, and has a small network of enforcement field offices throughout the US.

As of 2008, the FCC is organized into seven operating bureaux, which collectively handle the majority of the FCC's workload. This organizational structure is generally based on the different types of services the FCC regulates. For example, the Wireline Competition Bureau (formerly the Common Carrier Bureau) is concerned primarily with 'traditional' fixed and radio common carriers. It is responsible for the licensing of these entities, including the disconnection and reduction of services, and mandating minimum accounting standards and reporting methodologies. It also evaluates most merger applications. Other major bureaux include: the Media Bureau (a combination of the former Mass Media and Cable bureaux), which is charged with regulating AM and FM radio stations, television broadcast stations, multi-channel video providers, such as cable television entities; the Wireless Telecommunications Bureau, which regulates all aspects of mobile communications, including cellular services, personal communications services, paging, public safety radio frequencies, amateur and other personal radio services, specialized mobile and microwave radio services; and the International Bureau, which is responsible for the FCC's international telecommunications and satellite programes, implements international treaties concerning telecommunications, and licenses cable landings as well as satellite and earth stations. A 1999 reorganization created Enforcement and Consumer Affairs bureaux, both of which address matters that arise across different communications services (such as consumer complaints regarding television programming content and cellular service bills). In 2006, the FCC created the Public Safety and Homeland Security Bureau, consolidating many of the public safety and emergency communications functions that had been administered by different bureaux and mirroring a trend by US policymakers to reorganize government offices to focus on public safety and anti-terrorism interests.

The majority of the FCC's licensing and regulatory work continues to be conducted by service-specific bureaux. As a result, each bureau will often develop and recommend policy options that are designed to protect and promote the types of communications services overseen by that bureau. When an issue affects more than one service, such as when the FCC must decide what level of interference a new satellite service must be able to tolerate from terrestrial radio stations operating on an adjacent frequency, Commissioners often must consider competing proposals that have been developed by the different bureaux.

In addition to the work of its bureaux, the FCC is supported by nine offices. These offices, among other things, represent its legal interests, provide technology and economic advice, and offer general administrative support. Individual offices play a significant role in the FCC's policy-making activities. For example, the Office of General Counsel is involved in the review of all matters regarding the approval of mergers and acquisitions by FCC-regulated companies, and the Office of Engineering and Technology supports those rule-making proceedings that relate to the allocation of the electromagnetic spectrum to the different types of radio services (such as broadcasting, satellite, fixed and mobile terrestrial operations, etc.).

6.4.1.4 Enforcement powers
Under the Communications Act of 1934, the FCC enjoys broad and powerful enforcement mechanisms. The FCC may enforce the provisions of the Communications Act of 1934 directly, or request the US federal district courts to initiate enforcement proceedings. Breach of the 1934 Act's provisions may result in monetary fines, revocation of the underlying authorization, or obligations to take the necessary steps to remedy the breach. The FCC and the district courts may also require authorized carriers to produce documentation relevant to investigations upon request.

6.4.2 National Telecommunications and Information Administration

The National Telecommunications and Information Administration (NTIA) was created by executive order of the President in 1978 and by statute in 1993 (Executive Order 12046 and statute codified at 47 USC §901 *et seq.*) It is an agency of the Department of Commerce. Whereas the FCC manages 'public' spectrum, NTIA administers spectrum for exclusive government use, such as those radio frequencies used by the armed services. In addition, the NTIA advises the President on telecommunications policy. The NTIA also negotiates for greater market access in foreign countries for US companies and administers grant programmes related to telecommunications.

Collectively, the NTIA and FCC manage use of all electromagnetic spectrum in the US. This divided jurisdiction requires the two agencies to work cooperatively to determine the most efficient way to allocate spectrum resources and how best to resolve competing proposals for its use. One such approach is to allow for shared federal and non-federal use of a single frequency band, under a variety of 'primary', 'secondary', and 'co-primary' designations. The NTIA and FCC may also redesignate

spectrum from exclusive government use to exclusive non-government use (or vice versa), although this process can be time consuming and is often complicated by the necessity to relocate existing users. Thus, while the NTIA has no official power over non-governmental interests, the actions of the NTIA can have a substantial effect on the interests of private entities.

While the FCC is generally well known to the American public, the NTIA has traditionally operated with little public recognition. Industry leaders have also criticized the NTIA for its lack of openness. As part of the digital television transition, the NTIA gained a measure of public awareness by administering a programme by which households could obtain coupons to offset the price of analogue converter boxes. In addition, greater attention has been paid to developing long-range national spectrum planning. As part of this effort, there has been interest in finding ways to make the administration of the FCC and NTIA's joint spectrum management responsibilities more timely and efficient.

6.4.3 Competition authorities

Federal antitrust law has played a key role in the regulation of telephony and to a lesser extent in other areas such as broadcasting and television. The primary US antitrust laws are the Federal Trade Commission Act,[20] Clayton Act,[21] and the Sherman Antitrust Act. All of the legislation is enforced by the Federal Trade Commission's Bureau of Competition and the Antitrust division of the Department of Justice (DoJ). Technically, the jurisdiction of these two bodies overlaps, but the agencies have agreed that the DoJ has primary responsibility for the enforcement of US antitrust law in the telecommunications sector. Both the DoJ and the Federal Trade Commission (FTC) have been heavily involved in assessing the competitive effects of key industry mergers.

The FTC has traditionally worked to promote consumer rights, and these efforts continue despite the general trend of federal agencies toward deregulation and reliance on the free market to bring about robust competition. For example, it manages the Do-Not-Call Registry, which places limitations on telemarketing phone calls, and investigates complaints against businesses that violate the rules, even though such jurisdiction is shared with the FCC and state and local authorities. It is worth noting that although the FTC evaluates the potential anti-competitive effects of mergers and acquisitions, it lacks the jurisdiction to take action against unfair or deceptive acts or practices and unfair methods of competition by common carriers. This particular power is reserved to the FCC.

---

[20] Ch 311, 38 Stat 711 (1914) (codified as amended at 15 USC §§41–58).
[21] Ch 323, 38 Stat 730 (1914) (codified as amended at 15 USC §§12–278 and 29 USC §§52, 53).

6.4.4 Courts

The passage and implementation of the Telecommunications Act of 1996 triggered a flurry of legal challenges to the federal courts (and the DC Circuit Court in particular), resulting in several key decisions regarding federal pre-emption and unbundled network elements. Judicial intervention is not new in the telecommunications area, however. Where judicial authority has been exercised in the past, the courts have tended to adopt a more pro-competitive approach than the FCC.

6.4.5 Congress and the President

The FCC is an 'independent' agency established by Congress under the Communications Act of 1934. However, both Congress and the President exercise considerable influence over the agency. The Congress consists of the Senate and the House of Representatives. The Senate is composed of 100 members. Two are elected from each of the 50 states. Each member ('Senator') serves a term of six years. The House of Representatives, on the other hand, is composed of 435 representatives from all of the 50 states. The number of representatives for each state is determined by the population that resides there. Each state is entitled to at least one representative, who serves a term of two years. Broadly speaking, any proposed legislation must be approved by a majority of members in both the Senate and the House of Representatives before it is passed to the President, who will decide whether to sign the proposed legislation into law.

The FCC's budget is authorized by Congress, although nearly all of this amount (US $313 million in 2007) comes directly from regulatory fees and other FCC-collected funds, such as a portion of proceeds from the auction of electromagnetic spectrum. The FCC must account for its annual spending and file an annual report to Congress containing information to facilitate Congressional review of its performance. Congress can also pass legislation directing the FCC to implement specific policy objectives, such as to auction a designated frequency block by a set date. As Congress has become more interested in telecommunications issues in recent years, it has increasingly enacted this type of legislation. Such narrowly tailored legislation stands in contrast to the broad legislative mandates that are often given to the FCC (and other administrative agencies) and which afford such agencies wide discretion to establish specific policies within the scope of those mandates. In addition, Commissioners are frequently called to testify before Congressional committees. Congress is heavily lobbied by industry participants and consumer advocate groups, and the telecommunications sector is often listed among the top industries for both political lobbying activity and monetary contributions to Congressional interests. Members of Congress are not hesitant to criticize the FCC's actions publicly, particularly when they believe the FCC is implementing laws in ways that are inconsistent with Congressional intent.

The President (and his Administration) also exert influence over the FCC. The President appoints FCC Commissioners and names the Chairman, subject to approval

by the Senate, the majority of whom may represent his political party. Because the Chairman has the power to set the FCC's agenda and oversees the workings of the staff, the President can utilize his selection of a chairman as a means to influence the tone and direction that a particular Commission is likely to take on matters of interest to the Administration.

6.5 STATE BODIES

6.5.1 Public Utility Commissions

The 1934 Act conferred extensive interstate jurisdiction on the FCC, while at the same time explicitly reserving jurisdiction over intrastate communications services to the 50 states as well as the District of Columbia. The state Public Utility Commissions (PUCs) are responsible for telecommunications regulation at this level. State jurisdiction over telecommunications has, in some areas, been reduced by the Telecommunications Act of 1996 and the use of the federal pre-emption doctrine by the FCC (see section 6.7 below). The PUCs approve tariffs and interconnection rates for intrastate telephony, handle customer complaints, and issue intrastate licences.

In addition to regulating telecommunications, PUCs oversee all other public utility functions. The structure and size of the PUCs and each of their telecommunications policies differ (significantly in some cases) from state to state, but generally all PUCs are state-created agencies with a division specializing in telecommunications regulation. Historically, some PUCs, in states such as Illinois, New York, and California, embraced competition within local exchange markets; others thwarted competitive efforts by the FCC.

Although the Telecommunications Act of 1996 extends the FCC's authority to cover local competition, state regulators retain some jurisdiction over telephony issues. Their jurisdiction is limited, however, in many cases to ensuring compliance with federal regulations rather than developing policy. State regulators have the right to prohibit market entry of service providers if necessary to advance or preserve universal service, public safety, and telecommunications services. However, any regulation imposed by the states must be done so on a 'competitively neutral basis' and be consistent with the universal service obligations (USOs) set forth in §254 of the 1934 Act.

6.5.2 National Association of Regulatory Utility Commissioners

In addition to the PUCs, the National Association of Regulatory Utility Commissioners (NARUC) also plays a role in the development of US telecommunications. The Association is comprised of federal and state utility regulators and strives to coordinate action by state regulators and to develop cooperation between federal and state regulators. Despite these aims, in practice, the Association represents the interests of

state regulators and becomes publicly involved with issues only when consensus already exists among the PUCs. It has a standing committee on telecommunications.

6.6 PROCEDURAL PRINCIPLES AND MECHANISMS: THE ADMINISTRATIVE PROCEDURE ACT AND ADMINISTRATIVE LAW PRINCIPLES

Because the FCC is neither a judicial nor a legislative body, it operates under the general principles of administrative law. Administrative agencies such as the FCC are considered to have regulatory expertise in discrete subject areas, and Congress usually passes laws containing general guidelines as opposed to specific regulations. Under a theory of delegation, agencies exercise broad discretion to interpret and apply those laws and will use their authority to enact their own specific rules and regulations that are legally enforceable. For example, §303(a) of the 1934 Act gives the FCC broad authority to classify radio stations, prescribe the nature of service to be provided in each class, and to determine the location and frequency bands of such stations. The FCC has used this broad authority to establish different types of radio services, such as the Microwave Radio Service and Television Broadcast Stations, and to establish rules and regulations regarding their operation, such as channel plans that set forth where within the electromagnetic spectrum individual licensees will be permitted to operate, and prescribe power limits and other technical rules. Each agency's rules are compiled in the Code of Federal Regulations (CFR). The FCC's rules are contained in Volume 47. The CFR is published annually in book form by the US government. As a result, these print editions often fail to include an agency's most recently adopted rules or will list rules that have been rescinded or modified. Such rule revisions have full force and effect notwithstanding any inconsistencies with the print edition of the CFR. Accordingly, practitioners routinely consult updated online versions of the rules, such as those maintained by the US Government Printing Office or by private parties.

6.6.1 Administrative Procedure Act—rulemaking

Although administrative agencies such as the FCC have broad discretion to interpret and apply laws, they must act within established procedural guidelines. The Administrative Procedure Act sets forth the basic 'notice and comment' framework that the FCC uses in promulgating rules, and ensures both publication of proposed rules and the opportunity for the public to comment before a rule is adopted. Either on its own motion, or in response to a 'Petition for Rulemaking', the FCC typically issues a 'Notice of Proposed Rulemaking' that announces proposed rules, describes the legislative authority on which the rules are based, and provides the public with an opportunity to file comments addressing the proposal. The most common pleading cycle usually lasts 45 days from the time that the Notice (or a summary thereof)

is published in the Federal Register, which is the US government's daily compilation of actions taken by the FCC and other agencies: 30 days for interested parties to file comments and an additional 15 days for reply comments. The FCC may first issue a 'Notice of Inquiry' that contains no firm proposals in order to create public discussion of a subject that can aid the FCC in developing a proposed policy. A Notice of Inquiry is sometimes employed when the FCC seeks to introduce new and potentially controversial concepts which may or may not generate enough interest or support to actually be incorporated into the FCC's rules. In practice, this step is usually omitted. As a consequence, Notices of Proposed Rulemaking issued by the FCC can read like broad inquiries into a subject area. These Notices ask many questions, propose more than one course of action and often include few actual proposed rules. Unlike with a Notice of Inquiry, however, the FCC may proceed to adopt binding rules once a Notice of Proposed Rulemaking has been issued.

For the FCC to adopt binding rules, it must issue a decisional document called a 'Report and Order'. The Report and Order must take into account the record generated by the Notice of Proposed Rulemaking and the FCC's original proposals. A large body of case law exists that interprets how closely an administrative agency's action must correspond to its proposals or the comments that parties have filed. Although considerable leeway exists for an agency to adopt final rules that differ from those that were proposed, the agency's action must be 'based on the record' that has been generated for that proceeding. In addition, while the agency does not have to adopt proposals submitted by commenting parties, it cannot ignore them altogether. It must acknowledge those comments and explain why it has not adopted the parties' proposals.

The rules adopted in a Report and Order will typically take effect on a specified time after publication in the Federal Register (usually 60 days). The date of Federal Register publication can often be weeks after the FCC releases a decision, so new rules sometimes will not become effective until several months after the FCC adopts them. Also, in a typical proceeding, the FCC may issue a document adopting rules while simultaneously proposing additional rules. Thus, it is common for a docket in a proceeding to remain 'open' for years and for the FCC to issue decisions with a title such as the 'Second Report and Order and Third Notice of Proposed Rulemaking'. The majority of Commissioners' votes is needed to adopt an item, although it is typical for individual Commissioners to attach statements explaining their decisions.

6.6.2 Issuance of orders—adjudicatory action

Much of the FCC's day-to-day work involves the issuance of adjudicatory orders addressing individual applications and petitions brought under the existing rules. Although these orders generally relate to a discrete matter, they are significant in that they provide insight as to how the FCC interprets its own rules and may be cited as precedent in subsequent actions before the FCC. Many of these orders are issued

under delegated authority, either by a bureau chief or deputy, or by a division chief, although some orders are adopted by the FCC as a whole. FCC staff may also resolve matters by issuing a non-published letter, although this option is often used for routine processing matters, such as the dismissal of a defective application.

6.6.3 Review of FCC action

Review of FCC action is generally accomplished by the filing of a 'Petition for Reconsideration', or, if the action was taken under delegated authority (such as by a chief of a bureau or office), by an 'Application for Review'. A party must file its application or petition within a set time period (generally 30 days) to preserve its right of review. In addition, the FCC may set aside an action on its own motion within 30 days. The Commission will respond to an application or petition by issuing a 'Memorandum Opinion and Order'. If the Commission makes new determinations and also modifies, clarifies, or upholds prior decisions in a particular proceeding, it may combine a further 'Report and Order' and a 'Memorandum Opinion and Order' into one document. The document will, however, always list the relevant docket and include both titles.

Both the Administrative Procedure Act and the FCC's rules contain provisions for formal hearings. However, these procedures have become uncommon as a result of the FCC's review procedures. Instead, parties typically bypass formal hearings and appeal directly to federal courts, including the DC Circuit Court in particular.

When reviewing an FCC decision a court will consider whether the FCC acted within its powers, both within the broad powers of the Communications Act of 1934 and under the specific legislation upon which the FCC based its rule or action. In addition, a court may, under the Administrative Procedure Act, set aside the FCC's decision if it is arbitrary, capricious, an abuse of discretion, or unsupported by evidence in the record. Courts often invoke the Administrative Procedure Act when the FCC has not explained the basis for its decision in the written order it adopted. In many cases, the court will send the matter back to the FCC (remand), with instructions to adequately explain all or a portion of the decision.

6.7 THE PRE-EMPTION DOCTRINE AND FCC JURISDICTION

The 1934 Act created a two-tier system of regulators: (i) the FCC, which is responsible for regulating interstate and foreign commerce in wire and radio communications; and (ii) state PUCs, with implicitly reserved powers to regulate intrastate communications. Under the Tenth Amendment of the US Constitution, all powers not expressly given to the Federal Government are reserved to the states. The creation of dual regulators reflected the need to balance the interests of state and federal governments in the US federal system and, in theory, states retain complete control over common carriers providing telecommunications services within their borders.

The actual power states have to regulate intrastate commerce, however, has been reduced as a result of expansive interpretations of the Commerce Clause[22] powers by the Supreme Court and the use of the pre-emption doctrine based on the Supremacy Clause. Broadly speaking, the Supremacy Clause enables Congress and federal agencies, acting within the scope of their statutory authority, to pre-empt state law when, for example, state law frustrates the federal purpose of legislation. In the telecommunications sector, the Supreme Court has found that many seemingly *intrastate* activities directly and/or indirectly affect *interstate* commerce and, thus, fall within the ambit of the FCC.

The FCC's need to rely on the pre-emption doctrine did not arise until the 1960s, when it sought to stimulate competition in the intrastate telephony market and tension between state regulators arose over the funding of universal service. *North Carolina Utilities Commission v FCC*, 537 F2d 787 (4th Cir 1976), *cert denied*, 429 US 1027 (1976) (*NCUC I*) was the first in a series of cases that enlarged the jurisdiction of the FCC to include some power over intrastate communications via reliance on the pre-emption doctrine. *NCUC I* arose because several state regulators imposed conditions on the interconnection of non-AT&T telephone hardware to the local system in an effort to limit the scope of the FCC's *Carterfone* decision (*The Use of the Carterfone Device in Message Toll Service v AT&T*, 13 FCC 2d 420 (1968)), which permitted apparatus conforming to AT&T's system specifications to connect to the phone network. The Fourth Circuit reasoned that because the same handsets were used by customers to place interstate and intrastate calls, the state and federal regulations were incompatible with each other and that state regulation had to give way to federal law.

The case is significant as it attempted to define the ambiguous terms 'interstate' and 'intrastate' found in the 1934 Act. The Court held that §2(b) of the 1934 Act only limits the FCC from regulating matters that 'in their nature and effect are separable from and do not substantially affect the conduct or development of interstate communications' (*NCUC I* at 793). Under this two-prong test, state regulators retain jurisdiction over issues that are separable from interstate communications and that have no impact on interstate telecommunications. If separation of interstate and intrastate communications is impossible, the FCC has or acquires jurisdiction.

The Supreme Court modified the *NCUC I* test in *Louisiana Pub Serv Commission v FCC*, 476 US 355, in 1986. In *Louisiana*, the Court held that the FCC has jurisdiction only if the FCC can demonstrate that interstate and intrastate issues are inseparable and that the exercise of jurisdiction by the state frustrates the statutory authority of the FCC.

The Telecommunications Act of 1996 further augmented the scope of the FCC's jurisdiction. Under §251(d), the FCC is required to introduce competition into the

---

[22] The Commerce Clause of the US Constitution gives the federal government the power to regulate commerce 'among the several states' and with foreign nations.

local loop. Sections 251(d)(3)(A)–(C) expressly enable the FCC to pre-empt any state legislation that contravenes the purposes of local competition. In addition, the FCC may pre-empt any state regulation that may 'prohibit or have the effect of prohibiting the ability of any entity to provide interstate and intrastate telecommunications service'.

Attempts by the FCC to implement measures to introduce local competition were, however, challenged by incumbent local exchange carriers (ILECs) and PUCs on the grounds that the FCC lacked the requisite authority to promulgate rules on such issues as pricing of local services and dialing parity. The Supreme Court in *AT&T Corporation v Iowa Utilities Board*, 525 US 366 (1999), however, affirmed that the FCC had general jurisdiction to implement the provisions of the 1996 Act, notwithstanding the provisions of the 1934 Act which reserve jurisdiction over intrastate matters to the states.

6.8 THE LICENSING OF COMMON CARRIERS[23]

Subject to exemptions adopted by the FCC and limited statutory exceptions, the Communications Act of 1934 requires all operators and providers of interstate and overseas communications services to obtain the permission of the FCC before network operation and service provision. Providers of publicly available services or so-called 'common carriers' must therefore ensure they hold and comply with the relevant authorization(s). Carriers that wish to use radio broadcasting, such as microwave links, must also obtain authorizations from the FCC to use the radio spectrum. If carriers wish to provide intrastate services, they must obtain the requisite authorizations from the PUC in each relevant state.

6.8.1 Common carriers defined

The 1934 Act unhelpfully defines a 'common carrier' as 'any person engaged as a common carrier for hire, in interstate or foreign communication by wire or radio or in interstate or foreign radio transmission of energy'. However, under common law the term means any carrier that holds itself out to the public for hire on general terms. Examples of common carriers include AT&T, Verizon, and Sprint Nextel.

6.8.2 Common carrier authorization for provision of domestic fixed services

Prior to 1999, the FCC required persons wishing to provide domestic or interstate communications services over wire, or to construct related facilities, to apply to the FCC for an individual authorization under §214 of the Communications Act of 1934.

---

[23] See further Chapter 7.

Authorizations were granted on a case-by-case basis and applicants had to be able to demonstrate that a grant would serve the public interest, convenience, and necessity. The FCC now gives 'blanket' authority for all carriers to provide domestic services, so there is no longer a need to obtain individual authorizations. However, carriers must register their details with the FCC. All carriers who provide services and operate networks pursuant to the FCC general authorization must comply with the FCC's rules applicable to them or face revocation of the authorization. Carriers must also pay annual administrative fees levied by the FCC to recoup the costs of its regulatory activities. These regulatory fees (which are different from application processing fees and forfeitures that carriers may also have to pay) are calculated by reference to a carrier's revenue.

Dominant common carriers, such as incumbent local exchange carriers, must submit to the FCC all new tariffs and changes to existing tariffs 30 days prior to their implementation. Relevant carriers must provide an explanatory cover letter, FCC Form 159 (a fee-remittance schedule), the appropriate fee, and underlying cost justification. ILECs subject to price cap regulation must also submit annual price cap filings, detailing the costs of services falling within defined 'regulatory baskets'. Dominant common carriers may elect to file tariffs electronically.

6.8.3 Common carrier authorization for provision of international services

Persons wishing to provide international services, or to construct facilities, must apply to the FCC for an individual authorization in accordance with §214 of the Communications Act of 1934. Applicants must be able to demonstrate that the grant of the authorization will serve the public interest, convenience, and necessity. They must provide details of their state of incorporation, a company tree showing all parties who directly or indirectly own at least ten per cent of the applicant, and a description of the service(s) to be provided. In addition, they must certify any affiliation with a foreign carrier, the countries to which services will be provided, and the absence of any special concessions from foreign operators which have market power on a US international route.

As a result of its 1998 biennial regulatory review, the FCC streamlined the application process for granting §214 authorizations for the provision of international services. Provided an applicant is not (i) affiliated with a foreign carrier who possesses market power in the destination market, (ii) affiliated with a dominant US carrier, or (iii) requesting authorization to provide services over private lines to a country the FCC has not previously authorized, the FCC may grant the authorization 14 days after issuing a public notice. The applicant may provide services 15 days after the FCC's publication of the notice to the public. It takes up to 90 days for the FCC to process a filing made by an applicant caught by one of the above conditions or if the FCC otherwise deems an application ineligible for the streamlined procedure.

Pursuant to a §214 authorization, the applicant must file copies of all interconnection agreements with terminating foreign operators (if applicable). Carriers must

also file tariffs in accordance with 47 CFR §§61.31 to 61.59 if they have been classified as dominant on particular US international routes for reasons other than having an affiliation with a foreign carrier that possesses market power. In some cases, carriers must report the number of international circuits they lease.

6.8.4 Common carrier mobile and personal communications services (PCS) authorizations

As has become the trend in Europe, the FCC awards spectrum licences for mobile services, including PCS and 'third generation' advanced wireless services, by auction. The spectrum is typically allocated to the highest bidder, although successful applicants must also be able to demonstrate their technical, financial, and legal ability to provide the underlying service. Spectrum licences are usually for a period of ten years with an expectation of renewal, so long as the licensee has taken steps to meet the service requirements for its licence, such as building out facilities or meeting minimum service thresholds. Most services are licensed on a geographic basis—either nationwide, or in defined service areas. Licensees are permitted to partition (geographically split) their licences and/or disaggregate (divest a portion of the spectrum within their licensed areas). They may also lease spectrum to third parties or enter into private common arrangements (see 6.10). Roll-out obligations vary, with nationwide licences typically requiring construction of base stations to cover between one-third to 40 per cent of the US population within five years and two-thirds to 75 per cent of the US population within ten years. In other cases, the FCC has required that the carrier provides 'substantial' service upon renewal. This service level is purposely unspecific, and is intended to take into account the nature and scope of communications services that have developed in the radio band without requiring the carrier to meet a certain benchmark (such as coverage to a fixed percentage of population). The FCC attempts to prevent companies from obtaining market dominance through a variety of means, including setting auction rules that exclude bidding by licensees of like services, and allocating multiple frequency channels within a given market. The FCC has also mandated spectrum caps, but this means of control has fallen out of favour. The FCC eliminated its fixed spectrum cap for commercial radio services effective from 1 January 2003, opting instead to evaluate the competitive effects of spectrum aggregation by these carriers on a case-by-case basis.

6.8.5 Local entry licences

In addition to the above licensing requirements, facilities-based operators and resellers who wish to provide publicly available intra- and inter-LATA services must also apply for the requisite licences in each of the 50 states. The application forms and specific requirements differ for each state and are too detailed to summarize here. Broadly speaking, however, each PUC requires basic information about the applicant

240   6. US Telecommunications Law

(name and contact details), as well as information about the technical, administrative, and financial ability of the applicant to provide the service.

6.8.6 Foreign ownership requirements

Until the adoption of the WTO's telecommunications 'Reference Paper', the FCC had a long-standing policy of protecting its domestic markets as well as US carriers abroad under the guise of promoting effective competition. For example, it required all foreign carrier applicants to satisfy the 'effective competitive opportunities' (ECO) test when applying for international §214 licences, indirect ownership in a radio licensee in excess of the 25 per cent maximum in §310(b)(4) of the 1934 Act or a cable landing licence. This test required a showing that there were no legal or practical restrictions on US carriers' entry into the foreign carrier's domestic market.

On 15 February 1997, the US and 68 other countries adopted the WTO Basic Telecommunications Agreement in addition to specific market entry commitments contained in the telecommunications 'Reference Paper'.[24] In light of the requirements of the Basic Telecommunications Agreement, the US substituted the ECO test with an 'open entry' standard for applicants from WTO countries. The FCC now presumes that a licence should be granted to a foreign carrier unless it is shown that the foreign carrier poses a high risk to competition in the US. The FCC's decision to approve the transfer of radio licences from Voice Stream to Deutsche Telekom in 2001, demonstrated a further shift in its foreign ownership policy (*Applications of Voice Stream Wireless Corporation, Powertel, Inc, Transferors, and Deutsche Telekom AG, Transferee, for Consent to Transfer Control of Licences and Authorizations Pursuant to Sections 214 and 310(d) of the Communications Act and Petition for Declaratory Ruling Pursuant to Section 310(d) of the Communications Act*, Memorandum Opinion and Order, IB Docket No 00–187, FCC No 01–142 (2001)). In its decision, the FCC found that foreign control of radio licences was in the public interest. It held that §§310(a) and (b)(4) of the 1934 Act do not prohibit foreign governments from having indirect ownership of FCC radio licences in excess of 25 per cent unless the FCC finds that the public interest is otherwise served by prohibition. Notwithstanding this decision, applicants from non-WTO signatories must continue to satisfy the ECO test. Third parties and licensees entering into spectrum lease arrangements must also ensure they comply with foreign ownership requirements.

6.9 ACCESS, INTERCONNECTION, AND RELATED MEASURES

Access, interconnection, and related policy is a contentious area as it has a significant effect on revenue for both established operators and new entrants.[25] Historically,

---

[24] See further Chapter 15.
[25] See further Chapter 8.

the FCC's work relating to access and interconnection has focused on fixed networks, but increasingly wireless issues are coming to the fore. This section discusses important access, interconnection, and related measures taken by the FCC which apply to fixed and mobile networks.

6.9.1 Fixed networks

The 1996 Act required the FCC to introduce a number of network access, interconnection, and related measures on competitive local exchange carriers (referred to as LECs or CLECs) and incumbent local exchange carriers (ILECs) to facilitate network interoperability. ILECs have additional obligations, including a duty to provide unbundled network elements and co-location. Some of the key obligations are discussed below.

6.9.1.1 *Unbundled network elements*

To break the monopolies that ILECs had in the local access market for narrowband services, Congress enacted §251 of the Telecommunications Act of 1996, which imposed a broad duty on ILECs to provide any requesting telecommunications carrier 'non-discriminatory access to network elements on an unbundled basis at any technically feasible point on rates, terms and conditions that are just, reasonable and non-discriminatory'. The Act also required ILECs to provide unbundled network elements (UNEs) so that requesting carriers are able to combine UNEs to provide telecommunications services. Under the Act, all carriers (including resellers, facilities-based operators, and wireless providers) are entitled to UNEs.

The FCC had the responsibility of implementing §251, and, under the FCC's current unbundling rules,[26] ILECs must provide access to 'proprietary' network elements where access is 'necessary'. Access is deemed to be necessary if, taking into consideration the availability of elements outside the incumbent's network (e.g. self-provisioning and alternative suppliers), access to that propriety network element would, as a practical, economic and operational matter, preclude the requesting carrier from providing the services it intended to offer.[27] In certain limited cases, the FCC will mandate the unbundling of proprietary network elements even if access is not necessary, where, for example, lack of access may frustrate the purposes of the 1996 Act.[28]

Access to non-proprietary network elements is determined by reference to an 'impairment' standard. If a carrier can demonstrate that an inability to access a non-proprietary network element 'impairs' its capacity to provide a telecommunications service, then the relevant ILEC must make that element available to the requesting carrier. Impairment occurs when 'lack of access to that element poses a barrier or barriers to entry, including operational and economic barriers that are likely to make

---

[26] 47 CFR §§51.307–51.321.
[27] 47 CFR §51.317(a)(1).
[28] 47 CFR §51.317(a)(2)(iii).

entry into a market by a reasonably efficient competitor uneconomic'.[29] As occurs under the 'necessary' standard, when making this assessment, the availability of elements outside the incumbent's network (e.g. self-provisioning and alternative suppliers) must be taken into account. The scope of the term 'telecommunications services' as used in the Act is broad; however, the FCC has stipulated that a carrier cannot use unbundled network elements to provide wireless and long-distance services.[30] As these markets are competitive, no impairment arises.[31] The current FCC rules mandate that ILECs provide local loops, subloops, network interface devices, local circuit switching, dedicated transport, 911 and Enhanced 911 databases which enable calls to emergency services and operations support systems (OSS), although certain restrictions apply.[32] Access to these network elements is designed to facilitate competition in narrowband and broadband services. Prices for unbundled network elements are set by PUCs in accordance with a forward long-run incremental methodology mandated by the FCC.[33]

It is an understatement to say that, for the FCC, formulating the necessary and impair tests and determining the specific network elements to be unbundled was a fraught process. Implementation of §251 finally ended in 2006, a decade after the 1996 Act was adopted. The FCC's difficulty was in part due to the lack of guidance given in the Act about the factors it should take into account when determining which network elements should be unbundled. Section 251(d)(2) of the Act stated only that the FCC had to consider '*at a minimum*' if access to proprietary network elements was 'necessary' and if denial of access to non-proprietary network elements would 'impair' the ability of a carrier seeking unbundling to provide telecommunications services. Notwithstanding the weaknesses of the 1996 Act, the FCC also had significant difficulty developing rules which passed judicial scrutiny. The courts overturned the FCC's unbundling rules in whole or in part on three occasions. In 1999, the Supreme Court rejected the FCC's first formulation[34] of the necessary and impair standards.[35] In 2002, the US Court of Appeals DC Circuit[36] upheld the FCC's[37] revised necessary standard but overturned its new impairment test. In 2004,

---

[29] 47 CFR §51.317(b).

[30] 47 CFR §51.309(b).

[31] Unbundled Access to Network Elements, Order on Remand, WC Docket No 04-313, CC Docket No 01-338, FCC No 04-290, 20 FCC Rcd 2533 (2005).

[32] 47 CFR §51.319.

[33] 47 USC §252(d)(1); 47 CFR §§51.501–51.515. See also Review of the Commission's Rules Regarding the Pricing of Unbundled Network Elements, Notice of Proposed Rulemaking, WC Docket No 03-173, FCC No 03-224, 18 FCC Rcd 18945 (2003).

[34] Implementation of the Local Competition Provisions in the Telecommunications Act 1996, First Report and Order, CC Docket Nos 96-98, 95-185, FCC No 9-325, 11 FCC Rcd 15499 (1996). This report and order is also known as the *Local Competition Order*.

[35] *FCC v Iowa Utilities Bd*, 525 US 1133(1999).

[36] *United States Telecom Association v FCC*, 290 F3d 415 (DC Cir 2001) (*USTA 1*).

[37] Implementation of the Local Competition Provisions of the Telecommunications Act of 1996, Third Report and Order and Fourth Further Notice of Proposed Rulemaking, CC Docket No 96-98, FCC No 99-238, 15 FCC Rcd 3696 (1999). This report and order is also known as the *UNE Remand Order*.

the US Court of Appeals DC Circuit[38] was again critical of the FCC's third formulation[39] of the impairment standard. However, in 2006, the DC Circuit[40] upheld the FCC's new definition of impair developed in light of the 2004 ruling.[41] As the Court stated, 'the Commission's fourth try [was] a charm'.[42] One of the consequences of the extensive litigation has been the FCC's shift to a higher threshold for unbundling than the FCC had originally envisaged and CLECs had wished. The revised standards implicitly adopt an 'essential-facilities' type focus which favours ILECs.[43]

6.9.1.2 Co-location

An issue closely related to UNEs is co-location, which also proved to be highly contentious. Under §251(c)(6) of the 1996 Act, ILECs are required to provide physical co-location of equipment necessary for interconnection or access to UNEs at their premises. Where subject to technical and space limitations, ILECs must provide virtual co-location. The FCC's Local Competition First Report and Order specified where CLECs could locate equipment, the types of equipment they could co-locate, and the allocation of space if insufficient physical collocation space existed. For example, space within an exchange was allotted on a first-come, first-served basis. ILECs were not obliged to construct or lease additional space to facilitate co-location but had to take into account projected demand for co-location of equipment when planning construction work. In addition, ILECs who rejected co-location applications citing space constraints had to permit applicants to 'walk through' the relevant space so that they could confirm that no space was in fact available.

Three years later, the FCC modified its rules in its Advanced Services Order (Deployment of Wireline Services Offering Advanced Telecommunications Capability, Third Report and Order in CC Docket No 98–147 and Fourth Report and Order in CC Docket No 96–98, FCC No 99–355, 14 FCC Rcd 20912 (1999)) to enable CLECs to share co-location space at an ILEC's premises and to co-locate equipment without the need for a cage surrounding their equipment. In addition, if there were insufficient co-location space, ILECs had to permit co-location in adjacent controlled 'environmental vaults' or similar structures where technically feasible. The FCC's order was challenged before the DC Circuit Court in *GTE v FCC* (205F 3d 416 (DC Cir 2000)).

---

[38] *United States Telecom Association v FCC*, 359 F3d 554 (DC Cir 2004) (*USTA II*).

[39] Review of the Section 251 Unbundling Obligations of Incumbent Local Exchange Carriers, Report and Order and Order on Remand and Further Notice of Proposed Rulemaking, CC Docket Nos 01-338, 96-98, and 98-147, FCC No 03-06, 18 FCC Rcd 16978 (2003). This report and order is also known as the *Triennial Review Order*.

[40] *Covad Communications Co and DIECA Communications, Inc v FCC*, 450 F.3d 528 (DC Cir 2006).

[41] Unbundled Access to Network Elements, WC Docket No 04-313, CC Docket No 01-338, FCC No 04-290, 20 FCC Rcd 2533 (2005).

[42] *Covad*, 450 F3d at 531.

[43] For further background on the saga of the FCC's unbundling rules, see Karen Lee and Jamison Prime, 'Overview of US Telecommunications Law', *Telecommunications Law and Regulation* (2nd edn, OUP, 2005) 531–538.

Some of the order's provisions were upheld but the DC Circuit Court directed the FCC to reconsider rules requiring ILECs to permit the co-location of equipment which performs functions in addition to those strictly needed to interconnect or access UNEs and the cross-connection of CLEC equipment co-located at different ILEC premises. The right of CLECs to select the physical co-location space at an ILEC's premises and the prohibitions on ILECs requiring CLECs to use separate rooms for co-location were also overturned.

The FCC published its revised rules in 2001 in Deployment of Wireline Services Offering Advanced Telecommunications Capacity, Fourth Report and Order, CC Docket No 98–147, FCC No 01–204, 16 FCC Rcd 15435 (2001). It determined that ILECs had to permit CLECs to co-locate switching and routing equipment. Other multifunction equipment could be co-located only if its primary purpose was for interconnection and/or access. ILECs also had to provide cross-connection to CLECs co-located within the same premises as ILECs. The FCC's current co-location rules are set out in 47 CFR §51.323.

6.9.1.3 *Interconnection*

Section 251(a) of the Act imposes a duty on all telecommunications carriers to interconnect 'directly or indirectly' with the facilities and equipment of other carriers. ILECs must permit other carriers to interconnect to the PSTN at any technically feasible point in their networks to enable the transmission and routing of telephone exchange and exchange access services.[44] The rates ILECs charge must be 'just, reasonable and non-discriminatory,'[45] and any service provided by an ILEC must be equal in quality to the service it supplies to itself or any affiliate.

The responsibility for day-to-day interconnection issues, including determinations of whether or not rates are 'just and reasonable', falls to the PUCs. However, in the Local Competition First Report and Order, the FCC mandated that the states had to apply the same long-run incremental cost methodology (LRIC) pricing standard used for UNEs. ILECs challenged the FCC's decision but in *FCC v Iowa Utilities Bd* (525 US 1133 (1999)), the Supreme Court held that the FCC had the authority to direct states to adopt a uniform pricing methodology. The adoption of a LRIC standard was also attacked by ILECs but was ultimately upheld by the Supreme Court in *Verizon v FCC* (535 US 467 (2002)). The FCC may also directly intervene in interconnection disputes where a PUC fails to carry out its responsibilities under §252 of the Telecommunications Act of 1996.

In an important ruling for VoIP providers in March 2007,[46] the FCC affirmed that CLECs providing wholesale telecommunications services to VoIP service providers are entitled to interconnect with ILECs under §251(a) and (b) of the Act. Certain state

---

[44] 47 USC §252(c)(2)(A)–(B).

[45] 47 USC §252(c)(2)(D).

[46] Time Warner Cable Request for Declaratory Ruling that Competitive Local Exchange Carriers May Obtain Interconnection Under Section 251 of the Communications Act of 1934, as Amended, to Provide

PUCs had denied CLECs rights of access to ILEC interconnection services in 2005 on the ground that CLECs were not telecommunications carriers when providing wholesale services to VoIP service providers—they were not offering 'telecommunications for a fee directly to the public'. The FCC's ruling enables the exchange of voice calls between broadband networks and the PSTN when VoIP service providers procure interconnection services through CLECs. The FCC has yet to determine if VoIP providers are 'telecommunications carriers' and consequently permitted in their own right to rely on §251 of the Act to interconnect directly with ILECs.

6.9.1.4 *Intercarrier compensation*
Currently, interconnection rates are determined by two different arrangements. Access charges—the fees interexchange carriers (IXCs) and 'commercial mobile radio services' carriers pay to LECs for originating, terminating, and transporting long-distance calls—are governed by determinations of the FCC and PUCs. The FCC sets the rates for interstate access charges in accordance with §201 of the 1934 Act and a series of FCC rules contained in 47 CFR Part 69. Intrastate access charges are set by the PUCs. Reciprocal compensation—the fees for terminating and transporting local calls—are set by the state PUCs with reference to a framework adopted by the FCC.[47] PUCs can determine rates using LRIC methodology. In the event that a PUC lacks access to adequate cost information, it can determine a default rate. As a general rule, the rates for CLECs and ILECs have to be symmetrical, although asymmetrical rates can be used if certain conditions are met. PUCs can also select a 'bill and keep' arrangement, whereby neither carrier charges the other carrier for termination services, provided a roughly equivalent amount of traffic is exchanged between the two carriers. Section 251(b)(5) of the 1996 Act imposes a general requirement on all LECs to establish reciprocal compensation arrangements. Importantly, LECs do not receive any compensation for carrying ISP-bound traffic which originates on the networks of other carriers under the reciprocal compensation rules.[48]

Recognizing that the current arrangements can give rise to regulatory arbitrage and distort market incentives, the FCC issued a Notice of Proposed Rulemaking on 19 April 2001[49] in which it announced its intention to develop a unified intercarrier compensation scheme and solicited industry views on a proposed 'bill and keep' arrangement for all types of interconnection. It also adopted an interim arrangement, which excluded ISP-bound traffic, pending adoption of 'bill and keep'. Progress on the issue of intercarrier compensation, however, has been slow due to the complexity

Wholesale Telecommunications Services to VoIP Providers, Memorandum Opinion and Order, WC Docket No 06-55, DA 07-709, 22 FCC Rcd 3513 (2007).

[47] 47 CFR §§51.701–51.717.
[48] Implementation of the Local Competition Provisions of the Telecommunications Act 1996, Order on Remand and Report and Order, CC Docket Nos 96-98, 99-68, FCC No 1-131, 16 FCC Rcd 9151 (2001).
[49] Developing a Unified Intercarrier Compensation Regime, Notice of Proposed Rulemaking, CC Docket No 01-92, FCC No 01-132, 16 FCC Rcd 9610 (2001).

of the underlying issues which has been exacerbated by the deployment of Internet protocol technology. The FCC issued a Further Notice of Proposed Rulemaking in 2005 seeking views on a number of proposals for reform received from various industry groups.[50] In 2006, the National Association of Regulatory Utility Commissioners' Task Force on Intercarrier Competition also submitted to the FCC a plan referred to as the 'Missoula Plan' which has attracted significant industry backing.[51] The FCC sought comment on the plan in 2006–07 but a final decision on intercarrier compensation, which has been complicated by a number of petitions for regulatory forbearance from the interim scheme, has not been made. Pressure for some form of resolution, however, has now been applied by the US Court of Appeals for the DC Circuit. On 8 July 2008, it ruled that the FCC's interim intercarrier arrangement must be vacated on 6 November 2008 unless the FCC can find a legal basis on which it can exclude ISP-bound traffic from the interim compensation scheme.[52] Dashing hopes that the court's decision would provoke the necessary reform of the intercarrier compensation and universal service regimes, anticipated for over a decade, the FCC announced on 3 November 2008 that it will draft a narrow order to address the court's specific concerns and consult on the broader issues. The order and consultation published during the proof stage of this chapter can be found at High-Cost Universal Service Support, Order on Remand and Report and Order and Further Notice of Proposed Rulemaking, WC Docket Nos 05-337, 03-109, 06-122, 04-36, CC Docket Nos 96-45, 99-200, 96-98, 01-92 and 99-68, FCC No 08-262 (2008).

6.9.1.5 *Resale*

Section 251(b)(1) of the 1996 Act requires all LECs to make their telecommunications services available for resale on reasonable and non-discriminatory terms. All resale services must be of equal quality and provided within the same period of time as LECs provide to others.[53] The wholesale rates that incumbent LECs may charge are determined by PUCs, subject to directions from the FCC, and are calculated by reference to the retail rate for the relevant telecommunications service less 'the portion thereof attributable to any marketing, billing, collection and other costs'[54] avoided by the ILEC by not providing its services to retail customers. In its Local Competition First Report and Order, the FCC adopted a 'reasonably avoidable standard' to determine avoidable costs. However, the Commission's resale pricing rules were overturned by the Eighth Circuit Court of Appeals in *Iowa Utilities Bd v FCC* (219 F 3d 744 (2000)). The Court held that the FCC's interpretation was inconsistent with the plain meaning of the 1996 Act. The appropriate standard for determining avoided

---

[50] Developing a Unified Intercarrier Compensation Regime, Further Notice of Proposed Rulemaking, CC Docket No 01-92, FCC No 05-33, 20 FCC Rcd 4685 (2005).

[51] A copy of the plan can be found on the FCC's website at <http://www.fcc.gov/wcb/ppd/IntercarrierCompensation/history.html>.

[52] *In re Core Communications, Inc.,* 531 F3d 849 (2008).

[53] 47 CFR §51.603.

[54] 47 USC §252(d)(3).

costs was those costs that the ILEC will actually avoid incurring in the future, because of its wholesale efforts, not costs that 'can be avoided'. The Court also stated that PUCs must assume that ILECs are acting as both a wholesale and retail provider when they determine costs whereas previously the FCC's rules had treated ILECs as only wholesalers. No modifications to the resale rules have been made, although the FCC issued a Notice of Proposed Rulemaking in 2003.[55]

6.9.1.6 'Dialing parity'

LECs are required to provide 'dialing parity' (or carrier pre-selection, as it is known in Europe) for all originating telecommunications services. LECs must not cause unreasonable dialing delay and must provide customers with the option of using different carriers for local calls as well as inter- and intra-LATA services. 'Anti-slamming' measures prohibit carriers from changing a customer's designated carrier(s) without consent. In 2005, the FCC adopted rules governing the exchange of customer billing data between carriers to facilitate carrier pre-selection.[56]

6.9.1.7 Number portability

The 1996 Act requires LECs to provide number portability for fixed line numbers to the extent 'technically feasible' in accordance with requirements prescribed by the FCC. The FCC's requirements were adopted on 27 June 1996 and are set out in Telephone Number Portability (First Report and Order and Further Notice of Proposed Rulemaking, CC Docket No 95–116, FCC No 96–286, 11 FCC Rcd 8352 (1996)). Various technical and cost-recovery issues were subsequently clarified in later opinions and orders. The FCC permits carriers to recover certain costs associated with number portability from other providers which use a carrier's number portability facilities to process their own calls and from end-users. Charges paid by end-users are included in their monthly telephone bills. In 2003, the FCC clarified that wireline carriers must port numbers to wireless carriers where the coverage area of the wireless carrier overlaps with the geographic location in which a wireline number is provided.[57] On 8 November 2007, the obligations of local number portability were extended to providers offering interconnected VoIP services which enable customers using a broadband connection to receive calls from and terminate calls to the PSTN.[58]

[55] Review of the Commission's Rules Regarding the Pricing of Unbundled Network Elements and the Resale of Service by Incumbent Local Exchange Carriers, Notice of Proposed Rulemaking, WC Docket No 03-173, FCC No 03-224, 18 FCC Rcd 20265 (2003).
[56] Rules and Regulations Implementing Minimum Customer Account Record Exchange Obligations on All Local and Interexchange Carriers, Report and Order and Further Notice of Proposed Rulemaking, CG Docket No 02-386, FCC No 05-29, 20 FCC Rcd 4560 (2005).
[57] Telephone Number Portability, Memorandum Opinion and Order and Further Notice of Proposed Rulemaking, CC Docket No 95-116, FCC No 03-284, 18 FCC Rcd 23697 (2003).
[58] Telephone Number Requirements for IP-Enabled Service Providers, Report and Order, Declaratory Ruling, Order on Remand and Notice of Proposed Rulemaking, WC Docket Nos 07-243, 07-244, 04-36, CC Docket Nos 95-116, 99-200, FCC No 07-188, 22 FCC Rcd 19531 (2007).

6.9.2 Mobile networks

6.9.2.1 *Siting of wireless towers and antenna*

As mobile networks have proliferated, the number of communications towers and antenna sites have increased dramatically. However, the needs of carriers to add such facilities in order to build complete and comprehensive networks have increasingly conflicted with other interests, including concerns over the aesthetics, radio frequency safety, and appropriateness of individual tower and antenna sites. Traditionally, the construction of antenna towers and other physical facilities has been regulated at the local level, and has been subject to local zoning and land-use regulations. However, the Telecommunications Act of 1996 added §332(c)(7) of the Communications Act of 1934, which limits state and local authority over zoning and land use decisions for personal wireless service facilities. Under the 1996 Act, a state or local government may not unreasonably discriminate among providers of functionally equivalent wireless services and must not regulate in a manner that prohibits or has the effect of prohibiting the provision of personal wireless services. In addition, the Act requires state and local entities to act on applications within a reasonable period of time. These entities must also make any denial of an application in writing supported by substantial evidence in a written record. Furthermore, the Act expressly pre-empts decisions that are premised (either directly or indirectly) on the environmental effects of radio frequency (RF) emissions, so long as the provider complies with the FCC's RF rules.

Allegations that a state or local government has acted inconsistently with §332(c)(7) are to be resolved exclusively by the courts. The extensive record of court decisions developed in this area generally has found in favour of wireless carriers seeking to build towers, although municipalities have prevailed when they have accompanied their denials with a clear, written record, and when the courts have been convinced that they are not acting to effectively deny all new facilities. Moreover, courts have made it clear that local entities still retain powerful decision-making capabilities. In *AT&T Wireless PCS v Virginia Beach*, 155F 3d 423 (4th Cir 1998), the Court of Appeals for the Fourth Circuit found that the city of Virginia Beach did not violate the Act when it denied an application for approval to erect a communications tower on a church's roof despite the fact that the denial effectively precluded the provision of service to a part of the community. It is worth noting, however, that other courts have distinguished or explicitly rejected the *Virginia Beach* decision as not adequately recognizing the extent of pre-emption provided in the Telecommunications Act of 1996.

More recently, opponents of communications towers and antenna facilities have challenged the FCC's implementation of the National Environmental Policy Act (NEPA),[59] as well as the National Historic Preservation Act (NHPA),[60] and the Endangered Species Act (ESA),[61] in an effort to prevent the construction of proposed facilities. NEPA is a 'cross-cutting law' in that it applies broadly to federal undertakings, and therefore must

---

[59] Pub L No 91-190, 83 Stat 852 (1970) (codified as amended at 42 USC §§4321–4347).
[60] Pub L No 89-665, 80 Stat 915 (1966) (codified as amended at 16 USC §470 *et seq*).
[61] Pub L No 93-205, 87 Stat 884 (1973) (codified as amended at 16 USC §1531 *et seq*).

be considered by the FCC in its tower-siting decisions. NEPA requires federal agencies to implement procedures which consider the potential environmental effects within the agency's decision-making process. FCC licensees and applicants are required to review whether or not their proposed actions will have environmental consequences and, if applicable, prepare an environmental assessment that leads to a series of steps designed to evaluate the environmental effect of the proposed action and, if the impact is significant, to seek alternatives or mitigations. The filing of an environmental assessment is required, among other times, when a proposed facility may have a significant effect on historic properties, could threaten endangered species or critical habitats, or may affect Native American religious sites. Much of the FCC's recent efforts have been directed at establishing agreements with interested stakeholders (such as historical preservation officials) to streamline procedures for review of environmental matters under NEPA.

A more difficult issue has been migratory birds. Many parties, including the US Fish and Wildlife Service (FWS), have estimated that communications towers kill between four and five million birds per year, and have a potentially significant impact on migratory birds—including some 350 species of night-migrating birds that may be affected by tower lights. Moreover, FWS has suggested that provisions of the Migratory Bird Treaty Act[62] that allow for prosecution of individuals who kill migratory birds would apply when birds are struck and killed by flying into communications towers. Following publication of a Notice of Inquiry which sought to create a record on the effect of communications towers on migratory birds in 2003, the FCC issued a Notice of Proposed Rulemaking in 2006.[63] It proposed that new and upgraded communications towers subject to Part 17 of its rules—towers in excess of 200 feet (60.96 metres) or communications towers which may interfere with airport runways—must be installed with white lights rather than red lights to the maximum extent possible in order to minimize their impact on migratory birds. The FCC also sought comment on whether rules regulating the height and location of communications towers as well as the use of wires employed to support them were needed. The rulemaking proceeding continues but the decision of the US Court of Appeals for the DC Circuit[64] in February 2008 to strike down a 2005 FCC decision denying a petition of the American Bird Conservancy and the Forest Conservation Council which requested, among other things, that the FCC prepare an environmental impact assessment of communications towers on migratory birds in the Gulf Coast region of the US, complicates matters for the FCC. In order to comply with the court's order, for example, the FCC will have to correct an oversight in its rules, contrary to NEPA, which currently do not permit the public to comment on applications for registration of communications towers on the FCC's database until the FCC has approved them.

[62] Ch 128, 40 Stat 755 (1918) (codified as amended at 16 USC §703 et seq).

[63] Effects of Communications Towers on Migratory Birds, Notice of Proposed Rulemaking, WT Docket No 03-187, FCC No 06-164, 21 FCC Rcd 13241 (2006).

[64] American Bird Conservancy, Inc and Forest Conservation Council v Federal Communications Commission, 516 F 3rd 1027 (DC Cir 2008).

6.9.2.2 *Poles, ducts, conduits, and rights of way*

A related issue is the ability of wireless carriers to access the poles, ducts, conduits, and rights of way of utilities and ILECs. Prior to the 1996 Act, wireless carriers were not entitled to such access. However, §224(f)(1) of the 1996 Act requires 'utilities', which include ILECs and electric, gas, water, and other public utilities, to provide 'telecommunications carriers' with non-discriminatory access to any pole, duct, conduit, or right of way owned or controlled by them. In addition, the rates, terms, and conditions for such access must be 'just and reasonable'. The FCC has expressly recognized that providers of fixed services as well as providers of cellular service, mobile radio, and PCS are entitled to the benefits of §224.

Certain provisions implementing §224 were adopted in the Local Competition First Report and Order. The FCC later adopted rules dealing with pole attachments in three reports and orders. The complete set of rules is set out in §§1.1401 to 1.1418 of the CFR. Under these provisions, all requests for access must be in writing; utilities must either grant or reject the request within 45 days. Utilities must provide evidence why a request cannot be granted. In most cases, in the event of a dispute, the parties may refer the matter to the FCC for resolution. In certain cases, the states have jurisdiction to hear disputes.

The FCC's rules permit mobile operators to affix wireline and wireless equipment to utility poles. The decision to permit the attachment of wireless equipment to utility poles was adopted in Implementation of Section 703(e) of the Telecommunications Act of 1996 (Report and Order, CS Docket No 97–151, FCC No 98–20, 13 FCC Rcd 6777 (1998)). It was subsequently challenged before the Supreme Court, which upheld the FCC's decision in *National Cable & Telecommunications Association, Inc, v Gulf Power Co*, 534 US 327 (2002). In 2007, the FCC issued a Notice of Proposed Rulemaking[65] relating to rates and access procedures. Among other things, the Commission examined the different formulas used to determine the rates applicable to cable and telecommunications carriers (cable rates are lower), and asked how to account for increasing competition between these providers and how to treat pole attachments for the provision of information access services. However, because the right of access to poles, ducts, conduits, and rights of way is based on statutory requirements, it is unlikely that the FCC will make any fundamental changes to the existing rules and procedures.

6.9.2.3 *Number portability*

The FCC mandated that all cellular, broadband PCS, and specialized mobile radio (SMR) providers (collectively referred to as commercial mobile radio service (CMRS)) had to enable their subscribers to port their wireless telephone numbers to other wireless carriers in its 1996 Telephone Number Portability First Report and

---

[65] Implementation of Section 224 of the Act, WC Docket No 07-245, RM-11293, RM-11303, FCC No 07-187, 22 FCC Rcd 20195 (2007).

Order. Phased in over a number of years, wireless number portability has been available in all areas of the US since 24 May 2004. Wireless-to-wireline porting is also required in some cases, although the vast majority of porting has been away from wireline services.

6.9.2.4 Calls to mobile

The termination of calls to US mobile networks is not regulated. This is unlike the UK and Europe where a significant amount of regulatory resource has been directed to the prices mobile operators charge for terminating calls to their networks. In the US, the charges for calls to and from mobile phones are paid for by the mobile subscriber. This charging method enables cost-conscious customers to switch to alternative carriers when calls terminated to their network supplier are above a competitive level. Europe, on the other hand, has adopted a 'calling party pays' (CPP) principle where customers pay for only outbound calls. This principle creates less incentive for mobile operators to keep termination rates for incoming calls low; if someone wants to reach a mobile subscriber, the calling party has no choice but to pay the termination charges set by the operator.

The FCC was briefly interested in whether it should promote CPP in the US. In 1997, it issued a Notice of Inquiry exploring whether CPP could be used to promote and expand competition in the local exchange telephone market.[66] Two years later, the FCC adopted a Declaratory Ruling and Notice of Proposed Rulemaking 'to help facilitate' the offering of CPP in the US.[67] By 2001, however, the FCC had concluded that carriers were not precluded from offering CPP and that the evolution of the wireless market lessened the need to adopt CPP regulations, and ended its inquiry in the matter.[68]

The lack of interest in CPP is largely attributable to the low cost of wireless calls, including the continued reduction in the price per minute of use, the prevalence of pricing 'buckets' that offer extensive or unlimited calling at a flat rate, and contract plans that include free calls during certain hours or to and from subscribers on the same network. However, the US wireless market is dominated by a business model in which carriers discount the cost of handsets and provide generous bundles of voice minutes and, increasingly, text and data use, but require long-term subscriber contracts in return. Thus, the early termination fees charged for switching carriers before a contract has run are of much more interest to the general public than CPP.

[66] Calling Party Pays Service Option in the Commercial Mobile Radio Services, Notice of Inquiry, WT Docket No 97-207, FCC No 97-341, 12 FCC Rcd 17693 (1997).

[67] Calling Party Pays Service Offering in the Commercial Mobile Radio Services, Declaratory Ruling and Notice of Proposed Rulemaking, WT Docket No 97-207, FCC No 99-137, 14 FCC Rcd 10861 (1999).

[68] Calling Party Pays Service Offering in the Commercial Mobile Radio Services, Memorandum Opinion and Order on Reconsideration and Order Terminating Proceeding, WT Docket No 97-207, FCC No 01-125, 16 FCC Rcd 8297 (2001).

The FCC remains concerned that US subscribers pay too much to terminate their calls to mobile subscribers overseas as a result of the CPP principle adopted in Europe and elsewhere. In October 2004, the FCC initiated a Notice of Inquiry to gather information on foreign mobile termination rates, action by overseas regulators and the effect foreign termination rates were having on US consumers.[69] The mobile termination inquiry follows the FCC's detailed investigation into the rates US carriers had to pay for terminating calls to foreign fixed networks. In 1997, the FCC adopted its controversial Benchmarks Order (International Settlement Rates Report and Order, IB Docket No 96–261, FCC No 97–280, 12 FCC Rcd 19806 (1997)) in which it stipulated the principles by which US carriers had to negotiate their settlement rates for call termination to fixed foreign networks.[70] As of the time of writing, the FCC has not tried to regulate the termination rates for calls to overseas mobile networks.

6.9.2.5 Roaming

All carriers offering CMRS must permit subscribers of other CMRS networks to 'roam' onto or use their network facilities on a non-discriminatory basis.[71] Until August 2007, the FCC required CMRS carriers to offer only 'manual' roaming.[72] Manual roaming permits subscribers to originate calls on a 'foreign' carrier's network if they contact a foreign carrier and pay for its services by credit card. The FCC now requires all CMRS carriers to offer 'automatic' roaming which enables subscribers to use their handsets without the need to contact a foreign carrier directly.[73] Instead, subscriber networks and 'foreign' carriers must have a contract specifying roaming arrangements and subscribers move seamlessly across networks. All charges are billed to subscribers by their 'home' networks. While this requirement applies to real-time two-way voice and data services, including push-to-talk and text messaging, it does not apply where the networks are not technologically compatible (such as when the two carriers use different over-the-air network interfaces) and or for areas within the requesting carrier's home market. At the time of its decision, the Commission held open the possibility of expanding roaming requirements to non-interconnected services, such as wireless broadband internet service, but did not implement such a requirement.

---

[69] The Effect of Foreign Mobile Termination Rates on US Customers, Notice of Inquiry, IB Docket No 04-398; FCC No 04-247, 19 FCC Rcd 21395 (2004).
[70] See further Chapter 15.
[71] The obligation arises from the FCC's interpretation of §§201 and 202 of the 1934 Act.
[72] See, e.g., Interconnection and Resale Obligations Pertaining to Commercial Mobile Radio Services, Second Report and Order and Third Notice of Proposed Rulemaking, CC Docket No 94-54, FCC No 96-284, 11 FCC Rcd 9462 (1996) and Third Report and Order and Memorandum Opinion and Order on Reconsideration, CC Docket No 94-54, FCC No 00-251, 15 FCC Rcd 15975 (2000).
[73] Reexamination of Roaming Obligations of Commercial Mobile Radio Service Providers, Report and Order and Further Notice of Proposed Rulemaking, WT Docket No 05-265, FCC No 07-143, 22 FCC Rcd 15817 (2007).

6.10 SPECTRUM MANAGEMENT

Although US government-regulated radio frequencies represent but a small portion of the overall electromagnetic spectrum, these bands represent a vital and increasingly rich resource. First used for distress communications and, later, to provide over-the-air broadcasting of audio and video programming, radio frequencies are now an integral part of nearly all communications systems. For example, microwave radio links are used as part of the nationwide long-distance telephone network for the transport of calls over rugged and remote areas where the use of copper wire or fibre-optic cables would be impractical. Mobile phones, which are dependent on radio waves to connect subscriber handsets to the public switched telephone network, have supplemented and are increasingly serving as replacements for traditional wireline telephony in the US.

Spectrum management in the US has been based on the idea that spectrum is a scarce resource, and this scarcity rationale has served as one justification for government intrusion into areas of content and speech that would otherwise be constitutionally protected (as in matters relating to broadcast indecency). It is important to remember, however, that radio frequencies can be used to provide services that fall into any number of regulatory schemes, including common carrier, subscription, and mass media broadcasting models. Although technological innovation continues to expand the portion of the electromagnetic spectrum that is suitable for radio propagation and to reduce the amount of bandwidth necessary to transmit vast quantities of information, the increasing demand for radio services and the deployment of new bandwidth-intensive applications continue to make spectrum a valuable resource. The portion of the electromagnetic spectrum that is subject to government regulation extends from 3 kHz to 400 GHz, although only the portion between 9 kHz and 300 GHz is currently authorized for radio services.

Although the US has sovereignty to regulate the use of the electromagnetic spectrum within its borders, its spectrum management is heavily influenced by the decisions of the International Telecommunication Union (ITU), an international organization within the United Nations System where governments and the private sector coordinate global telecommunications networks and services.[74] The majority of the US lies within Region 2, although certain Pacific territories are part of Region 3. By following the international allocation for a particular band, the US can promote economies of scale in the development and manufacture of equipment and, in the case of non-geostationary satellite systems or terrestrial systems located near international borders, avoid harmful interference from the use of incompatible types of services. The US follows the same terms to designate categories of services and allocations as does the ITU in the international Radio Regulations.

---

[74] See further Chapter 15.

Within the US, spectrum may be allocated to either federal government or non-federal government use exclusively, or for shared use. As discussed in section 6.4.2, the NTIA regulates the use of federal government spectrum, the FCC has jurisdiction over the remaining 'public' spectrum, and the two bodies coordinate use of shared spectrum. The FCC publishes a table of frequency allocations at 47 CFR § 2.106 that lists the international allocation for each region, the US table of frequency allocations for both federal government and non-federal government use, and a list of the relevant FCC rules for each band. In addition, a spectrum band may have both primary and secondary allocations. Within a band, secondary services must not cause harmful interference to stations of primary services, nor may secondary services claim protection from stations of a primary service. Generally, however, a station operating on a secondary basis may claim protection from a secondary station that begins operation at a later date.

Once spectrum has been allocated for a particular purpose (e.g. fixed or mobile services, broadcasting, Earth-to-space satellite operations), the FCC may then designate a particular type of radio service to use that spectrum band and set forth appropriate licensing and operational rules for that service. For example, the 806 MHz–821 MHz band, allocated to fixed and land mobile services in the US, is used by the Cellular Radiotelephone Service under Part 22 of the FCC's rules. The FCC is generally required to authorize the use of spectrum by issuance of a licence of a set duration. However, provisions also exist for the use of the electromagnetic spectrum on an unlicensed basis. So-called 'Part 15' devices (named for the part of the FCC rules under which they are administered) generally must be operated at low power and cannot cause interference to licensed operations. Cordless telephones, garage door openers, and local wireless networks (WiFi equipment) are common examples of unlicensed devices. Users have no exclusive rights to use the spectrum, and must accept any interference caused by other unlicensed devices operating in the band. Aside from the establishment of technical standards, the FCC generally does not set forth particular rules for unlicensed operations as it typically does for licensed services. A third option used on a limited basis is to 'license by rule', in which an individual is considered to hold an FCC authorization and must abide by specific rules of operation for a radio service, but where the individual does not make an application with the FCC to obtain a physical licence document. The Citizens Band Radio Service is the most well-known radio service that is licensed by rule.

Until the 1980s, the traditional means of awarding spectrum licences was the competitive hearing (or 'beauty parades' as they are known in the UK), in which the FCC used an exhaustive administrative hearing to determine which applicant was best qualified to hold a licence under the FCC's broad public interest standard. This mechanism came under attack as inefficient and poorly suited to the rapidly evolving telecommunications market. The first alternative to competitive hearings, lotteries, quickly proved equally problematic. With little or no cost to apply for a licence, applicants often had neither the means nor the desire to build systems. Instead, winners would 'flip' (or trade) their licences to entities that truly wished to hold a

licence, and would reap considerable profits in the transaction. Those who were not selected often used administrative procedures, such as the filing of petitions to deny, that undermined one of the primary goals of lotteries—the quick issuance of licences. The FCC, in turn, was overwhelmed by the number of applicants. It is noteworthy that lotteries, authorized in 1991, lasted only two years before Congress granted the FCC authority to auction spectrum.

Section 309(j) of the 1934 Act, added in 1993, gave the FCC the ability to use competitive bidding (or auctions) as a means to allocate licences for mobile telecommunications services where there are 'mutually exclusive' applications (i.e. more than one entity is seeking a single licence). Although the billions of dollars in public revenue raised by spectrum auctions have attracted considerable attention, the 1934 Act (as amended) requires the FCC to consider efficient spectrum use and not the expectation of revenues as the dominant factor in designing and implementing auctions. An auction winner does not acquire a property right in the underlying spectrum, but can expect to hold and renew the licence without having to participate in subsequent auctions. However, auction winners are subject to all FCC rules, including fines and the possibility that the licence may be revoked for good cause. The FCC is also mandated to ensure that licences are disseminated among a 'wide variety of licensees', including small businesses, rural telephone companies, and women- and minority-owned businesses. The FCC has addressed this requirement by establishing bidding credits for 'designated entities'. Other methods which have been employed (and generally without widespread success) include the offering of FCC-sponsored financing for winning designated entities and the setting aside of specific spectrum blocks that only designated entities may bid on.

The current auction process promotes both efficiency and participation by serious applicants. Prior to an auction, each bidder must file a Form 175 'short form' application detailing its qualifications, and submit an upfront deposit in relation to the licences it wishes to bid on. The auction is conducted remotely via computer software, and consists of multiple rounds in which bids may be increased only by a set increment. Once bidding activity drops below a set level, the auction closes. Shortly thereafter, winning bidders must file a 'long form' application and submit payments. Bid withdrawal and default penalties are designed to ensure that only serious bidders participate. In addition, the FCC has adopted rules to prevent bidding collusion.

The spectrum auction policy is considered to be a success. Auctions can quickly allocate licences and promote the rapid deployment of service. In addition, the FCC has developed considerable expertise in designing and conducting auctions that have served as models for other countries considering their own spectrum auctions. The auction policy has not been without problems, however. The FCC has faced the greatest difficulties in implementing its designated entity procedures. Constitutional challenges undermined the FCC's women and minority bidding preference programmes, and some designated entities have either defaulted on instalment payments or declared bankruptcy. In addition to hindering the rapid deployment of service, these developments have pitted the FCC against federal bankruptcy courts and have

weakened the FCC's control over its licensing process. Policy makers have also struggled with the question of what is appropriate to auction. Broadcasters, who traditionally are required to 'pay' for their spectrum though public interest programming requirements, were not initially subject to auctions; public safety entities have also been exempt. However, Congress has endorsed auctions by expanding the FCC's authority and mandating the use of auctions in additional circumstances. For example, some private radio spectrum may now be subject to auction, even though spectrum auctions were originally authorized only for commercial subscription services.

The FCC's auction authority had been due to expire in 2007, but was extended to 2011 as part of the Deficit Reduction Act of 2005.[75] It is extremely unlikely that Congress will permit this provision to sunset in 2011, and there have been proposals to make the authority permanent. In addition, the Commission has expanded the types of auction models it employs. For example, the Commercial Spectrum Enhancement Act of 2004[76] established a mechanism for reimbursing federal agencies out of spectrum auction proceeds for the cost of relocating existing operations, which in turn allowed spectrum being used by federal government entities to be included in the first Advanced Wireless Services auction in 2006. The Commission has also introduced 'package' bidding in auctions, in which a bidder may choose to make a single bid for a group of multiple licenses or can follow the traditional method of submitting individual bids for individual licenses. Economists have promoted even more complex models, such as 'two-sided' auctions where existing licensees would be permitted to place their licences in an auction alongside compatible spectrum blocks that had not previously been licensed.

At the same time the auction model has enjoyed growth and widespread support, US regulators have also explored alternative spectrum allocation mechanisms that could supplement or even replace spectrum auctions in some circumstances. One concept would build on the benefit of low entry barriers to spectrum use associated with unlicensed operations, but would require an operator to obtain a non-exclusive licence to use the band and/or use so-called 'smart' radio technologies and other use protocols to allow multiple parties to use the radio spectrum in a cooperative manner. The non-exclusive licence would be widely available and not subject to auction as is the case with licences for exclusive use of spectrum. Variations of this idea are known by several labels, including the 'spectrum commons', 'hybrid', and 'license-light' models. In addition, the Commission has attempted to make it easier for licensees to engage in secondary market transactions and enter into other spectrum leasing arrangements. Another—and widely controversial—concept involves spectrum underlays and other models in which parties would be permitted to operate in portions of licensed spectrum bands on an exclusive basis or at power levels greater

---

[75] Pub L No 109-17, 120 Stat 4 (2006) (relevant provisions codified in scattered sections of 47 USC).
[76] Pub L No 108-494, 118 Stat 3986 (2004) (codified in various sections of 47 USC).

than currently permitted with unlicensed operations, so long as they did not interfere with pre-existing licensees on those channels.

Notwithstanding these ideas, the success of auctions makes it likely that the auction model will continue to be the dominant means of spectrum allocation in the US for some time to come.

6.11 BROADBAND

Section 706(a) of the Telecommunications Act of 1996 imposes a general duty on the FCC and the telecommunications commissions of each state to encourage the deployment of 'advanced telecommunications capability', which includes any high-speed, switched, broadband telecommunications capability that enables users to send and receive voice, data, graphics, and video on a reasonable and timely basis.[77] xDSL, cable modems, and third generation mobile services, for example, are classified as 'advanced telecommunications capability'. The 1996 Act permits the FCC and the state bodies to use a number of regulatory methods, such as price cap regulation, regulatory forbearance (an important de-regulatory tool used by the FCC and codified in the 1996 Act), removal of impediments to infrastructure investment, and the promotion of competition in local markets to fulfil their statutory duty. In accordance with the 1996 Act, the FCC must also regularly review the market for advanced telecommunications capability and identify the steps (if any) it needs to take to encourage deployment.[78] The 1996 Act does not specify the appropriate regulatory framework to encourage the rapid roll out of broadband technology but a framework developed by the FCC has emerged since the US Supreme Court upheld the FCC's cable modem decision in 2005.[79] Consistent with British and European regulators, the FCC has now adopted a deregulatory approach, avoiding the application of the detailed common carrier obligations of Title II of the Communications Act of 1934 (as amended), including access, interconnection, and universal service contribution, to broadband services. This approach has been driven by a desire to promote investment in network infrastructure across all delivery platforms. However, the FCC is increasingly concerned about the ability of users to access all applications and to connect all devices of their choice to broadband services. An access regime designed to protect 'net neutrality', underpinned by the Commission's powers under Title I of

---

[77] The FCC has defined this term to include access services having the capability to support upstream and downstream speeds in excess of 200 Kbp/s.

[78] See, e.g., Inquiry Concerning the Deployment of Advanced Telecommunications Capability to All Americans in a Reasonable and Timely Fashion and Possible Steps to Accelerate Such Deployment Pursuant to Section 706 of the Telecommunications Act of 1996, Notice of Inquiry, GN Docket No 04-54, FCC No 04-55, 19 FCC Rcd 5136 (2004), and Broadband Industry Practices, Notice of Inquiry, WC Docket No 07-52, FCC No 07-21, 22 FCC Rcd 7894 (2007).

[79] *National Cable & Telecommunications Association v Brand X Internet Services*, 545 US 967 (2005).

the 1934 Act, is therefore beginning to emerge. The FCC's treatment of broadband services provided over cable, wireline, wireless, and other networks is discussed below.

6.11.1 Cable networks

Following the decision of the US Court of Appeals for the Ninth Circuit in *AT&T v City of Portland* (216 F 3d 871 (2003)) which held that the conveyance element of cable modem services was a 'telecommunications service' and was therefore subject to the obligations set out in Title II of the 1934 Act, the FCC issued a Declaratory Ruling and Notice of Proposed Rulemaking[80] which ignored the Court's holding. The FCC determined that cable modem services were not 'telecommunications services', defined in the Act as an 'offering of telecommunications[81] for a fee directly to the public, or to such classes of users as to be effectively available directly to the public, regardless of the facilities used'.[82] For the FCC, a cable modem service entailed a single, integrated Internet access service which comprised computer processing, the provision of information, computer interactivity, and data transport. While the FCC conceded that cable modem services were provided via 'telecommunications', the conveyance service was not a standalone product being offered to the public for a fee. Rather, the conveyance service was seen as integral to and indivisible from other Internet services, such as email and access to content, offered by cable operators. As such, the conveyance element of the cable modem service was not a 'telecommunications service'. Instead, cable modem services were classified as 'information services'[83]—'the offering of a capability for generating, acquiring, storing, transforming, processing, retrieving, utilizing, or making available information via telecommunications, and includes electronic publishing, but does not include any use of any such capability for the management, control, or operation of a telecommunications system or the management of a telecommunications service'.[84] Information services are subject to the FCC's ancillary jurisdiction under Title I of the Act. However, the FCC found that, as the conveyance element of a cable service was indivisible from the other Internet services provided by cable operators, it did not need to be provided to competitors in accordance with the FCC's ruling in *Computer Inquiry II* (see section 6.2.6). The FCC's reading of the Act is arguably

---

[80] Inquiry Concerning High-Speed Access to the Internet Over Cable and Other Facilities, Declaratory Ruling and Notice of Proposed Rulemaking, GN Docket No 00-185 and CS Docket No 02-52, FCC No 02-77, 17, FCC Rcd 4798 (2002).

[81] 'Telecommunications' is defined as 'the transmission, between or among points specified by the user, of information of the user's choosing, without change in the form or content of the information as sent and received'. 47 USC §153(43).

[82] 47 USC §153(46).

[83] 'Information services' were previously called 'enhanced services', which were discussed in section 6.2.6. The terminology was amended slightly by the 1996 Act but the two concepts are essentially the same.

[84] 47 USC § 153(20).

strained but it was nevertheless upheld by the Supreme Court in *National Cable & Telecommunications Association v Brand X Internet Services*, 545 US 967 (2005). Even though cable modem services are free of the burdens of Title II regulation, the FCC has started to consider if it should exercise its powers under its ancillary jurisdiction under Title I of the Act to adopt 'open access' rules for these services and 'information services' more generally to protect consumer interests. A concern is that cable modem and other broadband Internet access services deploying IP-enabled technology (see section 6.15) allow providers to discriminate against data packets containing particular types of data or sent from application providers which may be competing directly with broadband providers or their affiliates, either by blocking access to them or giving them lower network priority. In 2005, the FCC adopted a broadband policy of 'net neutrality',[85] which set forth four broad principles, declaring that consumers were, among other things, entitled to access content, run applications, and use services and devices of their choice, subject to law enforcement and technical network concerns. In an effort to determine if further regulatory intervention is necessary, the FCC opened an ongoing Notice of Inquiry in 2007.[86] Meanwhile, the difficulty of differentiating between legitimate network management techniques and discriminatory behaviour has been highlighted by the FCC's investigation into Comcast, following allegations it interfered with or delayed peer-to-peer file sharing when its network was congested. The FCC issued an enforcement order against the cable operator on 1 August 2008 (Formal Complaint of Free Press and Public Knowlwdge Against Comcast Corporation for Secretly Degrading Peer-to Peer Applications, File No EB-08-1H-1518, WC Docket No 07-52, FCC No 08-183 (2008)). Comcast has appealed the FCC's decision on the basis that the FCC's open access policy is not enforceable under its Title I powers as it has never been formally adopted as a Commission rule.

6.11.2 Wireline networks

Shortly after the Supreme Court's decision in 2005, the FCC also determined that 'wireline broadband Internet access services' are 'information services'.[87] Thus they are not subject to Title II regulation. The reasons given for the FCC's decision, which was upheld by the US Court of Appeals for the Third Circuit in *Time Warner Telecom v FCC* (507 F 3d 205 (3rd Cir 2007)), were similar to those articulated in its cable modem decision. Although the service was provided via 'telecommunications', it was not being offered to the public for a fee. Rather, the service was 'a functionally

---

[85] Appropriate Framework for Broadband Access to the Internet over Wireline Facilities, Policy Statement, CC Docket Nos 02-33, 01-337, 95-20, 98-10, GN Docket No 00-185, CS Docket 02-52, FCC No 05-151, 20 FCC Rcd 14986 (2005).
[86] Broadband Industry Practices, Notice of Inquiry, WC Docket No 07-52, FCC No 07-31, 22 FCC Rcd 7894 (2007).
[87] Appropriate Framework for Broadband Access to the Internet over Wireline Facilities, Report and Order and Notice of Proposed Rulemaking, CC Docket Nos 02-33, 01-337, 95-20, 98-10, WC Docket Nos 04-242, 05-271, FCC No 05-150, 20 FCC Rcd 14853 (2005).

integrated, finished service that inextricably intertwines information-processing capabilities with data transmission such that the consumer always uses them as a unitary service'.[88] As a result of the FCC's decision, common carriers providing 'wireline broadband Internet access services' can escape the more onerous regulatory obligations of Title II but remain free to offer wireline broadband transmission on a Title II basis. Significantly, the FCC also decided that common carriers offering these services, including the BOCs, no longer had to comply with its *Computer Inquiry* rules. Although common carriers offering 'wireline broadband Internet access services' are no longer subject to Title II or the *Computer Inquiry* rules, the Commission's open access policy discussed above (see section 6.11.1) applies to providers of wireline broadband services and the FCC continues to evaluate if it should exercise its ancillary jurisdiction under Title I of the Act to impose measures to protect consumers.[89]

The FCC's decision with respect to 'wireline broadband Internet access services' does not mean that all wireline broadband services are exempt from FCC regulatory obligations. ATM, Frame Relay, and gigabit Ethernet services, for example, are classified as telecommunications services, and common carriers providing them remain subject to Title II and the *Computer Inquiry* rules unless the FCC has granted a petition for forbearance in their favour. The FCC has relieved Verizon[90] and AT&T[91] of many of the dominant common carrier obligations imposed under Title II and some of the *Computer Inquiry* obligations with respect to certain high capacity broadband services, such as Frame Relay and ATM, following forbearance petitions. Thus many broadband conveyance services and providers are in practice subject to 'lighter touch' regulation. The FCC's current approach to 'wireline broadband Internet access services' and high capacity broadband services is significantly different from its earlier policy. Previously, for example, the FCC had sought to require ILECs providing wireline broadband Internet access services using xDSL services to provide access to the high frequency portion of the local loop (or line share) in order to increase the roll-out of broadband services[92] on the basis that the conveyance element was a 'telecommunications service'.

---

[88] Ibid, para 9.

[89] Ibid, paras 146–159.

[90] FCC, 'Verizon Telephone Companies' Petition for Forbearance from Title II and *Computer Inquiry* Rules with Respect to Their Broadband Services Is Granted by Operation of Law' (Press Release, 20 March 2006).

[91] Petition of AT&T Inc. for Forbearance Under 47 USC §160(c) from Title II and *Computer Inquiry* Rules with Respect to Its Broadband Services, Memorandum Opinion and Order, WC Docket No 06-125, FCC No 07-180, 22 FCC Rcd 18705 (2007).

[92] Deployment of Wireline Services Offering Advanced Telecommunications Capability, Third Report and Order in CC Docket No 98-147 and Fourth Report and Order in CC Docket No 96-98, FCC No 99-355, 14 FCC Rcd 20912 (1999).

6.11.3 Wireless networks

In 2007, the FCC determined the regulatory framework applicable to wireless broad-band Internet access services. It decided that these services were 'information services',[93] using the same logic adopted in its cable modem and wireline broadband decisions. In its wireless declaratory ruling, the FCC also found that wireless broad-band Internet access services were not 'commercial mobile services'[94] on the basis that they do not involve the provision of an 'interconnected service'.[95] Operators providing these wireless broadband Internet services therefore can avoid the applica-tion of Title II but remain free to offer their services in accordance with Title II if they so wish. As for cable and wireline broadband services, ensuring net neutrality in the wireless context has become a concern, and the FCC has proposed that that winners of the upcoming advanced wireless services auction referred to below will be required to comply with explicit network access requirements as a condition of their authorizations.[96]

The vast majority of the FCC's activities in the area of wireless broadband serv-ices regulation since the late 1990s, however, has been dedicated to increasing the amount of spectrum allocated for wireless broadband services when the FCC real-ized that the increasing demand for wireless services would be likely to outstrip existing spectrum allocations. Policy makers have been particularly concerned that the US is falling behind other countries in broadband penetration. Thus, wireless broadband deployment has been viewed by many as an especially important policy objective. A difficult challenge in wireless broadband deployment has been how to promote service to the vast rural portions of the country, in which a limited customer base and higher deployment costs result in a lower rate of return than commercial service providers can realize in high-density urban areas.

As explained in section 6.2.9, the FCC auctioned the first 90 MHz of spectrum for advanced wireless services (AWS) in 2006. Since then, an additional 40 MHz of spectrum[97] has been allocated for AWS use, and the FCC is currently developing the

---

[93] Appropriate Regulatory Treatment for Broadband Access to the Internet Over Wireless Networks, Declaratory Ruling, WT Docket No 07-53, FCC No 07-30, 32 FCC Rcd 5901 (2007).

[94] These are defined in §332(d)(1) of the 1934 Act (as amended) as 'any mobile service . . . that is provided for profit and makes interconnected services available (A) to the public or (B) to such classes of eligible users as to be effectively available to a substantial portion of the public, as specified by regulation by the Commission'.

[95] 47 USC §332(d)(2) defines the term 'interconnected service' as a 'service that is interconnected with the public switched network . . . or service for which a request for interconnection is pending pursuant to subsection (c)(1)(B)'.

[96] Service Rules for Advanced Wireless Services in the 2155–2175 MHz Band, Further Notice of Proposed Rulemaking, WT Docket Nos 07-195, 04-356, FCC No 08-158, 23 FCC Rcd 9859 (2008).

[97] See Amendment of Part 2 of the Commission's Rules to Allocate Spectrum Below 3 GHz for Mobile and Fixed Services to Support the Introduction of New Advanced Wireless Services, including Third Generation Wireless Systems, Sixth Report and Order, Third Memorandum Opinion and Order and Fifth Memorandum Opinion and Order, ET Docket Nos 00-258, 95-18, RM-9498,-10024, FCC No 04-219, 19 FCC Rcd 20720 (2004), Eighth Report and Order, Fifth Notice of Proposed Rule Making and Order, ET Docket No 00-258, FCC No 05-172, 20 FCC Rcd 15866 (2005).

rules applicable to the available spectrum before it is auctioned.[98] Wireless broadband providers have also benefited from additional spectrum released as a result of the US's transition to digital television. The Digital Television and Public Safety Act of 2005[99] mandated that the FCC terminate all spectrum licences in the 698–806 MHz band (referred to as the 700 MHz band) held by analogue broadcasters by 18 February 2008.[100] The Act also required the FCC to commence an auction of the 60 MHz of spectrum recovered by 28 January 2008,[101] the proceeds of which will pay for the cost of issuing US households with coupons to be used toward the purchase of digital-to-analogue converters. The FCC's 700 MHz auction closed on 18 March 2008, raising in excess of US$19 billion.[102] With the exception of 10 MHz reserved for a novel partnership between public safety users, such as police, fire, and other emergency services, and private industry to create a nationwide broadband network which did not meet its reserve price, interest in the spectrum was high. Signals in the 700 MHz frequency travel much farther than in other bands, consequently making the deployment of broadband wireless services to rural areas, for example, much cheaper. The 700 MHz band is also ideal for the deployment of 4G mobile technology.

Finally, the FCC continues to take measures to support the deployment of WiMax technology in the 2.5 GHz band. On 10 June 2004,[103] the FCC restructured the 2495–2690 MHz band to create additional opportunities for the roll-out of low-power cellular broadband operations, going so far as to rechristen the Multichannel Distribution Service the Broadband Radio Service. The band, however, is encumbered by existing users, including high-power instructional television fixed service (ITFS) (also known as Educational Broadband Service) operators that in many cases consist of schools, churches, and other non-profit entities that have used their spectrum to, among other things, transmit broadcasts of educational programming to remote

---

[98] See Service Rules for Advanced Wireless Services in the 1915–1920 MHz, 1995–2000 MHz, 2020–2025 MHz, and 2175–2180 MHz Bands, Notice of Proposed Rule Making, WT Docket Nos 04-356, 02-353, FCC No 04-218, 19 FCC Rcd 19263 (2004) (also known as AWS-2) and Service Rules for Advanced Wireless Services in the 2155–2175 MHz Band, Notice of Proposed Rulemaking, WT Docket No 07-195, FCC No 07-164, 22 FCC Rcd 17035 (2007) (also known as AWS-3).

[99] The Act forms Title III of the Deficit Reduction Act of 2005, Pub L No 109-171, 120 Stat 4 (2005) (codified in scattered sections of 47 USC).

[100] Digital Television and Public Safety Act of 2005 §3002 (b).

[101] Digital Television and Public Safety Act of 2005 §3003.

[102] For more information about the rules adopted by the FCC applicable to the 700MHz licences, see Service Rules for the 698–746, 747–762, and 777–792 MHz Bands, Report and Order and Further Notice of Proposed Rulemaking, WT Docket Nos 06-150, 01-309, 03-264, 06-169, 96-86, CC Docket No 94-102, PS Docket No 06-229, FCC No 07-72, 22 FCC Rcd 9100 (2007) and Second Report and Order, WT Docket Nos 06-150, 01-309, 03-264, 06-169, 96-86, 07-166, CC Docket No 94-102, PS Docket No 06-229, FCC No 07-132, 22 FCC Rcd 15289 (2007).

[103] Amendment of Parts 1, 21, 73, 74, and 101 of the Commission's Rules to Facilitate the Provision of Fixed and Mobile Broadband Access, Education and Other Advanced Services in the 2150–2162 and 2500–2690 MHz Bands, Report and Order and Further Notice of Proposed Rulemaking, WT Docket Nos 03-66, 03-67, 02-68, 00-230, RM-10586, -9718, MM Docket No 97-217, FCC 04-135, 19 FCC Rcd 14165 (2004).

classroom sites. Although the FCC's original Report and Order provided a plan to separate such high-power use from new low-power broadband providers, the transition has been very slow. In 2006, the FCC modified its transitional arrangements to create additional incentives for incumbents to move to new band assignments.[104] Notwithstanding unresolved incumbent issues, the FCC announced in 2008 that it would auction all available BRS spectrum.[105] WiMax technology is also expected to be deployed in the 3650–3700 MHz band, which was made available for such use in 2005. This spectrum is unique in that it was not auctioned, but was instead licensed by way of non-exclusive nationwide licences and its users must work cooperatively to share use of the band.

6.11.4 Other

The take-up of broadband satellite services remains limited compared to xDSL and cable modem services but they remain a feasible alternative, particularly for rural areas, and the FCC has taken measures to facilitate its deployment. For example, in 2001, it authorized the deployment of new broadband satellite systems for use in the Ka-band and revised the Over-the-Air Reception Devices Rule so that it prohibits governmental and non-governmental restrictions that impair the installation, maintenance, and use of satellite antennas which are less than one metre in diameter or any size in Alaska and which receive and transmit fixed wireless signals, including those used to provide broadband services.[106]

The FCC has also supported the roll out of broadband services over power lines. In 2004, it made a number of changes to Part 15 of its Rules to accommodate and promote this new technology.[107] Further modifications to the rules were made in 2006.[108] The FCC also determined in 2006 that Broadband over Power Line-enabled

---

[104] Amendment of Parts 1, 21, 73, 74, and 101 of the Commission's Rules to Facilitate the Provision of Fixed and Mobile Broadband Access, Education and Other Advanced Services in the 2150–2162 and 2500–2690 MHz Bands, Order on Reconsideration and Fifth Memorandum Opinion and Order and Third Memorandum Opinion and Order and Second Report and Order, WT Docket Nos 03-66, 03-67, 02-68, 00-230, RM-10586, -9718, MM Docket No 97-217, IB Docket No 02-364, ET Docket No 00-258, FCC No 06-46, 21 FCC Rcd 5606 (2006).

[105] Amendment of Parts 1, 21, 73, 74, and 101 of the Commission's Rules to Facilitate the Provision of Fixed and Mobile Broadband Access, Education and Other Advanced Services in the 2150–2162 and 2500–2690 MHz Bands, Third Order on Reconsideration and Sixth Memorandum Opinion and Order and Fourth Memorandum Opinion and Order and Second Further Notice of Proposed Rulemaking and Declaratory Ruling, WT Docket Nos 03-66, 03-67, 02-68, RM-10586, -9718, IB Docket No 02-364, ET Docket No 00-258, FCC No 08-83, 23 FCC Rcd 5992 (2008).

[106] 47 CFR §1.4000.

[107] Amendment of Part 15 regarding New Requirements and Measurement Guidelines for Access Broadband over Power Line Systems, Report and Order, ET Docket Nos 04-37, 03-104, FCC No 04-245, 19 FCC Rcd 21265 (2004).

[108] Amendment of Part 15 regarding New Requirements and Measurement Guidelines for Access Broadband over Power Line Systems, Memorandum Opinion and Order, ET Docket Nos 04-37, 03-104, FCC No 06-113, 21 FCC Rcd 9308 (2006).

Internet access services are 'information services', thereby placing BPL operators on the same regulatory footing as cable, wireline, and wireless carriers providing Internet access services.[109]

6.12 UNIVERSAL SERVICE OBLIGATIONS (USOs)

The concept of 'universal service' was coined by Theodore Vail, then Chairman of AT&T, in 1907.[110] Vail first conceived the term to promote a public policy whereby a telephone company would provide all who wanted service in an area in return for continued regulation as the sole service provider in a given area. Later, as universal service came to represent the policy that all Americans should have basic telephone access at a reasonable rate, the primary issues related to the subsidy of high-cost users (such as rural and residential customers) by low-cost users (such as urban and business customers).

Some 80 years after the concept was first adopted, §254 of the Telecommunications Act 1996 finally wrote the principle of universal service into law. However, the 1996 Act declined specifically to define universal service, instead recognizing it as an 'evolving level of telecommunications services' that is based on seven broad principles, such as quality service at reasonable rates, and access to telecommunications services in rural and other high-cost areas. The 1996 Act also expanded the concept of universal service to include the principle that health care providers in rural areas, schools, and libraries should have access to advanced telecommunications services, such as the Internet and other broadband services. The 1996 Act directed the FCC and a Federal-State Joint Board established under the 1996 Act to adopt mechanisms to fund and support a universal service policy based on these seven principles. The Federal-State Joint Board, which is comprised of FCC commissioners, PUCs, and a state-appointed utility consumer advocate, continues to keep universal service policy and related mechanisms under review. It makes recommendations from time to time to the FCC which is required to implement them within one year of their receipt.

The FCC in conjunction with the Federal-State Joint Board adopted four distinct universal service programmes, which are administered by the Universal Service Administrative Company (USAC) in accordance with Part 54 of the FCC rules. USAC is an independent, not-for-profit corporation designated as the administrator of the federal Universal Service Fund by the FCC. Of the nearly US$7 billion in 2007 overall universal service fund support, nearly two-thirds went to the high-cost fund, which provides monies to providers to ensure that consumers in all regions of

---

[109] United Power Line Council's Petition for Declaratory Ruling Regarding the Classification of Broadband over Power Line Internet Access Service as an Information Service, Memorandum Opinion and Order, WC Docket No 06-10, FCC 06-165, 21 FCC Rcd 13281 (2006).

[110] Stated by Garnham, N, 'Universal Service', in Melody, WH (ed) *Telecom Reform* (Technical University of Denmark, 1997), at 207.

the nation have access to and pay rates for telecommunications services that are reasonably comparable to those services provided and rates paid in urban areas. The other funds are the lifeline/link-up programmes for low-income consumers (US$822 million), the schools and libraries fund (US$1.8 billion), and the rural health care fund (US$37 million).

Under the low-income scheme, PUCs designate which telecommunications carriers must provide and advertise a minimum list of services and functionalities, including, for example, access to the public switched network, emergency services, and directory assistance, to low-income users. The provision of broadband services is not mandatory. Qualified low-income consumers are entitled to discounts on the installation costs of these services and functionalities and they may also defer payment of any remaining charges. Additional discounts are available on calls and related services. In return for providing these services, eligible telecommunications carriers are entitled to federal financial support calculated to account for the revenue that they forego by providing these discounted services. By contrast, the high-cost programme does not target consumers of particular income levels, but instead is intended to provide affordable telephone service to those areas where the cost of providing such service, absent subsidies, would be much higher than the national average. This is the most costly and complex of the four programmes, and high-cost funds are used to support such costs as the provision of local loops and local switching costs, as well as providing other forms of long-term financial support. While the high-cost fund originally served to subsidize monopoly wireline voice networks that provided service to rural and other underserved areas, it has grown to include both incumbent and competitive carriers, including many wireless entities.

The 'e-rate' programme provides 20 to 90 per cent discounts on telecommunications services, Internet access, and internal connections to schools and libraries. The precise rate varies on the household income level of students in the community and the presence of the school or library in urban or rural areas. To receive the discount, schools and libraries must allow telecommunications carriers to bid on a contract for services. The schools and libraries then apply to USAC for a discount. If an application is successful, the carrier chosen by the schools and libraries provides the service at a discounted rate and the carrier is reimbursed the amount of the discount by USAC.

According to the FCC, more than 99 per cent of US public schools were connected to the Internet by 2002 as result of this scheme. The rural health care programme, which is designed to provide reduced rates to rural health care providers for the provision of 'tele-medicine' and 'tele-health' applications such as video links between remote clinics and specialist doctors in large urban hospitals, is administered in a similar way.

The universal service fund has been criticized as being susceptible to fraud and abuse. An inquiry in 2004 of the 'e-rate' programme found instances of improper or falsified purchases, unused equipment, and other substantial violations in nearly a third of the audits that were conducted. While the Commission has taken subsequent

steps to suspend and disbar from the programme persons who have been found to have been involved in such abuse, this has not completely stopped efforts to defraud the programme. In addition, a 2008 report by the Government Accounting Office was critical of both USAC and the FCC for failing to establish performance goals or similar measures for recipients within all four of the programmes, and for not conducting comprehensive audits once funds were awarded. This report came after a 2007 analysis by the FCC's Inspector General that found erroneous payment rates in the universal service programmes as high as 20.6 per cent. For these reasons, there is significant interest in providing increased oversight and review of universal service fund disbursements.

Prior to the 1996 Act, universal service was paid for predominantly by AT&T and other large long-distance providers. Under the 1996 Act, the FCC's universal service programmes are now paid for by charges levied by the FCC on all telecommunications carriers which provide interstate and international services to the public unless their contribution is less than US$10,000. The meaning of interstate and international services is broad and encompasses satellite, mobile, and payphone services. Telecommunications carriers pay quarterly charges toward universal service provision to USAC, which in turn makes payments in support of the four universal service fund programmes.

When §254 of the 1996 Act was first implemented, carriers paid a contribution based in part on their actual revenue earned from the provision of interstate services.[111] However, since 1 April 2003,[112] the charges paid are based on a carrier's projection of collected revenues derived from domestic end users for telecommunications or telecommunications services (less a carrier's projected universal service contribution) multiplied by a 'contribution factor'. The contribution factor is calculated by the FCC on a quarterly basis and is the ratio of projected costs for the universal service programmes for the quarter and projected interstate revenue from all carriers. The contribution ratio fluctuates. The ratio used for the third fiscal quarter in 2008 was 11.4 per cent. With the exception of low-income users, the FCC permits operators to recoup their contributions by charging their customers a universal service fee, which appears as a separate item in their phone bills. These fees must not exceed the FCC's contribution fee multiplied by the total amount of a customer's charges for interstate services.

The widespread substitution of non-wireline carriers for the provision of telecommunications services and evolving market practices have presented challenges for the universal service fund. Because many interstate telecommunications services are bundled with intrastate services and often non-telecommunications products, it can

---

[111] Federal-State Joint Board on Universal Service, Report and Order, CC Docket No 96-45, FCC 97-157, 12 FCC Rcd 8776 (1997).

[112] Federal-State Joint Board on Universal Service, Report and Order and Second Further Notice of Proposed Rulemaking, CC Docket Nos 96-45, 98-71, 90-571, 92-237, NSD File No L-00-72, CC Docket Nos 99-200, 95-116, and 98-170, FCC No 02-329, 17 FCC Rcd 24952 (2002).

be difficult to distinguish revenue derived from interstate and intrastate services. This problem creates a risk that not all revenue from interstate services is being counted. To address this problem in part, the FCC permits cellular, broadband PCS, and SMR providers to assume that no more than 37.1 per cent of their revenues is derived from the provision of interstate services, and their universal service contributions are assessed accordingly. This safe harbour figure has grown steadily from its original 15 per cent. In addition, the contribution methodology has to be considered in the context of the FCC's statutory and regulatory classifications of broadband services and of IP-enabled service (discussed in section 6.15). In 2006, the FCC required providers of interconnected voice-over Internet Protocol (VoIP) to contribute to the universal service fund.[113] In doing so, the Commission avoided determining if VoIP services by interconnected VoIP providers are a 'telecommunications service' or an 'information service', and instead found that such entities are 'providers of interstate telecommunications' for the purposes of §254 of the 1996 Act. This novel approach was designed to permit the Commission to obtain universal service support from VoIP providers without having to find that they were telecommunications carriers subject to onerous Title II common carrier requirements. The decision was challenged but upheld in 2007 in *Vonage Holdings Corp. v FCC* (489 F.3d 1232 (DC Cir 2007)), where the Court found that the FCC acted reasonably in exercising its permissive authority with respect to universal service obligations and that it did not have to reach the issue of how VoIP should be classified. Because the FCC's decision only addressed interconnected VoIP providers, an unresolved question is whether the FCC has the authority to regulate a larger class of IP-enabled services. To the extent that the FCC can and chooses to regulate such services, it still could be difficult to determine which portion of such services is sufficiently telephone-like to be subject to universal service obligations. Moreover, in cases where such service providers may be transitory or located in foreign countries, the FCC may find it difficult to collect charges that are due.

Despite the inclusion of additional sources of revenue, interstate revenue as a whole is declining as competition for long-distance services has intensified and as other IP-enabled technologies develop. This, in turn, reduces the funding available to the universal service fund. At the same time, costs have been increasing, particularly with respect to the high-cost fund.[114] Together, these factors create the possibility that the costs to provide universal service will not be met under existing arrangements and have led many to the conclusion that fundamental reform is needed to secure the long-term viability of universal service.

---

[113] Universal Service Contribution Methodology, Report and Order and Notice of Proposed Rulemaking, WC Docket No 06-122, CC Docket No 96-45 et al, FCC No 06-94, 21 FCC Rcd 7518 (2006).

[114] For example, in February 2004, the Federal-State Joint Board recommended that the FCC modify the funding available to designated carriers. See Federal-State Joint Board on Universal Service, Recommended Decision, CC Docket No 96-45, FCC No 04J-1, 19 FCC Rcd 4257 (2004).

At the time of publication, the FCC is considering three possible alternatives to its current contribution methodology and variations of them.[115] The first approach would require each interstate telecommunications carrier to pay a flat-rate monthly fee for each residential, single-line business, payphone, mobile wireless, and pager connection. A 'connection' for these purposes would be facilities that provide end-users with access to an interstate public or private network, regardless of the technology used to enable that access. These carriers would pay an additional contribution for multi-line business connections based on the maximum capacity of the connection. In addition, all carriers, even if they did not provide connections, would have to pay a minimum universal contribution based on a percentage of annual interstate telecommunications revenues. Another approach involves assessing contributions by reference to connections based solely on capacity with no distinction between residential, single-line business, payphone, mobile wireless, and pager connections. Local access providers and switched-transport providers would be responsible for these costs. The last option involves assessing universal service contributions based on the number of telephone numbers assigned to end-users and, for those customers without numbers, on the capacity of their connections. All of these changes are controversial due to the perception that they will unduly benefit or harm particular classes of consumers and types of service providers, and it has been difficult to build consensus in support of any particular approach.

Separately, and in order to contain what the Federal-State Joint Board on Universal Service characterized as 'explosive growth' in high-cost universal service support disbursements, on 1 May 2008, the FCC instituted an interim cap on payments made to competitive eligible telecommunications carriers.[116] This was designed as a temporary measure; in January 2008, the FCC had issued a Notice of Proposed Rulemaking seeking comment on comprehensive reform of high-cost universal service support.[117] That Notice incorporated a November 2007 recommendation by the Federal-State Joint Board on Universal Service that proposed sweeping changes to the programme, including an explicit recommendation that the nation's communications goals include achieving universal availability of broadband Internet services.[118]

[115] Federal-State Joint Board on Universal Service, Notice of Proposed Rulemaking, CC Docket Nos 96-45, 98-71, 90-571, 92-237, NSD File No L-00-72, CC Docket Nos 99-200, 95-116 and 98-170, FCC No 02-329, FCC No 01-145, 16 FCC Rcd 9892 (2001); Further Notice of Proposed Rulemaking and Report and Order, CC Docket Nos 96-45, 98-71, 90-571, 92-237, NSD File No L-00-72, CC Docket Nos 99-200, 95-116 and 98-170, FCC No 02-43, 17 FCC Rcd 3752 (2002); and Report and Order and Second Further Notice of Proposed Rulemaking, CC Docket Nos 96-45, 98-71, 90-571, 92-237, NSD File No L-00-72, CC Docket Nos 99-200, 95-116 and 98-170, FCC No 02-329, 17 Rcd 24952 (2002).
[116] High-Cost Universal Service Support, Order, WC Docket No 05-337, CC Docket No 96-45, FCC No 08-122, 23 FCC Rcd 8834 (2008). The Federal-State Joint Board had recommended a cap in May 2007. See High-Cost Universal Service Support, Recommended Decision, WC Docket No 05-337, CC Docket No96-45, 22 FCC Rcd 8998, 8999-9001 (Fed-State Jt Bd 2007).
[117] High-Cost Universal Service Support, Notice of Proposed Rulemaking, WC Docket No 05-337, CC Docket No 96-45, FCC No 08-22, 23 FCC Rcd 1531 (2008).
[118] Federal-State Joint Board on Universal Service, Recommended Decision, WC Docket No 05-337, CC Docket No 96-45,, FCC No 07J-4, 22 FCC Rcd 20477 (2007).

The Federal-State Joint Board envisioned the creation of three new funds with separate distribution mechanisms and separate funding allocations to provide high-cost support: a state-administered broadband fund to aid construction of facilities for new broadband services to unserved areas, a state-administered mobility fund for the dissemination of wireless voice services to unserved areas, and a federal-administered provider of last resort fund to support wireline carriers who provide this function. While the provider of last resort fund would represent approximately three-quarters of total expenditure, all three funds would operate within an overall funding cap roughly equivalent to the existing amount of high-cost funding. In addition, the FCC Notice asked about two other possible reform concepts. The first is elimination of the 'identical support rule', in which subsidies to certain competitive carriers that serve rural areas are based on the support that incumbent carriers receive per line instead of actual costs, even if actual costs are lower. The second proposal is to introduce 'reverse auctions', which would award contracts to provide local and regional service supported by universal service funding to the lowest bidder. Collectively, these proposals provided an opportunity for the FCC to consider comprehensive reform to universal service, although the FCC decided in November 2008 that it will not implement any of the Joint Board's recommendations. However, during the proof stage of this chapter, it began consultation on three alternative proposals to reform universal service. See High-Cost Universal Service Support, Order on Remand and Report and Order and Further Notice of Proposed Rulemaking, WC Docket Nos 05-337, 03-109, 06-122, 04-36, CC Docket Nos 96-45, 99-200, 96-98, 01-92 and 99-68, FCC No 08-262 (2008).

6.13 COMPETITION LAW

As discussed in section 6.4.3, the federal body primarily responsible for the enforcement of US antitrust law in the telecommunications sector is the Department of Justice (Telecommunications and Media Enforcement Section) (DoJ). The two key pieces of legislation enforced by the DoJ are the Sherman Anti-trust Act and the Clayton Act, both of which have been interpreted extensively by the courts. These Acts contain provisions which prohibit anti-competitive agreements, market abuse by monopolists, and other restrictive practices. The Clayton Act (as amended by the Hart-Scott-Rodino Antitrust Improvements Act of 1976[119]) and related regulations also require parties to mergers and other acquisitions to notify such transactions to the DoJ and the Federal Trade Commission (FTC) and to obtain clearance from the DoJ before their consummation. As a result, the DoJ has significant oversight of the structural changes occurring in the telecommunications sector. Third parties damaged by anticompetitive conduct also have rights to bring private actions against operators and others for alleged violations of antitrust legislation, and a number of claims have been made against operators.

---

[119] Pub L No 94-435, 90 Stat 1390 (1976) (codified at 15 USC §18a).

6.13.1 Anti-competitive agreements/monopolies

Section 1 of the Sherman Anti-trust Act mirrors the prohibitions of Article 81 of the EC Treaty.[120] Section 1 declares all contracts, combinations, and conspiracies that restrain trade between the 50 states of the US and foreign countries to be illegal. The Supreme Court has ruled that there are two types of conduct caught by §1: conduct that is 'per se illegal' and conduct which violates the so-called 'rule of reason'. An example of conduct which is 'per se illegal' is price fixing. Conduct is contrary to the rule of reason when it is otherwise lawful but unreasonably restrains trade. Such conduct is reviewed on a case-by-case basis and in light of its pro- and anti-competitive effects on relevant market(s).

In 2000, the DoJ and the FTC issued Antitrust Guidelines for Collaborations among Competitors which sets out the general principles that both agencies will use when reviewing agreements between competitors and the potential competition concerns likely to arise from collaboration. Section 1 of the Sherman Anti-trust Act does not expressly permit the DoJ to exempt anti-competitive behaviour from the Act where it 'contributes to the production or distribution of goods or to promoting technical or economic progress, while allowing consumers a fair share of the resulting benefit . . .'; nevertheless, in practice, the pro-competitive effects of agreements will be taken into account by the courts and the DoJ when assessing whether or not an agreement unreasonably restrains trade.

Section 2 of the Sherman Anti-trust Act makes it unlawful for natural persons and legal entities to monopolize any part of trade or commerce between the 50 states and foreign countries. Monopolies are not per se illegal but where a party has acquired or intends to acquire market power through anti-competitive means then a violation of §2 of the Sherman Anti-trust Act will occur. Where trade with foreign countries is involved, §§1 and 2 of the Sherman Anti-trust Act are not violated unless the conduct has a direct, substantial, and reasonably foreseeable effect on domestic trade or commerce, or on export trade or commerce of a person engaged in such trade or commerce in the US.

6.13.2 Price discrimination and other practices

The provisions of the Sherman Anti-trust Act are supplemented by §§2 and 3 of the Clayton Act. These provisions make it unlawful for persons involved in commerce to discriminate in price between similarly situated purchasers of like products where the effect of such discrimination may be 'substantially to lessen competition or tend to create a monopoly'. Discrimination is permissible, however, where price differences arise due to the cost of manufacture, sale, or delivery. Other provisions prohibit the payment or acceptance of bribes, discrimination in rebates, discounts or

---

[120] See further Chapter 9.

advertising services, and sales conditional on the non-use of goods or services of a competitor.

6.13.3 Penalties for non-compliance

A breach of §1 of the Sherman Anti-trust Act renders the underlying agreement void. The DoJ may also bring civil and/or criminal prosecutions in a federal court against offenders. If convicted, persons who participate in unlawful restraints of trade face severe fines and/or criminal penalties. Individuals may be fined up to US$1 million and be imprisoned for up to ten years. Corporations may be fined up to US$100 million for each offence. Similar penalties may be imposed by a court if §2 of the Sherman Anti-trust Act is violated. Violations of §§2 and 3 of the Clayton Act may result in fines but they carry no criminal penalties.

The DoJ has adopted leniency policies for corporations[121] and individuals[122] who report antitrust violations previously unknown to the DoJ. Corporations and individuals who confess their involvement, fully cooperate with the DoJ, and agree to other conditions will not be charged with criminal law violations.

Individuals who are injured as the result of conduct in contravention of antitrust law may also sue the offender(s) in a federal district court. If successful, they may recover three times the damages they suffered plus reasonable attorney's fees.[123] The possibility of treble damages provides a powerful incentive for private parties to enforce antitrust legislation, and a number of competitors to leading telecommunications operators and providers in the US have sought to enforce antitrust law directly through the courts. Over the last few years, individuals have filed suits alleging breaches of §§1 and 2 of the Sherman Anti-trust Act in a number of markets, including intrastate long-distance[124] and local telecommunications.[125] Most lawsuits have been unsuccessful but the option remains available for those who believe that a competitor or a supplier has acted in contravention of antitrust law.

6.13.4 Investigations

The DoJ initiates investigations into alleged anti-competitive practices following internal reviews by in-house economists and lawyers and complaints from industry participants, concerned citizens, informants, and other government agencies.

---

[121] Department of Justice, Corporate Leniency Policy, available at <http://www.usdoj.gov/atr/public/guidelines/0091.htm>.
[122] Department of Justice, Leniency Policy for Individuals, available at <http://www.usdoj.gov/atr/public/guidelines/0092.htm>.
[123] Clayton Act §4(a), 15 USC §15.
[124] See, e.g., *S&S Communications v Local Exchange Carriers Association, Inc*, 2006-1 Trade Cas. (CCH) ¶75,256 (DSD).
[125] See, e.g., *Bell Atlantic Co v William Twombly*, 425 F 3d 99 (2nd Cir 2005); *Cavalier Telephone, LLC v Verizon Virginia, Inc*, 330 F 3d 176 (4th Cir 2003).

The DoJ may compel legal and natural persons to produce information and other documentation relevant to a civil investigation by serving a Civil Investigative Demand (CID). The DoJ may request in a CID for a witness to give oral testimony or to answer DoJ questions in writing. Evidence in relation to criminal investigations is gathered pursuant to subpoenas issued by a grand jury. In both civil and criminal investigations, the DoJ may request assistance from the Federal Bureau of Investigations and other federal agencies.[126]

6.13.5 Regulatory double jeopardy?

The behaviour of telecommunications operators and service providers in the US is subject to antitrust law as well as the regulatory requirements set out in the Communications Act of 1934 and enforced by the FCC. In theory, certain conduct could violate both antitrust law and regulatory rules. However, in *Verizon Communications Inc v Law Offices of Curtis V Trinko, LLP* (540 US 398 (2004)), the Supreme Court stated that where a regulatory structure is designed to deter and remedy anti-competitive harm, it is less likely that antitrust law requires any additional scrutiny. In other words, no antitrust liability is likely to arise where regulation exists to prevent or remedy anti-competitive harm.

The case arose in the context of the Telecommunications Act 1996. Under §251(c) and related rules adopted by the FCC, Verizon, the incumbent LEC in New York, was required to provide unbundled network elements (UNEs), which included access to its operations support systems (OSS) necessary for interconnection, to its competitors. Verizon's competitors complained to the FCC and the New York State Public Service Commission (PSC) that Verizon did not provide the access they needed to its OSS. Each agency found Verizon in breach of its obligations and imposed financial penalties, remedial measures, and additional reporting requirements on Verizon. Subsequently, the law offices of Curtis V Trinko, a customer of AT&T, one of Verizon's competitors in New York, brought a class action against Verizon alleging that the denial of access to its OSS violated §2 of the Sherman Anti-trust Act.

The Supreme Court held that the law offices of Curtis V Trinko failed to substantiate a violation of §2 of the Sherman Anti-trust Act for several reasons. As an initial matter, the Court found that the Telecommunications Act of 1996 contained a 'savings clause' which did not preclude the application of antitrust law. However, it concluded that Verizon's refusal to deal with its competitors did not violate the antitrust standard set out in *Aspen Skiing Co v Aspen Highlands Skiing Corp* (472 US 585 (1985)). Also, because access to OSS was available pursuant to the Telecommunications Act of 1996 and the provision of access was compulsory, Verizon did not run afoul of the 'essential facilities doctrine' that had been adopted by lower courts. The Court

---

[126] For further information about the procedural matters surrounding a DoJ investigation, see the DoJ's Antitrust Division Manual available at <http://www.usdoj.gov/atr/foia/divisionmanual/table_of_contents.htm>.

stressed that Verizon was subject to the oversight of the FCC and the New York State PSC and each agency had taken enforcement action against Verizon. It also stated that the benefits of enforcing an antitrust violation must be weighed against its costs. In this case, the technical details surrounding interconnection and UNEs were difficult for a court to assess. By implication, alleged violations of telecommunications regulatory requirements are more expeditiously assessed by the FCC and PUCs and evaluated in accordance with regulatory law.

6.13.6 Mergers

Section 7 of the Clayton Act prohibits the acquisition of shares or capital in a natural or legal entity engaged in commerce or related activities affecting commerce where such acquisition may be 'substantially to lessen competition, or to tend to create a monopoly'. This provision covers mergers, asset and share purchases, joint ventures, and other acquisitions. The DoJ is responsible for ensuring that mergers in the telecommunications sector comply with §7.

The DoJ and the FTC have issued a number of guidelines relating to horizontal and non-horizontal mergers. The Horizontal Merger Guidelines were issued in 1992 and revised in 1997. The Guidelines focus on market definition and concentration, the potential adverse competitive effects of mergers, the ability of new participants to enter the relevant market(s), efficiencies resulting from the merger, and the likelihood of either party to the merger failing if the merger does not take place. The Guidelines were supplemented in March 2006 by Commentary on the Horizontal Merger Guidelines.[127] The Non-Horizontal Merger Guidelines were issued in 1984. Non-horizontal or vertical mergers are less likely to give rise to competition concerns but the guidelines set out the principal theories under which the DoJ would challenge non-horizontal mergers. These include the elimination of actual or potential competition, the creation of barriers to entry, and the ability of vertical mergers to facilitate collusion at retail levels and in downstream markets.

Since 1978, unless exempted by §7A(c) of the Clayton Act, mergers which meet specified criteria must be notified prior to the consummation of the transaction to both the DoJ and the FTC.[128] As a general rule, the purchaser and the target of the acquisition must notify the DoJ and the FTC if the following conditions[129] are satisfied:

1) if one person has sales or assets of at least US$100 million; the other person has sales or assets of at least US$10 million; and as a result of the transaction the

---

[127] See <http://www.usdoj.gov/atr/public/guidelines/215247.htm>.
[128] See Clayton Act §7A(a) and the Premerger Notification Rules found at 16 CFR Parts 801, 802, and 803.
[129] Note the monetary thresholds are adjusted annually.

acquiring person will hold an aggregate amount of stock and assets valued at more than US$50 million of the acquired person; or

2) as a result of the transaction, the acquiring person will hold an aggregate amount of stock or assets of the acquired person valued at more than US$200 million regardless of the sales or assets of the acquiring and acquired person.

Failure to notify may result in civil penalties or a court order requiring the parties to divest any assets acquired in violation of the Clayton Act if the transaction is already consummated.

Notifying parties must complete and have certified a Notification and Report Form. The Notification and Report Form requires the notifying parties to provide details about the transaction and information about acquisitions made in the last five years. The notifying parties must inform the DoJ and FTC if the acquiring person and acquired entity earn revenue from businesses that fall within any of the same industry and product codes in accordance with the North American Industry Classification System and, if so, the geographic areas in which they operate. Notifying parties may also voluntarily submit additional information to facilitate review of the transaction. They must also pay the appropriate filing fee. The fee is determined by reference to the value of the transaction.

After a Notification and Report Form is submitted, both the DoJ and the FTC review the Form. The notifying parties must usually wait a minimum of 30 days (15 days in the case of a cash tender sale or bankruptcy sale) before they may consummate a transaction. Parties may request early termination of the waiting period; however, requests for early termination are granted only where the DoJ and the FTC have completed their preliminary reviews and have concluded they will not take any enforcement action against the parties. Complex mergers which raise substantial antitrust concerns will usually not be eligible for early termination.

If either agency believes or both agencies believe that a transaction involving the telecommunications sector requires further analysis, then the DoJ becomes responsible for further investigation. If further information is necessary, the DoJ may request that additional information from the notifying parties. Such a request usually extends the waiting period for another 30 days (ten days in the case of a cash tender offer or a bankruptcy sale) from the date the parties comply with the DoJ's request. Interested third parties may submit written comments or make a presentation about the effects of the proposed transaction to the DoJ or the FTC at any stage of the review process.

If, at the end of its review, the DoJ concludes that the transaction does not substantially lessen competition, or does not tend to create a monopoly, then it recommends that no further action is taken. If the DoJ believes a transaction does raise concerns then it may discuss terms of settlement, such as divestiture of certain assets or businesses, with the notifying parties. Any settlement negotiated by the DoJ must be approved by the Assistant Attorney General and be published in the Federal Register. The DoJ must also publish a Competitive Impact Statement which explains

the nature of the proceedings and the reasons for and the effects of the proposed settlement terms. Third parties must also be given at least 60 days to comment on the proposed settlement terms. A US district court then enters the agreed settlement in accordance with the Antitrust Procedures and Penalties Act.[130] Alternatively, the DoJ may commence injunction proceedings in a US district court to stop the acquisition, and the federal district court will determine whether or not the acquisition complies with §7 of the Clayton Act.

The DoJ has agreed the terms on which a number of mergers could proceed in the telecommunications sector, including, for example: Cingular Wireless's acquisition of AT&T Wireless proposed in 2004, and SBC Communications' acquisition of AT&T and Verizon's acquisition of MCI, both of which were proposed in 2005. The DoJ has rarely sought to injunct an acquisition in the telecommunications sector but it did seek to enjoin MCI Worldcom's acquisition of Sprint in 2000. When it becomes clear the DoJ will oppose a transaction, the notifying parties usually abandon it.

6.13.7 Mergers and the FCC

The FCC also has a significant amount of oversight of structural changes occurring in the telecommunications sector brought about by mergers, corporate reorganizations, and other ownership transactions that result in the transfer of control or assignment of a 1934 Act licence. Under the 1934 Act, prior approval of the FCC is required before authorizations and licences relating to common carriers,[131] radio (both public and private),[132] satellite earth stations,[133] and submarine cable landings[134] may be transferred.

Failure to obtain the FCC's prior permission may result in fines and other enforcement action. In some cases, however, *pro forma* transactions (transactions that do not result in a change of ultimate ownership) are permitted without prior FCC approval. Licensees must notify the FCC within 30 days of completion of the transaction. In 2003, the FCC further streamlined its assignment and transfer of control procedures—particularly with respect to spectrum leasing schemes—as part of a comprehensive initiative to encourage the development of secondary markets in spectrum usage rights.[135]

In all cases where prior approval is required, the FCC must be satisfied that the 'public interest, convenience and necessity' are served by the transfer of the relevant FCC authorization. The impact of the proposed licence transfer on competition in

---

[130] 15 USC §16(b)–(h).
[131] 47 CFR §§63.03, 63.04, and 63.24.
[132] 47 USC §310(d).
[133] 47 CFR §25.119.
[134] 47 CFR §1.767.
[135] Promoting Efficient Use of Spectrum Through Elimination of Barriers to the Development of Secondary Markets, Second Report and Order, Order on Reconsideration and Second Further Notice of Proposed Rulemaking, WT Docket No 00-230, FCC No 04-167, 19 FCC Rcd 17503 (2004).

relevant markets is closely analysed by the FCC, although other factors, such as the potential effects of a transfer on universal service provision, national security, spectrum efficiency, and technical innovation, are also typically considered. Each licence transfer is assessed on a case-by-case basis, and the procedures followed vary depending on the specific licence. In all cases, the parties to a transaction are encouraged to discuss the merger with FCC staff in advance of submitting an application. The FCC tries to complete its review of major transactions within 180 days of the publication of the FCC's notice about the transaction; however, the 180-day timetable may be extended in light of the complexity of the transaction. Interested third parties are normally given 30 days in which to file comments with the FCC. The FCC issues its decision in writing. Unsuccessful applicants may challenge an FCC decision by way of judicial review. As FCC approval requires a majority vote of its commissioners, it is typical for controversial and large-scale mergers to be approved subject to a number of conditions that are either developed by the commissioners in order to reach consensus or proposed by the applicant in an effort to secure a majority vote.

The FCC also has powers under §§7 and 11 of the Clayton Act to block acquisitions of common carriers engaged in fixed and radio communications where the effect of the acquisition would be to substantially lessen competition or create a monopoly. In practice, these powers are rarely used and any action taken by the FCC is based on its powers set out in the Communications Act of 1934.

6.14 COMMUNICATIONS PRIVACY[136]

Federal communications privacy law seeks to protect individuals against intrusion from the government and against unsolicited communications from business entities and telemarketers. The law does not confer an absolute right to privacy to individuals. Instead, it seeks to balance privacy interests against other social interests, such as the desire to assist law enforcement agencies in their efforts to apprehend criminals for the public good, and the constitutional protections of commercial speech enjoyed by commercial businesses and telecommunications carriers.

The level of protection from government surveillance afforded to individuals varies, therefore, depending on a number of factors including the nature of the communication intercepted and the purposes for which law enforcement agencies require access to the communication. Among consumer protection matters, one problem that has generated intense interest is that of unsolicited communications from business entities. This issue is addressed via a number of mechanisms, including an 'opt-out' scheme whereby subscribers may request businesses not to ring them. The use of customer data by telecommunications carriers is also circumscribed and the rules dealing with customer data adopted by the FCC use 'opt-in' and 'opt-out' approaches

---

[136] See further Chapter 13.

depending on the circumstances when such data is to be disclosed and how it is to be used.

It should be noted that the regulatory measures taken by the FCC in the area of communications privacy contrast sharply with its decisions to embrace market forces in other areas. The FCC continues to attempt to balance the competing objectives of law enforcement, personal privacy, and business, and it is likely that further regulatory action by the FCC will be necessary in the future to ensure the balance remains appropriate. This balancing of what can often appear to be conflicting interests is likely to be among the most difficult and controversial policy matters that the FCC will face in the coming years.

6.14.1 Electronic surveillance and law enforcement

6.14.1.1 *History and development*
The ability of law enforcement agencies to engage in electronic surveillance is constrained by the Fourth Amendment of the US Constitution and by a number of statutory requirements. The Fourth Amendment protects citizens against unreasonable searches and seizures; however, it was not until 1967 that the Supreme Court held in *Katz v United States* (389 US 347) that electronic surveillance was a search and seizure for Fourth Amendment purposes. Prior to 1967, electronic surveillance was not considered to be a search and seizure as it did not involve trespass or the physical seizure of a material object.[137]

As a result of the Supreme Court's decision, and in an effort to meet law enforcement needs and privacy concerns, Congress passed the Omnibus Crime Control and Safe Streets Act of 1968[138] (the Omnibus Act). Title III of the Omnibus Act authorized the use of three principal techniques for the surveillance of voice conversations over fixed networks:[139]

1) content interception, such as wiretapping (18 USC §§2518–2519);

2) pen registers which permit the recovery and recording of the dialing information that addresses outgoing calls from a person under surveillance (18 USC §§3121–3127); and

3) trap and trace devices, which capture the incoming, originating number of a communication received by a person under surveillance (18 USC §§3121–3127).

Title III also allowed law enforcement to access telephone records held by third parties (18 USC §§2701–2709), and prohibited the use of electronic surveillance by private individuals (18 USC §2511). As described below, the standard required in

---

[137] *Olmstead v United States*, 277 US 438 (1928).

[138] Pub L No 90-351, 82 Stat 212 (1968) (codified as amended in scattered sections of 18 USC).

[139] The ability and procedures of federal investigators to use electronic surveillance in foreign intelligence investigations is set out in the Foreign Intelligence Surveillance Act of 1978, Pub L No 95-511, 92 Stat 1783 (1978) (codified as amended in scattered sections of 50 USC).

order to obtain permission to conduct wiretapping (also commonly known as a 'Title III authorization') is substantially higher than that required to implement pen registers and trap and trace devices.

The procedures that law enforcement agencies have to follow to engage in surveillance of voice communications are set out in the Omnibus Act. Wiretapping may be used only if approved by senior officials of the DoJ and if authorized by a federal judge. The intercepted conversations must concern one or more felony offences specified in the Act, and the law enforcement agency must have probable cause to believe the target of the surveillance has committed the applicable crime. The order given by a federal court specifies the duration and scope of the surveillance, the conversation(s) that may be recorded, and the steps the law enforcement agencies must take to minimize interference with unrelated conversations.[140] When the order expires, the court also notifies the target of the wiretap if any conversations have been recorded.

Law enforcement may be given access to telephone records pursuant to a warrant, court order, or *subpoena* in connection with any criminal investigation. Pen registers and trap and trace devices, by contrast, are easier for an agency to procure as they are viewed as less intrusive, and are much more common. An agency does not require a judge to find in its favour. Instead, the government certifies to the court that the use of a pen register or a trap and trace device is likely to produce information relevant to the investigation of any crime. Upon certification, a judge will give the necessary court order for the searches. Neither the courts nor the law enforcement agencies need to notify the targets of surveillance that they have been monitored or that any information was taken from them.

Due to the number of new technologies and services that emerged in the mid 1980s and the need for law enforcement to keep apace with these developments, Congress enacted the Electronic Communications Privacy Act of 1986.[141] The Act extended the scope of Title III of the Omnibus Act so that law enforcement could intercept voice and data communications transmitted by email, cellular phones, fax machines, and paging devices. Restrictions were imposed, however, on the interception of such communications in transit or stored on networks. The Act also permitted 'roving wiretaps'[142] which are used when a person is tracked from place to place. Law enforcement does not need to specify where a communication will be intercepted. It must, however, show probable cause that a suspect's conduct could potentially thwart an investigation from a specified location and it must obtain the prior approval of a high-ranking official of the DoJ and a federal court.

In response to the September 11 terrorist attacks in New York and Washington DC, Congress made further changes to Title III of the Omnibus Act by adopting the

---

[140] 18 USC §2518.
[141] Pub L No 99-508, 100 Stat 1872 (1986) (codified as amended at 18 USC §1367 *et seq.*).
[142] 18 USC §2518(11).

USA Patriot Act of 2001.[143] The purpose of the USA Patriot Act was to help capture the September 11 terrorists and to prevent further attacks. The Act was a sweeping piece of legislation that was passed soon after the September 11 attacks, and was designed to achieve its objectives by strengthening anti-money laundering legislation, tightening immigration law, imposing tougher penalties for acts of terrorism, and modifying the types of communications that law enforcement may monitor.

Specifically, the USA Patriot Act modified Title III of the Omnibus Act by enhancing the ability of law enforcement to engage in electronic surveillance in a number of significant respects. For example, §216 of the USA Patriot Act permits pen register and trap and trace orders for email, including email headings, and web browsers. The Act also gave law enforcement agencies access to stored email and other communication records, and treated voice mail like stored email so that agencies could access voice mail in accordance with a warrant or court ordered procedure rather than the more rigorous procedures required for content interception (18 USC §2703). Section 224 of the Act also added a number of terrorist and computer offences to the list of felony offences to which a communication must relate if content interception is sought. It is important to note that, while the USA Patriot Act modified the types of material subject to surveillance and adopted definitions of pen registers and trap and trace devices that are broad enough to encompass newer communications technologies such as email, it did not alter the fundamental distinction between wiretap authorizations, pen registers, and trap and trace devices. To obtain content information, a law enforcement authority still must obtain a wiretap authorization regardless of the medium in question. However, as a pen register or a trap and trace device permits the recording of 'dialling, routing, addressing, or signalling information', there is considerable leeway for policymakers to determine that information from new technologies is not content-related (and thus easier for law enforcement agencies to lawfully obtain). Although Congress made such a distinction for email and voice mail messages, the application of the content versus non-content distinction to other new technologies such as voice-over IP (discussed in greater depth in section 6.15 below) has become a difficult and challenging problem.

The USA Patriot Act has been criticized for conferring more tools with which to invade communications privacy on federal enforcement officials. The Act, however, includes some safeguards that were intended to address privacy concerns. For example, the USA Patriot Act supplemented existing provisions in the Omnibus Act for victims of unlawful wiretapping and victims of unlawful access to email and communications records held by third parties. Such victims may now sue the US if their claims are in excess of US$10,000 under §223 of the USA Patriot Act.

Many of the provisions of the USA Patriot Act were originally authorized to expire in four years, but passage of the USA Patriot Act Improvement and Reauthorization

---

[143] The full title of the legislation is Uniting and Strengthening America by Providing Appropriate Tools Required to Intercept and Obstruct Terrorism (USA Patriot Act) Act of 2001, Pub L No 107-56, 115 Stat 272 (2001).

Act of 2005 made permanent 14 of the 16 sections that were due to expire on 31 December 2005, and extended the roving wiretap provision, as well as a provision relating to access to business records, until 31 December 2009.[144] The legislation was controversial, particularly with respect to making the provisions permanent. Although the 2005 reauthorization expanded overall government anti-terrorism powers in some ways, it also made amendments designed to address lingering civil liberties concerns and bolster the likelihood that parts of the Act would be able to withstand constitutional challenge. For example, greater court oversight and review of certain provisions are now available, and federal authorities are obligated to periodically report how many times they have made use of specific USA Patriot Act provisions. The roving wiretap provisions continue to be particularly controversial, and the revisions increase the burden on law enforcement authorities to justify to a court that there is a reason to believe that each added place where electronic surveillance is conducted is related to the target of the investigation.

The physical and electronic surveillance of foreign entities and individuals is subject to the Foreign Intelligence Surveillance Act (FISA),[145] and subsequent amendments. FISA addresses the exchange of foreign intelligence information between foreign powers and their agents, which can include American citizens suspected of being engaged in espionage, and generally gives the President greater powers to engage in wiretapping and other forms of surveillance with limited public oversight than the laws discussed above. A special court, the United States Foreign Intelligence Surveillance Court, exists to oversee requests for surveillance warrants, when applicable. Due to the national security interests that underpin FISA, the court's proceedings are not open to the public. In 2005, it was disclosed that the Bush administration had engaged in a programme of warrantless domestic wiretapping carried out by the National Security Agency since at least 2002. Because of the scope of this activity, which is alleged to have included access to all fibre-optic communications passing through major interconnect locations that captured both domestic and foreign communications, numerous civil lawsuits were filed against telephone companies alleging that they allowed the government to listen in on their customers' phone conversations without obtaining the necessary court warrants. After considerable controversy, Congress granted telecommunications companies immunity from these suits in 2008.

6.14.1.2 Duties of telecommunications carriers

Section 705 of the Communications Act[146] prohibits persons assisting in receiving or assisting in transmitting any interstate or foreign communications by wire or radio from disclosing or publishing 'the existence, contents, substance, purport, effect or meaning' of such communications. Section 705 does, however, permit disclosure

---

[144] Pub L No 109-177, 120 Stat 192 (2005).
[145] Pub L No 95-511, 92 Stat 1783 (1978) (codified at 50 USC ch 36).
[146] 47 USC §605(a).

where authorized or mandated by Title 18 (Crimes and Criminal Procedure) of the United States Code.

In 1970, the United States Court of Appeals for the Ninth Circuit held in *Application of the United States for Relief*, 427 F 2d 639 (9th Cir 1970) that the Omnibus Act did not require, and that the courts did not have the authority to compel, communications providers to offer technical support to law enforcement agencies authorized to carry out surveillance. The Omnibus Act was quickly amended to impose a duty on providers of wire or electronic communications services to provide 'all information, facilities and technical assistance' necessary to accomplish court-ordered surveillance.[147] In exchange for their cooperation, providers are entitled to claim reasonable compensation and are given statutory immunity from any liability for facilitating authorized surveillance.

The extent to which providers had to offer technical assistance, and, in particular, the question of whether or not carriers had an affirmative duty to design or modify their network equipment to accommodate surveillance by law enforcement authorities, continued to be debated. In order to clarify the duties of communications providers, Congress adopted the Communications Assistance for Law Enforcement Act of 1994[148] (CALEA).

CALEA requires 'telecommunications carriers' to have the capability to 'expeditiously' isolate and to intercept communications content and 'call-identifying information'. Each telecommunications carrier must be able to deliver communications content and call-identifying information to a location specified by law enforcement other than its own premises. A carrier must also be able to carry out interception 'unobtrusively' while protecting the privacy and security of content and information not subject to interception. Section 105 of CALEA requires carriers to ensure that interception and access to call-identifying information can be activated only in accordance with lawful authorization and with the affirmative intervention of an officer or employee of the carrier.[149]

The term 'telecommunications carrier' is defined in §102(8) of CALEA and the FCC has determined that the following are 'telecommunications carriers' for the purposes of the legislation:[150]

1) any entity that holds itself out to serve the public indiscriminately in the provision of any telecommunications service;

---

[147] 18 USC §2518(4).

[148] Pub L No 103-41, 108 Stat 4279 (1994) (codified at 47 USC §1001 *et seq*).

[149] The FCC adopted a number of rules relating to the privacy duties of carriers in Communications Assistance for Law Enforcement Act, Report and Order, CC Docket No 97-213, FCC No 99-11, 14 FCC Rcd 4151 (1999).

[150] Communications Assistance for Law Enforcement Act, Second Report and Order, CC Docket No 97-213, FCC No 99-229, 15 FCC Rcd 7105 (1999).

2) entities previously identified as common carriers for the purposes of the Communications Act, including LECs, ILECs, competitive access providers, and satellite-based service providers;

3) cable operators and electricity firms and other utilities to the extent that they offer telecommunications services for hire to the public;

4) commercial mobile service providers;

5) providers of calling features such as call forwarding, call waiting, three-way calling, speed dialing, and the call redirection portion of voice mail;

6) private mobile service providers when their facilities offer interconnected services to public networks to the public or a substantial portion of the public;

7) resellers who own their own facilities; and

8) providers of information services, such as email and on-line service providers, where their facilities are also used to provide telecommunications services.

The FCC concluded, however, that pay telephone providers as well as private mobile radio service providers and information service providers who do not provide telecommunications services are not subject to the requirements of CALEA.

CALEA further stipulates that telecommunications carriers have to modify their network equipment and set aside network capacity to meet actual and projected surveillance requirements of law enforcement. The actual and projected surveillance requirements are set by the Federal Bureau of Investigations (FBI).

CALEA makes an important distinction between equipment that was deployed on or before 1 January 1995 and that which was deployed after that date. For the former class, a telecommunications carrier is not required to update its equipment to comply with CALEA unless it is replaced or 'significantly upgraded', or if the Attorney General agrees to pay the carrier to modify its equipment. A US$500 million fund to pay for such upgrades had largely been spent by 2003.[151] By contrast, a carrier is responsible for ensuring that equipment installed or upgraded after 1 January 1995 is CALEA compliant, unless it is not 'reasonably achievable', to meet the assistance capability requirements of CALEA (and even then, the legislation imposes an obligation on telecommunications equipment manufacturers and support service providers to make available upon payment of a reasonable fee by the Attorney General all features and modifications necessary for telecommunications carriers to satisfy their duties under CALEA).

CALEA is intended to be 'technology-neutral'. Section 103(b) expressly states that law enforcement agencies cannot dictate or prohibit specific network designs or system configurations. However, law enforcement agencies do have a right to consult with industry associations and standard-setting setting bodies about CALEA

---

[151] The FBI adopted a number of regulations dealing with the issue of cost recovery. See, for example, Implementation of Section 109 of the Communications Assistance for Law Enforcement Act, 62 Fed Reg 13307 (1997) (codified at 28 CFR Pt 100).

technical standards to ensure that the assistance capability requirements of the legislation are met. Under a safe harbour provision that applies to equipment installed after 1 January 2005, carriers using equipment that meets such standards will be found in compliance with CALEA's requirements. If industry cannot agree a standard or if an agency believes that a standard is 'deficient' then each may petition the FCC to adopt the appropriate technical requirements or standards. This process is triggered by the filing of a petition by a telecommunications carrier 'or any other interested person', and the FCC must make its determination within one year based on a number of factors, including whether compliance would impose 'significant difficulty or expense' on the carrier or users of the carrier's systems.[152] The current CALEA technical standard for mobile operators was set by the FCC under this process and is based on an industry-agreed standard with the addition of six of nine surveillance capabilities that had been requested by the DoJ and FBI.[153]

In March 2004, the DoJ, FBI, and the US Drug Enforcement Administration filed a petition for rulemaking asking that the FCC determine that broadband Internet access and some broadband VoIP services are covered by CALEA, and asking for clarification on a number of other matters related to the application of the statute. The DoJ claimed that the ability of federal, state, and local law enforcement to carry out critical electronic surveillance was being compromised by the rise of new technologies, such as voice communications through Internet facilities, for which CALEA standards had not been set. Parties who objected to the filing noted that, as a threshold matter, it had yet to be determined whether such services were even subject to the CALEA statute. A key argument of the DoJ was that the definition of 'telecommunications carrier' under CALEA may be interpreted more broadly than the definition of the term under the 1934 Act and, as a corollary, that the class of 'information services' that are afforded exemptions from CALEA are much more limited than the information services that have been identified by the FCC. In a 2005 decision, the FCC agreed with this reasoning.[154] After further finding that broadband and IP-enabled services can essentially replace conventional telecommunications services that were already subject to CALEA, the FCC required all facilities-based broadband Internet access and interconnected VoIP providers to meet a 14 May 2007 deadline to be compliant with CALEA's provisions. By making a distinction

---

[152] 47 USC §1008(b)(1).

[153] For further information about the standard ultimately adopted by the FCC, see Communications Assistance for Law Enforcement Act, Order on Remand, CC Docket No 97-213, FCC No 02-108, 16 FCC Rcd 6896 (2002). Upon release of the original industry standard, the FCC received petitions from multiple parties asking that additional provisions be required and that some industry-adopted provisions be stricken.

[154] Communications Assistance for Law Enforcement Act and Broadband Access and Services, First Report and Order and Further Notice of Proposed Rulemaking, ET Docket No 04-295, RM-10865, FCC No 05-153, 20 FCC Rcd 14989 (2005). The FCC upheld and clarified this decision in 2006. See Communications Assistance for Law Enforcement Act and Broadband Access and Services, Second Report and Order and Memorandum Opinion and Order, ET Docket No 04-295, RM-10865, FCC No 06-56, 21 FCC Rcd 5360 (2006).

between the 1934 Act and the CALEA statute, the FCC was able to support the broad application of CALEA while maintaining its general deregulatory approach to IP-enabled services.

6.14.2 Consumer privacy measures

The US Congress has adopted a number of measures to ensure that the privacy of subscribers is not invaded by telemarketers who solicit by fixed and mobile phones, faxes, and email. There are also measures directed at restricting the use of certain customer data by telecommunications carriers. However, because such provisions do not typically apply to customers using 'information services', the increasing numbers of consumers who are migrating away from traditional telecommunications carriers will give rise to new subscriber privacy concerns. The sections below discuss some of the key existing consumer privacy measures.

6.14.2.1 *Legal constraints on regulation of telemarketers*
In the US, solicitation by telemarketers is a type of commercial speech, which is protected by the First Amendment of the Constitution. Congress may regulate commercial speech, however, provided such regulation meets the four-part test set out in *Central Hudson Gas & Elec Corp v Public Service Commission* (447 US 557 (1980)). If the commercial speech concerns illegal activity or is misleading, then the government may freely regulate the speech. If, however, the speech is not illegal or misleading, then the government must be able to demonstrate that it has a substantial interest in regulating the speech, the regulation it seeks to impose directly and materially advances the government's interest, and is narrowly tailored. In *Cincinnati v Discovery Network, Inc* (507 US 410 (1993)), the Supreme Court held that a regulation is 'narrowly tailored' if it involves a careful calculation of the costs and benefits associated with the regulation and the burden on commercial speech it imposes.

6.14.2.2 *Unsolicited calls*
Congress addressed the problem of unsolicited calls by adopting the Telephone Consumer Protection Act of 1991[155] (TCPA). The TCPA gave the FCC the statutory authority to adopt regulations to stop unwanted telephone solicitations so that the privacy rights of residential telephone subscribers are protected. The legislation also gave the FCC the authority (but did not compel it) to establish a national database of telephone numbers of residential subscribers who object to receiving unsolicited calls by marketers. If adopted, companies were prohibited from making unsolicited calls to telephone numbers on the database. In addition, the TCPA imposed restrictions, subject to certain exceptions adopted by the FCC, on the use of automated telephone equipment.

[155] Pub L No 102-243, 105 Stat 2394 (1991) (codified at 47 USC §227).

When adopting regulations to implement the TCPA in 1992, the FCC declined to adopt a so-called 'national do-not-call list'. It mandated the use of company-specific do-not-call lists that allowed subscribers to indicate whether or not they wished to receive calls to their fixed home numbers from solicitors on a company-by-company basis. Each telemarketer was responsible for maintaining its own list. Moreover, if companies engaged in telemarketing, they had to ring subscribers no earlier than 8am and no later than 9pm. Exceptions were also available where there was an established business relationship and for tax-exempt non-profit organizations. The FCC thought that company-specific lists would better protect consumer privacy as there was no central list accessible by all telemarketers and the company 'opt-out' approach in conjunction with other restrictions would balance legitimate business interests and privacy concerns.

Despite these measures, public dissatisfaction over unsolicited phone calls continued to grow and, in 2002, the FCC was forced to revisit its approach to unsolicited calls. The FCC had received thousands of complaints about telemarketers and numerous inquiries about the TCPA and related rules. The public was concerned about the ever increasing amount of unsolicited calls and the use of new technologies, such as autodiallers which allowed the delivery of pre-recorded messages, and predictive diallers which allowed telemarketers to initiate phone calls when speaking to other customers. In the absence of further action by the FCC, the Federal Trade Commission (FTC) proposed a federal do-not-call list while several state legislatures established or were in the process of establishing statewide do-not-call lists. Telemarketers were also circumventing the requirements of the TCPA by hanging up before subscribers could ask them to add their numbers to company specific do-not-call lists.

Faced with this situation, Congress enacted new legislation, the Do-Not-Call Implementation Act,[156] in March 2003 that gave the FTC the authority to collect the funds necessary to implement its proposed do-not-call list, required the FCC to issue a final rule in its Telephone Consumer Protection Act rulemaking proceeding within 180 days, and made both the FTC and FCC submit annual reports addressing the implementation of the do-not-call provisions. The FCC quickly adopted a Report and Order on 26 June 2003 (Rules and Regulations Implementing the Telephone Consumer Protection Act of 1991, Report and Order, CG Docket No 02–278, FCC No 03–153, 18 FCC Rcd 14014 (2003)), that concluded that a single national database of fixed and mobile telephone numbers of subscribers who object to receiving telephone solicitations should be established from 1 October 2003. The registry was established in conjunction with the list adopted by the FTC. It is worth noting that the FCC's jurisdiction over the list is broader than the FTC's jurisdiction. The FTC has limited oversight of common carriers, banks, credit unions, savings and loans, insurance providers, and airlines. The FCC rules apply to all of these entities. Just as

---

[156] Pub L No 108-10, 117 Stat 557 (2003) (codified at 15 USC §6101 et seq).

the FTC was much more active than the FCC in establishing a national do-not-call registry, the FTC has effectively become the lead agency for administration and promotion of the registry, as well as the key source of public outreach and consumer support in this area. Because of the FCC's more extensive jurisdiction in this area, however, the FCC has taken a strong enforcement role.

As a result of the new scheme, subscribers now have three options to preserve their privacy by:

1) adding their numbers to the national do-not-call registry;

2) continuing to make do-not-call requests of companies on a case-by-case basis; or

3) registering on the national list and providing specific companies with permission to ring them.

The exceptions for established business relationships and for tax-exempt non-profit organizations continue to apply but all telemarketers are now obliged to provide caller ID information, not to abandon more than three per cent of calls answered by residential users, and to deliver a pre-recorded identification message when abandoning a call. Failure to comply with these rules may result in fines imposed by the FCC. Violation of the rules also gives subscribers a right to sue the offending party in state court.

Although consumers can register both wireline and mobile numbers on the do-not-call registry, separate FCC rules prohibit the use of automatic dialling machines or pre-recorded messages in calls to mobile telephones, pagers or any other service for which the called party is charged for the call. This restriction, in addition to the fact that public directories of wireless numbers have not traditionally been compiled in the US, serves to limit solicitations to mobiles.

In 2008, Congress made the registry of do-not-call numbers permanent.[157] The previous scheme established a limited validity for numbers placed on the registry and would have required consumers to periodically re-register their numbers.

6.14.2.3 *Unsolicited faxes*

The TCPA makes it unlawful for any person within the US to use any 'automatic telephone dialling system', such as fax machines or computers, to send advertisements to a subscriber's fax machine or fax server without the prior consent of the subscriber. The Act also requires telemarketers sending faxes to identify themselves to the intended recipient and to provide a telephone or fax number where they may be contacted. The FCC determined that prior consent must be in writing, include the signature of the recipient, and be clear. As is the case for unsolicited calls, failure to comply with these provisions of the TCPA may result in fines imposed by the FCC.

---

[157] Do Not Call Improvement Act of 2007, Pub L No 110-187, 122 Stat 633 (2008) (amending 15 USC §6101 *et seq*).

Violation of the fax rules also gives subscribers a right to sue the offending party in state court.

In 2005, Congress enacted the Junk Fax Prevention Act,[158] which amended the TCPA to create an exception to the prohibition on sending unsolicited faxes when business relationships have been established. In implementing the legislation, the FCC specified that a person sending a fax advertisement under the exception must obtain the fax number directly from the recipient or ensure that the recipient voluntarily agreed to make the number available for public distribution.[159] The rules also require senders to include specific notice and contact information that allows recipients to 'opt-out' of any future faxes. The revised rules took effect on 1 August 2006.

Public dissatisfaction with junk faxes, additional Congressional oversight, and renewed FCC interest in this area have resulted in a steady stream of FCC enforcement actions against violators. While forfeitures are often in the thousands of dollars, large-scale violations can be costly. In January 2004, the FCC imposed a US$5,379,000 fine on Fax.com, Inc (which it described as a 'fax broadcaster' whose business was faxing materials on behalf of others for a fee) for 489 separate violations of the TCPA.

6.14.2.4 *Unsolicited email*

The provisions of the TCPA do not apply to unsolicited email which advertises or promotes commercial products and services. To address the loopholes in the legislation and consumer concerns about 'spam', Congress enacted the Controlling the Assault of Non-Solicited Pornography and Marketing Act of 2003 or the CAN-SPAM Act of 2003.[160] The Act came into force on 1 January 2004 and makes it unlawful to send commercial email that contains deceptive or misleading subject headings or false information about the origin of an email. It requires senders of commercial emails to notify recipients that such emails are advertisements, to provide the sender's physical postal address, and to give recipients an opportunity to 'opt-out' of receiving commercial emails in the future. The opt-out notice must contain a return email address or other Internet-based mechanism by which email recipients can indicate they do not wish to receive future emails. The opt-out mechanism selected by a sender must remain active for 30 days. In addition, the Act prohibits senders and anyone acting on their behalf from sending commercial emails to a recipient who requests not to receive subsequent emails. The prohibition begins ten business days from the date of the recipient's request. Violation of the civil provisions of the Act may lead to injunctive relief and/or statutory fines. Breaches of criminal law may lead to imprisonment and fines up to US$6 million.

---

[158] Pub L No 109-21, 119 Stat 359 (2005) (codified at 47 USC §227).

[159] Rules and Regulations Implementing the Telephone Consumer Protection Act of 1991, Report and Order and Third Order on Reconsideration, CG Docket Nos. 02-278 and 05-338, FCC No 06-42, 21 FCC Rcd 3787 (2006).

[160] Pub L No 108-187, 117 Stat 2699 (2004) (amending scattered sections of 15 USC, 18 USC, 28 USC and 47 USC).

The FTC has primary responsibility for implementing and enforcing the legislation. In a report issued in June 2004, the FTC concluded that establishment of a 'do-not-email' registry would not only be ineffective but might actually compound the problem by giving unscrupulous email senders a comprehensive list of validated email addresses. In declining to establish a registry, the FTC continued to explore other means of enforcing the provisions of the CAN-SPAM Act. In addition, the FCC adopted rules that took effect in 2005 that prohibit the sending of unwanted commercial email messages to wireless devices without prior permission, and published a list of mail domain names used to send messages to wireless services.

6.14.2.5 Customer proprietary network information

Federal legislation also imposes duties on telecommunications carriers to respect the privacy of certain customer data. Section 222(c) of the Telecommunications Act of 1996, as amended by the Wireless Communications and Public Safety Act of 1999,[161] sets forth a framework for the use of 'customer proprietary network information' (CPNI) based on the sensitivity of the data acquired by telecommunications carriers, which include network operators and resellers of fixed and wireless services. CPNI is defined in §222(h)(1) of the 1996 Act and, broadly speaking, includes any information that relates to the quantity, technical configuration, type, destination, location, and amount of use of a telecommunications service by a subscriber and other information contained in a subscriber's bill. Such information includes phone numbers called by subscribers and the duration of calls. CPNI expressly excludes, however, 'subscriber list information'—information identifying the names of subscribers, their telephone numbers, or addresses that are published in a directory.

The 1996 Act affords protection to 'individually identifiable' CPNI. A telecommunications carrier may use, disclose, or permit access to 'individually identifiable' CPNI in accordance with the 1996 Act or with the approval of their customers. Section 222(c)(1) of the 1996 Act permits a carrier to use, disclose, and access 'individually identifiable' CPNI to provide the telecommunications service from which such information is derived, to provide services necessary to, or used in, the provision of that telecommunications service, including the publication of directories, or as otherwise provided by law.

The 1996 Act creates a number of exceptions to these restrictive rules. Use, disclosure, and access to CPNI is permissible by a carrier either directly or indirectly through its agents for such purposes as billing and debt collection, the protection of a carrier's rights and property, the provision of telemarketing and referral services requested by subscribers, and the provision of call location information concerning users of commercial mobile services in specified emergency situations. Disclosure of CPNI upon the affirmative written request by a customer is also permitted.

[161] Pub L No 106-81, 113 Stat 1286 (1999) (codified at 47 USC §615 et seq, 47 USC §222, 47 USC §251).

Unlike 'individually identifiable' CPNI, customer information that is 'aggregated' and does not contain individually identifiable CPNI may be disclosed to any party. Certain restrictions apply to aggregated data used, disclosed, or accessed by LECs. Subscriber list information may be disclosed to any person for the purpose of publishing telephone directories on reasonable, non-discriminatory terms. In 1998, the FCC adopted its second order dealing with the implementation of §222 of the 1996 Act and CPNI (Implementation of the Telecommunications Act of 1996, Second Report and Order and Further Notice of Proposed Rulemaking, CC Docket Nos 96–115, 96–149, FCC No 98–27, 13 FCC Rcd 8061 (1998)). In that order, the Commission clarified the scope of a carrier's right to use, disclose, and access 'individually identifiable' CPNI to provide telecommunications services from which such information is derived. The FCC adopted a 'total service approach' whereby carriers and their affiliates could use 'individually identifiable' CPNI without customer approval to market other products that were similar to or related to those already provided to a subscriber. For example, under the 'total service approach', a provider of local access services to a subscriber could use the subscriber's CPNI without prior approval to offer caller identification services. The Commission later clarified that all carriers could use CPNI to market customer premises equipment, and that certain carriers could use CPNI to market information services (Implementation of the Telecommunications Act of 1996, Order on Reconsideration and Petitions for Forbearance, CC Docket Nos 96–115, 96–149, FCC No 99–223, 14 FCC Rcd 14409 (1999)).

The Commission also adopted rules which set out the type of subscriber approval carriers had to obtain to use, disclose, or permit access to CPNI for purposes other than those specified in §222(c)(1). It stipulated that carriers had to obtain express written, oral, or electronic consent from their subscribers before they could use CPNI to market any additional services. On 18 August 1999, the US Court of Appeals for the Tenth Circuit in US West v FCC (182 F 3d 1224) held that the FCC's 'opt-in' requirement violated the First Amendment of the Constitution as it did not meet the test in Central Hudson and impermissibly regulated commercial speech.

In its Third Report and Order, the FCC reversed its findings in the Second Report and held that CPNI of subscribers could be used for intra-company purposes and by a carrier's agents, independent contractors, and joint venture partners to market and provide communications-related services.[162] However, subscribers had to be given the opportunity to 'opt-out' of such arrangements. Where a carrier wants to provide CPNI to third parties and affiliates that do not provide communications-related services, then subscribers must give their express consent to such disclosure.

A carrier's use of customer data for internal purposes is not without limits, however. In 2008, the FCC found that Verizon had violated Section 222(b) of the Act

---

[162] Implementation of the Telecommunications Act of 1996, Third Report and Order and Third Further Notice of Proposed Rulemaking, CC Docket Nos 96-115, 96-149, 00-257, FCC No 02-214, 17 FCC Rcd 14860 (2002).

by creating a customer retention programme that was triggered when Verizon received a local number porting request from a new phone company as part of a customer-initiated request to change phone carriers.[163] In the Verizon complaint, the activity clearly fell within the scope of the 1996 Act. A greater challenge to policy makers relates to how information service providers, which typically escape the provisions of the 1996 Act, can use customer data. For example, a 2008 test by Embarq (a local phone service spin-off of Sprint) that tracked Internet subscribers' web-surfing activities for advertising purposes generated concerns from privacy advocates and lawmakers.

The FCC further strengthened its privacy rules in a 2007 decision that imposed authentication requirements (such as use of a password) before a carrier is permitted to release phone call records to customers, extended the CPNI rules to providers of interconnected VoIP service, and took other steps to protect the personal telephone records of consumers from unauthorized disclosure.[164] These steps were taken in response to increasing concerns about 'pretexting', the practice of obtaining personal information under false pretences. The FCC sought comment on what further steps, if any, it should take to protect consumer privacy. Given the continuing illegal trade in personal information, it is likely that policymakers will continue to be active in this field.

6.15 IP-ENABLED SERVICES

More and more communications providers in the US, including cable, wireless, and wireline operators, have started to deploy Internet Protocol (IP) technology in their networks. IP technology is an innovative and more efficient way to enable two-way communication as it does not require the use of a dedicated transmission path as is the case with circuit-switched networks. Instead, data is divided into a series of packets, which are addressed and then transmitted across any number of different networks to their final destination. A router determines the path taken by each packet to reach its destination. With the greater deployment of and improvement in IP technology, the provision of IP-enabled services to customers, such as voice-over IP, has soared. Moreover, customers are beginning to replace circuit-switched services with IP-enabled services.

A fundamental question raised by IP-enabled services is whether or not the FCC has exclusive jurisdiction to regulate all types of IP-enabled services. Early on, certain states asserted they had jurisdiction to regulate services enabling users to make

[163] *Bright House Communications v Verizon California*, Memorandum Opinion and Order, File No EB-08-MD-002, FCC No 08-159, 23 FCC Rcd 10704 (2008).
[164] Implementation of the Telecommunications Act of 1996, Report and Order and Further Notice of Proposed Rulemaking, CC Docket No 96-115, WC Docket No 04-36, FCC No 07-22, 22 FCC Rcd 6927 (2007).

or receive voice calls using IP technology. However, in a 2004 decision, the FCC concluded that it had exclusive jurisdiction over these services.[165] Despite its assertion of jurisdiction, the FCC has thus far declined to determine if VoIP should be classified as a 'telecommunications service' which is subject to Title II of the 1934 Act or as an 'information service' which escapes Title II obligations. Instead, it has relied on its general ancillary powers under Title I of the 1934 Act and has, in a rather piecemeal fashion, imposed a series of obligations designed to promote public safety or advance the goal of universal service on what it has described as 'interconnected VoIP services'.[166] Many of these obligations have been introduced elsewhere in this chapter, and include compliance with the FCC's rules governing customer proprietary network information[167] and local number portability,[168] and duties to enable users to contact emergency services,[169] to ensure access by those with disabilities[170] and to contribute to the universal service fund.[171]

Although a regulatory framework for VoIP has now emerged, it remains largely unclear how IP-enabled services other than VoIP should be regulated and the FCC's role in the process. The FCC first began consideration of the complex legal and regulatory issues raised by IP-enabled services and their effects on the regulation of legacy systems in February 2004 when it opened a Notice of Proposed Rulemaking.[172] However, in July 2008, all of the issues raised in the notice remained unaddressed. The first is whether the states or the FCC has jurisdiction over all other types of IP-enabled services, including those where there is no voice element. Secondly, assuming the FCC has jurisdiction under the 1934 Act, it will need to determine if each service meets the statutory definitions of 'telecommunications', 'telecommunications service', or 'information service'. This, however, may be of less concern given

---

[165] Vonage Holdings Corporation Petition for Declaratory Ruling Concerning an Order of the Minnesota Public Utilities Commission, Memorandum Opinion and Order, WC Docket No 03-211, FCC No 04-267, 19 FCC Rcd 22404 (2004).

[166] These are services that satisfy four criteria: first, they enable 'real-time, two-way voice communications'; secondly, they require 'a broadband connection from the user's location'; thirdly, they require 'Internet protocol-compatible customer premises equipment'; lastly, they allow 'users generally to receive calls that originate on the public switched telephone network and to terminate calls to the public switched telephone network'.

[167] Implementation of the Telecommunications Act of 1996, Report and Order and Further Notice of Proposed Rulemaking, CC Docket No 96-115, WC Docket No 04-36, FCC No 07-22, 22 FCC Rcd 6927 (2007).

[168] Telephone Number Requirements for IP-Enabled Service Providers, Report and Order, Declaratory Ruling, Order on Remand, and Notice of Proposed Rulemaking, WC Docket No 07-243, FCC No 07-188, 22 FCC Rcd 19531 (2007).

[169] IP-Enabled Services, First Report and Order and Notice of Proposed Rulemaking, WC Docket Nos 04-36, 05-196, FCC No 05-116, 20 FCC Rcd 10245 (2005).

[170] IP-Enabled Services, Report and Order, WC Docket No 04-36, FCC No 07-110, 22 FCC Rcd 11275 (2007).

[171] Universal Service Contribution Fund, Report and Order and Notice of Proposed Rulemaking, WC Docket No 06-122 et al, FCC No 06-94, 21 FCC Rcd 7518 (2006).

[172] IP-Enabled Services, Notice of Proposed Rulemaking, WC Docket No 04-36, FCC No 04-28, 19 FCC Rcd 4863 (2004).

the FCC's efforts to sidestep classification of VoIP and to rely solely on its ancillary powers in Title I and the increasingly blurred distinction between Title I obligations and the requirements of common carriers using circuit-switching in Title II. Thirdly, the FCC must decide if some matters of public policy are of sufficient importance to warrant regulation of these services, regardless of the basis of FCC regulation. Some regulation may be necessary, for example, to promote public safety, including the ability of law enforcement agencies to conduct lawful surveillance of communications, to protect the privacy interests of users and to safeguard the universal service regime. The FCC expressed a desire in its 2004 Notice of Inquiry to keep regulation of IP-enabled services to a minimum; however, as discussed in section 6.11, it is becoming increasingly clear that access and interconnection-like obligations of some form may need to be extended to the new technological environment.

IP-enabled services clearly highlight the deficiencies of existing legislation to deal with them. The Communications Act of 1934 (as amended by the Telecommunications Act of 1996) assumes a market structure which is no longer relevant and sets forth a regulatory structure that is rapidly becoming obsolete as a result of IP technology. Continued FCC reliance on its ancillary jurisdiction in Title I of the Act may well lead to lengthy and costly litigation to determine the precise breadth and scope of the FCC's powers, and some policymakers have expressed discomfort with the FCC relying on the non-specific authority contained in Title I to make such important policy decisions. For these reasons, further legislative action by Congress is likely to be warranted. Given the complexity of the issues raised by IP-enabled services, however, lawmakers, the courts, the FCC, the 50 PUCs, and the industry will each have an important role to play in developing a new and appropriate regulatory framework.

Part III

KEY REGULATORY ISSUES

7

AUTHORIZATION AND LICENSING

Anne Flanagan

7.1 INTRODUCTION

Licensing is a key aspect of telecommunications regulation. At a basic level, a licence permits a telecommunications provider to offer specified equipment, networks, and/or services, and often conditions that permission on certain requirements. Licensing, however, can control market entry and, therefore, can be used to shape the market by limiting or not the number of players or the types of services that they are able to provide. It can create legal certainty for new entrants in markets where the telecommunications regulatory or general legal framework is not comprehensive or where there is not much history with telecommunications regulation. Under these circumstances, conditions imposed and rights accorded in licences can serve as a substitute for such frameworks. In similar situations, such as where private property rights might be uncertain, the licence can serve as a contract between the regulator and investors in the incumbent, a departure from the traditional legal nature of a government licence. As a binding contract, it can guarantee exclusivity, ensure due process[1] as well as impose performance obligations, e.g. in the form of enhanced

---

[1] This term is used here as shorthand for legal substantive and procedural requirements for fairness however they arise whether pursuant to statutory obligation or otherwise. It is suggested that a contract

market penetration or network roll-out requirements. Without such contracts, investors might otherwise be reluctant to commit the large amounts of capital required to update ageing networks or roll out new technologies and networks required to improve and update services. Without the performance obligations, countries might be unwilling to involve private parties in the running of the state-owned incumbent.[2] Licensing can also be used as a means to create competitive markets by imposing obligations on incumbents in order to level the playing field.

A licence is, therefore, an important regulatory tool in developing markets. In more mature markets, with emerged competition, the same considerations may not apply. One of the most significant changes in the current EU framework, discussed in the previous chapter, is that with the achievement of full competition, at least *de jure*, electronic communications providers no longer need to obtain individual licences requiring approvals to provide networks or services.[3] Instead, there is a scheme of general authorizations applied to all providers pursuant to the 2002 Authorization Directive.[4] EU Member States can subject these authorizations only to any of a defined and limited set of general conditions. Individual conditions can be applied only in certain circumstances, as will be explored further below. States may require individual licence grants only for scarce resources, now limited in the EU to radio spectrum and numbers.

Licensing as a means to manage and allocate radio spectrum for telecommunications and other uses is of growing importance in the EU, the US, and numerous other jurisdictions for a variety of emergent issues including digital convergence and the growing demands for radio spectrum. Spectrum licensing can have multiple, seemingly conflicting objectives and functions. It can be used to maintain market limits due to its scarcity and yet simultaneously open new markets. It can address the needs of both developing and very advanced markets. It can restrict usage while seeking to assure availability for more even yet to emerge uses as well as address

---

can provide these, including remedies such as early termination payments and what procedures will be used to resolve disputes or adjudicate breaches, e.g. arbitration procedures and rules as well as limitations on the reasons it can be abrogated or breached. The term 'due process of law' is a US constitutional law concept that implies certain guaranteed levels of procedural and substantive fairness. It is contained in the Fifth Amendment to the US Constitution that states, in part, that no person can be deprived of 'life, liberty, or property, without due process of law'.

[2] For an examination of issues arising in developing markets, see Chapters 16–17.

[3] This chapter focuses primarily on the nature and scope of approvals needed to provide communications networks and services. However, equipment intended to be attached to the network typically must also be 'authorized'. In many countries, it must meet type and safety requirements via an established approval process. Although Chapter 5 (at section 5.4.3) details the EU process and legislation governing this, this chapter's examination of the purpose and power of licensing, *inter alia*, to encompass public and consumer safety extends of necessity to the regulation of equipment used to provide communications networks and services. The discussion in this regard will make reference where applicable to this aspect of 'authorization'.

[4] Directive 2002/20/EC of the European Parliament and of the Council on the authorization of electronic communications networks and services, OJ L108/21, 24 April 2002 (the Authorization Directive).

the significant and ironic fact of spectrum underutilization. Spectrum licensing policy can as well regulate in order to deregulate, as with other markets.

In advanced information societies, the ever growing demands for communications mobility and other life style technologies, has spiked demand for spectrum to be made available for such use. Licensing can appropriately ration spectrum resources generally still considered 'scarce' and contain uses to those predetermined as safe, efficient, or effective (or socially or politically desirable) under a command and control regulatory model. Yet there is growing recognition that spectrum should wherever possible be made available on an untrammelled basis and its uses subject to market determination, and even possibly on an unlicensed basis. As advanced markets move to more efficient technologies such as the migration to digital TV, including in Europe and the US, spectrum will be freed for other uses in what has been called 'the digital dividend'. This is a significant issue as it entails a considerable swath of spectrum. As noted by the Office of Communications (Ofcom), the five analogue TV broadcasters in the UK use over half of the commercially important spectrum bands below 1GHz.[5] It is also a choice or a series of choices that can perhaps be viewed as a one-off event with decisions made now likely to govern its use for many decades to come. This is especially true given the considerable length of licences and the experienced difficulty of reallocating uses such as that encountered by the US in seeking to clear bands for advanced communications. How this and other spectrum is to be allocated and used in the EU, including via secondary spectrum trading markets, is therefore the subject of keen debate and consultation as well as near certain reform. Here the UK is leading the charge with its spectrum licensing and management reforms that include full and partial spectrum trading in many bands, limited technological-specific conditions to ensure greater neutrality, and reliance on the market to set spectrum value and 'best use'. It might be said that the EU is seeking to catch up here and address not only these issues but also how to ensure that its 27 countries' national borders don't pose a barrier to the effective development of pan-European mobile services of all kinds.

This chapter examines the current EU legal framework for authorization of electronic communications services and networks after a brief overview of the problems with the previous EU framework's implementation it was designed to address. It then outlines recent and other proposed reforms under consideration and arising from the Commission's (and others') view that the current framework still has failed to meet the needs of the Single Market, particularly in the markets for wireless and pan-European services. The chapter finally explores the UK's implementation of the EU regulatory scheme under the Communications Act 2003 and its spectrum reforms centred on the Wireless Telegraphy Act 2006. Before addressing these issues, however, the chapter will first briefly attempt to develop the history and jurisprudential underpinnings of licensing as it has evolved in the common law jurisdictions of

---

[5] Press Release, 'The Ofcom Digital Dividend Review' (Ofcom, London 5 November 2005).

England and the United States and how licensing has served as a tool both to limit and to open telecommunications markets to competition.

7.2 LICENCES: PRIVILEGES AND NECESSITIES

Telecommunications licensing, to a large extent, is a recent development: in most countries, telecommunications was provided as an essential public service, usually with posts, telegraph, and, sometimes, transport, by a government entity not subject to licensing. Yet the licensing of telecommunications providers did not emerge solely from the liberalization and privatization of State-owned incumbents that has swept the globe in the last 20 years. Rather, this modern development has much earlier foundations[6] and ties to historical events that are worth exploring to put a context and order in the study of today's telecommunications licensing laws.

7.2.1 Meaning and history of economic restrictions

A starting point for such exploration is the word itself. 'Licence' comes from the Latin 'licere', meaning 'to permit'.[7] This sense of a 'permission' to do an act or acts that would otherwise be unlawful or comprise a trespass or tort appears to apply in all legal meanings or contexts of 'licence',[8] such as a licence to enter onto land, to use a work protected by intellectual property, or to operate an automobile on public roads: licences under real property law, contract law, and government regulation, respectively.[9] This chapter deals primarily with the last grouping: licence under government regulation.[10] This has been defined as 'authority to do some act or carry on some trade or business, in its nature lawful but prohibited by statute except with the

---

[6] The focus here is primarily on law and principals derived from English common law; it does not suggest that there is not comparative historical precedent within civil law systems.

[7] See *Bouvier's Law Dictionary* (Baldwin WE, ed, Library Edition 1928), 711. Accord, *Black's Law Dictionary* (6th ed, 1979), 829–830. The other sense, noted to be merely secondary, is that of the document that embodies these permissions in writing. See, e.g. *State ex rel Peterson v Martin*, 180 Or 459, 474, 176 P2d 636, 643 (1947); *Mathias v Walling Enterprises*, 609 So2d 1323, 1332 (Fla App 1992); 53 Corpus Juris Secundum, *Licenses* § 2 (1983). Since in telecommunications licensing, the licensing document or certificate is often a complex writing with descriptions of grants, rights, networks, and approved equipment, as well as schedules of conditions and definitions, one must consider the two senses somewhat merged.

[8] See, e.g. Bouvier's Law Dictionary, n 7 above.

[9] See ibid.

[10] Even here, however, there is overlap with other contexts. It has been noted that with regard to US communications licensing that some state and local franchise and licence requirements have stemmed from the use of public lands by communications companies, see Quirk, WJ, 'A Constitutional and Statutory History of the Telephone Business in South Carolina', (2000) 51 South Carolina L Rev 290, 293. The use of public land is among the privileges that have been suggested as underlying the rationale for the imposition of regulation on common callings and undertakings granted privileges, see, Burdick, C, 'The origin of the peculiar duties of public service companies', (1911) 11 Columbia L Rev. 514, 616, 743.

permission of the civil authority or which otherwise would be unlawful'.[11] It examines this in the context of England and its derivative common law systems, most notably that of the US.

The public regulation of private parties in their provision of goods or services, such as telecommunications, stems in part from the common law's imposition of greater duties and legal obligations on so-called 'public' or 'common' callings.[12] These selected trades or undertakings, that changed over time according to their economic necessity[13] and often their scarcity, which frequently constituted a monopoly,[14] had imposed upon them a duty to serve all members of the public on reasonable terms and with reasonable care.[15] Inns and carrier coaches that were essential[16] to travel and travellers on the then few roads were soon included within this group that is today referenced primarily by the term 'common carriers' and is far more limited.[17] This is relevant for several reasons to communications licensing and regulation. Firstly, inns were the first post offices in Britain and, innkeepers, the first postmasters in a system that was the precursor to that ultimately governing telegraph and telecommunications in the UK. Secondly, the licensing of inns and common houses serves to illustrate the nature and scope of licensing jurisdiction, generally, as it has been exercised over time in the UK and the US. Finally, the classification of 'common carrier' continues to apply in the US today to telecommunications

---

[11] *Bouvier's Law Dictionary*, n 7 above.

[12] See Wyman, B, 'The law of public callings as a solution of the trust problem' (1904) 17 Harv L Rev 156, 156–159 (suggesting that akin to this common law theory, enhanced duties be placed on monopolies (then in the US often structured as a trust so that its competition law is called the Sherman Anti-trust Act) in light of their privileges and their economic necessity to society).

[13] That the scarcity of inns and their critical importance to development of Britain's emerging internal trade was a factor critical to their regulation is suggested by the fact that prior to their inclusion as a common calling, they could be indicted as a public nuisance 'if it was set up where it was not needed'. Webb, S and B, 'The First Century of Licensing' in *The History of Liquor Licensing in England* (Longmans, Green & Co, 1903), at 5, n 1.

[14] 'The rule that one who pursued a common calling was obliged to serve all comers on reasonable terms seems to have been based on the fact that innkeepers, carriers, farriers, and the like, were few, and each had a virtual monopoly in his neighborhood.' *Wilson v Newspaper and Mail Deliverer's Union of NY*, 197 A 720, 722 (NJ Ch 1938) (citing Wyman, n 12 above). Another commentator notes that the doctrine emerged from the Statute of Labourers in 1349 to prevent unjust wage demands in light of the labour shortages created by the Black Death and eventually to those few tradesmen or professionals who worked outside the feudal domain. See Cherry, B, 'Utilizing "essentiality of access" analyses to mitigate risky, costly and untimely government interventions in converging telecommunications technologies and markets' (2003) 11 Common Law Conspectus 251, n 31.

[15] See Speta, JB, 'A Common Carrier Approach to Internet Connection' (2002) 54 Fed Comm LJ 225, 251–257.

[16] The concept of an 'essential facility' under US competition law one to which access is an economic necessity was noted by the court in to have its roots in common carrier doctrine.

[17] It is noted that, in the US since the 19th century, 'common carrier' doctrine has been applied by courts to undertakings related to infrastructure such as docks, roads, railroads, telegraph, and ultimately telephone, and constitutes a narrower group. See, e.g. Candebub, A, 'Network interconnection and takings' (2004) 54 Syracuse Law Review 369, 381.

companies which are licensed[18] as such by and called 'carriers' under the US Communications Act of 1934.[19] Thus, the history and licensing of the inns within which the first postal system emerged evinces elements of law, economics, and social policy that continue to this day within the regulation and licensing of electronic communications providers.

The Tudor monarch established a system of posts at regular intervals along key routes outside of London to enhance the reach and efficiency of the King's messenger services.[20] Largely established at the few inns along each route, the innkeepers became the first postmasters with each responsible for forwarding the monarch's mail by horse dispatch to the next post. This system evolved into the General Post Office (its origins are detailed, above in Chapter 4), a government department that later came to encompass the telegraph and telephone systems. The Tudors' postal system was based on a daily retainer fee and a grant of a monopoly to the innkeepers for the letting of all horses for hire to all travellers on that road.[21] This linking of a grant of monopoly with a public benefit or service seems a requirement[22] by medieval common law courts for their legal recognition of restrictions on the freedom of any man to practice a trade even when these restrictions arose as the result of a royal

---

[18] In the US, telecommunication common carriers are not granted a licence certificate but rather, where required, approval to enter a market is made via an order by the FCC under s 214 of the Communications Act 1934. This individual approval process applies only to international service common carriers including facilities-based carriers, resellers, prepaid calling card providers and various wireless service providers offering calling between the US and foreign points., Some of these are entitled to an expedited processing of 14 days. However, since the decision to allow the market entry is made by the regulator on an individual basis, this chapter will consider this as licensing. For a discussion of the application and approval process as well as the four of international service common carriers not entitled to expedited processing, see, Crowe, TK, 'FCC 214 licensing in the post 9/11 environment'(July 2005), available at <http://www.tkcrowe.com/fcc_214_licenses.html>. Domestic, interstate services are now the subject of a blanket approval pursuant to s 214 powers, with all individual approvals now discontinued. This chapter will refer to this as an authorization or general authorization, a distinction in keeping with the classifications under the EU's regulatory scheme. The FCC imposes conditions and requirements for the performance of carriers' service and network provision by further orders, regulations, and approval of filed tariffs.

[19] 47 USC 151 et seq. These businesses are also categorized as 'public utilities' both falling under a larger category of businesses 'affected with a public interest' a doctrine expounded by Lord Chief Justice Hale and utilized by US courts to justify an exercise of economic regulation. See Munn v Illinois, 94 US 113, 125–6 (1776) (citing extensively Hale, De Portibus Maris, 1 Harg, Tracts 78 (1776)). The US courts for much of the early 20th century struggled to pin the boundaries of this doctrine in all sorts of scenarios, including minimum wage statutes, ticket brokers, and employment agencies. They failed to do so with any real cohesive analysis and appear to have largely turned away from the doctrine as a source of power for economic regulation. See Candebub, A, n 17 above.

[20] Postmaster General, 'The posts before 1711' in Monarchs of All they Surveyed: The Story of the Post Office Surveyors (HMSO, London, 1952), at 6–7. These 'surveyors' who originally surveyed the distance between and established these posts later oversaw the enforcement of the GPO's monopoly and proper collection of its postage rates. See generally, ibid. Over time, innkeepers remained the postmasters under new systems by bidding for the contract to provide such services which by then extended to private mail and for which these postmasters recouped their contract price and earnings from the postage charged.

[21] Ibid.

[22] It is, however, noted that the 'pretence d'un publike bien' had served as the basis for the grant of many privileges by the King. 4 Holdsworth, A History of English Law (2nd edn, 1938) 344 at n 6 (quoting YB Ed III Pasch pl 8).

franchise or privilege.[23] Other justifications at law were few. 'Custom' or 'prescription'[24] could legitimize royal privileges or franchises held since the time of memory that often had the result of restraining trade[25] such as the grants of political and commercial self-governance[26] to guilds and local authorities.[27] A national or public interest justified more recent grants. Beyond this, the principle of medieval common law, upheld by subsequent courts,[28] was that 'prima facie trade must be free, and that freedom could only be curtailed by definite restrictions known to and recognized by the common law'.[29] The prerogative to restrict economic liberty via limitations on trade, grants of intellectual property, etc., was subsequently vested in Parliament, although the royal prerogative did not disappear quickly or readily.[30] Hence, the source and nature of lawful restrictions on trade, while limited by these legal principles, were still numerous and varied. Moreover, it appears that the common law understanding of freedom to practice a trade without restriction was limited to the concept of freedom from arbitrary restriction not defensible by public policy.[31]

7.2.2 Licensing powers and historical purposes

Those defensible purposes could vary according to the grant and circumstance. How they applied in the context of inns is worth examining. The justifications for the limitations on the economic liberty of innkeepers in the form of a licence requirement may be seen to apply more generally to licensing of other common callings or common carriers, including, subsequently, telecommunications carriers. Inns and other public houses selling alcohol were very early on subject to licence by the local Justices of the Peace. They, by a grant of power from Parliament under 'the statute of 5 and 6 Edward VI c 25 (1552) . . . were authorized to select from time to time,

---

[23] See 4 Holdsworth, above, at 344. This commentator notes, ibid at n 4, that grants of the King could be contrary to the common law and public policy as restraints on trade. Accord, Webb S and B, above n 13 at 5, n 1 (quoting the King's 1604 circular letter to the Privy Council that 'By the law and statutes of this our realm, the keeping of alehouses and victualling houses is none of those trades which it is free and lawful for any subject to set up and exercise, but inhibited to all save such as are thereto licensed').

[24] Usage beyond the time of memory, defined as that before Richard I. 3 *Blackstone's Commentaries with Notes of Reference to the Constitution and Laws of the Federal Government of the United States and of the Commonwealth of Virginia* (St George Tucker, 1803), 36 at n 7 (reprinted Rothman Reprints, 1969).

[25] It is suggested that freedom from restraint according to common law standards meant freedom from arbitrary restraints, i.e. those not recognized by law. See Maitland, WH, *The Domesday Book and Beyond: Three Essays on the Early History of England* (CJ Holt, 1897), 261–264

[26] These grants, which were numerous and varied, often included not only the right to revenues collected in whatever undertaking it applied to but also jurisdiction over the persons and activities involved, or 'soke' and 'sake'. See Maitland, WH, above at 261–264. Hence trade and governance were often intertwined.

[27] 4 Holdsworth, n 22 above at 346.

[28] See, e.g. *Darcy v Allin*, (1602) Moore KB 671–675.

[29] 4 Holdsworth, n 22 above at 350.

[30] See generally, ibid, at 344–362. The English Statute of Monopolies of 1623, 21 Jac 1, ch 3, made void all privileges, commissions, and grants of monopoly not confirmed by statute.

[31] 4 Holdsworth, n 22 above at 350–352.

at their discretion, certain persons who were alone to exercise the trade of keeping a common alehouse'[32] and inns when they became subject to the legal regimen of common callings.[33] This regulation arose from a balancing of public interests: making available what was then seen to be a necessity of life, the beer consumed at every meal, and control over the disorder and problems produced by excessive drinking.[34] This grant was intended to strengthen earlier powers of the local Justices to eliminate any alehouses that went beyond that number required to serve the needs of the market,[35] perhaps an early example of natural monopoly theory that would serve to justify the virtually exclusive licensing of monopoly providers of telecommunications providers in the twentieth century.[36]

The powers that Parliament delegated here to the Justices of the Peace included 'three distinct forms of control: the power of selection, the power of withdrawal, and the power of imposing conditions',[37] all powers which might be said to describe accurately telecommunications licensing authority, until recently, in the EU. The broad purposes for which licensing might be imposed, were described over 100 years ago as follows:

The device of licensing—that is, the requirement that any person desiring to pursue a particular occupation shall first obtain specific permission from a governing authority—may be used to attain many different ends. The license may be merely an occasion for extracting a fee or levying a tax. It may be an instrument for registering all those who are following a particular occupation, in order, for some reason or another, to ensure their being brought under public notice. It may be a device for limiting the numbers of those so engaged, or for selecting them according to their possession of certain qualifications. Finally, the act of licensing may be the means of imposing special rules upon the occupation, or of more easily enforcing the fulfilment either of these special rules or of the general law of the land.[38]

As this chapter will later examine, these same purposes continue to apply to contemporary licensing as do some new ones. However, the source of the authority underlying the purposes is important for their legitimacy and scope. For example, the

---

[32] Webb, S and B, 'The First Century of Licensing' in *The History of Liquor Licensing in England* (Longmans, Green & Co, 1903), at 5, n 1.

[33] Ibid, at 5, n 1.

[34] Ibid, at 2–3.

[35] Ibid, at 5–6.

[36] Civil law countries in Europe seem to have had similar systems for authorizing and regulating transportation carriers as businesses affected with a public interest under a theory akin to that of common carriers and limiting their numbers within certain regions for reasons that seem premised on natural monopoly and public interest. See Fulda, CH, 'The regulation of surface transportation in the European Economic Community' 12 Am J Comp L (1963) 303, 308–313 (commenting that while Germany, Belgium, Italy, and others limited the numbers of competitors in trucking and railroads operations to ensure their continued availability and safe operation without the threat of unlimited competition that would cause more harm here than in other economic sectors, the limiting of numbers of business units by the US seems generally to have been confined to the liquor industry).

[37] Webb, S and B, n 32 above at 4–5.

[38] Ibid, at 4.

exercise of the regulatory or the 'police' power of the state ordinarily continues as the primary foundation of licensing requirements considered necessary for the public interest or general welfare such as public health, morals, or safety.[39] In the United States, a significant number of states take the position that licensing of legitimate businesses or occupations that do not involve such interests would be outside the limits of the police power.[40]

The source of the power underlying licence fees is less clear. While the sovereign's power to tax has sometimes been considered to underlie the imposition of licence fees, it has also been held that a true 'licence fee' is imposed under the police power and its characteristics are that it is applicable only to a type of business that is supervised or subject to regulation that does in fact occur, the expense of which is intended to be defrayed by the fees that are equated to the 'probable cost' of supervision.[41] Fees unrelated to the cost of regulation have been considered a 'tax' on occupations in the nature of an excise under the power to raise revenue, and in at least the US, subject to review under different standards from licensing fees.[42] It has been suggested that perhaps both powers can apply within the same fee and be valid. Licence fees for telecommunications providers appear to vary greatly within and across jurisdictions. However, under the EU's new framework, fees, other than those associated with scarce public resources, now must not only be based on the costs of licence issuance and enforcement, but must be demonstrably so or otherwise adjusted. They are then truly 'licence fees'.

A different source of authority may underlie the privilege, licence, or franchise involving the grant of a valuable resource belonging to the public, such as land,[43] or also in the case in telecommunications, radio spectrum.[44] Such have been considered to be administered by the state or local authority on behalf of the public under the

---

[39] See *Sharp v Wakefield* [1891] AC 173 (Bramwell, LJ noting that the licensing of public houses was largely police rather than economic regulation). Accord, 53 CJS, n 7 above at § 5.

[40] See 53 CJS, Licenses § 5.

[41] *National Biscuit Co v City of Philadelphia*, 98 A2d 182, 187–188 (Pa, 1953). Accord, *Hunt v Cooper*, 110 SW2d 896, 899–900 (Tex, 1937).

[42] See, e.g. *National Biscuit*, above at 187–189; *Hunt*, 110 SW2d at 899–901. Where the nature of the licence requirement is seen as revenue-raising rather than regulatory, it has been held that the licence is merely a receipt rather than an authority. See *Royall v State of Virginia*, 6 Sup Ct 510 (US 1886) (noting that a municipal occupation licence could not prevent an attorney licensed by the state to practise law in any part of the state from practising within the city limits, although it was a valid tax). Failure to obtain or comply with a licence that is seen as administrative or merely revenue producing may have lesser consequences at law than one which seeks to regulate skills or proficiency or is otherwise imposed for public safety or health. See, e.g. *Dubray v Horshaw*, 884 P2d 23, 28 (Wyo 2000) (noting that where statutory requirement for licence transfer was merely administrative rather than one intended to protect a class of persons from a particular harm, citing s 286 of the Restatement 2d of Torts, it created no duty of care to the plaintiff).

[43] See *Shively v Bowlby*, 152 US 1 (1984) (noting that public lands were traditionally held by the king for the benefit of the nation under *jus publicum*, with such vesting in the federal and state governments of the US upon the American Revolution).

[44] Corbett, K, Note 'The Rise of Private Property Rights in Broadcast Spectrum' (1996) 46 Duke LJ 611, 616–619.

doctrine of 'public trust', having roots in Roman law.[45] Here, a payment of a fee that reflects a value for the resource unrelated to its regulation, and that ensures its effective and efficient use, is therefore considered appropriate to be levied, although this is not always done.[46] In the UK, five third-generation (3G) mobile licences were auctioned by the Secretary of State for Trade and Industry resulting in nearly £22 billion in licence fees; the US FCC similarly sought to attain the highest possible returns, ultimately nearly $20 billion after 32 rounds of bidding, on what it termed 'beachfront' spectrum in the 700Mhz range with broadband capabilities.[47] Finland, in contrast chooses not to charge at all beyond a nominal administration fee and credits this policy with its mobile rates being among the lowest in the world.[48]

As will be further considered in the context of auctions, the revenue maximizing approach has been questioned for several reasons, not the least of which is the potential for incumbents in wireless telephony to bid beyond the prices that new commercial wireless telephony market entrants or those seeking spectrum for other uses could individually afford to pay despite the social benefits.

7.2.3 Purposes of contemporary telecommunications licensing

The historical purposes noted above for licensing underlie communications licensing not only historically but also currently. The following explores how these purposes can be traced in those few telecommunications markets where licensing existed before the recent liberalizations of the last 30 years and in modern telecommunications licensing regimes that have been put in place as a result.

7.2.3.1 Licenses as a control over market entry
Licensing as 'a device for limiting the numbers of those so engaged' has been very common in telecommunications in order to control the structure of the market. For example, in both the UK and the US, licensing was intended to limit the number of telecommunications providers which, in both cases, meant its extreme aspect of protecting a monopoly. In the UK, the Telegraph Act 1869 established 'exclusive privilege' in the General Post Office to operate telegraph services in the UK but itself not subject to licence or regulation as a government department. The Act exempted only certain entities such as railroads, canals, and limited other undertakings, such as Lloyds of London, providing these for their own use. However, a licence granted by the Postmaster General was required for other companies wishing

---

[45] See Institutes of Justinian 2.1 (T Cooper trans, 2nd edn 1841) positing that 'Things common to mankind by the law of nature, are the air, running water, the sea, and consequently the shores of the sea . . .'.

[46] See, e.g. Corbett, K, n 44 above.

[47] See, e.g. Gardiner, B., 'FCC's spectrum auction approaches $20 B in bids' (Epicenter 05/02/08), <http://blog.wired.com/business/2008/02/fccs-spectrum-a.html>.

[48] Pursiainen, H, 'The "lazy regulator" helps Finland's telecommunications boom' European Affairs, (Summer 2000). Also, see OECD, Communications Outlook 2007, 216–219 (OECD 2007).

to provide telegraph services.[49] This protective legislation was later extended to telephones when the definition of telegraph under the Act was construed to include telephony that could then no longer be provided by a private company.[50]

Historically, in the US, except for some small, rural carriers, American Telephone & Telegraph (AT&T) was the exclusive 'common carrier' licensed under the Communications Act of 1934 pursuant to a natural monopoly theory, after AT&T had acquired most of the other carriers in the country.[51] Licensing to limit the numbers of market entrants was neither exclusive to these two countries nor a mere historical curiosity. In 1999, the EU reported that the hurdle of the individual licence required by a majority of Member States with its ensuing complexities and, in some States, delay and expense, lack of transparency, and excessive regulatory discretion was a barrier to market entry.[52] Licensing had the effect, if not also the object, of limiting the number of market entrants and, therefore, of protecting the national incumbent and maintaining the near-monopoly market structure. This barrier to entry has yet to be fully resolved despite over five years since the implementation of the present EU framework with its requirement for general authorizations without the need for individual decisions or permissions. The current market access report card issued by the European association of companies competing with the former monopolists identifies only two of 18 EU national markets evaluated, the UK and Netherlands, with no serious barriers to entry in any of six specified access categories. All of the remaining States reportedly have at least two, and 12 of the States evaluated have three or more.[53] If some of the most liberalized markets in the world have residual licensing barriers to entry, the experience in other markets might be negatively extrapolated.

Licensing as a control against market entry must be contrasted with licensing as a tool to structure the market by introducing competition. This is done by licensing the incumbent that may or may not be still government-owned and/or granting licences to new entrant(s) that will offer services in competition with the incumbent. Here, to level the playing field, the conditions imposed on the incumbent, often via the licence, are generally more onerous than those on the new entrant. These can include, for example, requiring the incumbent to interconnect on a non-discriminatory basis and at regulated, sometimes cost-based rates and to maintain separate accounting to ascertain and verify such cost. A specific example of a licence as a market-opening

---

[49] Events in Telecommunications History, BT Group Archives, <http://www.btplc.com/Thegroup/ BTsHistory/ 1851–1880.htm>.

[50] *Attorney-General v The Edison Telephone Co of London, Ltd* [1880–81] LR 6 QBD 244.

[51] See Chapter 6 for a more detailed discussion of the early history of US telecommunications. For a further discussion of natural monopoly, see Chapter 3.

[52] Commission Communication, 'Toward a new framework for electronic communications infrastructure and associated services: The 1999 Communications Review' (1999 Communications Review), COM (1999) 539, 10 November 1999. Accord, Commission Communication, '5th Report on the implementation of the Telecommunications Regulatory Package' (1999).

[53] See, Regulatory Scorecard, 2007 at 3-4 (ECTA November 2007), <http://www.ectaportal.com/en/ basic651.html>.

tool was that authorized in the UK to Mercury under the British Telecommunications Act 1981 to provide a second fixed network in competition with British Telecommunications (BT), which was granted an 'exclusive privilege' under the same Act.[54] In the US there was the FCC's 1969 licensing of MCI to construct a microwave network and provide long-distance services to subscribers for their inter-office communications over it.[55] Both of these were, however, merely first steps with further action required in the form of additional legislation and court action to achieve what could be called a competitive market.

As noted, with wireless markets, licensing can serve simultaneously to limit and open markets. Limited spectrum availability and also the need to protect revenue flows of a state-owned or recently privatized monopoly incumbent (which may operate in both fixed and wireless markets) may cause countries to delimit the number of 2G and 3G wireless providers licensed in a market. Yet, wireless networks are less costly with potentially greater geographical penetration than is possible by installing new or upgrading aged fixed lines infrastructure. Wireless telephony has, therefore, in developing countries, been able to leapfrog this old technology to compete as an alternative infrastructure to fixed lines and enhance greatly the historically poor telephony penetration rates. Merely one example can serve to illustrate how dramatic the impact can be: in Pakistan mobile teledensity (phones per 100 persons) was 48.95 in January 2008, while that of fixed telephony including wireless local loops is reported at 4.45.[56] While that of there is considerable variation regionally in the rate of wireless roll out and take up, wireless growth has outstripped that of fixed in every region of the world.[57]

In a hybrid twist, one regulator has limited the number of market entrants but then used licensing conditions to open further the limited 3G markets. Hong Kong, seeking to increase both competition and innovation, set 'open network access' conditions on the four 3G licensees, requiring them to make a minimum of 30 per cent of their capacity available to virtual mobile network operators, effectively at least doubling the number of market entrants.[58] Some have questioned, however, whether the size of that market justified this and whether the attempted spur might not ultimately prove counterproductive.[59]

Limits on market entry can as well be imposed via requirements for multiple licences, i.e. different licences for different types of networks and services. Therefore, a provider might be required to have numerous licences, e.g. a mobile

[54] See Chapter 4.
[55] See Chapter 6.
[56] See 'Pakistan Reports 78.74 mln Mobile Subscribers in January' (Wireless Federation, February 14 2008), available at: <http://wirelessfederation.com/news/category/mobilink/>.
[57] ITU D 'Special Report: ICT and Telecommunications in Least Developed Countries 2001–2005' (ITU Geneva, 2006).
[58] See Press Release, 'Hong Kong: The Facts' at 6, (OFTA Hong Kong, September 2002), available at: <http://www.asia2002.gov.hk/press/HK-TheFacts.doc>.
[59] See Waters, P, 'Mobile competition: how many is too many?' Computer and Technology L Rev (2005), 11(3), 55–59.

licence limited to data, or for voice services over a small radio network such as that used by taxi companies, the types of licences more fully explored below. Before the last two rounds of EU reforms, the UK had as many as 22 categories of licences based on the network operated. In some countries a provider may be licensed for mobile voice telephony, but the country's economic policies may limit licensing of fixed voice or international voice to the national incumbent. Licensing with voice network and services markets exclusivity for a defined period, as mentioned previously, is not uncommon to attract strategic investors in a newly privatized incumbent in order to ensure a return on their investment. Voice services using Internet Protocols, however, have challenged such exclusivity. Wireless telephony using Voice over Internet Protocols (VoIP) may pose growing licensing and other regulatory challenges for jurisdictions with the growth of wifi hot spots providing broadband Internet access using unlicensed (possibly illegal) spectrum and the growing availability of wifi handsets and softphone software to convert mobile Internet access devices into phones.

7.2.3.2 Licensing to impose eligibility requirements
Licensing can be used to ensure professional and technical qualifications or other eligibility requirements, another of the historical 'ends' noted to justify the 'device of licensing'. To ensure that potential providers are solvent, able to deliver the services, complete the network they apply to provide, or use well the scarce resource they seek, it is not extraordinary to find licensing used for 'selecting them according to their possession of certain qualifications'. These qualifications can range from a 'fit and proper' standard applied to persons running the company[60] to the provision of an appropriate business plan[61] evincing expertise or the proof of a specific experience, such as numbers of years of provision elsewhere. This last licensing qualification is common in comparative licence award processes, often called 'beauty contests', where numerous providers compete for the licence to be awarded. Finland, for example, awarded four 3G mobile licences in 1999 based solely on a selection of the best applicants.[62] Sometimes minimum qualifications serve as the threshold for entry to auctions for licences, a process frequently used with spectrum licences. Price or some other criterion then becomes the deciding factor.[63]

7.2.3.3 Licensing as a means to impose special rules or operating controls
Licensing as a 'means of imposing special rules upon the occupation' can readily be seen in modern telecommunications regulation. Licences are used to impose all sorts

[60] See Application for Carrier or Service Provider Licence, Form I, sec G, Jamaica Telecommunications Act 2000, Telecommunications (Forms) Regulations 2000, <http://www.memt.gov.jm/PDF%20Files/MEMT/Telecommunications.pdf>.
[61] E.g. Belgium required a 5-year business plan to be filed. De Coridier, T, Van Dyck, J, 'Belgium: telecommunications—regulation' CTLR (2004), 10(3), N18–19.
[62] See Pursiainen, above n 48.
[63] Ibid.

of controls, especially regarding the provision of basic services.[64] Licences may impose technical requirements for equipment attached to or interconnected to the network for its protection as well as that of employees of providers and users. Conditions can also attempt to ensure the efficient use of numbers, spectrum, and other resources considered scarce by a jurisdiction. Indeed, it is not unusual for jurisdictions to condition all spectrum licences to ensure its efficient, effective, safe, and appropriate use, including conditions that mandate compliance with equipment non-interference standards and specifications for conforming use, as well as minimum roll-out and penetration requirements to justify the limited exclusivity. These can also mandate the specific service and/or a specific technology. These conditions and others premised on 'non-economic reasons in the general public interest' are called 'essential requirements' in the EU, a limited and harmonized set of conditions that has been honed over time to ensure that they are 'essential' and don't operate as barriers to entry.[65] These conditions can of course vary according to the nature of the equipment or service at issue.

Conditions imposed for specific technologies, however, run the risk of putting a regulatory burden on this technology that would not exist for others and which may undermine its development and use. Spectrum has been one area of licensing where conditions and rights granted under licences have tended to be technology specific in order to ensure non-interference and socially desirable uses, under the traditional command and control model. However, as the EU's regulatory framework is intended to be technology neutral, the UK has sought to deregulate and liberalize its spectrum to the extent presently possible. Allocations and conditions will be designed, wherever possible, to make spectrum available for any use not interfering with other users within that band. This will facilitate the ability to change use and, therefore, spectrum trading. It is Ofcom's ultimate target that, within the next few years, nearly 80 per cent of its managed spectrum be available on a technology neutral basis or with changed use generally not requiring any prior approval (not presently possible). To implement this policy, conditions will need to be only those light-touch, high-level conditions necessary to do that in light of the risk of interference according to the spectrum's physical characteristics. For example, where the risk was medium or high, there might be conditions such as requiring sensing capabilities in any devices used or compliance with a technological interface or mask designed to limit out of band emissions. It seems, however, that such a policy places greater reliance on the co-regulation of the marketplace or self-regulation by the licensee than on the standards developed for mandated uses by standards-making bodies,

Other non-economic conditions similarly imposed via licences are used to achieve social objectives, such as the funding or provision of some services on a non-competitive basis to ensure that all citizens, irrespective of location, have access

---

[64] Enhanced, or information services, in contrast, are unlicensed and not regulated in the US. See Chapter 6.
[65] See Chapter 5, European Union Communications Law at 5.4.2.

to at least a basic level of affordable service and to ensure consumer protections unique to telecommunications, such as the provision of emergency service operators on a toll-free basis. These, and other mandated services depending on the individual jurisdiction's policies, comprise the 'universal service obligation' (USO). Providing the USO ordinarily was the *quid pro quo* for the monopoly to provide all services. Imposing a USO obligation (or opportunity, as the right to be considered to provide such service is now viewed in the EU) in liberalized markets as well as the duty to contribute financially to its provision may now need to be governed via licensing conditions or rights. These can be individual conditions to provide the services necessary directly imposed on specific providers, often the former monopolist with its state-revenue-built networks and large market share. They can also be general conditions imposed on all or a defined group of providers, for example providers of public telecommunications networks and services. The conditions can exist even where yet to be triggered, such as the obligation to contribute to any USO fund that might be established but where there is not yet the perceived need, such as can be found in the UK general conditions of entitlement.

7.2.3.4 *Licensing as a means of enforcement*

Licensing as a means 'of more easily enforcing the fulfilment either of these special rules or of the general law of the land' is, or has been, true for telecommunications. Many sector-specific regulators rely on their licensing powers as their primary means of enforcement. Here the power to modify, revoke, or impose sanctions under telecommunications licences, even if subject to review by other bodies, is a way to ensure compliance with its obligations usually in the form of 'conditions' to the licence that may encompass not only requirements under telecommunications legislation but also other laws. An example of the latter was the UK. The UK telecommunications regulator imposed a duty to comply with competition law under a 'fair trade' condition in the licence. This condition was withdrawn when the 2002 EU telecommunications licensing reforms precluded conditions addressing compliance with general laws.[66] In the EU, therefore, this licensing purpose is thus delimited. EU law also further restricted the limited and specified sector rules that can be applied via licence conditions, as will be later addressed (see 7.3.2.5 below).

The use of conditions as a sector-specific means of enforcement does not preclude, of course the reliance on these other laws, which may indeed be necessary if the sector enforcement power is limited in scope or effectiveness. Thus, the UK regulator, Ofcom, is empowered under the UK Competition Act 1998, the Enterprise Act 2002, as well as the telecommunications laws and regulations. It can choose, therefore, which avenue will be more effective for specific anti-competitive behaviour. Most recently, it chose to address what it perceived as likely abuses of dominant behaviour in wholesale access and backhaul markets by British Telecommunications (BT),

---

[66] Authorization Directive, Art 6(3).

the former by means of the Enterprise Act. Pursuant to section 154 of that Act, Ofcom accepted a series of binding undertakings by BT to separate functionally its operations in order to provide access to its core network and to ensure product equivalence for downstream competitors, etc.[67] Section 154 of the Enterprise Act allows Ofcom, in lieu of proceeding with a formal referral for a full market investigation by the Competition Commission (which could have resulted in full structural separation of BT), to enter into binding undertakings for the purpose of remedying, mitigating, or preventing any adverse effect on competition concerned, or any detrimental effect on customers so far as it has resulted from, or may be expected to result from, the adverse effect on competition.

The possibility of taking corrective action for market abuses via sanctions under licence conditions remains a valuable tool, however. This could be especially true in emergent and developing markets where the need to control the former incumbents may be more acute than in more evolved competitive markets (although the serious regulatory intervention in the UK, one of the world's most evolved markets, belies this somewhat and suggests that control over the essential facility of the core telecommunications network always permits the ability to engage in exclusionary behaviour).

One scenario evidenced in contemporary telecommunications trends if not licensing historically is the use of a licence as a substitute for either and/or both special rules and the general law of the land. This is especially the case where there is the need to get outsiders to risk their money and time either to invest in the incumbent or competitors, but where the general legal framework might not be fully developed so as to protect that investment under known rules. It might also be helpful where there is not a general competition law framework that places duties on all players in the market or where the law exists but its enforcement agents are without expertise in telecommunications. Licences with obligations as well as rights may also benefit new entrants where the general competition law will not be enough and there are not adequate *ex ante* statutory requirements that ensure cost-based interconnection, something that competition law is unlikely to impose.

7.2.3.5 Licensing and fees
Considering a further cited historical purposes of licensing, it does not appear typically the case that telecommunications licensing is merely a device to extract a fee.[68]

---

[67] See, generally, Notice under s 155 (1) of the Enterprise Act 2002 Consultation on undertakings offered by British Telecommunications plc in lieu of a reference under Part 4 of the Enterprise Act (Ofcom, London, 2005) <http://www.ofcom.org.uk/static/telecoms_review/june05.htm>.

[68] But see 'Testimony of Barry M. Aarons before the Texas House of Representatives Committee on Regulated Industries' (30 June 2005)(stating that US municipality licence and franchise fees for telecommunications providers bear no relation to access to municipal rights of way (and therefore falling within the limited resource category) but are rather merely revenue raisers and ultimately a service tax on end users), <http://www.ipi.org/ipi/IPIPublications.nsf/IPI%20Congressional%20Testimony%5Cby%20Witness?OpenView>. Accord, Chapter 3.24, Municipal Telecommunications License Tax Code, Codification of General Ordinances of Midvale, Utah (1988 and amended 2002).

However, licensing fees are very common and not necessarily *de minimis* sums, even where based on the cost of regulation. The former individual licences under the UK regime for public telecommunications operators were as much as £40,000 annually, and were purportedly cost-based. There seems to be a trend of lowering licensing fees as has been the case in India, Zimbabwe, and other developing nations where there is growing recognition that lowering such costs may be key to more competitive markets and therefore ultimately lower costs to consumers.[69]

It is interesting to note that even where licences to provide services in a particular market are not formally limited numerically, the setting of prohibitively high licence fees has been used to limit the number of entrants to a lucrative market that is de facto being reserved for the incumbent former monopolist. This can be found, for example, in the fees set by numerous African countries for the provision of private international gateways which would compete with the national champion in international services.[70]

As earlier noted, in the case of spectrum licences for the second generation (2G) and 3G wireless technologies services, licensing fees in the multimillion and multibillion pound range were fairly common, although not always required.[71] There is a considerable debate about whether to make spectrum available at lower cost for various reasons, including the need to overcome the digital divide as well as to allow spectrum to be allocated for enabling new uses and devices. Where auctions based on highest price are the policy to maximize efficient use based on economic theory, it is unlikely that, without some form of aggregated bidding,[72] the potential developers of yet to be realized devices or low revenue potential uses will be able to compete on price against large wireless network owners.

Both the UK and the US prefer a market-based approach and do not ordinarily license available spectrum without bidding or some other market-based mechanism.[73] However, even here there are attempts to address some of these concerns, although how effective they will be remains to be seen. For example, while the US will not currently permit a gratis award of spectrum subject to licensing[74] for a 'spectrum commons' or free/low cost access model, in response to lobbying by Google

---

[69] Malakata, M, 'African telecom gateway costs to come down: UN agency intervenes to reduce prohibitively expensive international gateway license fees in order to lower the overall cost of telecommunications in Africa' (InfoWorld, 23 January 2007), <http://www.infoworld.com/article/07/01/23/HNafricantelecomcosts_1.html?TELEPHONY>.

[70] See ibid.

[71] Finland reasoned that to require payment of substantial fees for 3G spectrum, a public resource, would just mean that such costs would be passed on to consumers.

[72] See, e.g. Bykowsky, M, Sharkey, W, and Olson, M, Office of Policy and Planning Working Paper No 43, *A Market-Based Approach to Establishing Licensing Rules: Licensed Versus Unlicensed Use of Spectrum* (FCC, Washington, DC, 2008).

[73] Ofcom has addressed the 'seductive' lure of attempting to command the use of free spectrum to meet social policy goals

[74] In many jurisdictions including the UK and the US there are licence-exempt users/usages of spectrum usually in connection with low-powered devices.

and others, the FCC imposed the first 'open access' condition on blocks of the 700MHz band spectrum (the TV 'digital dividend') auctioned in early 2008. This requires the winners (such as Verizon and AT&T) to allow users to connect any device and download any software (e.g. a mobile softphone handset and Skype) in networks using that spectrum. As most US 'cellular' service carriers presently only allow mobile handsets which they sell to be connected to their networks, there were concerns that this condition would devalue the spectrum which had a minimum reserve bid of US$4.6 billion. It did not; bidding ultimately netted US$19.6 billion.

In contrast, a block reserved for a nationwide public safety access broadband network did not attract a single bid high enough to meet the minimum reserve of US$1.3 billion. Here the FCC attempted a hybrid 'commercial' approach that would have created a 'Public Safety/Private Partnership' between the licensee of one commercial spectrum block in this so called 'D Block' in the 700MHz range. This would have required the commercial licensee to build out a nationwide, interoperable broadband network to be shared with the public licensee for the use of public safety, facilitating more effective first responder emergency and planning communications; the commercial licensee, however, would have only pre-emptible, secondary access to the spectrum in non-emergency times and was precluded from participating in the management of the public safety licensee.[75] While the failure of this market-based approach may initially suggest that the FCC's insistence on auctions may need to be re-examined where other important public interests are involved, it may merely mean that the way the deal was structured was just not good enough to lure the private investor to put resources at risk without any possibility of participating in controls over the primary rights user.

In another approach to make low/no cost access available without giving up on its market value auction principles, the FCC is also currently considering a proposal that would require the winner of a new 25MHz band of spectrum to provide free broadband Internet access using at least 25 per cent of that spectrum.[76] Presumably, the winning bidder would use an advertising business model or reasonable access equipment charges which are not excluded from the definition of 'free' to recoup those costs. However, in a bit of social policy making, the FCC is considering requiring the licensee to filter the content of such free use to eliminate obscenity and pornography, etc.,[77] although it has been suggested that this is merely to mitigate political opposition from other ISPs.

---

[75] See 'Implementing a Nationwide, Broadband, Interoperable Public Safety Network in the 700MHz Band; Development of Operational, Technical and Spectrum Requirements for Meeting Federal, State and Local Public Safety Communications Requirements Through the Year 2010', PS Docket No 06-229, WT Docket No 96–86, Second Report and Order, 22 FCC Rcd 15289 (2007) (Second Report and Order).

[76] FNPR 08-158, In the Matter of Service Rules for Advanced Wireless Services in the 2155–2180MHz Band (FCC Washington, DC, 20 June 2008), <http://wireless.fcc.gov/>.

[77] The FNRP would require the licensee to use technology that 'filters or blocks images and text that constitute obscenity or pornography and, in context, as measured by contemporary community standards and existing law, any images or text that otherwise would be harmful to teens and adolescents' defined as children aged between 5 and 17.

Ofcom relied on 'market failure' to justify the non-auction of spectrum used on a large scale by one 'group' of spectrum users, the entertainment industry, for wireless microphones and other equipment used in programmes and special events. Finding that there was no possibility for this group to participate effectively in an auction in light of its great diversity, Ofcom concluded that it was necessary to reserve blocks of spectrum for which it would conduct a 'beauty pageant' and license the interleaved spectrum to a band manager who will make it available to such users on fair, reasonable, and non-discriminatory terms.[78]

The debate as to whether all or part of available spectrum should be licensed based on some 'macro economic' or societal benefit approach over a market, supply side one is not likely to be resolved any time soon.[79] Indeed, given the reality that only a very small percentage of spectrum is assigned or licensed via auctions,[80] a prior balance has already been achieved possibly based on uses now perceived as inefficient but which were based on social or public interest values at the time the allocation was made. Perhaps a bit ironically, in support of its decision to rely on market pricing allocations of spectrum as a primary policy tool, the UK regulator has identified an ultimate macroeconomic harm in the seemingly quick, easy, and cheap fix of commanding free spectrum to be made available to achieve public policy objectives.[81] Ofcom, however, is very forward thinking in its approaches to the issue. While it has thus far determined, based on usage patterns of licence-exempt spectrum, that demand does not now justify making more available and that innovation has not jumped licensing categories to date, Ofcom has undertaken a new consultation on possible future proposals for how a 'commons' of licence-exempt spectrum for channel sharing by multiple devices might be structured with reference to technical interference attributes and how 'politeness' rules to address interference might work.[82]

Issues of spectrum licensing pricing are clearly only part of the issue surrounding the management of spectrum that will need to be addressed more comprehensively by national regulators as well as forums dealing with international/regional spectrum allocations such as the EU and ITU. Other issues surrounding the auction licensing process are addressed further below, however.

---

[78] Statement 'Access to interleaved spectrum for programme-making and special events after the digital switchover' (Ofcom, London, 16 January 2008).

[79] See, e.g. RSPG 05-76, Chairman's Report of RSPG#6 at no 4, 'Economic Impact Assessment' (EU Commission DG InfoSoc Secretariat Brussels, 27 February 2005).

[80] As noted by a recent World Bank paper on spectrum reform: 'Auctions account for only about two percent of all spectrum assignments'. See Wellenius, B, and Neto, I, 'The Radio Spectrum: Opportunities and Challenges for the Developing World' (World Bank, 2008) at 4. While the cited percentage is based on a 2004 statistic and may not reflect the 2G and 3G, etc. auctions that have taken place since, the vast majority of spectrum allocation appears to be the subject of administrative assignment.

[81] See Strategic Spectrum Framework Review: Progress on Key Issues, 'Spectrum as a Policy Tool' at s 1.19 (Ofcom, London, 3 April 2008), <http://www.ofcom.org.uk/radiocomms/sfr/sfrprogress/>.

[82] See Consultation on Spectrum Commons Classes for Licence-Exemption (Ofcom, London, 6 May 2008), <http://www.ofcom.org.uk/consult/condocs/scc/SpecCommonsClasses.pdf>.

7.2.3.6 *Licensing and monitoring*

Returning to its historical justifications, the process of licensing does help ensure that those providing electronic communications networks and services are on the radar screen of the regulator who can oversee their compliance with laws and also make certain that the licensing fee and other payments, such as the contribution to a USO, are made where required. In the EU, although individual licensing requirements are now prohibited for such providers under the Authorization Directive, a Member State can still have a notification procedure or registry that will meet the historical role of 'ensuring their being brought under public notice'.[83] Thus, for example, while the UK regulator has eschewed this general register, it has put in place others such as the Communications Code registry that allows persons to check if an undertaking has code powers and if it has completed its annual financial security filing. It has also created a new registry to allow it and other possible spectrum users to know how spectrum is being traded and reused. These are discussed further in the UK implementation.

7.2.3.7 *Licensing as a binding agreement*

A final but contemporary purpose for licensing is to serve as a contract between the government and the provider.[84] This is the case, for example, where substantial strategic investment and expertise from the private sector is required to modernize large telecommunications infrastructure and provide new services or substantially improve services but where the government is not ready to or does not want to privatize or fully privatize the state-owned provider and transfer ownership. The relationship between the government and the private undertaking(s)[85] with its allocation of risk, rights, and obligations from a continuum of possible options is often spelled out in complex agreements. Just one example of this is found in build-operate-transfer (BOT) agreements whereby the private undertakings are given a concession to operate for a fixed time (often 15 to 25 years) the infrastructure that they have built[86] (say a new mobile network or a seriously upgraded fixed network) that is then turned over to the government at the end of the concession period. In addition to the project financing elements, the contract may also contain the conditions under which the service will be provided as well as the nature of the service and roll-out obligations. To ensure that the private parties' investment is protected, the BOT agreement may provide exclusive authority to the concessionaire to provide some or all services for some or all of the concession period. It may also limit the changes in national regulation that can affect the BOT operations and rights or apply

---

[83] See text accompanying n 38, above.

[84] See Wellenius, B, and Neto, I, *The Radio Spectrum: Opportunities and Challenges for the Developing World* (World Bank, 2008).

[85] More than one can be involved, for example, in a joint venture type of public/private partnership (PPP).

[86] The financing may come from a variety of sources including the host government and/or may, according to its nature as debt or equity, require sovereign obligations. See further Chapter 16, at 16.7.5.

a choice of law. In essence, the contract fulfils the purposes of licensing and may therefore effectively serve as the licence. However, there may be a separate licence which is included in or referenced within the BOT contract.

7.2.4 The legal nature of licences

The licence that gives rise to contractual obligations is contrary, however, to the traditional legal nature of government licensing. While a licence ordinarily does confer a right or a power to engage in a certain occupation or economic activity, or to use property that does not exist without the licence, subject to restrictions and revocaton, a licence has not historically been considered a contract between the issuing authority and the licensee.[87] Rather, courts in the US and the UK have considered them a privilege of an individual nature that created no property rights[88] and could not, therefore, be conveyed to third parties. Renewals had the same status as the initial licence and both were within the discretion of the granting authority to issue and revoke, and subject only to the jurisdictional limits of their authority.[89]

This would appear to be changing somewhat in telecommunications. In the EU, the Authorization Directive, discussed further below, makes the general authorization to provide electronic communications networks and services virtually automatic with its accompanying rights subject only to limited conditions and, possibly, a notification. It is also perhaps, perpetual as revocation is possible only in certain serious, limited circumstances. As the EU framework also requires that any decision that affects the interest of any party be subject to the right to comment and to appeal[90] ultimately to a judicial body, the removal of an authorization is entitled to such 'due process'.[91] Both aspects of the EU regime take the permission to provide telecommunications networks and services and its removal largely out of the discretion of the granting authority. Also, some Member States have exercised the option under the Framework Directive to permit the transfer by undertakings to other undertakings of rights in spectrum. The EU is itself exploring more extensive spectrum reform with trading as a cornerstone. These developments clearly comprise recognition of the great value of these rights of use and that the ability to trade or 'resell' spectrum rights may be important to their effective and efficient use. The nature of such greater rights seems a 'propertization', as one cannot ordinarily trade or sell something

---

[87] See Corpus Juris Secundum, n 7 above, at 3.

[88] See e.g. *Lap v Axelrod* 95 A2d 457 (NY App Div 3d Dept 1953), *appeal denied*, 460 NE2d 1360. Also see *Sharp v Wakefield* [1891] AC 173 ('The hardship of stopping the trade of a man who is getting an honest living in an honest trade, and has done so, perhaps, for years, with probably an expense at the outset, may well be taken into consideration; but it must be done so in conjunction with considerations the other way, and must be left to the discretion of the justices.' Bramwell, LJ, 182–183).

[89] See *Sharp v Wakefield* above (noting that, absent a provision in the enabling statute to the contrary, local justices had the same discretion to renew as to issue).

[90] Directive 2001/21/02 EC of the Parliament and the Council on a common regulatory framework for electronic communications networks and services (L108/33 24 April 2002), Art 4.

[91] See n 1, above.

without having a legally recognized property interest in it of some kind. This almost seems implicit in any creation of such secondary markets that need to make spectrum legally transferable. The FCC implemented a legal framework for trading that appeared structured to avoid this legal effect. It originally only permitted non-prior approval for spectrum leasing where the original licensee retained the full licence and remained responsible for compliance.[92] For transfers or assignments, the licence had to be returned to the FCC and new licence(s) issued with regulatory obligations running to the new licensee (or to both licensees if the spectrum was merely partitioned).[93] Clouding this prior legal distinction somewhat, the FCC has now, under its power of forbearance, streamlined this process once described as 'clumsy',[94] to allow certain transactions in both categories of leased and transferred/assigned spectrum to receive an 'instantaneous' (overnight), expedited processing based on parties' certification of compliance with various set criteria.[95]

Concerns that regulatory transactions could ultimately have an effect on the legal status of a licence are not unjustified. Courts have alluded to nature of the interests in 3G spectrum as property. For example, *dicta* by the court in *R (on the application of BT3G and others) v Secretary of State* [2001] 3 CMLR 61, noted that the contingent interest in the auctioned spectrum of a successful bidder which had to divest itself of another successful bidder prior to being issued the licence was different from that of the bidder which had to be divested. Similarly notable was the characterization by the court of the Secretary of State as a 'vendor' of spectrum with differing, potentially conflicting, interests, from that it has as regulator.

In the US, in a bankruptcy scenario, the Supreme Court considered a spectrum licence auctioned by the FCC to NextWave Communications under special rules to encourage minority and small business ownership to be in the nature of property and protected it from revocation by the FCC. The FCC sought to revoke the licence on NextWaves' default on its licence fee installment where that debt would be dischargeable under the bankruptcy law (*FCC v Nextwave Communications, Inc* 537 US 293 (2003)).

A regulatory approach that seems outright to deal with spectrum licences as a property interest can be found in New Zealand which sells 20-year, transferable spectrum management rights under the Radiocommunications Act 1989.

---

[92] See, generally, FCC 03-113, First Report and Order and Further Notice of Proposed Rulemaking that authorizes spectrum leasing in a broad array of Wireless Radio Services (FCC Washington, DC, 15 June 2003).

[93] Ibid.

[94] Judge, P, 'Ofcom to throw radio spectrum wide open' (Tech-World 23/11/04), <http://www.tech-world.com/mobility/features/index.cfm?featureid=1013>.

[95] See, generally, FCC 04-167, Second Report and Order, Order on Reconsideration and Further Notice of Proposed Rule Making (FCC Washington, DC 8 July 2004). For a good overview of the procedures and categories, see Wireless Telecommunications Bureau, 'Spectrum leasing' (FCC Washington, DC, 12 February 2008), <http://wireless.fcc.gov/licensing/index.htm?job=spectrum_leasing>.

7.2.5 Types of licences and licensing processes

7.2.5.1 *Licence form*

There is the possibility for thousands of licence types in telecommunications given the potential number of services, undertakings that provide them, and the number of countries in which they are sought to be provided. However, these can be generally be distilled into three primary overarching categories: individual provider/operator/ carrier licences; general authorizations (or class licences); and no licence requirement.

Individual licences are those that require an approval or exercise of discretion by the regulator or some other entity, including possibly the incumbent, concerning the ability of a specific undertaking to provide specified services or approved networks. Many countries require such individual authorizations that may be called by other names. For example, Trinidad and Tobago require all persons operating a public telecommunications network or providing a public telecommunications service or broadcast service to obtain a 'concession' from the minister responsible for telecommunications.[96] Such licences may be the subject of conditions that apply exclusively to a provider and possibly individually negotiated; or, individual licences may all have the same conditions. This was the case with the UK's former licensing scheme implemented under the EU's Licensing Directive.[97] Oftel harmonized licences and conditions by licence type, e.g. 'Standard Fixed PTO (with Code Powers) and 'Standard Fixed PTO (without Code Powers)'. The conditions were, therefore, applicable to all those running that kind of network or telecommunications 'system'. It was the running of that network or system that was the triggering event for the UK licence requirement as opposed to providing services. In these harmonized licences, there were very few unique conditions: those limited to BT and another small incumbent system, Kingston-on-Hull, and based on market power definitions.

With individual provider/operator/carrier licensing, there is usually an application and decision process that may vary by country as to the information required to be provided by the potential provider, the length of time that such decision and process can take, and the fee to be paid. However, with the WTO's transparency requirements for such information, evaluating the barrier that individual licensing represents in a specific country will be easier, if not the barrier itself ultimately lessened.[98]

General authorizations, formerly called 'class licences' in the UK, do not require such individual decisions. Rather, the undertaking is authorized to operate the network and/or services described by that authorization if it does so in conformity with its conditions. There may be an information, registration, or notification requirement, and the payment of a fee, which may be annual or otherwise. The authorization may be for a certain period, as were the UK class licences, but that has little

---

[96] Republic of Trinidad and Tobago Telecommunications Act, 2001, §21 (Act 4 of 2001).

[97] Directive 97/13/EC of the European Parliament and of the Council of 10 April 1997 on a common framework for general authorizations and individual licences in the field of telecommunications services, OJ L 117, 7 May 1997.

[98] See further Chapter 15, at 15.4.

consequence if the entitlement is virtually automatic. The general authorization does not mean simplicity, however. For example, under the UK's former system, there were 23 types of class licence, some of which had up to 115 pages of conditions in a template licence, although identical for each type of class licence. The general authorization is the foundation of the EU's current framework that is intended to further harmonize and simplify the licensing system throughout the Member States.

New Zealand does not require a licence for telecommunications or broadcast services. For, these, therefore, it has 'open entry'.[99] A provider of these services need not, but may, obtain a designation as a 'network operator' from the Minister of Communications.[100] Such designation is an individual grant of rights of access to land, and in particular the road reserve,[101] to lay or construct lines where this is required to commence and carry on a telecommunications or broadcast business.[102]

This designation also entitles the operator to approve all equipment connected to its network (section 106) and grants rights to recover damages for contravention of this process (section 110). It is, therefore, the only 'licensing' of equipment connected to networks except that regarding electromagnetic interference that is imposed by the national regulatory authority (NRA).

Europe would appear to have some free or 'open entry' jurisdictions. According to the EU, Denmark and the Netherlands have no licence, authorization or notification or declaration requirement for providers of all voice telephony networks; service providers are similarly unrestricted in other Member States such as Germany and Austria.[103]

7.2.5.2 Licensing procedures

The processes for obtaining licences are likely to be almost as varied as the types of licences. Countries will have unique aspects even if the general process is very similar. This chapter has already touched on what might be considered the primary procedures, such as an individual application with a review process and issuance. This can vary as to the information required to be submitted and the nature of the review which can be done by a different person or body from the issuing entity. For example, in Trinidad and Tobago, the Minister of Public Administration grants the above noted 'concessions' to authorize the operation of a public telecommunications network and/or the provision of any public telecommunications or

---

[99] NZ Ministry of Economic Development, 'Network Operator Designation for Telecommunications and Broadcasting Services' (Resources and Networks Branch Wellington 2003), <http://www.med.govt.nz/templates/MultipageDocumentTOC____22514.aspx>.

[100] Sections 102–105, NZ Telecommunications Act 2001 (SI 2001/103).

[101] Term used in New Zealand and Australia to define that area of land between the front boundary of private property and the road. For purposes of rights of access, this entails the road plus this area, a boundary-to-boundary concept.

[102] This grant would be called 'Code Powers' in the UK. See section 7.4.4.4 below.

[103] See Sixth Report on the Implementation of the Telecommunications Regulatory Package, COM (2000) 814 (7 December 2000) at Annex 1, Licensing, n 3.

broadcasting service. However, the application is made to the Telecommunications Authority which must review it and make its recommendation to the Minister within 90 days from its receipt, who then has 60 days to approve, reject, or modify the recommendation.[104] The review criteria and procedures are vague, however, and the Trinidad and Tobago Telecommunications Authority (TTTA) has asserted the right to change the procedures at any time. The applicant is required to submit information including *but not limited to*: company information, industry track record and expertise, financial stability, and the business plan viability, including specifics of the financial plan and risk analysis, the marketing and service plan, the technical plan, and manpower.[105] While of itself, this information might not be extraordinary, the specified evaluation criteria are somewhat subjective with the viability of the business plan worth 70 per cent or more of the total evaluation criteria to be used by the regulator whose own entrepreneurial expertise must be questioned.[106] The process is also cumbersome and not fully transparent. Separate network and service concessions are sometimes required since a Type 1 network concession does not grant the right to provide services over that network.[107] Also, the provision of virtual networks and services is a unique type of concession category (Type 2)[108] which is closed rather than on a first come first served basis as with other telecommunications service concessions. The key stated difference in this category is not that the service provider does not own the network, or the characteristic of pure telecommunications services, but rather the provision of multiple services over the network used.

If licences are to be limited, or there is demand beyond availability, there may be a comparative evaluative process, such as with the 'beauty contests' discussed above. The US was the first to use this process to assign cellular licences for various services to which it had allocated frequency. It set what it considered were appropriate standards for awarding available licences sought by multiple parties according to its statutory charge of 'public interest, convenience and necessity'.[109] The licences were awarded to the most 'worthy' candidate after a hearing process, which decision was often appealed for years in the US courts. This process was criticized for being too slow and costly and an impediment to the promotion of new services.[110] In addition to these specific criticisms, concerns with comparative processes generally have been raised regarding the objectivity of the selection criteria and their transparency.

---

[104] See Telecommunications Act, 2001 as amended 2004 at s 21. The Telecommunications Authority, in contrast, grants all licences for radio spectrum equipment or services pursuant to s 36 of the Act.

[105] See Eligibility and Evaluation Criteria for Concessions at 22 (TATT, 15 October 2007).

[106] See ibid, at 23.

[107] Ibid, at 11.

[108] Stated to be a service concession in one place, see ibid at 6, a network concession in another, see ibid at 10, and a network/service concession in another, see ibid at 18, adding to the confusion.

[109] 47 USC § 309.

[110] See Goodman, E, McCoy, S, Kumar, D, 'An overview of problems and prospects in US spectrum management', in *Telecommunications Convergence: Implications for the Industry & for the Practicing Lawyer*, 698 PLI/Pat 327 (Practising Law Institute, New York, 1 May 2002).

A random lottery with minimal pre-qualification standards was then used in the US, to assign spectrum licenses after the 'beauty contest' proved unsatisfactory.[111] This was intended to address the disputed decisions and promote the prompt roll-out of new services by eliminating delays, discretion, and determining factors beyond basic qualifying criteria. This was also criticized, however, as inefficient and promotive of speculation in spectrum. Many of those who won the lottery for cellular (mobile) licences immediately resold, or 'flipped' their licences to third parties who had to pay much more for them and then undergo an approval process with the FCC, resulting in unnecessary delays for their actual use.[112]

An auction process, often after a pre-qualification procedure to limit the bid to serious contenders intending to use the spectrum, has recently become the most common approach to awarding spectrum, with money and/or some other criteria meeting economic or social objectives, such as minority ownership, tariffs to be charged, service obligations to be met, or geographical roll-out of network and services as the determinants. The objectivity of the eligibility criteria remains a concern here. Multiple-round auctions having a series of bidding rounds with all licences remaining open to further bidding for the entire process are those currently favoured by the US and other countries. The process can vary from country to country but:

[t]ypical features of the rules governing such an auction include requirements that bidders make upfront payments; minimum opening bid requirements and increments for bid increases; activity rules to limit the ability of bidders to sit out rounds; rules regarding auction stages (points at which introduction of tighter activity rules may eliminate some bidders) and stage advancement designed to move the process along; stopping rules to determine when the auction closes; and rules and penalties for removal or withdrawal of bids.[113]

Auctions are not without their perceived flaws. The levels of debt incurred via competitive bidding for spectrum licences during the early part of this decade was a serious concern when ICT industries worldwide suffered financial reversals. Many spectrum licences had a subsequent loss of market value and some licensees were unable to obtain financing to pay for these devalued assets such as in the case of NextWave. Many were subject to obligations to pay these large fees upfront and prior to any ability to recoup the costs from new revenue streams as 3G spectrum involved technology and content that would not be rolled out for at least two years. This presented a significant hardship for many 3G market entrants. The general approach of maximizing fees for 3G spectrum has also been criticized beyond the issues discussed above regarding social objectives as perhaps slowing the investment necessary to use

---

[111] Congress approved this process in 1981 to expedite the granting of licences from the cited delays for some spectrum-based services. See Omnibus Budget Reconciliation Act of 1981, Pub L No 97–35, §1242, 95 Stat 357, 736 (codified as amended at 47 USC §309(i)(1988).

[112] Martin, MS, Cook Bush, A, 'The FCC's minority ownership policies from broadcasting to PCS', 48 Fed Comm LJ (1996) 423, 425–426. See generally Chapter 6.

[113] Goodman, E, et al, n 110 above at 341.

the spectrum and thereby delaying innovation.[114] Other research shows that in several advanced technology spectrum markets, market incumbents intentionally overbid,[115] possibly collusively to foreclose the market to new entrants.[116]

7.3 INTERNATIONAL LAW AND TELECOMMUNICATIONS LICENSING STANDARDS

Telecommunications has importance not only as an industry in its own right but as the platform over which other critical information society services are delivered. Thus, the effective opening of these services markets to trade is likely to depend on the modernization and upgrading of electronic communications networks, necessitating foreign direct investment and liberalization of communications markets for equipment, services, and networks.[117] Despite the global variation in licensing procedures and permissions ultimately obtained, the importance of telecommunications licensing as the means of market access and the need for some minimum harmonization of regulatory standards for licensing has been agreed to be a critical aspect of multilateral trade agreements. The most effective international accord for telecommunications regulation is the World Trade Organization's General Agreement on Trade in Services (GATS)[118] with its separate Annex on telecommunications, the Basic Agreement on Telecommunications, and the Reference Paper. Both the individually agreed, sector-specific provisions and general conditions of the GATS framework applicable to all Members have relevance for licensing, as the following details.

Under the overarching GATS framework:

- the 'Most-Favoured-Nation Treatment' (MFN)[119] general condition (Article II)[120] requires a Member's licensing regime to provide market access on terms and conditions 'no less favourable' than that accorded to providers of another country for all services even where no specific commitment is included in the Schedules;

---

[114] See, e.g. Convergent Communications Research Group, 'A submission on structural reform in spectrum management' (University of Adelaide 2003) at p 4, available at <http://archive.dcita.gov.au/__data/assets/pdf_file/0005/10868/Convergent_Communications_Research_Group.pdf>.

[115] See, Ozanich, G, Hsu, C, and Park, H, '3G wireless networks as an economic barrier to entry: the western experience', Telematics and Informatics (2004), 21(3), 225–234.

[116] See, generally, Rose, G, 'Spectrum auction breakdown: how incumbents manipulate FCC auction rules to block broadband competition', Working Paper 18 (New America Foundation 2007), available at: <http://www.newamerica.net/files/WorkingPaper18_FCCAuctionRules_Rose_FINAL.pdf>.

[117] Issues surrounding the complexities of opening emerging markets to competition are discussed in Chapters 16 and 17, below.

[118] TS 58(1996) Cm 3276; (1994) 33 ILM 44. See further Chapter 15.

[119] There are limited circumstances for reservations to the MFN condition. See Chapter 15.

[120] 'With respect to any measure covered by this Agreement, each Member shall accord immediately and unconditionally to services and service suppliers of any other Member treatment no less favourable than it accords to like services and suppliers of any other country.' Art II (1), GATS.

- the 'Transparency' general condition (Article III) requires all Members to publish their laws and regulations that affect trade in all services, scheduled or not. Licensing qualifications and conditions meet that criteria;

- the 'Domestic Regulation' condition (Article VI) requires where service or sector commitments have been made, that licensing, qualifications, and standards be based on transparent and objective criteria (4(a)) and not more burdensome than is necessary to ensure quality (4(b)). Licensing procedures must not restrict the service supply, (4(c)); Members must inform applicants of decision within a reasonable time after the submission of completed application and, upon request, advise of the status of the application, without delay (3);

- the 'National Treatment' condition (Article XVII) requires that there be no discrimination against a foreign service or suppliers of that service as compared to those domestic services or suppliers where the Member has included a scheduled commitment.

Under the sector-specific agreements:

- the Annex on Telecommunications requires transparency for access to and use of public telecommunications,[121] and requires that relevant information about conditions affecting access and use be made publicly available, including notification, registration, or licensing. Conditions imposed must be those necessary to safeguard the obligation of public telecommunications network and services providers to supply the general public and to ensure network integrity (5(e)). Conditions meeting these criteria that can be imposed include:
  - requirements for notification, registration, or licensing (5(f)(vi)),
  - limitations on resale or shared use of services (5(f)(i)),
  - use of interface or interoperability protocols (5(f)(ii), (iii)),
  - type approval of equipment that interconnects with the public telecommunications network (5(f)(iv)),
  - limitations on interconnection between private leased or owned circuits (5(f)(v));

- the 'Reference Paper' requires public availability of all licensing criteria and the normal time for a decision on an application as well as the terms and conditions for an individual licence. The reason for a licence denial is to be disclosed to the applicant upon request (4, Reference Paper);

- the 'Reference Paper' further requires transparency in procedures for allocating and using scarce resources which include spectrum, numbers, and rights of way, and that the procedures be timely, objective, and non-discriminatory. The current state of allocated frequency bands is to be made publicly available, except specific government frequency use (6, Reference Paper).

---

[121] This Annex is intended to encompass the provision of communications networks/services only to the extent of Members' scheduled commitments. See s 2 (c), Annex on Telecommunications.

One legal framework that is clearly compliant with the WTO standards for licensing and authorizations as well as allocation of scarce resources is that of the EU. The following examines this at length.

7.4 THE EU'S LICENSING REGIME

In 1999, the EU proposed a new framework to ensure equal regulation for converging markets and technologies. With respect to licensing, the new framework was to sweep under one scheme all public electronic communications and services, and not just those involving telecommunications networks.[122] The resulting Authorization Directive does this. It is not, however, an otherwise radically different scheme for permission to provide such networks and services from that under the prior Licensing Directive[123] at least as that was intended to work. Rather, the Authorization Directive is a further refinement of the Licensing Directive with provisions to ensure implementation of its intended light-touch regulatory scheme with individual grants of rights and conditions permitted only where justified. An examination of the former scheme is in order, therefore.

7.4.1 The Licensing Directive

Under the Licensing Directive, if Member States made the provision of telecommunications services subject to an authorization, the Directive's default requirement was for a general authorization requiring no explicit decision. Individual licences, in contrast, were to be limited to:

   i. public voice telephony where conditions had to be imposed, including USO;

   ii. the grant of rights to use of numbers and spectrum, both scarce resources;

   iii. where conditions had to be imposed on undertakings with significant market power (SMP) as previously defined by the EU; and

   iv. where rights of access to public or private land were granted (Article 7).

Member States could impose any of a limited set of conditions on all licences where justified and proportionate (but that comprised the 'least onerous system possible' for general authorizations) in the areas of: essential requirements, information required to verify compliance, prevention of anti-competitive behaviour and discriminatory tariffs, and efficient use of numbering capacity (Annex, 2). Conditions for general authorizations comprised a range of consumer protections, including billing and contract format (Annex, 3.1), provision of emergency services, provision of customer information needed for directory services, services for disabled

---

[122] See Chapter 5.
[123] Directive 97/13/EC, n 97 above.

people, compliance with interconnection, and contribution to universal services (Annex, 3.2–3.6). Beyond these conditions, Member States could further impose on individual licences only those conditions related to the circumstances justifying the requirement for an individual licence in the first place, as just discussed (Article 8). Thus, the list of additional conditions include those linked to the allocation of numbering rights, efficient use of radio spectrum, specific environmental or local planning requirements, maximum duration to promote certainty and planning ability, provision of universal service, quality and permanence of service/networks, mandatory provision of publicly available networks and services, and interconnection and leased lines obligations pursuant to other directives (Annex, 4).

Individual licences were to be granted pursuant to objective, transparent, and time limited procedures that applied to all unless objectively justified, and that were published in an appropriate manner (Article 9). Licences for any service or category of infrastructure could be limited in number only to the extent necessary to ensure efficient use of spectrum, or for the time needed to make available sufficient numbers, and only by means of a published decision that set forth the reasons for the limitation (Article 10). Detailed, objective, transparent, non-discriminatory, proportionate, and pre-published criteria for awarding the limited licences were required, and that gave due weight to the promotion of competition and maximizing the benefits of users (Article 10(3)). Procedures were also required to permit interested parties to comment on the limitation, as were invitations to parties to apply. Member States had to permit appeal from any denial of a licence to an independent body, and to review the limitations on licensing at reasonable intervals (Article 10(2)).

An undertaking complying with the conditions imposed on general authorizations could not be prevented from providing the relevant network or service, although there could be a requirement to notify the NRA of intent to provide these and to supply that information concerning the service needed to ensure compliance with applicable conditions (Article 5). A waiting period of four weeks could be imposed from receipt of this information prior to commencing service/network provision (Article 5(2)).

Fees for general authorizations could be based solely on administrative costs of controlling, managing, and enforcing the general authorization scheme and were to be sufficiently detailed and published in an accessible way (Article 6). Fees for individual licences were to encompass only those administrative costs incurred in the issuance, management, control, and enforcement of the applicable individual licences. Where spectrum or numbers were involved, charges could reflect their value to ensure their optimal use (Article 11), thus permitting Member States to auction spectrum. The Directive suggested further that all charges imposed had to be based on objective, non-discriminatory, and transparent criteria (Recital 12).

Where the holder of a general authorization failed to comply with any of its conditions, the NRA could notify it that it could no longer avail itself of the authorization 'and/or' impose specific measures to ensure compliance (Article 5(3)). Individual licensees that failed to comply with the conditions of their licence could have their

licences withdrawn, amended, or suspended, or have measures imposed by the NRA to ensure compliance. The undertaking had the opportunity to state its views on the condition's application and to remedy its breach within one month. The Directive imposed time limits for making and communicating that the decision had been confirmed, modified, or annulled, and procedures for appeal to an independent body (Articles 5(3), 9(4)).

The Directive, in an effort to facilitate the provision of Community-wide services, also established a 'one-stop shop' for obtaining licences from the Member States via a single application point (Article 13) and authorized a Commission charge to various European telecommunications regulatory groups, such as CEPT, to develop a harmonized regime for general authorizations (Article 12). Neither effort was very successful and was soon pre-empted by the current EU regulatory framework including the Authorization Directive proposed by the Commission only two years after the Licensing Directive's adoption. As the Authorization Directive notes, the 1999 Review indicated the need for more harmonized and 'less onerous' regulation of market access (Recital 1, 2002/20/EC). It was not generally a problem with the legal framework as promulgated but as implemented and enforced in many Member States. Rather than limiting requirements for individual licences to those circumscribed circumstances necessary to impose conditions, the flexibility under the Licensing Directive was exploited with individual licences mandated for many situations. The result was that the general authorization was the exception rather than the rule as the Directive intended. There also remained such marked divergence as to types of licences needed, time periods for decisions, costs, and information required, especially in connection with individual licences, that the EU licensing and authorization regime was considered to be a barrier not only to national market entry but to the Single Market.[124] As the EU premises its continued evolution and economic development on the implementation of dynamic and competitive information society services, including pan-European services, and infrastructure, this was a significant problem.[125] The following examines at length this 2002 authorization framework which sought to address this.

7.4.2 The Authorization Directive

Part of a new EU 2002 framework for electronic communications of five Directives and a Regulation intended to reform and replace existing regulation,[126] the Authorization Directive sought to achieve these objectives effectively by requiring Member States to implement what the Licensing Directive really intended. The Authorization

---

[124] See Communication from the Commission to the European Parliament, the Council, the Economic and Social Committee, and the Committee of the Regions, Towards a new framework for Electronic Communications infrastructure and associated services, [COM (1990) 539] at vii.
[125] Ibid.
[126] See further Chapter 5.

Directive does this by attempting to eliminate much of the discretion that the former Directive left to Member States. Some six years later, this approach has been fairly successful, if still in need of fine tuning in some areas and continued focus in others. The Commission's 13th Market Report notes continuing areas where divergent regulation, ineffective or insufficiently empowered NRAs, and new entrant's lack of access to market inputs have hindered market access and failed to address market concentrations. However, numbers of new entrants, market investment, generally lower consumer prices since 2002, the roll out of new services, higher penetration rates, and, in some Member States with previously entrenched monopolies, the build out of competitive alternative infrastructure are all evidence of growing sector competition.[127] The Commission has highlighted new challenges posed by the consolidation of markets via 'triple play' offerings and possible 're-monopolization' as well as new entrants' access to next generation networks. While this chapter will discuss these problems as they concern the Authorization Directive and what changes the Commission has made or proposes to make to address these concerns, it now first examines the Authorization Directive in some detail.

Let us begin by examining its scope and application. The Directive applies to the authorization of all public and private electronic communications networks and electronic communication services. The Framework Directive defines 'electronic communication services' as those:

normally provided for remuneration which consists wholly or mainly in the conveyance of signals on electronic communications networks, including telecommunications services and transmission services in networks used for broadcasting, but exclude services providing, or exercising editorial control over, content transmitted using electronic communications networks and services; it does not include information society services, as defined in Article 1 of Directive 98/34/EC, which do not consist wholly or mainly in the conveyance of signals on electronic communications networks. (Article 2(b), 2002/21/EC)

The electronic communications framework generally carves out from its application information society services, or those using the transmission services of networks. The Framework Directives wording 'electronic communications services' parallels that of the E commerce Directive (2000/31/EC) which governs 'information society services', i.e. those content services provided in the layers above network provision and transmission services. In both Directives, the other layer of services is defined and excluded by reference to that which it is not.

The qualification of 'normally provided for remuneration' in the framework's scope for regulation of electronic communications services derives from Article 95, the EU Treaty's freedom of movement protection for such services in the Single Market. Where this line is drawn is not clear since private networks are intended to be included under the Authorization Directive, according to its Recitals and without

---

[127] See Commission Communication 'Progress Report on the Single European Electronic Communications Market 2007 (13th Report)' 19 March 2008 [COM (2008) 153].

mention of the 'normally provided for remuneration' requirement. As self services may not be provided for remuneration, they would be beyond the Directive's reach. If those were, however, provided over a private network, an authorization for the network appears required. It may be that the Directive excludes only self-provided services over third-party networks.

The Directive also applies to 'electronic communications networks' which are defined in the Framework Directive as those:

transmission systems, and where applicable switching and routing equipment and other resources which permit the conveyance of signals by wire, by radio, by optical or by other electromagnetic means, including satellite networks, fixed (circuit- and packet-switched, including Internet) and mobile terrestrial networks, electricity cable systems to the extent that they are used for the purpose of transmitting signals, networks used for radio and television broadcasting, and cable television networks, irrespective of the information they convey. (Article 2(a), 2002/21/EC)

This intends a horizontal approach to regulation that governs irrespective of the technology used. According to the Directive, this is to ensure that all comparable systems are covered in a comparable way and have the same opportunity to benefit from the 'objective, transparent, non-discriminatory and proportionate rights, conditions and procedures' it required Member States to put in place by July 2003.

7.4.2.1 General authorization: procedures and rights
The Authorization Directive directs Member States to 'ensure the freedom' to provide electronic communications networks and services (Article 3(1)) that is limited only by its conditions[128] (Article 3(1)). Member States may subject the provision of these networks and services to a general authorization requirement (Article 3(2)) that does not require an explicit decision (Recital 8). The Directive permits the Member State to put in place a notification procedure before the provider can enter the market. This is limited to a declaration of intent to provide networks or services and the provision of information to enable the NRA to maintain a register of providers (Article 3(2)). The information is restricted to that needed to identify the provider, such as company registration numbers, location, contact details, and a brief description of the services and when they commence (Article 3(3)).

These mandates clearly limit the discretion of the Member States and remove the possibility of delaying the entry of the provider into the market. This 'least onerous' system was viewed as necessary to stimulate the development of new electronic communications services, including the pan-European services that are a significant focus of the new regulatory framework, and to permit the parties in the EU single market to benefit from its economies of scale (Recital 7), not possible under the

---

[128] This freedom is also subject to restrictions pursuant to Member States' power to legislate in defined areas under EU Treaty, Art 46(1), including public health, public policy, and public security. See Authorization Directive, 2002/20/EC at Art 3(1); Recital 3.

prior regime as implemented. This cross-border focus also underlies, in part, the requirement that certain rights be accorded to all undertakings providing networks and services within the authorization itself (see Recital 9). Such harmonization creates greater certainty about the ability to enter a new national market and, as the Recitals point out, ensure a level playing field throughout the Community. These are the right to:

- provide electronic communication networks and service (Article 4(1)a);
- apply for rights of way to install facilities on/over/under private and public land:
  - ○ to a competent authority separate from any provider,
  - ○ pursuant to procedures that are transparent, publicly available, and applied in a non-discriminatory and timely manner but that can differ for public and private communications networks, and imposes conditions only pursuant to principles of transparency and non-discrimination,
  - ○ with an effective appeal mechanism to an independent body (Article 4(1)b; Framework Directive, Article 11), including for undue delay.

The general authorization must further grant those persons providing public communications networks and services the right to:

- negotiate and obtain interconnection with and access to other publicly available networks as required by the Access Directive (Article 4 (2)(a));[129]
- eligibility to be designated to provide elements of universal service (Article 4 (2)(b)).

With the same right to negotiate and obtain interconnection and access largely now guaranteed in each Member State to those providing public networks and/or services, cross-border entry and the possibility for pan-European services is facilitated as there is no longer the need for an individual designation as an operator entitled to obtain such rights as was the case under the former regime. Here again, Member State discretion has been limited. Those not providing public networks and services are intended to negotiate interconnection on commercial terms. Member States are to provide declarations, either automatically on entry notification or upon request, and confirm rights under the general authorization to interconnection and rights of way in order to facilitate interconnection or negotiations with other authorities (Article 9). Such declarations, however, do not create or condition the exercise of rights.

7.4.2.2 *Rights to spectrum and numbers*
The only exceptions to the 'general authorization' mandate concern rights to use spectrum and numbers. This discretion, however, is not unlimited. The Directive directs Member States, wherever possible, to make spectrum available under the

---

[129] See further Chapter 8.

general authorization rather than requiring an individual grant of rights (Article 5(1)). It cites that this should be the case especially where the risk of harmful interference is small (e.g. low power uses). If individual rights must be granted for the use of spectrum and numbers, certain substantive and procedural safeguards are to be followed, which will be addressed shortly. Member States, however, may not restrict the numbers of individual rights granted to spectrum unless it is 'unavoidable' and dictated by their scarcity or efficient use.[130] Member States are to make available rights to use spectrum and numbers to both users and providers of electronic communications networks and services (Article 5 (2)).[131]

7.4.2.3 *Procedures for granting individual rights of use*
Member States must grant rights to use numbers and spectrum via open, transparent, and non-discriminatory procedures. They must inform the grantees of their ability, if any, to transfer such rights to third parties, and, as concerns spectrum, specify what conditions attach to that transfer. The time period allocated to grants of rights of use must be appropriate to the specific service if granted for a limited time (Article 5(2)). Decisions to grant rights of use should be made, communicated, and made public as soon as possible. For rights to use numbers from the national plan allocated to specific uses, three weeks from receipt of a complete application is specified; six weeks for similarly allocated spectrum (Article 5(3)).

This time period is extended by three weeks where the rights to use numbers of unique economic value (e.g., 1 800 FLOWERS) are granted by competitive or comparative procedures. This can only be done after a consultation that complies with Article 6 of the Framework Directive (Article 5(4)). Here any measures under this Framework that have a 'significant impact on the relevant market' can be taken only after interested parties have an opportunity to comment within a reasonable period. The consultation must be done pursuant to published procedures; all current consultations must be available through a single accessible point with their results made publicly available except where this involves confidential information according to either national or Community law (Article 6, 2002/21/EC).

---

[130] Both Art 5 and Recital 11 fail to make clear whether these two criteria for limitation apply to both kinds of rights to use due to unfortunate wording. However, this would make sense as both are considered scarce public resources, for which ensuring efficient use would seem commensurate under the 'public trust' theory discussed at section 7.2.2 above.

[131] There is a lack of clarity in the Directive that makes this provision a bit uncertain. Art 5(2) indicates that where an individual grant of rights to use numbers is made, that Member States 'shall grant such rights, upon request, to any undertaking providing or using networks or services under the general authorisation', 'shall' indicating that it is not a matter of discretion. In contrast, however, Recital 14 states that Member States are 'neither obligated to grant nor prevented from granting rights to use numbers from the national numbering plan . . . to undertakings other than providers of electronic communications networks or services', suggesting that it is totally a matter of discretion. A further cloud is created by the use in Art 5(2) of 'using networks or services under the general authorization' as the requirement for the general authorization only extends to providers of networks and services. While a user of networks could be a provider of services that might require a general authorization, this need not be the case.

Decisions to limit grants of rights to use spectrum and the granting of such limited rights must be done according to specified procedures that largely parallel those for granting individual licences under the Licensing Directive (see section 7.4.1, above). Limited individual rights to use to use spectrum are, as with all individual rights of use, to be granted pursuant to open, transparent, and non-discriminatory procedures (Article 5(2)). As previously noted, rights of use grants can be limited only where necessary[132] to ensure efficient use of spectrum (Article 5(5)). Member States, in determining whether to restrict the numbers of users, must:

  i. give due weight to the need to facilitate competition and maximize users' benefits;

  ii. permit interested parties, including users, to comment in transparent consultation procedures compliant with Article 6, as described above;

  iii. publish any decision to limit grants of rights to use with the reasons for that decision;

  iv. invite applications for these rights;

  v. grant the rights according to proportionate, objective, non-discriminatory, and transparent criteria that give due weight to the new framework's overarching regulatory objectives of promoting competition, contributing to the internal market, and promoting the interests of EU citizens[133] and under time-limited procedures that permit up to an additional eight months beyond the limit for other spectrum to ensure an open, transparent and fair process;[134]

  vi. review limitations at reasonable intervals or reasonable request of affected undertakings, and where further rights are possible, publish that conclusion and invite new applications (Article 7).

The Authorization Directive itself does not specify that there must be an appeal procedure from the decision regarding the granting of individual rights of use.[135] The Framework Directive, however, requires Member States to ensure effective mechanisms for any provider or user affected by any NRA's decision to appeal its merits to an independent body with appropriate expertise that must issue its decision in writing, if not a judicial body.[136] Further review to a court or judicial tribunal must exist.[137]

---

[132] Recital 11 indicates that 'necessary' is to be interpreted as 'unavoidable'.
[133] Article 8, 2002/21/EC. These objectives are to be sought by NRAs in carrying out all of their tasks under the new framework's Directives, all via reasonable and proportionate measures.
[134] Ibid, at Art 7.
[135] This is in contrast to Art 10, which requires an appeal procedure from the imposition of conditions. See 7.4.2.4, below.
[136] Article 4, 2002/21/EC.
[137] Ibid, at Art 4(2).

7.4.2.4 *Conditions*

Network and service providers may have three types of conditions imposed on them: (i) those under the general authorization, (ii) individual obligations that attach to the granting of rights of use of numbers and spectrum, and (iii) specific conditions to impose obligations under the Access and Universal Service Directives. Any condition imposed under any of these categories, however, must be objectively justified in relation to the service or network concerned, and proportionate, transparent, and non-discriminatory. The following examines each of the three categories of conditions in turn.

7.4.2.4.1 *Conditions under the general authorization*

Member States may only impose conditions under general authorizations falling within the Authorization Directive's maximum list of 18 condition categories.[138] NRAs may impose conditions on all providers of electronic communications networks and services under the general authorization, if justified. However, as the Directive cautions, in the case of networks and services not provided to the public, it 'is appropriate to impose fewer and lighter conditions' than are justified for public networks and services (Recital 16). The maximum list includes conditions or obligations regarding:

- administrative charges (Article 12, Authorization Directive);
- information requirements (Article 3(3), 11, Authorization Directive);
- general access obligations (Access Directive);
- interoperability of services, interconnection of networks (Access Directive);
- end-user accessibility to numbers under national plan (Universal Service Directive);
- conditions for spectrum use not under individual grant (Radio and Telecommunications Terminal Equipment Directive 99/5/EC);
- contributions to universal service obligations (Universal Service Directive);
- 'must carry' TV and radio broadcast obligations (Universal Service Directive);
- use during major disasters to ensure emergency services' and authorities' communications and public broadcasts;
- personal data/privacy protection (Electronic Communications Privacy Directive);[139]
- security of public networks against unauthorized use (Electronic Communications Privacy Directive);
- enabling lawful interception (Data Protection Directive (95/46/EC), Electronic Communications Privacy Directive);
- sector-specific consumer protection rules (Universal Service Directive);

---

[138] Part A, Annex, Authorization Directive. This lists the permitted subject areas that a general condition may govern.

[139] See further Chapter 13.

- illegal content restrictions (Electronic Commerce Directive (2000/31/EC), Television Without Frontiers Directive (89/552/EEC));
- standards and specifications (Article 17, Framework Directive);
- limiting public exposure to electromagnetic fields (Community Law);
- maintenance of public communications network integrity, prevention of electromagnetic interference (Universal Service and Access Directives, Harmonized Standards for Electromagnetic Compatibility Directives (89/336/EEC);
- environmental, planning, and other requirements for access to public/private land, conditions for co-location, facilities sharing (Framework Directive), financial and technical guarantees to ensure proper execution of installation.

General authorization conditions must be sector-specific and may not duplicate conditions applicable under national law.[140] This was a change from the Licensing Directive that, although it tried to create an exhaustive list of conditions, neither produced this result, nor could have done so. Due to its own jurisdictional limitation, a Member State was free to include any other licence condition that could be classified as falling under the very broad categories of defence, public interest, public policy, or security. The Directive provided that it was 'without prejudice to measures taken by Member States concerning defence and to measures taken by Member States in accordance with public interest requirements recognized by the Treaty, in particular Articles 36 and 56, especially in relation to public morality, public security, including the investigation of criminal activity, and public policy'.[141]

While these are areas where Member State action may fall outside the competence of the EU under the Treaty, not every action does. The Licensing Directive's carve out of these areas was somewhat broadly stated. It seems likely to have put beyond its reach any State action in these areas. The Authorization Directive does not have this limitation. Arguably, then, it can limit Member States to its sector-specific general conditions and Member States are free to impose obligations within their Treaty competences under national law.

7.4.2.4.2 Conditions and individual grants of rights
Individual obligations can be attached to the grant of rights of use of numbers and spectrum. Conditions for numbers are limited to those regarding:

- a service designation for a number;
- usage fees;
- efficient and effective use;
- providing public directory services;
- number portability;

---

[140] Article 6(3).
[141] Article 1(2), 97/13/EC.

- the grant's duration and transfer; and
- commitments made during competitive/comparative selection procedures.[142]

Conditions that Member States may attach to rights of use of spectrum include only those regarding:

- service or technology designations for granted frequency;
- effective and efficient use including coverage requirements;
- technical and operational conditions for avoiding harmful interference and public exposure to electromagnetic fields;
- usage fees;
- duration;
- transfer by the grantee; and
- commitments from selection procedures.[143]

These individual obligations are required, like those under the general authorization, to be objectively justified to the service, proportionate, transparent, and non-discriminatory. They may not duplicate the general conditions.

7.4.2.4.3 SMP and access-related individual conditions
Specific conditions under the Access and Universal Service Directives can only be imposed on network and service providers for a limited number of reasons.[144] These specific conditions can be divided into two overarching categories: (a) those imposed on undertakings found to have significant market power (joint or otherwise) in relevant markets after the analysis and pursuant to the procedures required by the Framework Directive; and (b) those imposed for other public interest reasons on non-SMP undertakings.

With respect to the first category under the Access Directive, the NRA must impose appropriate conditions on SMP operators where, after a market analysis (complying with Article 16 of the Framework Directive), it concludes that there is not effective competition in the relevant market.[145] Although there is the possibility for the NRA to apply other conditions in exceptional circumstances,[146] the SMP conditions specifically contemplated by the Access Directive govern, respectively, obligations of transparency,[147] non-discrimination,[148] accounting separation,[149]

---

[142] Section 6(1), Part C, Annex.
[143] Part B, Annex.
[144] Article 6(2).
[145] Directive 2002/19/EC at Art 8. See further Chapter 8.
[146] See ibid at Art 8(3). This, however, requires adherence to the comitology procedures set forth in Arts 5 and 7 of Decision 1999/468/EC by its cross-reference to the procedures in Art 14(2).
[147] Ibid, at Art 9.
[148] Ibid, at Art 10.
[149] Ibid, at Art 11.

access and interconnection,[150] and price controls and cost accounting.[151] Member States must publish the specific conditions imposed on undertakings pursuant to these Articles, identifying the specific product/service. Current and easily accessible, non-confidential information must be made available to all interested parties.[152]

Where the above SMP conditions will not achieve the Framework Directive's objectives,[153] the Universal Service Directive further requires that providers determined as SMP in relevant markets under the Framework Directive must also have imposed specific conditions regarding retail price controls,[154] minimum leased lines provision,[155] and carrier selection and pre-selection.[156] These must meet all the Framework Directive's requirements for transparency, objectivity, proportionality, and consultation as described with other conditions. Under the Framework Directive, Commission notification is required for retail price control conditions.

Within the second category of specific conditions, under the Access Directive, non-SMP providers controlling access to end-users by means of unique numbers or addresses can have conditions imposed to ensure end-to-end connectivity where justified. These may include mandatory interconnection imposed by the NRA where commercial negotiations, pursuant to the general authorization conditions, fail[157] as well as conditions imposing access to electric programme guides (EPGs) and application program interfaces (APIs) by providers of these associated facilities on fair, reasonable, and non-discriminatory terms where needed to ensure end-user accessibility to digital TV and radio services.[158] Technical and operational conditions to ensure interoperability and normal operation of networks can be imposed on beneficiaries of SMP access obligations.[159] The Directive also requires the imposition of conditions imposed on providers of conditional access services necessary for end-user access to digital TV and effective competition in such services.[160]

Interestingly, concluding that such Access Directive SMP conditions could not address a pan-European market failure in one of its recommended relevant markets, international mobile voice roaming, the Commission felt compelled to take action via regulation. Finding persistent and exceedingly high retail and wholesale roaming tariffs EU-wide and a lack of transparency to users about pricing structure after three

---

[150] Ibid, at Art 12.
[151] Article 13, 2002/19/EC.
[152] Ibid, at Art 15.
[153] Article 8, Framework Directive, states the objectives of promoting competition and the interests of EU citizens and contributing to the internal market's development.
[154] Article 17, 2002/22/EC.
[155] Ibid, at Art 18. The minimum set of service is to be provided (1) under harmonized specifications established by that must be published, and (2) pursuant to conditions of transparency, non-discrimination and cost orientation.
[156] Article 19, 2002/22/EC.
[157] Article 5(1)(a), 2002/19/EC.
[158] Ibid, at Art 5(1)(b).
[159] Ibid, at Art 5(2)).
[160] Ibid, at Art 6; see Chapter 8.

sets of consultations and a call to mobile operators to lower their rates voluntarily, the Commission determined that a pan-European solution was needed since any nationally set retail and wholesale price control conditions could not address the problem sufficiently or in a harmonized manner.[161] As these were a significant deterrent to EU-wide mobile use and not in any way justified by costs (retail rates, on average €1.10 per minute, were five times the wholesale costs) the Commission promulgated the Roaming Regulation.[162] This imposes, for each of three years, progressively lower maximum wholesale and retail price controls, called 'Eurotariffs' as the default to any other tariff offered by the provider together with transparency obligations.

Its recently launched May 2008 consultation considers the impact of the Regulation and the need for further action, including whether further price cuts are needed in light of the fact that there does not appear to be competition below the permitted rate and the possibility that providers are charging for full minutes when only seconds are involved in a call. A similar solution for mobile data roaming including SMS has been proposed[163] in light of the high retail roaming for those land prices and data downloads.[164] SMS sent from abroad have a proposed cap of 11 cents and wholesale data roaming, €1 per MB, effective 1 July 2009.

In another flexing of EU-wide muscle, backed by the DG Competition, the DG Information Society and Media has also launched a similar consultation (26 June 2008) on its draft Recommendation to ensure that national Access Directive conditions for voice call termination markets require efficient costing methods and ensure symmetrical[165] cost-based rates for voice call termination.[166] Prompted by differences in fixed and mobile termination rates the Commission considers not to be justified by the underlying costs, networks or national market characteristics (e.g. fixed operators pay mobile network operators nine times as much on average than the reverse for call termination), the proposal suggests that there is room for as much as a 70 per cent reduction in fixed to mobile termination rates. Citing significant regulatory divergences in the way cost-based price regulation has been effected with disincentives to efficiency, competition, and also a failure to apply technologically

---

[161] See Commission Staff Working Paper 'Impact Assessment of Policy Options in Relation to a Commission Proposal for a Regulation on Roaming on Public Mobile Networks Within the Community' SEC(2006) 925, 12 July 2006.

[162] Regulation (EC) 717/2007 of the European Parliament and of the Council on roaming on public mobile telephone networks within the Community and amending Directive 2002/21/EC, OJ L171/32 29, 27 June 2007.

[163] See DG Information Society and Media Working Document 'Public consultation on a review of the functioning of Regulation (EC) 717/2007 (the 'Roaming Regulation') and of its possible extension to SMS and data roaming services' (7 May 2008 Brussels), <http://ec.europa.eu/information_society/activities/roaming/docs/comments/public_consultation_may08.pdf>.

[164] Press Release 'High prices and lack of transparency source of anxiety for data roaming customers' IP/08/1048 27 June 2000.

[165] Symmetry meaning both among Member States and between fixed and mobile services.

[166] See Draft Commission Recommendation 'on the Regulatory Treatment of Fixed and Mobile Termination Rate in the EU' (26 June 2008).

neutral regulation as ascertained from its review of over 700 framework notifications, the Commission posits the need (and hence the justification) for EU-wide methods to be applied by the NRAs.

7.4.2.4.4 Universal Service Conditions

SMPs may also be likely to have USO obligations imposed on them under the Universal Service Directive. The uniform minimum set of services that are defined to fall within the USO in the EU consist of:

i. universal connection to the public telephone network and access to a defined, minimum set of publicly available telephone services (PATS)[167] at a fixed location (Article 4, 2002/22/EC);

ii. provision of public pay phones (Article 6, 2002/22/EC);

iii. provision of a printed or electronic directory, as required, comprising all PATS subscribers and directory enquiry services accessible to all end-users (Article 5, 2002/22/EC); and

iv. measures for disabled persons to ensure equivalent access to PATS, emergency services, directory enquiry (Article 7, 2002/22EC).

With respect to specific non-SMP conditions under the Universal Service Directive, non-SMP providers may seek to be considered to provide all or part of the USO, as described above. The Authorization Directive, therefore, allows non-SMP providers that are designated to provide all or part of the universal service obligation to have specific conditions imposed concerning its provision and tariffing.

Non-SMP specific conditions must also comply with the substantive and procedural requirements for imposing conditions under the Framework and Universal Service Directives[168] that here would include Commission reporting. Any specific

---

[167] The Universal Service Directive defines 'PATS' as 'service available to the public for originating and receiving national and international calls and access to emergency services through a number or numbers in a national or international telephone numbering plan, and in addition may, where relevant, include one or more of the following services: the provision of operator assistance, directory enquiry services, directories, provision of public pay phones, provision of service under special terms, provision of special facilities for customers with disabilities or with special social needs and/or the provision of nongeographic services'.

[168] The Access Directive imposes the requirement that such specific conditions comply with Arts 6 and 7 of the Framework Directive (Arts 5(3), 6(3)), governing transparency and consultation, as above described in connection with the granting of individual rights of use, above at 7.4.2.4.3 and the reporting requirements for certain NRA actions. The Universal Service Directive, in contrast, makes no specific reference in this regard to the Framework Directive, but rather, only to its own consultation requirements (Art 33) and Commission notification requirements (Art 36). While the notification requirements are in keeping with the Framework Directive, it requires only notification of all conditions maintained under Art 16 of the Universal Service Directive until a market review is complete. It would, however, seem likely that the consultation requirements of the Framework Directive (Art 6) would need to be complied with as the imposition/scope of universal service obligation is likely to have a significant impact on the market. It is likely, therefore, the Universal Service Directive's Art 33 is a refinement of the other to include manufacturers and end-user groups within interested parties.

condition must constitute a separate legal obligation from those in the general authorization. To ensure transparency, the criteria for imposing such obligations on individuals must, however, be referred to in the general authorization.[169]

7.4.2.5 *Amendments and modifications of rights and conditions*

Rights, conditions, and procedures concerning general authorizations, rights of use, and rights to install facilities can be modified only in objectively justified cases and in a proportionate manner.[170] Appropriate notice must be given of the intent to do so; interested parties must have at least four weeks to comment, except in exceptional circumstances.[171] Any such changes would need to fall within the Authorization Directive's substantive and procedural limitations for original conditions, e.g. fall within the exhaustive lists of parts A, B, and C of the Directive's Annex, and, where applicable, the other Directives that control conditions as described above.

Rights cannot be withdrawn before the end of the period for which they were granted except where justified. Where applicable, compensation must be made pursuant to national law.

One significant area where rights would be sought to be modified is that of the transfer of rights to spectrum via a spectrum-trading mechanism. Where it will not distort competition, the Framework Directive permits Member States to provide for the transfer of such rights from one undertaking to another limited only by notification and compliance with any publicized procedures set by the NRA.[172] The early movement by the UK and other Member States[173] to develop mechanisms for reallocating spectrum rights and permitting new uses prompted the Commission to consider whether a more harmonized EU-wide approach might not be advisable. In 2005, following a 2004 study commissioned by it and the conservative recommendation by the Radio Spectrum Policy Group for common trading procedures in phased bands of spectrum,[174] the Commission issued a communication rejecting the phased-band approach. It called instead for the establishment by 2010 of an EU-wide spectrum trading in bands suitable for mobile terrestrial communications and premised on some level of technological and service neutrality, adequate information disclosure, and harmonization (called 'approximation' here) of the nature of rights in spectrum and the formats for 'title' documents to address the varying notions of property interests under Member State law.[175] To date, these proposals, including one

---

[169] Article 6(2), Authorization Directive.

[170] Ibid, at Art 14(1).

[171] Ibid.

[172] Articles 9(3) and (4), Framework Directive.

[173] Identified by the Commission in its 2005 Communication as: DK, IT, NL, HU, AT, PT, SK, SI, and SE.

[174] See The Radio Spectrum Policy Group Opinion on Secondary Trading of Rights to use Radio Spectrum, RSPG04-54 at 4–5 (RSPG, 19 November 2004).

[175] See Commission Communication, 'A market-based approach to spectrum management in the European Union' at 7–10, 14 September 2005 [COM(2005) 400].

to repeal the GSM Directive that harmonized the 2G mobile standard in order to liberalize the use of the 900 and 1800MHz bands, are subsumed into a larger package of reforms that the DG Info Society is seeking to have implemented and which are only inching their way through the EU political processes.[176]

7.4.2.6 *Modifications to enable modifications*

The Authorization Directive will need to be modified to accommodate the revised procedures and nature of rights that spectrum trading and reuse liberalization would entail and conditions that could be attached to individual grants and regrants of spectrum. As proposed by the Commission these include a mandatory default for rights to use spectrum under the general authorization, removing the 'where possible' permissive language of the Directive; individual grants to use spectrum limited to two circumstances: avoiding serious harmful interference and fulfilling other objectives of general social interest. The granting of individual rights to radio spectrum would be required to be done pursuant to the proposed Framework Directive requirements under 9(b) governing mandatory ability to transfer rights without prior approval of the NRA for bands harmonized by the Commission under the proposed 9(c). These would be subject only to harmonized conditions and procedures for transfers, limitations, and identification of market conditions when competition would be restricted by such transfers.

Proposed Authorization Directive Articles 6(a) and 6(b) contemplate broad powers for the Commission, including the harmonization of procedures for granting the general authorization and individual grants of rights to use numbers and spectrum, and also not only the procedures used for individual selection of undertakings but also the actual selection of the undertaking taking into account the views of the NRA. Proposals contemplate a harmonized exception to the principle of technological and service neutrality. This is perhaps to continue to allow EU mandated standard uses across a band or to limit future challenges to any such designated standard like GSM, its national liberalization and deregulation of that spectrum without EU agreement as the UK essentially did). They further contemplate the ability to harmonize the scope of limitations not based on cultural diversity and media pluralism. An initial review of restrictions for current licensees and thereafter every five years for those not allowed to lease or transfer spectrum would be required. Many of these reforms, especially those enlarging the powers of the EU Information Society Commissioner as a super telecoms regulator, are controversial. Despite the undaunted efforts of the Commissioner, a virtual 'ever-Reding bunny',[177] these are likely to be subject to modification. The Commissioner signaled agreement to a proposed

---

[176] See Viviane Reding, Statement after the meeting of Council of EU Telecoms Ministers: 'Progress Made on the EU Telecoms Reform Package (Luxembourg, 12 June 2008), <http://ec.europa.eu/information_society/newsroom/cf/itemlongdetail.cfm?item_id=4181>.

[177] 'EU spokesman savages self-serving Ofcom' (PCPro, 31 October 2007), <http://www.pcpro.co.uk/news/134442/eu-spokesman-savages-selfserving-ofcom.html>.

compromise Body of European Telecoms Regulator ('BERT'), a smaller, but funded office replacing the National Regulators Group under a co-regulatory approach with the Commission. Its competence would be only telecoms and not spectrum and network security as sought. Disagreement remains on a range of other issues to be considered at the 27 November 2008 Council.

7.4.2.7 Reporting obligations

Information reporting to regulators can be costly and burdensome. Therefore, the Authorization Directive attempts to limit the information which undertakings must provide. To permit the NRA to monitor compliance with its conditions under the general authorization, for rights of use or specific obligations, NRAs may request, without additional justification, that proportionate and objectively justified information necessary to verify systemic or case by case compliance with:

i. payment obligations for USO contributions, administrative fees under the general authorization, and usage fees;

ii. those specific conditions permitted to be imposed under Article 6(2) of the Authorization Directive as described at section 7.4.2.4.[178]

Pursuant to the NRA's investigation or other reasons suggesting problems with compliance, NRAs may require proportionate, objectively justified information necessary to verify compliance with conditions on a case-by-case basis (Article 11(b)).

Such information can also be required for:

• procedures for and assessment of rights of use (Article 11(c));

• comparative quality/price reports for consumers (Article 11(d));

• clearly defined statistical purposes (Article 11(e));

• market analyses for effective competition pursuant to the Access and Universal Service Directives (Article 11(f)).

7.4.2.8 Compliance and enforcement

The Authorization Directive tempers the consequences that can occur where a provider fails to comply with conditions under the general authorization from those in the former Licensing Directive. It rather requires action 'commensurate with the infringement' (Recital 27). Unlike the Licensing Directive (see section 7.4.1 above), only in such exceptional circumstances where repeated breaches have failed to be remedied and financial and/or other proportionate sanctions have proved inadequate may an NRA preclude an undertaking from providing electronic communications networks and services and/or withdraw or suspend rights of use (Article 10). Where an NRA finds that the provider is not complying with any of the conditions of the

---

[178] Ibid, at Art 11(a).

general authorization, the rights of use, or specific conditions imposed under Article 6.2 of the Authorization Directive, the NRA shall notify the undertaking and give it a reasonable opportunity to state its views or a month to remedy such a breach (Article 10(2)). A shorter period may be agreed by the provider, or imposed where the breach is repeated; a longer period may be agreed by the NRA. Only after the provider fails to remedy the breach may the additional, proportionate measures be taken by the NRA.

Where evidence of a breach indicates a serious and immediate threat to public health, safety, or security, or poses operational or economic problems for users or other providers, the NRA may impose an interim, immediate measure as a remedy. The undertaking must then have a reasonable opportunity to be heard and propose other remedies prior to a final decision. NRAs may confirm the interim solution where it is appropriate (Article 10(6)).

The Authorization Directive mandates that undertakings have the right to appeal all measures to sanction or remedy breach of conditions under the appeal procedures mandated by Article 4 of the Framework Directive, which itself, however, provides that all providers of networks and services or users 'affected by a decision' of the regulator have an effective means of appeal to an independent body.

Proposed reforms to the Authorization Directive would tighten this flaccid enforcement framework. They contemplate a more streamlined enforcement process with tighter time limits and clearer, more decisive powers to fine and sanction, including the power to impose structural separation. The NRA's ability to order the breach in question be stopped immediately or within a reasonable time period is also proposed.[179] This should assist countries identified in the 13th Report as not having adequate powers to effect change. Indeed, one wonders what the UK's Ofcom could have done to BT realistically without its additional powers under the Competition and Enterprise Acts.

7.4.2.9 *Fees*

As did the Licensing Directive, the Authorization Directive mandates that administrative charges imposed under the general authorization be only those incurred in the 'management, control and enforcement' of that scheme (Article 12(1)).[180] This is extended under the new framework to encompass administrative charges for such activities in connection with rights of use and those specific conditions imposed

---

[179] See proposed amendments to Art 10, Authorization Directive in Commission Communication 'Proposal for a Directive amending Directives 2002/21/EC on a common regulatory framework for electronic communications networks and services, 2002/19/EC on access to, and interconnection of, electronic communications networks and services, and 2002/20/EC on the authorization of electronic communications networks and services' ('Reform Proposal') at 53, (COM(2007) 697, 13 November 2007).

[180] The Licensing Directive also encompassed the 'issue' of the 'applicable general authorization scheme', 97/13/EC, Art 6, as that Directive clearly contemplated that there could be different types of general authorizations, unlike the current framework.

under Article 6(2) (see section 7.4.2.4 above). Permissible activities to be included as costs are detailed by the Directive, a variation from the prior scheme, and include those incurred for international cooperation (e.g. radio frequencies, numbering schemes), harmonization and standardization, market analysis, monitoring compliance and other market control, as well as regulatory work involving preparation and enforcement of secondary legislation and administrative decisions, such as decisions on access and interconnection (Article 12(1)). As with the Licensing Directive (Recital 12), such administrative fees or charges are to be imposed in an objective, transparent, and non-discriminatory manner but, as further required here, one that also minimizes additional costs (Article 12(b)).

While the prior scheme required charges to be appropriately published and detailed (97/13/EC Article 6), the Authorization Directive additionally requires not only that the charges be published annually but that regulators provide an annual overview of their administrative costs for the permitted activities noted above, a requirement that effectively requires accounting separation for these, and an appropriate adjustment to be made when there is a difference between costs and charges (Article 12(2)). Accounting separation and cost justification are regulatory tools that previously in the EU regime for telecommunications, were limited to controls imposed on former monopolist incumbents that enjoyed special or exclusive rights and privileges and, subsequently, on SMP operators.

Finally, the Authorization Directive anticipates that non-cost related fees may be imposed that ensure the optimal use of numbers, spectrum, and rights to install facilities on public or private land (Article 13). In imposing these, Member States must ensure that they are objectively justified, transparent, and non-discriminatory, as well as proportionate to their intended use. This, combined with other articles in the Directive that permit a comparative/competitive procedure for granting individual rights of use, contemplate the possibility of usage fees determined by auction.

7.4.3 The EU Authorization Directive: the status quo and anticipated developments

Beyond the issues already identified, the Commission has introduced some reforms with relevance to the Authorization Directive.[181] The first of these is the consolidation and removal of several markets from the list of relevant markets to be reviewed for SMP, with the effect that only seven markets remain from the prior list of 18. Part simplification, part deregulation of some retail markets (although Member States are free to justify their own relevant markets as has the UK), it reinforces that the 2002

---

[181] See Commission Communication 'Proposal for a Directive amending Directives 2002/21/EC on a common regulatory framework for electronic communications networks and services, 2002/19/EC on access to, and interconnection of, electronic communications networks and services, and 2002/20/EC on the authorization of electronic communications networks and services' ('Reform Proposal') at 47–59, (COM(2007) 697 13 November 2007).

Framework has been a spur to competition since effective competition in a market is required to deregulate it. There are therefore fewer markets within which SMP conditions could be attached. However, the Roaming Regulation has eliminated the need for conditions in international mobile roaming so its removal from the list is prompted by greater regulation.

The 13th Implementation Report shows, however, that fixed line incumbents still have very high market shares and that, in light of this, the number portability condition is essential to competitiveness.[182] As part of the 2007 proposals, the Commission includes a change of the number portability condition to require that porting to the new carrier be effective in one day. This clearly will facilitate the use of this feature by users who might find the present five-day average to be too burdensome.

Other proposed amendments to the Directive are fairly innocuous of themselves: fine tuning amendments to general authorization conditions under other Directives where more substantial proposed reforms are contained. These would include, for example, the proposed amendments of the conditions to the general authorization to reflect the access for the disabled under the Universal Service Directive, the reflection of the current E Privacy Directive (2002/58/EC) rather than the earlier Telecommunications Privacy Directive (97/66/EC), as the former contains enhanced network security and data breach notifications, as well as a proposed amendment to the general condition for rights of end users to access not only numbers from the ETNS but also Universal International Freephone Numbers.

A significant change would have been the now rejected general conditions modification that comply electronic communications networks and service providers with the Information Society Directive and the IP Enforcement Directive.[183] This was objectionable as copyright, etc, are a national competence. It also flew in the face of the ban on conditions in the general authorization that mirror those under the general law, which clearly these IP provisions are in Member States. It also fell outside the scope of the Framework as regulating information society services. Rejection of content copyright regulatory authority by a telecoms regulator is not unprecedented. In *American Library Association v FCC* (DC Cir) (No 04-1037 March 15, 2005) the DC Federal Court of Appeals similarly clipped the wings of the FCC to impose technological requirements on digital equipment manufacturers to recognize 'broadcast flags', a digital rights management code that would permit content owners to limit redistribution.

7.4.4 The UK implementation of the EU 2002 Authorization Framework

The Communications Act 2003[184] and secondary legislation put in place the overarching UK framework for permissions to provide electronic communications

---

[182] See 13th Report, above at n 127.
[183] See Reform Proposal, n 181 above at 12.
[184] 2003, Chapter 21.

networks and services. It has been a work in progress with extensive, detailed market reviews and consultations completed not only by the legacy telecommunications regulator, Oftel, which served as the initial point of departure from the 1999 framework, but also that work done by the newly created convergence regulator, Ofcom which has continued trailblazing regulation now across the various electronic communications markets. Its spectrum deregulation and liberalization and its functional separation of British Telecom to require a totally independent operating division for the core network, including any next generation networks (NGN) that BT develops are perhaps the two most far-reaching. Notably, it can be said that these essentially were done outside of the EU framework. The former was undertaken pursuant to almost an aside in the Authorization Directive that says to Member States 'go ahead, do it as long as it does not distort competition and you have some procedures'; the latter pursuant to what might be called the UK's Enterprise Act's 'extreme' competition law-like powers, as previously noted. In both areas, the Commission is seeking to figure out a way to follow the UK's lead, as well as possibly to put the UK back on a lead, at least when it comes to spectrum trading, although in the UK it could all be a done deal before the EU gets its act together. The following examines the Act as well as its implementation and enforcement by Ofcom.

7.4.4.1 *The Communications Act 2003*

The Act, Part 2, Chapter 1 'Electronic Communications Networks and Services', governs the provision of electronic communications networks and services. It is lengthy and complex but puts in place the general authorization scheme requirement of the Directive by:

i. repealing those provisions of the Telecommunications Act 1984 governing the powers and requirements for licences, the provisions for their modification and enforcement, as well as those regarding designations of public telecommunications operators and governing the rights to access public and private land associated with that designation (section 147); and

ii. putting in place powers for Ofcom to set certain general and specific conditions (section 45) on specified persons providing electronic communications networks and services (section 46).

There is no 'general authorization' document or grant *per se*. Providers of electronic communications networks and services are merely now subject to a set of 22 General Conditions of Entitlement[185] notified and promulgated by the former regulator, the Director-General of Telecommunications, and continued with effect as modified by Ofcom, the successor regulator for all electronic communications including broadcast.

---

[185] Ofcom, 'Original Notification setting general conditions under section 45 of the Communications Act 2003' (Ofcom, London, 22 July 2003), <http://www.ofcom.org.uk/telecoms/ioi/g_a_regime/gce/>.

The consolidated, modified General Conditions of Entitlement,[186] comprising some 76 pages of rights, obligations, and definitions, implement sections 51–64 of the Act. These specify the permissible content and scope of general conditions which the Act permits to be applied 'generally' to every person providing an electronic communications network or service (section 46(2)(a)), or to every person providing those networks or services of a particular description as defined in the condition (section 46(2)(b)). While the UK's conditions will be examined below, a concern here is the source of the authorization to provide electronic communications networks and services.

Of course, this relates to the definition of these terms under the Act, which, as with much of the implementation of EU directives, have been done in the UK's own unique way. Thus, in contrast to the Framework Directive's definition of 'electronic communications network' (see section 7.4.2 above), the Communications Act defines it as:

(a) a transmission system for the conveyance, by the use of electrical, magnetic, or electro-magnetic energy, of signals of any description; and (b) such of the following as are used, by the person providing the system and in association with it, for the conveyance of the signals:

   i. apparatus comprised in the system;
   ii. apparatus used for the switching or routing of the signals; and
   iii. software and stored data (section 32(1)).

7.4.4.2 Notification procedure

The Communications Act 2003 requires that a person not provide a designated electronic communication network or service without advance notification to Ofcom, the NRA of his intent to do so (section 33(1)(2)). It also requires that any person 'making available a designated associated facility' similarly notify its intent to Ofcom (section 33(3)).[187] The Act also requires that Ofcom create a public register

---

[186] Ofcom, 'Consolidated version of General Conditions as at 15 August 2007 (including annotations), <http://www.ofcom.org.uk/telecoms/ioi/g_a_regime/gce/cvogc150807.pdf>.

[187] This separate listing of associated facilities in the Communications Act 2003 actually serves to address a gap in the EU framework that is caused by the fact that the Framework Directive defines its scope and aim at Art 1(1) as a 'harmonized framework for the regulation of electronic communication services, electronic communications networks, associated facilities and associated services'. It then proceeds to define these latter categories as 'facilities associated with an electronic communications network and/or an electronic communications service which enable and/or support the provision of services via that network and/or service. It includes conditional access systems and electronic programme guides' (Art 2(e)). The Authorization Directive's aim and scope, however, states only that it applies to 'authorisations for the provision of electronic communications networks and services' and carves out as unnecessary conditional access system/services authorizations at Recital 6 where it indicates that provision having previously been made for the free movement of providers of conditional access services in Directive 98/84/EC on the legal protection of services based on, or consisting of conditional access. It appears implicit in this, therefore, that associated facilities and services other than conditional access, while defined separately, are intended to be subsumed within electronic communications networks and services authorizations. This is not clear, however.

of notifying providers (section 44), and makes possible sanctions for failure to notify (sections 35–37). However, this notification requirement is premised on being a 'designated' network, service, or facility which the Act defines as being 'of a description of networks, services or facilities that is for the time being designated by Ofcom as a description of networks, services or facilities for which notification under this section is required' (section 33(2)). Ofcom, however, has not 'designated' any networks, services, or facilities for mandatory notification under these sections. Rather, while it originally planned to put in place a voluntary register for Public Electronic Communications Networks (PECN) to facilitate negotiation of interconnection pursuant to their rights under the general authorization, Ofcom subsequently determined that this was not in keeping with the permissive nature of the general authorization and decided not to proceed with it.[188] This would have been the implementation of the certificates under the Authorization Directive to facilitate interconnection and to obtain rights to access public and private land. Ofcom believed that this was unnecessary in light of the fact that there was sufficient guidance as to who comprised a provider of PECN in the 2003 Interconnection Guidelines[189] and that the register added nothing since it did not itself create or condition the exercise of rights.[190]

7.4.4.3 Conditions

Section 45 of the Act authorizes Ofcom to set conditions that must fall within either (a) general conditions (section 45(2)(a)), or (b) individual conditions of the following description: (i) universal service conditions; (ii) access-related conditions; (iii) a significant market power condition (section 45(2)(b)); and (iv) a privileged supplier condition. Each is considered in turn below.

7.4.4.3.1 General conditions

The Act authorizes 'general conditions' to be set within specified areas (section 45) that could probably be classified under the heads of 'consumer protection,' 'access and interconnection', 'essential requirements', 'universal service-related', and 'scarce resources'. Examining the specific areas that come within these, those falling within 'consumer protection' include:

- the protection of 'end-users' of public services (section 51(1)(a));

- procedures, standards, and policies of public network/service providers for:

  ○ handling of complaints from domestic and small business customers,

  ○ resolution of disputes between these customers and such providers,

---

[188] See Consultation 'Proposal that all provisions continued from licences made under the Telecommunications Act 1984 and all continued interconnection directions will cease to have effect except for specific provisions in specific markets listed in this document as exceptions' (Ofcom, London, 9 September 2004), <http://www.ofcom.org.uk/consult/condocs/Prop1984tele/provis_terminiate/>.

[189] Statement of DGT 'Guidelines for the interconnection of public electronic communications networks' (Oftel, London, 23 May 2003).

[190] See Consultation, above n 188.

  ° remedies and redress for complaints/disputes,

  ° making information about service standards and rights available to these
    customers (section 52).

'Service interoperability and network access' related conditions falls under 'access
and interconnection' (section 51(1)(b)). Conditions under 'essential requirements'
would be:

- proper and effective functioning of public networks (section 51(1)(c));

- prevention or avoidance of the exposure of individuals to electro-magnetic fields
  created in connection with the operation of electronic communications networks
  (section 51(1)(f));

- compliance with relevant international standards (section 51(1)(g)).

'Universal service-related' areas for general conditions are limited by the Act to:

- the assessment, collection, and distribution of financial contributions to any
  universal service obligation (section 51(1)(d));

- the provision, availability, and use, in the event of a disaster, of electronic communications networks, services, and associated facilities (section 51(1)(e));

- the broadcast or other transmission of 'must carry' services by electronic communications networks (section 64).

Finally, the Act's permitted general conditions for 'scarce resources' concern:

- access for end-users to numbers under the national numbering plan (section 57);

- the allocation and use of numbers by providers (section 58).

These track those permitted for general conditions under the Authorization
Directive.[191] Oftel originally promulgated 21 General Conditions of Entitlement to
provide electronic communications networks, services, and associated facilities.
There are now 22 with Ofcom's subsequent modifications. In putting these in place,
the regulator seems to have fully complied with the Act's procedural and substantive
requirements for publication, consultation, and approval of conditions, as well as
for notification of how conditions are to be set, approved, modified, and revoked
(sections 47–50). An outline of the General Conditions is provided in the Table 7.1
below. These are worth some consideration as they comprise the bulk of the regulatory framework for many providers of networks and services.

    The scheme generally distinguishes among three different categories of providers:
providers of electronic communications networks (ECN) or services (ECS), providers of public electronic communications services (PECS) and networks (PECN) and
providers of publicly available telephone services (PATS) and networks (PTN).
Some conditions to apply to all providers, a number are imposed only on providers
of public electronic communications networks and services, others, largely related to

---

[191] See 7.4.2 above.

consumer/end-user protection, imposed on the third group with the result that PATS providers are the most regulated under the general conditions.[192] Several conditions apply to subsets within these: Condition 3, regarding emergency scenarios applies only to fixed PTN and PATS; Condition 6 which governs standards for public pay phones applies only to such providers; and Condition 8 regarding public service TV broadcast obligations (i.e. 'must carry obligations') applies only to appropriate networks used for receiving TV.

Table 7.1 UK general conditions of entitlement

Condition 1: General access and interconnection obligations

- PECN providers to negotiate interconnection upon request by any PECN in EC with view to concluding agreement within reasonable time
- All ECN providers to keep confidential the information obtained in connection with access negotiations; use only for agreement

Condition 2: Standardization and specified interfaces

- All communications providers to comply with existing compulsory European standards or otherwise voluntary European or international standards/recommendations (ITU, ISO, IEC)
- Regulator can specify new compulsory standards for end-to-end connectivity

Condition 3: Proper and effective functioning

- Providers of fixed public telephone networks to take all reasonably practicable steps to maintain:
  - proper/effective functioning of network
  - availability to PATS/PTN in catastrophe, including to any emergency services organizations (ESO) by PATS

Condition 4: Emergency call numbers

- Provider of PATS/public pay phones to:
  - ensure end-user access to ESOs via '112' or '999' without charge and without coins or cards for pay phones
  - make available, to extent technically feasible, caller line identification to ESOs called on '112' or '999'

Condition 5: Emergency planning

- Providers of PTN/PATS to make arrangements to provide/restore reasonable and practicable services in a disaster on request of/in consultation with central and local government and ESO
- May seek compensation and be conditioned on indemnification from person seeking same

---

[192] See, Kemmit, H, 'The Regulation of VOIP Services in the UK' (2008)14(4) CTLR 87–91.

Condition 6: Public pay telephones

- Providers of these to ensure:
  - end-user access to operator assistance/directory inquiry
  - display of minimum connection charge, means of payment, location information for ESO, lack of charge for '112' and '999' calls
- Providers of public call boxes (PCBs) (installed on public land):
  - wheelchair accessibility minimums
  - additional minimums with receiving amplification
  - to cease PATS from PCB only on minimum notification requirement

Condition 7: Must carry obligation

- Providers of designated ('appropriate') networks over which public communications services provided and principal means for significant number of end-users to obtain television services to comply with direction to transmit service from must-carry list under section 64 of the Act.

Condition 8: Operator assistance, directories, and directory inquiry facilities

- Providers of PATS other than pay phones to:
  - provide end-users access to operator assistance, directory inquiry facility containing all UK subscribers not opting out
- Where assigns numbers, to provide directories of all local subscribers, updated at least yearly
- Reasonable fees

Condition 9: Requirement to offer contract with minimum terms

- Providers of public electronic communications services to offer contracts containing:
  - name, address of provider
  - service offered, service quality levels, connection time
  - maintenance service details
  - pricing, tariff particulars
  - duration, conditions for renewal and termination
  - details of compensation, if any, for quality level failures
  - dispute resolution means
- Modification material, detrimental to consumer only on one-month notice, right of cancellation

Condition 10: Transparency and publication of information

- PATS providers to publish clear, current information on prices, tariffs, standard terms, and conditions for access by end-users containing:
  - name, major office of provider
  - description of PATS offered
  - details of PATS in subscriptions/long-term rentals

- ○ details of standard tariffs/discounts, specially targeted schemes, concerning: access, all types of usage charges, maintenance
- ○ contract period, available dispute resolution mechanisms

Condition 11: Metering and billing

- Public Communications Services providers' bill to reflect service actually rendered
- Records of PCS to be maintained to prove same, but no longer than 15 months and subject to data protection requirements
- Designated PATS providers to have metering/billing systems approved by BAPT, NSI or NQA

Condition 12: Itemized bills

- PATS providers to provide subscriber itemized bills on request sufficient to verify charges and monitor service
  - ○ no or reasonable charge
  - ○ not to include calls to free phones
  - ○ not applicable to pre-paid services
  - ○ not required where alternative means

Condition 13: Non-payment of bills in fixed PATS

- Measures to effect payment for or disconnection to be proportionate and nondiscriminatory
- Due warning for interruption/disconnection; publication
- Interruption confined to concerned service if technically feasible

Condition 14: Codes of Practice, dispute resolution

- Providers of public electronic communications services to domestic (residential) and small business customers (not more than 10 employees, volunteers) to:
  - ○ provide on request a basic Code of Practice that:
    - at least states where Condition 10 information to be obtained
    - is in plain English and easily understandable
  - ○ establish, maintain procedures conforming to any applicable code of practice for handling complaints
  - ○ implement and comply with Dispute Resolution Scheme approved by Director under section 54's criteria re: ease of use, effectiveness, transparency, lack of charge:
    - own or existing Telecommunications Ombudsman Scheme
- Originating providers of premium rate services (PRS) to:
  - ○ establish and maintain code of practice for complaints and enquiries by domestic and small business customers to ensure they receive information about:

1. the nature of premium rate services, tariffs, how to bar access, number check services, complaint procedures, the role of Independent Committee for the Supervision of Telephone InformationServices (ICSTIS), the role of the Telephone Ombudsman schemes in PRS call disputes, provider contact information,
   including email, where to get information about nature of services billed
2. put in place processes and procedures for enquiry and help desk staff and distribution of consumer information.

- Originating providers of number translation services (NTS)[193] to establish and maintain code of practice to ensure reliable information to domestic and small business customers via:

  o publication of prices in pricelists, websites of calls to NTS with equal prominence to geographic, mobile and calling packages, including particularly:

    - details of when call charges to freephones apply
    - details of when NTS rates vary by time of day
    - details of any special offers, discounts schemes, bundled rates that apply to NTS services.

  o provision of customer advice in promotional materials and initial correspondence that refers to call pricing with maximum prices that apply, clear reference where complete published price list found.

  o processes and procedures for enquiry and help desk staff and distribution of consumer information.

- Providers of fixed line telephone services to establish small business and domestic customers code of practice for sales and marketing:

  o in plain English, free of charge/ prominent on website, advising that required by General Condition and applies irrespective of sales medium governing sales practices, recruitment and training, customer contact limitations and procedures, standards to avoid mis-selling, misrepresentation, sales to vulnerable persons, contract and customer information requirements, contract cancellation, advertising compliance, etc. (see text below for further discussion).

- Providers of PECS (to the extent it comprises conveyance of speech, music or sounds, i.e., VoIP) to comply with Code on the Provision of consumer information to Domestic and Small Business Customers for the provision of Services:

  o all, as applicable, to provide, during sales process/point of signature, in terms and conditions and in user guides, information about features and/or limitations different from PATS over the PTN with respect to:

    - service reliability (ceasing function during power failure, loss of broadband connection)
    - Emergency calls

---

[193] 'In the UK, Number Translation Service (NTS) is the service of routing a telephone call with a non-geographic number beginning with 07, 08, or 09 to a hidden geographic or mobile number. NTS numbers are called Freephone because callers are not charged for the call, just as with 800 and 888 numbers in the US. NTS is typically used by businesses and organizations to provide a single number for customers to call free-of-charge regardless of their geographic location. There are several fee-based subcategories of NTS, which are: Local Call Fee Access (LCFA), National Call Fee Access (NCFA), and Premium Rate Services (PRS)', Weiser, P, Definition, Searchnetworking.com (30 July 2002), <http://searchnetworking.techtarget.com/sDefinition/0,,sid7_gci841663,00.html#>.

- no access/reliability of access—clear information, acknowledgement by customer/ proof to Ofcom/labels/reminder cards
- access at single location—location registration prior to activation /update requirements
- access at multiple locations—registration and update requirements
- inability to Port Numbers; and,
- other information re: no operator assistance, directory inquiry, calling line ID, special disability features (condition 15), itemisation of calls free of charge (prospective customers/sales process only), and limitations on numbers/country code dialling clearly accessible.

Condition 15: Special measures for end-users with disabilities

- PATS providers to:
  - consult with consumer panel on such interests/requirements
  - provide alternative directory information and inquiry facilities with ability to connect end-user and free of charge
  - ensure access to text relay services where needed, at equivalent pricing
  - provide urgent repair services where needed
  - permit a nominee to safeguard service where user dependent on service
  - provide bills in alternative format for visually impaired
  - engage in publication/dissemination about services

Condition 16: Provision of additional facilities

- PTN provider to make available tone dialling, caller line identifications subject to data protection requirements, if technically feasible

Condition 17: Allocation, adoption, and use of numbers

- Provider of ECN, ECS not to adopt, use numbers under national numbering plan unless allocated to that provider or another who authorizes the adoption, use
- Provider of ECN, ECS to have numbering plan for allocated numbers for which it must make application, and ensure effective, efficient use within 6 months
- No undue discrimination for other provider's adoption/use of numbers
- Compliance with Annex of designated number usages
- Compliance with tariffing and notices for new numbering designations: 03 (public bodies, entities with national presence, not for profit) calling at same rates for geographical 01 and 02 calls without additional charges for all minutes; 07, personal numbering designation at no more that 20p a minute without free, pre-call notice.

Condition 18: Number portability

- Provider of ECN/ECS to provide number portability as soon as reasonably practical—but block transfers of less than 25 mobile numbers in two days
  - at subscriber's or other provider's request

- ○ on reasonable terms
- ○ at cost-orientated charging based on incremental costs, unless otherwise agreed or directed portability between like numbering codes, irrespective of actual service (geographic numbers irrespective of fixed or mobile service)
- ○ under revised PATS definition, portability for publicly available only for services originating and receiving national/international calls and access to emergency services through a normal telephone number

Condition 19: Provision of directory information[194]

- Providers of ECN, ECS and allocated numbers under Condition 17 to:
  - ○ meet all reasonable requests by any person for information re:
    - ■ its subscribers assigned those numbers
    - ■ other end-users assigned numbers originally allocated to it
    - ■ for the purpose of providing directories/directory inquiry service
    - ■ on fair, cost-orientated, non-discriminatory terms and in agreed formats
    - ■ in compliance with data protection requirements

Condition 20: Non-geographic numbers

- ECN, ECS providers adopting non-geographic numbers to:
  - ○ make available to end-users EC-wide where technically feasible
  - ○ limit access to end users in geographical areas where subscriber chooses for commercial reason

Condition 21: Quality of service

- Providers of public ECS to publish comparable, adequate, up-to-date information of quality of services on direction
- Not implemented except voluntary schemes, not to be imposed on small providers.

Condition 22: Service migrations

- Communications providers to provide authorization codes (MAC) upon request for broadband migration by end-user, customer, other provider (Not apply to service requiring fixed line provision with DSL (MPF)).
  - ○ within 5 working days by letter or email
- Exceptions for expired contract, can't validate user ID; valid MAC issued, wholesale provider refuses issue of MAC
- Compliance with MAC Process, including
  - ○ two contact methods for end-user

---

[194] A March 2008 consultation (closing June 2008) as to the Telephone Directory Service universal service obligations is proposing, *inter alia*, to remove GC8.2 and rely on normal market conditions to deliver directories without any regulatory requirement to do so. See 'Consultation on a proposal to remove and/or amend universal service obligations and general conditions relating to the provision of telephone directory information' (Ofcom, London, 10 March 2008).

- ○ details of MAC validity/service applicability
- ○ publishing information about availability of MACs
- ○ ability to reverse erroneous migration
- ○ facilitate migration in a fair and reasonable manner
- ○ ensure migration carried out within reasonable timescales; minimal loss of service

It is not perfectly clear that some of the General Conditions as promulgated and as implemented fall within the Authorization Directive's and the Communications Act's limitations for General Conditions. For example, both of these limit what might be called 'universal service-related' general conditions under the areas for general conditions to financial contributions to a universal service fund, radio and broadcast 'must carry' obligations, and disaster-related service/operation.[195] Specific obligations to provide universal service as permitted by the Authorization Directive and in the Universal Service Directive[196] are to be imposed on designated undertakings under specific conditions that are required by the Authorization Directive to be legally separate from conditions under the general authorization.[197] The UK General Conditions of Entitlement include conditions relating to the provision of public call boxes, directory enquiry, and disabled end-user services. These appear to fall within the USO categories to be addressed within specific universal service conditions,[198] albeit the actual requirements of these General Conditions of Entitlement are largely, but not entirely different from those ultimately imposed on the persons designated to provide the USO under specific conditions.[199] In light of this overlap in kind as well as the fact that these would seem both to be categories that fall only under areas for specific conditions, it is difficult to ascertain whether these general conditions fall within the statutory authorization. It is also difficult to ascertain whether the specific conditions are legally separate from the general conditions. For example, BT has a duty to provide call boxes under both the specific and, it would seem, the general conditions, with the latter governing wheelchair access, a service for disabled end-users. For this and other reason, the Conditions are not, therefore, models of clarity.

7.4.4.3.2 Modifications to the UK General Conditions of Entitlement
The General Conditions of Entitlement have not remained a static body of authorization controls since 2003. Rather, Ofcom has added to and modified the General Conditions since they were first promulgated. These changes have largely addressed evolutions in markets, technology, and the fall-out from competition. The last category has taken the form of controls on sales and other marketing conduct. Detailed codes for sales and marketing conduct to address 'slamming' (changing providers without permission) and high pressure sales to switch carriers and the greatly

---

[195] See 7.4.2 and 7.4.4.1 above.
[196] See 7.4.2.4.4 above.
[197] Ibid.
[198] See 7.4.2.4.4, above.
[199] See 7.4.4.3.3(i) above.

enhanced transparency requirements for premium rate services to enable customers to understand the difficult (and often very costly) tariffing structures were some of the key Condition 14 provisions in this regard. Condition 22 sought to ensure that competition in technologically evolving markets was enabled and that end-users' wishes for changing broadband service providers were not obstructed by communications providers not cooperating or by difficulties presented in changing residences.[200] A general condition is under consultation to address mobile service misselling, including such things as cash back schemes that deter the payment and slamming.[201]

Technological and market evolutions regarding VoIP-related services with their growing substitutability for circuit switched telephony prompted not only the promulgation of a code of practice under Condition 14 to ensure that consumers and end-users are fully aware of possible limitations to the reliability of these services, their access to emergency numbers and operator and other services in contrast to publicly available telephone services which by definition provide such services pursuant to other conditions,[202] but also the removal of prior regulatory forbearance with Conditions 3 (maintaining network integrity and access to emergency organizations at fixed locations) and 4 (use of 999 or 112 emergency numbers/caller location information) and clarification that the obligation/right to port numbers continues to be limited to providers of PATS whether VoIP or not, as redefined under Condition 18.[203] Essentially reversing an earlier position that allowed VoIP providers to opt to be PATS or not, Ofcom has applied the full spectrum of conditions to those providers of VoIP services that allow users to make calls to normal national phone numbers and who must now provide '999' and '112' access.[204] The restriction on number portability to PATS providers acts as an incentive for VoIP providers to provide such services/consumer protections. Ofcom has also intensified enforcement efforts with respect to emergency service access condition compliance.[205]

To address the confusion and association of 08 toll free numbers with revenue sharing numbers using the same initial prefix, harming the former, Ofcom created a new category of numbers to permit a sort of 'imprimatur' for groups like government agencies, non-profit organizations, and undertakings wishing a national presence without a further charge to consumers.[206] The new Condition 17.12 requires service providers to comply with the tariffing limitations placed on these number categories as within the National Numbering Plan.

---

[200] Statement and Notification 'Broadband migrations: enabling consumer choice' (Ofcom, London, 13 December 2006).

[201] Consultation, 'Protecting consumers from mis-selling of mobile telecommunications services' (Ofcom, London, 18 March 2008).

[202] Notification, 'Regulation of VoIP Services' (Ofcom, London, 29 March 2007), at 85–102.

[203] Ibid, at 103–108.

[204] News Release, 'Ofcom confirms VoIP providers must provide access to 999 to 112' (Ofcom, London, 5 December 2007).

[205] See Closed Cases; 'Own-initiative investigation against Virgin Media about compliance with General Condition 4 (Emergency Call Numbers)', Competition and Consumer Bulletin, CW/00974/11/07 (Ofcom, London, 11 June 2008).

[206] Notification, 'Raising confidence in telephone numbers: amending General Condition 17, (Ofcom, London, 31 May 2007) (inserting new condition 17.12 and renumbering 17.12 to condition 17.13).

In 2005, Ofcom triggered the 'Quality of Service' (QoS) General Condition 21 for certain communication providers providing voice services at a fixed location, requiring them to publish QoS information.[207] Those CSPs operating over the minimum threshold set at £4 million per quarter in gross revenue and 100 million minutes handled per quarter must publish information regarding: supply times, fault rates and fault repair times; billing complaints; and complaint resolution times. Condition 21 implements Article 22 of the Universal Service Directive and arguably falls within the permitted conditions under section 8, Annex A of the Authorization Directive.[208]

Previously, the only QoS reporting conditions[209] were those specifically imposed on BT for key performance indicator (KPI) reporting in connection with Ofcom's SMP wholesale market findings,[210] some of which now fall under the KPI 'undertakings' for BT Openreach following functional separation.[211] BT, as will be discussed further in the following sections, has had numerous specific conditions imposed on it by Ofcom due to findings of SMP and its designation as provider of universal service.

Finding that consumers have likely barriers to accessing alternative dispute mechanisms in order to address adequately unresolved consumers' complaints in light of their imbalance of power with communications providers, Ofcom, as set out in a July 2008 consultation,[212] is considering revising the general condition. The proposal would impose a mandatory Ofcom Code of Complaints Practice with high level minimum standard for complaints processing as has been done in other regulated

---

[207] Notification of Direction 'A Statement on setting quality of service parameters' (Ofcom, London, 27 January 2005).

[208] This provides that NRAs should be 'able to require undertakings that provide publicly available electronic communications services to publish comparable, adequate and up-to-date information for end-users on the quality of their services...' and that they can 'specify, *inter alia*, the quality of service parameters to be measured, and the content, form and manner of information to be published, in order to ensure that end-users have access to comprehensive, comparable and user-friendly information'. Universal Service Directive, Art 22. Recital 17 of this Directive makes clear that NRAs should be able to monitor QoS for providers of fixed PTNs and PATS other than those with USO conditions. However, this is not a specific condition under the Universal Service Directive but rather one under the General Conditions which must comport with Annex A of the Authorization Directive. There the only possible basis seems to be category 8 which permits sector-specific consumer protection rules including conditions in conformity with the Universal Service Directive.

[209] In early 2003, Oftel set a list of key performance indicators (KPIs) as a checklist against which BT could perform to attain relaxed retail price controls. Technically, therefore, these 15 KPIs against which performance was measured, while quality of service reporting, were voluntary and not conditions under the BT licence. See Statement 'Wholesale Line Rental' (Oftel, London, 11 March 2003).

[210] See Statement and Directions: Requirement on BT to publish Key Performance Indicators (Ofcom, London, 23 September 2004), <http://www.ofcom.org.uk/consult/condocs/bt_kpi/statement/statement_directions.pdf>. These comprised a range of month and/or quarterly reports regarding different performance parameters with regard to end user access (data stream), wholesale line rental, virtual path facilities, FRIACO, and specified interconnection circuits. The current BT Wholesale (products other than access) KPIs can be found at: <http://www.btwholesale.com/pages/static/Footer/About_BTW/Key_Performance_Indicators.html>.

[211] See 'Our Undertakings: Key Performance Indicators' (BT Group Plc London), <http://www.btplc.com/Thegroup/Regulatoryinformation/Ourundertakings/KeyPerformanceIndicators/index.htm>.

[212] Consultation, 'Review of Alternative Dispute Resolution and Complaints Handling Procedures' (Ofcom, London, 10 July 2008).

industries in lieu of the current individual provider codes that exist now, although Ofcom approved. This would also harmonize the definition of complaint to encompass all expressions of dissatisfaction with the products and services, including technological faults. Communications providers would be required to send letters to complainants advising of the existence of the ADR mechanism. The eligibility period would be reduced to matters still pending after 8 weeks rather than the current 12 weeks or earlier if a deadlock letter is sent. Providers would be precluded from using premium rate numbers to make complaints and would have record-keeping obligations for compliance monitoring. The proposal also includes possible evaluative standards for approving ADR schemes to ensure that such bodies are independent, impartial, and accessible.

7.4.4.3.3 Individual conditions
(i) Universal service conditions

'Universal service' is the first of section 45's conditions categories of permitted conditions. The Communications Act 2003 authorizes Ofcom to establish any specific condition it deems appropriate for securing compliance with obligations set out in the 'universal service order' by the Secretary of State for Trade and Industry (section 67).

The Secretary of State in the Electronic Communications (Universal Service) Order (SI 2003/1904)[213] defined the scope of the universal service obligation to include PATS, public pay telephones, directory and directory enquiry facilities, special measures for disabled end-users, and special tariff and billing options, including those for low income users, an obligation that remains unchanged in scope, to date, both in the UK and under the EU Directive which the Order partly implements. Pursuant to the Communications Act, section 66(1),[214] Ofcom then designated those persons to whom the universal service conditions were to apply. Ofcom imposed on BT and Hull (within its service area only) the specific USO obligations following the Order.[215] While the provision of universal service was reviewed in 2005–2006 by Ofcom,[216] the USO conditions, although slightly modified from those originally imposed[217] on BT (and on Kingston Communications in Kingston on Hull), still include the obligation to:

- provide a connection to the fixed telephone network at a uniform price[218] following a reasonable request, and provide a connection that allows functional internet access;

---

[213] 2003 c. 21.

[214] Implemented by The Electronic Communications (Universal Service) Regulations 2003, SI 2003/33.

[215] See Ofcom, Strategic Review of Telecommunications Phase 1 Consultation, Annex G (2003).

[216] See Ofcom's Annual Plan: April 2004–March 2005, at Table 8.7, E4 'Review of the Universal Service Obligation'.

[217] For example, new low income schemes, including a pre-pay option, were approved, as was the ability to modify some provision of public call boxes due to their cost and low utilization and the rules for removing them, including a 'local veto' for qualifying boxes. See Statement 'Review of the Universal Service Obligation' (Ofcom, London, 14 March 2006). None of these, however, alter the basic requirement in each of the areas, just the extent of the obligation or how it may be satisfied.

[218] Ofcom decided, in its 2006 review, that BT could charge non-uniform prices when the connection cost more than the standard charge of £3,400, recommending that it use the standard charge for particularly

- provide at least one scheme for consumers with special social needs who have difficulty affording telephone services;
- provide uniformly priced public call box services;[219]
- ensure that tariffs for universal services do not entail payment for additional unnecessary services;
- provide a basic level of itemized billing at no extra charge;
- provide universal services that accord with the defined quality thresholds;
- provide funds for a relay service for textphone users; and
- supply and maintain directories and databases for the provision of directory services.[220]

Ofcom has also, to date, concluded that both BT and KCOM should continue to bear the costs of the USO, in light of Ofcom's findings that the benefits to both of the USO continue to equal or outweigh the costs and that, therefore, no USO fund or other method is required.[221]

Some changes to the USO are, however, soon likely in light of Ofcom's provisional conclusions reached in a recent consultation on the directory service provision obligation that: (1) the current universal service Condition 7 imposed on BT is not lawful, and (2) market circumstances may justify no longer imposing others. The former, Ofcom concluded provisionally, was the consequence of the ECJ decision in *KPN Telecom BV v OPTA*.[222] This held that the only relevant information required to be provided pursuant to Universal Service Directive now Article 25(2) is the name, address, and telephone number of non-objecting subscribers. Thus, other information provided to other directory service providers can be subject to invoice. According to Ofcom, because the BT USO Condition 7 imposes an information obligation broader than such 'relevant information' and requires BT to provide all information contained in its OSIS database in machine readable form to any person seeking to provide publicly available directory enquiry services, this Condition does not implement the Directive's obligations. It, therefore, was an *ultra vires* act on the

---

vulnerable customers. See ibid at 29. Ironically, these charges involve those who are geographically remote and therefore at the heart of the purpose of the universal service obligation as originally conceived as a geographic averaging of costs in the context of the penny stamp. See National Post Museum, *The Queen's Own: Stamps that Changed the World* (Royal Mail Grp, London, 2003), <http://www.postal-museum.si.edu/queen%27s/postalreforms.html>.

[219] Ofcom granted BT a temporary waiver of the uniformity requirement while it engages in the process of replacing or re-engineering boxes to implement a new tariff scheme administered by the box itself rather than centrally.

[220] Ofcom's recent decision has provisionally concluded that the current USO Condition 7 imposed on BT to provide contents from the OSIS database is not lawful under a recent ECJ decision. It has, however, just concluded a consultation on the scope of the continuing directory service obligation as further discussed above.

[221] See Statement 'Review of the Universal Service Obligation' (Ofcom, London, 14 March 2006).

[222] Case C-109/03, ECR 2004, p I-11273.

part of Ofcom under the Framework.[223] The same is likely true of the obligation imposed on BT under General Condition 19 to provide data for the provision of directory information services by others,[224] hence requiring modification. Ofcom proposes to change BT's duty under the General Condition 19 to a more limited obligation to provide information only about its own subscribers. Ofcom is also considering revoking conditions for the mandatory provision of a written directory, having found that there is likely a competitive, profitable market in these. This would entail amendments to General Condition 8.2 that now requires providers who assign numbers to provide their subscribers with a printed directory and those in General Condition 14 imposing a similar obligation under a code of practice for information to consumers and small businesses would needed to remove any obligation to provide these to subscribers.[225] As with the EU, Ofcom has considered that the scope of the services provided should not be changed to include mobile or broadband.

(ii) Access conditions
Ofcom is authorized by the Act to impose conditions concerning the provision of network access and service interoperability appropriate to secure provider efficiency, sustainable competition, and the greatest possible benefit to end-users (section 73(2)). Where a person controls access to any electronic communications network, that person may have an access condition imposed on him without being a provider of a Public Electronic Communications Network (PECN) or of associated facilities (section 46(6)). Otherwise, specific access conditions must be imposed on providers of networks.[226] Sections 73 and 74 specify the permitted content of such conditions and include those relating to network access and service interoperability considered appropriate by Ofcom in light of the Framework Directive's regulatory considerations (section 73(2)). These include specific conditions to require interconnection of networks for the purpose of ensuring end-to-end connectivity for end-users of PECNs (section 74(1)), as well as those imposing obligations on a person providing facilities for the use of application programme interfaces or electronic programme guides (section 74(2)).[227]

---

[223] As stated by Ofcom: 'Universal Service USC 7 is, in effect, unlawful. The reason for this was essentially that USCs may be imposed only in order to secure compliance with Community obligations and, in particular for present purposes, the obligation in Art 5(1) of the Universal Service Directive and as USC 7 fails to impose an obligation on any undertaking (and, in particular, on BT as a designated provider) to guarantee that Article 5 Universal Service Directive services are made available then Ofcom was not empowered to impose USC 7. Accordingly, we consider that USC 7 should be revoked following the statutory process under the 2003 Act.' Consultation 'Consultation on a proposal to remove and/or amend universal service obligations and general conditions relating to the provision of a telephone directory service' at 10 (Ofcom, London, 10 March 2008), <http://www.ofcom.org.uk/consult/condocs/dirinfo/dirinfo.pdf>.
[224] See ibid, at s 2.6.
[225] See ibid, at Annex 6.
[226] Section 75 requires that Ofcom impose access conditions of providers of conditional access services for protected programmes.
[227] See further Chapter 8.

Initially, however, the only specific access-related conditions within the parameters of the Act were conditions which were imposed on Sky entities to provide conditional access and electronic programme guide services on fair and reasonable terms that are published, on a non-discriminatory basis, and maintaining accounting separation.[228] Other entities have since had similar conditional access conditions applied as the pay TV market evolved[229] and other types of specific access conditions have been imposed in connection with other PECS.

Notably, in 2006, in order to ensure end-connectivity for telephony,[230] Ofcom imposed an access condition on BT. As noted recently by the Competition Appeal Tribunal (CAT), before this time, no condition aimed at ensuring such connectivity had been imposed on BT but that it and the rest of the market had acted as if BT had such an obligation as a universal service operator and pursuant to earlier guidance in this regard.[231] Ofcom, however, reasoning that other providers would be ensured of call termination services either directly or indirectly (via transit), obligated BT to purchase both fixed and mobile narrowband call termination services from any requesting provider of PECN upon reasonable terms and conditions, including charges. BT could not unreasonably restrict or withdraw access to any normal telephone number under these specific section 73 and section 74 access conditions.[232] A series of disputes emerged from a collision between this condition and the rates that the mobile network operators sought to charge BT under the call termination price caps imposed on them as SMP in their own markets for mobile call termination. The SMP conditions and the disputes as resolved by a section 185 appeal to the CAT are discussed in the following section.

(iii) SMP obligations

The SMP conditions are the next group of the conditions permitted to be applied to specific providers. The Act authorizes Ofcom to impose specific conditions on persons designated as having dominance either alone or collectively with others (section 78). Dominance may be found as well in adjacent markets where they are so closely related as to permit the market power in one market to influence the other so as to strengthen market power there (section 78(4)). The Act directs that dominance be construed according to the Framework Directive as a 'position of economic strength

---

[228] See Explanatory Statement and Notice 'The Regulation of Conditional Access; Setting of Regulatory Conditions' (Oftel, London, 24 July 2003); Consultation 'Access Regulation, Regulation of Electronic Program Guides', s 3 (Ofcom, London, 18 August 2005), <http://www.ofcom.org.uk/consult/condocs/epg/epg/stat_provisions/>. Similarly, see Statement 'Technical Platform Services: Guidelines and Explanatory Statement' (Ofcom, London, 13 September 2006). Also, see Chapter 8.

[229] See Consultation 'The Setting of access-related conditions upon Top Up Tv' (Ofcom London 15 February 2007). The final statement expected in May 2007 has not been found on the Ofcom website.

[230] End-to-end connectivity ensures that retail customers can make calls to other customers on that same network or any other network.

[231] T-Mobile et al v Ofcom [2008] CAT 12, 28 (citing Guidance issued by the former Director General of Telecommunications on 'End-to-end connectivity' dated 27 May 2003).

[232] Statement 'End-to-End Connectivity' (Ofcom, London, 13 September 2006), <http://www.ofcom.org.uk/consult/condocs/end_to_end/statement/statement.pdf>.

affording it the power to behave to an appreciable extent independently of competitors, customers and ultimately consumers'[233] and apply the Framework's factors for determining dominance.

It further directs Ofcom to identify and review relevant markets according to the Framework and make determinations as to market power in conformity with all applicable guidelines of the Commission (section 79). Ofcom is to consult with interested parties by publishing notifications of the proposed determinations that either identify the markets or the parties determined to have SMP with the reasons for making these determinations (section 80). The Act mandates that Ofcom must notify the Commission of the proposed SMP conditions if they would affect trade between the Member States, in keeping with the Framework Directive's requirements (section 81).

Interestingly, the Act specifies Ofcom's duty to revoke any proposed condition that the Commission has indicated would create a barrier to the Single Market or that would not be compatible with Community obligations (section 82).

As noted by Ofcom, sections 87 to 92 implement the SMP-related provisions under Articles 9 to 13 of the Access Directive and Articles 17 to 19 of the Universal Service Directive.[234] The Act charges Ofcom with setting appropriate SMP conditions in markets where SMP findings have been made. It specifies the subject matter of these permitted SMP conditions in conformity with these Directives (sections 87–93). These include those conditions related to network access and use and network access pricing, undue discrimination, publication of such information as Ofcom directs to ensure transparency regarding any of these matters, publication of acceptable access terms and conditions (usually called a 'reference offer'), separate accounting, accounting methods, and, as permitted, access price controls (sections 87–88). Section 89 of the Act permits other appropriate access conditions outside those otherwise permitted to be imposed 'under exceptional circumstances' where dominance exists in a service market by a person who is a provider of electronic communications networks or associated facilities. These, however, must have the prior approval of the Commission (section 89(2)).

Conditions are also authorized where dominance is determined in service markets related to provision of carrier selection and pre-selection (section 90) and in an end-user public communications services market where access-specific conditions or any of the above SMP conditions fails to redress a failure of competition (section 91). Finally, Ofcom can set SMP conditions governing apparatus supply and leased lines provision, where dominance has been determined in related services markets (section 92). The Act requires Ofcom to apply requirements of cost orientation, non-discrimination, and transparency as required by the Universal Service Directive.

---

[233] 2002/21/EC, Art 14(2).
[234] Section 4.4, Review of Wholesale Broadband Access Markets (Ofcom, June 2004).

The Act further requires, after an initial review, that Ofcom at 'intervals they consider appropriate' carry out further analyses to determine whether the earlier SMP findings remain valid and whether the conditions imposed need to be modified. (section 85). Where Ofcom finds, in an apparatus market, that there is no one dominant, it is to advise the Secretary of State who may by order revoke Ofcom's power to impose SMP conditions in that apparatus market (section 85).

In the case of service conditions, the condition can be modified or revoked after such further market and market power review (section 86(3)) or if Ofcom determines that there has not been a material change in the market since that condition was set or last modified (section 86(4)), thereby allowing Ofcom some flexibility to try something else. With apparatus conditions, however, Ofcom may only modify/revoke conditions after the full relevant market/market power review (section 86(5)).

Since 2003,[235] Ofcom has engaged in ongoing market reviews and consultations as part of and in addition to the phases of its strategic review of telecommunications. The initial reviews to determine where it could peel-back old conditions retained under the transition regime and where the Framework Directive would require the imposition of new conditions took place from the end of 2004. Starting in 2005, Ofcom began what must be considered the section 84 and 85 reviews of markets wherein conditions were earlier set. BT (and in some areas KCom in Hull) has been found to have SMP in numerous wholesale and retail products and services markets with ensuing conditions regarding price controls,

For example, Ofcom after completing initial reviews and consultations in the wholesale broadband access and local access markets, determined that BT had SMP in the wholesale local access and asymmetric broadband origination markets outside of Hull and in the broadband conveyance market, but that Kingston Communications had SMP in the wholesale local access market and origination market in its service area of Hull. Ofcom imposed the following conditions on both providers in both these markets:

- to provide network access on reasonable request;
- not to discriminate unduly;
- to publish a reference offer;
- to notify terms and conditions;
- to notify technical information;
- to have accounting separation.[236]

---

[235] Oftel carried out much planning and part of the market analysis and review process leading up to the effective date of the new framework in July 2003.

[236] Explanatory Statement and Notification, 'Review of the wholesale local access market: Identification and analysis of markets, determination of market power and setting of SMP conditions' (Ofcom, London, 16 December 2004), pp 51–77.

A 2005 statement on the SMP non-discrimination condition indicates that Ofcom will presume that any non-price based transactional discrimination by a vertically integrated SMP provider is 'undue'.[237] This presumption, while rebuttable, is intended to tackle the subtle and difficult to prove effects of such discrimination, putting the burden on the SMP provider to justify the difference in treatment between its own and others' services.

In addition to the above, Ofcom imposed other conditions on BT. In both the above markets, BT has to provide quality of service information and to establish a statement of requirements for new access.[238] BT in connection with wholesale local access was ordered to provide a range of local loop unbundling services. These include:

• metallic path facilities/fully unbundled local loops;
• shared metallic path facilities/shared access;
• sub-loop unbundling;
• internal tie cables;
• external tie cables;
• site access;
• co-location;
• co-mingling; and
• ancillary services as may be reasonably necessary to use the other services.

In imposing these SMP conditions, Ofcom determined that a number of old BT licence conditions would be discontinued, including, e.g.:

• Condition 43—requirement to provide telecommunications services other than voice telephony services on request;
• Condition 45—SMP obligations to Interconnect;
• Condition 46—Requirement to publish reference interconnection offer;
• Condition 47—requirement relating to Interconnect Agreements;
• Condition 49—Requirement to send individual agreements to [Ofcom] and to publish them; and
• Condition 69—Charge Control for Standard Services.

A similar consultation and review of service and product markets conducted within the categories of retail and wholesale leased lines including all types of partial

---

[237] 'Undue discrimination by SMP providers: How Ofcom will investigate potential contraventions on competition grounds of Requirements not to unduly discriminate imposed on SMP providers' (Ofcom, London, 15 November 2005).

[238] See, e.g. Explanatory Statement and Notification, 'Review of the wholesale local access market: Identification and analysis of markets, determination of market power and setting of SMP conditions'.

private circuits concluded that BT was dominant in a significant number of the specific markets. Ofcom imposed SMP conditions analogous to those above,[239] but including for the leased lines market, obligations to supply, leased lines reference offers and service parameter information, and cost oriented pricing, etc.[240] However, Ofcom chose not to regulate the retail high and very high bandwidth markets. Here as well, there was commensurate peel-back of the old licence conditions as applied to these markets.[241]

Table 7.2 reflects the major markets in which Ofcom originally imposed SMP conditions on BT.

Table 7.2 Ofcom Phase 2 Consultation Document: Strategic Review of Telecommunications, slide 48 (18 November 2004)

Major markets where BT is subject to market-specific interventions

Retail markets	Wholesale markets
Residential analogue exchange line services	Call origination
Residential ISDN2 exchange line services	Local tandem conveyance and transit
Business analogue exchange line services	Inter-tandem conveyance and transit
Business ISDN2 exchange line services	Single transit
Business ISDN30 exchange line services	Termination
Residential local calls	Exchange line services
Residential national calls	Wholesale IDD
Residential calls to mobiles	Local access
Residential operator assisted calls	Asymmetric broadband origination
Residential IDD category A calls	Asymmetric broadband conveyance
Residential IDD category B calls (route-by-route)	Traditional interface line origination
Business local calls	<8 Mbit/s
Business national calls	Traditional interface leased line origination
Business calls to mobiles	8-155 Mbit/s
Business operator assisted calls	Alternative interface leased line origination
Retail low bandwidth leased lines	Leased Lines—trunk segments

Where conditions pertain to the access network (e.g. LLU and wholesale line rental), these are the responsibility of BT Openreach. This is the division of BT now functionally separate pursuant to the undertakings by BT to open this continuing bottleneck in lieu of a reference to the Competition Commission. Among SMP

[239] Review of the retail leased lines, symmetric broadband origination, and wholesale trunk segment markets, Final Statement and Notification, at s 13 (Ofcom, June 2004).
[240] Ibid, at s 17.
[241] Ibid, at Annex F.

conditions imposed on BT were various pricing and margin controls, including originally in both retail and wholesale markets. The limits on wholesale markets are called network charge controls (NCC). Both retail and wholesale controls were based on the RPI+/− x formula used by the UK regulator since price controls were introduced.

After easing the retail price cap formula (to RPI − 0%) as an incentive for meeting various targets, as discussed previously, in 2006 after the 2005 Strategic Review and a specific consultation, Ofcom removed retail price controls.[242] This ended over 20 years of price caps in the retail market. Voluntary assurances by BT were considered sufficient by Ofcom regarding pricing for vulnerable customers, although there remain the requirements under the USO, in any event. There has also been some deregulation of wholesale price and other controls.

After the Telecommunications Strategic Review, Ofcom deregulated the wholesale, narrowband inter-tandem conveyance and transit markets, having found that BT no longer has SMP there.[243] In addition to continuing NCCs for the remaining narrowband wholesale markets, including a revised cost-modelling method that incorporates 21CN components to reflect the ongoing transition to this kind of interconnection, Ofcom continued the other SMP conditions that include the requirement on BT to: notify charges; provide Network Access on reasonable request and for new Network Access; not unduly discriminate; publish a Reference Offer; notify technical information; be transparent as to quality of service; provide Carrier Pre-selection (CPS); provide Indirect Access (or 'Carrier Selection'); provide NTS (Number Translation Service) Call Origination; provide Flat Rate internet Access Call Origination (FRIACO); and have cost accounting systems and accounting separation.

Clearly the imposition of SMP conditions via market reviews and ongoing consultations is a complex and time-consuming process and one that providers are more willing to challenge than under the former regime. As previously mentioned, a recent decision by the Competition Appeal Tribunal illustrates this as well as the clash of different conditions and regulatory duties therewith. In *T-Mobile et al v Ofcom*,[244] numerous parties appealed to the CAT from a decision by Ofcom following a section 185 request to resolve a number of disputes between BT and the mobile network operators (MNOs). This involved the MNO's increased prices for call termination, some before and after BT had had imposed on it the end-to-end connectivity condition discussed above. Although the MNOs had been found to be SMP in their own call termination markets in 2004, Ofcom imposed price controls only on 2G call termination, leaving the 3G charging unregulated. The MNOs notified BT of price increases in 2G mobile call termination that were based on a blended rate of the

---

[242] Explanatory Statement 'Retail Price Controls' (Ofcom, London, 19 July 2006).

[243] Explanatory Statement and Notice of decisions on BT's SMP status and charge controls in narrowband wholesale markets 'Review of BT's Network Control Charges' (Ofcom, London, 18 August 2005).

[244] [2008] CAT 12.

regulated 2G and a 3G rate purportedly based on the pro-rated amount of calls terminated on their 3G networks.[245] The MNOs sought Ofcom's dispute resolution in 2007 when BT refused these increases. Ofcom, however, found that for the period before the end-to-end connectivity condition on BT, although there were price controls on the 2G call termination, there were no *ex ante* controls on the 3G rates.[246] These rates did not fall, therefore, under any *ex ante* regulation; Ofcom refused to take a position inconsistent with its 2004 3G pricing decision. Ofcom further concluded that for the period of the end-to-end connectivity condition, it could not alter the rates unless they failed to meet the 'reasonable' limitation of the condition, the only *ex ante* regulation that applied. Using a 'gains from trade' method, Ofcom found essentially that since BT did not lose money on these transactions or could have passed through the charges to customers to avoid losing money, they were not unreasonable.[247] This was despite the fact that during the period of this investigation Ofcom had imposed on the MNOs progressively lower mobile call termination price controls pursuant to a market review and effective from 1 April 2007 through 2011.[248]

All of the parties appealed the decision with various other intervenors, notably companies who purchase indirect interconnection with the MNOs from BT via transit arrangements and whose pricing would be affected. The CAT ruled in favour of the appellants, finding numerous errors of law by Ofcom. It concluded firstly that Ofcom had erred in failing to consider its broader powers and duties under sections 185 and 188 as a source of *ex ante* regulation whereby it could decide the matter. Ofcom erred in its position that there was only *ex post* competition law and the specific *ex ante* end-to-end connectivity condition already implemented as a basis to act. Rather the CAT concluded that sections 185 to 190 granted Ofcom the power to intervene in access-related matters in parallel with SMP regulation, even on own initiative and to set or modify conditions. Here, Ofcom as well had failed to consider the Article 8 regulatory objectives of the Framework Directive, as set forth in sections 3 and 4 of the Communications Act which should have been central to its determination. It failed to do this in refusing to take into account the likely harm to competition and consumers by virtue of the substantially increased rates for mobile voice call termination, including notably the harm to providers using indirect connectivity whose interests Ofcom did not at all address. The assertion that it had done so in connection with its 2004 findings and regulation was not sufficient consideration, according to the CAT, in light of the fact that considerable time had passed since then and that conditions had changed in that market, as evidenced by Ofcom's own market reviews. Even if this did comprise distinct market *ex ante* regulation,

---

[245] Vodaphone had earlier imposed these blended rates unknown to BT as there was not service cost transparency.
[246] [2008] CAT 12, paras 58–70.
[247] Ibid.
[248] Ibid, at 51.

Ofcom had a duty to consider the position of the parties, the state of the market, and to at least consider the costs as part of its separate regulatory dispute resolution duties under sections 3 and 4.[249] Ofcom was not bound to set a price that was based on the costs of providing the service. However, in disregarding entirely the relationship between such costs and prices, the CAT concluded that Ofcom had drawn too rigid a boundary between the exercise of its SMP and dispute resolution powers, assuming that only by virtue of a full market review could it consider these at all instead of perhaps allowing it to contribute to a conclusion that these prices were not reasonable. Further due to these boundaries between the different regulatory powers, although Ofcom posited that it acted with regulatory consistency, it further erred in not considering the need to be consistent with its 2007 SMP findings.[250]

Finally, the CAT considered that Ofcom had erred in applying an overly narrow construction of 'reasonable' under the end-to-end connectivity condition and in applying in connection therewith the gains from trade test.[251] This measure is not appropriate to test reasonableness. Ofcom either presumed in certain circumstances that BT would be content not to make a profit or to pass through enhanced costs to consumers as long as it did not make a loss. As Ofcom considered that consumer protection came from relevant market reviews and SMP conditions, it did not consider this relevant here despite the fact that numerous of the proposed increases, the H3G's especially, were indeed high, and possibly risked infringing both UK and EU competition law, including Article 82. Equally, the CAT found that the high rates put fixed-line consumers at a disadvantage to consumers of the MNOs as well as BT and the indirect connectivity fixed-line providers at a competitive disadvantage. Upholding the appeals as well founded, the CAT concluded that further evidence was needed to set the disputed rates and issue directions to Ofcom.[252]

Ironically, the CAT noted that the evidence it needed would be evidence that could overlap with challenges to Ofcom's 2007 Statement presently before the Competition Commission and that care would have to be taken not to prejudge that other investigation,[253] another example of the layered complexity here and the growing similarity with the US market with vast numbers of parties lined up on each side of the seemingly perpetual challenges to the FCC's regulatory measures.

(iv) Privileged operator

The final of the section 45 specific conditions relate to public communications providers that enjoy special or exclusive rights in connection with the provision of any non-communications services (section 77(2)).[254] Conditions to ensure transparency and that services are provided without cross-subsidies from the privileged business

---

[249] Ibid, at paras 175, 184–187.
[250] Ibid, at paras 107–113.
[251] Ibid, at paras 115–127.
[252] Ibid, at paras 194–199.
[253] Ibid, at para 196.
[254] This is not the case where this is solely in connection with associated facilities.

must be applied but are not mandated where revenues in connection with all communications activities are less than £50 million (section 77(4)). The conditions that must be applied to privileged operators may include:

i. requiring the provider to whom it applies to keep separate accounts in relation to his public electronic communications network or public electronic communications service and other matters;

ii. requiring the provider to submit the accounts of the different parts of his undertaking, and any financial report relating to a part of that undertaking, to a qualified auditor;

iii. requiring the accounts of the different parts of the undertaking to be published; and

iv. securing, by means other than separate accounts, the structural separation of the different parts of the undertaking (section 77(3)).

Ofcom does not appear to have made any designations of 'privileged operators'.

7.4.4.4 *Rights of access to install facilities: The Electronic Communications Code*

Rights to access private and public land to install and maintain electronic communications apparatus may be granted by Ofcom under the Electronic Communications Code (Code). Those eligible to seek a direction granting Code powers are providers of electronic communications networks and of conduit systems to be used by network providers (section 106(4)), such as water, gas, or transportation providers, or even local authorities that wish to make their infrastructure available for this purpose.[255] As noted by Ofcom:

the Code is designed to ensure that Code operators can deploy their networks rapidly, maintain them, and repair them as and when they need to do so without needing to seek specific authorisations. In the absence of the powers that Code operators benefit from, the ability for them to maintain their networks would be diminished and this would be of detriment to anyone using communications services of any description.[256]

Ofcom is charged with maintaining a public register of those providers to whom Code powers have been applied (section 108).[257] There are approximately 150 Code operators. As noted in a 2005 consultation, the vast majority had previously held code powers under the former regime (retained by virtue of the deeming provisions under Schedule 18 of the Communications Act).[258] While the new EU framework required this rights of way regime to be modified to address the regulatory expansion

---

[255] The Act defines 'conduit' to include 'a tunnel, subway, tube or pipe', s 106(7).

[256] Consultation 'Administrative charges for the electronic communications code: A change for Ofcom's charging principles at s 1.2 (12 December 2005).

[257] The register can be found at: <http://www.ofcom.org.uk/telecoms/ioi/e_c_c/cp_reg>.

[258] See Consultation, above n 256.

to all electronic communications networks and the elimination of individual licences within which Code powers were previously granted, the Code is substantively essentially unchanged from that which existed before the Communications Act 2003. To make the changes that it did effect, the Act primarily amended Schedule 2 of the Telecommunications Act 1984 that contains what was previously referred to as the 'Telecommunications Code'.[259]

To get a grant of code powers, a provider of networks or conduit systems for networks must now make a stand-alone application[260] to Ofcom that must contain the following:

- the identifying details and address of the provider which if a company, includes company number, the registered office and details of any subsidiaries, parents, and affiliates;

- a description of the electronic communications network or the system of conduits which the applicant intends to provide, including its location;

- the reasons for seeking Code powers and an explanation of why the network or conduit system could not practicably be provided otherwise;

- the purpose for which the network or system will be used, e.g., the type of service(s) and those likely to benefit; if a conduit system, written evidence of its availability for use by networks, evidence of the applicant's ability and willingness to share apparatus;

- a description of alternative arrangements to Code powers which have been sought, if any.[261]

Guidance indicates that the need for the grant should be evident from the provider's business plan, suggesting that one must be part of the application.[262] The applicant must also provide evidence of ability to meet fiscal liabilities under the Act, including letters from potential guarantors or company directors indicating willingness to ensure such arrangements are in place.[263] These information requirements are clearly related to those considerations Ofcom is required to consider by the Act in granting Code powers: the benefit of the network or system to the public, the practicality of providing the network or system without Code powers, the need to encourage sharing of apparatus, and the applicant's abilities to meet liabilities from the application

---

[259] See s 106(2), Sch 3 of the Communications Act 2003.

[260] Those who held a grant of Code powers under a PTO licence or another individual licence are deemed to have Code powers without the need for a new application. See Statement DGT, 'Statement: The Granting of Electronic Communications Code by the Director General of Telecommunications', 2.4 (10 October 2003).

[261] DGT, 'Notification under Section 107(2) of the Communications Act 2003: Requirements with respect to the content of an application for a direction applying the Electronic Communications Code and the manner in which such application is to be made' (10 October 2003).

[262] Statement, n 260 above, at s 9.

[263] Ibid.

of the Code and from the provider's conduct relating to matters under the Code (section 107(4)(a)–(d)). These, however, need to be balanced with the EU regulatory principles which include the need to promote competition. An example of the possible tension between the economic and social policies that underlie these mandatory factors is where Code powers are sought to facilitate the roll-out of alternative infrastructure presumed to promote competition and make access to new service available but where the building of that infrastructure will require significant highway disruptions and infrastructure sharing might alleviate this.[264]

As with the prior procedures, Ofcom must advertise that an application has been made and allow for consultation by interested parties. While all providers are eligible to apply, providers of essentially private networks are unlikely to be granted Code powers.[265] A preference will be given to those providers who are willing and able to share apparatus, but the inability or unwillingness is not a bar to the grant.

There is an administrative charge associated with a successful application and an annual charge to be paid, reflecting respectively the costs of processing the application and maintaining and administering the Code.[266] These are currently set at a £10,000 one-time charge for the application and a £1,000 annual charge as of 2006/2007.[267] No charge is made to unsuccessful applicants and the annual charge, as of 2005, reflects the cost of administering all grants of code powers to an undertaking. Ofcom found that its costs were largely related to the scheme as a whole rather than attributable meaningfully to any individual operator, some of which due to historical reasons had multiple grants of code powers.[268] Under the prior regulatory regime, there was no separate charge for Code powers which were granted only in connection with a licence, most commonly to PTOs. It has been suggested that this separate charging reflects not only a true 'licence fee' as previously discussed based on regulatory costs but also a measure to ensure that use of the public resources is by those that will maximize the benefit. It may cause providers to evaluate critically their need for code powers.[269]

The grant of Code powers is a personal benefit and may not be assigned to a third party.[270] The grant may, as per the Communications Act 2003, be limited geographically. This will be determined on a case-by-case basis and will likely be limited to circumstances dictated by the needs of the network, such as where the business plan indicates it is largely based on leased lines or that application of the Code is needed to facilitate only minor interconnections or installations.

---

[264] See Statement, n 260 above at 2.57 (noting the factors that will be considered in this balancing).
[265] Ibid, at s 9.
[266] These are authorized by s 36(1)(d) of the Communications Act 2003.
[267] Ibid.
[268] See Consultation, n 256 above.
[269] See section 7.2.2 above. Indeed, a significant number of code operators have requested that their code powers be revoked. See the 20 Directions revoking these at the A-Z Document List. <http://www.ofcom.org.uk/atoz/?letter=D&publication=All&sector=All>.
[270] Statement, n 260 above at 2.17.

The application of Code powers provides the following benefits to the grantee:

- simplified compliance with planning requirements due to exemptions for 'permitted development' under the Town and Country Planning framework;[271]
- the power to install apparatus in the streets without a 'street works' licence;
- the ability to obtain a court ordered right to enter private land and install, maintain, or remove apparatus if private negotiations have failed and upon proper notice by the provider.[272]

Regulations that replace the former licence conditions and restrictions have been promulgated by the Secretary of State in consultation with Ofcom and interested parties, pursuant to the Act. These, *inter alia*, detail requirements for providers exercising Code powers as regards works in connection with local planning. They are essentially unchanged from the former licence conditions. An example of their interaction with the planning regime, for example, is that while the installation of most apparatus does not require even notice to local planning authority under 'general permitted development order' or 'GDPO', the Regulations require a month's notice to local planning authorities and compliance with their reasonable conditions where the provider has not previously installed apparatus in the area or plans to install certain sized cabinets and boxes that don't require planning permission.[273] The Regulations also provide for notice to local planning authorities of 56 days, and other compliance requirements for works in connection with listed buildings and ancient monuments, conservation, and other protected areas.[274] The conditions imposed by the Regulations seek to minimize the aesthetic, environmental, and functional impact of the installation appropriate to the public or private land on which it is installed[275] by, for example requiring underground installations to be deep enough so as not to interfere with its use, such as agricultural land. They also require coordination between providers and others installing utilities[276] or coordinating public works such as highway and road authorities. They also impose inspection and maintenance obligations for safety to persons and property.[277]

The Regulations provide a more detailed procedure for 'funding liabilities' than the former licence conditions. These involve an annual section 16 certification

---

[271] See Part 24 of the Town and Country Planning, England and Wales (General Permitted Development) Order 1995, SI 1995/418 as amended. Planning (General Development) (Amendment) Order (Northern Ireland) 2003 SR No 98., Town and Country Planning (General Permitted Development) (Scotland) Amendment (No 2) Order 2001 SSI 2001/266.

[272] Telecommunications Act 1984, Sch 2 at s 5. For model notices, see <http://www.ofcom.org.uk/ telecoms/ioi/e_c_c/notices/models/>.

[273] The Electronic Communications Code (Conditions and Restrictions) Regulations 2003 (SI 2003/ 2553) s 5.

[274] Ibid, at ss 6, 7, 8.

[275] See, e.g. ibid, at s 3.

[276] Ibid, at s 14.

[277] Ibid, at s 10.

on 1 April by the provider, if an individual, or its board detailing amounts available and the procedures that permitted this representation to be made.[278] This also details 'relevant events' for requiring the availability of these funds, including a specified insolvency level.[279] Providers that have not exercised their code powers are to provide this certification two weeks prior to doing so. Ofcom maintains a list of providers that have filed such certifications.

This enhanced ability to enforce conditions for meeting obligations tracks enhanced powers to enforce Code conditions that the Act accords Ofcom. Under the 1984 Act, there were no powers for Oftel to take any specific action in response to a breach of a Code condition. The rationale was that such breaches would likely be in violation of private rights actionable in the courts or comprise breaches of other statutes such as unauthorized street works.[280] The Communications Act 2003, however, authorizes Ofcom to impose progressive but proportionate penalties, including financial, under procedures that are virtually identical for breach of other conditions as already described (see 'privileged operator' above). Suspension of the Code application to a provider is possible for repeated and serious contraventions of the Regulations but not for existing parts of the network or conduit system (section 113(4)(5)). Suspensions of Code powers can be imposed for suspensions of authorizations to provide networks (section 113(2)) or repeated, uncorrected failures to pay the administrative charge (section 113(1)). These would appear to apply to the entire network.

Absent such suspension, or revocation of the Code by request of the provider, the grant is considered to exist as long as the provider of the network or conduit system continues to do so.

7.4.4.5 *Rights to use spectrum*

In the UK, spectrum use is regulated under the Wireless Telegraphy Act 2006.[281] As noted by Ofcom, this Act brings together in one statute the legislation under which Ofcom manages radio spectrum, replacing, including by consolidating, six pieces of legislation prior applicable enactments, and repealing others.[282] Effective 8 February 2007, this Act replaces the Wireless Telegraphy Acts 1949, 1967, and 1998, the Marine etc Broadcasting (Offences) Act 1967, Part 6 of the Telecommunications Act

---

[278] According to Ofcom, the annual certificate shall, in the case of a company state: that in the Code Operator's Board's reasonable opinion, the Code Operator has fulfilled its duty to put funds in place in compliance with the Regulations, and shall state the systems and processes which enabled the Board to form that opinion; and the amount of funds which have been provided for. The certificate should be accompanied by a copy of the relevant instrument which will provide the funds.

[279] Ibid, at s 16.

[280] Ibid.

[281] 2006 ch 36.

[282] 'Consolidation of Legislation: the Wireless Telegraphy Act' (Ofcom, London, 2007), <http://www.ofcom.org.uk/radiocomms/ifi/wtact2006/>.

1984, and certain provisions of the Communications Act 2003 regarding the regulatory obligations with respect to the management of spectrum.[283]

7.4.4.5.1 The Act's scope and grant of powers

As with the prior acts, all persons must still be licensed to install and or use radio equipment.[284] It is an offence[285] to do so unless subject to an exception under the Act (section 8(3)) as specified in the Wireless Telegraphy (Exemption) Regulations 2003 as amended.[286] The Communications Act 2003 did not make major changes to the wireless telegraphy licensing regime but rather some adjustments to bring it into conformity with the new EU Framework and the new UK regulatory structure. The Act, however, transferred the power to manage spectrum from the Secretary of State to Ofcom.[287]

With only very limited exceptions, the new Wireless Telegraphy Act 2006 has exactly the same effect as the legislation it replaces, including various provisions of the Communications Act 2003. Thus, the following comprises a discussion of powers and duties originally granted under the latter that are now largely in the 2006 Act. References, therefore, will be to the Communications Act 2003 first, followed by the commensurate section in the WTA 2006.

7.4.4.5.2 Ofcom's Spectrum Management Duties

Under the Act, Ofcom now has the duty to develop and publish the UK Frequency Authorization Plan identifying what frequencies are allocated to a particular purpose and which are available for licensing[288] in the UK within the internationally agreed framework for spectrum allocation, i.e. the Radio Regulations of the International Telecommunications Union.[289] The Act requires Ofcom in making these determinations of spectrum management, to consider its availability for use, current and future demand, and the objectives of promoting: efficient management and use; economic and other benefits that may derive from its use; innovative services and competition in electronic communications services (section 154; WTA, section 3); the apparent

[283] See Joint Committee on Consolidation of Bills, First Report of Session 2005–2006 'Wireless Telegraphy Bill [HL], Vol II Minutes of Proceedings and Minutes of Evidence (House of Lords, House of Commons, London, 23 May 2006).

[284] Ibid, at s 8. A licence under the Broadcast Act may need to be obtained for certain TV and radio broadcasters.

[285] Ibid, at s 35. 1. See *R v Blake* [1997] 1 Cr App R 209.

[286] SI 2003/74. These are routinely updated. See, e.g. Wireless Telegraphy (Exemption)(Amendment) Regulations 2006 (SI 2006/2994). For a summary list of exempt uses see Annex 1, Licensing Policy Manual (Ofcom, 2007), <http://www.ofcom.org.uk/radiocomms/ifi/licensing_policy_manual_2/>.

[287] The Secretary still has residual powers to consult on policy and make a direction or order, in consultation with Ofcom and other persons, concerning reserving spectrum for specified uses and licensing exemptions and charges. Communications Act 2003, ss 156, 157; Wireless Telegraphy Act 2006, ss 1–5.

[288] Communications Act 2003, s 153; WTA 2006, s 2. The Frequency Authorisation Plan is available online at: <http://www.ofcom.org.uk/static/archive/ra/topics/eudirectives/fap/fapsearch.htm>.

[289] See Chapter 15, at 15.3.

implementation of the Framework Directive's mandate to ensure efficient use while operating under its overarching regulatory objectives.[290]

Where Ofcom determines to limit the allocation of certain spectrum frequencies due to their scarcity, the Act requires Ofcom to publish the criteria it will use to determine the number of available licences and the category of persons to whom they will be made available.[291] The criteria must be objectively justified, proportionate to the use, objective, and non-discriminatory in keeping with the requirements of the Framework Directive. The Act mandates a presumption, however, for the use without licence of equipment that will not produce undue interference,[292] implementing the Authorization Directive's requirement that rights to use spectrum be made under a general authorization wherever possible especially where harmful interference is unlikely to occur.[293]

7.4.4.5.3 Grants of recognized spectrum access

The Act creates an entirely new 'grant of recognized spectrum access' (RSA) (section 159) (WTA 2006, section 18). Persons using radio equipment (a station or apparatus) where a licence is not required but where transmissions occur within the UK may apply for such grant. Ofcom is to consider an RSA to the same extent as it would consider an existing licence when it allocates spectrum (section 160)(WTA 2006, section 20). Thus, Ofcom has indicated its intent to limit the levels of licensed emissions into spectrum and geographical areas covered by RSAs, as it would with licensed grants.[294] The RSA may be given for any use specified in the grant (WTA, section 3), and subject to any conditions that Ofcom may consider appropriate,[295] including for strength of signal and equipment, but cannot duplicate any conditions

---

[290] See 2002/21/EC, Art 8. In addition to the Act's specific inclusion here of these factors, the Art 8 factors are imposed on Ofcom generally to meet Community obligations in s 4 of the Communications Act.

[291] Communications Act 2003, s 164; WTA 2006, s 29. See also, The Wireless Telegraphy (Limitation of Number of Licences) (Amendment) Order 2006, SI 2006/2786; The Wireless Telegraphy (Limitation of Number of Licences) Order 2003, SI 2003/1902.

[292] Communications Act 2003, s 166; WTA 2006, s 8. While, previously stated policy indicated an intent not to exempt frequency that could have a change of use in the foreseeable future due to the difficulties associated with reallocating an exempt use where little if any data was available on who and where it was being used, Licensing Policy Manual (Radiocommunications Agency, July 2003), this has changed markedly with much broader exempt usage having been so classified, see Wireless Telegraphy (Exemption)(Amendment) Regulations 2008 (SI 2008/236, 6 February 2008), and Ofcom committed to exempting wherever possible. See 'Licensing Exemption', Licensing Policy Manual (Ofcom, 2007), <http://www.ofcom.org.uk/radiocomms/ifi/licensing_policy_manual_2/>.

[293] See 7.4.2 above.

[294] Statement 'Spectrum Framework Review for the Public Sector: Extending market mechanisms to improve how spectrum is managed and used', s 2.8 (Ofcom, London, 31 January 2008).

[295] The Communications Act referred to 'equipment' rather than 'use'. See s 159(2). RSAs and conditions could not, however, constrain the uses of public sector agencies, such as the Ministry of Defence. See Consultation, 'Spectrum Framework Review for the Public Sector: Notice of Ofcom's Proposal to make regulations on Recognized Spectrum Access for public bodies and consultation on technical conditions', s 4.7 (Ofcom, London, 20 June 2008).

that are already imposed under general conditions The Act provides for the grant to be converted to a licence or a licence to a grant.[296]

That RSA conditions could be also imposed under a general condition indicate that the Act here contemplates an exempt or similar use in the nature of a general authorization and where the exempt user might wish to preserve such use in future allocations. This is reinforced by the Act's reference to spectrum emissions originating from within the UK (section 159(1); WTA 2006, section 18(2)). Such a grant effectively reserving that particular usage might be sought by government agencies[297] whose spectrum use is currently largely 'licensed' only by a voluntary agreement called a 'side letter'[298] or providers of networks using equipment that is exempt from licensing as its risk of harmful interference is small, such as Wi-Fi.[299] Indeed, since 2007 Ofcom has been consulting on tradeability of RSAs for public sector entities.[300] As public entities hold a significant allocation of spectrum estimated to have a value of over £20 billion, Ofcom is seeking ways to improve its management and efficient use, including by such mechanisms as trading and licensing of traded RSAs where possible as part of its overall spectrum policy reforms. A consultation has begun on regulations and an order for the first band of public sector spectrum (from the MOD which holds 75 per cent of public sector spectrum) to be made subject to trading or converted to licences.[301]

With RSAs, the Act also contemplates unlicensed uses because they are outside the reach of the Wireless Telegraphy Act. The references to emissions from outside the UK (section 159(1)) as well as the use of a 'station' suggests a satellite operator whose emissions originate from orbit but which is not, itself, operating the receiving station. Although outside of the UK's licensing jurisdiction under the Wireless Telegraphy Act, this operator might wish to ensure continued frequency availability and interference minimization. Here, conditions would only be imposed under the grant notification procedures. The Wireless Telegraphy (Register)(Amendment) Regulations 2007 provide for the inclusion of RSA grants in the registry created by Ofcom to enable the spectrum of trading for whenever RSA trading is implemented.[302]

Radio astronomy was identified as a use where RSAs could be valuable to help limit interference. In 2007, Ofcom issued regulations for the granting of RSAs in

---

[296] Communications Act 2003, s 162; WTA 2006, s 27.

[297] This is limited to Crown bodies. That the Act contemplates this purpose for RSA is reinforced by the authorization to Crown agencies to pay for, *inter alia*, recognized grants of spectrum use. See Communications Act 2003, s 163; WTA 2006, s 28.

[298] This would seem a fairly unique UK example of a contract for a licence. See Licensing Policy Manual, Authorisation of radio use for Crown Bodies (Ofcom, 2007); <http://www.ofcom.org.uk/radiocomms/ifi/licensing_policy_manual_2/crown>.

[299] Ofcom Licensing Policy Manual, 'Licence Exemption' (Ofcom, London, 2004).

[300] See, generally, Statement, n 294 above.

[301] Consultation, 'Spectrum Framework Review for the Public Sector: Notice of Ofcom's Proposal to make regulations on Recognized Spectrum Access for public bodies and consultation on technical conditions' (Ofcom, London, 20 June 2008).

[302] SI 2007/38.

connection with radio astronomy uses in existing bands and in the six locations where presently carried out.[303]

The Act provides for charging for RSAs, including by auction.[304] Ofcom has issued initial regulations in connection with the radio astronomy RSA regulations regarding charges to be paid for RSAs which can vary according to the nature of the use and the frequency bands involved.[305] For example, for radio astronomy, Ofcom determined that it was appropriate to charge fees set by Administrative Incentive Pricing (AIP) based on the opportunity cost of denying the spectrum to alternative services. Thus, the opportunity costs for radio astronomy RSAs involving spectrum bands within which the alternative use would be broadcasting shared the AIP would involve fees comparable to broadcast uses, etc.[306]

7.4.4.5.4 Spectrum grants by auction and trading: market mechanisms and liberalization

The power to allocate spectrum licences and, now, RSAs by auction was introduced by the Wireless Telegraphy Act 1998.[307] The Communications Act 2003 modified this to add some flexibility to permit different payment methods, including by instalments.[308] This could enable Ofcom to moderate in future spectrum auctions any financial hardships created by large sums that spectrum auctions such as 3G have generated,[309] or allow new entrants to a market to pay for licences from future revenue streams, an approach that the US has recently taken in certain auctions.

The Communication Act's authority to Ofcom to introduce spectrum trading was one of the major new spectrum provisions. Phased implementation of spectrum trading combined with a program of increasing liberalization of spectrum via de-licensing bands and/or uses of compliant equipment as well as the removal of conditions specifying uses so that traded spectrum can be put to new uses comprises Ofcom's primary approach to spectrum management. After extensive study and consultation, Ofcom concluded that the traditional, top-down, command and control means of regulating spectrum did not promote efficient and effective use. Rather, full or partial trading of spectrum and the auction of returned bands or incentive-based pricing would facilitate such efficiency and effectiveness by allowing the spectrum to be transferred to and used by the user that valued it the most.[310] Starting in 2004,

---

[303] Statement on Regulations for Recognised Spectrum Access as applied to Radio Astronomy (Ofcom, London, 28 February 2007).

[304] Communications Act 2003, s 161; WTA 2006, ss 21, 23.

[305] Wireless Telegraphy (Recognised Spectrum Access Charges) Regulations 2007, SI 2007/392.

[306] See Consultation 'Notice of Ofcom's proposal to make regulations for Recognised Spectrum Access (RSA) for radio astronomy', ss 5.38–5.60 (Ofcom, London, 10 November 2006).

[307] Wireless Telegraphy Act 1998, s 3, ch 6.

[308] Communications Act 2003, s 167.

[309] Although, the desirability or need for doing this is counterbalanced by the likelihood that this hardship may have been self-imposed according to the previously discussed research that suggests intentional overbidding by 2G incumbents to pre-empt the market. See section 7.2.3.1, above.

[310] Statement 'A Statement on Spectrum Trading: Implementation in 2004 and beyond' (Ofcom, London, 6 August 2004).

it began a process of identifying classes of spectrum licences within which trading could take place, as well as liberalization that it expects to continue through 2012.

The Wireless Telegraphy (Spectrum Trading) Regulations 2004 set out the scope and procedures for spectrum trading.[311] Regulation 4(1) permits a licensee to transfer all rights and obligations under certain classes of wireless telegraphy licences applicable to equipment operating within frequency bands specified for that class in the Schedule, subject to certain exceptions and requiring application to and consent of Ofcom. Transfers include licences for the Public Mobile Operator, Private Business Radio (National, Regional), Common Base Station Operator, Fixed Wireless and Broadband Fixed Wireless, Point-to-Point Fixed Links, and Scanning Telemetry classes.

Regulation 6 authorizes the transfer of partial rights to spectrum (e.g. geographically, certain bands, partial channels) for certain licence classes and bands specified for that type of partial transfer. For example, the Fixed Wireless Access (including point-to-multipoint systems) and Broadband Fixed Wireless Access classes are permitted for spectrum apportioned by geographic area.

Two kinds of transfers are permitted: transfers of all rights and obligations from the transferor to the transferee, and transfers of rights and obligations that are concurrent to both the transferor and the transferee.[312] To enable and encourage spectrum trading, Ofcom has invited applications to change its approved use in connection with trading of rights, one avenue of its spectrum liberalization reforms.

Exceptions to the ability to trade spectrum include failure to pay the charges for the licence, lack of consent of any licensee/transferee, where Ofcom has given notice of revocation of the licence, and also where Ofcom has not yet consented to the transfer or made a requested variation or revocation of the licence.[313] If necessary or expedient, Ofcom can refuse consent in the interests of national security, compliance with EU and international obligations, or pursuant to an order of the Secretary of State under the Communications Act 2003's spectrum policy powers under sections 5 and 156.

In deciding whether to give consent, Ofcom may consider whether: the licensee is in violation of the terms of the licence; all the parties have consented; the transferee is able to meet the conditions and obligations of the licence as well as any criteria for persons to whom a licence of that class may be issued; and, in the case of partial transfers, whether the transfer hinders the ability of the transferor to meet the terms and limitations of the licence to be granted with the transfer.

There is an information requirement, including that to assist Ofcom in making the above determinations. When Ofcom determines that it has this information, it is to publish a notice of the transfer application, including the licence class and number, the parties' names, the date of its information determination, and, if a partial

---

[311] SI 2004/3154.
[312] Ibid, at ss 4 (1),(2) and 6.
[313] See ibid, at s 7.

spectrum transfer, a description of the rights to be transferred. On consent, the old licence is to be surrendered and a new licence issued to either the transferee in the case of a full transfer or to both parties in the case of concurrent rights and obligations.[314] There are currently no charges associated with a spectrum trade.

7.4.4.5.5 The spectrum licence

Spectrum licences are generally organized under a sector/class/system categorization scheme. The sector is a high level descriptor of the service sector the licence is intended to be used for; the class is a more particularized kind of service descriptor within that sector. The licence can be further narrowed to the particular system. Thus, for example, a licence could fall under Aeronautical/Radionavigation/Ground-based augmentation systems or Aeronautical/Aircraft/Transportable. This will usually dictate which schedules are attached to the sector/class licence.[315]

All licences for spectrum comprise the licence document granting the authority to a named person,[316] the terms and conditions, and a schedule or schedules. The licence document contains the licensee's name and address, the licence prefix number by sector/class/product, and its issue/start and renewal dates.

Ofcom has produced a generic set of 'Wireless Telegraphy General Licensing Conditions'[317] that is now attached to many classes of licence. This comprises seven conditions including:

- that the licence has effect until surrendered or revoked by Ofcom;
- that revocation is limited to a breach of condition, failure to pay fees, a breach of the trading regulations, national security, or Community/international obligations;
- a ban on transfer of the licence (while noting that rights and obligations under certain licences can be transferred pursuant to the trading regulations);
- the right of equipment access and inspection by Ofcom;
- the ability of Ofcom, on individual or class notice, to shut down, modify, or restrict the use of the radio equipment, permanently or temporarily, in whole or part, for breach of condition or causing/contributing to undue interference to the authorized use of other radio equipment;
- the obligation to construct and use the relevant radio equipment in accordance with the licence schedules and varied only with Ofcom's advance permission and after licence amendment/reissue;
- that the radio equipment is use only by authorized persons aware of the licence compliance obligations.

---

[314] Ibid, s 8(5).
[315] See Licensing Policy Manual, 'Different Classes of Licence' (Ofcom, London, 2007), <http://www.ofcom.org.uk/radiocomms/ifi/licensing_policy_manual_2/different_classes>.
[316] Ibid, at 'Persons who may be licensed', <http://www.ofcom.org.uk/radiocomms/ifi/licensing_policy_manual_2/who>.
[317] OF195 'Wireless Telegraphy General Licence Conditions Booklet' (Ofcom, London, February 2007), <http://www.ofcom.org.uk/radiocomms/ifi/wtf/#WTGLCBl>.

Other licences have either a separate booklet of conditions, such as Citizen's Band radio, or the conditions, generally including the above, are within the licence documents.[318] Ofcom has published templates for many licences.[319]

Schedules are attached according to the technical requirements of the service or services, with some licences having many services and, therefore, many schedules attached.[320] There are standard clauses defining the rules of use for all systems within the class and addressing such things as apparatus, inspection, and interpretation.[321] Individual clauses specifying the frequencies that may be used may be added to the schedules as well as a requirement for compliance with technical and operational conditions under an 'interface' requirement such as a block edge mask for in-block power or out of band emissions.[322] With complex systems involving hundreds of services, the licence can be many hundred pages long.

All wireless telegraphy licences currently fall within one of three types: 'pre-packaged', 'custom', or 'spectrum.'[323] Pre-packaged licences involve standard licences for uses and equipment with preset frequencies that typically do not require individual coordination or allocations, although this is not always the case. The licences are fairly simple and the fees typically low, flat rates to cover administrative costs, although there is the possibility for administrative incentive pricing which is a 'cost +' pricing to create financial incentives for spectrum to be utilized well under Ofcom's spectrum management policies. Certain Private Business Radio licences covering a range of shared frequency applications are examples of pre-packaged licences.

A customized licence may require coordination with other users to minimize interference or an individual allocation of frequency. An example of a use requiring this is fixed terrestrial (point-to-point) links, where the length of the link and its traffic capacity dictates the frequency assigned, with lower frequency bands reserved for longer, higher capacity links.[324] A customized licence might require a site visit to examine the physical characteristics of the location and equipment to be used. Fees can vary according to the spectrum used, geographical coverage, and other factors such as the number of stations, channels, and other users.

---

[318] See, e.g. The Aeronautical/Aircraft (Transportable) Licence, <http://www.ofcom.org.uk/radiocomms/ifi/wtf/#Aeronautical>.

[319] See Wireless Telegraphy Act Licenses (Terms, Provisions and Limitations), <http://www.ofcom.org.uk/radiocomms/ifi/wtf/>.

[320] See Licensing Policy Manual, 'What is a licence?' (Ofcom, London 2007), <http://www.ofcom.org.uk/radiocomms/ifi/licensing_policy_manual_2/what_is>.

[321] See ibid.

[322] See Manual, n 320 above.

[323] There are proposals for a revised Business Radio Licence scheme that would have a somewhat simplified framework also, however, with three kinds of licences that basically track the above groupings but which are more harmonized where possible and with greater built-in flexibilities.

[324] See Fixed Terrestrial and Satellite Links Licensing Procedure Manual (Radiocommunications Agency), <http://www.ofcom.org.uk/static/archive/ra/topics/fixedlnk/publictns/fixdlnkp-p/fixdlnkp-p.htm>.

Finally, the 'spectrum' licence is one that authorizes a whole block of spectrum usually for large geographical areas and that is used according to the licensee's determination, subject to conditions.[325] Correlated with the increasing complexity of these licences is the increasing complexity of the licences' procedures, time frames for their allocation, as well as the size of the fees, some which are determined at auction.

Prior guidelines indicated that licences for the simplest category take five days from submission of a completed application; 15 to 25 days for the second where no site inspection or international coordination was required, with most completed within 15 days.[326] These clearly meet the time frames of the Authorization Directive for the granting of rights of spectrum use that require a decision within six weeks for spectrum previously allocated for specific purposes within the national frequency plan.[327] This limit is without prejudice to where international agreements apply; the prior guidance suggested international coordination required up to 60 days.

Some licences under the final category involving whole blocks of spectrum indicated primarily as involving public networks may be awarded through licence auctions.[328] The Directive permits the six-week period here to be extended by up to eight months.[329]

7.4.4.5.6 A lack of transparency and effective consultation?

There is a Wireless Telegraphy Licence Policy Manual that explains licensing, transferring and variation procedures, terms and conditions, fees, and renewals for virtually all licence categories and classes. There are also some guidance notes, licence templates and general conditions booklets, and standard schedules available.[330] These, plus the numerous consultation documents and notices marking Ofcom's ongoing spectrum policy review and reform implementation, would appear formally to comply with the Framework and Authorization Directive's requirements for transparent and objective procedures, and proportionate and objectively justified conditions, given the complexity of the area, the numbers of licences, the technical nature of the conditions, as well as the need for individual conditions for particular systems.[331]

However, the information requirements necessary to achieve effective transparency of the UK spectrum licensing policies and procedures are great given the vast and technical nature of the spectrum management policy reforms that Ofcom has to

---

[325] See Licensing Policy Manual, n 320 above.
[326] Licensing Policy Manual (Radiocommunications Agency, July 2003)
[327] 2002/20/EC, Art 7(3).
[328] See, e.g. Public Mobile Operator for Cellular Radiotelephones (UMTS) 3G, UK Plan for Frequency Authorisation, <http://www.ofcom.org.uk/static/archive/ra/topics/eudirectives/fap/fapsearch.htm>.
[329] See 2002/20/EC, Art 7.
[330] See Spectrum, Information for Radiocommunications Licences: Wireless Telegraphy Act Licences (Terms, Provisions and Limitations), <http://www.ofcom.org.uk/radiocomms/ifi/wtf/>.
[331] Ofcom's website, however, remains a difficult one to negotiate for even an informed user.

date planned and implemented. To do this, since 2004, Ofcom has been engaged in a detailed and multilayered series of spectrum reviews and followed by the phased reform implementations, all with varying rounds of consultations, regulatory impact assessments, statements, and notifications required *inter alia* by the Framework Directive. Tracking developments can be a complex exercise even for an informed party. One example can be found in Ofcom's programme pursuant to the Communications Act 2003 charge that exempt spectrum usage is not likely to cause undue interference, Since then, Ofcom has progressively exempted equipment compliant with technical specifications for non-interfering use, this rather than additional exempt spectrum bands being Ofcom's preferred method for broader exempt uses. These exemptions have required a vast amount of secondary legislation (with all the preparatory consultations, etc.).[332]

Similar complexity exists in Ofcom's parallel reforms processes and consultations on a broad set of reforms to business radio class licences that will be implemented during 2008–2009. Ofcom recently published notice of its intent to put in place, by August 2008, the necessary legislation to do so.[333] These changes encompass all aspects of Ofcom's new spectrum management policies: simplification of licences (from 21 to 5 licence classes[334]), liberalization and technological neutrality (a limited set of equipment requirements especially for the three 'light' licence classes permitting market use determination), liberalization and spectrum trading (trading, at least partial, within all classes, including for new uses), and revised charging to enhance spectrum use efficiency (administrative incentive pricing varied according to a range of factors including demand, population density, sole or shared use, etc.), and harmonization of existing licences within the new formats. At the end of the day, this will be an effective, streamlined, and liberalized system for a vast array of business applications supported by a new licensing and fee payment computer system to implement it. However, despite the accomplishment and the online publication of the many documents, their full accessibility is limited by a poorly organized website that fails to track issues effectively by topic, Also, one must credit concerns that often Ofcom consultations seem fairly narrowly focused with

---

[332] The Wireless Telegraphy (Exemption) Regulations 2003 (SI 2003/74); The Wireless Telegraphy (Ultra-Wideband Equipment) (Exemption) Regulations 2007 (SI 2007/2084); The Wireless Telegraphy (Ultra-Wideband Equipment) (Exemption) (Amendment) Regulations 2007 (SI 2007/2440); The Wireless Telegraphy (Exemption) (Amendment) Regulations 2006 (SI 2006/2994); The Wireless Telegraphy (Radio Frequency Identification Equipment) (Exemption) (Amendment) Regulations 2007 (SI 2007/1282); Wireless Telegraphy (Radio Frequency Identification Equipment) (Exemption) Regulations 2005 (SI 2005/3471); The Wireless Telegraphy (Automotive Short Range Radar) (Exemption) Regulations 2005 (SI 2005/353); The Wireless Telegraphy (Automotive Short Range Radar) (Exemption) (No 2) Regulations 2005 (SI 2005/1585).

[333] Statutory Notice 'Notice of Ofcom's proposals to make Wireless Telegraphy Regulations: Relating to Business Radio licences' (Ofcom, London, 9 June 2008).

[334] These comprise Business Radio (Simple UK); Business Radio (Suppliers Light); Business Radio (Simple Site); Business Radio (Area Defined); and Business Radio (Technically Assigned).

comment sought on preformed Ofcom proposals in a sort of 'ticking the box' approach and sometimes dismissive responses.[335] There is also merit to views that in light of the fact that we are now in uncharted areas of convergence with unknown outcomes, there is a crucial need to ensure affirmatively that consultations have creative and broad input, including from such as other industries, economists, futurologists, and more individual consumers.[336] Others, in contrast, however, on occasion have voiced distress at the delays occasioned by perceived excessive consultations, called 'long winded and arduous' by one commentator.[337] This, however, seems to be more for self-serving reasons such as where the consultation is holding up plans to offer profitable services.[338]

It seems, on balance, that Ofcom could achieve a greater level of effective transparency and meaningful participation despite its seemingly limitless numbers of documents and consultations.

7.4.4.6 *Fees—administrative charges and licence fees*

Under section 38 of the Act, Ofcom may impose annual administrative charges on designated providers of electronic communications networks, services, or associated facilities, designated USO providers, SMP apparatus suppliers, and a person with a grant of Code powers who is not operating a network (section 38(2)). This is a much larger group than the licensees under the former regime who had to be running an applicable system to which the licence applied and would not have encompassed solely service providers. The Act requires that each year Ofcom publish a statement of charges in keeping with a current statement of charging principles. Ofcom established the current statement of charging principles in 2005 and annually, on or before 31 March, publishes a table of charges that allocate its costs by sector. According to its charging principles, Ofcom's cost allocation is based on the budgeted direct costs of individual projects and programmes, according to the relevant regulatory sector and regulatory categories within those sectors, to permit further particularization of regulatory fees. Overhead, projects and activities not directly attributable or allocated to specific projects, categories, and sectors are apportioned across these according to Ofcom's judgment as to time spent and levels of expenditure. Table 7.3 sets out the sector allocation of the costs of its £133.5 million budget for the year 2008–2009.

---

[335] See, e.g. Johnson, C, 'A Case Study: Ofcom and the Future of Radio' (July 2007), <http://www.estuaryfm.co.uk/casestudy.pdf>.

[336] See, e.g. ibid.

[337] Donegan, M, 'Ofcom denies spectrum bundling' (Unstrung 20 February 2008), <http://www.unstrung.com/document.asp?doc_id=146497>.

[338] See ibid. Also see, Wray, R, 'Ofcom angers BSkyB with surprise public consultation on pay TV' (Guardian.co.uk 27 June 2007), <http://www.estuaryfm.co.uk/casestudy.pdf>.

Table 7.3 Ofcom's Costs Allocated by Sector, Ofcom's Tariff Tables (31 March 2008)

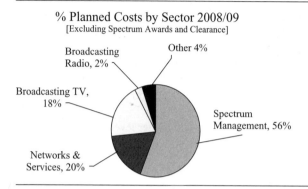

% Planned Costs by Sector 2008/09
[Excluding Spectrum Awards and Clearance]

Broadcasting Radio, 2%
Other 4%
Broadcasting TV, 18%
Networks & Services, 20%
Spectrum Management, 56%

The charging principles provide for administrative fees to be charged as a percentage of annual turnover, currently 0.0653 per cent,[339] in accordance with a system of revenue bands derived from 'relevant activities' under the Act but not for annual revenues of less than £5 million. The turnover data is based on the last but one calendar year, allowing for a bit of certainty and cross-market analysis. Relevant activities have been defined by the charging principles to include:

• the provision of public electronic communication services to end users;

• the provision of electronic communication networks, electronic communication services, and network access to communication providers; or

• the making available of associated facilities to communication providers.[340]

There is some complexity to determining what falls within the categories, especially in the separation of content services that are excluded and transmissions involving content layers that remain communications services. However, providers are to determine their revenue for 'relevant activities' and certify this information to Ofcom within 28 days of the publication of a general demand for such information.[341] Based on this information, Ofcom will calculate the individual administrative charge. Charges in excess of £75,000 per annum will be payable in monthly instalments, a change from Oftel policy.[342]

---

[339] See Ofcom's Tariff Tables, s 2.3 (31 March 2008).
[340] Guidelines, 'The definition of "relevant activity" for the purposes of administrative charging' (DGT, 29 July 2003), at 2.1 Ofcom has indicated that it intends largely to follow these guidelines.
[341] See Networks and Service, General Demand for Information (Ofcom, March 2004).
[342] Ofcom's Tariff Tables, s 2.4 (31 March 2008).

Ofcom committed to lower its costs from its original baseline costs figure of £144.9 million. Based on its current budget and the fact that in the 2007–2008 it paid back its origination loan to the government, it would appear that it has done that. While Ofcom notes that it came in under budget last year due to a range of things including deferred projects and that it is refunding the difference via lower administrative charges, not all sectors will experience fees lower than those for the last fiscal year due to the proportion of work allocated to that sector. Thus, networks and services fees are to increase by an average of 4.1 per cent while the television and radio sectors are to experience respectively lower fees by 2.4 and 6.3 per cent.[343] This detailed level of fiscal analysis in light of work plans with retroactive adjustment would appear to reflect full compliance with its Article 12, Authorization Directive requirements.

As previously noted, the administrative charge and costing for the application for and oversight of the Electronic Communications Code is separate from that of the administrative charge under the general authorization. Ofcom indicates that the annual Code charge is £1,000 irrespective of the numbers of sets of code powers with the one-off application fee at £10,000.[344]

Licence fees for spectrum are imposed under the Wireless Telegraphy Act 1998 via a determined administrative charging that substitutes for market forces, or is set by the market where spectrum is auctioned.[345] Administrative charging is the basis for most licence fees that are actually set by regulation after consultation with the user. They can be based on regulatory considerations such as cost recovery or incentive pricing to encourage efficient uses, with the latter indicated by Ofcom as its prevalent policy, even in connection with RSAs. Consultations for new charges require publication that sets the rationale for each fee with a month for interested persons to comment, procedures in keeping with the EU framework requirements.

Ofcom has conducted several auctions and a number are well in the line-up including the digital dividend, although some have had revised dates due to various issues including legal challenges to the sale of certain bands by 3G. Prices have ranged from the previously noted 3G auction highs to the L Band block award to a single highest bidder for under £9 million.

O2 and T Mobile, however, have launched legal challenges to the auction of 2.6GHz spectrum scheduled originally for 3Q 2008.[346] They contend that they cannot value the spectrum properly to bid on it until they know if and how much they will need. They claim that they cannot do this valuation before Ofcom completes a consultation on the 'refarming' of the 900MHz band, liberalizing its use to allow

---

[343] Ibid, s 1.8.
[344] Ibid, ss 2.5–2.7.
[345] See Licensing Policy Manual, 'Setting Prices for Licences' (Ofcom, 2007).
[346] Ofcom '2.6 GHz award update' (09 June 2008), <http://www.ofcom.org.uk/radiocomms/spectrumawards/awardspending/award_2010/update090608/>.

2G spectrum to be used for 3G purposes.[347] What is upsetting O2 and T Mobile is that part of the proposal contemplates taking back from these providers some of the 900MHz spectrum to auction to third other providers of 3G services.[348] This will clearly challenge Ofcom's powers to revoke or vary spectrum licences .and may present clarification as to the legal nature of a licence in the UK.

7.4.4.7 Compliance and enforcement

The Communications Act 2003 provides an enforcement scheme in connection with the requirement to pay the administrative charge, provide required information (sections 138–142) for the general and each of the specific conditions, and a premium rate service condition that falls outside of the Act's general and specific conditions. The following considers first the premium rate provider enforcement scheme.

7.4.4.7.1 Premium rate services enforcement

Section 120 of the Act authorizes a condition that is general in nature as it may be imposed on all or on persons providing a class of premium rate services. Premium rate services are those like chat lines, call-in contests, access to ring tunes and horoscopes, and more recently calling card-like services providing access to a block of long-distance minutes, all in exchange for an amount billed to your telephone or other communications service bill.[349] The Act essentially defines a premium rate service as one that provides the user with access to content or a facility via an electronic communications service where the charge paid to the communications service provider for that facility accessed or that content is included in the use of the service (section 120(8)). The condition applies to persons who provide the content, exercise editorial control, make available the facility, package the service, or provide the service over their network under an agreement with the provider or retain part of the service charge. It authorizes Ofcom to approve a code of conduct by such premium service providers, or, if none is arrived at, to enter an order regulating the provision and content of such services, including pricing and charge-sharing arrangements.

This is intended to continue a regulatory regime for these services established under the prior framework and continuing an industry-funded regulator, 'Phone-PayPlus'. This is the former Independent Committee for the Supervision of standards of Telephone Information Services (ICSTIS), recently rebranded, apparently in an effort to create a higher profile and eliminate the vagaries about its name. PhonePayPlus regulates controlled premium rate services on behalf of Ofcom and pursuant to the amended Eleventh Code of Practice (2006, as amended April 2008). After investigation of a complaint, it can impose sanctions for failure to comply with the Code that regulates such things as clear, accurate rate information, truthful and appropriate advertising, unreasonable delays in service, or service prolongation.

---

[347] Donegan, M, 'Ofcom delays 2.6GHz auctions' (Unstrung, 10 June 2008), <http://www.unstrung.com/blog.asp?blog_sectionid=414&doc_id=155970>.

[348] It has been suggested that an alternative motive is to delay the roll out of WiMax competitors.

[349] See further Chapter 13.

Sanctions can include reprimands, imposition of prior approval requirements, orders to reimburse complainants, fines, orders limiting access to services with requirements for compliance advice sought, and bans on named individuals from providing services.[350] A database of adjudicated sanctions is available on the PhonePayPlus website.[351] Where the premium rate services involve broadcasters, Ofcom can further sanction breaches of the Broadcast Code.[352]

7.4.4.7.2 Compliance with administrative charge requirement

Where, under the Communications Act, a person is reasonably believed by Ofcom to have failed to pay the administrative charge, it may issue a notification of non-payment. This must give the person a month within which to make representations or to remedy the failure, unless a longer period is determined by Ofcom, or a shorter period is agreed between the provider and Ofcom (section 40). Where no action is taken, a financial penalty that is proportionate and appropriate can be imposed (section 41). The penalty, however, is capped at twice the annual administrative charge (section 41(5)).

Only in serious or repeated instances of non-payment can Ofcom suspend or otherwise restrict the network or service provision (section 42). This may only be done with notice and opportunity to remedy or comment. These are procedures, as previously indicated, that are required by the Framework and Authorization Directive. They are the same procedures that pertain under the Act for the enforcement of conditions so that each need not be reviewed in turn. However, there are circumstances where the Act makes the failure to comply with a condition or authorization requirement a criminal offence. These include the provision of a network, service, or associated facility when the entitlement to do so is suspended for non-payment of administrative charges and failure to provide required information (section 143).

7.4.4.7.3 Market conduct enforcement

Sales practices and issues involved with 'slamming' have been the focus of considerable efforts by Ofcom to protect consumers. In one of the earliest investigations under the Communications Act 2003, BT was found to have breached General Condition 1.2 which requires that all electronic communication network providers keep confidential information obtained about another communications provider during access negotiations and use that information only for purposes of the agreement.[353] BT was found to have used, for marketing purposes, information provided by two

---

[350] For a list of barred service providers, see <http://www.phonepayplus.org.uk/pdfs1/barredsps_adjuds.pdf>.

[351] Board Service Provider Adjudications (PhonePayPlus), <http://www.phonepayplus.org.uk/service_providers/adjudications/default.asp?AD=13%2F07%2F2008&DateLookup=Search&SP=&ST=&Keywords=&cmd=2>.

[352] See Notice of Sanction 'Square 1 Management Ltd., Smile TV'(22 May 2007; 22:17), Broadcast Bulletin No 114-21/07/08, <http://www.ofcom.org.uk/tv/obb/prog_cb/obb114/>.

[353] See Competition Bulletin, 'Use of information for marketing activity directed at Wholesale Line Rental', (Ofcom, 2004), <http://www.ofcom.org.uk/bulletins/comp_bull_index/comp_bull_ccases/closed_all/cw_739/?a=87101>.

operators to process the transfers of customers under Wholesale Line Rental services provided by BT to the providers and pursuant to its SMP obligations within retail call origination markets.[354] BT used the customer-specific information it obtained from these other providers to arrange transfers to engage in 'customer save' activity to discourage its customers from making the switch to the alternative provider. Ofcom determined that BT could have properly used this information for a range of permitted purposes to facilitate transfer, including notifying BT Retail, the losing provider of the transfer, and sending appropriate confirming advice of transfer letters to ensure that the customer had properly authorized the change and, therefore that the winning provider had not engaged in 'slamming'. It was these varying uses which BT represented did not allow the information to be considered as falling within General Condition 1.2, as well as the fact that the customer information was provided not by the new provider but ultimately by the customer. It argued that only technical information necessary to the transfer could be considered to fall within the General Condition 1.2 bar. Ofcom, however, disagreed and concluded that BT had gone beyond permitted uses and called the customers to question their decisions and advise them of BT discounts and other incentives to dissuade them from changing providers. In addition, the advice of transfer letters to the customers went beyond the appropriate guidelines and contained similar marketing devices, urging the customer to contact BT. After the required notifications by Ofcom to BT and its responding representations, Ofcom ordered BT to comply with the General Condition 1.2 by not using customer-specific information acquired from another provider to carry out marketing activities by 14 June 2004 or face further enforcement and possibly a financial penalty under the Act's permitted sanctions.[355]

Fixed and, most recently, mobile slamming and misselling have also been the focus of much attention on the part of Ofcom and found by it to require intervention. Ofcom opened an investigation pursuant to its introduction of new rules to protect consumers from misselling and slamming in 2005, including General Condition 14.5. It took enforcement action against eight communications providers during this period which, it concludes, helped to reduce the number of fixed-line misselling complaints from a peak of 1,200 per month in 2005 to around 350 per month in January 2008. Also, finding that a voluntary code of practice in the mobile industry did nothing to lower the level of misselling, including deceptive cash back schemes, Ofcom has proposed a new general condition with a mandatory code of practice. What is interesting from a compliance perspective is that it creates due diligence and oversight obligations for mobile service providers with respect to those that retail

---

[354] See 'Notification of Contravention of General Condition 1.2 under Section 94 of the Communications Act' (Ofcom, 11 May 2004), <http://www.ofcom.org.uk/bulletins/comp_bull_index/comp_bull_ccases/closed_all/cw_739/notification.pdf>.

[355] Ibid.

their products[356] who could not otherwise be reached by Ofcom under sector-specific rules. Also, a breach could result in financial penalties of up to ten per cent of annual turnover, a sanction akin to those under competition laws.[357] It should be noted that it was the lack of adequate remedies to ensure effective consumer protection which led Ofcom to endorse the EU Commissioner's proposal to enhance the remedies that are available to regulators under the proposed Universal Service Directive reforms.[358]

Despite the possible over-compartmentalization of its framework powers identified by the CAT, Ofcom has appeared generally willing to act on its own investigation or following complaints and to use whichever legal remedies it found more effective in order to remediate breaches of conditions or abuses of consumers or the market by providers. These remedies have included those imposed outside the sector-specific powers, including under the Unfair Terms in Consumer Contract Regulations or the Enterprise Act. This strong level of enforcement should continue if the above misselling scenario is any indicator and Ofcom pursues its stated intent to seek additional sector-specific powers via new general conditions (within the applicable list) in order to control behaviours presently beyond its reach. The CAT also has added a level of enforcement oversight that is indeed activist.

7.5 CONCLUSIONS

For those new to telecommunications law, licensing and authorization might have seemed merely an administrative exercise. However, as the above analysis has demonstrated, while licensing and authorization might involve the procedural aspects of filling out the proper forms (if virtual), it is also an exceedingly complex area of telecommunications law concerned not only with the structure and nature of a particular telecommunications market but also the attainment of social policy objectives. Licensing and authorization can be used as a tool to implement important national economic priorities. This is true whether these are the preservation of a monopoly for the time being in order to, *inter alia*, permit investors to recoup their expenditures or continue a revenue stream for the government, or to open the markets for equipment, services, and networks to immediate or gradual competition. The EU experience with the latter objectives also shows that licensing is a tool that requires skill on the part of the regulator as well as inherent strength of conditions and sanctions to make the tool one that can address ongoing market failures inherent

---

[356] Consultation, 'Protecting consumers from mis-selling of mobile telecommunications services' (Ofcom, London, 18 March 2008).

[357] See, 2007–2008 Annual Report: Improving compliance and empowering citizens and consumers (2008).

[358] Despite this endorsement, it, at the same time, questioned the need for a central EU regulator to tackle pan-European licensing issues.

in a networked market where the former monopolist still controls the access network. We will be likely to see continuing efforts to forge a better tool via at least some of the EU's proposed Authorization Directive and other reforms.

This possible further fine-tuning (or is a sledge hammer being sought?) of the EU licensing regime shows that, despite the fact that licensing is a tool with old legal roots that appear to underlie the regulatory foundations for today's telecommunications markets, even if these are not always readily apparent, the law is an organic thing. It grows, evolves, and adapts as the societal conditions that produced it change. The evolution in telecommunications licensing especially in the UK and the US shows this clearly. The earliest providers, after the invention of the telephone, just entered the market and sold their apparatus and services, without the need for any formality. When telecommunications was deemed to be a service affected with a public interest, it was reserved to a single provider either under a licence or by requiring any others to have a licence. When this monopolist provider could no longer meet the economic and social needs in an increasingly computerized world that required creative and competitive communications networks and services, licensing was used as a tool to pry open markets and control the level of play. Finally, the removal of licensing requirements in the UK and the US for everything but access to spectrum brings us almost full circle. There, no licence is needed nor can be justified under the common law principles that limit the restrictions that can be placed on a person's economic freedom. At the same time, licensing law has also evolved in the EU to try to address the concerns about convergence in technologies and to provide a consistent, harmonized, and technology-neutral framework for any electronic communications network or service. More specifically and recently, in the UK and the US, spectrum licensing and liberalization policies have sought to meet the market's demand for mobile technologies in a way that does not limit what technologies these might be but that at the same time seeks to prevent *ex ante* any harm that could be caused by their use who knows how long in the future. This is clearly a further evolution that anticipates a future development, seemingly requiring a crystal ball to do so.

The EU's self-identified weaknesses in the implementation of the Authorization Directive and the further need for an effective spectrum trading and liberalization strategy show that it may need to change its authorization and licensing regime in order to hand out the crystal balls to some of the others whose regulatory 'vision' may not be as acute. Or perhaps the EU will only need one 'seer' whose joint vision will provide the harmonized way forward in a field of growing complexity. That will be a matter of considerable debate, although given the determination and achievements to date of the EU DG Information Society Commissioner, one should not bet excessively on that proposal's total defeat.

Whatever changes are realized, clearly some are necessary to overcome the continuing divergent implementation of the Directive since 2002 by Member States with

the noted less than full marks results of the 13th Market Implementation and other reports. We can no longer attribute the failures to the piecemeal implementation of the Framework or the lack of time passed to evaluate fairly the entire picture of licensing and authorization in the EU. While there are stars, there are also slackers. Therefore, the 'student' of EU licensing and authorization law for electronic communications providers will continue to witness the law in its dynamic evolution

8

ACCESS AND INTERCONNECTION

*Ian Walden**

8.1 INTRODUCTION

For the purposes of this chapter, and under the European Union's Access Directive,[1] the term 'access' encompasses all kinds of arrangements under which an operator or service provider acquires services from another operator in order to enable it to deliver services to its own customers. 'Interconnection' is a type of access right.[2] At its most basic level, interconnection involves the physical means of linking two different networks for the exchange of traffic, so that users on one network may communicate

---

* This chapter was originally written for the 2nd edition by Emma McCormack.
[1] Directive 2002/19/EC of the European Parliament and of the Council of 7 March 2002 on access to, and interconnection of, electronic communications networks and associated facilities, OJ L 108/7, 24 April 2002 (the 'Access Directive'). The definition of 'access' is in Art 2(a).
[2] Ibid. The definition of 'interconnection' is in Art 2(b).

with users on the other. Typically, interconnection arrangements provide for two networks to be joined together at a 'point of interconnection' and require each operator to carry messages received from the other operator at the point of interconnection across their network and to 'terminate' them with the relevant user.

The issues discussed in this chapter relate to the rights of operators to access each others' networks, not the rights of end-users to access telecommunications services.

The rationale in mandating different kinds of access in a liberalizing market is that it reduces the barriers to market entry, since a new operator will not have to build every network element before being able to offer an end-to-end service, and will be able to acquire services from an incumbent that it cannot feasibly duplicate. Access rights which are commonly regulated include network access (for example, access to the 'local loop'[3]), the provision of wholesale products for resale (for example, access to wholesale DSL products), and access to services and infrastructure necessary for the provision of a service (for example, access to co-location or number translation services).

There are obvious incentives for operators to enter into interconnection arrangements with operators in other territories. For example, an incumbent telephony operator in one country would want to interconnect with the incumbent telephony operator in another country, in order that its users could make calls to and receive calls from users in the other country.[4] Interconnection means the ability to extend an operator's reach and provide a wider range of (sometimes high-cost and very profitable) services to users.

There is, however, little commercial incentive for an incumbent operator to interconnect with another network operator who wants to compete in the same geographic market. Incumbent operators with a large number of customers may well determine, in the absence of appropriate regulation, that they bear little commercial risk if their users cannot contact the (initially very small number of) users on a new competitor's network. The new entrant, however, cannot survive without interconnection with the incumbent. Its network will be virtually useless to users unless they can contact users on the incumbent's network. An incumbent operator's refusal to interconnect, or the imposition of unfairly onerous terms in relation to interconnection, could therefore allow market entry to be obstructed, or even prevented altogether.

It is for this reason that interconnection has become a key regulatory issue and is recognized as being essential for creating and maintaining effective competition and any-to-any connectivity. Most jurisdictions now recognize that interconnection is so vital to the development of competition that specific *ex ante* rights and obligations for interconnection are considered necessary and proportionate, although some

[3] The 'local loop' is sometimes referred to as the 'local access network' and refers to the part of a telecommunications network that connects end-users premises with the nearest telecommunications exchange.
[4] Such international interconnection arrangements are examined further in Chapter 15, at 15.3.5.

jurisdictions, most notably New Zealand, have tried relying exclusively on competition law to bring about interconnection arrangements.[5]

As electronic communications markets have matured, and as communications
services have grown in sophistication, demand for other types of access has esca-
lated. Some of these demands were initially dealt with by regulators in the EU under
existing interconnection regulation, whereas in other cases access obligations were
developed and imposed outside of the interconnection regime. The Access Directive
consolidated many of these obligations and gave national regulatory authorities
enhanced powers to mandate access.

Access issues present regulators with significant challenges. If new entrants are
given insufficient rights to acquire interconnection and access from incumbents,
effectively competitive markets are unlikely to develop. Markets that are not effectively competitive are less likely to yield lower prices and high levels of innovation.
However, over-regulation can act as a strong disincentive to investment and innovation if incumbents fear that they will be made to give their competitors access to
their network without those competitors bearing any of the investment risk or cost
involved.

This chapter will review the regulatory regime impacting on access and interconnection, and discuss some of the contractual issues that arise when negotiating some
different types of access agreements.

8.2 BASIC CONCEPTS AND TERMINOLOGY

An understanding of some of the terminology used to describe access and interconnection arrangements greatly assists an understanding of the regulatory regime. This
section will explain some of the key concepts.[6]

8.2.1 Packet-switched and circuit-switched networks

There are some key differences between the interconnection arrangements for
'circuit-switched' networks and for 'packet-switched' networks.

Circuit-switched networks are networks which establish an end-to-end transmission path in order for a communication to be transmitted from one end to the other.
Telephone networks commonly use circuit-switched technology. When a call is made,
a dedicated channel is established over which the communication travels.

Packet-switched networks, by contrast, divide the data that comprises a communication into small packets. The packets are sent separately and reassembled at

---

[5] See *Telecom Corporation of NZ Ltd v Clear Communications Ltd* (1992) 4 NZBLC. However, such
issues are now subject to an *ex ante* access regime under the Telecommunications Act 2001, implemented
by the Commerce Commission of New Zealand.
[6] See further Chapter 2.

the destination. The internet is made up of interconnected or linked packet-switched networks. Packet-switched networks are increasingly being used to carry voice, as well as data. Two trends are apparent. First, telephony operators are increasingly using packet-switched technology when modernizing their network backbone, often referred to as Next Generation Networks (NGNs).[7] Thus, although circuit-switched technology may be used over the parts of the network where the call starts and the call ends, packet-switched technology will increasingly be used to carry the call over the operator's core network and to interconnect traffic between networks. The second trend is the emergence of 'voice over IP' (VoIP) technology, which involves packet-switched technology being used to carry voice traffic all the way across an operator's network.

8.2.2 Interconnection of circuit-switched networks—key concepts

8.2.2.1 *Call origination, call termination, and termination charges*
When a call is made between two interconnected circuit-switched networks, the operators must work out how the cost of carrying that call is to be divided between them. If the call is made within the same country, usually a wholesale charge known as a termination charge will apply. It is important to understand how this charge works.

This is most easily explained by thinking about a typical telephone call between different networks, like a call from a fixed line network (such as BT) to a mobile network (such as Vodafone). In this scenario the call is said to 'originate' on the fixed-line network where the user initiates the call by dialling the mobile telephone number. The call is carried over the fixed network to a point of interconnection with the mobile network. The mobile network operator will carry the call over their network from the point of interconnection to the relevant mobile user. When the call is connected, it is said to 'terminate' on the mobile network.

The concepts of origination and termination are relevant to the charges that flow between the fixed network operator and the mobile network operator.

We all know that telecommunications operators will charge us to make calls on their networks. Generally, the user who initiates a call will pay for that call. This is known as the 'calling party pays' principle, and is the charging model most widely used by telephony providers.[8] The fixed-line operator in the scenario described above would therefore charge their user for the call at the current retail rate.

An inter-operator charge would also apply in this scenario. The terminating operator, in this case the mobile operator, would charge the originating operator, in this case the fixed-line operator, for the termination of the call onto the mobile network.

---

[7] E.g. BT's next generation network, '21 CN', is an end-to-end IP-based network.
[8] The main alternative is a 'receiving party pays' regime, as operated in the US.

This charge is known as the 'termination charge'. This scenario is illustrated in Figure 8.1.

The termination charge will usually be a charge per minute (although there are some variations), and may vary depending on the time of day, i.e. congestion pricing. The level at which termination charges are set can be a controversial issue, and is addressed by regulators in a number of ways, as will be discussed later in this chapter.[9]

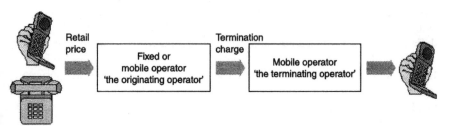

Retail price   Fixed or mobile operator 'the originating operator'   Termination charge   Mobile operator 'the terminating operator'

Figure 8.1

Source: Oftel, Review of the charge controls on calls to mobiles, 26 September, 2001.

8.2.2.2 *The international accounting rate regime*

Termination charges may be worked out in a different way to that described above where the interconnected networks are in two different countries. Under the international accounting rate model, the originating operator must pay the terminating operator 50 per cent of the pre-agreed cost of transmission of the call between the originating network and the terminating network. A net settlement is periodically made between the two networks.[10]

8.2.2.3 *Transit*

The basic scenario described above, where the two networks are directly interconnected, could be varied in a number of ways. For example, it may not be efficient for a small fixed-line operator to establish direct interconnection with every other operator. Instead, a small operator may rely on a third operator, often a large incumbent operator, to transit traffic across that other operator's network to the terminating operator's network. Provided that both the originating operator and the terminating operator are interconnected with that third party and the third party has agreed to transit calls across its network, the calls will be connected even though the parties have not established direct interconnection arrangements.

---

[9] See also Chapter 3, at 3.13.
[10] See further Chapter 15 at 15.3.5.

Even more complex arrangements have evolved. In the case of international calls or the exchange of internet traffic (discussed further in section 8.2.3), the messages or data may pass through many telecommunications networks.

8.2.3 Interconnection of packet-switched networks—key concepts

The interconnection of packet-switched networks is often referred to as 'IP interconnection', which describes the connection of computer networks that support packet-based communication controlled by a particular suite of software protocols known as transmission control protocol/Internet protocol (TCP/IP). The TCP/IP protocols define how packets of data are addressed, transmitted, tracked, and re-assembled by computers. TCP/IP is used by all computer networks which constitute the Internet. IP interconnection arrangements, therefore, are in place largely for the purpose of exchanging internet traffic between networks, and have been described as the glue that holds the Internet together.[11]

To understand how the contractual arrangements governing IP interconnection work, it is necessary to understand, at a basic level, the structure of the Internet carriage industry and the typical payment arrangements that operators adopt.

At a retail level, customers seeking access to the Internet will enter into a contract with an Internet service provider (ISP), like AOL or Orange Home. A diverse range of retail pricing models have been adopted by ISPs for internet access services, including volume and/or time-based charges, flat-rate charges for unlimited access, and combinations of these models. Many ISPs also often offer web-hosting services to their users, allowing them to put content onto the Internet. In other cases Internet content is hosted by specialist networks who do not themselves provide Internet access, for example eBay and Yahoo!.

In order that the users of an ISP can communicate with users on other networks, and access content (such as websites) hosted on other networks, ISPs must enter into IP interconnection arrangements with other IP networks. Sometimes direct interconnection is established, especially between networks which are close to each other geographically. However, it would obviously be both inefficient and virtually impossible from a practical point of view for every ISP to enter into direct IP interconnection arrangements with every other ISP and content provider around the world.

IP interconnection arrangements have evolved to overcome this problem. The primary way of avoiding the need to directly interconnect is by entering into transit arrangements, similar in principle to transit arrangements for voice telephony. Large, high-speed networks have developed which aggregate and transit traffic between

---

[11] Australian Competition and Consumer Commission (ACCC), *Internet interconnection: Factors affecting commercial arrangements between network operators in Australia* (2000) 30, quoting Jew B, M Reede and R Nicholls, 'Internet Connectivity: Open Competition in the Face of Commercial Expansion', paper presented to the Pacific Telecommunications Conference, January 1999.

numerous smaller networks, such as small retail ISPs. The operators of these networks are sometimes referred to as 'Internet access providers' or 'transit providers'. There is no strict definition of an Internet access provider, but it is generally an operator who can transit traffic to and from any other network on the Internet, through its own upstream transit agreements. The largest of these networks are often called 'backbone providers', or 'Tier 1 operators'. There is no strict criteria for defining a backbone provider, but they are usually the predominant IP infrastructure operator in a region, or one of a limited number of operators providing direct international Internet connectivity.[12]

The structure described above may give the impression of a neat series of tiered steps, with retail ISPs at the bottom, Internet access providers in the middle, and backbone operators, with international links, at the top. However, this would be an oversimplification. The prevalence of vertically integrated operators means that a large network may be both a retail ISP and a backbone provider. Furthermore, over-supply of international capacity, resulting in cheaper prices, has allowed some networks that would otherwise be described as ISPs or Internet access providers to bypass backbone providers and obtain international connectivity directly. Nevertheless, the analysis is helpful in understanding the structure of the industry and the reasons behind the different methods of charging.

8.2.3.1 *Peering and paying transit*
There are two main types of payment arrangements adopted in IP interconnection agreements, which will be referred to in this chapter as 'peering' and 'paying transit'. There are also a number of variations on these models.

The term 'peering' has sometimes been used as a generic term to describe the interconnection of any two computer networks.[13] However, the term is now generally understood to describe settlement-free IP interconnection arrangements; that is, arrangements where the interconnecting operators agree not to charge each other. Peering arrangements are commonly adopted between networks where the traffic flowing in each direction can be expected to be roughly equal.

Where the parties enter into 'paying transit' IP interconnection arrangements, by contrast, charges will be levied for traffic passing through the point of interconnection. Paying transit arrangements are generally entered into where the traffic flow is asymmetrical between the two networks. Transit providers may charge for traffic flowing in one or both directions over the point of interconnection. Whether parties enter into peering arrangements or paying transit arrangements will largely depend on their respective bargaining positions, based on factors such as size of subscriber

---

[12] See European Commission decision in Case IV/ M.1069 *WorldCom and MCI*, OJ L 116/1, 4 May 1999.

[13] Ibid, 33. The term 'peering' is used because for two or more networks to communicate, they need to use a common networking protocol, and can thus be described as 'peers'.

base ('eyeballs') or content hosted. These issues, and some of the other considerations that arise in negotiating IP interconnection agreements, are considered at section 8.7 below.

8.2.4 *Other access arrangements*

As noted in the introduction, the term 'access' encompasses a broad range of arrangements, of which interconnection is only one kind. These range from very intrusive arrangements involving physical access to another operator's facilities or network, to the mere provision of wholesale services. Many different kinds of arrangements lie in between these ends of the spectrum. Some examples, which are by no means at all an exhaustive list, are described below.

One of the most intrusive examples of network access lies in local loop access. 'Dial up' or 'narrowband' Internet users will be aware that such services have limitations, and in particular offer poor download speed. These limitations are partly due to the lack of capacity in the local loop network. It is possible, through digital subscriber line (DSL)[14] technology, to upgrade the local loop to provide high speed, 'broadband' Internet access services to users. By obtaining access to the local loop, operators obtain the right to locate equipment at a telephony operator's local exchange and to physically connect that equipment to end-users' local lines, in order to provide DSL broadband Internet services to those end-users. Where access to the whole line is obtained, the broadband operator controls the provision of telephony services to the end-user as well. More common is 'shared access', where the original operator continues to provide voice telephony services, with the alternative operator providing broadband services to the user.

Access arrangements may relate to facilities as well as network elements. An example of access to non-network facilities is the arrangement between the mobile operators O2 and T-Mobile to share mobile telephony masts and sites in Germany and the UK, as well as to provide reciprocal roaming services to each others' customers. These facility-sharing arrangements were achieved through commercial negotiations, and were subsequently cleared by the European Commission.[15]

The majority of access arrangements are not as intrusive as the ones described above, and are more like straightforward interconnection arrangements. An example is the provision of carrier pre-selection interconnect facilities, which allows users who are customers of one network to select an alternative operator in advance for particular calls (e.g. all national calls) without dialling additional digits on their telephone.

---

[14] There are many variants of DSL technology. The variant most commonly used for upgrading the local loop is, at present, asymmetrical digital subscriber line (ADSL) technology. ADSL provides fast download speeds, but comparatively slower speeds for sending data (ie the downloading and uploading speeds are 'asymmetrical').

[15] The parties asked the Commission for clearance, or, alternatively, an exemption of the arrangements under competition law. The Commission adopted favourable decisions; see *O2 UK Limited/T-Mobile UK Limited (UK network sharing agreement)* (2003) OJ L 200/59, 7 August 2003 and *T-Mobile Deutschland GmbH/Viag Interkom GmbH (Germany network sharing agreement)* (2003) OJ L75/32, 12 March 2004.

Unlike local loop access, carrier pre-selection only involves the interconnection of the two networks; it does not involve the alternative carrier taking physical control of the local loop.

Another example is the provision of flat-rate Internet access call origination (FRIACO). FRIACO is a wholesale product provided by BT to UK ISPs who provide dial-up Internet services to users. ISPs who obtain FRIACO from BT are charged a flat rate for calls made by their users who are BT customers to the telephone number dialled by the users' modems to obtain Internet access. Without FRIACO, it would be difficult for ISPs to offer flat-rate Internet access services to users.[16]

Some access arrangements are even less intrusive than the ones described above. For example, the provision of wholesale line rental requires the operator who owns a local access line to provide that line on a wholesale basis to another operator. This product is particularly useful for operators who have obtained carrier pre-selection, as it allows them to bill their customers for both calls and for line rental. In this case the incumbent operator will continue to service the customer's line, although the customer's contract will be with the other operator.

8.3 ACCESS AND INTERCONNECTION REGULATION

8.3.1 Introduction

The interests of new entrants in the telecommunications sector may be said to be protected by two distinct tiers of regulation in the EU. First, general competition law[17] prohibits certain anti-competitive agreements and the abuse of a dominant position. Secondly, measures have been implemented which apply only to the electronic communications sector. The 'sector-specific' rules are more specific, and have a greater reach than general competition law. Operators are required to comply with both competition law and the sector-specific rules.

EC competition law principally prohibits two types of practices: Article 81 of the EC Treaty prohibits anti-competitive agreements (which are also void as a matter of law), and Article 82 prohibits the abuse of dominance by an undertaking which holds a dominant position in a particular market, or a closely related one. Behaviour that may be challenged under Article 82 includes discrimination by an incumbent in favour of its own downstream business, and various pricing practices such as predatory pricing and margin squeeze. Article 82 may also prohibit an operator refusing to supply access or interconnection to another operator. This is particularly the case where the facility or service requested can be said to be an 'essential facility'. An essential facility is one which is essential in order for another operator to compete

---

[16] See further, section 8.3.4.1 below.
[17] In particular, through Arts 81 and 82 of the EC Treaty and domestic legislation like the Competition Act 1998 in the UK.

in the relevant market, where there is no alternative infrastructure that could be used for the same purpose, and where such infrastructure cannot feasibly be duplicated.[18]

Most regulators recognize that the general competition law rules discussed above are inadequate for fostering the emergence of competition in telecommunications markets. This is because the telecommunications sector may be said to have special characteristics which justify a more interventionist approach than is involved where general competition law is applied. These characteristics include the prevalence of previously state-owned and state-funded operators who have historically enjoyed a legal monopoly. These operators have often maintained very high market shares, even many years after the introduction of competition. Secondly, operators who wish to enter the market by building competing infrastructure face very high barriers to market entry; it may not be possible economically, for example, to build out an entire competing telephone network. Finally, the fact that competitor cooperation, in the form of access and interconnection arrangements, is essential for the operation of telecommunications markets is another factor which is said to justify the application of sector-specific rules.

The aim of sector-specific legislation is to foster competition. Therefore, as competition emerges, the arguments in favour of maintaining sector-specific rules lose their force. In the EU the sector-specific rules have already become more aligned with general competition law over time. It is mostly accepted, however, that sector-specific rules in the telecommunications sector are unlikely ever to disappear altogether due to certain innate features of the telecommunications market.

This chapter will focus on the sector-specific legislation on access and interconnection in the EU and the UK. Chapter 9, 'Competition Law in Telecommunications', deals with general competition law.

8.3.2 Regulation in the UK prior to the adoption of the Interconnection Directive[19]

Until the implementation of the Interconnection Directive in the Member States, there was no harmonized access and interconnection policy in the EU, and each Member State took a different approach. Because demand for interconnection at a local level only arises when competition is first introduced in a jurisdiction, the sector-specific legislation has developed largely in parallel with the history of liberalization of telecommunications markets.

---

[18] See European Commission, *Commission Guidelines on the application of EEC competition rules in the telecommunications sector* (1991) OJ C233/02, 6 August 1991, and *Notice of the application of the competition rules to access agreements in the telecommunications sector* (1998) OJ C265/2, 22 August 1998. See further Chapter 9.

[19] Directive 97/33/EC of the European Parliament and of the Council on interconnection in telecommunications with regard to ensuring universal service and interoperability through the application of the principles of open network provision (ONP), OJ L199/32, 26 July 1997 (the Interconnection Directive).

When Mercury Communications became licensed in the UK to provide fixed line telephony in competition with BT in 1981, BT was not required to interconnect with it—and in some instances refused to do so, arguing that Mercury customers should install an additional line (with an additional telephone) for making and receiving calls from other Mercury customers. Only with the commencement of the Telecommunications Act 1984 was the Director-General of Telecommunications (DGT)[20] empowered to mandate interconnection.[21] It was not long before the DGT was called upon to use these powers, and the first determination setting terms and conditions on which BT and Mercury were required to interconnect was made in October 1985.[22] This included a determination as to the charges which BT could levy, which were calculated on the basis of fully allocated costs, including a return on the capital invested.[23]

A number of further Mercury/BT determinations were made in the following years, as well as determinations in 1991 for the interconnection arrangements between Mercury and Vodafone and between Mercury and BT Cellnet (the two mobile network operators at the time).[24]

Further demands for interconnection arose when the first post-duopoly PTO licences[25] were issued in 1993, and when the first international facilities licences were issued in 1996. The new licensees were required to show that they had relevant connectable system (RCS) status in order to be entitled to interconnection. In practice, RCS status was defined in such a way that most PTO licensees were entitled to interconnection.

In 1994, Oftel commenced a major review of interconnection pricing. The review was needed to take account of the growing level in sophistication of the interconnection products needed and a growing requirement on the part of operators to purchase disaggregated interconnection services. In 1996/97 Oftel required that BT's interconnection charges be based on the forward-looking incremental cost of replacing capital assets, rather than the historic cost of what the assets cost when originally purchased.[26] This type of cost modelling in respect of interconnection pricing was finally adopted in an EU Recommendation in 1998,[27] although Member States still have discretion in whether they apply it.

---

[20] The functions of the Director General of Telecommunications now rest with Ofcom.

[21] Section 7(5) and (6) of the Telecommunications Act 1984.

[22] See Oftel, *A Brief History of UK Telecoms and Oftel* (Oftel, London, 1998). See also Chapter 4.

[23] See further Chapter 3, at 3.7.2.1.

[24] Ibid.

[25] Prior to the duopoly review, there were only two licensed fixed telecommunications operators, BT and Mercury (which became Cable & Wireless). See further Chapter 4.

[26] For further discussion on the costing of interconnection, see Chapter 3.

[27] European Commission, *Commission Recommendation 98/195/EC of 8 January 1998 on Interconnection in a liberalized telecommunications market*, OJ L 73 (1998) and *Commission Recommendation 98/195/EC of 29 July 1998 amending Commission Recommendation*, OJ L 228 (1998).

8.3.3 The Interconnection Directive

The Interconnection Directive brought about significant harmonization of interconnection policy in the EU. It introduced two different tiers of interconnection rights and obligations.

First, operators authorized to provide the public telecommunications networks and services set out in Annex I of the Interconnection Directive, or who enjoyed significant market power (SMP), were required to meet all reasonable requests for access to their networks (Article 4(2)). Three categories of networks/services were listed in Annex I: fixed telephone networks; mobile telephone networks; and leased line services. Member States were required to ensure the adequate and efficient interconnection of these networks to the extent necessary to ensure interoperability of these services for all users within the EC (Article 3(3)).

A rebuttable presumption of SMP arose where an operator had a 25 per cent market share. An operator with less than 25 per cent market share could be found to have SMP where the operator's ability to influence market conditions, its turnover relative to the size of the market, its control of the means of access to end-users, its access to financial resource, and its experience in providing products and services in the market were taken into account (Article 4(3)).

SMP operators were also subject to a range of other obligations under the Interconnection Directive.[28] These included adherence to the principle of non-discrimination, and a requirement to make interconnection agreements available to the national regulatory authority and to interested parties. SMP operators providing fixed-line networks and leased lines (but not SMP operators providing mobile networks) were also required to set transparent and cost-orientated interconnection charges, and to publish a reference interconnection offer.

The second tier of regulation under the Interconnection Directive required all operators authorized to provide the public telecommunications networks and services set out in Annex II of the Directive to negotiate interconnection with each other on request (Article 4(1)). The categories in Annex II were:

(1) organizations which provided fixed and/or mobile public switched telecommunications networks and/or publicly available telecommunications services, and controlled the means of access to termination points identified by numbers in the national numbering plan;

(2) organizations which provided leased lines into users' premises;

(3) organizations which were authorized in a Member State to provide international telecommunications circuits between the Community and third countries, for which purpose they had special or exclusive rights; and

---

[28] Such obligations may be found in Arts 6, 7, and 8 of the Interconnection Directive.

(4) organizations which provided telecommunications services which were permitted to interconnect in accordance with relevant national licensing or authorization schemes.

Where commercial negotiations failed to bring about interconnection, national regulatory authorities had a range of powers to intervene to settle disputes, to require specified conditions to be observed, to specify issues to be covered in interconnection agreements, and to set time limits for the conclusion of negotiations.

8.3.4 UK implementation of the Interconnection Directive and the imposition of other access rights

The Interconnection Directive was implemented in the UK through the Telecommunications (Interconnection) Regulations 1997, SI 1997/2931 (Interconnection Regulations), and through amendments to operators' telecommunications licences (both individual licences and class licences) in accordance with the Licensing Directive.[29] The Regulations and licence conditions largely replicated the provisions in the Interconnection Directive. This section will examine only some specific, important aspects of the UK implementation.

8.3.4.1 *Determinations of SMP and requests for access*
Oftel determined that Kingston Communications (in respect of the Hull area) and BT (for the remainder of the UK) had SMP in the provision of fixed networks and services and leased lines, and that Cellnet and Vodafone had SMP in the market for mobile networks and services. These operators were therefore required to meet all reasonable requests for access to their network from Annex II operators. BT and Kingston Communications were also required to publish a reference interconnection offer and to provide access services at cost-orientated prices.

A range of interconnection products were requested by Annex II operators, particularly of BT. Some examples that have proved particularly important for competing operators include the following:

i. FRIACO interconnection—as noted above, FRIACO stands for fixed-rate Internet access call origination. In simple terms, FRIACO is the service whereby ISPs are charged a flat rate for calls from BT customers to telephone numbers which are dialled by users' modems to access the Internet. FRIACO was first requested from BT in late 1999. When BT refused to provide FRIACO interconnection, a dispute was raised with the DGT by MCI Worldcom. The DGT directed BT to provide a FRIACO product at its digital local exchanges.[30] Further directions relating to

---

[29] Directive 97/13/EC on a common framework for general authorisations and individual licences in the field of telecommunications services; OJ L117/15, 7 May 1997 (the Licensing Directive).

[30] Director General of Telecommunications, *Determination of a dispute between BT and MCI Worldcom concerning the provision of a Flat Rate Internet Access Call Origination product* (2000).

FRIACO required BT to provide FRIACO interconnection at other levels in its network.[31]

ii. ATM interconnection—ATM interconnection refers to interconnection with BT's 'asynchronous transfer mode' network. Before BT provided ATM interconnection, operators wishing to purchase wholesale DSL products from BT were required to purchase an end-to-end service, consisting of DSL access, conveyance across BT's core network, and the connection between BT's network and their own network. ATM interconnection allows competing operators to use their own network for the conveyance of their customers' traffic wherever possible. This could allow operators to provide wholesale DSL products to other operators in competition with BT. BT was directed to provide ATM interconnection on a retail minus basis[32] in June 2002 following a dispute with Energis and Thus.[33]

iii. PPCs—PPCs are 'partial private circuits'. In effect, PPCs are circuits providing capacity between an end-user's premises and a point of interconnection between two operators' networks. PPCs allow competing operators to provide leased line services to end-users even if the competing operator's network does not reach the end-user's premises. BT was directed to provide PPC interconnection products in a series of decisions over 2001 and 2002.[34]

Another direction made by the DGT under the Interconnection Regulations concerned what are known as radio base station (RBS) backhaul circuits. RBSs are the base stations that transmit signals to and from mobile handsets. RBS backhaul circuits are functionally identical to PPCs, but they are used to link RBSs with the main part of a mobile operator's network. A dispute arose between BT and Vodafone as to the provision of RBS backhaul circuits. In June 2003 the DGT, using its powers under the Interconnection Directive and the Interconnection Regulations, directed

---

[31] Such as at its tandem exchanges. See DGT, *Determination relating to a dispute between British Telecommunications and Worldcom concerning the provision of a Flat-Rate Internet Access Call Origination product (FRIACO)* (2001).

[32] Retail minus pricing does not involve setting an absolute level of charge; it allows the operator to set the level of charges according to its commercial judgment. However, the operator is required to ensure that a sufficient margin exists between the charge in question and the relevant downstream price so as to allow the necessary additional costs of providing the downstream product to be recovered. Setting prices on a retail minus basis should ensure that no discrimination takes place between the downstream arm of the operator providing the product and competing operators.

[33] DGT, *Direction to resolve a dispute between BT, Energis and Thus concerning xDSL interconnection at the ATM switch* (2002).

[34] DGT, *Direction under condition 45.2 of the public telecommunications operator licence granted to BT under Regulations 6(3) and 6(4) of the Telecommunications (Interconnection) Regulations 1997* (2001), Director General of Telecommunications, *Phase 1 Direction to resolve a dispute concerning the provision of partial private circuits* (2002), Director-General of Telecommunications, *Partial private circuits, Phase 2—a Direction to resolve a dispute* (2002).

BT to provide RBS backhaul circuits to Vodafone on terms similar to those applying to PPCs.[35]

BT challenged the DGT's right to investigate the dispute on the basis that RBS backhaul circuits do not fall within the definition of 'interconnection' under the Interconnection Directive and the Interconnection Regulations. In May 2004 the Competition Appeals Tribunal handed down a decision holding that RBS backhaul circuits are not interconnection products, and, accordingly, the DGT had no jurisdiction over the Vodafone/BT dispute.[36]

The principal reason for the Tribunal's decision is that RBS backhaul circuits are, in effect, used by Vodafone to construct its own network—they link a *Vodafone* RBS with the main part of *Vodafone's* network. RBS backhaul circuits do not ensure connectivity between Vodafone customers and BT customers, or between Vodafone customers and customers on any other network. Indeed, for such connectivity to be established, points of interconnection would be needed.

The Tribunal was required to determine the appeal on the basis of the law in force in June 2003, when the direction was made. As will be seen below, the law now permits broader access rights to be mandated. The provision of RBS backhaul circuits has since been mandated under the new regime.

8.3.4.2 *Annex II list*

Oftel established a register of operators with rights and obligations to interconnect under Annex II of the Interconnection Directive. This list was known as the 'Annex II list'. To qualify for inclusion in the Annex II list an operator had to show that they were authorized to provide public telecommunications networks or publicly available services, that they were actually providing publicly available network services, that they were running a system with which to connect with others, and that they fell into one of the categories of operator set out in Annex II of the Interconnection Directive, as set out above. These categories were transposed into Schedule 2 of the Interconnection Regulations.

Oftel required operators to submit detailed information, such as network plans and copies of their customer contracts, to prove that they met the criteria for inclusion in the Annex II list. In recognition of the fact that some operators would need to establish interconnection before technically qualifying for Annex II status (which, for example, required that an operator was already providing publicly available network services), Oftel permitted operators to be added to the Annex II register on a 'provisional' basis. Such operators were required to show that they met the Annex II criteria within six months, otherwise they were removed from the register.

---

[35] DGT, *Direction to resolve a dispute between BT and Vodafone regarding wholesale connections between BT's and Vodafone's networks (radio base station backhaul circuits)* (2003).

[36] [2004] CAT 8. Although the DGT's determination was made before the Communications Act 2003 came into force, the appeal was made after that time, and so proceedings were brought before the CAT rather than the High Court.

Generally speaking, those operators in the UK who had RCS status before the implementation of the Interconnection Directive (mainly those with a PTO licence or international facilities licence) all qualified for Annex II status after its implementation. The main impact of the Directive was on those operators running a system under a class licence, such as the Telecommunications Services Licence. These operators, which included many ISPs, acquired rights and obligations to interconnect for the first time by obtaining Annex II status. The principal benefit in obtaining Annex II status was that operators became entitled to purchase network services from fixed-line SMP operators (particularly BT) at regulated cost-orientated prices.

8.3.4.3 *Licence conditions*
Obligations concerning interconnection, largely replicating the provisions of the Interconnection Directive and the Interconnection Regulations, were inserted into all telecommunications licences in 1999.[37] They included conditions requiring all Annex II operators to negotiate connection services, including co-location and facility sharing with each other, and for SMP operators to meet all reasonable requests for access, to not unduly discriminate, to publish a reference interconnection offer, and to charge cost-based prices for access services.

In addition, specific access conditions were at various times imposed on operators via their telecommunications licences. Some examples of these conditions are described below.

8.3.4.4 *Carrier pre-selection*
As noted earlier, where carrier pre-selection (CPS) is enabled, users can obtain call services from alternative operators (such as all national calls, or all international calls), without dialling any extra digits on their telephone. CPS was required to be implemented by an amendment to the Interconnection Directive in 1998.[38] It was implemented in the UK through amendments to all PTO licences, although the condition was only triggered where the operator had SMP in the market for fixed telephony, and thus only applied to BT and Kingston Communications.

8.3.4.5 *Wholesale line rental*
Following a review of the fixed telephony market which found that BT had market power in the provision of calls and access, BT's licence was modified in August 2002 to require it to provide line rental on a wholesale basis to other operators. This enabled operators who obtained both CPS interconnection and wholesale line rental

---

[37] Pursuant to the Telecommunications (Licence Modifications) (Standard Schedules) Regulations 1999, SI 1999/2450 and the Telecommunications (Licence Modification) (Mobile Public Telecommunications Operators) Regulations 1999, SI 1999/2453.

[38] Directive 98/61/EC of the European Parliament and of the Council of 24 September 1998 amending Directive 97/33/EC with regard to operator number portability and carrier preselection, OJ L 268/37, 3 Oct 1998.

from BT to offer their customers a single bill for calls and access, something that, previously, could only be done by those operators who owned the access line.[39]

8.3.4.6 *Access to the local loop*
In 2000 the European Council of Lisbon identified a pressing need to increase broadband Internet use across the EU. The EU was lagging behind the US in terms of penetration of such services, and it was perceived that it may miss out on the growth and employment potential of the knowledge economy. It was also perceived that increased competition in DSL broadband services would lead to lower prices and thus stimulate demand. Member States were therefore encouraged to ensure that new entrants were entitled to access to incumbent operators' local loop networks. Local loop unbundling was seen as the shot in the arm necessary for stimulating the broadband market.

The Commission adopted a Recommendation[40] in May 2000 recommending that Member States should mandate access to the local loop by the end of that year. It became clear, however, that many Member States were unlikely to meet this target. The European Parliament and Council then adopted a Regulation[41] requiring 'notified operators' to meet reasonable requests for unbundled access to their local loop and related facilities under transparent, fair, and non-discriminatory conditions, and to publish a reference offer for such access. National regulatory authorities were given powers to intervene to ensure non-discrimination, fair competition, economic efficiency, and maximum benefit for users, and to settle disputes. The 'Local Loop Regulation' remains the governing law, despite the new Access and Interconnection Directive; although the Commission has recently proposed its repeal as part of its 2007 Reform Proposals.[42]

'Notified operators' were those designated by their national regulatory authorities as having significant market power in the provision of fixed public telephone networks and services under the Interconnection Directive. This meant that BT and Kingston were 'notified operators' in the UK, and, accordingly, licence conditions consistent with the Commission Recommendation and the Regulation were imposed on them in August 2000.

In the months after the imposition of the licence condition a large number of operators expressed interest in obtaining access to BT's local access network. These operators signed confidentiality agreements with BT and joined an operator interest group established by Oftel to facilitate progress. However, the vast majority of these operators never obtained local loop access and withdrew their interest. This can be

---

[39] Oftel, *Wholesale line rental: Oftel's conclusions—statement* (2003).
[40] Recommendation 2000/417/EC of 25 May 2000 on unbundled access to the local loop, OJ L 156/44, 29 June 2000.
[41] Regulation 2887/2000 of the European Parliament and Council of 18 December 2000 on unbundled access to the local loop, OJ L336/4, 30 December 2000 ('Local Loop Regulation').
[42] See further Chapter 5, at 5.2.

attributed to many factors, including financial strains on the telecommunications industry at the time. Some in the industry, however, criticized the DGT and Oftel for failing to take swift and appropriate action against BT when faced with complaints by operators seeking access. To address this concern, Ofcom established a Telecommunications Adjudication Scheme in 2004, operated under the auspices of a Telecommunications Adjudicator, to facilitate competitor access to BT's local loop.[43] Over recent years, the availability and take-up of broadband Internet access has boomed, mainly through resale of wholesale DSL products obtained from BT.

8.3.4.7 Conditional access and access control services
Conditional access services and access control services are services provided to broadcasters and interactive service providers.

Conditional access services enable broadcasters to make access to their television or radio signals conditional upon prior authorization. Where conditional access is applied, users need a set top box and appropriately authorized access card to receive a broadcaster's channels in intelligible form. Access control refers to a range of services provided to broadcasters so that they can run interactive applications through a viewer's set top box.

Prior to the Access Directive, conditional access services were regulated by the Advanced Television Standards Directive.[44] The requirements in that Directive were implemented in the UK through the Advanced TV Services Regulations 1996, SI 1996/3151 and through the class licence for Conditional Access Services.[45] The licence required, amongst other things, that providers of conditional access services offered them on a fair, reasonable, and non-discriminatory basis.

Access control services were regulated in the UK under the class licence for Access Control services,[46] which required, amongst other things, that 'regulated suppliers' of such services offer them on fair, reasonable, and non-discriminatory terms. Sky Subscribers Services Limited was designated as a 'regulated supplier' for access control services supplied over its digital satellite platform.[47]

Oftel produced a number of policy statements and guidelines relating to the pricing and terms of supply of conditional access and access control services.[48]

---

[43] This now comprises Openreach. See further <http://www.offta.org.uk>.

[44] Directive 95/47/EC on the use of standards for the transmission of television signals, OJ L281/51, 23 November 1995.

[45] The Class Licence was issued under s 7 of the Telecommunications Act 1984 in January 1997 and re-issued in August 2001.

[46] August 1999.

[47] DGT, Decision as to the status of Sky Subscriber Services Limited as a regulated supplier in the market for access control services for digital interactive TV services (2000).

[48] These included the following: Oftel, The pricing of conditional access services and related issues (2002); Oftel, The pricing of conditional access services and related issues (2002); Oftel, Terms of supply of conditional access: Oftel guidelines (2002).

8.4 THE LEAD-UP TO THE ACCESS DIRECTIVE

The European Commission embarked on a review of regulatory policy in communications industries in 1999.[49]

The focus of discussion and debate about access and interconnection surrounded two issues. The first concerned the widening of the scope of access rights: the Commission considered that a broader scope of access obligations should be provided for. Apart from fostering competitive markets, the reasoning for the new approach included other public interest reasons, including the promotion of the common market and the protection of the environment (such as through mobile masts being shared rather than duplicated).

The second issue of focus involved when and how an operator should be determined to have SMP (and thus be subject to access and interconnection obligations, amongst other things). The Commission initially proposed a two-tier approach, with those operators with SMP, as defined in the Interconnection Directive, being subject to certain obligations, and those operators that were 'dominant', within the meaning of general competition law, being subject to more onerous access obligations.[50] The two-tier approach came under much criticism and was not implemented into the Directives.

8.5 CURRENT REGULATORY OBLIGATIONS IN RELATION TO ACCESS AND INTERCONNECTION

8.5.1 The access and framework directives

On 7 March 2002, the European Commission adopted a package of Directives establishing a new regime in respect of electronic communications networks, electronic communications services, and associated facilities. Member States were required to implement the Directives into local law by 24 July 2003, with the new rules commencing on 25 July 2003. The package included the Access Directive and the Framework Directive.[51] The Access Directive defines Member States' duties in relation to imposing access obligations. The Framework Directive is relevant in understanding these duties, in particular because it sets out the market analysis process which must be undertaken when imposing access obligations based on an undertaking's market power.

---

[49] See Commission Communication, 'Towards a new framework for Electronic Communications infrastructure and associated services: The 1999 Communications Review', COM (1999) 539, 10 November 1999.

[50] Ibid, p 27.

[51] Directive 2002/21/EC on a common regulatory framework for electronic communications networks and services, OJ L108/33, 24 April 2002 (the Framework Directive).

8.5.1.1 *Definitions of access and interconnection under the Access Directive*
The Access Directive defines 'access' as:

... the making available of facilities and/or services, to another undertaking, under defined conditions, on either an exclusive or non-exclusive basis, for the purpose of providing electronic communications services. It covers *inter alia*: access to network elements and associated facilities, which may involve the connection of equipment, by fixed or non-fixed means (in particular this includes access to the local loop and to facilities and services necessary to provide services over the local loop), access to physical infrastructure including buildings, ducts and masts; access to relevant software systems including operational support systems, access to number translation or systems offering equivalent functionality, access to fixed and mobile networks, in particular for roaming, access to conditional access systems for digital television services; access to virtual network services. (Article 2(a))

It is clear that the Commission has sought to define access very broadly, catching not only network access but access to physical infrastructure such as ducts and masts, and to related facilities such as software. The inclusion of 'virtual network services' in the definition also seems to imply that access obligations can be imposed on those who do not own the underlying network, but have other rights to use it, such as Mobile Virtual Network Operators.

Interconnection is defined in the Access Directive as:

... the physical and logical linking of public communications networks used by the same or a different undertaking in order to allow the users of one undertaking to communicate with the users of the same or another undertaking, or to access services provided by another undertaking. Services may be provided by the parties involved or other parties who have access to the network. Interconnection is a specific type of access implemented between public network operators. (Article 2(b))[52]

There is no question, then, that interconnection is considered to be a category of access under the European regulatory regime.

8.5.1.2 *Overview of the access conditions under the Access Directive*
The Access Directive envisages that Member States will have the power to impose several different types of access obligations These obligations can be summarized as follows:

i. Member States must impose a general obligation on all providers of public electronic communications networks to 'negotiate interconnection' with other such providers on request.

ii. National regulatory authorities may impose additional obligations on operators designated as having SMP on a specific market, requiring that they meet reasonable

---

[52] This definition is fairly similar to the definition of 'interconnection' used in the Interconnection Directive, except for the inclusion of the final sentence making it clear that interconnection is a type of access.

requests for access to, and use of, specific network elements and associated facilities.

iii. National regulatory authorities are to encourage and, where appropriate, ensure adequate access and interconnection and interoperability of services in a way that promotes efficiency, sustainable competition, and gives maximum benefit to end-users.

iv. National regulatory authorities must impose specific access obligations in relation to conditional access services.

These categories of obligations are explored in more detail below.

8.5.1.3 *General condition to negotiate interconnection: Article 4*
Article 4 of the Access Directive provides that operators of public communications networks shall have a right, and, when requested by other such undertakings, an obligation, to negotiate interconnection with each other for the purpose of providing publicly available electronic communications services to ensure the provision and interoperability of services throughout the European Community.

The categories of operators with rights and obligation to interconnect has thus been expanded under the Access Directive from those falling within one of the categories of Annex II (under the 1997 Interconnection Directive), to *all* providers of public electronic communications networks.

8.5.1.4 *Imposition of access obligations on operators with SMP: Articles 8–13*
The access obligations under Articles 8 to 13 of the Access Directive may only be applied to undertakings possessing SMP, except in exceptional circumstances.

8.5.1.5 *Determining SMP: market review procedure*[53]
A key difference between the access and interconnection regime under the Interconnection Directive and that under the Access Directive concerns the test that is applied to determine whether an undertaking is considered to have SMP. Whilst the Interconnection Directive created a presumption of SMP where an operator had 25 per cent market share, the Access Directive sets a higher hurdle by adopting a definition which is consistent with European competition case law. The Framework Directive provides that an undertaking is deemed to have SMP if:

... either individually or jointly with others, it enjoys a position equivalent to dominance, that is to say a position of economic strength affording it the power to behave to an appreciable extent independently of competitors, customers and ultimately consumers. (Article 14)

The process that national regulatory authorities are to undertake to determine whether any undertaking in a given market has SMP is set out in the Framework Directive.

---

[53] See further Chapter 5 at 5.6.

National regulatory authorities are required to take the 'utmost account' of two important documents: the Commission's guidelines for market analysis and the assessment of SMP[54] (EC Guidelines), and the Commission's Recommendation on the relevant product and service markets (Market Recommendation).[55]

The EC Guidelines were published in July 2002. They set out guidance on defining the appropriate product and services market and geographic market, for assessing whether any operator possesses market power in the defined market, and on deciding what remedies should be imposed on those that are found to have SMP. They are based on a number of documents, including existing case law of the Court of First Instance and the European Court of Justice and on previous EC competition law guidelines.

The final version of the Market Recommendation was adopted in February 2003. It sets out seven retail markets and eleven wholesale markets. Arguably, there is an underlying tension between the requirement that national regulatory authorities must on the one hand define markets according to general competition law, and the requirement on the other hand that they must take 'utmost account' of the 18 markets defined in the market recommendation. In 2007, the Commission adopted a revised version of the Recommendation,[56] reducing the number of markets to seven, one retail and six wholesale. If a national regulatory authority undertakes a study of part of the industry to determine the relevant market, and such study is undertaken strictly in accordance with the tests set out in general competition law, it is hard to see how taking the 'utmost account' of the Commission's list of markets is meant to change or influence that analysis.

If national regulatory authorities define markets that differ from those set out in the recommendation, they are required to undertake a consultation process with other national regulatory authorities and the Commission. The Commission may ultimately require a market definition which departs from the Market Recommendation to be withdrawn.[57]

The Framework Directive also provides for a procedure for analysing transnational markets. Such analysis would be conducted jointly by the relevant national regulatory authorities (Article 16(5)).

Based on its market analysis, each national regulatory authority must determine whether the market in question is effectively competitive. If the market is not effectively

[54] Commission Guidelines on market analysis and the assessment of significant market power under the Community regulatory framework for electronic communications networks and services, OJ C165/6, 11 July 2002.

[55] Commission recommendation on relevant product and service markets within the electronic communications sector susceptible to *ex ante* regulation in accordance with Directive 2002/21/EC of the European Parliament and of the Council on a common regulatory framework for electronic communications networks and services, OJ L114/45, 8 May 2003.

[56] Commission Recommendation (2007/879/EC) of 17 December 2007 (OJ L 344/65, 28 December 2007).

[57] Framework Directive, Arts 6, 7, and 15(3).

competitive, the national regulatory authority must identify the operators with SMP on that market and impose appropriate, specific, regulatory obligations, or maintain or amend obligations already in place (Article 16(4)). The decision to designate or not designate an operator as having SMP is subject to a consultation procedure under the Framework Directive. The Commission ultimately has the power to require that a particular decision be withdrawn (Article 7).

8.5.1.6 *The SMP conditions*

Where a finding of SMP is made, national regulatory authorities may impose one of the obligations in Articles 9 to 13 of the Access Directive (in the case of wholesale markets) or Articles 17 to 19 of the Universal Services Directive (in the case of retail markets).[58] This chapter will focus on the obligations in Articles 9 to 13 of the Access Directive.

The most important obligation for the present purposes is that which can be imposed under Article 12 of the Access Directive and which relates to the provision of access.

Under Article 12, national regulatory authorities may require an operator with SMP in a given market to meet reasonable requests for access to and use of specified parts of their network and associate facilities, particularly in situations where it is considered that denial of access or unreasonable terms and conditions would hinder the emergence of a sustainable competitive market at the retail level, or would not be in the interest of end-users.

The following types of access obligations are specifically envisaged in Article 12:

    i. giving of access to specified network elements and/or facilities, including unbundled access to the local loop;

    ii. negotiating in good faith with undertakings requesting access;

    iii. not withdrawing access to facilities already granted;

    iv. providing specified services on a wholesale basis for resale by third parties;

    v. granting open access to technical interfaces, protocols, or other key technologies that are indispensable for the interoperability of services or virtual network services;

    vi. providing co-location or other forms of facility sharing, including duct, building, or mast sharing;

    vii. providing specified services needed to ensure interoperability of end-to-end services to users, including facilities for intelligent network services or roaming on mobile networks;

---

[58] See further Chapter 5 at 5.8.

viii. providing access to operational support systems or similar software systems necessary to ensure fair competition in the provision of services; and

ix. interconnecting networks or network facilities.

The imposition of any of the obligations in Articles 9 to 13 must always be based on the nature of the problem identified, be proportionate, and be justified in light of the general policy objectives in the Framework Directive,[59] like consumer protection, the protection of privacy and ensuring network security and integrity. Where an access obligation is imposed under Article 12, additional factors must be taken into account. These factors are:

i. the technical and economic viability of using or installing competing facilities, in light of the rate of market development, taking into account the nature and type of interconnection and access involved;

ii. the feasibility of providing the access proposed, in relation to the capacity available;

iii. the initial investment by the facility owner, bearing in mind the risks involved in making the investment;

iv. the need to safeguard competition in the long term;

v. where appropriate, any relevant intellectual property rights; and

vi. the provision of pan-European services.

Apart from the access obligations in Article 12, described above, the other regulatory obligations that may be imposed on SMP operators are, in summary:

i. transparency (Access Directive, Article 9)—operators may be required to make public a range of information, such as accounting information, technical specifications, network characteristics, and terms, conditions and prices, or to publish a reference offer. Where an operator is required to give access to the local loop, the operator must be required to publish a reference offer which includes the provisions specified in Annex II of the Access Directive;

ii. non-discrimination (Access Directive, Article 10)—operators may be required to provide equivalent conditions in equivalent circumstances, and provide services and information of the same quality as it provides to its own downstream businesses;

iii. accounting separation (Access Directive, Article 11)—operators may be required to keep separate accounts in respect of interconnection or access services, and to provide them to the regulator on request; and

iv. price controls (Access Directive, Article 13)—in specific circumstances, operators may be subjected to price caps, including controls requiring that prices are 'cost orientated'.

---

[59] Access Directive, Art 8(4).

Subject to some narrow exceptions, the obligations above cannot be imposed on operators that have not been designated as possessing SMP. Also, the intent of the Commission is that these obligations should be exhaustive—no other obligations in respect of access and interconnection can be imposed unless the national regulatory authority first obtains authorization from the Commission.[60]

Article 7 of the Framework Directive envisages that national regulatory authorities in different Member States will work together to develop an agreed position on the imposition of remedies on operators with SMP so that the Directives are consistently applied. This work has been undertaken under the auspices of the European Regulators' Group.[61]

8.5.1.7 *Other access-related conditions: Article 5*

Article 5(1) of the Access Directive requires national regulatory authorities to encourage, and, where appropriate, ensure adequate access and interconnection, and interoperability of services, in a way that promotes efficiency, sustainable competition, and gives maximum benefit to end-users. The Directive specifically provides that this may include obligations:

i. on operators that control access to end-users, including in justified cases the obligation to interconnect their networks, to the extent necessary to ensure end-to-end connectivity; and

ii. to provide access to application programme interfaces (APIs) and electronic programme guides (EPGs) on fair, reasonable, and non-discriminatory terms, to the extent necessary to ensure accessibility for end-users to digital radio and television broadcasting services.

Article 5(1) goes beyond anything under the 1997 Interconnection Directive. It should be emphasized that it accords Member States the right to impose access obligations even on operators who do not have market power, where the national regulatory authority takes the view that such obligations are needed to ensure 'adequate access and interconnection, and interoperability'. It remains to be seen how far Member States will go in wielding these powers, which obviously have scope for being interpreted very broadly.

Conditions imposed under Article 5(1) must be notified to the Commission and other national regulatory authorities under Article 7 of the Framework Directive. This, at least, may prove to be a check on how these powers are used. Under the original proposal for the Access Directive, the Commission would have been entitled to require conditions set under Article 5(1) to be withdrawn, but this right was not included in the final wording. In 2006, the Commission again proposed an amendment

---

[60] Access Directive, Art 8(3).
[61] See ERG Common Position 'on the approach to appropriate remedies in the new regulatory framework', ERG (03) 30rev1 (April 2004) and revised Common Position 'on the approach to appropriate remedies in the ECNS regulatory framework' ERG (06) 33 (May 2006).

to require prior authorization from the Commission for Article 5(1) obligations,[62] but it is absent from the reform proposals published in November 2007;[63] which is illustrative on the ongoing political tussle over the best approach towards harmonization in the European Union.[64]

8.5.1.8 *Conditional access systems and other facilities: Article 6*

Article 6 of the Access Directive requires Member States to impose a range of conditions in relation to conditional access services for digital television and radio. As noted earlier, conditional access enables broadcasters to make reception of their television and radio signals conditional upon prior authorization such that viewers need descrambling equipment, usually in the form of an authorized access card inserted into a set top box, for viewing or listening to the transmission. These conditions include an obligation for providers of conditional access to offer services to broadcasters on a fair, reasonable and non-discriminatory basis, compatible with Community competition law.[65]

Member States may, where certain conditions are met, maintain, amend, or withdraw conditional access conditions if a market review is carried out and shows that one or more operators do not have SMP on the relevant market.[66]

8.5.1.9 *Proposals for reform*

In November 2007, the Commission published its proposals to reform aspects of the 2003 regulatory framework, including amendments to the Access Directive.[67] While a number of minor technical adjustments, repeals of outdated provisions, and clarifications are outlined, the only substantive proposal to amend the Access Directive is the inclusion of an additional remedy available for NRAs, the imposition of functional separation on a SMP operator.[68] Operators that voluntarily decide to transfer their local access network assets to a separate legal entity would be required to notify the NRA for assessment in respect of existing obligations.[69] These provisions reflect the experience in the UK with respect to BT[70] and a continued frustration with the ability of vertically integrated national incumbents to inhibit competition in certain

---

[62] Commission Staff Working Document 'on the Review of the EU Regulatory Framework for electronic communication networks and services – Proposed changes' COM(2006) 334 final, at 5.4.

[63] Proposal for a Directive 'amending Directives 2002/21/EC on a common regulatory framework for electronic communications networks and services, 2002/19/EC on access to, and interconnection of, electronic communications networks and services, and 2002/20/EC on the authorisation of electronic communications networks and services' COM (2007)697 rev 1.

[64] See further Chapter 5, at 5.7.1.

[65] The conditions are set out in full in Annex I, Part 1 of the Access Directive.

[66] Article 6(3) of the Access Directive. The amendment or withdrawal of conditions following a market review must not adversely affect the market for conditional access services, the retail market for digital television and radio services, or accessibility of certain specified television and radio services.

[67] Supra n 63.

[68] Ibid, at draft Art 13a.

[69] Ibid, at draft Art 13b.

[70] See further Chapter 4, at 4.3.8.1.

market sectors, particularly local access. In addition, the reforms would repeal Regulation 2887/2000 on unbundled access to the local loop, as its provisions are effectively subsumed within the Access Directive regime.

8.5.2 United Kingdom implementation of the Access Directive

Shortly after the EU review of telecommunications started in 1999, the UK also began a review of the regulatory environment governing the communications industry, starting with the Communications White Paper in 2000. This review led, eventually, to the passage of the Communications Act 2003, which implemented the Access and Framework Directives (and the other EU Directives which required implementation by July 2003), and brought about further sweeping changes, including the formation of Ofcom, which commenced its operations in December 2003.

The sections below look at the definitions of access and interconnection in the Communications Act 2003 and explain how the UK has implemented each of the four categories of access obligations in the Access Directive, discussed above.[71]

8.5.2.1 *Definitions of access and interconnection*
'Interconnection' is defined in section 151(2) of the Communications Act 2003 and largely replicates the definition in the Access Directive.

'Network access' is defined in section 151(3) and (4) of the Communications Act. It includes, apart from interconnection, access to a range of electronic communications networks, services, and facilities for the purpose of the provision of an electronic communications service. Whilst it is not as prescriptive as the definition of 'access' in the Access Directive, in that it does not give specific examples of the types of access covered, it is almost certainly as broad.

8.5.2.2 *Implementation of the general interconnection obligation*
One of the first tasks undertaken in preparation for the implementation of the Directives was the drafting of the General Conditions of Entitlement.[72]

Condition 1 of the General Conditions of Entitlement requires every person who provides a 'public electronic communications network' (PECN) to negotiate with other such providers 'with a view to concluding an agreement (or an amendment to an existing agreement) for Interconnection within a reasonable period'. This condition implements the obligation in Article 4 of the Access Directive (see section 8.5.1.3 above).

---

[71] Some of the determinations and guidelines discussed in this section were published by the DGT, others were published by Oftel, whilst those published since 29 December 2003 were published by Ofcom. To avoid confusion, this section will refer to Ofcom in the main text, whilst referencing the actual publishing body in the footnotes.

[72] See further Chapter 7.

The definition of PECN is such that it encompasses a transmission system, and the associated apparatus, software, and data used with the system for the conveyance of signals, where such system is provided wholly or mainly for making electronic communications services available to members of the public.[73]

As section 32(4)(a) of the Communications Act 2003 provides that the 'provision' of an electronic communications network includes references to 'its establishment, maintenance and operation', it is clear that the 'provision' of a PECN is not the same as ownership of the network, although some degree of control over it is clearly required. This issue is further explored in a statement issued by Ofcom in May 2003,[74] which states that the provider of a single network node who is willing to obtain transmission infrastructure that builds towards an electronic communications network will fall within the definition of a 'public electronic communications network'. Therefore, by way of an example used in the Statement, where provider A seeks interconnection from provider B, the links between provider A's node and provider B's node will constitute provider A's transmission system, whether the link is self-provided, leased from provider B, or leased from another provider altogether.[75]

Ofcom's statement is also helpful in analysing whether an electronic communications network is 'provided wholly or mainly for making electronic communications services available to members of the public'. The statement provides that a publicly available service is one that is available to anyone willing to pay for it and abide by the applicable terms and conditions.[76] A service with only one customer can be considered to be publicly available where it is genuinely available to others on good faith, but, conversely, a service with more than one customer would not necessarily be considered to be available to the public, such as a landlord providing services to tenants on a single premises where such services are not available except to those tenants. 'Members of the public' does not require that the service has to be useable by individuals—if a service is of such a scale that it is only useful to large corporate customers, it will be considered to be available to members of the public provided that it is generally available to such potential customers.

A service would not normally be considered to be available to members of the public where the provider earns a substantial proportion (i.e. 80 per cent or more) of its revenue from members of its corporate group. This is an important point, because it means that entities that only provide communications services to other members of their corporate group do not have a right to interconnection. Without this rule it would be open to large companies to obtain interconnection services from operators with SMP at cost-orientated prices (where cost-orientated prices have been imposed), and even to charge other operators for termination of calls onto their network. This would be intolerable from a public policy point of view, as interconnection rights and

---

[73] See Part 1 of the General Conditions and General Condition 1.4.
[74] Oftel, *Guidelines for the interconnection of public electronic communications networks* (2003).
[75] Ibid, para 4.8.
[76] Ibid, Chapter 6.

obligations should only accrue to those who invest in infrastructure used to provide truly public services, and who contribute to the competitive market.

8.5.2.3 *Ofcom's voluntary PECN Register*

The Interconnection Directive required operators to register with Oftel to be included on the 'Annex II list' in order to be acquire rights and obligations to interconnect. By contrast, under the new regime no registration is required—the only legal requirement is that of providing a PECN.

Ofcom initially decided to maintain a list, similar to the Annex II list, to simplify the process of negotiating interconnection. The list was known as the voluntary register of public electronic communications networks. To be included on the register, operators were required to submit an application form to Ofcom specifying details of how their network qualifies as a PECN. Inclusion on the register signified that on the facts and circumstances presented to Ofcom on the application form, it was reasonable for Ofcom to assume that the operator was providing, or intending to provide, a PECN. Ofcom subsequently decided to abandon the register on the grounds that it was difficult to administer and did not provide sufficient benefits to operators.

8.5.2.4 *Imposition of obligations on operators with SMP*

The Communications Act 2003 sets out the definition of SMP (section 78), the procedure that Ofcom must follow in reviewing markets (section 79(1)–(3)) and consulting and making determinations that one or more operators has SMP in a given market (sections 79(4)–81), and the conditions that Ofcom may impose on such operators (sections 87–91). The provisions in the Act largely correspond with the relevant Articles in the Framework and Access Directives.

National regulatory authorities were required to commence the enormous administrative feat involved in undertaking market reviews as soon as possible after the adoption of the Market Recommendation, in February 2003.[77] As the Communications Act was not in force at that time, special legislation was passed to ensure that the DGT had the power to undertake the tasks necessary to carry out the reviews required by the Framework Directive.[78]

8.5.2.5 *Assessment of SMP and regulatory option appraisals*

Ofcom published market review guidelines in August 2002.[79] These guidelines are used in conjunction with the EC Guidelines when assessing whether any undertaking in a given market possesses SMP. Although Ofcom's guidelines complement the EC Guidelines on most points, they also set out several pages of additional criteria that Ofcom considers should be taken into account when carrying out the analysis.

---

[77] Framework Directive, Art 16(1).
[78] See Electronic Communications (Market Analysis) Regulations 2003, SI 2003/330.
[79] Oftel, *Market review guidelines: criteria for the assessment of significant market power* (2002).

Ofcom will also undertake an analysis called a Regulatory Option Appraisal (ROA)[80] wherever it proposes imposing conditions on undertakings. In the case of wholesale markets, the aim of a ROA is to assess which, if any, of the remedies in the Access Directive are appropriate. The results of the ROA are annexed to the relevant market review consultation document.

8.5.2.6 *Ofcom's approach to the imposition of SMP access obligations*
In order to ensure that both SMP operators and competing operators would have a fair expectation of the kind of access obligations that Ofcom was likely to consider appropriate when conducting its market reviews, Ofcom also published guidelines (Access Guidelines)[81] explaining how it proposed to apply the conditions that it is entitled to impose on SMP undertakings under the Access Directive. The Access Guidelines indicate the nature of the products Ofcom would expect to be supplied as a result of such an obligation being imposed, and the conditions under which such products should be made available. The Access Guidelines are not legally binding but are, nevertheless, a useful analysis of the remedies that may be imposed on operators possessing SMP.

8.5.2.6.1 *Obligation to supply wholesale access products*
A key point in the Access Guidelines is the stated policy that, when imposing an obligation to provide access to wholesale products, in most cases Ofcom is likely to impose access obligations in the form of an obligation to 'meet all reasonable requests for access'. Importantly, the Access Guidelines state that Ofcom is likely to consider that a request which is technically feasible is 'reasonable' if the SMP operator can reasonably expect to receive at least a reasonable rate of return on any necessary investments when the access product is supplied at a price the requesting operator is willing to pay. Only in 'extreme examples' should a request for access be denied on the basis that the request is unreasonable.[82]

8.5.2.6.2 *New products and innovative products*
The Access Guidelines also provide guidance on the situation arising when a competing operator demands a new wholesale product, and the case of products that become available because of innovation on the part of the SMP operator.

In the case of a demand on an SMP operator to make a new or untested wholesale access product available to a competitor, it can be difficult to determine whether demand for the product will materialize. It is therefore difficult to determine whether the SMP operator can expect a reasonable rate of return on the investment that they will make, which (as set out above) is Ofcom's test for whether a request is 'reasonable'. The Access Guidelines state that if the SMP operator will incur significant development costs in supplying a product for which demand is uncertain,

---

[80] Oftel, *Regulatory option appraisal guidelines: assessing the impact of policy proposals* (2002).
[81] Oftel, *Imposing access obligations under the new EU Directives* (2002).
[82] Ibid, at 13.

the requesting operator may be required to take on an appropriate level of risk. This could involve:

i. the requesting operator committing to a level of demand at a price that would justify investment by the SMP operator in supplying the wholesale product; or

ii. allowing the SMP operator to specify a pricing structure based on forecast demand and/or specify a process of balancing payments between the SMP operator and the requesting operator at the end of a set period, based on actual demand.

The development costs would need to be incurred in a reasonable and efficient way by the SMP operator.[83]

In the case of products developed as a result of innovation (and, typically, significant investment) by an SMP operator, the Access Guidelines state that SMP operators should be required to supply an equivalent wholesale product when introducing innovative retail products. The same applies when an innovative wholesale product is made available by an SMP operator to its own vertically integrated retail business. The risk with this approach, obviously, is that SMP operators will be disincentivized from investing in the development of new services, because they will be required to share the results of their innovation with their competitors, rather than being able to gain a competitive advantage and increased market share by being 'first to market'. The Access Guidelines propose that this problem should be dealt with by allowing SMP operators to impose sufficiently generous terms in the supply of innovative wholesale products to other operators. Where a new or innovative product involves a high level of risk, cost-based price controls will normally be avoided, even if the SMP operator has very high market share. In such markets the Access Guidelines state that either no charge control, or a retail minus form of regulation may be more appropriate. A retail minus pricing model would in this case allow an element of supernormal profit to be built into the retail price to be retained by the SMP operator. The Access Guidelines consider that setting any kind of cost-based charge control risks distortion of commercial and investment decisions and discouragement of innovative market offerings, ultimately to the detriment of consumers.[84]

8.5.2.6.3 *Access to information protected by intellectual property rights*
The Access Guidelines state that if information which is protected by intellectual property rights is essential to allow competitors to the SMP operator to offer a competing product, the SMP operator would be expected to make the information available. The operator requesting the information would be expected to demonstrate that it is indeed essential.[85]

---

[83] Ibid.

[84] Ibid, 14, 33–35.

[85] Ibid, 35. See further Chapter 10. Note that this rule does not apply to standard network interfaces, which must be made available in all cases under the interface publication rules. Compare these rules to the essential facilities doctrine under general competition law: see further Chapter 9.

8.5.2.6.4 Terms and conditions governing access

The Access Guidelines indicate that Ofcom intends to attach conditions relating to
fairness, reasonableness, and timeliness to all obligations to provide access. This
means that the terms should be consistent with those which would be offered in a
competitive market, should be sensible and practical, should include obligations in
relation to timelines, such as reasonable service levels and penalties for non-delivery,
and should provide sufficiently unbundled services, so that a competing operator
pays only for what it needs.[86]

The Access Guidelines also envisage that conditions may be imposed on an SMP
operator in relation to the process under which competing operators request new
products. Ofcom expects SMP operators to deal with such requests within a reasonable timescale and to enter into discussions with competing operators if further
information or clarity is needed.[87]

8.5.2.6.5 Imposition of non-discrimination obligations

Non-discrimination obligations become particularly relevant where an SMP operator
is vertically integrated. The Access Guidelines state that there is a rebuttable presumption that discrimination by a vertically integrated SMP operator in favour of its
downstream business would have a material adverse effect on competition. Vertically
integrated SMP operators will therefore normally be required to ensure that they
provide services on equivalent terms and conditions as are available to subsidiaries
and partners, and that they can objectively justify any differentiation. The application
of different pricing may be justified on the basis of different underlying costs, or
different levels of risk. The Access Guidelines state that the non-discrimination rule
would not always prevent volume discounts from being applied, provided that they
are applied in a consistent manner. However, a volume discount that benefited the
downstream business of an SMP operator disproportionately, by virtue of its size,
would not be permitted.[88]

8.5.3.6.6 Imposition of transparency obligations

The Access Guidelines state that any new wholesale product offered by an SMP
operator will normally need to be published in the form of a reference offer. Initial
reference offers for new products, and changes and updates to a reference offer for
an existing product, should be released in a timely manner, allowing enough time for
a reasonably efficient operator to make necessary preparations. Information (including terms, conditions, and prices) must be supplied to any downstream business
at the same time that it is released to the market. Sufficient information should
be given at the time of or before the launch of a product to enable competitors to
make full and effective use of the product supplied, although the disclosure of such

---

[86] Oftel, n 79 above, 22–23.

[87] Ibid, 24.

[88] Ibid, at 16–17 and 30–31.

information can be made subject to a confidentiality agreement. A list of the mini-mum information that must be included in a reference offer is set out in Annex 2 to the Access Guidelines (although this list does not cover reference offers in respect of access to the local loop, which need to include the information set out in Annex II to the Access Directive).[89]

8.5.2.6.7 Imposition of charge controls

In general, Ofcom considers that in markets which are not effectively competitive, and where there is little prospect of this changing in the short-term future, the impo-sition of charge controls on SMP operators, in the form of cost-based prices, are generally appropriate. Prices subject to price control should still allow a return on capital that takes into account the level of risk involved. As competition evolves, price caps should be relaxed.

In markets which are not effectively competitive, but where market power is diminishing, the Access Guidelines propose that it may be sufficient to rely on the imposition of a general non-discrimination obligation, implemented by requiring that charges are based on a retail minus model. Whilst allowing the SMP operator to recover the same margin as it recovers when retailing the service itself, retail minus price models are intended to prevent the SMP operator from 'squeezing' its competitors' margins.[90]

8.5.2.6.8 Imposition of obligations relating to accounting separation

According to the Access Guidelines, the main purpose of obliging operators to pre-pare and publish regulatory financial information is to ensure compliance with the non-discrimination obligations (to prevent margin squeezing), and to prevent anti-competitive cross-subsidy. The information may also be used in setting charge controls, conducting sector reviews, and in specific case work. Typically, separate statements would be required in relation to the different activities of a vertically integrated operator. As it is generally not feasible for national regulatory authorities to continu-ally monitor prices, where there are incentives for SMP operators to impose a margin squeeze, it may be appropriate to also require publication of prices in the relevant downstream market, so that any margin squeeze would be highly visible.[91]

8.5.2.7 Market reviews

The process of identifying relevant markets, operators with SMP, and appropriate remedies was commenced in the UK soon after the publication of the Commission's Market Recommendation.[92] At the completion of each review a consultation docu-ment was published, setting out the relevant markets, proposed findings of SMP, and

---

[89] Ibid, 18–19, 30–31.
[90] Ibid, 19–21.
[91] Ibid, 21–22.
[92] See n 78 above in respect of the special legislation that was passed to empower the DGT to undertake this task.

any proposed SMP conditions, and inviting comments. After the consultation, final determinations of market power and SMP conditions are issued.

The size of this task should be appreciated. The UK market reviews totalled many thousands of pages of analysis. Much of the work was undertaken during the course of the handover of responsibility from Oftel to Ofcom, no doubt making the task even more difficult than it would otherwise have been.

Whilst a detailed analysis of each of the market reviews is beyond the scope of this chapter, some general trends have emerged which warrant particular attention. First, generally speaking, Ofcom has defined national markets more narrowly than recommended by the Commission in the Market Recommendation. By way of example, where the Commission recommended a single market for wholesale international call services, Ofcom found there to be a different market in wholesale international call services *to each country*, because calls to one country are not substitutable for calls to another country. Thus, Ofcom found there to be 235 different markets in wholesale international call services, 123 of which were found to be effectively competitive. Of the others, BT was found to have SMP in 108 and Cable & Wireless in the remaining four markets. Appropriate SMP conditions were imposed on these operators in respect of these markets.[93] When this market sector was reviewed for a second time in 2006, Ofcom reiterated its findings in terms of the number of markets, but also determined that no operator continued to have SMP, and therefore the previous obligations could be revoked.[94]

Another important trend in the way markets have been defined lies in the fact that Ofcom considers there to be different markets in call termination services to each separate fixed network and mobile network. By way of example, there is considered to be a market for call termination to Vodafone customers and a separate market in call termination to Orange customers. Again, this is mainly because the services are not substitutable for each other. The result of this approach is that every operator, no matter how small, is considered to have 100 per cent market share in the termination of calls onto their own network, and, accordingly, every operator has been determined to have SMP in that market.[95] Hutchison 3G UK ('3'), as the new entrant, appealed its SMP designation to the Competition Appeal Tribunal (CAT), on the grounds that Ofcom's analysis had been insufficient, in particular by failing to take into account the countervailing buying power of BT when negotiating with 3. The CAT upheld the

---

[93] Director General of Telecommunications, *Wholesale international services markets, identification and analysis of market and Determination on market power, final explanatory statement and notification* (2003).

[94] Ofcom, '*Wholesale international services markets*', 7 July 2006.

[95] Ofcom, *Statement on wholesale mobile voice call termination* (2004) and Director General of Telecommunications, *Review of fixed geographic call termination market* (2003).

appeal and remitted the decision back to Ofcom for reconsideration.[96] However, following the reassessment, Ofcom still found that 3 had SMP.[97]

Following the first market review, a range of SMP conditions were imposed which varied depending on the operator's market share in call origination. By way of example, the four established mobile network operators (Vodafone, O2, T-Mobile, and Orange) were required to comply with a range of conditions which include reducing their termination charges in line with charge controls. In contrast, the new entrant operator, 3, was only required to give advance notification of changes in its termination charges and supply Ofcom with details of call volumes.[98] However, following a second market review, charge controls were placed on all five operators, with 3 being given the ability to charge a slightly higher average charge to reflect its unique position.[99] Similarly, whilst BT is required to comply with a range of SMP conditions in the market for geographic call termination, including setting cost-based prices, its smaller competitors in this market are only subject to SMP conditions requiring them to provide termination services on reasonable request and to set fair and reasonable terms for such services.[100]

Where imposing an obligation on an SMP operator to provide network access, Ofcom has generally couched the condition as a requirement to provide network access to third party public electronic network and service providers on reasonable request, and, additionally, to provide such network access 'as Ofcom may from time to time direct'. A number of directions have already been issued in connection with these SMP conditions. Generally speaking, these directions preserve directions given by the DGT under the old regime. They include directions as to the provision of FRIACO interconnection, carrier pre-selection and wholesale line rental, ATM interconnection, and partial private circuits.[101]

Notably, a direction has also been issued in relation to the provision by BT of RBS backhaul circuits to mobile operators. This direction largely replicates the direction made in June 2003 that had to be withdrawn after BT's appeal to the CAT. This direction stands, therefore, as an interesting example of how the new regime may be more onerous in some respects that the old.[102]

---

[96] *Hutchison 3G (UK) Ltd v Ofcom* [2005] CAT 39.

[97] Ofcom, *Assessment of whether H3G holds a position of SMP in the market for wholesale mobile voice call termination on its network*, 27 March 2007.

[98] Ofcom, *Statement on wholesale mobile voice call termination* (2004).

[99] Ofcom, *Mobile Call Termination,* 27 March 2007.

[100] Director General of Telecommunications, *Review of Fixed geographic call termination market* (2003). As discussed in section 8.6.1.2, however, in practice all geographic networks are generally required to set their termination charges with regard to the principle of reciprocity.

[101] The directions made under the Interconnection Regulations 1997 are discussed above at section 8.3.4.1.

[102] Ibid.

8.5.2.8 *Article 5 access-related conditions*

As noted at section 8.5.1.7 above, apart from the general interconnection condition and SMP conditions, Article 5 of the Access Directive entitles national regulatory authorities to impose certain further access conditions.

The Article 5 conditions may be imposed where necessary to ensure adequate access and interconnection, and interoperability of services. In particular, national regulatory authorities may impose access-related conditions to ensure end-to-end connectivity, and to ensure accessibility for end-users to digital radio and television broadcasting through access to application programme interfaces and electronic programme guides. These provisions of Article 5 are reflected in sections 73 and 74 of the Communications Act. As in the Access Directive, these conditions can be imposed even where no operator possesses SMP in a market. Ofcom has indicated that it will construe its rights to impose such conditions restrictively, and expects the use of access-related conditions to be very limited.[103]

The sections below examine the circumstances where Ofcom has considered imposing Article 5 access-related conditions.

8.5.2.8.1 *End-to-end connectivity*

In guidance published in May 2003,[104] Ofcom considered the question of whether specific obligations were needed to ensure end-to-end connectivity, that is, connectivity enabling users to contact users and services on other networks as well as those on the same network. Achieving end-to-end connectivity would require that all operators both *purchase* call termination services from all other operators, and *provide* call termination services when requested. If imposed, operators would be positively required to ensure that they are directly or indirectly connected with all other operators and purchase call termination from those operators whenever one of their customers wants to reach a user or service on that other network, and positively required to ensure that they terminate any call received onto their network. These obligations would go beyond the obligation to negotiate interconnection on request, which all operators are required to do under Condition 1 of the General Conditions of Entitlement.

Ofcom concluded that the imposition of obligations to ensure end-to-end connectivity was not appropriate, for several reasons. In considering imposing an obligation to *purchase* call termination from other operators, Ofcom considered that the imposition of such an obligation on the universal service providers (that is, BT and Kingston) would be disproportionate. This is because those operators must in any case meet reasonable requests for access to publicly available telephone services, which, it is implied, includes being able to contact other customers and services, irrespective of

---

[103] Director General of Telecommunications, *National Roaming Condition, A consultation on proposals to set a national roaming condition after 25 July 2003* (2003), 4.

[104] Director General of Telecommunications, *End-to-end connectivity; Guidance issued by the Director General of Telecommunications* (2003).

the terminating network. For operators other than BT and Kingston, Ofcom considered that the commercial incentives to provide end-to-end connectivity were sufficiently strong to ensure that they seek to purchase call termination without any additional obligation to ensure that they do. This is clearly correct—it is almost unthinkable that an operator would seek to set up a new service that did not allow customers to contact users and services on other networks.

Ofcom considered that it was not necessary to impose any additional obligation on any operator to *provide* call termination services to other operators because almost all public electronic communications networks are already under an SMP condition requiring them to provide call termination to all other public electronic communications networks on fair and reasonable terms (see section 8.5.2.7 above).

8.5.2.8.2 National roaming

Before the auction for 3G mobile spectrum in 2000, the DGT sought to amend the PTO licences of the 2G operators who were bidding for 3G spectrum, requiring them to provide 'national roaming' to the new entrant who was awarded spectrum in the auction. In the end, because of the timing of a legal challenge, amendments were only made to the licences of O2 and Vodafone, who voluntarily accepted the condition. The national roaming condition required O2 and Vodafone to negotiate a national roaming agreement with the new entrant 3G operator, '3', allowing its users to roam onto their 2G network. The aim of the condition was to address the concern that 2G mobile network operators which won 3G licences would be able to offer basic 2G services to customers whilst building out their 3G network, whereas a new entrant would not have this advantage, and would not be able to compete.

With the abolition of telecommunications licences in July 2003, Ofcom had to consider whether to re-impose national roaming obligations on 2G operators under the new regulatory regime. The initial conclusion of its predecessor, Oftel, was that all four of the UK's 2G operators should be subject to a new access-related condition requiring them to provide national roaming on fair, reasonable, and not unduly discriminatory terms.[105] Ofcom has subsequently decided, however, that an access condition should not be imposed, on the grounds that the same result can be achieved by 'less intrusive regulation'.[106]

8.5.2.8.3 Access control services

As noted above, access control services are services that enable interactive applications to be run through a user's set top box. Access control services were previously regulated in the UK via the Access Control class licence.[107]

A consultation on the future regulation of access control services was issued in November 2003.[108] In it, Ofcom proposed imposing access-related conditions on

---

[105] Oftel, *National Roaming Condition*, 15 May 2003.
[106] Ofcom, *National Roaming*, 22 July 2004.
[107] See section 8.3.4.7 above.
[108] Director General of Telecommunications, *The future regulation of access control services* (2003).

Sky Subscribers Services Limited under sections 73(2) and 74(2) of the Communications Act. The conditions would require Sky Subscribers Services Limited to provide access control services for interactive television services on its digital satellite platform on fair and reasonable terms, conditions and charges, not to unduly discriminate, to keep separate financial accounts, and to publish terms, conditions, and charges for access control services. These conditions are broadly similar to the conditions in the former Access Control class licence. At the current time, however, the class licence continues in operation.

8.5.2.8.4 *Electronic programme guides*

An electronic programme guide (EPG) is a menu of channels and programmes accessible to viewers of multi-channel television services, allowing them to click through to particular channels using their remote control. Section 74(2) of the Communications Act specifically permits access-related conditions to be imposed for securing that EPG facilities are provided on fair and reasonable terms, without undue discrimination. Prior to the Access Directive, Oftel sought to regulate EPGs under the Conditional Access class licence.[109]

Ofcom consulted on the regulation of EPGs in January 2004.[110] It is proposed that access-related conditions under section 74(2) be imposed on British Sky Broadcasting Limited, the provider of the EPG on the digital satellite platform. The proposed conditions would require British Sky Broadcasting Limited to provide EPG services on fair and reasonable terms and without undue discrimination, and to keep separate accounts and publish its charges terms and conditions for EPG services. The proposed conditions are broadly similar to the conditions previously imposed under the Conditional Access class licence in relation to EPGs; although the latter continues to be the applicable conditions.

The consultation also included a new Code on Electronic Programme Guides, as required by section 310 of the Communications Act 2003.[111] The code includes guidance on matters such as giving appropriate prominence to public service channels and providing features to enable EPGs to be used by people with disabilities.

8.5.2.9 *Article 6 access-related conditions*

Article 6 of the Access Directive requires that the conditions set out in Part I of Annex I of the Access Directive must be imposed on providers of conditional access services. As noted earlier, conditional access services allow a broadcaster to make the receipt of its television and radio signals in intelligible form conditional on prior authorization. Sections 73(5) and 75(2) of the Communications Act require Ofcom to impose access-related conditions in relation to conditional access. Section 76 is concerned with the modification and revocation of such conditions.

---

[109] See section 8.3.4.7 above.
[110] Ofcom, *The Regulation of Electronic Programme Guides* (2004).
[111] Available at <http://www.ofcom.org.uk/tv/ifi/codes/EPGcode/epgcode.pdf>.

Following a consultation, Ofcom set access-related conditions in relation to conditional access on 24 July 2003, so that they were in place at the commencement of the new regulatory regime.[112] The conditions were applied to Sky Subscribers Services Limited and mirror the conditions required to be set under Part I of Annex I of the Access Directive. These include the requirement to provide conditional access services to broadcasters on a fair, reasonable, and non-discriminatory basis, to keep separate financial accounts, and to publish charges terms and conditions in relation to conditional access services. These conditions are broadly similar to the conditions imposed by the Conditional Access class licence.

8.5.2.10 *Dispute resolution*
Section 185 of the Communications Act 2003 empowers Ofcom to deal with certain disputes between operators in relation to network access. Sections 94 to 104 set out Ofcom's rights in relation to the enforcement of conditions which it has imposed (including SMP conditions and the General Conditions of Entitlement). Notably, civil proceedings can be brought by one operator against another where the first operator suffers loss occasioned by the other operator's breach of a condition. However, Ofcom's consent is required before such proceedings can be brought.[113]

Ofcom has issued guidelines for handling disputes and complaints. It is clear that in relation to both disputes and complaints Ofcom expects the party raising the issue with Ofcom to provide substantial evidence before Ofcom will consider taking action.[114]

8.6 PRACTICAL AND CONTRACTUAL ISSUES IN NEGOTIATING CIRCUIT-SWITCHED ACCESS AGREEMENTS

Every time that access arrangements are entered into there should, of course, be a contract in place setting out the parties' rights and responsibilities. This section will canvass some of the practical and contractual issues that are likely to arise when negotiating arrangements for access to parts of the public switched network. IP interconnection agreements are discussed in section 8.7.

Access agreements are by no means a generic set. For example, a complex agreement to establish a mobile virtual network[115] will have a little in common with a basic agreement to interconnect two networks. One factor that does act to distinguish

---

[112] Director General of Telecommunications, *The regulation of conditional access, Setting of regulatory conditions; Explanatory statement and formal notification pursuant to section 48(1) of the Communications Act 2003* (2003).

[113] Communications Act 2003, s 104.

[114] Ofcom, *Guidelines for the handling of competition complaints, and complaints about disputes and disputes about breaches of conditions imposed under the EU Directives* (July 2004).

[115] A mobile virtual network agreement gives one operator, usually with limited infrastructure of its own, and without a licence for radio spectrum, the right of access to parts of the network of a mobile

between different kinds of access agreements, however, is whether either party has SMP in the relevant market and, in particular, whether an SMP party is required to publish a reference offer for the access that is sought. This section will analyse first some aspects of those access arrangements not subject to a reference offer, with a particular focus on interconnection agreements. Some special considerations relevant to reference offers will then be examined.

8.6.1 Bespoke access contracts

Whilst a growing number of complex access arrangements exist, the most common arrangement that operators deal with on a day-to-day basis remains interconnection. With new telephony providers entering the market on a fairly regular basis, legal advisers and contract managers at telecommunications companies see a steady flow of interconnection agreements. A new entrant is likely first to seek to establish interconnection with the incumbent operator, in order to take advantage of transit services needed to establish connectivity with other operators. This agreement will usually be covered by the incumbent's reference offer; see section 8.6.2. The new entrant may then seek direct interconnection agreements with other operators.

Interconnection agreements are usually bilateral; that is, they govern the terms on which each party will terminate traffic onto the other party's network. Each party is usually subject to almost identical obligations, including identical warranties, and the same exclusions and limits on liability. For this reason, bilateral interconnection negotiations are often fairly harmonious. The parties should still ensure, however, that the contract gives them the legal protection they need. If it is unclear or poorly drafted, it will be of no help to the parties in the event of a later contractual dispute that the initial contract negotiations were not difficult.

Interconnection agreements will, of course, contain many of the terms that you would expect to see in any commercial agreement, including provisions setting out payment arrangements, confidentiality, limitations and exclusions of liability, and provisions relating to the whether the agreement can be assigned or transferred. The sections below describe some provisions that are particular to interconnection agreements.

8.6.1.1 *Location of the points of interconnection*
The interconnection agreement should set out the location of one or more points of interconnection. It will usually be appropriate to provide that the parties may also agree additional locations for additional points of interconnection at a later time. This way, the parties do not need to enter into another agreement just to establish another point of interconnection.

---

operator in order to provide mobile telephony services to its own customers. See further Chapter 11, at 11.2.5.

The most common place to locate a point of interconnection is at the site of a switch of one of the parties. This is commonly described as 'customer sited interconnection'. The location of the point of interconnection at some other location is commonly referred to as 'in-span interconnection'.

With customer sited interconnection arrangements, one party will need to locate (or 'co-locate') equipment inside the other's premises. The agreement should provide when and how the co-locating party is to get access to the other's premises to install and maintain such equipment. The party providing co-location may require the other to indemnify it for any damage caused in its premises.

8.6.1.2 *Termination charges*

The agreement will set out the charges levied by each party for the termination of calls onto its network. Termination charges are usually calculated on the length of the call, so the interconnection agreement will usually specify a charge per minute. The applicable rates may vary according to the time of day.

As noted in section 8.5.2.7, in the UK every public electronic communications network providing mobile call termination or geographic call termination has been determined as having SMP in the market for the termination of calls onto their respective networks.[116] Ofcom's approach in imposing SMP conditions in respect of call termination services has varied according to the structure of related markets, and whether each operator possesses market power in the related market for call origination. As a result, in the mobile market Vodafone, O2, T-Mobile, and Orange are required to comply with charge controls in respect of their 2G call termination services.[117] In the fixed market, BT is required to base its call termination charges on efficiently incurred long-run incremental costs, reducing each year in line with charge controls,[118] and each other operator providing call termination services is required to provide such services on terms, conditions, and charges that are fair and reasonable.[119]

New-entrant fixed telephony operators must, therefore, only levy fair and reasonable termination charges. However, as a dispute between BT and Telewest has demonstrated, in practice Ofcom requires that charges for fixed geographic call termination are calculated on the basis of 'reciprocal charging'.[120] This means that fixed geographic call charges will be calculated according to a formula based on BT's regulated charges. There is some room for the charges to vary if there are relevant differences between the terminating network and BT's network, but in practice reciprocal charging usually means that each party's termination rates are identical.

---

[116] See n 95 above.
[117] Ibid.
[118] Ibid.
[119] Ibid.
[120] Ofcom, *Resolution of a dispute between BT and Telewest about reciprocal charging arrangements for call termination rates* (2004). A reciprocal charging agreement for fixed geographic calls, setting out an agreed formula for calculating termination charges, has been in place in the UK since 1997.

8.6.1.3 *Forecasting and provision of capacity*

Interconnection agreements will provide how the parties determine the capacity requirements for each point of interconnection (port capacity), and may require that the parties try to ensure that sufficient capacity is maintained to meet 'busy hour' traffic demands. The parties will usually be required to give each other rolling traffic forecasts, on the basis of which orders for capacity at a particular point of interconnection are placed.

New entrant operators will have no historical data on which to base their traffic forecasts. Whilst there is an entire science dedicated to this area, some element of guesswork will be required. New entrants should therefore resist any provisions that impose penalties for incorrect forecasts, as they are much more likely to get it wrong than a party that has been running its network for some time.

8.6.1.4 *Interconnection circuits*

Interconnection circuits are links, such as leased lines, that connect a party's network with the point of interconnection. Each party will generally be responsible for ensuring that sufficient links are in place in order that it can terminate calls received via the point of interconnection.

8.6.1.5 *Technical requirements*

A minimum standard for the number of permitted 'dropped calls' (i.e. calls that are cut off) is common. Interconnection agreements usually also require compliance with a range of standards, as well as with detailed operational manuals developed by the parties.

8.6.2 Reference offers

Reference offers are standard contracts setting out the terms on which an operator will enter into access arrangements. As noted above, national regulatory authorities in the Member States of the EU are empowered by the Access Directive (and, to a more limited extent, by the Interconnection Directive before that) to require operators with SMP in a given market to publish a reference offer for network access.

As the largest SMP operator in the UK, BT is required to publish reference offers for a large number of different services. Rather than publishing a separate agreement for each different type of access, BT historically published a small number of agreements with schedules for each different service. However, with the operational separation of BT and the establishment of OpenReach, each SMP product now has a distinct reference offer.[121]

Regulators like reference offers because they can see exactly what terms an SMP operator is offering. The other principal advantage is that they eliminate the possibility

---

[121] Available from <http://www.openreach.co.uk>.

of the SMP operator unduly discriminating in the terms it offers different operators, because the terms are identical. For this reason, the terms set out in reference offers are usually not open to negotiation.

8.7 PRACTICAL AND CONTRACTUAL ISSUES IN NEGOTIATING IP INTERCONNECTION AGREEMENTS

The Internet is characterized by connected networks, and Internet users have come to expect close to full connectivity with every website and email address around the world. ISPs, therefore, need to ensure that they have direct or indirect connectivity in place with every other network which makes up the Internet. As identified earlier, there are two main ways of achieving IP interconnection: peering arrangements, and paying transit arrangements. A new-entrant ISP is likely to start with one or more paying transit arrangement to achieve world wide connectivity in one step, and then to pursue peering arrangements with local ISPs once it has established its business, in order to reduce costly transit charges.

Although some descriptions of Internet industries give an impression that they are unregulated (and unregulatable!), IP interconnection falls within the definition of interconnection under the Access Directive, and, as such, is regulated in the same manner as other forms of interconnection. As a consequence, those providing a public electronic communications network (which would catch all publicly available ISPs) must generally negotiate IP interconnection with each other on request.

IP interconnection agreements are also subject to the same dispute resolution mechanisms as other interconnection agreements, as set out in section 8.5.2.10 above.

8.7.1 Peering agreements

Whilst the term 'peering' is used in different ways, it usually describes an arrangement between two ISPs under which they agree to directly connect their networks to provide reciprocal access to each others' users, for no charge. To prevent networks taking advantage of this situation and sending all their traffic for free across the networks with which they are peering, peering agreements prohibit the exchange of traffic that has originated from, or is destined for, third party networks; that is, the agreements prohibit the exchange of 'transit traffic'.

There are some clear advantages with establishing peering. There are obvious cost advantages where the traffic flowing in each direction is approximately equal, as operators will not need to invest in the accounting infrastructure needed to bill each other for traffic passing over the point of interconnection. Another cost saving arises from the fact that neither party needs to pay a third party upstream transit provider for carrying the traffic between the two networks. One study showed that the cost of carrying traffic to the peering point of interconnection can be less expensive by a

factor of ten, than transit services which achieve the same connectivity.[122] There are also some technical advantages with peering, as compared with transit. As the traffic does not traverse third party networks, the connection can potentially be faster and more reliable, resulting in lower 'latency', meaning that fewer packets of data are lost. It is obviously in ISPs' interest to ensure faster traffic consumption, particularly if they are billing their users based on the amount of data downloaded!

Peering is not always the right solution, however. The most common reason why parties will not peer is that the traffic flow between them is asymmetrical, and one party will therefore bear a greater proportion of the cost of peering.[123] This is not only a question of the respective size of the networks, but also of whether the networks are content-rich. A network that is content-rich will have a small amount of inbound traffic (such as in the form of requests for data on the websites it hosts), but will generate a large amount of outbound traffic (in the form of the content from those websites being sent to the network from which the request was generated). The relative bargaining position of the parties will in this case influence whether a peering arrangement or a paying transit arrangement is established.

In considering a potential peering partner, an ISP is therefore likely to examine how much incoming traffic on its network originates from the potential peer, and how much outgoing traffic is addressed to the potential peer.[124] Calculations are then made to assess whether peering is likely to reduce the cost of the transit between the two networks. Peering will require investment in router capacity and interconnection circuits to carry traffic to the point of interconnection, so will only be justified if significant savings in transit costs will follow.

Some ISPs, particularly large ones, have peering policies which are freely available.[125] Any ISP that meets the criteria can apply to become a peering partner of that ISP. Backbone ISPs' peering policies can include requirements that the peering partner has presence in four or more regions where both parties have a presence, along with sufficient transport bandwidth and traffic volume to warrant direct interconnection.[126]

Once the parties have decided to establish peering arrangements, they will enter into negotiations on the contractual terms that will govern the relationship.

Whilst some peering agreements run to hundreds of pages, most are very short and informal documents compared with typical switched interconnection agreements. The agreements are usually 'bilateral', so that each party agrees to give the

---

[122] Norton WB, *Internet Service Providers and Peering* (2003), 3. Available from <http://www.cs.ucsd.edu/classes/wi01/cse222/papers/norton-isp-draft00.pdf>.

[123] For further discussion on the advantages and disadvantages with peering, see further ibid, 3–5.

[124] Internet traffic carries in it data that indicates which ISP the traffic originated from ('originating autonomous system' or 'originating AS') and is destined for ('terminating autonomous system' or 'terminating AS'). An ISP may therefore sample their inbound and outbound traffic and determine approximately how much of it originated from another ISP's network (in the case of inbound traffic) or is bound for routers on the other ISP's network (in the case of outbound traffic).

[125] E.g. Verizon Business 'Policy for Settlement-Free Interconnection with Internet Networks', available at <http://www.verizonbusiness.com/terms/peering/>.

[126] See n 122, 3–4.

other access to the users and content on its network. Because no charges are levied, peering partners do not treat each other as customers, but as equals. Sometimes this means that each party will be prepared to accept limited contractual undertakings from the other party (such as extremely limited warranties and no service level guarantees) on the basis that they want their own obligations to be as limited as possible. Many peering agreements may be said to lack teeth, but this is a reflection of the perceived low risks involved.

Notwithstanding this, there are a number of considerations that legal advisers reviewing peering agreements should be alert to. The sections below examine some of the issues that need to be addressed.

8.7.1.1 *Access to the peer's users*

A peering agreement should provide each party only with access to the other's users and should explicitly prohibit transit traffic being sent over the points of interconnection. Without this provision, operators could be required to carry any traffic originating from their peer across their network without receiving any payment for doing so—this would obviously go against the spirit of the peering arrangement.

The parties can normally identify and stop transit traffic because each party's AS numbers and router addresses will be included in the peering agreement. Packets of data with other AS numbers or originating from other routers can therefore be recognized.

8.7.1.2 *Location of the points of interconnection*

One of the first issues that the parties are likely to discuss and agree upon is the location(s) of the point(s) of interconnection. In some large cities, one option may be to interconnect at a public internet exchange, such as London Internet Exchange (LINX), where numerous network operators directly interconnect at one geographic location. Public internet exchanges manage the interconnection on their members' behalf and require their members to comply with common technical requirements. Some are run on a not-for-profit basis, with each member only contributing to the cost of running the exchange, whereas others are run by profit-making entities.

Internet exchanges such as LINX have hundreds of ISP members, and one or both parties negotiating peering may already have a presence at the exchange. In these circumstances establishing peering may take as little as a matter of hours once the agreement has been signed.

There are some clear advantages with interconnecting at a public internet exchange, a primary one being that each ISP will only need to have one single interconnection circuit between its network and the exchange in order to peer with many other networks. Some internet exchanges also have standard bilateral agreements on which their members contract, which can significantly simplify negotiations.[127]

---

[127] See, for example, the LINX bilateral interconnect agreement at <https://www.linx.net/good/bcp/peeringagreement_draftv4.html>.

Peering at a public internet exchange will not always be viable or desirable, however. For remote networks, the closest exchange may be far from any of the operator's network nodes,[128] or an operator may anticipate having few regional peering partners, meaning that peering at the exchange does not result in benefits from economies of scale. In these cases operators will enter into arrangements to peer at private peering points. Private peering points give the parties greater control over the interconnection, and, accordingly, much greater control over the quality of the service that can be expected.

Private peering is typically arranged by each party obtaining co-location services at a telecommunications exchange, and then establishing interconnection between the networks. The parties may find that they have points of presence[129] in common exchanges already, in which case establishing the physical interconnection can be achieved very quickly. If peering points are needed at further exchanges where the parties do not have points of presence, then they will need to agree which exchange(s) best suit their needs, and approach those exchange(s) to obtain co-location. Many cost and operational issues will influence the decision when choosing an exchange, including whether competitively priced interconnection circuits are available between the parties' respective networks and a particular exchange.[130]

It is not uncommon for large networks to establish peering at a variety of public internet exchanges and private peering points. Some peering agreements provide that the parties are required to investigate moving the location of a point of interconnection from a public internet exchange to a private peering point if and when the volume of traffic exchanged over the point of interconnection exceeds a certain level. This is intended to give operators greater control over the quality of service at those points of interconnection which carry the heaviest traffic.

8.7.1.3 *Compliance with peering criteria*

As noted above, many network operators have formal or informal criteria when choosing peering partners. What happens, however, when the parties have entered into a peering relationship and the peering partner subsequently fails to meet the criteria? For example, many operators will only be looking to peer with networks where the traffic flow between the two networks is relatively equal. However, the ratio of traffic transmitted from one network to the other may change over time, for example if one network operator develops its hosting business and becomes a net exporter of content.

Peering agreements sometimes deal with this by setting a traffic ratio (for example 4:1 outbound traffic to inbound traffic). The parties agree to peer (without settlement) up to the ratio, beyond which they must pay the other party, usually for each

---

[128] A network node describes a point in the network at which interconnection can be established.

[129] A point of presence is a point in the network from which users are connected.

[130] For a discussion on some of the criteria used by ISPs in selecting an exchange, see n 132 above, 8–10.

Megabyte of outbound traffic. This arrangement is a form of paid transit arrangement, discussed further in section 8.7.2 below. The issue of traffic ratios was brought into focus in 2003 in a dispute in the US between America Online and Cogent Communications Group. In enforcing its traffic ratio criteria, America Online began to charge Cogent for traffic that had previously been exchanged free of charge.[131]

Another example where peering criteria may be enforced is where one operator requires the other's network to have certain minimum characteristics. If the characteristics are not met, then sometimes transit charges are payable, such as if a minimum threshold for packet loss is exceeded.

Any provisions in a peering agreement that can potentially change the nature of the relationship to a paying transit relationship should be closely reviewed by legal advisors.

8.7.1.4 *Confidentiality and security*
As with switched interconnection agreements, there are two distinct confidentiality concerns: confidentiality of customer information and communications, and confidentiality of business information shared between the parties for the purpose of peering. Although limited, necessary traffic analysis may be permitted by the peering agreement, it will usually prohibit the capture of the content of any traffic exchanged between the parties' networks.

Standard confidentiality clauses should always be included to protect against the disclosure of business information learned through the peering relationship, and, importantly, against the use of such information for any purpose other than the performance of the agreement.

8.7.1.5 *Sharing of costs*
Where the parties interconnect at a public internet exchange, they will each have a separate agreement with the body that runs the exchange governing the costs of running the exchange, and so such costs will not need to be dealt with in the peering agreement. Where a private peering point is used, however, the parties must determine how costs are to be divided between them. Each operator may pay half, or the costs may be split based on the amount of traffic exchanged in each direction.

8.7.1.6 *Technical and operational schedules*
The information in the technical and operational schedules may include information such as the physical addresses of the points of interconnection, details of the parties' infrastructure, and the parties' contact details. Contact details will in most cases include details for a 24-hour network operation centre. Provisions for disaster recovery are also becoming more common.

---

[131] See Henderson, K, 'Power Shifting IP Peering', (*Phoneplus Magazine*, March 2003) available at <http://www.phoneplusmag.com/articles/331carrier2.html>.

8.7.2 Paying transit agreements

In this chapter, the term 'paying transit' is used to refer to any IP interconnection arrangements that are not settlement free. Historically, smaller ISPs would enter into paying transit arrangements with transit providers in order to obtain connectivity with third party networks that were beyond the smaller ISP's reach. The exchange of traffic between users of the small ISP and users of the transit provider was often governed by a peering arrangement, with points of interconnection often established at public Internet exchanges.

This changed, however, between 1996 and 1998, when many of the large US backbone providers radically changed their peering criteria. Within a very short time many pulled out of public internet exchanges and changed the majority of their peering partners into paying customers. Backbone providers now commonly only peer with a very small number of their largest competitors. Paying transit arrangements, therefore, now describe both the arrangement under which an operator transits traffic between two different networks for a fee, and the arrangement under which it charges for access to its own users and content hosted on its own network.[132]

Most ISPs are therefore now likely to find that they must pay their upstream Internet access provider or backbone provider a fee, often called a 'download fee' for inbound traffic received over a point of interconnection, whether the traffic has originated on a third party network or the Internet access provider/backbone provider's own network. The download fee will be charged, for example, when a user on the downstream ISP downloads a web page hosted on the backbone provider's network or on any network from which the backbone provider has agreed to provide transit.

Some Internet access providers/backbone providers also charge a fee, sometimes called a 'backchannel fee', for data received onto their network from the downstream network. A backchannel fee will be charged to the downstream network, for example, when a user on the backbone provider's network, or on any network to which the backbone provider has agreed to provide transit, downloads a web page hosted on the downstream network.[133]

ISPs can find, therefore, that they are paying for both inbound and outbound traffic carried by their upstream access provider. Although some content-rich networks are able to negotiate a more favourable position, many ISPs cannot. These arrangements have caused some disquiet amongst small and medium sized ISPs[134] and have attracted the attention of the competition authorities in Australia.[135]

---

[132] A detailed discussion of the series of events in the US in this period is included in Neil Cukier KN, 'Peering and fearing: ISP Interconnection and Regulatory Issues', <http://www.cukier.com/writings/peering-cukier-dec97.html>.

[133] A good explanation of the payment arrangements can be found in the ACCC discussion paper 'Internet Interconnection Service' (2003).

[134] See n 132, which reviews the arguments for regulatory control of IP interconnection in the United States.

[135] See n 133, in which the Australian Competition & Consumer Commission considers whether to 'declare' IP interconnection under Part XIC of the Trade Practices Act 1974. This would mean that providers

Unsurprisingly, in paying transit arrangements customers look for more detailed and more onerous contractual terms from their transit providers than they do from their peering partners. Some of these terms will be similar to those described for peering agreements, above. Some of the terms that are likely to differ are considered below.

8.7.2.1 *Access to all networks*
Unlike peering partners, who will only provide access to users on their own network, transit providers can provide access to virtually all other networks on the public Internet through upstream transit agreements. The paying transit agreement will set out which routes the agreement applies to. This will not, obviously, include those routes where the customer network has established private peering relationships or where other transit arrangements are in place.

8.7.2.2 *Location of the points of interconnection*
Whilst it is possible to establish paying transit arrangements at public internet exchanges, private interconnection arrangements are more common because the transit operator has better control over quality of service.

8.7.2.3 *Service levels*
Detailed schedules are likely to specify service level guarantees and may specify service credits or liquidated damages in the event that the service levels are not met.

8.7.2.4 *Charges*
Much detail is likely to be dedicated to how the charges payable are to be calculated, invoiced, and paid. Numerous different models may be used to calculate transit charges, including on a per byte basis or on a port basis (i.e. a flat-rate charge). Discounts may be applied based on volume or the perceived value of the content hosted on the customer network.

8.7.3 Emerging trends in peering and transit arrangements

Some recent trends may indicate a shift in power in the ISP/content network /transit provider hierarchy.[136]

The first such trend is an increase in peering arrangements between ISPs and content-only network operators, such as Yahoo! and Google. These network operators host extremely popular content, raising revenue from a variety of sources like advertising. They do not themselves provide Internet access. Instead of paying

---

would need to comply with certain access obligations and would empower the Commission to arbitrate disputes over the terms and conditions.

[136] See further n 131 above.

download charges to transit providers for content accessed from these networks, where peering is established, ISPs are able to access the content free of charge. The content networks also benefit, as they pay no backchannel fees to transit providers.

Another trend is that there has been an increase in large ISPs, such as AOL, offering to provide limited transit services between those networks with whom it has peering relationships. These services are different from the services provided by traditional transit providers because access is only provided to a small subset of networks making up the Internet, whereas traditional transit providers can provide worldwide connectivity, generally for a lower price than is offered by traditional transit providers. This type of transit arrangement is reportedly already common in Europe.[137]

Finally, emerging new content services may result in changes in the relationships between ISPs, transit providers, and content providers. For example, it is possible that new services such as streaming video will give content providers greater weight in arguing that they should be paid for outbound traffic originating on their networks. Bandwidth-hungry services could also alter ISPs inbound/outbound traffic ratios. Services such as voice-over IP and video conferencing, which are optimized where latency and packet loss are minimized, are also driving ISPs to seek greater control over their routing arrangements.

8.8 CONCLUDING REMARKS AND FUTURE TRENDS

The interconnection and access regime does not have a significant impact on interconnection and access arrangements between two operators who do not possess SMP. Although the regime requires them to negotiate interconnection with each other, there are commercial incentives for them to do so in any case. In this respect the regime may be said to merely reinforce rational market behaviour.

However, it is apparent that competing operators in the EU continue to rely heavily on the existence of sector-specific rules, particularly in the form of *ex ante* conditions and directions on network access, to obtain access rights from operators with SMP. This appears to be as much the case under the Access Directive as under the Interconnection Directive before that, and this looks unlikely to change in the near future. Although there is no doubt that general competition law would prohibit the refusal to supply access in many cases, it seems unlikely, for example, that general competition law would have resulted in competing operators obtaining rights access to FRIACO interconnection, ATM interconnection, and to wholesale line rental.

However, the gradual erosion of the market shares held by incumbents, and the emergence of new technologies in which they do not have a stranglehold, such as voice-over IP, is likely to prompt incumbents to argue for the retreat of the sector-specific rules. This is likely to be a future battleground between incumbent operators and their competitors.

---

[137] Ibid.

9

COMPETITION LAW IN TELECOMMUNICATIONS

Edward Pitt and Robin Morton-Fincham

9.1 REGULATION THROUGH COMPETITION LAW

It is a mantra of UK Government policy that the regulation of the telecommunications industry should, wherever possible, be achieved by applying general competition law rather than regulation specific for telecommunications.[1] Detailed, telecoms-specific regulation has been withdrawn in stages. A past Director-General

---

[1] See Communications White Paper, 2000. *A New Future for Communications* (Cmd 5010).

of the Office of Telecommunications (Oftel)[2] was described as making a 'bonfire of regulation' in pursuit of this policy.

The EU Commission also talks of rolling back regulation and relying on competition law. That policy—of using competition, and competition law, as the primary drivers and control mechanisms in the telecommunications sector—is now enshrined in the Communications Act 2003.[3]

In this chapter we will try to unpick the analysis which underpins that policy. Competition law (and its enforcement procedures) can provide a framework for effective regulation in the telecommunications sector, but competition law has, and always will have, considerable limitations as the only source of telecoms regulation. Regulations specifically designed for the telecommunications sector will still be needed, even after some of the special rules, put in place on privatization to stimulate market entry at the expense of the incumbent monopolist (in the UK that is BT), have been taken away.

The telecommunications market makes for an interesting competition law analysis: both in the UK and in most European countries (and, in a different way, in the US). It is not a market which developed 'naturally' from the beginning. In fact its development is still not 'natural' today. For over 90 years (since the local telephone companies were put together under the General Post Office in 1912) the UK has had a centrally planned and managed telecommunication system.[4] Certain elements were, and still are, key, for example: network integrity and compatibility throughout the UK; a universal service, available to all who need it or want it, on reasonable terms; and a robust system with high technical levels of service. Against that background the decision to privatize the telecommunications industry—both the domestic telephone business, run by the General Post Office (now BT), and the UK government's overseas telephone business, run by Cable & Wireless—was not simply a government decision to sell it off and walk away. The Telecommunications Act 1984, and other legislation passed to privatize BT and Cable & Wireless, ensured that the government, while it sold the ownership of the systems, retained a close and tight control over the way in which they were developed once in the private sector. For example, on privatization the number of licensed fixed network operators was at first limited to two; more operators were then allowed in, but only if first granted a licence to build and run a network. Only in 2003, nearly 20 years after privatization, was the need for a network operator to have a licence finally swept away. Yet the machinery of central government control, through Ofcom and the Communications Act 2003, remains firmly in place.

---

[2] In December 2003 the functions of Oftel, as UK telecoms regulator, were swept together into the Office of Communications (Ofcom), which also has responsibility for the regulation of radio, independent television broadcasting, and spectrum management.

[3] See Communications Act 2003, s 3(1): 'It shall be the primary duty of Ofcom, in carrying out their functions . . . to further the interests of consumers in relevant markets, where appropriate by promoting competition'.

[4] See further Chapter 3.

Since privatization there have been other attempts to redesign and manage the market, through evolving policies on issues such as entitlement to interconnection terms, number portability, indirect access, local loop unbundling and, now, functional separation into Openreach of BT's fixed line local access business. The Communications Act 2003 was not a revolution in the government's approach; some might even see the much-vaunted creation of a single regulator for the communications industry (Ofcom) as a mere cloak, behind which the government has been able to sharpen the instruments of regulation.

It is against this background that we will assess the competition rules, as they apply to telecommunications. Government management of the competitive process will be analysed under five headings: (i) management and manipulation of the market structure by government; (ii) control of behaviour through mainstream competition rules; (iii) special competition rules for telecommunications; (iv) market failure of competition—sector-specific rules; and (v) procedures for enforcement of the competition rules.

We also seek to show how these principles have been developed together with other EU Member States, and have been put in place throughout the European Community, through the EC Directives, as implemented in each Member State. At the end of this chapter we will show how these principles have been applied, both by the EU Commission and by the UK government, when approving structural changes (mergers and joint ventures) in the telecommunications sector.

9.2 MANAGEMENT AND MANIPULATION OF THE MARKET STRUCTURE BY GOVERNMENT

In order to understand how competition law is applied today in the telecommunications sector, it is useful to go back to 1984, the moment of privatization in the UK, when the ground rules for current telecommunications policy were laid. There were two premises underlying the Telecommunications Act 1984:

(1) consumer demand (tempered by the demands of shareholders) would be more efficient in the allocation and management of resources than the public owner; and

(2) to deliver real efficiency gains there needed to be competition between providers of physical telecommunication networks, not just competition between providers of services over one network.

All fixed line operators are now greatly more efficient than BT was, when it was a nationalized, monopoly supplier. The average cost of fixed line calls to both business and residential customers has consistently come down; it is now considerably less than half of what it was, in real terms, in 1984. The drop in broadband pricing to home consumers has been even more remarkable: from £50 per month when the service started to under £10 a month today. BT has made very considerable savings in costs, achieved partly through a great reduction in staffing and partly through

technological advances. The advance of broadband available to all has been remarkable. That process continues. The fall in prices of calls (and Internet access) has led to a huge growth both in the number of calls made and in use of the Internet. This in turn has spurred overall economic efficiency and growth across the economy as a whole.[5]

The second platform of policy, the building of competing physical networks, has happened more haphazardly. At the time of privatization the idea was that one competitor to BT in the provision of a fixed network would be enough to stimulate competition. Mercury, a subsidiary of Cable & Wireless, the UK's overseas telephone operator (which provided long distance international telecommunication cables, in particular to many Commonwealth countries), would provide competition to all BT's services. In practice, Mercury focused on supplying only to profitable segments of the market, in particular the business market.

In 1991, the government published the so-called 'Duopoly Review', as a White Paper.[6] It concluded that a competing network to provide mass consumer services with full national coverage was not being built. Therefore to encourage the building of fixed networks to provide telephony services to the mass consumer market, the government decided to franchise cable companies to build networks of fibre-optic and coaxial cable. For an exclusive period (typically 15 years) only those companies were entitled to use cable to broadcast screened entertainment (television programmes, feature films, etc.) to consumers in their franchised areas. Cable franchisees would be able to offer both telephony and broadcast services over the same network and, therefore, have two sources of revenue. As a further incentive to cable companies to build out new networks to reach mass consumers, BT was banned from broadcasting until 2005 (the ban was later lifted in 2001). The years 1989 to 1995 saw the award of some 140 franchise licences to some 70 different companies, who were granted exclusive franchises to provide broadcast services in their defined licensed areas. In those areas they were also free to provide telephony services.

Investment in these franchises was funded by investors, particularly from the US. However, by 1995 BT still had nearly 95 per cent of all residential telephone connections and 92 per cent of telephony revenues from domestic customers. It became clear that small cable companies would never have the commercial and financial muscle (or incentive) to be able to invest in national advertising campaigns and to invest in large networks using rapidly developing technology. Accordingly, after 1995 there was a fairly rapid period of consolidation between cable franchisees, which the government encouraged. The original 140 licensed cable networks are now subsumed in a single entity; the last cable merger was between NTL and Telewest, to form Virgin Media.

---

[5] See, e.g., 'Driving productivity and growth in the UK economy' (McKinsey Global Institute, October 1998).

[6] *Competition and Choice: Telecommunications Policy for the 1990s* (London, DTI, 1991).

The mass consumer market for fixed telephony access services is a concentrated market, i.e. there are now just two providers of fixed network services for mass consumers on a national basis—BT and Virgin Media. Other national networks—such as COLT and Cable and Wireless—focus on the business market, or providing backbone long-distance carriage for other carriers. There are very high barriers to entry; it is very expensive for a new entrant to enter the market by building its own network, especially one with national coverage. Further, all operators, including those providing fixed network services to the business market or 'backbone' services to other operators (the 'Carrier's Carriers'), are interdependent on each other for the delivery of each other's calls. These two factors have a major effect on the way in which competition law is applied and adapted in the telecommunications sector. It also means that special additional obligations, in the nature of telecoms sector-specific competition rules, are imposed: first, obligations to interconnect are imposed on all network operators; secondly, tougher obligations are placed on any network operator having significant market power (SMP),[7] which would not be imposed in other market structures.

The mobile market has been designed by the government with the same considerations as with the fixed telephony market, i.e. competition is most effective if there are the greatest feasible number of service providers who each build, own, and control their own networks. The first two analogue mobile licences were granted in 1985—to BT (now O2) and Vodafone. When digital technology became viable, allowing for more efficient use of the available spectrum, two further licences were issued, in 1993, to Orange and to One-2-One (now T-Mobile). The auction of so-called 'third generation' (3G) mobile telephony licences in 1999 was then designed to ensure that a fifth mobile network operator would be introduced to the market to further stimulate network competition between mobile operators. Thus the TIW consortium—now called '3'—was awarded the main licence in the third generation auction (although, interestingly, 3 has now been allowed to share part of its network with T-Mobile).

You might think that the fixed networks now face enough competition from mobile networks for there to be sufficient competition between networks. However, mobile telephony is still regarded by Ofcom as a separate product market from telephony services over fixed networks,[8] and indeed calls from a fixed line to a mobile line are a distinct market from calls from one mobile to another.[9]

More recently, local loop unbundling (LLU) then leading to BT's local access network being functionally separated from BT (as Openreach) is a practical example of encouraging competition in the broadband and voice markets though allowing competing networks to have access to BT's local access network on equivalent terms—or offer what is called 'equivalence of inputs', or 'EOI' for short, the idea

---

[7] See further, Chapters 5 and 8.
[8] See Ofcom website for texts of various telecoms market reviews, <http://www.ofcom.org.uk>.
[9] Ofcom statement—Mobile Call Termination 27 March 2007.

being that BT/Openreach must now provide inputs to other service providers on an equivalent basis.

Notwithstanding a policy of encouraging the building of competing networks, both the fixed and mobile networks are (at least as respects the mass consumer market) in the hands of a very limited number of operators—true 'oligopolists'.[10] Accordingly, to deal with those oligopolistic market structures special steps have been taken to micro-manage the structure further. These are analysed below.

9.3 CONTROL OF BEHAVIOUR THROUGH MAINSTREAM COMPETITION RULES

9.3.1 Basic principles of competition law

In July 1995, Oftel, as it then was, carried out a major review of the effectiveness of the rules contained in BT's licence and the conditions attached to it.[11] The licence conditions, especially those dealing with pricing, retail price control, network charge control, and interconnection, were extremely detailed. This involved continuous intervention by Oftel in relatively minor issues, normally in response to complaints from other operators. Consideration was therefore given to whether a broadly written competition rule could be used to substitute for the many detailed licence conditions. After a long battle between Oftel and BT (and, behind closed doors, between Oftel and the then DTI (now BERR)), BT eventually accepted the incorporation into its licence of the so-called 'fair trading condition', which was a 'look-alike' of the competition rules in Articles 81 and 82, EC Treaty.[12] A similar condition was then incorporated in all other important licences granted under the Telecommunications Act 1984. The fair trading condition has now been replaced by the Competition Act 1998, Chapter I (section 2) and Chapter II (section 18) which contain prohibitions in more or less identical terms to Articles 81 and 82, the EC Treaty. We record this piece of regulatory history because it highlights a central issue in telecoms regulation: how far is it practicable to use just the mainstream competition rules to regulate the telecoms industry?

A full analysis of Articles 81 and 82 of the EC Treaty, and of the Chapter I and Chapter II prohibitions in the Competition Act, is outside the scope of this work.[13] We will focus here, therefore, on the special issues which arise when applying

---

[10] E.g. in the UK three of the five mobile network operators are owned by fixed line incumbents from other European countries, i.e. Orange (France Telecom), T-Mobile (Deutsche Telekom AG), and 02 (Telefónica SA).

[11] *Effective Competition: Framework for Action* (London, Oftel, July 1995).

[12] BT appealed by way of judicial review, unsuccessfully, against the licence modification: *R v Director-General of Telecommunications, ex p BT* (unreported) [1996] EWHC Admin 391, 20 December 1996 (QBD).

[13] See generally: Roth, P (ed), *Bellamy and Child: European Community Law of Competition* (6th edn, Oxford University Press, 2008); Faull, J and Nikpay, A (eds), *Faull and Nikpay: The EC Law of*

competition law to the telecommunication sector. Section 2 of the Competition Act and Article 81, EC Treaty, are in almost identical terms. They both prohibit all agreements between undertakings which do or are intended to distort, restrict, or prevent competition. Section 18 prohibits any unilateral abuse by an undertaking of the dominant position it enjoys in a particular market.

There are two broad types of agreements between undertakings caught by Section 2 and Article 81:

i. 'horizontal' agreements between competitors—these include not only an agreement to sell at, or offer, common prices, and the sharing of customers; it extends to sharing of confidential commercial information—such as sales prices or sales figures (it may therefore also cover, for example, the practice of benchmarking—comparing your efficiency and costs against competing undertakings);

ii. 'vertical' agreements—between a supplier and its commercial customers, where there are restrictions, such as exclusivity of supply (exclusive dealerships) or restrictions on the commercial customer as to what it can do with the product supplied (such as resale price maintenance).

Article 81, EC Treaty, and section 2 of the Competition Act prohibit not only written contracts, but also decisions by trade associations and 'concerted practices' (a gentlemen's agreement, or the mere exchange of confidential commercial information without any agreement as to commercial behaviour). The anti-competitive nature of an agreement is judged according to its actual or intended effects on competition; its legal form is irrelevant. The rules are mandatory and apply regardless of what particular law applies to a contract. As said, the prohibition on restrictive agreements can apply both to agreements between competitors and to agreements between undertakings in a customer/supplier relationship.

Both the EC and the UK competition law systems provide a mechanism for some such restrictive agreements to be 'exempted', where the economic and social benefits of the restrictions outweigh the disadvantages. However the tests for exemption are quite precise, and do not give an enforcement agency—or a court—complete discretion to say 'this looks okay' (or not). The tests are that the agreement(s):

i. *either* improve the production or distribution of goods or services *or* promote technical or economic progress;

ii. allow consumers a fair share of the benefit;

iii. do not impose any restrictions which are not essential; and

iv. do not lead to elimination of competition in the field of the products or services in question.

Competition (2nd edn, Oxford University Press, 2007); or Whish, R, *Competition Law* (5th edn, Oxford University Press, 2003).

An agreement may fall within one of the EU Commission's so called 'block exemption' regulations, exempting agreements of common type, such as the Technology Transfer Block Exemption (TTBE)[14] or the Vertical Agreements Block Exemption (VABE).[15] In respect of agreements which could not be brought within a block exemption, until 1 May 2004 individual exemption could be granted by the Office of Fair Trading (OFT) (for agreements having purely national effects) or the EU Commission (for agreements which have a material effect on trade between EU Member States). The system of granting individual exemptions has now been swept away; it is now for the parties to make their own assessment—and carry the risk if they get it wrong. The block exemptions covering agreements in common form remain in place.

In practice in the telecoms sector there have so far been few allegations of cartel-type behaviour between telecoms suppliers. In an attempt to force down the cost of international calls on mobile the EU Commission sought to attack under Article 81 international roaming agreements between mobile operators. It abandoned this line when the EC Roaming Regulation was adopted. Similarly, many vertical agreements in the telecoms sector—very often interconnection agreements—by their nature tend to be non-exclusive. So there are relatively few cases which have been dealt with by the EU Commission or Oftel (now Ofcom) under these provisions (apart from a few early joint venture cases dealt with under Article 85 rather than under the European Community Merger Regulation (ECMR)—see section 9.8.2, on mergers, below). The more relevant provision—as an instrument of regulation—has been, and is, section 18 of the Competition Act and Article 82 EC Treaty, which prohibits any abuse by an undertaking of its dominant position. Yet even here, in practice there is much unilateral economic behaviour which distorts competition, or prevents its development, but is not an 'abuse' caught by section 18 and therefore needs to be dealt with by sector specific rules.

9.3.2 Competition law applied in an economic context: relevant markets

Sections 2 and 18 of the Competition Act (and Articles 81 and 82, EC Treaty) only bite if they have an appreciable effect on competition. To determine whether this is the case, the undertakings' economic position must be assessed. The tool for doing this is the concept of a 'relevant market' i.e. the market for goods or services which are reasonably substitutable with each other. Both the EU Commission and Ofcom have done a lot of work in this area, which has been published. The EU Commission has also published approximate definitions of telecoms markets.[16] These are both

[14] Commission Regulation (EC) No 772/2004 of 27 April 2004, OJ L 123, 27 April 2004, p 11.
[15] Commission Regulation (EC) No 2790/1999 of 22 December 1999, OJ L 336, 29 December 1999, p 21.
[16] Commission Recommendation of 11 February 2003 on relevant product and service markets within the electronic communications sector, (2003/311/EC), OJ L114, 8 May 2003, and Commission guidelines on market analysis and the assessment of significant market power under the Community regulatory framework for electronic communications networks and services, (2002/C 165/03), OJ C165, 11 July 2002.

quite refined; Ofcom has gone further and has identified considerably more markets than the 18 contained in the Commission recommendation.[17] Some examples of relevant markets include:

- providing fixed access to the network (the local loop);
- mobile network telephony (as distinct from fixed networks);
- pre-paid phone card indirect access business;
- individual routes to international destinations (e.g. UK to India; UK to North East USA; UK to France);
- termination of incoming calls onto an operator's own mobile network.

When you look at these market definitions you see that many are areas where a single undertaking has so-called 'market power' or dominance. Where a telecoms undertaking has 'market power' or (greater) dominance in specific telecoms markets the first approach is to see if mainstream competition law properly controls anti-competitive behaviour in that market. If not, there may be a need for specific regulation going beyond the basic competition rules. Examples of relevant markets where such specific regulation is needed are:

- BT has over 80 per cent of all local access connections; therefore other operators have access to those connections as a result of the EC Regulation on Unbundled Access to the Local Loop and now, through Openreach, a functionally separate part of BT;[18]
- each mobile network has a 'monopoly' on delivery of calls to its customers, i.e. call termination: there are tight price 'caps' on the rates which mobile network operators can charge for delivering calls to each of their networks.[19]

9.3.3 'Hardcore' anti-competitive behaviour—Enterprise Act 2002

UK competition law has been strengthened by the Enterprise Act 2002. UK government policy is that companies will only pay serious attention to the competition rules—in particular the ban on cartel-type behaviour—if there are serious penalties, including the risk of fines, and indeed imprisonment, for directors and senior managers. Accordingly, section 188(2) of the Enterprise Act creates—on pain of fine/imprisonment—four very special, so called 'hard core', cartel offences (i.e. criminal cartel behaviour). The cartel offence catches a narrower range of

---

[17] Within each market review, Ofcom has identified various separate sub-markets.

[18] Regulation (EC) No 2887/2000 of the European Parliament and of the Council of 18 December 2000 on unbundled access to the local loop, OJ L336/4, 30 December 2000.

[19] See summary of Competition Commission's recommendations: Vodafone, O2, Orange and T-Mobile Reports on references under section 13 of the Telecommunications Act 1984 on the charges made by Vodafone, O2, Orange, and T-Mobile for terminating calls from fixed and mobile networks, Competition Commission, 2003, vol 1, pp 3–6.

behaviours than is covered by section 2 of the Competition Act: fixing sale prices; sharing markets and/or particular customers; limiting or preventing supply, or production; and bid-rigging.

No enforcement proceedings have, yet,[20] been taken against companies in the telecoms sector under the Enterprise Act.

9.3.4 Mainstream competition rules: prohibition of anti-competitive agreements

We turn now to some examples of the kind of agreement in the telecommunications sector which may be caught by section 2 or Article 81.

9.3.4.1 *Agreements, between undertakings which compete with each other ('horizontal agreements')*

Agreements between competitors in the communications field which are likely to infringe the prohibition include (amongst others) those which:

    i. directly or indirectly fix purchase or selling prices, or other trading conditions—such as agreements between network operators as to prices, or discount levels, to be offered to business or domestic customers;

    ii. limit or control production, markets, technical development, or investment—such as an agreement to refuse to supply a particular type of telecommunications service provider, or only to supply them at particular rates;

    iii. share markets or sources of supply—such as agreements to allocate customers or types of customer between competitors, or between distributors or dealers (or service providers);

    iv. involve collusion with competitors when tendering for big contracts—such as contracts to outsource the telecoms requirements of a large bank;

    v. exchange otherwise commercially confidential information—such as swapping information on prices already charged or imminent price rises, or as to volumes of business done with particular customers, or even exchange of information as to costs;

    vi. form joint ventures to develop or provide goods or services jointly, which the undertakings could have offered separately.

There have so far been only a few competition law cases relating to coordination between competing providers of telecommunication services, or between network operators as to pricing. An investigation was carried out into the practices of mobile operators across Europe in respect of termination rates.[21]

---

[20] Summer, 2008.

[21] See Competition Commission 2003 report, see n 19. See also European Commission press release IP/99/298 Brussels, 4 May 1999.

Pricing arrangements under the umbrella of international organizations of tele-coms operators—such as the ITU—have been phased out. Thus a recommendation of the CEPT (European Conference of Postal and Telecommunications Administrations) that members make a minimum surcharge for carrying third party traffic was dropped.[22]

Many telecoms operators belong to international or national trade associations, who are alive to the need to ensure that members do not share commercially secret information, such as prices charged to individual customers or identity of customers. As the airline industry has done, national telecoms undertakings have formed inter-national alliances (such Uniworld, and, in the mobile sector, Freemove and Starmap). Each of these have systems in place to ensure that there is no exchange between members of commercially sensitive price information.

Cooperation between competing network operators in the practical operation of their networks raises more nuanced competition policy issues. The sharing between competitors of ducts and poles for cables is encouraged on environmental grounds.[23] In 2002 the EU Commission exempted arrangements under which O2 and T-Mobile would be allowed limited sharing of equipment on mobile masts. This was in response to claims by the mobile network operators that the cost of swift roll-out of 3G networks was proving much greater than expected, and that such costs could be cut by sharing parts of their networks. The terms of exemption were, however, tough-ened up after Oftel (now Ofcom) raised serious concerns that to allow sharing of some radio access networks (RANs) by two competing networks, cut across the EU (and UK) policy of ensuring full competition between independent networks.[24] Exemption to this network sharing was granted on the grounds that it speeded up mobile coverage throughout Germany and the sharing of masts involved only a small amount of shared, common costs. There was to be no sharing of backbone network capacity.

A more subtle form of horizontal coordination which may fall within section 2 (or Article 81) is where industry sets technical standards to enable interoperability of networks. The setting of industry standards which are not 'open' for all to use, or over which industry members seek to claim patent or copyright ownership of the

[22] CEPT Press Release 19/90/188 (6 March 1990).

[23] S 73(3)(b) of the Communications Act 2003 allows Ofcom to set conditions for securing that persons to whom the electronic communications code applies, participate in sharing the use of electronic communications apparatus. Paragraph 9 of the Introduction to the Oftel (now Ofcom) statement 'The Granting of the Electronic Communications Code by the Director General of Communications' (10 October 2003) gives 'the need to encourage the sharing of electronic communications apparatus' as a policy objective.

[24] Notice pursuant to Art 19(3) of Council Regulation No 17 Case COMP/C1/N.38.370—BT Cellnet & BT3G/One2One Personal Communications (United Kingdom Agreement) (2002/C 214/08) Case Comp/C1/N.38.370—Art 19(3): OJ C 214/17, 10 September 2002 and Commission Decision of 30 April 2003 relating to a proceeding under Art 81 of the EC Treaty and Art 53 of the EEA Agreement Case COMP/ 38.370—O2 UK Limited / T-Mobile UK Limited ('UK Network Sharing Agreement') (notified under document number C(2003) 1384) (2003/570/EC): OJ L200/59, 7 August 2003.

standard, or elements of it, or of the interface, have been considered under Article 81. The key point is that where technical interfaces or standards are developed by an industry to apply industry wide, they should be open to all who use them and made available on non discriminatory terms, whether as to payment or otherwise (so called FRAND terms).[25]

Agreements between competitors, or potential horizontal competitors, have been considered by the European Commission in the field of joint ventures to develop products and services which involve new, untested technologies or new selling techniques (see reference to Bertelsmann JV in Germany, at section 9.8.2 below).

Another type of joint venture agreement, often between competitors and common in the telecommunications sector, where substantive competition law issues do arise, is in consortium arrangements to build long-distance cables or networks, whether for large-capacity conveyance internally within the UK, or for international routes, whether to other EU Member States or internationally, outside the EU, for example to the US. Here, the following basic principles apply:

i. Two or more large operators can agree to share the cost of building an expensive cable (a new cable across the Atlantic may cost US$500 million, or more).[26]

ii. Normally, each participant in the joint venture, if it has an interest in a share of the capacity of the cable (for example, in the form of an Indefeasible Right of Use, or IRU), should be free to use its share of capacity as it wishes, including subleasing it to any customer on terms which that participant alone sets.

iii. Each operator should also be free to assign all or part of the benefit of the capacity—there should be no undue restrictions on a participant disposing of its share in capacity either outright, or by way of lease of capacity, subject to appropriate guarantees as respects ongoing liabilities, e.g. for maintenance.

iv. The parties should normally allow third parties (non-consortium members) access to the cable or network on reasonable terms.[27]

A case where the OFT sought to apply section 2 to an alleged arrangement between competitors, and failed completely, involved the members of the UK Cable Protection Committee (UKCPC). The UKCPC is made up of the major operators of cables across the Atlantic, the North Sea, and the English Channel. Its members also include companies and consultants specializing in laying subsea cables. The UKCPC exists to develop common rules for the management of the seabed, to develop cable laying technology and to act as the voice for the industry in its dealings with government, which also owns the foreshore and the seabed through the Crown

[25] ETSI (European Telecommunications Standards Institute)—ETSI Interim IPP Policy, *European Commission XXVth Report on Competition Policy 1995*, Brussels, Luxembourg: Office for Official Publications of the European Communities (1996), p 131. See further Chapter 10.
[26] See further Chapter 15, at 15.2.2.
[27] See *European Commission XXVIIth Report on Competition Policy* (1997), Brussels, Luxembourg: Office for Official Publications of the European Communities (1998), para 73.

Estate. OFT sought to argue that UKCPC acted as a 'purchasers' cartel', in negotiating with landowners (mainly State-owned bodies) a common form licence to use the
seashore and the seabed. UKCPC successfully showed that for an industry to adopt
a common negotiating position with the State falls wholly outside both Article 81
and section 2.[28]

Nevertheless, large operators need to be very alive to the risk that their common
approach to regulatory issues may be attacked as collusion in breach of Article 81
or section 2. For example, the new entrant mobile operator Hutchinson 3G UK
has brought an action against the four established mobile network operators that
they jointly ensured the regulatory rules on number portability favoured them as
incumbents and kept out the newcomer.[29]

9.3.4.2 *Agreements between suppliers and commercial customers*
('vertical agreements')

Vertical agreements, between suppliers and their commercial customers, may also be
caught by the prohibition in section 2 where they unduly exclude market entry by
competitors, or make this more difficult for them. A typical example of exclusion is
where a major supplier enters into a long-term (say 5–10 year) agreement to be the
exclusive supplier; during that period that customer is in effect 'out of bounds' to
competing suppliers.

Where a restrictive vertical agreement does or could affect trade between EU
Member States, Article 81, EC Treaty will also apply. This is especially the case if
an agreement, or a network of similar agreements, impedes entry to the UK market
or the market of another Member State. Common restrictions in vertical agreements
include: requirements to buy goods or services exclusively from the seller; obligations on a customer, who is a reseller of telecoms, or dealer, not to sell competing
products; and restrictions on the sourcing of components. Some (but not all) such
restrictions are exempted by VABE or TTBE (referred to above), the EC Block
exemptions for vertical (distribution/supply) agreements or technology transfer
agreements.[30] However, normally the VABE applies only where the supplier has a
market share below 30 per cent.[31] The TTBE also uses market share as a safe harbour
for agreements falling within its ambit.

Where either the supplier or the customer has a market share above 30 per cent
tougher rules apply, for example, as respects exclusivity requirements, non-compete,
or 'most favoured customer' clauses. Thus, a requirement by an operator with a

---

[28] *Cityhook Ltd v OFT and ors* [2007] CAT 18.
[29] As to substance, the claim is as yet undecided—see *Hutchinson 3G UK Limited v 02 (UK) Limited,
and others* [2008] EWHC 50 (Comm).
[30] Commission Regulation (EC) No 772/2004 of 27 April 2004 on the application of Art 81(3) of the
Treaty to categories of technology transfer agreements. OJ L 123/11, 27 April 2004.
[31] Commission Regulation (EC) No 2790/1999 of 22 December 1999 on the application of Art 81(3)
of the Treaty to categories of vertical agreements and concerted practices. OJ L 336/21, 29 December
1999.

market share above 30 per cent that its commercial customer should buy all its telephony requirements from it, or locking in that customer for an unduly long period (say, over two to three years) may be prohibited.

Note that section 2 and Article 81 can only catch agreements *between undertakings*. For example, a decision by a telecoms operator, in its offering to end consumers (who are not undertakings), to bundle several services together (e.g. by offering customers a quadruple play package of fixed, mobile, broadband, and content) in order to give it an advantage over its competitors, or even to exclude them, cannot be attacked under section 2/Article 81. (If, however, a dominant undertaking bundles its consumer offerings, this could amount to a unilateral abuse of a dominant position, if it unfairly excludes smaller competitors.)

9.3.4.3 *Exemption from the prohibition in Article 81 and section 2*

Some agreements which do restrict competition may, however, offer greater benefits both to economic efficiency and to consumers, which more than offset their anti-competitive effect. These agreements may be capable of exemption. However, the restrictions in such agreements must be essential in order to generate such benefits.

Exemption can be obtained in one of three ways:

i. Until 1 May 2004, we still had a formal exemption (clearance) procedure administered by the competition authorities. Undertakings could apply to the OFT (or to the EU Commission, where the agreement affected trade between EU Member States) with a view to obtaining a declaration of non-infringement (negative clearance), or an individual exemption, if no block exemption applied e.g. VABE or TTBE. Under the so-called 'modernization' of the competition rules the system of individual negative clearance or exemption has been swept away. It is now for the parties to an agreement to make their own assessment that the exemption tests are met.

ii. Alternatively, the parties can ensure that their agreements fit within the terms of an EC or UK 'block' exemption, which then gives certainty that the exemption tests are met. In essence, a block exemption sets out lists of terms in standard types of agreement which are on balance beneficial and hence acceptable, even though they are or may be restrictive of competition. The main EC block exemptions now in force cover: vertical agreements (distribution, etc.); technology transfer agreements (patent licences, etc.);[32] agreements for joint research and development;[33] specialization agreements.[34] Other block exemptions which are sector-specific: (insurance, motor vehicle dealerships, shipping) are generally being withdrawn. An agreement which falls within an EC block exemption is automatically exempt under the UK Competition Act, even if it has no effect on trade between Member States.

---

[32] See n 30.
[33] Commission Regulation (EC) 2659/2000 of 29 November 2000 on the application of Art 81(3) of the Treaty to categories of research and development agreements, OJ L304/7, 5 December 2000.
[34] Commission Regulation (EC) 2658/2000 of 29 November 2000 on the application of Art 81(3) of the Treaty to categories of specialization agreements, OJ L304/3, 5 December 2000.

iii. In limited circumstances it may be possible to apply to the Directorate General of Competition of the EU Commission for guidance or a 'business review' letter. Similarly, the OFT offers 'opinions' on particular cases. So long as the behaviour is as described to the competition authority, no action will be taken by the competition authority against it.

The essence of 'modernization' of the competition law system is that it is for the parties to the agreement to work out for themselves if restrictions in an agreement are essential to make the agreement work, and are, overall, beneficial to efficiency and the consumer. In effect, we now have a system of 'self certification' for exemption, rather than an authorization system.

Many restrictions will be exempted in this way. However, there are two restrictions in a vertical agreement between a supplier and its commercial customer which will never be exempted, however small an undertaking's market share:

i. a restriction imposed by a supplier on its commercial customer (such as a dealer or a telecoms service provider providing service using another's network) as to the price at which it resells the products (or services)—Resale Price Maintenance (RPM);[35]

ii. an absolute restriction as to the export of products (or services) from one EU Member State to another.

A practical example of attempted resale price maintenance in the telecoms sector would be a restriction by a network operator as to the price at which an indirect access operator should resell on the latter's own branded services; this would be prohibited. Similarly, a restriction imposed by a mobile network operator on the price at which a mobile virtual network operator (a MVNO is a services provider which does not have a physical network) resells its own branded airtime, or on how it packages airtime, would be prohibited.

9.3.5 Mainstream competition rules: prohibition of abuse of a dominant position

Both the EC Treaty and UK competition law have special rules to prohibit anti-competitive behaviour in the form of an abuse by an undertaking of its dominant position on a particular market. An undertaking (i.e. a corporate group taken as a whole) may be dominant if it has a market share of more than 40 per cent of a relevant product market. (In some very limited circumstances an undertaking with a lower market share can be dominant, for example, where there are economic or

---

[35] Although, interestingly, the US Supreme Court, in a recent case *Leegin* says that RPM imposed by a supplier with a small market share may lead to economic efficiency; we wait to see if this thinking crosses the Atlantic and softens European enforcement agencies approach to RPM (*Leegin Creative Leather Products, Inc v PSKS, Inc* 127 Supreme Court 2705 (2007)).

contractual links between two large companies neither of which individually has a dominant position, but together they are what is called 'collectively' dominant.[36])

An abuse is much more than the exercise of commercial muscle by a powerful undertaking. In essence, abuse is behaviour which an undertaking knew, or should have known, was likely either to push competitors from a market ('exclusionary abuse') or unfairly exploit customers (or suppliers) ('exploitative abuse'). There may also be a latent moral test—is this behaviour which an ordinary person would call vicious behaviour? However, before you get to analysing whether a particular form of behaviour might be abusive, you need to identify the relevant product market in which the undertaking may be dominant.

A relevant product market exists where one product directly substitutes for, or is interchangeable with, another, especially from the perspective of the user. It is often narrowly defined. For example, the European Court of Justice held, in *United Brands*, that bananas are a separate product market from other fruits, such as apples or pears;[37] and vitamins A, B, and C are each separate product markets.[38] In the telecoms sector, relevant product markets, as previously defined by the EU Commission or the EU courts, have also traditionally been narrowly defined: For example, the mobile market is separate from the market for services over fixed networks; the wholesale interconnection market is separate from the retail market; local leased lines are a separate product market from long-distance leased lines; there are distinct markets for wholesale services over particular international routes, e.g. London to the north-east coast of the US; the business market is distinct from the mass consumer retail market; London is different from the rest of the UK; access (line rental) is a separate market from call conveyance.[39]

In the communications market there are two other factors relevant to assessing dominance:

   i. economies of scale and scope—the idea that once a network is built the cost of supplying each new piece of business or each new customer becomes progressively less and less;

   ii. other advantages as the network increases; so called 'network effects' and 'network externalities':

Network effects mean that the greater the number of customers, the more everyone will want to join a particular network. Indirect Network Externalities refers to the advantage gained through being able to offer closely related complementary products, each reducing the cost of the other (telephone access, directory enquiries, long-distance calls, national calls, Internet access—all in a single offering).

---

[36] See the concept of joint dominance in *Società Italiana Vetro SpA, Fabbrica Pisana SpA and PPG Vernante Pennitalia SpA v Commission of the European Communities* [1992] ECR II-1403.

[37] *United Brands v Commission ('Chiquita')* Case 27/76 [1978] ECR 207.

[38] *Hoffmann-La Roche & Co AG v Commission of the European Communities* ('Vitamins') [1979] ECR 461.

[39] See Commission Recommendation, n 16 above.

Further, a related symptom appears in the computer industry, where a particular process or concept becomes the uniform accepted standard. There comes a point at which the developer of a new concept grows its business so successfully that the business 'tips' in its direction, and it scoops the pool. The concept of a 'tippy' market which suddenly tips in favour of the market leader is well understood in the field of computers—see how IBM (for main frames) and Microsoft (for PC software) have become the standard industry solution. However the concept has some relevance in the telecoms field, and we will come back to this when dealing with some EU Commission decisions on mergers in the telecommunications field (see sections 9.8.2 *et seq.* below).

Relevant markets are also geographic: just one EU Member State, or an area within the UK. Thus there are national markets for mobile voice telephony, local area markets for leased line capacity, or regional markets (for example that enjoyed by Kingston Communications in its home base of Hull).

In telecoms, as in other sectors, dominance is also assessed over time. A transient high market share is unlikely to give rise to dominance concerns (interestingly, high market shares arising out of bidding markets tend not to generate too many competition law concerns because there is normally a competitive tender process, unless there is a very long duration period). Once an undertaking is dominant in a relevant market, competition law imposes higher standards of responsibility as regards its economic behaviour—the so called 'special responsibility' of the dominant undertaking. Its conduct may be an abuse, where the same conduct of a non-dominant undertaking would not be. Typical examples of an abuse include:

 i. predatory pricing—selling at below the marginal cost of production with the effect (even if not intended) of driving a competitor from the market, or severely damaging it economically;

 ii. discriminatory pricing—charging different prices to customers in comparable positions, where the costs of supply do not differ;

 iii. purchasing of a patent for a product which provides the only practical alternative to the product made under the patent of the dominant supplier;

 iv. refusing to supply a product or service which is an essential or important raw material or input to an undertaking competing in another market;

 v. in telecoms, putting a commercial customer in a 'margin squeeze'—i.e. supplying an essential service (such as access to end customers) at a wholesale price which does not leave the downstream commercial customer (such as an indirect access operator) enough headroom to compete with the dominant supplier in the downstream market.

Interestingly, pure excessive pricing—pricing which bears little or no relationship to the costs of supply—is rarely attacked as an abuse, unless the high prices exclude competitors.

Some of the tests used to determine whether behaviour is an abuse have been specifically refined for telecommunications. For example, price predation typically occurs where sales are made at below 'average variable cost'. Prices are presumed to be predatory if they are set at below 'average marginal cost' (the costs of direct labour, power, and raw materials, with no attribution for overheads). The marginal cost of conveying one more telephone call is often very close to zero. Accordingly, in telecommunications network cases average variable cost is replaced by the concept of long-run average incremental costs (LRAIC); broadly, this involves linking the cost of each additional service to the additional cost of providing a further unit of capacity.[40]

The majority of abuse cases brought against dominant telecoms companies have involved some form of price predation or margin squeeze. In practice in the UK it is most often BT which is dominant in certain market segments, and consequently has been attacked for abuse of dominance. For example, BT has been alleged to have abused its dominant position through predatory pricing (see for example the *Freeserve* case, referred to below). However, in practice, mounting 'an abuse of dominance' case against an incumbent based on price predation is quite difficult. This is especially because:

    i. in pricing cases (e.g. allegations of margin squeeze) cost allocation is very complex; and

    ii. many of the costs (or their methodology) have themselves been regulated, so BT (as has Deutsche Telecom before the EU Commission) has sought to argue that setting prices at levels which are determined by costs/other prices which are themselves in turn regulated cannot or should not be an abuse.

Oftel's decision in the FRIACO case[41] illustrates neatly the limitation of the concept of '*abuse*' (and in particular a 'margin squeeze' as a typical form of abuse) and how the interconnection rules, not the concept of abuse of dominance, were used to resolve the issue.

Internet service producers offered dial-up Internet services to end customers who paid for the services on a 'per minute' basis. They used smaller carriers (such as COLT and Thus) to bring the traffic to their servers. Those carriers charged the ISPs a wholesale per minute rate for carrying the calls from the BT local exchange to the ISP servers, and made a per minute 'outpayment' to BT to bring the call from the customer as far as the BT local exchange.

BT suddenly started to offer an unmetered Internet retail service—its charge to its retail customers was not based on minutes of usage. The ISPs wanted to offer the

---

[40] See further Chapter 3.

[41] See Oftel (now Ofcom) Determination relating to a dispute between British Telecommunications and Worldcom relating to the provision of a Flat Rate Internet Access Call Origination product (15 February 2001), and Oftel (now Ofcom) Direction amending the requirements for provision of a Flat Rate Internet Access Call Origination product (15 May 2002). See further Chapter 8.

same type of retail tariff, but BT refused to offer a wholesale unmetered outpayment for carrying the traffic from the customer as far as the BT local exchange. The ISPs (and the smaller carriers) complained to Oftel that this was an abuse by BT of its dominant position. It put both ISP and smaller carriers in a 'margin squeeze'; they had to pay out to BT at a (wholesale) per minute rate but could only charge their customers an unmetered retail rate. BT denied this was an abuse. That issue was never decided; BT was made to offer a wholesale unmetered tariff to get the calls from the end customers to the local exchange as an interconnection tariff, i.e. the complaint of an abuse by BT was settled instead by a determination of the smaller carriers' request for interconnection on unmetered terms.

A decision of the Competition Appeal Tribunal (CAT) in the UK provides a good example of both the complexity of bringing allegations of abusive pricing within section 18 and the overlap between competition rules and regulatory rules. *Freeserve* complained to Oftel that BT had, in the pricing and marketing of its broadband services, abused its dominant position contrary to section 18 of the Competition Act. BT Wholesale provided wholesale narrow and broadband services both to ISPs, including Freeserve, and to BT's own ISP business, called BT Openworld. In other words, BT and Freeserve were competitors on the downstream retail market for the provision of Internet services.[42]

Freeserve complained that BT was abusing its dominant position. Oftel concluded that there was no merit in any of the four allegations of abuse made against by BT by Freeserve (now called Orange Home), which related to BT's pricing of the wholesale inputs which Freeserve needed from BT to provide service. Freeserve appealed all aspects of Oftel's decision to the CAT. The CAT dismissed the appeal, with the exception of Oftel's reasoning in answer to Freeserve's pricing allegations. Freeserve had claimed that there was *prima facie* evidence of both unlawful cross-subsidy of BT Openworld and of predatory pricing by BT Openworld, on the basis that BT's ISP business could not be generating sufficient revenues to cover its variable and incremental costs.

On the cross-subsidy allegation, Oftel had relied on its findings in earlier cases involving breaches by BT of its licence conditions and found that the evidence provided by Freeserve was not sufficient to reopen the case. The CAT held Oftel was wrong to apply the principles used in assessing whether a 'cross subsidy' was unfair under BT's then licence conditions, when looking at an allegation of abusive price predation under section 18. The concepts of predatory pricing, and margin squeeze, are abuses distinct from unfair cross subsidy in breach of BT's licence condition. On those aspects of Oftel's decision that were set aside for lack of reasoning, Oftel adopted a further decision,[43] in which Oftel considered that the pricing issues raised were most appropriately addressed in the context of a margin squeeze under BT's

---

[42] *Freeserve.com.plc v Director General of Telecommunications* [2003] CAT 5.
[43] November 2003. See link at <http://www.ofcom.org.uk/bulletins/comp-bull-index/com-bull-ccases-all/cw-613/cw-613.pdf>.

licence (rather than as abusive predatory pricing). It concluded that BT was not acting contrary to section 18.[44]

The EU Commission has also considered abusive pricing by a dominant operator in the provision of telecommunications services and has applied Article 82 with greater success than Ofcom. In May 2003 the Commission found that Deutsche Telekom (DT) was dominant in both the provision of wholesale local loop access and in the corresponding downstream market for the provision of retail access services to end customers.[45] DT therefore competes with those operators who purchase DT's local loop services on wholesale terms so as to be able to provide retail services to their own customers.

DT was charging new entrants higher prices for wholesale access to the local loop than the price DT was charging its own retail subscribers to be connected to DT's network. This resulted in DT's downstream (retail) competitors not being able to make a margin—they could not effectively compete with DT. DT was subsidizing its retail activities through revenues made in the upstream market.

DT argued that its conduct was not an abuse contrary to Article 82 because its wholesale and retail prices were already subject to sectoral regulation by the German telecoms regulator, Reg TP. The Commission disagreed and imposed a (albeit lenient) fine of €12.6 million. On appeal, the European Court (CFI) upheld the Commission's decision that regulatory obligations are in addition to, not instead of, competition law obligations.[46]

In another decision, the EU Commission fined Telefonica €152 million for what the Commission described as 'a very serious abuse' over a five-year period of dominance in the Spanish wholesale LLU market. Telefonica charged its wholesale LLU product to its downstream competitors at such a high price that those competitors could not offer an ADSL based broadband retail product and make a profit.[47]

One interesting development is that in determining whether a dominant telecoms network operator is applying a margin squeeze the European Court confirmed that the dominant operator should offer downstream prices which a competitor 'equally efficient' as itself could offer, rather than the prices of a 'reasonably efficient' competitor. This is important, because the dominant operator can take a better view—on whether its prices are abusive—by using its own costs, rather than having to guess what the costs of a reasonably efficient competitor might be. Abuse cases involving the application of a margin squeeze in other regulated sectors rely on the same 'equally efficient competitor' test—see *Albion Water*.[48]

---

[44] This is now the subject of a further appeal.

[45] Commission Decision relating to a proceeding under Art 82 of the EC Treaty, case COMP/C-1/37.451, 37.578, 37.579—Deutsche Telecom AG, OJ L263/9, 14 October 2003.

[46] *Deutsche Telekom AG v Commission*, CFI Judgment, 10 April 2008.

[47] Commission Decision, 4 July 2007, Case Com/38.784.

[48] *Dwr Cymru Cyfyngedig v Albion Water* [2008] EWCA Civ 97.

9.3.6 A special form of dominance: control over 'essential facilities'

Much academic comment has focused on an enhanced form of dominance which can arise in telecoms—the concept of an 'essential facility', for example the control of a bottleneck on the national system, through which all other operators must pass, such as the local network covering the whole country controlled by BT/Openreach. The concept of an 'essential facility', which gives rise to a position of 'super dominance' enjoyed by the undertaking which controls the facility, arose as an attempted device to force dominant companies to share their networks.[49] The thinking was that normally it is only an abuse for a dominant undertaking not to make its network available to others if it has already done so (since then not to do so would be discriminatory), but that if it has never shared its infrastructure with anyone in the first place it is not obliged to open it up to others. The EU Commission argued that if an undertaking is 'super dominant' and controls an essential facility it must share it, even if it has never offered it to anyone before. The essence of the EU Commission's position is that an 'essential facility' is more than mere dominance, but covers a close or total monopoly over a particular part of the network. Where an operator enjoys such ownership or control it should be obliged to supply all who request passage of traffic over it—whether an existing 'dependent' customer or a newcomer. Any refusal to supply over an essential facility would be an abuse.

The essential facilities concept as applied to telecoms has never been properly tested before a court. In practice obligations to supply are imposed by other rules, specific to telecommunications. Thus the obligation to offer interconnection arises under the Interconnection Directive; the obligation to supply conditional access and related services flows from the Access and Interconnection Directive, and regulations made under it. The concept of an 'essential facility' (and the related concept of an absolute obligation to supply on reasonable terms) has also been severely curtailed by the European Court in *Oscar Bronner*.[50]

The concept of 'super dominance' through control of an essential facility has probably been dealt a further blow by an important anti-trust ruling by the Supreme Court of the United States, in *Verizon v Trinko*.[51] The scope of EU competition law is very influenced by academic thinking and cases in North America. The US Supreme Court ruled that an incumbent local operator (the erstwhile Baby Bell company for New York State, formerly Nynex and Bell Atlantic, now called Verizon) had no obligation under US anti-trust law to make available parts of its network on an 'unbundled' basis. Such obligations only arise under the (US) Telecommunications Act of 1996. In short, the US court found that administrative agencies were better

---

[49] See US case, *MCI Communications v AT&T* 708 F 2d 1081 (7th Cir 1983).

[50] *Oscar Bronner GmbH & Co v Mediaprint Zeitungs and Zeitschriftverlag GmbH & Co KG, and others* (Case C-7/97 [1998] ECR 1-7791 of 26 November 1998).

[51] *Verizon Communications Inc v Law Offices of Curtis v Trinko LLP*, (02-682) 540 US 398 2004. The Court said 'Enforced sharing requires anti trust courts to act as central planners, identifying the proper price, quantity and other terms of dealing—a role for which they are ill suited.'

placed to enforce network sharing arrangements than the courts enforcing anti-trust law. This ruling confirms our basic thesis set out at the opening of this chapter—competition law is a useful tool for regulation in the field of telecoms, but it does not solve every problem.

For further guidance on how the competition rules apply to the particular circumstances of telecommunications, reference can be made to two sets of guidelines issued by the European Commission,[52] and also to the guidelines on the application of Chapter I and Chapter II prohibitions published by Oftel jointly with the OFT.[53]

The upshot of the above analysis is that in practice the concept of 'abuse of a dominant position' does not arise as easily in telecoms as some regulators (such as DG Comp/Ofcom) might hope; it is not impossible to apply, but not easy to do so. In the author's view the reason for this is plain. The concept of an 'abuse' involves nasty behaviour, which the dominant operator knows, or should have known, would drive a smaller competitor from the market—or at least seriously weaken it. An abuse is more than the mere exercise of commercial muscle by a powerful undertaking. In some cases, behaviour is only an abuse if it amounts to 'wrong' behaviour: intention to harm a competitor has to be shown.[54] Yet, in telecommunications much of the behaviour of a monopolist or incumbent may have a distorting effect on competition, but it is not 'abusive'. The correct course can only be chosen after careful economic analysis and the application of sector-specific rules, which only apply going forward.

9.4 MAINSTREAM COMPETITION LAW: THE LONG STOP—THE ENTERPRISE ACT 2002

Under EC competition law, Articles 81 and 82 are the complete system. Any further steps to deal with market failure or failure of competition require primary legislation—an EC Directive or an EC Regulation. A good example is the EC Roaming Regulation, introduced in 2007,[55] which sets maximum retail prices for mobile calls made abroad from one EU Member State to another.

Unlike the EC system, UK competition law recognizes that the national equivalent of Articles 81 and 82 (sections 2 and 18 of the Competition Act) cannot deal

---

[52] See *Guidelines on the application of EEC competition rules in the telecommunications sector* (1991) OJ C 233/02 and *Notice on the application of the competition rules to access agreements in the telecommunications sector—Framework, relevant markets and principles* (1998) OJ C 265/02.

[53] Application of the Competition Act in the Telecommunications Sector (Oftel, London, January 2000).

[54] See *AKZO Chemie BV v Commission of the European Communities* [1991] ECR I-3359, Case C-62/86.

[55] Regulation (EC) No 717/2007 of the European Parliament and of the Council of 27 June 2007 on roaming on public mobile telephone networks within the Community and amending Directive 2002/21/EC, OJ L 171/32.

with every competitive failure. Under the Enterprise Act 2002 the OFT (or Ofcom) can conduct market studies, to see if there is some structural failure in the market. If there is, a reference can be made to a separate body—the Competition Commission— which can then, if needed, order structural remedies—including divesture. It was this mechanism which was used to secure the Undertakings which BT gave in order to set up Openreach—the functional separation of its local access network to allow all operators access on equal terms—including BT's retail arm. This is discussed further below.

Under the EC system this long stop mechanism to deal with market failure of competition does not exist—so, for example, to enable other Member States to force national incumbents to functionally separate their local access networks would require an EC Regulation.

9.5 SPECIAL COMPETITION RULES FOR TELECOMMUNICATIONS (SIGNIFICANT MARKET POWER)

The telecommunications sector has two features which distinguish it from many other markets:

i. in most EU Member States it has (or had) an entrenched fixed line incumbent, with a very high share of the residential market; and

ii. the barriers to market entry to build a national fixed (or mobile) network are very high.

This means that both fixed and mobile network markets are supplied by just a very few operators.

Given these two unique factors, mainstream competition rules have three weaknesses or gaps:

i. An abuse can only be committed by an undertaking which is dominant in a relevant market. Normally only one undertaking is dominant in any market. Telecoms markets are often dominated by two, three or four operators (an oligopoly) whose unilateral, but also parallel, behaviour needs to be controlled.

ii. As mentioned above, an abuse is 'nasty' economic behaviour—acts designed to, or likely to, drive a competitor out of a market, or seriously weaken it. Not all behaviour that weakens competition is abusive, in that sense.

iii. The concept of 'abuse of a dominant position' is not enough where, as a matter of policy, you wish to deliberately stimulate competition, and encourage new entrants to the market.

In many telecommunications markets no single undertaking is dominant, but just a few big operators service the market. Attempts have been made to extend the concept of dominance to cover 'joint' or 'collective' dominance, where just a very few

(two, three, or four) companies control a market. However, the courts have been reluctant to do this. Normally, 'joint' or 'collective' dominance only arises in limited circumstances where there are contractual or other economic links between them; simply being members of an obligopoly is not enough (see: *Flat Glass* case referred to at footnote 64 below). For this reason the concept of significant market power, while based on the idea of dominance, has been expressly widened to include undertakings which enjoy a 'position equivalent to dominance jointly with others'.[56] Further, some behaviour of the incumbent or dominant operator can only be said to be socially or economically undesirable after a close study of the facts; in other words, there is some economic behaviour which it would be unfair to call abusive before such study, but which may need correcting or in response to which rules need to be put in place to encourage new entrants to the market.

Accordingly:

i. special competition rules were put into BT's licence (as the ex-monopolist incumbent) to positively assist market entrants;

ii. the rules originally developed (in the UK) to cover BT have been developed at European level; now any operator which has SMP is subject to additional obligations, in particular not to discriminate in its dealings with other operators and to charge cost orientated prices.

9.5.1 Special competition rules—prohibition on undue discrimination

Where an undertaking has a dominant position in a market, an abuse of that position can take several forms, including: predatory pricing (pricing below cost) and discriminatory pricing to force out a competitor. However the concept of abuse does not in fact cover all behaviours which may be harmful to competitors or simply unfair to customers. Further, an abuse must be an abuse of the competitive process, and of competing undertakings. Typically, the concept of abuse does not deal with unfair treatment of end customers.

Accordingly all regulated utilities in the UK which operate under a licence—water, gas, and electricity industries, for example—are subject to a broad obligation not to unduly discriminate, or unduly prefer any class of person. This provision has been a very flexible tool for all utility regulators to control inefficient or unfair behaviour by the monopoly utility provider.

This prohibition was also in BT's original licence granted in 1984 under the Telecommunications Act 1984. Although BT no longer, since 2003, operates under a licence, the prohibition on undue discrimination still applies to BT in those markets where it still enjoys SMP. The same prohibition has been extended to all

---

[56] See Art 14 of Directive 2002/21/EC of the European Parliament and of the Council of 7 March 2002 on a common regulatory framework for electronic communications networks and services (Framework Directive), OJ L108/33, 24 April 2002.

operators who have SMP in any market—as do, for example, the mobile network operators in the 'markets' for mobile call termination on each of their networks. This broadly written prohibition on undue discrimination and undue preference (and the related obligation to publish tariffs) goes beyond 'normal' competition rules.

A short look at how this prohibition has been enforced against BT shows how it differs from the mainstream competition rules against abuse of dominance. Condition 57[57] of BT's licence provided that BT 'shall not' show undue preference to, or exercise undue discrimination against, particular persons or persons of any class or description' as respects the provision of certain of its key services. Undue preference or discrimination extends to BT unfairly favouring any other business which it carries on. The prohibition on undue discrimination still applies to BT, even though BT no longer formally has a licence.[58]

The prohibition of undue discrimination covers not only the extremely low ('predatory') price offered on a selective basis, but also prevents BT from offering prices which discriminate more generally according to, for example, the size of customer or the geographical location of the customer, even if sales are made at a profit and cover BT's costs. Not every instance of price discrimination, even when exercised by a dominant operator, is inevitably an 'abuse' of its dominant position; it is too simplistic to say that once an operator is dominant it must justify all price differences on the basis of differences in the costs of supply. For example, even a dominant operator is able to, and frequently does, without committing an abuse, respond to price competition with a price which is still above fully allocated cost, but it will not necessarily be the same price charged to other customers in the same position. In practice, the prohibition of undue discrimination, previously in BT's licence, and now imposed on operators with SMP, can be a harsh rule. In effect it means that if BT, say, faces price competition in just one segment (say, business lines to large customers), it may have to reduce its tariff across the board, so that there is still some cost relationship between services supplied to different classes of customer.

Since the condition covers any discrimination, not just price discrimination, it is also a very flexible regulatory tool: between 1996 and 1999, some 12 orders for enforcement of the then condition in BT's licence prohibiting undue discrimination were made against BT. An analysis of those orders shows that they did not all cover behaviour which was 'abusive' in an Article 82 sense. For example, mere inefficiency by BT in connecting up a new entrant's pay phones (when BT had an installed base of 80,000 pay phones) was determined to be discriminatory against the new entrant; it probably was not 'abusive' applying Article 82 tests.[59]

---

[57] The successor to Condition 57 continues to have effect on BT in all those markets in which BT has been found to have SMP.

[58] See Condition 57 of the BT Continuation Notice of 25 July 2003.

[59] See Director-General's Determination on 15 April 1997 as respects Maintel Communications Ltd (case ref: BX/112/033).

Whether discrimination is 'undue' is a very broad rule. For example, it catches the case where the incumbent operator is obliged to sell certain services at a published, non-discriminatory tariff, but as part of a 'deal' with a major customer it offers certain other services (e.g. advice on how to set up its own private network) at a low cost. Although a broad rule, whether discrimination is 'undue' is normally decided according to one of two tests:

    i. is the difference in treatment between two customers in a comparable position just too great; or, more normally,

    ii. does the discrimination have a significantly adverse effect on competition?[60]

The prohibition forbids not only undue discrimination against or between third parties, but also undue preference by the operator in favour of its own downstream business. Thus, where BT supplies an essential input (e.g. local leased lines) to its own downstream business, providing network-management for large corporates, it must do so on identical terms to those terms on which it supplies third-party competitors. Further, it must not price the downstream business too low; it must allow an equally efficient competitor in the downstream market enough 'headroom' to make a living.

The obligation not to discriminate is backed up by a price publication rule. Broadly, BT has to publish its retail (residential and business) tariffs. The purpose of this rule is so that customers can check that they have the same tariff as is applied to others in the same or comparable position—that there has been no discrimination.[61]

9.5.2 Special competition rules for operators with significant market power

The UK was the first European country to privatize its telephone networks. A regulatory concept to come out of Oftel, the then regulator, was the idea that larger operators who were 'well established' or had 'market power' should be subject to obligations going beyond the obligations imposed on normal telecoms operators. From this grew the regulatory concept of an operator having 'significant market power' (SMP). An operator has SMP 'if, either individually or jointly with others, it enjoys a position equivalent to dominance, that is to say a position of economic strength affording it the power to behave to an appreciable extent independently of competitors, customers and ultimately consumers'.[62] The concept is aligned to the

---

[60] See, e.g., UK Access Guidelines, 'Imposing Access Obligations under the new EU Directives', Oftel statement of 13 September 2002.

[61] See Condition 58 of BT's Licence Conditions ('Publication of Charges, Terms and Conditions') (reference to continuation notice).

[62] The Framework Directive at Art 14(2). For detailed application of Art 14(2), see: Commission guidelines on market analysis and the assessment of significant market power under the Community regulatory framework for electronic communications networks and services, OJ C 2002 165/6, 11 July 2002 and *Oftel's market review guidelines: criteria for the assessment of significant market power*, 5 August 2002, London: Director General of Telecommunications.

concept of dominance used in Article 82, but it is not the same. In particular there are these important differences:

i. A national competition authority (NRA) can determine a single operator to have SMP where its market share is as low as 25 per cent;[63] under Article 82 dominance is hard to show where an undertaking has a market share of less than 40/50 per cent.

ii. More than one operator may have SMP in the same market. The EU Commission tried to develop the concept of a small group of undertakings having 'joint' dominance or 'collective' dominance under Article 82, but the European Court has, in effect, said that only very rarely can more than one undertaking have dominance in a relevant market.[64] Accordingly Article 14 of the Framework Directive plainly extends the concept of dominance so that an undertaking has SMP if 'either individually, *or jointly with others*, it enjoys a position *equivalent to dominance*'. A good example of several operators having SMP in the same market is the determination by the Spanish Regulator in March 2006 that three mobile network operators have collective dominance and imposed SMP obligations on all of them. This included an obligation to allow all mobile virtual network operators (MVNOs) access to their networks and provide services over them on equal terms.[65]

iii. An operator only has SMP if a NRA has first determined that it has SMP and issued a notice to that effect; under Article 82 an undertaking has to work out for itself whether it is dominant, and, if so, what it needs to do to avoid abusing that dominant position.

The special rules imposed on those operators having SMP is a recognition of the fact that, unlike other economic sectors, the provision of network infrastructure

---

[63] See para 75 of the *Commission guidelines on market analysis and the assessment of significant market power under the Community regulatory framework for electronic communications networks and services* (OJ C165/6, 11 July 2002) which states that 'undertakings with market shares of no more than 25 per cent are not likely to enjoy a (single) dominant position on the market... The Commission may in some cases have concerns about dominance with even lower market shares [less than 40 per cent], as dominance may occur without the existence of a large market share'. See also *Oftel's market review guidelines, criteria for the assessment of significant market power* which states in the 'market shares' box in Table 1 at clause 2.3 that 'suppliers with market shares below 25% are not likely to enjoy single dominance... There may still be concerns about dominance where an undertaking has less than 40%, according to the size of that undertaking's market share relative to its competitors'.

[64] See joined cases T68/89, T77/89 and T78/89 *Societa Italiana Vetro SpA, Fabbrica Pisana SpA and PPG Vernante Pennitalia SpA v Commission* of 10 March 1992 (*Italian Flat Glass* case). As a matter of policy, the Commission tried to develop the concept of joint/collective dominance so as to extend the number of mergers it could catch (and prohibit) under the EC Merger Regulation (see *Airtours plc v Commission*, Case T342/99 OJ 2000/C79/69, (2002) ECR II–2585). The ECMR now uses a wider test to see whether a merger is undesirable: will it lead to a significant impediment to effective competition? Before, the test was: would the merger lead to the creation or strengthening of a dominant position? Given the change to the ECMR, I suspect that further attempts to extend the scope of joint dominance under Art 82 will fade away—which will reinforce the need to keep special rules for oligopolists with SMP in place.

[65] See European Commission press release IP/06/97, Brussels, 31 January 2006.

(which is very expensive to build) may be in the hands of only two or three operators, none of whom are dominant. Article 82 of the EC Treaty and the Competition Act may not catch abusive behaviour on their part.

Accordingly, additional obligations are placed on providers of electronic communication networks or services once they have been held to have SMP in any market segment. The policy purpose is to impose stricter and specific obligations on operators who, while not necessarily 'dominant' in Article 82/Chapter II terms, nevertheless enjoy market power because they are members of an oligopoly. The scheme under which operators are designated as having SMP and its obligations are set out in the Access Directive. Those operators designated by an NRA as having SMP can be made subject to various obligations (Access Directive, Articles 8 to 13 inclusive):

i. to offer 'cost orientated' interconnection prices;

ii. not to discriminate as to the terms and conditions of interconnection which they offer;

iii. to offer to supply services to all who request them, unless there is a 'good' commercial reason not to (such as that they have not paid their bills!);

iv. transparency obligations—to publish interface specifications, network characteristics, and prices;

v. accounting separation—to keep accounts so as to clearly identify the costs (for example) of running the fixed network, or of major routes;

vi. obligatory access to, and use of, specific network facilities.

The process for deciding which operators have SMP and should then be subject to additional obligations has been harmonized at community level under the Access Directive. However the practical operation of the system is firmly in the hands of each NRA.

Broadly, it is for each NRA to carry out regular market reviews and then set out which are the relevant product or service markets in its Member State. In doing so the NRAs should have regard to the EU Commission's recommendation on relevant markets.[66] In the UK, Ofcom has determined that BT has SMP in some 18 markets. Mobile network operators also have SMP on the 'markets' for termination of calls on each of their own networks. The number of markets in which operators have SMP obligations is slowly reducing. BT is subject to SMP obligations in 18 markets, but reducing. The reduction in the number of markets in which SMP may arise results from increasing competition at the retail level, especially as respects international calls. However, some wholesale markets and the markets for local access remain uncompetitive and those designated as having SMP will be subject to constraints for some time to come.

---

[66] Commission Recommendation 2003/311/EC of 11 February 2003 on relevant product and service markets within the electronic communications sector OJ L 114 of 8 May 2003, p 45. Now revised by Commission Recommendation 2007/879/EC.

9.6 MARKET FAILURE OF COMPETITION—
SECTOR-SPECIFIC RULES

In addition to the competition rules which are sector-specific to telecoms (such as the rules imposed on those having SMP and which may even tilt the playing field against the incumbent, and assist or protect the new entrant), there are other special rules which are needed to deal with market failure in the telecommunications sector to ensure that the competitive process works properly. These rules go further than the rules set out above.

9.6.1 The limitations of competition rules (general and sector-specific) as instruments of regulation: some general points

The two main extra mechanisms used to deal with the limitations of competition rules are the interconnection rules and price control. A third is the forced structural separation of parts of an operator's network to which all operators need equal access i.e. to force companies to share parts of the network.

9.6.2 Special rules on interconnection[67]

9.6.2.1 *Interconnection*
Under normal competition rules (Article 82, EC Treaty, or section 18 of the Competition Act 1998) only a dominant operator may be obliged to supply services to another undertaking. In telecommunications, all operators are to a degree interdependent. They must be able to deliver their own customers calls on to other networks and their customers will need to receive calls from other networks. However, any one operator might hold others to ransom by refusing to deliver calls. The obligation for one operator to interconnect with, and deliver the calls of, another operator cannot be 'shoe-horned' into the framework of Articles 81 and 82 or the Chapter I and Chapter II prohibitions of the Competition Act 1998; nor is it an obligation which can only be imposed on operators with SMP—it needs to be imposed on all or most operators for a national network, based on the 'all to any' principle, to work best. Some attempts were made to argue that ownership of a part of the network, and control by an operator of access to its own customers, is in some sense an 'essential facility', or bottleneck, to which the operator must allow others access; to refuse to do so would be an abuse of that operator's 'dominant' position in the 'market' made by the bottleneck. An often-cited example is the need for an operator to be able to deliver calls to a customer of another network operator. It is, however, very artificial to say that every operator (not just BT) which owns or controls the 'local loop' to its own customer is 'dominant', in competition law terms, in a 'market' which is access to each of its customers. Hence, the rules to require interconnection and delivery of

---

[67] See further Chapter 6.

calls, which apply to all operators providing services to the public, will always be needed.[68] Accordingly all communications network providers are obliged to provide interconnection. These obligations are set out in the Access Directive[69] and implemented in the UK General Conditions of Entitlement[70] so that all network operators must offer to negotiate interconnection on reasonable terms.[71] The main purpose of the interconnection rules is to foster interdependence: to ensure that all operators are able to deliver each of the calls, originating from their customers both nationally and overseas, over systems run by other operators.

The interconnection rules are explained in Chapter 8. Those rules and the competition rules overlap but it is useful to bear in mind the following principles:

i. only a dominant undertaking can (and then only under certain circumstances) be obliged to supply services to a commercial customer. An undertaking which is not dominant can normally refuse to supply another without giving any reason. Therefore, to ensure interconnection you need a special set of rules to ensure this happens—competition law will not ensure universal interconnection;

ii. even where an operator is dominant (as, for example, mobile network operators are in the markets for termination of calls on their networks) competition law is a clumsy mechanism for fixing the actual price at which calls are terminated.

9.6.2.2 *Price control*
This is also outside the scope of normal competition rules. There have not been any decisions under Article 82 of the EC Treaty, involving simple excessive pricing, i.e. an operator overcharging because there is no competition. The EC cases on excessive pricing (which in themselves are few and far between) have all involved some form of exclusionary or discriminatory behaviour[72] which has weakened or diminished a competitor. Broadly, the concept of 'abuse' under Article 82 or section 18 may catch excessive pricing which is exclusionary (as in a margin squeeze case) but cannot normally be used to catch exploitative, excessive pricing. In 2003 the EU Commission started infringement proceedings against Vodafone, 02, and T-Mobile as respects their excessive roaming charges in the UK and Germany. The Commission asserted that those charges were excessive, and hence abusive in breach of Article 82.[73]

---

[68] See further Chapter 6.

[69] Directive 2002/19/EC of the European Parliament and of the Council of 7 March 2002 on access to, and interconnection of, electronic communications networks and associated facilities (the Access Directive), OJ L 108/7, 24 April 2002, at Art 4(1).

[70] Article 5(1) of the Access Directive is implemented by ss 45 and 46 of the Communications Act 2003, which is in turn implemented by the General Conditions of Entitlement.

[71] See Condition 1 of the General Conditions of Entitlement (22 July 2003).

[72] See e.g. *United Brands v Commission ('Chiquita')* Case 27/76 [1978] ECR 207 and *General Motors Continental NV v EC Commission* Case 26/75 [1975] ECR 1367, [1976] 1 CMLR 95.

[73] The EU Commission abandoned its cases when the Roaming Regulation was adopted.

The European Commission tried to use Article 82 as a means to reduce the termination rates charged by mobile networks, but with little success. The EU Commission's proceedings in 1997 against Deutsche Telecom in respect of its leased-line prices show that Article 82 is an inadequate instrument of price control.[74] In practice there is a big difference between an abusive price—a price which is grossly excessive, bearing little or no relationship to the cost of supplying it—and prices which are just unnecessarily high. Further, with termination rates there is a particular feature of the market which leads to prices rising to excessive levels; there is 'market failure' in the way in which a price is reached. With a mobile termination rate the immediate customer (the fixed network) is not actually paying the bill; it passes it on to its own customer. The fixed network has little commercial incentive to negotiate hard to reduce the termination rate. It was for this reason that in the UK the sector-specific rules are used to impose price controls on termination rates of calls to mobiles.[75]

It is reasonable to assume that it will rarely be possible to use the 'abuse of dominance' concept to control simple excessive pricing, unless there is evidence of exclusionary behaviour or some form of price discrimination which has no objective justification and a clear adverse effect on competitors.

9.6.2.3 *The Roaming Regulation*

This is a good example of the need for specific rules to control excessive pricing. For many years the costs of making international mobile calls were much higher than mobile calls within each Member State. International mobile calls were so high because mobile operators charged very high prices to terminate calls coming in from abroad. Attempts to get the industry to reduce their international termination, or 'roaming', rates voluntarily failed. Attempts to use Article 82 (abuse of dominance) to push down rates also petered out. It was because Article 82 cannot in practice be used to push down or control excessive prices that the EU Commission adopted the Roaming Regulation.[76] Even though each mobile network operator and fixed operator is dominant in the 'market' for termination of calls to its customer in its network, a specific regulation is needed to control what are seen to be 'excessive' prices. Abuse of dominance does not achieve that result. The EU Commission abandoned its 'test case' to see if Article 82 could be used to control excessive roaming tariffs.[77] The EC Roaming Regulation fixes maximum prices which a network operator can charge for an incoming call to its network. The interesting part is that it applies to *all* mobile network operators, not just those operators having SMP.

---

[74] See *European Community XXVIIIth Report on Competition Policy 1998*, Luxembourg: Office for Official Publications of the European Communities, 1999.

[75] See Competition Commission Report referred to at n 19 above.

[76] Regulation (EC) No 717/2007 of the European Parliament and of the Council of 27 June 2007 on roaming on public mobile telephone networks within the Community and amending Directive 2002/21/EC, OJ L 171/32, 29 June 2007.

[77] See Commission Press Release IP/07/1113, Brussels, 18 July 2007.

9.6.2.4 *Price control—joint dominance*

As we have seen above, Article 82 (and the Chapter II prohibition) is also not apt to control misuse of market power by a small group of companies, no one of which is dominant, but which together control the market—so-called joint dominance. It has been suggested that in certain situations two or three telecoms operators might have joint dominance. For example, BT and one cable operator might be the only two operators offering a fixed line service to residential customers in a particular area. We suggest that the idea that those two might be 'jointly' dominant is an artificial construct; if there are elements of behaviour, e.g. overpricing, which need to be dealt with, they should be dealt with sector-specific legislation (as in telecoms) or under the residual competition rules in the Enterprise Act 2002. These latter provisions have been deliberately left in place to deal with so called 'complex monopoly' behaviour. This is exactly the route used to control the mobile termination rates on the four main networks. Following the Competition Commission's report the price which each mobile network may charge for each incoming call to its customers is capped; it reduces further over the next five years on the RPI − X formula. Similarly BT's retention—its charge for originating a fixed-to-mobile call—has been capped. General competition law did not do this; a special investigation and rule was needed.[78]

9.6.2.5 *Functional separation*

We deal below with the rules imposed on BT to ensure equal access to its local networks. Suffice it to say here that even if a dominant undertaking is 'abusing' its position by refusing access to its networks on fair and reasonable terms, forced divestiture, of that part of the network, or other structural changes, cannot be a 'remedy' under Article 82.

9.6.2.6 *Intellectual property rights in telecoms network technology*

Some elements of a network may enjoy intellectual property rights. Further common standards used in interfaces may enjoy IP protection. The question then is how best to ensure that all operators can use those IP protected elements, i.e. have access to IP rights needed in the running of networks—patents, copyright, or design rights. The use of general competition law to force rights owners to licence their rights to

---

[78] See Chapter 7 of the Oftel 'Review of mobile wholesale voice call termination markets—EU market review, 15 May 2003' which follows the recommendations of the Competition Commission's 'Reports on references under section 13 of the Telecommunications Act 1984 on the charges made by Vodafone, O2, Orange and T-Mobile for terminating calls from fixed and mobile networks' (December 2002). The Competition Commission's reports of December 2002 were also followed in Oftel's 'Notice under section 15(3) of the Telecommunications Act 1984 (proposed modifications to the licences of Vodafone, O2, T-Mobile and Orange)' (February 2003). That Notice was implemented by added Conditions 70A and 70B of the Continuation Notices of T-Mobile and Orange (dated 25 July 2003) and by added Conditions 70B and 70C of the Continuation Notices of Vodafone and O2 (dated 25 July 2003). Those added conditions are preserved in the Continuation Notices for all four operators.

others is fraught with difficulty.[79] The EU Commission's case against Microsoft has taken years to conclude. Only now is Microsoft obliged to licence its copyright and other rights in interoperability to others on fair and reasonable terms.

In the telecoms, conditional access is a good example of the need for a special rule to make IP rights widely available. Conditional access is the technical means of access to a particular service—the 'set-top box'—which enables you to unscramble a television signal or a digital message. The Access Directive[80] lays down detailed rules as to the terms on which other broadcasters can reach their customers through the set-top box and on which manufacturers can require a licence to make the boxes. It is not at all clear that general competition law (in particular Article 82, EC Treaty) could have been used to achieve the same result.

9.6.3 The limitations on competition rules (general and telecoms sector-specific) as instruments of regulation: some specific examples

Against this background of the limitations of both mainstream competition law and of telecoms specific competition law rules, there are specific rules put in place to correct those limitations. Given the particular features of the telecommunications market, some additional rules have been put in place to deal with market failure, i.e. where neither market forces, nor competition law, nor competition law-type rules specific to telecoms, provide a solution. We highlight below, in particular, the rules relating to:

- indirect access;
- number portability;
- network charge control on BT;
- interconnection obligations;
- price control over mobile termination rates;
- local loop unbundling and 'functional separation' of the local network; and
- consumer protection legislation.

---

[79] See, e.g., joined Cases 241/91P and C242/91P, OJ 95/C137/05, (1995) ECR I-743 *(1) Radio Telefis Eireann (2) British Broadcasting Corporation (3) Independent Television Publication Ltd v Commission Magill*; see also Case 418/01 (2004) *IMS Health Gmbh & Co OHG v NDC Health Gmbh & Co*, which develops the principles laid down in the *Telefis* case.

[80] Access Directive at Art 6 and Annex 1. See also Art 4(2) which requires digital television transmitters/re-distributors to transmit in wide-screen format (16:9 aspect ratio dictated by whereas (4)); paragraph 1 of Annex VI to the Universal Service Directive (Directive 2002/22 EC (2002) OJ L108/51) which requires all television sets to be able to descramble the common scrambling algorithm; para 2 of Annex VI to the Universal Service Directive which creates technical standards for analogue and digital televisions. Directives 2002/19/EC and 2002/22 EC are implemented in the UK by SI 2003/1901 (the Advanced Television Services Regulations 2003). In addition, Oftel (now Ofcom) has set regulatory conditions for conditional access (see Oftel document *The regulation of conditional access, setting of regulatory conditions, Explanatory statement and formal notification pursuant to section 48(1) of the Communications Act 2003* (24 July 2003).

9.6.3.1 *Indirect access and carrier pre-selection*[81]

Indirect access through another service provider (IA) is the facility which enables the customer of one fixed network operator (typically BT) to make calls using another service provider by dialling a four- or five-digit access code before making the call. The fixed operator provides 'access' (the line carrying the call to the local exchange) and the IA provider arranges for the rest of the call to be delivered. IA was brought in to encourage competition between service providers, which would in turn put pressure on BT to reduce its wholesale prices. The BT line provides the access, but the call is managed, once it leaves the BT network, and is billed to the customer, by the IA operator. The calls pass over BT's fixed network and then, normally via the IA operator's switch, to its terminating destination. The IA operator pays BT, as the network operator, for the carriage of the originating call at wholesale interconnection rates. It then charges its customers a retail rate and it makes money on the 'turn'.

IA was introduced as a means of forcing BT to reduce its retail prices; it allows a BT customer to have a choice as to which operator should carry each call, the choice being made on a call-by-call basis, even if the underlying final line connection is provided by BT. It was a successful policy—in effect resellers competed both with each other and with their network supplier—forcing down the cost of calls. IA was particularly successful in allowing IA operators to offer cheap calls to overseas destinations; as a result the price of calls abroad has tumbled—calls to Australia have fallen from 40p a minute in 1998 to 3p a minute today. As a technique to stimulate competition it has been greatly supplemented by local loop unbundling.

Carrier pre-selection (CPS) is a variant of IA. With CPS a customer is able to use a fixed operator for access (i.e. for the right to use the line against payment of a fixed monthly or quarterly rental fee), but his or her telephone is pre-programmed to use another carrier for carrying all outgoing calls; it is not necessary to dial the four- or five-digit prefix, as it is with IA. The pre-selected carrier makes its money in the same way as an IA operator, i.e. it carries the traffic over BT's and other networks at their wholesale interconnection rates and charges its customer a retail price.

Only BT and Kingston Communications are obliged to allow their customers the freedom to use CPS if they wish.[82] The introduction of CPS had a similar economic purpose as IA. CPS is designed to give customers a greater choice over which operator carries their calls, thus further stimulating competition between operators.

9.6.3.2 *Number portability*

The need to have a new telephone number if you moved to a new network or service provider was found to discourage customers from changing supplier, thus reducing competition between network and service providers.

---

[81] Also referred to as 'easy access'.

[82] See continued Condition 50A in the Continuation Notices for BT and Kingston (both having effect from 25 July 2003).

Number portability is the right of a customer, when moving to a new operator, to retain his or her existing number, thus not needing to have a new number allocated to him or her by the new operator. All operators are now obliged to offer this facility. The costs of providing it are shared between the old operator and the operator taking over the customer. The purpose of mandating number portability is to make it easier for customers to switch supplier without the trouble (or loss of business) caused by their change of number, hence sharpening competition between network operators and service providers for new customers.

9.6.3.3 *Price control generally in BT*

Price control still has a large place in Ofcom's regulation of the telecoms sector. In the early years, following the privatization of BT in 1984, price control was the major part of the then Oftel's work. As competition has developed, so the need for price control has reduced as competition forces down prices. Ofcom has come to spend more time enforcing competition law and similar regulatory rules, less on price control.

However, price control still has an important place in Ofcom's, and other NRAs', work. In some segments of the market BT (or other operators) has a monopoly or dominant position. Lack of competition means price remains too high—well above the rate you would expect to find in a competitive market.

There are two broad principles behind the price controls still in place:

i. prices should be capped at a level which 'mimics' what the price would be if the relevant market were fully competitive;

ii. price controls should give an incentive to the operator to continually improve efficiency. Typically this efficiency has been achieved by offering the carrot of 'RPI − X' price increases—if the operator can reduce its costs by more than X during the period of the price control (say five years), it can keep the profit for the rest of that period.

The controls on BT's retail and network charges last came up for renewal in 2006. Control on retail prices was not extended—so 22 years after the privatization of BT competition has done its work—competition from other operators has meant retail price control is no longer required. Removal of price control at the retail level also reflects the decision to reduce, from 18 to 7, the markets in which any operator may have SMP. Those remaining 7 markets are all wholesale markets, not retail markets.

However there are two ongoing constraints on the retail price which BT charges to its end customers:

i. The Universal Service Obligation—that all customers anywhere in the UK can get a service from BT. The USO has the practical implication that BT has a single national tariff—a 'geographically averaged' tariff. This has a knock-on effect on other operator tariffs, so national tariffs—the same price countrywide—are the norm.

ii. The fact that the tariffs, at least in the past, were 'unbalanced'—the cost of having a phone ('access') was kept low (below BT's cost) so everyone could afford a phone, with the loss on providing access being recovered from the charge for individual calls.

9.6.3.4 *Network charge control on BT*

Under the network charge control, which applied until 2006 to the charges which BT makes to other operators for interconnection, a cap of RPI – 8 per cent was applied for three baskets of non-competitive services and a safeguard cap of RPI + 0 per cent for services which were deemed to be prospectively competitive. Network price controls have now been aligned with the regime of designation of SMP, so a separate price control is imposed in each market in which BT has been designated as having SMP. Thus, for example, an RPI – X (X being between 4.0 per cent and 8.9 per cent) cap has been imposed on BT for its Partial Private Clients (PPC) product.

Network (or 'wholesale') charge/price control is only imposed in those segments where Ofcom has determined BT to have SMP—at present in 18 segments, shortly reducing to seven.

No control is applied in segments which are judged to be fully competitive; again BT is constrained, however, in relation to markets which are not fully competitive by the obligation not to discriminate between one category of wholesale customer and another (an obligation reinforced by the terms of the Interconnection Directive (see Chapter 6)).

9.6.3.5 *Mobile termination rates*

As said above, the prohibitions in the Competition Act 1998 on restrictive agreements and abuse of a dominant position were thought by some to be sufficient as a complete set of national domestic competition rules, because they parrot Articles 81 and 82, EC Treaty. The reality is that the EC competition rules are not a perfect template for national competition legislation. There still needs to be a mechanism to be able to look at unexpected anti-competitive behaviour, which is not automatically prohibited under Article 81/82-type rules, and be able to order remedial action on a case-by-case basis. The price of calls to mobiles is such a case.

Following references by Oftel and then Ofcom to the Competition Commission, the Commission concluded that the market for delivering calls on to mobile networks is not competitive, if only because the terminating mobile operator's immediate customer (another fixed or mobile network operator, which has a call to deliver) was not actually paying the bill—it merely passed it on to its own customer. Accordingly, obligations were put on all four network operators so that the prices which the mobile network operators can charge for delivering each call to their network customers are controlled. Similarly BT's 'retention', i.e. the bit of money which it keeps as respects calls which start on its fixed network, has been forcibly

reduced.[83] The charges for mobile calls termination are now also fixed for the fifth mobile operator H3G. Calls from a fixed line to a mobile line are treated as a separate market from calls from one mobile network to another; separate rates are capped for such calls.

9.6.3.6 *Interconnection obligations*

As said above, the view has been put forward that each operator has a monopoly, and is hence 'dominant', in a market which is comprised by the access which that operator has to each and every one of its customers for incoming calls. If that hypothesis had stood up to close analysis, Ofcom and the other NRAs could have relied on the competition rules to force each operator to allow other operators to deliver calls to the terminating operator's customers and on reasonable terms, since a refusal by the latter to do so would be an 'abuse' of each operator's dominant position in the 'market' for terminating calls on its own network.

This adventurous thinking has never been tested; the obligation to connect and deliver calls does not arise under the competition rules but under the interconnection rules. Once an operator has its own network which allows it to deliver its own customers' outgoing calls over other networks, it *must* deliver the incoming calls to those customers. The interconnection rules are explained in Chapter 6.

9.6.3.7 *Local loop unbundling*

In economic terms BT, as the incumbent fixed network operator, has a bottleneck monopoly over allowing access to its customers over the 'final mile' of the national fixed line (as distinct from mobile) network—the last part of the network from the local exchange to someone's house or business. Oftel, and then Ofcom, made various attempts to allow competitors to use that final mile to provide services to their customers. BT's wholesale prices of access to other operators were controlled; IA and CPS forced BT to allow other operators access to BT's network.

Fixing the price at which other operators could have access to BT's local circuits was not enough to stimulate competition. BT exercised all sorts of subtle forms of non-price discrimination which main stream competition law and sectoral behavioural rules could not stop.

Local loop unbundling (LLU) was the next attempt to stimulate competition from smaller network operators. LLU means forcing the incumbent (BT in the UK) to allow other operators to put their equipment in BT's exchanges and compete with BT; 'LLU' is the jargon term for forcing BT to allow other operators to take over and run the copper pair 'local loop' connection between the BT local exchange and the

---

[83] Vodafone, O2, Orange, and T-Mobile: Reports on references under s 13 of the Telecommunications Act 1984 on the charges made by Vodafone, O2, Orange, and T-Mobile for terminating calls from fixed line networks, *Oftel and Competition Commission document presented to the Director General of Telecommunications*, December 2002.

end customer. 'Unbundling' means that the wires are physically connected from BT's main frame at the exchange directly to another operator's network and then the latter's switch. The new operator then pays BT a set, price controlled, fee for the use and management, for its own benefit, of the line. The new operator then bills its customer for use of the line (access) as well as for the calls.

For a long time the UK government was opposed to mandatory LLU, fearing it would mean that other operators would have less incentive to build competing infrastructure to reach mass consumers and to connect each home. Other European countries (notably France and Germany) favoured LLU as a 'quick fix' to introduce competition at the mass retail level. Eventually, after the UK government had decided to mandate LLU, the EU issued a Regulation which required all Member States to put in place rules to ensure that the incumbent operator in each Member State offered LLU.[84]

The UK government changed its policy to allow LLU, partly as a result of EU Commission pressure, but also in part because of the need to speed growth of use of the Internet and the implications for broadcasting. Developments in DSL, and in particular ADSL (asynchronous digital subscriber line) technology, now mean that it is possible to send not only high-speed data down a traditional local line made of copper pairs, but also broadcast material. ADSL allows BT and others to provide a comparable broadcast, high-speed data, and voice service to that provided by Virgin Media over their coaxial and fibre optic cable networks. BT is now itself able to broadcast. To stimulate competition, other providers of telephony and broadcast services would be able to have access to BT's 'local loop'—the last line connection from the local exchange to the end customer.

In theory, LLU forces competition in the 'local loop' by enabling customers to switch between operators. However, initially LLU met only partial success as a policy to inject more competition into the market for local access—i.e. use of the line to the customer's home or place of business.

Firstly, it is very expensive for another operator to go into BT's exchange, take the final line from BT's main frame, and link it to its own equipment, which is in its own room or cabinet in BT's exchange. Take up by other operators of LLU, across the whole of the European Community, was slow. In practice, it is often only economic to take advantage of LLU in an area where an operator other than BT wants to supply services to customers with a high volume of traffic.

Secondly, Ofcom had to deal with endless complaints from other operators that BT delayed in providing LLU in practice; BT for ever raised seemingly unnecessary difficulties. The bans on discrimination by BT were ineffective, partly because detection was difficult, and time consuming for Ofcom.

---

[84] Regulation (EC) No 2887/2000 of the European Parliament and of the Council of 18 December 2000 on unbundled access to the local loop, OJ L 336/4, 30 December 2000.

Accordingly, the LLU regime has been 'beefed up', so that BT's local access network has now been moved across to a separate line of business (called *'Openreach'*) which deals at arms length with the rest of BT. This process has been referred to as the *'functional separation'* of BT's Access Service Division. It was the result of Ofcom's 2004 Strategic Review of Telecommunications (a market study carried out by Ofcom using its competition law powers under the Enterprise Act 2002). In essence, Ofcom found that BT's control over the local access network acted as a bottle-neck in terms of opening up, in particular, the downstream broadband market in the UK. In order to remedy this bottleneck BT undertook to separate out its local access network into a new line of business to be run separately and independently from the rest of BT. BT did this in order to avoid a reference to the Competition Commission, the outcome of which was uncertain, and could have ended in an order to BT completely divesting its local network.

Openreach now owns, operates and maintains all the local access networks from the local exchange, as well as some back haul circuits to the core node (district exchange). Openreach is still owned by BT, but there is now full functional separation. In practice, this means: separate engineering and administrative staff; separate financial accounting; separate technical and computer systems; blocks on the flow of commercial information between Openreach and the rest of BT. Openreach is based on the idea of requiring 'equivalence of access' to other operators, servicing the downstream market (it is also known as providing 'equivalence of inputs' i.e. BT must provide the same product and services to all operators on the same timescales and terms and conditions by means of the same systems and processes, including its own downstream business).

BT is now on notice that running Openreach as a separate entity must be made to work; if not, BT is likely to be made to sell of Openreach, and its business altogether i.e. have complete structural and ownership separation of the national local access network.

Normal competition rules did not oblige BT to offer LLU. Nor could the competition rules be used to order functional separation of Openreach. Each of the above measures is an obligation to supply imposed on BT, which it would not have been obliged to do under normal competition rules. Other countries within Europe, with similar local access network issues, are looking closely at whether functional separation will work in the UK, with a view to adopting it in their own countries.

9.6.3.8 *Other co-location*

In order to run interconnecting networked systems, it is often necessary for competing operators physically to place equipment or lines on the same premises, or in common ducts, i.e. to 'co-locate' them. Some thought has been given as to whether the ex-monopoly national incumbent, which is dominant, by owning sites for equipment (footway line boxes, local exchanges, distinct exchanges, etc.) controls access to an 'essential facility'. In order to avoid being in breach of Article 82 of the EC

Treaty, or the Chapter II prohibition, it must (so the argument went) share these sites with other operators, i.e. allow co-location. This view has never been tested before a court. In practice in the UK, if there is an obligation on an operator (not just BT) to allow another to co-locate on its premises or elsewhere on its network this results not from Article 82 or Chapter II,[85] but from its interconnection obligations, under the rules requiring BT to offer LLU (under Condition [83] of the BT Continuation Notice and under EC Regulation 2887/2000) or under other obligations on BT to allow co-location.

9.6.3.9 *Consumer protection legislation*

Before turning to the processes for enforcement of competition law it also useful to remind ourselves that competition, and competition law, do not produce the complete, perfect outcome for consumers. In telecoms, the greatest welfare for the consumer is reinforced in two ways: specific rules to deal with the protection of the consumer (on billing, contract terms, etc., dealt with in Chapter 5, at 5.9) and applying the benefits of competition and competition law by requiring some operators to offer the same benefits countrywide—such as the Universal Service Obligation imposed on BT or the 'roll out' obligations imposed on mobile operators—to ensure their networks have reception which covers most of the country.

9.7 PROCEDURES FOR ENFORCEMENT OF THE COMPETITION RULES

In the UK, Ofcom supervises the telecommunications market, relying on both the general competition rules contained in the Competition Act 1998 and on the 'competition' and regulatory rules specific to operators of telecommunications networks and providers of telecoms services made under the Communications Act 2003 or using powers in the EC Directives. The EU Commission has jurisdiction to enforce the EC competition rules, where the arrangements or conduct in question have a real effect on trade between EU Member States.

Both the EC and UK general competition rules are also self-executing, i.e. affected third parties can enforce them by issuing proceedings before the national courts, i.e. in terms of bringing an action for damages, or of seeking an injunction (see *Garden Cottage Foods v Milk Marketing Board*[86]). Failure by an undertaking to comply with section 2 (restrictive agreements) or section 18 (abuse of dominance) is a breach of statutory duty to obey the law (although, curiously, this is not spelled out in the Competition Act). Accordingly, third parties who suffer loss from the breach (say the victims of a predatory pricing scheme) can claim damages. Claims for

---

[85] See, e.g. Access to Bandwidth: Delivering Competition in the Information Age (Oftel, London, November 1999), para 7.7.

[86] *Garden Cottage Foods Ltd v Milk Marketing Board* [1984] AC 130, [1983] 3 CMLR 43.

damages are made easier by section 58 of the Competition Act, which, in effect, says that findings of fact by the OFT (or Ofcom, in a communications case) may be relied on in civil proceedings for damages (referred to as follow-on actions).

In practice, the majority of competition cases before the national courts are applications for injunctions. These are normally both a swift and effective remedy.[87] Some telecoms companies have had similar success in getting injunctions against powerful or dominant network operators.[88] In brief, we have what is called a mixed enforcement system—important cases are investigated by Ofcom; but breaches of competition law can also be pursued by injured parties through the courts by bringing a claim for damages or by seeking an injunction.

Competition rules specific to telecommunications, on the other hand, may, or may not, be enforceable by third parties before a court. However, they can always be enforced by Ofcom. Under the Competition Act 1998, Ofcom has jurisdiction to enforce the Chapter I and Chapter II prohibitions (and investigate alleged breaches of them) where the conduct in question 'relates to activities connected with communications matters'. Under the Communications Act 2003, Ofcom has power to enforce all regulation (e.g. the rules applicable to operators with SMP) in the telecoms sector. Ofcom thus has two distinct sets of powers to deal with allegations of anti-competitive behaviour in the telecommunications sector: (i) powers under the Competition Act 1998; (ii) powers to enforce sector-specific rules.

Telecoms specific rules are sometimes called *'ex ante'* (before the event) rules, the application of the competition law to telecoms being described as *'ex post'*— after the event. This is misconceived. Competition law applies to a telecoms operator at all times; it has to observe the competition rules, now, and work out how they apply to its commercial services. It is quite wrong to think that the competition rules, as *ex post* rules, only apply after the operator has been forced to change its practices by an enforcement agency. Competition law is not applied *ex post*—after the event: in telecoms, as in all other sectors of the economy, it applies immediately without the need for action by Ofcom or any other NRA. The only thing which is *ex post* is the fine or claim for damages if the telecoms operator has failed to observe the competition rules.

9.7.1 General competition law—enforcement mechanisms

Under the Competition Act 1998, Ofcom has 'concurrent' powers of investigation and enforcement in the field of communications—i.e. the same powers as the OFT has across the economy as a whole. Thus Ofcom has the power to:

i. require any person (an individual or a company) to produce any document or information which is relevant (Competition Act 1998, section 26(1));

---

[87] See *Adidas Salomon AG v Lawn Tennis Association & Others* [2006] EWHC 1318 (Ch).
[88] See *Software Cellular Network Ltd v T-Mobile (UK) Ltd* [2007] EWHC 1790 (Ch), [2007] UKCLR 1663.

ii. enter a company's premises on notice and require the production of documents and an explanation of what is in them (Competition Act 1998, section 27(5));

iii. enter a company's premises forcibly, with a warrant issued by a judge, to search for such documents (Competition Act 1998, section 28(2));

iv. fine a company up to 10 per cent of its group's turnover where it has intentionally or negligently infringed either of the prohibitions.

Where there is sufficient evidence of ongoing infringement of the Chapter I or II prohibitions in the 1998 Act, Ofcom has powers to:

i. give directions to bring the infringements to an end (Competition Act 1998, sections 32 and 33);

ii. order interim measures to protect the position of affected parties or to preserve the position pending completion of the investigation (Competition Act 1998, section 35).

These are extensive and, in the case of fines, severe powers.

Increasingly important is the real risk of significant claims for damages from undertakings which have suffered loss through breach by others of the competition rules. Breach of both EC and UK competition law is a breach of statutory duty, giving rise to claims for damages. In the past such claims were few; it was difficult to get the evidence and bring the claim before the High Court. A major change to the enforcement regime is to be able to bring a 'follow-on' action, under section 58 of the Competition Act. If an enforcement agency (OFT, Ofcom) makes an infringement decision the injured party can bring a follow-on action before the High Court or the Competition Appeal Tribunal (CAT).[89] This avoids the need to bring a fresh claim; you can rely on the infringement decision.

The purpose of competition law is to encourage economic efficiency by eliminating cartels and stopping abuse of dominance. However, that policy objective will only be achieved if the rules are observed and enforced. Modern thinking on enforcement recognizes that compliance with competition law goes up, the higher the risk of being caught out.[90] Accordingly various techniques to improve the risk of being caught have been brought in, many based on the experience of the enforcement agencies in the US (the Anti-Trust Division of the Justice Department and the Federal Trade Commission). Such modern techniques include:

i. financial rewards to 'whistleblowers';

ii. leniency—if a company comes forward voluntarily to admit to an infringement, it can secure total, or partial, immunity from fines;

iii. rewards (reduced fines) for cooperation with the enforcement agencies;

---

[89] Competition Act, s 47A.

[90] Note: Parallels can be drawn with the setting up of a modern police force under Home Secretary Sir Robert Peel in the 1850s—crime decreased as the risk of being arrested rose; simply making the penalties more draconian was ineffective in reducing crime.

iv. 'follow on' actions for damages—an injured party can rely on the OFT/ Ofcom's finding of infringement to bring a claim for damages—it does not have to prove the whole case again.

Even more severe are the powers of enforcement under the Enterprise Act 2002, which prohibits so-called 'hardcore' cartels—bid rigging, price fixing, and customer allocation between competitors. These are more limited classes of behaviour than those prohibited by section 2 of the Competition Act; the Enterprise Act does not catch many things caught by the Competition Act, such as information exchange between competitors, any restriction in a 'vertical' agreement, abuse by a single undertaking of its dominance position, or agreements between purchasers of goods or services. However, the penalties for directors and senior managers caught in such 'hard core' cartels—such as bid rigging and pricing cartels between sellers—are severe: personal fines and imprisonment.

The Enterprise Act draws on experience in the US that more effective compliance with competition (anti-trust) laws happens when directors and senior managers face the real risk of personal fines and imprisonment. The first directors in the UK to go to prison were directors of companies involved in the marine hoses cartel. It is an open question whether, in such a highly regulated industry such as telecoms, where companies are very alert to compliance with competition law, an Enterprise Act criminal prosecution is likely.

9.7.2 Enforcement of sector-specific rules

Where there is an alleged breach of a sector-specific regulatory rule, Ofcom's powers, both of investigation and enforcement, are weaker. Thus, Ofcom has no power to enter and search the premises of a network operator or a service provider for evidence of a breach of licence condition. However, Ofcom's powers to enforce licence conditions are stronger than Oftel's powers were under the Telecommunications Act 1984, thus:

i. 'where Ofcom determine[s] that there are reasonable grounds for believing that a person is contravening, or has contravened',[91] a General Condition of Entitlement or a Specific Condition, it may give a notification which states that the relevant Condition has been breached and sets out[92] the other steps to be taken;

ii. if that notification is not complied with, Ofcom may issue an 'enforcement notification' requiring compliance with the initial notification;

iii. an injured third party can, in some cases, sue for damages for breach of licence condition—it need not ask Ofcom to enforce the condition. Now you can sue for damages for, amongst other things, breach of certain conditions: those imposed

---

[91] Communications Act 2003, s 94(1).
[92] For the requisite content of the notification, see s 94(2) of the Communications Act 2003.

under section 45 (General and Specific Conditions); a (section 95) enforcement notification; or a Direction (section 100).[93] However proceedings cannot be brought for breach of condition without the consent of Ofcom (section 104);

    iv. in extreme cases of breach of enforcement notice Ofcom can order a network to be closed down;

    v. Ofcom has power to fine following a notification for breach of condition.

In general Ofcom uses its powers under the Competition Act 1998 less than its regulatory powers, which latter are probably more flexible and easier to enforce. Further, experience of the way in which the EU Commission enforces the EC competition rules suggests that a great many complaints are settled informally. Certainly the majority of complaints to Oftel alleging breaches by a licensee of a licence condition (about 80 per cent of which have, at least in the past, been levelled against BT) were settled. From 1995 to 2003 the DGT made a mere 16 orders for enforcement (again, mostly against BT), using powers under the Telecommunications Act 1984.

The practice of settling cases is supposed to free up Ofcom's resources to handle more serious infringements. It may have the reverse effect—'soft' enforcement takes up more administrative time than a 'short, sharp shock'. It is also still relatively rare for injured parties to seek to enforce their rights under the Competition Act 1998 directly, by action before the courts, whether by way of an action for damages or injunction. The action for injunction to enforce section 2 or 18, or Articles 81/82 (as distinct from a long drawn action for damages) remains the most effective (and exciting) means. Some have been successful—(see *Adidas v Lawn Tennis Association & Others*).[94] Closer to telecoms an interesting example of a new entrant being able to rely on mainstream competition law to obtain an injunction is *Software Cellular Network*.[95] This company, trading as Trufone, offered a voice over Internet protocol (VOiP) service, which required activation of network numbers which had been allocated by Ofcom. T-Mobile refused to activate the numbers. The court ordered it to do so on the grounds that T-Mobile is dominant in the market for termination of calls to its customers. However inefficient the process, the least expensive (and most effective) course remains, as before, a complaint to Ofcom in the first instance. Another technique available to the complaining party is to generate adverse publicity for the undertaking against which a complaint is made.

Ofcom may make claim to be a competition authority, with special expertise in telecommunications. In reality it is much more than that; it is a regulatory agency with powers to manage the market going way beyond those of a normal competition authority.

---

  [93] A Direction under s 100 of the Communications Act 2003 is a direction from Ofcom to a provider to suspend provision of an electronic communications network/services.

  [94] See n 88.

  [95] See n 89.

9.8 STRUCTURAL CONTROLS: REGULATION THROUGH MERGER CONTROL

9.8.1 EU policy: main themes

The formal legal position of the EU Commission is that mergers (which are suffi-ciently large to be dealt with under the EC Merger Regulation)[96] are assessed accord-ing to whether they will materially lessen competition and hence have an adverse effect on competition.[97] The same principles apply to the approval of joint ventures (whether they are set up as autonomous entities on a long-standing basis and need clearance under the Merger Regulation, or fulfil the criteria for exemption under Article 81(3) of the EC Treaty under the 'modernization' procedures under Regulation 1/2003). In practice, the Commission's approach to mergers is consider-ably more nuanced. The following are the key features of the European Commission's approach to mergers in telecommunications and related sectors:

i. The EU Commission has a policy of encouraging network infrastructure competition wherever possible, as does the UK government. In order to gener-ate competition, competing physical networks should be built; however, the EU Commission places a greater emphasis than the UK government on stimulating competition between service providers.

ii. The EU Commission is vigilant to ensure that the national incumbent ex-monopolist in each Member State does not use a merger as a means further to protect and restrict entry into its national market.

iii. Vertical integration between a telecommunications network operator and an operator in another sector (e.g. a broadcaster) can be as great a threat to competition as consolidation between network operators.

iv. Mergers involving US investment into the European Community raise par-ticular issues, including the related issue of EU operators' access to US markets.

Each of these features is now discussed below.

A detailed explanation of the scope of the EC Merger Regulation, and its proce-dures, is outside the scope of this work.[98] For the purposes of the analysis which follows, it is sufficient to bear in mind these key features of the European regime:

i. The EC Merger Regulation applies to mergers where the combined turnover, in their last financial year, of all the parties involved in the concentration exceeds

---

[96] Council Regulation 139/2004 of 20 January 2004 on the control of concentrations between under-takings OJ L 24, 29 January 2004.

[97] The original EC Merger Regulation 4069/89 has been replaced, with effect from 1 May 2004, by EC Regulation 139/2004 on the control of concentrations between undertakings. Much of the Regulation is merely consolidation of previous amendments in one text. A material change is that it is no longer neces-sary to show that a merger will create a dominant position enjoyed by the newly merged undertaking. It is sufficient for the Commission to show that there will be a significant impediment to effective competi-tion (i.e. a significant lessening of competition).

[98] See again, Roth, Faull and Nikpay, and Whish, cited at n 13 above.

€5 billion. In such cases Member States cannot apply their own national merger controls. However the regulation does not apply to mergers whose economic effects are likely to be felt in just one Member State. Even if the combined turnover of the undertakings concerned does exceed €5 billion, the EC merger regulation does not apply where the combined turnover of the parties within the Community (disregarding turnover elsewhere in the world) arises as to at least two-thirds in one and the same Member State; in that case the merger control procedures of that Member State apply.

ii. To avoid the need for multiple merger clearances in several Member States the EC Merger Regulation will also apply where the turnover in at least *three* Member States of at least *two* of the undertakings concerned in the concentration is above certain thresholds, and the combined worldwide turnover of all the undertakings concerned exceeds €2.5 billion; in such a case the national rules of any Member State will also not apply.

iii. Article 21.3 of the EC Merger Regulation says that Member States may not apply their national *competition* rules to a merger falling under the Regulation. They may, however, take measures to protect their 'legitimate interests' as a result of a merger (Article 21.4). These interests include 'public security', 'plurality of the media', and 'prudential rules'. The second criterion is particularly important for Member States wishing to ensure a wide variety of choice in broadcasting and newspapers; this exception to the otherwise clear division of responsibility between Brussels and the Member States has an impact on the approach to mergers in the telecommunications sector.

iv. So-called 'concentrative' or 'full function' joint ventures (where the parties give up independent activity in the field of the joint venture) are normally dealt with under the EC Merger Regulation; where the parties both remain as independent suppliers in this field, or related fields, clearance is dealt with under Article 81(3) EC Treaty. (See, the joint ventures between France Telecom, Deutsche Telecom, and Sprint.)[99]

v. The test which the Commission applies in deciding whether to block or approve a merger is whether it would lead to a significant impediment (lessening) to effective competition. In practice this means that wherever one undertaking has a market share of 20 per cent or more, you need to start looking carefully to see if the merger proposed has an adverse effect in its or related markets.

9.8.2 EC merger and joint venture clearances

9.8.2.1 *Encouragement of network and service competition*
Generally, the European Commission has adopted a positive approach to structural mergers and joint ventures which lead to the building of significant new infrastructure.

---

[99] Commission Decision 96/546/EC (1996) OJ L 239/23 (*Atlas Decision*, Case IV/ 35.337); and Commission Decision.

In 1999, the Commission cleared a joint venture to build a long-distance back-bone network, alongside the French railways lines. It was exempted under Article 81 of the EC Treaty, rather than under the Merger Regulation—but the EU Commission applies the same principles to permanent structural changes (as distinct from behavioural cases) whether technically they fall under the Merger Regulation, or are joint ventures which fall outside the ECMR, but need exemption under Article 81(3). The joint venture was set up by SNCF, which has control of the French rail network, and Cegetal, itself a joint venture owned by Mannesmann, Vivendi (originally the French water utility), BT, and SBC International.[100] The main benefit of the joint venture would be to provide a second wholesale network operator in France, to compete with France Telecom. The joint venture was therefore cleared without any conditions being attached.

Encouraging competition between networks also means that mergers must not lead to a reduction in an already small number of network operators. While there is no objection to putting together a European network by merging several national operators, this must not be done at the expense of reducing the number of networks in each Member State. The merger of Vodafone and Mannesmann on 12 April 2000 is a good illustration of this point.[101]

In order to build out a pan-European network Vodafone needed a market leading presence in Germany. In a highly contested bid Vodafone bought Mannesmann, which operated the Mannesmann Mobilfunk network in Germany. However, as the price for merger clearance:

i. Mannesmann had to sell its minority holding in Orange to France Telecom (because Vodafone already had its network in France and was not allowed to own or control two);

ii. France Telecom had to sell a minority interest which Orange had in Belgium, because France Telecom already had an existing mobile network in that country.

The net effect was to ensure that in each Member State there were still at least four competing mobile networks, each wholly independent with no cross shareholdings between them (since a cross holding of shares between competitors leads to the presumption that they do not in fact compete with each other!).

Other mergers have been cleared, but subject to conditions, to ensure the structure of supply in each Member State includes four, or five, major mobile network operators. Thus, more recently, in Austria T-Mobile, with a market share of 22 per cent, merged with tele.ring (13 per cent). The merger was allowed only on condition that

---

[100] Commission Decision of 20 May 1999 relating to a proceeding under Article 81 of the EC Treaty (Case IV/36.592—Cégétel 4), OJ L218/14, 18 August 1999).
[101] See EC Notice of non-opposition dated 12 April 2000 in Case No COMP/M.1795—*Vodafone Airtouch/Mannesmann*.

the parties offloaded some network and spectrum assets to the fifth, new entrant, operator—H3G.[102]

At least in mobile, the structure of supply may reduce to as few as three network operators, at least in cases where MVNOs offer real competition to the network operators.[103] The presence of MVNOs as a real alternative to the underlying network operator has been a factor in deciding to clear other mobile mergers. Thus, in Portugal the Portuguese Competition Authority allowed the merger between two mobile networks operators (between Sonaecom and Portugal Telecom Mobile) but on condition that the merged entity must offer contracts to anyone who wants to run a MVNO service over of their merged network, on reasonable terms.[104]

When Telefonica acquired O2 a similar pattern was applied. Telefonica ran mobile networks in Spain and the Czech lands; 02 in the UK, Germany, and Ireland. Both operated through networks ('Freemove' and 'Starmap') to obtain roaming services in EU Member States where neither had its own network. As a condition of clearance, Telefonica had to leave the Freemove alliance to ensure that there was no commercial or geographic overlap between the roaming networks. It also ensured that Freemove was less likely to become a club of powerful networks. In cases where a mobile operator is completing its European coverage by buying an operator in another Member State, where it has no presence, mergers have been cleared without condition.[105]

9.8.2.2 *National incumbent must not block ease of entry to national markets*
Several EU mergers and joint ventures have involved link-ups between one or more national, ex-monopolist, incumbent network operations. When these have occurred, particular concerns have been:

i. where a national incumbent seeks to enter a downstream market on a joint venture basis with another national incumbent, either in its home market or abroad, it must make available its own network facilities on equal terms to competitors in that downstream market;

ii. national incumbents must not link arms to impede market entry in other ways.

---

[102] Commission Decision of 26 April 2006 declaring a concentration to be compatible with the common market and the EEA Agreement (Case No COMP/M.3916—*T-Mobile Austria/tele.ring*).

[103] See e.g. acquisition of Orange Netherlands by T-Mobile, European Commission Case No COMP/M.4748, 20 August 2007.

[104] Portuguese Autoridade da Concorrencia Decision of 22 December 2006

[105] See e.g. acquisition of One (Austria) by France Télécom and Mid Europa Partners, European Commission Case No COMP/M.4809, 21 September 2007; acquisition of Amena (Auna Operadores de Telecomunicaciones), mobile operator in Spain, by France Télécom SA, European Commission Case No COMP/M.3920, 24 October 2005; acquisition by Weather Investments SpA of Hellas Telecommunications (Greece), European Commission Case No COMP/M.4591, 4 April 2007; acquisition Vodafone/Oskar Mobile, European Commission Case No COMP/M.3776, 25 October 2005.

Both the *Infonet* case (*Infonet* (1992) OJ C7/03) and the *Atlas* ((1995) OJ C 337) and *Phoenix* ((1996) OJ L 239) joint ventures between France Telecom and Deutsche Telekom (which latter two have ended in tears) show these points.

Infonet is a company that provides value-added services—managed networks for large corporate users, primarily for data transmission. To do this it uses leased lines to build private or virtual private networks for its customers, based on the X25 packet switch. In 1987, 25 per cent of the company was owned by Computer Sciences Corporation of the US, and the remaining 75 per cent was held in varying proportions by 12 national telephone companies—including, in the EU, France Telecom, Deutsche Telekom, and the Dutch PTT. As its 'price' for exemption, under what is now Article 81(3), EC Treaty, the Commission required that:

i. the telecommunications operator shareholders in Infonet established in the Community had to make available leased lines to third parties on the same terms and conditions as they were made available to Infonet;

ii. where a European national incumbent telecommunications operator, which was also a shareholder in Infonet, acted as the Infonet distributor in its national territory, that operator must not cross-subsidize its business as the Infonet distributor.

The terms of the commitments given by the national telecommunications operators based in EU Member States were designed to ensure that new entrants could come into the national market to provide competing corporate data transmission services. However the commitments were very loosely drafted. The Commission learned, not for the first time, how difficult it is in practice to impose, monitor, and properly enforce behavioural undertakings, as distinct from requiring structural change as a condition for clearance.

Atlas/Phoenix/GlobalOne, the joint venture of the respective overseas businesses of France Telecom and Deutsche Telekom, raised the same policy issues as *Infonet*, but written much larger. Atlas was a joint venture set up on a 50:50 basis by France Telecom and Deutsche Telekom to provide corporate value-added services in Europe. In turn, Phoenix/GlobalOne was set up by Atlas, with a participation by Sprint, to provide corporate telecommunications services, and traveller and carrier services for other operators on both a regional and a global basis. Exemption of both joint ventures was conditional:

i. Deutsche Telekom and France Telecom could not offer leased-line or PSTN/ ISDN services to Sprint or any joint venture entity on more favourable terms than those offered to third parties;

ii. telecommunications services must also be offered on non-discriminatory terms; and

iii. there should be no discrimination between the joint ventures and third parties as to the timing or manner of introduction of new network interfaces. Many of the principles developed and applied to the joint venture partners in these cases

are now applied generally to all operators designated as having SMP (see further Chapter 5).

9.8.2.3 *The threats posed by vertically integrated telecommunications operators*
This book is *primarily* about telecommunications; it is not about broadcasting.[106] However, in order to understand EU (and UK) policy towards structural change in the telecommunications sector, it should be borne in mind that telecommunications businesses look for the opportunity for a second revenue stream from their networks, for example by providing broadcast material as well as just transmitting it.

Telecommunications is about conveying messages; a telecommunications operator makes its money from conveying millions of messages. In the UK, the cable companies (now Virgin Media) have a dual source of revenue from conveying both telephone messages and broadcast material (feature films, news programmes, and other screened entertainment). Significant extra revenue can be earned by providing the message itself; network operators may therefore look for additional revenue through providing their own programme material, or that of other people.

Several telecommunications operators have sought to maximize revenue by integrating backwards into content provision—providing the message—and integrating downstream to provide various types of value added services. The EU Commission has had to consider several such cases.

British Interactive Broadcasting ('OPEN') (BIB) was a joint venture set up by BT, BSkyB (owned as to 39 per cent by News Corporation), HSBC, and Matsushita.[107] Its purpose was to provide digital interactive television services, so that banks, travel agents, and supermarkets can interact directly with customers. The services would be integrated with other services such as broadcast programmes (which could also be interactive, such as voting in quiz shows) and Internet services, such as email, downloading music or games, or Internet access.

The primary concern, in competition policy terms, was that these services had to be accessed through the set-top box, for which BSkyB, or related companies, own the intellectual property rights. BT, through using other technology, was at least a potential competitor to BSkyB to provide interactive digital services. The joint venture therefore at least restricted potential, rather than actual, present competition between them. The EU Commission imposed a series of detailed conditions to the exemption it granted to the BIB joint venture for seven years.

A good example of a merger control authority imposing conditions on a vertical acquisition was when New Corporation bought Hughes TV (DBS/Direct TV).[108]

---

[106] However, see further Chapter 11.

[107] British Interactive Broadcasting/Open (Case IV/36.539), Commission Decision of 15 September 1999 relating to a proceeding under Article 81 of the EC Treaty, OJ L312/1, 6 December 1999.

[108] Apollo/DirecTV/Hughes Network Systems (Case No COMP/M.3708) European Commission decision of 23 March 2005.

Bertelsmann/Kirch/Premiere[109] brought into sharp focus the Commission's understandable objections to excessive market power in the telecommunications sector through vertical integration of technology and network operation. The proposals would have brought together a variety of interests to provide a package of digital Pay TV services: set-top box technology, broadcasting facilities (Bertelsmann), access to cable and/or satellite networks (Bertelsmann and Deutsche Telekom), and programming content (Kirch). The Commission blocked both proposals. The contribution of technologies would, the Commission held, lead to bottlenecks in the provision of Pay TV and similar programme services. The mergers would have further strengthened, to an unacceptable extent, Kirch's dominant position in the provision of Pay TV services.

Another area where the Commission has objected to proposed mergers which involve vertical integration is where the owner or maker of key equipment used in building networks gets to acquire shares in a network operator. For this reason the Commission carried out an in-depth investigation into Microsoft and Liberty's proposed (and ultimately aborted) acquisition of a minority share in Telewest and other European cable companies.[110] Microsoft could have used such minority shares in cable companies to influence or control their choice of new software systems and gain the benefit of 'network effects' for Microsoft systems being used in several Member States.

9.8.2.4 *Transatlantic market entry*

In *BT/MCI*,[111] the proposed merger between BT and MCI in the event did not go ahead (MCI merged with WorldCom instead—see below). Nevertheless, the proposed merger raised some interesting issues of transatlantic trade policy where there would have been a link up between a major European and a major American telco. MCI's position in the UK market (and in other EU Member States) was weak. In the UK there was no overlap between BT's and MCI's respective businesses in the residential market; there was little overlap in the business market. Nevertheless, BT and MCI would have had a powerful joint position in a distinct market, namely, the provision of wholesale capacity on transatlantic routes. Accordingly, as the price for letting this merger go through, the EU Commission would have imposed requirements on access to that capacity, and in particular it would have required BT and MCI to dispose (by outright sale or grant of IRUs) of overlapping capacity in the eastern end of the transatlantic routes, which the Commission saw might be a bottleneck.

---

[109] Deutsche Telekom/Beta Research, Case No IV/M.1027, European Commission decision of 27 May 1998, OJ L 53/1, 27 February 1999.
[110] See Commission press release of 22 March 2000 (IP/00/287).
[111] British Telecom/MCI, Case No IV/M.856, European Commission Decision 97/815/EC of 14 May 1997, OJ L 336/1, 8 December 1997 (lapsed).

There were two other interesting features in this proposal:

i. The fact that the merger needed approval under the EC Merger Regulation did not stop the UK regulator (then Oftel) seeking to place additional controls on BT on non-competition grounds (which Article 21.4 of the EC Merger Regulation, referred to at section 9.8.1 above, allows a Member State to do) to protect the legitimate interest of consumers in the UK. In this case (had the merger gone ahead) Oftel would have placed a 'ring fence' around BT's UK business, so that it would not have been unduly exposed to improvident overseas investment by BT, to the detriment of the UK consumers (see *Domestic Obligations in a Global Market*, Oftel, 1997).

ii. Some other US operators appear to have used the EC merger clearance process to seek to secure other concessions from BT. Thus it appears that they sought to lean on the US regulatory agencies to approve the merger under US merger control rules only provided the UK government were to change its then policy on local loop unbundling, thereby hoping to gain greater access to the UK market for US operators.

The Vodafone/Airtouch merger[112] led to the creation of the largest worldwide mobile network operator, supplying service in many EU Member States and in the US. Since there was no overlap between the two groups' geographic coverage (EU and US respectively), the merger was cleared without the EU Commission imposing any conditions.

MCI/WorldCom was the first case where the Commission looked specifically at the position of operators in the provision of Internet, as distinct from conventional switched voice telephony.[113] It looked like it was possibly not just a European market, but a global one. The Commission made, over several months, an in-depth investigation of the various submarkets of the Internet. It concluded that the merger would result in a dominant position in the provision of top level or universal Internet connectivity. As a condition of the merger, MCI was forced to dispose of various parts of its Internet-related businesses. The Commission did not stand in the way of a merger which would give global coverage to two merged American companies, which coverage would extend to the whole of the EU.

However the later proposed merger between MCI/Worldcom (as it had become) and Sprint raised greater concerns, and greater sensitivity in the EU relationship across the Atlantic with the US. The EU Commission blocked this proposal, since both competitors and customers would have been dependent on the merged entity to get universal Internet connectivity. Fortunately the US merger control body took the same view, and the cross-Atlantic tensions caused by differences between EU and US merger policy did not arise, as has happened in other cases.[114]

---

[112] *Vodafone/Airtouch*, Case IV/M.1430 (1995) OJ C 295/2. declaring a concentration to be compatible with the common market and the functioning of the EEA Agreement (- (II)).

[113] See *WorldCom/MCI*, Case IV/M.1069, Commission Decision 1999/287/EC, 1999, OJ L 116/1.

[114] E.g., during the merger of General Electric and Honeywell (Case COMP/M.2220) when the EU Commission and the US merger control bodies took opposite positions.

The BT/AT&T[115] joint venture was set up to provide global telecommunications services to multinational companies and international carrier services to other tele-communication network operators. The EU Commission, in a Phase II investigation lasting four months,[116] looked closely at these markets and the distinct markets for traffic on the UK/US routes and international voice telephony markets in the UK. On the main markets it found that, although the parties had a high share of the relevant markets (between 30 per cent and 50 per cent), they had a much lower combined share of capacity and such surplus capacity was causing prices to fall. The joint venture, as originally structured, would nevertheless have adversely affected some specific UK markets. As a condition, some UK businesses were disposed of and Oftel imposed some additional conditions in BT's licence.

The common thread in each of these cases is that where operators are based on both sides of the Atlantic, the EU Commission will not raise substantive objections to mergers designed to give the combined entity global coverage.

9.8.3 UK policy towards mergers and joint ventures

At section 9.2 above, we discussed how the UK government has sought to 'design' the structure of the UK telecommunications market to deliberately stimulate or intro-duce competition and how it has adapted that design over time in the light of experi-ence. The legal instruments to control mergers have been also used to support this policy of market management and manipulation.

9.8.3.1 Enterprise Act 2002 (UK merger control provisions)

Where a merger falls under the EC Merger Regulation, the UK government has no jurisdiction to block the merger, or to impose conditions before it can be allowed to go ahead. The UK merger control provisions will, however, cover mergers below the turnover financial thresholds, when the EC Merger Regulation does not apply. The OFT will have jurisdiction to review mergers either where the turnover in the UK of the undertaking to be acquired exceeds £70 million, *or* where both parties are in the same product market (which can be narrowly defined) and the merger will bring their combined market share in the UK to, or increase it above, 25 per cent. The test applied is almost identical to the EU Merger regulation: will the merger lead to a significant lessening of competition (SLC). The OFT cannot itself block a merger which is likely to substantially lessen competition; however it can refer such a merger to the Competition Commission to rule on whether this will be the case.

---

[115] Commission Decision 99/765/EC of 30 March 1999 declaring a concentration to be compatible with the common market and the functioning of the EEA Agreement (Case IV/JV.15—*BT/AT&T*).

[116] The ECMR has two stages in its procedure. A first assessment lasting five weeks. If the merger clearly does not give rise to a significant lessening of competition, the merger is cleared. 90% of mergers within the ECMR thresholds are so cleared. In a few cases the merger may give rise to significant impediment to competition, and in such cases the Commission carries out a much more in depth Phase II investigations.

9.8.3.2 *UK policy themes*

Vertical integration is of particular concern to the OFT when deciding whether to clear a merger under the Enterprise Act 2002.

Another concern of the UK government has been to ensure that UK-based companies are able to compete effectively in overseas markets, to take advantage of the head start which they had as a result of privatization occurring earlier in the UK than elsewhere.

As stated in Chapter 4, the basic thrust of UK government policy since the White Paper Duopoly Review in 1991 (and indeed before that) has been to encourage the building of competing physical networks. Although obvious, it should be stated that BT, as the incumbent ex-monopolist in the UK, has never been allowed to buy significant further capacity by acquiring a competitor.[117] There has, however, been no restriction on BT building further capacity. By the same token, after 1995 there was no restriction on the merger of franchised cable licensees, where the franchisees did not compete in the same exclusively franchised areas. Equally, the OFT has raised no objection to further consolidation between indirect access (IA) providers of services over the fixed networks of others.[118]

A clear example of UK merger policy in telecoms focusing on ensuring that there are competing networks is in the broadband market. We are now going through a period of consolidation—the number of suppliers of broadband to end consumers is falling; several smaller broadband suppliers have been mopped up by more powerful suppliers.[119] We are left with a few big groups—BT, Carphone Warehouse, Tiscali, BSkyB, Virgin Media (what was NTL/Telewest). Following Tiscali's purchase of Pipex in 2007 it has become clear that it will be difficult for any of the two or three leading players to materially increase that market share by acquisition.

9.8.3.3 *Consolidation of cable operators*

In the late 1980s, about 140 exclusive regional franchises were granted to some 70 different companies. By 1998, a process of consolidation had reduced the number of cable franchise operators to three—Telewest, CWC (Cable & Wireless), and NTL. This happened with government encouragement. NTL has since acquired CWC's cable business, and Telewest.

NTL's acquisition of CWC was the first acquisition by one cable company of another to be referred to the Competition Commission. The reasons for the referral to the Competition Commission were not because of the combined market power of NTL and CWC in the retail fixed network telecommunications market, but because of the merger's potential effect on the wholesale market for Pay TV content. In the

---

[117] A limited exception to that was when, surprisingly, the OFT raised no objection to BT buying a small broadband service provide Plusnet (OFT Case No ME/2755/07; decision of 31 January 2007).

[118] See e.g. Carphone Warehouse's acquisition of Onetel (OFT Case ME/2259/06, 23 June 2006).

[119] See e.g. Carphone Warehouse acquisition of AOL UK, European Commission Case No COMP/M.4442, 7 December 2006.

event the merger of the NTL and CWC cable franchise businesses was cleared without conditions, partly because the Competition Commission felt that Oftel and the ITC together had sufficient regulatory powers to handle any misuse of market power in the broadcasting markets. NTL have now merged to form Virgin Media.[120]

9.8.3.4 *Vertical integration with a telco*
Vivendi, the French water utility and communications conglomerate, which also has a 49 per cent interest in Canal Plus, bought 24.9 per cent in BSkyB, the leading UK supplier of Pay TV services. The merger was referred to the Competition Commission because of concerns as to (i) the acquisition of broadcasting rights for sports and films, and (ii) the control and supply of conditional access technology.

The Competition Commission concluded that BSkyB's position as the acquirer of national sports rights was a strong one, but the merger would not materially enhance it. It also concluded that the respective interests of BSkyB and Vivendi in the NDS and SECA set-top box technology would not materially restrict the availability of such technology to third parties.

More recently the OFT looked at the ability of a network operator to increase its market power through the ability to 'bundle' the provision of fixed, mobile and broadband services. NTL, which offered content, internet access and fixed line services (so called 'triple play'); it was allowed to merge with Virgin Mobile on the basis that the ability to offer mobile as well ('quadruple' play) would still not give the combined entity market power through integration of contact and emergency services.[121]

9.9 EC STATE AID RULES AND TELECOMS

The EC Treaty contains strict rules on when Member States can grant financial state aid from state resources to industrial or commercial enterprises. The state aid rules are an integral part of the EC Treaty framework, which together with competition law, is focused at creating a truly European Common Market based on undistorted competition. The state aid rules serve two purposes: to stop EU Member States giving national champions, or national industries, an unfair advantage over competitors in other Member States and, secondly, to ensure that state aid is not given which leads to prolonged inefficiency or delays modernization of a particular sector.

There are several instances where the EU Commission has had to consider, and on occasion block, Member States' attempts to grant state aid in the telecommunications sector.

[120] OFT decision given on 30 December 2005 (full text published 10 January 2006) of 10 January 2006—Case No ME/2033/05.
[121] NTL Incorporated/Virgin Mobile Holdings: OFT decision of 22 May 2006, Case No ME/2311/06.

A full analysis of the EC State aid rules can be found in specialist books on the subject.[122] Suffice it to set out here the basic principles.

The basic rule is that any aid granted by a Member State from state resources which distorts or threatens to distort competition is incompatible with the idea of a Common Market if it affects trade between Member States. The concept of an '*aid*' covers any form of financial assistance which has the effect of a subsidy; aid thus includes not only grants of cash, but making loans available on favourable terms (which an undertaking would not have been able to obtain on the market); the issuing of state guarantees in relation to an undertaking's debts; and exemption from obligations to pay tax targeted at certain undertakings.

However, certain types of aid, such as that given to deal with natural disasters or aid having a social character granted to individual consumers (such as financial assistance for people on low incomes to enable them to have a telephone line) are automatically compatible with the EC Treaty.

While some aid is automatically compatible with the Common Market, certain types of aid may or may not be, under Article 87.3, EC Treaty, depending on the circumstances surrounding the provision of the aid. For example:

i. aid given for economic development in areas where the standard of living is abnormally low or there is serious unemployment;

ii. aid to promote the execution of an important European project;

iii. aid 'to facilitate the development of certain economic activities . . . where such aid does not adversely affect trading conditions to an extent contrary to the common interest';

iv. aid for cultural purposes;

v. such other categories of aid as the EU Council of Ministers may decide.

In essence, all state aid must be notified and receive prior approval of the European Commission. However, some aid schemes may not need individual approval, if they meet the terms of one of the block exemption regulations—for example, those which apply to certain small aid schemes or regional aid schemes. If a Member State fails to seek prior approval for the provision of aid, the risk is that the aid in question must be repaid by the recipient (therefore the risk lies with the recipient receiving the aid to ensure that the Member State has sought and received the appropriate approval for the aid). The fact that a commercial enterprise's accounts may be qualified by its auditors, with the risk that aid may have to be repaid, is a strong incentive for such prior approval to be obtained.

---

[122] See e.g. Biondi, A, Eeckhout, P, and Flynn, J, *The Law of State Aid in the European Union* (Oxford University Press, 2004); Hancher, L, Ottervanger, T, and Slot, PJ, *EC State Aids* (Sweet & Maxwell, London, 1999).

In practice, aids which have been granted in the telecommunications sector have been either aid for the improvement of poorer regions (87.3(a) above) or aid to encourage economic development (87.3(c) above).

Thus in order to promote economic development throughout of the community the EU Commission has approved many schemes in poorer and more remote regions of the Community for improving local broadband access. For example, the EU Commission has approved schemes in the mountainous areas of Cumbria,[123] as well as for bringing broadband to remote rural areas of Scotland.[124] Similar schemes have been approved in other Member States, for example in France and Spain.[125]

Relying on Article 87.3(c), under which aid schemes may be approved where they stimulate economic development, the UK government has been allowed to introduce schemes for the development of broadband infrastructure schemes for business parks[126] and also the setting up of a broadband business fund to encourage broadband access for small and medium sized (SME) businesses.[127]

However, not all schemes to stimulate broadband access for businesses have been approved. For example, the EU Commission ordered the repayment of grants given to a broadband development scheme in the Netherlands (since the aid was focused not on the provision of broadband, but on upgrading the existing broadband infrastructure); similarly it imposed changes on a scheme put forward by the City of Amsterdam to assist with the building up of a Fibre to the Home (FTTH) network.[128]

9.10 OUTSTANDING POLICY ISSUES

The shape of telecommunications markets is still changing. A few comments on the enforcement of competition law and merger control policy in the communications control field can be made:

(i) It is extremely difficult for merger control agencies (in the UK or the EU Commission) to predict or plan market structure, even a few years ahead. Just as politicians are charged with being slaves to the outdated theories of dead economists, so merger control agencies need to be very wary of focusing too heavily on the problems of last year (cross-subsidy by the ex-monopolist of one service by another, market access, price control, etc.).

---

[123] Cumbria Broadband—Project Access, State Aid No 282/2003.

[124] Broadband in Scotland—remote and rural area, State Aid No 307/2004.

[125] Cases: Haut débit en Pyrénées-Atlantiques—France, State Aid Case No 381/2004 and Broadband in rural and ultra-remote areas, State Aid No 583/2004.

[126] Project Atlas; broadband infrastructure scheme for business parks, State Aid Case No213/2003.

[127] Broadband Business Fund, State Aid Case No 199/2004.

[128] Cases: Tax exemption for bio fuels used as motor fuel, State Aid Case No 59/2005 and Citynet Amsterdam, State Aid Case No 53/2006.

(ii) At the other extreme, many say that the Internet has developed free of regulation and therefore telecommunications regulation can move in the same direction. This view is probably misguided. As the Internet increases in reach and becomes a mass consumer service, various issues come sharply into focus: universal service obligations, pricing of bottlenecks, interoperability of systems and networks. All of these are real, practical issues which regulatory merger control agencies will always need to control carefully in order to be seen to be protecting the public consumer interest.

(iii) On privatization many thought that telecoms-specific regulation would fade away as BT faced ever greater competition. When that did not happen, general competition law was seized on as the framework for regulation in the sector; sector-specific rules would be phased out; it would be enough for people knowledgeable about the sector to apply general competition law. Now, there is general acceptance that sector-specific rules will be with us for a long time, even if their concepts (such as the rules imposed on undertakings having SMP) are based on competition law principles. Thinking is now developing on what controls will be needed over new sources of market power: digital rights management; online navigation tools; the position of Next Generation Core Networks (NGN) and those service providers also effectively able to bundle content with communication services ('triple play', 'quadruple' play, etc.).

(iv) Government policy for the last 25 years has been that full competition will provide the best telecommunications system for the nation. If perfect competition does not (yet) exist, regulation is put in place which mimics what would happen if there was such full competition. Ofcom now has a much wider remit over broadcasting as well as telecoms. As the regulator for independent broadcasting it has social as well as economic objectives. The open question is whether that social thinking applies in the telecoms area. It raises the question: does perfect competition, and regulation which seeks to mimic perfect competition, really deliver all the social outcomes society needs?

10

TELECOMMUNICATIONS, INTELLECTUAL PROPERTY, AND STANDARDS

Alan Cunningham and Gary Lea

10.1 INTRODUCTION

The purpose of this chapter is to explore some of the issues surrounding the intersection of technical standards in telecommunications and intellectual property (IP) in telecommunications.

The central conceptual controversy between the two is quite simple. Both standards and IP are important to the telecommunications industry. Standards are required in order to produce certain technological, social, and economic benefits; IP rights are

also required in order to produce *other* technological, social, and economic benefits. As in all difficult relationships, they both want different things; even to the extent that the same things are wanted, they are certainly achieved in very different ways. The nature and object of standards is such that they are expected to be widely promulgated without excessive restriction or exclusive control. Conversely, any items protected by IP rights *are* exclusively controlled in order that the owner of such rights can benefit from the licensed use of that which they protect. True, there may be situations where the licensed use is free or at low cost but that decision is, subject to what is said below in relation to overrides from competition law and related regulatory fields, largely a matter for the owner.

This conceptual conflict is illustrated by the practical issue of recurrent controversy between standards and IP in the telecommunications standardization process. Here, certain standards that are required to advance the telecommunications industry are constrained by the ownership of IP considered 'essential' for the standard. IP is becoming increasingly protected from being free-ridden on as a part of an industry standard, or is being used as a strategic tool in the standardization process. The industry requires standards; IP owners want compensation for the use of their IP, or want the freedom to use their property as they wish. Resolution is not always easy and seldom 'clean'.

The difficulty of resolving such problems is most acute for those nongovernmental or quasi-governmental bodies which are responsible for or involved in coordinating the development of standards. These 'standard development organizations' (SDOs) face the sometimes impossible task of ensuring that industry gets the standards it needs, but also that the legal rights of their members are respected. Issues faced during such diplomacy include the strategic use of IP to either hold up the standardization process or direct it to the favour of individual companies, the licensing of IP for use in a standard on unreasonable and unfair terms or the simple denial of allowing what is considered an essential IP to be used at all.

The focus of this chapter is how SDOs have attempted to resolve such issues. However, prior to dealing with that subject, some contextual understanding is required. First, the area of standards in general, and technical standards in particular, will be discussed. The importance of technical standards in the telecommunications industry will also be briefly explored. Next, the chapter examines the technical standard-setting process for the telecommunications industry, highlighting some prominent SDOs. IP is then discussed, first in the context of the difficulty it presents to standards and secondly in the context of the importance it has in the telecommunications sector. Focus will then be placed on how some SDOs have attempted to resolve difficulties. Finally, the chapter will also briefly discuss the issues of compulsory licensing and also the emergence of new non-traditional SDOs and the problems they face.

10.2 STANDARDS

10.2.1 Standards in general

Standards are an essential aspect of effective existence. Imagine society without the agreed standard of a common and well-defined language.[1] Imagine legal affairs without the agreed standard of criminal or civil process. Without standards, life would become unbearable; as a result of the virtue of standards, however, society can operate in an effective and beneficial manner. In this respect, and generally speaking, a standard can be understood as 'an agreed way of doing something'.[2] This is the virtue of the standard; the effect is surety and conformity in the practice in hand, resulting in a direct net economic gain from R&D and related investment and, less directly but still importantly, the possibility of developing additional value-adding products and services. In the telecommunications context, this economic value enhanced by the so-called 'network effects' is discussed below.

Standards emerge from a number of different sources. The basis of a standard agreement might have emerged, for example, over a period of time in society, without a formal consensus on the matter, but becoming generally accepted as a standard (i.e. common and repeatable) way of doing a certain thing. It may have been given some type of *imprimatur* as 'standard' by an agreed body with the ability and competency to decide on such matters.[3] Or it might be a standard as 'law', laid down from on high by one or more governments with an interest in or responsibility for the practice in question.[4] However, irrespective of how standards are developed, be

---

[1] Although the idea of a common and well-defined language might be less true today than in earlier times: for example Schumpeter, commenting on the effect of the standardized intellectual, linguistic, and social system advanced by Christendom during the early medieval period, points out that 'St Thomas was an Italian and John Duns Scotus was a Scotsman, but both taught in Paris and Cologne without encountering any of the difficulties that they would have encountered in the age of aeroplanes'. Schumpeter, JA, *History of Economic Analysis* (Routledge, London, 1997), 73–74. See also Aitchison, J, *The Seeds of Speech: Language Origin and Evolution* (Cambridge University Press, Cambridge, 1996), 60–61.

[2] Spivak, SM and Brenner, FC, *Standardization Essentials: Principles and Practice* (Marcel Dekker, New York, 2001), 1. A rather more formal definition of the term standard is provided by the International Standard Organization (ISO), who suggest a standard is 'a document, established by consensus and approved by a recognized body, that provides, for common and repeated use, rules, guidelines or characteristics for activities or their results, aimed at the achievement of the optimum degree of order in a given context', ISO/IEC Guide 2: 1996.

[3] Sometimes, however, bodies with the ability and competency to agree on standards can miss out on the innovative standards advanced through *de facto* evolution. For example, the useful hyper text transfer protocol (HTTP) standard that revolutionized Internet communications was not recognized by the Internet Engineering Task Force (IETF) until 1999, by which stage, of course, the success of HTTP was secured and it was well established as a *de facto* standard.

[4] For example, in the US, the Federal Communications Commission (FCC) establishes standards for interconnection between telephone networks and standards governing the use of products that might interfere with broadcast communications (see further Chapter 13); similarly, the US Advanced Research Projects Agency (ARPA) was instrumental in developing the early standards for the Internet.

they market/society/committee-based (*de facto*) or government/official bureau-based (*de jure*), they represent an attempt by society to ensure a common point of reference for conformity, similarity, compatibility or adaptability.[5]

In addition to howsoever standards emerge, they may also relate to a number of different activities. Standards can be socio-cultural, for example relating to activities such as fashion or social etiquette. Standards can be economic, for example an agreed way of doing things within an economic or financial sphere. They can be political, concerned with methods of governmental, democratic, or other process.[6] Finally, although not exclusively, standards can be technical, required to ensure harmony and organization in the creation and use of technology.

The aspect of a standard that determines its success in providing organization, compatibility, and harmony, is the fact that it is available, and expected, to be freely used. The term 'free' is not necessarily meant here as in 'free beer', however. Rather, it references the 'viral' nature of a standard; it is free as in 'minimal restrictions'. Standards only become standards because they are common, widely promulgated, and free from the excessive restrictions that would subvert their 'standard-ness'. Even where a standard is essentially proprietary, such as is built in to much of what Microsoft produces, the market will only accept a *de facto* standard if it is not excessively controlled. Witness, for example, the availability of Microsoft IP in the early days of their development, and the way in which they allowed the free downloading of products such as Internet Explorer (later 'bundling', of course, raising somewhat different issues of 'product tying'). Standards, whether they are *de facto* or *de jure*, can only fulfil their purpose if control is minimal and exposure vast.

A further distinction can be made about standards. Not only can they emerge from differing sources, and deal with different areas of activity, but they can also be categorized as to function. Such a categorization isolates the relevant objectives of a standard within the contextual framework of the origin and general purpose of the standard. Swann,[7] for example, has characterized standards as having four distinct functions. For example, he suggests that standards can be concerned with compatibility or interfacing or they might be concerned with quality. They can also be concerned with variety reduction or with information standards. As such, one might thus distinguish between a *de facto* technical standard that has as its main concern the coordination of quality in a certain area and a *de facto* technical standard that has as its main concern the coordination of compatibility (at the expense of quality).

---

[5] See the typological hierarchy of standards proposed by leading US authority Ken Krechmer: Krechmer, K, 'The Fundamental Nature of Standards: Technical Perspective', 38(6) IEEE Communications Magazine (2000), 70–73.

[6] See, for example, the standards developed for parliamentary behaviour that emerged from the Nolan Committee, established in response to continual 'sleaze' allegations levelled at the Conservative government.

[7] Swann, P, 'The Economics of Standardisation, A Report for the DTI' (2000) <http://www.berr.gov.uk/files/file11312.pdf>.

There is no correlative link between the area that a standard deals with, the method of its formation, or its particular function. Socio-cultural standards tend to emerge organically, becoming standards in a *de facto* manner, but formal bodies may have a role in their development. Economic standards may be developed and imposed by a body designed to establish such standards, or they may also emerge over time without a formal influence.[8] Technical standards may similarly be the result of either *de facto*, *de jure*, or soft law development. It is to the technical standard that we now turn our focus.

10.2.2 Technical standards

Standards have a particularly useful role in coordinating the use of technology and assisting and advancing technological development. Schmidt and Werle[9] highlight standards as a coordinating aspect in the process of technical development. As they point out, lack of coordination, or bad coordination, can result in the incompatibility of various technical devices and the failure of technology. Successful standards and their promulgation can lead to the successful accommodation of diverse technological gadgets. They see this coordinating role of standards as especially important in large technical systems—not only with regard to the construction and maintenance of such systems, but also with regard to their operation and use. In this respect, technical standards are the medium of coordination—the 'technical rules that specify the relational properties of artefacts'.[10] If actors comply with these rules they are ensured compatibility and the smooth operation of the technology, benefiting both those who create and sell the technology and also those who use it.

Prior to effective and organized standardization in technology, the impact of technology on society was diminished, and the ability to effectively and efficiently create technology reduced. However, irrespective of the qualitative effect of modern standardization, standardization has, it seems, always played some role in how society uses and/or develops technology. Spivak and Brenner highlight some early instances of standards being used in relation to technology and technological development.[11] For example, they point out that as early society left the fields and founded cities, standard measures of length were required for construction purposes. Similarly, as agriculture became more developed, standard measures of volume were required for the distribution and tithing of produce. In Roman times, a set of weights and measures that were used as the national standard were kept in temples for reference

---

[8] Interestingly, modern formal commercial law evolved out of the mediaeval *lex mercatoria*, which was merely an organic set of market-based standards developed over time by merchants and used in order to organize and run their businesses efficiently over the great distances opened up by sea travel.

[9] Schmidt, SK and Werle, R, *Coordinating Technology: Studies in the International Standardization of Telecommunications* (MIT Press, Cambridge, MA, 1998).

[10] Schmidt and Werle, n 9 above, 26.

[11] Spivak and Brenner, n 2 above, 7–8.

and protection.[12] During the medieval period, the practice of using the king's body as a source of standard dimensions was common—Spivak refers to the instance of Henry I of England, in 1120, as decreeing that the ell, a traditional cloth measure, was the distance from his left shoulder to the tip of his extended hand. In this respect, as long as technology, defined in its most inclusive sense,[13] has been an aspect of civilization, standards have been required for its beneficial and organized use.

Industrialization was *the* major organizing influence on the use and development of technical standards; in a sense, it provided the impetus for the standardization of technical standards themselves. The rationale for this new stage in the evolution of standards was the increasing role that technology was playing in the life of everyday society, the health and safety risks of non-standardized technology, and, most importantly, the financial benefits that could be accrued by both ensuring efficient methods existed for creating technical products, and that those technical products themselves would be compatible.[14] The efficient release of products into society, and their beneficial compatibility, meant that they became efficient, effective, and more valuable to the public at large. Hesser and Inklaar[15] provide some examples of how standardization was both (i) a response to the difficulties encountered by societies' increasing use of technology and making technology efficient and effective, and (ii) somewhat differently, a desire to streamline production processes, i.e. make more profit. In some respect it was increasingly this latter desire for high productivity rates that led to the increased sophistication of standards and the standards process.

However, by the end of the eighteenth century the burgeoning need for technical standards threatened to outstrip the means to create them as the old reliance on personal knowledge, contacts, or contracts alone was simply no longer possible; this shortfall was cured by the emergence of professional bodies for engineers. In the UK, following in the wake of the Smeatonian Society,[16] the first of these bodies to emerge was the Institution of Civil Engineers (ICE); this was founded in 1818 with Thomas Telford taking on the presidency in 1820.[17] Thus it was that the first modern era technical standard was issued in 1841 when Joseph Whitworth, a pioneer in the field of micrometry, issued a memorandum to the ICE on screw threads in which he

[12] They were kept in the Temple of Dioscuri, Castor, and Pollux; also a standard model of the Roman Amphora Quadrantal, or Amphora, the measure of capacity for fluids, was kept in the Temple of Jupiter.
[13] That is, as an art or craft of use to humankind.
[14] Compatibility is used here to mean compatible for both industry and society in general. The compatibility in industry ensured the more speedy release of goods on to the market, while keeping costs low; the compatibility of the goods used in society ensured that demand for such goods continued, due to their usefulness.
[15] Hesser, W and Inklaar, A, *An Introduction to Standards and Standardization* (Beuth Verlag, Germany 1998).
[16] An informal private body of pioneering civil (as distinct from military, originally) engineers established in 1771 by John Smeaton (1724–1792): Watson, JG, *The Smeatonians: The Society of Civil Engineers* (Telford Press, London 1989).
[17] The ICE acquired a permanent establishment in 1833 and, after Telford's death in 1834, funds for training and publishing activities: Watson, JG, *The Civils: The Story of the Institution of Civil Engineers* (Telford Press, London 1988).

proposed a system based on defining the profile of the peaks and valleys comprising the thread, a consistent number of threads per inch for a given screw size and a uniform 55° slope from the peak to the valley of the thread helix.[18]

The development of industry and technology during the nineteenth century saw many more advances in the development of technical standards. The simple clarifying philosophy of having a standard process for every activity led to an assuredness in life and business that not only safeguarded the profits of industry, but that also revolutionized the use of technology in society. During this period of increased standardization, and increased technological innovation, the development of technical standards was undertaken by a variety of different actors, dependant on the technical activity in question. Natural monopolies, such as the telegraph, electrical, or postal systems, would have had standards developed either by government, or by the government-controlled operators of the system in question. Lack of competition in such national industries kept controversial standardization issues to a minimum. Other less centralized industries or activities saw technical standards developed mainly by market players.

The creation and use of technology has certainly not diminished in the centuries subsequent to the nineteenth, but the philosophy created then regarding the necessity of technical standards has remained, if not grown stronger. New technologies have emerged, old ones developed, but the desire for standards remains. One element that has changed, however, is how technical standards are developed. As technological diversity increases, previously closed markets open and governments try to remove themselves from regulating technology, the SDO, a non-governmental body developed to standardize the standardization process itself, has emerged. The role of this type of body in the context of telecommunications standards will be discussed latterly.

10.3 TECHNICAL STANDARDS AND TELECOMMUNICATIONS

The telecommunications sector is one which has always relied upon technical standards, those generally agreed and defined ways of doing things, in order to succeed. In many respects, the development and use of technical standards is a defining characteristic of a successful telecommunications sector. Telecommunications (from the Greek *tele* meaning 'far away' and the Latin *communicare* meaning 'impart', or 'share with') is all about interconnectivity, about communication. If communication is to succeed, as linguistic development and use throughout civilization has illustrated, a set way of doing things is required. This is no less so in telecommunications,

---

[18] Hemenway, D, *Industrywide Voluntary Product Standards* (Ballinger Publishing, Cambridge MA, 1975), 3–4. Hemenway also catalogues the rise of the US Sellers screw standard (1864) and the resulting problems of lack of interchangeability (including the near collapse of the British Eighth Army in WWII when the wrong screws were shipped and used).

although the rationale for standards is also teleologically purely technical. Standards are important in telecommunications because they allow technical compatibility and interoperability across technical networks. This simple technical requirement, of ensuring that things fit, subsequently satisfies the social end of telecommunications: communication everywhere, for all people. This significance is principally evident in the atypical institutional development of SDOs in telecommunications and its sister network electrical and electronic industries; very early on, the dominant demands of interoperability meant that *international* efforts had to be made to accommodate it in the shape of the International Electrotechnical Committee (IEC) and the International Telecommunications Union as discussed below.

More important, though, are the economic effects arising from networks in the telecommunications context. The development of technical standards that promote compatibility and increased connectivity allows both for more users to become attached, and for such attachment to be undertaken easily. Standards therefore increase the benefit that can be accrued from the network. If all telecommunication companies offered what are considered unique products and used discrete, unique standards relevant only to a particular company, not only would the idea of an efficient and easily connected network cease to exist, but certain economic benefits would also be lost. This is because standard products, or uniform products, produce greater economic 'externalities' in that they allow people to communicate across a greater network with greater ease. Such increased network externalities lead to a higher value of external relationships on the network. Standards, in the context of telecommunications, therefore have a technical and practical effect, but they also have an important economic effect in increasing network externalities, and increasing the value of telecommunications networks. This effect is the direct result of the non-exclusive nature of standards; developing exclusive standards for separate use in individual companies would not only prevent the ease of technical and social assimilation, it would also minimize externalities.[19]

A consequential economic effect of standards in the telecommunications industry is that they can create advantages for economic actors involved in their development; what one might call the 'strategic importance' of standards. It is once strategic importance is considered that the common nature of standards becomes an element of controversy and the desire to, in a sense, 'own' or 'control' standards becomes understandable. For example, at a meeting of the US House of Representatives Committee on Science in 2000,[20] Raymond G Kammer, Director of the National Institute of Standards and Technology, stated that estimates that Europe's mobile

---

[19] See, for more detail, Lea, G and Hall, P, 'Standards and intellectual property rights: an economic and legal perspective' 16(1) Information Economics and Policy, 67–89 (2004).
[20] Statement of Raymond G Kammer, Director, National Institute of Standards and Technology, Technology Administration, Department of Commerce, before the House Committee on Science Subcommittee on Technology, 13 September 2000 'The Role of Standards in Today's Society and in the Future', <http://www.nist.gov/testimony/2000/rkstds.htm>.

phone systems were 18 to 22 months ahead of those in the US had attributed Europe's fast start, at least in part, to the adoption of common standards. Having a key role in the development of a successful standard can thus present a company with a highly desirable lead-time in a market. The desirability of such a lead-time is obviously increased if the role involves a telecommunications company's IP. When the line between a common technical standard and a company's IP becomes blurred, and when the prize at stake might be a considerable lead-time in innovative practices and resultant profits, one can begin to appreciate some of the problems that can occur.

10.3.1 Telecommunications and technical standards development

As previously mentioned, standards can emerge from a number of sources. They can be market-based, law-based, or committee-based. Within the telecommunications sector, standards arise from all such sources. For example, a number of firms can group together, or one firm can innovate, to establish a standard. Alternatively, telecommunications standards can be developed through the governmental system; for example, the 'New Approach' to standardization taken by the EC established a number of essential requirement standards, concerning health, safety, the environment, and general interests, which must be adhered to.[21] However, this chapter wishes to focus on the particular role in standard development that is undertaken by standard committees or SDOs. Some history of the role of standards development in telecommunications can assist in appreciating the current status and focus of SDOs.

Prior to the trend of market liberalization that swept across developed countries during the 1980s, standards in the telecommunications industry were largely set either by government as owner of the telecommunications provider, or by the monopoly provider itself, if privately owned. In this respect the standards process was reasonably constrained and restrained. Existing without competition in their field, telecommunication providers only had to ensure conformity and coordination across their own networks; there was little need for consensus building or agreement among companies. The only requirements in deciding what a standard would be were issues of technological efficiency and effectiveness, and cost.[22] The additional factor of minimal transnational telecommunication prior to the middle half of the twentieth century meant that not only were monopolistic telecommunication companies responsible for setting their own standards (without national difficulty), but they also had little to worry about regarding international telecommunication standard-setting.

---

[21] The 'New Approach' emerged from Council Recommendation 84/5410 of 12 November 1984, concerning the implementation of harmonization in the field of telecommunications, (1984) OJ L298/49. See further Chapter 4. The New Approach emerged because the lack of speed of the standardization process was perceived by the EC to be restricting European harmonization. See also, Bekkers, R and Liotard, I, 'European standards for mobile communications: the tense relationship between standards and intellectual property rights' [1999] EIPR, 110–126.

[22] Although, for monopolistic companies, even the issue of cost was not really an issue; see, for example, the phenomenon of the 'gold-plating' of technical systems by monopolies.

As a result of such factors, Schmidt and Werle suggest that in the telecommunications sector the pure market-driven process of standardization, the *de facto* method, has been historically of minor importance. They point out that due to the historical high infrastructural, and military significance of the industry, national governments played a strong role in the development of its evolution, and subsequently its standards. Prior to the liberalization process of recent decades, one central organizational paradigm emerged and dominated—the single network operator, owned or controlled tightly by the State. As Schmidt suggests 'the close affiliation of the network operator to the government resulted in a hierarchical quasi-imposition of technical standards as regulations'.[23]

However, the increasing requirement for transnational telecommunications instigated the modern telecommunications standards process, as it is now known. Removing the domineering influence of government, and lessening that of the national monopolies, Schmidt marks out the requirement for international coordination as the major starting point of the development of the modern standards process in telecommunications: that of the telecommunications SDO. Bilateral agreements between national telecommunications operators were the first substantiation of the process; such arrangements included technical and operational specifications for the network interconnection points as well as more commercially orientated regulations. It was due to this process that the International Telegraph Union (ITU) was established in 1865, one of the earliest international standardization organizations. It was conceived as an institutional umbrella under which the principles for bilateral and multilateral trans-border telecommunications agreements would be established.

In this respect, the nascent telecommunications sector missed out on coordination being provided by the market, shifting largely from standards set by government, or, as a personification of government, the national telecommunications provider, to standards set by international standardization committee.[24] As transnational communication increased and the telegraph was replaced by sophisticated telecommunications technology, the International Telegraph Union became the International Telecommunications Union, currently the most prominent international telecommunications standards body.[25] Prior to 1993, the ITU consisted of two separate units, the Comité Consultatif International des Radiocommunication (CCIR) and the Comité Consultatif International Télégraphique et Téléphonique (CCITT). CCITT had historical responsibility for the development of standards, although it was established in 1956 at a time when international telecommunication standards were not a major issue in telecommunication policy. Another early SDO, similarly established due to the requirement for standards for international communication (albeit with regional European significance), was the Conférence Européenne des Administrations des Postes et des Télécommunications (CEPT).

---

[23] Schmidt and Werle, n 9 above, 44.
[24] Although the standard-setting body could be supported by government.
[25] See further Chapter 12, at section 12.3.

However, although these SDOs had emerged, their realm of responsibility was still largely the development of technical standards for international communications between national telecommunication monopolies. As such, both CEPT and CCITT were largely constructed of national telecommunication network operators, otherwise known as PTTs (post, telegraph, and telephone) or PTOs (public telecommunications operators). In this respect, while international telecommunications resulted in a new regulatory paradigm for the telecommunication standard-setting process, the change was hardly revolutionary. New organizations were required to accommodate agreement on international standards development, but monopolies still constituted a major part of their make up and true competition had yet to affect the process.

Two factors acted to change the development of the telecommunications standardization process. First, in the late 1980s and 1990s, both national and international telecommunications markets truly opened up, and liberalization began the process of separating the monopolies. Secondly, there was a specific technological change; the transition from analogue to digital. Bekkers and Liotard[26] suggest that this change in technological paradigm led to a major change in the telecommunications manufacturing process, including concentration, acquisitions, and cooperations. Such changes meant that the standardization process also had to change. ITU and CEPT had been developed in order to develop standards primarily for international telecommunications between monopolists. They were required because neither Government nor markets had the ability to develop standards in line with the needs of the international telecommunications environment. Eventually, however, ITU and CEPT came to lack the ability to deal with subsequent changes. Liberalization of national markets and digitization created new problems for such SDOs.[27] Their members were primarily monopolistic operators. They had to evolve in the face of the difficulties posed by a post-digital and post-liberalization world. In this context, the ITU effected change internally in order to accommodate these economic and technological changes. In 1993, the issue of standardization was concentrated in a new section of the ITU, the ITU-T, one of three new sectors of the union, the other two being the radiocommunications sector and the telecommunications sector.

Standardization issues were transferred to the ITU-T at this time and it now deals with all such issues. Standards development in Europe was to change also. Concern at a Community level could be traced back as far as the 1960s when the issue of incompatible Member State technical standards and technical regulations arose in the context of 'technical barriers to trade' (TBT) as a block on the free movement of goods and free provision of services.[28]

---

[26] Bekkers and Liotard, n 21 above.

[27] Tang, P, 'Institutional Instability, Governance and Telematics' (1995) 2 *Review of International Political Economy* (1995), 567–999.

[28] See the General Programme of 28 May 1969 for the elimination of technical barriers to trade and the Council Resolution drawing up a programme for the elimination of technical barriers to trade

The difficulty was that, in addition to the problem of technical and other barriers to trade created by Member States, perhaps the biggest obstacle that the then-EEC faced in making the Common Market a reality was itself; in so far as the Community institutions had taken any initiatives to promote harmonization of rules and procedures affecting trade, these had often taken the form of highly detailed technical regulations which were both time-consuming to prepare and required unanimous voting in the relevant institutions. Indeed, it was the vast logjam caused by this so-called 'maximalist' approach to harmonization that was largely responsible for the stagnation and near-collapse of the EEC in the 1970s.

The first means to escape from the *cul de sac* described above were provided by the European Court of Justice in the *Cassis de Dijon* case.[29] In its decision, the Court enunciated a principle of mutual recognition whereby, even in the absence of technical harmonization, products lawfully produced and marketed in one Member State could circulate throughout the Community in accordance with the relevant free movement provisions of the EEC Treaty[30] unless a specific objection could be raised on the basis of mandatory requirements relating to 'the effectiveness of fiscal supervision, the protection of public health, the fairness of commercial transactions and the defence of the consumer'.[31] Following *Cassis de Dijon*, the other Community institutions considered what could be done positively to accelerate harmonization: in the specific case of technical standards and technical regulations, the European Parliament resolved in 1980 to call upon both the Council and the Commission to come up with concrete measures to improve the situation.

In response, the European Telecommunications Standards Institute (ETSI) was established by CEPT. ETSI is an SDO with specific European significance; its creation in 1987–88 was instigated by the European Commission,[32] as they considered that CEPT could not accommodate all the relevant new players in the rapidly changing telecommunications arena. Prins and Schiessl also suggest that a rationale for ETSI was the specific potential risk of IP in standards being used to create obstacles to open access in the telecommunication field, the threat of which was already being identified by the Commission at that time as acute.[33]

This threat was probably recognized as the logical outcome of the requirements of a truly competitive market competing with the requirements of the

(OJ 1969 C76/1); these mark the origins of the former approach to harmonization and were supplemented by a further programme in 1973 covering foodstuffs and industrial products.

[29] Case 102/78 *Rewe Zentrale v Bundesmonopolverwaltung für Branntwein* [1979] ECR 649.

[30] Articles 30–36 (now consolidated and recast as Arts 28–30, EU Treaty).

[31] *Rewe Zentrale v Bundesmonopolverwaltung für Branntwein* at 662.

[32] As a result of recommendations given in the Green Paper on the Development of the Common Market for Telecommunications Services and Equipment, COM (87) 2100 final, 13 June 1987. This resulted in the so-called new approach to standardization, which distinguished between essential requirements and voluntary standards. The essential requirement is a health, safety, or environmental issue standard. A voluntary standard is usually a technical specification. The new approach does not provide for the drawing up of voluntary standards by the EC, but by private European standardization bodies. ETSI is one such body recognized by the EC for this purpose.

[33] Prins, C and Schiessl, M, 'The new telecommunications standards institute policy: conflicts between standardization and intellectual property rights' [1993] 8 EIPR 263.

standardization process. Long points out that the tradition among SDOs had long been to act on a purely voluntary basis, leading to codes and guidelines that were simply advisory.[34] In this respect, SDOs respected the principle of the freedom of IP rights holders to exploit them or not at their own discretion, and exerted no obligation on IPR holders to release proprietary information or to grant licences over rights utilized or embodied in a standard.

Such a bucolic environment must surely have been aided by the lack of real competition amongst telecommunication providers. In the absence of real competition, one would expect that the inclusion of IP in standards would not have presented much difficulty, because markets were assured. As the free market was emerging, however, and competing telecommunication companies began to realize that market strength could depend vitally on their role in the standardization process, the role of IP in standardization became much more pertinent. What other, historically non-monopolized sectors had already experienced, and dealt with largely through *de facto* standardization (thus largely removing the IP/standard conflict issue), telecommunications was now experiencing.

The organic development of telecommunications SDOs has now entered a third stage. As Walden and many others[35] point out, the work of the 'established' telecommunications SDOs is coming under pressure because of the combined effects of convergence with IT and the rise of other bodies, such as industry associations and *de facto* standards bodies. These new bodies develop standards at a much quicker pace and also focus on specific issues that require resolution. Although considerable efforts to 'match pace' have been, and continue to be made by established SDOs, there is still a sentiment that the new SDOs are a more efficient way of getting standards developed. One might also view these next generation bodies as representative of the desire to side-step competitive restraints implicit in the traditional standardization process. The traditional arena for standards still advances the soft law process. Telecommunications companies, operating in a competitive environment, may perceive that technical standards are less beneficial than in the monopolized past. Their desire is now, frequently, to develop *de facto* proprietary standards, such as those that emerged in the computing sector. The new, non-traditional bodies will be discussed further below.

10.4 A DIFFICULTY FOR THE STANDARDS PROCESS: INTELLECTUAL PROPERTY

The regulatory environment surrounding the development of technical standards for the telecommunications industry has evolved to accommodate new technological and economic factors, but it appears that the accommodation of such factors has

---

[34] Long, CD, *Telecommunications Law and Practice* (2nd edn, Sweet & Maxwell, London, 1995) 173–175.
[35] At Chapter 12; see also Schmidt and Werle, n 9 above.

created additional problems. In particular, the liberalization of telecommunication markets has led to normal competitive circumstances amongst firms. Because of this, SDOs must now recognize the impact of IP on the standard-setting process. Previously, standard-setting bodies were operating in the context of a lacuna of competition, so IP rights were not a major problem in the process of standard development. Now that telecommunication firms are competing nationally and internationally, IP rights are an important aspect of their arsenal, and as such now come to impinge on the standard setting process.

What is the difficulty? Consider, respectively, the standard and the IP right. The most important aspect of standards, and technical standards in particular, is that they are expected to be widely promulgated and used, without undue restriction. The idea that a standard is available for common and reasonable use is essential to the success of a standard and central to the idea of something being or becoming standard. In the telecommunications sector, this idea of a standard being available for common and reasonable use has ensured the growth of the industry, the creation of vast network externalities, and communicative benefits for society. It is unlikely that such events would have occurred if, instead of standards, the industry operated solely with IP on normal commercial terms.

In turn, the fact that the telecommunications sector has historically been a monopolistic sector has probably assisted the role of standards. On the other hand, the rationale behind and practice of vesting exclusive rights in the stuff that standards are created from, in information, stands in stark contrast with the philosophy and rationale of standards. Seen purely from the perspective of standards, and leaving aside the countervailing interests of intellectual property for a moment, to be granted exclusive rights of use concerning a technical process that can be patented could allow restrictions to be placed on the use of the process. The owner of such exclusive rights of use might deny, for example, the general and free use and promulgation of information that could contribute to the useful coordination of a certain technological practice. Such restrictive behaviour would conflict with the benefit that could be collectively gained from promulgating the technical process as a standard. In the context of the modern standardization process, certain protected technical processes are sometimes considered as integral aspects of a developing standard. The fact that someone has exclusive rights of use concerning that essential technology allows for the potential restriction of the standardization process, or the disruption of it, undermining its role for the purpose of private pecuniary gain at the expense of the common good that standards are supposed to promote.

Of course, the other perspective here is that the granting of IP rights serves as an important incentive in the development of the telecommunications industry *and* as a central aspect of a free and competitive market, which the telecommunications sector has only recently become. As such, IP rights should be respected. In the context of a competitive and free market, it is not difficult to appreciate the rationale behind the granting of exclusive rights for informational goods.

10.4.1 The rationale behind IP rights

IP rights are a remedy to a particular problem. The problem stems from certain natural economic characteristics of information. First, information is non-scarce; once created, and if suitably stored, it cannot be used up like a tangible product could be. Secondly, information is non-rivalrous; if one person makes use of information, another person can make use of it without rivalling the first use. This is in contrast to an apple, for example, for if one person eats it, that's that. Finally, while information is certainly not non-excludable, it is more prone to non-exclusion than tangible goods. Being more prone to non-exclusion means being less prone to being valuable; this is especially so in the case of informational goods, because exclusion could create the scarcity and rivalry necessary for the creation of value.

Because of these natural characteristics, it would be very difficult for a for-profit company to suggest spending time and money on developing informational goods, because the natural economic characteristics of such goods would suggest that value could not be obtained from them. If, unlike an apple, they are *not* scarce, who would be prepared to pay for them? Once the information is created, anyone can make use of it without lessening the amount of it; such abundance would make payment ridiculous. If, unlike an apple, they are *not* rival, who will pay for it? Simply use someone else's, they will not mind since you are not rivalling their use. However, the most important aspect of many modern businesses is the intangible aspect. This is certainly so in the telecommunications industry, as certain inventions, for example, are the defining aspect of a business's service. In addition, in the competitive telecommunications industry, creating new informational goods can provide a competitive advantage. Who will undertake R&D regarding patentable inventions if, once created, they become valueless?

In response to the difficulties presented by the use of informational goods, the granting of exclusive rights of use surrounding such goods can act as a remedy. The granting of IP rights allows for the exclusive appropriation of certain types of information, and applies resultant property rules to regulate the use of such appropriated information. The catch-all phrase 'intellectual property law' is actually used in order to describe what are a number of discrete areas of law; patents, copyright and neighbouring rights, design rights, and trademarks. Patents, for example, protect inventions; copyright creates exclusive rights in expressions of ideas; design rights protect the man-made appearance of certain goods; trademark law offers protection to man-made signs used to differentiate goods for sale. Intellectual property is a similar catch-all term used to describe those things so protected. By creating these artificial conceptual exclusionary effects through the application of concepts of exclusive ownership and property rules, information goods acquire value. If a company is granted the exclusive right to do certain things with an invention, it will spend time and money creating that invention, because it realizes that it will now be valuable. In this respect a conceptual exclusionary effect is created in order that the information becomes conceptually scarce and conceptually rival and realistically valuable

(as long as the rule of law is respected). One can suggest that the current conflicts between IP and telecommunications standards has been the result of a previously exclusionary effect being removed: the monopoly. IP is, of course, a limited monopoly. Given this, it is not difficult to appreciate the nature of the conflict. IP provides remembrance of things past.

Of course, another point is that society requires access to information goods to develop and innovate. Implicit in the justification for granting IP rights is the rather worrying idea of information being excessively protected from use; that is, the problems of monopolization. Even if one accepts that creators of information goods (i) require protection from free-riding, and (ii) may not have created such goods if such protection did not exist, the idea that society can be prevented from using such goods freely for an indefinite period is not pleasant, and not useful for human development. In this respect, IP law also tries to create a balance between protecting products and ensuring such products can be used for the benefit of society. Within this balancing act, one finds the essential kernel that influences the larger debate between standards and IP in telecommunications. If IP is exclusively controlled by one individual, the possibility of that important innovation becoming unreasonably lost to society is high. In response to this, the grant of an IP right is limited in time and remit. It is argued that this provides a balance between the exclusivity required for people to create, and the freedom required for society to benefit from the creation.

This conflict within IP, between 'the desire for the widespread diffusion of new products and processes and the need to create sufficient incentives for firms to engage in innovation',[36] is reflected in the conflict between standards and IP. The conflict arises simply because a standard, in the truest understanding of the word, can be considered a public good. A public good is one that is non-excludable and non-rival. As information goods, standards have come to satisfy such criteria by conceptual design rather than natural effect. As previously suggested, the natural non-excludability of informational goods is a point of debate. Information is naturally non-scarce and non-rival, once created. However, while not suited to excludability, it is certainly excludable. Standards have thus acquired public goods status only because they are allowed to be considered standards. They have acquired it because of the particular purpose of standards; in their role as standards, conceptual exclusivity cannot be applied. As implied, this is not to suggest that informational goods cannot be excluded. For example, in contrast to this idea of the ideational public good, is the idea of the ideational private good, as represented by the existence of IP rights. Both ownership systems deal with the same subject matter, informational goods. However, they require different results and thus apply different systems. This explains their essential conflict.

[36] Shurmer, M and Lea, G, 'Telecommunications Standardization and Intellectual Property Rights: A Fundamental Dilemma?', *Standards Policy for Information Infrastructure* (MIT Press Cambridge, MA, 1995).

Given the problems associated with the natural economic characteristics of information, and the fact that such characteristics are allowed to flourish in the concept of the standard, one might ask why parties are involved in developing standards if, unlike those items capable of IP protection, no one can claim ownership of them, and profit from such ownership. Schmidt and Werle point out that an interest in coordination motivates parties so that they will 'voluntarily engage in negotiation with others on an appropriate solution'.[37] Any costs involved in such engagement are compensated by any utility that they believe will result. That utility can be viewed as, for example, increased network externalities for all companies involved. In this respect, developing standards, and allowing certain information to be considered as a standard, is justified. The only problem is that other informational goods can justify the application of exclusive ownership.

10.4.2 Telecommunications and IP

The incentive argument that can act to justify allowing the exclusive ownership of informational goods is an integral aspect in appreciating the vital role of IP in the telecommunications industry. Indeed, the history of the telecommunications industry as an industry can be traced back to the grant of a patent to Alexander Graham Bell. Bell was granted a patent for his invention of a process for transmitting and receiving the sound of the human voice over wire. The grant of the patent meant that the invention was commercialized free from competition,[38] and allowed the Bell Telephone Company to grow quickly. Just as that initial patent allowed telecommunications to grow and foster without the pressures of competition, the existence of IP rights currently allows modern telecom companies to undertake daring research and innovation, secure in the knowledge that the time and money spent will be recouped by the exclusive rights conferred by IP law. Without such security, it is arguable that innovation and R&D would suffer, telecommunication companies not being prepared to take risks which are not assured financial reward. The importance of IP in telecommunications was further enhanced by the process of liberalization, which removed the protection offered in many countries by telecommunications monopolies—in such an economic climate, technical innovation and a strong IP portfolio are essential for commercial success. In addition to fostering innovation and strengthening competitive ability, IP rights can have other interesting economic effects. One of the main alternative functions of IP is its use as a strategic weapon, both generally and in the standardization process.

The ways in which IP rights can be used as a strategic weapon in the standards process broadly reflect the ways in which IP can be of general strategic importance

---

[37] Schmidt and Werle, n 9 above, 59.
[38] Although it is interesting to imagine what innovative effect competition might have had on the development of the telephone system if such a patent had not been granted, and how the lack of a monopoly might have led to an early telecommunications industry free from the problems of monopoly.

to any company. Invariably, two strategic standardization issues will present themselves to the telecommunications company with a large and important IP portfolio. First, because of the interconnected nature of the telecoms industry, and the benefits of large network externalities, controlling one's IP too strongly may lead to others succeeding. Such strong control might allow those who release their IP either freely, or on more relaxed terms, to prevail. The computing industry provides a perfect example of this type of strategic failure.

In the 1980s and 1990s, Apple arguably pioneered much of the technological innovation of personal computing, producing many radical and successful concepts which are now ubiquitous in computing. However, at the end of 2007, its US market share consisted of approximately 8.1 per cent of the personal computer market, with Microsoft and the generic personal computer accounting for the rest. Although now recovering market share from a low in the 1990s, the inability of Apple to benefit from technological superiority is in no small fashion the result of its strategic (mis-) management of IP during the 1980s and early 1990s. For example, the important process of early acceptance and mass promulgation of a technology largely bypassed Apple Macintosh. Why? Product distribution was hampered by the lack of application software, a deficiency partly compounded by Apple's strict rules on distribution of materials for software developers; in other words, the result of how it controlled its IP. Apple was refusing to allow mail-order companies to sell Macintoshes, it also forbade mail order distribution of *Inside Macintosh*, the guidebook to the Macintosh architecture which was the programmer's bible for the system. Apple also put very tight restrictions on the Apple Certified Developer Program, by which software developers were able to obtain Macs at a discount and receive informational materials. A few daring employees worked around these restrictions to get development materials into the hands of every software programmer possible, with the sensible idea that each Mac out in the field would help sell additional Macs simply through its presence. They might do so because if companies are encouraged to select their IP, the network effects theory would lead to it becoming a *de facto* standard. Customers would want to stay with the technology that provides them with the greatest reach, and can also become locked into a standard. Even if the other technology is better, the fact that its release into the market was delayed because of an overly protective perspective regarding IP could spell its doom. In the computing arena, the case of Apple and Microsoft is a prominent example of the importance of this continual strategic choice, although there are many other examples. Interestingly, Apple appears to have learnt from this early strategic mistake in their utilization of IP; subsequently, it placed some of the technology of its iPod music system into the hands of actual or potential rivals in order to create network effects and attempt to establish a *de facto* proprietary standard[39] and, after a cautious start, it is likewise 'opening up' the iPhone.

---

[39] London, S, 'Product to platform: the iPod's big play', *Financial Times*, 19 January 2004. Lewin, P (ed), *The Economics of QWERTY: History, Theory and Policy. Essays by S.J. Liebowitz & S.E. Margolis* (Palgrave, New York, 2002).

Conversely, not controlling one's IP strongly enough may lead to the loss of perfectly entitled revenue or a position of market strength. While Microsoft's policy makers, for example, are extremely astute in freeing their rein over their IP when it suits them, they generally assert very tight control over their IP, and this is reflected in their financial situation and market position. Although initially predicating its IP activities on software copyright since the late 1990s, Microsoft has dramatically increased both its patenting and patent acquisition activities, reaching its 5,000th US patent granted in March 2006; this can be viewed in terms of 'buttressing' the IP position in such a way as to give greater leverage in licensing negotiations, whether licensing in or out.

In sum, the two basic choices regarding how to use IP rights become acutely relevant in the context of telecommunications standards. A company can choose to restrict the freedom surrounding its IP and risk missing an opportunity to influence the standards process. A company can allow their IP to be used (either with compensation or without) and benefit from its inclusion in a standard. A further choice that is sadly becoming more prominent is a mixture between the two: allowing use, but on what might be deemed unreasonable or unfair terms. These, then, are the three options that face a telecommunications company when dealing with the use of their IP in a standard.

10.5 ILLUSTRATING THE DIFFICULTY BETWEEN IP AND TELECOMMUNICATION STANDARDS

Bekkers and Liotard have pointed out that, in a sense, *both* IP rights and standards are ultimately created to serve the public interest. Standards 'can overcome many disadvantages related to too wide a variety of products, services or methods', while 'a framework of property rights is deemed necessary to ensure that individuals or companies can employ innovative activities'.[40] However, in addition they admit that standards and IP will conflict because of the essentially public[41] character of standards, which is looking for equal access for all, and the private nature of property rights, providing exclusive ownership to individuals. This conflict between the public good nature of standards, and the private interest personified in an IP right, has become the predominant issue of difficulty surrounding the post-liberalization and post-digital standardization process.

Competitive markets now mean that owners of IP may want to engage in either of two problematic scenarios: either protect their rights exclusively, or allow the use of their IP in standards for strategic purposes. They might decide that they do not want to allow their property to be used in the development of standards, or they do want it to be used, but under what others might consider unfair and unreasonable

---

[40] Bekkers and Liotard, n 21 above.
[41] Bekkers and Liotard call this a quasi-public character because not all parties have equal access to the standard and to the standardization process, n 21 above.

(or anti-competitive) terms. Such behaviour, especially when the IP in question is considered technologically necessary in the development of the standard, is understandably problematic. Two practical examples illustrate this.

10.5.1 The GSM example

Bekkers and Liotard have provided an excellent overview of the process of developing the Global System (or standard) for Mobile (GSM) standard. Some of the issues raised during this process are a practical illustration of this conflict between telecommunication standards and telecommunication IPR. A brief description of the GSM process provides some pertinent examples of the importance of IP as a strategic implement used by the telecommunication companies to strengthen their positions in the standardization process. The role of SDOs in addressing such conflict is also illustrated here.

GSM was first mooted as a standard when CEPT, the forerunner of ETSI, asked manufacturers and operators for proposals for a new telecommunications standard for mobile telephony. Eight different proposals were submitted. Four were the result of a Franco-German alliance, and used what, at the time, were new technologies, CDMA (Code Division Multiple Access) or hybrid designs. Four were of Scandinavian origin, based on the contrasting TDMA (Time Division Multiple Access) technology. By 1986 a choice had to be made, but CEPT had difficulty in reaching a consensus. A majority of country delegations judged the most innovative Franco–German design as too proprietary. Only when the German manufacturer Siemens coordinated with Ericsson, exchanging technology, was the deadlock released, with Germany now supporting the Scandinavian designs as a result of their new-found friendship.

In 1988 the responsibility for coordinating the development of GSM transferred to the newly created ETSI. Manufacturers involved in the process from the start had proclaimed that their IP was available on fair, reasonable, and non-discriminatory conditions. As from 1987, the operators of the GSM standard began the procurement procedure for GSM, but soon realized that a number of essential IP rights were used in basic GSM technology, some patents being held by US companies. This procurement of such essential patented technology would involve the separate negotiation of licences. The risk that companies would refuse to grant licences was a continual threat during the development of the GSM standard, and indeed, as Bekkers and Liotard point out, Motorola lost a number of procurement contracts on the basis of non-compromise over licence conditions.

Much later, further IP issues arose. In the US a company called InterDigital Technology Corporation claimed patent infringement relating to TDMA-based systems, including GSM. In 1995, the US Federal Court ruled such claims invalid.[42]

---

[42] *Motorola, Inc v Interdigital Tech Corp*, 1030 F Supp 1052, 1086 (D Del 1996).

Confusingly, in the German Federal Court in 1996 the Court upheld one of the InterDigital patents found invalid in the US. Subsequently, InterDigital identified other alleged infringements of other of its patents by Ericsson and Nokia and took action accordingly. However, interestingly, whilst resisting Inter Digital's various claims, the three major players in the GSM standardization process subsequently came to hold large market shares for mobile phone handsets, with a combined market share of 80 per cent.

In the event, although basic GSM technology is now being superseded and the relevant patents are expiring, the infringement cases and appeals rumble on: as late as 2006, Nokia, by then the world's largest mobile phone producer, settled one of its patent disputes with InterDigital for US$253 million and, even as of April 2008, there is still a significant final dispute to resolve.

10.5.2 The Qualcomm example

A more recent example[43] of how standards and IP can detrimentally intersect is the behaviour of Qualcomm in the context of the WCDMA (wideband code division multiple access) standard.[44] This standard was to be the successor of GSM, and again IP issues came to the fore. ETSI, by this stage fully in control as regards standard development in the EU, had selected a radio access technology based on the WCDMA system, sponsored by Ericsson and Nokia, for its third generation (3G) wireless system. The issue of 3G mobile systems had been a pertinent one for telecommunications SDOs for some time. In 1985 the ITU began studies on global personal communications which resulted in a system referred to as international mobile telecommunications in the year 2000 (IMT-2000). ETSI developed, in parallel, a 3G mobile system called universal mobile telecommunications systems (UMTS). IMT-2000 is essentially a family of systems, of which UMTS is a subset, ensuring 3G systems are compatible and provide uniformity in communications. The standardization process that surrounded this technology was affected, however, by a dispute between ETSI and Qualcomm Inc regarding the use of IP in the development of this particular standard.

After much work regarding the development of the standard by various standards bodies and consortia, in 1998 Qualcomm informed ETSI that unless the UMTS standard proposal provided retrospective compatibility with another standard, IS-95,

---

[43] Some other examples of conflicts between intellectual property and standards development are the conflict with the ITU concerning the 56 Kilobit per second modem and the conflict over the discrete multi-tone (DMT) and carrier-less amplitude/phase modulation (CAP)/quadrature amplitude modulator (QAM) line codes for asymmetric digital subscriber line (ADSL) in the US's Committee T1.

[44] A fine description of this issue is provided in Hjelm, B, 'Standards and Intellectual Property Rights in the Age of Global Communication—A Review of the International Standardization of Third Generation Mobile System'. A Paper presented at 5th IEEE Symposium, Computers and Communications, Antibus—Juan Les Pins, France, 3–6 July 2000. Available online at <http://arxiv.org/ftp/cs/papers/0109/0109105.pdf>.

it would prevent the use of IP which it claimed was essential in the development of the 3G standard. Qualcomm stated that the standard proposed by ETSI, WCDMA, was specifically designed to exclude Qualcomm technology. Qualcomm stated that this was a violation of free trade laws between US and Europe, and claimed patent infringement on key technology required for the WCDMA standard. In 1998, Qualcomm also formally invoked claims of IP rights to five standard proposals pending before the ITU and stated that it would refuse to license under any ITU terms unless the desired converged and IS-95 compatible standard emerged via the IMT-2000 standard process.

As a further backdrop to this developmental process, Qualcomm had been involved in litigation since 1995 with Ericsson over IP rights surrounding CDMA technology. Ericsson brought a suit against Qualcomm alleging patents taken by Qualcomm regarding CDMA technology infringed Ericsson patents. Ericsson had focused on TDMA technology, but stated that they had several patents that applied to the Qualcomm technology. In 1996 Qualcomm countersued, stating breach of nondisclosure agreements and seeking declaration of non-infringement and invalidity. The conflict between the two emerged as a result of the Qualcomm technology being adopted by the Telecommunication Industry Association as a standard, IS-95. The inclusion of their technology in their standard allowed Qualcomm to contend that technology compliant with the standard implicitly infringed their patents. Ericsson suggested that the WCDMA standard did not infringe any of the IP rights suggested by Qualcomm. Their suit was based on the perception that Qualcomm's refusal to license was simply a way of protecting vested interests and expanding market share in Europe. As a result of such activities the development of the standard itself was delayed. In conclusion, the 3G issue was resolved with the inclusion of the Qualcomm technology, but not until they gained a position of strategic strength and delayed the standard process for others.

As at April 2008, Qualcomm is in dispute with Nokia over both 3G and other mobile telecommunications patents. At the heart of the dispute is the royalty sum payable but, ostensibly to strengthen its negotiating position, Qualcomm has initiated patent infringement proceedings in several countries, including the US, the UK, Germany, France, Italy, and China. So far, Nokia has successfully defended and counterclaimed in relation to some patents in the US and UK; it has also filed papers showing royalties payable under the previous licensing scheme in excess of US$1 billion over approximately 15 years. In its most recent US filings, Qualcomm has 'upped the stakes' by alleging a conspiracy by Nokia, Broadcom and others to undermine its 3G patents portfolio through various blocking tactics, including co-ordinated litigation.

10.5.3 Lessons?

The lesson of the Qualcomm and GSM affairs is that IP can very much become a bargaining tool and strategic point from which to direct the standardization process.

Even though standards themselves are not automatically exclusionary *per se*, they can be developed in fashions which suit certain parties to the disadvantage of others. If an owner of what is considered essential IP can command the fact that it is considered essential and use that command strategically, the standard itself can subsequently provide other benefits that might alleviate the cost involved in the licensing of the essential technology on fair, reasonable, and non-discriminatory terms, which the IP owner might not have been willing to do otherwise.

That is one lesson; the other is more simple—that the bargaining process or decision to refuse to licence technology can stonewall the standardization process itself, leading to losses for those dependant on or waiting for a standard and those who want to benefit from new technology. This is especially so when dealing with the development of new technology in telecommunications because the manufacturers want to be sure of what the standards are before they begin product development. If there is uncertainty, the manufacturer will have to wait.

This, then, opens up two main possibilities: first, that, to the extent possible, SDOs will have to improve internal processes to try to prevent 'patent ambush' or other malpractice and, second, hard law, in the shape of provisions against abuse of IP rights, abuse of a dominant position (monopolization) or anti-competitive tactics (cartelization) will be brought up, front and centre. These issues are examined more closely in the following sections.

10.6 ATTEMPTING TO SQUARE THE CIRCLE: THE ROLE OF THE SDO

A perceived solution amongst those bodies involved in developing and promulgating telecommunication standards has been to develop policies which attempt to ensure that conflicts regarding IP owned by telecommunication companies and standards developed for the benefit of telecommunication companies do not occur. The predominant method now employed by the typical SDO is the creation of *ex ante* IP regulatory policies by which members must abide.

10.6.1 International standard setting

10.6.1.1 *ISO/IEC*
Before focusing on the IP policies of some specific telecommunications SDOs, it is worth noting that the overarching international standardization organization, the International Organization for Standards (ISO) and its sister organization the International Electrotechnical Commission (IEC) have common IP Policies, which, since March 2007, have also been linked to the ITU's Patent Policy as well. It is true that ISO and the IEC do, admittedly, play a rather general role in the development of technical standards for the telecommunications industry, but given their status it is worth exploring their policy.

ISO's most relevant unit in relation to the setting of standards in telecommunications is Technical Committee 107 (TC 97) created in 1960. The scope of this section is the standardization of information processing systems 'from the perspective of freestanding computer systems, office machinery and data communication implementation'. For example, the TC 97 and the CCITT both operated in 1984 toward the development of the Open System Interconnection reference model, a seven-layer protocol architecture, that has importance in the area of telematics standards and computer communications. According to Schmidt, the IEC has less of an overt role in telecommunications standards, but its work covers all spheres of electrotechnology, including power, electronics, telecommunications, and nuclear energy. Whilst being involved in the development of telecommunications standards, the jurisdiction of ISO and the IEC in the matter of standards is much broader than that of bodies such as ITU or ETSI.

10.6.1.2 *International Telecommunications Union*
The International Telecommunications Union is a specialized standardization body, focusing explicitly on the telecommunications sector. The ITU has a specialized subunit that specializes in the development of standards for the telecommunications industry, ITU-T. ITU-T actually has two separate IP Policies, a Patent Policy and a Software Copyright Policy. The Patent Policy was originally described as a code of practice regarding the intersection of IP rights (patents) and the subject matter of ITU-T Recommendations. The Policy as formulated began by stating that the ITU-T Recommendations were non-binding international standards, with the objective of ensuring compatibility of international telecommunications on a worldwide basis. In meeting this requirement, the policy stated, it must be ensured that Recommendations, their application, and use should be accessible to everybody. Thus 'a commercial (monopolistic) abuse by a holder of a patent embodied fully or partly in a Recommendation must be excluded'.

10.6.1.3 *The new common policies*
Taking effect from March 2007, wherever possible, the ITU, ISO, and IEC Patent Policies have been harmonized with a view to requesting early disclosure by parties of patents necessary to practise or implement a relevant standard. Common patent declaration and licensing forms have been established, along with, crucially, a widely accessible patent information database.[45]

10.6.2 European standard setting

ETSI was one of the first SDOs to attempt to radically change the approach of such organizations regarding the role of IP in standards development.[46] Shortly after

---

[45] See details at <http://isotc.iso.org/livelink/livelink/fetch/2000/2122/37707101/Common_Policy.htm>.
[46] Long, n 34 above, 173–175.

its establishment, it began serious work on developing a code of practice to regulate members' behaviour when IP and standards came into conflict. In 1993, two documents were adopted by ETSI, an IPR policy and an IPR undertaking. However, the development of ETSI's IP policy has been the subject of considerable debate and controversy, based on its original *de facto* compulsion to license,[47] and ETSI has since developed a new IP rights policy in order to attempt to reconcile the difficulties that have emerged as a result of IP becoming involved in the telecommunications standards process.

The current policy (as revised to March 2007) has three stated objectives at Clause 3. The first is that standards and technical specifications developed by ETSI will best meet the technical requirements of the European telecommunications sector. In order to further this primary objective, the policy states that ETSI wishes to reduce the risk to ETSI members and those who apply ETSI standards that any investment in the preparation, adoption, and application of standards might be wasted as a result of an 'essential' IP right being unavailable. In the achievement of this reduction of risk, ETSI wants to create a balance between the needs of standardization for public use in the field of telecommunications and the rights of owners of IP. The second major objective of the policy is stated as being that IPR holders, whether members of ETSI or affiliates or third parties, should be adequately and fairly awarded for their use of IPR in the implementation of standards and technical specifications. Finally, the policy states that ETSI shall take reasonable measures to ensure, as far as possible, that its activities which relate to the preparation, adoption, and application of standards and technical specifications enables such standards and specifications to be available to potential users in accordance with the general principle of standardization.

The ETSI IP policy, at Clause 4, obligates members to use their reasonable endeavours to inform ETSI of essential IPR in a timely fashion. In particular, on a good faith basis, those members who are submitting technical proposals for standards or technical specifications must draw the attention of ETSI to any of their IP rights which may become essential if the standard is adopted. This is not an obligation to undertake IP searches. Interestingly, the definition of IPR used excludes confidential information and trade secrets; to the extent that a member can and does deliberately manipulate what is disclosed in its patents, this may represent a loophole that needs to be revisited.

Under Clause 6, once an essential IP right is identified and brought to the attention of ETSI, the Director-General (DG) is obliged to immediately request that the owner of the IP in question give, within three months, an undertaking in writing that it is prepared to grant irrevocable licences on fair, reasonable, and non-discriminatory terms and conditions. Such licences must at least allow the following in relation

---

[47] See, for example, Tuckett, R, 'Access to public standards: interoperability revisited' (1992) 12 EIPR 423; Good, D, 'How far should IP rights have to give way to standardization: the policy positions of ETSI and the EC' (1992) 10 EIPR 2105; Prins and Schiessl, n 33 above; and Long, n 34 above.

to the IP: the manufacture, including the right to make or have customized components and subsystems to the licensees own design for use in manufacture; the sale, leasing, or otherwise disposal of equipment so manufactured; the reparation, usage, or operation of equipment; and usage methods. The above undertaking may be made subject to the condition that those who seek licences agree to reciprocate.

At the request of the European Commission and/or EFTA, with regard to a specific standard or specification, ETSI can be obliged to arrange to have carried out in a competent and timely manner an investigation including an IPR search, with the objective of ascertaining whether IPRs exist or are likely to exist, which may be or may become essential to a proposed standard or specification, and the possible terms and conditions for such licences.

Under Clause 8, where a member informs ETSI that it is not prepared to licence an IPR in respect of a standard or technical specification, ETSI's General Assembly undertakes a review of the requirement for that standard or technical specification in order to satisfy themselves that a viable alternative technology is available which is not blocked by that IPR and which satisfies ETSI's requirements.

Where no such viable alternative technology exists, work on the standard or technical specification shall cease and the DG requests that the member reconsiders its position. If the member decides not to withdraw its refusal to licence the IPR it informs the DG of its decision and provides a written explanation of its reasons for refusing to licence the IP right in question. The DG sends the members an explanation, together with relevant extracts from the minutes of the General Assembly, to the ETSI Counsellors for their consideration.

Where ETSI becomes aware that licences are not available from a third party with the terms set out above, the standard or specification is referred to the DG for further consideration. The DG first requests full supporting details from members complaining that licences are not available. He then writes to the IP owner concerned for an explanation and requests that licences be granted in accordance with ETSI requirements. Where the IP owner refuses this request, or does not answer the letter within three months, the DG informs the General Assembly.

A vote is taken in the General Assembly on an individual weighted basis to refer the standard or technical specification immediately to the relevant committee to modify it so that IPR is no longer essential. Where such a vote does not succeed the General Assembly consults ETSI Counsellors with a view to finding a solution to the problem; they may also request appropriate members use their good offices to find a solution to the problem. If this does not lead to the solution, the General Assembly can request the European Commission to explore what further action might be appropriate including non-recognition of the standard or technical specification in question.

It is worth pointing out that, under Clauses 13 and 14, no decision can be taken by ETSI in relation to the implementation of the IP Policy unless supported by 71 per cent majority of the weighted individual votes cast by members. Also, any violation of the policy by a member shall be deemed to be a breach by that member of its

obligations to ETSI and the ETSI General Assembly has the authority to decide the action to be taken, if any, against the member in breach in accordance with the ETSI statutes, which includes removal.

10.6.3 US standard setting

The Alliance for Telecommunications Industry Solutions (ATIS) is a leading US telecommunications SDO which now covers the operational activities of the Committee T1 which was a part of the general US standards body, the American National Standards Institute, ANSI.[48] The Patent Policy used in ATIS' activities directly derives from, and incorporates parts of, the general Patent Policy of ANSI (see Clause 10.4, ATIS Operating Procedures). The Policy, as adopted by ATIS at Clause 10.4.2 of its Operating Procedures, begins by stating that there is no objection in principle to drafting a proposed American National Standard in terms that include the use of a patented item, if it is considered that technical reasons justify this approach. If such a proposal is submitted, however, various procedures need to be followed by members. First, and prior to the approval of such a proposed American National Standard, ATIS must receive from the identified party or patent holder either:

(1) assurance in the form of a general disclaimer to the effect that such party does not hold and does not currently intend holding any invention whose use would be required for compliance with the proposed standard; or

(2) assurance that:

    a. a licence will be made available without compensation to applicants desiring to use the licence for the purpose of implementing the standard; or

    b. a licence will be made available to applicants under reasonable terms and conditions that are demonstrably free of any unfair discrimination.

If either of these licences are to be granted, ATIS includes with the promulgated standard a note stating that attention should be given to the possibility that compliance with the standard may require the use of an invention covered by patent rights. A disclaimer states that by publication of the standard, no position is taken with respect to the validity of this claim or of any patent rights in connection therewith.

Finally, the notice points out that the patent holder has filed a statement of willingness to grant a licence under these rights on reasonable and non-discriminatory terms and conditions to applicants desiring to obtain such a licence. ATIS states that it accepts no responsibility for identifying all patents for which a licence may be required or for conducting inquiries into the legal validity or scope of those patents which are brought to its attention.

---

[48] The name Committee T1 came from its full title, ANSI: Accredited Standards Committee for Telecommunications—One.

10.6.4 The approach of standard development organizations

Essentially, irrespective of the differing administrative approach adopted to minimize conflict, SDOs can normally only rely on what is called the 'soft law approach', given their legal status. They can do their best to identify controversial IP, and try to persuade IP owners to commit to offering the IP on RAND terms. However, they do all this without the weight of legal force. The standards bodies have evidenced an exceptionally thorough policy on IP and standards issues, trying to minimize problems in an *ex ante* fashion, by attempting to ensure, so far as is possible, that those organizations that come to the table do so 'with clean hands'. They also attempt *ex post* resolution, where IP is being constrained.

One suggested method for improving matters would be to ensure that stronger, contractually-binding membership agreements are used; as envisaged, these should be in the form of 'club contracts' so that members can enforce them *inter se* and they should contain post-termination covenants to keep restraints on the activities of former members. However, there are a number of difficulties with this approach, key amongst them being:

    i. quite apart from any suspicion of compulsion over IPR licensing, compulsion in general would be viewed with suspicion in a setting where members donate time voluntarily;

    ii. actual enforcement could prove expensive and time-consuming if prior 'cease and desist' requests failed; and

    iii. there would be significant consequential issues to resolve in terms of allocation of risks/liabilities, copyright ownership, etc. which many SDOs, rightly or wrongly, prefer to leave untouched at the present time.

The present problem remains, though, that SDOs often have no measures available by which to enforce the actions suggested by the policies, other than, of course, expulsion.

Another problem that emerges when one considers the scope of the IP policies is that they are not typically inclusive of all types of IP; the ITU-T has led the way on this issue by drafting software copyright guidelines. With more areas of IP becoming important to technology, some fresh thinking on the part of SDOs might be timely; at the very least they should include a policy relating to software copyright. However, when the only censure that can be provided by the SDO is the removal of the member, the resolution of conflicts between standard and IP will continue to be *ad hoc* and problematic. Unfortunately, without the stick of the law, the only carrot that can ensure complete buy-in to the process is where some financial or competitive advantage is to be gained. In a competitive environment, agreement and reasonable compromise are not easy to achieve. In many respects, competition in the telecommunications sector has both exacerbated the conflict between IP and standards and weakened the relative power of the SDOs to respond to this growing conflict. Without the protection and security offered by a monopoly, telecommunication companies

are more likely to try to deny or unfairly control the use of IP in the standards process and less likely to compromise in the non-governmental scenario created by the SDOs. However, there may be scenarios where both the law and new non-governmental action can step in to the regulatory breach left absent by the increasing irrelevancy of the traditional standards development system.

10.7 THE INFLUENCE OF HARD LAW

While the soft law approach of the SDOs is only as effective as the intention of the parties (now in question due to competitive pressures), a number of traditional hard law remedies are available in cases concerning conflict between IP ownership and telecommunications standards. As Bekkers and Liotard have pointed out, a most interesting issue surrounding the standards/IP process is to what extent the owner of an essential IPR, perceived as required for a standard, can be forced by law, as opposed to persuaded by an SDO, to licence it to others. Competition law provides us with the most insight here.

In a European context, the presence of abusive behaviour by the owners of IP rights who also have a dominant position in the telecommunications market might speak of anti-competitive behaviour.[49] In addition, Article 81 regulates agreements between companies, so patent pooling or cross-licensing activities in standards development might come under scrutiny. The response to such activities might even be compulsory licensing or similar.

Previous European case law regarding similar circumstances provides us with some assistance. In *Volvo v Veng* (Case 238/87 [1988] ECR 6211), it was decided that a refusal to licence does not necessarily constitute an abuse. In *Magill* (Case T-70/89 [1991] CMLR 669), however, famously, television broadcasters were held liable for refusing to license programme information to *Magill* magazine. Here the Court of First Instance held that the exercise of an IPR constitutes abuse if it is used in a manner falling outside the specific subject matter of the IPR claimed. Two situations were mentioned where claiming exclusivity of an IPR might constitute abuse. First, where a company is 'preventing the production and marketing of a new product, for which there is potential consumer demand'. Secondly, if the right is used in 'order to secure a monopoly in the derivative market'. As Prins and Schiessl point out, 'assuming that the language of the CFI is sufficiently general, the first exception might be relevant in standard setting cases'.[50]

More recently, the European Court of Justice decided in *IMS Health Gmbh & Co OHG v NDC Health GmbH & Co KG* (C-418/01, Judgment delivered 29 April 2004) that the refusal by an undertaking in a dominant position to grant a licence for

---

[49] Article 82 of the EC Treaty
[50] Prins and Schiessl, n 33 above.

a copyright *can* constitute an abuse of a dominant position, but only in certain circumstances. This case involved two companies, IMS and NDC, who were both involved in the tracking of pharmaceutical and healthcare product sales. IMS provided pharmaceutical laboratories with sales data, formatted in a particular fashion: a structure of numbered 'bricks' was used, each corresponding to a particular geographical area (of, in this case, Germany). The IMS data model became, pertinently, in some sense a standard, as it was not only sold, but also distributed free of charge to medical institutions in Germany. As a result, these medical institutions became 'locked-in' to the use of the IMS methodology, changing their processes and systems to accommodate it. However, a separate company, Pharma Intra Information, began to distribute medical sales data using a similar 'brick' methodology. PII was subsequently purchased by NDC. IMS sought an injunction preventing NDC from using any structure derived from the 'brick' method it used, asserting its copyright in this database structure. The German national court was of the initial opinion that IMS could not refuse to grant a copyright licence to NDC permitting them to use the database structure, since such a refusal would constitute an abuse of a dominant position under EU law. It referred the case to the ECJ looking for particular clarification on the issue of when such a refusal to licence could be considered an abuse of dominance.

The ECJ first suggested that the national court must assess the issue of indispensability of the product or service, looking at the existence of alternative solutions as evidence either way. In the case of the 'brick' method, the ECJ pointed out that there might have been a high degree of 'lock-in', since the medical institutions that used it modified their systems to do so, but also acted to modify the structure by their use, improving it by their participation. These factors led to high dependency, making the cost, in both time and money, of changing, impractical. The ECJ then asserted that a refusal to licence cannot, in itself, constitute an abuse of dominance, since exclusive rights to reproduction are part of the copyright granted. However, the manner in which a right is exercised can, in exceptional circumstances, lead to abusive conduct. Specifically, the ECJ suggested that in order for a refusal, by an undertaking which owns a copyright, to give access to a product or service indispensable to carry on business to be considered as an abuse, three criteria must be satisfied. First, the undertaking requesting the licence must intend to offer new products or services not offered by the copyright owner, and for which there is a potential customer demand. Secondly, the refusal cannot be justified by objective consideration. Thirdly, the refusal must be such as to reserve to the copyright owner the relevant market by eliminating all competition.

In the US a number of cases have also been decided on analogous issues. In *Wang v Mitsubshi* 41 USPQ 2d 1263 (Cir Ct App 1997), the Court of Appeal for the Federal Circuit found that a patentee's conduct, including that in a standard-setting group, gave rise to a perpetual, royalty-free implied licence to Mitsubshi. In *Stambler v Diebold* 11 USPQ 2d (NY Dist Ct 1988), the plaintiff continued to sit on an American National Standards Institute Committee even after realizing that a proposed standard might infringe his patent. Stambler subsequently quit the committee

without notifying it of the alleged infringement. When Stambler attempted to enforce his patent, the District Court for Eastern District of New York considered that Stambler could not remain silent while an entire industry used the convention. The court ruled that he could not do so, on grounds of equitable estoppel and laches, finding that Stambler's course of conduct had reasonably allowed other members to believe that he would not assert any patent covering the standard's subject matter. Finally, the Federal Trade Commission also took action against Dell Corporation for unfair competition under the Federal Trade Commission Act.[51] The action was based on Dell's failure, while at table, to disclose patents as required by an SDO's rules and Dell's later conduct in trying to enforce patent rights against users of a standard adopted by the group. The result in this case was a consent order entered into whereby Dell agreed not to enforce its patent against computer manufacturers incorporating the so called VL bus design in their products.

10.8 NEW STANDARD DEVELOPMENT ORGANIZATIONS: SOME ISSUES

This chapter has focused on a number of reasonably well-developed SDOs and their regulatory policies for dealing with IP rights. However, many new SDOs have emerged which have some relevance regarding the development of telecommunications standards. Although their remit is not solely inclusive of telecommunications, their relevancy is apparent due to the increasing interconnection between the telecommunications, Internet, and computing industries, the important synergies between the three, and the momentum behind such bodies.

Of these new bodies, at least one can be considered to follow in the tradition of the established SDOs previously described. It was, initially, the Internet Society (ISOC), which took on responsibility for the Internet. The rationale for its establishment in 1992 was the supporting of the technical evolution of the network. Its role regarding standard setting and coordination then became concentrated in the Internet Engineering Task Force (IETF), a sub-committee established for developing standards. However, outside of this new, but traditionally flavoured standards body, a vast number of more informal, market or vendor driven bodies are also establishing themselves. An expected response to the laggard nature of the traditional body, one major argument in their favour is that they are able to compromise on IP issues very quickly. There are still, however, problems concerning their actions.

10.8.1 Consortia, pools, and all that

In the late 1980s and 1990s many new non-traditional technological SDOs were established, mainly in response to the technological advances of those decades.

---

[51] *Re Dell Corporation* (20 May 1996) doc #C-3685 [unreported].

In telecommunications, for example, the Asynchronous Transfer Mode (ATM) forum and the Frame Relay Forum were established. In the broader computing arena, we have the X-Window Consortium and the Open Software Foundation. Arguably, the most prominent of these new SDOs is the W3 Consortium, established in order to develop and promulgate the protocols for the World Wide Web, and illustrating that even the relatively new ISOC was already perceived as a neo-traditional SDO.

The main new actor to emerge in this standard-setting process is the consortium. A consortium is usually developed in order to effectively and efficiently commit an industry to a particular standard that is considered rapidly required, utilising stakeholder influence, and the commitment of a number of essential or major IP holders. As Wilkinson points out, 'the difference between the traditional organisations and consortia is the difference between regulatory duty and business opportunism'.[52] The most concentrated example of consortium action is the patent pool,[53] where, usually, those who own a number of essential patents for a particular standard will join up with the intention of balancing non-discriminatory and non-exclusive access to the essential patents while ensuring that adequate reward is gained for the IP owners. Such activity can be viewed as a commercial response to the perceived bureaucratic slowness of the more established SDOs. Consortia and patent pools are also rapid responses to specific and important technological issues, as was illustrated by the 3G Patent Platform Partnership. If such commercial standard-developing activity continues as now, the market-based *de facto* era of standard setting that telecommunications largely bypassed will undoubtedly come to dominate.

The main rationale for these new types of SDO is that they are a response to an increasingly technological society, and a diverse technological society at that. So much new technology requires bodies appropriately specialized to further the development of standards in these new areas, and traditional bodies might not have the ability to cope with such a rapidly changing technological landscape. As a result of this, the incumbents are feeling the pressure of bodies that are market and vendor driven and which appear to be able to develop standards at a much quicker rate. Interestingly, these new bodies might also be able to compromise on IP issues in a much quicker fashion. That is not to suggest that there is no potential for difficulty emerging regarding standards set by such new bodies and any IP owned by their members. On the contrary, aside from previously discussed issues regarding the use of IP as a bargaining tool in the standards process, a major problem with such organizations is that they might be more prone to fall foul of competition or anti-trust law. Given that such organizations are comprised of market players trying to resolve standards, there is much more potential for the problematic strategic use of IP rights.

[52] Wilkinson, S, 'The evolving relationship between patents and standards: the diamonds are safe', *Canadian Intellectual Property Review* (1999).

[53] Another example of the business consortium is the patent forum. The patent forum is more of an experts' panel which decides on issues of the essential nature of patents.

10.8.2 Consortia and competition

The idea of patent pooling organizations, or telecommunication consortia, coming together to maximize the strategic importance of their IP in the context of standards development, can have implications in competition law, especially in the EU. In the US, similar considerations apply under antitrust legislation, and with a limited form of 'safe harbour' afforded to those complying with the requirements of the Standards Development Organization Advancement Act 2004. Under Article 81 of the EC Treaty, horizontal agreements relating to IP can be incompatible with the common market, restrictive of competition, and subsequently void.[54] If the action of the patent pool or consortium is to group their IP and strategically decide not to grant licences for the purpose of advancing the standardization process to their liking, they may be acting anti-competitively, especially if the final aim is the earning of supra-competitive profits. A number of European cases illustrate this possibility.

In *Video Cassette Recorders Agreements* (OJ [1978] L 47/42, [1978] 2 CMLR 160), the Commission prevented a patent pooling scheme, citing Article 5 of the old Regulation 240/96 on Technology Transfer Agreement Block Exemptions. Article 5 prevented the cross-licensing and pooling of patents and know-how from being exempted under Article 81(3). Article 81(3) allows certain activity if it contributes to technical or economic progress. If such type of activity is allowed under Article 81(3) of the EC Treaty, as seen as contributing to technical or economic progress, an exemption can be obtained.

In the context of competition law impinging on patent pools it is important to note that in May 2004, a *new* technology transfer block exemption agreement Regulation[55] was issued which established new rules for the granting of exemptions under Article 81(3). This Regulation explicitly impacts on the establishment and practice of patent, or (as the Regulation calls them) technology, pools. The influence of the Regulation on patent pools can be distinguished between what it states regarding agreements establishing patent pools and what it states regarding licences issued by such bodies to third parties subsequent to their establishment.

First, the agreements establishing the pooling of intellectual property rights are not covered by the Regulation itself. Instead, the important Regulation Guidelines lay out in great detail the principles to be applied by the Commission and national competition authorities[56] regarding such agreements. In general, the Guidelines suggest that the attitude towards agreements establishing patent pools is to be based on the relationship between the pooled technologies and technologies outside of the pool. The Guidelines distinguish between technological complements and substitutes, and

---

[54] See further Chapter 8.

[55] Commission Regulation (EC) 772/2004 of 27 April 2004 on the application of Art 81(3) of the Treaty to categories of technology transfer agreements, OJ L123, 27 April 2004.

[56] It is also worth noting that as a result of the Council Regulation 1/2003 on the implementation of rules laid down in Arts 81 and 82, national competition authorities will have responsibility for the implementation of European competition law.

essential and non-essential technologies. To briefly explain, technologies are complementary if they are both required to produce the product or carry out the process to which they relate. Technologies are substitutes if either of them can produce the product or carry out the process in question. Essential technologies, for the purpose of the Guidelines, are those for which there is no substitute either inside or outside the pool and which are considered integral for producing the product or carrying out the process in question. Distinguishing the technologies included in a pool is the basis of any subsequent analysis of the anti-competitive intentions or effect of the pool.

For example, the Guidelines suggest that the inclusion in a pool of substitutive technologies would be restrictive of inter-technology competition and, essentially, collective bundling. If the pool is substantially composed of substitutive technologies, the arrangements are also suggestive of price-fixing. In this respect, the Guidelines suggest that the inclusion of substitute technologies in a pool is in violation of Article 81(1). In addition, they suggest that it is unlikely that the condition of Article 81(3) would be fulfilled to mitigate such violation, in the case of a pool comprising substitutive technologies. Where a pool is comprised of essential technologies, and, as the Guidelines suggest, thereby also complementary technologies, the establishment of the pool would fall outside Article 81(1) irrespective of the market position of the parties. The conditions on which any subsequent licences are granted may, however, be caught under Article 81(1), as pointed out below. The Guidelines also address certain restraints that they suggest are commonly found in technology pools and which require assessment in the context of such pools, and certain institutional issues surrounding the creation of pools.

The second role of the Regulation regarding patent pools relates to their licensing activity. Individual licences issued by patent pools to third parties are treated like any other licence agreement for the purpose of the block exemption Regulation. In this respect such licences will be exempted when the conditions established in the Regulation are fulfilled, including the requirements of Article 4 of the exemption containing the list of hardcore restrictions. The new Regulation has changed certain rules regarding the exempt or non-exempt status of technology transfer licences. First, the definition of technology transfer agreement has been extended to include the licensing of software copyright, an area becoming more relevant in the telecommunications/standards arena. Secondly, when attempting to ascertain the ability of a technology transfer licensing agreement not to fall under Article 81(1), market share thresholds are now used. Where the undertakings party to the agreement are competing undertakings, any exemption will only apply if the combined market share does not exceed 20 per cent of the relevant technology and product market. Where they are not competing undertakings, the market share condition is raised to 30 per cent.

Other sections of the Regulation outline hardcore restrictions which are not allowed (Article 4) and excluded restrictions (Article 5) which are not automatically exempted, but if excluded from the rest of the agreement will allow it to continue. Irrespective of the state of the particular rules associated with the exemption of technology transfer licences, the general policy behind any exemption is that embodied

in Article 81(3); that a licence, for example, is seen as improving the production or distribution of goods or contributing to the economic or technical progress of the Community. One might imagine that it is highly unlikely that a consortium or pool pooling their patents in order to influence standards development, could be seen as contributing to economic or technical progress, especially considering the purpose of standards. In *MPEG-2* (Case No IV/C-3/36.849, OJ C 229/19, 22 July 1998), however, the pooling of essential patents that were required for the development of the MPEG–2 video-signal standard was allowed by the Commission. Here, however, the pool had agreed to allow access to the pooled technology on a non-discriminatory and non-exclusive basis. Obviously, the objective of this pool *was* to contribute to technical and economic progress, so it can be considered as being in compliance with competition law, but it also acted in keeping with the objectives of standardization and SDOs. A similar patent consortium relating to 3G mobile telephony technologies, the 3G3P (3G Patent Platform Partnership) was established in order to allow for the systematic and organized granting of essential patents for 3G standardization. The Commission, in exploring this consortium, sent a comfort letter, distinguishing the 3G3P from a more conventional, and one assumes, anti-competitive pool, accepting that that 3G3P was not established on an anti-competitive basis, but rather allowed for extensive freedom and individuality of patents.[57] Similarly, in *X/Open*,[58] the Commission approved the activities of a group of computer companies in establishing a common application environment for the Unix operating system.

However, even if a patent pool or analogous consortium is not acting in an anti-competitive fashion, but is detrimental to the standardization process, it is unlikely that the Commission will intervene. As Whish points out, 'pooling agreements may be permitted where they are a necessary response to someone else's superior bargaining power';[59] he provides the analogous example of collecting societies. It is envisaged that if a patent pool was established in order to subvert the superior bargaining power of one operator, the rationale might be commendable, but the resultant bargaining power gained by the previously strategic minnows should not invest them with the desire to be as equally odious in their strategy as their initial combatants.

Overall, as Wilkinson has suggested, the anti-competitive effect of a consortium may well be minimal.[60] The establishment of consortia is usually undertaken to counter the strong influence of another competitor whose extensive IP portfolio might be used unconscionably. The European Commission also appears to be in favour of adopting a rule of reason approach exploring the loss of competition and the effect of the activities of the consortium in establishing a standard in balance against any losses in freedom to compete. Consortia and other *de facto* bodies are simply necessary reactions to the problems facing the traditional SDO. The difficulty

---

[57] Commission Press Release IP/02/1651, 12 November 2002.
[58] Commission Decision of 15 December 1986, OJ 1987 L 35/36.
[59] Whish, R, *Competition Law* (5th edn, Butterworths, London, 2003), 756.
[60] Wilkinson, n 52 above.

for such bodies is that competition simultaneously created problems for them, but weakened their ability to tackle the problem. The consortium has simply stepped into the breach.

10.9 CONCLUSION

The advent of competition can be viewed as the centre point around which all other issues discussed in this chapter turn.

Before competition, the telecommunications SDOs had the implicit, and possibly explicit, agreement of all parties involved. Protected from competitive pressure by national monopolies, their role in developing standards for international communications rarely conflicted with their ownership of IP.

After the introduction of competition, however, matters changed radically. Bereft of the advantages of monopolies, telecommunications providers had to turn to anything that would provide competitive advantage, and strengthen it. Naturally, IP rights were the obvious answer. Created in large numbers, given the nature of the telecommunications sector, these limited monopolies were seen as, if not replacing the leverage and benefits of their historic monopolies, then at least reflecting them.

When reminded of the important role of standards in the telecommunications industry, and of their role in helping develop them, companies began to realize that:

i. the old principles applied in the standardization process might undermine the benefits that IP now provided them; and

ii. scope existed for strategic use of IP in the standards process that might support their competitive advantages.

Allowing their IP to be subsumed into a standard, even with due compensation, was viewed by many telecommunications companies as a weakening of competitive advantage. Using the benevolent advantages of the standard to their own advantage was a natural competitive response.

Of course, the latter perspective was anathema to the principles of the SDO and to the notion of standards themselves. The SDOs were still, correctly, advancing the traditional benefits of standardization to the public and to industry. In light of this they have developed their IP policies to attempt to prevent the conflict of interests between IP and standards. However, without the force of law, they rely on consensual agreement to prevent and resolve such conflicts. Ultimately, because of competitive pressures, telecommunication companies cannot act in a truly consensual way. Unless there is some benefit to be gained, it is difficult to envisage companies readily compromising for the good of industry standards. As such, while competition elevated IP, and brought it into conflict with standardization, it also degraded the ability of parties to come together and suitably resolve such issues consensually.

As has been illustrated, hard law and new SDOs are emerging as possible reme-dies, or at least responses, to the difficulties created by competition. Hard law, mostly in the shape of competition law, can potentially require the compulsory licensing of IP. New non-traditional SDOs can accommodate the competitive pres-sures of the telecommunications industry and hopefully advance standardization without unduly conflicting with IP. The only problem with the non-traditional SDO is that, without the benefit of non-commercial interest, its actions can be, or be directed towards, anti-competitive practice, designed only to advance proprietary interests rather than the broader public good. It is even possible now, especially given IT and telecoms convergence, that proprietary *de facto* standards might emerge as predominant in the telecommunications industry. In this respect, the irony is that the standardization process will have removed IP conflicts, by making standards IP, rather than using IP in standards.

Part IV

TELECOMMUNICATIONS TRANSACTIONS

11

CAPACITY AGREEMENTS—FROM MICROWAVES TO MOBILE VIRTUAL NETWORK OPERATORS

Rhys Williams and Graeme Maguire*

11.1 INTRODUCTION

11.1.1 What are capacity agreements?

In a competitive communications environment, capacity agreements enable operators at every level to offer their customers more choices, to develop innovative new product offerings, and to increase revenue. This in turn encourages increased competition and enhanced efficiency in communications facilities.

In the broadest sense, capacity relates to the ability of a communications network to carry information. It can be measured in a number of ways, from the number of bits per second that can be transferred over a line or the number of calls that can be carried simultaneously to the bandwidth of a coaxial cable.

Electronic communications operators require capacity in order to sell services to their customers. Accurate capacity planning is essential for operators seeking to

* The authors would like to thank Richard Graham, associate, Bird & Bird, for his assistance with this chapter.

establish themselves in the market. If they have too little capacity, calls will fail and transfer times will slow down. Excess capacity, however, will simply lead to wasted costs. Having access to a wide range of capacity agreements enables operators to ensure they have sufficient capacity for all their customers' needs when they need it.

It should be noted that in this chapter, the term 'capacity agreement' is used to denote the contractual arrangements between different communications operators. The term can be (and often is) used to describe the contractual relationship between an operator and its customers, especially in relation to business-to-consumer (B2C) leased lines and IPLCs (discussed briefly further below). However, the primary focus of this chapter is on business-to-business (B2B) capacity agreements.

11.1.2 History

Capacity agreements have developed since the liberalization of the communications market and the introduction of competition. Originally, when there was only one incumbent operator in each market, that operator built and operated its own network and determined how much capacity each element of the network required.

With the introduction of competition, however, it soon became apparent that operators were not going to build complete competing infrastructures. Some competing networks were established, in particular in the major metropolitan areas, but substantial areas of the country continued to be served by one or perhaps two networks. In addition, other operators entered the market without owning any infrastructure at all, and these 'reseller' operators instead purchased capacity from other operators at wholesale prices, then on-sold that capacity at retail prices or used it for particular services or applications.

As new services were developed, so demand for capacity grew, encouraging the network operators to design, build and deploy new networks with ever greater capacity. Fibre-optic systems began to replace the traditional copper wire systems, not least because of the advantages they offered over the old systems, such as cost, digital signalling functionality, and reduced signal degradation. Fibre-optic systems are basically thin filaments of glass through which light beams are transmitted. The light beams carry information in digital form, sent through the fibre strand over a predetermined wavelength. Because light can only travel in one direction, fibre-optic systems are often (but not always) deployed in fibre pairs to enable simultaneous two-way communication.

As the communications industry developed into an international then a global industry, so operators became more willing to purchase capacity from their competitors. This was particularly true of capacity on undersea cables, which were originally constructed by consortia of incumbents, who quickly realized the opportunities for profit from the hoards of new entrants to liberalizing markets in the late 1980s and early 1990s.[1]

---

[1] See further Chapter 15, at 15.2.2.

By the late 1990s, at the peak of the first telecoms/e-commerce boom, a number of operators began using capacity swaps as a means of boosting their sales figures. The basic idea of a capacity swap, whereby Company A provides capacity to Company B in exchange for similar amounts of capacity in a different geographic location, was sensible and logical for operators having different capacity requirements in different places and building out their own networks at differing times. However, a number of capacity swaps were also recorded internally as sales, apparently boosting revenues and/or profits for companies whose internal auditing processes were perhaps not as robust as they should have been. The bursting of the dotcom bubble that followed shortly afterwards resulted in a number of these companies entering Chapter 11 bankruptcy proceedings, although not necessarily directly as a result of having swapped capacity with each other. Capacity swaps still take place today but there are fewer of them and the appropriate accounting treatment is now clear.

As technology evolved, so communications companies developed new methods of increasing capacity on optical fibres, for example through wavelength division multiplexing (WDM). WDM increases the capacity of a cable by transmitting multiple signals simultaneously over the same optical fibre but at different wavelengths. Lit optical fibres traditionally supported one light stream, using one frequency of light. First introduced in the 1980s, WDM technology was originally limited to two wholly discrete frequencies on the same fibre. Since the 1990s, however, and the introduction of dense wavelength division multiplexing (DWDM), communications companies have been able to support an increasing number of separate wavelengths through constantly expanding channel counts and faster supported TDM (time division multiplex) rates within the individual wavelengths.[2]

The potential bandwidth in optical fibres is vast, with over 160 channels capable of being run through a single fibre, enabling operators to provide large amounts of capacity with an advanced degree of product differentiation. Each wavelength can carry any communications protocol containing voice, data or video traffic, with bandwidth rates up to 40Gb/s.

This constantly increasing capacity has coincided with the exponentially increasing demand for capacity from end-users due to the growth of the Internet and longer connection times for data traffic. Interestingly, after a number of years in which commentators have suggested that there was a substantial surplus of bandwidth, novel bandwidth-hungry applications such as video-content services are once against driving the demand for capacity especially in the fibre-to-the-home market across Europe. This in turn will drive the continued evolution of the capacity agreement market.

In today's market, capacity agreements represent a substantial element of legal practice in the sector, for the same reasons as before: they facilitate increased and

---

[2] See further Chapter 2, at 2.1.3.

efficient use of communications networks. Agreements range from simple deals for voice minutes and gigabits, through to satellite transponder capacity and complex mobile virtual network operator (MVNO) arrangements.

11.2 TYPES OF CAPACITY AGREEMENT

11.2.1 Leased lines

Wholesale leased lines, also known as private lines, dedicated lines or permanent circuits, are perhaps the simplest form of capacity agreement. A leased line is basically a fixed circuit linking two locations, rented from another communications provider for a specific period of time. The circuit or line is usually provided at a number of different speeds, ranging from 64Kbps to 155Mbps or even higher.

The availability of leased lines was a key enabler to facilitating the effective establishment of competition in the communications marketplace. The early EU communications regulatory regime required ex-incumbent operators to make available leased lines to the new entrants.[3]

In most jurisdictions, leased lines have become commoditized. If the purchaser does not like what is being offered by one operator, it can ask another operator to provide a competing quote.

Traditional leased lines using analogue or digital circuits and SDH (synchronous digital hierarchy) and PDH (plesiosynchronous digital hierarchy) transmission are now being superseded in many instances by alternative methods of transmission, notably ethernet technology.[4]

In addition, partial private circuits (PPCs), which provide dedicated transmission capacity between an end-user's premises and an operator's point of handover, with the remainder of the circuit being provided by the operator from whom the PPC is rented, offer purchasers a further alternative solution. The key to the attraction of PPCs, indeed the key to the attraction of all capacity agreements, is ownership of the end-user. The operator that rents the PPC retains billing control over and controls the relationship with its own customer.

PPCs, as a microcosm of leased lines, offer an economic solution to not having a fully national network, enabling operators to obtain extensive national coverage with minimal investment costs and the ability to configure the circuits to provide required capacity (and security) requirements.

A further sub-set of leased lines comprises International Private Leased Circuits (IPLCs or International Private Line Circuits in the USA). An IPLC is a point-to-point circuit line offered by operators to end-users to provide a communications link between two (or more) offices of the same organization based in different parts of

---

[3] See further Chapter 5, at 5.6.
[4] See further Chapter 2, at 2.1.7.

the world. The ending of the BT/Mercury international facilities duopoly by Oftel in 1996, which enabled new entrants to provide International Facilities Based Services, including facilitating the use of IPLCs to do so, played a key part in the development of international communications as other countries followed the UK's lead.

Unlike a traditional leased line, however, an IPLC is not a single dedicated circuit. Rather, it is a service offering termination services between two (or more) pre-defined points, although the operator may route traffic through a variety of different networks between those points. This has the benefit of a lower cost, but has the potential problems of different traffic engineering processes or unexpected traffic volume surges impacting on transmission speeds.

11.2.2 Indefeasible rights of use

Historically, indefeasible rights of use (IRUs) developed as a term of art to describe certain long-term leases of part of the capacity of an international submarine cable. The capacity is specified in numbers of channels of a given bandwidth. Many of the original IRU arrangements were for very long terms (25 years was typical), which led to a number of significant implications later on which we discuss below.

As noted earlier in this chapter, the original undersea cables were constructed by consortia of incumbents. The original consortia have now largely been replaced by individual companies or joint ventures, although it is not uncommon for new consortia to be formed to construct systems. The membership of the consortia has changed, however. Global liberalization, enabling operators to hold licences or be authorized to operate in multiple jurisdictions, has removed the original need for foreign partners, and many operators have experienced the difficulties of managing by committee, as a consortia requires.

The first 'undersea' cable was actually laid under the River Thames in 1840, and by 1850 a cable connected England to France. An undersea telegram cable linked Ireland and Newfoundland in 1858. The first transatlantic telephone cable system, TAT-1, was constructed in 1956 and the first transatlantic fibre-optic system came into service in 1988. The oceans of the world are now dotted with submarine cables.

The success of subsea and long distance cables also drove the development of bandwidth technology, in particular the invention of bi-directional analogue technologies in the early 1960s, superseding the requirement for a separate cable for each 'direction' of traffic.

In order to ensure resilience, IRUs can be purchased in pairs, on two separate cables (operators may have other contingency arrangements in place—for example a satellite link). The intention is that if one is accidentally cut, for example by a ship's anchor in shallow water, the built-in redundancy of the design will permit uninterrupted service because all traffic can be automatically routed via the surviving cable. Usually, this works well: simultaneous cuts on two separate subsea cables are a relatively rare—if still alarming—event. As a general rule, once a subsea cable is laid, the only risks it faces are if it is in an earthquake zone or a heavy fishing activity area.

IRUs can be purchased in pre-existing systems. More commonly, however, they are purchased in systems that are being built or that have just been built. This acknowledges the fact that technology continues to develop at a very fast rate, and even relatively new subsea cables are quickly superseded by faster and cheaper designs.

Early purchasers of IRUs in a planned subsea cable system are often granted capacity bonuses on the basis that their committed participation makes initial funding by the cable owner far simpler and may also encourage other operators to become involved.

The term 'indefeasible' is something of a misnomer, given that IRUs are not indefeasible and no legal title passes to the purchaser. Rather, an IRU is a long-term 'lease' that cannot be terminated by the cable owner (or other superior rights holder) other than in particular specified and limited circumstances, for example the insolvency of the purchaser, or the purchaser's failure to contribute to maintenance costs.

Unlike a traditional leased line, whereby the renting operator pays fixed periodic charges (usually either monthly or quarterly), an operator purchasing an IRU historically paid a substantial upfront sum on execution of the agreement, but then is only liable for ongoing maintenance costs. The single upfront payment has advantages for both the purchaser and the seller. The latter is able to book revenue earlier than it would be able to for a normal leased line. The former can take advantage of specific capital allowances for IRUs, enabling them to obtain tax deductions for depreciation. This was not an issue when those providing the IRUs were incumbent or ex-incumbent operators and credit risk was not even perceived as an issue. However, after the significant expansion of communications operators and the bursting of the 'bubble' in early 2001 many of these arrangements looked far from sound with hindsight. Fundamentally, IRUs are usually, from a legal perspective, contractual rights. Having paid significant sums up front for a contractual right is not necessarily an argument that takes you very far in discussions with an insolvency practitioner trying to maximize value from the assets of a failed operator. A lot of time and effort was spent in attempts to characterize IRUs as property rights, but to little or no avail.

The term IRU now has a much wider usage than the original IRU arrangements on undersea cables discussed above. Many capacity arrangements are characterized as IRUs, including arrangements that might be considered to be leased lines (see above) or dark fibre arrangements (see below). It is important to look below the label and understand the reality of the arrangements that are being put in place and the associated risks and how these are most appropriately addressed.

11.2.2.1 Tax treatment of IRUs
From the perspective of purchasers of IRUs, it is worth noting briefly the UK tax treatment of the cost of acquiring IRUs after 21 March 2000. Broadly, for UK tax purposes, the acquisition of an IRU (or rights derived from an IRU) from the owner of a cable system is treated for income tax purposes as an allowable revenue deduction for the purchaser and not as capital expenditure. The relevant legislation for

income tax purposes was set out in Schedule 23 to the Finance Act 2000 but this has now been rewritten into Parts 2 and 5 of the Income Tax (Trading and Other Income) Act 2005 (ITTOIA) with effect from 5 April 2005. In ITTOIA, IRUs are defined as 'indefeasible rights to use a telecommunications cable system'. Any IRU relating to a cable or to a system a part of which comprises a cable will therefore by caught by ITTOIA. IRUs in any medium other than a cable (e.g. a duct) will fall outside the relief. For corporation tax purposes, the rules on the taxation of intangible fixed assets as set out in Schedule 29 to the Finance Act 2002 apply to IRUs with effect from April 2002 (subject to transitional rules), so that profits and gains in respect of IRUs acquired by a corporate purchaser are chargeable to corporation tax as income in accordance with their accounting treatment. Under Schedule 29, a deduction would be afforded to a company in respect of expenditure on the IRU on an amortized basis i.e. over the life of the IRU. In either case, any income or proceeds derived from the purchaser's subsequent exploitation, disposal, or revaluation of the IRU will be taxable income. If the purchaser of an IRU does not have a trading activity, it will be subject to tax on income derived from the IRU but, in calculating the amount of net income which is chargeable, it would still be able to make a deduction for the acquisition costs of the IRU. However, this treatment may differ where the non-trading income consists of 'annual payments' against which no expenses or deductions may be made, since this form of payment would instead be subject to deduction of tax at source under the UK's withholding tax regime.

From the perspective of the owner of a cable system, the grant of an IRU by the cable-owner is not affected by the tax treatment of IRUs for purchasers. For UK tax purposes, the grant of an IRU by a cable-owner might be considered as either giving rise to (i) a trading receipt where the grant is part of the owner's normal exploitation of the cable system, or (ii) a capital receipt derived from the use or exploitation of its cable system. Where the receipt is a capital sum, the cable-owner will not be regarded as having disposed of the cable network itself, and neither will it be treated as having disposed of absolute ownership of the rights to use the cables. Instead, the cable-owner will only be taxed on the capital sum (less any allowable costs) on the basis that it has received consideration for granting a right of use of part of the cable system to the person acquiring the IRU. Similarly, for UK capital allowances purposes, since the grant of an IRU is not treated as a part 'disposal' of the cable system itself, the owner continues to be entitled to capital allowances on its original cost of installing the system.

11.2.3 Dark fibre

As a general rule, one of (if not) the largest expenses faced by any communications network provider is installing that operator's cables in the ground. It is commonly estimated that between 60 per cent and 80 per cent of the entire cost of a fibre optic network can be spent on the civil engineering work necessary to design, construct, and connect it. The actual infrastructure itself is relatively cheap. As such, it makes

obvious commercial sense for operators to install more fibre than actually currently required at time of build in its ducts and channels, in order to provide for future network development, resilience, and on-sale opportunities of leased lines and dark fibre (this, of course, is part of the reason for the bandwidth surplus noted above).

The term dark fibre has been defined in a variety of different ways over the years. Some have argued that it is any optical fibre that is not attached to transmission equipment at all. Others have suggested it is fibre that is not attached to transmission at only one end, so is awaiting additional work before it can be utilized. Certainly, there appears to be common consensus that it is optical fibre through which no light and thus no signal is being transmitted. Fibre through which light is being transmitted, and which is carrying a signal, is known as lit fibre. There is also something of a halfway house known as 'dim fibre', which is a term used in DWDM. DWDM supports as many as 160 wavelengths, each of which is a different frequency of light. Thus, when some wavelengths are left 'dark' and some are 'lit', the resulting fibre is 'dim fibre'.

11.2.4 Satellite capacity agreements

Satellite capacity or transponder leasing agreements are increasingly becoming a more important option in respect of both telecommunications and broadcast capacity in circumstances where terrestrial arrangements offer no practical solution, where there are temporary surges in demand requirements, or as a back-up method of service provision. In a global telecommunications network, satellites can provide key links to the Internet backbone and multiple fibre networks. The commercial value of satellite communications technology extends beyond traditional telecommunications services, and satellites play a fundamental role in a wide range of services, including high-speed Internet and multimedia, direct-to-home high definition television, radio, GPS, maritime, defence, and private VSAT network solutions.[5]

One of the key areas of activity in the satellite communications sector is the practice of transponder leasing. Transponder leasing allows satellite operators to lease and allot segment capacity on their satellites to customers, either on a permanent or an occasional-use basis. A transponder, basically a microwave relay circuit, on a satellite receives signals from earth stations, amplifies them, changes the frequency, and then relays the signals back to earth. The advance in compression and multiplexing technology has allowed transponders to carry multiple types of voice, data, audio, and video transmissions on one transponder. By leasing capacity to numerous telecommunications operators, broadcasters, and corporate customers, satellite operators are able to generate significant revenue. Associated contractual arrangements include up-linking services and facility arrangements.

The key providers of transponder leasing capacity in the satellite industry include Inmarsat, SES, Eutelsat, Intelsat, AsiaSat, Intersputnik, and COMSAT. As with all

---

[5] See further Chapter 15, at 15.2.1.

capacity providers, satellite operators view the ability to book and manage redundant capacity as an integral part of generating revenue. They are therefore willing to invest significantly in developing systems that allow both themselves and their customers to choose their capacity to suit their requirements as and when they arise.

11.2.5 MVNO Agreements

A mobile virtual network operator (MVNO) is a telecommunications service provider that offers mobile telecommunications services to customers, but which does not itself have a network or the licence to use an allocation of spectrum.[6] It is the mobile equivalent of the 'resellers' discussed above. An MVNO does this by procuring wholesale services from a mobile network operator and then reselling such services to its own customers. The classic MVNO model is a business with a well known consumer brand leveraging its brand into mobile communications such as Virgin and Tesco. A number of MVNOs have also positioned themselves to appeal to specific target customer groups, for example cost-sensitive customers who do not require any value added service elements. Some have used the MVNO model as a way of expanding their product portfolio from a pure fixed telephony offering to also include mobile telephony.[7] Others have adopted innovative business models such as relying significantly on advertising revenues.

There are various attractions for commercial entities wishing to set up such ventures. Most significantly MVNOs will not be required to invest in infrastructure assets. This significantly reduces the capital expenditure required to enter the mobile marketplace and provides a potentially shorter route to profitability. The downside is an MVNO's margins can be significantly more exposed when retail prices fall. A typical MVNO will own and activate its own SIM cards, a key differentiator between an MVNO and the pure service providers that played an important part in the early development of the mobile market in the UK. It will also set off its own tariffs (against the backdrop of the wholesale tariffs it pays the mobile network operator), manage billing and account authentication, own its subscriber database, and control customer service, distribution, branding, and marketing.[8] Some deploy significant intelligent network infrastructure to enable them to offer a broader range of differentiating value added services.

There are also benefits for the mobile network operator providing the services to the MVNO in terms of gaining additional usage of capacity on its network, thereby generating further revenues; though there will clearly be a potential risk of loss of customers to the MVNOs. There has consequently been a lot of debate around the part regulation needs to play in facilitating MVNOs. However, the light regulatory touch currently applied in the UK seems to have been the right approach; at least so far. The EU has been keen to encourage the development of MVNOs and has issued

---

[6] Ofcom, 'The International Communications Market 2006'.
[7] See Ofcom 'The Communications Market—Interim Report, February 2006', section 11, p 86.
[8] See Ofcom 'The Communications Market—Interim Report, February 2006', section 11.

a recommendation to NRAs to examine the competitiveness of the market for call termination on individual mobile networks.[9] In the UK, the MVNO arrangements are not facilitated by regulation requiring mobile network operators to enter into MNVO arrangement but rather are very much left as a commercial matter to be negotiated between the mobile network operator and the potential MVNO. Further, an MVNO is not required to comply with any specific MVNO regulations in addition to the general requirements set out in the General Conditions of Entitlement.[10] The approach does vary in certain European jurisdictions and a number of regulators have introduced measures requiring mobile network operators to open up their networks to MVNOs.[11] All regulators are keeping a keen eye on how this important market continues to develop within their respective jurisdictions.

There are now a number of successful MVNO arrangements in place in the UK, with Virgin Mobile's telecommunications supply agreement with T-Mobile being the most notable with over four million UK customers.[12] The number of MVNOs has increased significantly over the last decade with the new EU communications regime, and across the globe there are well in excess of 200 such arrangements in place. With service providers increasingly offering bundled products to their customer base, the addition of mobile products to their portfolio will increase the attractiveness of MVNOs.

The backbone of any MVNO arrangement is the ability of the MVNO to resell the airtime it has purchased from the mobile network operator under its own branded service. This ability to purchase wholesale extends beyond the basic purchase of minutes to SMS, MMS, GRPS, and 3G/HSDPA capacity as well.

For mobile network operators, there are a number of reasons for allowing MVNOs to use their networks. MVNOs offer an ability to lease excess capacity on the operator's purchased spectrum, with the responsibility for marketing and customer support often being dealt with by the MVNO. MVNOs provide the mobile network operator with an opportunity to generate economies of scale in respect of its network utilization. MVNOs may also provide the mobile network operator with the ability to reach market niches that would not otherwise be reached under its own branding strategy.

11.3 KEY CONTRACTUAL ISSUES

11.3.1 Introduction

Although some types of capacity agreement, such as leased lines and IRUs, have in effect become commoditized, thus leaving little scope for negotiation of individual terms, there remain a number of key issues to bear in mind in every capacity agreement.

---

[9] Commission Recommendation of 17 December 2007 (2007/879/EC).
[10] <http://www.ofcom.org.uk/telecoms/ioi/mnvo/>.
[11] E.g. see Commission Press Release IP/06/97 of 31 January 2006 re Spain.
[12] <http://www.virginmobile.com>.

As with any written contract, certain provisions will usually be included in a capacity agreement, in particular payment terms, limitations on and exclusions of liability, termination, confidentiality, and traditional boilerplate provisions. In addition, the following provisions will need particular attention in any bespoke capacity agreement.

11.3.2 Service level agreements

As with any commercial contract, service level agreement (SLA) response times often have a bearing on the charges paid for the service. Clearly, one party's commitment to provide services of a specified standard and within a specified period will cost a purchaser more than a promise to use reasonable endeavours to achieve those standards with a light service credit regime. In addition, many providers will argue that SLAs are non-negotiable because they have to provide the same level of service to all their clients. This is fine, but the charges therefore may be negotiable.

One particular issue under capacity agreements, however, is repair times. Does the offering provide for network redundancy to ensure resilience? Put another way, can traffic be switched instantly to a diverse path in the event that the primary traffic path fails? What is the guaranteed speed of restoration? This is particularly important for subsea capacity in that it will always take longer to send a ship to repair a cable breakage at sea than it will to repair a cable break on land. Equally, the speed of restoration on subsea cables can be faster if a party owns and staffs facilities such as cable landing stations or other access points itself, and so does not require consent to access such premises. This is also clearly the context behind the discussion below in relation to the options under the pre-emption regime in relation to transponder capacity on satellites.

Negotiations tend to focus around key definitions such as 'availability' and how planned and emergency maintenance is to be dealt with. It is also important to understand the balance between the margin a supplier may be making on providing the services and the potential impact on the customer if the services are not provided. Clearly resilience and diversity have roles to play here in appropriate circumstances. Many SLAs will be backed up by service credit regimes which will provide some limited redress if the contracted availability is not achieved without the customer having to claim and prove its loss.

It is widely acknowledged that leased lines play a vital role in business communications in the UK, at both a retail and a wholesale level. It is therefore important that the markets for these services operate effectively and competitively. As such, it is not surprising that Ofcom has focused regulatory attention on the markets.

Where an operator has had an SMP determination made against it by Ofcom,[13] its SLAs may be open to regulatory analysis. For example, in late 2007, a number of operators complained to Ofcom that Openreach's SLAs for wholesale line rental (WLR), local loop unbundling (LLU), and ethernet services were ineffective because

---

[13] See further consideration of SMP obligations in Chapter 8.

they did not provide Openreach with sufficient incentives to provide or repair services. As a consequence, the operators argued Openreach's service performance had been unsatisfactory. Ofcom considered the complaint and found for the operators, directing that amendments be made to Openreach's SLAs.[14]

Dark fibre raises interesting SLA issues in that the apparatus attached to each end of the fibre is the user's responsibility, but the connection may be the fibre owner's (or a third party's) responsibility. It is important that this is clearly addressed in any dark fibre agreement to ensure clarity of obligations.

Further, there are a number of different product specifications for dark fibre at an ITU level. The capacity of an optical fibre to accept transmission technology (such as WDM) depends upon its specifications. Thus, given the speed with which technology is developing, purchasers should be conscious of the risks of entering into any long-term contract for dark fibre without being certain that the fibre is 'future-proofed' and comfortable that its transmission properties are sufficiently clarified in the contract.

11.3.3 Term

The ideal term of an agreement will obviously vary depending on a number of factors. In relation to capacity agreements, particular factors to bear in mind include:

- security—a longer term contract provides more security than a shorter term, in that on-going costs are known and the purchaser will have the comfort of knowing that it will not have to find replacement capacity on short notice;

- cost—a longer term can usually be purchased more cheaply (relatively speaking) than a short term. If the capacity being purchased is a fundamental part of the purchaser's service offering, the purchaser may want a longer term contract to ensure continued supply;

- scalability—if an operator is expecting to expand quickly, it will want an option to increase capacity quickly and simply. In which case, it may be sensible to seek to tie all related capacity agreements to the same termination/expiry date for ease of internal administration;

- risk aversion—short-term contracts lower the barriers to exit in the event of a market downturn. During the dotcom boom, operators entered into very long-term contracts, but then struggled to exit those contracts when the bubble burst. This is the obvious counterpoint to the issue of contractual security noted above;

- competition—in a competitive market, prices will be driven down as innovation and technology develops. Short-term contracts enable purchasers to take advantage of new service offerings such as enhanced speed or lower latency.

---

[14] See Ofcom, 'Service level guarantees: incentivising performance', 20 March 2008.

11.3.4 Access

Like simple leased lines, the majority of dark fibre agreements are now commoditized standard terms. Key issues to bear in mind, however, remain the same as when early dark fibre agreements were negotiated. Given that the purchasing operator is responsible for attaching electronic communications equipment and lasers to light the fibre at each end (unless the vendor is providing a managed service), the purchaser will want to ensure that it has appropriate and sufficient access rights at each end. The seller will usually want as long a term as possible, but with the option of early termination should it decide to alter the physical architecture of its network.

11.3.5 Relocation of apparatus

Even with the protection of Code Powers, and in particular paragraph 21 of the Telecommunications Code,[15] there is always a risk that an operator will have to relocate its apparatus at some point during the term of a capacity agreement. The seller will therefore want to address this possibility in the capacity agreement. Equally, the purchaser will want to ensure that if any relocation is required, its access to the capacity and its costs will remain unaffected through a temporary (or permanent) re-routing of traffic.

11.3.6 Testing

The IRU agreement itself may or may not contain testing procedures for the entire cable system. It should certainly contain testing and acceptance provisions for the IRU circuits themselves. ✓

11.3.7 Satellite capacity contractual issues

Transponder leasing arrangements tend to be on standard terms offered by the satellite operator and scope for any significant negotiation is often limited. The contracts contain the general terms that you would expect to find in B2B commercial arrangements. However, certain key terms require more attention to deal with the nature of satellite capacity.

Transmission plan: The transponder leasing agreement will ordinarily contain a detailed transmission plan setting out a detailed description of the usage and technical parameters of the signals to be transmitted to the satellite.

Compliance with laws: Although an obligation to comply with all necessary laws is common in general commercial arrangements, transponder leasing arrangements tend to focus particular attention on the laws that the satellite operator and customer must comply with. The satellite operator will generally be required to

---

[15] Sch 2 to the Telecommunications Act 1984. See further Chapter 7, at 7.4.4.4.

ensure that all approvals and consents are obtained in respect of the leasing of the satellite capacity. On the other hand, the customer will often be burdened with the requirement to ensure that it complies with all laws in force in the country of transmission of the up-link signal and, more onerously, in the countries where the footprint from the satellite is able to be received (usually referred to as 'landing rights'). The Audiovisual Media Services Directive (previously the Television Without Frontiers Directive) can be highly relevant here to lightening some of the regulatory burdens, but any detailed discussion is beyond the scope of this chapter.[16]

Force majeure and exclusions of liability: The relationship between force majeure and unavailability is particularly important in transponder leasing agreements. With the risks of adverse atmospheric conditions such as solar flares and sun outages being highly relevant, the satellite operator will be keen to ensure that the definition of force majeure and exclusions of liability provide appropriate protection for the satellite operator. It is important that the customer understands the implication of these and what arrangements are available to mitigate the consequences.

Rights of pre-emption and restorability: As the ultimate aim of any satellite operator is to ensure that all its capacity is used, there will be scenarios where capacity cannot be offered to those requesting it, whether due to excess capacity requirements on the allotted transponder or by the downtime of alternative transponders. The satellite operator therefore has to prioritize allocation of capacity and, where designated capacity is not available, offer alternative capacity. The relevant terms used to describe the prioritization are whether there is a right of pre-emption over the capacity and whether the capacity is restorable:

- where there is a right of pre-emption over a customer's satellite capacity, the satellite operator can use the allocated capacity to restore other customers' services;

- where there is no right of pre-emption then the satellite operator cannot use the allotted capacity for other customers;

- where the satellite capacity is deemed to be fully restorable, then should the customer's allocated transponder fail, the customer will be provided with an alternative transponder on the same satellite. If the satellite fails, then the customer will be provided with capacity on an alternative satellite to the extent possible; and

- where the satellite capacity is not restorable, then in the event the transponder or satellite fails, the customer will not be provided with alternative capacity.

The customer's needs and what it is willing to pay together with the strength of the customer's negotiating position will ultimately dictate what priority it has over other customers. The following scenarios illustrate the hierarchy of customer rights:

1) the satellite capacity is non pre-emptible and fully restorable;

2) the satellite capacity is non pre-emptible and non-restorable; and

---

[16] See further Chapter 14, at 14.3.3.2.

3) the satellite capacity is pre-emptible and non-restorable.

It is very important to look carefully at how these terms are used in different transponder leases including whether pre-emption rights are in favour of the satellite operator or the customer.

Earth stations: It will be usual for satellite operators to require its customers to ensure that the earth stations used for transmitting the signals to the satellites meet certain requirements. The customer will generally take the risks arising from non-compliance with these requirements.

Right to resell: The extent to which the customer under a transponder leasing arrangement may resell any allotted capacity, if at all, is clearly a key issue.

Fixed/occasional-use capacity: Historically satellite capacity tended to be leased on a permanent basis. However, the requirement for the occasional use of satellite capacity has become increasingly important in the satellite capacity sector. In respect of broadcasting, the transmission of live broadcasts away from the studio (e.g. Anfield or the Millennium Stadium) has contributed to an increase in the number of occasional-use satellite capacity arrangements.

Rights of cancellation: The customer's right to cancel any allotted capacity will ultimately depend upon the negotiated position. It is unusual for a customer to be able to terminate allotted capacity once it has entered into a long-term supply arrangement without paying significant early termination charges. In respect of occasional-use capacity, there are general rights to withdraw capacity on agreed notice provided that a minimum commitment is achieved over the term of the agreement.

11.3.8 MVNO contractual issues

The contractual arrangements in place with the MVNO and the mobile network operator will vary significantly depending on the nature of the network and the size of the MVNO. The telecommunications regulation in the particular territory may also impose certain requirements. Certain key terms contained within the MVNO arrangements include the following:

Pricing: The MVNO will want to be able to work independently of the mobile network operator and set its own pricing structures, though clearly it will need to pay the charges it has agreed to pay to the mobile network operator, and competition law will clearly be relevant where the mobile network operator tries to dictate what prices must be charged.

Branding: This is clearly a key issue given in many cases it is leveraging a well known consumer brand that is at the heart of the MVNO business plan. Many Tesco Mobile subscribers may not know that the underlying network used is the O2 network.

Term/exclusivity/minimum commitment: As you would expect these issues are at the heart of the commercial deal. The MVNO will need to ensure that it has the ability to move to a different mobile operator or at least use this possibility as leverage when terms are renegotiated and extended.

Promoted services: Contractual provisions will apply in respect of the services that the MVNO is able to provide and promote. In the field of mobile communications, new services are regularly developed as a way of creating extra revenues. MVNOs will require flexibility to procure and offer these services to their own customers. However, the mobile network operator will be keen to ensure that the MVNO does not profit from these opportunities to the detriment of the mobile network operator's customer base.

Customer services and billing: The MVNO agreement will document who will be responsible for customer services and billing. If the MVNO has such responsibility, the contractual arrangements will need to document how information is passed between the systems and how customer service issues are ticketed and resolved.

Handset procurement: The arrangements in place dealing with the procurement of handsets will ultimately vary depending on the nature of the relationship with the mobile network operator. The MVNO may have independent arrangements in place with the handset manufacturers or may be able to benefit from the mobile network operator's bulk purchasing arrangements.

11.4 REGULATORY ISSUES

As the electronic communications market has liberalized, so the regulatory burden on operators in the sector has become lighter. Today's market is a long way from the market of the 1990s, when specific individual licences were required by operators offering services either in the UK or in undersea capacity internationally. In jurisdictions outside the UK, of course, different regulatory regimes will apply though there is now significant harmonization throughout the EU Member States as a result of the EU communications regulatory regimes. The focus of this chapter, however, has been on the UK capacity market.

As discussed further in Chapter 7, under the Communications Act 2003, General Conditions of Entitlement apply to anyone who provides an electronic communications service[17] or an electronic communications network.[18] The General Conditions replaced the previous regime of individual licences granted under the Telecommunications Act 1984. A capacity agreement, depending on the type of capacity being purchased and the other provisions of the contract, may be a contract for an electronic communications service or an electronic communications network. In either case, both the buyer and the seller of the capacity will have to ensure that they comply with the relevant General Conditions that apply to them, and these will vary on a case-by-case basis, because differing conditions apply to operators, depending on what services or networks they are providing. The consolidated General Conditions are set out on Ofcom's website.[19]

---

[17] Defined in s 32(1) of the Communications Act 2003.
[18] Defined in s 32(2) of the Communications Act 2003.
[19] <http://www.ofcom.org.uk/telecoms/ioi/g_a_regime/gce>.

Many capacity agreements, such as PPCs, are also access services and as such regulated under the Access and Interconnection Directive.[20] Access agreements are addressed further in Chapter 8, but in brief, if an operator has been found by Ofcom to have significant market power (SMP)[21] in any relevant market, Ofcom may impose conditions on those operators, in particular in relation to ensuring that charges are on cost-orientated terms and are not unduly discriminatory.

In its market review of 2004, Ofcom found that Kingston Communication had SMP in the Hull area and BT had SMP in the rest of the UK for the retail market for low bandwidth 'traditional interface' (TI) markets (such as analogue circuits or digital circuits using SDH and PDH transmission), the wholesale markets for low and high bandwidth TI terminating segments and the 'alternative interface' (AI) market (e.g. ethernet) for terminating segments at all bandwidths. BT was also found to have SMP in the UK market for trunk segments.

As a result of these findings, a number of obligations were imposed on BT and Kingston, including obligations to supply, requirements not to discriminate unduly between customers, requirements to publish prices, terms, and conditions, and, in some cases, price controls.

In a further market review in early 2008,[22] Ofcom found that progress towards more effective competition had varied considerably by market. It proposed that:

- outside the Hull area, a separate market now existed for wholesale AI services at bandwidths over 1Gbps and that this market was effectively competitive, so no SMP regulation was required;
- a new geographical market in high bandwidth wholesale terminating segments existed in Central and East London and that again it was competitive and no SMP regulation was required; and
- the market for low bandwidth TI retail leased lines in Hull was now competitive and so could be deregulated.

Ofcom found other markets also to be effectively competitive and so no longer subject to SMP regulation, but others were still less competitive than they had been two years previously. SMP regulation has therefore been retained in a number of markets where operators are purchasing capacity.

In the same review, Ofcom also considered whether or not BT should be required to provide dark fibre in the access network (that is to say, from a business customer site to the Local Serving Exchange) as a means of promoting more effective competition in the downstream market for leased lines. Ofcom's initial view was that a dark fibre product would fall within the definition of an Electronic Communications

---

[20] Directive 2002/19/EC on access to, and interconnection of, electronic communications networks and associated facilities (OJ L 108/7, 24 April 2002).
[21] Defined in s 78 of the Communications Act 2003.
[22] Ofcom Business Connectivity Market Review Consultation, 17 January 2008 <http://www.ofcom. org.uk/consult/condocs/bcmr>.

Network under the Communications Act 2003, so Ofcom could therefore find that an operator has SMP in that market (and thus impose obligations on that operator). Ofcom was not persuaded, on initial view that any operator did have SMP in the relevant market. Ofcom invited interested parties to provide their views by the end of March 2008 on whether or not BT (or any other provider) might have SMP in the relevant market and, if so, whether the benefits of mandating a dark fibre access product would outweigh the costs. At the time of writing, Ofcom has not yet made a final determination.

As noted above there has been a lot of debate around the part regulation needs to play in facilitating MVNOs. However, the light regulatory touch currently applied seems to have been the right approach at least so far. In the UK, an MVNO is not required to comply with any specific MVNO regulations in addition to the general requirements set out in the General Conditions of Entitlement. As noted earlier, however, several countries do impose regulatory requirements on MVNOs aimed at facilitating the access MVNOs require.

There are significant regulatory issues in relation to the provision of satellite services, including under the International Telecommunications Union's Radio Regulations.[23] These are mainly an issue for the satellite operator but if a customer under a transponder lease and associated arrangements is providing its own uplink service it will need to comply with the relevant requirements set out in the General Conditions of Entitlement and the Wireless Telegraphy Act 2006 and regulations issued under it. Consideration will also need to be given to any regulation relevant to the landing of the signal in relevant jurisdictions.

In addition, of course, operators are also bound by the rules of general competition law, in particular Articles 81 and 82 of the EC Treaty. Further details on this can be found in Chapter 9, but the Articles are targeted at prohibiting two types of practice: anti-competitive agreements and abuse of dominance by a dominant undertaking.

11.5 EMERGING TRENDS

It is possible to identify a number of trends from considering the experience of the UK market in relation to capacity agreements.

The UK has historically been at the forefront of market liberalization and technological development in the communications sector. Thus, the current market in the UK may provide some useful guidance on emerging trends internationally.

Novel regulatory or technological developments, such as fibre to the corner (FTTC), fibre to the home (FTTH), and digital subscriber line access multiplexer (DSLAM) open up a range of potential new capacity arrangements that operators can negotiate between themselves.

---

[23] See further Chapter 15, at 15.3.4.

In addition, operators today widely acknowledge the cost and difficulties inherent in constructing competing infrastructures. This is particularly true in the mobile market, where 3G networks (as a result of the higher frequency range and the requirement to transmit large amounts of information) require smaller cells, more base stations, and additional macrocells, microcells, and picocells than the 2G network. This results in a corresponding increase in build and maintenance costs. As a result, some operators are entering into infrastructure sharing agreements (which may take a variety of forms, from creating a JV vehicle to building/running/maintaining the infrastructure, to the simple sharing of space, masts, or buildings). However the parties agree to divide their respective responsibilities, there will be a requirement for each to enter into capacity agreements with the other.

Lastly, it is clear that one of the major themes emerging from the Framework Review[24] is the continued drive at EU level for further deregulation across Europe. From the perspective of capacity agreements, it is very likely that this will result in a reduction in the number of regulated markets. As such, certain obligations will be removed from operators previously deemed to have SMP within such markets (although general competition law will of course continue to apply to deter any anti-competitive practices).

---

[24] 2007 Review of the EU Regulatory Framework, dated 13 November 2007.

12

COMMUNICATIONS OUTSOURCING

Michael Sinclair

12.1 INTRODUCTION

12.1.1 What is outsourcing?

12.1.1.1 *General*

Outsourcing has recently come to mean sourcing externally anything that would otherwise have to be provided internally in order to support business operations. However, the traditional conception of an outsourcing is somewhat narrower than this contemporary meaning. It connotes two elements:

1) the transfer out of the business of some kind of infrastructure into the new outsourced service provider; and

2) the provision by the new outsourced service provider of some kind of service back to the business.

12.1.1.2 Transfer of infrastructure

The infrastructure to be transferred may be made up of a combination of one or more of employees, land and buildings, other physical assets, the benefit of contracts, licences (including for software and intellectual property rights), other intangible assets (such as intellectual property rights), documentation, and other information and data. The infrastructure transferred usually consists of everything owned or used by the customer in order to provide the service itself prior to the outsourcing.

The transfer is usually effected by a transfer agreement under which the customer transfers ownership of all assets owned by it and assigns the benefit (or novates) contracts and licences to the outsourced service provider. The transfer agreement is usually entered into for a nominal consideration and often resembles a sale of business agreement. The outsourced service provider may push for the inclusion of warranties in relation to the condition of assets included in the infrastructure. Such warranties are very often resisted by a customer on the basis that the infrastructure is required merely for use by the outsourced service provider for a temporary period before the infrastructure is supplemented or entirely replaced (by a new and improved infrastructure in order to achieve enhanced service provision).

In the most basic kinds of outsourcing there may be little or no transfer of infrastructure. This may be because no infrastructure is required in order to provide the service, the supplier intends to use its own infrastructure to provide the service, or because the infrastructure will be entirely replaced by a new and improved infrastructure.

Where no infrastructure is transferred or used in the provision of the service, the boundary between outsourcing and a mere services agreement is difficult to draw, and the blurring of this distinction explains the contemporary use of the word 'outsourcing' to cover services agreements as well as the more traditional infrastructure/service back outsourcings. In this chapter 'outsourcing' refers to the traditional meaning of that word.

12.1.1.3 Coupled with service back

Once the infrastructure has been transferred to the outsourced service provider, it uses that infrastructure to provide a 'service back' to the customer. The service will fall somewhere in the continuum between a 'process outsourcing' and what can (for want of a better expression) be called a 'functionality outsourcing'.

A functionality outsourcing, in simple terms, means the provision of a function formerly provided in-house by the business to itself. A classic example might be the provision of IT and IT support. Process outsourcings, in contrast, do not involve the provision of a discrete function used in the operation of the business, but rather involve the outsourced service provider performing a business process or range of

processes formerly performed by the business itself. An example is accounting and related business processes, human resources, payroll, and supply chain management.

Process outsourcings depend upon mapping the processes used to achieve the result required. Functionality outsourcings, on the other hand, rely on providing the function itself.

12.1.2 Rationale for outsourcing

12.1.2.1 Concentrating on core business

The decision to outsource as a business strategy gained considerable support from economic arguments underlying national privatization policies implemented by various governments, both in the UK and abroad. Underlying these policies is the idea that governments should concentrate on their core activities and divest themselves of functions and processes which are not truly governmental in character.[1] Similarly, the economic rationale for outsourcing is that it allows a business to concentrate on its core activities, leaving functions and processes in respect of which it is not an expert to be performed by an expert (the outsourced service provider).

The outsourced service provider, in supplying similar services to numerous customers, achieves economies of scale and is able to pass the resulting savings back to the customer in the form of reduced costs for the provision of the service.

12.1.2.2 Application to communications arena[2]

The core business of most companies is not, of course, communications, but communications networks are at the core of many of their daily operations. Because communications services are inherently technology-dependent, a business's communications infrastructure may quickly become outdated. This is one reason why outsourcing is attractive, because the outsourced service provider, through benefits obtained from economies of scale, may be able to implement regular technology refreshes.

The growth in the dependence on computers in business has also led to the convergence of computer and communications technology in the areas of data transfer and data networks that (in the case of a large business) may be national or global in scale. Because of the difficulties in maintaining the integrity of a national or global network, businesses increasingly look to outsource the provision and maintenance of such networks.

---

[1] See Sinclair, M, 'Common Constraints in Public and Private Law Over the Exercise of Privatised Functions' (PhD dissertation held in the Cambridge University Library, 1994).
[2] See, generally, Sinclair, M and Durie, R, 'Telecommunications Outsourcing', in *Outsourcing Practice Manual* (Sweet & Maxwell, London, 1998), chap I; Sinclair, M, 'IT and Telecoms Outsourcing In Europe and the Law', in *The Strategic Guide to Outsource IT and Telecoms* (World Trade Magazines, London, 1999) at 42; Sinclair, M, 'Telecommunications Outsourcing', in *Technology Outsourcing—A Practitioner's Guide* (Law Society Publishing, London, 2003), chap 4.

In a traditional outsourcing the customer is concerned only with the service or the outcome, and not with the method by which it is achieved. However, communications services present challenges for this traditional model because a business wanting an outsourced communications solution, while caring about the standard of service it receives, may also care about the technology platform upon which that service is delivered. It is for this reason that a communications outsourcing tends to raise more technology-related issues than other types of outsourcings.

12.1.3 Issues applying to all outsourcings

12.1.3.1 *Improved service*
Outsourcings often involve the transfer of functions and processes that, to the business, have been problematic in terms of service delivery and that have led to dissatisfaction with that service. The business will frequently look to the outsourced service provider to improve upon that service. This finds its most basic expression in the fact that many outsourcings involve a gradual (or even immediate) replacement of existing infrastructure with an improved infrastructure designed to enhance service delivery.

There may be a migration period during which the service provider is given grace before improving service levels, but it is almost always the case that the customer will expect improved service levels over time. This is certainly true of communications outsourcings, where the customer will expect existing communications infrastructure (such as handsets, switches, routers, leased lines, and cabling) to be replaced very quickly after service commencement. Service levels (for example, successful call connections, repair of defective equipment, network down time) will also be expected to improve.

12.1.3.2 *Decreased involvement of management*
All outsourcings are characterized by decreased involvement of a business's management in the daily operations of the outsourced service. Indeed, the relevant management personnel may themselves be transferred to the outsourced service provider as part of the infrastructure transfer.

12.1.3.3 *Reserving strategy/policy decision-making function*
A business outsourcing services to an outsourced service provider will generally wish to reserve certain high-level policy or strategic decision-making powers to itself. In the context of communications, this might include decisions about matters as simple as the required functionality for handsets, up to sophisticated policy decisions about the extent to which the service provider ought to be required to use certain types of network technology. Reserving policy decision making may also extend to technology refresh and replacing technology infrastructure over time. A customer certainly would not wish to be locked into a type of technology that

quickly became outdated, or that made it difficult for the customer to bring the service back in-house at the end of the outsourcing agreement.

12.1.3.4 *Transfer of assets*
As mentioned at section 12.1.1.2 above, most outsourcings involve the transfer of some form of infrastructure. At its most sophisticated, this will be by way of a transfer agreement resembling a sale of business agreement. At its most simplistic, it could be by way of one or two clauses in the outsourcing agreement that transfer ownership of assets referred to in a schedule. The question of consideration should always be dealt with, as the transfer of assets may involve stamp duty or other tax implications. In the context of communications, the transfer of assets may also involve obtaining certain consents in relation to software or other licensed rights used in relation to the assets transferred. This issue is discussed in detail at section 12.4 below.

12.1.3.5 *Transitional arrangements and migration to new service*
Most outsourcings involve a grace period during which the supplier prepares to migrate to the new service levels. This is normally by way of a migration plan, which is essentially a time line with stepped service levels. Very often transitional arrangements will be required during which there is a handover of the infrastructure from the customer to the supplier as and when consents for the transfer of certain assets or licences are obtained. The outsourcing agreement will have to provide for the allocation of responsibility during such transitional arrangements.

The received wisdom is that customers should not enter into outsourcing agreements without having final service levels and the date at which they are to apply. This is because, once the outsourced service provider has had transferred to it the infrastructure, it in effect holds the customer as a 'captive audience' because the customer will not easily (without considerable cost and effort) be able to take the service back in-house. Accordingly, unless the customer has agreed the final service levels prior to the outsourcing taking effect, it will have little bargaining power to push for final service levels that are acceptable to it after that time.

12.1.3.6 *Council Directive 2001/23/EC—allocating liability*
Outsourcings frequently involve the transfer of personnel from the customer to the outsourced service provider along with the accompanying infrastructure. At the end of the outsourcing those personnel, if used primarily for the provision of services to the customer, may find that the supplier no longer requires their services. In the interim the personnel may have changed over time, as the supplier may have taken on additional personnel to meet the new service levels required.

The provision of the service may be transferred back in-house to the customer, or it may be sourced from a new service provider. In either case, the personnel used by the incumbent service provider may make claims for redundancy or unjustified dismissal against the incumbent service provider, the customer, or successor service provider under regulations implementing Council Directive 2001/23/EC on the

approximation of the law relating to business transfers. In the UK these regulations are the Transfer of Undertakings (Protection of Employment) Regulations 2006 (SI 2006/246).

The Directive and the implementing regulations are intended to provide protection to employees who, because of an outsourcing (or at the end of it), find their terms and conditions of employment have changed to their disadvantage, or who find that they are now without employment as a result of an outsourcing (or at the end of it). For example, a communications expert retained by a business that subsequently outsources its communications infrastructure to a communications service provider may find that, if the parties have not agreed that the service provider will employ the communications expert, he or she is without employment. In these circumstances the employee may claim that the communications 'undertaking' has transferred to the new service provider and that the 2006 Regulations therefore deem the new service provider to be his or her employer. Because the new service provider has disclaimed responsibility for employing that communications expert, the communications expert has a claim against the new service provider.

The Directive and the implementing regulations have the effect, by automatic operation of law, of deeming an employee to be employed by one or other of the parties. Because the parties are unable to avoid this effect by agreeing contractual provisions to the contrary, it is usually the case that they will agree to allocate liability by way of indemnities under the outsourcing agreement. For example, a customer might agree to indemnify the supplier for all claims made against the supplier by employees arising prior to the date of transfer, and the supplier may agree to give a similar indemnity for all post-transfer liabilities.[3]

12.1.3.7 Technology refresh

Many outsourcings are to a greater or lesser extent technology-dependent. Where the technology is key to the provision of an adequate service, it will be important for the customer to negotiate obligations on the part of the outsourced service provider to update the technology from time to time. If the customer does not do this there will be no incentive for the service provider to update the technology over time, as this will be a cost that it cannot recoup.

Technology refresh is particularly important in communications and IT outsourcings, where the rapid pace of technological change means that systems and networks quickly become outdated. Communications service providers will frequently argue that it should not matter to the customer what form of technology platform is used to deliver the service as all the customer should be concerned about is the standard of service received. However, as mentioned at section 12.7 below,

---

[3] See Sargeant, M and Vassell, R, 'Employment Issues' in *Technology Outsourcing—A Practitioner's Guide* (Law Society Publishing, London, 2003), chap 9.

frequently customers will have certain minimum technology platform requirements to which they require outsourced service providers to adhere.

12.1.3.8 *Network security (IT security and data security)*

If the outsourced service provider provides or has access to the customer's networks and systems, and has access to or stores or processes the customer's data, the outsourcing agreement should provide for IT and data security. Generally, there should be a provision which requires the outsourced service provider to take all steps in accordance with best industry practice to prevent the introduction of viruses into the customer's systems and networks, and to prevent corruption of the customer's data; and provision for an indemnity if it fails to take such steps and the customer suffers damage as a result.

If the outsourced service provider is storing or processing the customer's data then, if those data are commercially sensitive or otherwise confidential in nature, the outsourced service provider should be required to store them logically and physically separate from the data it holds in relation to its other customers. Protections such as these become very important in the case of communications outsourcings, because communications networks may be used to transfer data which, if corrupted, may cause business losses to the customer and the customer will wish to ensure that its voice and other networks are not being hacked. For this reason, it may be necessary to require the outsourced service provider to implement monitoring systems against breaches of security and promptly to inform the customer if it becomes aware of any breaches of security.

12.1.3.9 *Exit management and successor supplier*

Early outsourcing agreements very often did not provide for what would happen at the end of the outsourcing relationship. The outsourcings they implemented were characterized by a protracted negotiation towards the end of the relationship during which the customer would sometimes be 'held to ransom' by the existing supplier who, because it knew that it would be losing the contract, wished to extract maximum revenues for any handover or termination services it had to provide.

The infrastructure and existing know-how very quickly come to reside with the existing outsourced service provider. Accordingly, unless the outsourcing agreement provides for obligations on the outsourced service provider to provide handover services, the customer will be in a weak position to negotiate for such services at the end of the relationship. For this reason an outsourcing agreement should provide for a detailed exit management plan which the existing supplier must implement and follow during the final stages of the relationship. This could include (in the case of a communications outsourcing) requiring the outsourced service provider to:

  i. undertake an audit or inventory of all existing handsets, switches, and other equipment used by it to provide the services;

  ii. provide a list of all leased lines and other contracts used by it in providing the services;

iii. provide details as to the numbering plan used for the customer's networks;

iv. provide a database of the configurations and a database of helpline call resolutions; and

v. provide all other documentation and process maps used by it in providing the services.

The outsourced service provider should be required to provide all cooperation and assistance reasonably requested by the customer to achieve a smooth transition from the existing outsourced service provider to the customer or a successor supplier as the new supplier of the services. Although it might be reasonable for the existing outsourced service provider to charge for such services, generally these rates should be agreed in advance, or they should be at no more than the outsourced service provider's existing consultancy rates. The outsourced service provider should also be required to assist the customer in porting the existing telephone numbers to any new supplier (this is discussed in detail at section 12.5.3 below).

As the customer may wish to buy back certain infrastructure, or to send it on to a successor supplier, the pricing principles and obligation to sell such equipment should be prescribed in the outsourcing agreement. Generally, outsourced service providers are only too willing to sell existing infrastructure back to customers because, of course, second-hand IT and communications infrastructure is not particularly valuable. It is also a way of recouping certain costs which would otherwise be sunk costs not able to be recovered by the outsourced service provider.

The exit provisions in the outsourcing agreement might also need to provide for the grant of any intellectual property rights or software licences owned or used by the outsourced service provider in providing the services.

12.2 TYPES OF COMMUNICATIONS OUTSOURCING

12.2.1 Voice

Voice is the most common type of communications outsourcing and involves the outsourcing of standard telephony infrastructure to the outsourced communications service provider. This may include transferring handsets to the outsourced communications service provider which it will subsequently update. The outsourced service provider then provides standard voice lines at agreed PSTN tariffs.

12.2.2 Voice over Internet protocol

Voice over Internet protocol (VoIP) refers to packet data transmission of voice using Internet protocols (IP). Transmission is most commonly over the Internet, although IP can equally be used as part of a dedicated leased line infrastructure. The uptake of VoIP has for quite a long period been slow because of concerns about quality,

resilience, and integrity of carriage across the Internet but quality has been improving steadily. VOIP is already in use on trunk routes by carriers to provide traffic between PSTN networks, especially internationally, and has, with the advent of widely available broadband, made inroads into the consumer mass telephony market.

A VoIP outsourcing is most likely to be considered where the customer is migrating to a data IP network and wishes to include voice within the data carried.

12.2.3 Data

It is also very common to outsource the carriage of data traffic. Data communications outsourcings are distinguished from voice outsourcings by virtue of the increased need for bandwidth capacity.

There is, of course, no sharp distinction between voice and data outsourcings, because increasingly voice data packets are sent across the data network. Similarly, facsimiles sent via the voice network blur the distinction between the two. With VoIP the distinction has blurred further by the sending of voice packets or data across the Internet (and then into communications connections linked to the Internet).

12.2.4 Mobile data—WAP applications

Customers in communications outsourcings may now ask their outsourced service provider to provide an option for the customer to request mobile data functionality. This involves the use of a wireless application protocol (WAP) which is the radio frequency spectrum equivalent to protocols used for the Internet.

WAP does not increase the bandwidth or data carrying capacity of a mobile network but allows that network to carry information otherwise carried through wires in accessing the Internet. WAP has increased in relevance with the commercial availability of third generation (3G) mobile telephony (discussed at section 12.2.6 which offers the greater bandwidth capacity required for its application.

12.2.5 Networks

The outsourcing of the carriage of voice and data traffic invariably involves outsourcing of the accompanying networks. This can include switches, routers, leased lines, other dedicated lines, cabling infrastructure, and associated software. Networks can include local area networks (LANs) and wide area networks (WANs) (discussed below).

12.2.5.1 *LANS*
At its most simple, a LAN consists of a local network of computers linked to central servers. The most common type of LAN is a computer network used within a single building. WLAN is the wireless (WiFi) variant of this network type.

12.2.5.2 *WANs*

A WAN consists of the communications links linking LANs. It may link buildings, local offices in an entire country, or be global in nature. A WAN can cover both voice and data, but it is normally used for data.

12.2.5.3 *Virtual private networks*

A virtual private network (VPN) is a software-driven dedicated communications network designed to act as if it were dedicated to the particular customer (even though at any time lines used by a VPN may carry the traffic of more than one customer). A VPN is private in the sense that it is intended to guarantee the provision of bandwidth capacity required by the customer at any time, allowing the customer to 'burst' above its usual capacity requirements and have the network meet such requirements. It is a 'virtual' network in the sense that the software driving it does not depend upon a dedicated route for the data.

12.2.6 Mobile telephony

A mobile telephony outsourcing in many respects looks just like a mobile communications services agreement, except that existing handsets and user contracts in relation to those handsets may need to be transferred to the outsourced service provider.

Mobile telephony outsourcings will become more important with the advent of 3G mobile telephony, which brings with it the ability of mobile telephony to provide increased bandwidth capacity (allowing faster and greater access to the Internet in conjunction with WAP). Third-generation mobile telephony licences allocating the new frequencies to be used by 3G in the UK were awarded to five operators in June 2000, but uptake has been relatively slow.

12.2.7 Audio and video conferencing

With various pressures giving rise to efforts to reduce air travel, suppliers of audio and video conferencing services have seen an increase in the demand for their services from large business customers. Many large organizations see the advantages of costs savings and of an enhanced service by outsourcing their audio and video conferencing requirements. This will usually involve the transfer of the existing in-house equipment to the supplier, followed by the replacement of such equipment over time. There will often be a migration plan to migrate the service to IP and the supplier will usually provide a managed service under which calls may be booked and connected electronically or through human agency.

The increasingly wide and relatively inexpensive availability of web-based conferencing (relying on IP service), including desk-to-desk conferencing, may cause the volume of such audio and video conference outsourcing to level off or even decrease over time.

12.2.8 Call centres

Although not strictly communications outsourcings as such, call centre outsourcings tend to involve numerous communications-related issues. This is because call centre outsourcings may often involve the outsourced service provider taking over communications infrastructure to provide call centre services.

12.2.9 Maintenance

In a full communications outsourcing, the provision of network maintenance will be part of the service. For example, the outsourced service provider will be required to fix network down time and call failures within time frames specified in the service level agreement. However, a customer might wish to maintain ownership and operation of, say, its data network, but outsource the maintenance of that network to an outsourced service provider. Here the service levels will relate to fix times.

12.2.10 E-commerce-related infrastructure

With increased use and reliance by business on the Internet as an accepted basis for conducting business, Internet and e-commerce-related infrastructures are being outsourced. These very often involve communications infrastructures. Some examples are set out below.

12.2.10.1 *Dedicated trading information exchanges*
Dedicated trading information exchanges can take various forms over the Internet. A common example is where a service provider provides a customer and its suppliers with access to a dedicated server containing information posted there by the customer and its suppliers. In this way the customer and suppliers can exchange information on a secure basis over the Internet without the need to use more complicated electronic data interchange (EDI) arrangements which had, until the advent of the Internet, been the general way of exchanging supply chain information electronically in a secure fashion.

The information exchange is 'dedicated' in the sense that passwords are given out by the customer to its suppliers and no one else may (in the absence of hacking) access information held on the server without such passwords. The customer may also seek additional security comfort by requiring the service provider to provide the data in encrypted form when they are released from the server.

12.2.10.2 *IP tunnelling*
IP tunnelling uses encryption technology for the creation of what are, in effect, dedicated lines of communication maintained through communications networks into and across the Internet and out into the communications network on the other side between nodes of a WAN. The most common example is a business wishing to

exchange information internally to other offices across the globe through the use of the Internet. IP tunnelling can be used for both voice and data, and the technology both overlaps and relies upon encryption software.

12.2.10.3 *Encryption*
Because technology in the communications and Internet arenas is converging, communications service providers providing data traffic carriage across communications lines into the Internet are often being asked to provide a 'one-stop shop' through secure encryption of the data transferred. This can apply also to voice transmissions.

12.2.10.4 *Application Service Provider (ASP) applications*
'ASP' is commonly referred to as 'renting software' or 'bureau use' of software over the Internet. Put simply, it means that a customer does not itself need to be licensed to use software in order to have its data processed by that software, but instead pays a subscription fee to a service provider who provides or 'rents' access to the software over the Internet. The use of ASP applications generally involves large bandwidth capacity, and it is for this reason that communications service providers are particularly interested in this kind of technology.

12.2.11 Cabling and related infrastructure

The outsourcing agreement will need to define the boundary (if any) between the network and services provided by the outsourced service provider and any retained network held by the customer. For example, the customer might wish to outsource everything from the exit terminal from its private automatic branch exchange (PABX) to the outsourced service provider. This would mean that it would retain responsibility and ownership of the PABX, cabling, and related physical infrastructure, including handsets, within its building. However, the more common type of outsourcing involves the outright transfer of the entire infrastructure, including cabling and handsets.

The Electronic Communications Code (the Code) provides that, as between the owner of land and the operator of electronic communications apparatus (the operator), the operator owns the cabling installed on, under, or attached to land or any building.[4] In this way, the Code overcomes the outcome that would result from the law of fixtures.

Under the Code, an operator is required to remove cabling when it ceases to provide a service and there is no prospect of the cabling being used by the operator.[5]

---

[4] As set out in Sch 2 to the Telecommunications Act 1984 as amended by Sch 3 to the Communications Act 2003. The Electronic Communications Code gives operators the right to carry out works of specified kinds, to install and keep installed, and to have access to any installations and apparatus on land belonging to others (often referred to as Code Powers) if certain conditions are satisfied. In addition, operators with Code Powers benefit from some important exemptions from the Town and Country Planning regime. Ofcom is the body responsible for the administration of the Electronic Communications Code under the Communications Act 2003. See further Chapter 5, at section 5.3.3.4.

[5] Clause 22 of the Code.

Therefore, if, at the end of an outsourcing, a customer wishes to retain cabling, etc. installed by the operator (this will be important where the customer wishes to take the service back in-house, and to achieve a smooth transition to a new operator), the outsourcing agreement should provide that the operator shall not have the right to remove any cabling installed by it and that it shall permit the customer or its successor supplier to use it to provide the services.

12.2.12 Co-location/hosting

At the edges of the outsourcing spectrum are co-location/hosting arrangements under which an incumbent operator hosts or permits a competitor to site its own equipment at, say, the incumbent's local exchange so that the competitor can send and receive traffic directly from the local loop.

12.3 REGULATORY ISSUES SPECIFIC TO COMMUNICATIONS OUTSOURCING

An outsourced service provider running an electronic communications network is regulated under the Communications Act 2003 just like any other similar service provider. The shift away from licensing is perhaps the most significant change to the communications sector under the new regime.[6] However, changes have been ushered in across the sector and the regulator, Ofcom, continues the consultation and review process in respect of the many aspects of the operations of communications providers.

The operations include, in the UK, price regulation, number portability, data protection, carrier pre-selection, the provision of a universal service, the availability of certain information (including technical interface specifications for network access), and the provision of leased lines with specific capacity and transparent pricing. This regulatory framework is discussed in other chapters of the book and is beyond the scope of this chapter.

12.4 TRANSFERRING THE INFRASTRUCTURE

12.4.1 Transferring physical assets

Physical assets include PABXs, switches, routers, cabling, and handsets. If owned by the customer, they are usually listed in a schedule to the transfer agreement and transferred by way of sale to the outsourced service provider (usually for a nominal consideration).

---

[6] See further Chapter 3.

It is important to agree a consideration for these assets, as there may be stamp duty implications. There are also VAT concessions available if physical assets, together with all other assets comprised in the undertaking, are transferred in a way that enables the transfer to be viewed as the transfer of a business as a going concern. Article 5 of the Value Added Tax (Special Provisions) Order 1995 has the effect that, if the transfer is not a supply of goods or services but a sale of a business as a going concern, it is not subject to VAT.

As assets transferred may include embedded software, it is important to check any documentation under which such assets were originally supplied for restrictions against on-sale or for obtaining consent for on-sale.

12.4.2 Novating existing service contracts

Where a business conducts its business operations at a range of sites in one country or in more than one country, it may well be the case that it has existing service contracts with suppliers on a regional basis which cannot be terminated before the implementation of the new outsourcing arrangement. Where that is the case, unless these overlapping contracts can be terminated with the agreement of the existing supplier, the customer will be left paying twice for the service after the outsourcing.

In such circumstances the new outsourced service provider should be required, either before or as part of the migration process, to enter into negotiations with existing suppliers for the novation of existing suppliers' service contracts to the new outsourced service provider. These contractual provisions can appear either in the outsourcing agreement or in the accompanying transfer agreement. They normally provide for the allocation of costs, responsibilities, and for pre- and post-transfer indemnities for existing service contracts novated.

Where existing service contracts cannot be novated the customer may wish to oblige the outsourced service provider to take on the role of contracts manager (this is discussed at section 12.4.8 below).

12.4.3 Novating leased-line contracts

Just as with other types of existing service contracts, where the customer uses leased lines in providing itself a communications network prior to the outsourcing, it will be necessary to have these terminated or transferred to the outsourced service provider. There are very often fixed costs associated with terminating leased lines. A comparison will need to be made as to the relative cost of terminating or transferring leased lines.

12.4.4 Novating managed switches

The customer may, prior to the outsourcing, have already outsourced the provision and maintenance of switches to one or more service providers. In an entirely 'managed

service' outsourcing the customer will wish to relinquish responsibility for managing these relationships and will wish the outsourced service provider to take over the switches themselves (or to supply replacement switches). Accordingly, the provisions dealing with novation of existing contracts should also cover managed switches.

12.4.5 Novating network software licences

In a very limited number of circumstances the customer may be using free-standing diagnostic or other network software in the operation of its network (an example is Novell software). If the existing infrastructure is to be used for a time after the outsourcing is to take effect, the licence for the use of the software will need to be novated to the outsourced service provider or it will need to obtain its own licence to use this software. The principle is the same as the novation of other existing service contracts.

12.4.6 Obtaining consent

The contractual provisions in the outsourcing agreement or the transfer agreement need to allocate various responsibilities to the customer and the outsourced service provider for obtaining consent to the assignment or novation of the various contracts and licences referred to above.

If the customer is in a particularly strong bargaining position it may be able to get the outsourced service provider to assume sole responsibility for obtaining such consent (and for implementing replacement systems and services at its own cost if such consent is not obtained). The circumstances in which a customer might achieve this position are relatively rare.

It is more usual that the obligation to obtain consent is a shared responsibility, and the real issue becomes who should bear the cost of procuring replacement systems if consent is not obtained. This is something which should be specifically provided for in the contractual provisions.

12.4.7 Procedure if consent is not obtained

The contractual provisions relating to consent should say that if consent is first refused, the relevant party should continue to attempt to procure such consent for a period (to be specified) and the other party should provide reasonable assistance in procuring such consent. The provisions should be clear about whether efforts to obtain such consent and to provide such assistance include the payment of money. If consent is not obtained after a certain period of time, the contracts or licences at issue should fall into the class known as 'managed contracts'. Sometimes the parties agree from the outset that certain contracts will not be novated but will be managed (as 'managed contracts') on an ongoing basis by the outsourced service provider.

12.4.8 Managing suppliers not novated

Where contracts and licences cannot be novated, or it is agreed that they will not be novated, the customer should require the outsourced service provider to assume the role of managing agent in relation to those contracts. This will mean that the outsourced service provider, and not the customer, will be responsible for their day-to-day administration and for liaising with the existing suppliers in relation to the customer's requirements. This will enable the customer to receive a seamless service (called a 'managed service') and a one-stop shop from the outsourced service provider.

12.4.9 Allocation of liability—novated and managed contracts

As mentioned at section 12.4.2 above, the contractual provisions should provide for a pre- and post-transfer indemnity in relation to existing contracts and licences which are novated to the outsourced service provider. For example, claims relating to a contract novated which relate to the period prior to the novation should generally be borne by the customer, and it should indemnify the outsourced service provider if such claims are made against the outsourced service provider.

Similarly, where the outsourced service provider manages existing contracts and licences which are not novated, the customer should ask for an indemnity for claims made against it arising out of the outsourced service provider's activities beyond the scope of its authority to manage those contracts.

12.5 CONTRACTUAL ISSUES SPECIFIC TO COMMUNICATIONS OUTSOURCING

12.5.1 Restrictions on network use

The outsourced service provider will generally require the customer to agree in the outsourcing agreement that the customer shall not use the services for the transmission of any material which is defamatory, offensive or abusive, or of an obscene or menacing character, or in a manner which constitutes an infringement of the intellectual property rights of any person.

12.5.2 Security and network access

The customer will want to ensure that the outsourced service provider maintains high standards of security to protect the outsourced network from unauthorized access, which could lead to breaches of confidentiality and loss and/or corruption of the customer's business critical data. Therefore the outsourcing agreement should contain provisions in respect of the key elements needed to ensure the network remains secure.

12.5.2.1 *Access codes*

Authorization codes and passwords will need to be classified as confidential information, and both the customer and outsourced service provider should be obliged to notify the other if they know or have reason to believe that such codes have been obtained or used by unauthorized third parties. The customer will want the agreement to provide that it will not be liable for service charges in relation to network access obtained by use of access codes which it has instructed to the outsourced service provider to be withdrawn.

The agreement should also contain adequate provisions detailing specific security measures required of the outsourced service provider to protect the confidentiality of the access codes.

12.5.2.2 *Security policies*

The outsourcing agreement should provide that the outsourced service provider must comply with agreed security policies, including those in respect of:

    i. outsourced service provider personnel access being limited to those persons whose access is necessary in connection with the service delivery;

    ii. relevant industry standards such as ISO9001, ISO20000, and ISO 27001; and

    iii. industry best practice measures regarding virus detection software and virus prevention generally.

The customer will wish to include indemnities in respect of losses caused by the outsourced service provider's breach of such provisions.

12.5.2.3 *Customer data*

The customer will wish to ensure that the outsourced service provider observes detailed, industry best practice rules to protect the confidentiality, integrity, and security of the customer's data. The outsourcing agreement should include provisions with respect to data back-ups, data storage and encryption standards, password routines, and treatment of personal data. The customer will wish to impose an obligation on the outsourced service provider to report any unauthorized access to the customer's data.

The customer should insist that the cost of restoration measures, when data is lost or corrupted due to the outsourced service provider's acts or omissions, is borne by the outsourced service provider, and that the customer is entitled to take any such restoration measures itself if reasonably required.

12.5.2.4 *Security audits*

The customer will want to include a provision in the agreement that entitles it to have access, on short notice, to the outsourced service provider's systems and premises in order to audit the security and integrity of the outsourced service provider's systems

and procedures, and to establish compliance with the security provisions of the outsourcing agreement.

12.5.2.5 Unauthorized access and service charges

The customer will want comfort in the outsourcing agreement that it will not have to pay any service charges arising out of hacking of the network by unauthorized third parties. Accordingly, the outsourcing agreement should provide that, where there is such unauthorized use of the network, the customer shall not be liable to pay service charges unless such authorized use results from:

    i. the negligence, fraud, or failure by the customer to keep equipment physically secure from unauthorized use; or

    ii. the disclosure by the customer of passwords supplied to it by the outsourced service provider for accessing the network.

12.5.3 Number portability

As explained in detail elsewhere in this book, in the UK and within the European Union, the Universal Service Directive,[7] implemented in the UK by the Communications Act 2003, requires that service providers should provide number portability. This obligation is imposed on providers of both fixed and mobile telephony, although not between the fixed-line and mobile networks themselves.

Article 30(1) of the Universal Service Directive provides that 'Member States shall ensure that all subscribers of publicly available telephone services, including mobile services, who so request can retain their number(s) independently of the undertaking providing the service (a) in the case of geographic numbers, at a specific location; and (b) in the case of non-geographic numbers, at any location'. This provision is implemented into UK legislation through the imposition of General Conditions of Entitlement, Condition 18 (entitled Number Portability) which is contained in the Notification.[8]

For both fixed and mobile telephony, the customer may have specific requirements for number portability that go beyond rights conferred by legislation. For example, the outsourcing agreement might provide for the following in relation to number portability:

    i. That the outsourced service provider shall, in accordance with a migration plan, at its own cost take all reasonable steps to enable the customer to port the then current telephone numbers supplied through existing suppliers so that the customer can continue to use them as part of the outsourced services.

---

[7] Directive 2002/22/EC on universal service and users' rights relating to electronic communications networks and services, OJ L 108/7, 24 April 2002, the 'Universal Service Directive'.
[8] Notification under s 48(1) of the Communications Act 2003. See further Chapter 5.

ii. That the customer shall have the right to apply for registration and to register telephone numbers allocated to it under the agreement as trade or service marks, whether on their own, or in conjunction with some other words or trading style or device, or represented as words. In *1–800 Flowers Inc v Phonenames Ltd* [2001] EWCA Civ 721, Phonenames Limited owned a number of telephone numbers (such as the phone number 0800 356 9377 corresponding to the UK freephone number 0800 Flowers) and opposed an attempted registration by 1–800 Flowers Inc of the trademark '800-Flowers' in the UK in relation to flower services. In the first hearing of the case, Jacob J held that '0800 Flowers' (and 0800 word numbers in general) did not have any inherent capacity to distinguish the goods and services of any one business and so was not registrable as a trademark. An appeal by Phonenames Limited at the Court of Appeal failed. Although this case may not be the last of its type, it means that, at least so far as the law exists at the moment, a customer wishing to reserve a specific right to apply for the alpha-numeric representation of a phone number as a trademark may face considerable difficulties in obtaining such a registration.

iii. That the supplier shall not be entitled to withdraw or change any telephone number, or code, or groups of codes designated for the customer once such numbers have been allocated to it, except in order to comply with any provision of a licence or any applicable numbering scheme, or if required by law or the relevant regulatory authority. Where such change is required, the outsourced service provider should be required to give the customer the maximum period of notice practicable and indemnify the customer if it fails to do so. This is important because, for large business organizations, costs involved in publicizing and changing telephone numbers can be extremely high.

iv. That on termination or expiry of the outsourcing agreement, the outsourced service provider shall at its own cost take all reasonable steps to enable the customer to port the then current telephone numbers allocated to it so that it can continue to use them with a successor supplier.

v. That the outsourced service provider shall comply with the provisions of the Numbering Directive and relevant domestic implementations of the same.

12.5.4 Ownership of intellectual property in network software

If the outsourced service provider is, as part of the service, to develop software for use in operating the network, and such software would be required by the customer or a successor supplier in order to operate the infrastructure at the end of the outsourcing, the outsourcing agreement should provide for a perpetual royalty-free licence to use such software at the end of the agreement (and an obligation on the outsourced service provider to deliver a copy of the software to the customer).

In the relatively rare circumstances in which software is developed specifically for an infrastructure and part of the service charges includes the development of that software, the customer might wish to own the intellectual property rights in it rather

than merely be licensed to use it on termination. Here the outsourcing agreement should provide for obligations in relation to assigning the intellectual property rights in the software to the customer.

12.5.5 Business continuity plans—network down

Because communications and data infrastructures are business critical to the operation of most (if not all) businesses, it is essential that any outsourcing agreement in relation to communications includes provisions for business continuity and disaster recovery. This should include:

    i. requiring the outsourced service provider to have in place at all times a business continuity plan approved by the customer;

    ii. requiring the outsourced service provider to comply with such plan;

    iii. requiring the outsourced service provider to provide alternative networks and infrastructure if the network is down for a specified period of time;

    iv. allowing the customer to terminate the agreement if such business continuity plans are not complied with and a replacement service is not quickly implemented.

Sometimes business continuity plans include requiring the outsourced service provider to have contractual arrangements in place with a disaster recovery network service provider for the implementation of business continuity network services on short notice. This, of course, has cost implications which are inevitably borne by the customer.

12.5.6 Capacity planning

The customer will need comfort that the outsourced service provider shall maintain sufficient capacity to accommodate the customer's requirements. This will frequently have to include provisions that require that the outsourced service provider has the capability to handle temporary peak requirements which exceed the normal service capacity agreed.

Because it is likely that the customer's capacity requirements will change over time, the outsourcing agreement should provide that the customer and outsourced service provider should regularly consult with each other. This should be part of a formal capacity planning and development procedure that ensures timely adaptation to the customer's evolving needs, and a formula or change control procedure to provide for updated charge levels that may need to result from a different capacity being made available.

12.5.7 Customer premises equipment

The outsourcing agreement should contain provisions that specify the customer's and the outsourced service provider's responsibilities in connection with supplier

equipment physically located at customer premises and used in the provision of the services. Frequently these provisions will address:

i. the customer's responsibility to provide suitable accommodation, facilities, and environmental conditions, and how failure to do so may affect the outsourced service provider's service delivery obligations;

ii. the outsourced service provider's obligation to leave the customer's premises in a clean and tidy state after removal of any equipment during the term of the agreement and/or at termination;

iii. the effect of any unauthorized connections to the equipment by the customer if these have a detrimental effect on the service delivery; and

iv. the outsourced service provider's obligations as to any licences and permissions required for placement of the equipment at the customer premises and its responsibility as to operating the equipment.

12.6 GUARANTEEING SERVICE LEVELS

12.6.1 Service level agreement

12.6.1.1 *General*

Although called a service level 'agreement', the service level agreement is actually just a definition of the service and the performance levels required in relation to that service—it is not a contract separate from the outsourcing agreement.

The service level agreement should include a detailed description of the service to be supplied together with the service levels applicable to that service. The service description should include a description of the carriage part of the service, the managed component of the service (i.e. for full managed services, it should prescribe the obligations in relation to the hardware and equipment estate) and all other services to be provided. Outlined at sections 12.6.1.2 to 12.6.1.7 below are some communications-specific issues which should be dealt with in a communications outsourcing service level agreement.

12.6.1.2 *Network availability*

Obviously the customer will wish the network to be available for use 24 hours a day, seven days a week. However, recognizing that there may need to be a very limited latitude for down-time, many customers for outsourced communications solutions are prepared to agree that the service level for network availability shall be something less than 100 per cent. Normally it is something like 98.5 or 99.5 per cent availability. This will, of course, differ according to the nature of the customer's business.

12.6.1.3 *Platform fix*

The service level agreement should also provide for fix times for errors or faults in the technology platform—for example, for fixing a defective switch or router. These are

generally specified in terms of hours for critical faults, and possibly hours or even days for non-critical faults.

12.6.1.4 *Logical and physical moves*

Logical moves are software-implemented moves relating to the configuration and ability of a switch to recognize a call as a numerical extension number and route it to the appropriate physical extension. A physical move, on the other hand, relates to the physical relocation of handsets connected to the PABX.

Most communications outsourcing agreements which cover handset and extension infrastructure permit the customer to request a certain number of logical and physical moves for free, allowing the customer to relocate offices and personnel as part of its daily business operations. Beyond certain limits the customer will be charged. Because the customer will have requirements to have logical and physical moves implemented quickly, service levels for the implementation of them should be specified. These should be expressed as a number of hours or days from the date and time of the request.

12.6.1.5 *Hot-desking and virtual extensions*

Hot-desking and virtual extensions refer to flexible call routing (often required by businesses whose personnel operate from an unfixed location or from out of the office from time to time).

In the most simple PABX configuration, a virtual extension requires a notional extension number which is allocated to a specific user. This is sometimes referred to as an analogue or digital '0' extension number. This does not include the supply of a handset, but may include PABX features and facilities, calls within the same site, on net calls, and PSTN access to the outsourced communications service provider's network. The analogue or digital 0 extension service can be used alone, or in conjunction with voicemail or hot-desking services.

Hot-desking, on the other hand, includes the supply of the analogue or digital 0 extension number, but, unlike a virtual extension, to work hot-desking requires the allocation of a DDI (direct dialling inward; or DID, direct inward dialling) number. Hot-desking therefore consists of the analogue or digital 0 number with an accompanying DDI number.

The service level agreement should provide for the response times for implementing hot-desking and virtual extensions when requested by a user.

12.6.1.6 *Call failure rates*

The service level agreement should provide for the customer's requirements in relation to successful calls and call failure rates. It will provide something like: 'The service provider shall provide a grade of service of 1:100 from the handset to any PSTN number between the required maintenance cover times for all category A sites across the countries [or sites] covered by the agreement.' The service level '1:100' means that, in the busy hours, not more than one call in 100 is not available. It is sometimes described as 'PO1'. Therefore, PO2 would mean two out of 100 calls are not available in busy hours.

12.6.1.7 *Data integrity*

The service level agreement should also provide for the procedures and processes that the outsourced service provider should follow in order to maintain integrity of voice and data carried across the network. This should include maintaining operational surveillance of the network and undertaking appropriate diagnostic and analytical software scans.

12.6.2 Best industry practice and total quality management

The outsourcing agreement should provide that, in providing the services, the outsourced service provider must comply with best industry practice. Sometimes a service provider will even agree to comply with world best practice in relation to communications.

A customer may also require the outsourced service provider to comply with certified total quality management (TQM) procedures in the provision of the service or in managing the service.

12.6.3 BS standards

A customer may also require the outsourced service provider to comply with certain BS standards in relation to such matters as caller resolution and other processes. A typical example is requiring the outsourced service provider to comply with BS 7799 security protocols.

12.6.4 User satisfaction surveys

Apart from cost savings, the main factor in judging the success of a communications outsourcing is user satisfaction. Accordingly, it is increasingly the case that customers wishing to embark on communications outsourcings require their outsourced service providers to undertake periodic user satisfaction surveys based on criteria prescribed in the outsourcing agreement.

The outcome of such surveys can be measured according to objective criteria which may be linked to rewards or performance incentive bonuses payable to the outsourced service provider.

A customer with strong bargaining power may also reserve to itself the right to terminate the agreement if user satisfaction surveys fall below certain measurable thresholds of satisfaction.

12.6.5 Helpline—caller triage and call resolution

Certain kinds of communications-related outsourcings require the outsourced service provider to implement and follow certain mapped processes in providing services. A classic example is call centre services, where caller resolution is process mapped as part of the development of the service level agreement. Similarly, time

frames to achieve call resolution can themselves be measured and be made subject to service levels.

12.6.6 Service level and network audit rights

In order to monitor the outsourced service provider's compliance with the service level agreement, a customer may reserve to itself in the outsourcing agreement a right to send in technical auditors to audit compliance with the service level agreement and to examine the integrity of the network. Such rights are invariably resisted by network service providers, but, provided they are limited by reasonable notice periods and obligations to respect confidentiality, they are sometimes agreed to.

12.6.7 Remedies for breach of service levels

12.6.7.1 *Service credits and non-exclusive remedies*

There are several contractual routes a customer might choose to use in order to motivate an outsourced service provider to comply with the service level agreement. The most commonly used is the right to receive service credits if the outsourced service provider fails to comply. The service credits regime is usually coupled with key performance indicators and a formula for calculating the quantum of service credits according to the magnitude of the breach.

There is always a risk, of course, that service credits could constitute a penalty, and therefore that they may not be enforceable. However, from a customer's perspective, it should not allow the outsourced service provider to use service credits as a *de facto* cap on the service provider's liability. If, for example, a breach of the service level agreement resulted in a total quantifiable loss to the customer of £100,000 (only £50,000 of which was attributable to sourcing a replacement service, with the remainder constituting other direct losses), there should be no reason why the customer cannot recover the remaining £50,000 as damages (assuming it has recovered the first £50,000 as service credits).

In order to reserve such a right, the outsourcing agreement should provide that service credits are in addition to, and not in replacement for, any rights or remedies available to the customer under the agreement or at law, including the right to claim damages.

12.6.7.2 *Breach constituting a persistent breach or material breach*

Most services agreements provide that the customer has the right to terminate for 'material' breach of the agreement. Just what constitutes a material breach may depend on the circumstances, and it is certainly not free from doubt that a breach of the service level agreement will always constitute a material breach.

It is therefore best (from the customer's perspective) to provide in the outsourcing agreement that, for the avoidance of doubt, a breach of the service level agreement constitutes a material breach. This, of course, will be of little comfort to the customer

if the breach can be remedied in time by the outsourced service provider (generally rights of termination in relation to material breach are coupled with a right on the part of the supplier to remedy the breach if it is able to do so). Accordingly, the customer should also negotiate for the inclusion of the right to terminate if there is a *persistent* breach. The agreement should prescribe what constitutes a persistent breach. For example, it may constitute all of the following:

i. a single non-compliance with the service level agreement continuing over, say, two months; or

ii. more than, say, three unrelated non-compliances with the service level agreement occurring in one month (obviously the range of options here is considerable).

12.6.7.3 *Termination rights*
If the outsourcing agreement covers more than one site or country, the customer should consider reserving to itself the right to terminate the agreement in so far as it relates to that site or country, but to keep the remainder of the agreement in full force. In this way if the customer suffers from poor service at one site or country, it can remove that site or country from the scope of the agreement without having to terminate the whole agreement. Generally termination of the whole agreement would relate to very serious breaches, and non-compliance in one country or site may not be enough to persuade the customer to exercise such right.

The outsourced service provider will wish to reserve to itself the right to terminate the agreement if for any reason its licence to operate a communications system is revoked and a substantially similar licence cannot be obtained.

12.7 TECHNOLOGY PLATFORM

12.7.1 Generic requirements—equipment and network

Earlier in this chapter it was mentioned that it is best practice in communications outsourcings to impose certain minimum requirements on the outsourced service provider in relation to the technical performance of the technology platform (including equipment and the network). This is because, although an outsourcing is mostly service based, the equipment and network used in the outsourcing impact upon the quality of service delivery. Therefore it is not unusual for a customer to ask for an obligation on the outsourced service provider to ensure that the equipment and the network (and anything else used as part of the technology platform) comply with agreed technical specifications (which would consist of certain minimum technical specifications set out in a schedule to the agreement). These might include such things as the type of operating platform, switches, routers, and switching protocols used.

The customer may also require the outsourced service provider to adhere to a 'common platform architecture' described in the outsourcing services agreement.

It will include elements that overlap the respective technology architectures of the customer and outsourced service provider.

12.7.2 Heritage/legacy platform

Where the service provider inherits (as part of the infrastructure transferred) heritage or legacy technology platform, it will normally argue that it should not be required to make the heritage or legacy platform comply with any minimum specifications or other requirements. From a customer's perspective this may be acceptable if there is a short migration period to a new technology platform. However, where it is envisaged that the existing platform will be used for some time, the customer may well argue for certain minimum safeguards. These might include requiring the outsourced service provider to meet the same specifications or other performance criteria as existed prior to the outsourcing.

12.7.3 Resilience of the technology platform

A major issue in communications outsourcings is the resilience of the technology platform used. This relates to the ability of the system to carry traffic uninterrupted and without corruption over sustained periods.

With voice traffic it is immediately apparent when resilience has not been achieved, but this can be less obvious in the case of data traffic. Accordingly, the obligation on the outsourced service provider to ensure that the technology platform meets certain minimum requirements should include requirements in relation to resilience.

12.7.4 Compatibility with in-house systems

One of the difficulties with communications outsourcings (as with all outsourcings involving a transfer of infrastructure) is that the customer may be faced with difficulties in bringing the system back in-house at the end of the outsourcing relationship. This problem will be particularly acute if the systems used by the outsourced service provider are incompatible with any residual systems retained by the customer. For this reason a customer may wish to specify in the technology platform specification (in relation to both equipment and the network) that the systems and network used by the outsourced service provider must remain compatible with the customer's remaining systems.

12.7.5 Restriction on changing the technology platform

For the same reason, the outsourcing agreement may need to provide that the outsourced service provider must adhere to the common platform architecture unless the customer consents. Sometimes outsourced service providers see such an obligation as unduly restrictive on their power to supply the services by whatever means they choose, and therefore this issue often turns on the respective bargaining strengths of the parties.

12.7.6 Testing the technology platform

The customer may require the outsourced service provider to test components of the technology platform before rolling it out to the customer. Such testing should generally be coupled with a report mechanism allowing the customer to see the results of the tests and allowing it to observe such tests if requested.

12.7.7 Technology refresh

The efficacy and benefits of communications outsourcings can be quickly eroded through advances in technology if those advantages are not quickly made available to the customer. From the outsourced service provider's perspective, however, there is little incentive to make new technology available to a customer once an outsourcing has started, as this will represent a further sunk cost that the outsourced service provider cannot then recoup. Accordingly, a customer wishing to 'future proof' itself in relation to advances in technology has two options:

i. to insist that the agreement be of a relatively short duration—this will inevitably have adverse pricing consequences for the customer;

ii. to agree a procedure by which the customer can insist upon technology refresh, if necessary by shouldering additional costs itself.

Technology refresh can include anything from replacement of existing handsets and PABXs up to increasing bandwidth and the technology used for transmitting data packets across the network.

Generally, the customer should require the outsourced service provider to report to it, say, on a three-monthly basis about any technological advances available in the marketplace in relation to the services provided by the outsourced service provider.

12.8 ENSURING CHARGES REMAIN COMPETITIVE

12.8.1 Basis of charging determines method of monitoring costs

If pricing is transparent then the customer will want to be able to monitor the basis for calculating charges. Although numerous charging models are available, some of the more common for communications outsourcings are set out below.

12.8.2 'Cost plus'

'Cost plus' is a transparent pricing basis under which the outsourced service provider provides the service at the raw cost of providing the service, plus a percentage reward on such raw costs for its management of the service and to account for the supplier's return on investment.

12.8.3 'Per seat'

'Per seat' pricing is generally non-transparent and is set according to the number of users receiving the service.

12.8.4 'Open book'

'Open book' pricing may or may not be on the basis of cost plus, and involves complete transparency of all costs incurred by the outsourced service provider in providing the service. It is generally coupled with rights of financial audit.

12.8.5 Benchmarking PSTN tariffs

There are numerous ways in which to benchmark pricing for outsourced communications services. Benchmarking can range from an obligation to pass savings back to the customer to sophisticated arrangements involving an external indicator (by which to adjust the pricing).

For mobile telephony, benchmarking tends to focus on the most cost-effective tariff on a per user basis. This is because user/caller patterns in the case of mobile telephony can more easily be linked to an individual tariff than those in relation to fixed voice or data services.

For fixed voice or data telephony services, benchmarking may occur once or twice yearly, and the purpose of such benchmarking is to provide a mechanism to review the PSTN tariff rate element of usage charges. It will involve comparing the PSTN tariff rates as a whole with PSTN tariff rates offered by similar suppliers in the marketplace.

Although the types of benchmarking may range from informal to formal, the strongest kind from the customer's perspective is to use a benchmarking agency to undertake the comparison. The criteria and methodology used by the agency should be agreed in advance (to make sure that there is a comparison of like with like). The procedure should prescribe whether the benchmarking can result in increases, or merely in decreases in the PSTN tariff rates. Obviously, current market trends indicate that generally benchmarking should result only in decreases.[9]

12.9 PAN-EUROPEAN AND OTHER INTERNATIONAL CONSIDERATIONS

12.9.1 Scope of coverage

If the outsourcing agreement provides for service in more than one country, the outsourced service provider may need to use other service providers in countries

---

[9] See, e.g. *Cable & Wireless Plc v IBM United Kingdom Ltd* [2002] 2 All ER (Comm) 1041.

where it itself does not have an operating presence. This will have consequences in terms of the service it can provide, and some of the issues relevant to international coverage are as set out below.

12.9.2 Direct and indirect models of supply

Where the indirect model of supply is used (subcontracting), the outsourced service provider should not be excused from supplying the service in accordance with the service levels merely because it subcontracts the provision of the service. Moreover, reporting obligations in relation to compliance with service levels should be on a per country basis in order to detect non-compliance on a per country basis. Service credits and rights of termination should similarly be linked on a per country basis.

12.9.3 Liability allocation on a per country basis

If the outsourced service provider is subcontracting in various countries, it may be appropriate to divide liability upon country lines so that there is a separate cap on liability for claims arising in each country. This will mean that if the customer suffers variable service in one country, but consistent service in another, the outsourced service provider's total liability cap will not be 'used up' in relation to other countries because of exceptionally poor performance in one particular country.

12.9.4 Varying service levels internationally

Where the outsourced service provider is using other suppliers in various countries in order to provide a global solution, it may well push for service levels which vary between countries. Although from a supplier's perspective this might seem reasonable, it may not be acceptable to a customer wishing to implement a globally consistent service.[10]

12.10 FUTURE TRENDS IN COMMUNICATIONS OUTSOURCING

The technologies associated with communications outsourcings have been characterized by convergence with those used in relation to the Internet, broadcasting (particularly radio), and cable. This is particularly so in the case of data traffic (which could equally be carried through the Internet or on cable infrastructures).

Convergent technologies have resulted in regulators having to coordinate a consistent response to the technologies. One of the important principles accepted by the European Union is that regulation of the technologies associated with communications

---

[10] In relation to varying service levels internationally, see Sinclair, M, 'IT and Telecoms Outsourcing in Europe and the Law', n 2 above, at 42.

should be technology-neutral, and the convergence in the regulatory framework bears witness to this.

As technologies converge, so the industry itself also faces a period of consolidation. Increased emphasis on achieving cost-savings will mean that operators may be forced to move aspects of their operations off-shore (customer relationship management and billing are but two examples). Outsourcing off-shore presents technical and legal challenges to the operators (although these are not peculiar to the communications sector). It therefore remains to be seen how much off-shore outsourcing will feature in future rationalizations of the sector.

Part V

COMMUNICATIONS CONTENT

13

COMMUNICATIONS PRIVACY

Christopher Millard

13.1 INTRODUCTION

13.1.1 Scope of this chapter

The jurisprudence of privacy has a fragmented history. Privacy, as a distinct legal concept, probably has its origins in an essay published in the *Harvard Law Review* in 1890. In 'The Right to Privacy',[1] Samuel Warren and Louis Brandeis reviewed the long history of protection under the English common law for various individual liberties and private property, and extrapolated a general 'right to privacy'. Ironically, more than a century later, the US still does not have a privacy law with general

---

[1] (1890) 4 Harvard Law Review 193.

application to the private sector. Instead, it has a patchwork of sector-specific laws and regulations covering a diverse range of subject matter.[2]

Even in jurisdictions that have specific privacy or data protection legislation, various other rights and obligations may exist that are analogous to privacy rights and have an impact on communications activities. For example, in the UK, telecommunications privacy is regulated primarily under the Data Protection Act 1998 (the DPA 1998) and the Privacy and Electronic Communications (EC Directive) Regulations 2003 (SI 2003/2426)[3] (the PEC Regulations).[4] In addition, however, various other statutes have a direct impact on telecommunications privacy, including the Wireless Telegraphy Act 2006, the Communications Act 2003, and the Anti-terrorism Crime and Security Act 2001. Moreover, the Human Rights Act 1998 and the Regulation of Investigatory Powers Act 2000 are now of significant importance in this field. More tangentially, individuals may also be able to assert unrelated common law rights, such as confidentiality, or unrelated statutory rights, such as copyright or defamation, as a means of controlling, for example, the use of recordings of telephone conversations or the dissemination of email messages. Following an overview of the international context, this chapter will focus on current UK legislation that has a direct impact on communications privacy. A considerable body of new legislation has been introduced both in the UK, and in Europe generally, following the implementation of a number of new EU directives designed to harmonize national laws relating to the protection, processing, transfer and use of personal data. The complex and overlapping rules in this area will be analysed by reference to specific activities, such as interception of communications and use of telecommunications services for direct marketing purposes. Common law and statutory rules affecting message content but only indirectly having an impact on privacy, such as confidentiality, copyright, and defamation, are beyond the scope of this chapter.[5]

---

[2] Examples include: consumer video rental records (Video Privacy Protection Act of 1998, 18 USC §2710 (1994)), consumer financial services (e.g. Fair Credit Reporting Act of 1970, 18 USC §1681 (1988); the Fair Credit Billing Act of 1976, 15 USC §§1601, 1602, 1637, 1666 (1988); the Right to Financial Privacy Act of 1978, 12 USC §§3401–3422 (1994); Gramm-Leach-Bliley Financial Modernization Act of 1999, 15 USC §§6801–6810, 6821–6827), interception of electronic communications (Electronic Communications Privacy Act of 1986, §2510 et seq.), the online privacy rights of children (Children's Online Privacy Protection Act of 1998, 15 USC §6501 et seq.; Children's Online Privacy Protection Rule, 16 CFR Part 312) and health records (e.g. Health Insurance Portability and Accountability Act of 1996 ('HIPAA'), Public Law 104-191 of which the Privacy Rule came into force for most purposes in 2003). Some recent US privacy laws are extraordinarily focused. For example, on 1 January 2008 California joined Wisconsin and North Dakota in banning the forcible implantation of identification devices, such as RFID chips, in human beings (an act to add Section 52.7 to the Civil Code, relating to identification devices, Senate Bill No 362 – now Cal Civ Code Section 52.7).

[3] The PEC Regulations have been supplemented by the Privacy and Electronic Communications (EC Directive) (Amendment) Regulations 2004 (SI 2004/1039).

[4] The PEC Regulations implemented the Privacy and Electronic Communications Directive (02/58/EC) (the Privacy and Electronic Communications Directive) and superseded the Telecommunications (Data Protection and Privacy) Regulations 1999 (SI 1999/2003).

[5] See generally Reed, C and Angel, J (eds), *Computer Law* (6th edn, Oxford University Press, 2007).

13.1.2 Jurisdictions with and without privacy laws

Eighty years after Warren and Brandeis's seminal article, popular concerns about the implications of widespread use of computers in the public and private sectors led to the adoption of data protection laws in various European jurisdictions. The first was the German state of Hessen in 1970.[6] Since then over 50 countries around the world have enacted data protection legislation intended to protect individuals' rights to privacy by restricting the manner in which information about them may be processed in the private sector.[7] A number of other countries have enacted legislation regulating the processing of personal data in the public sector (e.g. in the US, the Privacy Act of 1974, 5 USC, §§552 *et seq.*).

Most of the existing data protection laws with general application to the private sector are in Europe. Almost all of those laws are based on the Data Protection Directive and the Privacy and Electronic Communications Directive (see section 13.1.3.3 below) both of which have now been implemented by all 27 EU Member States. While the majority of countries in the world do not yet have data protection laws, a number of jurisdictions either have general privacy rights, sometimes entrenched in a constitution, or have sector-specific privacy rules that have an impact on communications.

13.1.3 International initiatives to harmonize data protection rules

13.1.3.1 *OECD privacy guidelines*

The proliferation of national data protection laws has given rise to various transnational initiatives to limit the emergence of inconsistent national rules that might become obstacles to cross-border trade. In 1974, the Organisation for Economic Co-operation and Development (OECD) established an Expert Group, the Data Bank Panel, to study various aspects of computers and privacy.[8] A second Expert Group, established under the chairmanship of Mr Justice Kirby, chairman of the Australian Law Reform Commission, developed Guidelines on basic rules to facilitate harmonization of national data protection laws and pre-empt unnecessary restrictions on transborder data flows. A Recommendation containing the Guidelines was adopted by the OECD Council and became applicable on 23 September 1980.[9] The Memorandum accompanying the OECD Guidelines contains a recommendation that Member countries 'take into account in their domestic legislation the principles

---

[6] Hessisches Datenschutzgesetz (HDSG), 30 September 1970, Hess. GVOBL I 1970, P 625. The first national law was the 1973 Swedish Data Act, as amended in 1997.

[7] For details of existing national data protection laws, see Millard, C and Ford, M (eds), *Data Protection Laws of the World* (Sweet & Maxwell, London, 1998). In addition to such national laws, there are many state and provincial privacy laws in various federal countries.

[8] In 1977 the Data Bank Panel organized a symposium in Vienna, out of which came *Transborder Data Flows and the Protection of Privacy* (OECD, Paris, 1979).

[9] OECD, *Transborder Data Flows and the Protection of Privacy* (OECD, Paris, 1981).

concerning the protection of privacy and individual liberties set forth in the Guidelines . . . [and that] . . . Member countries endeavour to remove or avoid creating, in the name of privacy protection, unjustified obstacles to transborder flows of personal data.'

The OECD Guidelines represent an attempt to balance the conflicting priorities of data protection and the free flow of information. The most fundamental limitation of the Guidelines is that they have no legal force. They are not embedded in any convention. Moreover, the open-textured nature of the Guidelines means that they can serve only as a loose framework for the harmonization of national laws.

In January 2003 the OECD released a report (which formed the basis for a further publication in November 2004), providing practical guidance for OECD member countries, businesses, industry, and individual users on the implementation of its privacy guidelines online for the purpose of 'ensuring global privacy and the free flow of information'.[10] During 2006 the OECD examined cross-border aspects of privacy law enforcement and issued a report of its findings in October of that year.[11] This led to the adoption in June 2007 by the OECD Council of a *Recommendation on Cross-border Co-operation in the Enforcement of Laws Protecting Privacy*.[12]

13.1.3.2 *Council of Europe Convention*

Unlike the OECD, which is essentially concerned with the economic development of its Member States, the Council of Europe has a broader political mandate. In 1968, the Parliamentary Assembly of the Council of Europe expressed concern over the adequacy of the European Convention on Human Rights in securing privacy protection in the context of information technology. As a response, the Committee of Ministers conducted a study and subsequently passed two Resolutions establishing data protection principles, one for the private sector (Resolution (73) 22), the other for the public sector (Resolution (74) 29). The Committee of Experts that prepared the Resolutions called for the development of an international data protection agreement. After many drafts, the final text of the Convention for the Protection of Individuals with regard to Automatic Processing of Personal Data[13] was adopted by the Committee of Ministers and was opened for signature on 28 January 1981. The Convention came into force on 1 October 1985 after five states had ratified it. The UK ratified the Convention on 26 August 1987, with effect from 1 December 1987. At the time of writing, 40 States had ratified the Convention.[14]

---

[10] OECD, Privacy Online: Policy and Practical Guidance and Privacy Online: OECD Guidance on Policy and Practice (OECD, Paris, 2003).
[11] Available at: <http://www.oecd.org/sti/privacycooperation>.
[12] Ibid.
[13] European Treaty Series No 108.
[14] These were Albania, Andorra, Austria, Belgium, Bosnia and Herzegovina, Bulgaria, Croatia, Cyprus, Czech Republic, Denmark, Estonia, Finland, France, Georgia, Germany, Greece, Hungary, Iceland, Ireland, Italy, Latvia, Liechtenstein, Lithuania, Luxembourg, Malta, Moldova, Montenegro, the Netherlands, Norway, Poland, Portugal, Romania, Serbia, Slovakia, Slovenia, Spain, Sweden, Switzerland, the former Yugoslav Republic of Macedonia, and the UK.

The Convention deals with the automatic processing of any information relating to an identifiable individual. Ratifying states must place obligations on controllers of files to comply with various principles and to grant various rights to data subjects. In relation to transborder data flows, the Convention prohibits the imposition, on the grounds of privacy protection, of restrictions on the transfer of data from the territory of one Convention party to that of another. Two exceptions are permitted. One is where the first party gives special protection to a particular category of data and the second party does not. The other is where the data are to be re-exported to a non-Convention state.

In 2001 the Council of Europe adopted an additional protocol to the Convention for the Protection of Individuals with regard to Automatic Processing of Personal Data regarding supervisory authorities and transborder data flows.[15] The Protocol was adopted in response to the vast increase in the volume of international transfers of data and considerable technological development since the date on which the Convention came into force. It is intended to improve the application of the principles set out in the Convention by introducing two new provisions: one relating to the establishment of supervisory authorities to monitor compliance with the Convention, and the other relating to transborder data flows to countries or organizations which are not parties to the Convention. At the time of writing, 21 states had ratified the additional protocol.[16]

From time to time the Council of Europe's Committee of Ministers adopts Recommendations relating to specific sectors or issues. In 1995, the Committee of Ministers adopted a Recommendation 'on the protection of personal data in the area of telecommunication services, with particular reference to telephone services'.[17] This recommendation contained an appendix setting out detailed principles covering such things as directories, direct marketing rules, itemized billing procedures, and use of calling-line identification. Many of these principles were subsequently carried over into the EU's Telecoms Data Protection Directive (see 13.1.3.3 below).

In 1999, the Committee of Ministers adopted a Recommendation 'for the protection of privacy on the Internet'.[18] This Recommendation contained, in an appendix, 'Guidelines for the protection of individuals with regard to the collection and processing of personal data on information highways . . .' It was intended that the Guidelines might be used as, or incorporated into, codes of conduct. With the benefit of hindsight, the Guidelines look somewhat unrealistic with, for example, a very restrictive approach to international data transfers. Users were also encouraged to request, and indeed ISPs to promote, anonymous Internet access and the use of pseudonyms.

---

[15] European Treaty Series No 181.
[16] These were Albania, Andorra, Austria, Bosnia and Herzegovina, Croatia, Cyprus, Czech Republic, France, Germany, Hungary, Latvia, Lithuania, Luxembourg, Netherlands, Poland, Portugal, Romania, Slovakia, Sweden, and Switzerland.
[17] Recommendation No R (95) 4, 7 February 1995.
[18] Recommendation No R (99) 5, 23 February 1999.

Nevertheless, although the Guidelines were not widely adopted as a model code of conduct, they highlighted a number of important security and privacy issues that had not previously been given much attention. In particular, the Guidelines drew attention to the risk that people might be profiled without their knowledge or consent based on their online activities and that web sites might be used to collect excessive amounts of personal data. Ironically, a decade or so later, both of these risks often seem to be forgotten as millions of people seem remarkably eager to share their own personal data, and often that of others, via social networking sites such as Facebook and MySpace.

13.1.3.3 *European Union data protection initiatives*

In 1981, the same year that the Council of Europe's Convention was opened for signature, the European Commission recommended that the EC Member States that had not already done so should sign the Convention and seek to ratify it by the end of 1982.[19] The Commission indicated in its Recommendation that it would engage in a compulsory harmonization programme if Member States were too dilatory in ratifying the Council of Europe Convention. In July 1990, the Commission submitted to the Council of Ministers a series of proposals, including two draft Directives intended to harmonize data protection laws. The first dealt in general terms with data protection and transborder data flows;[20] the second specifically with data protection aspects of public digital telecommunications network.[21]

After five years of protracted debates in the European Parliament and European Council, a substantially revised version of the first proposal was finally adopted as Directive 95/46/EC of the European Parliament and of the Council of 24 October 1995 on the protection of individuals with regard to the processing of personal data and on the free movement of such data (the Data Protection Directive). It took a further two years before the adoption of Directive 97/66/EC of the European Parliament and of the Council of 15 December 1997 concerning the processing of personal data and the protection of privacy in the telecommunications sector (the Telecoms Data Protection Directive). The deadline for the (then) 15 European Member States to implement both directives was 24 October 1998. At the time of writing, the Data Protection Directive had been implemented by all of the (now) 27 EU Member States.

The European Commission issued its first report on the implementation of the Data Protection Directive on 16 May 2003.[22] The Report concluded that the Directive broadly achieved its aim of ensuring a high level of protection for personal data

---

[19] Recommendation of the Commission 81/679/EEC, (1979) OJ L 246/31.

[20] Proposal for a Council Directive concerning the protection of individuals in relation to the processing of personal data, (1990) OJ C 277/3, s 11.

[21] Proposal for a Council Directive concerning the protection of personal data privacy in the context of public digital telecommunications networks, in particular the Integrated Services Digital Network (ISDN) and Public Digital Mobile Networks, (1990) OJ C 277/12, s 11.

[22] IP/03/697 16 May 2003.

while allowing the free flow of personal data within the European Union. However, it noted that late transposition by Member States, and differences in the way in which the Data Protection Directive had been implemented at a national level, had prevented Europe's economy from maximizing the benefit of the directive. The Report proposed a number of ways to address and reduce those differences including the modification of national legislation and practices as regards the application of the rules.

On 24 February 2004, the European Parliament issued a report in response to the Commission's report on implementation of the Directive.[23] The Parliament shared the view of the Commission that the Directive should not be amended for the time being. In a Communication to the Parliament and the Council dated 7 March 2007, the European Commission reviewed the current implementation of the Directive and concluded that it 'constitutes a general legal framework which fulfils its original objectives' and that consequently it had no plans to propose any amendments.[24] This conclusion was a considerable disappointment to many observers, including several EU privacy regulators. Indeed, just two days after the Commission's Communication was published, the UK Information Commissioner, Richard Thomas, issued a press release calling for a 'greater global consensus on privacy'. Thomas suggested that 'European laws may need some revision to achieve a closer consensus' and stressed that 'the European Union [must] be ready to consider changes'.[25]

The provisions of the Telecoms Data Protection Directive that relate to direct marketing activities were implemented initially in the UK by means of the Telecommunications (Data Protection and Privacy) (Direct Marketing) Regulations 1998 (SI 1998/3170) (the 1998 Regulations). The 1998 Regulations came into force on 1 May 1999, but on 1 March 2000 were revoked and superseded by the Telecommunications (Data Protection and Privacy) Regulations 1999. The 1999 Regulations implemented the entire Telecoms Data Protection Directive, with the exception of Article 5. Article 5, which deals with monitoring and interception of communications, has since been implemented in the Regulation of Investigatory Powers Act 2000 (RIPA), which came into force in October 2000. The 1999 Regulations have since been revoked and superseded by the PEC Regulations (see section 13.1.1 above). The PEC Regulations came

---

[23] Report (24 February 2004) on the First Report on the implementation of the Data Protection Directive (95/46/EC) A5-0104/2004.
[24] Communication from the Commission to the European Parliament and the Council on the follow-up of the Work Programme for better implementation of the Data Protection Directive, Brussels, 7 March 2007, COM(2007) 87 final.
[25] 'UK Information Commissioner calls for greater global consensus on privacy', Press Release, 9 March 2007, available at <http://www.ico.gov.uk>. The Information Commissioner's Office announced subsequently that it had appointed a consortium led by RAND Europe to review European data protection law and make recommendations for reform. 'UK privacy watchdog spearheads debate on the future of European privacy law', Press Release, 7 July 2008, available at <http://www.ico.gov.uk>. Perhaps in response to this apparently *ultra vires* initiative by its UK Information Commissioner, the European Commission subsequently appointed a group of experts 'to reflect on the Data Protection legal framework in the European Union'. See Register of expert groups, available at <http://www.ec.europa.eu>.

into force on 11 December 2003 and implemented Directive 02/58/EC of the European Parliament and European Council concerning the processing of personal data and the protection of privacy in the electronic communications sector (the Privacy and Electronic Communications Directive). The Directive was adopted on 12 July 2002 and the deadline for Member States to implement it was 31 October 2003. All 27 EU Member States have now implemented the Directive but they have not done so in a consistent manner.[26] It is likely that the Commission will take the same approach as it has taken in relation to the Data Protection Directive to improve implementation and consistent application of the Directive amongst Member States.

The Privacy and Electronic Communications Directive is intended to complement rather than replace the Data Protection Directive. It contains provisions relating to the security and confidentiality of electronic communications, the processing of location and traffic data, the use of itemized billing and of calling, and connected line identification, automatic call forwarding, directory services, and unsolicited communications (see section 13.3 below). On 13 November 2007, the European Commission adopted a Proposal for a Directive that would amend the Privacy and Electronic Communications Directive.[27] The most significant change would be the introduction of an obligation on providers of publicly available communications services to provide notice of security breaches to 'subscribers'. This would result in a degree of alignment between the EU and the US where at least 44 states, the District of Columbia, Puerto Rico, and the Virgin Islands have enacted laws requiring notification of security breaches involving personal information.[28] However, whereas US breach notification laws tend to be of broad application to businesses regardless of the sector in which they operate,[29] the European Commission's proposals, at least in their original form, would apply only to providers of publicly available electronic communications services. More specifically, an obligation to notify the national regulatory authority and the subscriber concerned would be triggered by:

a breach of security leading to the accidental or unlawful destruction, loss, alteration, unauthorised disclosure of or access to personal data transmitted, stored or otherwise processed in connection with the provision of publicly available electronic communications services.[30]

---

[26] For example, in relation to unsolicited communications (direct marketing) some Member States require 'opt-in' consent to send direct marketing emails to both corporate and individual subscribers while others only require 'opt-in' consent for individual subscribers; some Member States take a broad interpretation of the 'similar goods and services' exception to permit communications in relation to a wide range of the sender's own related goods and services, while others have adopted a more restrictive approach.

[27] Proposal for a Directive of the European Parliament and of the Council amending Directive 2002/22/EC on universal service and users' rights relating to electronic communications networks, Directive 2002/58/EC concerning the processing of personal data and the protection of privacy in the electronic communications sector and Regulation (EC) No 2006/2004 on consumer protection cooperation COM (2007) 698.

[28] National Conference of State Legislatures, State Security Breach Notification Laws as of 4 November 2008. Current status report available at: <http://www.ncsl.org/programs/lis/cip/priv/breachlaws.htm>.

[29] For a detailed analysis of the US breach notification landscape, see P M Schwartz and E J Janger, 'Notification of Data Security Breaches', (2007) 105 *Michigan Law Review* 913.

[30] Commission Proposal, n 27, above, Art 2(3)(b).

Both the European Data Protection Supervisor and the Article 29 Working Party welcomed the proposed introduction of a breach notification obligation but recommended that it be broadened in two respects.[31] First, they called for the new breach notification obligation to apply not just to providers of publicly available information services but also to 'providers of information society services such as on-line banks, on-line businesses, on-line providers of health care services etc'.[32] Secondly, they proposed that the scope of recipients of security breach notifications should be broadened to include 'all persons concerned' or 'all persons whose data has effectively been compromised' and not merely the narrowly defined group of 'subscribers' to a particular service.[33] While it is easy to see the appeal of these arguments, there are also difficulties with each. In the first case, an extension of the obligation to, say, online banks but not, for example, off-line banks might still seem arbitrary. In the second case, an extension of the obligation to notify so as to encompass anyone affected by a breach might lead to considerable uncertainty and be unduly onerous.

On 26 June 2008, the European Parliament's Committee on Civil Liberties, Justice and Home Affairs published an opinion on the proposed directive that appears to represent an attempted compromise between the Commission's original position and the broader approach proposed by the European DP Supervisor and the Article 29 Working Party.[34] The European Parliament's Opinion supports the widening of the breach notification obligation to encompass providers of information society services such as online banks and other e-commerce businesses. Significantly, however, the Opinion proposes restricting the notification obligation to cases where the breach 'is likely to cause harm to users'. Moreover, the Opinion would amend the Commission's proposal so that, normally, only a regulatory authority would need to be notified in the first instance. The exception to this rule would be where the service provider deems it necessary to notify individuals first 'to avoid imminent and direct danger to consumer's rights and interests'.[35] Once notified, the 'competent authority' would evaluate the breach and, if it deems it to be serious, would require an appropriate notification to be given to the affected persons. The notification might,

---

[31] Opinion of the European Data Protection Supervisor on the Proposal for a Directive of the European Parliament and of the Council amending, among others, Directive 2002/58/EC concerning the processing of personal data and the protection of privacy in the electronic communications sector (Directive on privacy and electronic communications), issued 10 April 2008; Art 29 Data Protection Working Party Opinion on the review of the Directive 2002/58/EC on privacy and electronic communications (ePrivacy Directive), 00989/08/EN, WP 150, adopted on 15 May 2008.

[32] Article 29 Working Party Opinion, WP 150, at 3.

[33] Article 29 Working Party Opinion, WP 150, at 3.

[34] Opinion of the Committee on Civil Liberties, Justice and Home Affairs for the Committee on the Internal Market and Consumer Protection on the proposal for a directive of the European Parliament and of the Council amending Directive 2002/22/EC on universal service and users' rights relating to electronic communications networks, Directive 2002/58/EC concerning the processing of personal data and the protection of privacy in the electronic communications sector and Regulation (EC) No 2006/2004 on consumer protection cooperation, 2007/0248(COD).

[35] European Parliament Opinion, footnote 34, Amendment 20.

however, be postponed if appropriate in the context of a criminal investigation.[36] This more nuanced approach, which would include a risk-assessment process and take into account enforcement activities, would be likely to avoid the problems of excessive and inappropriate notification that have led to criticism of simplistic US breach notification laws such as the original Californian statute.[37]

In January 1995, the EU Council of Ministers adopted a Resolution on the lawful interception of telecommunications.[38] This Resolution addressed various technical issues in relation to interception of communications by law enforcement agencies. The privacy implications of the Resolution were discussed in detail in a May 1999 Recommendation of the EU Data Protection Working Party.[39] The Working Party expressed concern at the scope of the interception measures envisaged by the Resolution and stressed the need for the national law of the EU Member States to specify the precise circumstances and manner in which surveillance should be authorized.

The Working Party has also adopted various other recommendations and opinions on privacy issues relating to telecommunications[40] and the Internet.[41] In November 2000, the Working Party adopted a substantial Working Document entitled: *Privacy on the Internet: An Integrated Approach to On-Line Data Protection.*[42] This contained a detailed discussion of Internet technologies and services, perceived privacy risks and the application of the Data Protection Directive and the Telecoms Data Protection Directive. It called for the development of privacy-compliant web-browsers

---

[36] European Parliament Opinion, footnote 34, Amendment 21.

[37] See Schwartz and Janger, n 29, above. At the time of writing, the proposed directive still faced several remaining procedural steps. Final adoption was not expected until mid-2009. In the UK, in 2007 the government cited uncertainty as to the benefits of US breach notification laws as a justification for rejecting a call from the House of Lords Science and Technology Committee for a UK data breach notification law (The Government Reply to the Fifth Report from the House of Lords Science and Technology Committee Session 2006–07, HL Paper 165, Personal Internet Security, Cm 7234. October 2007). In a follow-up report in July 2008, the same House of Lords Committee acknowledged the importance of 'setting the correct level of notification' but reaffirmed its view that 'data security breach notification legislation would have the twin impacts of increasing incentives on businesses to avoid data loss, and should a breach occur, giving individuals timely information so that they can reduce the risk to themselves.' (House of Lords Science and Technology Committee, 4th Report of Session 2007–08, Personal Internet Security: Follow-up, HL Paper 131, published 8 July 2008).

[38] (1996) OJ C 239/1.

[39] Recommendation on the respect of privacy in the context of interception of telecommunications, 5005/99/final, WP 18, adopted on 3 May 1999. The Working Party is established under Art 29 of the Data Protection Directive.

[40] These include an Opinion on the general review of the telecommunications legal framework (5009/00/final, adopted on 3 February 2000), and an Opinion on the storage of traffic data for billing purposes (12054/02, adopted on 29 January 2003).

[41] These include a Recommendation entitled: *Anonymity on the Internet,* (XV D/5022/97/final, WP 6, adopted on 3 December 1997), a Working Document on *Processing of Personal Data on the Internet,* (5013/99/final, WP16, adopted on 23 February 1999), a *Recommendation on Invisible and Automatic Processing of Personal Data on the Internet Performed by Software and Hardware,* (5093/99/final, WP25, adopted on 23 February 1999), and a *Recommendation on the preservation of traffic data by Internet Service Providers for law enforcement purposes* (5085/99/final, WP25, adopted on 7 September 1999).

[42] 5063/00/final, WP37, adopted on 21 November 2000.

and the promotion of Privacy-Enhancing Technologies (PETs). This was followed, six months later, by a *Recommendation on certain minimum requirements for collecting personal data on-line in the European Union.*[43] In this document the Working Party stressed the importance of providing detailed information to individuals on-screen prior to data collection, with simple opt-outs where appropriate, and also the need to limit the collection of information to that required for specific and legitimate purposes.

In May 2002, the Working Party issued a *Working Document on determining the application of EU data protection law to personal data processing on the Internet by non-EU based web sites.*[44] This paper considered the application of the jurisdictional rules in Article 4 of the Data Protection Directive and concluded that where a non-EU data controller places a cookie on the hard drive of an EU user's PC and uses that cookie to collect personal data, the data controller must comply with the relevant requirements of the national data protection law, via a designated local representative if it has no establishment in the EU. A 2006 *Opinion on privacy issues related to the provision of email screening services*[45] analysed services provided by ISPs and others that screen emails for viruses and spam. The Working Party concluded that although the European Convention on Human Rights, the Data Protection Directive and the Privacy and Electronic Communications Directive might all place restrictions on such activities, there would also be justifications for providing such services, subject to appropriate safeguards. Most recently, a 2008 *Opinion on data protection issues related to search engines*[46] has provoked some vigorous lobbying from affected players in the industry. The Opinion argues that non-EEA providers of search engines are regulated under national laws implementing the Data Protection Directive either because they have an EEA establishment (e.g. a sales office) or because they use equipment in the EEA (e.g. cookies). This effectively gives the Directive global reach in relation to such businesses. The Opinion proposes a broad application of the 'personal data' concept to search engine log files, IP addresses and web cookies and calls for data retention to be minimised and proportionate, with six months as a suggested maximum.

The Working Party has also published an opinion on unsolicited communications for marketing purposes under Article 13 of Directive 02/58/EC (Privacy and Electronic Communications Directive).[47] This opinion examines the concepts underlying Article 13 (unsolicited communications) of the Directive which have been the subject of different interpretations by various Member States. These include practices relating to electronic mail, prior consent, direct marketing, opt-in, and communications to legal persons.

---

[43] 5020/01/final, WP43, adopted on 17 May 2001.
[44] 5035/01/final, WP56, adopted on 30 May 2002.
[45] 00451/06, WP118, adopted on 21 February 2006.
[46] 00737, WP148, adopted on 4 April 2008.
[47] 5/04/final, WP90 adopted on 27 February 2004.

An area of significant controversy in which the Working Party has been actively engaged since 11 September 2001 has been the extent to which it is appropriate or justified for providers of public communications services to be required to retain communications traffic data for a variety of purposes, including anti-terrorism activities. In October 2002, The Working Party adopted an Opinion on mandatory systematic retention of telecommunications traffic data.[48] In this Opinion, the data protection commissioners expressed 'grave doubts as to the legitimacy of such broad measures'. In 2005, in response to a proposed directive on data retention, the Working Party voiced its concerns again in a more strongly worded Opinion.[49] While acknowledging that '[t]errorism presents our society with a real and pressing challenge', the commissioners argued that 'data retention interferes with the inviolable, fundamental right to confidential communications' and that 'any restriction on this fundamental right must be based on a pressing need, should only be allowed in exceptional cases and be the subject of adequate safeguards'. Of particular concern were the proposals that data should be retained for up to two years (this was considered excessive) and that it should be available for use for the investigation of any 'serious crime' and not merely for anti-terrorism purposes.

After considerable political controversy,[50] the Data Retention Directive was finally adopted on 15 March 2006.[51] The Directive requires EU Member States to ensure that certain categories of communications data are retained for a minimum of six months and a maximum of two years (Article 3, Article 6). The relevant categories of data, which are specified in detail in Article 5 of the Directive, are those deemed necessary 'to trace and identify the source', 'to identify the destination', 'to identify the date, time and duration', and 'to identify the type' of a communication. In addition, 'data necessary to identify users' communications equipment or what purports to be their equipment' and 'data necessary to identify the location of mobile communication equipment' must also be retained (Article 5(1)(e),(f)). The Directive stresses that it is not to be used as a justification for retaining any 'data revealing the content of the communication' (Article 5(2)). The deadline for implementing the Directive in national law was 15 September 2007 (Article 15(1)). This deadline was, however, subject to postponement by way of Declaration to 15 March 2009 for communications data relating to Internet Access, Internet telephony and Internet e-mail (Article 15(3)). No fewer than 16 EU Member States, including the UK, made such

---

[48] 11818/02/final, WP64, adopted on 11 October 2002.

[49] Opinion 4/2005 on the Proposal for a Directive of the European Parliament and of the Council on the Retention of Data Processed in Connection with the Provision of Public Electronic Communication Services and Amending Directive 2002/58/EC (COM(2005)438 final of 21 September 2005) 1168/05/EN, WP 113, adopted on 21 October 2005.

[50] See Walden, I, *Computer Crimes and Digital Investigations* (Oxford University Press, 2007) at 4.230 *et seq.*

[51] Directive 2006/24/EC of the European Parliament and of the Council of 15 March 2006 on the retention of data generated in connection with the provision of publicly available electronic communications services or of public communications networks and amending Directive 2002/58/EC.

declarations with the result that the initial implementation deadline was operative for only a minority of the Member States.

Not surprisingly, the Article 29 Working Party was far from happy with the final form of the Data Retention Directive. In an Opinion issued on 25 March 2006, the Working Party described the decision to retain data for the purpose of combating serious crime as 'an unprecedented one with a historical dimension. It encroaches into the daily life of every citizen and may endanger the fundamental values and freedoms all European citizens enjoy and cherish'.[52] With this in mind, the privacy commissioners stressed the 'utmost importance that the Directive is accompanied and implemented in each Member States by measures curtailing the impact on privacy'. Among other things, the Opinion called for a constrained interpretation of 'serious crime', that data to be retained should be kept to a minimum and that there should be no large-scale data mining.

13.1.3.4 *APEC Privacy Framework*

In November 2004, the members of Asia-Pacific Economic Co-operation (APEC) adopted a Privacy Framework.[53] This contains Information Privacy Principles that overlap to a large extent with those found in the Organisation for Economic Cooperation and Development (OECD) Guidelines, the Council of Europe Convention, and the EU Directive. The APEC Principles cover harm prevention, notice, collection limitation, restrictions on use, choice, integrity, security safeguards, access and correction, and, finally, accountability. This last principle encompasses the concept of consent or due diligence in relation to international transfers of data. Notably absent from the Framework is the requirement to appoint an independent regulator. Moreover, the APEC Principles are, in general, perceived as a somewhat weaker framework than that set out in the OECD Guidelines or established by the Council of Europe Convention. Nevertheless, APEC's focus on harm prevention, together with increasing dissatisfaction with the highly bureaucratic approach adopted by many privacy regulators in the EU, has led to significant and growing interest in the APEC model.[54]

---

[52] Opinion 3/2006 on the Directive 2006/24/EC of the European Parliament and of the Council on the retention of data generated in connection with the provision of publicly available electronic communications services or of public communications networks and amending Directive 2002/58/EC. 654/06/EN WP 119, adopted on 15 March 2006.

[53] Available from <http://www.apec.org/>.

[54] See Millard, 'The Future of Privacy (part 1)—Privacy 1.0 and the need for change', Data Protection Law & Policy, Vol 4, Issue 11, Nov 2007; Millard, 'The Future of Privacy (part 2)—What might Privacy 2.0 look like?', Data Protection Law & Policy, Vol 5, Issue 1, Jan 2008.

13.2 INTERCEPTION, MONITORING, AND RECORDING OF COMMUNICATIONS

Since the early days of communications networks, technology has been available for, and has indeed been used for, surveillance purposes and, in particular, for interception, monitoring, and recording of communications.[55] With the advent of mass communications and the use of surveillance techniques on a systematic basis by both public and private sector organizations, concerns have grown as to the appropriateness of such practices in democratic societies. The UK Information Commissioner, for example, in 2006 launched a major report entitled *A Surveillance Society* and put out a press release stating: 'Two years ago I warned that we were in danger of sleepwalking into a surveillance society. Today I fear that we are in fact waking up to a surveillance society that is already all around us.'[56] The report noted, among other things, widespread monitoring in the workplace of telephone calls, email, and Internet use.

Many justifications can be made for the interception, monitoring, and recording of communications. These range from prevention and investigation of terrorism and other serious crimes through to ensuring that proper records are kept of commercial transactions that take place entirely via phone conversations or email exchanges. For historical and cultural reasons, public attitudes to surveillance can vary significantly from country to country, and there are marked differences in popular levels of trust, or distrust, of public and private sector organizations. This can be problematic for multinational businesses that wish, for example, to adopt common standards for managing their email or other internal communications systems. At the EU level, only limited progress has been made to date in developing a common approach to these issues.[57] Moreover, as development of technology and services continues apace, new issues emerge. For example, there has been considerable controversy in the UK regarding the piloting by a company called Phorm of targeted Internet advertising services based on the browsing habits of users.[58]

For students and practitioners seeking to make sense of the law in this area from a UK perspective, the statutory position has unfortunately evolved on an *ad hoc* basis over many years and is now rather chaotic. To form a complete picture it is necessary to look in a number of places and to consider various provisions, the practical application of at least some of which is far from certain.

---

[55] See, for example, <http://www.recording-history.org/HTML/surveillance1.php>.

[56] <http://www.ico.gov.uk/upload/documents/pressreleases/2006/waking_up_to_a_surveillance_society.pdf>.

[57] For example, the Article 29 Working Party's Opinion on the processing of personal data in the employment context contains only a superficial discussion of the issues. 5062/02/En/final, 13 September 2001.

[58] For the case against Phorm see, e.g. < http://www.theregister.co.uk/2008/02/29/phorm_roundup/>. For Phorm's defence, see: <http://privacy.phorm.com/>.

13.2.1 Wireless Telegraphy Act 2006

Under section 48 of the Wireless Telegraphy Act 2006 (which largely reproduced section 5(b) of its predecessor, the Wireless Telegraphy Act 1949), it is an offence if a person, without official authority, either:

(i) uses wireless telegraphy apparatus with intent to obtain information as to the contents, sender, or addressee of a message (whether sent by means of wireless telegraphy or not) . . . or,
(ii) he discloses information as to the contents, sender, or addressee of such a message.[59]

This provision has a very broad scope. Not only is the entire wireless sector covered, regardless of whether a communication is via a public or a private telecommunications system, but disclosure in the wake of interception may also constitute a criminal offence.

13.2.2 Telecommunications Act 1984

In marked contrast to the broad reach of the privacy provisions in the Wireless Telegraphy Act 1949, the privacy provisions in the Telecommunications Act 1984 (the 1984 Act) (now repealed) were much narrower in scope. Section 44(1) of the 1984 Act provided that '[a] person engaged in the running of a public telecommunications system who otherwise than in the course of his duty intentionally modifies or interferes with the contents of a message sent by means of that system shall be guilty of an offence'. Similarly, under section 45(1) of the 1984 Act, it was an offence for a person engaged in the running of a public telecommunications system (otherwise than in the course of his duty) to disclose intentionally to any person:

(a) the contents of any message which has been intercepted in the course of transmission by means of that system; or
(b) any information concerning the use made of the telecommunication services provided for any other person by means of that system . . .

These provisions only applied to employees of public operators and did not apply to modification, interception, or disclosure of messages in the context of private telecommunications systems.[60] The 1984 Act was largely repealed by the Communications Act 2003. Specifically, the provisions that made it an offence to modify and interrupt messages were repealed. RIPA (see section 13.2.6 below) contains provisions relating to the interception of communications.

---

[59] See further Chapter 7.
[60] A system is a public telecommunication system if it is designated as such by the Secretary of State: s 9(1) of the Telecommunications Act 1984.

13.2.3 Communications Act 2003

The Communications Act 2003 replaced (most of) the 1984 Act, Broadcasting Act 1990, and Broadcasting Act 1996 with a new framework for the regulation of electronic communications networks, services, and associated facilities. The new framework implemented a significant proportion of the harmonized framework for the regulation of electronic communications networks and services which was established by the four EU Communications Directives—the Directive on a common regulatory framework for electronic communications networks and services (the Framework Directive) (02/21/EC), the Directive on access to, and interconnection of, electronic communications networks and associated facilities (the Access Directive) (02/19/EC), the Directive on the authorization of electronic communications networks and services (the Authorization Directive) (02/20/EC), and the Directive on universal service and users' rights relating to electronic communications networks and services (the Universal Service Directive) (02/22/EC).[61]

The monitoring and recording of phone calls on private networks was previously regulated by the class licences granted by the Secretary of State pursuant to section 7 of the Telecommunications Act 1984 (subject to various conditions). Almost all telecommunications users ran their telecommunications systems under these licences. The two main class licences covering non-public telecommunications systems were the self-provision licence (SPL) and the telecommunications services licence (TSL). Both class licences contained a condition entitled 'Privacy of Messages'. In the SPL this was Condition 7; in the TSL it was Condition 10, but the content of the two conditions was identical. This licensing regime was abolished by the Communications Act 2003[62] in favour of an automatic entitlement to provide electronic communications networks, services, or facilities, subject to notification to the Office of Communications (Ofcom) and compliance with specified regulatory conditions (conditions of entitlement).[63]

13.2.4 Interception of Communications Act 1985

Section 1 of the Interception of Communications Act 1985 (now repealed) provided that '. . . a person who intentionally intercepts a communication in the course of its transmission by post or by means of a public telecommunication system shall be guilty of an offence'. This was subject to various exceptions, notably that the interception had been authorized by a warrant issued by the Secretary of State, or that the interceptor had reasonable grounds for believing that the sender or recipient of the message had consented to the interception. The only grounds for issuing a warrant were that it was '. . . necessary (a) in the interests of national security; (b) for the

---

[61] See further Chapter 5.

[62] The Communications Act 2003 provides for transitional provisions and savings provisions that apply to certain existing licensing agreements under the 1984 Act.

[63] See further Chapter 5.

purpose of preventing or detecting serious crime; or (c) for the purpose of safeguarding the economic well-being of the United Kingdom (s 2(2))'.[64] The Secretary of State was required to consider whether the information that was sought could reasonably be acquired by other means (section 2(3)).

With regard to its scope, it became clear that the Interception of Communications Act 1985 (the 1985 Act) had no application to an interception that took place outside a public network (see, for example, *R v Effick* [1994] Crim LR 832, 99; Cr App Rep 312, 158, in which the court held that interception by the police of telephone conversations on a cordless telephone was not subject to the 1985 Act). RIPA repealed the 1985 Act and replaced it with a much broader regime covering all types of communications via both public and private networks (see section 13.2.6 below).

13.2.5 European Convention on Human Rights and Human Rights Act 1998

In *Halford v United Kingdom* [1997] IRLR 471, the European Court of Human Rights ruled that interception of telephone calls made on an internal telecommunications system operated by Merseyside police was an infringement of Article 8 of the European Convention on Human Rights. Article 8(1) provides that 'Everyone has the right to respect for his private and family life, his home and his correspondence'. Article 8(2) adds that public authorities may interfere with this right only 'in accordance with the law'. The Court considered the scope of the Interception of Communications Act 1985 and concluded that, because it did not apply to interception via a private network, such interception could not be 'in accordance with the law'.[65] Partly in response to that ruling, in June 1999 the Home Office issued a Consultation Paper entitled *Interception of Communications in the United Kingdom* (Cm 4368), in which it proposed, among other things, that the regime in the Interception of Communications Act 1985 should be widened to cover all communications networks.

The Human Rights Act 1998, which received Royal Assent on 9 November 1998, incorporated the European Convention on Human Rights into UK law. It did so by indirect means, among other things by requiring courts to interpret UK legislation, so far as possible, in a manner compatible with the Convention.[66] Section 19 of the Act came into force on 24 November 1998, and has since then required the government to make a written statement in relation to any proposed legislation as to whether the Bill in question is or is not compatible with the Convention.[67] The remaining provisions of the Act were brought into force on 2 October 2000.[68]

---

[64] The economic well-being justification is available only in relation to 'information relating to the acts or intentions of persons outside the British Islands' (s 2(4)).

[65] More recently, the European Court of Human Rights ruled in *Khan v United Kingdom*, The Times, 23 May 2000, that use by the police of a covert listening device breached Art 8 of the Convention as there existed at the time no statutory system to regulate the use of such devices.

[66] Human Rights Act 1998, s 3.

[67] Human Rights Act 1998 (Commencement) Order 1998 (SI 1998/2882).

[68] Human Rights Act 1998 (Commencement No 2) Order 2000 (SI 2000/1851).

13.2.6 Regulation of Investigatory Powers Act 2000

The Regulation of Investigatory Powers Act (RIPA) was enacted on 28 July 2000 and most of its provisions were brought into force in 24 October 2000 (Regulation of Investigatory Powers Act 2000 (Commencement No 1 and Transitional Provisions) Order 2000 (SI 2000/2543)). RIPA replaced the Interception of Communications Act 1985 (see section 13.2.4 above) and section 45 of the 1984 Act (see section 13.2.2 above) and, among other matters, regulates 'intrusive investigative techniques', empowering the police and other authorized persons to compel individuals or organizations to disclose information necessary to decipher encrypted messages. While these encryption-related provisions clearly have an impact on telecommunications privacy, a detailed discussion of those rules is beyond the scope of this chapter.

With regard to interception of communications, section 1(1) of RIPA makes it 'an offence for a person intentionally and without lawful authority to intercept, at any place in the United Kingdom, any communication in the course of its transmission by means of (a) a public postal service; or (b) a public telecommunication system'. Section 1(2) creates a similar offence in relation to private telecommunication systems, with the exception that no offence is committed if the interception is either made by a person with the right to control that system, or is made with the consent of the system controller (section 1(6)). The Explanatory Notes to the bill that preceded RIPA give examples of activities within this exception, such as the use of a second handset in a house to monitor a call, and routine recording of calls by a financial institution to provide evidence of transactions. Section 5(1) permits the Secretary of State to issue a warrant authorizing or requiring the interception of communications in specified circumstances.

In addition to the criminal offences created by section 1(1) and (2), section 1(3) has created the following new tort of unlawful interception on a private network:

(3) Any interception of a communication which is carried out at any place in the United Kingdom by, or with the express or implied consent of, a person having the right to control the operation or the use of a private telecommunication system shall be actionable at the suit or instance of the sender or recipient, or intended recipient, of the communication if it is without lawful authority and is either—

(a) an interception of that communication in the course of its transmission by means of that private system; or

(b) an interception of that communication in the course of its transmission, by means of a public telecommunication system, to or from apparatus comprised in that private telecommunication system.

Thus, a system controller who is protected from criminal liability under section 1(2) may nevertheless face civil proceedings for breach of section 1(3). As the Explanatory Notes to the bill that preceded RIPA observe, 'where an employee believes that their employer has unlawfully intercepted a telephone conversation with a third party, either the employee or the third party may sue the employer' (paragraph 21). However, the key issue will be whether the employer has 'lawful authority' to intercept

the communication. There are two main grounds on which lawful authority might be based. First, on the fact, or reasonable belief, that both the sender and the intended recipient of the communication in question have consented to its interception (section 3(1)). This may lead to employers inserting consent clauses in employee contracts, and possibly also in customer or other individual third party contracts. There may be many situations, though, where the consent of both parties to a communication cannot be obtained. This is likely, in particular, to be a problem in relation to senders of communications, as an employer usually cannot predict who will send communications to its employees. As a result, considerable reliance will in practice have to be placed on an alternative ground for lawful authority, as set out in the Telecommunications (Lawful Business Practice) (Interception of Communications) Regulations 2000 (SI 2000/2699), issued pursuant to section 4(2) and (3) of the Regulation of Investigatory Powers Act (Lawful Business Practice Regulations).

The Lawful Business Practice Regulations authorize the interception of a communication if it is effected by or with the express or implied consent of the system controller (e.g. an employer) for specific purposes relating to monitoring or keeping a record of communications relevant to the system controller's business (regulation 3). Communications are relevant if they are transactional, otherwise relate to the business, or otherwise take place in the course of carrying on the business (regulation 2(b)). Qualifying business purposes include establishing the existence of facts, ascertaining compliance with regulatory or self-regulatory practices or procedures, and ascertaining or demonstrating that standards have been achieved (e.g. quality control or training). In addition, such interception may be justified in the interests of national security, for crime prevention or detection purposes, for investigating or detecting unauthorized use, and for purposes related to effective system operation (regulation 3(1)).

Furthermore, the Lawful Business Practice Regulations authorize monitoring for the purpose of distinguishing business from non-business-related communications (regulation 3(1)(b)).[69] In every case, however, the system controller must have made 'all reasonable efforts' to inform every user of the system that communications may be intercepted (regulation 3(2)(c)).[70] Rather curiously, the Lawful Business Practice Regulations state that interception for business purposes is authorized only to the extent permitted by Article 5 of the Privacy and Electronic Communications Directive. This perhaps suggests that a challenge was anticipated to the pragmatic way in which the power to override the confidentiality rule in that Article has been used.

---

[69] The Regulations also permit monitoring of 'communications made to a confidential voice-telephony counselling or support service which is free of charge (other than the cost, if any, of making a telephone call) and operated in such a way that users may remain anonymous if they so choose' (reg 3(1)(c)).

[70] The Information Commissioner and Department of Trade and Industry have taken the view that external third party callers or senders of email will not be persons who 'use the telecommunications system' in question. It is arguable that an external third party caller or sender will fall into that category but the more important issue will be what constitutes 'reasonable efforts' in terms of the obligation to inform such users of the possible interception.

The Regulation of Investigatory Powers (Communications Data) Order 2003 came into force on 5 January 2004 (SI 2003/3172). It specifies additional public authorities for the purposes of section 25(1) of RIPA that are entitled to acquire communications data from telecommunications companies or Internet service providers. It specifies which individuals within those public authorities are entitled to acquire communications data, and places restrictions on the grounds on which they may acquire such data and the types of data they may acquire.

On 11 June 2003 the Information Commissioner released the third part of a four-part Employment Practices Data Protection Code entitled 'Monitoring at work'.[71] It describes the way in which organizations can comply with the requirements of the DPA 1998 if they wish to monitor the activities of their employees. Broadly speaking, the DPA 1998 requires any adverse impact on employees to be justified by the benefits to the employer and others.

The Code includes special provisions for electronic communications (including telephone calls, fax messages, emails, and Internet access). Monitoring which involves an interception and results in the recording of personal information must comply with the Lawful Business Practice Regulations and the DPA 1998. The Good Practice Recommendation 3.2, relating to monitoring electronic communications, encourages employers to promulgate a clear policy, and sets out key points to be addressed when enforcing such a policy.

13.2.7 Anti-Terrorism, Crime and Security Act 2001

The Anti-Terrorism, Crime and Security Act 2001 (the Anti-Terrorism Act) amends the Terrorism Act 2000 to provide, among other things, for the retention of communications data. Sections 102 to 104 of the Anti-Terrorism Act permits the Secretary of State to issue codes of practice, enter into agreements with communications providers, or give directions, as necessary, for the purpose of safeguarding national security, or preventing or detecting crime, or the prosecution of offenders which may relate directly to national security. The wide ambit of the terms 'communications provider' and 'communications data' mean that these provisions are broadly applicable to service providers such as telephone companies, Internet service providers, and postal companies, and any data they transmit and receive (communications data has the same meaning as set out in RIPA and includes anything transmitted by means of a postal service, anything comprising speech, music, sounds, visual images, data, and signals).

A voluntary code of practice was issued under the Retention of Communications Data (Code of Practice) Order 2003, pursuant to section 102(1) of the Anti-Terrorism Act. The Code came into effect on 5 December 2003.

As regards data relating to voice calls, the data retention provisions of the Anti-Terrorism Act have been superseded by the Data Retention (EC Directive)

---

[71] In June 2005 the Code was reissued in updated form with all four parts in a single document, together with a summary 'Quick Guide' for small businesses. Both documents are available at <http://www.ico.gov.uk>.

Regulations 2007 which transposed into English law the 2006 Data Retention Directive (SI 2007/2199).[72] The Regulations came into force on 1 October 2007. As a result of a Declaration made at the time the Directive was adopted, the UK Government has until 15 March 2009 to apply the Directive to communications data relating to Internet Access, Internet telephony, and Internet email.

Under regulation 4, public communications providers must normally retain specified data relating to voice (but not Internet telephony, i.e. VoIP) and mobile calls for 12 months from the date of a communication. Under regulation 5, the data which must be retained include the number from which the call was made and the name and address of the subscriber and registered user, the number dialled, the date and time of the call, and the service used. For mobile calls, additional information relating to the mobile user and network equipment (including geographic location) must also be retained.

13.3 PRIVACY AND ELECTRONIC COMMUNICATIONS (EC DIRECTIVE) REGULATIONS 2003

13.3.1 Restrictions on use of cookies, traffic, billing, and location data

Regulation 6 of the PEC Regulations concerns the confidentiality of communications. It regulates the circumstances in which electronic communications networks may be used to store or gain access to information stored in the terminal equipment of a subscriber or user. The provision applies to all such activities and not merely those involving the processing of personal data. Where, however, the use of a cookie, for example, involves the processing of personal data, service providers must also comply with the DPA 1998, including the fair information provisions and the requirement not to process excessive personal data. Regulation 6 specifies the information to be provided to subscribers or users about the purposes of the storage of, and access to, the information and requires that subscribers or users be given an opportunity to refuse such storage or access. Limited exceptions exist where information storage or access is for narrow communications purposes or is strictly necessary for the provision of an information society service.

Regulation 7 concerns the processing of traffic data. Traffic data is defined as any data processed (i) for the conveyance of a communication on an electronic communications network, or (ii) for the billing in respect of that communication. This Regulation provides protection for both individual and corporate subscribers with regard to the processing of traffic data. Such data must be erased or modified so that they cease to be personal data, where the data is no longer required for the purpose of transmitting the communication. Traffic data may be processed and stored by a public communications provider if (i) it is for the purpose of marketing electronic

---

[72] The Directive and its legislative history are discussed in 13.1.3.3, above.

communications services or the provision of value added services to the subscriber or user; (ii) consent has been provided; and (iii) such processing and storage is limited to the duration necessary for the purpose of the marketing activity. Data required for the purposes of a bill can only be retained for as long as the period in which the bill may lawfully be challenged or payment pursued. Regulation 7 also outlines the purposes for which traffic data may be processed and the circumstances in which consent must be obtained, as well as general provisions relating to the processing of traffic data.

Regulation 14 deals with restrictions on the processing of location data. Location data is defined as any data processed in an electronic communications network indicating the geographical position of the terminal equipment of a user of a public electronic communications service (it includes data relating to the latitude, longitude, or altitude of the equipment, direction of travel, and time recorded). Such data may only be processed where (i) the subscriber or user cannot be identified from that data, or (ii) where it is necessary for the provision of a value added service with the consent of the relevant user or subscriber. Location data may only be processed by the communications provider, the third party provider of the value added service, or a person acting on their behalf.

13.4 ITEMIZED BILLS

Regulation 9 provides that, if requested by a subscriber, a provider of a public electronic communications service must provide bills which are not itemized. This reflects a concern expressed in the Privacy and Electronic Communications Directive that fully itemized bills may 'jeopardize the privacy of . . . users' (Recital 33). A relevant scenario might be where a phone line at particular premises is shared by several residents.

13.5 CALLING OR CONNECTED LINE IDENTIFICATION

The PEC Regulations deal with the use of calling or connected line identification (CLI) for incoming and outgoing calls. The Regulations cover both call return and call display facilities.

As regards outgoing calls, an electronic communications service provider must provide, free of charge, a 'simple means' of preventing the presentation of the identity of the calling line on the connected line. This facility must be offered to users and subscribers originating a single call (PEC Regulations, regulation 10(2)), and to subscribers to a line who should be able to bar identification with respect to all calls made from that line (PEC Regulations, regulaton 10(3)). Given the wide meaning of 'user' (any individual using a public electronic communications service), the right to withhold calling number identity must be offered on calls from pay-phones and other telephones to which the public have access.

The corollary right from the perspective of incoming calls is that where presentation on the connected line of the identity of the calling line is available, the electronic communications service provider shall ensure that the called subscriber has a 'simple means' to reject the calls in question (PEC Regulations, regulation 11(3)). Similarly, the subscriber can also reject calls where the identity of the calling party is not revealed.

Further, as regards incoming calls on a line, where presentation of the identity of the calling line on the connected line is available, the called subscriber must be provided with a 'simple means', without charge, of preventing the presentation of the identity of a calling line on the connected line (PEC Regulations, regulation 11(2)). Lastly, where presentation on the calling line of the identity of the connected line is available, the electronic communications service provider must provide the called subscriber with a 'simple means' to prevent, without charge, the presentation of the identity of the connected line on any calling line (PEC Regulations, regulation 11(4)).

Exceptions to these rules exist in relation to emergency calls and malicious or nuisance calls (PEC Regulations, regulations 15 and 16). In order to facilitate responses to emergency calls, there is no right to withhold the identity of the calling line. Indeed, there is a prohibition on preventing such presentation with respect to calls made to the national emergency number (999) or the single European emergency call number (112). As regards unwanted calls, where subscribers inform an electronic communications service provider that they require the tracing of malicious or nuisance calls, an electronic communications service provider may override anything done to prevent the presentation of the identity of the calling line on the affected subscriber's called line, in so far as it appears to the provider necessary or expedient. An electronic communications service provider may hold and make available to those with 'a legitimate interest therein' data containing the identification of a calling subscriber, if the data were obtained during the period in which it was attempting to trace malicious or nuisance calls.

13.6 DIRECTORIES

The PEC Regulations contain provisions relating to directories (both printed and electronic) of subscribers to publicly available electronic communications services (PEC Regulations, regulation 18(1)). As regards entries relating to individuals, unless a subscriber has been informed and given the opportunity to determine whether his or her personal data should be included, a directory may not contain personal data (PEC Regulations, regulation 18(2)). Furthermore, where an individual's information is included, a producer of a directory must allow the individual to verify, correct, or withdraw the data free of charge at any time. In addition, subscribers must be informed of the consequences of choosing particular directory options. The Regulations do not specify whether subscribers should be required positively to

'opt in' to inclusion in a directory or whether it is sufficient for them to 'opt out'. The Information Commissioner has commented that 'it is not unreasonable for inclusion in the directory to be the default position provided that subscribers are made fully aware that this is the case and it is simple and straightforward for them to opt out if they choose'.[73] If a directory has already been produced before the request is made, the request applies to the next edition of the directory (PEC Regulations, regulation 18(6)).

The Regulations prohibit reverse searching unless the prior informed consent of the data subject has been obtained.

Corporate subscribers' rights are limited as compared to those of individual subscribers, although a corporate subscriber may request that its number be excluded from the directory.

13.7 USE OF TELECOMMUNICATIONS SERVICES FOR DIRECT MARKETING PURPOSES

13.7.1 Automated calling systems

The PEC Regulations replicate the 1999 Regulations, in that they prohibit the use of automated calling systems to make direct marketing calls to individuals or corporates, except where the prior consent of the subscriber concerned has been obtained (PEC Regulations, regulation 19). The system regulated is a system which is capable of automatically initiating a sequence of calls to more than one destination in accordance with stored instructions and transmitting recorded sounds for receipt to some or all of the destinations called. Although somewhat unclear, this is likely to apply only to a call that is initiated and completed without human intervention. An automated dialling system that sets up calls that are taken over by a live operator when answered would not appear to be covered by this rule.

13.7.2 Voice calls

In relation to voice calls, the PEC Regulations replicate the 1999 Regulations but also allow corporate subscribers to register their numbers with the telecommunications preference service (the TPS). It is open to any individual or corporate subscriber to put his or her telephone number on the TPS's register. The PEC Regulations prohibit direct marketing calls to individuals whose numbers appear on the TPS's register, or who have previously notified the caller that they do not wish to receive such unsolicited calls for the time being (PEC Regulations, regulation 21). It is possible for an individual to object to the receipt of direct marketing calls generally, but to agree

---

[73] Guidance to the Privacy and Electronic Communications (EC Directive) Regulations 2003, Part 2. Available at <http://www.ico.gov.uk>.

(perhaps by accepting an organization's terms and conditions) that a particular organization may, nevertheless, make direct marketing calls to him or her.

13.7.3 Fax

As regards the sending of unsolicited communications by fax, the PEC Regulations continue the arrangements in relation to the faxes that were operating already under the 1999 Regulations. Regulation 20 prohibits the sending of unsolicited direct marketing materials by fax to corporates that have notified the sender that they do not wish to receive such faxes or to subscribers who have registered with the fax preference service (FPS). Again, it is possible to bypass a general opt-out by a subscriber if that subscriber has notified a particular caller that he does not object to receiving direct marketing communications from that caller.

Regulation 20 also prohibits the sending of unsolicited direct marketing materials to an individual subscriber by fax without obtaining the prior consent of the subscriber.

13.7.4 Email

The PEC Regulations define electronic mail as 'any text, voice, sound or image message sent over a public electronic communications network which can be stored in the network or in the recipient's terminal equipment until it is collected by the recipient and includes messages sent using a short message service'. Accordingly, email and text/picture/video marketing messages are all likely to be treated as electronic mail for the purposes of Regulation 22. Moreover, given the breadth of the definition, even simple voicemail and answering machine messages appear to constitute 'emails' for the purposes of this Regulation. This may not have been intended and is probably frequently overlooked when live voice calls are being made for marketing purposes. Regulation 22 applies to individual subscribers but not to corporate subscribers.[74]

Regulation 22(2) prevents a person from transmitting, or instigating the transmission of, unsolicited communications for the purposes of direct marketing by means of email unless the recipient of the email has previously notified the sender that he or she consents for the time being to such communications being sent by, or at the instigation of, the sender. The individual subscriber is required to 'opt in'. The Information Commissioner has commented that such 'opt-in' consent may be demonstrated in a variety of ways, including ticking a box, clicking an icon, sending an

---

[74] The view of the Article 29 Working Party (<http://ec.europa.eu/justice_home/fsj/privacy/docs/wpdocs/2004/wp90_en.pdf>) appears to conflict with the current guidance published by the UK Information Commissioner ('UK Guidance') (available at <http://www.ico.gov.uk>). The Working Party considers that a marketing email sent to a 'personal' email addresses at a corporate subscriber should be considered the same as marketing to natural persons.

email, or subscribing to a service. The crucial consideration is whether individual subscribers fully understand both that they are consenting and what it is that they are consenting to. The Article 29 Working Party has recently published guidance (see section 13.1.3.3 above) which asserts that a general email requesting consent is not sufficient, nor is it sufficient for a website to contain pre-ticked boxes. This appears to be a rather stricter approach than that currently adopted by the Information Commissioner and may be cumbersome in practice.

13.8 GENERAL APPLICATION OF THE DATA PROTECTION ACT 1998 TO THE COMMUNICATIONS SECTOR

13.8.1 Jurisdictional reach

The DPA 1998 applies to 'data controllers' in respect of particular 'personal data' only if the controller either is established in the UK and the data are processed in the context of that establishment, or the controller is established outside the EEA 'but uses equipment in the United Kingdom for processing the data otherwise than for the purposes of transit through the United Kingdom' (section 5(1)). A data controller who falls into the second category must nominate a representative in the UK in relation to its obligations under the DPA 1998.

This apparently straightforward statement of territorial scope is fraught with difficulty in the telecommunications context. For one thing, due to the breadth of the establishment concept in the DPA 1998 it is possible that, for example, a telecommunications operator or an ISP will be established in multiple states within the EEA.[75] Similarly, a commercial organization may find that it is subject to multiple, and in certain respects inconsistent, national rules in relation to its internal cross-border Intranet. Even where a data controller is not established in multiple EEA states, it may at least use equipment in multiple states. The EU Data Protection Directive makes it clear that 'when the controller is established on the territory of several Member States, he must take the necessary measures to ensure that each of these establishments complies with the obligations laid down by the national law applicable . . .' (Article 4(1)(a)).

The second problematic aspect of the territoriality rule is the exception for the processing of data using equipment in the UK that is merely 'for the purposes of transit through the United Kingdom' (DPA 1998, section 5(1)(b)). What if, for example, a website on a server in the US is 'mirrored' by a UK-based ISP on a server in the UK to facilitate access to that site by UK-based customers of the ISP? Will the ISP in the UK become a data controller in relation to any personal data contained in

---

[75] Section 5(3) of the DPA 1998 provides that, in addition to UK individuals, companies, and partnerships, '. . . any person who maintains in the United Kingdom—(i) an office, branch or agency through which he carries on any activity, or (ii) a regular practice' will be treated as established in the UK.

that website? Will the ISP in the US be treated as established in the UK merely because an ISP in the UK has chosen to make a copy of the site (quite possibly without the site controller's knowledge)? What if a website on a server in the US plants a 'cookie' on the PC of a UK-based visitor to the site and subsequently interrogates that cookie remotely each time the visitor returns to the site? Is the data controller in the US using equipment in the UK (i.e. the visitor's PC) to process data about that visitor? Given that 'processing' includes 'obtaining, recording or holding . . . information or data' such a construction is possible. This would, however, be an absurd result as the website operator in the US would presumably have to appoint the UK visitor as its representative for the purposes of compliance with the DPA 1998!

13.8.2 Notification obligations

Subject to various exemptions, under the DPA 1998 it is a strict liability offence for a data controller to process personal data without first giving a notification to the Data Protection Commissioner (sections 17(1) and 21(1)). The DPA 1998 lists various 'registrable particulars' which must be included in a notification, including the controller's name and address, or that of any nominated representative; a description of the personal data to be processed; the purposes for which the data are to be processed; the recipient(s) to whom the data may be disclosed; and details of countries outside the EEA to which the data may be transferred. In addition, a notification must specify 'a general description of measures to be taken for the purpose of complying with the seventh data protection principle' (section 18(2); see section 13.8.6 below).

13.8.3 Information provision requirements

The first data protection principle provides that '[p]ersonal data shall be processed fairly and lawfully. . .' (DPA 1998, Schedule 1, Part I, paragraph 1). The interpretation provisions make it clear that personal data 'are not to be treated as processed fairly unless' certain information is provided, or made readily available, to the individual concerned (Schedule 1, Part II, paragraph 2(1)). The information to be given to data subjects must include the identity of the data controller and any nominated representative, the purpose or purposes for which the data are intended to be processed, and 'any further information which is necessary, having regard to the specific circumstances in which the data are or are to be processed, to enable processing in respect of the data subject to be fair' (Schedule 1, Part II, paragraph 2(3)).

13.8.4 Justification for processing data

Personal data must not be processed unless one of a number of conditions is satisfied. These are set out in Schedule 2 to the DPA 1998. In summary, processing is legitimate if the data subject has given his or her consent; or if it is necessary for the performance of a contract to which the data subject is a party or for taking steps to

enter into a contract, for compliance with a legal obligation (other than contractual), or for certain public sector purposes.[76] In addition, processing is justified if it is 'necessary for the purposes of a legitimate interest pursued by the data controller or by the third party or parties to whom the data are disclosed, except where the processing is unwarranted in a particular case by reason of prejudice to the rights and freedoms or legitimate interests of the data subject'.

More stringent conditions apply to processing of sensitive data. These are set out in Schedule 3 to the DPA 1998. The DPA 1998 defines 'sensitive personal data' as 'personal data consisting of information as to' a data subject's racial or ethnic origin, political opinions, religious beliefs, or other beliefs of a similar nature, membership of a trade union, physical or mental health or condition, sexual life, or commission or alleged commission or proceedings in relation to any offence (section 2). Processing of sensitive data will be legitimate only if the data subject has given his or her 'explicit consent'; the processing is necessary in relation to an employment right or obligation; the processing is necessary to protect the vital interests of the data subject or another person in circumstances where consent is not obtainable; the processing is by a charitable body in relation to its members; the data subject has made the data public; the processing is necessary in relation to legal proceedings or advice; or the processing is for certain public sector purposes. In addition, processing may be legitimate in the public or private sectors where it is carried out for medical purposes by a health professional, or where it is carried out, with appropriate safeguards, for ethnic monitoring purposes to promote or maintain equality. The Data Protection (Processing of Sensitive Personal Data) Order 2000 (SI 2000/417) has established various additional circumstances in which sensitive data may be processed. Of potential significance in the telecommunications context is an exemption covering certain processing activities for the purposes of preventing or detecting any unlawful act (Schedule, paragraph 1(1)).

13.8.5 Data subject rights

The sixth data protection principle requires data controllers to process personal data 'in accordance with the rights of data subjects under this Act' (DPA 1998, Schedule 1, Part I, paragraph 6). An interpretation provision states that a person will be regarded as contravening this principle only if he fails to provide access to data as required, fails to comply with a notice from a data subject requiring him to stop processing data for certain purposes, or fails to comply with the procedures relating to automated decision making (Schedule 1, Part II, paragraph 8). This restrictive statement should, however, be read in conjunction with the general right which an individual has under section 13 of the DPA 1998 to compensation where he or she has suffered

---

[76] Broadly, these are that the processing is necessary for the administration of justice, in relation to any statutory or government function or other public function exercised in the public interest.

damage as a result of contravention by a data controller of any of the requirements of the Act. The difference between these provisions is that a breach of the sixth principle may trigger the service on the data controller by the Data Protection Commissioner of an enforcement notice, whereas breach of section 13 may form the basis for a civil claim for compensation for damage and, possibly, distress.

13.8.6 Security obligations

The seventh data protection principle provides that '[a]ppropriate technical and organizational measures shall be taken against unauthorized or unlawful processing of personal data and against accidental loss or destruction of, or damage to, personal Application of Data Protection Act 1998 to Communications Sector 399 data' (DPA 1998, Schedule 1, Part I, paragraph 7). Given the degree of public concern regarding the security, or otherwise, of communications and transactions via the Internet, this principle needs to be considered carefully, notwithstanding that public concerns may be overstated.

The DPA 1998 contains some interpretation of this principle from which a number of practical conclusions can be drawn. The first is that what constitutes 'appropriate' security will vary widely depending on the circumstances. Relevant factors include the nature of the data to be protected, an assessment of the harm that might result from unauthorized or unlawful processing or accidental loss, destruction or damage, the state of technological development and the cost of any security measures (Schedule 1, Part II, paragraph 9). This suggests, for example, that whereas publication on a website of information that is already in the public domain might require little or no security cover, the collection via email or the web of medical or other sensitive data might necessitate adoption of rigorous security measures.

Secondly, data controllers are required to 'take reasonable steps to ensure the reliability of any employees . . . who have access to the personal data' (Schedule 1, Part II, paragraph 10). Again, the use of the word 'reasonable' suggests that a range of steps may be appropriate depending on the circumstances, ranging from minimal supervision to positive vetting.

Thirdly, where a data controller uses a data processor, the controller will automatically be in breach of the seventh principle unless the following criteria are satisfied:

1) the processor provides 'sufficient guarantees in respect of the technical and organizational security measures governing the processing to be carried out' and the controller takes 'reasonable steps to ensure compliance with those measures' (Schedule 1, Part II, paragraph 11); and

2) the processing is governed by a written contract requiring the processor to act only as instructed by the controller and to comply with security obligations equivalent to those imposed on the controller (Schedule 1, Part II, paragraph 12).

This requirement to document arrangements between controllers and processors is clearly of broad significance to the telecommunications industry, characterized as it is by numerous interconnection, outsourcing, and service provider relationships. Specifically in the Internet context, data controllers will need to ensure that they have appropriate, and properly documented, contractual arrangements in place with any ISPs or other third parties which process data on their behalf, for example by hosting websites.

13.8.7 Transborder data flows

The eighth data protection principle provides that '[p]ersonal data shall not be transferred to a country or territory outside the European Economic Area unless that country or territory ensures an adequate level of protection for the rights and freedoms of data subjects in relation to the processing of personal data' (Data Protection Act 1998, Schedule 1, Part I, paragraph 8). The interpretation provisions add that adequacy depends on 'all the circumstances of the case', including the nature of the data, the country or territory of origin and final destination of the data, the law in force and international obligations of those jurisdictions, the purposes and duration of the intended processing, 'any relevant codes of conduct or other rules which are enforceable in that country or territory', and any security measures taken in the destination country or territory (Schedule 1, Part II, paragraph 13).

The Data Protection Directive, Article 25(6), envisages that the European Commission may find that particular countries outside the EEA provide an adequate level of protection for personal data. Following a procedure involving a Committee of Representatives of the Member States (Article 31(2)), such countries may be added to what is, in effect, a 'white list' of approved destinations. At the time of writing, such adequacy findings had been made only in relation to Switzerland,[77] Hungary,[78] the 'Safe Harbor Privacy Principles' issued by the US Department of Commerce,[79] Canada,[80] Argentina,[81]

---

[77] Commission Decision 2000/518/EC of 26 July 2000 pursuant to Directive 95/46/EC of the European Parliament and of the Council on the adequate protection of personal data provided in Switzerland, (2000) OJ L 215/1.
    [78] Commission Decision 2000/519/EC of 26 July 2000 pursuant to Directive 95/46/EC of the European Parliament and of the Council on the adequate protection of personal data provided in Hungary, (2000) OJ L 215/4. This decision became redundant when Hungary acceded to the European Union on 1 May 2004.
    [79] Commission Decision 2000/520/EC of 26 July 2000 pursuant to Directive 95/46/EC of the European Parliament and of the Council on the adequacy of the protection provided by the safe harbor privacy principles and related frequently asked questions issued by the US Department of Commerce, (2000) OJ L 215/7. See the European Commission's website (<http://www.ec.europa.eu>) for other documentation relating to the US Safe Harbor arrangements and also to documentation relating to the transfer to the US of Air Passenger Name Record (PNR) data.
    [80] Commission Decision 2002/2/EC pf 20 December 2001 pursuant to Directive 95/46/EC of the European Parliament and of the Council on the adequate of the protection of personal data provided by the Canadian Personal Information Protection and Electronic Documents Act, (2002) OJ L 2/13.
    [81] Commission Decision C(2003) 1731 of 30 June 2003 pursuant to Directive 95/46/EC of the European Parliament and of the Council on the adequate protection of personal data in Argentina, (2003) OJ L 168.

Guernsey,[82] the Isle of Man,[83] and Jersey.[83a] In addition, the Article 29 Working Party has issued favourable opinions in relation to the adequacy of the data protection laws of Jersey and the Faroe Islands and it seems likely that those jurisdictions will be added to the 'white list' in due course.[84] The detailed arrangements relating to the Safe Harbor are complex and beyond the scope of this chapter. In general terms, however, the benefit of the Safe Harbor is available only to organizations that are regulated either by the Federal Trade Commission or by the US Department of Transportation[85] and that publicly commit to adhere to a set of principles that are broadly similar to the principles of the Data Protection Directive. Details of organizations that are within the Safe Harbor are available on a public website.[86] The Data Protection Act 1998 provides that 'Community findings', such as those relating to the countries outlined above, are conclusive for the purpose of demonstrating adequacy under the eighth data protection principle (Schedule 1, Part II, paragraph 15).

Although over time the list of 'adequate' destination countries is expected to grow, the 'white list' is currently very short and rather eclectic. Consequently, it is likely that there will remain many situations in which it cannot be demonstrated that a destination country ensures an adequate level of protection. To overcome the eighth principle's prohibition on transfer in such cases, it will be necessary to rely on one or more of the exemptions listed in Schedule 4 to the DPA 1998. There are nine exemptions, the first seven of which apply 'automatically', in the sense that no prior regulatory approval is needed. The remaining two exemptions are not automatic and require the prior approval of the Data Protection Commissioner.

Probably the most straightforward automatic exemption is that the data subject has consented to the transfer (Schedule 4, paragraph 1). Although the Internet is perceived by some as a threat to privacy, it may in fact prove to be a particularly effective medium for obtaining data protection consents. An individual can be provided, by email or via a web page, with the requisite information to make an informed decision about an international transfer. The consent of that individual can then be captured via a return email or a 'click-through' on a website.

The second and third automatic exceptions to the prohibition on transfer relate to contracts which a data controller might enter into with or for the benefit of a data subject, as well as preparatory steps in relation to such contracts (Schedule 4, paragraphs 2 and 3). Again, there may be many instances in the telecommunications and Internet contexts where one of these exemptions will justify the transfer of personal data to inadequate countries. Obvious examples would be the various transfers

---

[82] Commission Decision of 21 November 2003 on the adequate protection of personal data in Guernsey (2003) OJ L 308.

[83] Commission Decision of 28 April 2004 on the adequate protection of personal data in the Isle of Man, (2004/411/EC), (2004) OJ L 151/48.

[83a] Commission Decision 2008/393/EC of 8 May 2008 pursuant to Directive 95/46/EC of the European Parliament and of the Council on the adequate protection of personal data in Jersey, (2008) OJ L 138/21.

[84] Opinion 8/2007 on the level of protection in Jersey, WP 141, adopted on 9 October 2007; Opinion 9/2007 on the level of protection in the Faroe Islands, WP 142, adopted on 9 October 2007.

[85] This means, for example, that regulated financial institutions cannot enter the Safe Harbor.

[86] The Safe Harbor List can be found at <http://www.export.gov/safeharbor>.

necessary to set up and complete an electronic commerce transaction. These might include payment arrangements with credit card issuers and fulfilment arrangements with suppliers and shippers.

The remaining automatic exemptions are likely to be of much more limited relevance in the telecommunications and Internet contexts. The fourth covers transfers that are necessary for reasons of substantial public interest (Schedule 4, paragraph 4). The fifth applies to transfers that are necessary in connection with legal proceedings, legal advice, or for establishing, exercising, or defending legal rights (Schedule 4, paragraph 5). The sixth is available where the transfer is 'necessary to protect the vital interests of the data subject' (Schedule 4, paragraph 6), and the seventh covers transfers of personal data from a public register (Schedule 4, paragraph 7).

This leaves the two non-automatic exemptions to the prohibition on transfers. These are the only other grounds on which personal data may lawfully be transferred to a non-EEA country that fails to ensure adequate protection for data subjects. The first covers transfers that are 'made on terms of a kind approved by the Commissioner as ensuring adequate safeguards for the rights and freedoms of data subjects' (Schedule 4, paragraph 8). The second covers transfers that have been 'authorized by the Commissioner as being made in such a manner as to ensure adequate safeguards for the rights and freedoms of data subjects' (Schedule 4, paragraph 9).

The European Commission has approved three sets of contractual clauses for transborder data flows. Two of these relate to a transfer out of the EEA to a Data Controller.[87] The third relates to a transfer out of the EEA to a Data Processor.[88] It is intended that contracts based on the clauses will be entered into by data exporters based in the EEA and data importers based outside of the EEA. The clauses require the receiving party to establish adequate standards of protection over personal data and, subject to limited compliance and administration exceptions, guarantee that the parties have fulfilled their obligations in respect of transborder data flows set out in the Data Protection Directive. The standard contracts contain a number of provisions that commercial organizations may consider onerous. In particular, they state that the governing law is the place of establishment of the data exporter, liability is joint and several as between the data exporter and data importer, onward transfers from the data importer are not permitted, and the contracts confer rights on individuals who are not parties. Moreover, the standard clauses appear to have been designed for use in simple situations where two entities wish to make point to point transfers of data for one, or at least limited, purposes. In reality, many organizations operate in multiple jurisdictions, have complex legal structures, and need to transfer vast amounts

[87] Commission Decision 2001/497/EC of 15 June 2001 on standard contractual clauses for the transfer of personal data to third countries under Directive 95/46/EC, (2001) OJ L181/19; Commission Decision 2004/915/EC of 27 December 2004 amending Decision 2001/497/EC as regards the introduction of an alternative set of standard contractual clauses for the transfer of personal data to third countries, (2004) OJ L 385/74.

[88] Commission Decision 2002/16/EC: 'on standard contractual clauses for the transfer of personal data to processors established in third countries'; (2002) OJ L 6/52.

of data for many different purposes and in different capacities (i.e. potentially as controller and/or processor). Some national regulators have been willing to accommodate creative uses of the standard clauses by organizations, including multi-party, multi-jurisdictional, hybrid arrangements incorporating both controller and processor clauses. Some other regulators have tended to adopt a rather literalist, bureaucratic approach and have insisted that organizations implement the standard clauses in their original form with as few variations as possible. Moreover, whereas the standard clauses are supposed to be pre-approved, some regulators insist on a filing procedure and, in some cases, a positive approval procedure before they recognize them as valid in their national EU jurisdiction.[89]

As an alternative to the standard contracts, the Data Protection Directive also envisages transfers taking place pursuant to a custom contract. While a custom contract enables parties to deal with the transfer of personal data in compliance with the Directive on a more flexible basis, in principle it does not have the advantage of automatic recognition by regulators that the standard contracts are supposed to have. Many jurisdictions require bespoke contracts to be submitted to local data protection authorities for approval and very few organizations have made such submission.[90] In practice, however, this distinction may have little substance now that many national data protection regulators also require contracts based on standard clauses to be filed and, in some cases, approved.

Detailed guidance on international transfers has been published by the Working Party. In addition to general guidance on the subject,[91] the Working Party has on several occasions considered the appropriateness of 'binding corporate rules' (BCRs) as an alternative to the standard contractual clauses. The question is whether an internal code of conduct for international transfers would allow an organization to adopt a set of common standards or policies relating to data privacy that would be binding on members of the group, without the need to adopt an intra-group agreement based on the standard contracts. In that context, the Working Party has made a number of suggestions including provisions to guarantee a good level of compliance, self and/or external audits, complaint handling procedures, rules on jurisdiction, and cooperation.[92] Based on that particular working document from the Article 29

---

[89] See Millard, n 54 above.

[90] Commission Staff Working Document of 20 January 2006 on the implementation of the Commission decisions on standard contractual clauses for the transfer of personal data to third countries (2001/497/EC and 2002/16/EC).

[91] See, in particular, the Working Party's working document entitled, Transfers of personal data to third countries—applying Articles 25 and 25 of the EU Data Protection Directive, adopted on 24 July 1998 (DG XV D/5025/98/final, WP 12).

[92] See the Working Party's working document entitled, Transfers of personal data to third countries: Applying Article 26(2) of the EU Data Protection Directive to Binding Corporate Rules for International Data Transfers, adopted on 3 June 2003 <http://ec.europa.eu/justice_home/fsj/privacy/docs/wpdocs/2003/wp74_en.pdf>.

Working Party, the UK Information Commissioner issued a checklist detailing required contents for a submission for approval of BCRs in the UK.[93]

On 14 April 2005, the Working Party adopted two documents that were intended to facilitate the process for applicants for BCR approval. Working Party 107 established a 'Co-Operation Procedure for Issuing Common Opinions on Adequate Safeguards Resulting From "Binding Corporate Rules"'. Working Party 108 established a 'Model Checklist Application for Approval of Binding Corporate Rules'. Take up of the BCR process remained slow and on 10 January 2007, the Working Party adopted a Recommendation 'on the Standard Application for Approval of Binding Corporate Rules for the Transfer of Personal Data' (Working Party 132). In the 18 months that followed, the number of BCR applications increased only slightly and the information commissioners met again in June 2008 to consider further steps to simplify and streamline the application and approval process.

At its meeting in June 2008, the Working Party adopted three further documents relating to the BCR process. The first is a detailed table setting out the essential content to be included in a set of Binding Corporate Rules, together with a description of additional information to be provided by an applicant for BCR approval.[94] The second document provides a 'framework', though 'not a model BCR', to give guidance as to how a company might structure its privacy standards so as to meet the criteria for BCR approval.[95] The third document is a set of Frequently Asked Questions relating to BCRs.[96] This is based on the experience to date of the national regulators in dealing with BCR applications and is intended to be updated as required.

The Working Party has also considered the transfer of Passenger Name Record (PNR) of air passengers to the United States Bureau of Customs and Border Protection (US CBP) and to the US Department of Homeland Security[97] and the

---

[93] The checklist has since been superseded by the standard EU BCR checklist issued by the Article 29 Working Party. See n 94.

[94] Working Document setting up a table with the elements and principles to be found in Binding Corporate Rules, 1271-00-00/08/EN WP 153, adopted on 24 June 2008, <http://ec.europa.eu/justice_home/fsj/privacy/docs/wpdocs/2008/wp153_en.pdf>.

[95] Working Document setting up a framework for the structure of Binding Corporate Rules, 1271-000-01/08/EN, WP 154, adopted on 24 June 2008.

[96] Working Document on Frequently Asked Questions (FAQs) relating to Binding Corporate Rules, 1271-00-02/08/EN, WP 155, adopted on 24 June 2008.

[97] The European Commission's Decision of 14 May 2004 on the adequate protection of personal data contained in the Passenger Name Record of air passengers transferred to the United States Bureau of Customs and Border Protection can be found, along with various related documents, on the Justice and Home Affairs pages of the Commission's website at: <http://www.ec.europa.eu>; Article 29 Data Protection Working Party Opinion 5/2006 on the ruling by the European Court of Justice of 30 May 2006 in Joined Cases C-317/04 and C-318/04 on the transmission of Passenger Name Records to the United States, 1015/06/EN, WP 122, adopted on 14 June 2006; Opinion 7/2006 on the ruling by the European Court of Justice of 30 May 2006 in Joined Cases C-317/04 and C-318/04 on the transmission of Passenger Name Records to the United States and the urgent need for a new agreement, 1612/06/EN, WP124, adopted on 27 September 2006; Opinion 5/2007 on the follow-up agreement between the European Union and the United States of America on the processing and transfer of passenger name record (PNR) data by

level of protection ensured in Australia and Canada for the transmission of PNR data from airlines.[98] Article 26 of the Data Protection Directive, on which the exemptions to the transborder data flow restrictions are based, provides that a Member State which grants any special authorization must provide details to the European Commission and the other Member States. If a Member State or the Commission raises a valid objection to the authorization, the Commission must 'take appropriate measures' and the national regulator would be required to 'take the necessary measures to comply with the Commission's decision' (Article 26(3)).

Even that may not be the end of the story, however. Article 31 of the Data Protection Directive has established a further committee, comprising representatives of the Member States. The European Commission is required to submit to this committee drafts of any measures to be taken in relation to special international transfer authorizations. The committee may disagree with the Commission's approach, resulting in suspension of the relevant 'measures' and referral to the EU Council of Ministers that may ultimately 'take a different decision' (Article 31).

The transborder data flow rules in the Data Protection Directive and the Data Protection Act 1998 seem to be based on a presumption that international data traffic always follows precise and predictable routings. This assumption is fundamentally at odds with the way in which information is in fact conveyed via digital telecommunications networks and, in particular, the Internet, for at least two reasons. First, the Internet, which is a vast and dynamically configured network of networks, has what is sometimes called a 'self-healing' architecture. Messages, or data representing information of any other kind, are split into 'packets' that are sent to their intended destination via the most efficient routing at any given instant. A technical obstacle to the transmission of particular packets will be bypassed automatically and the packets concerned will be forwarded via a different route. Transfers are thus not predictable in geographical terms.

Secondly, because Internet email can be downloaded, and web pages can be viewed anywhere on the planet where an individual or organization has a connection to an ISP, the sender of a message or operator of a website has no effective control over where a particular message will be downloaded or web page viewed. Even where, for example, there are rigorous access controls on a particular website that enable a website operator to verify conclusively the identity of a particular visitor to that website, it is not possible currently for the website operator to be sure of the

air carriers to the United States Department of Homeland Security concluded in July 2007, 01646/07/EN, WP 138, adopted on 17 August 2007; Opinion 2/2007 on information to passengers about the transfer of PNR data to US authorities, 00345/07/EN, WP 132 / 00345-01/07/EN WP 151, adopted on 15 February 2007 and revised and updated on 24 June 2008.

[98] Opinion 1/2004 on the level of protection ensured in Australia for the transmission of Passenger Name Record data from airlines and Opinion 3/2004 on the level of protection ensured in Canada for the transmission of Passenger Name Records and Advanced Passenger Information from airlines; Opinion 1/2005 on the level of protection ensured in Canada for the transmission of Passenger Name Record and Advance Passenger Information from airlines, 1112/05/EN, WP 103, adopted on 19 January 2005.

physical location of that visitor. Consequently, it must be assumed that data contained in Internet email messages and web pages potentially may be transferred to any country in the world, without regard to the adequacy or otherwise of the local data protection safeguards, if any.

Moreover, the sheer volume of personal data that is conveyed via the Internet and the vast number of data transfers make it inconceivable that more than a tiny minority of transfers can be regulated in any meaningful way under the cumbersome rules established by the Data Protection Directive and the Data Protection Act 1998.

13.9 CONCLUDING REMARKS

Data protection laws continue to evolve and issues relating to communications technology and services are at the forefront of the debate as to how best to strike a balance between privacy, on the one hand, and a range of competing factors such as national security and various commercial interests. The stakes are now high, as can be seen from the following recent examples. The first concerns SWIFT, an international organization that handles payments messages for more than 7,800 banks and other financial institutions. Apparently in response to an opinion issued by the Article 29 Working Party that was critical of disclosures of personal data to the US government,[99] SWIFT announced in October 2007 that it was undertaking a radical redesign of its global messaging architecture.[100] The second is a pre-emptive strike by the UK privacy regulator against an anticipated invasion of privacy by the UK government. Speaking in London on 15 July 2008, Richard Thomas, declared that 'Any government run database holding the telephone and internet communications of the entire population would raise serious data protection concerns . . .'[101] Interestingly, he admitted that he was merely 'Commenting on speculation that the government is considering the development of such a database . . .' Meanwhile, businesses and other organizations will continue to face the challenge of navigating a minefield of complex rules governing, for example, the monitoring and recording of communications and the transfer of data throughout international networks.

---

[99] Opinion 10/2006 on the processing of personal data by the Society for Worldwide Interbank Financial Telecommunication (SWIFT), 01935/06/EN, WP128, adopted on 22 November 2006.

[100] 'SWIFT Board approves messaging re-architecture', Press Release available at <http://www.swift.com>.

[101] 'A communications database would be "a step too far"', ICO Press Release, 15 July 2008, available at <http://www.ico.gov.uk>.

14

CONTENT REGULATION

Nicholas Higham

14.1 INTRODUCTION

14.1.1 Meaning of content

This chapter discusses the regulation of content carried over any type of electronic communications network, and of those who provide content (content service providers). The electronic network in question might be a wired or wireless telecommunications network (including the Internet), a terrestrial multiplex, or a satellite broadcasting system.

In discussing content, we mainly mean material of an audiovisual nature or sound broadcasting. The transmission of the BBC 1 Channel is a content service, as are the transmission of Sky News, Classic FM, the Disney Channel, video downloads from the Internet, and football clips on the third generation mobile network '3'. Certain forms of paid-for text or email services may also be content services but a person

who facilitates simple voice telephony, whether carried on a fixed or mobile network, or over the Internet using voice over Internet protocol (VoIP), or enables emails, 'chats', or consumer-to-consumer (peer-to-peer) SMS text messages would not be the provider of a content service as the service provided commercially is limited to the carriage of the messages rather than the provision or editing of the content[1] of the messages.

'Content services' are defined under the Communications Act 2003 (the 2003 Act), but only so as to exclude them from the definition of 'electronic communications services'. Content services are brought back into regulation under the 2003 Act only if they are also licensable under specific provisions of Part 3 of the Act.

14.1.2 Impact of technology on content delivery

Historically, content has been delivered by different service providers using distinct networks: television was broadcast from terrestrial broadcasting stations (and more recently, satellites); telephone calls were carried by telecommunications operators over plain old-fashioned telephone networks; and cable television services over cable networks. Until recently, mobile telephone networks carried little more than voice, and television reception was passive. Almost all of that has already changed, or will change soon, and the factors that have brought about the change include:

- digitization;
- dramatic increases in the capacity of the means used for the conveyance and storage of information in digital form;
- equally dramatic reductions in the cost of network and consumer equipment;
- advances in micro-engineering of wireless devices;
- the desire for access on the move.

Digitization and data compression are the enabling technologies behind modern means for conveying content. In essence, digitization involves using a sampling process to break down complex information—like a film, a conversation, or a music recording—into a series of simple instructions (noughts and ones) that a computer processor can understand, process, and then transmit to one person or to many. Audio CDs, DVDs, Sky Digital, DSL, and the Internet all carry or store information in digital form.[2]

Older media, including traditional voice telephony over fixed line networks, terrestrial broadcasting in the UK (but not the Freeview service, which is digital), and

---

[1] The formal definition of content is set out in section 14.2 below.

[2] If a household does not have a DSL-enabled local access line, data must be carried over the local loop in analogue form, and a modem will be needed to convert digital output generated by the user's home computer into analogue form before it is carried over the local access line, and vice versa in respect of information to be carried from the local switch to that user.

vinyl LPs contain or carry information in analogue form—where the information is in the form of changes in a continuous signal. However, digital technology is replacing analogue in almost all media. By 2011, most voice and data in the UK will be carried over digital Next Generation Networks (NGNs[3]); most homes in the UK already receive digital television signals (using Freeview, Sky, or cable) and digital personal video recorders (PVRs) are replacing video recorders. Analogue television is to be switched off completely in the UK by 2012. The switch-off of analogue television in favour of the spectrally more efficient digital will release valuable frequencies for reuse, often called the 'digital dividend'.

Some examples help show the dramatic improvement in the performance or price/performance of digital devices:

- the capacity of a submarine cable under the Atlantic was 280Mbytes/sec in 1988, but one can now achieve data transfer rates on a single optic fibre of 10 trillion Bytes/sec;

- the first iPod cost £349 and held 1,000 songs; now an iPod costing half as much can hold 40,000 songs, and by 2015, at least in theory, one will be able to hold every song ever written;

- there are more than 110 million blogs in the world;

- more than 2,000,000 people thought it worthwhile to download a video clip of a gorilla playing a drum on YouTube.

14.1.3 Impact of convergence

The process by which different media are converted to digital form with common formats and protocols and are carried over the same networks to a wide variety of different consumer devices is commonly known as 'convergence'.

At first, convergence was most evident at the network or conveyance levels—in message switching and increasingly in broadcast, for example in Sky television, Freeview, and Digital Audio Broadcasting.

Today, consumers have embraced digital technology and convergence is happening in their own homes:

- more than half of UK homes have access to broadband Internet services, which transfers data packets under a digital format known as Internet Protocol;

- most music recordings are now downloaded to personal computers and MP3 players instead of being purchased on an audio CD; and with the introduction

---

[3] Next Generation Networks are often defined as being capable of delivering data at rates in excess of 20 Mbytes/sec, which enables delivery of high definition video and video telephony among other services.

of greater bandwidth, the phenomenon is now extending to films—lawfully or unlawfully;[4]

- many mobile handsets can receive full motion video and, while the clips may be short and the images small, they are perfectly formed and can provide a sufficient 'experience' of live action to viewers;

- 3G services are becoming mainstream, allowing users better Internet access on the move;

- mobile television to handsets using the DVB-H format is being rolled out in a number of countries;

- there has been rapid development in interactive television (iTV')[5] where a viewer can send messages via his telephone line back to the broadcaster of the programme he is watching using his handheld controller and set-top box. Use of iTV has expanded as a result of the popularity of reality shows and other programmes where viewers can vote, although there have been recent set-backs.[6]

The Office of Communications (Ofcom) has shown the developments vividly in a timeline included in its submission to the Convergence Think Tank in February 2008, which is reproduced in Figure 14.1.

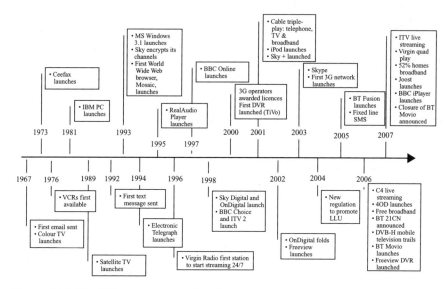

Figure 14.1 The UK convergences timeline

---

[4] See <http://www.ZML.com>; lawful distribution of videos will grow when download speeds are faster and if better links become available between PC and TV in the home—some studios are trialling special movie-download kiosks.

[5] Not to be confused with ITV, or Independent Television PLC.

[6] See the discussion on Premium Rate Services at section 14.10.

As long ago as 2001, it was widely predicted that, by now, broadcast television channels and audiovisual works carried over the Internet would be commonly viewed on a single device in the home or on the move. This remains the exception rather than the rule, but this outcome is already possible, is growing (especially now with 'Catch-up TV', a facility that allows viewers to stream over the Internet a programme they missed for up 30 days after it was broadcast), and may be expected to develop further.

Convergence, as manifested in technology and consumer devices, has already led to changes in consumer behaviour. Texting is already universal and immensely popular (though multi-media messages are less popular). More than three quarters of a billion people now use the Internet worldwide, music downloads have ravaged the CD audio market, and more general Internet shopping has now taken firm hold.

14.1.4 Social networking

Beyond that, there is the 'Web 2.0', which offers 'mashups' (the blending of non-linear content of various types) and greater participation and interaction. Within the scope of Web 2.0 are 'blogs' (web logs) of a personal diary-type nature, 'social networking sites' such as MySpace, Bebo, and Facebook, virtual world sites like Second Life, and hybrid file-sharing sites such as Limewire and YouTube. Facebook has in excess of 60 million users. Among other features, it allows the creation of personal profiles, listing of interests, and uploading of these details, with photographs—60 million photographs are uploaded every week—to what Facebook call 'The Wall'. Bebo allows its users to explore various types of entertainment and provides users with a new way of distributing content and of receiving some financial return from their content through monetization of the advertising that downloaders see when receiving it. MySpace allows users to upload selected personal details and to specify the characteristics of persons they would like to meet. It also allows musicians to upload a limited number of songs in MP3 format.

Limewire is of a rather different nature; it offers a fast file-sharing program that enables its users (lawfully or not) to exchange audio files. YouTube is a rather similar service to Limewire, but more focused on video; users may offer home-made videos mixed, controversially,[7] with clips from commercial music videos and movie clips.

All these sites in their own way allow empower consumers by enabling them to remix works and to upload them with their own material, which may comprise 'user-generated' content and·clips of third party commercial content (where copyright law is often disregarded). Use of social networking sites may also disempower commercial media providers, or at least reduce their revenues, because of fragmentation

---

[7] Copyright owners have established certain basic 'Principles' for User Generated Content Services aimed at eliminating infringing content (<http://www.ugcprinciples.com>).

of the market and because a growing number of users spend an increasing amount of time on these sites at the expense of consuming regular broadcasting or DVDs.

A new generic phrase has been coined for the mixed content on social networking sites: 'lifestyle media'—where media content is 'packaged' with social interaction providing consumers with greater personal choice on what they consume and on when, where, and how they do so.

The interest of younger consumers in video-on-demand and lifestyle media, which can even lead to a degree of addiction,[8] has profound implications for the future funding model of broadcasting, which relies heavily on advertising revenues. The problem is all the greater because of the increasing use of personal video recorders, which allow viewers to speed through advertising breaks. Users are more resistant to conventional advertising, but also reluctant to accept excessive new wave advertising, in the form of general or targeted pop-ups on screen. Presently, broadcasters rely on a mix of licence fees (a national tax), sales of advertising space,[9] and subscriptions, but all these methods face their own challenges, are 'in play', and will need to be rethought. Bill Gates has said of broadcasting that 'The biggest thing with video [today] is taking all of television and putting it on the Internet, creating a video experience that blows away the broadcast model.'[10]

Good content will always have a market of course, but the way in which it will be financed, delivered, and consumed will not be quite the same in five years' time as it is today. Television companies are beginning to see themselves, not as traditional broadcasters, but as media-neutral publishers of audiovisual material. They will in future make their programmes available, according to customer choice, over different media: digital terrestrial television, satellite, Internet, or mobile television.

14.1.5 The political dimension to content

Readers should recognize the political dimension to the regulation of content. This arises from:

(1) a long legacy, even in European liberal democracies, of government direction or control over radio and television broadcasting based on reasons partly connected with the scarcity of spectrum for broadcasting and partly on the legitimate wish of governments[11] to ensure a wide range of 'acceptable' entertainment, and informational and educative content for all citizens—which underpins the concept of public service broadcasting;[12]

---

[8] See <http://www.ofcom.org.uk/media/news/2008/04/nr_20080402>.

[9] There is evidence of resistance to over-aggressive pop-up and targeted personal advertising on social interaction sites.

[10] <http://www.microsoft.com/presspass/exec/billg/speeches/2006/01-04CES.mspx>.

[11] Not all governments are so altruistic in their objectives, and some would argue against aspects of the balanced approach adopted in the UK.

[12] See section 14.6.4 below.

(2) the understandable desire to promote and protect national cultural traditions and language; and

(3) evolving views of the correct balance between the right of free expression and the duty of the government to protect citizens, and particularly children, from harmful material and (a recent revival) from exposure to terrorism.

These high-level political concerns underpin the thinking behind the regulation of content services and help explain why, to this day, even within the European Community, there remain important cultural differences in the way in which nation states regulate content. Other countries, notably China, the United Arab Emirates (UAE), and Singapore, are considerably more restrictive.

It is useful to remind ourselves that freedom of expression is not an absolute right under the European Convention for the Protection of Human Rights and Fundamental Freedoms, now incorporated into English Law by the Human Rights Act 1998. Under Article 10(2) of the Convention, the right is balanced by a notion of social responsibility when issues of national security, public safety, health and safety, and the protection of the rights of others are at stake. Nor, despite the importance of the First Amendment, is freedom of speech an absolute right in the USA, where there is some continuing control on obscenity, libel, and 'fighting words'.[13]

14.1.6 Impact of convergence on regulation

Convergence in the means of distribution and home delivery, and in the utility of home devices, has inevitably led to a need to refresh the way in which different media and different delivery channels are regulated and converge the regulatory bodies. In the medium term, any distinctions between the mode of regulation of content and different delivery mechanisms become less justifiable, and might even become undesirable, impracticable, or absurd.

That progressive thinking informed the policies underlying the 2003 Act; Ofcom itself is a creature of the concept of 'convergence', but the regulatory framework is evolving more slowly than technology and behaviour. The government stood back in 2003 from creating a level playing field for content carried by means of broadcasting and content available over the Internet, arguing in part that they produced different 'viewer experiences'. However, convergence is an irresistible force and important changes to the regulation of some Internet-borne works are now imminent under the new Audiovisual Directive.[14] This measure extends broadcasting-type regulation to certain lookalike services of European origin available over the Internet.

In parallel with this, there is a renewed debate on the responsibilities of Internet Service Providers (ISPs), particularly in relation to the hosting and carriage of material that infringes copyright and undesirable content; and a debate about how, if at all,

---

[13] See *Chaplinsky v New Hampshire* 315 US 568 (1942).
[14] See section 14.3.3 below.

to regulate users of social networking sites who upload material of every kind on a non-commercial basis.[15]

Beyond these evolutionary changes there is a prospect of continuing and perhaps more fundamental change. The Audiovisual Directive will increase the regulatory burden on certain types of ISPs, yet the longer term trend could be in the opposite direction—towards a lighter-touch regulatory framework in which controls prior to or at the point of broadcast or transmission are largely abandoned. What, some people ask, is the rationale for heavy-handed regulation of broadcasts when there is little or none for other audiovisual material freely available over the Internet? Is there a real risk of public harm and does that justify regulation at the point of broadcast or transmission? Is such regulation proportionate?

Under a lighter-touch regulatory model, the emphasis would shift towards individual responsibility, for oneself or one's family. This would involve promoting Codes of Practice for content aggregators on labelling and filtering the audiovisual material they made available for broadcast or transmission. Codes might be adopted under self- or co-regulatory schemes. Such an approach would take Europe more in the direction of the US, where the Federal Communications Commission has a much reduced role in the regulation of content.[16]

14.1.7 Use of technology for self-regulation

There is a recognition that regulation of content in an age of convergence cannot be made perfect and that different approaches may be required. Thus:

- by using software embedded in the browser of a PC or a network, or propriety software from an ISP, or controls in digital decoders for television, a user can decline to receive emails or files from nominated sources;

- by using 'parental control' software, such as 'Net Nanny', users may block material that is labelled as sexually explicit or violent, or which uses bad language, or which is not labelled and is therefore unknown;

- using anti-spam programs, users may, more or less successfully, screen out or trash bulk or spam emails they do not want to receive.

Technology of this nature is developing all the time. Systems for rating content are becoming more sophisticated and more used. The Internet Contents Rating Association (ICRA), an independent non-profit organization established in 1999, develops, implements, and manages a voluntary self-rating system which provides end-users with a means to limit access to content that they consider to be harmful.[17] The ultimate objective is to develop a system that is acceptable internationally.

---

[15] See section 14.3.5 below.
[16] See section 14.3.2 below. See further Chapter 6.
[17] Visit <http://www.icra.org>.

ICRA has built upon the pre-existing RSACi system[18] which is intended to provide users with credible, objective information on the levels of sex, nudity, violence, and offensive language on websites (and in software games). The system relies on self-rating of content by content providers and the provision of a software tool on an end-user's PC or, at the network level, a filter to impede delivery of material that exceeds levels preset by or for the user.

Other means of control exist. Telephone calls can, to some extent, be filtered at the point of reception or delivery using features in calling line identifier (CLI) technology to warn of, or to block, calls from unwelcome numbers or calls which do not carry or display the number of the caller. A UK user has a right to register, free of charge, with the Telephone Preference Service and with the Fax Preference Service that he or she does not want to receive sales and marketing calls. Other forms of marketing using electronic communications services may be unlawful under Communications Privacy Regulations.[19]

Within the home, television viewers have always had an off button, and may program a DVD player not to play X-rated disks.

Means of control of the type discussed above all involve delegation of responsibility to viewers. Viewers, informed by rating and filtering schemes and protected by Notice and Take Down procedures, clearly have a greater part to play in the regulation of content even if none of the current arrangements can deliver 100 per cent certainty. On the other hand, there is evidence that a majority of television viewers would prefer the existing system of controls on broadcast content to be maintained; they continue to distinguish watching television (often carried out in a family environment) from computer use, which is usually private in nature.

There is a need for clear thinking to identify the principles and objectives that justify content controls. These issues will lead to an intriguing public debate over the coming years.

14.1.8 The continuing demand for public service broadcasting

One difference between the future European regulatory framework (and particularly in the UK) and the framework in the US will be the abiding desire in Europe to see the continuation of public service broadcasting as epitomized by the BBC today.[20] While there is a current debate about the future of public service broadcasting in the UK, including whether the BBC should receive 100 per cent of the licence fee, the future of public service broadcasting in one form or another is assured, even if it is financed a little differently in future.

---

[18] The Recreational Software Advisory Council, based in Washington DC, which was folded into ICRA in 1999/2000.
[19] See further Chapter 13.
[20] See section 14.9 below.

14.1.9 Scope

This chapter will focus on the regulation of certain forms of content and of certain types of service providers. This chapter will not cover:

- the regulation of electronic programme guides (EPGs);[21]
- the 'must carry' rules imposed on certain broadcasters;
- the obligations on ITV companies to make programmes available to the entire ITV network;
- the regulation of Channel 4 as a carrier;
- the obligations imposed on broadcasters in relation to services for deaf or disabled persons.

Other sections of Part 3 of the 2003 Act are mentioned only in passing: these include access to broadcast rights in respect of major sporting events, and rules bearing on programming quotas, news provision, and programme commissioning.[22]

The chapter also ignores the law of gaming in the UK, recently relaxed to allow gaming online.[23]

14.2 DEVELOPMENT OF THE UK LICENSING FRAMEWORK

14.2.1 The significance of licences and codes of practice

While the skeleton of the regulatory framework for content is formed by EU measures and UK statutes, the flesh is contained in licences and self- or co-regulatory codes of practice.[24] A number of self- and co-regulatory schemes are discussed later in this chapter. The significance of licences and codes should not be underestimated: they are often the most important instruments governing the regulation of content.

Finally, it is important to recognize that, even after the significant changes before and after the 2003 Act, the regulatory framework for content regulation remains in a state of flux. The passing into law of the Audiovisual Directive and the ongoing march of convergence will inevitably lead to further changes in the legal and regulatory framework over the next years.

---

[21] See further Chapter 8, at 8.5.2.8.4.
[22] See further the Ofcom website at <http://www.ofcom.org.uk>.
[23] See the Gambling Act 2005, available at <http://www.opsi.gov.uk>.
[24] Self-regulation is where industry players themselves set standards and enforce them on their members, while co-regulation is a form of collaboration between industry and a government agency in which the latter sets or approves the framework or a minimum set of standards which it expects the industry to observe, and sometimes acts as enforcer of last resort.

14.2.2 Regulation of broadcasting before the 2003 Act

The old saw that 'the past is the key to the future' applies strongly to the regulation of content. This chapter therefore provides an overview of the separate regimes that applied to the regulation of content under the UK Broadcasting Acts and under the Telecommunication Act 1984 (1984 Act), aspects of which, like parts of the Acts themselves, survive. It then moves on to an analysis of relevant EU measures, the UK regime for the 'main' television channels, the regime for television and radio services under the 2003 Act, including the newer digital channels, the regulation of the Internet, and the regulation of sound broadcasting. The chapter also looks at arrangements for the regulation of premium rate calls, the voluntary arrangements for regulating content on mobile telephones, and other specific issues.

The history of legislation in broadcasting dates back to the Wireless Telegraphy Act 1904 and to the grant of the Licence and Agreement from the Post Office to the BBC on 18 January 1923. In this chapter, however, we shall jump to 1990 and the enactment of the Broadcasting Act in that year.[25]

Under the 1990 Act, the Independent Television Commission (ITC) was created with responsibility for licensing and regulating all commercial television services, but ITC did not regulate the BBC, where other arrangements applied.[26] In addition, the 1990 Act provided new procedures for the award of licences to run Channel 3 franchises and the then newcomer, Channel 5, and for a reorganization of the ownership of Channel 4. The 1990 Act also created a new Radio Authority to regulate radio broadcasting stations.

Initially, the licensing process for Channel 3 franchises (Granada, Carlton, etc.) was such that, provided a quality threshold was met, the licences would be awarded to the persons making the highest cash bid. This was controversial at the time and a political compromise was subsequently reached under which the award could be made to a lower bidder if his bid promised exceptional quality.

The functions of the ITC under the Broadcasting Act 1990, as amended by the Broadcasting Act 1996, were to regulate the provision of:

- television programme services by persons other than the BBC and the Welsh Authority;
- additional services (which is to say teletext);
- multiplex services;[27] and
- digital additional services (teletext linked to digital transmissions),

all provided from places within the UK.[28]

---

[25] For a full chronology, see Macdonald, B, *Broadcasting in the United Kingdom, a Guide to Information Sources* (2nd edn, Mansell, 1994).
[26] Under the aegis of the erstwhile Broadcasting Standards Commission.
[27] See section 14.4.5 below.
[28] Broadcasting Act 1990, s 2.

The 1990 Act contains many detailed provisions concerning the award of licences and the contents of those licences, including obligations to comply with high standards and a code on 'undesirable' material. These standards and codes have been superseded, but they informed the new arrangements adopted by Ofcom under the 2003 Act.

14.2.3 Regulation of the BBC before the 2003 Act

At the time of the enactment of the 2003 Act, the BBC was a body corporate formed under a Royal Charter dated 1 May 1996, which had replaced an earlier Charter of Incorporation 'under Letters made Patent under the Great Seal' dated 20 December 1926. The BBC was further regulated under a Deed, usually referred to as the Agreement, dated 25 January 1996, made between the Department of National Heritage, then the relevant sponsoring Ministry, and the BBC, which has since been further amended.[29]

The affairs of the BBC were directed by its Governors, who were required, among other things, to monitor and review how the BBC fulfilled its several legal and contractual obligations (including, therefore, its obligations under the 1996 Agreement) and to ensure that the BBC complied with relevant standards and practices. In particular, the Governors had to ensure that the BBC complied with lawful directions of two bodies established under the 1996 Act: the Broadcasting Complaints Commission (BCC) and the Broadcasting Standards Council (BSC).

The functions of the former body, the BCC, involved the investigation of complaints; those functions were subsequently transferred to the latter body, the BSC, whose own functions included the preparation of codes in relation to unjust and unfair treatment and broadcasting standards. The functions of the BSC have now been assumed by Ofcom.

14.2.4 Regulation of content on telecommunications networks before the 2003 Act

The approach to the regulation of content carried on telecommunications networks was entirely different. The previous regulator for telecommunications, Oftel, had no general statutory responsibility for the regulation of content carried over telecommunications networks. Instead, the 1984 Act focused on the misuse of telecommunications systems, establishing offences for either the sending of messages that are 'grossly offensive or of an indecent, obscene, or menacing character, or which caused annoyance, inconvenience or needless anxiety to another';[30] or the fraudulent use of a telecommunication system.[31]

---

[29] See section 14.9 below.
[30] Section 43, replaced by s 127 of the 2003 Act.
[31] Section 42, replaced by ss 125–126 of the 2003 Act.

An innovation under the 2003 Act is the establishment of a administrative procedure for Ofcom to take enforcement action against those that 'persistently misuse' an electronic communications network or service, where a person uses a network or service on a sufficient number of occasions to cause another person 'unnecessarily to suffer annoyance, inconvenience or anxiety'.[32]

14.2.5 Regulation of the Internet

The development of Internet services in the early 1990s gave rise to intense debate within international institutions and groupings such as G7, UNESCO, WIPO, IGU and ICRT, and OECD. It also gave rise to considerable activity amongst European Union institutions who were forced to consider whether it was necessary to develop a wholly new framework to address the special properties of the Internet, including in particular its international character, or instead to rely on making incremental changes to the existing regulatory framework for content on other media.

Regulation of the Internet may be broken down under a number of heads:

- governance issues, including the respective future roles of the Internet Corporation for Assigned Names and Numbers (ICANN),[33] a private US not-for-profit organization that administers allocation of domain names and IP addresses, the Internet Society, the World Wide Web Consortium, and the formal international organizations such as the International Telecommunications Union (ITU) and the World Intellectual Property Organization (WIPO);

- security issues, including the increasing emphasis on combating spam, viruses, and other 'malware', which are outside the scope of this chapter;

- issues of network neutrality—that is ensuring that all data is transported on an equal footing regardless of the nature of its content;

- protection of intellectual property rights, such as infringement of copyright (particularly film and music);

- regulation of content to prevent or constrain access to illegal and harmful material, such as child sexual abuse images or racist material; and

- issues concerning civil liberties and freedom of speech, where regulation of content extends beyond the control of illegal and harmful material into censorship of content that is considered sensitive for religious or political reasons, as happens in some countries today, notably China, the UAE, Singapore, and North Korea.

---

[32] Sections 128–131.
[33] Nominet administers domain names within the UK country code space: .uk.

14.3 THE COMMUNITY DIMENSION AND
INTERNATIONAL PRACTICE

14.3.1 Early moves in the EC

On 16 October 1996, the Commission adopted a Communication on Harmful and Illegal Content on the Internet[34] and a Green Paper on the Protection of Minors and Human Dignity in Audiovisual and Information Services.[35] The former measure concluded that, despite some siren voices in industry, existing laws should apply to the Internet and that it was clearly the responsibility of Member States to ensure that they did so. The latter paper was designed to engender a debate focused on particular types of illegal material, notably anti-semitic and racist material. This paper was later endorsed by the Council of Ministers and European Parliament.

The Commission called for cooperation and coordination at a European and international level to assist in the enforcement of relevant laws. The Commission also recommended the development of a regulatory framework combining self-control by Internet service providers, the adoption of technical solutions such as rating and filtering software, and the provision of monitoring intelligence by Internet users themselves.

The call for existing laws to be applied to activities carried on over the Internet did not lead to an immediate and comprehensive review of UK statutes, although a reasonable amount of legislative change was in fact required. It was often an accident of language whether any particular law covered activities carried on over the Internet in the same way as it covered activities carried on in traditional ways. To take just one example, it was hard to determine whether gaming on the Internet was, or was not, illegal under the then current laws. Following media concern, amending legislation was introduced, in the form of the Sexual Offences Act 2003, to update the Protection of Children Act 1978.[36]

At this time, in the UK as in other countries, different media had traditionally been regulated by distinct regulatory bodies, and no regulator had been created or taken responsibility specifically for controlling content on the Internet, although some regulators begun to regulate elements of it.[37] The debate on whether and if so how content on the Internet should be regulated was protracted and hard-fought. Many industry players continued to argue strongly that the Internet was something so apart from any other form of media or content delivery service and that it should not be regulated at all—or only in the same limited manner as print publishing.

It was also argued, with more force, that any country that attempted to regulate the Internet was doomed to failure because of its international character. If a regulator closed down a website or server in one country, the same material would in all

---

[34] COM (1996) 487.
[35] COM (1996) 0483.
[36] See also Part VII of the Criminal Justice and Public Order Act 1994.
[37] E.g. the Advertising Standards Authority.

probability become available on another server in the same or a different country. The protagonists of this line of argument pressed their case, not just because of the special nature of the Internet, but also on the basis of the right to free expression, in some cases forgetting or deliberately overlooking that this never has been an absolute right.

People on the other side of the argument, concerned in particular about the Internet's growing ability to deliver audiovisual material, wanted to introduce much the same type of 'heavy-handed' *ex ante* control over Internet content as applied to traditional broadcasting content, arguing that it was irrelevant to the consumer whether the material was conveyed to the home by terrestrial or satellite broadcasting and viewed on a television set there, or conveyed over a public telecommunications system using Internet Protocol and delivered on a screen on a personal computer or web-enabled television.

Debate continued for some time, and indeed has revived, but the broad approach adopted in most countries in relation to the Internet centres around four propositions:

i. What is illegal off-line is illegal on-line.

ii. Specific legislation should be brought forward to protect against a small handful of harms, particularly propagation of child sexual abuse images and racial material.[38]

iii. Means to label content should be developed alongside filters that enable users to elect what they do and do not want to see at the point of reception.

iv. Self-regulatory schemes among ISPs and content service providers should be encouraged.

Note the distinction in (i) above between the illegal (for example child sexual abuse images) and material which some would find offensive (for example pornography involving only adults). Offensive material is not necessarily illegal, but access to it may perhaps be controlled.

14.3.2 Initiatives in other countries

Not every country in the world has taken this approach. For example, in Australia, a more interventionist approach has been taken. In 1999, the Broadcasting Services Amendment (Online Services) was enacted to amend the Broadcasting Services Act, 1992 by introducing a system of co-regulation that would enable the Australian Broadcasting Authority (ABA) (as then was) to investigate and make decisions about Internet content, and issue interim or final take-down notices. The Act also provided for industry bodies, or the ABA itself, to develop codes or standards. This framework

---

[38] Specific legislation may also be required in other fields, such as Distance Selling and Betting and Gaming.

was significantly changed, first in light of the merger of the ABA with the Australia Communications and Media Authority (ACMA) in July 2005, and secondly by the passage of the Communications Legislative Amendment (Content Services) Act 2007.

The 2007 Act regulates stored and live content services when accessed by means of an electronic carriage service. A content service is defined as 'a service that delivers content to a person having equipment appropriate for receiving that content . . .'[39] but Internet search engines and voice calls are explicitly excluded from its scope.

Subject to some exceptions, *content with an Australian connection*,[40] is prohibited under the 2007 Act if it has been classified by the Australian Classification Board as:

- RC[41] or X18+;[42]

- R18+ and not subject to a restricted access system;

- MA15+,[43] not subject to a restricted access system and provided as part of a commercial content service;

- MA15+, not subject to a restricted access system and provided as part of a mobile premium service.

Content may also potentially be prohibited if it is unclassified and likely to be prohibited were it classified.

The 2007 Act places obligations on specified classes of service provider:

- Hosting Service Provider—who hosts stored content;

- Live Content Service Provider—who provides live content to the public;

- Links Service Provider—who provides links to content for the public;

- Commercial Content Service Provider of Live Content—who provides live content for a fee;

- Commercial Content Service Provider of Stored Content—who provides stored content for a fee;

The 2007 Act authorizes the ACMA to issue 'take-down' notices in respect of prohibited or potentially prohibited stored or static content; 'service cessation' notices in respect of live services or 'link detachment' notices for links to such content. The notices may require that the content is removed or put behind age-restricted access systems. Notices must be complied with by 6pm on the following day, and there are sanctions for non-compliance.

---

[39] This would include a computer or a mobile phone.
[40] Hosted in Australia or, if live, provided from Australia.
[41] Refused Classification.
[42] Restricted to those aged 18 or more.
[43] Mature Accompanied (person) aged 15 or more.

Some countries with the tradition of authoritarian government, including China and Singapore and some Middle Eastern States, have attempted to control access to Internet content, with greater or lesser success, by requiring that all users access the Internet through a government-controlled server, by the use of which material deemed unacceptable to the State may be blocked.

There are also some differences in approach within Europe. In Germany, section 4 of the States Treaty on Media Youth Protection, among other things, censored the portrayal of children or adolescents in unnatural sex-focused postures, 'infringements of human dignity', pornography, the glorification of the war, and anti-Semitic propaganda, such as holocaust denial.

In France, there have been a number of cases, notably one involving the ISP Yahoo!, which held that the promotion and sale of Nazi memorabilia on its US-based website was illegal under French law[44] on grounds that the material could be accessed by users of the Yahoo service in France. The court held that Yahoo! Inc had permitted the visualization of the objects in France and, on advice from international experts, and despite criticism, ordered that Yahoo! Inc take all necessary measures to make any access via Yahoo.com to the auction service for those memorabilia difficult for persons accessing from France. In the US however, the courts quickly found an immediate threat to the legal and constitutional rights of Yahoo!, Inc and granted a declaration that the First Amendment precluded enforcement within the US of a French court order intended to regulate the content of its speech over the Internet.[45] The French courts are also notable for the way in which they protect the rights of trademark owners in cases where there are references to brands on the Internet.[46]

The US represents the high water mark of freedom of speech, though even there, there is no absolute right. Obscene material, on any medium, is not protected by the First Amendment to the US Constitution which otherwise guarantees freedom of speech, The test of obscenity is high: the average person applying contemporary community standards, must find that the material as a whole appeals to the prurient interest; the material must depict or describe in a patently offensive way sexual conduct (defined by applicable law) and it must lack serious literary, artistic, political, or scientific value.[47] Material that does not rise to this level may be 'indecent' instead and may be restricted from *broadcast* during times of the day when children may be in the audience, although the Federal Communications Commission (FCC) does not regulate subscription cable or satellite channels in respect of indecent or profane material or any material available over the Internet.

---

[44] *Association Union des Etudiants Juifs de France v Yahoo! Inc. 2000*; the case was brought under Art 24 *bis* of the Act of 29 July 1881 and Art 645–1 of the French criminal code.

[45] *Yahoo!, Inc v LICRA* (169 F Supp 2d 1181 (ND Cal 2001)).

[46] E.g. Tribunal de commerce de Paris 1ère chambre B Jugement du 30.6.08 *Parfums Christian Dior et autres/eBay Inc, eBay International AG*.

[47] <http://www.fcc.gov/cgb/consumerfacts/obscene.html>.

644 14. Content Regulation

Title 18 of the United States Code, section 1464, addresses wireless communication (and not therefore Internet over wireline) and prohibits the utterance of 'any obscene, indecent or profane language by means of radio communication. Moreover, Rules and Decisions of the FCC prohibit the transmission of indecent or profane material during the period from 6am to 10pm. Civil enforcement of these requirements lies with the FCC, but sanctions are set low.[48]

The FCC does not regulate violence on television, nor other standards of the type brought under control in the UK Broadcasting Code.

Returning to the UK, interesting research was carried out in 2001 on the acceptability of content, and the results of this research are discussed in and informed the Communications White Paper which paved the way for the 2003 Act. The research study, which was commissioned jointly by the BSC, the BBC, the ITC, the British Board of Film Classification, and the programme producer Flextech, showed that audience groups were inclined to apply different standards to explicit sexual material according to the nature of the service, the means of its access, and whether reception involved payment. Similarly, expectations of the use of swearing and offensive language suggested a clear difference between various media, including a difference in expectations according to whether viewers were watching free-to-air services or subscription channels. Viewers tended to be more tolerant of 'challenging' material on Channel 4 than on BBC1 and there were fewer complaints about subscription channels than free-to-air channels.[49]

The Department of Trade and Industry (DTI) and the Department for Culture, Media and Sport (DCMS) (as they then were) concluded from this research, influenced also perhaps by political reality, that while the convergence of different systems, including particularly the convergence of Internet broadcasting, was challenging the framework, nonetheless differences in the expectations, power, context of use, and intrusiveness of different services remained, and those differences could justify taking a different regulatory approach in relation to, say, terrestrial public service broadcasting than in relation to the Internet, at least in the immediate future.

It was the acceptance of these arguments that, in part, led to the very different framework for television and radio broadcasting on the one hand and the Internet on the other under the 2003 Act. Radio and television remain subject to extensive regulation. The Internet is not presently regulated in this way,[50] but that is not to say that the Internet is completely unregulated. As we have seen, it does not operate in a legal vacuum: material on the Internet may be libellous or in breach of copyright[51]

---

[48] *The Commission's Forfeiture Policy Statement and Amendment of Section 1.80 of the Rules to Incorporate the Forfeiture Guidelines*, 12 FCC Rcd 17087, 17100-01 (1997), *recon denied*, 15 FCC Rcd 303 (1999) (*'Forfeiture Guidelines'*).

[49] BBC, BSC, and ITC, *Striking a balance—The control of children's media consumption*, September 2002.

[50] But remember the future impact of the Audiovisual Directive.

[51] See section 14.11.1 for the position of ISPs in relation to liability for Internet content.

(where indeed the regime may be strengthened) and it may contravene other laws. Other important initiatives bear on regulation of Internet content:

- the work of the Internet Watch Foundation;[52]
- the self-regulatory code established by the Internet Service Providers Association;[53]
- the legislative framework for premium rate telephone calls.[54]

14.3.3 European Community measures on broadcasting

It will be useful at this point to refer to other Community measures that bear on the regulation of content. First, we should mention the Framework Directive[55] which puts in place the definitions of Electronic Communications Networks (ECNs) and Electronic Communications Services (ECSs), which are discussed below only in the context of content, and the Authorization Directive[56] which limits the types of conditions that may be imposed on providers of ECNs, and in particular disallows imposition of them of any general condition relating to content. These measures are to be reformed under proposals recently issued by the Commission.[57] Secondly, we must mention the Television Without Frontiers Directives and the Audiovisual Directive, which are discussed below. Thirdly there are further important measures in relation to the Internet, which are also discussed below.

14.3.3.1 *The Television Without Frontiers Directives*

Council Directive 89/552/EEC of 3 October 1989, the so-called Television Without Frontiers (TWF)[58] Directive, was the first substantive Community measure in the field of broadcasting. The origins of this Directive lay in the promotion of the free movement of services and, in particular, the freedom to transmit broadcasts across frontiers by various technologies, including retransmission over cable networks.

The approach taken under Directive 89/552/EEC was that Member States must ensure that all television broadcasts transmitted by broadcasters under its jurisdiction, or by broadcasters who make use of a frequency or satellite capacity granted by, or a satellite up-link situated in, their jurisdiction, should comply with the law applicable to broadcasts for the public in that Member State (Article 2). Building on this, under Article 2(a), Member States should ensure freedom of reception, and therefore

---

[52] See section 14.10.2.
[53] See section 14.11.1 below.
[54] See section 14.10 below.
[55] Directive 2002/21/EC of the European Parliament and of the Council of 7 March 2002 on a common regulatory framework for electronic communications networks and services; OJ L 108/33, 24 April 2002. See also Chapter 5 on European Law.
[56] Directive 2002/20/EC of the European Parliament and of the Council on the authorization of electronic communications networks and services; OJ L 108/21, 24 April 2002.
[57] Com (2007) 697 and 698.
[58] OJ L 298/23, 17 October 1989.

should not restrict retransmission, on their own territory, of television broadcasts lawfully transmitted from other Member States, except in limited circumstances (see the comment on Article 22 below). This is a common European Community approach, often known as 'home-regulation'—if the product or service is lawful in the Member State in which it is produced or initiated, it should not be prevented from being resold or used in a second EC Member State.

The 1989 TWF Directive provided for harmonization of national rules concerning a number of matters including:

- the time reserved for 'European works';
- the proportion of material produced by independent producers that must be broadcast;
- the rules concerning the separation of advertising and sponsorship from programming;
- the types of television advertising that may be included in programming and the total advertising time.[59]

The 1989 Directive also contains provisions for the protection of minors and provision for a right of reply.[60] Article 22, for example, requires Member States to take appropriate measures to ensure that television broadcasts by broadcasters under their jurisdiction do not include programmes that might seriously impair the physical, mental, or moral development of minors, in particular those that involve pornography or gratuitous violence. The same prohibition extends to other programmes which are likely to impair the physical, mental, or moral development of minors, except where it is ensured, by selecting the time of the broadcast or by any technical measure, that minors in the area of transmission will not normally hear or see such broadcasts (this gives rise to the '9pm threshold' or 'watershed').

A right of reply is given under Article 23, which provides that, without prejudice to other provisions adopted by Member States under civil, administrative, or criminal law, any natural or legal person, regardless of nationality, whose legitimate interests, in particular reputation and good name, have been damaged by an assertion of incorrect facts in a television programme must have a right of reply or equivalent remedies.

Member States are permitted, under Article 3, to lay down more detailed or stricter rules in areas covered by the TWF Directive. This opens the door to diverse national rules and is one of a number of reasons why this Directive has never fully met the high hopes of those who introduced it in achieving a single market for broadcasts. Other, and perhaps more important, reasons are languages and culture.

Council Directive 89/552/EEC was substantially amended by the second TWF Directive (97/36/EC).[61] The 1997 Directive clarified the rules on the rights of

---

[59] Chapters III and IV.
[60] Chapters V and VI.
[61] OJ L 202/60, 30 July 1997.

Member States to derogate from the obligation not to restrict retransmission. They may do so only if:

    i. a television broadcast coming from another Member States manifestly, seriously, and gravely infringes Article 22 of the 1989 Directive;

    ii. during the previous 12 months, the broadcaster has infringed the provisions referred to above on at least two prior occasions;

    iii. the Member State concerned has notified the broadcaster and the Commission in writing of the alleged infringements and of the measures it intends to take should any infringement occur again; and

    iv. consultations have not produced an amicable settlement.[62]

The 1997 Directive also included additional powers to prevent broadcasters from broadcasting events of major social importance for society on an exclusive basis, for example a sports cup final, if that would deprive a substantial proportion of the public of the possibility of following the event by a live coverage or deferred coverage on free television. Member States may draw up lists of designated events, national or non-national, which it considers to be of major importance, but must do so in a clear and transparent manner in due and effective time (so-called 'listed events').

Additional restrictions are placed on advertising on television and, in particular, television advertising and tele-shopping for cigarettes and other tobacco products were prohibited, and programme sponsorship by undertakings whose principal activities comprised the manufacture or sale of cigarettes and other tobacco products was disallowed.[63] There are other controls on tele-shopping, which is defined as direct offers broadcast to the public with a view to the supply of goods or services, including immovable property, rights, and obligations in return for payment.[64] Member States are required to ensure that broadcasts do not include any incitement of hatred on grounds of race, sex, religion, or nationality.

Under Article 22(b) of the 1997 Directive, the Commission was required to carry out an investigation of the possible advantages and drawbacks of further measures with a view to facilitating control by parents or guardians over the programmes that minors may watch. Article 22(b) particularly directed that the study should address the possibility of equipping new television sets with a technical device that allowed the filtering out of certain programmes, the setting up of appropriate rating systems, and the encouragement of family viewing policies and other educational and awareness measures. Under Article 26, the Commission was required to submit biennial reports on the application of the Directive, having particular regard to Article 22(a).

---

[62] Article 2(2).
[63] Article 13.
[64] Article 11.

Article 22(a) was interesting because it began to contemplate the introduction of controls at the point of reception, rather than at the point of transmission. However, technology has moved on from that point.

14.3.3.2 *The Audiovisual Directive*

Many of the provisions of the 1989 and 1997 TWF Directives are to be replaced under Directive 2007/65/EC of 11 December 2007 (the Audiovisual Directive)[65] when it is transposed into national law by Member States.[66]

The Audiovisual Directive follows the structure and approach of the 1989 TWF Directive but has two main effects: first it extends the EC regulatory framework for television broadcasting into all audiovisual media services transmitted by media service providers established in Member States, and others which use satellite uplinks or satellite capacity appertaining to Member States; secondly, it makes detailed changes to the rules on content and advertising contained in the current TWF Directives.

Under Article 1 of the Audiovisual Directive, an audiovisual media service is defined as:

a service as defined by Articles 49 and 50 of the Treaty which is under the editorial responsibility of a media service provider and the principal purpose of which is the provision of programmes in order to inform, entertain or educate, to the general public by electronic communications networks within the meaning of Article 2a of Directive 2002/21/EC. Such an audiovisual media service is either a television broadcast as defined [in Article 1(c)] or an on-demand audiovisual media service as defined in [Article 1(g)].

This definition contains a number of terms defined in their own right and needs to be unpacked. An audiovisual media service is one that provides 'programmes'. Programmes are defined as:

a set of moving images with or without sound constituting an individual item within a schedule or a catalogue established by a media service provider and whose form and content is comparable to the form and content of television broadcasting. Examples of programmes include feature-length films, sports events, situation comedies, documentaries, children's programmes and original drama.[67]

The programmes must be delivered by way of a television broadcast or an on-demand audiovisual media service. The former is:

an audiovisual media service provided by a media service provider for simultaneous viewing of programmes on the basis of a programme schedule',[68] which would include conventional

---

[65] Directive 2007/65/EC of the European Parliament and of the Council amending Council Directive 89/552/EEC on the co-ordination of certain provisions laid down by law, regulation or administrative action in Member States concerning the pursuit of television broadcasting activities.

[66] The deadline for adoption is 19 December 2009 (ibid, Art 3(1)).

[67] Ibid, at Art 1(2)(b).

[68] Ibid, at Art 1(2)(e).

television channels, while the latter is 'an audiovisual media service provided by a media service provider for the viewing of programmes at the moment chosen by the user and at his individual request on the basis of a catalogue of programmes selected by the media service provider.[69]

which would include an on-demand service provided over air or by means of the Internet.

To qualify under the Directive, the services in question would need to be under the editorial responsibility of an identifiable media services provider,[70] who selects and then either schedules or catalogues them; although this does not necessarily imply that the media service provider would have to have legal liability under national law for the content or the services provided.[71]

Two other important definitions in the Audiovisual Directive should be mentioned:

- 'audiovisual commercial communication', which is 'images with or without sound which are designed to promote, directly or indirectly, the goods, services or image of a natural or legal entity pursuing an economic activity. Such images accompany or are included in a programme in return for payment or for similar consideration or for self-promotional purposes . . . [72] Audiovisual commercial communication includes television advertising, sponsorship, teleshopping and product placement.'

- 'European works', which are:

  ° works originating in Member States;

  ° works originating in European third states party to the European Convention on Transfrontier Television of the Council of Europe;

  ° works co-produced within the framework of agreements related to the audiovisual sector concluded between the Community and third countries and fulfilling the conditions defined in each of those agreements.[73]

The definition then goes on to set out more detailed rules on how these rules apply where works involve residents of countries within and outside of Member States or

---

[69] Ibid, at Art 1(2)(g).
[70] A 'natural or legal person who has editorial responsibility for the choice of the audiovisual content of the audiovisual media service and determines the manner in which it is organised'.
[71] Ibid, at Art 1(2)(c).
[72] Ibid, at Art 1(2)(h).
[73] Ibid, at Art 1(2)(n)(i). This class of works, and the ones described in the previous bullet point, are subject to the further condition that works originating in Member States should not be the subject of discriminatory treatment in the third county concerned.

such third states: essentially works will be deemed to be 'European works' if they are mainly made, or production is mainly supervised and controlled, by residents of one or more such States or where the production costs are preponderantly contributed by co-producers in such States and the co-production is not controlled by persons outside of such States. The definition is also extended to certain co-produced works.[74]

The Audiovisual Directive substitutes new Articles into the 1989 TWF Directive, as amended by the 1997 TWF Directive. New Article 2, when adopted, will require each Member State to ensure that all *audiovisual media services* (which are defined to include television broadcasts and on-demand audiovisual media services) transmitted by media service providers (see the definition above) under its jurisdiction comply with the rules of the system of law applicable to audiovisual media services intended for the public in that Member State. This repeats the language of the 1989 TWF Directive, but is extended to on-demand audiovisual media services.

The definition of on-demand audiovisual media services has been written with care following extensive consultation and debate. It would extend to a video-on-demand service but only where, as with catch-up TV or a film library, the viewer is selecting from a catalogue of programmes offered by the media service provider; and, of course, for the requirement to apply, the media service provider must be under the jurisdiction of the Member State concerned, which, for example, would exclude on-demand audiovisual media services streamed from the USA.

Article 2(3) contains detailed rules to determine whether a media service provider is under the jurisdiction of a Member State: the tests include whether the head office is there, or whether editorial decisions are taken there, and where the majority of the workforce is based. As with television broadcasters under the 1989 TWF Directive, media service providers are also deemed to be under the jurisdiction of a Member State if they use a satellite up-link in or satellite capacity appertaining to that Member State.

Article 2(a) of the 1989 TWF Directive, which requires Member States to ensure freedom of reception and not restrict retransmission, on their own territory, of television broadcasts lawfully transmitted from other Member States, is extended to audiovisual media services, and the right to derogate from this obligation is to be different in television broadcasts and on-line audiovisual media services. In the former case, derogation may take place only if the broadcast manifestly, seriously, and gravely infringes Article 22(1) or (2)[75] and/or Article 3(b)[76] of the 1989 TWF Directive. In the latter case, on-demand audiovisual media services, which are inherently riskier,

---

[74] 'Works that are not European works (as defined above) but are produced within the framework of bilateral co-production treaties concluded between Member States and third countries provided that the co-producers from the Community supply a majority share of the total cost of production and that the production is not controlled by one or more producers established outside the territory of the Member States'—ibid, at Art 1(2)(n)(iii).

[75] That they might impair the physical, mental, or moral development of minors.

[76] That they contain incitement to hatred based on race, sex, religion, or nationality—a new provision.

a Member State may derogate if necessary for public policy reasons, including investigation and prosecution of criminal offences, protection of public health, public security, or protection of consumers), but subject also to the requirements that:

- the content in question prejudices these objectives or presents a serious and grave risk to them, and is proportionate;
- the Member State has (except in cases of urgency) first asked the other Member State under whose jurisdiction the media service provider falls to take measures, and has notified that Member State and the Commission if it fails to have done so.

The Commission may ask the Member State seeking to exercise a right of derogation in respect of an on-demand audiovisual media service to desist if, after investigation, it concludes that it is acting in contravention of Community law.

The right of Member States (under Article 3 of the 1989 TWF Directive) to impose stricter rules is preserved under the Audiovisual Directive, but where it does so and assesses that a broadcaster under the jurisdiction of another Member State is providing a broadcast 'wholly or mostly directed towards its territory',[77] it must consult the other Member State concerned to try to find a solution, and must most notify that Member State and the Commission of its intention to take action and allow the Commission three months in which to decide if the proposed measures are compatible with Community Law.

The Audiovisual Directive inserts a new Chapter IIA into the 1989 TWF Directive. This Chapter requires Member States to ensure that all audiovisual media service providers provide users with details of their names and addresses and the name of the authority which regulates them. It also imposes on Member States the obligation to require media service providers:

- not to transmit material that incites hatred based on race, sex, religion, or nationality (Article 3b);
- to make their services accessible to persons with a visual or hearing disorder (Article 3c)—this is expressed only as an encouragement;
- not to transmit cinematograph works outside of the licence period agreed with rights holders;
- to comply with a number of specific obligations in relation to 'audiovisual commercial communications', a term that is defined to include television advertising, sponsorship, tele-shopping and product placing, each of which terms is also defined in Article 1 of the Audiovisual Directive. These obligations include prohibitions of 'surreptitious advertising', general provisions on human dignity, discriminatory material, and health and safety and specific provisions in relation

[77] The phraseology is taken from the Court of Justice decision in *TV10* Case C-23/93, ECR (1994) I-4795.

to pharmaceuticals, tobacco, and alcohol. Member States are also encouraged to develop Codes in relation to the promotion of unhealthy foods.

Article 3f includes additional rules on programme 'sponsorship', defined as 'any contribution made by a public or private undertaking or natural person not engaged in providing audiovisual media services or in the production of audiovisual works, to the financing of audiovisual media services or programmes with a view to promoting its name, its trade mark, its image, its activities or its products'.[78]

Article 3g prohibits 'product placement', defined as 'any form of audiovisual commercial communication consisting of the inclusion of or reference to a product, a service or the trade mark thereof so that it is featured within a programme, in return for payment or for similar consideration',[79] subject to limited derogations in relation to cinematograph works, films, and series made for audiovisual media services and sports programmes and light entertainment programmes and where no payment is made for the provision of certain types of goods and services.

The obligations on Member States under Chapter IIA are evolutionary, in that they replace quite similar provisions included in Chapter IV of the 1989 TWF Directive. They will need to be imposed on media service providers at national level. In the UK, this will be achieved by means of the issue of the new edition of the Broadcasting Code.

The Audiovisual Directive also inserts a new Chapter IIB into the 1989 TWF Directive. This Chapter, which relates only to on-demand audiovisual services, requires Member States to:

- take appropriate measures to ensure that on-demand audiovisual media services provided by media services providers under their jurisdiction which might seriously impair the physical, mental, or moral development of minors are only made available in such a way that ensures that minors will not normally her or see the same—Article 3(h) (this, it is suggested, will be a harder test than is currently the case for television);

- ensure that providers within their jurisdiction of on-demand audiovisual media services promote the production of and access to European works, but only 'where practicable' and 'by appropriate means', some of which are suggested—Article 3(i) (this is a new and rather unclear obligation, and manifestly something of a political 'fudge').

The Audiovisual Directive also inserts a new Chapter IIC into the 1989 TWF Directive concerning exclusive rights and short news reports in television broadcasting, which will replace existing Article 3a of the 1989 TWF Directive.

Finally, the Audiovisual Directive inserts a new Chapter VIIB into the 1989 TWF Directive concerning cooperation among Member States regulatory bodies.

---

[78] Directive 07/65/EC, Art 1(2)(k).
[79] Ibid, Art 1(2)(m).

14.3.4 European measures relating to the Internet

The 1989 Directive, as amended by the 1997 Directive, defined 'television broadcasting as 'the initial transmission by wire or over the air, including that by satellite, . . . of television programmes intended for reception by the public',[80] and defines 'broadcaster'[81] as 'a natural or legal person who has editorial responsibility for the composition of schedules of television programmes [82]. . . and who transmits them or has them transmitted by third parties'.

The TWF Directives do not therefore apply to content transmitted over the Internet unless the content could be said to be 'television programmes'. This is changing— hence the adoption of the Audiovisual Directive.[83]

Other measures do, however, apply to the Internet. There are of course the early measures described in 14.3.1 above and, in addition, in 1998 the European Council issued Recommendation of 24 September 1998 (98/560/EC).[84] This measure, which is only a recommendation and therefore not mandatory on Member States, was aimed at fostering a climate of confidence to promote the development of the audio-visual and information services industry within Europe. Member States were recommended, as a supplement to the existing regulatory framework, to establish on a voluntary basis national frameworks for the protection of minors and human dignity in audio-visual and information services. The Annex to this Recommendation contained a number of 'indicative guidelines' for the implementation at national level of a self-regulation framework, and includes reference to the preparation of codes of conduct, particularly in relation to protection of minors, support for parental control, the handling of complaints, and the discouragement of content that is offensive to human dignity.

Recommendation 98/560/EC was followed by three Council Conclusions dated 27 September 1999, 17 December 1999, and 23 July 2001 respectively, in which the Commission was invited to take account of self-regulatory initiatives, to encourage greater dialogue among industry players and users on the evaluation and rating of audiovisual material, to support the protection of minors through increased media literacy, and to promote best practice across the Community.

More recently, a Proposal for a Decision of the European Parliament and of the Council[85] has called for greater protection of children using the Internet and other communications technologies, in particular in areas of child grooming, child abuse,

---

[80] This definition is to be changed under the Audiovisual Directive to 'an audiovisual media service provided by a media service provider for simultaneous viewing of programmes on the basis of a programme schedule'.

[81] Article 1(1).

[82] The term 'television programmes' is not defined under the Directives.

[83] Neither the TWF Directives nor the Audiovisual Directive apply to sound broadcasting, although sound broadcasting is emphatically regulated in the UK.

[84] OJ L 298, 17 October 1989.

[85] Com (2008) 106 Final of 27 February 2008.

and cyber-bullying. The Proposals build on earlier work under the EC safer Internet programs and establish four action lines:

* reducing illegal content and tackling harmful content online;
* providing a safer online environment;
* ensuring public awareness;
* establishing a knowledge base.

And, of course, on-demand audiovisual media services, but no other Internet-delivered services, are now to be regulated under the Audiovisual Directive.

14.3.5 Other relevant EC measures

We should also briefly mention three other important measures that have a material impact on the liability of ISPs for content. They are Directive 2000/31/EC of the European Parliament and of the Council 'on certain legal aspects of information society services, in particular electronic commerce, in the Internal Market', better known as the 'Electronic Commerce Directive';[86] and Directive 2001/29/EC of the European Parliament and of the Council 'on the harmonization of certain aspects of copyright and related rights in the information society', the 'Copyright Directive';[87] each of which has been transposed into English law by Regulations issued under the European Community Act 1972.

14.3.5.1 The Electronic Commerce (EC Directive) Regulations 2002
These Regulations[88] transpose the Electronic Commerce Directive into English law. They are directed to 'information society services' which are summarized in Recital 17 of the Electronic Commerce Directive as:

any service normally provided for remuneration, at a distance, by means of electronic equipment for the processing (including digital compression) and storage of data, and at the individual request of a recipient of a service.[89]

The Regulations are subject to some exclusions under:

* paragraph 3 in relation to taxation, the data protection regime, questions relating to cartel law, activities of a public notary (or holder of an equivalent office), legal representation of a client, and betting, gaming, and lotteries;

---

[86] OJ L 178/1, 17 July 2000.

[87] OJ L 167/10, 22 June 2001.

[88] SI No 2013/2002. They are part of a package of Regulations issued in 2002, the others relating to financial services.

[89] Also see the original measure that defined the term: Directive 98/48/EC of the European Parliament and of the Council of 20 July 1998 amending Directive 98/34/EC laying down a procedure for the provision of information in the field of technical standards and regulations; OJ L 217/18, 05 August 1998.

• paragraphs 4(4) and (5), which provide that they do not apply to the fields of copy-right,[90] neighbouring rights, and other intellectual property rights, to contractual obligations concerning consumer contracts or certain other matters.

Under paragraph 3(2), the Electronic Commerce Regulations do not apply to any future Act of Parliament or Regulations so, in order to apply the same exclusions to legal liabilities created after adoption of the Electronic Commerce Regulations, further Regulations would need to be drawn up at the time when the new legislation is passed into law.[91]

There are four main objectives under the Electronic Commerce Regulations:

i. To provide that any requirement that falls within the 'co-ordinated field' shall apply in relation to the provision of 'information society services' by a service provider established within the UK, irrespective of the Member State within the service is provided, and to require any relevant enforcement authority within the UK to secure compliance. (The coordinated field means general or specific requirement on information society service providers or information society services regarding establishment, qualifications, and the quality or content of the service including rules on advertising and contracts and rules on liability).

ii. To set out minimum levels of information that the service provider of an electronic information service must provide and includes basic matters such as the name and address of the service provider, its email contact address, the identity of any regulatory body which supervises the service provider, and, in the case of a registered company or other entity, its registration number; and also requires the service provider to make it clear when the service is provided on a commercial basis or is unsolicited.[92]

iii. To provide a clear explanation of the information to be provided in relation to the formation of a contract by electronic means and a right for the consumer to identify and correct input errors prior to placing his order. These rights may only be excluded in the case of an agreement between parties who are not consumers; in case of non-compliance, the consumer may rescind the contract.[93]

iv. The last objective, and the one most relevant to this chapter, is to specify the cases in which providers of information society services are, and are not, liable for material included in services that they provide.

On this last point, a distinction is drawn between liability in a case where the service provider takes a passive role as a mere conduit, and where he is more directly

---

[90] But see the Copyright Regulations referred to in the next section below.
[91] E.g. Electronic Commerce Directive (Racial and Religious Hatred Act 2006) Regulations 2007 (SI 2497); Electronic Commerce Directive (Terrorism Act 2006) Regulations 2007 (SI 1550); Criminal Justice and Immigration Act 2008, s 68, Sch 14.
[92] 2002 Regulations at paras 6 and 8.
[93] Ibid, at para 11.

responsible for the origination or propagation of the material. Thus, under paragraph 17(1) of the UK Regulations:

where an information society service is provided which consists of the transmission in a communications network of information provided by a recipient of the service or the provision of access to a communication network, the service provider (if he otherwise would) shall not be liable for damages or for any other pecuniary remedy or for any criminal sanction as a result of that transmission where the service provider—

(a) did not initiate the transmission;
(b) did not select the receiver of the transmission; and
(c) did not select or modify the information contained in the transmission.

Note that the requirements under (a) to (c) are cumulative.

Paragraph (2) provides that:

the acts of transmission and of provision of access referred to in paragraph (1) include the automatic, intermediate and transient storage of the information transmitted where:

(a) this takes place for the sole purpose of carrying out the transmission in the communications network; and
(b) the information is not stored for any period longer than is reasonably necessary for the transmission.

The intent here is that, where the service provider is merely a conduit, he should not be liable. The ISP cannot, however, rely on this defence if he 'caches' information, that is to say if he automatically and temporarily stores the information, unless the sole purpose of this caching is the more efficient onward transmission of that information to other recipients of the service at their request, and provided that four other conditions are satisfied:

• he does not modify the information;
• he complies with conditions on access to the information;
• he complies with any rules regarding the updating of the information, specified in a manner widely recognized and used by industry;
• he does not interfere with the lawful use of technology, widely recognized and used by industry.

A service provider who stores information on his own servers, or servers under his control, has a yet narrower defence available to him. Under paragraph 19, he has a defence only if he has no actual knowledge of the unlawful activity or information and:

• 'is not aware of facts or circumstances from which it would have been apparent that the activity or information was unlawful'; or
• 'upon obtaining such knowledge or awareness acts expeditiously to remove or to disable access to the information.'

The act of removing or disabling access is generally known in the industry as 'Notice and Take Down' and is a common requirement under a number of Codes.[94] Notice and Take Down appears an elegant solution to a largely intractable problem and indeed it is much invoked. However, not all copyright owners are happy with the position for, effectively, responsibility for policing unlawful content on websites, including social networking sites, is transferred to rights or brand owners. But ISPs and owners of websites cannot necessarily be insouciant and just sit back and wait for a Notice to Take Down. In a recent case in France, eBay was fined nearly €40,000,000 for allowing online auctions of fake copies of luxury branded goods.[95]

An ISP might, but for the provisions of these Regulations, have been held liable for information carried by means of the service it offers under a number of heads, including defamation, obscenity, a breach of financial services regulations, or any other law or regulation that may make the carrier or publisher of information liable. The effect of the Regulations is therefore to provide a qualified defence to ISPs whose activities are limited to the operation of a communications network and who have no control over or knowledge of the information that is stored or transmitted.

There is an important right of derogation under paragraph 5, which permits an enforcement authority to take measures in respect of an information society service where it considers that it is necessary (and proportionate) to do so for reasons of a serious and grave risk to:

• public policy, in particular the prevention, investigation, detection, and prosecution of criminal offences, including the protection of minors and the fight against incitement on grounds of race, sex, religion, or nationality;

• the protection of public health;

• public security;

• the protection of consumers, including investors.

Any enforcement authority must first ask any other Member State which regulates the service provider in question to take action and notify the Commission and the Member State in question of its intention to take measures. PhonepayPlus, as an enforcement authority in the UK, has taken advantage of this derogation to enforce against premium rate service providers in other EU Member States.[96]

14.3.5.2 *The Copyright and Related Rights Regulations 2003*
These Regulations[97] transpose the EC Copyright Directive into English Law. They are lengthy and address an array of matters from folksongs to educational establishments

---

[94] E.g. the IWF Code, see section 14.11.2 below.
[95] Decision of La Tribunal de Commerce de Paris June 2008, now under appeal.
[96] PhonePayPlus, Report No 93, October 2002, available at <http://www.phonepayplus.org.uk/pdfs_news/IMR93.pdf>.
[97] SI No 2498/2003.

and from performers' rights to the sub-titling of broadcasts. For the purpose of this chapter, we are most interested in paragraph 8, which inserts a new section 28A into the Copyright, Designs and Patents Act, 1988, providing that:

copyright in a literary work, other than a computer program or a database, or in a dramatic, musical or artistic work, the typographical arrangement of a published edition, a sound recording or a film, is not infringed by the making of a temporary copy which is transient or incidental, which is an integral part of a technological process and the sole purpose of which is to enable—

(a) a transmission of the work in a network between third parties by an intermediary; or
(b) a lawful use of the work,

and which has no independent economic significance.

Similar language is added as a new paragraph 1A in Schedule 2 of that Act.[98]

Section 28A of the Copyright, Designs and Patents Act 1988 has a similar effect in relation to copyright[99] as does paragraph 17 of the Electronic Commerce Regulations in relation to liability in general in the sense that it extends protection to service providers in relation to certain acts that might otherwise infringe third party rights, but they are not identical in effect. The amendment to the Copyright Act provides a complete defence to a claimed infringement, while the Electronic Commerce Regulations only relieve the ISP from pecuniary loss, so allowing a claimant to continue to seek an injunction.

Any advantage under this part of the new copyright regime is partly eroded under new section 97A of the Copyright, Designs and Patents Act 1988, which gives back to the court a power to grant an injunction against an ISP where it 'has actual knowledge of another person using their service to infringe copyright'. This language led to an extended debate on where actual knowledge existed—for example did it arise merely because a person had claimed infringement, whether or not that claim was disputed by the third party concerned? The new section, like paragraph 22 of the earlier Electronic Commerce Regulations, provides that, in determining whether the ISP had actual knowledge, the court will take into account 'all matters which appear to it in the particular circumstances to be relevant and, amongst other things, shall have regard to whether or not the ISP has received a notice through a means of contact made in accordance with Regulation 6(1)(c) of the Electronic Commerce (EC Directive) Regulations 2002[100] and the extent to which the notice includes the full name and address of the sender of the notice and details of the infringement'. Unfortunately, this leaves ISPs in a state of some uncertainty as to whether or not an injunction might be granted in any given case.

---

[98] Paragraph 8(2) of the regulations.
[99] Note the exclusion in relation to copyright under para 4(4) of the Electronic Commerce Directive.
[100] This requires publication of details of the service provider, including his electronic mail address, which make it possible to contact him rapidly and communicate with him in a direct and effective manner.

There has been a remarkable absence in UK case law in this area, although one defamation case[101] reinforces the view that, as long as the ISP complies with the Take Down Notice, it should escape liability for its users infringing actions.[102] However, this remains to be seen and, if the UK courts decide to follow their French neighbours, the result may not be as favourable for the ISPs.

In a recent French decision *Zadig v Google*,[103] Zadig a production company sued Google for uploading one of their videos. In an email, Google informed Zadig that it had removed access to the documentary in question. However, the film was made available on the site several times by other Internet users. Each time, the broadcasting was notified, Google removed the content concerned, but Zadig considered that Google had not taken all necessary steps to stop the broadcasting of the film. The High Court of First Instance of Paris ('Tribunal de Grande Instance') held, with regard to the first broadcast, that Google had complied with these provisions by expeditiously removing the film. However, as regards the following broadcasts, the court considered that since Google had already been notified of the illegal nature of the content, it had the obligation to do everything necessary in order to prevent a further broadcast. The court ruled that Google had not proved that it had implemented such means, as the technical means that Google alleged it had developed had manifestly been ineffective. Google could not therefore benefit from the liability limitation provided by French legislation and was condemned for copyright infringement. Many legal commentators expect this decision to be overruled as being in contravention of Article 15 of the EC Regulations which provides for a general principle of 'no monitoring' by an ISP of the information they store, nor a general obligation actively to seek facts indicating illegal activity. The decision has also been criticized as leaving service providers too vulnerable to litigation.

If the Zadig decision is set as a precedent, service providers which host material may need to develop technical means capable of searching for specific content, a task that many argue is near impossible since the Internet is borderless and constantly evolving.

14.4 UK REGULATION OF CONTENT

14.4.1 The Communications Act 2003

The 2003 Act substantially changed the landscape for the regulation of content and content providers, but it was not a fully consolidating measure and has not displaced everything that has gone before. Parts of the 1984, 1990, and 1996 Acts remain in

---

[101] See *Bunt v Tilley* [2006] 3 All ER 336.
[102] See also *Sheffield Wednesday Football Club Ltd and others v Hargreaves* [2007] All ER (D) 270 (Oct) the author of anonymous defamatory postings was ordered to be revealed, which might curb the enthusiasm of these 'bloggers'!
[103] 19 October 2007 (TGI Paris)—Google Video.

force and, while the BBC now operates under a new Charter and Agreement,[104] both documents build on the earlier 1996 arrangements and the interim amendments made in 2003.

The 2003 Act is long and hard to navigate. Content issues are addressed in Part 1, under the title of 'Functions of Ofcom', and again in Part 3, 'Television and Radio Services'. We will start our analysis by looking at the definition of content services under the 2003 Act and follow on by providing a roadmap to the several provisions within the 2003 Act that may bear on specific types of content.

14.4.1.1 *Content services*

In the UK, 'content services' are explicitly carved out of the definition of electronic communications services (ECS) under section 32(2) of Part 1 of the 2003 Act. ECS, and their manner of regulation, are addressed in Chapter 7, but it is convenient to recall the definition of ECS here, which is:

a service consisting in, or having as its principal feature, the conveyance by means of an electronic communications network of signals, except in so far as it is a content service.

This definition of ECS uses the word 'conveyance', which is a quite distinct activity from the provision of a contents service, which is defined under section 32(7) as:

so much of any service as consists in one or both of the following—

(a) the provision of material with a view to its being comprised in signals conveyed by means of an electronic communications network;

(b) the exercise of editorial control over the contents of signals conveyed by means of such a network.'

Note the phrase 'so much of' which underlines the fact that services may need to be 'unpacked' into separate carriage and content elements.

The word 'signal' in the definitions of an ECS and a content service is defined widely to include speech, music, sounds, visual images or communications, or data of any description (section 32 (10)). Any form of material comprised in a 'signal' conveyed over an electronic communications network is therefore capable of being content within the meaning of the 2003 Act. However there is a limitation: the definition of a content service requires that a service exists under which material is provided or edited by some person, who will usually do so on a commercial basis. In the case of simple voice calls or emails or SMS texts, no third party is providing material or editing it so no content service is provided. The only *service* being provided here would be the carriage of the message, which of course is an ECS and not a content service. On the other hand, the provision of audiovisual works for an on-demand service or a television or radio channel is likely to fall within the definition

---

[104] Issued in 2006.

of a content service and hence be excluded from the definition of an ECS. However, such services may be regulated under Part 3 of the 2003 Act, as we shall see below.

As a result of the carve out of content services from ECS, the regulatory regimes for ECS and for content services are wholly different. However, a company, for example an ISP, may be supplying both services and sometimes it can be difficult to assess whether a particular service is an ECS or a content service. The heart of the distinction, as we have said earlier, is whether the service is primarily the carriage, or conveyance, of signals or is instead the provision or editing of material that is intended to be carried over an ECN. The provision of basic Internet access would be an ECS; but the compilation of video or football clips intended for streaming over the Internet would be a content service. Virgin Cable provides an ECS by carrying the channels of third party providers like Disney and UK Gold over its cable system. UK Gold provides a type of content service, but does not provide an ECS, as it is not a carrier.

14.4.3 The nature of television broadcasting

As television broadcasting remains the most important source of audiovisual content, we need to examine the nature of modern broadcasting. Like everything else in technology, it has moved on from what it was.

At the present time, viewers may receive television broadcasts in one or more of six ways:

- conventional analogue broadcasts from terrestrial transmitters;
- newer digital broadcasts from terrestrial multiplexes;
- direct-to-home satellite broadcasts (notably Sky);
- transmissions over cable television networks;
- streamed data over fixed or mobile telecommunications networks using Internet Protocol (this is used for video-on-demand services and increasingly for 'catch-up television' where viewers who missed a conventionally broadcast programme may have it streamed to them over the Internet within a period of time following the original broadcast);
- broadcasts to mobile handheld devices using DVB-H standards (and other standards are also possible).

Broadcast television is improving in quality with the introduction of High Definition TV standards. The same standards cannot yet be achieved for programming streamed or downloaded over the public Internet, but already the quality of IP transmissions is far better than in the past, thanks in part to increases in broadband speeds. The quality of video-on-demand services and catch-up television will undoubtedly improve further in the medium term.

The government will switch off analogue transmissions in the UK by 2012, and indeed one region has already switched. In parallel with this the signal strength of digital transmissions is to be increased to provide a more robust service.

In recent years, the UK has moved from a limited number of television channels to a multi-channel world, with a majority of the population now having access to additional channels over and above the 'main' broadcast channels, i.e. BBC 1, BBC 2, ITV, Channel 4, and Channel 5. Some additional channels are broadcast by these same broadcasters and others are transmitted by Sky, the cable companies, and digital Multiplexes. However, the five 'main' channels remain at centre stage and are regulated differently from other channels. In particular they are subject to public service obligations that are not imposed in relation to other channels.

14.4.4 Business models and the value chain

Just as television (and radio) channels are now delivered over different media, so too the business models of broadcasters have evolved. A few short years ago, a broadcaster was vertically integrated; it produced the programmes (or bought in films), edited and ordered programmes into a channel, carried out the technical steps required to enable the channel to be broadcast, and then broadcast it from its own broadcast stations, probably using analogue terrestrial broadcasting equipment. Now, at least in the UK, this simple model has gone and has become much more complex. The main broadcasters commission much of their output from independent producers (or producers abroad), and the BBC and ITV have disposed of their broadcasting station assets.

In parallel with this, new companies have entered the market as independent producers of programmes, as 'aggregators', companies which acquire rights to programmes from third party producers and package these into new channels, and companies that operate the broadcasting stations or multiplexes, in some cases having first acquired the assets from the BBC or ITV.

The new business model is best depicted in a 'Value Chain'—see Figure 14.2.

Activity 1 on the Value Chain is programme origination, or programme making, which is not in and of itself a regulated or licensable activity under the 2003 Act.[105] Activity 2 is the packaging of programmes into channels by an aggregator, which, as we shall see, is likely to be licensable as a 'Television Content Licensable Service' or a 'Digital Television Programme Service'. Activity 3 is the further technical activity under which a channel is prepared for transmission and then conveyed to the

Figure 14.2

---

[105] But customers of programmes will want to ensure that programme makers comply with all relevant provisions of the Broadcasting Code, and include contractual terms to that effect.

broadcasting station; this again is likely to be a regulated activity; typically Activity 3 operations will be undertaken alongside channel aggregation by one of the main broadcasters and will be licensable as a 'Television Broadcasting Service'.

Activity 4 is the broadcast of the channel to the public from the broadcasting station or multiplex. This involves the operation of an ECN which, under the 2003 Act, does not of itself need a licence unless it is a multiplex, which requires a special licence under section 7 of the Broadcasting Act 1996.

14.4.5 The nature of multiplexes

The conventional analogue broadcasting stations will be switched off between now and 2012 and replaced by multiplexes. Indeed the multiplexes are already in use. Today, there are six national multiplexes in the UK and another is to be established to allow further digital radio broadcasting. In addition, there are other regional multiplexes for sound broadcasting. Multiplexes are facilities that combine the information within two or more programmes and broadcast them together in digital form at the same time using a single wavelength. Multiplexes are therefore more efficient, but require a modem, in the form of a 'set-top box', in the home to convert back the signals into a form that is intelligible to the current generation of television sets.

The first multiplex was allocated to the BBC and is not licensed by Ofcom. A second, known as Multiplex A, was licensed to a joint venture company then controlled by NTL, S4C, and United News and Media;[106] the third was awarded to Channels 3 and 4. Following the collapse of ITV Digital, the fourth, known as Multiplex B, is now used in part by the BBC for the additional digital channels it offers, and the last two, known as Multiplexes C and D, were awarded to a private operator.

The licensees of Multiplexes B, C, and D and, in relation to unreserved capacity, the licensee of Multiplex A, may contract with licensed providers of digital programme services for the provision of programmes for broadcast over their respective multiplexes. Under the conditions attached by ITC (as was then) to the licences that were awarded, multiplexes B, C, and D are not required to carry any of the so-called 'qualifying services', which is to say the digital broadcasts provided by Channels 3, 4, and 5 that are 'simulcasts' of their analogue programming. Radio broadcasts are still primarily received in analogue form, particularly by car drivers, but the BBC and some independent stations now also broadcast their programmes, and in the case of the BBC additional programmes, in digital form over multiplexes. There are rather similar provisions in relation to simulcast radio services as there are in relation to simulcast television.[107] Interestingly, digital radio broadcasts now support text so 'steam radio' has now become an audio-visual service, if only in a modest way!

---

[106] Part of the capacity on this is reserved for Channel 5, S4C in Wales, and for Gaelic programming.
[107] 2003 Act, ss 256–261. The challenging economic times may well impact the future ownership and use of multiplexes for sound broadcasting.

Digital radio programming is also carried over the Internet. This is less common for television broadcasts, mainly because of bandwidth limitations, but is changing with catch-up television, such as the BBC's iPlayer.

14.5 DUTIES OF OFCOM

14.5.1 General duties of Ofcom

After setting the context in the previous section, we can now turn to the role of Ofcom in the regulation of 'content services' under the Communications Act 2003.

Section 3 of the 2003 Act sets out the general duties of Ofcom which, only in the context of content regulation, include:

- furthering the interests of citizens;
- furthering the interests of consumers in relevant markets, where appropriate by promoting competition.[108]

The significance of the duality of citizen and consumer was described by Ed Richards, then a senior partner at Ofcom before being made Chief Executive, as lying at the very heart of Ofcom:

Consumer choice backed by effective competition captures a significant element of our needs: but it does not capture the whole picture . . . Our concerns, our needs as citizens are exemplified by many of the characteristics of public service broadcasting [including being] part of an informed democracy, spreading educational opportunity and engaging in our diverse culture . . .[109]

This theme is reflected in the 2003 Act. Section 3(2) requires Ofcom to secure, in the carrying out of their functions, each of the following:

- the availability throughout the UK of a wide range of television and radio services which (taken as a whole) are both of high quality and calculated to appeal to a variety of tastes and interests;
- the maintenance of a sufficient plurality of providers of different television and radio services;
- the application of standards that provide adequate protection to members of the public from the inclusion of offensive and harmful material in such services;
- the application, the case of all television and radio services, of standards that provide adequate protection to members of the public and other persons from both unfair treatment and unwarranted infringements of privacy.

---

[108] See further Chapter 4, at 4.3.7.2.
[109] Speech to the Royal Television Society dinner on 4 December 2003.

This, and the section that follows, substantially echo earlier provisions under the 1996 Act in relation to public service broadcasting and broadcast standards, but have been brought up-to-date.

Again in the context of content regulation, section 3(4) of the 2003 Act required Ofcom to have regard, in performing their duties, to such of the following matters as appear to them to be relevant in the circumstances:

- the desirability of promoting the fulfilment of the purposes of public service television broadcasting in the UK;
- the need to balance obligations to provide protection against offensive and harmful material with an 'appropriate level of freedom of expression';
- the vulnerability of children and others whose circumstances appear to Ofcom to put them in need of special protection;
- the desirability of preventing crime and disorder.

Ofcom is also required, in the case of a conflict, to give priority to overarching European Community measures. Otherwise, where any general duty conflicts with another, it must secure that the conflict is resolved in the manner they think best in the circumstances (section 3(7)). This provides Ofcom with a broad discretion, but one that, as with any administrative act, must be properly based.

Section 6 of the 2003 Act supports light-touch regulation. Subsection (1) provides that Ofcom are required to keep the carrying out of their functions under review with a view to securing that regulation by Ofcom does not impose burdens which are unnecessary or maintain burdens which have become unnecessary. Ofcom must also, under subsection (2):

have regard to the extent to which matters which they are required to further or to secure or are already furthered or secured, or could be, by effective self-regulation and, in light of that, to consider to what extent it would be appropriate to remove or reduce regulatory burdens imposed by Ofcom.

This is a significant development which positively encourages the development of self-regulatory regimes over statutory regulations, and which we already see in the context of regulation of advertising on television and radio.

Sections 7 and 8 and 14 to 21 of the 2003 Act provide for impact assessments, set promptness standards, and provide for consultation, research, and the creation of a consumer panel and advisory committees, all of which, obviously, could have some bearing on how content is regulated.

Section 11 addresses the topic of media literacy, which we discuss in more detail below. Sections 12 and 13 provide for the Content Board and its functions, which again are discussed below.

14.5.2 The Ofcom Content Board and media literacy

The Content Board is a committee of Ofcom, acting under the main Ofcom Board and makes recommendations to the main board. The Content Board has the functions that Ofcom confers upon it under powers contained in the Act that paved the way for Ofcom, the Office of Communications Act 2002. Under section 13 of the 2003 Act, Ofcom must confer functions on the Board in relation to matters concerning the content of anything which may be broadcast or otherwise transmitted by means of ECNs and to 'the promotion of public understanding or awareness of matters relating to the publication of matter by means of the electronic media' (section 13(2)(b)).

In the light of its principal statutory function, the Content Board has a central role in the regulation of content. Indeed, Ofcom has delegated to the Content Board all decisions relating to content except where these:

    i. would have a significant economic impact on the whole industry, or a significant section of it;

    ii. would have a direct effect on the value of an individual licence; or

    iii. relate to Ofcom's own governance responsibilities.[110]

The Content Board's functions in relation to the content of broadcasts also means that the Content Board takes the major role in determining the Broadcasting Code for television and radio services.[111]

In carrying out its functions, the Content Board is required to ensure that Ofcom is made aware of the different interests and of other factors which, in the Board's opinion, need to be taken into account as respects different parts of the UK.

The second statutory function of the Content Board is interesting; it is a truism that many people in the UK are confused by the complexity of media offerings today, and fail to get all that they might want or need from new media. At its simplest level, there are those who cannot programme a video recorder (and who may never learn to do so before that technology is altogether replaced by personal video recorders); at other levels, substantial numbers do not use or sufficiently understand PCs, the availability of information and entertainment on the Internet, iTV,[112] digital TV, or digital radio. There is a digital divide within the population, and both Ofcom and the Content Board have roles to play in bridging this.

Section 10 of the 2003 Act requires Ofcom to take steps calculated to encourage others to secure that easy-to-use domestic electronic apparatus is developed, and section 11 provides that Ofcom have a special role (in at least part of which the Content

---

[110] Speech by Stephen Carter, Chief Executive, Ofcom, 'The Communications Act: Myths and Realities', 9 October 2003, available at <http://www.ofcom.org.uk/media/speeches/2003/10/carter_20031009>.

[111] See section 14.7.7 below.

[112] Interactive television.

Board also has functions) in the promotion of media literacy. This role includes duties (but few powers) to help bring about or encourage better public understanding of:

- the nature and characteristics of material published on electronic media and the processes by which such material is selected, or made available, for publication on electronic media;
- consumer equipment and delivery means;
- means to control what is received and the uses to which systems may be put;
- the use of effective and easy technologies and systems to control access to material.

Ofcom are also obliged to encourage the development of access technologies and systems.

There is no single agreed definition of media literacy, but Ofcom uses the, rather oblique, interpretation: 'Media Literacy is the ability to access, understand and create communications in a variety of contexts.' Media literacy, say Ofcom, should 'provide some of the tools that people need to make full use of the opportunities offered, to manage their expectations and to protect themselves and their families from the risks involved. Through confident use of communications technologies people will gain a better understanding of the world around them and be better able to engage with it'.[113]

Ofcom have recognized the need to take a leadership role and to work with content producers, broadcasters, platform and network providers, educators, government departments, parents, children's charities, and other organizations in promoting media literacy. Ofcom focus their work on research, awareness, and the promotion of labelling of content.

14.5.3 Ofcom and over-arching Community obligations

Section 4(1) sets out certain overarching Community obligations that arise under the package of measures adopted by the European Union in relation to electronic communications networks and services.[114] The most relevant to content regulation are, perhaps:

- the requirement to promote the interests of all persons who are citizens of the European Union;
- the obligation, so far as practicable, not to favour one form of ECN or ECS over another.

---

[113] Ofcom, *Strategy and Priorities for the Promotion of Media Literacy*, November 2004, at paras 2–3.
[114] See Chapter 5.

But section 4(1) does not paint the full picture: there are other important Community measures in relation to television, notably the two TWF Directives and the new Audiovisual Directive and the UK Regulations made or to be made under them, and also other measures in relation to the Internet. These are discussed elsewhere in this chapter.

14.5.4 Functions of Ofcom in relation to television and radio services

Having looked at the nature of television broadcasting today and at Ofcom's general duties, we can now look at the functions of Ofcom in relation to television and radio services.

Section 2 of the 2003 Act provided for the transfer to Ofcom of functions of the 'pre-commencement regulators', and in particular for the takeover by Ofcom of:

• the functions of the ITC in respect of the award of licences and the function of securing the provision of nationwide television broadcasting services known as Channel 3 and Channel 5;

• the functions of the ITC in relation to Gaelic broadcasting, C4C, and the National Television Archive;

• the functions of the Radio Authority;

• certain functions of the BSC, which previously had had responsibility for broadcasting standards for independent television, and which had assumed the functions of the old BCC in 1998.

One of Ofcom's most important functions is the award and subsequent enforcement of licences. One does not require a licence for every activity that falls within the definition of a content service but, depending on their nature, activities that fall within the scope of that definition may require one or other of the several types of licence provided for under Part 3 of the 2003 Act. The licences of most importance in the regulation of content (and which are discussed in greater detail below) are:

• Television Broadcasting Licences;

• Television Licensable Content Licences;

• Digital Television Programme Services Licences;

• Television Multiplex Licences,[115]

and equivalent forms of licences in respect of radio broadcasting.

It is worth reminding ourselves that, under English Law, a licence essentially permits a person, or a company, to do something that is inherently lawful but which, but for a licence, is prohibited by a law in the country concerned. Beyond being the

---

[115] Restricted Television Licences and Ancillary Television Licences are also awarded.

formal permission to carry on a particular activity, a licence can fulfil a number of other possible governmental objectives. It may:

- allow the government to remain informed of who is carrying out the licensed activities and to supervise them;
- be used as a barrier to competitive entry, for example where a single or a limited number of licences is awarded;
- impose positive obligations on the licensee, for example in terms of the provision of particular types of programming;
- impose conditions on the licensee, for example as to programme standards;
- protect consumers in a market in which there is no true competition, by regulating quality and terms of supply and by capping prices;
- allow the government, or a regulatory agency, to enforce against a licensee and impose sanctions for breach or, as an ultimate sanction, to revoke the licence altogether;
- allow the imposition of a levy or fee.[116]

Ofcom's main function in television and radio is to license and regulate independent broadcasters but, under sections 198 to 210 of the 2003 Act, Ofcom are given various further functions in relation to the BBC, C4C, the Welsh Authority, and the Gaelic Media Service.

Ofcom's functions in relation to the BBC and the other broadcasters mentioned above are considerably more limited than the functions Ofcom currently enjoy in relation to the independent broadcasters of Channels 3, 4, and 5. Thus, under section 198(2) of the 2003 Act, Ofcom has the function of regulating the BBC only to the extent that there is provision for them to do so under the 2006 BBC Charter and the BBC Framework Agreement and also under the 2003 Act and Part 5 of the 1996 Act.[117]

For completeness, we should mention that Ofcom also have limited functions in relation to the Welsh Authority under section 203 of the 2003 Act. The Welsh Authority continues in existence with important functions in relation to the provision of high quality television services in Wales. The Gaelic Media Service, now renamed Seirbheis nam Meidhanan Gaidhlig, has continuing, but modified, functions in relation to broadcasting in the Gaelic language.

We should also mention that the position regarding Channel 4 is a little different from that of other independent broadcasters. Channel 4 is broadcast by the Channel 4 Corporation (C4C) which used to enjoy a licence under the 1990 Act. That licence was terminated immediately before the 2003 Act came into effect and was replaced by a licence granted by Ofcom pursuant to statutory requirements set out in section 231

---

[116] See further Chapter 7.
[117] See section 14.9 below.

of the 2003 Act. The primary functions of C4C are to secure the continued provision of Channel 4 and the fulfilment of its public service remit.[118]

14.6 THE REGULATORY FRAMEWORK FOR TELEVISION AND RADIO

14.6.1 The three tiers of regulation

The UK approach to the regulation of television content under the 2003 Act is to distinguish between three tiers or types of service providers:

• certain 'public service broadcasters' providing 'relevant television services' must comply with significant public interest requirements and controls; these are sometimes referred to as 'Tier 3' regulations;

• all public service commercial broadcasters must comply with quantitative requirements concerning the source of television programmes and the amount of news programming and original material they carry; these are sometimes referred to as 'Tier 2' regulations;

• all persons (whether or not they are public service broadcasters) providing more widely defined 'television and radio services' must comply with certain standards in relation to the content of programmes and advertising they carry; these are sometimes referred to as 'Tier 1' regulations.

Tier 3 regulations applied to 'public service broadcasters' providing 'relevant television services'. Both these expressions are defined under the 2003 Act:

• 'public service broadcasters' are defined as the BBC, the Welsh Authority, 'licensed public service providers', and the public teletext provider (section 264(12)). Licensed public service providers are in turn defined as the broadcasters holding any Channel 3 franchise, and Channel 4, and Channel 5 (section 362). The public teletext service is defined as the service that is required to be secured in accordance with section 218 of the 2003 Act, which must consist of a single teletext service provided in digital form for broadcast by means of a television multiplex service and also, for so long as Channel 4, S4C and one or more Channel 3 services are broadcast in analogue form, an analogue teletext service (section 362). Ceefax is the current public teletext service on BBC and Teletext on the ITV channels;

• 'relevant television services' are defined as:

   ○ the television broadcasting services provided by the BBC; note that these would *not* include any services provided by BBC Free to View Limited as services

---

[118] As defined under the 2003 Act, s 265(3).

provided by a BBC subsidiary are specifically deemed not to be provided by the BBC itself;

○ public services provided by the Welsh Authority;

○ every Channel 3 service and Channels 4 and 5 and the public teletext service (section 264(11)).

When looking at Tier 3, we need also to consider another defined expression: 'television and radio services are defined as:

(a) programme services apart from those provided by the BBC; and

(b) services provided by the BBC in relation to which Ofcom have functions (section 405).

We will deal with Tiers 1, 2, and 3 in sequence.

14.6.2 Regulation of providers of television and radio services (Tier 1)

Any person providing television or radio services, whether or not he is a public service broadcaster, will be required, under his licence, to comply with Codes relating to standards, fairness, privacy, and sponsorship, now integrated under the Broadcasting Code.[119]

The underlying objectives of the Broadcasting Code include that persons under 18 are protected, that material likely to encourage or to incite the commission of crime or to lead to disorder is not included in television and radio services, that there is adequate protection for the public from the inclusion of offensive material, that unsuitable sponsorship is avoided, that news is reported with accuracy, and that no subliminal techniques are used (section 319).

In setting or revising standards, Ofcom must have regard to a number of statutory requirements (which can, however, be modified by the Secretary of State) including the degree of harm or offence that may be caused, the likely size and composition of the audience and their expectations, the risk of unexpected exposure to the content, and the desirability of maintaining editorial control over content.

Under section 320, the views of the person providing the relevant television or radio service on matters of political or industrial controversy and current public policy must be excluded. In addition, Ofcom are required to include in their Broadcasting Code provisions intended to preserve due impartiality within a television programme or a series of television programmes, and to prevent, in local radio services and radio licensable content services, giving undue prominence to particular persons or bodies.

Section 321 sets out the objectives for advertisements and sponsorship, and disallows political advertising, other than advertisements 'of a public service nature' or party political broadcasts required under section 333 or Schedule 12 of the 2003 Act.

---

[119] See section 14.7.7 below.

Section 322 allows Ofcom to issue directions to providers of television programme services, the public teletext service provider, and providers of additional television services (analogue or digital). Under these directions, Ofcom may set limits on the amount of advertising that may be included in any hour of broadcasting and the intervals between advertising; these limits are imposed on licensees under conditions in their licences.

Sections 324 and 325 address how the Code (on advertising standards) is to be set and published, and provide for licences issued by Ofcom to require licensees to comply with the Code and with directions issued by Ofcom concerning the exclusion of particular advertisements, advertising methods or sponsorship.

Finally, for the purposes of this chapter, sections 326 and 327 address the Code on fairness, responsibility for which transferred from the BSC to Ofcom under Part 1 of the 2003 Act; and modify the rules under which complaints will be adjudicated.

These requirements flow into the conditions of the licences issued by Ofcom under the 2003 Act and into the Broadcasting Code itself.

14.6.3 Quantitative regulation of the source and types of programming (Tier 2)

Sections 277 to 289 of the 2003 Act impose a number of quotas on 'licensed public service channels', which is to say ITV and Channels 4 and 5, but *not* the BBC or the Welsh Authority.[120] Licensed public service channel providers are therefore more narrowly defined than public service broadcasters.

The quotas concern volumes of independent and original productions, news and current affairs programming, and regional programme making, and they also provide for a Code relating to the commissioning of programmes. The requirements in relation to the news, current affairs, and regional programme making differ as between ITV, Channel 4, and Channel 5.

Currently, every licensed public service channel must ensure that a minimum time is allocated to 'qualifying programmes' and to the broadcasting of a range and diversity of independent productions. The nature of 'qualifying programmes'[121] and 'independent productions' is specified, not by Ofcom, but by the Secretary of State; but Ofcom specifies the quotas for original productions (section 277).

Under section 279, licensed public service channels must carry a sufficient quantity of high quality, national and international news and current affairs programmes; Ofcom sets the minimum requirements for the duration of those programmes and determines how much news programming should be in prime time.

---

[120] The BBC is subject to obligations, but the source document for these is the BBC Framework Agreement—see section 14.9 below.

[121] Defined as programmes of such description as the Secretary of State shall order.

Finally, Tier 2 broadcasters must also comply with a number of important Codes of Practice approved by Ofcom regarding:

- the commissioning of independent productions (section 285), and the arrangements between the broadcaster and independent producer, for example in relation to rights ownership;
- the broadcast of certain 'listed events', which include important national sporting events (section 299);
- provision for the deaf and visually impaired (section 303).

14.6.4 Regulation of public service broadcasters (Tier 3)

The purposes of public service television broadcasting are specified in section 264(4) as being:

(a) the provision of relevant television services which secure that programmes dealing with a wide range of subject-matters are made available for viewing;
(b) the provision of relevant television services in a manner which . . . is likely to meet the needs and satisfy the interests of as many different audiences as practicable;
(c) the provision of relevant television services which . . . are properly balanced; and
(d) the provision of relevant television services which . . . maintain high general standards, particularly with respect to contents, quality of programme making, and professional skill and editorial integrity.

These purposes reflect the TWF Directives, and build on similar language in the 1996 Act. Quite what public service television may be, who should provide it, and whether it is required at all, are intriguing issues at this time, when spectrum scarcity is less of a limiting factor, most homes have multi-channel television,[122] and Internet use is growing fast. For all that, the concept of public service television is firmly embedded within the 2003 Act and in the public mind, and any changes are likely to be evolutionary.

Ofcom has a duty, under section 264(3), to carry out periodic reviews of the extent to which the current public service broadcasters have provided relevant television services that fulfil the purpose of public service television broadcasting. In the course of its first review, Ofcom took account of the matters specified in section 264(6), which included whether the services:

- comprised a public service for the dissemination of information and for the provision of education and entertainment;
- reflected the cultural activity and its diversity in the UK and facilitate understanding and well-informed debate on news and current affairs;
- satisfied a wide range of different sporting and other interests;

---

[122] This phrase connotes the ability to receive more than Channels 1 to 5.

- included programmes of an educational nature and a suitable quantity and range of programmes dealing with science, religion and other beliefs, social issues, international issues, and matters of special interest.

The regulatory regime for every licensed public service broadcaster, and for the public teletext service provider, includes a condition requiring the channel or service provider to fulfil the given public service remit for that channel or service concerned. The public service remit for every Channel 3 service and for Channel 5 is the provision of high quality and diverse programming (section 265(2)), while the public service remit for Channel 4 is the provision of a broad range of high quality and diverse programming which in particular:

- demonstrates innovation, experiment and creativity in the form and content of programmes;
- appeals to the tastes and interests of a culturally diverse society;
- makes a significant contribution to meeting the need for the licensed public service channels to include programmes of an educational nature and other programmes of educative value; and
- exhibits a distinctive character (section 265(3)).

The public service remit for the public teletext service is the provision of a range of high quality and diverse text material (section 265(4)).

The BBC falls outside these requirements, but has obligations under the BBC Framework Agreement to meet extensive public service criteria.[123]

Providers of licensed public service channels must, under section 266, prepare a statement of programme policy and, having regard to guidance given by Ofcom, must monitor their own performances in carrying out that policy. If a licensee wishes to change its programme policy it must consult Ofcom before doing so.

Subject to certain constraints, and following a public consultation, the Secretary of State has the right, by order, to modify the public service remit for any licensed public service channel or for the public teletext service or the purposes of public service television broadcasting (section 271).

Public service broadcasters are also subject to a number of obligations including a must-offer obligation under section 272, intended to secure that every licensed public service channel which is in digital form, and the public teletext service, are made available for broadcast or distribution over every appropriate network,[124] and that they may be viewed in intelligible form by as many members of its intended audience as practicable without any charge for reception.

---

[123] See section 14.9.3 below.

[124] This is defined to mean an ECN used by a significant number of end-users as their principal means for receiving television programmes.

14.6.5 The exemption in favour of webcasts

Content intended to be webcast is excluded from these arrangements under section 233(3), which provides as follows:

a service is not a television licensable content service to the extent that it is provided by means of an electronic communications service if—

(a) it forms part only of a service provided by means of that electronic communication service or is one of a number of services access to which is made available by means of a service so provided; and

(b) the service of which it forms part, or by which it may be accessed, is provided for purposes that do not consist wholly or mainly in making available television programmes or radio programmes (or both) for reception by members of the public.

This subsection is central to the proposition that packaging of content intended to be provided over the Internet requires no licence from Ofcom and is generally unregulated under the 2003 Act.[125] The provision of Internet access is the provision of an electronic communications service, and is regulated as such. However, information and entertainment 'channels' provided by ISPs form only part of the total range of services provided by those service providers, and their services do not consist wholly or mainly in making available television programmes or radio programmes for reception by members of the public. It follows therefore that the entertainment channels provided by ISPs are not television licensable content services and are not regulated as such.

Up until this point of the convergence cycle, the language of this exemption has served, but, as we saw in section 14.3.3 above, it will now need to change in relation to certain audiovisual material when the Audiovisual Directive is transposed into English law. This need was appreciated under the 2003 Act and, under section 234, the Secretary of State has the authority to modify any of the provisions of sections 232 or 233 having regard to any one or more of the following factors:

(a) the protection which, taking account of the means by which the programmes and services are received or may be accessed, is expected by members of the public as respects the contents of television programmes;

(b) the extent to which members of the public are able, before television programmes are watched or accessed, to make use of facilities for exercising control, by reference to the contents of the programmes, over what is watched or accessed;

(c) the practicalities of applying different levels of regulation in relation to different services;

(d) the financial impact for providers of particular services of any modifications of the provisions of that section; and

(e) technological developments that have occurred or are likely to occur.

---

[125] Remember also that, if the content is not 'broadcast', which is to say not transmitted by means of wireless telegraphy, its transmission will not be a television broadcasting service under s 362.

Section 234 is likely to be relied upon to implement the Audiovisual Directive. Beyond that, we are likely to see amendments to the 2003 Act itself in 2011 or 2012 to accommodate changes in technology and evolving consumer expectations in the area of fair use. A review has already commenced.

14.7 TELEVISION LICENSING

14.7.1 Licensing of television under the 2003 Act

We may look now in more detail at the way in which the statutory framework for the regulation of television,[126] and 'the Tiers' of regulation discussed in section 14.6, have been implemented through licences and codes.

It is a function of Ofcom to regulate the services specified in subsection 211(2) of the 2003 Act when provided by any person other than the BBC or the Welsh Authority. The services are:

- television broadcasting services broadcast otherwise than *only* from a satellite;[127]
- television licensable contents services;[128]
- digital television programme services;[129]
- restricted television services;
- additional television services;
- television multiplex services provided otherwise than by the BBC; and
- digital additional television services,

which, in each case, are provided from places in the UK or which, in the case of television licensable content services and digital additional television services, are provided by persons under the jurisdiction of the UK.[130] Regulation is effected through the issue of licences and codes of practice.

The definitions in the 2003 Act are important. Unfortunately they are also complex and scattered around. Perhaps the best starting point is the definition of 'television programme', which is defined, in section 405(1), as:

any programme (with or without sounds) which—

(a) is produced wholly or partly to be seen on television; and
(b) consists of moving or still images or of legible text or of a combination of those things.

---

[126] Ofcom have a similar function in relation to sound broadcasting, which is discussed in section 14.8 below.

[127] See section 14.7.2 below. Channels, compiled in the UK but broadcast only from a satellite, are likely still to be regulated as digital television programme services.

[128] See section 14.7.4 below.

[129] See section 14.7.5 below.

[130] Of course, broadcasters operating within, or coming under the jurisdiction of, other Member States would be regulated in a rather similar manner in their home jurisdictions by virtue of the TWF Directive.

Note that the use of the phrase '*to be seen on television*' in paragraph (a) does not dictate whether it is to be broadcast to the home or transmitted over an alternative type of ECN provided, in each case, that it is *intended* ultimately to be seen on a television receiver. A programme specifically intended both for television broadcast and Internet distribution would clearly fall within the definition; but a programme only ever intended to be shown in a cinema would fall outside it. A programme intended to be distributed over the Internet and viewed only on a personal computer could also fall outside the definition on the grounds that a personal computer is not a television receiver.[131] However, at a time when we are moving towards dual-function screens which may be used for viewing conventional television programming alongside video material on the web; and when an increasing number of personal computers are fitted with a device enabling them to receive television broadcasts; and when we are on the threshold of mobile TV, the question what is or is not a television receiver becomes more interesting.[132] The phrase 'television receiver' is already widely defined under the Statutory Instrument[133] that sets out the licence fees that are payable on installation and use of televisions in the UK,[134] but this definition will need to evolve as technology marches on.

14.7.2 Television broadcasting services

The first type of service regulated by Ofcom under section 211(2) of the 2003 Act is a 'television broadcasting service'. This is defined in section 362, which in turn builds on the definition of a television programme. A television broadcasting service is defined in section 362 as:

a service which—

(a) consists in a service of television programmes provided with a view to its being broadcast (whether in digital or in analogue form);
(b) is provided so as to be available for reception by members of the public; and
(c) is not—

   (i) a restricted television service;
   (ii) a television multiplex service;
   (iii) a service provided under the authority of a licence under Part 1 of the 1990 Act to provide a television licensable content service; or
   (iv) a service provided under the authority of a licence under Part 1 of the 1996 Act to provide a digital television programme service.

---

[131] There is no statutory definition of a television under the Communications Act 2003.
[132] See the discussion on the definition of broadcast in the context of 'television broadcasting service' immediately below.
[133] SI 692/2004, The Communications (Television Licences) Regulations 2004.
[134] Any apparatus installed or used for the purpose of receiving any television programme service.

Note the use of the word 'broadcast' in paragraph (a). A service in which the television programmes are intended to be delivered by means other than a *broadcast* (a word defined in section 405 (1) as 'broadcast by wireless telegraphy') would not be television broadcasting.

Perhaps surprisingly, the definition of television broadcasting service does not explicitly link to the definition of a 'contents service' under Clause 32(7) of the Act. A television broadcasting licence probably *is* a contents service, but is only licensable if and when it satisfies all elements set out in section 362.

Under section 215 of the 2003 Act, Ofcom was obliged to issue digital replacement licences to companies holding Channel 3 and Channel 5 licences at the date on which the 2003 Act came into effect. The Channel 4 licence was replaced under section 231.

Television broadcast licences have been issued to the ITV companies and to Channel 4 and Channel 5. These licences include Tier 1, Tier 2, and Tier 3 responsibilities. The licences may be seen on the Ofcom website.[135] They are in broadly standard form varying only in the details contained in parts of the Annex, which set out matters such as the regions in which coverage must be provided, the obligations to produce original and regional programmes, and list the analogue broadcasting stations to be used.

Condition 2 takes us into the digital age by *requiring* the licensee concerned to provide the licensed service to the holder of the C3/C4 multiplex, and stipulates that this service is to be equivalent in all material respects to the analogue form of the service, as authorized under the licensees' previous analogue-only licence, unless otherwise agreed by Ofcom. Licensees are prohibited from charging fees for the reception of programmes; the broadcasters must therefore rely primarily on advertising and sponsorship income.

Condition 7 requires the licensees to fulfil the public service remit agreed in respect of the channel and to prepare a statement of programme policy, having regard to guidance drawn up by Ofcom in accordance with section 266 of the 2003 Act. Section 8 applies to Channel 3 companies and requires the licensee to ensure networking arrangements among them are in force.

Obligations to provide a minimum amount of regional programming, independent productions and news (Tier 2 obligations) appear in Conditions 8–16, and are detailed in parts of the Annex. Condition 14 requires the licensee to observe the Broadcasting Code and the Code on advertising, and this is supplemented in Conditions 33 and 34 which mandate additional requirements in relation to complaints made in respect of standards, fairness, and privacy. Condition 21 requires the licensee to comply with rules relating to the transmission of certain listed (mainly sporting) events, and to carry a teletext service, described as an 'additional service' under the Act.

---

[135] Available at <http://www.ofcom.org.uk/tv/ifi/tvlicensing/>.

Television broadcasting licences also contain detailed provisions on technical standards, retention and production of recordings, provision of information to Ofcom, change of control and ownership restrictions, and assisting digital switchover. Ofcom has power to vary certain licence conditions, subject to due process.

Looking quickly now at the four other types of services that are excluded from the definition of a television broadcast services licence under section 362(c):

    i. a 'restricted [television] service' is defined under section 42A of the 1990 Act as 'a service which consists in the broadcasting of television programmes for a particular establishment or other defined location, or a particular event, in the United Kingdom'—that is to say a special, and usually short-term, service;

    ii. a television multiplex service, discussed in section 14.7.3 below;

    iii. a television licensable content service, discussed in section 14.7.4 below; and

    iv. a digital television programme service, discussed in section 14.7.5 below.

14.7.3 Nature of television multiplex service

A television multiplex service, a concept first introduced under the 1996 Act, is a carrier service which is defined, under section 241 of the 2003 Act, as a service:

consisting in the packaging together of two or more services[136] which include at least one relevant television service and are provided for inclusion together in the service by a combination of the information in digital form.

Multiplex service licences are discussed in section 14.7.6 below.

This super-abundance of complex and scattered definitions is not easy to grasp on first reading, but hold in mind that the main independent broadcasters hold television broadcasting licences, because they not only make television programmes but also make them available for reception by the public (two steps in the value chain), while companies that merely aggregate programmes into channels without taking the added step of providing them so as to be available to the public are likely to be licensable only as providers of a television licensable content service or of a digital television programme service. Mere production of a television programme is not licensable—it is only when programmes are packaged together into a channel that a licence will be required under section 211.

For example, UKTV Interactive Limited, the company that produces the UKTV History channel, packages together the several television programmes comprised within that channel for broadcast over Multiplex B as part of BBC Free to View

---

[136] Although a service can still fall within the definition where, for the time being, it is the only one so included.

Limited's[137] 'Freeview' offering (and on other platforms). UKTV Interactive Limited is a packager and requires a digital television programme service licence; but it does not need a television multiplex service licence nor a television broadcasting service licence. BBC Free to View Limited requires a multiplex service licence to operate Multiplex B for carrying the UK History channel (and other channels), and also requires a digital television programme service licence in its own right because it packages other programmes together for its own digital channels, such as BBC 3 and BBC 4.

These distinctions in scope between a television broadcasting service on the one hand and a television licensable content service or a digital television programme service appear slight, but they lead on to important differences in the applicable regulatory regime.

14.7.4 Regulation of television licensable content services

Television licensable content services are defined in section 232(1) as meaning, subject to section 233:

any service falling within sub-section (2) insofar as it is provided with a view to its availability for reception by members of the public being secured by one or both of the following means—

(a) the broadcasting of a service (whether by the person providing it or by another) from a satellite; or
(b) the distribution of the service (whether by that person or by another) by any means involving the use of an electronic communications network.

Note that the definition, up to this point, captures any service available for broadcast or for distribution by any form of ECN. However, subsection (2) then goes on to limit the definition by providing that:

a service falls within this sub-section [only] if it—

(a) is provided (whether in digital or in analogue form) as a service that is to be made available for reception by members of the public; and
(b) consists of television programmes or electronic programme guides, or both.

This definition is curiously back-to-front. Unravelled, it means, in effect, that a 'television licensable content service' is a service consisting of the provision of television programmes (or EPGs) for broadcasting or transmission over an ECN.

There are some clarifications of the definition within the remaining subsections of section 232. Section 233 then contains important exceptions, providing

---

[137] Note that this multiplex is operated by BBC Free to View Limited (BBC FtV), and not the BBC directly. BBC FtV requires a digital multiplex licence from Ofcom; the BBC does not.

that the following services are *not* to be treated as television licensable content services:

- any service to the extent it is provided for broadcast by means of a television multiplex service;
- any service to the extent it consists of a service authorized by a licence to provide a television broadcasting service (which comprises the additional element of providing them so as to be available to the public);
- the public teletext service or additional television services;
- a 'web service' (which exemption is discussed in section 14.6.5 above);
- a two-way service;
- certain services provided to closed user groups and on single premises.

The first bullet point will exclude a number of television channel providers from regulation as television licensable content services, but two points should be made: first the exclusion applies if and only if the channels are carried *only* over digital multiplex channels broadcast from within the UK, and secondly, in that case, they are likely to be regulated as digital television programme services.

Under section 235 of the 2003 Act (which refers also to section 13 of the 1990 Act), a person requires a licence to provide a television licensable content service, and indeed as many licences as the number of distinct services that he provides. Under subsection (3), applications may be refused on strictly limited grounds.

A licence to provide a television licensable content service is awarded subject to a number of conditions.[138] These licences include Tier 1 responsibilities. Licensing is 'normally straight-forward', and the target time for award is four weeks.[139] Ofcom require to be satisfied, however, that the applicant is a fit and proper person, that he is not disqualified from holding such a licence, and that the service is not likely to contravene the standards objectives set out in section 319 of the 2003 Act or the Fairness Code. A licence will not include positive obligations in relation to quality, news coverage, or balance—those are obligations imposed on broadcasters under television broadcasting licences, not on the holders of television licensable content service providers.

Under section 236, Ofcom has statutory powers to:

a. direct the licensee to include a correction or a statement of findings if it considers that to be an appropriate remedy; or

b. require any particular programme to be excluded from the service.

In case of a breach of a condition in a television licensable content service licence, Ofcom may impose a fine of up to the greater of £250,000 or 5 per cent of the

---

[138] Available at <http://www.ofcom.org.uk/tv/ifi/tvlicensing/guidance_notes_and_apps/tlcs/>.
[139] Guides to the licence award process are available on <http://www.ofcom.org.uk>.

'qualifying revenue' of the licensee (section 237). However, the Secretary of State must be notified of any case taken against the BBC, and may substitute a different sum for the fine imposed by Ofcom.

Under section 234 of the 2003 Act, Ofcom may serve notice on the licensee of a television licensable content service licence if it is satisfied that the licensee has included in the service one or more programmes that contain material likely to encourage crime or disorder in breach of licence conditions. If such a notice is served, the licence is suspended until the matter has been fully resolved.

Ofcom also enjoys ultimate powers under section 238 of the 2003 Act to revoke a television licensable content service licence, but only after the licensee has been notified that Ofcom is contemplating doing so and the licensee has failed to remedy the breach.

Much of Part 1 of the 1990 Act continues to apply to television licensable content services, but with amendments made under the 2003 Act. These provisions cover, for example, the imposition of general licence conditions and restrictions on holding of licences.

The conditions under a television licensable content service licence reflect those contained in television broadcasting licences except that a number of requirements are omitted, in particular the prohibition on charging fees for reception, the public service remit, regional, original, and news production requirements, networking arrangements, and obligations in respect of digital switch-over.

14.7.5 Digital programme television service licence

A digital television programme service is defined, in section 362 of the 2003 Act, by way of a cross-reference to section 1(4) of the 1996 Act, as 'a service consisting in the provision by any person of television programmes . . . with a view to their being broadcast in digital form for general reception, whether by him or some other person . . .' (but subject to certain exclusions). The key word here is 'digital'. A digital television programme service is similar in nature to, and the licence is in broadly similar terms as, a television licensable content services licence but, unlike the former, it is directed to the provision of television programmes with a view to their being broadcast in digital form from a multiplex.

The form and conditions of a digital programme television service licence is substantially the same as that of a television licensable service licence.

14.7.6 Multiplex service licences

Multiplex service licences were first awarded by ITC under the Broadcasting Act 1996. Licensees are authorized and indeed required to provide the core services identified in their responses to the Invitation to Apply, which are not detailed in the licences on grounds of commercial confidentiality. The services are to be provided

by means of wireless transmission from the several stations or sites listed in the licence (which will allow national or regional coverage as the case may be) using any of the radio frequency bands which the licensee has been authorized to use.

The licences are generally for an initial period of 12 years and, if granted within six years of the 1996 Act, may be renewed on one occasion only. Ofcom has the power to make limited variations to technical conditions on renewal.[140]

The licences contain a number of technical requirements in relation to transmissions and the electronic programming guides included within the licensed services.

Condition 10 requires licensees to act fairly and not to discriminate between one customer and another, and not to enter into tying arrangements. Condition 14 requires licensees to ensure that digital programme providers whose channels are carried over the multiplex are duly licensed.

14.7.7 The Ofcom Broadcasting Code

Ofcom is required under the 2003 Act to draw up a Code for television and radio broadcasting covering standards in programmes, sponsorship, fairness, and privacy. The objectives behind the standards are set out in numerous sections of the 2003 Act.[141] The standards also need to reflect the TWF Directive (as amended) and must comply with the Human Rights Act 1998, which guarantees freedom of expression but 'subject to restrictions proscribed by law and necessary in a democratic society' (section 10).

Broadcasters of television and radio programmes, including licensees holding television broadcasting licences, television licensable content services licences, and digital television programme services licences, are required by their licences to observe the Broadcasting Code. In addition, the BBC is required under the BBC Agreement to observe parts, but not all, of the Broadcasting Code.

Ofcom's Broadcasting Code[142] applies to all radio and television broadcasting and addresses, in a single document, programme and sponsorship standards, fairness and privacy.[143] The Code is evolutionary rather than revolutionary: it builds on earlier codes developed by the erstwhile ITC, except where change was mandated by specific provisions of the 2003 Act. However, the new unitary Code is better organized and provides a measure of simplification, which is always welcome.

The foreword to the Broadcasting Code emphasizes that freedom of expression is at the heart of any democratic State, but that with rights come duties and responsibilities. The focus is on adult audiences making informed choices within a regulatory framework which gives them a reasonable expectation of what they will receive,

---

[140] Ofcom decided against varying conditions on renewals due in 2010.

[141] Including ss 3, 310–321, 326, and also in s 107 (1) of the 1996 Act (see section 14.6.2 above).

[142] Available at <http://www.ofcom.org.uk/tv/ifi/codes/bcode/fwd/>.

[143] See Consultation on the proposed Ofcom Broadcasting Code dated 14 July 2004, available at <http://www.ofcom.org.uk>.

while at the same time robustly protecting those too young to exercise fully informed choices for themselves.

The Broadcasting Code therefore emphasizes protection for children (people under 15) and for young people (those under 18), and is structured into the following sections:

1. Protecting the under-18s: These provisions constrain the broadcasting of material that might impair the physical, mental, or moral development of people under the age of 18, and require 'appropriate scheduling', including the 9pm watershed, which survives, and continues to receive public support, despite personal video recorders, catch-up TV, and the Internet. There is guidance on coverage of sexual offences, drugs and alcohol, violence offensive language, sex, and exorcism and the occult.

2. Harm and offence: There must be adequate protection against material that, according to generally accepted standards, would be considered harmful and offensive. Any material of this nature must be justified by its context. Examples include anything that glamorizes violent, dangerous, or seriously anti-social behaviour, or shows methods of suicide or self-harm.

3. Crime: Material should not encourage the commission of crime or lead to disorder.

4. Religion: Broadcasters must exercise a proper degree of responsibility with respect to the content of religious programmes, must not solicit people to join a religious denomination.

5. Due impartiality and due accuracy and undue prominence of views and opinions: News in whatever form must be reported with due accuracy and presented with due impartiality. Significant mistakes should be acknowledged and corrected on air and the political allegiances of persons should be made clear.

6. Elections and referendums: Special rules on the coverage of political, policy, and industrial issues apply in the sensitive periods prior to elections and referendums.

7. Fairness: These rules apply to how broadcasters treat the individuals or organizations affected by programmes rather than the general public. Broadcasters must avoid unjust or unfair treatment and not 'ambush' interviewees or edit interviews unfairly. Guarantees on anonymity should be honoured. People criticized should be given an opportunity to respond.

8. Privacy: Again, these rules apply to how broadcasters treat the individuals or organizations affected by programmes rather than the general public. The Broadcasting Code entrenches the right to respect for private and family life under Article 8 of the European Convention on Human Rights. There should be no *unwarranted* invasion of privacy. A broadcaster must be able to show that the public interest outweighs the right to privacy. Information which discloses the location of a person's home or school should not ordinarily be disclosed. Means used to obtain information should be proportionate, and use of surreptitious filming or recording is constrained. Broadcasters should not broadcast footage of persons in distress unless warranted.

9. Sponsorship: Unsuitable sponsorship is prohibited and all sponsorship should be transparent, sponsors' message should be separated from programming, and programmes should not be distorted for commercial purposes.

10. Commercial references and other matters: Editorial control should be preserved and products and services should not be promoted in programmes, including by being given undue prominence. There are detailed rules on product placement within programmes. Broadcasters must comply with the PhonepayPlus rules.[144] There are special rules on charities and financial services and recommendations.

Issues ebb and flow in the public mind, but there is always something about which the general public, or governments, have passionate views. Today, use of bad language is perhaps more of an issue than nudity or explicit sexual material, although that position could reverse. The government has emphasized public health issues, and we have seen new rules on advertising of high fats, salt, and sugar foodstuffs. The recent Report by Lord Hutton[145] touched on issues of harm and offence, although that was not the focus of the enquiry. Terrorism, and perhaps more so, anti-social behaviour, and how these should be portrayed, are significant current issues.

Many complaints are made to Ofcom alleging breaches of the Broadcasting Code. Complaints are considered fortnightly by a Committee comprising members of the Content Board and Ofcom, and are published as Broadcast Bulletins.[146] Looking at four successive Bulletins in January and February 2008, complaints were raised under sections 1 (the most) and 2, 5, 9, and 10.

Apart from the broadcasting PRS cases, one recent case brought under the Broadcasting Code merits particular comment. In the case against Sumo TV,[147] Ofcom found that Sumo had not performed sufficient checks on user-generated clips incorporated into its broadcasts.[148] Ofcom make it clear that broadcasters promoting user-generated material into publicly broadcast programmes will not be allowed to ignore the Code.

Ofcom has published new outline procedures[149] for the imposition of statutory sanctions in content and content-related cases, which took effect as from 18 January 2008.

The procedures explain that, under the 2003 Act, Ofcom has power to impose the following sanctions in cases of a breach of Ofcom's Codes by a broadcast licensee or (in more limited cases) the BBC or S4C:

- issue a direction not to repeat a programme;

- issue a direction to broadcast a correction or a statement of Ofcom's findings;

---

[144] See section 14.10.6 below.
[145] Report of the Inquiry into the circumstances surrounding the death of Dr David Kelly CMG by Lord Hutton, 28 January 2004, HC 247.
[146] Available at <http://www.ofcom.org.uk/tv/obb/>.
[147] Broadcast Bulletin 101, available at <http://www.ofcom.org.uk/tv/obb/prog_cb/obb101/>.
[148] Some unpleasant sexual material in a rap song and other material in which a child was shown to be distressed by adult behaviour had been included.
[149] <http://www.ofcom.org.uk/radio/ifi/ifiguidance/sanctions>.

- impose a financial penalty;
- shorten a licence (in some cases);
- revoke a licence (not applicable to the BBC, S4C, or Channel 4).

Ofcom also has a more general power under broadcasters' licences to issue Directions in respect of 'any matter, subject or thing'.

The outline procedures set out Ofcom's intended approach, and provide for a hearing (if requested) before a committee comprising members of the Content Board and Ofcom, due process, and an opportunity for the broadcaster to comment on the proposed sanctions before they are imposed. A fast track process may also be invoked if Ofcom considers there is a risk of ongoing material harm, or in certain other cases.

14.7.8 Regulation of advertising on television and radio

Following a formal delegation of authority by Ofcom, the Committee of Advertising Practice (CAP) is the industry body responsible for the advertising codes of practice in the UK. CAP's Broadcast Committee contracted with Ofcom to write and enforce the codes of practice that govern the content of all television and radio commercials on channels licensed by Ofcom, and advertising on interactive television services, television shopping channels, and teletext services. Ofcom retained responsibility for programme sponsorship, the amount and distribution of permitted advertising, and judgments about whether advertising is 'political' (and therefore generally prohibited).

The Committee comprises representatives of broadcasters licensed by Ofcom, advertisers, agencies, direct marketers, and interactive marketers. Delegation is consistent with the principle of promoting self-regulation.

Two sets of rules apply to broadcast advertisements—a set for television and another for radio. In broad terms, they state that no broadcast advertising should mislead, offend, or cause harm.

In practice, in the UK almost all broadcast advertisements are vetted as a matter of course before transmission by Clearcast, previously the Broadcast Advertising Clearance Centre (BACC).[150] Similarly, almost all national radio commercials and certain special categories of local and regional radio advertisements are vetted before broadcast by the Radio Advertising Clearance Centre (RACC).[151]

Complaints about advertising may be addressed to the Advertising Standards Authority (ASA), an independent body responsible for handling and resolving complaints about both broadcast and non-broadcast advertisements.[152] Decisions on complaints are taken by the ASA Council, which is split into two groups—12 members

---

[150] See <http://www.clearcast.co.uk/clearcast>.
[151] See <http://www.racc.co.uk/>.
[152] See <http://www.asa.org.uk>.

adjudicate on non-broadcast complaints and 12 on broadcast complaints. Although some have relevant industry experience, most Council members come from outside the advertising industry.

ASA also keeps a watching brief on tele-shopping channels, ensuring they are complying with the Broadcasting Codes and resolving any complaints that arise.

The ASA's work in regulating broadcast advertising is funded by the advertising industry through a 0.1 per cent levy on advertising airtime—this mirrors the way in which non-broadcast self-regulation is funded. The money is collected by a separate body, the Broadcast Advertising Standards Board of Finance (Basbof)[153]—so there is no question of the amount of an advertiser's contribution influencing the ASA's decision making.

The ASA carries out research on subjects related to advertising regulation to ensure that the Codes are kept up to date, meet the needs of consumers and society, and reflect latest developments in the advertising world, technical or otherwise.

For every complaint, the ASA follows a strict process designed to be fair and reasonable and considers all points of view. ASA begins by deciding if there is a case to answer under the Codes. Some complaints can be resolved quickly by the ASA. But if the complaint cannot be resolved so easily, a formal investigation may be necessary.

In a formal investigation, evidence must be submitted in writing. If a breach of the Codes seems to have occurred, the ASA executive responsible for handling the complaint writes a recommendation, and, after complainants and broadcasters have been allowed to comment on its factual accuracy, this is passed to the Council of the ASA. The Council then decides if there has been a breach of the Code and, if so, orders the advertisement to be changed or withdrawn, or that its scheduling be altered.

An advertisement would be suspended before an investigation and adjudication only in rare and very serious cases, for example if harm or detriment could be caused to the public by leaving it on air.

About 10 per cent of complaints each year come from competitors or consumer or pressure groups. They are handled in the same way as consumer complaints, except that a complainant which is a competitor needs to provide very compelling grounds for the challenge, and the complainant company or organization will be named in the report.

Once the Council has made a decision, the broadcasters must ensure that the ruling is been followed.

The ASA's adjudications are published and are made available to the media. An independent review procedure is in place to ensure that matters are conducted fairly. In the rare instance where a substantial flaw of process or adjudication is apparent,

---

[153] See <http://www.basbof.co.uk/>.

or where additional relevant evidence becomes available, the independent reviewer can ask the Council to reconsider its original decision.

Broadcasters are obliged by a condition of their Ofcom licences to enforce ASA rulings. If they persistently run advertisements in breach of the Code, broadcasters risk being referred by the ASA to Ofcom, which can impose fines and even withdraw their licence to broadcast.

14.8 THE REGULATORY FRAMEWORK
FOR SOUND BROADCASTING

14.8.1 Sound broadcasting services

In an echo of the position that applies for the regulation of independent television, it is a function of Ofcom, under section 245 of the 2003 Act, to regulate:

* sound broadcasting services provided for broadcast otherwise than only from satellite and which are national, local, or 'restricted' services;
* radio licensable content services;
* additional radio services;
* radio multiplex services;
* digital sound programme services; and
* digital additional sound services,

unless these services are provided by the BBC[154] and, in each case, only if they are provided from places within the UK or by a person whose principal place of business is in the UK.

Radio licensable content services up-linked from the UK and provided for broadcast by satellite are also regulated under this section unless authorized under the laws of another EU State—in which case the laws of that State will apply.

Under section 247 of the 2003 Act, a radio licensable content service is defined as a service consisting in sound programmes provided (in digital or analogue form) as a service to be made available for reception by members of the public if that service is to be provided 'with a view to its availability for reception being secured by broadcasting [by that person or any other] or by distribution over an ECN'.

As with television licensable content services, a number of services are excluded from this definition under section 248. Services that are excluded services are:

* services provided with a view to being broadcast by means of a multiplex service;
* national, local, or restricted sound broadcasting services provided with a view to their being broadcast otherwise than only from satellite (see also section 245(3));

---

[154] Services provided by subsidiary companies of the BBC may, however, be regulated by Ofcom.

- a television licensable content service;
- a two-way service;
- a service distributed over an ECN to persons within a single set of premises;
- a service provided only to persons with a business interest in receiving the programmes within it.

Once again, the Secretary of State has the power to modify the definition of radio licensable content services under section 249 of the 2003 Act.

14.8.2 Sound broadcasting licences

A person wishing to provide a radio licensable content service in the UK will require a licence under the 1990 Act, which may be awarded by Ofcom on an application made to it under section 250 of the 2003 Act. The licence may contain such conditions as Ofcom may consider to be appropriate, particularly regarding the duties imposed on Ofcom under the 2003 Act, technical standards, and adherence to relevant Codes,[155] which of course enables the application of the Broadcasting Code and the Code on advertising content.

As we have seen in relation to television (see 14.7.2), providers of national and local sound broadcasting services[156] are obliged to meet certain statutory requirements bearing on the content of their programming; in particular requirements as to the character of their radio station and the coverage of local and national radio services. These requirements, originally laid down in section 106 of the 1990 Act, substantially amended under section 312 of the 2003 Act, require a sound broadcaster to preserve the character of his service, and not to depart from this without the approval of Ofcom. For its part, Ofcom must hold a public consultation before allowing any service provider to change the character of a service (section 313). Applications to change the character of a service are commonplace. Ofcom also have duties to secure that local material is included in local sound broadcasting services, and must draw up guidance on this issue (section 314).

14.9 THE BRITISH BROADCASTING CORPORATION

14.9.1 The nature of the BBC

The BBC remains the largest broadcaster in the UK and, uniquely, it is funded by a licence fee imposed on every household[157] with a 'television receiver'.[158] It is a body

---

[155] Provisions relating to the award of, and licence conditions in, sound broadcasting licences are set out in ss 86 and 87 of the 1990 Act.
[156] There is also provision for restricted service licences—short or long term—to cover special events, or to serve establishments such as hospitals or universities.
[157] Or office or public house.
[158] See SI 692/2004, discussed earlier.

corporate established under letters Patent by Her Majesty the Queen. Its governance was reformed under a Charter issued on 19 July 2006. The 2006 Charter[159] confirmed the continuation of the BBC and provided that the members of two new bodies, the BBC Trust and the Executive Board (of the BBC) were to become the members of the BBC.

Except for some transitional provisions, the 1996 Charter came into effect on 1 January 2007 and continues in force until 31 December 2016.

The BBC broadcasts seven national television channels, an equal number of national radio channels, and a large number of local radio channels. It also has an important and popular website,[160] and publishes many books and journals. It has recently launched a catch-up TV service.[161]

14.9.2 The BBC Charter

The 2006 Charter states, in Article 3, that the BBC exists to serve the public interest and that its main object is not chasing audiences as such but the promotion of its 'public purposes'. The BBC is also authorized to establish and maintain subsidies through which it may undertake commercial activities, to the extent permitted by the BBC Framework Agreement.[162] The public purposes of the BBC are defined in Article 4 as high-level aspirations, namely:

- sustaining citizenship and civil society;
- promoting education and learning;
- stimulating creativity and cultural excellence;
- representing the UK, its nations, regions, and communities;
- bringing the UK to the world and the world to the UK;
- in promoting its other purposes, helping to deliver to the public the benefit of emerging communications technologies and services and, in addition, taking a leading role in the switchover to digital television.

Article 5 explains that the BBC should promote its public purposes mainly through the provision of output consisting of information, education, and entertainment, supplied by means of television, radio, *and online* services—or by newer technologies as they are developed. This has mandated the BBC to develop its significant web-presence. The means by which the BBC is to promote its public purposes are elaborated under the BBC Framework Agreement.

---

[159] <http://www.bbc.co.uk/bbctrust/framework/charter.html>.

[160] See <http://www.bbc.co.uk>.

[161] See <http://www.bbc.co.uk/iPlayer>.

[162] Framework Agreement is defined as the agreement between the BBC and DCMS, and which is discussed in section 14.9.3 below.

All other activities are to be 'peripheral, subordinate or ancillary', a demarcation which is a continuing sore with some commercial providers.

Article 6 provides for the independence of the BBC, subject to any express provisions of the Charter or BBC Framework Agreement.

The BBC Trust sets the overall strategic direction of the BBC according to the public interest and the interests of licence fee payers; it also exercises general oversight over the Executive Board. The nuances of the relationship between these two bodies are explained in Article 9. Members of the BBC Trust are not treated, in any legal sense, as being trustees of property or as being subject to the laws relating to trustees.

Further details relating to the qualifications and appointment of members of the BBC Trust and the Executive Board, and their proceedings, may be found in Articles 13 to 23 and Articles 28 to 37 of the Charter respectively. A post of Director General of the BBC is created under Article 40.

Articles 25 to 27 require the BBC Trust to adapt and publish 'Protocols' which set about a detailed framework within which the Trust will discharge its functions and address in greater detail the relationship between the BBC Trust and the Executive Board. The Trust is also to prepare Protocols on engaging with licence fee payers and on transparency.[163]

Article 24 is important; it sets out the general functions of the BBC Trust and bestows on it the tasks of:

- setting multi-year 'remits' and approving strategies which include high-level budgetary allocations;
- defining suitable performance criteria and measures against which the effective promotion of the public purposes will be judged; and
- issuing 'service licensees' for BBC Services and monitoring compliance with them.

The Trust has developed detailed remits for each of the public purposes set out in Article 3 of the Charter.[164]

Following the order in which the public purposes are listed, the remits include targets to produce independent journalism of the highest order; stimulating informal learning and promoting educational goals for children; encouraging participation in cultural activities—drawing on talent from across the UK's creative community; building a global understanding of international issues; and helping audiences understand and adopt new technologies.

For the BBC Channels, the service licences are in some ways analogous to the public service provisions contained in television broadcasting licences issued by Ofcom to ITV companies and Channels 4 and 5.

---

[163] See <http://www.bbc.co.uk/bbctrust/>.
[164] Available at <http://www.bbc.co.uk/bbctrust/framework/purpose_remits.html>.

Service licences have been issued by the BBC Trust in respect of each of the BBC Channels.[165] The service licence for BBC 1, for example, clarifies the remit for that channel—it is mandated to be BBC's most popular mixed-genre television service across the UK. The service licence requires that BBC 1 is available 24 hours a day, sets its budget, and requires a particular mix of high quality programming ranging from drama and comedy through news and documentaries to religion, arts, and children's programming. Service licences for other BBC channels have different emphases.

14.9.3 The BBC Framework Agreement

The BBC Framework Agreement complements the Charter and includes, in Clauses 5 to 20, further detail on how the remits and service licences described above are to be drawn up and consulted on.

Clause 21 of the Framework Agreement requires the Executive Board to prepare, and later publish, statements of programme policy in respect of all services provided by the BBC other than commercial services,[166] the BBC World Service or services produced for government departments primarily aimed at users outside of the UK.

There is provision for future changes to the BBC's UK public services under Clauses 23 to 33, but changes that are significant require the application of a 'Public Value Test', which involves several elements:

• a 'public value assessment' to assess the likely public value of the proposed change in terms of its value to licence fee payers and society as a whole and the value of money;

• a market impact assessment, to be conducted by Ofcom, but according to a methodology agreed with the BBC Trust;

• public consultation.

After addressing digital switchover (in Clauses 34 to 41) and efficient use of the radio spectrum (in Clause 42), the Framework Agreement sets out arrangements for the development of guidelines to secure appropriate standards in the BBC's UK Public Services. These appear in Clauses 44 to 46, and include an obligation on the BBC (in Clause 46) to observe 'Relevant Programme Code Standards', set by Ofcom under section 319 of the 2003 Act; but only those that relate to the objectives set out in five of the paragraphs of subsection 319(2). These standards are the ones relating to:

• protection of persons under the age of 18 (paragraph (a));

• omission of material likely to encourage or incite any crime or disorder (paragraph (b));

---

[165] Available at <http://www.bbc.co.uk/bbctrust/framework/bbc_service_licences/tv.html>.
[166] Commercial services are defined in Clause 101.

- exercise of responsibility with respect to the content of religious programmes (paragraph (e));

- application of generally acceptable standards so as to provide adequate protection for members of the public from the inclusion of offensive and harmful material (paragraph (f));

- refraining from the use of subliminal techniques that might influence minds (paragraph (l)).

Enforcement of other standards under paragraphs 319(2)(c) and (d) (impartiality and accuracy of news) are for the BBC Trust alone and the standards under paragraphs (a), (b), (e), (f), and (l) are applied to the BBC subject to the overriding condition that they should not be used to make judgements on the accuracy or impartiality of any programme included in the UK's Public Broadcasting Services.

As a result of this, the BBC's UK Public Broadcasting Services are regulated by Ofcom only in respect of the subject matter of the five parts or paragraphs identified above; and even here the complaints procedures are different,

Clause 47 sets out detailed rules for the provision of news and current affairs programmes; these form a vital part of the BBC's public service broadcasting and go towards fulfilling the BBC's public purposes. The BBC is also required to broadcast certain party political broadcasts.

Clauses 49 to 59 set out the proportions of programmes that must be made in-house or by independent producers, and in the nations and regions. These have some parallels with similar rules on quotas for independent broadcasters[167] and can be considered as Tier 2 obligations. Ofcom contributes in this area, for example by proposing common definitions.

Clauses 65 to 74 address the sensitive issue of the position of the BBC in the marketplace. As a vast, multi-dimensional organization funded out of a compulsory licence fee (which is admitted to be a tax) the BBC is in a position to dominate the television and radio sectors if unconstrained. This part of the Framework Agreement therefore imposes some constraints on the BBC, including the adoption by the BBC Trust of a policy on fair trading and the obligation to issue a formal statement on the BBC Trust's policy on the competitive impact of the BBC's activities on the wider market, and an obligation on the BBC only to carry on commercial services where they support the BBC's Public Purposes and always through separate subsidiaries.

Clause 75 provides for payment to the BBC of the licence fee, and Clause 76 sets out restrictions on the BBC raising additional monies whether by means of sponsorship of its programmes or by providing subscription services, which require Ministerial approval. Other sections address matters such as Ministerial broadcasts, training,

---

[167] See section 14.5.4 above.

equal opportunities, and archives.[168] There are provisions regarding value for money and borrowing.

Towards the end of the Framework Agreement are two parts that address complaints and the relationship between the BBC and Ofcom. The BBC Trust establishes the complaints procedures after a public consultation, and the procedures must reflect overriding principles set out in Clause 90.

Under Clause 91, the BBC is formally required to cooperate with Ofcom and provide information reasonably required in connection with the performance of Ofcom's functions. The BBC is also required to do all it can to secure an agreement with Ofcom in relation to matters required to be agreed with Ofcom under the 'relevant provisions' of the BBC Framework Agreement,[169] which relate to news and current affairs, programming quota, and national and regional programme making, facilities for the deaf and visually impaired, programme commissioning, and the retention and production of recordings. Matters regarding Party Political Broadcasts are omitted from this list.

In addition, the BBC Framework Agreement lists separately a number of 'Relevant Enforceable Requirements', being requirements imposed on the BBC under the following Clauses of the BBC Framework Agreement:

• Clause 45: the Fairness Code

• Clause 46: Programme Code Standards

• Clause 47: News and Current Affairs

• Clause 49: Programme Quotas for original productions

• Clauses 50 and 51: Programming for, and programme making in, the nations and regions

Clause 93 of the BBC Framework Agreement states that, if Ofcom is satisfied that the BBC has contravened a Relevant Enforceable Requirement, then Ofcom may require the BBC to include a correction or statement of finding in the service concerned. Clause 94 also authorizes Ofcom to fine the BBC for breach of a Relevant Enforceable Requirement.

14.9.4 The future of public service broadcasting

Ofcom considers that public service broadcasting (PSB) programmes should increase our understanding of the world, stimulate our interest in arts, science, and history, reflect and strengthen our culture identity, and help make us aware of different cultures and alternative viewpoints.[170] Public service broadcasting programmes

---

[168] Sections 81–88.

[169] Defined as Clauses 47, 49–52, 59, 61, and 62.

[170] Ofcom, *Review of Public Service Television Broadcasting: Phase 1—Is television special?*, April 2004.

should be original, innovative and challenging, of high quality, engaging, and widely available. When it considered the future of PSB in 2006, Ofcom concluded that:

- the existing analogue PSB model, under which ITV companies notionally received a soft subsidy worth up to £400 million in the form of free spectrum, helped finance PSB, will not survive digital switchover;

- ITV companies should maintain most current programme quotas but be relieved of the obligation to provide regional non-news programming, which is expensive;

- Channel 4 will come under increasing pressure to replace current PSB programming with more commercial content, and further initiatives may be necessary;

- Channel 5 has a smaller, but still important, role in PSB, mainly through its commitment to original UK productions and news programming;

- the BBC is best placed to continue with PSB, but must 'sharpen' its sense of purpose;

- the BBC Charter should be renewed until 2016, but the BBC's performance should be made subject to a vigorous mid-term review;

- independent production quotas should continue to be supported.

Ofcom's big idea has been that, in order to create 'competition' in PSB, the government should consider establishing a new Public Service Publisher (PSP), operating as a small commissioning unit for PSB programming, and funded at around £300 million out of tax revenues (as a substitute for the soft subsidy), the licence fee, or a levy on the turnover of UK licensed broadcasters. However, this idea has not commanded unanimous support. The House of Commons Select Committee on Culture, Media and Sport concluded that:

given the huge amount of public service content currently available on new media, we believe that the creation of a new public service publisher, as currently envisaged by Ofcom, is unnecessary. The creation of a new public service content institution for new media would run the risk of distorting the market and impeding innovation. We also believe that an approach that attempts to impose the institutional interventions of the past in the new media world is misguided. At a time when technological change and digital uptake strengthens the case for the withdrawal of existing intervention, the introduction of new public institutions does not appear to be merited.[171]

There has also been discussion of a 'top-slicing' approach under which some of the proceeds of the BBC licence fee will be paid instead to other broadcasters who provide public service broadcasting.

---

[171] House of Commons, Culture, Media and Sport Select Committee Report on Public Service Content (HC 36-1) Session 2007-08, at para 132. Ofcom has now produced voluminous reports on PSB, but the final decision on its future rests with Parliament.

14.10 PREMIUM RATE SERVICES

14.10.1 Regulation of premium rate services

Premium rate services (PRS) first came into view as 'audio text services'—value-added information services supplied over conventional telephone lines, usually as a result of the user calling a so-called 'premium rate' number (now) in the 09xx xxxxxx format. Chat services quickly followed under which a caller could call one or many persons to 'chat' about anything, and these chats were often flirtatious or sexual in nature. A series of highly publicized scandals took place typically involving high telephone charges and what would now be called 'grooming' by paedophiles of children who rang child chat lines, usually without their parents' knowledge. Faced with substantial bills, parents who could not or would not pay faced the loss of their essential telephone service and children were put at risk. There were calls for the telecommunications industry to grasp the situation and introduce a self-regulatory scheme.

Led by BT, network operators agreed to help establish, and to fund, an independent regulatory body with the name of The Independent Committee for Standards in Telephone Information Services (ICSTIS).[172] Initially, the self-regulatory scheme was set up under a framework of contracts between ICSTIS and participating network providers which required those network providers to enter into further contracts with their premium rate service provider customers. In time this was supported by a condition, included in licences issued to operators of telecommunications systems under the 1984 Act, requiring licensees not to provide certain (controlled) PRS unless and until an appropriate Code had been put in place. The Code set standards for controlled PRS, and premium rate service providers were bound to adhere to the Code under agreements entered into with the network providers with whom they contracted and by whom their respective shares of the revenues would be paid. In 2007, ICSTIS was renamed PhonepayPlus.[173]

With a credible regulatory framework in place (which is not the case in all other countries), premium rate services over fixed and mobile telecommunications networks became big business in the UK. Until recently, the value of the industry was in excess of £2 billion. Premium rate services notoriously continue to include 'adult' chat lines, but they also extend to a wide range of other services from benign technical advice lines (often on information technology and car maintenance) through fun advice lines (horoscopes and tarot) and weather forecasting to chat lines, fax back services, cheap rate international calls and competitions, and now to reverse-charge SMS and to participation television, as discussed below.

---

[172] For further information, visit <http://www.phonepayplus.org.uk>.
[173] See <http://www.phonepayplus.org.uk>.

Although not accessed through a 09xx number, the 118xxx directory enquiry services, which have now replaced BT's 192 service, fall within the definition of controlled premium rate services and have further extended the market.

14.10.2 Recent developments in premium rate services

Recently, there has been enormous growth in reverse-charged SMS messaging over mobile phone lines, which has accelerated further with the adoption of five-digit short codes. Under reverse charging, the subscriber or user is charged for receiving a message from the service provider. If he pays for use by monthly payments, the charge will be added to his bill; if he pre-pays by buying cards, it will be deducted from the credit on the card. Reverse charge SMS is used as a payment mechanism for ring tones and alert services, and sometimes these take the form of monthly subscription services, where again there have been a number of abuses, mostly because the user was unaware that he had entered into a long-term subscription service.

Other recent factors fuelling growth of premium rate services have been the use of reverse charged SMS and premium rate telephone calls to enter quizzes ('Quiz TV'), to deliver votes for television reality shows like Big Brother and I'm a Celebrity, Get Me Out of Here!, and to part-pay for the prizes in shows like Millionaire. Use of premium rate calls in relation to allow viewers to 'participate' in television programmes has created a significant new income stream for television broadcasters.

14.10.3 Scope for abuse

Premium rate may be considered as being a payment mechanism, with the charge appearing on a bill delivered by the user's Electronic Communications Service provider.[174] Premium rate calls may be charged at up to £1.50 per minute or a £2.00 one-off (or 'drop') charge.

Most premium rate calls are benign but there is considerable scope for abuse, either because subscribers may unexpectedly run up high telephone charges, which can put their basic telephone service at risk, or because, in a few cases, content is misleading, inappropriate for the audience (particularly children), or downright dishonest. There is therefore a clear, continuing need for consumer protection in the field of premium rate services, but also limitations on what can be achieved within the ambit of the overarching EC framework of regulation.

---

[174] This has led some to ask whether use of pre-paid airtime on mobile handsets to buy goods or services using the premium rate mechanism makes the pre-paid cards a form of electronic money, and subject to regulation by the Financial Services Agency (FSA). However, the FSA does not consider this to be the case—see CP 172, Electronic Money: Perimeter Guidance.

14.10.4 Impact of the EC measures

The 2003 Act implements the new EC Authorizations Directive.[175] Under the Authorizations Directive, there are strict limits on the types of conditions that may be imposed on providers of telecommunication networks and telecommunication services under general authorizations. In the context of premium rate services, it became impossible to include obligations in general conditions[176] analogous to the condition in earlier telecommunications licences that had underpinned the UK regulatory regime for premium rate services. It was therefore concluded that a new statutory foundation for the regulation of premium rate services had to be created within the 2003 Act in order to maintain the regulatory arrangements. The relevant sections are sections 120 to 124.

14.10.5 The new legal framework

Under section 120 of the 2003 Act, Ofcom has power to set conditions for regulating the provision, content, promotion, and marketing of premium rate services. The conditions may be applied to any person who provides a premium rate service or to persons providing specified types of premium rate services. But the only provision that may be made by the conditions is that the relevant person comply with any Code approved by Ofcom under section 121 (or, in the absence of an approved Code, any Order issued under section 122). The conditions imposed by Ofcom are described below.

Under complex tiered definitions in subsections 120(7) to (15), PRS are now defined as services which consist in:

• the provision of content of communications transmitted by means of an ECN; or

• allowing the user of an ECS to make use of a 'facility' made available through that service (a typical facility might enable voting, entering a competition or the purchase of goods or services);

and which are charged on a bill for the ECS over which the PRS is carried.

A person provides a PRS if, broadly speaking, he:

i. provides, edits, or packages the content of the PRS, or makes available the facility within that service;

ii. provides the ECS used for delivery of the PRS and shares in the revenue earned by that service;

iii. is the provider of the ECN used to deliver the PRS and has a direct agreement with the provider of the PRS in respect of the use of that network for that purpose; or

---

[175] See further Chapter 7.
[176] Under s 45 of the 2003 Act.

iv. is the provider of the ECN used to deliver the PRS in a case in which use of that network for PRS (or services that may include PRS) is authorized by an agreement between (a) the network provider and (b) an intermediary service provider or a person who is a PRS provider under paragraphs (ii) or (iii) above.

Apart from paragraph 1, the language is not easy to follow but, in essence, paragraph 2 is designed to catch and label as a regulated service provider the person first in line to hold a direct contract with the operator of the ECN on which the premium rate is terminated; while paragraphs 3 and 4 are intended to catch operators of the ECNs on which services are terminated and who enter into a contract with a PRS provider (or an intermediary).

Figure 14.3 shows the relationships in a typical case.

*In this case, which is common, the service provider is an 'aggregator' of many premium rate calls. The service provider provides the 'platform' by means of which a variety of content services are made available to be paid for by premium rate calls. The service provider is the primary target for regulation. The person in the right hand box is called an information provider by Phonepay Plus.

Figure 14.3 The value chain for premium rate calls

14.10.6 Who is brought under control for premium rate services?

As stated earlier, under section 120(1) of the 2003 Act, Ofcom may set conditions for regulating the provision, content, promotion, and marketing of PRS and may apply these to any person who provides a PRS or to persons providing specified types of PRS.

The conditions imposed by Ofcom[177] have been applied to defined 'Communications Providers' and require them to comply with directions made under a Code approved by Ofcom under section 121 of the 2003 Act in relation to 'Controlled Premium Rate Services'. These are defined as premium rate services charged at more than 10p a minute, chatline services, services operated through the use of Internet dialler software,[178] and sexual entertainment services.

Section 121 of the 2003 Act requires Ofcom to be satisfied that any proposed Code is objectively justifiable, non-discriminatory, proportionate, and transparent, and that it provides for a sufficiently independent person to administer and enforce it.

---

[177] E.g. see Ofcom statement re: the PRS condition and mobile services (October 2006) available at <http://www.ofcom.org.uk/consult/condocs/prsconditions2/statement/prsconditions.pdf>.

[178] Where software downloaded over the Internet replaces one dial-up number with a different number.

PhonepayPlus has submitted a Code and Ofcom has approved the current (the 11th) edition of the PhonepayPlus Code.[179]

The PhonepayPlus Code has become more elaborate over time, particularly in recent years because of the arcane and obscure language contained in sections 120 to 124 of the Act. The Code regulates three groups of persons:

  i. the main body of the Code applies to 'service providers' as to which see below;

  ii. additional provisions bear on so-called 'information providers', as to which again see below; and

  iii. certain network providers[180] involved in the value chain are also brought under a degree of control under the Code and must carry out due diligence; provide information to PhonepayPlus; maintain records on premium rate numbers they deal in; terminate access to premium rate services or numbers, or withhold payments due to service providers, when so instructed; delay payments to service providers (under the so-called 30-day rule); and remit the levy that funds its activities direct to PhonepayPlus. Moreover, where a network provider is itself the service provider through one of its own divisions, it is subject to the full force of the Code rules.

'Service providers' under the Code are defined as:

the first person who falls within Section 120(9)(a) to (d) of Section 120(10) of the [2003] Act who, not being a network operator himself, contracts with, or enters into arrangements with, a network operator for use of the network operator's facilities in the provision of the relevant premium rate service.

To emphasize the point, service providers are therefore some, but not all, of the persons who might be brought under regulation under section 120 of the 2003 Act. Paragraph 3.3 of the Code imposes some general obligations on service providers. These include use of particular number ranges for particular types of premium rate services (such as 0909 or 0908 for sex entertainment services), provision of information to PhonepayPlus, and an obligation to inform their own information provider customers (if any) of Code obligations.

Paragraph 5.1 provides that PayphonePlus may require the service providers of particular categories of service to obtain prior permission from PhonepayPlus before they are provided. Prior permissions are required, for example, for 'live services' (defined as including two-way or multi-way voice conversation—which includes the type of service that enables people to buy cheap international calls through use of prepaid cards), remote gambling services, counselling services, and PRS used in television broadcasting. PhonepayPlus' powers here are constrained by the Electronic Commerce Directive which generally precludes any Member State from requiring

[179] Available at <http://www.phonepayplus.org.uk/pdfs_code/PhonepayPlus11CoP_Apr08v3.pdf>.
[180] These network providers are defined under para 11 of the Code as either 'lead networks', whose billing and metering systems fall to be approved by Ofcom, or who have entered into prescribed arrangements with a lead network.

that a person wishing to provide 'information society services' must obtain prior permission.[181] The services that do require prior permission from PayphonePlus are therefore ones falling outside of the definition of 'information society services'.

Paragraphs 5.2 to 5.14 contain the principal rules. These require that all services are legal, avoid causing harm and offence, and are fair. The rules also require that services, and all promotional material for them, are clearly and accurately described, that details of the service provider are provided, and that pricing information is clear and legible, especially where the user is to be entered into a subscription service. PhonepayPlus takes a hard line on those who describe premium rate services as being 'free'—they are not: the user always pays a relatively high premium above a conventional telephone call charge.

For some services, including live services, competitions, contacting and dating, sexual entertainment and subscription services, and services involving Internet diallers, there are additional detailed requirements.

There are important provisions requiring service providers to ensure that users are able to terminate services by the use of a simple 'STOP' command and for automatic cut off after preset expenditure.

14.10.7 Information service providers

A number of persons who fall to be defined as service providers under the 11th Code do not themselves produce the content of the premium rate service, but instead act as 'aggregators' of third party services. The role of the service providers in this case is to provide the facilities and technology required to allow the third party services to be made publicly available. In the parlance of the industry the persons providing the content at one remove through aggregators are referred to as 'information providers'. The 11th Code introduced new provisions relating to 'Information Providers', who are defined as 'any person falling within section 120(9)(a) to (d) of the 2003 Act not himself being a service provider for the purposes of the Code'.

Paragraph 4.1 of the Code requires information providers to comply with the provisions of the Code where applicable to them or to the service and/or promotion with which they are concerned. Paragraph 4.2 reiterates that PhonepayPlus deals primarily with service providers and network operators, but provides that PhonepayPlus may, under procedures elaborated in paragraph 8.1.4, deal direct with an information provider where he accepts full responsibility for the service and undertakes to accept any sanction imposed on him by PhonepayPlus. Even in this case, however, the service provider remains responsible for compliance and for the sanction if the information provider does not comply or make any payment due.

PhonepayPlus has also issued a number of Statements of Expectations and Helpnotes which explain the criteria it applies in granting permissions or interpreting and enforcing Code provisions.

---

[181] Directive 00/31/EC, at Art 4(1).

14.10.8 Proceedings of PhonepayPlus

PhonepayPlus is funded through a levy on the revenues due to service providers from networks in relation to premium rate services.[182] This levy is deducted at source by providers of the ECNs on which users' premium rate calls are terminated and paid by them direct to PhonepayPlus. The amount of the levy is calculated by reference to the cost of running PhonepayPlus' operation and the forecast revenues of each ECN derived from premium rate services. PhonepayPlus draws up an annual budget which is published as part of a consultative process; the budget must then be approved by Ofcom; and there is provision for adjustment of the levy if there is overpayment or underpayment to PhonepayPlus.

A Code Compliance Panel appointed by PhonepayPlus meets to adjudicate on breaches of the Code. Other more minor cases are resolved by the Secretariat informally under delegated authority. Typical complaints include excessive costs, unsolicited promotions using SMS, misleading services, misleading competitions with bogus or highly-conditioned prizes, fax-back services that are inappropriate to businesses, and 'adult' chat lines promoted in magazines targeted at children.

PhonepayPlus generally acts against UK-based service providers. Where the service may be accessed in the UK but the service provider is outside the jurisdiction, PhonepayPlus' powers will depend on whether or not the service provider is based in another Member State of the European Community. Article 3 of the Electronic Commerce Directive provides for home-country regulation so that, where a service provider is based in another Member State of the European Community, it is generally for the regulatory authority in that 'host' country (also referred to as the country of origin) to take action to curb any unlawful activity on the part of the service provider, and not for a regulatory authority in the country to which services are provided. However, very often regulators in other Member States do not take action against premium rate service providers established there and, in that case, PhonepayPlus, working with the Department for Business, Enterprise and Regulatory Reform, may seek to take advantage of a derogation under Article 3 (4) of the Directive, allowing a regulatory authority outside the host country to take urgent action for the protection of consumers. Where the service provider is outside the European Community these concerns do not arise and, even if the service provider is in a remote location and does not engage with it, PhonepayPlus always has the possibility of instructing the UK-based network provider to terminate the service.

Paragraph 8 of the Rules sets out how complaints are investigated and provides for informal procedures, a standard procedure, and an emergency procedure if a case is serious and requires an urgent remedy. Remedies include a formal reprimand, a fine,

---

[182] There was, at the time this book went to press, a question over whether the MNO's new Payforit service is or is not a premium rate service.

barring use of the number or the service (or indeed in an extreme case, the provision of all types of premium rate services), and the payment of refunds to end-users.

Under the Rules, any person against whom a complaint is raised may request an oral hearing or a review of a panel decision by another panel. Members of the Code Compliance Panel exercise independent judgement, and do not always support recommendations of the Executive. Nevertheless, they are considered too close to the Executive to have the degree of independence formally required of an appeals body under the Human Rights Act. The PhonepayPlus Code therefore provides for an Independent Appeals Body, to which appeals from certain panel decisions may be made.

During 2007, there were a number of revelations concerning inappropriate behaviour by certain service providers and broadcasters in relation to competitions and voting within programmes broadcast on television. Three instances caught public attention:

- a competition broadcast by GMTV in which many entrants were effectively disenfranchised as a result of winners being selected before voting lines closed;
- the 'You Say, We Pay' programme broadcast by Channel 4 in which the chances of winning were not always equal;
- the 'Blue Peter' programme on BBC, where the BBC pretended that a viewer was a winner, when he was not.

In the first two cases, PhonepayPlus found a breach of the Code and imposed fines on the service providers concerned.[183] Ofcom instituted separate proceedings against the BBC[184] and GMTV and imposed fines on these broadcasters.

The BBC Trust took the complaints against the BBC extremely seriously and commissioned a Report on Premium Rate Telephony which exhaustively reviewed BBC practices in the area and made a number of recommendations for future training and working practices in the area.[185]

PhonepayPlus has always been accountable to Ofcom and required the approval of Ofcom to its Code and budget. However, following the problems with broadcast PRS services described above and criticisms in some quarters that, with at least two regulators involved, it was unclear who was in charge, further changes have been made.

---

[183] The maximum fine being £250,000, under the Communications Act 2003 (Maximum Penalty and Disclosure of Information) Order 2005 (SI No 3469).

[184] Regulating the BBC in relation to this part of the Broadcasting Code is one of the areas in which Ofcom has powers over the BBC.

[185] Available at <http://www.bbc.co.uk/bbctrust/assets/files/pdf/review_report_research/premium-rate>.

The problems in broadcast PRS were attributable in part to systemic failures on the part of certain (but not all) broadcasters[186] and in part to poor practices on the part of (some but not all) telecommunications service providers;[187] Ofcom regulated the former,[188] PhonepayPlus the latter. As a result of a review carried out by a non-executive director of Ofcom, Richard Eyres, Ofcom took two initiatives. First it has moved to assert greater control over PhonePayPlus and, on 4 December 2007, Ofcom agreed a formal Framework Agreement with PhonepayPlus[189] setting out the new relationship between the two bodies. This affirmed the right of PhonepayPlus to deliver day-to-day regulation of the premium rate market place but included a formal right for Ofcom to approve policy matters, objectives and the strategic direction of PhonePayPlus, and also to approve its directors.[190] Given that premium rate now contributes to the funding of some broadcasting activities, these new arrangements can perhaps be seen as a logical and inevitable step, though they do move the arrangements further away from self-regulation.

The second step was to publish proposals for the variation of Television Broadcasters' Licences to make them explicitly and directly responsible for communications with the public in cases where 'the mechanism of communication' features in programmes', and to publish new, detailed guidance[191] on the practices Ofcom expects broadcasters to observe, particularly in relation to selection of winners, puzzle methodologies and pricing information. The new rules[192] provide for independent verification of technical and administrative compliance procedures in relation to controlled PRS.

Separately, PhonepayPlus has now established a prior permissions regime for service providers providing premium rate services to broadcasters.

14.11 OTHER BODIES

14.11.1 The Internet Service Providers Association (ISPA)

The ISPA is a trade body whose main activities include promoting competition, self-regulation and the development of the Internet industry.[193] This includes making representations on behalf of Internet Service Providers (ISPs) to government bodies, such as the Home Office and the Department for Business, Enterprise and Regulatory Reform, and to Ofcom to advance the interests of ISPs.

---

[186] See the cases brought by Ofcom for breach of the Broadcasting Code against GMTV Issue 94 and the Final Report from the BBC Director general to the BBC Trust.

[187] See the Adjudications of PhonePayPlus against Opera and Eckoh on <http://www.phonepayplus.org.uk>.

[188] Under Section 10.10 of the Broadcast Code, licensees must comply with the PhonepayPlus Code.

[189] <http://www.ofcom.org.uk/consult/condocs/phonepayplus/formalframework.pdf>.

[190] This had always happened but informally.

[191] <http://www.ofcom.org.uk/consult/condocs/participationtv/statement/>.

[192] <http://www.ofcom.org.uk/consult/condocs/participationtv/statement/>.

[193] See <http://www.ispa.org.uk>.

However, there are consumer benefits because each ISP that chooses to become a member of ISPA must adhere to the ISPA UK Code of Practice,[194] which sets out basic requirements on members to:

- use reasonable endeavours to ensure that the content of the services they provide (but not third party content where no such obligation is undertaken) is legal and honest and does not contain child abuse images or material inciting violence, cruelty, or racial hatred;
- act fairly and reasonably at all times in their dealings with consumers, other businesses, and each other;
- comply with advertising codes and the PhonepayPlus code;
- ensure that charges for services are clearly stated in relevant promotional material;
- comply with UK legislation relating to data protection;
- notify ISPA of a single point of contact who is authorized to deal with ISPA complaints.

ISPA is careful to say that, unless expressly provided, nothing in the Code shall be taken to suggest that the Code regulates and/or that the Council will adjudicate on the legality or otherwise of material accessible on the Internet.

ISPA membership does not automatically confer Internet Watch Foundation (IWF) membership.[195] However, members are encouraged to consider direct IWF membership, must provide ISPA with a point of contact to receive notices from the IWF and must remove web pages and/or Usenet articles notified to them by IWF unless it is not technically possible, when they must notify the IWF of the reasons as soon as reasonably practical.

The Council may also issue Best Common Practice statements but these are not binding on members.

All ISPA members must belong to an Alternative Dispute Resolution (ADR) scheme approved by the ISPA Council. The Code lays down a procedure and timetable for dealing with a complaint against an ISPA member for breach of the ISPA Code. If a complaint is not resolved between the customer and the member, the complainant will be advised to contact the appropriate ADR scheme for adjudication. The Secretariat of ISPA also has power to refer issues falling within the ambit of a particular regulatory or self-regulatory body (such as IWF, PhonepayPlus, or Ofcom) to that body.

If the Council decides that a Member has breached the Code, the Council may:

i. require the Member to remedy the breach; and/or

ii. require an assurance from the Member, or any associated individual, relating to future behaviour, in terms determined by the Council; and/or

---

[194] Available at <http://www.ispa.org.uk/about_us/page_16.html>.
[195] See further section 14.11.2 below.

iii. suspend the Member from ISPA without any reimbursement of membership fees in whole or in part; and/or

iv. convene a General Meeting of ISPA for the purpose of considering an extraordinary resolution for the expulsion of the Member, in accordance with Articles 2 to 9 of the Articles; and

v. at its absolute discretion publish part or all of its decision.

14.11.2 The Internet Watch Foundation (IWF)

The IWF is a charitable body, with a trading arm.[196] It was formed in 1996 under pressure from the government and police to do something about child pornography on the Internet. It is substantially controlled by ISPs and has more than 80 members.

Originally IWF was scantly funded and enjoyed limited independence from its ISP owners. Its accountability was also ambiguous: was it a trade organization or a public body? In recent years, there has been material change in governance, including the appointment of more outside directors. This has helped move IWF in the direction of becoming a more independent public body.

The IWF aims 'to foster trust in the Internet', to 'assist service providers to combat abuse of their systems', and to 'assist law enforcement in the fight against criminal content on the Internet'. The IWF deals with reports of potentially illegal content, but limited to content that contains:

i. images of child sexual abuse hosted anywhere in the world;

ii. criminally obscene images hosted in the UK; and

iii. incitement to racial hatred content hosted in the UK.

Complaints may be made through an online reporting system (the Hotline) and all content found to be potentially illegal is reported to law enforcement authorities.

Under the Protection of Children Act 1978, it is an offence for a person:

to take, or permit to be taken, or to make any indecent photograph or pseudo-photograph of a child[197] or to distribute or to show such indecent photographs or pseudo-photographs; or to possess indecent photographs or pseudo-photographs, with a view to their being distributed or shown to himself or others; or to publish or cause to be published any advertisement likely to be understood as conveying that the advertiser distributes and shows such indecent photographs or pseudo-photographs or intends to do so.

There can be a question mark over whether the person is or is not 'apparently' under the age of 18, but otherwise establishing an offence under the Protection of Children

---

[196] See <http://www.iwf.org.uk>.
[197] That is to say a person apparently under the age of 18 involved in sexual activity or posed to be sexually provocative.

Act is relatively straightforward.[198] By contrast, proving an offence under the Obscene Publications Acts 1959 and 1964[199] is more difficult, since matters of taste and judgement are involved. An 'article' is deemed obscene under those Acts only if:

its effect or (where the article comprises two or more distinct items) the effect of any one of those items is, if taken as a whole, such as to deprave or corrupt persons who are likely, having regard to all relevant circumstances, to read, see or hear the matter contained or embodied in it.[200]

This definition of 'obscene' has been held to be narrower than common usage of the word, which is filthy, lewd, or disgusting.[201] In addition, a defence is available under the 1964 Act if, *inter alia*, publication can be said to be in the interests of science, literature, art, or learning.

Publishing[202] an obscene article is an offence, but many juries are unwilling to find that the legal test of obscenity is met; being reluctant to accept that the article could corrupt *them*.

As for the third head, racism, it is an offence under the Public Order Act 1986 to stir up racial hatred against any person or persons in Great Britain defined by reference to colour, race, nationality (including citizenship), ethnic, or national origins.

There is clear case law that downloading indecent images of children is an act of 'making' an indecent photograph under the Protection of Children Act 1978.[203] However, in the recent case of *R v Ross, Warwick & Porter*[204] it was held that a person could not be in possession of indecent photographs of children under the Criminal Justice Act 1988, section 160(1) if he no longer had custody or control of the images. In the case of deleted computer images if a person could not retrieve or gain access to an image then he no longer had custody or control of it.

Full members of the IWF, being those who host on-line content, are bound by the IWF Code and agree to provide contact details for employees who are authorized to receive notifications from IWF.

The principal regulatory tool used by the IWF is service of a formal Notice on its members alerting them that specified material is illegal and recommending that it be taken down. Full members agree to act, 'within an acceptable time' after receipt of a notice from IWF, to take down the relevant content, unless there are reasonable grounds for not doing so or they believe an error has been made. IWF may also issue recommendations that its members do not carry certain newsgroups.

[198] See generally Walden, I, *Computer Crimes and Digital Investigations* (Oxford University Press, 2007).
[199] The Acts were further amended in 1977 so as to include films.
[200] Section 1 of the 1959 Act.
[201] *R v Anderson and others* [1971] 3 All ER 1152.
[202] This is widely defined under s 2 of the 1959 Act.
[203] *R v Bowden* [2001] QB 88; *R v Jayson* [2002] EWCA Crim 683; *R v Fellowes and Arnold* (1997) 1 CAR 244.
[204] [2006] EWCA Crim 560.

If there is a dispute as to the nature of the content, it will be referred to law enforcement officers who will make the final judgement.

If a full member does not comply with the Code, the IWF reserves the right to suspend it from membership. A member may appeal a warning or suspension from membership, and this appeal will be heard by a subcommittee of the IWF Board.

14.11.3 The Independent Mobile Classification Body (IMCB)

Recent generations of mobile handsets have a significant larger memory and more intelligent software and now support colour, picture messaging, and faster Internet browsers. Mobile network operators (MNOs) naturally want to take advantage of this increased functionality, and of upgrades at the network level enabled by the roll-out of '2.5 G' and 3G technology, as a springboard for carrying more data to users and for increasing the average revenue per user (ARPU) by charging for enhanced services either on a subscription or a pay-per-view basis.

One obvious application is providing video clips, whether in the form of anodyne sports and film clips or more controversial 'adult material', a type of product that has always been included in the first wave of use of most new electronic media. Other opportunities include gambling and chat rooms which, enhanced by video or images, may present a yet greater risk of 'grooming' of children by adults, unless controlled.

MNOs now make available over their networks content services which they themselves provide or which are provided by third parties. Some content services include 'adult material' and gambling or gaming services. This immediately created a potential problem: the majority of young people in the 14 to 17 age bracket, and an increasingly large percentage of children in the 10 to 13 age bracket, have mobile handsets; indeed they are more likely than older customers to have the advanced models best equipped for these type of data applications.

MNOs have therefore established a Code of Practice for the Self-regulation of Content on Mobiles.[205]

The approach adopted by the MNOs under the Code is not to deny the service, but put in place arrangements under which:

• a third party content provider must self-rate his material as being suitable for general viewing or only by those who are 18+ according to objective criteria set by an independent classification body; and

• each MNO must provide filtering tools which can deny access to 18+ material if the registered owner of the handset concerned has not verified that he is at least 18 years old.

---

[205] For the full text of the Code, visit <http://www.t-mobilepressoffice.co.uk/company/content-code.pdf>.

The Code required the creation of a new independent body to classify content, and the MNOs appointed the Independent Mobile Classification Body (IMCB), a subsidiary of PhonepayPlus, to this role.[206] ICMB has drawn up a classification framework by reference to the frameworks developed by other bodies for content in other media, notably the British Board of Film Classification's (BBFC)[207] framework for films and the Interactive Software Federation of Europe's framework for computer games.[208] Material that would be classified as being for the 18+ age group in these media, such as actual or realistic depictions of sexual activity, graphic violence, drugs use, or sustained or detailed infliction of pain, is similarly classified as being for the 18+ age group under the ICMB framework. There are no separate thresholds for lower age groups.

MNOs disclaim any responsibility for classifying content on the public Internet accessible by mobile handsets, but offer parents and carers advice and a filter that may be used to screen out unwanted Internet content. MNOs will also work with law enforcement agencies to report illegal content, and will put in place Notice and Take Down Procedures.

If a consumer considers that commercial material has been incorrectly self-classified by the service provider according to the classification framework, he must complain in the first instance to the MNO concerned, but there is a right of appeal to the IMCB if the MNO does not respond within 28 days or if the MNO disagrees that the classification was incorrect. In this case (only), the consumer may complain to the ICMB. Content providers also have a right of appeal to the ICMB if they consider that an MNO has incorrectly decided that their material should have been classified as 18+.

Ofcom has recently launched a review of the Mobile Content Code which was due for publication in 2008. Dr Tanya Byron has also recently delivered a Report[209] on the risks to children's safety and wellbeing of exposure to potentially harmful or inappropriate material on the Internet and in video games, which calls for 'a shared culture of responsibility' among families, industry, government, and others in the public sector, and more specifically to the need to provide better information on the content of some material and to reform the classification of games. A UK Council for Child Internet Safety is to be established with a remit to establish a Code of Practice on moderation of user generated content, to develop kite-marking for filtering software, and to encourage search engines to increase the visibility of safety settings. Measures are also to be taken to increase 'e-safety' at schools.

---

[206] See <http://www.imcb.org.uk>.
[207] See <http://www.bbfc.org.uk>.
[208] See <http://www.isfe-eu.org/>.
[209] A copy can be found on <http://www.gamepolitics.com/images/legal/ByronReview.pdf>.

14.11.4 Association for TV on Demand (ATVOD)

The Association for TV on Demand (ATVOD) is a self-regulatory body committed to protecting consumers of on-demand audio visual content services delivered via a platform which allows the user to select content and view it at any time.[210] This can be:

    i. streamed or downloaded to a device, set-top box, or personal computer;

    ii. pushed to a device or set-top box either by means of broadcasting or use of IP over wired or wireless networks; or

    iii. delivered by any other means so that a programme or other prepared content can be viewed at any time of the viewer's choosing.

Content may be paid for or offered free. It can be provided by public service enterprises or supported by commercial organizations.

ATVOD is led by an independent Chairman, who ensures that its members adhere to its Code of Practice, adjudicates on consumer queries, and helps promote greater understanding of, and trust in, on-demand services as they differ from conventional broadcast television.

Its members have put in place and maintain means of protecting children and other customers from material that may be inappropriate for them. It does this through a Code of Practice which requires that:

- children and young people are protected from unsuitable content;
- all users are protected from advertising and other commercial communications which are not legal, decent, honest, and truthful;
- adequate information about the nature of content is available before it is viewed;
- service providers keep their promises to users.

14.11.5 Conclusion

Starting with the invention of Caxton's printing press, developments in technology have always driven copyright law, literary works starting with / and extending later to photographs, moving images, television, and now the Internet.

So too technology drives development in the regulation of content. When television was limited, and often broadcast by state-controlled companies, governments were able to influence what was broadcast and the volume of broadcasting. They have no such ability with the Internet, and so, in the main, the place and time of control has changed from the point of transmission to the point of reception.

The Internet has enabled new ways of working, trading, and interacting to a scale never seen before. The Internet has radically improved choice, very much a mantra

---

[210] See <http://www.atvod.org.uk>.

of the nineties and noughties; but of course, as with every new invention, from the car to nuclear fission, it has capacity for some bad alongside much good. There are those who are concerned for our children and seek new ways of controlling or filtering some of the most egregious content, and in particular to ensure we are not opening a doorway to child abusers and grooming. That debate will continue, and will perhaps lead to stronger codes of practice and higher expectations of ISPs.

The role of public service television in a crowded marketplace will continue to be fiercely debated; need public service extend across the board from popular to high culture and from reality TV to documentaries? How can local communities be best served?

What is certain is that the Internet, refuelled and enhanced by Next Generation Access and broadband mobile, will continue its triumphant, transformational, and disruptive march, empowering consumers and citizens alike, but leaving regulators facing new, and perhaps unpredicted, challenges.

Part VI

INTERNATIONAL REGULATORY REGIMES

15

INTERNATIONAL
TELECOMMUNICATIONS LAW

Ian Walden

15.1 INTRODUCTION

Telecommunications is an inherently transnational technology. As such, the development of telecommunications has always required substantial cooperation and
agreement between nation states. Cooperation can be seen at a number of different
levels, including the need for adherence to certain standards, both technical and
operational. Historically, the need for ongoing cooperation between states has meant
the establishment of inter-governmental organizations, of which the International
Telecommunication Union (ITU) lays claim to the oldest pedigree of any such organization. These inter-governmental institutions have been responsible for laying down much
of the framework that comprises international telecommunications law and regulation.

In addition, the nature of the industry demands the construction of communications
links across jurisdictions subject to both domestic and international law. As such, the
telecommunications industry has been subject to treaties and conventions established under public international law for the treatment and use of common natural
resources, specifically the law of the sea and outer space law.

Over recent years, the sources of international telecommunications law has diversified
as the industry and national markets have undergone fundamental change. At a technical
level, the need for internationally agreed standards has expanded exponentially with the

growth of data communications and the range of services being made available over communication networks. The rate of technological change has required more flexible and dynamic decision-making procedures and institutions. Historically, standards-making bodies comprised monopolistic operators that were part of a national public administration. With market liberalization, the numbers of participants in the stand-ards-making process has risen dramatically, whilst conversely the effective role of governments has diminished significantly. As a consequence, we are witnessing a period of change in those international institutions to which the attention of telecom-munications lawyers has traditionally been focused. International industry associa-tions have emerged to challenge the primacy of intergovernmental organizations. At the same time, governments, particularly among developed nations, are increasingly looking to scale-down their involvement in the governance of the telecommunica-tions sector, driven both by a desire to reduce demands on public finance, as well as through a recognition that they are not necessarily best placed to make appropriate decisions in such a rapidly evolving environment.

International telecommunications organizations such as the ITU are also experienc-ing institutional competition from other intergovernmental bodies, particularly the World Trade Organization (WTO). While the associated multinational trade agree-ments have focused on telecommunications as a distinct economic activity, a tradable service, rather than simply as a medium or conduit for conducting trade. As the indus-try undergoes fundamental structural shifts, with operators merging to become global entities as well as pondering the consequences of convergence, attention has shifted to issues of market access as the primary concern in international telecommunications law. The ITU has experienced a loss of status in the face of such new priorities and is therefore engaged in a re-examination of its role in the changing environment.

Despite the global trend towards market liberalization, there continues to be an inevitable divergence of view between developed nations and developing nations towards the telecommunications sector. Whilst all nations recognize the critical role of telecommunications in a nation's economic infrastructure and development, many countries continue to see telecommunications as a public resource and even a natural monopoly in which governments have a right and obligation to intervene. Developing countries are experiencing considerable pressure to embrace the credo of market liberalization from a number of directions. First, the need to attract foreign invest-ment into the domestic telecommunications market. Secondly, developments in technology, particularly Internet-related, increasingly erode the ability of states to exercise effective regulatory control over the sector. Thirdly, developmental organi-zations, such as the World Bank and the European Bank of Reconstruction and Development (EBRD), have imposed liberalization conditions as part of their loan programmes for infrastructure investment projects in telecommunications.

This chapter broadly examines three substantive aspects of international telecom-munications law:

- the construction of international telecommunications network infrastructure, both satellites and submarine cables;

• the structure and operation of the ITU and its rule-making activities, and

• the impact of the WTO and its trade agreements on national telecommunication markets and legal regimes.

15.2 INTERNATIONAL NETWORK INFRASTRUCTURE

As at a national level, the physical construction of telecommunications networks is subject to a particular regulatory framework not applicable to the provision of services over such networks. For example, issues concerning rights of way across public and private property are a central element in the licensing of a public telecommunications operator.[1] At an international level, similar issues arise concerning the rights and obligations of those wanting to construct either wireless (i.e. satellite) or wireline (i.e. cable) networks between sovereign jurisdictions. This section reviews the law governing the launch and operation of communication satellites[2] and the laying of submarine cables.

15.2.1 Satellite regulation

The launch of TELSTAR I in 1962 marked the beginning of satellite technology for use in telecommunications, broadcasting, and for military purposes. Satellites are now also used for weather forecasting, earth observation and navigation purposes, such as GPS technology. Satellites operate as a radio relay station, receiving and retransmitting signals on specific frequencies, through so-called 'transponders', from and to receivers and transmitters on earth.

Satellite systems can be distinguished into geostationary and non-geostationary systems. A geostationary system (GEO) is based above the equator (around 36,000kms) and revolves at the same speed as the earth, thereby appearing to be stationary (i.e. a synchronous orbit). An advantage of GEOs is the ability to provide continuous and relatively comprehensive coverage of the earth with only three satellites,[3] although providers may operate more.[4] Disadvantages of such systems include the fact that the equator can only accommodate a limited number of systems; while the quality of communications is diminished somewhat by the transmission delay caused by the substantial distance travelled by signals to and from such satellites, particularly for voice telephony.

---

[1] See further Chapter 7, Authorization and Licensing.
[2] Issues relating to the assignment of frequency spectrum and orbital slots are discussed in section 15.3.2 below.
[3] An idea published by Arthur C Clarke in Wireless World in 1945. Coverage does not really extend to regions above latitudes 75° north or south. The angle of elevation in northern Europe does significantly limit reception.
[4] Inmarsat, at 15.2.1.2, for example, has a constellation of 4 satellites, with 5 providing back-up services.

Recent developments in the satellite market have been in the proliferation of non-geostationary systems operating in medium earth orbits (MEOs), operating at around 10,000 kms above sea level, and low earth orbits (LEOs), operating at around 1,500kms above sea level. Such systems require a considerably greater number of satellites than GEO systems to ensure continuous coverage.[5]

The launch and operation of satellites is subject to international space law. Historically, satellite systems were developed under international conventions between States, such as INTELSAT, INMARSAT, and EUTELSAT. However current non-geostationary systems are multinational private consortia operating under private agreement and subject to national legal regimes.

15.2.1.1 *International space law*

International space law comprises a set of agreed principles embodied in a series of treaties and conventions. These principles encompass the launch and operation of satellites, particularly in respect of liability for any damage caused by the satellite or any other space object.

In 1962, the UN General Assembly adopted a declaration comprising nine fundamental legal principles governing the use to be made of 'outer space'.[6] This declaration formed the basis of the 'Outer Space' Treaty agreed in 1967.[7] This Treaty continues to be the primary international legal instrument governing the launch and operation of telecommunications satellites.

In terms of economic exploitation, the Treaty declares that outer space and celestial bodies may not be subject to national appropriation (Article II). States are also responsible under international law for their activities in outer space, whether carried out by governmental or non-governmental authorities; the latter requiring authorization and ongoing supervision (Article VI). Liability for damage caused by any object placed in space would rest jointly with the State that launches, or procures the launch of, the object, and the State 'from whose territory or facility an object is launched' (Article VII). Jurisdiction and control over any object in outer space remains with the State that has registered the object, whilst ownership is unaffected by the presence of the object in space or its return to Earth outside of the registering State (Article VIII). To facilitate international cooperation in the use of outer space,

---

[5] E.g. the ICO International MEO system will use some 10 satellites; while Globalstar uses 48 satellites.

[6] Resolution 1962 (XVIII)), adopted at UN General Assembly, 13 December 1963 (GAOR Annexes (XVIII) 28, p 27). The physical boundaries of outer space are somewhat unclear, although 100km above sea level, representing the boundary between the lower and outer atmosphere, is a generally accepted figure: see 'The legal regime of airspace and outer space: the boundary problem', pp 425–456, in Cheng, C, *Studies in International Space Law* (Clarendon Press, Oxford, 1997).

[7] Treaty on Principles Governing the Activities of States in the Exploration and Use of Outer Space, including the Moon and Other Celestial Bodies (London, Moscow, and Washington, 27 January 1967; TS 10 (1968); Cmnd 3519).

States are required to provide information to the United Nations regarding their activities in, and use of, outer space (Article XI).

The liability provisions of the Outer Space Treaty were elaborated further in a 1972 Convention on International Liability for Damage Caused by Space Objects.[8] The concept of 'damage' is defined in the following terms:

... means loss of life, personal injury or other impairment of health; or loss of or damage to property of States or of persons, natural or juridical, or property of international intergovernmental organisations (Article I(a)).

Consequential losses, such as future traffic revenues, do not seem to be encompassed within this definition.[9] Reflecting the terms of the 1967 Treaty, liability lies with the 'launching state'; this encompasses both the state that launches or procures the launch of the space object and the state from where it was launched (Article I).[10] In certain circumstances, this definition could result is there being three potential 'launching states'; for example, where a satellite supplier based in the UK arranges for the launch of satellite for a customer based in France, under a 'delivery in-orbit' arrangement, from a launch service provider based in Kazakhstan.[11] Where a launch has involved two or more states, then liability is joint and several (Article V), unless agreed otherwise privately by the parties.[12]

Under the Convention, liability is *absolute* where the damage is caused on the Earth or to an aircraft (Article II).[13] The only formal claim that has been submitted under article II was by Canada in 1979, claiming US$6 million from the Soviet Union for damage caused by the radioactive debris from the re-entry of Cosmos 954 in January 1978. The claim was settled for US$3 million, without liability being acknowledged.[14] Liability is limited to fault-based liability where the damage is to the space object of another launching state caused elsewhere than on the Earth (Article III). A state may claim damages either on behalf of itself; its natural or legal persons (i.e. the state of nationality); or for those sustaining damage whilst in its territory (Article VIII). Claims for compensation are subject to certain time limits and, where diplomatic settlement is not achieved, may be decided upon by a 'Claims Commission' established at the request of either party (Articles XIV–XX).

Underpinning the 1962 Declaration and the Outer Space Treaty was the concept that each State would maintain a register detailing the space objects for which the

---

[8] London, Moscow, and Washington 29 March 1972; TS 16 (1974); Cmnd. 5551. The Treaty entered into force for the UK on 9 October 1973.

[9] See generally Beer, T, 'The specific risks associated with collisions in outer space and the return to earth of space objects—the legal perspective', pp 42–50, Air and Space Law, vol XXV, no 2, 2000.

[10] Launching includes any attempts.

[11] BNSC, 'Registry of space objects' available at <http://www.bnsc.gov.uk/content.aspx?nid=5975>.

[12] E.g. an agreement between Russia and Khazakstan.

[13] Unless it can be shown that the damage is the result of 'gross negligence or an act or omission done with intent to cause damage' by the claimant state (Art VI).

[14] Beer, at p 48.

state claimed jurisdiction and control. Such registration procedures were formalized under the 1975 Convention on the Registration of Objects Launched into Outer Space.[15] Under the Convention, the launching state accepted an obligation to maintain a register (Article II), although the contents and conditions of use could be determined by the 'state of registry'. In the UK, the Registry is maintained by the British National Space Centre (BNSC).[16] Certain information is required to be furnished to the Secretary-General of the United Nations for general publication (Articles III, IV).[17] This information should be distinguished from that maintained under the auspices of the ITU in respect of the allocation of frequency spectrum and orbital slots.[18]

Aspects of the treaties comprising international space law have been transposed into UK law by the Outer Space Act 1986 (OSA), which is administered by the BNSC on behalf of the Secretary of State for Innovation, Universities and Skills. The Act applies to the 'launching or procuring the launch of a space object'; 'operating a space object' or 'any activity in outer space' (section 1), which are all licensable activities.[19] However, a licence is not required for the leasing or use of space segment capacity, i.e. on a transponder, from an existing satellite operator.[20] Under the terms of any such licence, a licensee is subject to a number of obligations, including supplying certain information for inclusion in a register to be maintained by the Secretary of State and to 'avoid interference with the activities of others'(section 5). In terms of liability, the licensee is obliged to obtain third-party liability insurance for any loss or damage arising from the authorized activities (section 5(2)(f)), currently up to a value of £100 million,[21] as well as indemnifying the government against any claims (section 10). As part of the licensing process, the BNSC will also ensure that the applicant has made appropriate ITU filings for frequency and orbital slots through Ofcom.[22] The OSA licensing regime is currently under review, with a view to updating it to reflect 'the evolving international situation, and the challenges posed by future space projects'.[23]

In terms of jurisdiction, a satellite system can be distinguished into two components: the 'earth segment' and the 'space segment'. The 'earth segment' comprises

---

[15] New York, 14 January 1975; TS 70 (1978); Cmnd 7271. The Convention entered into force for the UK on 30 May 1978.

[16] See n 11 above.

[17] The information to be supplied is: the name of the launching state or states; an appropriate designator or registration number for the space object; the date, territory or location of launch; basic orbital parameters and the general function of the space object (see generally <http://www.oosa.unvienna.org>).

[18] See section 15.3.2 below.

[19] An example of a typical licence can be obtained at <http://www.bnsc.gov.uk/assets/channels/industry/OSA2008Example.pdf>.

[20] BNSC, 'Revised Guidance for Applicants—Outer Space Act 1986'.

[21] Ibid, at p 2.

[22] See Ofcom, 'Procedures for the Management of Satellite Findings', 27 March 2007.

[23] BNSC, 'Review of licensing regime', available at <http://www.bnsc.gov.uk/content.aspx?nid=5976>.

those stations that send ('uplinks') and receive ('downlinks') transmissions from the satellite and which are subject to the laws of the jurisdiction in which they physically located.[24] The 'space segment' has been defined in the following terms:

. . . the telecommunications satellites, and the tracking, telemetry, command, control, monitoring and related facilities and equipment required to support the operation of these satellites. (INTELSAT Agreement, Article 1(h))

Jurisdictional responsibility for the 'space segment' can be sub-divided between the State that launched the satellite and the State from where the satellite is controlled. If control is distributed between multiple sites, then it is the operator's principal place of business.

15.2.1.2 International satellite conventions
With the successful launch of Sputnik I in 1957, the operation of satellite systems was initially a highly charged political arena with important military and therefore 'Cold War' implications. However, the 1962 UN resolution represented an important acceptance by the international community that space should be treated as a common resource of 'all mankind'. In addition, the industry then consisted of national, generally state-owned, monopoly operators. With these factors in mind, it was therefore perhaps inevitable that the first satellite systems were the subject of international treaty, rather than private endeavour.

The first international satellite organization (ISO) was established in 1964 under 'Interim Arrangements for a Global Commercial Communications Satellite System'[25] and, subsequently, the Agreement Relating to the International Telecommunications Satellite Organization (Intelsat).[26] Intelsat had legal personality (Article IV) and operated in accordance with the inter-governmental Agreement and an 'Operating Agreement'. Member countries were required to grant Intelsat, and certain of its officers and employees, legal and taxation privileges and immunities (Article XVII). Intelsat's stated prime objective was:

. . . the provision, on a commercial basis, of the space segment required for international public telecommunications services of high quality and reliability to be available on a non-discriminatory basis to all areas of the World. (Article III)

Intelsat comprised 147 member countries and signatories, as well as over 200 'investing entities', in 2001. In the UK, British Telecommunications was the designated signatory to Intelsat, reflecting the governmental origins of the organization; although prior to privatization, more than 20 other UK-based operators were designated as

---

[24] The geographical coverage of a satellite's transmissions is known as its 'footprint'.
[25] Washington, 20 August 1964–20 February 1965; TS 12 (1966); Cmnd 2940.
[26] See the Agreement relating to the International Telecommunications Satellite Organization 'INTELSAT' (with Operating Agreement), (Washington, 20 August 1971; TS 80 (1973); Cmnd 5416).

'investing entities'. In July 2001, Intelsat became a private company and in 2005 was acquired by four private equity companies.

The International Mobile Satellite Organization (Inmarsat) was established in 1979 as an intergovernmental organization providing satellite services for the maritime and aeronautical sectors, particularly communications in situations of distress and safety.[27] In 1994, it established a separate private company, I-CO Global Communications Ltd, to build and provide a non-geostationary mobile satellite-based telecommunications system.[28] Until 1999, Inmarsat's organizational structure was very similar to Intelsat. The vast majority of its operations were privatized in 1999 and it floated on the London Stock Exchange in 2005.

A third international satellite organization to which the UK was a member signatory is the European Telecommunications Satellite Organization (Eutelsat), established in 1977 and comprised of 48 member countries.[29] Whilst the Convention and Operating Agreement were modelled closely on the Intelsat texts, in contrast to Intelsat only one operator per member is a shareholder, which for the UK was British Telecommunications plc. The prime objective of Eutelsat was 'the provision of the space segment required for international public telecommunication services in Europe' (Article III(a)). As with Intelsat and Inmarsat, Eutelsat was privatized in 2001, providing services through a private company (Eutelsat SA), whilst the intergovernmental organization continues to operate in order to 'ensure that basic principles of pan-European coverage, universal service, non-discrimination and fair competition are observed by the company'.[30]

With market liberalization, concerns arose that the treaty-based satellite systems could be utilized by incumbent operators to restrict access to space segment capacity and satellite services. In particular, a service provider wanting to purchase satellite capacity was generally required to procure the capacity via their local signatory, i.e. the incumbent operator. Not only did this generate revenue for the signatory, but associated 'coordination procedures' required details of the proposed service to be widely disclosed: e.g.

To the extent that any Party or Signatory or person within the jurisdiction of a Party intends individually or jointly to establish, acquire or utilize space segment facilities separate from the INTELSAT . . . such Party or Signatory, prior to the establishment, acquisition or utilization of such facilities, shall furnish all relevant information to and shall consult with the Assembly

---

[27] See the Convention on the International Maritime Satellite Organization (INMARSAT) (with the Operating Agreement), London, 3 September 1976; TS 94 (1979); Cmnd. 7722. It changed its name in 1994.

[28] See generally Case No IV/35.296—Inmarsat-P, OJ C 304/6, 15 November 1995.

[29] See the Convention establishing the European Telecommunications Satellite Organization (EUTELSAT) (Paris, 15 July 1982; TS 15 (1990); Cmnd 956, as amended by a Protocol of 15 December 1983, Cmnd 9154). The UK instrument of ratification of the Convention was deposited on 21 February 1985 and the Convention, Operating Agreement and Protocol entered into force on 1 September 1985.

[30] See <http://www.eutelsat.com>: 'Introduction to Eutelsat'.

of Parties . . . to ensure technical compatibility . . . and to avoid significant economic harm to the global system of INTELSAT. (Article XIV(d))

Such procedures could obviously be abused to restrict competition either directly, by blocking the provision of a service, or indirectly, by the incumbent operator commencing a competing service.

As part of the EU's liberalization programme, Member States party to any of the international satellite organizations, i.e. Intelsat, Inmarsat, Eutelsat, and Intersputnik, were required to notify the Commission of any measures which could breach European competition law.[31] In addition, a 1994 Council Resolution called for the rules of the international satellite organizations to be adjusted to ensure strict separation between regulatory and operational aspects; as well as separation or flexibility between ownership of investment shares and usage of the systems.[32]

To minimize the potentially anti-competitive operation of the satellite organizations, the European Commission believed it was necessary to ensure that 'users obtain direct access to space segment capacity, while providers of this space segment should obtain the right to market space capacity directly to users'.[33] Such direct access has subsequently been implemented in most of the Member States, although through separate ancillary agreements rather than amendments to the provisions of the international agreements.[34] However, the Commission did not consider such developments to be sufficient to ensure a fully liberalized market in the provision of satellite-based services. Therefore, Member States now have an obligation to 'take all appropriate steps to eliminate' incompatibilities between the international conventions and the EC treaty.[35]

In the US, the government took a much more proactive stance towards the anti-competitive position of the ISOs. In 2000, Congress adopted the Open-Market Reorganization for the Betterment of International Telecommunications Act,[36] with the express purpose of ensuring that Intelsat and Inmarsat became independent commercial entities with a pro-competitive ownership structure. The Federal Communications Commission was required to determine whether Intelsat, Inmarsat, or any of their successor entities 'will harm competition in the telecommunications markets of the United States' and condition or deny any applications or authorizations

---

[31] Commission Directive 94/46/EC of 13 October 1994 amending Directive 88/301/EEC in particular with regard to satellite communications (OJ L 268/15, 19 October 1994), at Art 3.

[32] Council Resolution on further development of the Community's satellite communications policy, especially with regard to the provision of, and access to, space segment capacity; OJ C379/5, 31 December 1994.

[33] 'Towards Europe-wide systems and services—Green Paper on a common approach in the field of Satellite Communications in the European Community', Communication from the Commission, COM(90)490 final, 20/11/1990. See also the 1991 Guidelines, at paras 122–128.

[34] See Communication from the Commission, 'Fifth Report on the Implementation of the Telecommunications Regulatory Package', November 1999.

[35] Commission Directive 2002/77/EC 'on competition in the markets for electronic communications networks and services' (OJ L 249/21, 17 September 2002) at Art 8(2).

[36] The 'ORBIT Act', Pub L 106–180, 114 Stat 48 (2000), codified at 47 USC § 761 et seq.

where such harm is found to be present or potential. Such a unilateral move was in breach of the US's international treaty obligations under the Intelsat agreement,[37] but acted as an effective spur to the privatization process.

With the progressive moves towards full commercialization and privatization, the treaty-based satellite systems are no longer relevant as a feature of international telecommunications law. From a competition law perspective, the process of privatization has raised a number of issues, including the need to ensure that the private operating entities do not retain any of the legal immunities granted to international organizations; and opening up the shareholding to non-participant entities, preferably through a public offering.[38] Such operators are now subject to the scrutiny of competition regulators in the same way as other multinational satellite ventures.[39] However, the ISOs also had a public service remit, both in general terms of offering services on a non-discriminatory basis, as well as specific service offerings, such as Inmarsat's maritime distress and safety services. Whether the privatized entities will continue to adequately fulfil such public service obligations in a commercial environment, only time will tell.[40]

15.2.2 Submarine cables

Submarine cables have been a component of the international telecommunications infrastructure since 1851, when the first submarine cable for telegraphy was laid between England and France. The first commercially successful transatlantic telegraph cable was operational in 1866; the first transatlantic coaxial copper telephone cable (TAT-1) in 1956, and the first transatlantic fiber optic cable (TAT-8) in 1988.[41] The emergence of satellite technology was generally seen as signalling the demise of submarine cable as a transmission medium. However, submarine cable has continued to prosper and expand as the dominant medium for international traffic due to its superior transmission quality, reliability and security, carrying over 95 per cent of international voice and data traffic.[42]

---

[37] Sagar, D, 'Privatisation of the Intergovernmental Satellite Organisations', paper presented at the ECSL Tenth Summer Course on Space Law and Policy, Nice, 27 August–8 September 2001.

[38] Ungerer, H, 'The transformation of the International Satellite Organisations—some aspects from a European perspective', 11 April 1999: published on the Competition Directorate-General website. See also Press Release, 'Commission gives green light to Inmarsat restructuring', IP/98/923, 22 October 1998.

[39] E.g. Commission competition decisions: Case IV/34.768—International Private Satellite Partners (OJ L 354/75, 31 December 1994) and Case IV/35.518—Iridium (OJ L 16/87, 18 January 1997).

[40] Sagar, n 37 above.

[41] See generally Wagner, E, 'Submarine cables and protections provided by the law of the sea', pp 95–109, *Open Governance: Strategies and Approaches for the 21st Century* (ed Mensah) (Proceedings of The Law of the Sea Institute, 28th Annual Conference, 1994).

[42] ICPC Presentation, 'About submarine telecommunication cables: Communicating via the ocean', kindly made available to the author, July 2008.

The expense of laying submarine cables has meant that, historically, consortia of operators from different jurisdictions have carried out such projects under private agreement, often referred to as 'cable clubs'. Such 'clubs' usually comprized the monopoly operators from each jurisdiction connected to the cable. In contrast to the first satellite systems, such consortia were not the subject of international conventions. During the telecommunications boom of the late 1990s, the 'club' model was replaced by single private ventures, such as Global Crossing and FLAG, who were able to raise sufficient investment from the capital markets without consortia. However, with the subsequent downturn in the sector, a number of these companies experienced financial difficulties and numerous submarine cable systems have been taken out of service.[43] As a consequence, we have seen a return of cable 'clubs' as a financing vehicle for submarine cable systems. Cable laying projects are driven by the perceived growth in demand for bandwidth to carry data traffic, which reflects in part general economic activity around the world.

In terms of regulatory issues, submarine cabling can be divided into:

- the laying of the cable itself;
- the provisioning of capacity in the form of IRUs (Indefeasible Rights of Use) and, subsequently, as International Private Leased Circuits (IPLCs);[44]
- the operation of the cable landing station; and
- the facilities required to connect the operator's domestic network to the cable landing station, commonly referred to as 'backhaul'.[45]

The issue of cable laying concerns issues of public international law and national marine law, in respect of landing rights. The establishment of cable landing stations usually involves a complex array of national and (or) local planning and environmental laws. The provisioning of capacity and 'backhaul' facilities, as well as access to landing stations, has come to the attention of telecommunications regulatory authorities in terms of competition concerns.

In similar fashion to satellites, the international law of the sea governs the laying of submarine cable and associated liabilities for damage, where such cable lies outside the territory of a state. The primary international treaty governing ownership of the seas is the United Nations Convention on the Law of the Sea 1982 (UNCLOS), which only came into force in November 1994.[46] The UK instrument of accession was deposited on 25 July 1997 and the Convention came into force in the UK on 24 August 1997.[47] In March 1998, the European Community acceded to the Convention in

---

[43] See Burnett, R, 'The legal status of out-of-service submarine cables', Maritime Studies, No 137, July/August 2004.
[44] For a consideration of the commercial aspects of IRUs, see Chapter 11, at 11.2.
[45] See Hogan & Hartson, Submarine Cable Landing Rights and Existing Practices for the Provision of Transmission Capacity on International Routes, Report to the European Commission, August 1999.
[46] See UN General Assembly Resolution A/48/263 of 28 July 1994.
[47] Treaty Series No 81 (1999), Cm 4524.

respect of those matters for which competence has been transferred to it by those Member States that are parties to the Convention.[48]

The Convention divides the sea into five different zones, each subject to different legal regimes:

- *internal waters* are 'on the landward side of the baseline of the territorial sea' and are part of a state's sovereign territory (Article 8);

- *territorial waters* extending 12 nautical miles in breadth and over which the coastal State has sovereignty (Article 3), subject to the right of 'innocent passage' (section 3);

- *continental shelf*, comprising 'the sea-bed and subsoil of the submarine areas that extend beyond its territorial sea' up to 200 nautical miles (Article 76), and over which the coastal state exercises 'sovereign rights for the purpose of exploring it and exploiting its natural resources' (Article 77);

- *exclusive economic zone* extending over a 200 nautical mile zone, where the state has the right to declare exclusive economic interests in the resources (Part V); and

- *high seas* which are open to all states, both coastal and land-locked (Article 87).

A coastal state is entitled to lay submarine cables in its territorial waters, provided that they do not obstruct the rights of use of others, such as innocent passage (Article 21(c)). Any state is entitled to lay cables on the continental shelf, subject to the rights of other users already present; as well as the right of the coastal state to take reasonable measures in respect of exploitation, controlling pollution, and the imposition of conditions on cables entering its territory or territorial waters (Article 79). States are also free to lay cables in the exclusive economic zone (Article 58) and the high seas (Article 87), subject to an obligation to respect existing cables and pipelines (Article 112).

The need to protect submarine cables from damage caused by other uses of the sea, such as fishing, dredging, or anchoring, gave rise to the Convention for the Protection of Submarine Cables in 1884,[49] which is applicable outside of territorial waters.[50] The Convention was implemented in English law by the Submarine Telegraph Act 1885, although any contradictory provisions within the 1982 Convention supersede its provisions (Article 311.2). Under the Submarine Telegraph Act, it is an offence to unlawfully and wilfully, or by culpable negligence, break or injure a submarine cable under the high seas (section 3), attracting a maximum tariff of five years' imprisonment. Conversely, where a ship owner can prove damage to his equipment in order

---

[48] Council Decision of 23 March 1998 concerning the conclusion by the European Community of the United Nations Convention of 10 December 1982 on the Law of the Sea and the Agreement of 28 July 1994 relating to the implementation of Part XI thereof; OJ L 179/1, 23 June 1998: at Annex II.

[49] Paris, 14 March 1884 (75 BFSP 356; C 5910).

[50] Primarily in the continental shelf zone: Wagner n 41 above, at p 100.

to avoid damaging a submarine cable, then the ship owner may claim compensation from the cable owner, provided that all reasonable precautionary measures were taken.[51] In 1958, the International Cable Protection Committee was established as an industry body comprising owners and operators of submarine telecommunications cables, including government administrations, in order to promote the protection of submarine cables against man-made and natural hazards.[52] It has produced a number of recommendations on issues such as 'Cables Crossing Criteria', concerning the placing of new cables near existing systems, which members comply with on a self-regulatory basis.

Although recognition of the value of submarine cables can be seen to date back to the 1884 Convention, our increasing dependence on cable infrastructure, especially for Internet traffic, has led some authorities to implement additional protective measures within territorial waters. In Australia, for example, the Australian Communications and Media Authority (ACMA) has declared a number of protection zones over submarine cables recognized as being of vital significance to the national interest, particularly in terms of the economy.[53] If carriers want to lay new cables within the zone, they are required to obtain a permit from the ACMA; while certain types of activity are prohibited, such as trawling, or restricted, such as navigational aids.[54] Conduct resulting in damage to a submarine cable constitutes an offence, attracting a maximum tariff of ten years, on the basis of strict liability if the cable is within a protection zone.[55] Similar protection schemes have been adopted in New Zealand, Indonesia and Singapore.[56]

In similar fashion to the international satellite organizations, the cooperative nature of the 'cable clubs' has raised competition concerns.[57] In a liberalizing environment, competing operators will want to purchase capacity on the cable and may need access to the cable landing stations to physically connect their networks to the international circuits. Cable owners, historically incumbent operators, may delay the provisioning of capacity on the cable, levy excessive tariffs, or make landing station access difficult, in order to obstruct a competitor's entry into the market.

In some EU Member States, national regulators have imposed access and interconnection obligations upon incumbent operators to their submarine cables.[58]

---

[51] Continental Shelf Act 1964, s 8(1). See *Agincourt Steamship Co Ltd v Eastern Extension, Australasia and China Telegraph Co Ltd* [1907] 2 KB 305, CA.
[52] <http://www.iscpc.org>. There are also national committees, such as the UK Cable Protection Committee (<http://www.ukcpc.co.uk>).
[53] See, for example, ACMA media release 126/2007: 'Protection zone declared for submarine telecommunications cable off the coast of Perth', 4 October 2007.
[54] Telecommunications and Other Legislation Amendment (Protection of Submarine Cables and Other Measures) Act 2005, No 104.
[55] Ibid, at Sch 1, Pt 1, ss 36–37.
[56] E.g. New Zealand, Submarine Cables and Pipeline Protection Act 1996.
[57] See also Chapter 9, at 9.3.3.1.
[58] See Hogan & Hartson, n 45 above and the Commission Communication, 'Fifth Report on the Implementation of the Telecommunications Regulatory Package', COM(1999)537, 10 November 1999.

While the Access and Interconnection Directive does not expressly refer to cable landing stations or 'backhaul' circuits, such facilities clearly fall within the concept of 'access', and operators could be required to provide access, either where the operator is designated as having SMP or as a general measure.[59] In the UK, the Office of Fair Trading (OFT) has investigated accusations made against the UK Cable Protection Committee that it engaged in a collective boycott of an operator, Cityhook plc, and the collective setting of 'wayleave fees' paid to UK landowners for landing cables. The OFT eventually decided not to proceed with the case; although the decision was made on the grounds of administrative priority rather than non-infringement.[60] At an international level, US operators have complained in the past about access to submarine cable systems in the Indian market, particularly access to cable landing stations owned by VSNL the dominant international carrier, which has resulted in changes in national rules.[61]

15.3 INTERNATIONAL TELECOMMUNICATIONS UNION

The International Telecommunications Union (ITU) was founded in 1932, through the merger of the International Telegraph Union and the International Radiotelegraph Union; although its origins can be said to date back to the establishment of the International Telegraph Union by 20 European states in 1865.[62] As such, the ITU is one of the oldest of the intergovernmental organizations, which illustrates the inherently international nature of the telecommunications industry, both in terms of the scope of services being demanded and the nature of the physical resources involved, specifically radio spectrum. It became a specialized agency of the United Nations system in 1947.[63] Based in Geneva, the ITU exists to further the development of telegraph, telephone, and radio services, to promote international cooperation for the use of telecommunications and the development of technical facilities, and to allocate radio frequencies. The basic principles for the conduct of international telecommunication services, the basis for membership of the ITU and its organization and

---

[59] Directive 2002/19/EC on access to, and interconnection of, electronic communications networks and associated facilities (OJ L 108/7, 24 April 2002), under Art 12 and Art 5(1)(a) respectively.

[60] *Cityhook Ltd v OFT and ors* [2007] CAT 18.

[61] See USTR, 'Results of the 2007 Section 1377 Review of Telecommunications Trade Agreements', at p 14–15. Available from <http://www.ustr.gov/Trade_Sectors/Telecom-E-commerce/Section_1377/Section_Index.html>.

[62] For a history of the ITU, see Lyall F, 'Communications Regulation: The Role of the International Telecommunication Union', 1997 (3) The Journal of Information, Law and Technology (JILT) <http://www2.warwick.ac.uk/fac/soc/law/elj/jilt/1997_3/lyall/>.

[63] International Convention on Telecommunications, Atlantic City, 2 October 1947; 1950 UK Treaty Series No 76, Cm 8124.

permanent organs, are contained in the International Telecommunications Convention and Constitution, to which the UK is a party.[64]

The Constitution contains the fundamental principles of the ITU, while the Convention details the operational procedures, which may be subject to periodic review. The 'supreme organ' within the ITU structure is the Plenipotentiary Conference, which comprises every Member State and meets every four years (Constitution, Article 8), the last being held in Antalya, Turkey, in 2006.[65] Between meetings, a Council, comprising no more than 25 per cent of the total membership, acts on behalf of the Plenipotentiary (Constitution, Article 10(3)). The work of the Union is sub-divided into three sectors:

• the Radiocommunications Sector (ITU-R);

• the Telecommunication Standardization Sector (ITU-T); and

• the Telecommunication Development Sector (ITU-D) (Constitution, Article 7).

The work of each sector is carried out by a series of organizational entities: world and regional conferences, boards, assemblies, and numerous study groups examining particular topics. An administrative 'Bureau', within the General Secretariat, supports each sector, and the General Secretariat is headed-up by the Secretary-General, currently Dr Hamadoun Touré.

The ITU comprises two categories of membership:

• 'Member States', i.e. national governments, of which there are currently 191, although governments may designate national regulatory authorities as their representative;[66] and

• 'Sector Members', representing all the various categories of player within the telecommunications industry, including regional and international organizations, such as the GSM Association, and the intergovernmental satellite organizations, such as ARABSAT.[67] In total, these entities number over 700.

Sector members have been involved in the work of the ITU since the Rome Telegraph Conference in 1871, with the sponsorship of a Member State (Convention, Article 19(1)(a), (b)). In 1998, the Convention was amended to enable Sector Members to apply directly to join the ITU; although the applicant's Member State must approve such a procedure (Convention, Article 19(4*bis*)-(4*quater*)). However, despite being eligible for membership, it was not until the Plenipotentiary in 1994 that Sector

---

[64] See the Constitution and Convention of the ITU, Geneva, 22 December 1992 (Treaty Series No 24, 1996, Cm 3145); as amended by the Final Acts of the Plenipotentiary Conferences of the ITU, at Kyoto (1994), Minneapolis (1998) and Marrakesh (2002). See generally <http://www.itu.int/>.

[65] The next will be in Veracruz, Mexico, in 2010.

[66] E.g. Ofcom in the case of the UK, as directed by the Secretary of State under the Communications Act 2003, s 22.

[67] Note that the historic satellite organizations discussed in section 15.2.1.2 above, such as Inmarsat, now fall under Member State listings, according to where they are established.

Members were able to formally participate in the decision-making processes of the ITU; and only in 1998 that Sector Members were recognized as having formal rights of participation under the Constitution:

In respect of their participation in activities of the Union, Sector Members shall be entitled to participate fully in the activities of the Sector of which they are members, subject to relevant provisions of this Constitution and the Convention:
(a) they may provide chairmen and vice-chairmen of Sector assemblies and meetings and world telecommunication development conferences;
(b) they shall be entitled, subject to the relevant provisions of the Convention and relevant decisions adopted in this regard by the Plenipotentiary Conference, to take part in the adoption of Questions and Recommendations and in decisions relating to the working methods and procedures of the Sector concerned.' (Article 3(3)).

A Sector Member may also be authorized to act on behalf of a Member State (Convention, Article 19(9)), which may be he case where an operator continues to be part of the government, often under a specific ministry, or has been conferred with certain special or exclusive rights within the jurisdiction. Sector Members participate in those sectors of the ITU for which they apply, e.g. ITU-R, so participation in one sector does not confer authorization to participate in another.

Despite the enhanced status of the Sector Members, the fundamental legal instruments of the ITU, the Constitution, Convention, and Administrative Regulations,[68] continue to be under the exclusive jurisdiction of the Member States.

An industry player may also be invited by a Sector of the ITU to participate as an 'Associate' within a study group (Convention, Article 19(12)), with more limited rights of participation, although with an obligation to help defray the costs of the group in which they participate (Convention, Article 33(5)(4bis)). This category of participants was established within the ITU system in 1988, as a means of enabling participation by small entities in the work of the ITU.

With the liberalization of the telecommunications industry and the proliferation of commercial operators, tension has grown within the ITU over the position of industry members within the ITU structure. On the one hand, governments are wary of relinquishing their historic rights to control the organization; whilst on the other hand, they recognize industry's legitimate interests in the work of the Union, as well as wanting industry to contribute any ever greater proportion of the costs associated with its operations and activities.[69] The issue of industry involvement dominated the 1998 Plenipotentiary Conference in Minneapolis, where a single category of industry membership was finally recognized:

Sector Member: An entity or organization authorized in accordance with Article 19 of the Convention to participate in the activities of a Sector. (Constitution, Annex)

---

[68] See section 15.3.4 below.
[69] See Resolution 110 (Marrakesh, 2002): 'Review of the contribution of Sector Members towards defraying the expenses of the International Telecommunication Union'.

In terms of financing the work of the ITU, the Constitution was amended to place Sector Member contributions on an equal footing to those of Member States (Article 28). In addition, new 'Advisory Groups' were established for each Sector, with a broad remit to review the 'priorities, programmes, operations, financial matters and strategies' of the various bodies within each Sector (Convention, Article 11A, 14A, 17A). These new bodies should increase the influence of Sector Members within the ITU as Member States and industry will participate on an equal footing.

As part of a broad review of the ITU's role and strategy for the future, an ITU Reform Advisory Panel was established at the end of the last decade, comprising both governmental and private sector members,[70] and made the following recommendation in 2000 with respect to the balance of influence between Member States and Sector Members within the ITU:

> The decision-making functions of the ITU should reflect the modern, competitive telecommunications environment in which the private sector plays the lead role while the regulatory agencies act as an arbitrator for the wider public interest.[71]

Whilst such sentiment was welcomed by the telecommunications industry, the degree to which Member States continue to intervene in the sector in the 'public interest' may give cause for concern. Currently, there are no institutional procedures to enable Sector Members to appeal against a decision made by Member States or arbitrate in a dispute with a Member State.

The work of the ITU can be distinguished into three major areas: standardization, spectrum management and orbital slots, and development issues.

15.3.1 Standards[72]

It was the issue of technical standards that gave rise to the establishment of the International Telegraph Union in 1865, when governments recognized the need for standards to extend the telegraph network throughout Europe. Standards represent the cornerstone of the global telecommunications industry, and the ITU is one of the leading international institutions for *de jure* standards-making. The ITU's remit extends not only to technical issues, but also operational and tariffs[73] structures for international telecommunication services.

Over recent years, the ITU's pre-eminent position in the standards-setting field has somewhat diminished in the face of regulatory competition from regional

---

[70] For a full list of members, see <http://www.itu.int/newsroom/reform/rapmembers.html>.

[71] ITU Reform Advisory Panel (RAP), Observations and Recommendations for Reform, 10 March 2000.

[72] See further Chapter 10, at 10.6.1.2.

[73] See further section 15.3.5 below.

organizations,[74] industry bodies[75] and, most significantly, *de facto* standards organizations such as the Internet Engineering Task Force (IETF) which are able to develop standards much more rapidly that formal bodies such as the ITU. Recognizing such developments the ITU is examining ways to reposition itself:

ITU-T could become a facilitator for collaboration, convening meetings among different standards bodies and industry forums, in particular on interworking between the Internet and telecommunications networks, both fixed and mobile.[76]

As such its standards-development role would be focused on those areas where it currently leads: optical transmission, voice services, numbering, signalling, and network management.

15.3.2 Radiocommunications

The development of radiocommunications at the beginning of the twentieth century also gave rise to the need for international cooperation to avoid harmful interference. The International Radiotelegraph Union, established in 1906, adopted operating principles that have continued to form the basis of the ITU's regulation of radiocommunications: Member States were required to give notify each other of any new service utilizing the radio spectrum and were obliged to ensure that such services did not interfere with other uses of the frequency.[77]

The Radiocommunications Sector of the ITU, primarily operating through the Radio Regulations Board, exercises a regulatory function in respect of the use of two scarce resources, radio-frequency spectrum and orbital slots, both of which require management in order to maximize utilization, as well as prevent interference between services and space objects.[78] The ITU is responsible for the allocation of bands of the radio-frequency spectrum and orbital slots to Member State administrations and then registers the assignment of particular radio frequencies by an administration to a specific operator in the 'Master International Frequency Register' (the 'Master Register'). The ITU records all satellite filings, both geostationary and non-geostationary, as well as the earth stations that communicate with those systems.[79]

---

[74] E.g. the European Telecommunications Standards Institute (ETSI): <http://www.etsi.org>.

[75] E.g. the GSM Association: <http://www.gsmworld.com>. It comprises some 449 member companies from 149 countries.

[76] RAP n 71 above at. 3.

[77] See Allison, A, 'Meeting the challenges of change: the reform of the International Telecommunications Union', Federal Communications Law Journal, vol 45, no 3, 1993, at 498.

[78] Constitution, Art 1(2)(a), (b); Chapter II (Arts 12–16) and Convention, Section 5 (Arts 7–12). The ITU's procedures cover both geostationary and non-geostationary satellite systems.

[79] See the ITU 'Space Network Systems Online', at <http://www.itu.int/sns/>.

Such procedures are designed 'to eliminate harmful interference . . . and to improve use made of the radio-frequency spectrum'.[80] The overriding objective of the ITU regulatory regime is the efficient use of the spectrum, while ensuring that public safety and emergency communication services, the only other policy concerns directly addressed in the Radio Regulations, are not adversely affected:

Any emission capable of causing harmful interference to distress, alarm, urgency or safety communications on the international distress and emergency frequencies established for these purposes by these Regulations is prohibited. Supplementary distress frequencies available on less than a worldwide basis should be afforded adequate protection.[81]

The ITU regime should not, therefore, be viewed as a comprehensive governing framework for the provision of radiocommunication services, since national and regional policies and laws on radiocommunications will generally encompass a much broader remit of issues, including environmental concerns.[82]

The ITU and Member States have the difficult task of reconciling, on the one hand, that these limited natural resources be used 'rationally, efficiently and economically' with, on the other hand, being expected to bear in mind that countries should have 'equitable access to [the resources], taking into account the special needs of the developing countries and the geographical position of particular countries'.[83] The latter phrase provision was introduced to reflect the interests of developing countries who were concerned to reserve a portion of the relevant resources until such time as they were in an economic position to exploit them. To address this tension, the ITU distinguishes between planned and non-planned spectrum bands. The former are subject to a plan developed at ITU regional or world conferences, against which administrations then submit their requirements and the spectrum is shared out; while spectrum in the unplanned bands is distributed on a first-come-first-serve basis. The planned bands enable equitable access, but at the expense of rigidity and tied spectrum that is potentially unused; against the flexibility of non-planned bands that can exclude 'latecomers'.[84]

Despite these coordination procedures, one of the dominant issues of concern in the Radiocommunications Sector over the past two decades has been the problem of overfiling of requests for orbital slots with associated frequencies for satellite systems. In particular, Member State administrations have been accused of filing for 'paper satellites' that have little or no real prospect of becoming operational. The filing is

[80] Harmful interference is defined as 'Interference which endangers the functioning of a radionavigation service or of other safety services or seriously degrades, obstructs or repeatedly interrupts a radiocommunication service operating in accordance with the Radio Regulations.' Constitution, para 1003. See also the Radio Regulations, at Art 1(1.169). 'Harmful interference' is distinguished from 'permissible interference' (i.e. interference which falls within certain parameters) and 'accepted interference' (i.e. interference greater than certain parameters, but accepted by two or more administrations).

[81] Article 4, at 4.22. See further section 15.3.4 below.

[82] See further Chapter 7, at 7.4.4.5.

[83] Ibid, Art 44(2). Introduced in the 1973 ITU Convention.

[84] ITU, 'Overview of the Radio Regulations', available at <http://www.itu.int/sns/radreg.html>.

designed to pre-empt competing claims to what is perceived as an ever-diminishing resource in the face of multinational private satellite consortia, such as Globalstar and Iridium. The administration may then be expected to realize the value of the allocation by reselling or leasing the slot to the highest bidder at some later date. In the early 1990s, for example, Tonga applied to the ITU for 31 orbital slots and was awarded 6. Tonga then leased one of the slots to Columbia and auctioned off the remaining slots for US$2 million each.[85] Such warehousing practices not only subject orbital slots to financial speculation and give rise to disputes,[86] they substantially lengthen the procedure for genuine satellite systems to obtain the necessary allocations.[87]

To address the problem of overfiling, it was proposed at the World Radiocommunications Conference (WRC) in 1997 that administrations be required to provide specific evidence of the proposed satellite system, referred to as administrative and financial 'due diligence'. Administratively, the Member State administration would be required to make regular submissions on the implementation of the system, including the contractual date of delivery, the number of satellites procured, and the proposed launch date.[88] Financial constraints would include an annual coordination and registration charge, as well as a refundable deposit. The latter financial proposals were rejected over concerns that this would effectively represent a spectrum usage charge. Instead, it was agreed that the ITU would be able to recover its full costs for processing such applications.[89] Such procedures have helped reduce the filing backlog; although ongoing wrangles are taking place between the ITU and satellite operators about the true costs involved and the resulting high fees. This has lead to substantial non-payment and arguments over the consequences, namely cancellation of the filing, and who bears the liability for the outstanding invoice, either the operators or the Member States with whom the ITU has a formal legal relationship.[90]

In terms of the spectrum bands, the ITU is also the forum for Member States to debate the allocation or reallocation of newly or prospectively available spectrum. In November 2007, for example, at the ITU's WRC, it was agreed that spectrum within the UHF band, which has traditionally been the exclusive preserve of broadcasters,

---

[85] Jasentuliyana, N, *International Space Law and the United Nations* (Martinus Nijhoff, 1999), at pp 309–310.

[86] Indonesia placed one of its satellites in a slot registered with Tonga on the basis that the 'assignment' was 'wrong in law'. Ibid, at 310.

[87] See ITU Press Release, 'Scrambling for Space in Space' (Geneva, 16 September 2002), where it is stated that the backlog of satellites awaiting coordination stood at 1200, with between 400–500 new requests each year.

[88] RRs, Resolution 49, at Annex 2.

[89] See ITU Resolution 91 'on cost recovery for some products and services of ITU' (Minneapolis, 1998) and Resolution 88 'on the implementation of cost recovery for satellite network filings' (Marrakesh, 2002).

[90] Sung, L, 'ITU's cost recovery: the satellite factor', *Satellite Today*, 1 September 2004.

would be opened up for use by mobile broadband services.[91] Such spectrum is becoming available worldwide as a consequence of terrestrial television shifting from analogue to broadband signals, which use considerably less bandwidth; commonly referred to as the 'digital dividend'.[92] Such spectrum is highly sought after because of the quality of signal available and their propagation characteristics, which means the signals travel further and are more capable of penetrating buildings. The signal range means the cost of rolling out wireless broadband networks is considerably reduced, which is obviously beneficial for developing countries.[93]

15.3.3 Telecommunications development

From 1947, membership of the ITU expanded rapidly among developing nations. As their numbers grew, so did their share of the votes and ability to influence the direction and activities of the ITU. At the Nairobi Plenipotentiary Conference in 1982, such increasing influence resulted in development issues becoming one of the basic purposes of the ITU:

to promote and to offer technical assistance to developing countries in the field of telecommunications, and also to promote the mobilization of the material and financial resources needed for implementation. (Constitution, Article 1(1)(b))

Therefore, since 1982, the ITU has given equal priority to telecommunications development with standards-setting and radiocommunications. The Telecommunication Development Sector operates through a Telecommunication Development Bureau, Telecommunication Development Conferences and associated Study Groups.

In particular, the ITU has worked with other development agencies, such as the World Bank and the International Bank of Reconstruction and Development, to improve the flow of technology, funds and expertise into developing countries. The Reform Advisory Panel has proposed that the ITU's development focus should be expanded 'from technical assistance towards helping developing countries establish pro-market regulatory frameworks',[94] which would seem to reflect the influence of the WTO in the telecommunications sector.

15.3.4 Legal instruments of the ITU

As an international treaty, the Constitution and Convention of the ITU are legal instruments to which Member States are bound in respect of all telecommunications activities that 'engage in international services or which are capable of causing

---

[91] ITU Press Release, WRC-07, 'ITU World Radiocommunications Conference concludes after four weeks: International treaty sets future course for wireless', 16 November 2007.
[92] See further Chapter 7 and Chapter 14.
[93] Financial Times, 'Radio spectrum freed for mobiles', 19 November 2007.
[94] RAP, n 71 above.

harmful interference to radio services of other countries' (Constitution, Article 6(1)). Whilst primarily detailing the rules governing the establishment and operation of the ITU, the Constitution also embodies certain fundamental legal principles governing international telecommunications in Chapter VI. Members give recognition to certain rights of users, i.e. the 'right of the public to correspond by means of the international service' (Article 33). Member States also have an obligation for 'ensuring the secrecy of international correspondence', although subject to the right to ensure compliance with national laws (Article 37). The majority of the principles represent reservations that Members have the right to exercise, such as in respect of the 'stoppage of telecommunications' for reasons of national security, public order, or decency (Article 34) and the 'suspension of services' (Article 35). Member States are also protected from any liability arising from the use of international telecommunication services (Article 36).

There are three unique features of the ITU Constitution and Convention, which differ from traditional public international law. First, the private sector has a specified role in decision-making activities of the ITU, as noted above. Secondly, to ensure legal certainty, Administrative Regulations have a fixed date for implementation and have immediate provisional application unless the revision is formally refused by a Member State (Constitution, Article 54, 3*penter*). In addition, a Member State is deemed to have consented to be bound by the revision to the Administrative Regulations, after a period of three years, if it fails to notify the Secretary-General otherwise (Constitution, Article 54, 5*bis*). Thirdly, any reservations by a Member State have to be notified prior to the signing of the final acts of a plenipotentiary, since subsequent reservations are not possible. These provisions are designed to ensure legal certainty, which impacts directly on technical implementation issues.

Complementing the Constitution and Convention are Administrative Regulations, sub-divided into:

• International Telecommunications Regulations; and

• Radio Regulations.

The Administrative Regulations comprise the general principles to be observed in the provision of international telecommunication services and networks and the assignment and use of frequencies and orbital slots. Such Regulations 'shall be binding on all Member States' (Constitution, Articles 4(3), 54). At the time of accession to the Constitution and Convention,[95] a Member State may make reservations in respect of any of the existing Administrative Regulations (Article 54(2)). Any subsequent partial or complete revision of the Administrative Regulations requires a Member State to indicate their consent to be bound, by depositing an instrument of ratification, acceptance or approval or by notifying the Secretary-General (Article 54(3)*bis*);

---

[95] I.e. 27 June 1994 in the case of the UK.

although a Member State will be provisionally bound from the entry into force of the revision, if the Member State has signed the revision (Article 54(3)*penter*).

Under the Constitution, Member States are also required to:

take the necessary steps to impose the observance of the provisions of this Constitution, the Convention and the Administrative Regulations upon operating agencies authorized by them to establish and operate telecommunications and which engage in international services or which operate stations capable of causing harmful interference to the radio services of other countries. (Article 6(2))

However, this blanket provision is qualified by the concept of a 'Recognized Operating Agency' (RAO):

Any operating agency . . . which operates a public correspondence or broadcasting service and upon which the obligations provided for in Article 6 of this Constitution are imposed by the Member State in whose territory the head office of the agency is situated, or by the Member State which has authorized this operating agency to establish and operate a telecommunication service on its territory. (Constitution, Annex)

Historically, ROAs were generally the state-owned incumbent operator. However, in liberalized markets, the categories of ROAs could potentially extend to any provider of international services, including resale services. In the UK, for example, some ten operators are categorized as ROAs.

The current applicable International Telecommunications Regulations are those adopted at Melbourne in 1988; comprising 10 substantive articles and a series of appendices (ITRs).[96] Reiterating the Constitution, the Regulations are only binding on 'administrations' (i.e. Member States and recognized operating agencies). Administrations do, however, have the freedom to enter into 'special mutual arrangements' for the provision of international telecommunications networks and services (ITRs, Article 9), which provides considerable flexibility for countries such as the US and the EU Member States, which have regulated to ensure liberalization: e.g. the application of interconnection regulations to intra-EU international traffic. Over the years, there have been inevitable calls for the International Telecommunications Regulations to be revised, driven, in part, by the considerable changes that have occurred in the market since 1988, but also by developing country concerns that the ITRs are too favourable towards richer nations and the dominant global players they represent.

At the 1998 ITU Plenipotentiary, a resolution was adopted instructing the Secretary-General to establish an Expert Group to advise on the future of the ITRs.[97] No consensus on the way forward was reached by the following Plenipotentiary in 2002, or again by the 2006 Plenipotentiary, and therefore the review process continues.[98] However, the 2006 Resolution does, for the first time, put a prospective

---

[96] Available at <http://www.itu.int/ITU-T/itr/files/ITR-e.doc>. They entered into force on 1 July 1990.
[97] Resolution 79 (Minneapolis, 1998): 'International Telecommunication Regulations'.
[98] See Resolution 121 (Marrakesh, 2002) and Resolution 146 (Antalya, 2006).

end date on the negotiations, by resolving that the ITU convenes a conference in 2012 to decide on recommendations to amend the ITRs. One proposal for reform, representing the perspective of certain developing countries, is to give greater granularity to the ITRs by incorporating references to various ITU recommendations in the ITRs, which would then become de facto mandatory upon Member States. Such an approach is being strongly resisted by countries such as the US, however, who believe that such intervention in a liberalized market would be inappropriate.

The current applicable Radio Regulations (RRs) were published in 2008, with the provisions from the WRC-07 entering into force on 1 January 2009. The RRs are contained in four volumes; comprising some 59 articles, 25 appendices, and various resolutions and recommendations. The RRs distinguish between three distinct acts in relation to frequency: 'allocation', 'allotment', and 'assignment' (RRs, Article 1, 1.16–1.18). 'Allocation' consists of an entry in the 'Table of Frequency Allocations' for use in respect of one or more terrestrial or space radiocommunication service. Such services may be categorized as 'primary' or 'secondary' services, on a regional or global basis; with the latter being required to comply with the interference rules laid down for the former, as well as being unable to claim protection from interference from the former. 'Allotment' indicates the use of a designated frequency by administrations for a service in certain countries or geographical areas and under specified conditions. The 'assignment' of frequencies is carried out by Member State authorities through an authorization or licensing procedure, such as under the UK's Wireless Telegraphy Act 2006.[99] Such assignment is then notified to the ITU for recording in the Master Register.[100] When granting an assignment, Member States are free to derogate from the ITU allocation, but only to the extent that it does not cause harmful interference to others operating in accordance with the RRs (Article 4.4).

To ensure compliance with the RRs, particularly the elimination of harmful interference, an international monitoring system has been established (RRs, Article 16). The scheme comprises the operation of a network of monitoring stations, operated by Member States, either alone or in conjunction with others, and international organizations. The system is voluntary in nature.

In addition to the binding legal instruments, the various bodies of the ITU adopt recommendations, resolutions, and decisions. Whilst the Administrative Regulations comprise the general principles to be complied with, the manner in which they are to be implemented are detailed in ITU-T and ITU-R Recommendations, which represent the bulk of ITU rule-making.[101] Such recommendations do not have 'the same legal status as the Regulations' (ITR 88, Article 1.4), although 'administrations' 'should comply with, to the greatest extent practicable, the relevant' recommendations (Article 1.6).[102] Draft recommendations are prepared within the various sectoral

---

[99] See further Chapter 7.
[100] E.g. Ofcom, Procedures for the Management of Satellite Filings, 27 March 2007.
[101] E.g. over 2600 ITU-T Recommendations are currently in force.
[102] However, see also the opinion of the Advocate-General in *Italy v Commission* [1985] 2 CMLR 368, 373.

'Study Groups' and enter into force either through approval at the relevant assemblies or conferences, or through direct correspondence with Member State administrations (Convention, Articles 11(2), 14(1)).

In the event of a dispute regarding the interpretation of any of the legal instruments, Constitution Convention or Administrative Regulations, settlement will either be achieved through mutually agreed bilateral or multilateral arrangements or, if not settled by such means, via an arbitration procedure (Constitution, Article 56). The decision of the arbitrator(s) shall be 'final and binding upon the parties to the dispute' (Convention, Article 41), although no enforcement mechanism is available in the event of non-compliance. A compulsory arbitration procedure is also provided for under an Optional Protocol to the Convention, between Members that are party to the Protocol.[103]

15.3.5 International accounting rates

As discussed above, the origins of the ITU in the International Telegraph Convention was the need to extend the operation of telecommunication networks beyond national borders. As well as the need for common standards for the transmission of messages between different networks, such international traffic also raised the issue of payments to be made between national operators for the carriage of each other's traffic. The historic regime established for the making of such payments is known as the 'International Accounting Rate system' and the principles of its operation are contained in the ITU's International Telecommunications Regulations (Article 6).

The International Accounting Rate system comprises a series of related rates that are intended to provide for an equitable payment to the terminating operator for the termination of an international call and, where relevant, to any transit operators that have handled the call.[104] The 'collection charge' (ITRs, Article 2.9) is the retail price levied on the originating customer by the originating operator. The 'accounting rate' is essentially a wholesale rate representing the agreed cost of transmitting each unit of traffic between the calling parties.[105] The 'settlement rate' is the payment made by the originating operator to the terminating operator and is usually 50 per cent of the accounting rate. Obviously, such payments are made on a net settlement basis between operators, since traffic generally flows in both directions and therefore it is the operator that originates the most traffic that is required to make the periodic payments.

Although the system is embodied in the International Telecommunications Regulations and has been elaborated as a series of recommendations from the ITU, the

---

[103] Constitution, Art 56(3).The UK has ratified the Optional Protocol, 27 June 1994.
[104] Either direct transit or switched transit.
[105] Usually expressed in terms of Special Drawing Rights (SDR), under the International Monetary Fund, or the gold franc: Convention, Art 38; ITRs 88, Art 6.3.1.

system operates through a series of bilateral agreements between telecommunication operators in each jurisdiction:

For each applicable service in a given relation, administrations (or recognized private operating agencies) shall by mutual agreement establish and revise accounting rates to be applied between them. (ITRs, Article 6.2.1)

As noted below, however, these bilateral agreements may still be considered state measures subject to consideration under public international law, such as the General Agreement on Trade in Services.[106]

Whilst the essential elements of the international accounting rate system have remained the same over many years, the system was in fact designed to operate under certain conditions, which are no longer present in most telecommunications markets:

• jurisdictional symmetry with respect to both call origination and traffic flows;

• collection charges higher than the accounting rate;

• relatively constant inflation and exchange rates; and

• monopoly operators in each jurisdiction providing the international service.

As these conditions have either disappeared or altered, the international accounting rate system has given rise to substantial payment flows between operators, representing invisible trade imbalances between countries. In 1996, for example, US operators were obliged to pay around US$6 billion to operators in other jurisdictions, of which it was estimated that 70 per cent constituted 'an above-cost subsidy from US consumers to foreign carriers'.[107]

Indeed, under the current regime, the coexistence of liberalized telecommunications markets with traditional monopolistic environments can actually reward the latter at the expense of the former. In particular, a practice know as 'whipsawing' has arisen, whereby monopolistic operators in one country are able to negotiate with competing operators in other countries to achieve substantially lower accounting rates for the termination of traffic originating in the monopoly country. Alternatively, the monopoly operator may lease their own circuit in the liberalized terminating regime, therefore bypassing the accounting regime for outbound transmissions (commonly referred to as 'one-way bypass').

The payment imbalance is exacerbated by the fact that, historically, accounting rates have not been based on actual cost, but were often priced at a premium. For some countries, such as the US, the accounting rate system has therefore come to be seen as an unacceptable regime that positively disadvantages the introduction of competitive markets. However, countries which are net creditors under the accounting rate system, often although not exclusively developing countries, usually view the

---

[106] See further 15.4.1 below.

[107] Federal Communications Commission, In the matter of International Settlement Rates, Report and Order, IB Docket No 96–261, 7 August 1997 ('Benchmark Order'): para 13.

system as constituting an important source of foreign 'hard currency' revenue for investment into the domestic market, either in the form of network rollout or through subsidizing the cost of access (e.g. line rental). In effect such revenues have been seen as contributing to a universal service policy, at a global level as well as for individual countries.[108] Indeed, the ITU's Secretary General has noted that developing countries receive more revenue from the accounting rate system in one year than they have received from development banks, such as the World Bank, for telecommunications programs during the first half of the 1990s.[109]

Over recent years, there has been significant pressure for the international accounting rate system to be reformed.[110] Such pressure has arisen from governmental concern to reduce trade deficits, as well as bringing benefits to end-users through a reduction in the cost of international telecommunications. In addition, technological developments have resulted in a proliferation of alternative calling procedures designed, either directly or indirectly, to avoid the normal operation of the international accounting regime. Such procedures can be broadly distinguished into two categories:

• 're-origination' techniques, which take advantage of asymmetric rates on particular routes to minimize the cost of the accounting rates, e.g. call-back,[111] country-direct, calling cards, refile;[112]

• 'bypass' techniques, which completely circumvent the international accounting regime, e.g. international simple resale services, VSATs,[113] Internet telephony.

These practices inevitably lead to a reduction in the revenues of the monopoly provider of international telecommunication services and, in some cases, are infringements of national law.[114] However, whilst re-origination techniques represent a loss in collection revenues, the concurrent increase in settlement payments may significantly offset the impact for the incumbent and will encourage the maintenance of high

---

[108] See Tyler, M, *Transforming economic relationships in international telecommunications*, Chapter 8, Briefing Report for ITU Regulatory Colloquium No 7 (1997). Also, Stanley, K, 'International settlements in a changing global telecom market'in Melody (ed), *Telecom Reform*, pp 371–394 (Technical University of Denmark, 1997).

[109] Tarjanne, P, 'Reforming the international accounting rate system', 2 ITU News (1998).

[110] See ITU Report of the Informal Expert Group on International Telecommunications Settlements, March 1997.

[111] Various forms of 'call-back' exist but it essentially involves a reversal in the direction of the call, e.g. a call from a country with high originating international tariffs is manipulated to appear to come from the terminating country which has low originating international tariffs, using features of call signalling systems.

[112] 'Refile' involves routing a communication from country A to country B via a third country, C, where the sum of the tariff rates for calls between A–C and C–B are less than A–B.

[113] Very Small Aperture Terminals, used for satellite-based telecommunications direct to home.

[114] See ITU Resolution 21 of the Plenipotentiary Conference, Kyoto, 1994: 'Special Measures concerning Alternative Calling Procedures on International Telecommunication Networks' (revised at the Minneapolis Plenipotentiary, 1998), noted that 86 Member States prohibit 'call-back' (as of October 1998).

accounting rates.[115] The ITU is in an uneasy position in respect of such activities and has called upon Member States to take appropriate action against operators in their jurisdiction who are breaching the laws and regulations of other Member States.[116]

Proposals to reform the system take two main forms. First, there have been moves within the ITU to lower accounting rates towards the actual cost of terminating international calls. Such cost-based tariffing is designed to reflect the regulatory position adopted in liberalized markets, such as that applicable to interconnection agreements.[117] It also reflects existing obligations under the 1988 International Telecommunications Regulations, where Member States are required to revise accounting rates 'taking into account relevant [ITU-T] Recommendations and relevant cost trends' (Article 6.2.1). The main relevant Recommendation, D.140, 'Accounting rate principles for international telephone service', calls upon administrations to move accounting rates towards a cost-based approach, by identifying those operational elements that are considered to be legitimate components within the accounting rate:

- international transmission facilities;
- international switching facilities; and
- national extension.

The direct costs of utilizing these facilities, with some allocation of the associated common costs, should comprise a cost-based settlement rate.[118] Despite Recommendation D.140 and a fall in accounting rates by 12 per cent over the past three years, many ITU members have viewed progress towards cost-orientated rates as too slow. As a result, an Annex E to D.140 has been adopted containing indicative target rates and specified deadlines for each country.[119]

The second approach to address the present accounting rate system is through the adoption of a range of alternative rate systems, which are designed to reflect the different conditions present in many markets. Five alternative models have been suggested:[120]

- *call termination charges*, where a single rate charged to terminate into a country from any other country, as is currently operated for the international

---

[115] See Secretary General's Paper on Accounting Rate Reform, ITU-T, COM 3-2-E (November 1996).

[116] Resolution 21, n 114 above.

[117] See Chapter 3.

[118] See D.140, Annex F: 'Principles to be applied by Administrations in developing and using a cost model'.

[119] D.140, Supplement 2 (06/2003): 'Updated teledensities and indicative target settlement rates' (1 January 2003).

[120] E.g. ITU-T Recommendation D.150, 'New system for accounting in international telephony', June 1999.

telegram service. The primary advantages of such a system are transparency and non-discrimination;

- *facilities-based interconnection charge*, as already required under European Union law[121] and generally in operation for mobile roaming;

- *'sender keeps all'*, where no payments are made between national operators, historically the system adopted between the UK and Ireland. Such an approach also reflects the 'peering' arrangements present in the Internet.[122] However, as with peering, it does operate on a presumption of equality in traffic flows;

- *international private leased circuits*, where the charge will reflect the cost of leasing such capacity;

- *volume-based payments*, fixed per traffic unit carried, as currently used in Internet-based transit arrangements.

The ITU's developmental role has created problems when addressing the reform of the international accounting rate system, since the system is perceived in many Member States as contributing funds to the broader development of telecommunications in their jurisdiction. Indeed, the ITU specifically recommends that accounting rate apportionment in favour of a developing country should be used for telecommunications improvements.[123]

Pressure to reform the system is also being driven, in part, by decisions made by regulatory authorities in certain jurisdictions. In particular, the Federal Communications Commission (FCC) created considerable consternation in certain countries when it issued its International Settlement Rates Order in 1997.[124] The Order represented a fundamental policy shift from the previous Uniform Settlements Policy (USP), which had been operating since 1980.[125] Under the USP approach, all US licensed operators were required to operate under the same accounting rate with foreign correspondents, which addressed the problem of 'whipsawing', as well as obliging operators to maintain proportionate inbound and outbound traffic volumes.

However, the FCC recognized that the WTO 'basic agreement' had the potential to sharply worsen the US's balance of payments deficit on international services, since incumbent operators in non-liberalized markets would be free to establish

---

[121] See further Chapter 8.

[122] Ibid.

[123] Resolution 22: 'Apportionment of revenues in providing international telecommunication services' (Kyoto, 1994).

[124] Benchmark Order, n 107 above. The Order was reformed in 2004, to remove its application from routes where US carriers had negotiated benchmark compliant rates. See *International Settlements Policy Reform: International Settlement Rates*, IB Docket Nos 02–324 and 96–21, First Report and Order, FCC 04–53 (rel 30 March 2004).

[125] Uniform Settlement Rates on Parallel International Communications Routes, 84 FCC 2d 121 (1980); applicable to international telephone services since 1986: See Implementation and Scope of the International Settlements Policy for Parallel Routes, CC Docket No 85–204, Report and Order, 51 Fed Reg 4736 (7 February 1986).

US-based operations subsidized from their monopolistic international revenues. The progress of reform within the ITU was slow, therefore the FCC decided to take unilateral steps to drive the pace of change towards cost-based settlement rates.

The Order lays down benchmark 'settlement rates that carriers subject to our [FCC] jurisdiction may pay for termination of US-originated traffic' (paragraph 312). Countries were categorized into three tiers, representing different stages of economic development. The rates are to be implemented over a transition period, over one to four years, and operators were able to appeal against a rate determination (paragraph 74). The regime came into effect on 1 January 1998 and the first targets were to be achieved by 1 January 1999. The rates were based on a methodology known as 'tariffed components pricing' (TCP), which comprised the three elements specified in Recommendation D.140: international transmission, international exchange, and national extension. All US-licensed carriers were subject to the order, while for foreign-affiliated operators compliance was a condition of obtaining approval for the provision of long-distance services to the home jurisdiction (paragraph 207).

The Benchmark Order generated opposition in many countries, such as the Caribbean region, over the potential impact the order would have on domestic operator revenues. In addition, the European Commission and Japan raised concerns about the compatibility of the Benchmark Order with the US's commitments under the General Agreement on Trade in Services, specifically the principle of 'most-favoured-nation'.[126]

In 1998, Cable & Wireless brought an action before the US courts challenging the legality of the Benchmark Order. Over 100 other petitioners and intervenors, comprising national governments, regulators, and operators, soon joined the case on both sides. The main thrust of the complaint was that the FCC had exceeded its authority through the extraterritorial nature of the Order's provisions.[127] The court found overwhelmingly in favour of the FCC, holding that it had the requisite powers to make decisions regulating the actions of US-licensed operators, including the contractual arrangements entered into for international settlement rates:[128]

the Commission does not exceed its authority simply because a regulatory action has extraterritorial consequences.

Objections to the use of the TCP methodology were dismissed on the grounds that the FCC had acted reasonably, whilst the petitioners were criticized for withholding actual cost data which could have been used as well as failing to propose alternative methodologies.

During the course of the proceedings, the Australian operator Telstra entered a petition against the Benchmark Order on the grounds that it did not address the issue of international Internet connections. Telstra complained that the Order was based

---

[126] Ibid, at para 109. See also section 15.4 below.
[127] *Cable & Wireless et al v FCC*, No 97–1612, DC Cir, 12 January 1999.
[128] See 47 USC §205(a), 211(a).

on a circuit-switched environment, where traditionally each correspondent operator is responsible for the provision of half of the international circuit. Telstra argued, however, that in an Internet environment non-US operators were effectively forced to purchase a full-circuit in order to connect to the Internet exchange points based primarily in the US.[129] As a consequence, US carriers were obtaining significant financial benefits from the current arrangements for international Internet connections. The court denied Telstra's petition as constituting insufficient grounds for overturning the FCC Order, but the issue has subsequently been pursued within the ITU.

In April 2000, ITU-T Study Group 3 approved a draft Recommendation on International Internet Connection that had been proposed by Australia. Draft Recommendation D.120 was presented to the World Telecommunication Standardization Assembly (WTSA) for adoption in October 2000:

Noting the rapid growth of the Internet and Internet based services: It is recommended that administrations negotiate and agree bi-lateral commercial arrangements applying to direct international Internet connections whereby each administration will be compensated for the costs that it incurs in carrying traffic that is generated by the other administration.

For many Internet-based services, such as the World Wide Web, traffic flows are asymmetric, as an individual request for a page generates large flows of data towards the requester. Such data is generally from servers based in the US and connected to the Internet by US operators. Under the draft Recommendation, US operators would have been required to pay transit and termination fees to operators in other jurisdictions, such as Australia, to which the individual requester is connected; rather than the current settlement-free 'peering' system, with operators such as Telstra having to pay for full international circuits.

The draft Recommendation generated significant opposition from the US and Europe, but was supported by many developing nations members. An amended version was eventually adopted at WTSA:

recommends that administrations involved in the provision of international Internet connections negotiate and agree to bilateral commercial arrangements enabling direct international Internet connections that take into account the possible need for compensation between them for the value of elements such as traffic flow, number of routes, geographical coverage and cost of international transmission amongst others. (Recommendation D.50 (10/00) *International Internet Connection*)

The shift from mandatory to voluntary compensation enabled the proposal to be adopted, although the US and Greece made reservations and stated that the Recommendation would not be applied in their jurisdictions. Despite the agreed position, it can be expected that the ITU will be required to address this issue again over the

---

[129] See further Chapter 8, at 8.7.1.2.

coming years, as Internet-based data communications continue to expand as a proportion of total international traffic.

The international accounting rate system is gradually disappearing in its current form to be replaced by a multitude of different arrangements reflecting the state of liberalization in Member States, technological developments, and the commercial positions of the respective parties. Political pressure to accelerate such change has shifted somewhat in recent years from the ITU to the WTO. A moratorium was agreed between certain Member States not to pursue a legal action before the WTO on accounting rates,[130] although that has not prevented accounting rate-related issues being argued before the Dispute Settlement Body.[131]

15.4 WORLD TRADE ORGANIZATION

The WTO was established in 1994 as part of the final act embodying the results of the Uruguay Round of multilateral trade negotiations.[132] The function of the World Trade Organization is to facilitate the implementation, administration and operation of certain multilateral trade agreements (Article III(1)). The unique feature of the WTO is the establishment of a dispute settlement body to enforce the obligations accepted by Member States within the context of the agreements.[133] The existence of an enforcement mechanism has been a key factor in pushing the WTO to the forefront of intergovernmental organizations.

For the telecommunications industry, the accelerating process of market liberalization coincided with the GATT Uruguay Round, which commenced in 1986. A key feature of the Uruguay Round was that for the first time trade in services was included within the scope of the multilateral negotiations. With the increasing importance of trade in services, particularly for developed nations, telecommunications was recognized as a critical element both as a facilitator of trade in services, as well as an increasingly tradable service in its own right. Such recognition ensured that telecommunications issues moved towards the top of the agenda for countries such as the US and the UK.

At the conclusion of the 'Uruguay Round' at Marrakesh in 1994, a series of trade agreements were adopted, of which only some are of relevance to the telecommunications sector. The GATT[134] is concerned with trade in goods and, as such, potentially impacts on trade in telecommunications equipment. In 1996, the major developed

---

[130] See WTO Report of the Group on Basic Telecommunications (S/GBT/4), 15 February 1997.
[131] See the Telmex case discussed below at 15.4.4.1.
[132] See the Agreement, Establishing the World Trade Organisation with Understanding on Rules and Procedures Governing the Settlement of Disputes and Trade Policy Review Mechanism (Marrakesh, 15 April 1994; TS 57 (1996) Cm 3277; 33 ILM (1994); OJ L 336/1, 23 December 1994). The Treaties entered into force on 1 January 1995.
[133] See section 15.4.3 below.
[134] TS 56 (1996) Cm 3282; 33 ILM 28 (1994).

nation Member States adopted a further agreement within the context of GATT on 'Information Technology Products', which directly encompasses most forms of tel-ecommunications equipment. The Agreement on Trade-Related Aspects of Intellectual Property (TRIPS)[135] is also of obvious importance to an industry so heavily depend-ent on its investments in research and development.[136] Other agreements which can and have impacted on the sector include the Agreement on Subsides and the Agreement on Government Procurement.[137] However, this section will examine the General Agreement on Trade in Services (GATS)[138] as the primary WTO-agreement establishing a framework for international telecommunications law.

15.4.1 General Agreement on Trade in Services

In terms of the scope of GATS, a 'Services Sectoral Classification List' places 'Com-munications Services' as the second category, which is then subdivided into five sub-sectors: postal services, courier services, telecommunication services, audio-visual services, and other. Category C, 'Telecommunication services', is then further sub-divided into 15 further sub-categories, including 'packet-switched data transmission services' and 'electronic data interchange (EDI)'. However, those 15 services are also distinguished into 'basic' and 'value-added' services:

all telecommunication services, both public and private that involve end-to-end transmission of customer supplier information for which suppliers 'add value' to the customer's informa-tion by enhancing its form or content or by providing for its storage and retrieval.[139]

The nature of telecommunication services mean they can be further distinguished into a number of categories on the basis of geographical scope (i.e. local, long-distance, and international); mode of transmission (i.e. wire and wireless or radio-based); the use and ownership of infrastructure (i.e. facilities-based or resale), and to whom the services are provided (i.e. public or non-public).[140]

The GATS is concerned with four modes of supplying services:

(1) from one territory to another, i.e. cross-border supplies;[141]

(2) the provision to foreign consumers in the service provider's territory, i.e. consumption abroad;

(3) the establishment of a commercial presence in another state; and

[135] TS 10 (1996) Cm 3046; 33 ILM 81 (1994).
[136] See further Chapter 10.
[137] For a complete list of WTO Legal Texts, see generally: <http://www.wto.org/english/docs_e/legal_e/legal_e.htm>.
[138] TS 58 (1996) Cm 3276; 33 I.L.M 44 (1994).
[139] <http://www.wto.org/english/tratop_e/serv_e/telecom_e/telecom_coverage_e.htm#basic>.
[140] Ibid.
[141] This concept was examined in the *Telmex* case at para 7.25 *et seq*.

(4) through the presence of a natural person in another state.[142]

In terms of the telecommunications sector, modes (i) and (iii) are most relevant in terms of business practice.

The GATS contains an annex on telecommunications and, subsequently, a protocol establishing commitments in basic telecommunications. Taken together, these agreements have required Member signatories to substantially open up their telecommunication markets to international competition.

The GATS comprises a number of fundamental 'General Obligations and Disciplines' to which all Members are required to comply from the moment the agreement entered into force (Part II). These general obligations are then supplemented by specific commitments accepted by a Member in a Schedule of commitments appended to the GATS (Part III and IV). Each schedule specifies:

(a) terms, limitations and conditions on market access;
(b) conditions and qualifications on national treatment;
(c) undertakings relating to additional commitments;
(d) where appropriate the time-frame for implementation of such commitments; and
(e) the date of entry into force of such commitments. (Article XX)

These schedules represent a baseline or codification of conditions in a specific national market upon which a foreign service provider can rely. In addition, they constitute the starting-point for future negotiations to further liberalize the sector. A commitment may only be modified or withdrawn by a Member after three years from the date it entered into force (Article XXI).

The best known general obligation upon Members is the Most-Favoured-Nation (MFN) Treatment:

... each Member shall accord immediately and unconditionally to services and service suppliers of any other Member treatment no less favourable than that it accords to like service and service suppliers of any other country. (Article II(1))

However, a Member may specify that this principle shall not be applicable to certain measures listed in an Annex on Article II Exemptions.[143] Such MFN exemptions are subject to review after a five-year period and should not exceed a period of ten years.[144]

There is some debate whether the MFN principle should operate in respect of the international accounting rate regime, since in many non-competitive markets the amount an incumbent operator charges for the termination of international calls will vary significantly between different originating jurisdictions. Member States have an obligation to ensure that any 'monopoly supplier of a service' does not act in a manner inconsistent with either the MFN principle or any of the specific commit-

---

[142] GATS, Art I(2).
[143] GATS, Art II(2).
[144] GATS, Annex on Art II Exemptions, paras 5–7.

ments made by the Member (Art VIII(1)). However, settlement rates are the subject of bilateral contractual agreements between operators, therefore, it is questionable whether such agreements fall within the jurisdiction of the GATS. The MFN principle would seem to be applicable only if accounting rate agreements were considered to be a 'measure by Members', i.e. taken by governments and authorities or by 'non-governmental bodies in the exercise of powers delegated by central, regional or local government or authorities' (Article I(3)(a)). Where an operator falls into the latter definition, it may then be unclear whether a bilateral agreement constitutes the exercise of a delegated power, even if in compliance with an ITU recommendation to which the Member State administration has accepted.

Article VI of the GATS addresses 'domestic regulation'. It requires Members to ensure that any authorization procedures are handled 'within a reasonable period of time' (Article VI(3) and are capable of 'objective and impartial review' by a judicial or administrative body (Article VI(2)). Such commitments are obviously applicable to licensing procedures for the provision of telecommunication services. In addition, there is an on-going commitment to develop disciplines to ensure that 'qualification requirements and procedures, technical standards and licensing requirements do not constitute unnecessary barriers to trade' (Article VI(4)).

Competition law issues are addressed under Part II, 'General Obligations and Disciplines', in Articles VIII 'Monopolies and Exclusive Service Suppliers' and IX 'Business Practices'. Such rules may be used to prevent an abuse of dominant position or restrictive trade practices. These provisions can be seen as being of particularly interest to telecommunication operators trying to provide services into countries whose legal systems have historically had no legal rules addressing general competition issues.[145]

In contrast to the GATT, the principle of 'national treatment' constitutes a specific commitment applicable to particular service sectors and detailed in a Members' Schedule to the GATS:

. . . each Member shall accord to services and service suppliers of any other Member, in respect of all measures affecting the supply of service, treatment no less favourable than that it accords to its own like services and service suppliers.' (Article XVII)[146]

The other key specific commitment under the GATS concerns 'market access' (Article XVI), under which Members detail those service sectors into which service suppliers from other Members may enter.

---

[145] E.g. Asian countries.
[146] See GATT (1947), Art III, 'National Treatment on Internal Taxation and Regulation'.

15.4.2 Telecommunications Annex

At the time of the GATS, Members also adopted a supplementary Annex on Telecommunications. Its objective was to clarify the position of Members 'with respect to measures affecting *access to and use of* public telecommunications transport networks and services' (paragraph 1). The Annex is therefore concerned with the supply of value-added telecommunication services over such public networks and services rather than any right to provide the networks and services. These obligations are incurred, therefore, whether or not the Member has liberalized the provision of basic networks and services.

The Annex imposes obligations of transparency of conditions of access and use, including tariffs, terms and conditions, and specifications of technical interfaces with the public networks and services (paragraph 4). The first draft of the Annex stated that access and use should be on cost-orientated terms, but this was removed in the face of opposition.[147] Access should be 'non-discriminatory', a term which embraces both the MFN and national treatment principles. Service providers should be permitted to attach terminal equipment to the public network; interconnect private circuits and utilize any operating protocols that do not interfere with the availability of the public network (paragraph 5(b)). In terms of restrictions, Members may only impose conditions that are necessary:

- to safeguard the public service responsibilities of the suppliers of public networks, i.e. the universal service obligation;
- to protect the integrity of the network; or
- to comply with a Member's commitments in its Schedule (paragraph 5(e)).

Such conditions may include restrictions on the resale of such services, compliance with any 'type-approval' regime,[148] or licensing and notification obligations. In addition, developing countries may impose conditions 'necessary to strengthen its domestic telecommunications infrastructure and service capacity and to increase its participation in international trade in telecommunications services' (paragraph 5(g)). To assist the growth of telecommunications in developing countries, developed Members are encouraged to make available information and opportunities concerning the transfer of telecommunications technology and training to the least-developed countries.

15.4.3 Fourth Protocol

At the conclusion of the 'Uruguay Round', ministers adopted a decision to enter into further voluntary negotiations on the liberalization of trade in the provision of basic

---

[147] Stated in Zutshi, B, 'GATS: Impact on developing countries and telecom services', p 24, *Transnational Data and Communications Report*, July–August 1994.
[148] See Chapter 5, at 5.4.3.

telecommunication networks and services.[149] Pending the conclusion of these negotiations, Members were granted a MFN exemption for measures affecting the provision of such basic telecommunications.[150] These negotiations, carried out under the auspices of the 'Group on Basic Telecommunications', were scheduled to conclude no later than 30 April 1996. However, by the deadline there had been insufficient offers from Members to enable a conclusion to be reached; therefore negotiations were continued until an agreement was finally reached on 15 February 1997.[151]

This agreement is commonly referred to as the 'Basic Agreement on Telecommunications', although the term is somewhat misleading since the agreement consists primarily of a series of 'Schedules of Specific Commitments and a List of Exemptions from Article II concerning basic telecommunications' submitted by some 69 Members.[152] These commitments supplement or modify any existing submissions made by Members and are annexed to the existing schedules through a device referred to as a Protocol, which becomes an integral part of the GATS (Article XX). As such, these submissions constitute the fourth Protocol to have been entered into by certain Members of the WTO. The Fourth Protocol was intended to enter into force on 1 January 1998; however, further delays meant that it became effective on 5 February 1998.

Supplementary to the Schedules, the Chairman of the Group on Basic Telecommunications issued two explanatory notes clarifying certain issues applicable to the scheduling of commitments. First, a 'basic telecom service' was defined in the following terms:

(a) encompasses local, long distance and international services for public and non-public use;
(b) may be provided on a facilities-basis or by resale; and
(c) may be provided through any means of technology (e.g., cable, wireless, satellites).[153]

Second, any qualifications referring to market access being limited due to the availability of spectrum/frequency were compatible with the GATS and did not need to be specifically noted.[154]

The 'Basic Agreement' has been seen as the most significant development in the global liberalization of the telecommunications market. It has been estimated

---

[149] 33 ILM 144 (1994).

[150] GATS, Annex on Negotiations on Basic Telecommunications.

[151] For a detailed history of the negotiations, see Sherman, L, '"Wildly enthusiastic" about the first multilateral agreement on trade in telecommunications services' (1999) 51(1) *Federal Communications Law Journal* 61–110.

[152] The initial 69 governments have since been joined by 8 further governments. See the WTO Secretariat compilation available at <http://www.wto.org/english/tratop_e/serv_e/recap_e.xls>. The 15 EU Member States submitted one schedule: see Annex to Council Decision (97/838/EC) of 28 November 1997 concerning the conclusion on behalf of the European Community, as regards matters within its competence, of the results of the WTO negotiations on basic telecommunications services; OJ L 347/45, 18 December 1997.

[153] Note by Chairman, S/GBT/W/2/Rev.1, 16 January 1997.

[154] Note by Chairman, S/GBT/W/3, 3 February 1997.

that the Member countries represent over 90 per cent of global revenues in telecommunications.[155] The commitments made by Members encompassed market access, foreign direct investment and, for the majority of Members, adherence to a set of pro-competitive regulatory principles. The Protocol addressed the introduction of competition into the four biggest bottleneck markets within telecommunications: satellite services, international public voice telephony, domestic long distance, and the provision of the local loop.

In respect of the MFN exemptions, a number of countries specified accounting rates as outside the scope the 'Basic Agreement', including India, Pakistan, Sri Lanka, and Turkey. The US maintained a MFN exemption for DTH and DBS satellite services to enable the continuation of existing 'reciprocity' regulations.

15.4.3.1 Reference paper

One unique feature of the Fourth Protocol was the adoption of a 'Reference Paper' by 57 of the 69 Member signatories as an additional commitment incorporated into the Schedules. The Reference Paper comprises a set of definitions and principles on the regulatory framework governing the provision of basic telecommunications.[156] The principles address particular objectives for the establishment of a pro-competitive regulatory regime, rather than the mechanisms or processes for their achievement. As such, the Reference Paper represents an important body of international legal principles for the telecommunications sector, of considerably greater significance than the ITU constitutional principles.[157] In addition, where a Member State has incorporated the Reference Paper into its Schedule of Commitments, the principles are enforceable before the WTO Dispute Settlement Body.

In terms of competition law, the Reference Paper firstly defines two key concepts, 'essential facilities' and 'major supplier':

Essential facilities mean facilities of a public telecommunications transport network or service that

(a) are exclusively or predominantly provided by a single or limited number of suppliers; and

(b) cannot feasibly be economically or technically substituted in order to provide a service.

A major supplier is a supplier which has the ability to materially affect the terms of participation (having regard to price and supply) in the relevant market for basic telecommunications services as a result of:

(a) control over essential facilities; or

(b) use of its position in the market.

---

[155] See Spector, PL, 'The World Trade Organisation Agreement on Telecommunications', pp 217–222, The International Lawyer, vol 32, no 2, Summer 1998.

[156] Council Decision, n 152 above, p 52.

[157] See section 15.3.4 above.

The concept of 'essential facilities' originates in US antitrust law, although it has also been embraced within European Union competition law.[158] The concept of 'major supplier' is similar to the traditional competition concept of dominance, and is similar to the current EU concept of an 'organization with significant market power'.[159] The perspective of the Reference Paper is the supplier's ability to affect access to the market by others, which reflects its international trade origins.

The first two substantive issues addressed in the Reference Paper concern controls to be placed upon the ability of a 'major supplier' to be able to restrict competition. First, a supplier who, alone or with others, constitutes a 'major supplier' must be subject to 'appropriate measures' to prevent anti-competitive practices, whether current or future. Three specific anti-competitive practices are then listed:

- cross-subsidization;
- the use of 'information obtained from competitors with anti-competitive results', such as the forecast traffic volumes in interconnection arrangements; and
- 'not making available to other services suppliers on a timely basis technical information about essential facilities and commercially relevant information which are necessary for them to provide services' (paragraph 1.2)

Second, interconnection with a major supplier should be 'ensured at any technically feasible point in the network'. Such interconnection should be on non-discriminatory terms and conditions, on the basis that such terms and conditions should be no less favourable that that provided for its own 'like services', echoing the 'national treatment' principle under the GATS. The interconnection must be achieved in a timely fashion and on 'cost-oriented rates that are transparent, reasonable, having regard to economic feasibility, and sufficiently unbundled so that the supplier need not pay for network components or facilities that it does not require for the service to be provided'. Interpretation of this critical concept of 'cost-oriented' is already the subject of international dispute. Finally, the request for interconnection may be in respect of points which are not offered to the majority of users.

Building on the Annex on Telecommunications, the procedures and arrangements for interconnection with a major supplier must be transparent, including publication of 'either its interconnection agreements or a reference interconnection offer'. A service supplier must have recourse to an independent domestic body to resolve any disputes that may arise in respect of interconnection.

The other four issues covered in the Reference Paper address broader aspects of a pro-competitive telecommunications market:

- defining a 'universal service obligation' will 'not be regarded as anti-competitive *per se*', provided they are addressed in a transparent and non-discriminatory

---

[158] For US law, see *MCI Communications v AT&T*, 708 F 2d 1081 (7th Cir 1983), 464 US 891 (1983); for EU law, see Case C-7/97 *Oscar Bronner GmbH & Co KG v Mediaprint Zeitungs-und Zeitschriftenverlag GmbH & Co KG and Others* [1998] ECR I-7791.

[159] See further Chapter 5.

manner and are necessary to achieve the universal service defined by the Member State (paragraph 3);

- reflecting Article VI of the GATS, any licensing criteria must be publicly available, as well as 'the terms and conditions of individual licences'; and the reasons for any licence denial must be made known to the applicant (paragraph 4);

- although the need for, and form, of any regulator is not addressed, the Reference Paper imposes an obligation upon a Member State to ensure that any such regulator(s) are 'separate from, and not accountable to, any supplier of basic telecommunications services' (paragraph 5);

- the allocation and use of scarce resources, 'including frequencies, numbers and rights of way', should be carried out in an objective, timely, transparent, and non-discriminatory way (paragraph 6).

Whilst the Reference Paper addresses 'ends' rather than 'means', its influence is likely to be considerable at both a national and international level. First, as part of the Schedules of Commitments, the Reference Paper represents a Member State commitment to which foreign service providers may refer. Second, over time national legislators are likely to reflect and incorporate such principles into domestic law. Third, the Reference Paper represents a baseline from which any future multilateral negotiations will depart.

15.4.4 Status of WTO law

The Reference Paper, as a unique set of international legal principles for the telecommunications sector, is not only pro-competitive, but would also seem sufficiently detailed to constitute possible grounds upon which to instigate legal proceedings in the event that a Member State failed to comply. However, this begs the question of the status of the WTO agreements in the legal order of those some 60 nations that have incorporated it into their Schedule of Commitments. This issue can be further distinguished into two questions:

- whether the WTO agreements, and in particular the Reference Paper, may be used in the interpretation and application of national or regional (e.g. EU) telecommunications regulations; and

- whether the Reference Paper could be used as the basis for initiating proceedings before a court in the event of a conflict with existing regulations, i.e. have direct effect?

Within the European legal order, the Court of Justice has addressed the first issue, that of interpretation, on a number of occasions. In *Commission v Germany (International Dairy Agreement)* [1996] ECR I-3989, it was held that where the Community has entered into an international agreement, the provisions of secondary Community legislation 'must, as far as possible, be interpreted in a manner that is consistent with

those agreements' (paragraph 52). Further, in *Hermès International v FHT Marketing* [1998] ECR I-3603, the Court held that national courts, when interpreting a Community measure that falls within the scope of a WTO agreement, must apply national legislation 'as far as possible, in the light of the wording and purpose' of the agreement (paragraph 28). Therefore, a court should consider the principles contained in the Reference Paper when interpreting the application of European telecommunications laws implemented in national law.

With regard to the second issue, that of direct effect, the final recital in the Community Decision adopting the WTO agreements states:

. . . by its nature, the Agreement establishing the World Trade Organisation, including the Annexes thereto, is not susceptible to being directly invoked in Community or Member State courts.[160]

Despite this, the European Court of Justice has been required to consider the issue of the status of WTO agreements on a number of occasions, most significantly in *Portugal v Council* [1999] ECR I-8395.[161] First, the Court addressed the status of the WTO agreements in the legal order of the Member States, concluding that:

. . . the WTO agreements, interpreted in the light of their subject-matter and purpose, do not determine the appropriate legal means of ensuring that they are applied in good faith in the legal order of the contracting parties. (paragraph 41)

Second, their status within the Community legal order was examined. The Court considered that the WTO agreements were based on the 'principle of negotiation' which distinguished them from other international agreements that were recognized as having direct effect (paragraph 42). The Court also noted that the EC's major trading partners did not give direct effect to the agreements, which would effectively disadvantage the Community in future negotiations. Therefore, the Court concluded that:

the WTO agreements are not in principle among the rules in the light of which the Court is to review the legality of measures adopted by the Community institutions. (paragraph 47)

The Court's reasoning in this case has been heavily criticized for undermining the status of the WTO agreements.[162] However, the Court did confirm its previous jurispru-

---

[160] Final recital in Council Decision 94/800/EC, of 22 December 1994, concerning the conclusion on behalf of the European Community, as regards matters within its competence, of the agreements reached in the Uruguay Round multilateral negotiations (1986-1994) OJ L336/1, 23 December 1994.

[161] See also Case C-93/02 *Biret International v Council* [2006] 1 CMLR 17, where the court confirmed the existing position, but did leave open the possibility of private claims against EU institutions based on EU measures that are found to violate WTO law by the Dispute Settlement Body, a position which had been suggested by Advocate General Alber [2003] ECR 10, at para 24.

[162] See generally Zonnekeyn, G, 'The status of WTO law in the EC legal order' (2000) 34(3) *Journal of World Trade Law* 111–125; and Griller, S, 'Judicial enforceability of WTO law in the European Union: annotation to Case C-149/96, *Portugal v Council*' (2000) 3(3) *Journal of International Economic Law* 441–472.

dence that the GATT rules could have direct effect where either the adoption of the measures implementing obligations assumed within the context of the GATT is at issue; or a Community measure refers expressly to specific provisions of the general agreement (para. 111).[163] In this regard, it is interesting to note that the European Commission's 2002 package of measures in the telecommunications sector, make explicit reference to the commitments made by the Community and its Member States in the context of the Fourth Protocol to the GATS.[164]

In terms of UK law, the general applicability of the WTO agreements is somewhat uncertain due to the lack of clarity as to which aspects of the agreements fall within the competence of the Community, as opposed to the individual Member States. The problems raised by such joint competence were examined inconclusively in a dispute brought by the US against the Community, the UK, and Ireland, in 1997, in respect of the tariff classification of Local Area Network equipment.[165] In terms of the regulation of the provision of telecommunications services and networks, it would seem that the Community has competence in all aspects addressed in the Reference Paper.[166]

In the absence of direct effect, either under European or national law, the only mechanism under which a party could seek enforcement against a Member State for failure to comply with their obligations in respect of the telecommunications sector is through the WTO Dispute Settlement Body.

15.4.5 Dispute resolution

One unique feature of the multinational trade negotiations concluded in 1994 was the establishment of a dispute settlement mechanism applicable to the trade agreements.[167] For the first time, disputes between Member governments about compliance with an international treaty can be submitted to an independent body, the Dispute Settlement Body (DSB), and a defaulting party may be made subject to enforcement procedures.[168] The 'Understanding' encompasses the GATS and therefore is applicable to disputes concerning commitments made in respect of national telecommunications markets.[169]

---

[163] See Case C-280/93 *Germany v Council* [1994] ECR I-4973, paras 103–112.

[164] E.g. Directive 02/21/EC on a common regulatory framework for electronic communications networks and services (OJ L 108/33, 24.4.2002) at Recital 29.

[165] Customs Classification of Certain Computer Equipment, WTO doc. series WT/DS62, WT/DS67 and WT/DS68. See also Heliskoski, J, 'Joint Competence of the European Community and its Member States and the Dispute Settlement Practice of the World Trade Organisation', in *The Cambridge Yearbook of European Legal Studies*, Vol 2, 1999, pp 61–85.

[166] See Opinion 1/94 of the Court of Justice [1994] ECR I-5267.

[167] See generally, Merrills, JG, *International Dispute Settlement* (3rd edn, Cambridge University Press, 1998).

[168] The dispute settlement system under GATT 1947 was essentially a conciliation procedure.

[169] Ibid, at Appendix 1.

Under the agreed procedures, a Member government may request the establishment of a Panel by the Dispute Settlement Body with the following terms of reference:

To examine, in the light of the relevant provisions in (name of the covered agreement/s cited by the parties to the dispute, the matter referred to the DSB by (name of party) in document . . . and to make such findings as will assist the DSB in making recommendations or in giving the rulings provided for in that/those agreement/s. (Article 7.1)

However, it would not seem appropriate to characterize the DSB as a judicial body. The Panel shall comprise three individuals chosen by the DSB secretariat with the consent of the parties. In the absence of agreement, the Director-General may appoint the panellists. After an investigation, the Panel submits a report to the DSB for consideration, detailing the Panel's findings and conclusions. The DSB will usually adopt the panel report unless one of the parties notifies the DSB of its intention to lodge an appeal to the Appellate Body (Article 17). The Panel or Appellate Body will decide whether a particular Member State measure is inconsistent with the terms of the relevant agreement and may recommend ways of overcoming the issue. A Member, against whom a decision has been reached, is obliged to implement the recommendations and rulings of the DSB within a reasonable period of time (Article 21).

In the event that a Member fails to comply, the Understanding allows for the payment of compensation or the suspension of concessions (Article 22). The ability to suspend trade concessions granted to an infringing Member is the real stick within the dispute settlement procedure under the WTO. A complaining party may be able to suspend concessions or obligations not only in the sector of dispute (e.g. telecommunications), but also, where appropriate, in other sectors under the same agreement (e.g. GATS), or even under another covered agreement. Any such concession must be authorized by the DSB and should be 'equivalent to the level of the nullification or impairment' (Article 22.4).

Whilst the WTO dispute procedures are between governments, industry obviously plays an important role in bringing such matters to the attention of governments. Under European law, complaints may be submitted in writing to the Commission and a formal examination procedure may be invoked prior to the decision to pursue a dispute.[170] In the US, the Office of the United States Trade Representative (USTR) is required to annually solicit comments from industry on the implementation of the 'Basic Agreement' pursuant to the Omnibus Trade and Competitiveness Act of 1988.[171]

---

[170] See Council Regulation (EC) No 3286/94 of 22 December 1994 laying down Community procedures in the field of the common commercial policy in order to ensure the exercise of the Community's rights under international trade rules, in particular those established under the auspices of the World Trade Organisation; OJ L 349/71, 31.12.1994.

[171] 19 USC s 1377. A determination that a foreign country is either not in compliance with a telecommunications-related agreement that it has entered into with the US; or denies US companies the market

The dispute settlement procedures have so far been invoked in respect of very few disputes in the telecommunications sector. Formal proceedings before the DSB have been pursued by the European Commission against Korea[172] and Japan in respect of preferential trade practices in favour of US suppliers of telecommunications equipment, both of which were resolved by agreement.[173] Proceedings have also been brought by the US against Belgium, regarding telephone directory services,[174] which was settled. The only case to reach a Dispute Panel and a formal decision was a claim made by the US against Mexico, the so-called 'Telmex case', discussed below.

In the vast majority of situations, however, it is the threat of WTO proceedings that is used as a stick to encourage resolution through negotiations. The US has been particularly willing to issue such threats, such as against Canada, regarding discriminations against US-based carriers transmitting international traffic,[175] and Germany, regarding Deutsche Telekom's failure to meet interconnection obligations and discrimination against foreign carriers for call completion.[176]

Both the European Commission and the US have threatened to take action against Japan over the introduction of the Long-Run Incremental Cost methodology for interconnection rates, as current rates are not considered to meet the 'cost-orientated' principle required under the Reference Paper.[177] Such threats underpinned on-going bilateral negotiations, which reached a successful conclusion in July 2000.[178]

15.4.5.1 Telmex

The *Telmex* case concerned a preferential arrangement between Telmex, the Mexican incumbent, and the US operator Sprint. Other US operators, such as AT&T and MCI, complained to the US government that this arrangement was discriminatory, and therefore in breach of Mexico's commitments under the GATS, the Telecommunications Annex and the Reference Paper. Following the lodging of a formal complaint before the WTO, the Mexican regulator, Cofetel, issued new regulations requiring Telmex to terminate the preferential arrangement and provide non-discriminatory treatment to all foreign long-distance operators. Despite this, the US decided to proceed with

---

opportunities provided for under the agreement, is treated as a violation of a trade agreement under the Trade Act of 1974, s 304(a)(1)(A), 19 USC §2101.

[172] WT/DS40 'Korea—Laws, regulations and practices in the telecommunications procurement sector', 5 May 1996. See also Agreement on telecommunications procurement between the European Community and the Republic of Korea; OJ L 321/32, 22 November 1997.

[173] WT/DS15 'Japan—Measures affecting the purchase of telecommunications equipment', 18 August 1995.

[174] WT/DS80 'Belgium—Measure affecting commercial telephone directory services', 13 May 1997.

[175] See 1998 Annual Report of the President of the United States on the Trade Agreements Program, at 257.

[176] See 'US warns on German telecoms', Financial Times, 12 August 99. See also 1999 Annual Report, at 293.

[177] E.g. 'US uses WTO threat to challenge Japanese pricing' (20 September 1999): <http://www.totaltele.com>.

[178] See USTR Press Release: 'United States and Japan agree on interconnection rates', 18 July 2000.

its request to the DSB for the establishment of a panel, which was duly formed in August 2002. The Panel was required to make determinations on a number of issues, both of fact and law, interpreting the various WTO agreements, as well as broader issues of international telecommunications law.[179]

In terms of findings of fact, the 'relevant market' was disputed, with Mexico arguing that the operation of a traditional accounting rate regime for international calls meant that the 'relevant market' had to be two-way traffic, not just the termination of communications into Mexico, as argued by the US.[180] The Panel accepted US evidence that demand substitution was essential to the market definition process and that an outgoing call was not a substitute for an incoming call.[181] In terms of market power, the Panel concluded that Telmex was a 'major supplier' on the basis of its position under applicable domestic rules, which granted Telmex the right 'to negotiate settlement rates' for the entire Mexican market.[182]

On matters of law, one fundamental issue to be determined was whether conduct of a major supplier could be considered 'anti-competitive' if such conduct was required by law. Surprisingly, the European Commission, as a third party to the proceedings, supported Mexico's position that state rules could not be considered an anti-competitive practice. However, the Panel held that 'a requirement imposed by a Member State under its internal law on a major supplier cannot unilaterally erode its international commitments' made under GATS and related measures.[183]

The Panel concluded that Mexico has failed to meet its commitments under both the Annex on Telecommunications and the Reference Paper. Under the Annex, Mexico had failed to comply with Articles 5(a) and (b) in respect of access to and use of the 'public telecommunications transport networks', on a facilities basis, on reasonable and non-discriminatory terms. Under the Reference Paper, Mexico's obligations to maintain 'appropriate measures' preventing anti-competitive practices (at 1.1) were held to have not been met, as well as its obligations to ensure that Telmex provided interconnection at 'cost-orientated rates' (at 2.2(b)). However, since Mexico had not made commitments for non-facilities based services, it was found not to have violated any of its obligations in respect of such services.

Both sides in the dispute had reason to be unhappy with aspects of the Panel's conclusions, but neither party chose to appeal and, in June 2004, the parties reached an agreement resolving the dispute;[184] with Mexico subsequently amending its resale regulations in August 2005 in full compliance with the DSB's recommendations.

---

[179] See 'Mexico—Measures affecting Telecommunication Services', Report of the Panel, WT/DS204/R, 2 April 2004.

[180] Ibid, at paras 4.151–4.158.

[181] Ibid, at paras 7.149–7.152.

[182] Ibid, at paras 7.153–7.155.

[183] Ibid, at para 7.244.

[184] WT/DS204/7, S/L/162, 2 June 2004.

15.4.6 The Doha round

As already noted, the process of trade liberalization under the WTO regime is an ongoing one, with multinational negotiations attempting to broaden and deepen the commitment of Member States to free trade. The current round of negotiations formally commenced at Doha, Qatar, in November 2001.[185] In parallel with these negotiations, Member States are negotiating and entering into bilateral trade agreements with trading partners, at a level which generally goes beyond that which states are prepared to commit at a multinational level. Telecommunications forms a component of the current round, with the major industrialized countries calling upon other countries to make commitments to fully liberalize and the 'elimination of MFN exemptions for telecommunication services'.[186] Other than such calls for adoption, however, there is little by way of substantive proposals to amend the existing agreements; which is illustrative of how far and successful the current agreements have been in terms of fundamentally changing national and international telecommunications law.

15.5 CONCLUDING REMARKS

The international regulatory regime for the telecommunications industry can be seen to comprise a substantial body of principles, rules, and regulations. At the highest level, the international trade agreements address issues of market access, promoting competition throughout the telecommunications sector. The treaties governing the use of space and the sea determine the obligations of operators, through their respective governments, when utilizing common resources in the provision of telecommunications services.

At the next level down, the ITU continues to represent the primary source of rules and regulations detailing the manner and means by which operators in different jurisdictions cooperate to achieve international telecommunications services. Industry consolidation through global mergers and joint ventures are likely to have minimal impact on the need for such rule making. As such, the ITU is likely to continue to be one of the main international forums for the telecommunications industry.

The process of liberalization has resulted in the demise in importance of the international satellite conventions, which may eventually disappear as instruments of international telecommunications law, though not as operating entities. The rise of

---

[185] WTO Ministerial Declaration, 14 November 2001 (WT/MIN(01)/DEC/1). See also Chapter 17, at 17.4.1 for a discussion of competition policy within the Doha Round.

[186] TN/S/W/50, 'Communications from Australia, Canada, the European Communities, Japan, Hong Kong China, Korea, Norway, Singapore, the Separate Customs Territory of Taiwan, Penghu, Kinmen, and Matsu and the United States', 1 July 2005.

the WTO as *the* forum for telecommunications law over recent years has been very significant. However, over time its role may diminish, as open competitive markets become the international norm. A similar process can be seen within Europe, where the Commission is currently in the process of overhauling the existing regulatory framework to reflect the end of the phase of liberalization, enabling moves towards a less detailed competition-based regulatory regime.

16

TELECOMMUNICATIONS REFORM IN DEVELOPING COUNTRIES

Ann Buckingham, Camilla Bustani, David Satola,[1] and Tim Schwarz[2]

16.1 INTRODUCTION

The past ten years have seen a transformation of the telecommunications sector in the developing world. Governments have established new regulatory regimes and institutions, corporatized and privatized their state-owned telecommunications operations and liberalized markets by issuing licences to new entrants. During the

---

[1] The author is Senior Counsel, the World Bank. The views expressed are those of the author and not necessary those of the World Bank, its Board of Directors, or the countries they represent.

[2] The authors would like to thank Mr Christian W Liedtke, who is currently reading law in Bonn Germany (specializing in intellectual property), for his research contributions to the chapter during a four-week placement at Linklaters.

same period, global telephone subscribers quadrupled from 1 billion to 4 billion (mostly due to the widespread adoption of mobile services), world teledensity increased from 15 per cent to more than 60 per cent, and world mobile penetration reached almost 50 per cent.[3]

The economic downturn that began in 2000 had a substantial impact on the developing world, both changing the competitive landscape and influencing the types of transaction that took place. Despite the downturn, sector reform continued unabated, as many governments continued to pursue aggressive liberalization polices. However, traditional strategic investors (both fixed and mobile) from developed countries largely lost interest in the telecommunications sectors of developing countries, focusing instead on core markets, cutting costs, reducing debt, and rehabilitating credit ratings. Consequently, governments in the developing world found the traditional privatization routes of strategic sale to developed country operators and international initial public offerings (IPOs) increasingly difficult. Where strategic sales were successfully held, the strategic investor was more likely to be an operator from the developing world seeking to develop a regional presence. In some cases, governments resorted to alternative approaches such as local listings, management contracts, and trade sales to private equity funds.

With respect to sector liberalization, during the downturn, developing countries had to work harder to attract investors and new entrants, and consequently focused more on the design of competitive processes and on regulatory refinements to enhance the attractiveness of newly liberalized markets to investors. Bidders in auctions for new entrant licences tended to be operators from emerging markets looking to expand beyond their home markets and capitalize on the often exponential growth in the mobile sector, rather than traditional strategic investors from developed countries.

These changes resulted in the emergence of a new breed of large, dynamic regional operators, particularly in Asia and the Middle East. Post-downturn, strategic investors from the developed world have shown renewed interest in developing markets, particularly as opportunities for growth in their home markets slow, but have increasingly found themselves competing against these new powerful regional operators for a shrinking number of investment opportunities.[4]

The retreat of developed country operators during the downturn and the emergence of these new regional players has caused a geographic shift in investment flows in the global telecommunications sector: instead of the traditional uni-directional

---

[3] ITU World Telecommunication/ICT Indicators Database.

[4] E.g. in December 2007, when a consortium led by Vodafone won the bid for the second mobile licence in Qatar, the six other qualified bidders comprised ACE Consortium (which included Airtel), Argos Consortium (which included Verizon), AT&T Bahrain-based Batelco, UAE-based Etisalat, and Kuwait-based Zain (formerly MTC). See 'Seven Bidders Selected for Qatar's Second Mobile Licence', *Global Insight*, 19 September 2007 and 'Vodafone Consortium Wins Second Qatari Mobile Licence', *Global Insight*, 11 December 2007. Similarly, the three winners of the new fixed-line licences in Saudi Arabia were Bahrain's Batelco, Hong Kong's PCCW, and US firm Verizon Communications ('Saudi Fixed-Line Winners to Receive Licence in July', *Global Insight*, 16 June 2007).

investment flows (primarily from the US and Western Europe to the developing world), investment flows are now regional and multi-directional.

Yet despite the significant changes in global telecommunications markets, the reform agenda in developing countries has remained remarkably constant: establishing a new regulatory authority, enacting a modern regulatory regime, modernizing the incumbent state-owned operators, and attracting new entrants. In addition, those countries that have undertaken reforms have placed increasing emphasis on ensuring that such sector reforms are implemented effectively. and have sought to enhance the effectiveness of national regulatory authorities by investing in capacity-building. Where resources and skills are limited, some countries have sought to achieve efficiencies and higher quality regulation through the creation of multi-sectoral regulators, which pool expertise across multiple industries. Regional initiatives to coordinate regulatory approaches and to share expertise have emerged, which are intended to improve the quality and predictability of decision-making.

Following liberalization and privatization, as the number of market participants grows and the range of services provided multiplies, so too do the number of potential disputes, and their complexity increases. Thus, in the aftermath of liberalization and privatization initiatives, the successful management and resolution of disputes assumes even greater importance.

This chapter will address the following issues:

• characteristics of telecommunications markets pre-reform;

• the impetus for, and objectives in, undertaking sectoral reforms;

• the components of a comprehensive reform package; and

• managing sector disputes in the aftermath of liberalization and privatization.

This chapter deals generally with the impetus for and content of sector reform processes, while the specifics of the design and content of telecommunications regulatory frameworks in developing countries is discussed in Chapter 17.

16.2 CHARACTERISTICS PRE-REFORM

Prior to reform, telecommunications and postal activities in most developing countries are combined and provided by the same parastatal or State-owned entity, operating under a government department or ministry, commonly-known as the PTT ('posts, telegraph, and telecommunications'), usually with no accounting or structural separation between its different activities.[5] Often a single ministry or administrative agency undertakes the simultaneous and indistinct roles of operator, regulator,

---

[5] There were a few exceptions, such as in the Caribbean, where in most of the English-speaking islands Cable & Wireless until the early part of the 21st century enjoyed a private monopoly.

and policy maker, and military and national security agencies often have significant influence.[6] The military sometimes also control large parts of the radio spectrum, some of which may need to be relinquished as part of the liberalization process.

PTTs, pre-reform, generally enjoy monopoly rights of varying scope and duration, covering, at a minimum, fixed voice telephony services and telecommunications infrastructure, but sometimes including all telecommunications services and even internet services.[7]

State-owned incumbents often operate pursuant to a (politically motivated) five-year plan rather than a licence, and enjoy special property rights (such as the use of public property for no, or minimal, payment), special radio spectrum rights, and special customs duties, and tax exemptions. Employees have civil servant status, making internal restructuring difficult; over-staffing and inefficiencies are commonplace. Management of the state-owned incumbent is often unprepared to face the challenges of a commercially driven, competitive environment.

Regulatory controls are usually exercised either on a *de facto* basis by the PTT itself or by the ministry or department responsible for the PTT. As a result, political imperatives often drive sector policy, such as overstaffing state-owned incumbents to reduce unemployment, or causing the incumbent to build out its network in certain regions for strategic political advantage.

Prior to reform, the state-owned monopoly is generally subject to no, or minimal, service obligations, usually resulting in low fixed-line penetration (historically often below 1 per cent in sub-Saharan African countries), little network investment, poor quality of service, long waiting lists for telephone lines, inaccurate and late billing, and a limited range of services.

The tariff structure of the PTT in developing countries pre-reform is typically unbalanced, with revenues generated from high international and long-distance tariffs typically used to subsidize cheap, below-cost installation, line rental, and local call rates, which are often kept low for political and social reasons. However, this model has become untenable even without sector reforms, as voice over Internet protocol (VoIP) and international call-back services (whether or not authorized) have provided *de facto* competitive alternatives to the incumbent's expensive international services. Still, politically captured and inefficiently run incumbents who are unable to meet the most basic communications demands of the population, typically hinder both sector and general economic development.

Perhaps for this reason, examples of pre-reform countries have become increasingly rare. One example is Azerbaijan, where the Ministry of Communications and

---

[6] See, e.g., Smith, Warrick, 'Utility Regulators—Roles and Responsibilities', *Viewpoint Note No 128*, the World Bank (October 1997).

[7] The scope of Cable & Wireless' private monopolies in the Caribbean was also extremely wide, covering in many cases fixed, mobile, data, value-added, Internet, and satellite services as well as infrastructure. In the case of Dominica, Cable & Wireless's monopoly was effectively 'future-proofed' from technological developments, so that any future telecommunications service would automatically fall within its scope.

Technology currently has a triple role as policy-maker, regulator, and investor (owning both the wholly state-owned incumbent and significant stakes in most of the competing operators). The conflicts of interest that this creates have significantly hampered the development of the sector.

16.3 IMPETUS FOR UNDERTAKING REFORM

Although the impetus for reform in the telecommunications sector has evolved over time and varies from country to country, there are a number of common drivers. The impetus to undertake wholesale sector reform does not always originate with national government. Occasionally, it is the result of collective political and economic will at a regional level. Alternatively, it may derive from international pressure. For example, World Trade Organization (WTO) membership may be conditional upon applicants making commitments to sector reform. Similarly, reforms may be required as a condition to receiving access to credit facilities from international financial institutions. Other institutions may simply promote, encourage, or finance sector reforms. In a post-conflict situation, reforms may be instituted by an external agency with interim authority, or may be necessitated by the need to support reconstruction and stabilization efforts. That said, even where the catalyst for sector reform is external, the process is widely regarded as being in a government's own interest given the role of communications services as an engine of wider economic growth.

16.3.1 The role of the World Trade Organization (WTO)[8]

In the past ten years, the WTO has played a pivotal role in furthering telecommunications liberalization and encouraging regulatory reform in developing countries, as membership of this global trading system has required applicants to make liberalization commitments relating (*inter alia*) to the telecommunications sector, and to adopt a set of best-practice regulatory principles.

Telecommunications was put on the WTO's agenda during the 1990s, when it was recognized that the sector has a special status as an engine for economic growth generally, as well as being a distinct sector of economic activity. The WTO conducted a series of negotiations in relation to the liberalization of trade in the telecommunications sector, under the umbrella of the General Agreement on Trade in Services (GATS).

Prior to the mid 1990s, few governments had offered commitments under the GATS to liberalize 'basic' telecommunications (i.e. fixed voice telephony and other core telecommunications services), and in the vast majority of countries these were

---

[8] See further Chapter 15, at 15.4.

subject to long-standing monopolies. In 1998, the Agreement on Basic Telecommunications was annexed to the Fourth Protocol of the GATS to extend previous sector liberalization commitments to 'basic' telecommunications. The Agreement consists of a set of schedules of specific, binding commitments by WTO members to provide market access and national treatment in basic telecommunications. At its inception, 69 countries committed to open their telecommunications markets immediately or by a specified implementation date. Ten years later, more than 100 countries had committed to open some or all telecommunications markets. While in some cases liberalization commitments were made voluntarily (with some existing members offering to improve their existing sector commitments), in some developing countries the nature and scope of commitments was the result of political pressure from developed country WTO Member States, eager to open foreign markets to their own investors and to reduce restrictions on cross-border communications. In some cases, acceding members were given a grace period before being required to open up basic telecommunications services to competition. Cambodia and Nepal, for instance, acceded in 2004 and were each given five years to liberalize basic telecommunication services.[9] New Eastern European/CIS members, such as Moldova, Georgia, Croatia, and the Kyrgyz Republic, were required to make market access commitments that open up basic telecommunications services to competition within two to four years of WTO entry.[10]

In addition to making commitments on market access and national treatment for telecommunications services, Member States were encouraged to adhere to a common set of regulatory principles as part of their telecommunications sector commitments. These principles set out the agreed elements of a telecommunications regulatory framework, covering competition safeguards, interconnection, universal service, licensing, independent regulation, and management of scarce resources, and are set out in the 'Reference Paper' appended to the Agreement on Basic Telecommunications.[11] Most WTO members who have made liberalization commitments have also committed to implementing the Reference Paper, usually by incorporating it in their schedules.

Although simply a high-level statement of principle rather than a detailed 'shopping list' of regulatory provisions, the Reference Paper nonetheless provides guidance

---

[9] Cambodia's and Nepal's schedule of commitments require them to liberalize fixed voice telephony services by January 2009 (WT/ACC/KHM and WT/ACC/NPL). In addition, Nepal's schedule of commitments required Nepal to license a second mobile operator in 2004 and to remove all limitations on the number of mobile operators by January 2009.

[10] Moldova's schedule of commitments entered on 21 December 2001 required the Moldtelecom monopoly to be removed by 31 December 2003 (WT/ACC/MOL). The Republic of Croatia entered commitments on 22 December 2000, which required HT-Croatian Telecommunication's monopoly to be lifted no later than 1 January 2003 (WT/ACC/HRV). Georgia, whose commitments were also entered in December 2000, was permitted one year longer: until 1 January 2004 (WT/ACC/GEO). The Kyrgyz Republic's commitments entered on 22 April 1999 required the monopoly over international and long distance communications to be lifted from 1 January 2003 (WT/ACC/KGZ).

[11] The Reference Paper is available at <http://www.wto.int/english/tratop_e/serv_e/telecom_e/tel23_e.htm>.

to governments around the world (including those who are not currently WTO members) on internationally accepted regulatory practice.

16.3.2 The role of multilateral development institutions

The WTO is not the only multilateral agency that has been involved in shaping the evolution of developing countries' telecommunications sectors. Multilateral development institutions, through their lending and advisory activities, have also played an important role. In this section, we use the term 'multilateral development institution' to cover both international financial institutions (IFIs)[12] and national bilateral aid agencies or programmes providing grant funding for technical assistance and other forms of support. In addition, of course the International Telecommunication Union (ITU), a United Nations specialized agency, has broad responsibility for and impact on telecommunications development.

While each multilateral development institution pursues its own development mandate according to its own constitution or agenda, each can play an important part in providing credibility to a country's reform process. Some institutions (such as the IFC and the EBRD, for example) can play a role in the reform process by making path-breaking investments in a country's telecommunications sector. While the World Bank deals almost exclusively with governments and parastatals, the IFC's activities are almost entirely with private sector entities, or entities in the process of being privatized, mainly in the form of making debt or equity investments in operators (though the IFC also provides transactional advisory services). Some institutions (such as MIGA) can provide comfort to investors by providing guarantee instruments in connection with certain commercial transactions. IFIs may also work alongside each other, such as in Central Asia, where the World Bank, the Asian Development Bank (ADB), the EBRD, and the European Union (through the TACIS programme) are all active.

Apart from making financial investments in and otherwise providing financial support to operators (e.g. through guarantees), multilateral development institutions can also play an important role in sector reform by providing funding for technical assistance in the sector reform process, and increasingly are providing the technical assistance directly to countries on a reimbursable basis. Such assistance can take the form of policy advice, advice on legal and regulatory reform, privatization transactional assistance, engineering services such as frequency monitoring, and capacity building for the newly created regulators in the sector. Multilateral development

---

[12] These include (i) the members of the World Bank Group (International Bank for Reconstruction and Development (IBRD); International Development Association (IDA); International Finance Corporation (IFC); the Multilateral Investment Guarantee Agency (MIGA); and the International Centre for the Settlement of Investment Disputes (ICSID)); (ii) the European Bank for Reconstruction and Development (EBRD); (iii) the European Investment Bank (EIB); (iv) the African Development Bank (AfDB); (v) the Asian Development Bank (ADB); and (vi) the Inter-American Development Bank (IADB). When referred to in this chapter, the World Bank means the IBRD and the IDA.

institutions can play a catalytic role in sector development, by working with governments to create transparent legal and regulatory environments, and to mobilize private capital and management.

The World Bank and other IFIs may also be involved indirectly in sector reform (i.e. other than through providing funding for advisory services) through so-called 'policy-based' lending (similar to what were once known as structural adjustment operations) that incorporates certain conditions or targets involving reform. In such a case, the disbursal of a non-telecommunications loan or a credit (even though geared to achieving macroeconomic objectives) may be made conditional upon, for example, the recipient government introducing market-liberalizing legislation or offering for sale a strategic stake in the incumbent.

The World Bank also co-finances projects with other IFIs, and, as a Bretton Woods sister institution of the WTO, cooperates with the WTO in its areas of competence. In this sense, the World Bank played an instrumental role in providing encouragement and funding (through *info*Dev)[13] to some 20 of the nearly 70 countries that submitted offers on the WTO telecommunications agreement in 1997, assisting them in the preparation of their offers. Since that time, the World Bank has assisted countries in implementing their offers into national legislation. Other examples of cooperation among multilateral institutions in the sector include joint products of the World Bank and the ITU, for example, the updated, on-line ICT Regulation Toolkit and the online database of regulators' decisions.[14]

Other IFIs include the EBRD which, like the IFC, makes investments in operators, but also provides funds for advisory services in the sector reform process, either as stand-alone legal reform projects, or in conjunction with its investment activities. In addition, several countries have their own national aid agencies which have been active in telecommunications sector reform, including the Canadian International Development Agency (CIDA), the Danish International Development Agency (DANIDA), the Swedish International Development Agency (SIDA), the UK Department for International Development (DfID), the US Agency for International Development (USAID), and others. The European Union, through its PHARE and TACIS programmes, has also provided many of the same kinds of support.

Looking ahead, in recognition of market changes, the focus of IFI assistance is being re-oriented from a narrow focus on the traditionally defined telecommunications sector towards a more comprehensive approach reflecting the convergence in

---

[13] *info*Dev is the Information for Development Grant programme, a multi-donor grant programme administered by the World Bank, whose purpose is to promote projects on the use of information and communications technologies for economic and social development, with special emphasis on the needs of the poor in developing countries. More information is available at <http://www.infodev.org>.

[14] The ICT Regulation Toolkit, funded by *info*Dev, is available at <http://icttoolkit.infodev.org/en/index.html>. The Regulators' decisions database can be accessed at: <http://www.ictdec.org/>. It is a multilingual, searchable database of decisions of regulators from around the world. It gives regulators and other decision-makers involved in resolving disputes access to sector 'precedent' from other jurisdictions. Access to such precedent is aimed at facilitating better informed decision-making in resolving disputes and regulatory questions in other jurisdictions.

the telecommunications, broadcasting, and information technology sectors globally, and the challenges posed by the 'digital divide'.

16.3.3 Other multilateral initiatives

The issue of the development of sector regulation (and its impact on wider economic development) has also been the subject of discussions at other global fora, including at the UN's two-phase World Summit on the Information Society (WSIS), which demonstrated a global acknowledgment of the importance of a well-regulated information society to development.

The first phase of WSIS was concluded in December 2003. The second phase was concluded in late 2005, with the issuance of the so-called 'Tunis Commitment' and the 'Tunis Agenda for the Information Society' (Tunis Agenda).[15] Notable among the many statements, declarations, and other provisions of the summit documentation are the following two outcomes: the formation of the Internet Governance Forum (IGF) (under the auspices of the UN Secretary General) and the WSIS Action Line Items that flow from the Tunis Agenda.[16] The IGF—though focusing on the internet—covers many issues traditionally thought of as being in the telecommunications sector. In *de facto* recognition of convergence, issues such as access to communications infrastructure, data security, and the right to receive and impart information—traditionally thought of as telecommunications issues—are now being discussed in the IGF.[17] Similarly, the WSIS Action Line Items, conducted under the auspices of the ITU,[18] include such issues as information infrastructure, access to information, critical infrastructure security, the legal and regulatory enabling framework, and other related issues previously thought of as 'telecommunications' issues.

Certain of the issues addressed in the WSIS context might at first blush appear to be somewhat abstract or theoretical. For example, one of the issues identified at WSIS was the question of access to communications as a constitutional right; a novel argument, yet one which has had real application in the Caribbean for a major global operator (see box below).

Dominica: *Marpin*, telecommunications and constitutional freedoms

In the Organisation of Eastern Caribbean States (OECS), various arguments had been made on whether the Cable & Wireless (C&W) monopolies in the individual countries were unconstitutional.

---

[15] The Tunis Commitment and Tunis Agenda can be found at: <http://www.itu.int/wsis/documents/doc_multi.asp?lang=en&id=2266|0>.

[16] The IGF website can be found at: <http://www.intgovforum.org>.

[17] The 'right to receive and impart information' is inherent in Art 19 of the Universal Declaration of Human Rights.

[18] <http://www.itu.int/wsis/documents/doc_multi.asp?lang=en&id=2266|0>.

In Dominica, C&W had a 25-year telecommunications licence expiring in 2020 containing a broad exclusivity (including national and international telecommunications services). Marpin was granted a licence in 1996 to provide cable TV services and associated telecommunications services. Marpin then decided to provide email and Internet services offering international communications. In early 1996 it was told by the government that it could do this using C&W's network. In early 1997 it entered into an agreement with C&W for access to the Internet via C&W leased lines and using C&W terminating equipment, and for an allotment of 1-800 numbers for customers' Internet access. In March 1998, Marpin gave notice that it was terminating the agreement, and it began to use VSAT to bypass the C&W network for international access. C&W responded by withdrawing the numbers.

Marpin brought an action in the Dominican High Court, claiming that C&W's exclusive licence to provide national and international telecommunications services infringed that country's constitutional guarantee of freedom of communications. Both the High Court and the Court of Appeal found for Marpin, and C&W appealed to the Judicial Committee of the Privy Council, the court of final appeal.[19]

The Privy Council allowed the appeal, but sent it back to local courts on the basis that, while theoretically a monopoly could contravene the constitutional freedom of communications, the question of whether the monopoly was reasonably required to ensure universal access to telecommunications services should be determined by local conditions. Ultimately the 2001 agreement between the five members of the OECS and C&W settled the dispute. Marpin was licensed to provide voice services within Dominica, but its customers were not permitted access to C&W international circuits. Without such a settlement, C&W's monopoly would have remained vulnerable to constitutional challenge in the Dominican courts, which could then have been used as a precedent for similar suits in other OECS countries.

The role that the efficient provision of communications infrastructure and services plays in this regard is also reflected in the Millennium Development Goals (MDGs), a set of development targets developed during the 1990s and adopted by the Member States of the United Nations in 2000, in the form of the Millennium Declaration.[20] Indeed, the MDGs and WSIS put the economic and social imperatives

---

[19] *Marpin*, privy Council Appeal No 15 of 2000.
[20] The MDGs can be found at: <http://www.developmentgoals.org/>. In terms of the MDGs, telecommunications most obviously supports MDG 8, target 18 (working with the private sector to make the benefits of Information and Communication Technology (ICT) available to all). Moreover, a recent analysis of how telecommunications and ICT support all of the MDGs which was presented at the first phase of WSIS can be found at: <http://www.un.org/millenniumgoals/bkgd.shtml>.

front and centre of the reform debate and arguably give the imprimatur of the international community to these objectives.

16.3.4 Conflict and post-conflict rebuilding

In a post-conflict situation, the impetus for reform may come from an external agency exercising interim authority. Such interim occupying or governing authority is likely to place development and reform of the communications sector high on the post-conflict reconstruction agenda, due to the importance of communications in enabling other rebuilding efforts, restoring order, and supporting humanitarian initiatives. In contrast, in countries where conflict is enduring, entrepreneurs and operators may develop market-based or pragmatic solutions to enable communications infrastructure to be built and telephony services to be deployed in the absence of a functioning government or regulatory framework.

While communications is recognized as a vital platform for the restoration of social and economic order and development, large investments are generally required to rebuild or replace network infrastructure destroyed in the conflict. Yet sovereign governments may not yet have been reinstated, and in any event are likely to be financially weak and dependent on donor aid. Private sector investment is therefore generally required to rebuild the sector. Still, striking the balance between profitability, affordability, and the need to swiftly restore communications services nationwide is usually fraught with difficulty.

In some cases, private investors may flock to post-conflict countries, even where a sovereign government and an enabling regulatory environment have not been established. A country emerging from conflict may be seen as a *tabula rasa*, with the potential to rebuild a sector from scratch and to provide high-margin communications services—particularly a country which is perceived to have great potential given its location and demographic. Some such investors may see the opportunity for quick profit, given the unmet need for communications services and lack of competing alternative providers. Others may see a longer-term advantage from being first to market. Usually such investment has centred on wireless technologies, given the ease and lower cost of rolling out wireless networks and the lower security risks entailed.[21] By contrast, private investors have shown little interest in rebuilding fixed networks, given the generally dilapidated and damaged state of existing infrastructure, the high costs of fixed network installation and the lack of enforceable property rights to protect wireline installations.

---

[21] See, e.g. 'Progress Made in Iraq's Wireline Reconnection, But the Future is Wireless', *Global Insight*, 27 February 2004, and 'Sierra Leone: Opportunity Outweighs Risk in Cellular Market', *Global Insight*, 4 August 2002. See also the post-conflict reconstruction in Lebanon, which in the communications sector centred on the award in 1993 of two build-operate-transfer contracts for GSM mobile networks rather than the rebuilding of the fixed network.

For example, in Iraq, an interim occupying authority, the Coalition Provisional Authority (CPA), was put in place following the defeat of the Baa'thist regime in the 2003 Iraq war. The CPA regarded the resuscitation of the communications sector as a high priority: robust communications services were needed to support reconstruction efforts, underpin economic redevelopment, and promote law and order, as well as to provide a tangible benefit to the general public in an attempt to increase popular support for the occupation. The CPA therefore conducted a mobile licence auction within months of the official end of the war. The regulatory environment was far from satisfactory: not only was no governing regulatory framework put in place, but the CPA's authority to grant licences was also in question. Moreover, the auctioned licences were limited to a term of two years, and the CPA emphasized that successful bidders had no guarantee that issued licences would be recognized or upheld following the transfer of power to a sovereign Iraqi government.[22] Despite this fundamental regulatory uncertainty, however, interest in the auction was tremendous, with at least 35 bidder consortia (both regional and international) vying for the three available licences.[23] Their eagerness to participate in the Iraqi telecommunications sector reflected not only the strategic location of Iraq itself (and the perception that there would be foreign interest in the country for years to come), but also the unmet demand among the well-educated and technically literate population. While two years was unlikely to be sufficient time for the successful bidders to recoup their investments, they saw the benefit in being first to market and gambled (correctly) that a future sovereign Iraqi government would recognize and renew their licences on the basis of their performance. Despite tougher than expected operating conditions and extremely high security and other operating costs, being first to market (with an existing subscriber base and network infrastructure) had its rewards, as the Iraqi government duly extended the CPA-issued temporary licences and in 2007 ultimately awarded two of three 15-year nationwide mobile licences to operators that held CPA-issued licences (Zain (formerly MTC-Atheer) and AsiaCell)). The third CPA licensee, Orascom's Iraqna, withdrew from bidding in the 2007 auction, citing the high licence price (US$1.25 billion), and subsequently agreed to sell its existing operations to Zain.[24] Despite the considerable risks, the Iraqi market continues to be regarded as having among the highest growth potential in the Middle East, particularly given the lack of fixed-line infrastructure and the acute need for communications services.

Afghanistan tells a different story. Like Iraq, the existing communications network infrastructure had been largely destroyed, following decades of conflict and under-investment. A mobile licence auction was held by the fledgling new Afghan

---

[22] See, e.g. 'Iraq awards mobile phone licences' 'The CPA Mobile Tender: A Risky Proposition, But One Not to Be Missed', *Global Insight*, 28 October 2003.

[23] 'Regional Bidders Successful in Iraq's Mobile Licence Tender', *Global Insight*, 7 October 2003.

[24] 'Three Iraqi Mobile Licences Awarded to MTC-Atheer, Asiacell and Korek', *Global Insight*, 17 August 2007 and 'Orascom's Nine-Month Profit Up 116%, Sells Iraqna for US $1.2 bil.', *Global Insights*, 3 December 2007.

government less than a year after the ousting of the Taliban, but the auction failed to attract the levels of interest seen in Iraq. Interestingly, the winning bidder consortium was a joint venture between a development aid agency, two foreign operators, and an equipment manufacturer, in an apparent attempt to spread the investment risk.[25] Yet even Afghanistan, which has one of the lowest mobile penetration rates in the region and an ongoing conflict, has seen interest in its mobile sector grow, as opportunities to acquire mobile licences become increasingly scarce globally (a testament to the wave of liberalizations in recent years) and regional operators see home markets become increasingly competitive and reach saturation. Two further GSM licences were auctioned in 2005, which were purchased by Lebanese-owned Investcom and UAE-based Etisalat for US$40 million.[26] To rebuild the fixed network infrastructure, however, the Afghan government has had to rely on financial support from donor countries, including India, Iran, and Russia,[27] as well as the World Bank and the ITU, and consequently investment in the rebuilding of infrastructure has been low.[28]

In Somalia, on the other hand, reconstruction occurred organically without any formal or organized sector reform or reconstruction. There, the state-owned PTT administration collapsed in the early 1990s when the country was plunged into civil war. Today, much of the country remains in the control of rival faction leaders and attempts to re-impose central authority have largely failed. Despite the lack of any regulatory framework or government authorization, more than ten small- to medium-sized telecommunications operators offering a variety of fixed-line, mobile, and internet services using various technologies have been established by local entrepreneurs keen to fulfil unmet demand. However, the continuing conflict has hampered the expansion of telecommunications services in volatile areas where the risks of investment are perceived to be too great.[29]

---

[25] The winning bidder, Roshan (formerly the Telecom Development Company of Afghanistan), was owned by a consortium that includes the Aga Khan Fund for Economic Development, Vivendi (through Monaco Telecom International), MCI and Alcatel. See 'Competition Introduced to Afghan Mobile Market', *Global Insight*, 30 June 2003 and 'Afghans get Second Mobile Phone Network', *Total Tele.com*, 28 July 2003.

[26] See 'Etisalat buys Afghan mobile licence—reports UAE-based company signs 15-year US$40.1m deal for GSM licence', *Total Telecom*, 23 May 2006; 'Investcom, Saudi-US Consortium Win Afghanistan's Two GSM Licences', *Global Insight*, 16 September 2005; and 'Etisalat Awarded Afghan Mobile Licence', *Global Insight*, 24 May 2006.

[27] 'India to Help Rebuild Afghan Telecoms Infrastructure',*Global Insight*, 31 March 2003; 'Iran to Aid Afghanistan in Telecoms Development', *Global Insight*, 9 May 2003.

[28] 'World Bank lends Afghanistan $22m for Telecoms', *Total Tele.com*, 8 October 2003 and 'ITU to provide US$0.5m Funding for Afghanistan', *Total Tele.com*, 6 December 2002. This financial assistance was also intended to cover technical support in designing and implementing a new regulatory framework for the sector.

[29] Bray, J, 'International Companies and Post-Conflict Reconstruction Cross-Sectoral Comparisons', p 19, <http://www-wds.worldbank.org/servlet/WDSContentServer/IW3P/IB/2005/03/30/000012009_20050330161732/Rendered/INDEX/31819.txt>; 'Somalia: Somali Operators Agree to Interconnect Networks', *Global Insight*, 2 November 2005; and 'Telsom Mobile Links Somalia and Somaliland, Awards GSM Contract to Tecore', *Global Insight*, 26 September 2003.

It is perhaps still too early to tell whether the rewards gained by the new operators in each of these countries are sufficient to reflect the levels of investor risk taken. These new players lack the security of market protectionism, and are likely to face significant competition in the short to medium term if retail tariffs are set too high. In stark contrast, in Lebanon, the two mobile operators awarded the build-operate-transfer (BOT) contracts in 1993 following the end of the civil war had a contractual right to an extended mobile duopoly and consequently their initial invest-ment proved highly profitable. See sections 16.7.4 and 16.7.5 below.

Enduring and sustainable development in a post-conflict country is likely to be contingent upon the enactment of a modern regulatory framework to manage the development of competition and to balance the objective of investors to recoup their initial investment with wider economic and social interests. Without such frame-work, sector development may be sub-optimal and *ad hoc* government intervention may be needed to manage operator interaction. A good example is Somalia, where, in the absence of any formal legal framework, operators have formed self-regulatory bodies to coordinate their operations and manage disputes. For example, in 2005, five operators in the self-declared republic of Somaliland in northern Somalia were able to reach agreement on direct interconnection between their networks for the first time, working together under the aegis of the Somaliland Telecom Operators Association. Prior to this agreement, it was not possible for subscribers of one network to make direct calls to a subscriber on another.[30]

Bosnia and Herzegovina: role of the OHR

The Dayton Peace Agreement, which marked the end of the military conflict in the former Yugoslavia in 1995, established the Office of the High Representative (OHR) to act as the primary civilian peace implementation agency in Bosnia and Herzegovina. The High Representative was tasked with overseeing the imple-mentation of the civilian aspects of the Peace Agreement on behalf of the inter-national community, and coordinating the activities of the civilian organizations and agencies operating in Bosnia and Herzegovina. The OHR's mission is defined as 'ensuring that Bosnia and Herzegovina is a peaceful, viable state on course to European integration.'

To this end, among its various activities, the OHR promulgated the BiH Tele-communications Law in 1998, which not only provided a regulatory framework for the BiH telecommunications sector, but also established the regulator (the Communications Regulatory Authority, or CRA). In the first few years of its exis-tence, the CRA was staffed with OHR-appointed international staff members, but during 2003 control of the CRA shifted to BiH nationals, as part of the pro-cess of disengagement from those areas where they have fulfilled their mandate.

---

[30] 'Somalia: Somali Operators Agree to Interconnect Networks', *Global Insight*, 2 November 2005.

Other recent post-conflict countries include Liberia, East Timor, and the Solomon Islands. These countries are all currently involved in various stages of reform processes, attempting to balance the interests of private incumbents with exclusive rights against the benefits of competition (as a driver of sector reform and as a basis for economic development). As reform efforts in these countries are still in progress, it is too early to tell as of this writing what the outcomes will be.

16.3.5 Economic and social pressures

It is widely accepted that an efficient and competitive communications sector is key to enhancing productivity and driving economic growth and development. Moreover, modern communications networks and services are seen as vital to participation in the global economy, to attracting foreign direct investment, and to overcoming the 'digital divide'.[31] For these reasons, even in the absence of external pressures to undertake reforms, many countries have nonetheless chosen to liberalize markets and introduce modern regulatory frameworks.

Examples include Bahrain, the UAE, and Qatar, each of which has in recent years introduced a new regulatory framework, fully liberalized all telecommunications markets, and established a sector regulatory authority. Yet none of these countries made WTO commitments in the telecommunications sector,[32] and none receives credit or financial assistance from IFIs or other multilateral development agencies. Instead, each recognized that sector reforms were required to improve service quality and reliability, to lower communications costs, and to facilitate the growth of the high-tech sector and introduction of new convergent services, in order to maintain a position as a financial hub, and to compete in global markets.

This trend can be compared to the reform effort in the EU in the 1990s: the European Commission similarly recognized that the legal and regulatory environment had a direct impact on sector development, and that the emergence of sophisticated and competitive pan-European services would require community-wide sector reforms.

16.4 GOVERNMENT OBJECTIVES

Whatever the overriding impetus for undertaking a process of sector reform, the reform agenda will reflect the relevant government's own policy objectives, both short- and long-term. Common government objectives are summarized below.

---

[31] Also, see, generally, Kessides, I, *Reforming Infrastructure—Privatisation, Regulation and Competition* (The World Bank, 2004).

[32] Commentators, however, suggest that the UAE's decision to abolish Etisalat's fixed monopoly in 2004 was prompted, at least in part, by an expected review by the WTO of its exemption from telecom deregulation commitments. Country Report: United Arab Emirates', *Global Insight*.

16.4.1 Attracting foreign investment

Governments usually wish to encourage foreign investment in the domestic communications market, typically as investors in (or managers of) the incumbent state-owned telecommunications operator and new entrants. Foreign investors generally bring with them capital, know-how, and technology, and their presence can be pivotal in management and service improvements.

In the mobile sector, the role of regional foreign investors and the level of mergers and acquisitions activity have increased significantly in recent years, resulting in substantial industry consolidation in the developing world. Examples of active regional investors are Etisalat, Orascom, and Zain (formerly MTC) in the Middle East; MTN in sub-Saharan Africa; Hutchison, SingTel, and Telekom Malaysia in Asia; America Móvil in South America; Mobile TeleSystems in Eastern Europe and Central Asia; and Digicel in the Caribbean. Each of these operators has operations or significant investments in more than five countries. Facing increasing competition and market saturation in home (and neighbouring) markets, operators have looked increasingly further afield to capitalize on remaining mobile markets with high growth potential and access a larger customer base. For example, Zain acquired African mobile telecoms giant Celtel in 2005 for US$3.4 billion, thereby adding another 14 countries to its global operations. Similarly, in recent years, both Western and Middle Eastern operators have acquired direct and indirect stakes in operators in fast-growing mobile markets in South and South East Asia.[33] Some, like Millicom, have become global players with mobile operations spanning Africa, Latin America, and Asia.

16.4.2 Building local investment institutions and attracting local investors

Privatization initiatives may involve the flotation of shares in the incumbent state-owned operator on a national stock exchange as a means of encouraging citizens and local financial institutions to invest in equity securities, and of expanding and strengthening local securities markets. Governments can also achieve the same objective by requiring new entrants to list on the national stock exchange. For example, in Saudi Arabia the terms of the auctions for the second mobile licence (won by Etisalat) in 2004[34] and the third mobile licence (won by Zain) in 2007[35] required the newly licensed entity to list a specified percentage of its shares on the national stock

---

[33] See e.g. 'AT&T Eyes Indian Mobile Market', *Global Insight* 28 September 2007, 'Etisalat Mulling Doubling PTCL Stake in Pakistan', *Global Insight*, 10 September 2007, 'Saudi Telecom Strikes US$3.01-bil. Deal with Malaysia's Maxis; Gains Foothold in India, Indonesia', *Global Insight*, 27 June 2007, 'India: Vodafone Wins Control of Hutchison Essar with US$11.1-bil. Bid', *Global Insight*, 12 February 2007.
[34] 'Saudi Arabia: European Operators Lose Out Again in Saudi Mobile Licence Competition', *Global Insight*, 15 July 2004.
[35] 'Saudi Arabia: MTC Kuwait Wins Third Mobile Licence for US$6.1 bil.', *Global Insight*, 26 March 2007.

exchange, with certain shares to be reserved to the Saudi Social Security Fund and the Saudi Pension Fund. In Kuwait's 2007 auction of a third mobile licence, participants were required to bid for a 26 per cent stake in the third operator, with a further 24 per cent stake retained by the government and the remaining shares to be floated on the Kuwaiti stock exchange.[36]

In addition, governments may seek to encourage domestic investors (such as local utilities or entrepreneurs) to invest in new entrants. This was the case in South Africa, where in licensing a second national operator (SNO) in 2005, the government allocated 30 per cent of the shares in the SNO to a consortium of two utility companies, TransTel and Eskom, and required a further 19 per cent stake in the SNO to be issued to a 'Black Empowerment Group' (a consortium of local entrepreneurs) following a tender process.[37]

16.4.3 Generating revenues

Government coffers usually benefit from privatizations and liberalization. Receipts from the sale of a government stake can amount to billions of dollars, and therefore can be used to cover a budget deficit, retire external debt or finance government projects. Between 1990 and 2006, some US$83 billion was raised through privatizations of incumbent telecommunications operators in developing countries.[38]

Licence fees from new licences issued to new entrants by way of auction can also generate substantial revenues, as can radio spectrum fees. In Kuwait, STC (Saudi Telecom) paid US$900 million in the 2007 auction of a 26 per cent stake in the third mobile operator.[39] In the same year, Zain paid over US$6 billion for the third mobile licence in Saudi Arabia.[40]

Lastly, governments can anticipate increased tax revenues, both from the telecommunications sector and from the rest of the economy (which is likely to grow as the telecommunications sector develops).

16.4.4 Increasing penetration and improving quality of service

Governments typically wish to increase penetration of telephone lines and access to communications services, and to improve service quality. Investors or bidders in a privatization or licence auction are frequently required to make commitments regarding network roll-out, service coverage, increases in subscriber lines, and quality of service. Sometimes new licences may be auctioned for a fixed price, thereby focusing

---

[36] 'Kuwait: Tender Document Released by Third Kuwaiti Mobile Operator', *Global Insight*, 25 September 2007.
[37] 'South African Regulator Awards SNO Licence', *Global Insight*, 12 December 2005.
[38] 'Trends in Telecommunication Reform 2007: The Road to Next-Generation Networks (NGN)', (ITU, Geneva, 2007).
[39] 'STC Wins 26% Stake in Kuwait's Third Mobile Operator', *Global Insight*, 27 November 2007.
[40] 'MTC Kuwait Wins Third Mobile Licence for US$6.1 bil.', *Global Insight*, 26 March 2007.

licence 'bids' on commitments to network roll-out, service coverage, and quality of service. In Bahrain, for example, the second mobile licence was offered in 2003 for a fixed sum of BHD100,000 (US$265,000), and consequently bidders were incentivized to submit aggressive bids in respect of network roll-out timetables and quality of service levels in order to secure the offered licence.[41] However, this is rare in auctions for mobile licences, with the return of high sector valuations and fierce competition for increasingly rare opportunities to acquire rights to scarce radio spectrum.

16.4.5 Bridging the 'digital divide'

Access to knowledge and information systems, particularly through the medium of the internet, is increasingly regarded as a fundamental driver for improved productivity and economic growth. Communications transmission networks and technologies form the core of the information infrastructure needed to obtain such access. Participation by developing countries in the burgeoning global 'information-based' economy may be impeded where the national communications infrastructure is inadequate to secure that access, or where the necessary communications services are inefficient, low-quality, or costly. This disparity in access and in the ability to use information services has given rise to an internet-driven phenomenon known as the 'digital divide' between those economies with advanced information technology infrastructure, and those without. The rapid growth in this 'divide' poses significant developmental challenges and opportunity costs for governments in developing countries. In particular, the lack of information technology infrastructure in those countries hinders the introduction of more efficient internet-based mechanisms for the delivery of educational, health, agricultural, and even governmental services, and the dissemination of market information.[42] The desire to help 'bridge' this divide has spurred governments to create facilitating regulatory and investment environments, with special emphasis on infrastructure liberalization, in order to diffuse usage and understanding of the internet and information technologies more widely.[43]

---

[41] The winning bidder, Zain, committed to provide services as at the date of commercial launch with at least 95% population coverage, and to comply with high quality of service levels in respect of service availability and call completion rates. See the terms of the Mobile Telecommunications Licence granted to MTC-Vodafone Bahrain BSC on 22 April 2003, available at <http://www.tra.org.bh>.

[42] See Wellenius, B, 'Telecommunications Reform - How to Succeed', *Viewpoint Note* No 130, the World Bank (October 1997); Braga, CP, 'Inclusion or Exclusion?', *UNESCO Courier* (1998); *Can Africa Claim the 21st Century* (Washington DC, the World Bank, 2000), at 1–2, 4, 137–9. See also Analysis, 'The Networking Revolution and the Developing World', *infoDev*, the World Bank (2000), Box 1, at vii, 18. Indeed, it has been suggested that '[From a developmental perspective] in the emerging knowledge-based economy of the 21st century, information and communications technology will likely assume an importance that dwarfs other types of infrastructure' (ibid, at 153).

[43] See 'Information and Communication Technologies: A World Bank Group Strategy', the World Bank Group (Washington DC, April 2002).

16.4.6 Regional communications hubs

A country with a modern and functioning communications sector in a region still lagging behind can act as a regional hub for transit traffic, resulting in revenues from incoming transit and from directing the traffic onwards to termination points. A healthy communications sector attracts related industries, as well as businesses and industries that rely on communications, including telemedicine, banking, and call centres.

In Sri Lanka, restrictions and the ambiguous exclusivity in international communications services granted to Sri Lanka Telecom Limited arguably denied Sri Lanka the jobs and growth that neighbouring India derived from the business process outsourcing industry in recent years.[44] Since international facilities and services were liberalized in 2003 with the licensing of new External Gateway Operators (EGOs), VSNL Lanka (a new EGO licensee) has been able to offer high-quality connectivity over the SEA-ME-WE submarine cable, which in turn is thought to be a significant contributor to HSBC Bank plc's decision to establish a 1,500-seat call centre in Sri Lanka in 2005.[45]

One more recent example of this dynamic is the acquisition of Maltacom by Tecom and Dubai Investment group for EUR220 million. The Maltese government stated that one of the reasons for selecting the Tecom consortium was its proposed 'Smart City' project, which accompanied its proposed acquisition of Maltacom. Smart City Malta is modelled on the Dubai Internet and Dubai Media Cities and is intended to create a high-tech hub in the Mediterranean.[46]

16.5 CONTENT OF THE REFORM PROCESS

Reform of the telecommunications sector typically comprises a series of interrelated measures, which together are intended to enhance the attractiveness of the sector for new investors, improve the performance of the state-owned incumbent and promote wider economic and social development.

16.5.1 Sector policy statement

Any reform process should begin with the preparation of a statement of government objectives, preferably in the form of a well-articulated sector policy statement.

---

[44] Samarajiva, R, 'Sri Lanka's Telecom Reforms of 2002–2003', *Public Interest Program Unit of the Ministry for Economic Reform, Science and Technology*, Sri Lanka (2004); Dharmawardena, S, 'Sri Lanka's Experience in Interconnection and Liberalisation of International Telecom Segment', *Newsletter Issue 15*, South Asia Forum for Infrastructure Regulation, February 2004.

[45] 'HSBC Opens 31 Mln USD Call Centre in Sri Lanka', <http://www.forbes.com> (12 June 2005).

[46] See <http://www.bi-me.com/main.php?c=34&cg=&id=4042&t=1>; <http://www.telegeography.com/cu/article.php?article_id=12669>; and <http://www.smartcity.ae/malta/index.html>.

This document then helps to promote public discussion and consultation on the proposed changes, helps secure government commitment to reform at the highest level, and provides a 'roadmap' for the reform process moving forward.

Sector policy statements typically cover the social, economic, and even political objectives to be achieved, the liberalization agenda and timetable, desired market structure, the incentives to private (and probably foreign) investment, plans to enhance the reliability and utility of communications services, a redefined role for State participation in the sector, regulatory separation and independence, and the core regulatory principles to underpin sector reforms. Publishing a formal policy statement of this nature both increases the transparency and consistency of policy-making, and facilitates public awareness and investor understanding of the proposed reform process. Moreover, addressing these issues upfront ensures that difficult policy decisions (such as the timing of reforms and market liberalization) are taken early on in the reform process, thereby improving the coordination and sequencing of the different components of reform. That said, in practice, sector policy statements are often vague, unclear, and non-committal.

Some countries use their communications law to spell out in detail their sector policy objectives (e.g. to sell a certain percentage of the incumbent operator or to issue a certain number of national mobile licences). Indeed, in some countries this primary legislation is used to impose an obligation on the government to privatize the incumbent operator or to issue certain licences by a certain date.[47] Many investors welcome this approach because it provides them with greater assurance that the sector policy will in fact be implemented. However, governments rarely like to constrain their discretion, and so it is more common for a country to set out its sector objectives in a legally non-binding government policy statement.

Iraq: limitations of investor reliance on sector policy

An example of a highly uncertain regulatory regime where key investor protections were set out in sector policy statements only is Iraq. In October 2003, prospective bidders in the auction held by the Coalition Provisional Authority (CPA) for three regional mobile licences in Iraq had to factor into their investment decision the fact that the licence would be granted by an interim authority, with no guarantee that the licence would be respected or upheld following the transfer of sovereign power to an Iraqi government. Absolute commitments regarding network roll-out and service quality were required, subject to hefty penalties and forfeiture of a large performance bond if not met, with no exemption where the failure to meet those targets was caused by outbreaks of hostilities,

---

[47] See e.g. the statutory timetable for liberalization and licensing in the 2002 Bahraini Telecommunications Law (<http://www.tra.org.bh/en/pdf/Telecom_Law_final.pdf>), and the 1999 Telecom Act in Mozambique, which required the monopoly over basic telephony services to be lifted five years after the privatization of the incumbent.

terrorist attack, or civil war. In return for accepting those risks, bidders were promised a regional monopoly for a period of at least one year in order to recoup their network investment. However, the tender authorities did not include undertakings regarding the sanctity of the monopoly in the licence. Instead, these were presented as sector policy.

Just six months after those licences were awarded, the CPA gave permission to two mobile operators in the northern region of Iraq (SanaTel and Korek) to continue their existing mobile operations in competition with AsiaCell, the holder of the new CPA-issued licence for the northern region.[48] In the absence of a formal undertaking or commitment not to grant further licences, AsiaCell was left with little or no avenue for legal redress. AsiaCell struggled to fulfil its network coverage obligations under its CPA-issued licence, citing difficulties in accessing areas in the north due to alleged obstructive behaviour from one of these two operators.[49] AsiaCell was unable to prevent SanaTel and Korek, who held licences issued by Kurdish authorities, from continuing their operations, and Korek was ultimately one of the three successful bidders for the 15-year nationwide mobile licences granted by the Iraqi government in 2007.[50]

Where multiple government ministries or agencies have overlapping spheres of authority, care must be taken to avoid the issuance of inconsistent or conflicting policy statements. This commonly occurs where the policies of the telecommunications ministry differ from the policies of a ministry or government agency promoting information technology and e-commerce.[51]

16.5.2 Liberalization

A core component of a sector reform strategy is the liberalization of communications markets, which subjects market participants to the disciplines of product and service competition. In 1999, 73 per cent of basic telecommunications markets remained closed to competition.[52] Today, more than 100 countries have liberalized basic telecommunications services, partly in response to commitments made under

---

[48] 'CPA Awards Second Licence to SanaTel', *Global Insight*, 22 April 2004.
[49] 'AsiaCell Facing Obstruction From Kurdish Mobile Operator in Northern Iraq', *Global Insight*, 4 April 2005 and 'MTC-Vodafone Operations Under Way in Iraqi Capital', *Global Insight*, 4 April 2005.
[50] See n 24.
[51] Compare e.g. Bangladesh's 1998 National Telecommunications Policy issued by the Ministry of Post and Telecommunications, with the 2002 National Information and Communication Technology (ICT) Policy issued by the Ministry of Science and Information & Communication Technology. Similarly, in Sri Lanka, the policies of the Telecommunications Regulatory Commission are not always consistent with those espoused by the Information & Communications Technology Agency through its e-lanka initiative.
[52] 'Trends in Telecommunication Reform 2003: Promoting Universal Access to ICTs' (ITU, Geneva, 2003), at Figure 1.3.

the WTO Agreement on Basic Telecommunications, and many more have liberalized the mobile sector.[53]

In some cases, all markets are liberalized immediately; usually, however, countries adopt a phased approach, whereby the incumbent operator retains a monopoly over so-called basic telecommunications services or international/long-distance fixed voice services, and the corresponding network infrastructure. In a few developing countries such as Ghana and Uganda, a more radical approach was taken to the liberalization of basic telecommunications services, where licences for a second network operator were awarded prior to, or at the same time as, the sale of a strategic stake in the incumbent operator, leaving the latter with no exclusivity period.

Liberalization has had a dramatic impact on sector growth. For instance, in Latin America, the benefits of full competition were evident, with telephone connections growing twice as quickly in Chile (where the government retained the right to issue competing licences at any time) as in Argentina, Mexico, and Venezuela (where incumbents enjoyed monopoly privileges for six to ten years). Chile also enjoyed higher rates of private investment and rural penetration.[54]

In many cases it is important to grant the incumbent a period of adjustment during which it can gradually eliminate cross-subsidies between its services and rebalance its tariffs so that they reflect true cost—but this period should not be allowed to be excessively long. Although it may be difficult to identify the operator's true costs (and so establish the rebalancing level at which tariffs should be set), international benchmarks from competitive markets may provide some guidance. Once competition is introduced, these tariff levels are bound to fall further. The experiences of the past ten years have shown that, while rebalancing initially increases local call prices, consumers have benefited from a dramatic decrease in the price of international, mobile, and internet tariffs. Even in the absence of formal liberalization, the incumbent's ability to continue to cross-subsidize below-cost local call tariffs with very high long-distance and international call tariffs has been significantly eroded in recent years, with the proliferation of VoIP and international call-back services.[55] Even in circumstances where VoIP and international call-back are not authorized, the difficulty in policing those services, combined with the relatively low entry costs and ease of deployment (not to mention low cost relative even to cross-subsidized

[53] ITU World Telecommunication Regulatory Database.

[54] See Wellenius, B, 'Telecommunications Reform—How to Succeed', *Viewpoint Note No 130*, the World Bank (October 1997).

[55] In Argentina, partly thanks to the adoption of a currency board making indexation for inflation illegal, it took the incumbent and the government over six years to resolve the issue of rebalancing. During this period, the price of long-distance calls was up to 50 times the cost, and international calls were four times more expensive than in other countries in Latin America. This stimulated the use of foreign call-back and calling card services, resulting in a fall in Argentina's international telephone revenues of about 25 per cent. See Smith, P and Wellenius, B, 'Mitigating Regulatory Risk in Telecommunications', *Viewpoint Note* No 189, the World Bank (July 1999). Today these pressures on high prices would have been made even worse by the use of VoIP.

services of incumbents), mean that incumbents are experiencing competitive market pressures.

Unlike fixed voice telephony markets, the mobile sector has generally been opened to private sector new entrants immediately, often as a duopoly. In 2006, nearly 90 per cent of countries had competitive cellular markets.[56] Most other market segments (e.g. terminal equipment, data, internet, and value-added networks and services) have been opened up to competition immediately.

While it is true that many developing countries have now taken significant steps towards market liberalization, adopting new sector legislation providing for the introduction of competition and issuing new entrant licences (predominantly mobile licences), full market liberalization often requires more. Often countries that purport to have fully liberalized their telecommunications markets retain regulatory instruments and licences that contain market restrictions, such as prohibitions on new entrants establishing and operating backbone networks, or tight limits on the types of service or network that may be operated. For instance, VoIP services may be prohibited. Regulatory regimes may have a multiplicity of licences, so that a mobile operator may require separate data and value-added-services licences in order to provide mobile content and data services, or a fixed licence to operate its backbone network. The need for separate licences is administratively burdensome even when such licences are freely available on demand, and tantamount to a restricted unliberalized market when the government limits the number of these licences or seeks to preserve the national incumbent's exclusive rights to operate data or backbone services. See Chapter 17, at 17.5.3, for a more detailed discussion of licensing limitations and moves towards 'unified' technology- and platform-neutral licensing regimes.

16.5.3 A new regulatory framework

An effective legal and regulatory framework is essential in order to regulate the sector once state control (through ownership of a monopolist incumbent) is relinquished, and to attract private investment into the communications sector. Typically this framework is introduced through the enactment of new communications legislation, which generally covers the creation of a new regulatory authority, market liberalization, and core regulatory principles. The design of the new framework will have a material impact on sector development: a regime that permits substantial regulatory discretion, government interference, arbitrary decision-making, unilateral licence modification and revocation, or draconian remedies (such as network asset confiscation) entails substantial regulatory risk—and that risk will be priced into investors' investment decisions.[57]

---

[56] 'Trends in Telecommunication Reform 2007: The Road to Next-Generation Networks (NGN)' (ITU, Geneva, 2007), at Figure 1.9.

[57] For a discussion of the design of regulatory frameworks in developing countries, see further, Chapter 17.

In addition, it may also be desirable to make changes to non-communications legislation and the wider legal framework, in order to provide the necessary regulatory security for investors.[58] Existing laws on foreign investment, foreign exchange control, tax, company formation, corporate governance, insolvency, investor protection, competition,[59] intellectual property, broadcasting, data protection, and privacy—or the lack thereof—may have a significant impact on the attractiveness, development, and growth of the communications sector, and in some cases may even conflict with the approach taken in the new communications legislation. Ideally, sector reforms should also be coordinated and undertaken in conjunction with wider economic reforms.

16.5.4 Modernizing the incumbent

A key part of many reform packages will be the modernization of the incumbent state-owned fixed operator. As is discussed further in section 16.7 below, modernization can involve a number of different, sequential reforms. In the (now relatively rare) cases where telecommunications operations still form part of a ministry or government department, the incumbent will need to be restructured as a separate corporate entity. By subjecting the business to company laws of general application, the incumbent operator will have to adopt corporate disciplines and to respect generally applicable accounting principles. By transferring ownership in, or management control of, the incumbent, in whole or in part, to the private sector, the incumbent may experience significant gains in productivity and efficiency, improved access to investment capital, and a marked reduction in political interference in its operations and management strategy.

16.5.5 Attracting new entrants

Liberalization in developing countries is not simply a question of abolishing any existing exclusive rights. New entrants must also be permitted, and sometimes encouraged, to enter the newly liberalized market. However, this process sometimes lags considerably behind the formal 'abolition' of the monopoly.

For example, when Oman acceded to the WTO in 2000, it committed to fully liberalizing mobile markets by January 2003 and voice telephony markets by January 2004.[60] However, a second mobile licence was not awarded until June 2004, and

---

[58] Ibid, at 13–16. See also Smith, P and Wellenius, B, 'Mitigating Regulatory Risk in Telecommunications', *Viewpoint Note* No 189, the World Bank (July 1999).

[59] See Ungerer, H, 'Access Issues under EU Regulation and Anti-trust Law: The Case of Telecommunications and Internet Markets', Incidental Paper, *The Program on Information Resources Policy*, Harvard University and the Center for Information Policy Research (2000) (available at <http://www.pirp.harvard.edu>) for a comprehensive discussion of the increasingly important interplay between sector-specific legislation and general competition legislation in the converging telecommunications and internet markets.

[60] WT/ACC/OMN.

Omantel's fixed-line monopoly in practice remains in place as no competing fixed-line licence has to date been awarded by the Omani regulator—and probably will not be until after the sale of a strategic stake in Omantel has been successfully concluded. In Saudi Arabia, although STC's monopoly over all telecommunications sectors was legally abolished in 2001, it was April 2007 before three new fixed licences were issued, and therefore STC continued to have a *de facto* monopoly for a further six years.

As examined further in section 16.8 below, governments and regulators typically introduce competition by holding a tender process to issue licences. During the downturn, governments in developing countries sometimes needed to go further and actively to encourage investors and foreign operators to enter a newly liberalized communications market. This was in stark contrast to many developed countries; for example, when all telecommunications monopolies were abolished in the European Union at the height of the telecommunications boom in the late 1990s, there was no shortage of investors and foreign operators eager to establish a presence in what were identified as key strategic markets.

16.6 CREATING A REGULATORY AUTHORITY

Central to almost all sector reform efforts has been the creation of an independent regulatory authority, upon which day-to-day regulatory responsibility for the communications sector is conferred. The number of regulatory authorities for the communications sector worldwide has mushroomed from just 14 in 1990 to 148 in 2007.[61] Interestingly, Africa has the highest percentage of countries with regulatory authorities (91 per cent), followed by the Americas (89 per cent) and Europe (80 per cent).[62] However, regulatory authorities differ widely in form, jurisdiction, powers, resources, and degree of autonomy.[63] Indeed, there is no single model of regulator design, and its composition, powers, scope of authority, and institutional form will need to reflect the legal, political, and institutional backdrop of the country concerned.

In this section, we consider the key principles that underpin the design and creation of a regulatory authority.

16.6.1 Position of regulator within government

The first question to be addressed when designing a regulatory authority is its form and position within the executive branch of government. There is no single 'global

---

[61] ITU World Telecommunication Regulatory Database.

[62] 'Trends in Telecommunication Reform 2007: The Road to Next-Generation Networks (NGN)', (ITU, Geneva, 2007).

[63] See e.g. the survey of different regulator models in Northfield, D., 'Global Trends in Communications Regulatory Structures', *Global Regulatory Strategies vol 1 Nos 5–6*, the Yankee Group (September–October 2001).

standard' for the design of regulatory authorities; even in the developed world regulatory models vary widely.

In the US, for instance, the Federal Communications Commission (FCC) is essentially a rule-making body, which is fully independent from the government. By contrast, in the UK, the Office of Communications (Ofcom) is a quasi-independent issue-specific advisory, investigative and enforcement body with strong links to the government. In much of continental Europe, the regulator is located within the relevant ministry, separated only by 'Chinese walls'.

Despite this variety in developed markets, investors into developing countries will prefer the regulatory authority to be as independent as possible from the government, as the risk of political interference or capture is generally higher. Therefore, international regulatory best practice in developing countries is to create a regulatory authority which is entirely separate from the ministry responsible for communications, and which is accountable instead to parliament or a ministry responsible for economic development generally. However, this ideal is rarely attained in practice: regulators in developing countries often include strong ministry representation or the government retains broad political powers of appointment.[64] It is worth noting that the concern with the political independence of regulatory authorities is not, however, limited to developing countries. The European Commission has proposed, as part of its review of the regulatory framework for the sector applicable to the Member States of the European Union, to mandate the political independence of national regulatory authorities (who are currently required only to be independent of regulated industry). In some respects it is surprising that this is not already a requirement in Europe, when it has been considered international best practice in developing countries for many years.

16.6.2 Role of the communications ministry

Typically, regulation of the sector is undertaken by a ministry of communications prior to the creation of the regulatory authority. The legislation creating the new regulatory authority must therefore provide for a transfer of powers and authority from that ministry to the new regulatory authority.

The choice as to which functions should be the responsibility of the minister and which should be the responsibility of the regulator will be a political one, and will vary from one country to the next. Usually, the role of the ministry following the transfer of regulatory powers is limited to the formulation of sector policy, oversight of liberalization and privatization initiatives, and responsibility for any intergovernmental matters arising in relation to the sector. Separating the policy and regulatory functions between the ministry and the regulatory authority allows sector regulation to be implemented in a neutral and impartial manner, whereas government policies

---

[64] See e.g. Mustafa, M, 'Benchmarking Regulators: Making Telecom Regulators More Effective in the Middle East', *Viewpoint No 247*, the World Bank (June 2002).

may be perceived to prefer the interests of one constituency over another (whether consumers or industry).

Where the incumbent is wholly or partly state-owned, it is preferable to transfer responsibility for the state-held shares to a different ministry, such as the ministry responsible for the economy or finance. By separating the policy function from ownership of the incumbent, sector policy is more likely to be formulated in the wider national interest, even where this conflicts with the interests of the incumbent in retaining exclusivity or market power.

Once reform processes (including major privatization or licensing initiatives) are concluded, it is questionable whether a separate ministry to oversee the sector is needed at all: general policy formulation may be better left to a department of a general development or economic ministry to ensure coordination of policy objectives and approaches across different industries and sectors. Proponents of a sector-specific ministry argue that this may dilute the understanding of the peculiarities and specificities of the sector; but the counter-argument is that this detailed sector knowledge is needed primarily by the regulatory authority rather than the ministry.

16.6.3 Independence and autonomy

The key benchmark against which regulatory authorities in developing countries are assessed is their actual and perceived independence from both government and industry. The term 'independence' is to some extent a misnomer; no regulatory authority is truly independent and free of any supervision from the executive, legislative and judicial branches of government. Rather, the concept is used to describe the degree of autonomy the regulatory authority enjoys from political influence and control, and the safeguards in place to protect the authority from political and industry capture.

An independent regulator increases investor confidence in the objectivity and stability of regulatory processes, by providing a measure of comfort that regulatory decisions will be impartial and that all market players (whether state-owned, dominant, or new entrant) will be treated fairly. This is widely believed to encourage greater foreign and domestic investment in the communications sector.

Where independence is lacking, investors in new entrants in particular will be worried that a government, as both owner of the incumbent and its regulator, might discriminate against new entrants, or resolve disputes in favour of the incumbent. The regulatory authority might also implement an interconnection policy that favours the incumbent (e.g. through the use of historic rather than incremental cost-based interconnection tariffs), or fail to ensure equivalent access to numbering and spectrum resources. On the other hand, political capture of regulatory decision making could also result in politically motivated decisions that have a detrimental impact on the incumbent, such as a refusal to allow the incumbent to rebalance artificially low local call tariffs.

The main disadvantage of independence (from the point of view of the government) is the loss by the government and the relevant ministry of some influence over the sector and over regulatory decisions that affect voters (e.g., the ability to keep local call prices of the incumbent below cost in order to appease the electorate).

Where a country has a history of 'independent' regulation, there is no difficulty in conceiving of an entity that is independent of the government and the political process, despite being a government institution. However, in the developing world, one should not take for granted the existence of an environment supportive of the creation of a fully independent regulatory institution. Instead, a degree of independence may be secured through institutional design. In particular, provisions on the appointment, removal, conflicts of interest, and remuneration of individual commissioners, and on the financing and accountability of the regulatory authority, should all be developed with a view to maximizing the regulatory authority's freedom from undue political and industry influence.

16.6.4 Multi-sectoral or sector-specific?

The remit of the new regulatory authority must also be set. By far the most widely adopted approach is to create a regulatory body with responsibility solely for the communications sector. That said, a few countries have established a cross- or multi-sectoral regulator, including Latvia, Costa Rica, Gambia, Jamaica, Niger, and Panama.[65]

Multi-sectoral models are more common in smaller countries, particularly where human and financial resources are scarce. The resultant increased size of the regulatory body enables it to take advantage of economies of scale and scope. Indeed, significant cost-savings may be achieved through sharing both a common pool of legal, regulatory, financial, and economic expertise, and administrative overheads. Multi-sectoral models may also be useful in countries where industries are dominated by a single player; the influence of dominant players on regulation in any given industry may be diminished where the responsible regulatory authority has jurisdiction over multiple industries. Moreover, where the sectors regulated fall within the responsibility of different line ministries, the use of a multi-sectoral model may reduce the risk of political capture. However, it is also possible that sectoral line ministries oppose the concept of a cross-sectoral regulator, and the diversity of their interests could hamper the operation of such a regulator through conflicting government policies.

If a multi-sectoral regulatory model is selected, the first question to be addressed will be what industries to cover, and how to allocate regulatory costs across those industries. On the one hand, a multi-sectoral regulator might be responsible for a range of unrelated utility sectors. A good example is the Public Utilities Commission

---

[65] Kerf, M, and Smith, W, 'Privatizing Africa's Infrastructure: Promise and Challenge', *World Bank Technical Paper No 337* (Washington DC, the World Bank, 1996).

of Latvia (PUC), which has jurisdiction over the telecommunications, postal, railway transportation, gas, and electricity sectors.[66] Similarly, the US has had multi-sector public utility commissions at the state level for many years, which often regulate telecommunications, natural gas, and electric power supply. Arguably, such network industries share significant commonalities. For example, the PUC has introduced a unified price-cap mechanism to control the tariffs of major utility providers in regulated industries.[67] In addition, the spread of jurisdiction across multiple utility sectors could help protect the regulatory authority from capture from large companies within a particular industry. Of course, where there is a determined national industrial policy in favour of a national champion, in whatever the regulated sector, the spreading of jurisdiction across sectors through a multi-sector regulator will have little discernible effect.

Where the industries covered are unrelated, the structural design of the regulatory authority should take into account the need to ensure sufficient technical expertise exists to carry out what are often sophisticated, complex technical functions (such as the resolution of interconnection disputes and radio frequency management). This may be achieved through the establishment of sector-specific departments within the regulatory authority. However, structural separation of individual industry regulators may undermine one of the objectives of having a multi-sectoral approach, namely achieving real cost-savings through pooled resources.

Alternatively, multi-sectoral regulators may have responsibility for related but discrete sectors brought together by the phenomenon of 'convergence'. A leading example is the Malaysian Communications Multimedia Commission (MCMC), created under the Malaysian Communications and Multimedia Commission Act 1998. The MCMC is responsible for regulating the communications, broadcasting, multimedia, e-commerce and postal sectors, and it is also the certification authority for digital signatures. Other examples include Saudi Arabia (where the regulatory authority is responsible for communications and IT) and South Africa (where the regulatory authority is responsible for telecommunications, broadcasting, and postal services).

A 'converged' regulator of this type facilitates the implementation of a truly technology-neutral regulatory framework, avoids any dispute over delineation of regulatory authority in related sectors, and encourages the development of specialist expertise crossing all convergent sectors. Given the quickening pace of convergence, such a regulator may seem better equipped to adapt to the changing regulatory requirements, to regulate the provision of bundled services, and to coordinate regulatory requirements between related sectors.

---

[66] Law on Regulators of Public Services 2001, s 2.
[67] See 'Method for Tariff Setting—Price Cap', <http://www.sprk.gov.lv/index.php?id=605&sadala=133>.

16.6.5 Scope of authority and powers

The legislation creating a regulatory authority should detail its primary objectives, and scope of authority and powers. Typical objectives may include encouraging competition and minimizing barriers to entry, improving sector efficiency and quality of service, protecting consumers, and attracting sector investment. Sector-specific powers include: licensing, interconnection, and network access (in particular, approving model or reference offers, setting the terms of interconnection and access in the event of a dispute, and regulating wholesale tariffs), retail tariff controls, numbering and spectrum management, implementation of universal and rural access strategies, and general market monitoring. General powers will include the rights to acquire and dispose of property and to borrow funds (sometimes subject to governmental approval), and general powers of enforcement.

The regulator should in particular have robust information-gathering powers. These, together with sanctions available to it, will give the regulator teeth as a regulatory body. The type of information-gathering powers granted will depend on the institutional and legal framework of the individual country, although they might be 'benchmarked' to the information-gathering powers of another national organization (such as regulators in other sectors, or the High Court).

In many countries, a plethora of existing regulatory bodies may have jurisdiction over aspects of the communications sector. These include governmental agencies responsible for spectrum management, broadcasting, equipment approval, customs, consumer welfare, and (less commonly) competition. If such existing agencies are not included in consultative processes, and if demarcation lines between spheres of authority are not made clear (with guidelines or processes for inter-working and cooperation, where appropriate), reform initiatives can rapidly become mired in a 'turf war' which can paralyse the wider reform effort.

Sri Lanka: supplanting an existing regulatory authority

The Sri Lankan Telecommunications Regulatory Commission (TRC) was established under the Sri Lankan Telecommunication (Amendment) Act 1996. This agency was the successor body to the Office of the Director General of Telecommunications (ODGT), a department of the Ministry of Telecommunications, and assumed the staff, policies and procedures of the ODGT.

Recognizing the pivotal role of the telecommunication sector in economic development and in supporting initiatives to create employment in new outsourced services and IT-enabled service industries in the early years of the 21st century, the Wickremesinghe government proposed a radical overhaul of the telecommunications regulatory framework, and the creation of a new, independent regulatory authority (the Information and Communications Commission) with responsibility for all electronic communications networks and, potentially, postal services, data protection and e-commerce. It was envisaged that this new,

revamped regulatory authority would operate very differently from the existing authority: with regulatory discretion and intervention kept to a minimum, new staff, processes streamlined, and the emphasis on building the capacity needed to meet all regulatory challenges without the assistance of external consultancies.[68]

Clearly, the abolition of an existing regulatory authority, and its replacement with a new authority to which existing staff and practices are not simply transferred, is likely to become highly politicized and difficult to implement. Indeed, although the legislation to create the new regulator and accompanying regulatory framework was drafted in 2003, the proposed legislation was abandoned following a subsequent change in government.

16.6.6 Composition and appointment

The actual and perceived independence of a regulatory authority will be influenced most heavily by its composition and appointment processes.

The trend in regulator design is for regulatory decisions to be made through a regulatory board or commission as opposed to by a single individual. Use of a commission structure reduces the risk of arbitrary and subjective regulatory decisions being made, although it may also slow down the decision-making process. Prior to 1998, 70 per cent of new telecommunications regulators were headed by a single individual,[69] whereas today most regulatory authorities have a commission structure. In principle, individual commissioners or board members should be appointed on the basis of their professional qualifications rather than political allegiances, by a body other than the line ministry (such as by the country's top executive or by a cross-party Parliamentary committee), and by reference to certain predetermined appointment criteria. In practice, many commissioners or board members are simply political appointees or ministerial representatives, which can greatly reduce the independence and credibility of the regulatory authority. Sometimes government officials will be appointed as commissioners to the regulator as of right on an *ex officio* basis. The risk of resultant political influence can be mitigated, however, by ensuring that such *ex officio* commissioners have reduced voting power, or simply observer status, on the board of the regulator. In addition, *ex officio* commissioners can come from such organizations as the Chamber of Commerce, the Law Society, or a group representing consumer interests.

Where the incumbent has only recently been structurally separated from the ministry, the regulator may in practice be staffed by people who had only recently been employed by the incumbent. This inherent regulatory bias may be to the significant

---

[68] See Samarajiva, R, 'Sri Lanka's Telecom Reforms of 2002–2003', *Public Interest Program Unit of the Ministry of Economic Reform, Science and Technology*, 2004.

[69] 'Trends in Telecommunication Reform 2003: Promoting Universal Access to ICTs' (ITU, Geneva, 2003).

disadvantage of new entrants. The more independent the regulator is from political processes and possible industry capture, the more a prospective new entrant is likely to be attracted to making an investment in the domestic communications market.

As important to the independence of the regulator are the conditions of removal. Again, to enhance the independence of the regulatory process, commissioners should only be removable for cause, with the grounds specified in the enabling legislation and limited to articulated forms of gross misconduct or conflict of interest. Furthermore, the ministry should not have decision-making power over the level of remuneration of individual commissioners, so as to avoid indirect ministerial influence on commission decisions.

Ideally, commissioners' terms should be staggered so as to reduce the influence of any one government over their appointment, and to encourage policy continuity and preserve institutional memory. Full-time members are preferable to part-time members, to ensure that individual commissioners are able to give sufficient time and focus to their regulatory duties. However, staffing difficulties and poor remuneration may render a part-time structure more practicable.

16.6.7 Transparency of decision-making

Investors will be concerned about the transparency of the environment in which they are about to invest. Transparency, predictability, and impartiality of regulatory decision making is enhanced considerably where the regulatory authority adopts an approach of wide public and industry consultation prior to making regulatory decisions, thereby allowing all interested parties to contribute their views and perspectives to the decision-making process, or publishes advance guidelines setting out the regulatory authority's proposed approach.

A good example of a new regulatory authority that has purposefully adopted a culture of transparency and consultation is the Telecommunications Regulatory Authority of Bahrain (TRA).[70] Prior to making material regulatory decisions, the TRA typically publishes a consultation paper on its website and invites industry comment and submissions. On occasion, it has held public workshops or other discussion fora as a means of canvassing industry opinion and building consensus for regulatory change. All significant rules, licences, orders, and regulations are published on its website.

16.6.8 Conflicts of interest

The independence of the regulatory authority can be enhanced by ensuring that individual commissioners or board members have no actual or perceived conflict of interest. This is generally achieved by including conflict of interest provisions in the

---

[70] See <http://www.tra.org.bh>.

law (applicable to both commissioners and their direct families), which bar appointment and authorize removal of commissioners with a clear conflict of interest due to political involvement or material investments or involvement in market participants. To help enforce these provisions, it is common for commissioners to be required to file a statement on conflicts of interest on an annual basis. That said, conflict of interest provisions should not be so broad as to prevent skilled and experienced individuals from being selected. This will be a particularly difficult balance to achieve in a country lacking a pool of experts in the field of telecommunications, and indeed in many cases the initial staff of the regulator and possibly some of its board members will have come directly from the incumbent.

Conflicts may also arise on a day-to-day basis, where an individual matter before the regulatory authority raises a potential conflict of interest with a staff member. In these circumstances, the procedures of the regulatory authority should require affected commissioners and staff members to disclose this conflict and to abstain from any related decision-making.

16.6.9 Financing the regulator

An effective regulatory authority requires sufficient financial resources to support its day-to-day operations. A regulatory authority requires adequate and reasonably assured financing resources to be operationally effective and to invest in training and capacity-building. Independence will be enhanced if the regulator is financially autonomous from the communications ministry and from government budget allocations. Therefore, regulatory authorities are most commonly financed through an industry-wide levy, typically imposed on sector participants through an annual licence fee.

At the same time, efficiency and transparency is fostered by requiring the regulator to prepare formal budgets and audited accounts, which may be filed before parliament or another overseeing authority, and by requiring the regulator to limit industry levies and licence fees to no more than the level needed to finance its budgeted running costs.

16.6.10 Capacity-building

The process of establishing a credible and effective regulatory authority does not end with the enactment of enabling legislation. Regulatory decision-making often requires sophisticated multi-disciplinary skills, and the regulatory authority will need to draw heavily on legal, economic, financial, and technical expertise. In addition, leadership skills may need enhancement. As a result, a critical issue for many developing countries is often the need for capacity building within the newly created regulatory authority.

Often regulatory positions are poorly paid, and staff may have little or no experience of dealing with sophisticated regulatory structures or techniques. New regulatory

authorities may in practice be dependent upon external consultants to provide the necessary high-calibre professional expertise.

From the standpoint of investors in the incumbent, a short-staffed and inexperienced regulatory authority may mean that in practice the incumbent will be able to engage in anti-competitive practices unchecked, thereby helping to ensure its continued market dominance. From the perspective of investors in a new entrant, the inability of the regulatory authority effectively to control the incumbent or to enforce sector regulation may significantly undermine the viability and prospects of their fledgling business.

To help minimize this reliance on external expertise, a programme of training and workshops should be put in place immediately following the regulatory authority's creation, to enable the transfer of any necessary skills and to ensure staff have a full understanding of the issues and techniques involved.

Areas where training is often needed include: institutional development, design of regulatory procedures, training and skills (particularly in relation to interconnection and tariffs), analysing financial and market data, and use of financial models. Workshops or one-on-one sessions run by former regulators from other countries that have themselves undergone reform can be particularly helpful or insightful. Preparation of detailed practice manuals and internal guidelines can also assist new or inexperienced regulators in applying regulatory techniques and rules moving forward. Finally, where regulatory controls are based on cost analysis (e.g. retail and interconnection tariffs), assistance may be required initially—particularly in countries where data is difficult to obtain—to undertake a rigorous quantitative financial and economic analysis and to prepare full cost models for all operators, which can be utilized by the regulatory authority moving forward.

Specialist expertise on particular regulatory functions can be obtained by outsourcing regulatory functions (such as market analysis and financial audits) where appropriate. However, outsourcing may be a luxury an under-funded regulatory authority may be ill able to afford. In some cases, foreign nationals who have worked as regulators in other parts of the world, or who have practised in the field of telecommunications regulation, have been appointed as Commissioners, or even as heads of new regulatory authorities, in order to provide the necessary sector expertise. This is the case in Bahrain, where the regulatory authority is currently headed by a British telecoms consultant, whose deputy comes from the Lithuanian regulator and whose predecessor came from the Greek regulator. Similarly, the new Qatari regulatory authority is currently led by a former Legal and Regulatory Officer at Ireland's Chorus Communication Limited, and until recently Samoa's Office of the Regulator was led by an Australian expatriot.

16.6.11 Maximizing regulatory stability

A well-designed regulatory authority, with strong mechanisms to reinforce its autonomy, is widely believed to reduce regulatory risk. However, it is difficult to

build mechanisms into the regulatory regime to prevent the regulator itself from arbitrarily changing its regulatory approach or adopting inconsistent decisions, particularly where an effective appellate body is lacking.

One approach that has been adopted in some countries, which has the effect of reducing the risk of arbitrary regulatory decision-making, is to adopt a supra-national regional structure or regulatory agenda. The key advantage of a regional initiative is that, by de-nationalizing the process, decisions may be made on more rational and less politicized grounds. The most famous example of a regional structure is of course the European Union, which through its directives and regulations sets the parameters within which Member States regulate the electronic communications sector.[71] However, other regional structures have been adopted in the developing world. Regional fora include initiatives undertaken by REGULATEL (Latin America), ECOWAS (West Africa), and the Organisation of Eastern Caribbean States (OECS). Governments and regulators in the Middle East have also proposed a more coordinated regional approach.[72] Through the MEDA programme, the EU's principal financial instrument for the implementation of the Euro-Mediterranean Partnership between the EU and MEDA beneficiary countries, a selection of Middle Eastern countries[73] benefit from technical assistance, including through cooperation with Europe's European Regulators' Group (ERG), the forum of national regulators from the EU Member States.

The OECS: a regional approach to regulatory reform and liberalization

The Eastern Caribbean Telecommunications Authority (ECTEL), the regulator created by the OECS, was one of the first supra-national, regional telecommunications regulatory bodies created. The original objective of the regional grouping in telecommunications in the OECS was to create a collective critical mass in order to increase bargaining power when negotiating with the incumbent, Cable & Wireless (C&W), which had held exclusive operating rights in the English-speaking Caribbean for 130 years. However, ECTEL still serves an important function at the OECS level.

Regional cooperation
ECTEL was established by Treaty on 4 May 2000, and describes itself as a 'regional telecommunications regulatory advisory body for its Member States.'[74]

---

[71] See further Chapter 5, European Union Communications Law.
[72] See 'Bahrain and Jordan to Co-Operate in Regulatory Development', *Global Insight*, 10 July 2003; 'Saudis Lead Gulf Regulatory Initiative', *Total Tele.com*, 1 November 2002.
[73] Namely, Algeria, Egypt, Jordan, Lebanon, Morocco, Syria, Tunisia, Turkey, and the Palestinian Authority.
[74] See 'Developing a better, competitive telecommunications environment,' ECTEL (available at <http://www.ectel.int/ectelnew-2/Liberalisation_files/Media.pdf>).

ECTEL is responsible for ensuring a harmonized and coordinated approach to telecommunications regulation in the OECS Member States. It makes recommendations to the individual national regulators on regional telecommunications policy, and monitors its implementation. It also works together with these national regulators in relation to the management and regulation of spectrum use. As stated in the preamble to the Treaty, the Member States recognized that 'a harmonised and co-ordinated approach by the Contracting States is required to achieve a liberalised and competitive telecommunications sector'.[75] Such a regional approach creates economies of scale, reducing the regulatory burden on individual Member States (both in terms of cost and personnel), and harnessing technical and regulatory expertise for the benefit of all.

Strength in numbers

By the mid 1990s, most countries around the world were beginning the process of liberalizing their telecommunications sectors, but in some countries in the Caribbean C&W was still being issued with licences conferring on it long monopolies. It was recognized by the countries of the OECS that the regulatory framework in each country was woefully inadequate. Governments held minimal regulatory powers, telecommunications regulation (in licences where they existed, and in any legislation or agreements) was vague, ambiguous, and outdated, and the governments were not benefiting from royalties, licence fees, dividend payments from joint venture arrangements, spectrum fees, customs & excise taxes, and the use of government property.[76] In some cases the lack of regulation meant that C&W was able to charge very high prices for its services, without effective control, and by 1996, the very high cost of access to telecommunications services (including leased lines and bandwidth-intensive data services, as well as international telephony) was found by the OECS to be hindering economic development.

In 1998 the members of the OECS commenced the OECS Telecommunications Reform Project with financial assistance from the World Bank, to introduce competitive reforms in the telecommunications sector (which included the establishment of ECTEL).[77] The OECS countries had already been in negotiations with C&W with a view to reducing the latter's monopoly and putting in place a regulatory regime that would promote economic development and competition, and be consistent with the WTO regulatory framework (even though only three of the OECS States had made any previous commitments to liberalization[78]).

[75] The Treaty establishing ECTEL is available at <http://www.oecs.org/Documents/treaties/ECTEL%20Treaty-2000.pdf>.
[76] OECS Telecommunications Reform Project Information Sheet, available on OECS website, <http://www.oecs.org/proj_telecoms.html>.
[77] See 'UK: Caribbean—Region moves to liberalise telecom sector,' *Global Information Network*, 23 May 2000.
[78] 'UK: C&W challenges Caribbean reform plans', *Communications Week International*, 17 July 2000.

After very difficult and protracted negotiations, the five OECS countries (acting together) and C&W reached an agreement on 7 April 2001 setting out the timetable for liberalization of the telecommunications sector, and the consequent reduction and eventual removal of C&W's monopoly position in those countries.

The West African countries making up ECOWAS looked at the example of the OECS, but have not yet accomplished true regional regulatory reach. However, ECOWAS members have begun focusing on the policy environment, with a view to eventually achieving region-based regulation.

In Latin America, REGULATEL is the grouping of 19 regulators from the region, which is also examining ways of introducing interoperability and harmonization in regulatory approaches in that region.[79] REGULATEL has shown particular interest in the European regulatory framework, and has a relationship with Europe's European Regulators' Group (ERG), through which they are able to access regulatory expertise and draw from the experiences of European regulators.

In the South Pacific, the Pacific Islands Telecommunications Association (PITA) of the Pacific Forum provides a structure similar to that of REGULATEL.[80] PITA is emerging as a regional force as telecommunications markets in the South Pacific become more interdependent (through roaming agreements and potential undersea cable projects linking the islands), and as their markets become more competitive and operators become more sophisticated in their service offerings.

While the field is still quite new, experience is already showing that some features contributing to the success of regional regulation initiatives include the collective political will to formulate regional policy, and the existence of underlying regional institutional structures to implement that policy. In the OECS, for example, the existence of the OECS Secretariat at the political and institutional level allowed the rapid establishment of ECTEL's institutional structure. The governments participating in the telecommunications reform project there also had a clear motivation for pursuing regulation on a regional level: that of building a common negotiating position against C&W. While ECOWAS also enjoys a pre-existing political structure, REGULATEL and PITA, by contrast do not. Moreover, a common motivating force for agreeing a regional approach is less clearly identifiable in both the ECOWAS and REGULATEL examples—and accordingly progress in formalizing true cross-border regulatory harmonization through an international legal mechanism like a treaty is less advanced.

---

[79] The members of REGULATEL are Argentina, Bolivia, Brazil, Colombia, Costa Rica, Cuba, Chile, Ecuador, El Salvador, Guatemala, Honduras, Mexico, Nicaragua, Panama, Paraguay, Peru, Dominican Republic, Uruguay, and Venezuela. See <http://www.regulatel.org>.
[80] For information about PITA see, <http://www.pita.org.fj/>; and for information about the Pacific Islands Forum, see <http://www.forumsec.org.fj/pages.cfm/economic-growth/ict/>.

16.6.12 Role of industry self-regulation

The idea of industry self-regulation is that the market players know best how they should be regulated, and in certain circumstances (particularly where there is no large power disparity between the dominant and other operators) it may be an effective and efficient way for industry to be regulated.

In Malaysia, the Malaysian Communications Multi-Media Commission (MCMC) is expressly required by its enabling legislation to promote and encourage industry self-regulation to the extent possible.[81] Accordingly, it has been promoting self-regulation in the communications and multimedia industry through the establishment of industry self-regulatory bodies. These bodies are made up of industry and consumer representatives, and have the aim of working together to produce voluntary industry codes to guide industry conduct. There are currently four designated industry self-regulatory bodies in Malaysia: the Access Forum, Consumer Forum, Content Forum, and Technical Forum.

An example of the work of one of these bodies is the General Consumer Code of Practice (GCC) for service providers in the communications and multimedia industry, which was drafted by the Communications and Multimedia Consumer Forum of Malaysia after its designation as an industry self-regulatory body. The aim of the GCC is to provide model procedures for reasonably meeting consumer requirements, handling consumer complaints and disputes, creating an inexpensive mediation or alternative dispute resolution process other than the court and procedures for compensation of the consumer in case of a breach of the code, protection of consumer information, and benchmarks for the communications and multimedia service providers for the benefit of consumers. The MCMC registered the Code on 17 October 2003.[82]

Another example where industry self-regulation came to the fore is New Zealand. Prior to the introduction of a sector-specific regulatory regime in 2001, the telecommunications sector in New Zealand was regulated only through generic competition law and the courts. As a result, industry self-regulatory bodies took a more prominent role in an attempt to reach industry-wide agreement on regulatory issues such as number portability and interconnection, thereby increasing sector efficiency and reducing the risk of expensive and time-consuming litigation. Industry bodies included the Telecommunication Numbering Advisory Group, the New Zealand Telecommunications Industry Association, and the Telecommunications Users Association of New Zealand. Experiments with industry self-regulation in New Zealand suggest that four elements are required for an industry body to be effective in resolving sector issues: namely, a majority-based decision-making process (to avoid the incumbent exercising a veto power), full industry membership, focused

---

[81] The MCMC is required 'to encourage and promote self-regulation in the communications and multimedia industry', s 16(g) of the Malaysian Communications and Multimedia Commission Act 1998.

[82] Mohamed, Harme, 'Regulating for Convergence: Malaysia's Perspective', Malaysian Communications and Multimedia Commission, 6 October 2003. See also <http://www.mcmc.gov.my/mcmc/consumer/consumer.asp>.

agenda of issues to be targeted, and a transparent process.[83] In New Zealand, competition authorities were wary of the possibility of anti-competitive collusion occurring within industry groups. Ultimately, the self-regulatory tools failed, and reliance on a generic competition law regime proved insufficient, resulting in the belated establishment of a sector-specific regulatory framework.

16.7 MODERNIZING THE INCUMBENT

In many developing countries, the state-owned incumbent suffers from a history of inefficiency, poor management and under-investment, and is not well placed to meet the challenges of a competitive market. Therefore, a comprehensive strategy for sector reform must include steps to modernize both the management and operations of the incumbent operator.

16.7.1 Regularizing the incumbent's legal status

Pre-reform, state-owned incumbents are typically authorized to provide telecommunications services on the basis of existing communications legislation, concession arrangements, or often simply the state prerogatives related to public administration. Telecommunications licences or authorizations are considered unnecessary. Once communications markets are liberalized, it is vital that the incumbent is not afforded special treatment and permitted to continue to provide services outside the ambit of the general licensing and regulatory framework. Therefore, the new regulatory framework will generally require the incumbent to hold communications licences like any other operator. In practice, the incumbent may be resistant to the new communications licence, particularly where it operated freely without administrative restriction prior to the reforms.

In some countries, the incumbent has been required to pay an initial licence fee upon grant of the new licence. In other countries, the fee has been waived on the basis that the new licence simply formalizes its existing implied or statutory authorization to operate its network and provide telecommunications services. In contrast, where a new mobile licence has been reserved for or allocated to the incumbent, it is more usual (and usually equitable) to charge the incumbent a fee equivalent to that paid by other new entrant mobile operators.

Finally, where there are other existing operators, the incumbent may lack formal interconnection agreements governing its interconnection arrangements. These will need to be put in place in conformity with the interconnection rules in the new regulatory framework.

---

[83] See, 'Telco Forum Hopes to Cut Costs, Delays', *Computerworld*, 20 October 1997.

16.7.2 Corporatization

Where the incumbent is part of a government ministry or department, a critical initial step in the reform process is the 'corporatization' of the incumbent; that is, the transformation of the entity owning and operating the fixed telecommunications network from a government body to a corporate entity, usually incorporated under local company laws.

Corporatization of the incumbent subjects it to corporate disciplines, as the new corporate entity will need to comply with company accounting and reporting requirements. Corporatization also has the effect of separating ownership and management functions, thereby promoting the appointment of professional managers instead of political appointees. This encourages decision making based on the interests of the business, rather than a politically motivated agenda focused on wider social or economic goals. Corporatization may also free the business from public sector borrowing and procurement constraints.

The trend in most developing countries has been to separate the postal and telecommunications commercial activities of the relevant government body. The telecommunications assets and business are then transferred either to a newly formed joint-stock company governed by ordinary company laws, or alternatively to a statutory corporation established under special legislation which can serve as the legal basis for reserving to the state certain rights which may not be available under ordinary company law, and also confer special privileges on the statutory corporation (e.g. exemptions from taxation and from legal liability for deficient performance). The postal activities are generally transferred to a statutory corporation.

In some countries, the legal aspects of separating the telecommunications, postal, and regulatory activities of the operator (including the transfer of assets, and the establishment of new corporate entities and the new regulator) are addressed in the general communications law. However, a number of countries have preferred to address these aspects of the separation in discrete legislation, on the basis that these issues are 'one-off' (i.e. with little continued relevance once the separation has taken place).

The corporatization process can be complex: assets of the telecommunications business will need to be identified and separated from government assets, and the new entity's legal ownership or right to those assets will need to be formalized or verified. Staff will need to be allocated between the new corporate entity and the remaining ministerial or departmental function. This due diligence and verification process then enables an initial balance sheet for the new corporate entity to be prepared.

Where the government plans to privatize the incumbent shortly following its corporatization, the government may also engage in some balance sheet strengthening and organizational changes such as divesting non-core operations, closures, or workforce reductions, in order to make the incumbent more attractive to investors.

Today, most incumbent fixed operators have undergone the corporatization process. An example where this process is yet to be undertaken is Bangladesh, where a

tender was recently issued for consultants to advise on the restructuring of the Bangladesh Telegraph & Telephone Board.

16.7.3 Privatization

The term 'privatization' is generally used to refer to the divestiture of state-owned shares in the incumbent operator to private parties, either through a bilateral share sale or a flotation of shares on a domestic or international stock exchange. Often privatization of the incumbent will occur in staged phases, with tranches of shares sold sequentially by way of strategic or trade sale or IPO—or by a combination or through multiple iterations of the three. In 1991, less than 20 per cent of countries had fully or partly privatized their incumbent telecommunications operator. By 2007, this had risen to more than 60 per cent, with 123 countries having a private or privatized national fixed-line incumbent. While this might sound impressive, this figure includes countries where the government retains a significant or even majority equity stake in the incumbent, and this still leaves about 70 countries with fully state-owned incumbents.[84] Africa, South East Asia, and the Middle East are the regions where full State ownership is most likely to have been retained.[85] Fully private or privatized incumbents tend to be limited to the Americas, with very few exceptions.

Governments may wish to privatize the incumbent for a number of reasons. Most obviously, a privatization will, in the short-term, generate revenue for the government through the sale of its shares in the incumbent to private investors, which may in turn be applied to reduce fiscal deficits and retire external debt. Privatization may also provide much needed budget relief and access to the necessary investment where major network upgrading or development is overdue. Privatization involving sales to foreign investors is also a method of attracting foreign direct investment.

Where revenue generation is at the forefront of the government's objectives, policy makers may be tempted to limit post-privatization competition and protect the privatized company's future revenues (e.g. by conferring a monopoly over core telecommunications services) with a view to maximizing revenues from the sale. However, numerous studies have been undertaken showing that, while the grant of a monopoly may significantly increase the sale price in a privatization, it is likely to substantially decrease investment in network infrastructure and to be economically harmful to consumers.[86]

In the longer term, some forms of privatization may improve the performance and efficiency of the incumbent: the sale of a strategic shareholding to a foreign operator

---

[84] 'Trends in Telecommunication Reform 2007: The Road to Next-Generation Networks (NGN)', (ITU, Geneva, 2007), p 8.
[85] ITU World Telecommunication Regulatory Database. 'Trends in Telecommunication Reform 2003: Promoting Universal Access to ICTs', (ITU, Geneva, 2003).
[86] See e.g. Wallsten, S, 'Telecommunications Privatization in Developing Countries: The Real Effects of Exclusivity Periods', AEI-Brookings Joint Center for Regulatory Studies (2000).

allows the transfer of management expertise and provides access to the capital needed to expand and upgrade network facilities. Corporate governance may be improved by subjecting the company to the monitoring and discipline of profit-oriented investors, and reducing political interference in business planning and management strategies. A foreign listing allows the company to tap international capital markets (and subjects it to capital market disciplines), and enables management compensation to be linked to company performance. Governments may also wish to develop and expand market capitalization of local securities markets, and promote wider investment participation by local citizens and financial institutions, through a listing on the national stock exchange. Indeed, in both developed and developing countries, privatized firms account for a sizeable fraction of total capitalization of national stock markets. However, a lack of liquidity and transparency in the national stock market may limit the attractiveness of a local listing. Finally, governments may wish to reward employees of the incumbent or the wider citizenry through a form of voucher programme (though this technique, widely used in the 1990s by former Soviet-bloc countries, is now widely discredited).

The 1990s were the hey-day of privatizations, with many State-owned incumbents partially or fully privatized, typically through a strategic sale to Western operators.

In a strategic sale, the government sells a minority or majority shareholding in the incumbent operator to a 'strategic investor'. The government typically transfers to the strategic investor a degree of 'management control', such as shareholder voting rights, the right to appoint a majority of the directors on the Board, and the right to control the day-to-day operations of the company in exchange for the technical expertise and experience of the strategic investor. The government may nevertheless wish to retain a right of veto over specified corporate actions, for example through the retention of a government-owned 'golden share' with special veto or voting rights.[87]

Between 2002 and 2004, privatization attempts were more likely than not to be unsuccessful.[88] This was in part due to the global economic downturn, but also to a sharp reduction in appetite for investment in the sector following the collapse in the valuations of telecommunications operators in the developed world, a refocusing of Western operators on home markets rather than risky investments in developing countries, and the perceived over-exposure of financial institutions to telecommunications sector debt. Indeed, of the privatizations that took place between 2005 and 2007, only three involved strategic investors from developed countries (Telefónica of

---

[87] Strategic sale privatizations are usually run as a form of competitive tender. Bidding is typically restricted to investor consortia that meet specified pre-qualification criteria, such as a minimum level of operating experience (or minimum subscriber numbers) and financial worth. Investor consortia may also be required to include domestic investors, and total foreign equity participation may be subject to a cap.

[88] Privatization tenders for strategic investors held during this period were cancelled in Nigeria, Ethiopia, Kenya, Malawi, and Albania due to insufficient interest, failure to meet the reserve price, or inability to pay the bid amount. Similarly, the proposed privatization of Ukrtelecom in the Ukraine was postponed due to unfavourable market conditions. See further, 'Trends in Telecommunication Reform 2003: Promoting Universal Access to ICTs' (ITU, Geneva, 2003).

Spain in Colombia, the US's Terracom in Rwanda, and Telecom Italia in Turkey—albeit in a consortium with Saudi Oger). Instead, where a strategic sale was successfully completed, the strategic investor was more likely to be a developing country operator seeking to establish a regional presence. For example, Maroc Telecom acquired majority stakes in Mauritania's Mauritel in 2001, in Burkina Faso's ONATEL in December 2006, and in Gabon Telecom in February 2007.

The retreat of traditional operator-investors from developed countries during the downturn opened the way for increasing involvement by private equity houses in privatizations in the developing world, which were more likely to assume sector and country risks with a view to acquiring undervalued assets during a downturn. In some cases, but by no means all, the government will insist that these private funds enter into a consortium with an operator in order to ensure the operational experience necessary to provide appropriate quality of service and compliance with build-out and customer service obligations in the licence of the target operator. In addition, these funds on occasion bring in an operator to acquire operations that are not required or desired by the financial investor.

In Israel, the privatization process for the incumbent operator, Bezeq, began in 2001 and was originally intended to be in the form of a strategic sale of a majority stake to a foreign operator. When this proved impossible, due in part to the downturn in the global telecommunications sector and the commencement of the *intifada*, proposals were made to sell the company to domestic investors and banks or through an initial public offering, but these were blocked partly due to security concerns regarding the risk of hostile interests potentially acquiring control of Bezeq in the after-market. Eventually, a 30 per cent stake in Bezeq was sold to a private equity syndicate for almost US$1 billion in 2005.[89]

Bahamas: disadvantages of sales to purely financial investors

The case of the Bahamas provides an interesting example of the importance of technical expertise, even when governments are open to financial investors. There, JP Morgan and Citigroup Venture Capital led a consortium of foreign and local financial investors (known as BahamaTel), which initially won the tender for a 49 per cent stake in BTC (formerly BaTelCo), the national incumbent operator. A few months later, however, the Tenders Commission determined that its business plan was deficient.[90] Notably, BahamaTel was the only bidder consortium that consisted solely of financial investors, on the face of it lacking the necessary technical expertise.

---

[89] 'Bezeq Ownership Transferred to Saban-Apax Consortium', *Global Insight*, 12 October 2005.
[90] 'Govt. drops Bahamatel as BTC bidder', *Business News Americas*, 31 October 2003.

More recently, high commodity prices and trade surpluses have resulted in the emergence of large sovereign wealth funds in the Middle East and East Asia, who have shown increasing interest in the telecommunications sector in the developing world as a means of diversifying and generating high investor returns. Two recent examples of sovereign wealth funds' activities are the 2007 acquisition of the fifth Nigerian mobile licence by Abu Dhabi-based fund Mubadala (in which UAE's Etisalat subsequently acquired a 40 per cent stake) and the 2006 acquisition of Ceske Radiokommunikace by a consortium comprising Al Bateen (another sovereign wealth fund based in Abu Dhabi), Mid-Europa, and Lehman Brothers.[91]

Instead of, or in addition to, a sale to a strategic or financial investor, a government may elect to divest shares in the incumbent through an IPO on either an international or a local stock exchange, sometimes in multiple, staged tranches. These IPOs almost always comprise a secondary offering of the government's own shareholding rather than the issue of new shares (i.e. the sale receipts flow to the government rather than to the company), and include domestic retail offerings and foreign and domestic offerings to institutional investors. The ability of the public to participate in an offering can be an important factor in reducing public opposition to a privatization process.

Between 2000 and 2004, with foreign and institutional investor interest in the communications sector in decline and with telecommunications securities commanding low values on international capital markets, governments increasingly turned to local listings to part-privatize the incumbent. Successful examples include the IPOs of 10 per cent of Jordan Telecommunications Company (in 2002) and 30 per cent of Saudi Telecommunications Company (in 2003), which raised US$90 million and US$4 billion respectively. China Mobile's IPO on the New York Stock Exchange in 2002 raised US$1.4 billion.

Even after the downturn, some countries have preferred a domestic IPO over other forms of privatization, as a means of raising capital and strengthening local securities markets without ceding operational control. For example, in 2005, the Sultanate of Oman sold 30 per cent of the share capital of OmanTel in an offering limited to domestic investors and pension funds on the local Muscat bourse, whereas plans to sell a strategic stake in the company have been repeatedly shelved since 2000.[92]

Speculation on the secondary markets can inflate share prices of a privatized telecommunications operator after an IPO, making a subsequent strategic sale more costly and therefore less likely.[93] In those circumstances, an IPO is more likely to

[91] See <http://www.telegeography.com/cu/article.php?article_id=15546>; and <http://www.altassets.com/news/arc/2006/nz9845.php>.

[92] 'Omantel IPO Closes, Nearly 2.5 Times Oversubscribed', *Global Insight*, 12 July 2005. The government has announced renewed plans to sell a strategic stake in Omantel in late 2008.

[93] See e.g. the experience in Poland: the Polish national operator, Telekomunikacja Polska (TPSA), was first privatized through a public offering of 15% of the shares of TPSA in 1998. Subsequently, the government launched a tender for a strategic investor. Eventually only one bidder emerged, a consortium

occur *after* a strategic sale (allowing the strategic investor first to bring capital and technical/management expertise to improve the company's performance and hence its share price upon flotation).[94] For example, in 2007, a consortium led by France Télécom acquired 51 per cent of Telkom Kenya for US$390 million. Under the terms of the privatization, the consortium is required to subsequently launch an IPO for the sale to the public of 30 per cent of the company (11 per cent deriving from the consortium's shareholding, and 19 per cent from the government's shareholding), which will result in 40 per cent of the company being owned by the strategic investor, 30 per cent by the Kenyan government, and 30 per cent by public shareholders.[95]

In the current environment, strategic sales again hold promise, both for operators from developed countries and for regional operators with healthy balance sheets looking for opportunities for expansion in faster growing markets. In 2007, strategic sale privatizations were successfully completed in Kenya, Rwanda, and Nigeria, with privatizations in Algeria, Ghana, Botswana, and Vietnam continuing or anticipated in 2008. Notably, some of these privatizations are 'repeat' privatizations, where the government had re-nationalized or re-acquired previously privatized stakes, often due to a souring of relations with the strategic investor.

Foreign investor interest appears to remain strong, particularly where the privatization opportunity includes mobile operations. Both Kuwait's Zain and UAE's Etisalat have expressed interest in the Algerian government's proposals to partially privatize Algérie Télécom (which has both fixed and mobile operations) in 2008 for US$2–3 billion,[96] and SingTel, Japan's NTT DoCoMo, Vodafone, France Télécom, and Telenor all anticipated to be bidders in the proposed privatization of Vietnam's second largest mobile operator in 2008.[97]

However, the attractiveness of privatizations of fixed wireline incumbents without a mobile arm is questionable, as fixed wireline businesses are typically seen as being a far less attractive investment opportunity than mobile businesses. This is in part

---

led by France Télécom, which purchased 35% of TPSA's shares for US$4.3 billion, plus an option for an additional 16% of TPSA's shares.

[94] At this stage, the company will be worth more than it was when the strategic investor initially came in, and the government may decide to make an IPO of its shares (or part of its shares) to realize this increase in value. In the privatization of Teléfonos de Mexico (TELMEX), for instance, the Mexican government first sold only 20% of its interest to a strategic investor in 1990, for the price of US$1.8 billion. In 1991 and 1992, it sold another 31% through two IPOs, for the price of US$4.5 billion, representing an appreciation of 70% per share. However, the recent experience in Poland stands in stark contrast to that generally accepted convention of transaction structure and sequencing. The Polish national operator, Telekomunikacja Polska (TPSA), was first privatized through a public offering of 15% of the shares of TPSA in 1998. Subsequently, the government launched a tender for a strategic investor. Eventually only one bidder emerged, a consortium led by France Télécom, which purchased 35% of TPSA's shares for US$4.3 billion, plus an option for an additional 16% of TPSA's shares.

[95] 'Kenya: France Télécom Consortium Wins 51% Stake in Telkom Kenya', *Global Insight*, 16 November 2007.

[96] 'Algérie Télécom to Be Privatised by H1 2008', *Global Insight*, 6 March 2008.

[97] 'No Let Up for Growth in South-East Asian Mobile Markets', *Global Insight*, 26 February 2008.

due to increasing effective substitution of mobile for fixed telephony services,[98] and the erosion of formerly high-profit markets such as long-distance and international telephony due to competition from cheaper VoIP and call-back services. Moreover, in many cases, the incumbent fixed wireline network requires considerable capital investment due to a legacy of under-investment. In contrast, mobile networks are relatively cheap and quick to install, pose fewer security concerns, and have typically experienced far greater growth and profitability. Therefore, increasingly private sector investment has focused on acquiring a mobile licence or existing mobile business rather than investing in fixed incumbents. In some cases, governments have sought to address this bias by permitting the fixed-line incumbent to acquire a mobile licence or mobile division prior to privatization. In Botswana, for example, the Botswana Telecommunications Authority unveiled a new service-neutral licensing regime in the lead-up to the privatization of Botswana Telecommunications Corporation, and granted BTC the first service-neutral licence in 2007, thereby allowing it to provide any service wirelessly.[99] In Kenya, meanwhile, before the privatization of Telkom Kenya in 2007, the government bought back the company's 60 per cent stake in Safaricom, Kenya's mobile operator, thereby allowing Telkom Kenya to undertake needed restructuring and to establish its own (wholly owned) mobile division to compete directly in the mobile sector.[100]

16.7.4 Management contracts

Instead of divesting state assets, governments may engage foreign operators to take over the management of a state-owned operator for a specified period by way of a management contract.

Management contracts were, until recently, relatively rare. The mechanism was used primarily where there was political opposition to divestment: it allowed the government to retain full ownership of the incumbent, while importing management expertise. Management contracts with major capital expenditure obligations (but without an equity investment) had been in awarded in the 1990s in Thailand, Indonesia, the Lao People's Democratic Republic, Yemen, and the Ukraine.

---

[98] According to the ITU, in 1993 global telecommunications traffic consisted predominantly of calls between fixed networks (fixed-to-fixed traffic). According to ITU statistics, 87.9% of global calls were fixed-to-fixed, with only 10.3% of calls involving mobile networks, and approximately half of those involving calls between fixed and mobile networks. In other words, approximately 95% of global telecommunications traffic either originated or terminated on a fixed network in 1993. By 2003, over 75% of global traffic involved mobile networks, and less than 75% originates and/or terminates on a fixed network. See <http://www.itu.int/interconnect>. Developing countries around the world have felt the impact of this trend, with fixed-rate penetration stagnating or even falling, and mobile penetration rising dramatically. In India, for example, the number of mobile subscribers is expected to exceed the number of fixed subscribers in 2004.

[99] 'Botswana: BTC Awarded New Operating Licence', *Global Insight*, 26 March 2007.

[100] 'Kenya: France Télécom Consortium Wins 51% Stake in Telkom Kenya', *Global Insight*, 16 November 2007.

Management contracts without investment commitments were even more uncommon; examples include Kiribati and Mongolia.[101]

Management contracts, however, have recently become more prominent, and are now viewed as useful alternative tools where privatization is not a feasible option (e.g. due to lack of investor interest or poor market conditions), enabling the incumbent to reap the benefits of foreign management expertise and international facilities.[102] Moreover, a management contract can be combined with an IPO to obtain the benefits of a strategic sale (access to capital and management expertise) without the permanent loss of management control.[103]

Nigeria: combined management contract and local IPO

In Nigeria, the government attempted to privatize the incumbent, Nigerian Telecommunications Limited (NITEL) in 2001, through the sale of a 51 per cent stake for US$1.317 billion to a consortium (Investors International Limited, or IIL) that included Portugal Telecom and KPN. When IIL failed to pay the agreed purchase price by the March 2002 deadline, and the reserve bidder withdrew, the government cancelled the strategic sale privatization. Instead, it elected to adopt a combined management contract/IPO strategy.

The government duly launched a management tender, and in March 2003 awarded Pentascope International (a Dutch consultancy) a three-year management contract intended to enhance the value of NITEL. The contract required Pentascope to oversee the modernization of NITEL, and included stringent network roll-out and performance targets.

The government finally privatized NITEL in its fourth attempt in 2006 through the sale of a 51 per cent stake to a local consortium, Transcorp, which partnered with British Telecommunications to provide technical services[104] However, at the time of writing, the government and Transcorp had announced their intention to conduct a bidding process for the joint sale of a 51 per cent

---

[101] Izaguirre, Ada Karina 'Private Participation in Telecommunications—Recent Trends', *Viewpoint Note* No 204, the World Bank (December 1999).

[102] A good example is the management contract awarded to France Télécom in 2003 for the management of Teleyemen: the management contract will enable Teleyemen to access France Télécom's capacity on the SEA-WE-ME3 submarine cable system and to France Télécom's international satellite connectivity services.

[103] Management contracts are also increasingly appearing as purely private sector transactions. A telecommunications operator (whether an incumbent or a new entrant) may contract with an international operator with greater operating expertise to provide temporary management services. This may be in order to secure international expertise and the right to use an internationally recognized brand, without requiring the international operator to assume the risk or capital requirements of an equity stake in the venture. In the case of prospective new entrants, a management contract may be needed to meet the pre-qualification criteria where these include a substantial level of operating expertise (for example, measured in relation to the number of operating licences held or total subscriber numbers).

[104] 'Nigeria: Transcorp Takes Formal Ownership of NITEL', *Global Insight*, 15 November 2006.

stake in the company in an effort to secure a new core strategic investor, leaving each with a holding of approximately 25 per cent. The government indicated it intended to subsequently sell its remaining shares in a listing on the Nigerian Stock Exchange.[105]

As managers under a management contract do not take any investment risk, management contracts need to be carefully designed in order to ensure that public policy objectives are respected and realized and that the manager is given incentives for good performance and is subject to penalties for sub-standard performance. Moreover, the balance of decision-making power between the government and the manager, and the power of the government to terminate the management arrangements, need to be carefully worked out.

Lebanon: management contracts as interim 'bridge'

In Lebanon, management contracts have been used as a 'stop gap' measure pending full privatization. The two GSM mobile networks in Lebanon were built and operated under BOT contracts (see below, section 16.7.5). When these contracts were terminated, the mobile assets vested in the Republic of Lebanon. Interim management contracts were put in place with the BOT operators to provide for the continued management of the networks pending their 're-privatization'.

In 2001, the government engaged an investment bank to conduct an auction for the sale of the two networks and associated mobile licences. Following political resistance to an outright sale and concerns about relinquishing the mobile sector completely to private sector control, the Council of Ministers in 2002 decreed that a second tender for two three-year management contracts should be grafted on to the auction process, as an alternative bidder 'option'. In the end, after considerable delays and rule changes, when the first round of the auction and tender was held in January 2004, only two bidders submitted qualifying bids. These bidders coincidentally happened to be the investors in the former BOT operators, and were linked to members of the government. Amid claims of political interference in the outcome and a general public outcry, the auction and tender process was aborted; instead, in February 2004, the government ran a new international tender (excluding the two previous bidders) to manage the two networks.[106] Management contracts were duly awarded to Detecon and the Mobile Telecommunications Company of Kuwait in April 2004,

---

[105] 'Nigeria: Government and Transcorp Plan to Sell Stake in NITEL', *Global Insight*, 13 February 2008.
[106] 'Qordahi Gets Green Light to Re-Start Mobile Tender', *The Daily Star* (Beirut, 4 February 2004).

in an attempt to introduce impartial, foreign management expertise for an interim period, following which the government would hold a new, fairer auction of the two mobile businesses. In 2007, the Lebanese government announced its intention to auction both mobile networks in 2008, with bidders eligible to buy up to two-thirds of the new mobile operators, with the remaining third to remain with the government for a subsequent listing on the Beirut Stock Exchange.[107] However, the proposed auction was subsequently shelved due to political tensions in the country, and instead the two mobile networks continue to be operated pursuant to these management contracts.

16.7.5 BOTs, BOOs, and BTOs

A 'build-operate-transfer' (BOT) contract is a form of concession or commercial agreement between private investors and a state. Under a BOT contract, an investor (or a consortium of investors) will be granted the rights to build a telecommunications network and to operate it pursuant to the terms of the concession, usually sharing a portion of the revenues with the state. At the end of the concession term, network assets are transferred back to the state. This arrangement allows private sector participation where a state wishes or is required by law to retain infrastructure ownership, and has been used in India, Lebanon, and, in a slightly different form, in Indonesia.[108] Rare examples of an ongoing BOT-type arrangement are the two mobile networks in Syria (MTN and SyriaTel), which commenced operations in 2001 and operate under 15-year BOT concessions from the incumbent state-owned fixed-line operator, Syrian Telecommunications Establishment, and the concession granted to Timor Telecom (owned by Portugal Telecom) in East Timor.[109] Under the Syrian concessions, STE is entitled to a share of billed gross revenues.[110]

It was thought that a BOT-type arrangement encouraged investment by reducing investor risk: the investor's 'exit strategy' is guaranteed at the date of expiry or termination of the BOT. However, in practice, BOTs used in the communications sector can be much more problematic than BOTs used in other infrastructure projects (such as toll roads and power plants), and the investor's exit can be exceedingly complex, acrimonious, and protracted.

---

[107] <http://www.lebanonmobileauction.com>; 'Etisalat To Bid In $6.8B Lebanon Tel Sale Amid Election Doubt', *Dow Jones Newswires*, 24 December 2007 and 'Qtel To Bid In $6.8B Lebanon Tel License Sale', *Dow Jones Newswires*, 26 December 2007.

[108] 'Trends in Telecommunications Reform: Convergence and Regulation 1999' (Geneva, ITU, 1999), at p 45.

[109] Bray, J, 'International Companies and Post-Conflict Reconstruction Cross-Sectoral Comparisons', p19, <http://www-wds.worldbank.org/servlet/WDSContentServer/IW3P/IB/2005/03/30/000012009_20050330161732/Rendered/INDEX/31819.txt>.

[110] 'Zain Considers Acquisition of MTN Syria', *Global Insight*, 16 December 2007 and 'Syria: Two New GSM Networks Activated', *Global Insight*, 26 April 2001.

This is because, at the end of the BOT contract, it is not just the physical network infrastructure that needs to vest in the state: without complex system IT systems and software to manage and monitor the network, the system will be inoperable. Whereas title to physical equipment and sites can be transferred readily, the assignment of contracts covering equipment supply, rental and maintenance, site rentals, rights of way, software licensing, employees, distributors, resellers, and customers may each require individual third party consents. Network, frequency, and planning permissions and authorizations will need to be transferred. Even the task of creating an 'asset inventory' is impossible given the difficulties of defining what is in fact included in the 'network' to be transferred and what should be retained by the BOT operator,[111] and reflecting the continual changes to the network. Intellectual property rights associated with the network service, or contained in critical network or billing software systems, may well belong to the BOT operator or its parent company, who may be unwilling to allow their use by the State or a new successor operator. Some of these issues may be alleviated by the enactment of a law vesting contractual and other rights in the state, although such action could be perceived as amounting to a form of expropriation and may have limited or no legal effect on contracts governed by foreign law.

The state will also need to incorporate a vehicle to which assets can be transferred in order to avoid subjecting the business to government procurement and civil service restrictions. The state and the BOT operator will need to agree on a valuation of the transferred assets, as valuation procedures in the BOT contract are likely to be capable of differing interpretation. On a practical level, the termination or expiry of BOT-type arrangements may cause significant industrial relations issues, as existing employees seek guarantees of employment security or simply resign following the ending of the BOT arrangement. As a result, the state may have to provide substantial employment indemnities to retain key employees to operate and manage the network. Procedural matters may in practice prove time-consuming and difficult.[112] The vesting of assets may also need to be coordinated with tax authorities in order to avoid the levying of stamp or transaction duty on the asset transfer. To complicate matters further, network performance is likely to have deteriorated in the years preceding BOT expiry, as the BOT operator has little incentive to continue to invest in network maintenance and upgrades as the expiry date approaches. In the (highly likely) event that the transfer results in systems failures or network outages, the consequent public outcry may have political repercussions for the government concerned.

---

[111] For example, standard office facilities, computer terminals, servers, and company vehicles may not be thought of as part of a 'telecommunications system' as such, but these items will still be necessary for the continued and uninterrupted running of the system. The BOT operator and the government are also likely to disagree as to who should own items on the periphery of the network.

[112] For example, re-assigning network codes and transferring GSM Association memberships, or changing SIM card information.

Countries considering establishing a BOT-type arrangement would do well to recall the three ICC and UNCITRAL arbitrations commenced by the BOT mobile operators following the termination of their BOT contracts by the Lebanese government in 2001,[113] and the difficulties subsequently suffered by the Lebanese government in its attempts to auction to third-party bidders the 'network assets' it acquired following the termination of the BOT arrangements.

Less common but also in existence are 'build-transfer-operate' (BTO) and 'build-operate-own' (BOO) contracts. Under BTO contracts the investors build the network and transfer title to the government, but continue to operate the network and share revenues from its operation with the state. This allows the state to retain ownership and control over the network, typically reflecting a reluctance of the state to relinquish control of key infrastructure, but is detrimental to the investors, who bear most of the costs without the benefit of ownership. In Thailand, BTO concessions were introduced in the 1980s to ensure the build-out and operation of networks for fixed, cellular, and value-added services. Although since 2000 the Thai government has proposed the conversion of the BTO arrangements into licences as part of wider sector reforms and in order to facilitate the proposed privatization of the state-owned incumbents, to date the resolution of the existing concessions has not been resolved.

A BOO contract is, essentially, the contractual equivalent of a licence, in that it simply authorizes an entity to build and operate its own network. However, unlike many licences,[114] it typically includes a revenue sharing obligation similar to those found in BOTs and BTOs. An example is the grant in 2001 of a BOO contract in Egypt for the construction of a major wireless local loop network, which required the winning consortium to share operating revenues with state-owned Telecom Egypt.[115]

16.8 ATTRACTING NEW ENTRANTS

Liberalization is not simply a matter of abolishing any existing exclusivities enjoyed by the incumbent. In addition, governments must ensure that investors and operators are willing to enter the sector and compete. In part, the attractiveness of a newly liberalized sector to new entrants will turn on the design of the regulatory framework regulating the transition from monopoly to competition.

While certain forms of licence (such as ISP licences or value-added services licences) may be available 'off-the-shelf' on request from the licensing authority,

---

[113] 'Libancell Banned from Arbitration', *Global Insight*, 19 July 2001.
[114] Although licences may also contain revenue sharing obligations: see, for example, the 20% revenue share obligation in the mobile licence won by a consortium led by Turkcell in Iran. See 'Turkcell Enters Iranian Mobile Market', *Telecom Worldwide*, 19 February 2001.
[115] 'Wireless Local Loop Project to Reduce Fixed-Line Bottleneck', *Global Insight*, 15 March 2001.

typically governments use a more structured (and often competitive) licensing process where licence numbers are limited (for example, due to scarcity of radio spectrum) or where the government wishes to license a core market (such as fixed or mobile) or to encourage new entrants to make binding commitments, such as to build out networks in certain areas or to deploy high-speed data services. Where licences are awarded through competitive tender, entry decisions may be determined by the form and conditions of the tender process itself. Governments will need to balance any revenue-raising objective against the need to ensure the winning bidders are able to enter the market on a sustainable basis and retain sufficient funds to devote to network deployment and service delivery.

16.8.1 Types of competitive selection process

The two principal competitive selection processes are beauty contests and auctions. The term 'beauty contest' refers to a method of comparative selection whereby the relative merits of bids are assessed based on a subjective evaluation of specified qualitative and quantitative criteria. The government sets the appropriate criteria on the basis of which the winning bid is selected (for example, commitments for network deployment and coverage, network service quality, the introduction of high-speed and multimedia services, or investment commitments). Beauty contests can be a useful licensing method where a government wishes to allocate licences to the bidders whose business plans most closely align with government objectives for sector development, and is prepared to forego competition on licence price. However, the use of qualitative and subjective evaluation criteria in the selection process can significantly diminish transparency and can open the government to accusations of bias or political interference.

In contrast, in an auction, the selection process is based on financial bids. Compared to beauty contests, auctions offer three key advantages: the ability to allocate licences efficiently, and consequently maximize revenue (in that licences are awarded to the bidders that value them most, and who therefore offer the highest purchase price), and greater transparency of process. However, auctions need to be carefully designed to ensure that the licensing process itself does not cause inefficient or undesired outcomes.

Auctions vary significantly in structure and design. The main auction types are: (i) ascending (or 'English') auction, (ii) descending (or 'Dutch') auction, (iii) sealed bid auction, and (iv) hybrid (or 'Anglo-Dutch') auction, although there are many other variants.[116] Auctions can also be split into two broad categories; continuous auctions, such as ascending and descending auctions, where bidders may alter their bids according to the action or inaction of other bidders, or sealed bid auctions,

---

[116] The hybrid Anglo-Dutch model was first proposed in Klemperer, PD, 'Auctions With Almost Common Values' (1998) 42 *European Economic Review* 757–69.

where the bidder has one chance to bid and does not know how much other bidders are offering.

16.8.1.1 *English auctions*

In an English auction, the auction begins with a financial bid, sometimes set as a 'reserve' price by the auctioning authority, and continues with each higher bid that is made, concluding when no further bids are forthcoming. The item is then sold to the highest bidder at the final price bid. It is also possible to sell several items at the same time using an English auction, in which case the price rises on each item (e.g. each licence) independently, and none of the objects is finally sold until all bidding on all objects is completed.

English auctions are vulnerable to collusion, where participants agree to avoid excessively raising the bidding price. Bidders can use the early stages when prices are still low to signal who should win which items, and then tacitly agree to stop driving prices up. Operators can also group together into bidding coalitions, thereby reducing competition in the auction, and then split up the licences between them after the auction closes. For this reason, English auctions are typically accompanied by stringent anti-collusion rules for the duration of the auction.

English auctions can encourage predatory and entry-deterring behaviour. For example, if only a small number of licences is available, incumbent operators may try to intimidate new entrants into not bidding by indicating that they will top all bids. English auctions can, in this way, allow strong or dominant bidders to deter the entry of rival bidders altogether, who may not participate at all if they do not anticipate standing a good chance of obtaining a licence. This may result in the auction being unprofitable or failing to attract the desired variety of bidders.

English auctions can also be affected by the 'winner's curse'. This refers to the situation when two bidders make similar bids in an auction but have different information about the value of the item, and the winner is the bidder who has most overestimated the value. As bidders are keen to ensure they do not overestimate the value of an object in this way, this can cause them to bid overly cautiously. Moreover, because weak firms will fear this outcome more than other, stronger bidders, the stronger, more dominant bidder wins most of the time—and it also generally pays a relatively low price because its rivals will have bid extremely carefully.[117]

---

[117] For example, in 1995, in the bidding for the Los Angeles mobile-phone broadband licences, the value of the licence was hard to estimate, but it was probably worth similar amounts to several bidders. However, Pacific Telephone, which already controlled the local fixed-line telephone business, had clear advantages from its database on potential local customers, its familiar brand-name, and its experience with doing business in California. The auction was an ascending auction and the result was that the bidding stopped at a very low price, yielding only US$26 per capita. In Chicago, by contrast, the main local fixed-line provider did not participate and it was therefore not obvious who would win, so the auction yielded US$31 per capita even though Chicago was thought less valuable than Los Angeles (See Klemperer (1998) and Bulow, JI and Klemperer, PD, *Prices and the Winner's Curse*, Discussion paper, Nuffield College, Oxford University (2000), available at <http://www.nuff.ox.ac.uk/economics/people/klemperer.htm>).

16.8.1.2 *Dutch auctions*

In a true Dutch auction (so called because of its historical antecedents in the Dutch flower industry), the bid price is set high by the auctioning authority, and progressively lowered until accepted by a bidder. While this is the historically correct use of the term, current financial trade literature is more likely to define the Dutch auction as the competitive or uniform price (sealed bid) auction described below.

16.8.1.3 *Sealed bid auctions*

Auctions can also take the form of simultaneous sealed bids, where each bidder simultaneously makes a single 'best and final' offer and each object is sold to the highest bidder at the price it bid for that object. These can be run either as first price or second price auctions. In a first price auction the highest bidder receives the goods for the amount it offered, whereas in a second price auction the highest bidder receives the goods for the price tendered by the second highest bidder.

16.8.1.4 *Anglo-Dutch auctions*

The disadvantages of English auctions, including collusion and predatory behaviour, can be mitigated by including a sealed bid stage in an otherwise ascending auction. This type of hybrid auction is termed an Anglo-Dutch auction.[118] The participants bid in an open ascending auction until there is one more bidder than there are units for offer and the remaining bidders then make a final sealed bid that is not lower than the current asking price. This model was used successfully in the auction of British 3G spectrum licences.

The Anglo-Dutch auction design is particularly valuable if one bidder (for example, an incumbent operator) is considered to be significantly stronger than other potential bidders, as it helps to level the playing field. The sealed bid at the final stage introduces some ambiguity over which of the final bidders will win, and operators, especially weaker ones, may therefore be attracted to the auction by the knowledge that they have a chance to make it to this final stage and the overall outcome is not a foregone conclusion. However, by providing weaker bidders with a greater chance of victory, sealed bid auctions may not be appropriate when the government's foremost objective is to maximize revenues. Notwithstanding this risk, the overall bids may actually be higher by the end of the first, ascending, stage of an Anglo-Dutch auction, than if a pure English auction were used, because participants may perceive their chances of winning as being greater.

The Anglo-Dutch auction also incorporates the advantages of sealed bid auctions. Collusion is discouraged because the final sealed bid round allows bidders to exit any collusive agreements without fear of reprisal. Tacit collusion is also reduced since firms are unable to use the sealed bidding round to signal bidding strategy to

---

[118] First proposed by Paul Klemperer (ibid). Note the use by Klemperer of the contemporary meaning of the term 'Dutch' auction in his description of this hybrid as an Anglo-Dutch auction. The reference to 'Dutch' is to a sealed bid auction as opposed to the traditional 'descending' Dutch auction.

each other and any consortium formed between two strong bidders will always be vulnerable to being challenged by other (weaker) bidders at the final sealed bid stage.

A form of Anglo-Dutch auction was used in Nigeria in 2001 when the government issued three GSM mobile licences. Initially, an attempt had been made to award the licences by way of beauty contest, but this process had failed due to allegations of corruption, and therefore the greater transparency afforded by an auction was considered preferable and more likely to have credibility in the eyes of international investors. Ultimately, a type of Anglo-Dutch auction (a hybrid of an ascending clock auction[119] and a sealed bid auction) was chosen to ensure, *inter alia*, that collusion was deterred and also to ensure that, if the number of bidders fell, the auction could be tailored appropriately and ended quickly by moving to the sealed bid phase.

16.8.2 Design of competitive selection processes

A successful competitive selection process must always be designed to take into account the context in which it operates, for example, the number of licences on offer compared to the number of expected bidders.[120]

The choice of process will also depend on the aims of the government in the licensing process. An auction designed to raise as much revenue as possible will inevitably differ in form from one in which the government has other social aims. For example, if the key motivation is to attract a variety of competitors or to achieve strategic licence commitments (such as aggressive network roll-out or modernization targets, substantial investment in the infrastructure, network deployment in remote or rural areas, or even job creation), then the choice and design of the process will need to reflect these requirements and should dilute price competition accordingly.

Attention must also be paid to the quality of the design of an auction, as poorly designed auctions can leave wide loopholes for bidders to game the auction process and consequently distort the auction outcome. For example, in 2000, the Turkish government auctioned two mobile licences in succession, stating that the reserve price for the second licence would be equal to the selling price of the first. One bidder bid far more for the first licence than it was realistically worth, assuming that no rival would be willing to bid that high for the second licence. The second licence remained unsold, and the winning bidder of the first licence was left without a rival operating the second licence.[121]

---

[119] Where the *auctioning authority* announces prices to the bidders that increase over time and bidders choose whether to accept or reject the announced prices.

[120] In the Netherlands' auction for the 3G mobile-phone licences, the Government simply followed the auction design which was used for 3G mobile-phone licences in the UK. This caused severe problems, as the Netherlands had an equal number of bidders who were incumbent operators and licences on offer. This meant that very few new entrants turned up, and those who did made deals with the incumbent operators, resulting in just one new entrant being left to compete with five incumbents for the five licences, producing a poor financial result for the government.

[121] 'Turkey: GSM 1800 Licence Victor Pays High Price', *Global Insight*, 13 April 2000. Indeed, it was suggested that the winning bidder, a consortium of Telecom Italia and Isbank, deliberately attempted to price its competitors out of the race for the second GSM licence to be auctioned to the losing bidders.

The credibility of auction process and rules is also important. Although in some circumstances it may not make sense for a government to punish a bidder violating the auction rules (for example, when excluding the offending bidder would end the auction immediately), or it might be difficult to impose fines large enough to have a serious deterrent effect on strong bidders, a failure to enforce the rules can aggrieve other bidders, who may decide to quit the auction as a result.[122]

Government coffers inevitably benefit from the sale of assets, such as licences, through competitive selection processes. Indeed, receipts can amount to hundreds of millions of dollars. However, if the price paid by an investor for a stake in the incumbent or for a new licence is too high, then, although government coffers benefit, ultimately consumers may not. High prices may result in less money being available for investment to build out or improve networks and increase penetration, and in higher tariffs to be paid by users. Perhaps a good example is Nigeria, where mobile subscribers suffered from high call tariffs following the initial auction of mobile licences, as the newly licensed mobile operators sought to recoup investment costs quickly. Another example is India, where second fixed operator licences were sold for what were perceived to be exorbitant prices in 1996. This meant that projected revenues were modest, and the licence holders had great difficulty in obtaining debt financing for necessary capital expenditures.[123]

Investors will also need to determine whether the regulatory environment places any restrictions on their ability to participate in the sector. Some countries, such as Saudi Arabia, prohibit foreign investment in the communications sector, and special exemptions to this prohibition are required to permit foreign participation in newly liberalized markets. Sweeping exemptions have generally been granted to increase the range and quality of potential bidders in licensing processes.[124] In other countries, foreign investment may be permitted only if local investors or the government hold an equity stake in the licensed entity. For example, in April 2004 the monopoly of state-owned Etisalat in the UAE was abolished, but the Supreme Committee responsible for the communications sector has indicated that a government

[122] In the Netherlands, for example, six bidders competed for five 3G mobile-phone licences in an ascending auction in which bidders were permitted to win just one licence each. When the government failed to take any action to punish one bidder who threatened another by demanding that it cease bidding, the threatened bidder quit the auction. The sale raised less than 30% of what the Dutch government had forecast based on the results of the UK's similar auction just three months earlier.

[123] Wellenius, B, 'Telecommunications Reform—How to Succeed', *Viewpoint Note* No 130, the World Bank (October 1997).

[124] The Saudi foreign direct investment legislation requires amendment to allow foreign ownership in the telecommunications sector, as this has been included in a list of 'sensitive' sectors in which foreign investment is barred. In February 2003, the bar on foreign investment in internet access and some data transmission services was lifted; the bar on foreign investment in the mobile sector is expected to be lifted as part of the mobile auction process in 2004. However, the mobile auction rules require bidders to team up with at least five Saudi companies in a bidding consortium, and foreign ownership will be restricted to 49%. See 'Announcement of Saudi Mobile Licence Bidder Shortlist Postponed', *Global Insight*, 29 March 2004.

shareholding will be required in any new entrant.[125] Similarly, in Azerbaijan, the Ministry of Communications and Information Technology until recently held major shareholdings in all fixed and mobile operators.[126]

Governments also need to consider the right balance between competing policy objectives. Proposals to grant sweeteners to some operators or investors (e.g. reserving a mobile licence for the incumbent operator, as was done in Nigeria) must be weighed against overall policy objectives of attracting (and retaining) investment in the sector generally and the risks of creating unfair competitive advantages. In developing countries whose markets are in transition, issuing multiple licences in high-margin segments of the market (such as the mobile segment) that can be effective substitutes for other, more costly segments (such as the fixed-line segment), may preclude or pre-empt investment in those costlier segments, thereby distorting market development.

16.8.3 Selection processes for fixed-line licences

Given the often exponential returns witnessed in the mobile sector, attracting bidders to a competitive bidding process for the award of mobile licences is usually not difficult. By contrast, fixed licences are often considered significantly less desirable. Investment costs in a fixed network are high, margins low, and new entrants typically face fierce competition from mobile operators for basic voice services (as a result of fixed-mobile substitution) and increasingly, with the roll-out of wireless broadband and 3G networks, for broadband services. Thus, even though a fixed market may have been liberalized (in that legal barriers to competition have been removed), a lack of interest in any fixed licences on offer may result in a *de facto* continued monopoly in the fixed-line market. Therefore, to successfully attract new entrants in the fixed-line market, governments may need to develop strategies to encourage investor interest or to offer prospective licensees 'sweeteners,' such as encouraging the deployment of cheaper fixed wireless technology, offering a 'unified' licence that is technology-neutral and permits full or limited mobility services, opting for service-based competition rather than requiring duplication of expensive fixed network infrastructure or giving winners certain priority rights (e.g. in future spectrum auctions). Governments may also opt to offer fixed licences in a 'beauty contest' for a nominal fee rather than through an auction process, in order to reduce entry barriers and to reflect the lower value investors may place on a fixed licence.

In Morocco, an attempt to license a second national fixed operator through a competitive auction process failed in 2002, after none of the 12 groups who had

---

[125] See 'United Arab Emirates Opens Telecoms to Competition', *Total Telecom*, 12 April 2004, and 'Government to Take Stakes in New UAE Telecoms Entrants', *Global Insight*, 19 April 2004.

[126] Aztelecom, the incumbent fixed operator, is wholly state-owned; its fixed competitors are all at least 50% owned by the state. In the mobile market, the government owns 37% of Azercell and in January 2004 sold its 51% stake in Bakcell to Motorola GTIB.

requested bidder documentation submitted a bid. Among the reasons suggested for the lack of interest was the falling demand for fixed services in Morocco: the fixed incumbent was suffering from negative growth while mobile telephony established itself as the primary voice platform (with the mobile market growing five times faster, in terms of subscribers, than the fixed market).[127] The regulatory authority re-launched an auction for fixed licences in 2005, but this time in a bid to increase interest from smaller niche players, offered a total of six local loop, two national/long-distance and two international gateway licences (with bidders bidding for all three given more favourable weighting), accompanied by a more favourable regulatory framework (including a more detailed interconnection regime and a substantial reduction in required universal service fund contributions and roll-out obligations). Licences were 'technology-neutral,' allowing operators to adopt more cost-effective wireless technologies to deploy networks and, on request, to offer 'limited mobility' services. In addition, winners of the new fixed licences would, along with the existing GSM operators, receive priority in the upcoming 3G auction. Two companies ultimately took up local, long-distance, and international licences, with one also obtaining permission to offer limited mobility services in a 35-kilometre radius.[128] Notably, both companies also hold mobile licences in Morocco.

Prospective investors in fixed licences might also be discouraged from participating in a tender process if the reserve price is too high and does not reasonably reflect the value of the relevant market segment. In South Africa, for example, the government began the process of licensing a second national (fixed) operator (SNO) in 2002, by holding a competitive bidding process to select the strategic investor for the SNO. It took three failed attempts to select a winner for the strategic stake in the SNO before a bidder was finally selected in 2005; prior bidders had been rejected for submitting 'financially deficient' bids, possibly reflecting the disjuncture between their evaluation of the future value of the fixed market and the government's own revenue objectives.

Meanwhile, recognizing the fact that fixed licences are significantly less attractive than mobile licences and offer much less opportunity for financial reward or growth, the regulatory authority in each of Bahrain and Jordan successfully introduced fixed-line competition in 2005, not by conducting an auction or other competitive tender process, but by simply making fixed licences available 'off-the-shelf' for a fixed fee. In Bahrain, fixed licences are available on demand, with no restrictions placed on the number of licences that can be granted, for an initial fee of less than US$100,000 and an annual licence fee of one per cent of the licensee's annual turnover attributable to the licensed activity.[129] In Jordan, a prospective fixed operator not wanting to use radio frequencies or access public rights of way can acquire a class licence on demand for less than US$50,000 that authorizes the operation of a

[127] 'Morocco: Government Re-evaluates Morocco's Fixed Liberalisation,' *Global Insight*, 27 March 2003.
[128] 'Morocco: MediTel Wins Fixed-Line Licence', *Global Insight*, 11 July 2005.
[129] See <http://www.tra.org.bh/en/licensingTypes.asp>.

public telecommunications network and provision of public telecommunications services.[130]

By contrast, larger markets with perceived greater growth potential may have greater success in auctioning fixed licences. In Saudi Arabia, the tender for new fixed licences to end the *de facto* monopoly of the incumbent, STC, attracted substantial interest (even though the new fixed-line licences carried obligations to cover at least 3 per cent of the country with fibre-optic networks or 15 per cent with wireless local loop or wireless broadband networks within seven years), and in 2007 the regulatory authority successfully awarded three fixed-line licences to consortia led by Bahrain-based Batelco, US-based Verizon Communications, and Hong Kong-based PCCW, respectively.[131] Winning bidders separately applied for spectrum rights to deploy wireless local loop access. Successful bidders such as PCCW are expected to deploy high-quality value-added and broadband services such as IP TV (successfully deployed by PCCW in its home market).

A similar outcome appears likely in Egypt, where, at the time of writing, at least seven operators were vying for the second national fixed licence. This licence would permit the holder to offer a range of services, including triple play, international gateway, WiMax, data and internet, local, international fixed voice, and other value-added services.[132] The government also invited interested parties to explore infrastructure options with the state electricity and railways authorities. Licence contenders included both developed and developing world heavyweights such as France Télécom, UAE's Etisalat, and Orascom.[133]

16.9 MANAGING DISPUTES IN THE AFTERMATH OF PRIVATIZATION AND LIBERALIZATION

Once the state-owned incumbent has been separated from government and new entrants have established operations, mechanisms will need to be in place to resolve any disputes that may arise between operators or with the government. Disputes have existed in the communications sector for decades. Historically, disputes in the sector have revolved around the nature and duration of exclusive rights granted to incumbents, licensing of new entrants, the technical, operational, and pricing aspects of interconnection arrangements, spectrum matters including harmful interference and licensing, and disputes between service providers and customers.[134] However, as the number of service providers grows (particularly following the introduction

---

[130] See <http://www.trc.gov.jo>.

[131] 'Saudi Arabia: Saudi Fixed-Line Winners to Receive Licence in July', *Global Insight*, 16 June 2007.

[132] See <http://www.tra.gov.eg>.

[133] See 'Egypt to auction 2nd fixed-line license June 19', *Reuters*, 24 February 2008.

[134] For a more thorough discussion of innovations in telecommunication dispute resolution, on which this section is based, see, e.g., *Dispute Resolution in the Telecommunications Sector: Current Practices and Future Directions*, World Bank/ITU, 2005, currently available at: <http://www.itu.int/md/D02-RGQ18.1-C-0020/en> (ADR Study).

of competition), and as the range of services provided (and technologies used to provide them) multiplies, so too do the number of potential disputes, and their potential complexity increases. Successful dispute resolution is crucial for liberalization and reform efforts to succeed.

16.9.1 Local dispute resolution mechanisms

Like any other part of the regulatory process, the manner in which, and speed with which, disputes in the sector are resolved, and the finality of, or ability to appeal, those decisions, is a key factor that needs to be taken into account in regulatory design. Disputes can cause delays in sector liberalization, distort costs by diverting both regulator and operator resources, create uncertainty, and limit the effectiveness of competition.[135] Indeed, regulatory policy, including dispute resolution and enforcement, can shape markets through the incentive structures it creates. Where the incentives are for operators and service providers to seek resolution of disputes, rather than seeking to create disputes or prolong them, stakeholders in the sector should benefit from the resulting efficiencies. In particular, sector development will benefit from a regulatory environment that encourages prevention, early identification, and resolution of disputes. Where the local judicial system is perceived to be inadequate (e.g. due to a lack of competency over technical issues, or concerns regarding impartiality, or delays inherent in court processes), investors may prefer to have access to alternative dispute resolution fora, or a specialist sector appellate body (see box below).

India: a specialist appellate tribunal

India has a bifurcated institutional structure, with both a 'regulator', the Telecommunications Regulatory Authority of India (TRAI), and a separate institution for settling disputes, the Telecommunications Dispute Settlement and Arbitration Tribunal (TDSAT). The TDSAT was originally established as a separate institution in part due to concerns that granting dispute resolution, or quasi-judicial, competencies to the same body that issues and controls licences would create a conflict of interest.

In 2003, a decision of TDSAT over so-called 'limited mobility' of fixed wireless local loop (WLL) operators had the effect of reshaping the entire Indian mobile market, and resulted in an explosion of subscriber growth. The dispute concerned the practice of WLL operators of allowing their customers limited mobility at tariffs far lower than mobile tariffs, to which the licensed mobile operators objected on the grounds, *inter alia*, that the WLL operators had not paid the equivalent to mobile licence fees, resulting in unfair competition to the

---

[135] Ibid.

mobile operators. TDSAT found in favour of the WLL operators, permitting them to offer limited mobility services.[136] The decision was upheld on appeal, and ultimately resulted in the TRAI's decision in November 2003 to adopt a unified licensing regime covering both basic (fixed local) and mobile services. This enabled the WLL operators to migrate to the new regime and provide full mobility services over their CDMA WLL networks in direct competition with the existing GSM mobile operators. However, disputes continue over the distinctions between limited and full mobility. For example, in 2005, Tata brought an appeal to the TDSAT challenging a decision by the TRAI ordering the CDMA WLL operators to withdraw advertising campaigns that portrayed limited mobility services as mobile services with a landline tariff.[137]

Notably, the creation of a specialist dispute resolution tribunal has not prevented decisions being routinely appealed to the local courts. A recent example is the attempt by India's GSM mobile operators to prevent the TRAI from issuing dual-technology (CDMA and GSM) spectrum licences. Having failed to win their case through the TDSAT, they simply moved their case on appeal to the high court.[138] It should be noted that the Indian approach is criticized for inconsistent verdicts by regulators and courts (explicitly including the TDSAT).[139]

Indeed, although disputes have traditionally been resolved through the courts, regulatory frameworks are increasingly providing for disputes to be referred to alternative dispute resolution mechanisms (ADR), ranging from industry self-regulation to mediation and arbitration.[140] The design and operation of such dispute resolution mechanisms varies, but in all cases a key area of concern for regulators and policy makers is to balance the need for speedy resolution of disputes with the need to develop a reliable body of precedent to ensure consistency and predictability of regulatory decision making.

[136] *Cellular Operators Association of India v Union of India*, Petition No 1 of 2001 (TDSAT, 8 August 2003).
[137] 'Fixed Wireless Operators Accused of Marketing Services as Mobile in India', *Global Insight*, 13 January 2005.
[138] 'GSM Operators File to Block New Spectrum Awards in India', *Global Insight*, 24 December 2007.
[139] See 'India: The GOM Tackles Reform', Global Technology Forum, Economist Intelligence Unit, 22 October 2003 (<http://www.ebusinessforum.com/index.asp?layout=rich_story&doc_id=6772&categoryid=&channelid=&search=tdsat>).
[140] Although a full discussion of ADR is beyond the scope of this chapter, it is worth noting some distinguishing features of different dispute resolution techniques for the purposes of the discussion in this chapter. At one end of the continuum, litigation is of course the most formal and adversarial. At the other end is negotiation, which is the most consensual. Regulatory adjudication and arbitration can also have elements of formal, adversarial processes. Mediation (and conciliation) as well as arbitration also have consensual aspects. Negotiation, mediation/conciliation, and arbitration can all be conducted confidentially, which limits the ability of decisions to act as precedents in future disputes. Mediation/conciliation, arbitration, and regulatory adjudication all may have the possibility of appeal, and are 'facilitated' by third parties. Regardless of the form of dispute resolution, each takes time and resources, although the conventional wisdom is that, as a process becomes more adversarial, it also consumes more time and resources.

16.9.2 International dispute resolution mechanisms

Investing and operating in the developing world typically carries a higher degree of political, economic, and security risk, which may not be adequately addressed by local avenues for dispute resolution. For example, if there is a change in government policy, such as the abolition of existing rights or a nationalization of core communications infrastructure, the affected foreign investor may find local courts or regulatory bodies unsympathetic. Accordingly foreign investors may seek to protect their investments in high-risk markets by requiring disputes relating to their investments to be resolved through international arbitration in a neutral venue (e.g. through the World Bank's International Centre for Settlement of Investment Disputes (ICSID),[141] the International Chamber of Commerce,[142] or according to the United Nations Commission on International Trade Law (UNCITRAL)[143]) or by relying on a bilateral investment treaty (see further, section 16.9.3 below). These solutions may have an adverse effect on the local regulatory framework, by hampering the development of local jurisprudence or causing inconsistent regulatory outcomes that do not reflect local norms. However, launching an international arbitration can also be extremely costly, and may be of limited effect if the relevant government refuses to recognize the arbitration and the plaintiff investor is unable to enforce an arbitral award. For example, when France Télécom brought an international arbitration claim against the Lebanese government following the government's termination of its BOT contract in 2001, the Lebanese government was able to secure a judgment from a sympathetic local court that the arbitration provisions in the BOT contract were unlawful and of no legal effect, and used this as a basis to ignore the arbitration proceedings.

Bolivia: limitations of international arbitration

In 2006, following the re-nationalization of former state-owned companies in the oil and gas industry, Bolivia's new government announced plans to re-nationalize the incumbent fixed-line operator, Entel. The 47 per cent of the shares in Entel held by Bolivian citizens reverted to state ownership, and the government threatened that, if Telecom Italia (which had acquired a 50 per cent stake in Entel for US$600 million in the 1995 privatization) did not agree to sell its shares, the government would use executive powers to regain control of the company.

In October 2007, Telecom Italia sought international arbitration to block Bolivia's efforts to take over Entel. The suit was filed at the World Bank's International Centre for Settlement of Investment Disputes (ICSID).[144] However, the Bolivian government has refused to recognize ICSID's jurisdiction, claiming

---

[141] For further information see <http://icsid.worldbank.org/ICSID/Index.jsp>.
[142] For further information cf <http://www.iccwbo.org/policy/arbitration/id2882/index.html>.
[143] For further information re see <http://www.uncitral.org/uncitral/en/about_us.html>.
[144] Case no ARB/07/28. For further information such as the present status of the case see <http://icsid.worldbank.org/ICSID/FrontServlet?requestType=CasesRH&reqFrom=Main&actionVal=ViewAllCases>.

that Bolivia had withdrawn from the organization in May 2007. It appears that, amid speculation that Telecom Italia would pursue redress under ICSID and against the backdrop of another conflict with a Dutch water supplier, Bolivia had sent a formal notice to the organization declaring its withdrawal from the ICSID convention.[145] At the time of writing, the Telecom Italia case was currently pending before the ICSID but a panel had not yet been constituted.

This followed the Venezuelan government's successful re-nationalization of privately owned incumbent CANTV and its mobile unit, Movilnet, in May 2007 through a tender offer and the acquisition of the strategic stake held by US-based Verizon, which had acquired a 40 per cent shareholding in CANTV in its 1991 privatization. In this instance, Verizon preferred to take the cash offered in exchange for a swift exit from the country, rather than attempting to halt the proposed re-nationalization.[146]

16.9.3 Bilateral investment treaties

Bilateral investment treaties (BITs) codify the reciprocal agreement of two countries to encourage, promote, and in particular protect investments in each other's territory. Most BITs provide for the jurisdiction of the dispute to be either at the investor's principal place of business or subject to international arbitration.[147] Currently there are approximately 2,265 BITs between developing and industrial countries. Particular centres for these agreements are Eastern Europe, the Americas, and Asia.[148]

One of the most recent cases in the telecoms sector involving a BIT was *France Télécom v Lebanon*. France Télécom's Lebanese subsidiary had provided GSM mobile services in Lebanon pursuant to a BOT contract since 1994. In 2002, France Télécom filed a suit with the International Chamber of Commerce, as well as according to the UNCITRAL rules (the first suit was ultimately abandoned), claiming that its subsidiary had been expropriated, not treated equally and that the BOT had been prematurely terminated. France Télécom's claim amounted to US$771,000,000. Lebanon countersued for US$840,000,000. In February 2005 the arbitration panel returned a verdict, awarding US$266,000,000 to France Télécom. Lebanon countered by asking the Federal Supreme Court of Switzerland to withdraw

---

[145] See 'Bolivia: Entel to be nationalised', *Financial Times*, 31 January 2007; 'Bolivia Telecoms: Nationalisation Moves Ahead', *The Economist Intelligence Unit*, 13 April 2007; and 'Bolivia: Entel Nationalization', *Business News Americas*, 3 March 2008.

[146] 'Nationalisation sweeps Venezuela', *BBC News*, 15 May 2007; See: <http://www.cantv.com.ve/Portales/Cantv%5Cdata%5CPR%20-%2020070409%20-%20Tender%20offers%20launched.pdf>; and 'Venezuela: Government buys control of CANTV', *International Herald Tribune*, 10 May 2007.

[147] For more detailed information concerning bilateral investment treaties as well as digital versions of more than 1800 BITs, see <http://www.unctadxi.org/templates/Startpage____718.aspx> and <http://www.iisd.org/pdf/2004/trade_bits.pdf>.

[148] See <http://www.unctadxi.org/templates/Page____1007.aspx>.

the panel's decision and to annul the amount awarded to France Télécom. The Swiss Federal Surpreme Court rejected Lebanon's motion and upheld the judgment of the arbitration panel.[149]

Telekom Malaysia v the Government of Ghana

Another recent BIT dispute which went to international arbitration was that between the government of Ghana and Telekom Malaysia. In 1997, the G-Com consortium, in which Telekom Malaysia (TM) holds an 85 per cent stake, bought a 30 per cent stake in Ghana Telecom (GT) for US$38 million. TM was given a five-year management contract to run the company for the duration of GT's fixed-line duopoly with new entrant Westel. But by the end of this five-year term, TM had provided only 275,000 of the 400,000 fixed lines it had been mandated to bring into service, as a result of which the government chose not to renew its contract. TM tried to sell back its stake to the government, recover its deposit, and claim damages for 'unfair treatment,' beginning arbitration proceedings under the UNCITRAL Rules before the Permanent Court of Arbitration at The Hague, Netherlands under the Malaysia-Ghana bilateral investment treaty. In May 2005, the parties reached an amicable settlement, with the government paying TM the sum of US$50 million over two years, after which TM's stake in GT would revert to the government.

16.9.4 WTO dispute resolution

USA v Mexico, a dispute over the interconnection rates between Mexico and the US charged by Telmex, is the first (and so far only) case of WTO dispute resolution regarding telecommunications services under the GATS.[150] The dispute was lodged by the US in 2000 and a decision was issued in 2004, pursuant to which the parties agreed to remedial steps recommended by the WTO's dispute resolution panel. This case established that the international interconnection services in question were cross-border services covered by the GATS. While the WTO dispute resolution process can be complex, this case showed that the new dispute resolution mechanisms provided in the GATS were effective. The panel's decision confirmed the principles set out in the Reference Paper as relevant in international telecommunications, particularly the pro-competition protections. It also made clear that the fact that a

---

[149] For the Swiss judgment in full text (French), see <http://jumpcgi.bger.ch/cgi-bin/JumpCGI?id= 10.11.2005_4P.98/2005> (case reference no: 4P.98/2005).

[150] See 'Mexico—Measures affecting Telecommunication Services', Report of the Panel, WT/DS204/ R, 2 April 2004 (available at <http://www.wto.org/english/tratop_e/dispu_e/cases_e/ds204_e.htm>). See further Chapter 15, at 15.4.5.1. See also, Wellenius, Galarza, and Guermazi, 'Telecommunications and the WTO: The Case of Mexico', World Bank Policy Research Working Paper 3759, November 2005, The World Bank (Wellenius).

country that had submitted its schedule of commitments was not excused from performance of those commitments merely because it had not yet adopted the necessary implementing regulations. Following the decision, Mexico agreed to promulgate the necessary regulations to give effect to its commitments.

16.10 CONCLUSION

Reform of the communications sector can lay the foundations for the reform of other sectors of the economy, attracting new (foreign and domestic) investment, facilitating transactions and reducing transaction costs, and fostering the dissemination of information. As such, it can be one of the most important factors in the economic development of developing countries.

A comprehensive reform agenda will cover the formulation of a clear sector policy statement, managed liberalization of all communications markets, the enactment of a modern regulatory framework, the creation of an autonomous regulatory authority, modernization and privatization of the state-owned incumbent, and the holding of transparent competitive selection processes to ensure new licences (where licence numbers are limited) are allocated to the most appropriate candidates. Successful design and implementation of such reforms, however, will ultimately depend on there being the requisite political support at the highest levels of government.

In many respects, the recent global downturn in the telecommunications sector created a 'new world order'. During the downturn, the appetite for investment in developing countries diminished dramatically, as major operators from developed countries refocused on strengthening balance sheets, reducing debt, and rehabilitating credit ratings. These market changes had a significant downstream effect on sector reforms in the developing world. No longer could governments rely on traditional approaches to privatization (such as a strategic sale to a developed country operator or an international listing), and attracting new entrants to newly liberalized markets proved more difficult, thereby denying reforming countries the benefits of competition. Nonetheless, the core building blocks of the reform agenda have remained relatively constant. That said, the increased difficulties in attracting foreign investment have led governments to focus their energies more on establishing investor-friendly regulatory environments, and on finding regional or local solutions to attain reform objectives.

At the same time, technological advances, witnessed by what is generically referred to as 'convergence', effected changes on the telecommunications landscape by eroding technology-specific barriers among telecommunications, broadcasting, and computing infrastructure and among different types of service. The new emphasis on 'digital bits' is also slowly changing the way in which the sector is regulated, as discussed in Chapter 17.

Today, most developing countries have made considerable progress in completing sector reforms: most have enacted modern sector legislation, created an industry

regulator, and both corporatized and at least partially privatized the state-owned incumbent operator. Consequently, the reform agenda in the developing world has begun to move from instituting the basic programme of reforms discussed in this chapter towards new generation of reforms aimed at strengthening existing frameworks, attracting new investment, and building capability and capacity in regulatory institutions.

17

DESIGNING REGULATORY FRAMEWORKS FOR DEVELOPING COUNTRIES

Ann Buckingham and Mark Williams

17.1 INTRODUCTION

For much of the latter half of the twentieth century, the provision of telecommunications services in developing countries was the responsibility of the state. Penetration rates were low, service quality was poor, and the incumbent operator was often in financial difficulties. Government attempts at improvement focused on securing investment, technical assistance, and financial support. However, in the late 1990s, three factors dramatically changed attitudes to communications markets in developing countries.

The first was the widespread reform of communications markets in Europe, driven by a series of EU directives requiring liberalization and regulatory harmonization in all Member States. The experience of regulatory reform in some southern European markets was particularly relevant, because it showed that competition

could be successfully introduced into markets with less-developed networks, a legacy of state ownership and structural imbalances—characteristics often shared by developing countries.

The second factor was the licensing of mobile operators in developing countries, and the ensuing explosion in the number of mobile subscribers. This dramatically increased teledensity,[1] thereby indicating the extent of unmet demand for telecommunications services, and forced governments to establish regulatory frameworks to manage the development of competition.

Finally, the requirements of membership of the World Trade Organization (WTO) have prompted many developing countries to commit to liberalizing the telecommunications sector, providing access to foreign operators and instituting basic regulatory reforms.

These events shifted the sector agenda in developing countries from one of securing investment to one of liberalization and regulatory reform. It also prompted developing countries—and those working with them—to look for a regulatory model that was at the same time robust and appropriate to developing countries. Unsurprisingly, most have looked to developed countries for models to emulate, in the hope that replica regulatory structures will act as a catalyst or spur to the same sector development and growth seen in the developed world. Of the various models applied around the world, the wholesale reform of electronic communications regulation in the EU has emerged as the *de facto* global standard, and has successfully provided the basis for reforms around the world.

There are many aspects of the EU model that can be applied in other countries, and it provides a sound platform on which to build a comprehensive package of sector reforms. Consequently, the temptation in reform efforts has sometimes been to seek to transplant EU regulatory models directly into developing countries. However, developing countries are typically very different from those in Europe, both in the way in which markets have developed and in the nature of government institutions. It is unlikely that a simple transposition of models from developed countries will be either feasible or successful, and this is reflected in the experience of reform in developing countries.

The key to successful implementation of a new regulatory framework in developing countries is to combine the lessons learned from international experience, of which the EU is an essential part, with a deep understanding of local circumstances and priorities. A bespoke approach should be adopted for each developing country, reflecting its specific market environment, legal system, institutional capacity, and political realities.

---

[1] Developing countries achieved nearly 34% mobile penetration by 2007, with mobile penetration growing at a compound annual growth rate of 53% (and over 90% in the 50 least developed countries) during the period from 1996 to 2006. By the end of 2006, there were nearly 4 billion mobile and fixed line subscribers, of which only 1.3 billion were fixed telephone lines—a number that has barely increased since 1996, and over 60% of world mobile subscribers were located in developing countries. See 'Trends in Telecommunication Reform 2007: The Road to Next-Generation Networks (NGN)', (ITU, Geneva, 2007).

This chapter will discuss the building blocks of a robust regulatory structure for developing countries, illustrating the way in which regulatory detail can be adjusted or changed to reflect the individual circumstances of a country undergoing reform and some of the issues that may arise during regulatory design and implementation.

At the outset, we acknowledge that all countries are different and it is difficult to make general statements about developing countries which apply to all of them in the same way. However, we have concentrated this discussion on features of regulatory systems that are common in many developing countries and can be considered to be broadly representative of the issues faced by governments, regulators, and operators in these countries.

17.2 MODELS FOR REGULATORY REFORM: LOOKING TO THE DEVELOPED WORLD

The WTO has had a pivotal role in securing the liberalization of telecommunications markets around the world, primarily through countries' commitments under the Agreement on Basic Telecommunications.[2] The WTO, recognizing the need for liberalization to be accompanied by regulatory reform in order to manage the transition from monopoly to competition, also appended to this Agreement a regulatory 'Reference Paper' that sets out the core requirements of a telecommunications regulatory framework, which countries 'adopt' as part of their sector commitments.

However, the text of the Reference Paper is brief and abstract: it is limited to six high-level core principles (covering competitive safeguards, interconnection, universal service, licensing, allocation and use of scarce resources, and the creation of an independent regulator), most of which can be interpreted and applied in a variety of ways. Very little guidance is given on the design or content of regulatory structures, or on how to implement the required reforms in an individual country. This reflects both its status as a document agreed by consensus, and its purpose, which is simply to spur countries to undertake a process of regulatory reform meeting minimum standards of international good practice. Consequently governments embarking on reforms have had to look elsewhere for assistance.

Liberalization, competition, and regulatory reform have been at the heart of the success of the communications industry in Europe, North America, and elsewhere in the developed world. It is therefore unsurprising that many developing countries have looked to this success story as a model for their own development.

In this section, we compare four different regulatory models that have been applied in the developed world, and explain why the EU regulatory framework has been the most commonly used model for reforms in developing countries over the past decade.

---

[2] This Agreement is annexed to the GATS Fourth Protocol, and came into force on 1 January 1998. The Agreement contains schedules of commitments to market access and national treatment with respect to basic telecommunications services. See further Chapter 15, at 15.4.

17.2.1 The EU regulatory model[3]

As a preliminary point, it is perhaps worth noting that there is no specific EU 'regulatory text' which can simply be reproduced in a given country. The EU regulatory models discussed below comprise a series of directives, which comprise directions to individual EU Member States to enact compliant national legislation by a specified implementation date. Individual Member States and national regulatory authorities are in many instances given considerable latitude as to how they implement the specific requirements of the EU directives under the rubric of 'subsidiarity': the directives simply set out the parameters within which Member States must operate. Indeed, Member States have often interpreted and applied the provisions of the EU directives described below in divergent ways.

EU regulation of the electronic communications sector can usefully be divided into two discrete phases: transitional market regulation and mature market regulation. The first phase covers the period 1987 to 2001, during which a series of directives and regulations were adopted to regulate the shift from monopoly to full competition; this regulatory framework is known as the '1998 package' (referring to the date of full market liberalization). The second phase began in 2002, when the EU issued a new package of directives designed to regulate now fully liberalized and increasingly mature electronic communications markets, known as the '2002 package'.[4]

17.2.1.1 *The 1998 package*

Historically, European telecommunications markets were generally regarded as natural monopolies, best operated by government departments or state-owned companies in the public interest. In the late 1980s, the European Commission launched an investigation as to whether telecommunications monopolies were in breach of the EC Treaty (as they restricted the freedom to provide services in Member States), and advocated widespread sector reform. These reforms were of two types: 'liberalization' initiatives designed to open up telecommunications markets to full competition; and 'harmonization' initiatives designed to introduce a common approach to telecommunications regulation across the European Union. Central to these reforms was the establishment of a national regulatory authority, independent of market participants.

The liberalization directives adopted a phased approach to market liberalization, abolishing exclusive rights progressively across all market segments.[5] In parallel with these liberalizing measures, the harmonization directives required Member

---

[3] See further Chapter 5.

[4] In this chapter, we do not address the European Commission's November 2007 proposals for regulatory review, which are expected to result in a new regulatory package in 2010, as these assume a level of market maturity and competition rarely found in the developing world. That said, discrete regulatory tools, such as the proposals to allow a regulator to require 'functional separation' between wholesale and retail divisions of the incumbent, may have application in specific cases.

[5] Liberalization began with the market for terminal equipment, and was followed sequentially by markets for data and value-added services, satellite services, service provision over cable TV network infrastructure, mobile services, and finally fixed voice telephony and network provision.

States to adopt a common approach to telecommunications regulation, on the basis that the establishment of pan-European networks and services would best be promoted by the rapid introduction of consistent regulatory frameworks across the EU. The regulatory principles in the harmonization directives were designed to control anti-competitive conduct by the incumbent, and to manage the transition from monopoly to full competition. The core concept of these directives was 'open network provision', which emphasized that access to and use of public telecommunications networks and services should be unrestricted, except where limited by non-economic reasons in the general interest such as network integrity and security.[6] The harmonization directives also laid out abstract concepts that are required to underpin Member State regulatory frameworks, namely: objectivity, proportionality, transparency, non-discrimination, and regulatory independence.

17.2.1.2 *The 2002 package*

By 2001, all telecommunications markets in the EU had been opened to competition,[7] and therefore the liberalization process was complete. Recognizing that in many Member States telecommunications markets were now competitive and maturing (with the notable exception of local fixed voice telephony), the EU adopted a new regulatory package in 2002 designed to reinforce competition by increasing market freedom. In particular, the new package created a regulatory 'exit strategy' by authorizing national regulatory authorities to 'roll back' many of the detailed regulatory controls in the 1998 package once a market is perceived to have effective competition. Greater emphasis is therefore given to generic competition law as a means to control anti-competitive market behaviour. The 2002 package also takes into account convergence by regulating all types of electronic communications transmission network consistently.

17.2.2 The US Regulatory Model[8]

Telecommunications regulation in the US has evolved very differently. The US model, while often reaching the same regulatory outcome as the EU model, uses very different tools and approaches.

In part, this is due to the complexities caused by the federal nature of the US system and a tradition of deference to state utility regulators. The powers of federal government are limited by the US Constitution, and, as a result, a complex system has evolved which allocates regulatory responsibility for inter-state and international

---

[6] Specific requirements were laid out in a series of directives relating to interconnection, leased line availability, ISDN, and voice telephony (covering universal service, tariff controls, and the availability of public payphones).

[7] Most Member States were required to liberalize by 1 January 1998, but Member States with less developed networks were granted derogations to enable them to make necessary structural adjustments. The last country to liberalize (Greece) introduced full competition on 1 January 2001.

[8] See further Chapter 6.

communications to a federal agency (the Federal Communications Commission, or FCC), and local communications to State public utility commissions. This has led to diverging and sometimes inconsistent regulatory approaches, and a multiplicity of regulatory requirements across different states. Disputes over the boundaries of federal and state jurisdiction have also hampered the FCC's ability to coordinate nationwide reforms in the manner that was achieved by the European Commission across all EU Member States. Jurisdictional difficulties are compounded by the overlapping antitrust enforcement powers of the Department of Justice, and the power of federal courts to impose binding interpretations of law and to dictate structural remedies in response to antitrust litigation. Indeed, regulatory reforms in the sector have at times been achieved only through forced structural industry changes and been influenced more by judicial rather than administrative decision-making.[9]

While the local monopolies of the incumbent local exchange carriers (ILECs) were declared invalid by the federal Telecommunications Act of 1996,[10] the US model has had only marginal success in promoting the emergence of facilities-based local exchange competition. Today, the ILECs still dominate local access and service markets[11] and the original seven Regional Bell Operating Companies (RBOCs) and GTE have now been consolidated to just three major operators.

The development of a modern and sophisticated technology-neutral approach in the US has also been hampered by legacy statutory distinctions between 'telecommunications services', 'information services', and 'cable television services', whose definitions are ill suited to the categorization of new, convergent services such as voice over Internet protocol (VoIP) and broadband.[12]

Moreover, the US had no legacy of state ownership in the sector. This means that US regulatory structures have not had to contend with many of the issues and complications associated with separation of government ownership and regulatory functions, which typically must be addressed in developing countries.

That said, the general principle of 'forbearance' in the 1996 Telecommunications Act (and its predecessors) is one that has been emulated in some regulatory frameworks in developing countries. In essence, this principle directs the FCC to forbear from applying any provision of the Act where analysis of the relevant market leads the FCC to conclude that forbearance does not harm the consumers and is generally

---

[9] Judicial regulation occurred most famously through the forced divestiture of AT&T following an antitrust complaint filed by the Department of Justice, which resulted in structural separation of local and long-distance markets, but see also the relatively frequent judicial overturning of FCC regulatory decisions on appeal.

[10] Codified at 47 USC §§171 *et seq*. This Act permitted local operators to access long-distance markets and vice versa, but only on a highly regulated and state-by-state basis.

[11] As of 31 December 2007, the ILECs controlled 82% of all end-user fixed switched access lines, <http://www.fcc.gov/wcb/iatd/comp.html>.

[12] See further, Marcus, J Scott, 'The Potential Relevance to the United States of the European Union's Newly Adopted Regulatory Framework for Telecommunications', *Federal Communications Commission, OPP Working Paper No 36*, July 2002, and FCC decisions on distinctions between PSTN and VoIP services.

in the public interest. However, the discretion implicit in such a general concept is often ill suited for use in developing countries, where the existence of such discretion can be a cause of arbitrary and uneven decision making, corruption, or a lack of transparency.

Thus, although the pro-competition aspirations of the US model are relevant to all, the model itself is *sui generis*, and arguably not suitable for adoption elsewhere.

17.2.3 Australasian regulatory models

Two very different regulatory models were adopted by Australia and (until 2001) New Zealand.

In Australia, regulation of the telecommunications sector is split between the generic competition regulator (the Australian Competition and Consumer Commission, the ACCC) and a sector-specific regulator (the Australian Communications Authority, the ACA). For example, the ACCC has jurisdiction over interconnection regulation, whereas the ACA has responsibility for licensing, technical regulation, spectrum allocation, and consumer protection. This approach is not suited to developing countries: not only do they usually lack a generic competition regulator, but a split regulatory approach requires a level of coordination and coherency in regulatory policy generally lacking between different government agencies and regulatory authorities in developing countries. Moreover, duplication of regulatory bodies is likely to raise regulatory costs, thereby exacerbating the already acute problem of securing adequate regulatory funding.

New Zealand initially adopted a unique strategy of eschewing sector-specific regulation and relying instead on generic competition law and the courts to regulate the sector. This approach is widely regarded as having been unsuccessful, and consequently in 2001 a new sector-specific regulator was created within the existing competition regulatory authority. That said, despite the oft-cited shortcomings of the pre-2001 approach,[13] the level of competition achieved in New Zealand communications markets in 2000 (some ten years after liberalization) was not dissimilar to that achieved in countries with sector-specific regulation—at a far lower regulatory cost to the government.[14] However, the lack of generic competition laws and the inadequacy of judicial institutions in most developing countries clearly preclude imitation of this regulatory model elsewhere.

---

[13] Such as the length, cost, and lack of clarity of dispute resolution through the court system, and the lack of an effective remedy following a judicial ruling that the incumbent has abused its dominant market position (a declaratory ruling of that nature simply sent the parties 'back to the drawing board', causing yet further delays in agreeing on the terms of a fair and reasonable interconnection contract).

[14] Although the lack of regulation may have in practice imposed higher transactional costs on market participants.

17.3 DIFFERING CHARACTERISTICS
IN THE DEVELOPING WORLD

Although the EU model is typically touted as the best regulatory model to emulate in the developing world, it is in practice not suitable for direct transposition in developing countries. This is because communications markets in developing countries differ in a number of important ways from those found in developed countries. In particular, both the market composition and the wider institutional framework found in developing countries will significantly affect the way in which the sector should be regulated. Consequently, the principles underpinning the EU regulatory framework are the most relevant to the design of regulatory structures in the developing world, rather than the detailed regulatory requirements themselves.

17.3.1 Differences in market composition and development

One of the most important differences between communications markets in developed and developing countries is the relative importance of mobile networks. In developed countries, the rapid growth of mobile network subscriptions reflects user preference for mobile technologies due to the added functionality of mobility. However, mobile services continue to coexist with fixed telephony services. In contrast, in many developing countries, the lack of capacity, low penetration, and poor quality of service of fixed networks means that mobile networks have tended to become the primary means of access to communications services.

This dominance of the mobile networks in developing countries has implications for many aspects of the regulatory framework. Because of the historical legacy of 'national champion' incumbent fixed operators dominating European telecommunications markets, EU telecommunications regulation from its inception has had an inherent focus on controlling this dominance. This focus can be seen in the EU regulatory approach to interconnection, tariffs, quality of service, local loop unbundling, and liberalization.[15] As mobile operators typically play a much more significant and dominant role in developing countries, certain regulatory provisions usually reserved for dominant fixed incumbents in Europe may need to be extended or applied to mobile operators in developing countries if such mobile operators are, in practice, more likely to be able to exert anti-competitive pressure. Similarly, regulations specific to fixed networks such as local loop unbundling, while an important

---

[15] E.g. the 1997 Interconnection Directive (Directive 97/33/EC) set out a series of requirements for interconnection, with more onerous obligations attaching to operators determined to have 'significant market power'. Although the Directive placed rights and corresponding obligations on both fixed and mobile operators, the full weight of a determination of significant market power fell only on fixed operators. For example, only *fixed* operators were required to publish reference interconnection offers, to offer transparent and cost-oriented charges, and to make available unbundled interconnection services. These requirements were carried through to the 2002 package in Directive 2002/19/EC on access to, and interconnection of, electronic communications networks and associated facilities. See further Chapter 8.

part of EU and US regulatory models, may serve no useful purpose in developing countries where the primary means of access is through wireless technology. Instead, the major challenges faced by regulatory authorities in the developing world are more likely to relate to the interconnection of mobile networks and service quality.

A second important difference lies in the application of the concepts of universal service and rural access. Teledensity in developing countries is typically much lower than in Europe and North America.[16] Large segments of the population often do not have ready access to a fixed telephone line due to the lack of network coverage in the areas in which they live or because they simply cannot afford the cost of available services. Governments traditionally attempted to improve network coverage through public ownership of the incumbent operator and cross-subsidies between urban and rural parts of the business. However, this approach was unsuccessful in most developing countries and network coverage and service penetration rates remained very low. By contrast, liberalization of mobile markets has resulted in rapid network roll-out, and coverage has extended into small towns and, in many countries, into rural areas. Mobile networks have also made it easier for the poor to get access to services through call centres and the resale of services on a call-by-call basis. However, despite these dramatic improvements in the availability of telecommunications services, some segments of the population, particularly in remoter rural areas, remain underserved. Universal access policy is therefore increasingly focusing on these peripheral areas where population density is low and costs are high.

Policy makers are also increasingly turning their attention to other ICT services. Broadband penetration in the developing world remains very low with limited availability and very high tariffs. Increasing the availability of broadband at affordable prices is therefore emerging as a major challenge facing governments and regulators across the developing world. The approach taken in the developed world, which has focused on liberalization through access to the incumbent's fixed network infrastructure, is not relevant in many developing countries where the incumbents are often weak with only limited network infrastructure.

A third difference lies in the degree of market liberalization in developed and developing countries. In many developing countries, despite the wave of liberalization efforts over the past five years, elements of monopoly still remain in parts of the fixed network. Core backbone infrastructure often remains a monopoly controlled by the incumbent operator and, in some cases, this is also true of international gateways. Competing operators may require access to these facilities if they are to function, but even if the incumbent is willing to provide access, it may lack the technical capacity on its network to provide a reasonable quality of service. Regulatory issues such as unfair discrimination also arise when the incumbent monopoly provider of essential services such as international connectivity also has a mobile business that may

---

[16] Within the Euro-zone, the total number of fixed and mobile subscriptions in 2006 was 173 per 100 inhabitants. This compared to just 17 per 100 inhabitants in low-income countries (source: World Bank, World Development Indicators, 2008).

be given priority access and preferential treatment. Greater regulatory intervention may therefore be required in developing countries to attempt to achieve a more level playing field.

Finally, foreign exchange controls are an institutional feature of some developing countries that may have a direct impact on market development. In such countries, it can be difficult for operators to purchase the equipment needed to upgrade and expand network infrastructure. This raises particular issues for the regulatory authority, which must take such constraints into account when calculating costs, assessing claims that operators have been unwilling to provide interconnection capacity, and monitoring quality of service.

17.3.2 Institutional differences

Regulatory reforms in developing countries must also be sensitive to the wider legal, political, and institutional environment. In many developing countries, the basic framework of a functioning legal and judicial system may be lacking or dysfunctional and consequently there may be no effective check on arbitrary decision making. Even where the courts do function adequately, it is unlikely that there will be a judiciary that is sufficiently skilled or experienced in technical regulatory matters to be able to effectively apply the regulatory framework or resolve technical disputes. Moreover, reliance on the courts to challenge or appeal regulatory decision making may create inconsistencies in regulatory approach in countries whose legal systems lack the concept of binding judicial precedent.

Developing countries often lack a clear and coordinated strategy for reforming the sector. This means that the sequencing of reforms may not always be coherent. In contrast, the regulatory reforms in the EU were introduced in a systematic and coordinated way. An example of this difference is the implementation of tariff rebalancing. An important accompaniment to sector liberalization, it ensures that market entry is both possible and efficient without threatening the financial viability of the incumbent operator. Tariff rebalancing in the EU therefore occurred in parallel with market liberalization. In contrast, the political will for similar rebalancing in developing countries is often absent, because it is likely to increase significantly the price of line rentals and local calls and therefore engender public opposition. The result is that, in some developing countries, markets have been liberalized but the incumbent has been prevented from aligning its tariffs to cost. This can threaten the financial viability of the incumbent.

Although by mid 2007, 123 International Telecommunications Union (ITU) member countries had privatized their incumbent fixed operator,[17] many governments in developing countries still retain (often significant) stakes in the incumbent fixed

---

[17] 'Trends in Telecommunication Reform 2007: The Road to Next-Generation Networks (NGN)' (ITU, Geneva, 2007).

operator, and sometimes in one or more mobile operators. While this is also true in many developed countries, the institutional separation between government and operational functions is usually less clear in developing countries, and political involvement in operational decision making is often more pervasive. The independence of the regulatory authority from political interference may also be in doubt. This political interference in both the operation and the regulation of the sector raises many issues for the application of the EU model. The power of the regulator to make decisions that may adversely affect a (wholly or partially) state-owned operator may be limited by political constraints; where a state-owned operator is directly contributing to government finances, it may be even more difficult to make decisions that either reduce revenues or increase costs. Privately owned operators may find themselves at a severe disadvantage *vis-à-vis* operators that are politically well-connected or still owned in whole or in part by the state. In practice, taking legal action against an operator with powerful political support may be impossible. One approach to address these difficulties is to make legislation more prescriptive, leaving less room for discretion by the regulator. This may help to reduce political interference in regulatory decision making. However, there is a limit to how far this can be taken without adversely limiting the freedom of the regulator to make necessary or appropriate decisions.

Implementation of the EU framework also requires a level of sophistication and expertise in the regulatory authority that may be lacking in developing countries, particularly given legal and institutional limitations and lack of resources. Similarly, a lack of available and reliable market and cost data may preclude the use of sophisticated regulatory techniques commonly used in the developed world. EU regulatory authorities have developed considerable experience and expertise in the application of regulatory frameworks, which have been developed over the course of over 20 years. A pan-European market in professional legal, economic, and technical regulatory advice has also developed, providing resources to regulatory authorities where required and encouraging the harmonization of approaches and standards across the continent. No such equivalent pool of local skilled resources exists in most developing countries, and regulatory authorities are often under-staffed, under-skilled, and under-resourced. Consequently, an overriding principle governing regulatory design in developing countries should be simplicity: the more straightforward a regulatory procedure or control, the more likely it will be implemented and enforced.

A related problem is that, in developing countries, sector reforms have often been undertaken on an *ad hoc* piecemeal basis, resulting in conflicting regulatory approaches and inconsistent operating licences. This legacy of partial and incomplete reform initiatives can significantly hinder future sector development and reform, and constrain the regulator's freedom to act. As a result, regulatory compromises may need to be brokered with existing operators in order to overcome legal and structural barriers to reform. This contrasts with most developed countries, where regulatory change is typically highly planned and coordinated, and transitions between evolving and changing regulatory structures are relatively smooth.

The EU model also assumes an underlay of general competition law, which can be utilized to regulate competitive markets once sector-specific regulatory controls are lifted or reduced. Generic competition rules and regulators typically do not exist in most developing countries. Therefore, regulatory regimes in such countries must be adapted to compensate for this absence.

Corruption among government authorities, the judicial system, and the private sector is a fact of life in many developing countries. This can affect both the substance of regulatory decisions and the way in which they are perceived by the market and the general public. The framework for establishing regulatory authorities, the powers given to the authority, and the modalities by which regulatory decisions are made should all take this into consideration. It may therefore be preferable in developing countries to have a more transparent directive regulatory framework, even if this is at the cost of reduced flexibility. For example, if corruption is of serious concern in a country, the regulatory regime could 'automate' decisions and regulatory consequences in order to reduce the possibility for corrupt decision making. Moreover, where approval or a decision of the regulatory authority is required, the regulatory regime could deem a decision to have been adopted if no contrary decision is taken within a specified period of time. In contrast, the EU model gives the regulator considerable latitude to make decisions on the scope of its own regulatory powers and to exercise broad discretion in regulatory decision making. The considerable flexibility, latitude, and discretion built into the EU and other developed country regulatory models can be detrimental if transported to countries suffering from endemic corruption.

17.4 ROLE OF COMPETITION LAW

A second important source of regulation in the electronic communications sector in the developed world is competition law: telecommunications regulation is in fact a combination of sector-specific and generic competition regulation. Competition rules covering anti-competitive market concentrations and behaviour both supplement and complement sector-specific regulatory frameworks, and should not be overlooked as a critical component of the regulatory environment in developed countries.[18] Indeed, it is this detailed and highly complex underlay of competition law that allows both the European Commission and EU national regulatory authorities to 'roll back' regulatory controls, and the FCC to exercise regulatory forbearance.

Developing countries, in contrast, typically lack any history of antitrust jurisprudence and regulation, and therefore caution must be exercised when both designing appropriate regulatory frameworks and advocating a more 'light-handed' regulatory approach.

---

[18] See further Chapter 9.

To overcome this lacuna, regulatory 'work-arounds' have emerged in developing countries that build competition law concepts and constructs into telecommunications regulatory regimes. This solution has had limited success, given the lack of capacity of most sectoral regulators in developing countries. Regulators typically have insufficient resources to investigate complex competition complaints, and both regulators and courts may lack the jurisprudence and expertise to handle competition disputes effectively.

17.4.1 The WTO and the 'Singapore Issues'

The lack of adequate competition regulation in the majority of developing countries became the subject of discussion at the First Ministerial Conference[19] of the WTO, which took place in Singapore in December 1996. An EU initiative at this Ministerial Conference introduced four new policy areas for discussion, relating to investment, competition policy, transparency in government procurement and trade facilitation, which areas subsequently became known as the 'Singapore Issues'.

In relation to competition policy, proponents of the proposal (most notably, the EU, US, Canada, and Korea) argued that a multilateral framework would enhance the contribution of competition policy to international trade and development, and that developing countries need enhanced technical assistance and support in capacity-building in this area. Core principles could form the basis of a multilateral agreement (not dissimilar to the telecommunications regulatory Reference Paper included as part of the WTO Agreement on Basic Telecommunications), which would require Member States to establish competition policies and rules conforming to the stated principles. Although the proponents did not agree on the principles for inclusion, suggested items included: transparency; non-discrimination and procedural fairness; provisions on 'hard-core cartels';[20] modalities for voluntary cooperation; and support for progressive reinforcement of competition institutions in developing countries through capacity building.[21]

Detractors (led by Brazil, India, China, Malaysia, and Indonesia) argued that multilateral competition rules favour developed countries and were of dubious value to themselves. Some argued that their development needs differed from developed countries, and that 'national champions' may need protection through national industrial

---

[19] Under the governance structure established by the WTO Agreement, the WTO's highest decision-making body is the 'Ministerial Conference'. This body is, in essence, a meeting of all WTO members that must take place at least every two years. The Ministerial Conference has the power to take decisions by consensus on all matters relating to multilateral trade agreements.

[20] Defined by the OECD as anti-competitive agreements, anti-competitive concerted practices, or anti-competitive arrangements by competitors 'to fix prices, make rigged bids (collusive tenders), establish output restrictions or quotas, share or divide markets by allocating customers, suppliers, territories or lines of commerce' (see *OECD Recommendation of the Council Concerning Effective Action Against Hard Core Cartels*, 25 March 1998).

[21] See the Doha Ministerial Declaration, 14 November 2001 (WT/MIN(01)/DEC/1), para 25.

or competition policy in order to build up the capacity needed to compete success-fully with foreign firms. Domestic firms, they claimed, should be treated differently from multinationals. If, however, the core WTO principles of non-discrimination and national treatment were applied to a multilateral competition policy, foreign firms would be entitled to equal treatment with domestic firms, and would have access to a free competitive environment in the host country. Others objected to the failure to include on the agenda issues such as anti-dumping measures or the obligations of foreign firms to host countries, which arguably would benefit developing countries at the expense of developed countries. Some countries have argued that restrictive business practices are better dealt with under the auspices of other international agencies, such as the United Nations Conference on Trade and Development. Finally, concerns were expressed about the lack of common understanding about the proce-dural and substantive content of the Singapore Issues, and the capacity of developing countries meaningfully to negotiate the issues involved with stronger negotiating counterparts.

The Ministerial Declaration issued at the conclusion of the First Ministerial Conference in Singapore agreed simply to establish working groups to study further the issues in these four policy areas in order to identify areas that merit further con-sideration in the WTO framework.[22] By the time of the Fourth Ministerial Conference in Doha, Qatar, held in November 2001, the Singapore Issues had become increas-ingly prominent. The majority of developing countries had made public their opposi-tion to the commencement of formal negotiations on the Singapore Issues, stating that they should continue to be studied by working groups only. The compromise reached in the Doha Ministerial Declaration was that, in relation to each of the Singapore Issues, 'negotiations will take place after the Fifth Session of the Ministerial Conference on the basis of a decision to be taken, by explicit consensus, at that Session on modalities [i.e., scope and timeframe] of negotiations'.[23] No default option was proffered should consensus not be reached in that Session of the Ministerial Conference. Meanwhile, over 100 developing countries (including 68 WTO members) had made it clear they did not want the Singapore Issues on the agenda at the Fifth Ministerial Conference,[24] and many countries made it clear that any concessions on Singapore Issues would be contingent upon making tangible and significant progress on negotiations for the removal of agricultural subsidies in the US and EU.

Against this acrimonious backdrop, the Fifth Ministerial Conference was held in Cancún, Mexico in September 2003. Few were surprised when the Ministerial

---

[22] Singapore Ministerial Declaration, 13 December 1996 (WT/MIN(96)/DEC).
[23] Doha Ministerial Declaration, 14 November 2001 (WT/MIN(01)/DEC/1).
[24] See e.g. the ACP Declaration on the Fifth Ministerial Conference of the WTO, Brussels, 1 August 2003 (77 members of the Asia, Caribbean, and Pacific group of countries); the Declaration of Second LDC Trade Minister's Meeting, Dhaka, May–June 2003 (49 least-developed countries); Africa Trade Ministers' Meeting, Mauritius, June 2003 (53 African countries); and the WTO Submission by Group of Developing Countries, 4 July 2003.

Conference collapsed in apparent disarray, with WTO members failing to agree on either the future agenda of negotiations on agriculture and services (the Doha Development Agenda), or the basis and timing for negotiating the Singapore Issues. In July 2004, the General Council of the WTO agreed to proceed with negotiations on only one of the Singapore Issues, trade facilitation, and the remaining three (including competition policy) were dropped from the Doha agenda as part of attempts to salvage the Doha round of negotiations.

The failure to make progress on the Singapore Issues at the Cancún Ministerial Conference was no doubt inevitable, but still disappointing: a basic agreement on core competition principles and a commitment to capacity building in developing countries would, if implemented, provide a valuable counter-point to sector-specific regulatory reforms.

17.4.2 Regulatory solutions in the absence of generic competition rules

If a country lacks a framework of generic competition law, the architect of an electronic communications regulatory regime will need to consider strategies to incorporate core competition law principles into the sector-specific regulatory framework. This has become particularly important in developing countries with the increase in private market participation and the emergence of competition. We describe some strategies commonly deployed below.

17.4.2.1 *Two-tier regulation*
Regulatory frameworks in developing countries frequently incorporate a 'two-tier' structure, whereby greater regulatory controls are placed on an operator who is determined to have dominance or significant market power in a particular market. This mechanism can be used to constrain anti-competitive market behaviour by dominant players, while minimizing the regulatory burden on both new entrants and regulators, and is based on the EU concept of 'significant market power' and the US concept of 'dominant carrier'.

The first question to address in developing two-tier regulatory structures is market definition. In the EU, the European Commission consults both with market participants and national regulatory authorities, and then adopts a recommendation on product and service markets within the electronic communications sector whose characteristics justify the imposition of regulatory obligations under the various directives. This market definition exercise is undertaken in accordance with principles of EU competition law, and is reviewed regularly. National regulatory authorities, taking account of this recommendation, then define relevant markets appropriate to national circumstances.[25]

---

[25] Directive 2002/21/EC on a common regulatory framework for electronic communications and services, Art 17.

This approach is arguably not suitable for transposition into most developing countries: the EU system assumes that regulators are familiar with and well versed in complex competition law concepts. It is not realistic to expect a nascent regulatory authority in a country with no history of generic competition regulation to apply sophisticated competition law theories to determine market definitions and parameters. An alternative could be for developing country regulators simply to adopt the markets defined in the European Commission's recommendations. However, EU markets are defined narrowly. For example, the Framework Directive specifies six different interconnection markets for different call origination, transit, and termination services.[26] This is likely to be needlessly complex for developing countries that simply wish to impose heightened controls on interconnection on major operators. Instead, it may be preferable to develop straightforward and appropriate market definitions in conjunction with the design of the new regulatory regime. Ideally, the regulatory experts responsible for its design should prepare initial market definitions, which can then be adopted and reviewed by the new regulatory authority moving forward.

The second issue is how the concept of 'dominance' should be defined. In the EU, 'significant market power' is now defined by reference to the ability to act independently of competitors, suppliers, and customers.[27] This concept is derived from the competition law concept of 'market dominance', and requires a sophisticated analysis of market characteristics such as market share, relative turnover, the nature and extent of barriers to market entry, availability of reasonably substitutable services, control over essential facilities, and the power to raise and sustain prices above competitive levels. In addition, the 2002 EU regulatory package permits a finding of 'joint dominance', again through an assessment of detailed and complex market characteristics.[28] Competition authorities in the EU are well versed in those concepts, and the considerable jurisprudence in competition case law guides the required market analyses.

In contrast, imposing a complex definition of 'dominance' on a newly created regulatory authority in developing countries with no competition law experience and limited resources can be impractical. It may also encourage reliance on retained external consultants to apply the required analytical techniques. It may instead be appropriate to incorporate a more 'rough and ready' approach, such as benchmarking 'dominance' to a specified market share: while not perfect, at least this may enable a regulatory authority readily to apply the concept and provides some guidance as to which entities will be determined to have dominance. This approach is similar to that adopted in the EU 1997 Interconnection Directive, which created a

---

[26] Ibid, at Annex I.

[27] Ibid, at Article 14.

[28] Ibid, at Annex II states that 'joint dominance' is likely to occur where the market exhibits a number of characteristics: mature market, stagnant or moderate growth on the demand side, low elasticity of demand, homogenous product, similar cost structures and market share, lack of technical innovation, absence of excess capacity, high barriers to entry, lack of countervailing buying power, lack of potential competition, informal links between operators, retaliatory mechanisms, and reduced scope for price competition—which list is also stated to be non-exhaustive.

rebuttable presumption that an operator had significant market power when it had more than 25 per cent of a particular telecommunications market.[29]

Thirdly, the regime must specify what obligations flow from a determination of dominance in a particular market. These may include retail and interconnection tariff regulation, more extensive interconnection and access obligations, and stricter regulatory scrutiny generally. Although based on the EU concept of 'significant market power', more detailed and comprehensive obligations and restrictions may flow from such a determination in developing countries in order to compensate for the lack of a general competition law prohibition against abuse of a dominant position and other anti-competitive behaviour. Typically, these obligations are outlined in the primary legislation with the detail specified in regulations or licences.

17.4.2.2 *Incorporating generic competition rules in primary legislation*

The emergence of competitive mobile markets in developing countries means that competition regulation, rather than monopoly control, is the priority for regulators. Indeed, it is becoming increasingly common to include provisions for competition regulation in new electronic communications legislation, sometimes in the form of an additional chapter on competition law.[30] This can be a helpful tool where a country lacks a general competition law regime. However, the usefulness of including a sector-specific competition law regime should not be overstated: jurisdiction over such competition matters is usually given to the new communications regulatory authority. This authority typically lacks the time, resources, and experience in complex competition cases to enforce these general competition rules. Moreover, usually no systems or processes are put in place to detect or investigate possible anti-competitive behaviour, and therefore such legislative provisions tend to be ignored rather than applied.

Moreover, in the absence of a generic competition framework, there is unlikely to be any institutional experience of defining or regulating anti-competitive practices. To strengthen the effectiveness of a new sector-specific competition law regime of this nature, it is generally advisable to prepare or incorporate a list of market action that is deemed to be anti-competitive or that raises a presumption of anti-competitive behaviour. This list should be prioritized to indicate the types of activity that are considered to be the most damaging to the market, and should indicate the types of evidence (e.g. predatory pricing, refusal to serve, and discrimination) that the regulatory authority might take into account in assessing whether the competition rules have been breached. Definitions or guidelines of key types of anti-competitive behaviour, and an indication of how the regulator would enforce the prohibitions and demonstrate that such behaviour has taken place, could be contained in regulations or guidelines issued by the regulatory authority.

---

[29] Directive 97/33/EC on interconnection in telecommunications, Art 4.3.

[30] See e.g. the Nigerian Communications Act 2003, Chapter VI, Part I. See also, the Public Utilities Commission of Sri Lanka Act and Sri Lankan Electronic Communications Networks and Services Bill.

17.4.2.3 *Including 'fair trading' conditions in licences*

Licences often include specific provisions designed to control anti-competitive behaviour. These may take the form of generic prohibitions of anti-competitive agreements and abuses of a dominant position, and restrictions on mergers and market concentrations, similar to those discussed above.

More specific controls may also include prohibitions on unfair cross-subsidization or undue discrimination. Other controls include dividing services provided by an incumbent into two or more separate and independent companies or business streams, and requiring transparency and non-discrimination in dealings between the two businesses. In some countries, the government has also limited the lines of business into which the incumbent might enter (e.g. by precluding the incumbent from holding a mobile licence), although this is unusual where the government stands to gain from the incumbent's profitability.

17.4.2.4 *Greater ex ante regulatory control and intervention*

A fourth method of seeking to control anti-competitive behaviour in the absence of a generic competition law regime is to increase regulatory intervention. For example, the regulatory regime might require approval of all tariffs or interconnection agreements before they can take effect. This approach is particularly common in countries with a history of state control or collusive market behaviour, which may have little confidence in the ability of other regulatory techniques to prevent or control anti-competitive market behaviour. However, this approach should be avoided wherever practicable: it greatly increases regulatory uncertainty for market participants, increases the bureaucratic burden and delay, and may hamper market development.

17.5 BUILDING BLOCKS FOR REGULATORY FRAMEWORKS IN DEVELOPING COUNTRIES

In communications regulation in developing countries, there is no such thing as a 'one-size-fits-all' approach. Rather, each individual country must be analysed carefully in order to assess its specific market characteristics, legal foundations, regulatory and institutional capacity, and any political realities or tensions that may influence or shape a particular regulatory approach.

In this section, we do not propose or espouse any particular model or regulatory construct. Rather, our aim is simply to consider in more detail the different aspects of communications regulation when applied to developing countries,[31] highlighting

---

[31] Central to any reform initiative is usually the creation of an independent or autonomous regulatory authority to regulate and oversee the development of the communications sector. The key theories and principles underpinning the creation of this regulatory authority, and the various forms that such authority may take (whether regional or national, sector-specific, or multi-sectoral) are discussed in Chapter 16, at 16.6.

particular issues, challenges, and pitfalls that may arise in different circumstances and exploring the possible options or regulatory solutions in response.

17.5.1 'Consensus-building' pre-reform

A critical initial step when undertaking reforms is to engage in a process of 'consensus building' to secure broad support for the proposed reforms. Undertaking sector reforms is frequently a politically charged issue. Maximizing ground support for the reform process is likely to facilitate its introduction and implementation.

Clearly, meetings with all key players (including interested ministries, regulatory authorities, operators, and consumer agencies (if any)) are desirable: they provide an opportunity to explain the rationale behind the proposed reforms and the overall benefits that regulatory reform would deliver. Regulatory reforms typically have considerable impact on existing operators' businesses and revenues. Some reforms, taken individually, may be beneficial to an individual operator, others prejudicial. As a result, one often encounters considerable resistance to reform, as individual operators and existing regulatory agencies will contest any individual regulatory change likely to have a significant adverse impact on their sphere of operation or revenues. Industry-wide workshops and consultations are best complemented by bilateral meetings with key players, which provide interested parties with an opportunity to express freely, on a confidential basis, their views on what they perceive to be the most difficult or challenging issues that must be addressed.

In addition, when designing the regulatory framework, it is preferable to ensure that all interested parties derive some visible or tangible benefit from the reform. If the impact of a reform is seen as being purely negative (e.g. all powers of the existing regulatory agency are removed, or an operator receiving preferential treatment under the existing regime simply loses its special status while deriving no benefit), one can expect to encounter greater resistance or lobbying against the reform process. This negative perception, however, may be due to a lack of understanding of the wider benefits of reform or a lack of confidence in the way in which reforms would be implemented: if so, these concerns may be alleviated through effective consultation and consensus-building.

17.5.2 Regulatory architecture

An important initial question in designing a regulatory framework will be the respective roles and importance of primary legislation, regulations, orders, guidelines, and licences. In particular, decisions will need to be taken as to which document will contain which regulatory principles and controls.

17.5.2.1 *Legislation v regulations*
In preparing new primary legislation to govern the communications sector, one must determine what to include in the legislation, and what to consign to

supporting regulations. The preferred approach is to enshrine the core principles and basic framework of the regime in the primary legislation, leaving the detail to secondary legislation, which can then be readily adapted and evolve as markets develop. For example, in relation to interconnection, one would expect to see in the legislation: the basic right and obligation to interconnect on fair, reasonable, and non-discriminatory terms, an outline of the consequences flowing from a determination of dominance, basic procedural requirements (such as an obligation to file or publish agreements), and the regulator's right to intervene in the event of a dispute. However, details on the calculation of the cost of interconnection, accounting and settlement principles, approval processes, technical specifications, and procedures are best relegated to a supporting regulation of general applicability. Policy cornerstones, such as a liberalization timetable or reform agenda could be included in the legislation to give market participants confidence in the future shape of reforms, although governments typically prefer to document such matters in sector policy statements that can be more readily changed.

17.5.2.2 *The role of licences*
Investors in developing countries where the regulatory environment is uncertain often attempt to protect their interests by seeking detailed, self-contained licences that purport to cover all key regulatory controls, and to secure limitations on the regulatory authority's freedom to amend those licence terms. This approach has been adopted extensively in privatizations and licence auctions in the developing world and is thought to provide investors and lenders with the regulatory comfort needed to undertake major investments in the sector, and to give all stakeholders clarity as to the licensed entity's rights and obligations.

There are three problems with this approach. First, the protection granted to investors is not watertight. Unless the licence is in the form of a concession or franchise agreement giving the investor enforceable contractual rights of redress, a licence in most countries is simply an administrative instrument and its terms can usually be amended by any legislative and regulatory instrument having primacy under local law. Even a contractual arrangement confers only limited protection if it lacks an adequate dispute resolution mechanism. In addition, an investor who wishes to continue its presence in a given country may prefer not to institute a direct challenge to government.

In reality, the investor's main protection against adverse regulatory change lies in a regulatory authority or government's desire to appear credible and investor-friendly. This desire exists whether regulatory controls are contained in licences, regulations, or legislation. That said, arbitrary intervention in an individual entity's licence may well attract greater adverse international attention than an amendment of a subsidiary regulation. However, in a high-risk country, arbitrary licence change and revocation may well occur notwithstanding any licence constraints on such action.

Niger: arbitrary revocation of 'codified' licences

A good example of the limited protection afforded by an 'unchangeable' comprehensive licence is the repeated and politically motivated revocation of Telecel's mobile licences in Niger in the late 1990s—the government of the time was determined to revoke Telecel's licences irrespective of any restriction contained in its licences.

In June 1996, the Minister of Communications, Culture, Youth and Sport issued Telecel-Niger SA a *Convention de Concession d'Exploitation du Reseau Cellulaire du Niger*: a 25-year mobile licence terminable only for breach. In February 1997, the Prime Minister ordered the Minister to treat Telecel-Niger's licence as null and void. Subsequently, Telecel-Niger sought a new mobile licence, which was granted in October 1998. Just as Telecel-Niger was preparing to launch commercial service, this licence was again unilaterally cancelled by the government without apparent cause.

Secondly, this approach may hamper the development of a modern regulatory framework. International good practice dictates that licences should be standardized and harmonized to the extent possible. This means that subsequent licences[32] should, in theory, adopt the same regulatory approach and format as the highly tailored lengthy licences issued previously in order to avoid creating unjustified asymmetric and discriminatory regulation. Yet, detailed licences granted as part of a privatization or auction tend to be heavily negotiated with bidders. The result may be that the applicable sector rules are skewed in favour of the entity that negotiated the licence terms, to the detriment of later, often smaller, market entrants.

Moreover, in an attempt to promote certainty for the initial investor, highly tailored licences of this nature are likely to specify in great detail the requirements and procedures the regulatory authority must apply in relation to interconnection, tariff, and other key decisions. As these controls are difficult to change due to the restrictions on licence modification, this may pose a major stumbling block to any future attempts at regulatory reform. Furthermore, the licence may result in a misallocation of scarce regulatory resources if the licence terms do not reflect appropriate regulatory priorities in the interests of the sector as a whole. Such licences typically allow licence modification in the public interest, within which category the regulatory authority could argue such regulatory reforms fall. However, this term is by nature amorphous and capable of multiple interpretations; any licensee opposing such

---

[32] This applies both to licences issued in tranches (e.g. where there is an initial licence auction, with additional licences issued later) and to different forms of licence with significant areas of commonality (such as national infrastructure and international gateway licences, or fixed, data, and mobile licences).

change may be able to delay or derail reform by threatening legal action to challenge the legality of the proposed licence modification, or (in the case of major investors) by threatening to withdraw its investment in the country. This has happened in many developing countries, particularly in the Caribbean and the Pacific where operators have engaged governments in protracted legal disputes over changes to licences. This has created a burden on government resources and delayed implementation of sector reforms.

Thirdly, the use of such all-encompassing licences also encourages investors to look no further than the terms of the licence in assessing a regulatory environment, in the mistaken assumption that this forms an exhaustive regulatory code. This may cause the unwary investor to overlook key issues arising in sector-specific and generic legislation, regulations, decrees, and other regulatory instruments.

In theory, it is preferable to limit licence terms to fundamental, investor-specific requirements (e.g. the scope and duration of the authorization, commitments related to network roll-out and quality of service, rights to radio frequencies), with generally applicable regulatory controls relegated to primary legislation and regulations.[33] To provide investor confidence and certainty, the core concepts and principles underlying key aspects of the regulatory regime should be enshrined in legislation, with detailed regulatory mechanics set out in regulations, orders, and sector guidelines. Greater use of secondary legislation allows regulatory approaches to evolve, as the market requires. Comprehensive, detailed licences should instead be limited to those countries where licences are issued in advance of regulatory reform, and where no reasonable sector-specific regulatory framework is in place. However, in practice, stakeholders commonly prefer the use of detailed licences, despite the limitations and pitfalls described above.

17.5.2.3 *Convergence and technological neutrality*
The regulatory scheme should be technology-neutral in order to ensure that the development of new, 'converging' services is not impeded by regulatory constraints on the form of service delivery. Recognizing the agility and complexity of the telecommunications sector, the EU 2002 package moved away from distinctions based on technology or network type. Instead, the starting point under this regulatory package was that all electronic communications transmission networks (whether fixed, mobile, satellite, Internet, or broadcasting transmission) should be regulated consistently. The theory underpinning this approach is that, in a 'converged' world, distinctions between technologies and transmission structures are artificial and distort incentives for investment. This approach also avoids confusion as to which regulatory framework (telecommunications, broadcasting, or information services) and which regulatory institution would apply to new 'hybrid' services such as video

---

[33] This approach is not dissimilar to the approach taken in the US, where traditionally regulatory terms and conditions were imposed through decisions, orders, and regulations rather than through telecommunications licences.

conferencing, cable television, video-on-demand, or internet services. Many developing countries, in contrast, have continued to license and regulate technologies, networks, and services in differing and sometimes conflicting ways and to have multiple regulatory institutions with overlapping or poorly defined jurisdictions.

The most obvious regulatory response to the challenge of convergence is to draft primary legislation that is technology-neutral and covers all electronic communications transmission networks. Examples include Malaysia's 1998 Multimedia Act, and the communications convergence legislation recently proposed in Sri Lanka and India (the 2003 Sri Lankan Electronic Communications Networks and Services Bill and the 2001 Indian Communication Convergence Bill), although neither were ultimately enacted.

However, in a true technology-neutral regulatory system, operators should be free to use the most appropriate technology for the conveyance of traffic and service delivery. This requires more than technology-neutral enabling legislation; in addition, the licences and service authorizations themselves must not constrain the method of service provision (see below, section 17.5.3.2). Too often, regulatory regimes in developing countries have generated multiple regulatory agencies, with sometimes overlapping jurisdictions and inconsistent approaches to regulation, and a myriad of different licences, which define in narrow detail the technologies permitted and the scope of networks and services authorized. Therefore, in practice, the introduction of a 'convergent' regulatory regime will require an overhaul of the existing regulatory architecture and the licensing system to ensure that the development of the markets are not constrained. However, this may be possible only if markets are fully opened to competition: the continued existence of monopoly rights in discrete market segments may dictate the issuance of narrowly drawn licences reflecting that monopoly.

17.5.3 Licensing

Regulatory frameworks typically require operators of communications networks and/or providers of communications services to obtain some form of licence or authorization, or alternatively to register with or notify the regulatory authority, prior to commercial service launch (which, for simplicity, we collectively refer to as 'licences' in this section). These documents or procedures provide the necessary authorization for an operator to participate in telecommunications markets, often set out an operator's rights and obligations, and are a means of enabling regulatory authorities to keep track of market participants.[34]

---

[34] See further Chapter 7.

17.5.3.1 *Licensing processes*

As licences control market entry, good regulatory practice dictates that both the licensing procedures and licence documents be straightforward, clear, and streamlined. The EU 2002 package seeks to minimize barriers to market entry by simplifying licensing procedures, and keeping licensing documents as straightforward and short as possible with no limit on licence numbers unless required by radio spectrum constraints. In particular, all electronic communications networks and services are to be licensed using a mechanism that requires no explicit decision or administrative act by the national regulatory authority; that is, new entrants must *at most* be required only to notify the regulatory authority of their intention to operate a network or provide services.[35] This notification is simply intended to allow the regulatory authority to maintain a list of network and service providers. Regulatory authorities may grant 'individual rights of use' where the right to use radio frequencies or numbering ranges is conferred, but only where a departure from the ordinary notification procedures is warranted in the circumstances (e.g. due to a material risk of harmful interference).

In contrast, developing countries often suffer from confusing, long-winded, and arbitrary licensing procedures, or complicated and overly narrow or prescriptive licences may deter new entrants, hamper sector development, or increase the risk premium attached to investment in a country's communications sector.

Bangladesh: licensing pitfalls

The history of licensing in Bangladesh has left operators with a legacy of highly uneven and inconsistent licences. For example, some operators are prevented from engaging in direct interconnection, while others are prevented from carrying other operators' long-distance traffic. Similarly, some GSM operators are entitled to construct their own network backbone infrastructure, whereas others are required to use that of the State-owned fixed operator. These differences may stem both from a piecemeal and uncoordinated approach to licensing, and from the differing bargaining power of licensees when negotiating licence terms.

Separate licences are also required for network operation and frequency usage. While operating licences tend to be of long duration, frequency licences must be renewed annually. In the case of mobile networks, delays in frequency licence renewals have forced some mobile operators to operate their networks without a valid frequency licence. Uncertainty over the continued renewal of frequency licences may disincentivize operators from engaging in long-term planning and investment.

---

[35] Directive 2002/20/EC on the authorization of electronic communications networks and services.

While the licensing obligation under the 2001 Telecommunications Act in Bangladesh is extraordinarily broad (requiring, for example, equipment maintenance, construction work, and using any form of radio apparatus to be licensed, with no apparent authority to grant exemptions from licensing requirements), the scope of the individual licences on offer has tended to be narrowly drawn. For example, an Internet service provider may require as many as six different telecommunications licences to provide Internet service. The requirement to hold multiple licences raises the barriers for market entry and increases the regulatory burden. The regulator is also permitted to charge licensees a multiplicity of different fees and to introduce new fees at any time, which creates significant regulatory uncertainty and cost.

However, despite the urgent need for licensing reform, implementing such reform can be difficult in the absence of clear authority to amend existing licences, particularly in a litigious environment like Bangladesh.

Ideally, licensing should be as simple and streamlined as possible, with published and objective licensing criteria. While investors in and lenders to major operators in the developing world have generally required some form of formal 'licence' with a defined scope and duration, regulatory bottlenecks can be reduced by limiting formal licences to key public networks (e.g. fixed and mobile network infrastructure licences, international gateways, and frequency usage). Entities wishing to provide value-added, Internet, or data services or to operate private networks could be under an obligation simply to register with the regulatory authority of their activities, or even be exempted from licensing requirements altogether.

Licensing processes should be designed to reflect government liberalization policy. As a general principle, licence numbers should be unlimited and available upon request, except where there are real constraints, such as availability of radio frequency spectrum. Temporary bottlenecks due to numbering or spectrum issues should be resolved by a revision of the relevant numbering or spectrum plans, rather than by curtailing market entry.

Regulatory authorities in developing countries may also prefer a more structured licensing process than the EU notification regime in order to impose more rigorous licensing criteria due to concerns regarding fraud, consumer protection, or national security. As a general principle, however, the lower the barriers to market entry, the more likely that competition will take root and flourish. This principle holds true in both developed and developing countries, although typically there is a greater diversity of market barrier in developing countries (e.g. in the form of restrictions on foreign ownership and the movement of capital). That said, a pure EU-style notification regime may assume a degree of market liberalization and maturity, and confidence in the regulatory environment, which may not yet exist.

Regulatory discretion in licence allocation, however, should be kept to a minimum, with licensing occurring automatically upon filing the required information. This helps protect the licensing system from the possibility of corruption, and also minimizes delays in awarding licences where regulatory resources are limited.

17.5.3.2 *Licence categories and unified licences*

To ease regulatory burdens associated with market entry, and to encourage the introduction of new converging services, licences should be kept technology-neutral to the extent possible. An encouraging trend is the emergence of 'unified licensing' regimes in India and in a number of African countries. The idea behind a unified licensing regime is that licences authorize the provision of services and/or operation of network infrastructure, but do not constrain the type of services or infrastructure that may be provided or operated. As adoption of IP-based next-generation networks increases, a unified licensing regime is arguably the best way to overcome the difficulty of delineating and categorizing types of networks and services and to allow operators and customers to benefit from greater choice in means of service delivery and use. For example, should the operator of a wireless local loop network be permitted to offer limited or full mobility services? Should a mobile operator be allowed to operate 'femto' cells which enable mobile subscribers to use their mobile phone as a landline phone in their home? A licensing regime which seeks to distinguish fixed from mobile services may need to draw artificial distinctions to preserve the boundaries between the two types of service, thereby preventing a fixed operator from providing any form of mobility or a mobile operator from allowing mobile handsets to be used as a fixed line within the home area. Thus, the regulator may set geographic limits on the amount of mobility a wireless local loop subscriber may enjoy, or may ban the use of technologies which allow a mobile handset to replace a landline service. These arbitrary distinctions often give rise to operator disputes and ultimately diminish competition and customer choice.

In practice, some countries who purport to have adopted a 'unified' licensing regime still restrict the types of networks or services operated and provided. Although the governing legislation or regulations may give the impression that licensing is technology and service neutral, the actual licences themselves may place limitations on the licensee's field of use, commonly in the form of licence annexes which define the types of service that may be provided or networks or technology that may be deployed. For example, in 2005, Jordan introduced a 'unified' or 'integrated' licensing regime that introduced a single form of 'public telecommunications individual licence' authorizing the operation of public telecommunications networks and provision of public telecommunications services. The existing fixed and mobile operators were transitioned to this new form of licence, thereby removing historical anomalies between licences issued at different times and for different services. At first blush, this 'integrated' licence appears to allow a licensee to operate any network and provide any service. However, the licence attaches detailed schedules which specify the types of service covered and specifically prohibit the provision of

certain services (e.g. mobile wireless services) unless this is authorized in a separate licence agreement.

A true 'unified' licensing regime should not seek to draw distinctions between types of network and service (with spectrum rights granted through a separate frequency licence, authorizing use of a frequency for a general use consistent with ITU allocations, but not seeking to delineate technologies used). Categories of licence, if used, should be kept to a minimum to avoid unnecessary licence duplication. The scope of licence authorization also should be clearly drawn, preferably as broadly and technologically-neutral as possible in order to support the emergence of new convergent service types.

India: unified licensing regime
In November 2003 the Indian Department of Telecommunications introduced a 'Unified Access Services Licensing Regime', whereby fixed and mobile operators would hold a 'unified access service licence' authorizing licensees to provide all telecommunications services using any technology. This meant that both mobile and local fixed operators were free to implement GSM, CDMA, and other wireless technologies to provide any voice, data, or inter-net service, whether on a full or limited mobility or a fixed basis. This move followed a challenge by GSM mobile operators to the legality of the provision by local fixed operators of limited mobility services across their CDMA wire-less local loop systems, and resulted in an explosion in mobile subscriptions as the existing wireless local loop operators deployed full and limited mobil-ity services across their CDMA networks, making low-cost mobility services to large, previously underserved segments of the population.

17.5.3.3 *Issuing authority*
In some legal systems, it may be that only a minister has constitutional authority to issue a licence—or some form of ministerial control may be sought for political reasons. Ministerial discretion over licensing is highly undesirable, and creating another layer in the licensing process is likely to delay further the granting of licences. Where this additional layer is unavoidable, the scope of the ministerial power to veto licence grant should be specified explicitly and be limited to matters of genuine governmental concern (e.g. where matters of national security are involved), and time limits for ministerial intervention should be set.

17.5.3.4 *Licence fees*
Licence fees are typically imposed for the initial licence grant, and on an annual basis thereafter. The fees for most categories of licence should be kept to a minimum in order to avoid creating unnecessary barriers to market entry. Ideally, the initial fees for the grant of such licences should simply reflect the administrative cost of

processing the application. However, licenses that give an operator the right to use a scarce resource (such as radio spectrum) are often very valuable. Governments typically charge substantial fees for the award of such licences. In some cases, these are paid upon licence award while, in others, they are spread out over a several years. These licences (together with the accompanying right to use the associated radio spectrum) have sometimes proved to be so valuable that governments have attempted to raise licence fees retrospectively. This happened, for example, in Benin in 2007 when the regulator unilaterally imposed an additional licence fee of over US$50 million on Benin's three mobile operators (tantamount to a 500 per cent increase to the initial licence fee paid). Only the state-owned mobile operator 'paid' the fee, causing the regulator to suspend the licences of the two privately owned mobile operators and shut down their networks. This prompted the intervention of the President of South Africa to negotiate a deal with the President of Benin, under which the operators were permitted to resume service upon payment of the increased fee, in exchange for certain concessions.[36]

Annual licence fees typically form the main source of funding for the regulatory authority and help to ensure its freedom from undue political interference. The amounts of these annual fees are typically specified in the licence, usually as a percentage of the business's total revenues. However, ideally this should be specified as a cap and the regulatory authority should adjust the fees according to the costs incurred in regulating the sector. The level and method for calculating annual fees should in this case be set out in a regulation or order of general application.

The scope of the regulator's responsibilities may extend beyond the major network operators and include small market participants such as Internet Service Providers (ISPs). The imposition of significant licence fees on these providers is likely to act as a disincentive to market entry and therefore may have the effect of stifling competition. Therefore, regulators often include turnover thresholds in licence fee structures, below which small companies are either exempted from fees or charged only a nominal amount.

In some jurisdictions, governments have established multi-sectoral regulatory authorities that have responsibility for regulating more than one industry. This has the advantage of economies of scope (since much of the required expertise is common across industries), particularly in countries where the supply of skilled staff is limited. It also has the advantage of increasing the institutional independence of the regulatory authority from both line ministries responsible for individual sectors and from the market participants in each sector.

Where a regulatory authority is multi-sectoral with jurisdiction over more than one industry, regulatory costs may need to be allocated between the regulated industries. This can be done by allocating the regulatory budget between participants in all regulated industries on the basis of their total relevant revenues. This approach

---

[36] 'World Dialogue on Regulation for Networked Economies', 18 September 2007.

has the advantage of simplicity and transparency. However, it may also create imbalances, since both profit margins and the cost of regulation may vary significantly between industries. An alternative approach is to separate the regulatory cost attributable to each industry; licence fees for each industry are then set accordingly. However, this process may become complex where the majority of regulatory costs are common across industries. On the other hand, if there are few common regulatory costs, this raises the question of whether there are any cost-savings from having a multi-sectoral regulator.

Where a regulator also has responsibility for information services, data protection, and e-commerce, these areas of regulation may in practice also be financed by the licensees in the communications sector because of the difficulties in identifying and taxing all the beneficiaries of such regulation.

17.5.4 Retail tariffs

In the absence of effective competition in the market, a dominant operator has little commercial incentive to keep tariffs low, and therefore regulatory controls are required to keep tariffs in check. Where the incumbent operator is owned by the state and the operator pays a dividend to the government, controls on tariffs may also affect public sector revenue. In addition, tariff controls directly affect operator revenue streams, and consequently their ability to finance new investment in infrastructure, switching, and interconnection capacity. Control of retail tariffs has therefore traditionally been seen as one of the most important functions of the regulatory authority.[37] This is frequently reflected in the sector legislation, which often spells out the responsibilities of the regulatory authority with regards to tariff control in some detail.

17.5.4.1 *Application of tariff controls*
The first issue which needs to be addressed is to whom tariff controls will apply. The regulatory systems of developing countries regulate retail tariffs of operators in different ways. It is not uncommon for the fixed incumbent operator to be required to obtain regulatory approval of any changes to its retail tariffs. This is often a legacy from the time when the fixed operator was a monopoly and regulatory controls on its retail tariffs were essential for protecting customers. Mobile operators and ISPs, on the other hand, usually face no regulatory controls of their retail tariffs. This differential treatment of retail tariffs increasingly looks anachronistic for two reasons. First, as the market share of the fixed operators dwindles, a system of focusing regulatory retail tariff controls on fixed operators becomes increasingly irrelevant as a way of protecting customers. Secondly, where incumbent fixed operators have been privatized and are in genuine competition with other operators and ISPs, retail tariff controls limit their ability to compete with other operators.

---

[37] See further Chapter 3.

Regulatory frameworks in developing countries are beginning to recognize this inconsistency of approach, and as a result a two-tier system of regulation based on the concept of market dominance is increasingly being applied in developing countries. This provides a more systematic way for regulators to decide which licensees will be subject to retail tariff controls. This approach was adopted in Bahrain, where licensed operators with significant power are subject to tariff controls in relation to any telecommunications service for which the regulatory authority determines that insufficient competition exists.[38] However, in the majority of developing countries, this mechanism is rarely applied in a rigorous and systematic way.

In practice, therefore, the retail tariffs for the majority of telecommunications services in developing countries are unregulated because they are provided by mobile operators. This has not been regarded as a major problem to date, since the retail tariffs of mobile operators have fallen over time as competition has intensified. However, as mobile operators are becoming the dominant players in many developing countries, regulators will increasingly need to consider the implications of market structure and the effectiveness of competition on their decisions about whether or not to regulate their retail tariffs.

Finally, the framework should also ensure that the regulator is encouraged to withdraw regulatory tariff controls when this is appropriate. This is provided for under the EU 2002 package through regular market reviews and determinations of significant market power. However, in developing countries, such reviews are likely to represent an undue burden on the regulatory authority. Instead, one option could be to allow operators to apply for a removal of their designation as a dominant operator if they believe this is warranted due to a change in market conditions. Alternatively, regulators could be required to review tariff controls where there is *prima facie* evidence that an operator is no longer in a dominant position.

17.5.4.2 *Forms of tariff control*

Once the regulator has determined which operators and which services are to be regulated, it must also determine the form of the tariff control. There are a number of options for this.

It is common in developing countries to see a requirement that all regulated tariffs be pre-approved. This system was designed when the sector was dominated by a monopoly provider and there were typically only a limited number of different services. However, with the introduction of new technologies, new operators, and a proliferation of new tariffs, these arrangements have become increasingly unworkable.

Not only does it impose an impossible burden on the regulatory authority, but it also creates unnecessary delays for operators seeking to introduce new tariffs plans and to respond to competitive threats. It also hampers the ability of operators to make medium-term strategic plans due to uncertainty as to regulatory approval of

---

[38] Section 58 of the 2002 Telecommunications Law, <http://www.tra.org.bh>.

future tariff changes and future revenue streams. Indeed, the governing legislation may not give any guidance on the basis upon which tariffs will be approved or rejected, which exacerbates this uncertainty. Even where regulatory frameworks do identify costs as the basis of tariff approval, there is usually no guidance on the form of costs or how they should be calculated. Also, this system leaves operators vulnerable to short-term political influences on tariffs, particularly during an election year. The overall effect may be to stifle the development and beneficial effects of competition.

There are also disadvantages to this system from an economic efficiency point of view. The basis for tariff approval is usually cost. Where regulators are required to approve all new tariffs, tariffs are continually being revised to match costs. As a consequence, operators do not receive any of the benefits arising from an improvement in efficiency and a reduction in costs, and they therefore do not have any incentive to increase the efficiency of their operations.

In order to counter both the administrative and economic problems associated with a tariff approval system, regulators in Europe across all sectors have introduced price-cap formulae as an alternative tariff control system. This system sets price trends over a period of three to five years, allowing regulated companies to retain the benefits of any efficiency improvements that they may make, and therefore gives them an incentive to invest in cost-saving technologies and more efficient working practices.

In the telecommunications industry, price caps usually apply to a basket of services. This means that the average price of a selection of telecommunications services must decline over time. However, operators are free to set the price of specific services in order to respond to competition as it emerges. Another advantage of a price-cap system is that of administrative simplicity. There is no need for prior approval of tariffs since tariff changes must comply with a pre-defined formula and this compliance can be verified *ex-post* at the end of the year.

This approach has a number of advantages for developing countries. The simplicity and transparency of a formula-based system makes the process of price regulation much clearer and more predictable for market participants. In addition, as price-control formulae are set only periodically, the whole process of cost modelling becomes less onerous. Indeed, regulatory authorities may hire external expertise to assist in setting the formula, allowing higher-quality decisions to be made. The disadvantage of price-control formulae is that the modelling required can be complex. However, this can be simplified through the use of international benchmarks for some of the parameters.

In some developing countries, as competition has emerged in segments of the market, regulators have faced a new challenge in regulating retail tariffs: preventing operators from under-pricing (also known as 'predatory pricing') in an attempt to stifle the growth of competition. An increasingly important priority for regulators, this market behaviour can be difficult to control in the absence of effective generic competition law controls.

17.5.4.3 *Calculating the cost of provision*

Most forms of tariff control require some form of cost-orientation. Regulatory frameworks in developing countries vary in the degree to which they specify exactly which tariffs are to be based on costs and the cost concepts to be used. However, whether the system being used is a tariff approval system or a price cap, an estimate of costs will have to be carried out, either by the regulatory authority or the operator. In doing so, regulators in developing countries will face a number of difficult issues.

Operators in developing countries are generally unlikely to collect data on the cost of service for commercial reasons. When submitting tariff applications, they must therefore carry out an explicit cost-of-service estimate. The simplest way of doing this requires the allocation of high-level costs across the different services. This requires costs to be broken down by asset categories and allocated using information from the network on traffic routing. To do this correctly is a major undertaking and operators often lack the required expertise.

In order to ensure that operators can earn a 'reasonable' rate of return on their business, it is necessary for them to include this in their calculations of costs. The estimate of what constitutes 'reasonable' is very difficult because it reflects a number of factors including interest rates, country risk, and the commercial risk associated with the business. In developed countries, data from financial markets is used to make a quantitative estimate of these parameters. However, in the majority of developing countries, these markets simply do not exist and, even where they do, there is insufficient data to make robust estimates of the parameter values.

A major issue in the cost-calculations used in tariff approval is the efficiency with which the operators' costs were incurred. If the regulator deems that the operators have been inefficient and therefore require higher tariffs than would otherwise be the case, they may reject a tariff application or reduce the tariffs in a more or less arbitrary way. In developing countries that have only limited competition and a long history of state ownership of the incumbent, objective benchmarking of operator efficiency is very difficult.

Regulators in developing countries will be required to address all of these issues if they are to make robust decisions on the cost-orientation of tariffs. They can take a number of steps to ensure that these decisions are made in the most objective way possible. Central to these is the development of a cost model which both the regulator and the regulated operators are agreed on. This usually takes a significant period of time and will typically require external support. The basic principles for modelling the cost of service in telecommunications networks are well established and the key issue in developing countries is the data that is used. The use of international benchmarks for some of the cost-calculation parameters can be useful and provides an effective solution where data is not available locally. The use of industry consultation can also be an effective way to ensure that models are developed in a clear and transparent way, and provides a check on some of the key parameters used in the model.

17.5.4.4 *Tariff rebalancing*

In developing countries, the incumbent's tariffs are typically highly unbalanced—charges for line rental and local calls have historically been set well below cost, with charges for national and international calls set well above cost. Incumbents have often retained monopolies over international gateway services, which has allowed them to continue to cross subsidize the losses made the other services. However, innovations such as VoIP and call-back have (lawfully or otherwise) reduced the incumbents' market shares in these profitable markets and this system of cross-subsidy is becoming increasingly unsustainable, forcing governments and regulators to review their policies on rebalancing.

Rises in rental or local call charges disproportionately affect low-income or low-volume users. Tariff control is therefore usually very politically sensitive and, in practice, regulators have often found it very difficult to raise and rebalance the incumbent's tariffs, even where they have the statutory power to do so. However, as fixed operators lose market share to the mobile operators, this is becoming less politically sensitive.

17.5.5 Interconnection

New operators will not be able to enter the market unless their subscribers are able to call subscribers on other existing networks. The terms and conditions of interconnection between networks therefore have an important role in promoting competition in the sector.[39]

Nigeria: the importance of interconnection regulation

Econet, MTN, and the state-owned incumbent NITEL were each awarded a GSM mobile licence in Nigeria in 2001, prior to the enactment of regulatory reforms in the sector. As Econet and MTN were both new entrants, almost all calls made by their subscribers had to be terminated on NITEL's fixed network. However, Econet and MTN were initially permitted to access only a fraction of the capacity they needed to interconnect to NITEL's fixed network, thereby constraining the ability of Econet and MTN subscribers to make 'off-net' calls (i.e. calls from one network to another).[40] In August 2003, when a fourth mobile licence was issued to Globalcom, MTN and Econet adopted similar tactics. The lack of effective interconnection had a significant effect on the ability of operators to develop their business and provide effective competition, and eroded the 'head start' Econet and MTN hoped to secure over slower-moving NITEL through the earlier launch of their mobile networks.

---

[39] See further Chapter 8.
[40] 'Interconnection Bedevils Mobile Operators', *Global Insight*, 12 October 2001.

This situation did not improve until after the enactment of the 2003 Nigerian Communications Act, which set out mandatory principles for interconnection and empowered the regulator to intervene and issue regulations controlling the negotiation and terms of interconnection, including the timeframe and procedures for negotiations, service levels, rate methodologies, and provisioning of facilities.[41] By threatening operators with enforcement action under the Act (and, ultimately, the sanction of licence revocation), the regulator was able to secure operator agreement to improved and more equitable interconnection arrangements.[42] This illustrates the importance of interconnection regulation to a regulatory regime and of undertaking regulatory reforms in parallel with market liberalization.

17.5.5.1 *Which operators should be regulated?*

Direct regulation of interconnection in the EU has traditionally focused on the fixed incumbent, as high termination charges were seen as a potential barrier to entry at the outset of market liberalization. In 1998, however, the UK began regulating mobile interconnection charges, and this approach has subsequently been followed by other EU countries. The primary concern in mobile termination charge regulation in the EU has been to prevent operators from setting excessively high retail prices through collectively raising termination charges (which costs are carried through to the retail price), rather than the creation of barriers to entry for new competitors.

The same issue applies in developing countries where mobile termination charges, when not subject to regulatory controls, have been set at high levels and these have fed through into high retail prices. In these countries, controlling mobile termination charges is therefore seen as a key consumer protection issue since the mobile operators usually provide the majority of telecommunications services in the country. Where individual operators have achieved very large market shares, this also raises the issue of their ability to use their termination charges to create barriers to entry and to constrain the development of effective competition. Although the underlying issues facing regulators in approaching regulation of interconnection charges may be similar in both developing countries and the EU, the EU approach to selecting the operators to which regulatory controls of interconnection charges apply (through the EU definition of the market for mobile termination, which by definition means that every mobile network operator is deemed to have 'significant market power' and therefore subject to regulation) may not be appropriate. This EU system of regulating all mobile termination charges may be too great a burden for regulators in developing countries and may create undue risks for investors entering risky

---

[41] The Nigerian Communications Act 2003, Chapter VI, Part II.

[42] 'Pressure Mounts to Conclude GSM Interconnection in Nigeria by December 2003', *Global Insight*, 11 November 2003.

markets. Instead, it may be preferable to adopt a simpler framework of market definition, which limits these more extensive regulatory controls to the dominant fixed and mobile operators.

17.5.5.2 *How should interconnection be regulated?*

The mechanisms for regulating interconnection are established through all four elements of the general regulatory framework—the law governing the sector, subsidiary regulations, operator licences, and the interconnection agreements themselves.

The law typically sets out the basic obligations to interconnect, the 'two-tier' regulatory structure (if used) that distinguishes dominant from non-dominant operators, the powers of the regulator with regard to interconnection regulation, and the basic principles for setting interconnection charges. Licences may contain similar provisions but often include greater detail. However, care should be taken to avoid unnecessary regulatory duplication.

The regulator may also issue interconnection regulations that apply to all operators, typically with more onerous provisions attaching to those that are dominant. These regulations may include detailed provisions for the calculation of the cost of interconnection, where physical interconnection should be available, rules and principles for interconnection product development and specification, rules for ordering and provisioning, rules and principles for interconnection pricing, regulatory accounting and costing, interconnection accounting and settlement principles, and dispute resolution mechanisms. Regulations may be a better tool than licences for this purpose because of the need to ensure that all operators are subject to the same regulatory controls, and to allow the detail to be updated as markets develop.

However, most of the detailed implementation of interconnection arrangements is done through interconnection agreements, which contain the specific commercial, technical and operational terms between two interconnecting operators. Dominant operators may be required to publish a reference interconnection offer (RIO), which is typically approved by the regulatory authority and forms the basis of interconnection arrangements with other operators. Historically these 'reference' interconnection offers were required only of dominant fixed operators, but the current market dominance of mobile operators may require them to be subject to the same obligation.

An alternative approach adopted in some jurisdictions is for the regulatory authority to encourage the use of a model interconnection agreement by all operators, which assists in standardizing the interconnection environment in a country and in ensuring that interconnection is undertaken in accordance with international norms. In small countries in particular, the use of model agreements or a shorter, streamlined form of RIO, with greater emphasis on interconnection regulations and guidelines for detailed regulation, may be more appropriate: by including more detail in interconnection regulations or guidelines and less in the RIO or model interconnection agreement itself, this should reduce the time required to negotiate or approve interconnection agreements and reduce the scope for operator disagreement on the terms of interconnection.

Where interconnection agreements or RIOs require regulatory approval, procedures should be designed to minimize regulatory discretion and delay. For example, the regulatory regime could specify that, in the absence of a contrary decision of the regulator within a specified time period, an agreement is deemed to have been approved. The grounds upon which a regulator can reject an agreement or RIO should be clearly specified, and be limited to objective and proportionate criteria.

17.5.5.3 Interconnection payments

Interconnection payment arrangements vary around the world. In some countries, operators make no payments to each other for interconnection, while in others they do. This difference is primarily based on two factors: the retail tariff structure in the relevant country and the pattern of inter-network traffic flows. If a country has a Receiving Party Pays (RPP) retail tariff system (where customers pay to receive calls), then there is no need for an interconnection payment to be made for an inter-network call since the cost of terminating a call is covered by the person receiving the call. The alternative system, known as Calling Party Pays (CPP), requires the person that initiates the call to pay the full cost of the call and the person receiving the call pays nothing. Under this system, the network that terminates the call incurs a cost but receives no revenue from its customer. In this case, the terminating network would typically expect to receive an interconnection payment from the originating network to cover the cost of carrying the call from the point of interconnection to the receiving party. However, if the traffic flows between networks are approximately symmetrical, the network operators may decide to waive the charges on the basis that the net payments would be too insignificant to justify the administrative cost of an interconnection payment system. Where no interconnection payments are paid (either because of an RPP retail tariff system or because the operators waive payments due to the expected symmetry of inter-network traffic flows), this is known as a 'bill and keep' system.

The RPP system is in force in only a few countries around the world, most notably the US. Instead, a large majority of countries, including nearly all developing countries, have adopted the European CPP model. In developing countries, where markets are developing rapidly, it is rare for traffic flows to be sufficiently stable and symmetrical to justify a 'bill and keep' system, and therefore, in practice, systems of interconnection payment are generally in operation. This necessitates an active role for the regulator in controlling charges, adjudicating disputes, and monitoring quality of service.

In some countries, however, interconnection payment arrangements between operators may be inconsistent. For example, in Bangladesh, payment arrangements among operators range from revenue sharing, 'bill and keep', and straight payments for services provided. These different payment structures cause inequity between operators, as different operators pay different charges for the identical interconnection service. Moreover, these bilateral arrangements provide little or no incentive for operators to invest in increased interconnection capacity, as they confer 'free'

interconnection on some operators while charging high tariffs to others. In such circumstances, the commercial payment arrangements would need to be regularized in order to create the right incentives for network investment and to ease bottlenecks in interconnection facilities created by market distortions.

There are a few countries which have attempted to switch from RPP to CPP systems. Where this takes place, regulators face a number of important economic and financial issues. Termination charges will have to be introduced into interconnection arrangements. Retail tariffs for outgoing calls will have to rise to compensate the introduction of these charges, and the impact of this increase is often difficult to manage. Where retail tariffs are also regulated, these controls will have to take into account this change. This may have significant implications for regulators, particularly where retail tariffs are set for a period through a price cap.

Sri Lanka: implementing interconnection payments reform

Historically, in Sri Lanka, the industry used a system of RPP. However, it was believed that this was constraining the development of the mobile market as it encouraged subscribers to switch their phones off to avoid incoming calls. As a result, mobile operators lobbied for a switch to CPP. The regulator (the TRC) decided to implement this change and to introduce new interconnection charges (fixed and mobile) based on cost. However, a lack of consensus between operators on the structure of costs had delayed implementation for a number of years. To resolve this issue, the TRC commissioned a modelling exercise to facilitate operator agreement on cost-based interconnection charges.

The key issues that arose during this exercise included agreement on a methodology for cost allocation for operators, the value of the cost of capital to be used in the modelling, and de-averaging of tariffs by the time of day and for different products.

The introduction of termination charges and the CPP system required a revision of retail call prices. The introduction of the new interconnection tariffs, which included an increase in the price of fixed-to-mobile calls, and the CPP system were scheduled by the TRC to take place in 2004. However, these changes were put on hold upon a change in government and have not been subsequently implemented.

17.5.5.4 *Calculating the cost of interconnection*

It is now generally accepted by regulatory authorities around the world that, where networks charge for the provision of interconnection services, the applicable tariffs should be based on cost. This ensures that the provider of interconnection receives some compensation for the costs that it incurs and is given an incentive to invest in interconnection capacity. A number of different ways of calculating the cost of

interconnection have emerged, the two most common methods being fully allocated costs and Long-Run Incremental Cost (LRIC).[43]

LRIC has emerged as the global regulatory standard. However, its calculation can be complex. Even in developed countries, it is rarely carried out in-house by regulators. Indeed, its implementation in developing countries is particularly difficult for a number of reasons.

First, considerable network engineering and financial data is required for a 'bottom-up' model and detailed management accounting information is required for a 'top-down' model. This data may simply not be available over a reasonable timescale for operators in developing countries. Secondly, the LRIC methodology calculates the efficient cost of providing the specified services and therefore termination charges based on LRIC are intended to encourage providers to be as efficient as possible. However, in developing countries, the incumbent is frequently owned by the state and has a legacy of publicly determined investments and overstaffing. As a result, it may be difficult to improve efficiency in the short term and this limits the degree to which the regulator is justified in setting interconnection charges based on efficient costs. Finally, LRIC cost estimates should be forward-looking and are therefore based on traffic forecasts. These may be particularly unreliable in the volatile markets typical of developing countries.

The complexity of calculating the cost of interconnection means that regulatory authorities have sometimes used benchmarking to set interconnection tariffs instead. The experience of regulating interconnection in the EU has provided a substantial body of evidence on the cost of interconnection, and this has been used to set interconnection rates in developing countries for both mobile and fixed operators.

Botswana: use of international benchmarking to set mobile termination charges

In February 2003 and September 2003, the regulator in Botswana (the BTA) issued two determinations on interconnection disputes that covered the setting of termination charges. Although the BTA expressly recognized LRIC as the best methodology for setting interconnection charges, benchmarking was used due to the lack of available cost data.

In the first decision, the charge for termination on the fixed network was calculated as the average of the equivalent charges across the 15 EU Member States. However, in the second decision, the BTA stated that it was 'not confident that most of the EU countries have reached or are in the process of reaching efficient cost-oriented termination charges'[44] and therefore set the termination charge for fixed-to-mobile calls on the basis of the average of the current best practice range set by the EU.

---

[43] See further Chapter 3, at 3.13.1.
[44] 'Ruling on Interconnection Charges Dispute between Botswana Telecommunications Corporation and Mascom Wireless (Pty) Limited', BTA Ruling No 1 of 2003, 26 February 2003.

17.5.5.5 *Indirect access and access deficit charges*

Indirect access allows customers to receive communications services, most commonly long-distance and international calls, from a provider other than the operator that provides the access line. Under these arrangements, subscribers are able to choose to route calls via their preferred provider by dialling prefix codes on a call-by-call ('carrier selection') or on an ongoing basis ('carrier pre-selection'). Typically, regulatory intervention is required to oblige the incumbent operator to provide competitors with indirect access. These arrangements are not common in developing countries. That said, they potentially offer a viable means of introducing limited competition and may therefore be useful in smaller markets, provided this benefit is not outweighed by implementation costs.

Where indirect access is mandated, the alternative operator purchases origination services from the access provider. The charge for this service is usually set by the regulatory authority on the basis of cost. Where the incumbent's tariffs are unbalanced, this may cause a problem because the incumbent is required to maintain its call charges above cost in order to compensate for the losses that it makes on line rental. However, an alternative provider has no such constraints and can therefore undercut the incumbent. This potentially results in inefficient entry and could threaten the financial viability of the incumbent operator. In order to minimize the risk of this happening, regulators have set up systems of charges called Access Deficit Contributions (ADCs). These are mark-ups on interconnection which the alternative operator pays to the incumbent as compensation for the profits it forgoes when entry in the long-distance/international markets occurs.

This system is only appropriate while the incumbent's tariffs are unbalanced. Once rebalancing is complete, the system should be withdrawn. If a universal service fund is also established, it is important to avoid double-counting of costs between access deficits and universal service costs. This is a difficult exercise and a regulatory authority in a developing country would typically require external advice on the design and implementation of such a scheme.

The Bahamas: access deficits and universal service[45]

The tariffs of the incumbent operator in the Bahamas (BTC) are unbalanced and, in particular, local calls are provided free of charge. The legal framework in the Bahamas provides for the establishment of both Access Deficit Contributions and Universal Service Fund payments but does not specify how these should interact with each other.

Indirect access is not mandated in the Bahamas, so any alternative provider has to supply a means of access as well as long-distance/international calls to its customers. Entrants are free to set their own tariffs (unless they are deemed to be dominant) and therefore do not face an access deficit as a result of regulatory

---

[45] The USO consultation document containing a discussion of these issues is available at <http://www.pucbahamas.gov.bs/consultations.php>.

controls on tariffs. However, the incumbent offers access and local calls below cost and therefore entrants must also offer similar tariff structures if they are to be successful.

BTC clearly makes a loss on providing services to some of its customers. However, it continues to do so because of its Universal Service Obligation. The law provides for the establishment of a Universal Service Fund which would provide some compensation to BTC for the cost it incurs in meeting this obligation.

In the absence of regulatory mandated indirect access and given the presence of a Universal Service Fund, there is no economic justification for a system of Access Deficit Contributions. However, the regulator faces considerable pressure from stakeholders who will be affected by its decision on these issues and faces the possibility of legal action if any of the operators feel their point of view is supported by the law.

17.5.6 Facility sharing and co-location

Under the EU model, national regulatory authorities are entitled to encourage co-location and facility sharing between operators, but the clear regulatory preference is to leave these to normal commercial agreement. In contrast, local loop unbundling of the copper local access network is mandatory.

In developing countries, local loop unbundling may have little or no relevance, particularly where fixed network infrastructure is inadequate and the primary form of communications access is via mobile networks. On the other hand, a more active approach may be appropriate toward tower and mast sharing between wireless operators of all descriptions, as this should lower the cost of network roll-out (thereby lessening the costs passed on to consumers) and may alleviate environmental concerns where a country lacks an adequate generic environmental law regime. The telecommunications laws in many developing countries contain a requirement for operators to share infrastructure for these reasons. However, in practice, these requirements are rarely enforced, particularly in rapidly developing markets. On the other hand, where network roll-out has achieved nationwide coverage, operators have more of an incentive to share tower facilities and agreements are made on tower-sharing for commercial reasons.

A key emerging issue in developing countries in this area is the sharing of facilities and co-location related to landing points for submarine cables. As telecommunications markets develop and broadband services become more widespread in developing countries, the demand for international bandwidth is increasing rapidly. Traditionally, in developing countries, this has been provided primarily by satellite links but the cost of this is high and the technical capacity of the satellite infrastructure is not sufficient to support the high demand for bandwidth. Access to the international submarine cable infrastructure is therefore becoming increasingly important in developing countries.

There are many such cables but the landing points in each country are often controlled by the incumbent operator. Obtaining access to these facilities at reasonable terms is therefore a key issue for the development of the telecommunications market. Regulators have historically found it very difficult to enforce effective cost-based access to these facilities and this is particularly difficult in developing countries where the capacity of the regulatory authority is often low. The best long-term solution to this problem is to ensure that there is more than one cable landing point in a country and that they are owned by different operators. However, in the meantime, regulators should engage in consultation with concerned parties to ensure that sound regulations are established and that they are effectively enforced.

17.5.7 National roaming

Where mobile operators are licensed on a sequential or regional basis, it is not uncommon for an incumbent mobile operator to be required to provide roaming services to the newcomer on its existing mobile network. Except in large or sparsely populated countries where network roll-out would be particularly expensive or onerous, or in countries (such as Iraq) where roaming occurs in regions where the new entrant is not licensed to install its own network infrastructure, national roaming may in practice be of limited value.

In the early stages of commercial launch, new entrants are typically keen to build a strong brand and market reputation as quickly as possible. While national roaming may be seen as a relatively easy method of introducing competition or attaining rapid network roll-out, the ability of the incumbent 'host' network to affect adversely the newcomer's performance and quality of service and thereby damage a fledgling brand, combined with the lack of recourse to effective commercial courts should a dispute under roaming agreements arise, may render roaming too risky a proposition. Rather than expending its energies in putting in place the necessary legal, commercial, and technical roaming arrangements, the newcomer is more likely to prefer instead to concentrate on building out its own network infrastructure.

For example, in Bahrain, the Mobile Telecommunications Licence granted in 2003 to the new entrant mobile operator (Zain, formerly MTC Vodafone Bahrain) included a right to roam on the incumbent Batelco's mobile network while it completed its network roll-out. Zain's licence also contained stringent roll-out requirements: with 95 per cent population service coverage required from the date of commercial launch. However, Zain did not exercise its option to implement national roaming, preferring simply to expedite its roll-out programme.

17.5.8 Universal service and rural/peri-urban access

Most developing countries do not have the luxury of imposing EU-style universal service obligations (USOs), which require every person to have access to a fixed telephone line and basic (fixed) telecommunications services at affordable prices

regardless of geographic location. Instead, they seek to attain the objective of giving all inhabitants some form of access to telecommunications facilities and services. In rural areas, this may take the form of telecentres or community phones, or special subsidized 'rural access' network licensing schemes. In peri-urban areas, the focus may be more on ensuring affordability of basic services or some form of communications access for households falling below the poverty line.

Low fixed penetration rates, the uneconomic cost of fixed network roll-out, lack of access to necessary capital for network investment, years of under-investment in existing fixed network infrastructure, and the need to rebalance local and line rental tariffs may all pose substantial obstacles to basing a universal access strategy on the fixed network. Regulators in developing countries have therefore often looked beyond the incumbent fixed operator to address universal access issues.

17.5.8.1 *Defining universal access*

The first issues that must be addressed in designing a universal access strategy are the definition of the access objective and which body will be responsible for its formulation. Typically, the government will be responsible for sector policy and the regulatory authority for its implementation. The definition of the universal access objectives often falls somewhere in between these two remits. Access to telecommunications services in rural areas is often a politically sensitive issue and governments therefore usually want to be in charge of defining universal service objectives. However, this may result in unrealistic or poorly defined requirements, which the regulator is then responsible for implementing. This is particularly so in developing countries where rural poverty is a major issue and regulators often do not have sufficient influence to ensure that government decisions are practical. An alternative approach is leave the regulatory authority or universal access implementing agency to define the specific objectives.

Universal access strategies typically focus on improved teledensity, access to communications services, telecentres and initiatives to improve rural connectivity, and increased Internet usage.[46] It is important to ensure that sufficient flexibility is built into the definition to allow it to be changed when conditions warrant. A good example of this is the requirement to provide public payphones, which was appropriate before the widespread adoption of mobile phones but which has become increasingly irrelevant in many countries.

Finally, it is important to avoid specifying technologies for the provision of universal access. What is of interest to customers in these areas is the provision of services and they are likely to be indifferent as to how those services are delivered (i.e. whether voice telephony services are provided over mobile or fixed networks).

---

[46] See e.g. Wellenius, B, 'Sustainable Telecenters: a Guide for Government Policy', *Viewpoint Note No 251* (the World Bank Group, January 2003), and the extensive discussion in 'Trends in Telecommunication Reform 2003: Promoting Universal Access to ICTs' (ITU, Geneva, 2003).

17.5.8.2 *Designing universal access programmes*

Once objectives have been determined, a strategy or programme for their attainment must be developed. There is substantial international experience of designing universal access programmes in developing countries. These often revolve around establishing funds to finance roll-out programmes and may sometimes include innovative auction-based systems to select providers. However, simply licensing new entrants to provide rural access will be insufficient: without effective, cost-oriented, and non-discriminatory interconnection, timely and non-discriminatory access to radio frequencies, numbering ranges and rights of way, and confidence in the fair enforcement of regulatory controls, such initiatives are unlikely to succeed.[47]

Network roll-out and coverage obligations in mobile licences, while traditionally not regarded as a universal access obligation, may in practice have the same effect. Since they are contained in licences as obligations, these coverage requirements are not explicitly funded. However, since operators take them into account during the licence award process, they are implicitly financed by both the government and subscribers through higher retail tariffs, and initial licence fees that are lower than might otherwise have been the case.

However, the rapid roll-out of mobile networks in developing countries, which often exceeds licence requirements, show that competitive forces by themselves will ensure that wide areas of the country are served. Indeed, the success of the mobile networks in even very low-income developing countries has raised questions about whether the distortionary effects on the market and the administrative burden on the regulatory authority caused by the introduction of a formal universal access programme in fact outweigh the benefits of the scheme.

Bangladesh: market-based initiatives

There has historically been no formal universal service/access obligation in Bangladesh. However, mobile operators have rolled out their networks throughout the country and some are providing services to the poor for essentially commercial reasons. For example, Grameen Phone provides credit to women in rural areas through a related company, allowing them to buy a handset, connect to the network, and resell calls.[48] The initial loan is approximately US$500 and a pilot study showed that the women could earn, on average, US$2 per day after all costs. This annual income is approximately twice the country's GDP per capita. Grameen selects candidates for loans on the basis of their credit history, location, and their ability in English, and provides a one-day training session.

---

[47] See Prof Rohan Samarajiva, 'Sri Lanka's Telecom Reforms of 2002–2003', *Public Interest Program Unit of the Ministry for Economic Reform, Science and Technology*, 2004, at p 5.

[48] 'Trends in Telecommunication Reform 2003: Promoting Universal Access to ICTs' (ITU, Geneva, 2003) at p 43, and 'Bringing Cellular Phone Service to Rural Areas'. Lawson, C and Meyenn, N, *Viewpoint Note No 205* (The World Bank Group, March 2000).

The rapid roll-out of the mobile networks in Bangladesh and the penetration of services into rural areas through commercial initiatives in the mobile sector contrasted with the low number of lines rolled out by the specialist rural operators (Sheba Telecom and the Bangladesh Rural Telephone Authority). This suggests that market-based initiatives may sometimes be more effective than a formalized rural access programme, and that universal service funds may not always be necessary. However, the Grameen Phone initiative in Bangladesh was aided considerably by its connection to Grameen Bank, a financial institution that provides micro-credit facilities in rural areas.

17.5.8.3 *Funding universal access*

Funding of universal access programmes is a very significant issue for regulators. The traditional approach is to create a 'Universal Service' or 'Rural Access' fund, to which licensed operators contribute on a regular basis. This operates as a tax on the sector and, in some countries, this may have an adverse impact on operators and potential investment in the sector.

The size of the funds and the political sensitivity of the way in which they are used do raise significant issues for the regulatory authority. They require careful design, efficient and transparent management, auditing, and rational fund allocations. Corruption can be an issue in some countries, so the rules and operating procedures for the funds should be designed to minimize the risk of this occurring. One method of improving transparency is to engage in consultation on the allocation of resources and the operation of the fund. Beneficiaries of the fund will have a clear incentive to ensure that resources are not misused and that they are allocated in a sensible and equitable way. They therefore have an interest in participating in any such consultation exercise. Regular publication of auditors' reports is also a useful way of enhancing transparency.

In practice, the track record of Universal Service Funds in developing countries is poor. In most cases, funds have not been fully disbursed or, where they have, they have not been effective at increasing widespread coverage of the networks. In some countries, funds contributed to Universal Service Funds by private operators have been used to support loss-making state-owned enterprises. It is possible that, in future, they will be used to support backbone networks funded by governments but which are not financially viable.

17.5.8.4 *Broadband access*

Governments in developing countries are increasingly focusing on securing widespread access to broadband technologies at affordable prices. From a regulatory perspective, improving broadband access will require full market liberalization (with operators able to obtain the necessary licences as needed to roll out broadband wireless access technologies, backbone infrastructure, and international gateways), robust

access regulation (enabling operators to access and share domestic, cross-border and undersea backbone infrastructure on fair and reasonable terms), access to spectrum to support wireless access technologies, and minimal barriers to entry (with any necessary licences or other approvals available on demand and at minimal cost).

Some countries have also attempted to improve the availability of core broadband infrastructure through licensing operators in that segment of the market. Nigeria and Kenya are both examples of such an approach. The regulator may also have a role to play in the establishment of Internet exchange points (IXPs) which allow traffic originating in developing countries to remain within the region, rather than transiting through hubs in Europe or North America.

In addition to these regulatory measures, governments seeking better broadband network services have also begun to intervene directly in the provision of core network infrastructure. Mobile operators in developing countries have traditionally found it cheaper and more reliable to build out their own backbone transmission networks using wireless and satellite technologies rather than rely on securing access from the incumbent fixed operator. However, governments are now becoming involved in network development through investing in fibre-optic cable infrastructure, either directly or through state-owned incumbent operators.

The stated objective of these investments is to provide widespread access to wholesale capacity at reasonable prices which, it is expected, will reduce the price and increase the coverage of broadband services. In practice, much of this activity has been promoted by equipment manufacturers and financed through supplier credit. In Africa, for example, contracts totalling over US$1 billion for more than 30,000 kilometres of fibre-optic transmission networks were awarded to governments or State-owned enterprises in the 18 months leading up to January 2008.[49] Contracts for such networks have been commissioned by governments in the Democratic Republic of Congo,[50] Ghana,[51] Kenya,[52] and Uganda,[53] and by state-owned incumbent fixed operators in Botswana, Ethiopia, Malawi, Togo, and Zambia. A related approach is the one taken by the government of South Africa which, in 2006, combined the telecommunications assets of electricity provider Eskom and transport parastatal Transet to create a new broadband infrastructure company to provide national backbone transmission capacity on a cost-plus basis.[54]

This development has interesting policy implications since these networks are being developed by governments in a post-privatization, post-liberalization market.

---

[49] 'Sub-Saharan Africa: Broadband, Regulation and International Bandwidth Pricing Drive National Backbone Roll-Out', *Global Insight*, 29 January 2008.
[50] 'China Telecom Construction Corporation Wins National Fibre-Optic Backbone Contract in DRCongo', *Global Insight*, 10 January 2008.
[51] 'Ghana Launches National Fibre Backbone Project' *Global Insight*, 18 May 2007.
[52] 'Kenya: Huawei, ZTE and Sagem Win National Fibre Backbone Project in Kenya', *Global Insight*, 16 October 2007.
[53] 'Uganda: Chinese Government Gives Uganda Loan for Fibre Backbone', *Global Insight*, 31 May 2007.
[54] 'South Africa: Infraco Plans New Submarine Cable', *Global Insight*, 3 August 2007.

In some ways, this is turning the clock back ten years with governments again investing in network deployment where previously they had divested all of their activities in the telecommunications sector. A second implication is whether governments will be able to utilize these networks effectively without distorting the market through preferential treatment of this network. Operators may, for example, find themselves under increasing political pressure to purchase backbone transmission capacity from the new government-owned backbone networks in order to provide financial support to the State-owned entity.

Where government-owned backbone networks exist and are offering adequate quality of service at the right price, operators may be willing to use these networks to increase the capacity of their networks. Access to such backbone services may significantly increase the ability to roll out 3G and other high-speed technologies on a more widespread basis. However, to secure real benefits from the substantial investments in fibre-optic backbone infrastructure, these initiatives should be accompanied by complementary steps to liberalize the market, ensure that access networks are developed (through, for example, making available spectrum and licences to provide broadband wireless access), and that access to international connectivity is also available. These interventions also come at a cost to the public sector—both in potential distortion of the market and the fiscal costs of repaying loans made to finance network construction.

17.5.9 Radio spectrum allocation

The regulatory framework will need to contain the principles and procedures governing the allocation of radio spectrum to ensure that resources are allocated between operators in a fair, non-discriminatory, and efficient manner. Usually, the communications regulatory authority is given the power to maintain a national frequency plan and to assign frequency ranges to operators of electronic communications networks.

There are three models of spectrum regulation: a 'command and control' model, where the licensee is given strict operating parameters and rules defining spectrum rights; an 'exclusive rights' model, where the licensee is given rights that are generally transferable and flexible to use specified spectrum within a defined area during a fixed period of time (with spectrum use rules largely technical in order to manage interference issues; and a 'commons' model, where spectrum is unlicensed and users share a frequency block subject only to limited technical requirements, e.g. with respect to power emissions (a well-known example of the latter being the use of Wi-Fi technologies in WLANs).[55] The 'command and control' model is the model most commonly used for most spectrum blocks in the developing world, but creates administrative burden and restrictions through the need to acquire specific radio

---

[55] 'Trends in Telecommunication Reform 2006: Regulating in the Broadband World' (ITU, Geneva, 2006).

frequency licences for specific uses governed by bureaucratic defined spectrum allocations, thereby discouraging innovation and technological evolution. An 'exclusive use' model provides more flexibility, but may encourage spectrum 'hoarding' as operators may seek to acquire large blocks of spectrum for unspecified uses in order to deny spectrum opportunities to competitors. On the other hand, a 'commons' model for most spectrum uses does not sufficiently manage over-crowding and interference issues, particularly where the spectrum use is not highly localized.

Arguably, a variant of the 'exclusive use' model is generally the most effective way to regulate spectrum while conferring the flexibility to allow the rapid deployment of new radio technologies, while safeguarding the interests of other spectrum users and minimizing the regulatory burden on spectrum regulators, provided that prospective spectrum licensees are required to demonstrate a genuine need for the spectrum licensed and are subject to appropriate usage restrictions to ensure efficient and non-interfering spectrum use.

17.5.9.1 *Allocation between different industries*
Radio spectrum is used by multiple government agencies and industries, including telecommunications, broadcasting, civil aviation, shipping, emergency services, national security and law enforcement agencies, and the military. Allocation of spectrum between different uses is, at a high level, governed by the the the ITU.[56] However, specific allocations between different uses and spectrum coordination with neighbouring countries will need to be undertaken at a national level.

In practice, spectrum usage allocation may be negotiated informally between the relevant responsible ministries; alternatively, a formal inter-ministerial body may be established for this purpose. In Nigeria, for example, a National Frequency Management Council was established, containing representatives of all interested ministries and the security agencies, to determine spectrum allocation issues and to publish a national frequency allocation table.[57] Spectrum that has been allocated for use by electronic communications networks is then assigned to operators and end-users by the Nigerian Communications Commission.

17.5.9.2 *Allocation within communications sector*
Radio spectrum is a scarce resource and needs to be allocated carefully to ensure spectrum is available for future needs. In practice, spectrum grants have tended to be *ad hoc*, with first-comers often granted large blocks of spectrum, often in an attempt to maximize interest and licence value. Today, many developing countries are looking to deploy broadband access, typically using wireless technologies such as broadband fixed wireless access and WiMax. If prior spectrum grants were inefficient or over-extensive, regulators may find new broadband wireless technologies require

---

[56] See further Chapter 15, at 15.3.
[57] The Nigerian Communications Act 2003, Chapter III, Part 2.

relocation of existing spectrum users. Additionally, balancing the use of licensed and unlicensed spectrum remains a challenge.

17.5.9.3 *Interrelationship with operating licences*

Licences to use frequencies for electronic communications may be separate from or incorporated in a network operating licences and authorizations. Rights to use frequencies that are an essential adjunct to the operating licence (such as the uplink and downlink frequencies for satellite and mobile networks) should ideally be incorporated in the operational licence. In practice, they can simply be attached to the operational licence, thereby allowing the use of a consistent, standardized format for frequency licences. If a separate frequency licence is granted for such 'essential' frequencies, then the frequency licence should not contain duration or revocation provisions separate to or different from those contained in the accompanying operating licence: if a frequency licence for essential frequencies is revoked or expires, this will obviously render the accompanying operational licence worthless. In contrast, where the licensed frequency range is non-essential (e.g. frequencies for microwave transmission links), the frequency licence should always be separate from the operating licence. This helps ensure efficient frequency use, as operators incur additional fees for the right to use such frequencies and are therefore encouraged to apply for frequency ranges only when needed. Frequency licences for non-essential frequencies may also be for a term shorter than the operator's operating licence.

17.5.9.4 *Frequency fees*

Frequency fees should encourage efficient frequency use, to reflect the fact that radio spectrum is a valuable, limited public resource. Thus, fees should be high enough to prevent operators from 'hoarding' unused spectrum, but low enough so as not to discourage smaller operators from entering the market or using wireless transmission media. There are various market-based mechanisms for ensuring that spectrum fees are appropriately set, and the approach taken should reflect the availability of the particular frequency range, current and likely future demand, and the need to promote efficient use.

For example, where efficient use of spectrum is not a priority (e.g. frequencies for amateur radio and other private, non-commercial use), frequency fees should simply cover the cost to the regulatory authority of managing the spectrum and should not reflect the value of usage. In contrast, if the relevant frequency range is for commercial use, becoming congested, or in high demand, a market-based pricing mechanism such as marginal value pricing or spectrum auctions may be appropriate. In spectrum auctions, spectrum fees are set according to the value ascribed to the frequencies by bidders. This method is commonly used to allocate licences for frequencies integral to mobile networks.

Under marginal value pricing, the spectrum fee reflects the marginal value to the user of such frequencies. This approach is most suitable frequencies used for non-essential commercial purposes such as microwave or satellite transmission links.

Where spectrum is auctioned, the price is set by the market. However, for other types of spectrum in which the regulator sets the price, care should be taken to ensure that frequency charges are not inappropriately high. If they are, this will act as a barrier to entry to new investors and these higher costs may get passed through to customers. In the case of spectrum for services that are new and innovative in developing countries such as broadband wireless, regulators should set spectrum fees simply to cover administrative costs so that investment and innovation is encouraged.

17.5.9.5 Frequency monitoring

Monitoring the use of radio spectrum is an increasingly important function of regulatory authorities in developing countries. Wireless technologies are taking a central role in the provision of services in developing countries because of their natural advantages (e.g. lower cost and relative ease of network roll-out). However, wireless networks rely on the availability of clear spectrum and operators therefore depend on the regulator to enforce regulatory controls on harmful interference and frequency usage. Developing countries may also face a legacy of unauthorized use of transmitting equipment and frequency interference.

Regulators in developing countries typically lack the resources to purchase expensive monitoring equipment and the skills necessary for its operation. Moreover, the regulation of spectrum usage depends on the regulator being able to take effective enforcement action against those who use spectrum unlawfully.

There are no simple solutions to these issues. The cost of spectrum monitoring equipment can be minimized by ensuring that the optimum equipment configuration is used and that contracts with suppliers are reasonable. There is significant scope for sharing of international experience in this area and potentially the use of procurement advisors. As pressure on spectrum increases, operators may also see it as being in their interests to ensure that spectrum is monitored effectively and may therefore be prepared to contribute to the costs of monitoring, thereby easing the financial burden on the regulator.

17.5.9.6 Spectrum trading

Spectrum trading allows holders of frequency licences to sell their rights to use radio frequencies, thereby promoting efficient spectrum use. Market-based approaches have a general advantage in developing countries because they minimize the opportunities for poor decision-making, political influence, and corruption. However, in the case of spectrum trading, they require a sophisticated structure of administration, regulation, property rights, and enforcement. This often does not exist in developing countries and therefore spectrum trading is unlikely to be a realistic proposition.

17.5.10 Numbering

Historically, numbering plans were usually 'owned' by the incumbent fixed operator. As part of a new regulatory framework, 'ownership' and management of the numbering

plan is generally transferred to the new regulatory authority, and all operators are afforded non-discriminatory and timely access to numbering blocks.

Numbering is sometimes classified in telecommunications legislation as a scarce resource. As this may have the effect of limiting the number of licences available for voice telephony services, this approach is not advocated. Instead, regulatory authorities should be mandated and encouraged to make managed changes to the existing numbering plan to free up sufficient numbering ranges to meet demand.

17.5.10.1 *Asymmetric rights to numbering blocks*
Mere transfer of management of the numbering plan to the regulatory authority may be insufficient to level the playing field. Frequently, the incumbent may have secured large numbering blocks for its own use prior to the transfer. Not only does this encourage inefficient use of numbers, but this puts the incumbent at a competitive advantage, as the incumbent will have access to many more so-called 'golden' or premium numbers than new entrants. Ideally, limited numbering blocks should be allocated to each operator on the basis of forecast need, with the rest reclaimed by the regulatory authority. This approach helps ensure that numbering resources remain sufficient without the need for repeated and frequent changes to the numbering plan (which are disruptive and costly to implement), and ensures that new operators requiring numbering capacity are treated fairly and equivalently.

17.5.10.2 *Charging for number usage*
Efficient use of numbering resources is fostered by charging for number use. These charges can be levied on operators per number block. The power to impose such charges should be expressly conferred on the regulatory authority in its enabling legislation.

17.5.10.3 *Number portability and carrier pre-selection*
Number portability refers to the ability of subscribers to retain their number when they change service provider. Carrier pre-selection refers to the ability to route calls, on an ongoing basis, using a provider other than the operator supplying the access line. Both are intended to reduce the cost to customers of switching between providers and therefore promote competition. However, both require software and hardware upgrades and therefore impose a significant cost on operators.

Regulators in developing countries should consider whether the benefits of such measures are likely to outweigh the cost of implementation. In particular, it may be better for regulators in developing countries to prioritize reducing barriers to entry and encouraging the establishment of viable alternative providers. Imposing additional costs on these operators may not further this. Indeed, it is worth noting that end-users in developing countries are likely to be more price-sensitive that those in developed countries. This means that the cost to consumers of switching provider are likely to have a less detrimental effect on competition than in developed countries. Therefore, the incremental benefit of introducing number portability and carrier pre-selection may be more limited in developing countries.

17.5.11 Equipment testing and certification

Network development in developing countries can be hindered by slow and expensive local equipment testing and certification processes. Developing countries commonly have their own equipment testing and approval centres, which may significantly burden the introduction of new technologies and import of network equipment through added bureaucratic 'red tape', costs, delays, and the possibility for abuse and corruption. Coordination and consistency of approach may also be lacking between communications regulatory authorities and customs officials in the interpretation and application of equipment import rules. Given the concentration of network equipment manufacture among a relatively small group of companies with international or regional presence, such a degree of regulatory interference is unlikely to be warranted.

It is often desirable to make radical changes to existing equipment type approval procedures in order to minimize these effects. Ideally, local equipment and testing and certification programmes should be limited only to those types of equipment that may have a special detrimental effect in the local environment (e.g. because of interference with sensitive radio frequency usages), with equipment requiring certification identified through means of a 'negative list'. In all other cases, it would be preferable for the regulatory framework simply to recognize equipment approvals from designated international and foreign testing centres. However, the loss of jobs in existing test centres may encounter political resistance.

Sri Lanka: removing cumbersome local type approval processes

The existing Sri Lankan 'type approval' regime is set out in the 1991 Telecommunications Act. This Act requires all terminal equipment to be approved by the Telecommunications Regulatory Commission, and the manufacture, trade, sale, import, and repair of equipment to be separately licensed.

Under the reforms proposed in the 2003 Electronic Communications Networks and Services Bill (which was ultimately not enacted following a change in government), this cumbersome type approval regime was to be replaced with a streamlined 'apparatus compliance' regime. Under the new provisions, apparatus placed on the market or put into service in Sri Lanka need only comply with a recognized standard, being a specification or standard published by a standards body recognized by the new regulator or published by the regulator itself. No additional restrictions would be placed on radio apparatus, unless such radio apparatus fell within the ambit of a published negative list of restricted apparatus.

The intent behind the proposed significant deregulation of equipment approvals was to remove the cumbersome and time-consuming process of local approvals, to facilitate the import of telecommunications equipment into Sri Lanka, and to limit the role of customs officials in controlling such imports.

17.5.12 Property rights

New entrants to a liberalized telecommunications sector in developing countries will require certain property rights in order to construct, maintain and operate their networks. They will need reassurance that they will enjoy real property rights which are adequate—both substantively and procedurally—to meet their build-out and service obligations under their licences, and which are no less favourable than those granted to the incumbent. Necessary property rights in respect of both public and private land may include: rights of way to install and maintain infrastructure, fast-track zoning procedures, compulsory purchase powers to obtain key sites needed for network roll-out (e.g. to erect microwave transmission towers or base stations), and rights to access and share 'bottleneck' facilities (which are generally included in the network access regime). Operators may also require rights to cut trees, fly lines, or erect network infrastructure in state-owned land or environmentally sensitive areas. In some cases it may be necessary to coordinate the property rights exercised by different utilities, particularly in respect of network construction, so as to minimize disruption.

Clearly, the importance of property rights to any particular new entrant will depend to a large extent upon the property rights it previously enjoyed and the technology proposed. Thus, new entrants deploying wireless technology will generally have less need for rights of way and compulsory purchase powers than operators of wireline networks. Similarly, existing utility companies entering telecommunications markets may already enjoy sufficient rights of way.

The design of appropriate property rights will depend heavily on the property law system and land ownership structures in the relevant country. Moreover, the availability of and procedural constraints on compulsory purchase orders will need to be considered carefully in weighing operator needs against the interests of land owners. In addition, the ease with which an operator can access public and private land and install infrastructure will have a material impact on new entrants' decisions to roll out duplicating network infrastructure (which may be both economically inefficient and environmentally disruptive) or simply to lease the necessary infrastructure from existing market players (which may hinder market development).

Bahrain: facility duplication v leases

During development of the new telecommunications regulatory framework in Bahrain, the issue of property rights and the rights of licensees to install new infrastructure was debated at length.

The incumbent, Batelco has significant amounts of surplus fibre and duct capacity. It was therefore argued that it was unnecessary to give new entrants the right to install their own network infrastructure with all the disruption that this would entail. Instead, Batelco would be obliged to lease capacity to entrants. The alternative view was that this would make entrants dependent on both Batelco's cooperation and the ability of the regulatory authority to set fair and equitable

terms for access. In practice, providing access to Batelco's duct and fibre infrastructure on regulated terms was a failure and these entrants instead developed their own wireless-based infrastructure. Five years after the initial liberalization of the market, the regulator is revisiting the legal and regulatory framework that provides competitors with access to Batelco's wireline infrastructure.

17.5.13 Consumer protection

It may be necessary to ensure that the electronic communications regulatory framework contains appropriate mechanisms to protect consumers, particularly where a country lacks generic consumer protection rules and organizations. Consumer protection mechanisms may include requiring approval of operators' standard customer contract, although the relevance of this measure is diminishing with the growth in mobile pre-paid subscriptions in developing countries. Instead, it may be more useful to require operators to publish a (binding) customer charter and to establish consumer complaints procedures meeting minimum regulatory standards. The latter, if effectively implemented, can help relieve the burden on the regulatory authority by promoting industry resolution of consumer complaints wherever possible. Other consumer measures may include provisions for directory and operator assistance and requirements for per second and itemized billing.

17.5.14 Offences

Telecommunications legislation often includes numerous criminal offences, including the unlicensed operation of telecommunications networks, unauthorized interference with communications, unauthorized use of radio spectrum, and the connection of unapproved terminal equipment, to name but a few. Applicable penalties usually include a term of imprisonment. The practical relevance of such criminal sanctions is questionable.

For example, the 1991 Sri Lankan Telecommunications Act contains an 'Offences and Penalties' section listing numerous criminal offences, ranging from operating a telecommunications system without a licence to the commission of an act of drunkenness by a telecommunication officer, climbing up a telecommunication post, and the tendering for transmission at a telecommunication office of a 'scurrilous' message. Yet no single instance of a criminal prosecution of these offences has occurred since the Act's enactment. In Bangladesh, criminal penalties are harsh: the mere act of operating or constructing a network or providing any service without a licence (a state of affairs which may not be uncommon given bottlenecks in licence renewal processes) could result in ten years' imprisonment.[58]

---

[58] The Bangladesh Telecommuniation Act 2001, s 35(2).

In relation to most regulatory obligations, administrative sanctions are likely to be a more useful or practicable enforcement tool than criminal prosecution. Accordingly, the emphasis in new sector legislation should be placed on regulatory rather than criminal sanctions.

17.6 CONCLUSION

Markets in developing countries have changed dramatically over the last ten years. The explosion in the demand for and supply of mobile services has increased teledensity throughout the developing world. The emergence of new technologies such as fixed wireless access, limited mobility services, and VoIP has changed the economics of the industry, allowing competition to flourish in what was previously considered a natural monopoly. Developing countries have recognized this and many have undertaken reform of their regulatory frameworks to match these developments and take advantage of the potential for private sector involvement.

The emerging global standard for regulatory reform is the EU regulatory framework. However, the market and institutional characteristics in developing countries are very different from the EU and other developed countries, which in turn prevent a direct transposition of models from the developing world. Thus, while many of the guiding principles underlying the EU framework remain relevant, the actual components of a new regulatory framework must be tailored to the circumstances of the individual country undertaking reforms.

In this chapter, we have discussed the various building blocks that together comprise a regulatory framework, and explored some of the issues that may arise in developing countries during its design and implementation.

Index

Journey from the North